ROUTLEDGE HANDBOOK
OF RADICAL POLITICS

Successive waves of global protest since 1999 have encouraged leading contemporary political theorists to argue that politics has fundamentally changed in the last twenty years, with a new type of politics gaining momentum over elite, representative institutions. The new politics is frequently described as radical, but what does radicalism mean for the conduct of politics?

Capturing the innovative practices of contemporary radicals, *Routledge Handbook of Radical Politics* brings together leading academics and campaigners to answer these questions and explore radicalism's meaning to their practice. In the thirty-five chapters written for this collection, they collectively develop a picture of radicalism by investigating the intersections of activism and contemporary political theory. Across their experiences, the authors articulate radicalism's critical politics and discuss how diverse movements support and sustain each other. Together, they provide a wide-ranging account of the tensions, overlaps and promise of radical politics, while utilising scholarly literatures on grassroots populism to present a novel analysis of the relationship between radicalism and populism.

Routledge Handbook of Radical Politics serves as a key reference for students and scholars interested in the politics and ideas of contemporary activist movements.

Ruth Kinna is a professor of Political Theory at Loughborough University where she specialises in nineteenth- and early twentieth-century socialist thought and contemporary radical politics, particularly anarchism and the utopianism of prefigurative politics. Since 2007, she has been the editor of the journal *Anarchist Studies*. She is the co-founder of the Anarchism Research Group and co-convenes the Anarchist Studies Network. She is the author of *Kropotkin: Reviewing the Classical Anarchist Tradition* and *The Government of No One*.

Uri Gordon is formerly the co-convenor of the Anarchist Studies Network and has taught political theory at universities in Britain and Israel. He has been active in climate justice, Palestine solidarity and anticapitalist movements in both countries. Uri is the author of *Anarchy Alive! Anti-Authoritarian Politics from Practice to Theory* and the co-editor of the monograph series *Contemporary Anarchist Studies*. His recent publications include a conceptual genealogy of prefigurative politics and a collaborative article on co-production in social and political theory. His work has been translated into thirteen languages.

ROUTLEDGE HANDBOOK OF RADICAL POLITICS

Edited by Ruth Kinna & Uri Gordon

Routledge
Taylor & Francis Group

NEW YORK AND LONDON

First published 2019
by Routledge
52 Vanderbilt Avenue, New York, NY 10017

and by Routledge
2 Park Square, Milton Park, Abingdon, Oxon, OX14 4RN

Routledge is an imprint of the Taylor & Francis Group, an informa business

Library of Congress Cataloging-in-Publication Data
Names: Kinna, Ruth, editor. | Gordon, Uri, 1976– editor.
Title: Routledge handbook of radical politics / edited by Ruth Kinna &
Uri Gordon.
Other titles: Handbook of radical politics
Description: New York, NY: Routledge, 2019. | Includes bibliographical
references and index.
Identifiers: LCCN 2018056329 (print) | LCCN 2019003869 (ebook) |
ISBN 9781315619880 (Master) | ISBN 9781317215288 (Adobe) |
ISBN 9781317215271 (ePub3) | ISBN 9781317215264 (Mobi) |
ISBN 9781138665422 (hardback) | ISBN 9781315619880 (e-book)
Subjects: LCSH: Radicalism. | Radicalization. | Right and left
(Political science)
Classification: LCC HN49.R33 (ebook) | LCC HN49.R33 R68 2019 (print) |
DDC 303.48/4—dc23
LC record available at https://lccn.loc.gov/2018056329

ISBN: 978-1-138-66542-2 (hbk)
ISBN: 978-1-315-61988-0 (ebk)

Typeset in Bembo
by codeMantra

MIX
Paper from
responsible sources
FSC www.fsc.org FSC™ C013985

Printed in the United Kingdom
by Henry Ling Limited

CONTENTS

Contents

Contents

TABLES

CONTRIBUTORS

Bürge Abiral is a PhD candidate in the Department of Anthropology at Johns Hopkins University. She received her bachelor's degree from Williams College, USA, with Honours in Anthropology, and her master's degree in Cultural Studies from Sabancı University, Turkey. She is currently working on her dissertation project on the ecological agriculture movement in Turkey, and her interests include human-environment relations, multispecies ethnography, food studies, value and social movements.

Liat Ben-Moshe is a scholar-activist based in Chicago. Her books include *Politics of (En)Closure: Deinstitutionalization, Prison Abolition and Disability* and the anthology *Disability Incarcerated: Imprisonment and Disability in the United States and Canada* (edited with Allison Carey and Chris Chapman).

Will Boisseau researches the place of animal advocacy within the British left, particularly the relationship between the anarchistic/direct action and the legislative wings of the movement. His work explores the class and gender issues influencing this relationship, the marginalisation of animal rights in mainstream labour politics and a range of concepts including speciesism, total liberation and intersectionality. He completed his PhD at Loughborough University in 2015.

Lydia X. Z. Brown is an activist/organiser, writer and educator focused on state violence against multiply-marginalised disabled people, especially institutionalisation and incarceration. They have worked to end restraint, seclusion, and adversives; challenge police violence; close institutions; and disrupt social justice communities.

Bonnie Burstow is a professor at the University of Toronto, an anarchist, a philosopher, a long-time antipsychiatry activist and a prolific author. She teaches in courses in community organising in alliance with disenfranchised populations. She is the chair of such activist organisations as Coalition Against Psychiatric Assault. Her books include *Psychiatry and the Business of Madness*, *Psychiatry Interrogated*, and *Psychiatry Disrupted,* with her latest book being a novel called *The Other Mrs Smith*, where we not only see the horrific experiential effects of electroshock, but see activists organising against it.

Emily Charkin is writing a PhD about self-build and radical education at the UCL Institute of Education. Her previous research and writing has been about children's experiences of the Peckham Health Centre (1935–1950), Whiteway Colony (1926–today) and the educational ideas of Colin Ward (1924–2010), Leila Berg (1917–2012) and the US deschoolers in the 1970s. She also runs a community woodland in East Sussex with her husband and three flexi-schooled children, where they try out some of these ideas (http://www.wildernesswood.org).

Alexandre Christoyannopoulos is a senior lecturer in Politics and International Studies at Loughborough University. He is the author of *Christian Anarchism: A Political Commentary on the Gospel* and *Tolstoy's Political Thought* as well as a number of articles, chapters and other publications on religious anarchism and on Leo Tolstoy, including the multi-volume collection of *Essays on Anarchism and Religion*. A full list of publications is available via http://orcid.org/0000-0001-5133-3268.

Laurence Cox is a senior lecturer at the National University of Ireland, Maynooth where he co-directs the MA on Community Education, Equality and Social Activism and runs a PhD-level programme of participatory action research in social movement practice. He co-founded the practitioner-oriented social movement studies journal *Interface* and the Council for European Studies' social movements research network. Cox is the co-author of *We Make Our Own History: Marxism and Social Movements in the Twilight of Neoliberalism* and has also published extensively on contemporary Buddhism in the west, including *Buddhism and Ireland: From the Celts to the Counter Culture and Beyond*.

Patrick G. Coy is a professor of Political Science and the director of the Center for Applied Conflict Management at Kent State University. He has taught both academic and practitioners' courses in mediation, negotiation and conflict resolution, and has served as an international observer and as a member of Peace Brigades International during the ethnic conflict in Sri Lanka. Coy is the author of over 30 peer-reviewed articles and book chapters, and co-author of *Contesting Patriotism: Culture, Power and Strategy in the Peace Movement*. He has also edited eleven books including *Social Conflicts and Collective Identities* and *A Revolution of the Heart: Essays on the Catholic Worker Movement*.

Rachel da Silva Gorman is an academic and an artist working in dance theatre and curating. Her work focuses on political economy and anticolonial aesthetics. She teaches choreographic process in disability and queer arts communities, and is a long-time organiser in feminist, antiracist and anti-occupation movements.

Claire Delisle is an activist-scholar and critical pedagogue who focuses on power, resistance and leadership. Her labour, Irish republican and abolitionist activism are central to her research on social movement organising. Claire teaches criminology and sociology at the University of Ottawa. She also teaches at Discovery University, where she engages with students who were at one time homeless. She has been taking part in ICOPA since 2008, and co-organised ICOPA 15 on Algonquin territory. She is the founder and co-lead of a lifers' liaison group that collaborates with life-sentences prisoners at a maximum-security penitentiary in Ontario.

Ruth A. Deller is a reader in Media and Communication at Sheffield Hallam University, UK and is a senior fellow of the Higher Education Academy (HEA). She has published widely on a range of topics including: identities and media representations; audience and fan studies and the relationships between 'old' and 'new' media. She is currently writing a monograph, provisionally titled *Religion on Television: Broadcasting Belief in the 21st Century*.

Jim Donaghey is a sometime anarchist agitator with a limited range of dance moves. Jim's PhD 'Punk and Anarchism: UK, Poland, Indonesia' was completed at Loughborough University in 2016, and he is currently a postdoctoral research fellow at Queen's University Belfast. He is also a member of the collective that runs Just Books radical bookshop at the Belfast Solidarity Centre. He has been involved with Do-It-Yourself (DIY) and anarchist music for the last sixteen years, playing hundreds of gigs around Ireland, the UK, Europe and South East Asia, and helping to produce dozens of records and zines. He is keeping his musical oar in with an anarcho-riot-folk outfit called Gulder.

Francis Dupuis-Déri is a professor of political science at Université du Québec à Montréal (UQAM); has been part of many radical collectives in Québec, France and the United States; and since 2003, has published many books in French, including *The Black Blocs* (which was subsequently translated into English and Brazilian Portuguese) and *Anarchy Explained to My Father* (translated into English and Greek). The author wishes to acknowledge the financial support of the Observatoire sur les profilages (CRSH) and the translator Ellen Warkentin, who helped him with regard to the English language.

Claire English is a feminist mother, agitator and organiser, presently working as an associate lecturer in Organisational Behaviour at Queen Mary University of London. Claire's research explores the workings of gender and race in transnational migrant solidarity activism in the UK and Europe, particularly at the French/British border of Calais. She helped to form Calais Migrant Solidarity in 2010 and is a member of Plan C, a group that looks at the social reproduction of social movements.

Loree Erickson is a porn star academic and organiser. Her work is focused on transforming cultures of undesirability through creating, theorising and supporting others in the production of queercrip porn. She also organises and theorises on collective care and transformative justice.

Mel Evans is an artist and campaigner part of Liberate Tate. Her book *Artwash: Big Oil and the Arts* was published in 2015. Her play *Oil City* was produced by Platform and presented as part of the Two Degrees Festival in 2013. Her writing has been published in *Contemporary Theatre Review*, *Performance Research Journal*, *Internationale Online*, *The Guardian*, *The Independent*, *New Internationalist*, *Dissent!*, *Red Pepper* and others. She regularly speaks about art and politics at events, which have included Economic Exceptionalism at the Institute of Contemporary Arts London, D&AD President's Lecture, Performing Protest Conference Leuven University, Artwash Book Tour UK and Ireland, Curating Conflict at the V&A Gallery London and Question Everything at the Cambridge Festival of Ideas.

Anthony T. Fiscella, born and raised in Virginia and currently living in Sweden, completed his doctorate in 2015 at Lund University in the history of religion where he also obtained his master's degree. His doctoral dissertation 'Universal Burdens' focused largely on what might be considered a decolonisation of the concept of 'freedom'. With a general interest in social change, dissemination of power and the role of life-organising stories, he has written about follower-power, Islam and anarchism, the MOVE Organization, taqwacore and the Daoist-like anarcho-primitivism of Lynyrd Skynyrd.

Rebecca Fisher was until recently a researcher at Corporate Watch, an independent research and publishing group, providing critical information on the social and environmental impacts of corporations and capitalism. Fisher's work has focused mainly on issues of democracy and consent, including in relation to the 2003 invasion and subsequent 'reconstruction' of Iraq, and as the editor of the Corporate Watch publication *Managing Democracy, Managing Dissent*. She has also been active in various grassroots movements, especially in alternative media and against border controls.

Uri Gordon is formerly a co-convenor of the Anarchist Studies Network and has taught political theory at universities in Britain and Israel. He has been active in climate justice, Palestine solidarity and anticapitalist movements in both countries. Uri is the author of *Anarchy Alive! Anti-Authoritarian Politics from Practice to Theory* and the co-editor of the monograph series *Contemporary Anarchist Studies*. His recent publications include a conceptual genealogy of prefigurative politics and a collaborative article on co-production in social and political theory. His work has been translated into thirteen languages.

Margherita Grazioli is a postdoctoral research fellow in Urban Studies (Social Sciences) at the Gran Sasso Science Institute (L'Aquila, Italy). Her research interest in urban geography, housing policies and social movements is rooted in her activism in the Movimento per il Diritto all'Abitare in Rome. She completed her PhD ('The right to the city in the post-welfare metropolis. Community building, autonomous infrastructures and urban commons in self-organised housing squats in Rome, Italy') at the University of Leicester.

Sandra Jeppesen researches with autonomous media and antiauthoritarian social movements from an intersectional queer, trans★, feminist, antiracist, anticapitalist and decolonising perspective. She is the co-founder of the Media Action Research Group (MARG, mediaactionresearch.org), and was a member of the former *Collectif de Recherche sur l'Autonomie Collective* (CRAC) in Montreal. Currently, she is an associate professor in Interdisciplinary Studies/Media Studies at Lakehead University Orillia, Canada, where she holds the Lakehead University Research Chair in Transformative Media and Social Movements.

Ramsey Kanaan founded AK Press as a young teenager out of his bedroom in Scotland. He's been wrestling with the eternal question 'if ideas actually matter, how do we disseminate them' for almost four decades now. He's currently the publisher of PM Press in Oakland, California.

Ruth Kinna works at Loughborough University and writes on nineteenth- and early twentieth-century socialist thought and contemporary radical politics, particularly anarchism. Since 2007, she has been the editor of the journal *Anarchist Studies*. She is co-founder of the Anarchism Research Group and co-convenes the Anarchist Studies Network. She is the author of *Kropotkin: Reviewing the Anarchist Tradition* and *The Government of No One*.

Luca Lapolla was awarded his PhD in History at Birkbeck, University of London, in January 2018. He researched post-1968 libertarian communities in Britain and Italy reflecting on the importance that memory, space and representation have in influencing the theory and praxis of anarchist movement(s). He is interested in social and cultural history and takes an interdisciplinary and comparative approach. After a BA in Modern Foreign Languages and an MA in Modern and Contemporary History, his master's thesis on the

1970s anarcho-communist organisation ORA was published in Italy. Luca aims at producing academic historical research of practical significance for present and future radical activists.

Talila A. Lewis is a social justice engineer, attorney, educator and organiser whose liberation struggle centres around prison abolition, correcting and preventing wrongful convictions of deaf and disabled people, and ending all forms of violence against multiply-marginalised individuals and communities.

Michael Loadenthal is a visiting professor of Sociology and Social Justice at Miami University, and the executive director of the Peace and Justice Studies Association. Michael holds a PhD in Conflict Analysis and Resolution (George Mason University), and a master's degree in Terrorism Studies from the Centre for the Study of Terrorism and Political Violence (University of St Andrews, Scotland). His research has involved ethnographic studies with abortion providers, Rastafarians, Mexican revolutionaries, 'eco-terrorists' and Palestinian guerrillas. His latest book, *The Politics of Attack: Communiqués and Insurrectionary Violence*, focuses on a discursive and analysis of insurrectionary anarchist networks.

Josep Lobera is a lecturer in the Department of Sociology of the Autonomous University of Madrid (Spain) and in the joint programme of Tufts University and Skidmore College (USA). His research focuses on the institutionalisation of protest movements and on attitudes towards immigration. He is the co-editor of the *Spanish Journal of Sociology* and scientific editor of the biannual report on Social Perception of Science and Technology.

Martina Martignoni has completed her PhD at the School of Management, University of Leicester. Her thesis, *Postcolonial Organising: An Oral History of the Eritreans in Milan*, explores the politics of self-organising of the Eritrean community in Milan and investigates the interconnections between postcoloniality, migration, difference and organising. Her research interests move across migrations, oral history and autonomous political practices in Italy. She has co-authored with Dimitris Papadopoulos the paper 'Genealogies of Autonomous Mobility' for the *Routledge Handbook of Global Citizenship Studies*.

Lateef McLeod is a disability justice activist who published a poetry book, *A Declaration of a Body of Love*, and is working on a novel, *The Third Eye Is Crying*. He is a doctoral student at California Institute for Integral Studies in their Anthropology and Social Change Program.

Mia Mingus is a writer, public speaker, educator and community organiser for disability justice and transformative justice responses to child sexual abuse. Her writings can be found on her blog, Leaving Evidence.

Pamela Palmater is a citizen of the sovereign Mi'kmaw Nation on the unceded territory of Mi'kmak'i (Atlantic Canada) and a member of Eel River Bar First Nation. She is a lawyer, author, social justice activist and former spokesperson and educator for the Idle No More movement. She currently serves as an associate professor and chair in Indigenous Governance at Ryerson University.

Diego Parejo is an anthropologist and researcher at the Autonomous University of Madrid (Spain). His research focuses on the new European populist movements and on immigration in highly diverse urban contexts.

Sean Parson is an assistant professor of Politics and International Affairs at Northern Arizona University. He is the editor of the book *Superheroes and Critical Animal Studies: The Heroic Beasts of Total Liberation* and the forthcoming book *Cooking Up Revolution: Food Not Bombs, Anarchist Homeless Activism, and the Politics of Space.* When not writing, teaching or grading, he mostly spends his time hiking the mountains and forests of Northern Arizona with his four-legged best friend Diego.

David Naguib Pellow is the Dehlsen chair of Environmental Studies and the director of the Global Environmental Justice Project at the University of California, Santa Barbara. His teaching and research focus on environmental and ecological justice in the US and globally. His books include *What Is Critical Environmental Justice?*; *Total Liberation: The Power and Promise of Animal Rights and the Radical Earth Movement*; *Resisting Global Toxics: Transnational Movements for Environmental Justice* and *Garbage Wars: The Struggle for Environmental Justice in Chicago.* He works with numerous organisations focused on improving the living and working environments for people of colour and other marginalised communities.

Maia Ramnath is a writer, historian, artist and activist based in New York City. The author of two books and numerous articles, she has previously taught world history, modern South Asian history and Asian studies at New York University and Pennsylvania State University. Both in writing and in action, she focuses upon the intersection of anarchism and anticolonialism. She is currently a board member of the Institute for Anarchist Studies.

Chris Rossdale is a lecturer in Politics and International Relations at the University of Bristol. His research focuses on social movements, resistance and international political theory. He has published in *International Political Sociology, Millennium Journal of International Studies* and *Globalizations,* and his book *Resisting Militarism: Direct Action and the Politics of Subversion* was published in 2019 with Edinburgh University Press.

Peter Seyferth. Dr. phil., political philosopher from Munich, tried to get elected to the German Bundestag as a candidate of the Anarchist Pogo Party (APPD) in 1998 while finishing his MA in Political Science. The party's slogan, 'work is shit', did not attract enough voters, so he did a PhD on Ursula K. Le Guin's utopias. Since then, he has taught political theory and philosophy at universities and adult education centres. His last publication is an edited volume on anarchist understandings of the state (*Den Staat zerschlagen!*).

Jeff Shantz is a long-time activist in varied radical projects from the Ontario Coalition Against Poverty to the Red Sparks Union. He currently teaches community advocacy, critical theory and corporate crime at Kwantlen Polytechnic University in Metro Vancouver, and Unceded Coast Salish Territories (British Columbia). He is a founding member of the Critical Criminology Working Group radicalcriminology.org and The Social Justice Centre, Surrey. Jeff has written several books including *Insurrectionary Infrastructures, Crisis States: Governance, Resistance, and Precarious Capitalism*, and *Cyber Disobedience: Re://Presenting Online Anarchy,* with Jordon Tomblin.

Speaking of IMELDA is an intergenerational, London-based collective, which includes former members of Irish Women's Abortion Support Group (IWASG), who supported women travelling to England for abortions between 1980 and 2000. The name Imelda was originally used as a code name for abortion by IWASG, who also often wore a red skirt so as to be identified by women travelling. In reclaiming the name IMELDA and wearing red in their actions, they pay homage to previous reproductive rights activists. They deploy interventionist style performance to upend the pretence that Ireland is 'abortion free' by highlighting that people travel daily to Britain to access abortion. Their actions have been aimed at breaking down the barriers that prevent women from speaking freely about abortion. They operate against the shaming and silencing of those who have abortions, challenging the stereotypes of the quiet and pure Irish woman. Sometimes audacious and often uninvited, their actions unapologetically declare the right to bodily integrity and reproductive autonomy. They campaign to Repeal the 8th Amendment to the Constitution of Ireland, which in 1983 legislated that the unborn foetus has equal rights to life as the mother. They also campaign to enable access to free, safe, legal and local abortion services in Northern Ireland where, unlike the rest of the UK, abortion remains illegal under the 1861 Offences Against the Persons Act. They have been featured extensively in high-profile newspapers and other publications and have presented in universities, conferences, events, exhibitions and on radio.

Judith Suissa is professor of Philosophy of Education at UCL Institute of Education, London. Her research interests are in political and moral philosophy, with a focus on the control of education, social justice, libertarian and anarchist theory, the role of the state and the parent-child relationship. Her publications include *Anarchism and Education: A Philosophical Perspective* (Routledge, 2006) and (with Stefan Ramaekers) *The Claims of Parenting: Reasons, Responsibility and Society*.

Leah Temper is a transdisciplinary researcher, activist and filmmaker with a degree in communications science and a doctorate in Ecological Economics from the Autonomous University of Barcelona. She is a deputy scientific coordinator of EJOLT, a global research project that brings activists and scientists together to catalogue and analyse ecological distribution conflicts and confront environmental injustice, and the editor of *The Global Atlas of Environmental Justice* (ejatlas.org). Temper has published in numerous journals and is the co-editor of the book *Ecological Economics from the Ground Up* (Routledge). Her media work includes short films such *Life After Growth* and *Delhi Waste Wars*, as well as blogs and newspaper articles.

M. Testa, undercover antifascist blogger, has analysed the changing fortunes of the British far right since 2009. He is the author of *Militant Anti-Fascism: 100 Years of Resistance* and has written for the anarchist magazine *Freedom* and for *Anarchist Studies*. His blog is at: malatesta32.wordpress.com.

Jim Thomas is the co-executive director at the Action Group on Erosion, Technology and Concentration (ETC), which works to address the socioeconomic and ecological issues surrounding new technologies that could have an impact on the world's most vulnerable and marginalised people. His background is in communications, writing on emerging technologies and international campaigning. For the seven years previously, he was a researcher and campaigner on genetic engineering and food issues for Greenpeace International. Thomas has extensive experience on issues around synthetic biology, geoengineering, transgenic crops, data-driven technologies and nanotechnologies. He has written articles, chapters and technical reports in the media and online as well as participated extensively in UN-level technology governance processes.

Lisa Trocchia-Baḻ̣ḵīts, PhD, serves as Scholar-in-Residence at Green Mountain College in Vermont, USA, where she teaches and is engaged with curriculum design in two graduate-level programmes: Sustainable Food Systems (MSFS) and Resilient and Sustainable Communities (RSC). Dr. Trocchia-Baḻ̣ḵīts researches and writes about horizontal, decentralised social structures, the diverse economies of bioregional food systems, the performance of cultural food-ways, and self-organised, community-based food system social networks as sites of radical social change.

Aurora Trujillo has a passion for the role that cycling can take as a motor to change the world. As part of her PhD, she researched the political and cultural barriers to cycling becoming mainstream in the UK. She was also part of setting up and running Freewheelers Bicycle Co-op in Lancaster, was a member of Bicycology and worked at the London Cycling Campaign. She is currently taking a break from research and activism.

Bart van der Steen is a lecturer in Modern History at Leiden University, the Netherlands. His research focuses on interwar labour movements and New Social Movements from 1968 to the present. His published works include *Party, State, Revolution: Critical Reflections on Žižek's Political Philosophy* (with M. de Kesel), *A European Youth Revolt: European Perspectives on Youth Protest and Social Movements in the 1980s* (edited with K. Andresen), *Een Banier waar geen Smet op Rust: De Geschiedenis van de Trotskistische Beweging in Nederland* (with R. Blom) and *The City is Ours: Squatting and Autonomous Movements in Europe, 1980–2014* (edited with L. van Hoogenhuijze and A. Katzeff).

Matthew Wilson makes beer with Bartleby's Worker Co-op and is currently based at Nottingham Business School, researching other worker co-ops. His published work includes *Rules Without Rulers*, published by Zero Press.

A. J. Withers is a queer, trans and disabled antipoverty activist and organiser who's worked with the Ontario Coalition Against Poverty since 2000. He is the author of *A Violent History of Benevolence: Interlocking Oppressions in the Moral Economies of Social Working* (co-authored with Chris Chapman), *The Healing Power of Domination: Interlocking Oppression and the Origins of Social Work* (with Chris Chapman), *Disability Politics and Theory* and creator of stillmyrevolution.org. He is a PhD student in social work at York University and receives support from the Social Sciences and Humanities Research Council of Canada.

ACKNOWLEDGEMENTS

Enormous thanks to Natalja Mortensen for proposing this project and Maria Landschoot and Charlie Baker for guiding us through the production process. Thanks, too, to Bernadette Buckley and Giorgos Katsambekis for very helpful and encouraging comments on various drafts of the introductory text. We'd also like to acknowledge the feedback we received from one anonymous reviewer whose trenchant critique, while not encouraging, helped us sharpen the arguments set out in the introduction. Above all, we would like to thank our contributors, for their dedication, insights, engagement and forbearance.

INTRODUCTION

Uri Gordon and Ruth Kinna

Aims and Scope

This collection is dedicated to the dynamic radical social movements that have mushroomed since the late 1980s, and the social and political critiques and alternatives they have inspired. The radicalism of these movements is broadly defined by the advancement of a politics that challenges existing institutional arrangements, by an ethics supporting the disruption of the status quo, and by the interaction of theory and practice. We do not explore frames of action or cultures of protest, nor do we examine the socio-economic, cultural and political contexts in which activism takes place, or the spaces allowed for the expression of transgressive ideas. These are all well documented in a substantial and growing body of work (Flesher Fominaya, 2014; della Porta, 2015) and across the movement-facing research of academic journals like *Interface, Antipode, Social Movement Studies* and *The Journal for the Study of Radicalism*. Instead, the collection concentrates on the ways that radical politics is theorised through practice, and on the perspectives of the actual groups who participate in radical politics.

The majority of our contributors are academic activists, who combine considerable experience of movement practices with scholarship and research. Our primary concern was to invite specialists who are also participants in, or intimately connected with, the movements and projects they discuss. While we have attempted to contextualise the radicalism of our contributors' essays, the ideological content of radical politics is deliberately left open. Thus, rather than focus on conceptual or methodological debates, for which there is already a substantial literature, we invited our contributors to define their radicalism and to do so with reference to movement activism. Contributors to this volume sometimes identify or locate their positions or frameworks (for example, ecological, anarchist, feminist) but not typically in order to focus on the elaboration of the conceptual markers that define them. For example, in the case of feminism, contributors explore the campaigns that they are engaged with: pro-abortion politics and safer spaces are two areas. As a result, the volume captures the plurality and diversity of political activism, while weaving together ideas that are often linked narrowly to particular currents of thought in conceptual and methodological studies. In this way, the collection will hopefully give readers a sense of radical movements' scope while also outlining a set of responses, critiques, proposals and reflections on topics central to radical politics today.

Many of our contributors are based in Western Europe or North America, but not exclusively so. We have tried to make sure that different voices are well represented in the collection and we have not systematically mapped voice to issue (women are not restricted to areas of feminist politics). Nevertheless, while the scope of the collection is international, the perspectives tend to be rooted in the North America and Europe. We hope that this limitation has been offset by the inspiration that authors draw from the global movements they discuss. The diversity of radical politics, the transnational character of protest cultures, the internal complexity of global movements and the rapid shifts within radical politics all rule against the presentation of a definitive or exhaustive collection. Our ambition is to present a snapshot rather than a portrait of contemporary radical politics. The result is that we pass over the analysis of some important inspirational movements such as Occupy or Black Lives Matter and cover some less well-known political activities (for example, antipoverty campaigning, antipysch politics, biketivism) alongside more familiar campaigns, for example, climate politics and antimilitarism.

We have prioritised areas of politics that we believe have a significant presence or influence in activist movements. As well as thinking about the longevity of particular issues, we are interested in highlighting the ways that movement practices have contributed to the theorisation of radical politics – in highlighting how normative political theory inspires activism and continues to feed back into it. Decolonisation and border politics are examples. In order to capture the levels at which contemporary radical politics operates, we look both at the politics of transnational networks and the activism of micropolitical organisations. Similarly, we examine radicalism as it is practised in transgressive, antipolitical activism and by groups seeking to achieve legislative changes through direct action: bed-pushing, art and antipoverty activism.

In order to capture the dynamism and innovative practices of contemporary radical politics, the collection is structured around four themes: *Critiques*, *Solidarities*, *Repertoires* and *Transformations*. Our aim is to introduce readers to some of the major issues motivating radical activism and to show how these issues support a range of projects and networked practices, before discussing the diverse and creative activities that activism involves and the aspirations that it embraces. The sections are roughly equal. Because we asked our authors to address common questions, there are some overlaps between the sections. Given the intersectional focus of the collection, we welcome this and believe that the interplay perfectly captures the dynamic, interlocking character of contemporary radical politics.

RADICALISM

Situating Contemporary Movement Practices

Uri Gordon and Ruth Kinna

Situating Contemporary Movement Practices

Our aim in this chapter is to discuss some of the specific forces pulling on the concept of radicalism. The view that radicalism is a chameleon concept is well established in the history of ideas. As Glenn Burgess puts it, there are 'as many radicalisms as there are radicals' (Burgess, 2006–7). Our central premise is that while the meaning of radicalism has always been context-dependent and ideologically fluid, anarchism has stepped out of the shadows to become the beating heart of contemporary left radical networks. The story we relate below tells how anarchistic politics has moved from the margins to the centre of radical politics. Our argument is that radicalism has the conceptual breadth to include anarchist currents and that these have been sidelined because of the way that radicalism has taken its content from particular historical movements. The recognition that anarchism is a key ingredient in radicalism, associating radical politics with anticapitalist direct action movements, is a seismic political shift.

An important body of recent scholarship has explored the construction of substantive radical traditions (Burgess and Festenstein 2007; Calhoun 2012). We instead survey the evolution of the concept, asking how radicalism was theorised at the cusp of the transition from the age of ideology to the age of party politics and how anarchist ideas intersected with it. The age of ideology usually describes the period following the American and French Revolutions when a political left-right spectrum began to take shape. The age of party politics is used here to describe the reduction of the spectrum to three dominant ideologies, liberalism, conservatism and socialism at the cost of other historically significant currents of ideas including republicanism, Bonapartism, anticolonialism, feminism and anarchism (Aiken, 1956; Schwartzmantel, 1998). Examining this transition enables us to recover an anarchistic strand within the framework of radicalism and identify its hallmarks.

We then examine the post-war history of social movement activism to explore the associative principles that left radicalism articulates. These have been shaped by a set of events that have stimulated the rediscovery of a left-libertarian radical tradition. In sketching this brief history, we note that democratisation is now a central theme in left radical politics and that the practice of direct, deliberative, participatory democracy has been identified as one of its outstanding features. The 2011 Occupy movement has helped cement this association

(Graeber, 2013; Szolucha, 2017). We want to make two points in respect of this analysis. First, that the concerns of the contemporary left radicalisms we examine are not wholly encompassed in a populist democratic framing. And second, that the theorisation of populism as a left radical politics helps highlight the ideological divisions within it and the fracturing of democracy along anti-elitist lines.

To do this, we first identify three associative principles of left radicalism. These are intersectionality, horizontalism and direct action. We then turn to recent scholarship on left populism. This adds another layer of complexity to the discussion of radicalism; yet, the tendency of protest movement analysts to discuss anarchism as the major component of radial left populism (Grattan, 2016; Gerbaudo, 2017) makes the populist-radical nexus difficult to ignore. The populist lens narrows the scope of radical politics because it elevates concepts of sovereignty and democracy to the forefront. In populism studies, the primary issues under discussion are how 'the people' is or should be theorised and what values of democracy populist movements promote (Kioupkiolis and Katsambekis, 2014: 1–15). It also leaves the ideological distinctions between left and right populism unclear.

To explore the conceptual framing of left-leaning radicalism within populism, we examine three thick descriptions advanced by Margaret Canovan, Ernesto Laclau and Federico Finchelstein. We abstract an anticonstitutional framing from Canovan, a concept of leadership pertinent to the construction of 'the people' from Laclau and an organisational model from Federico Finchelstein. By looking at the ways that populism can be radicalised, through the anarchistic model we develop, we attempt to make the nature of this distinction clear. Illustrating ideological distance between the populist left and right, we also seek to show where normative thrust of the currents of ideas that animate contemporary radical activist networks lies without enforcing rigid and distorting political designations upon them.

Radicalism

Kai Artzheimer notes:

> Like many other concepts in political science, the notion of radicalism harks back to the political conflicts of the late 18th and 19th century. Even then, its content was dependent on the political context and far from well defined. Consequentially, being 'radical' has meant different things to different people in different times and countries. Moreover, radicalism is closely related, if not identical to a number of (equally vague) concepts such as extremism, fundamentalism, and populism. As of today, there is no universally accepted definition of radicalism, and, by implication, radical attitudes.
>
> *(Sage, 2011)*

As some of our contributors mention, standard dictionaries define radicalism as pertaining 'to the root or origin; original; fundamental; as a *radical* truth or error; a *radical* evil; a *radical* difference of opinions or systems' (Webster's 1828). Radicalism is equally about starting points, novelty and extremes. In both common parlance and politics, the responses that radicalism provokes often reflect subjective judgements about the promise or threat that radical prescriptions imply. As a political discourse, it is often associated with change, upheaval and upset. Considering eating as a 'kind of proselytising', the Victorian novelist and satirist Samuel Butler warned against radicalism, advising that all 'thoughts are more easily assimilated that have been already digested by other minds'. Just as indigestion could be explained by the 'naughtiness of the stiff-necked things that we have eaten', he suggested that it 'may also arise from an attempt on the part of the stomach to be too damned clever, and to depart from precedent inconsiderately'. Butler concluded, 'the healthy stomach is nothing if not conservative. Few radicals have good digestions' (Butler, 2014 [1912]: 112–13).

In political theory, radicalism is linked strongly to the progressive programmes of pre-socialist democrats and the reform agendas of the early nineteenth-century utilitarians (Halévy, 1928; Thomas, 1979; Scriven, 2017). Yet, the turmoil and upset modelled by the great eighteenth-century revolutions account for the early and still common association of radicalism with left politics. Radicalism had acquired this reputation by the early nineteenth century, if not before, as self-described radical movements variously calling for democratic reforms, civil liberties and the extension or protection of republican values sprang up across Europe and in America. By the 1840s, radicalism was linked with programmes of social as well as political change and as its exponents fled Europe, radicalism took root in this form in the new worlds as well as the old (Gollan, 1967: 15). In 1881, the antisocialist liberal academic Maurice Block[1] observed that 'radicalism and radicals are applied to democratic doctrines more or less advanced, and to their adherents' (1884). Five years later, the journalist Henri Rochefort defined '*Radicalism*' as that 'body of political doctrines which the Republican party has constantly professed, and … [the] social reforms which it has unceasingly demanded' (1886: 11). Like Block, Rochefort linked radicalism to a set of principles forcefully elaborated in 1789 and believed that it had a stable ideological content. Even if radicals subsequently adopted different labels and called themselves socialists, for instance, for as long as they faithfully advanced the ideals expressed in the Revolution, they were radicals. Still listing 'radicalisme' as a neologism, the 1873 *Dictionnaire De La Langue Française* similarly connected radicalism to the progressive programmes advanced by those who called themselves radicals. Radicalism described the 'system of the radicals, advocates of the complete reform of political society'.

Yet, the relationship of radicalism and post-revolutionary progressive or left politics was always contingent. The emergence of European socialist and social democratic parties after 1848 caused self-styled radicals to reassess their convictions and as new currents of ideas entered into the political fray, radicalism fractured. Nietzsche and Dostoevsky are often credited with stimulating a rightward drift in radical politics and with the radicalisation of conservatism. From the late nineteenth century, the term radicalism became as firmly attached to antidemocratic aristocratic political values as it had previously been to liberal-egalitarian philosophical movements and progressive democratic traditions (Detwiler, 1990; Dahl, 1999: 51–59). Boulangism and Randolf Churchill's Tory radicalism were two of its earlier European manifestations; Rochefort was one of those who moved across the spectrum while still remaining radical. In the 1870s, he had participated in the Paris Commune. Twenty years later, he backed General Boulanger.

In the twentieth century, demands for root and branch change increasingly emanated from both the left and the right. The 1932 *Dictionnaire de l'Académie Française* defined radicalism blandly as the 'system or party of radicals'. Kurt Zube's[2] German-language interwar almanac *Radikaler Geist* spoke to a progressive politics shaped by the embrace of new ideas and subversive thinking in politics and the arts. Zube was radical in the sense that he encouraged social innovation and change. His aim was to open up 'new perspectives' and help readers give 'them completely different content'. Before the Nazis shut it down, his magazine promoted the work of (amongst others) Brecht, Freud, Silvio Gesell, Herman Hesse, Lenin, Rosa Luxemburg, Marx and Engels, Romain Rolland, Margaret Sanger, Max Stirner and Stefan Zweig. As a radical, Zube endorsed critique, reflection, pluralism and socialistic change (Zube, 1930). However, by this time, the far right was fully mobilised against the liberal-social democratic centre and the revolutionary socialist left in large parts of Europe, and it was better-positioned to initiate fundamental radical transformations. Historians and political scientists argue about the closeness of the relationship between nazism, fascism and the religious right, but however the boundary-lines are drawn, all varieties of reactionary politics are commonly labelled 'radical' (Copsey, 2016).

Early political scientists struggled to differentiate one type of radicalism from another. Block introduced two measures for comparison. The first placed radicals as opponents of absolutism at the extreme left of a political spectrum that centred on a tolerant, liberal core. The second was based on political style or convention. On this scale, a radical was someone '*absolute*, in all opinions' including those 'in the monarchical as well as in the republican party'. Pursuing a line of thought that appeared perfectly designed to muddle the politics of radicalism, Block further noted that radicalism was 'characterized less by its principles than by the manner of their application'. Radicalism had the 'character of the boy'. It was 'enthusiastic, imaginative, to a certain extent generous, lives in an ideal world, pursuing a single idea, and pursuing it frantically, without regard to the evils caused by the efforts to realize it' (1884). Block believed that the juvenile politics radicals practised were tempered by the reforming programmes they promoted. But in the absence of any more precise measures, this perceived overlap with liberalism could never be more than a happy coincidence. Block's contention that radicalism was as much about dogma and the manner in which change was promoted as it was about policy innovation made it difficult to determine radicalism's limits and decide where the convergence with liberalism began and ended.

Radicalism remains a chameleon concept and the fuzziness of the correlation of style and substance still resonates in modern scholarship. Familiarly contrasted with reformism, radicalism is used normatively to assess change agendas by exposing gaps between the perception and the actuality of political programmes. Dolowitz et al. (1996: 455–70) use radicalism as one of three 'R's' to dissect Margaret Thatcher's brand of conservatism and question the novelty of the changes she introduced. Downey (2007: 108–90) similarly deploys radicalism to assess radical democracy, finding that recent articulations can appear 'piecemeal and pragmatic' and 'naive and timid rather than radical' (2005: 109).

The idea that radicalism describes politics on the margins also still resonates in contemporary scholarship. There are two common trends here. First, radicalism is used as a synonym for extremism. Specifically, radicalism is used to describe the combative politics of (usually right-wing) political parties that compete for power to destabilise liberal-democratic regimes (Capoccia, 2005: 233). In a secularised, securitised world, radicalism is also tied to religiously inspired terrorism. For example, the Islamic Supreme Council of America defines Islamic radicalism as a form of 'fundamentalism' built 'on the concept of political enforcement of religious beliefs' (n.d.). Second, it describes the activism of right-leaning antiglobalisation and left-leaning alterglobalisation activists that are either partially or fully detached from the institutional mainstream: marginal in another sense. As Cristina Flesher Fominaya notes, radicalism is a moniker for complex political groupings that express fears about national identity and diminished national sovereignty as well as those that rally around anticorporate, anti-austerity and pro-democracy campaigns (2014: 3–4).

The link between radicalism and antisystem grassroots activism, while not conceptually essential, opens up new perspectives on the familiar histories. Often bypassed in accounts that focus on the radicalisation of emergent political systems, the antisystem currents that Flesher Fominaya finds in today's political landscape were nevertheless deeply rooted in nineteenth-century radical movements influenced by anarchists. Craig Calhoun notes that the first self-designated anarchist, Pierre Joseph Proudhon, found a following with nineteenth-century American radicals, 'artisans, outworkers and others' who conjoined 'economic grievances' with 'appeals for social inclusion, and approaches to solidarity rooted in craft and community' (2012: 7).

In the early age of party politics, pro-anarchist ideas were frequently voiced by socialists critical of those who identified as radicals, and so appeared to be antiradical and rightly placed beyond its traditions. Yet, the distinctive marker of the pro-anarchist critique was the focus on the elite institutionalisation of revolutionary values and their parliamentary disappointment. These activists were critical of the political systems that radicals inhabited, not the values that they claimed to advance. In this respect, they deserve to be placed within the frame.

Unlike other radicals, those influenced by anarchism championed extra-parliamentary action and were wary of campaigns that turned on demands for more political rights or greater representation. Their view was that a narrow focus on institutional politics distracted radicals from the real issues that confronted them. Joseph Lane[3] explained: 'the Radical stands helpless, shouting loudly about the cost of Monarchy and the pension list' and fails to see 'that this is a drop in the ocean compared to the robbery of the landlord and the capitalist class' (Lane, 1887). Similarly, admitting that radicalism was a byword for 'the best and most advanced opinion' William Morris[4] argued that radicals were deluded in thinking that they could realise their demands for education, 'a steady and tolerable livelihood undisturbed by disgraceful wars abroad, or ruinous commercial crisis at home' by 'persisting in pushing' for change 'at the polling booth'. Radicalism would only be worth something when the Radical Party became the 'Party of the People'. Yet, this was hardly a realistic prospect because it entailed a complete reversal of practice: Morris urged radicals to work outside parliamentary institutions and give up dreams of universal suffrage. He told their constituents to 'take part in affairs yourselves and don't look on while your leaders pretend to work for you'. Leaders and their rivals were either tyrants or hypocrites who would only manage exploitation rather than fight for its abolition (Morris, 1994 [1884]: 47–49).

For most of the nineteenth and twentieth centuries this anarchist-inflected critique of parliamentary radicalism confined its exponents to the political wilderness. Today, the tables have turned. The anarchistic commitment to organise outside the institutional framework and coordinate activity through grassroots social movements and associations is an established current within radical politics. In what follows, we plot some of the shifts that have propelled anarchism from the sidelines to the centre ground of radical politics and identify its conceptual markers.

Radicalism and Anarchism

It would be disingenuous to say that left radicals have habitually traced their roots back to late Victorian radicalism, but not inaccurate to say that the traditions that left radicals have constructed in the last fifty years chime with the forms of left-libertarianism that Morris and others articulated. In the 1960s, *Radical America*, the iconic mouthpiece of the Students for a Democratic Society (SDS), found one of the antecedents of their movement in the early twentieth-century syndicalist union, the Industrial Workers of the World (IWW). Not everyone agreed about the IWW's record, but even those who judged it most harshly acknowledged that it had left a potent anticapitalist, revolutionary legacy that fed into sixties radicalism. The IWW was celebrated as 'a brave and imaginative labor organisation that once seemed as though it might pose a threat to the stability of American capitalism'. The reason why New Leftists joined it in the 1960s was 'primarily because it seems to offer a heritage of militant, dramatic warfare against the rules of America' (Buhle, 1967: 6).

Voices in the Occupy movement located themselves in longer histories. Tom Paine, the great radical who 'galvanized the attention, hopes and enthusiasm' of eighteenth- and nineteenth-century democrats (Calhoun, 2012: 6), re-emerged as a champion of 'real democracy' in literature on Wall Street (Graeber, 2013). Perhaps more immersed in the traditions E.P. Thompson discussed in *The Making of the English Working Class*, occupiers in London variously found the lineages of their movement in the Magna Carta, the Levellers and the Putney debates. Yet, Morris, too, interpreted the Magna Carta as a declaration against tyranny and argued that it had contributed to the struggle against domination and arbitrary authority (Morris, 1887).

Constructing histories is fraught with problems. In the case of Occupy, the identification of 'the people' with the revolutionary campaign for American independence had the effect of sidelining Indigenous groups in the struggle against re-colonisation. Yet, leading figures within left radical movements have argued that their construction is an essential part of transformative struggle. C.L.R. James, in a talk delivered in Detroit in 1967 and reprinted in *Radical America* said: 'when I was a boy I lived in Trinidad. My parents were Trinidadian. We knew nothing about Africa except what we learned from the British. And what they taught us was what they themselves believed about Africa – or perhaps what they wanted us to believe' (James, 1968: 24). For James, the discovery and recovery of history was a tool for empowerment. Following James, we argue that movement history tells us something about the continuities of the currents contained within radicalism and the political aspirations of left-leaning radicals.

The current convention is to treat the emergence of the New Left in the 1960s as the noteworthy reference point for contemporary radicalism (Maeckelbergh, 2012). However, as Dan Berger remarks of the North American movement, this rendering of radicalism's modern history creates a misleadingly dichotomous picture of the 1960s as an era of creative ferment and the 1970s as one of political quiescence, even desolation (Berger, 2010: 4). Casting aside this decade-based periodisation, Berger recommends taking a long view, stretching the 'sixties' into a period extending from the 1950s to the 1970s. This not only makes better sense of the innovative transnational anticapitalist, antinuclear, antiwar and antiracist initiatives that flourished after the evaporation of mass student and worker protests, but also foregrounds shifts in liberal democratic politics that mobilised left radicals into action.

For Berger, the election of Ronald Reagan in 1980 is the watershed moment for contemporary radicalism. Perceived as the culmination of a struggle that had raged throughout the long sixties, his presidency marked the full retrenchment of post-war progressive politics. As Berger argues, the attempt to 'wipe out radical protest' by the adoption of liberal domestic politics during the 1970s gave way to the adoption of a fully reactionary programme of economic neo-liberalism, nationalism and 'aggrandized militarism' (Berger, ibid.: 2–3). A commentary in *Radical America* reinforces this analysis. The journal described the long-feared 1980 election result as a confirmation of the 'impact of the New Right [and] the strength of a reaction that has been growing for some time'. The election meant that the 'antigay, antifeminist, and racist campaigns of recent history have now been legitimized under the banner of states' rights, military supremacy, free enterprise, and religious fundamentalism' (*Radical America*, 1980: 2).

On this reading, the ascendancy of the New Right did not represent a disappointment of libertarian aspirations. Rather, it reaffirmed a familiar critique of power while simultaneously drawing attention to the significance of the global policy shift Reaganism represented. In 1966, the American anarchist and pacifist Paul Goodman had rejected the idea that politics is 'prudent steering in difficult terrain'. His view was that politics was a craft shaped by Machiavellianism: 'how to get power and keep power, even though the sphere of effective power is extremely limited and it makes little difference who is in power' (Goodman, 1966: 61). Reagan's victory reinforced the anti-elitist thrust of this critique but cast Goodman's casual dismissal of the liberal democratic consensus in a new light. *Radical America* (1981: 4) declared itself numbed and 'chilled' by the 'scope of the electoral gains of the conservatives and the frightening prospects – national and international, personal and collective – that their program portends'. The contributors had found the lesson of the sixties in constant activist vigilance: 'when social movements have been able to bring about progressive legislation, leaving the protection of the newly-won "rights" up to the government can render the movement passive and make the reforms vulnerable to the shifting winds of electoral politics' (1980: 3).

The mobilisation against the conservative reaction led to the widely, if belatedly, acknowledged anarchistic turn in radical movement organising and ethics (Epstein, 2001; Blumenfeld, Bottici and Critchley, 2013). It also involved significant shifts in the cultures of left radicalism. Central to these was the increasing importance of radical democratic practices, recently seen in global movement activism through affinity groups, networks, consensus decision-making and horizontal leadership cultures (Cornell, 2010). Murray Bookchin captured the mood. Radicalising meant developing 'libertarian institutions' and 'democratizing the republic and radicalizing the democracy'. It meant stopping 'the centralization of economic and political power' by means of building a 'free municipal confederation of towns and cities and villages structured in a libertarian form' (Bookchin, 1985: 29). If the Zapatista insurrection of 1994 was not the seminal event for this reimagining of radical politics, the global protests it inspired were certainly an incubator for democratic practices through the social justice campaigns in the early 2000s.

Resisting the attempt of the Mexican government to remove land rights from Indigenous peoples (demanded as condition of Mexico's entry to the North American Free Trade Agreement (NAFTA)), the Zapatistas declared war on the Mexican government 'and the neoliberal economic politics implemented since 1982' (Gómez, 2016: 205). The demands they made against the government brought forth assemblages that self-consciously refused uniformity, championed autonomy and created global horizontal, leaderless networks based on affinity. As Gómez notes, the Zapatista demands for 'democracy, liberty, respect, land, dignity, and autonomy' that 'resonated throughout Mexico and the world' were not demands made of elites or even against them. In mobilising against the 'neoliberal Mexican state' the Zapatisatas importantly redefined 'their relationship to the state', the 'balance between politics, culture and rights and most notably, the meanings of citizenship and indigenous identity' (Gómez, 2016: 205). Drawing attention to the imperial and colonial drives of Western politics, liberal and socialist alike, the Zapatistas openly rejected the vanguard models of politics embedded in Western liberalism and orthodox socialism. As Staughton Lynd explains, the Zapatista's spokesperson, Subcomandante Marcos, refused to step into the shoes of the enlightened elite and also rejected the other dominant vanguardist model, proletarian dictatorship. Refusing to 'occupy the place from which all opinions will come, all the answers, all the routes, all the truth', Marcos denied the possibility of speaking and acting for 'the people' at all (quoted in Lynd and Grubacic, 2008: 8). His blunt message was 'I shit on all the revolutionary vanguards of this planet'. This was the message he gave to the 'Zapatistas' critics'

> We know that the Zapatistas don't have a place in the (dis) agreement of the revolutionary and vanguard organizations of the world, or in the rearguard. This doesn't make us feel bad. To the contrary, it satisfies us. We don't grieve when we recognize that our

ideas and proposals don't have an eternal horizon, and that there are ideas and proposals better suited than ours. So we have renounced the role of vanguards and to obligate anyone to accept our thinking over another argument wouldn't be the force of reason.

(Marcos, 2003)

'By the 1970s', Eladio Gómez argues of Chicana/o movements, 'the language of civil rights no longer sufficiently represented the political desires and demands of political movements'. These movements were 'now composed of constituencies that had new goals and targets and employed a range of different tactics' (Gómez, 2016: 4). Radicalism not only rediscovered its antiparliamentary roots but also asserted an antiprogrammatic politics.

What are its significant features? We think that there are three: one is intersectionality, a second is horizontalism and a third is direct action.

Associated with the work of Kimberlé Crenshaw, intersectionality has been understood in terms of the ways that formal power – notably law – operates to reinforce social oppressions (Crenshaw, 1989). In contrast, movement critique often involves contesting structural, but often informal and/or normalised, hierarchical relationships which marginalised groups experience as domination. The altered dynamic was apparent in the general statement of the Combahee River Collective. This talked about the commitment to struggle against 'racial, sexual, heterosexual and class oppression' and defined the Collective's 'particular task' as the development 'of integrated analysis and practice based upon the fact that the major systems of oppression are interlocking' (Combahee River Collective, 1977). At the moment of Reagan's victory, *Radical America* argued in a similar vein that the success of the radical left was that it had 'fumbled toward an understanding of the ways that class, race, and sex interact in American society, and the ways that the quality of individual lives reflects the contradictions of society as a whole' (1981, 3).

For left radicals, these relationships reflect historical power advantages that are entrenched in existing institutions. To give an example: in the late 1990s, activists involved in a wider US 'reclaim the media' campaign produced *The Declaration of Media Independence* in order 'to build meaningful participation from communities of color and indigenous communities to claim the undeniable right to communicate – to liberate our airwaves, networks and cultural spaces' (McGee et al., 1997: n.p.). The document emphasises the systematic exclusion of non-white and non-male voices from public communications, and the undemocratic character of existing constitutional provisions. The authors explain: 'We are interested in more than paternalistic conceptualizations of "access," more than paper rights, more than taking up space in a crowded boxcar along the corporate information highway'. Because media justice takes 'history, culture, privilege, and power' into account, the authors also seek 'new relationships to media and a new vision and reality for its ownership, control, access, and structure'. They continue:

> At the heart of our work is a rigorous power analysis, with race, class and gender at the center … We need a unique space so that our communities can move forward the visions and strategies for this work that are grounded in their own reality, which we believe will lead our society towards a truly free and democratic media.
>
> *(ibid.)*

The ambition, then, is not just to reconstitute formal decision-making bodies, but to reconstruct social relations within grassroots institutions.

The second feature is horizontalism. This, as Laura Grattan argues, is a term adopted from workers' movement in Latin American, *horizontalidad*, to describe 'experiments in constituting popular power' (Grattan, 2016: 163). Democracy is a central component of horizontalism, but as Maria Sitrin explains, it is distinguished by the quality of the relationships that flat organising fosters and entails.

> Horizontalidad is a new way of relating, based in affective politics and against all the implications of 'isms'. It is a dynamic social relationship. It is not an ideology or political program that must be met so as to create a new society or new idea. It is a break with these sorts of vertical ways of organizing and relating, and a break that is an opening.
>
> *(Sitrin, 2012: 32)*

Because of its antiprogrammatic bent, horizontalism is also associated with movement diversity. This was the idea that David Solnit (2004) advanced in the late 1990s: radicalism 'is a movement of movements, a network of networks, not merely intent on changing the world, but – as the Zapatistas describe – making a new one in which many worlds will fit'.

> Its common-sense principles and rebellious spirit have always been with us, but this new radicalism is a dramatic departure from previous efforts to effect change. It transcends simplistic generalizations about form or method: It has no international headquarters, no political party, no traditional leaders or politicians running for office, and no uniform ideology or ten-point platform. Rather, it takes many forms and expresses itself differently in different places and communities across the globe.
>
> *(Solnit: xii)*

The final component is direct action. Like intersectionality and horizontalism, this can be interpreted in different ways. The rejection of representative politics ties it to late nineteenth-century anarchistic radicalism. The Do-It-Ourselves ethics that direct action is also associated with is another feature common to historical and contemporary left radicalism. The innovation of modern radicalism, now one of its key components, is the idea that activists create the social relationships they want to promote directly by their activism. David Graeber describes it like this:

> When protestors in Seattle chanted 'this is what democracy looks like', they meant to be taken literally. In the best traditions of direct action, they not only confronted a certain form of power, exposing its mechanisms and attempting literally to stop it in its tracks: they did it in a way which demonstrated why the kind of social relations on which it is based were unnecessary. This is why the condescending remarks about the movement being dominated by a bunch of dumb kids with no coherent ideology completely missed the mark. The diversity was a function of the decentralized form of organization, and this organization *was* the movement's ideology.
>
> *(Graeber, 2004: 84)*

Solnit explained that this 'common theme' of the new radicalism is 'the practice of letting the means determine the ends'. He continued:

> Unless the community or world we want is built into and reflected by the struggle to achieve it, movements will always be disappointed by their efforts. Groups political parties, or movements that are hierarchically structured themselves cannot change the antidemocratic and hierarchical structures of governments, corporations, and corporate capitalism.
>
> *(Solnit, 2004: xiv)*

To conclude this section, our argument has been that there are strong continuities between the pro-anarchist forms of radicalism that emerged as antiradical movements in the late nineteenth century and the currents of ideas that emerged in the 1960s as self-consciously radical movements and which feed existing grassroots radicalism. Articulated as a response to Reaganism and animated by insurrections against the imposition of neo-liberal policies in degraded liberal democratic regimes, twenty-first-century left radicalism is a democratic movement. In this, it diverges from nineteenth-century pro-anarchist antiparliamentary, antiradical radicalism. Yet, it operates through associative principles that challenge the fundamental elitism of representative liberal democratic systems, as those pro-anarchist movements also did.

Radicalism and Populism

If present-day radicalism is frequently linked to a type of activism that is positively shaped by mistrust of elite politics and politicians, recent literature on populism demonstrates that such mistrust continues to have purchase on the right as well as the left. Populism describes an anti-elite politics that manoeuvres for power within existing institutional frameworks as well as for its dispersal without them. Populism, Grattan remarks, defies 'firm theoretical grasp' (2016:9). Tapping into a similar vein, Margaret Canovan notes that populism diverges from other 'ism's' in lacking a 'common history, ideology, programme or social base' (2004: 243). Like 'radicalism', it has often taken its meaning from its alignment with a shifting left-right political axis. Conflating radicalism with populism has often muddled political terminology. Yet, the observed closeness of the relationship between the two offers a useful framework for assessing contemporary left radicalism and facilitates consideration of what is at stake in the pro-democracy politics that left leaning radicals promote. In this section, we explore some recent approaches to populism in order to tease out the conceptual markers that will allow us to further these tasks.

One driver for recent analyses of populism is the desire to detach the concept from its specific manifestations. As Katsambekis explains, ideological conceptions derive core characteristics of the phenomenon from particular instances of it. Since the 1980s, populism has consequently been associated first and foremost with right-wing authoritarian movements that issue highly personalised appeals to advance illiberal or antiliberal social agendas. Canovan (2004: 242) acknowledged that her view of populism could be extended to include Tony Blair's New Labour and the regime of Hugo Chavez but she also took as her starting point Ross Perot, the 1992 US presidential candidate, Pim Fortuyn's List, Pauline Hanson's One Nation Party in Australia, Preston Manning's Reform Party in Canada, Jean Marie Le Pen's *Front National*, Jörg Haider's Freedom Party and Umberto Bossi's Northern League.

For Katsambekis, this approach wrongly attributes 'a predominantly moralist and homogenizing character' to populism (2016: 391). In order to provide a 'high level abstract' definition, he theorises populism discursively, employing Ernesto Laclau's work to identify two 'operational criteria' (Katsambekis, 2016: 391). Populism is 'articulated around the nodal point of "the people"' and it is rooted in a perception or 'representation of society' as 'predominantly antagonistic' and divided into 'two main blocs: the establishment' or elite and 'the people' (Stavrakakis and Katsambekis, 2014: 123). Kioupkiolis and Katsambekis similarly observe that a central concern of populist research is to discover the degree to which 'the people' emerges as a hegemonic or unified force and a second, related to it, turns on the character of the antagonisms that democratic politics is expected to negotiate (2014: 1–15).

This approach facilitates the close analysis of populist groups and parties and detaches populism from the exclusive association with antidemocratic mobilisations. It also facilitates the inclusion of movements within the populist family that do not rely on charismatic leaders or adopt top-down organisational structures. It frees populism from the contingent shifts in the left-right spectrum, and so alleviates the problems that arise from the default classifications of the phenomenon. Observing that 'populism' is often applied as a term of abuse by critics standing outside the movements they brand, Margaret Canovan was moved to designate the illiberal and antiliberal far right parties that had mushroomed in recent decades as 'New Populist', precisely in order to distinguish them from other pro-socialist or liberal progressive manifestations (ibid.: 243; 247). However, the discursive approach does not overcome entirely the tendency to moralise populism. For example, Roman Gerodimos's discourse analysis of Greek anarchist movement publications concludes that 'far left populism' is a 'vengeful, violent response' to representative systems that appropriate 'agency from the individual citizen' by appealing to a 'proto-totalitarian utopia' (Gerodimos, 2015: 622). Moreover, it risks leaving open the identification of the ideological trends within populism and their distinctive theoretical commitments.

Rather than present an abstract conception of populism, social movement historians have opened up its history to identify ideological trends within it. The driver here has been to challenge dominant associations with reactionary politics and models of charismatic leadership. Nineteenth-century Russian populism is a familiar touchstone for theorists casting about for an attractive alternative (Gerbaudo, 2017: 72–74),[5] though apart from the clue in the name, the links between this diverse set of revolutionary movements and contemporary activist groups are far from obvious. Populism's backstory has also been related more broadly as a history of radicalism. Dating the association back to the European wars of religion, 'the anti-Roman Catholic or Protestant agitations of the late middle ages and early modern period', Terrell Carver suggests that there is a long-standing relationship 'between radical politics and populist anti-elitism' (2009: 53). English Chartism is identified as another important early expression of radical populism (Canovan, 243). Calhoun describes nineteenth-century American radicalism as a 'populist politics' (ibid.: vii). Examining the history of the American People's Party which emerged in the late 1870s as the progenitor of modern US populism, Grattan uses the idea of 'aspirational populism' to ground populist politics in radical democracy (2016: 4). This form of populism is 'openly premised on its ability to reach ordinary people' and mobilises around a notion of democracy that 'is not defined by the existing institutions and procedures of liberal, capitalist governance' (ibid.: 11). Gerbaudo coins the term 'anarcho-populism' to draw radicalism and populism together.

This blending of radicalism with populism can be slotted comfortably into the discursive framework that Stavrakakis and Katsambekis propose, and it shines a light on the distinctive organisational features of modern left populist movements. Yet, the radical politics we discuss in this collection emerges as a form of anti-elitis politics that promotes special modes of participation and pursues particular logics of action to standard models of populism. When it is collapsed into populism, this difference is lost and the problem of conceptualising radicalism is only referred back to other ideologically contested ground.

To remedy this problem, we explore the models of populism that Margaret Canovan, Ernesto Laclau and Federico Finchelstein have developed. Not all these models fit within the high-level definition that Katsambekis recommends. Indeed, Finchelstein defines populism as a reactionary authoritarian politics. Yet in different ways, each reveals something about the ideological gap between left and right populisms and helps reveal how populism intersects with the radical traditions we want to explore.

Like Katsambekis, Canovan argues that populism's signature tune is the invocation of 'the people' to expose the illegitimacy of established elite power and the demand for its return to its rightful custodians (Canovan, 2004: 247). The demand springs from a commitment to the idea of popular sovereignty, an idea that lies at heart of democracy. Yet in populism, the demand picks at a tension between citizens and their representatives. Canovan argues that this tension is almost unavoidable because the mechanisms intended to integrate citizens into democracy are so complex and removed from everyday life that they appear designed to rob the people of its power. Populism thus expresses a disappointment in the existing political order and populists perpetually return to it in order to expose the variance between the promise of empowerment and the experience of representative democracy, and to assert the people's legitimate power against the sectional interests which appear to usurp it.

Canovan uses this general conception to argue that populism is at once antivanguardist and redemptive. Antivanguardism encapsulates a rejection of progressive liberal agendas, but it is systemically rather than ideologically specified: vanguardism is 'built into liberalism, socialism and feminism and is present even in modern conservatism' (ibid.: 246). Populist antivanguardism thus represents a rejection of the view that 'in the long run everyone is going to be liberated and made better off' because the experts who occupy positions of power are capable of 'showing the way to the rest' (ibid.). Populism redefines the progressive agenda by challenging the vanguard, preaching renewal through the replacement of the dishonest, inauthentic and self-serving professionals. This is populism's redemptive quality.

The second model, Ernesto Laclau's analysis of populism, centres on the construction of 'the people' as a social agent (Laclau, 2007: 118). While Canovan identifies three political meanings extending from the Latin, *populus* (the people as sovereign, as nations and as the commoners distinct from the ruling elite (2004: 247–8)), Laclau focuses on the antagonistic relationship between a *populus* and a *plebs*. A *populus* is the 'body of all citizens' and a *plebs* is the 'underprivileged'. Their relationship is not fixed either juridically or ideologically. For in populism, 'the people' has no given unity. Rather, Laclau argues, it is an identity in formation, which comes into being when 'a *plebs* claims to be the only legitimate *populus*', and 'wants to function as the totality of the community' (ibid.: 81).

The identity that populism brings about proceeds from the demands that the *plebs* advances. This can be understood both as a request and a claim; the dynamics of populist politics is explained by the transformation of one into the other (ibid.: 73). The process is driven by the failure or inability of institutions to meet a plurality of individual demands. The frustration bred by this failure hastens the symbolic unity of the people by triggering its identification of the existing order as the institutionalised 'other'. Laclau rejected the criticism that this account of populism reifies the people. Responding to Slavoj Žižek's accusation that it does, Laclau explained: where 'there is a more permanent tension between demands and what the institutional order can absorb ... requests tend to become claims, and there is a critique of institutions rather than just a passive acceptance of their legitimacy'. At the same time,

> when relations of equivalence between a plurality of demands go beyond a certain point, we have broad mobilizations against the institutional order as a whole. We have here the emergence of the people as a more universal historical actor, whose aims will necessarily crystallize around empty signifiers as objects of political identification.
>
> *(Laclau, 2006: 656)*

'The people' does not exist. It is constructed through its negativity in common opposition.

Leadership plays a central role in the process, but not in a conventional manner. Stating that populism 'concerns the centrality of the leader' (Laclau, 2007: 99), Laclau dismissed the familiar idea that leadership amounted to an elaborate form of stage-management or crowd manipulation. Structural analysis shows that when institutions collapse, the glue that once held society together also dissolves. New assemblages come into being but only through their naming. In other words, Laclau's contention was that the unity of 'the people' does not result from the internal development of the heterogeneous movements that coalesce around unfulfilled demands. Rather, it comes from its symbolic identification. In Laclau's words, 'the popular symbol or identity actually *constitutes* what it expresses through the process of its expression' (Laclau, 2007: 99).

Unlike Canovan and Laclau, Federico Finchelstein presents an explicitly ideological conception of populism. He examines the dominant modes of participation promoted in post-war populist governments. Historicising populism, Finchelstein distinguishes a pre-populist phase (running from Boulangism to the ascendancy of Karl Lueger, the early twentieth-century Viennese champion of political anti-Semitism) from its proto-populist expression in post-war Latin America. On this view, populism describes 'a form of authoritarian democracy for the post-war world; one that could adapt the totalitarian version of politics to the post-war hegemony of democratic representation' (Finchelstein, 2014: 467). The experience of fascism is central to populism's appearance and so too is the perceived threat of communism. But it differs from both. For Finchelstein, Peronism is populism's exemplar. The more-or-less marketised, egalitarian, participatory and nationalist regimes and movements that have emerged since the 1980s, not only in Latin America but also across Europe, are variations on this theme, often 'crude imitations of the original' capable of mimicking populism's 'rhetoric and rituals' but unable to produce the 'autarkic industrialisation' that once mobilised 'multiclass urban coalitions' (Schamis, 2006: 21; 34).

These three thick descriptions illuminate a facet of populism that can suit both left and right political agendas, but also help tease out the distinctiveness of the radicalism we explore.

To begin with Canovan, Benjamin Arditi has already drawn out the illiberal politics that extend from populist antivanguardism. As it plays fast and loose with established norms, using the idea of the people as its nodal point, Arditi argues that populism rounds on 'the political and economic establishments *and* elite values of the type held by opinion-formers in the academy and the media' (Arditi, 2004: 136). As it does so, it 'slips all too easily into authoritarian practices' by demonising the existing elite while keeping the concept of elitism intact. It brings 'a quasi-Hobbesian theory of political obligation' into play (ibid.: 142). The insight Arditi draws from Canovan's analysis is that elitist and anti-elitist populists easily turn a 'classic exchange of obedience for protection' into a 'passionate allegiance to a political grouping in exchange for jobs and security'. The people's champions become 'infallible sovereigns' whose decisions are 'unquestionable because they are theirs' (ibid.: 143).

As we have already seen, radical politics contains another option, an anarchistic option that distinguishes elite rule from egalitarian and democratic norms. The left-libertarian radicalisation of Canovan's antivanguardist thesis turns on the generalisation of the critique of the ruling class or elite. Instead of fixating on the disappointment with the progressive agendas that Canovan associates with vanguardism, left radicals challenge its technocratic premises. In this version of anti-elitism, there can be no replacement of corrupt elites with peoples' new, authentic champions, since the anarchistic option entails the eradication of the power distributions that elitism assumes. From this perspective, elitism does not represent the factional degeneration of democracy or the corruption of the constitution, but an

unacceptable alternative to democracy. A.J. Bauer's (2012) reflections on the incommen-
surability of Tea Party populism with the populism of the Occupy movement capture the
difference:

> The fundamental debate between the Tea Party and Occupy ... has little to do with
> the economy, per se, and even less to do with the horse race of contemporary electoral
> politics. Rather, it is a debate in which two movements, each responding to a perceived
> crisis in state legitimacy, seek to advance contrary alternative models of authority – one
> rooted in the historical founding of the nation (i.e. the Constitution) and the other in
> the contemporary and quotidian performance of political action in concert.

Laclau's account of populism and the construction of 'the people' illuminate a second
conceptual fracture. Arditi's work on Laclau's concept of leadership fleshes out one pole.
Recalling Laclau's arguments that 'the symbolic unification of the group around an individuality ... is inherent to the formation of a "people"', Arditi explores the relationship
between the *populus* and the *plebs* to theorise the concept of leadership. In accordance with
Laclau, he acknowledges that the naming of the people does not refer 'to actual persons but
to the name of the leader as a structural function' (Arditi, 2010: 490). Nevertheless, naming
points in the former direction for the name is necessarily a singularity, and singularity, as
Laclau put it, leads to 'identification of the unity of the group with the name of the leader'
(Laclau, 2007: 100). Likewise, populism does not 'lead automatically' to 'actual ruling',
but naming positions the *plebs* as the *populus*-to-be. The theorisation Arditi develops paints
populism as a contest for the right to rule in the name of the people, hinting at a process
of replacement rather than transformation. Indeed, Arditi compares the constitution of the
'signifying totality' to the formation of Hobbes' sovereign. Arditi notes that for Laclau, as
for Hobbes, 'without a leader there can be no "people" and therefore no politics either'
(Arditi, 2010: 490).

Miguel Vatter's analysis of plebeian politics captures an alternative to this conception of
leadership, one which resonates with anarchistic radicalism. This reconfigures the relationship of the *plebs* to the *populus*. While Laclau described the power relationship between the
populus, the 'body of all citizens' and a *plebs*, the 'underprivileged' as a rivalry for right to
function as the 'totality of the community', Vatter recovers a classical conception that recasts
this relationship philosophically as a disagreement about power and the rights it entails. In
a review of modern and classical republican democratic theory, Vatter admits the rivalry
between the *plebs* and the *populus* but argues that the *plebs* 'distinguish themselves from the
populus because they struggle for a form of power ... called "no-rule"'. This 'is exercised
in the absence of the distinction between those who govern and those who are governed'
(ibid.: 244) and it points to a distinctive form of anti-elitism. Plebeian politics 'understands
the constitution, and its division of powers, as that which makes possible a political life that
lies "beyond" the rule of the state and which places the achievement of equal law above the
achievement of unitary order'. Rejecting the 'consensus of the law', it advances the right to
'an equal power to make law' but not 'an equal right to rule' (Vatter, 2012: 256). The sovereignty that Arditi detects in Laclau's notion of leadership is absent in this conceptualisation.

The third fracture emerges from Finchelstein historical modelling of populism. This
usefully outlines an ideal type that has seven features:

> (i) an extremely sacralizing understanding of the political; (ii) a political theology that
> considers the people as being formed by those who follow a unique vertical leadership;

(iii) an idea of political antagonists as enemies who are potentially (or in fact) traitors to the nation; (iv) a understanding of the leader as a charismatic embodiment of the voice and desires of the nation as a whole; (v) a strong executive and the discursive, and often practical, dismissal of the legislative and judicial branches of government; (vi) a radical nationalism and an emphasis on popular culture, as opposed to other forms of culture that do not represent "national thought," (vii) and, finally, an attachment to a vertical form of electoral democracy that nonetheless rejects in practice dictatorial forms of government.

(ibid.: 468)

Finchelstein suggests that these features define populism. Scholars of populism like Katsambekis may disagree, yet the organisational model is instructive for our purposes. It is also possible to treat it as the institutional foil against which grassroots social movements have mobilised in the last fifty years. Insofar as the alternatives they advance can also be described as populist, as Katsambekis, Grattan and others argue, Finchelstein's ideal represents only one possible type. Either way, the associative principles practised by current radicals turn this model on its head.

Neither Grattan nor Gerbaudo lists the essential characteristics of an alternative model of populism; yet, both outline some of its key features. Grattan uses Occupy to think about aspirational democratic populism and identifies its hallmarks in the aversion to making demands, a commitment to horizontalism, a refusal to 'define the boundaries of *peoplehood*' and the adoption of consensus decision-making. Ploughing a similar furrow, Gerbaudo describes anarcho-populism as 'libertarian, participatory, or leaderless populism' that 'articulates the neo-anarchist method of *horizontality* and the populist demand for *sovereignty*, the mass ambition of populist movements, with the high premium placed on individual participation and creativity' (Gerbaudo, 2017: 7). Our construction of contemporary radicalism suggests a different theorisation, pointing to the rejection of sovereignty and the promotion of intersectionality consistent with horizontalism.

To sum up, populism can be understood as a discursive strategy that turns on the idea of 'the people' and which is rooted in a perceived antagonism between it and the elite. Yet, it can be inflected in different ways to advance conflicting normative principles. There are ideational trends within populism that resonate with the concerns and expressions of radical movements, but attention to the distinctly anarchistic strain in left radicalism helps us identify three lines of fracture. One turns on normative values, a second on the constitution of power and the third on the structure of governance. As will become clear from reading the chapters in this collection, these associative principles can be understood and applied in diverse ways. They do not exhaust the theoretical ground of contemporary left radicalism. Our argument is that they underpin the politics of contemporary radicalism and the democratic, egalitarian aspirations that analysts of populism have explored.

Notes

1 Maurice Block was an economist and member of the l'Académie des sciences morales et politiques. His publications include the *Dictionnaire de L'Administration Française* (2nd edn. Paris: Berger-Levrault, 1877); *Les Progès de la Science Économique Depuis Adam Smith* (Paris: Gullaumin, 1890); and 'The Progress of Economic Ideas in France', *Annals of the American Academy of Political and Social Science* (July 1893), pp. 1–33.
2 Kurt Zube (1905–91) also wrote under the name of Soleman. He was the author of *An Anarchist Manifesto* (1977) online at www.panarchy.org/solneman/solneman.html.

3 Joseph Lane (1851–1920) was involved in a number of radical clubs and projects before turning to socialism and anarchism in the 1880s. See Nicholas Walter's biography at https://libcom.org/history/lane-joseph-1851-1920.
4 William Morris (1834–96) founded the Socialist League in 1884 to advance revolutionary socialism. Influenced by anarchism, he identified as communist. See the biography at https://williammorrissociety.org/about-william-morris/.
5 Franco Venturi's *The Roots of Revolution* (1983 [1960]) is the seminal history of the nineteenth-century Russian movements which shaped revolutionary politics in the period between the 1825 Decembrist Revolt and the assassination of Tsar Alexander II in 1881.

References

Aiken, Henry D., *The Age of Ideology* (New York: Mentor, 1956).
Arditi, Benjamín, 'Populism as a Spectre of Democracy: A Response to Canovan', *Political Studies*, 52, (2004): 135–143.
Arditi, Benjamín, 'Populism is Hegemony is Politics? On Ernesto Laclau's *On Populist Reason*', *Constellations*, 17, (2010): 488–497.
Artzheimer, Kai, 'Radical Attitudes', in Bertand Badie, Dirk Berg-Scholsser and Leonardo Morlino (ed.) *International Encyclopedia of Political Science* (Thousand oaks, CA: Sage, 2011), pp. 2199–2202.
Bauer, A.J., 'This is What Democracy Feels Like: Tea Parties, Occupations and the Crisis of State Legitimacy', *Social Text Periscope* (December 2012) https://bit.ly/2IVS0ui [accessed 4 July 2018].
Berger, Dan, 'Exploding Limits in the 1970s', in Dan Berger (ed.) *The Hidden 1970s. Histories of Radicalism* (New Brunswick, NJ: Rutgers University, 2010), pp. 1–17.
Block, Maurice, 'Radicalism', in John Joseph Lalor (ed.) *Cyclopaedia of Political Science, Political Economy, and of the Political History of the United States*, vol. 3 Oath – Zollverein (Chicago: Melbert B Cary, 1884) https://bit.ly/2MIZof1 [accessed 4 July 2018].
Blumenfeld, Jacob, Bottici, Chiara and Critchley, Simon, *The Anarchist Turn* (London: Pluto, 2013).
Bookchin, Murray, *Radicalising Democracy*. A Timely Interview with Murray Bookchin conducted by the editors of *Kick It Over* magazine (Vermont: Green Program Project, 1985), pp. 1–10.
Buhle, Mari Jo, 'Wobblies and Draftees: The I.W.W.'s Wartime Dilemma, 1917–1918', *Radical America*, II (1), 1967: 6–18.
Burgess, Glenn, 'A Matter of Context: "Radicalism" and the English Revolution' in Mario Caricchio and Giovanni Tarantino (eds.) *Cromohs Virtual Seminars. Recent Historiographical Trends of the British Studies (17th – 18th Centuries)*, 2006–2007. https://bit.ly/2z6uBqE [accessed 4 July 2018].
Burgess, Glenn and Matthew Festenstein (eds.), *English Radicalism, 1550–1850* (Cambridge: Cambridge University Press, 2007).
Butler, Samuel, *The Notebooks of Samuel Butler*, ed. Henry Festing Jones (Auckland: The Floating Press, 2014 [1912]), pp. 112–113.
Calhoun, Craig, *The Roots of Radicalism. Tradition, the Public Sphere, and Early Nineteenth-Century Social Movements* (Chicago and London: Chicago University Press, 2012).
Canovan, Margaret, 'Populism for Political Theorists?', *Journal of Political Ideologies*, 9 (3), (2004): 241–252.
Capoccia, Giovanni, *Defending Democracy: Reactions to Extremism in Interwar Europe* (Baltimore and London: The Johns Hopkins University Press, 2005).
Combahee River Collective, 'Combahee River Collective Statement' (1977) https://combaheerivercollective.weebly.com/the-combahee-river-collective-statement.html [accessed 4 July 2018].
Copsey, Nigel, 'The Radical Right and Fascism', in Jens Rydgren (ed.) *The Oxford Handbook of the Radical Right* (2016) https://bit.ly/2IS38sc [accessed 4 July 2018].
Cornell, Andrew, *Unruly Equality: U.S. Anarchism in the 20th Century* (Oakland: University of California Press, 2010).
Crenshaw, Kimberlé, 'Demarginalising the Intersection of Race and Sex: A Black Feminist Critique of Antidiscrimination Doctrine, Feminist Theory and Antiracist Politics', *University of Chicago Legal Forum*, 140, (1989): 139–167.
Dahl, Göran, *Radical Conservatism and the Future of Politics* (London: Sage, 1999).
della Porta, Donatella. *Social Movements in Times of Austerity* (Cambridge: Polity, 2015).
Detwiler, Bruce, *Nietzsche and the Politics of Aristocratic Radicalism* (Chicago and London: Chicago University Press, 1990).

Dictionnaire de la Langue Française v. 4 (Paris: Hachette, 1873) online at https://artflsrv03.uchicago.edu/philologic4/publicdicos/navigate/17/713/?byte=1074813 [accessed 4 July 2018].

Dolowitz, David, David Marsh, Fiona O'Neill and David Richards, 'Thatcherism and the 3 'R's': Radicalism, Realism and Rhetoric in the Third Term of the Thatcher Government', *Parliamentary Affairs*, 49, (1996): 455–469.

Downey, John, 'Participation and/or Deliberation? The Internet as a Tool for Achieving Radical Democratic Aims', in Lincoln Dahlberg and Eugenia Siapera (eds.) *Radical Democracy and the Internet* (Basingstoke: Palgrave Macmillan, 2005), pp. 108–127.

Epstein, B., 'Anarchism and the Anti-Globalization Movement', *Monthly Review*, 53 (4), (2001): 1–14.

Finchelstein, Federico, 'Returning Populism to History', *Constellations*, 21 (4), (2014): 467–482.

Flesher Fominaya, Cristina, *Social Movements and Globalization: How Protests, Occupations and Uprisings are Changing the World* (Basingstoke: Palgrave/Macmillan, 2014).

Gerbaudo, Paolo, *The Mask and the Flag: Populism, Citizenship and Global Protest* (London: Hurst and Company, 2017).

Gerodimos, Roman, 'The Ideology of Far Left Populism in Greece: Blame, Victimhood and Revenge in the Discourse of Greek Anarchists', *Political Studies*, 63, (2015): 608–625.

Gollan, Robin, *Radical and Working Class Politics: A Study of Eastern Australia, 1850–1910* (Victoria: Melbourne University Press, 1967).

Gómez, Eladio, *The Revolutionary Imaginations of Greater Mexico: Chicana/o Radicalism, Solidarity Politics, and Latin American Social Movements* (Austin: University of Texas Press, 2016).

Goodman, Paul, *The Moral Ambiguity of America. The Massey Lectures for 1966* (Toronto: CBC Publications, 1967).

Graeber, David, *Fragments of an Anarchist Anthropology* (Chicago: Prickly Paradigm Press, 2004).

Graeber, David, *The Democracy Project* (London: Allen Lane, 2013).

Grattan, Laura, *Populism's Power: Radical Grassroots Democracy in America* (New York: Oxford University Press, 2016).

Halévy, Elie, *The Growth of Philosophic Radicalism*, trans. Mary Morris (London: Faber & Faber, 1928).

James, CLR, 'Document: CLR James on the Origins', *Radical America*, II (4), (1968): 20–29.

Katsambekis, Giorgos, 'Radical Left Populism in Contemporary Greece: Syriza's Trajectory from Minoritarian Opposition to Power', *Constellations*, 23 (3), (2016): 391–403.

Kioupkiolis, Alexandros and Giorgos Katsambekis (eds.), *Radical Democracy and Collective Movements Today. The Biopolitics of the Multitude versus the Hegemony of the People*, (London: Routledge, 2014), pp. 1–15.

Laclau, Ernesto, 'Why Constructing a People Is the Main Task of Radical Politics', *Critical Inquiry*, 32, (2006): 646–680.

Laclau, Ernesto, *On Populist Reason* (London: Verso, 2007 [2005]).

Lane, Joseph, *An Anti-Statist Communist Manifesto* (1887), https://libcom.org/library/an-anti-statist-communist-manifesto-joseph-lane [accessed 4 July 2018].

Lynd, Staughton and Andrej Grubacic, *Wobblies & Zapatistas. Conversations on Anarchism, Marxism and Radical History* (Oakland, CA: PM Press, 2008).

Maeckelbergh, Marianne, 'Occupy the US: Musing on Horizontal Decision-Making and Bureaucracy', reprinted from *STIR* in *Kosmos Journal for Global Transformation* (Spring 2012) https://bit.ly/2tSGoU7 [accessed 4 July 2018].

Marcos, Subcomandante, *I Shit on all the Revolutionary Vanguards of this Planet*, Communique from the Zapatista National Liberation Army, Mexico to Euskadi Ta Askatasuna, Basque Country (January 2003) https://bit.ly/2Ad2Uvd [accessed 4 July 2018].

McGee, Art, Thenmozhi Soundararajan, Mekani Themba-Nizon, Malkia Cyril and Jeff Perlstein, 'Declaration of Media Independence. Media Justice: Media for All the People', in chickpea (comp.) *Radical Ladies and Media Justice*, (n.p., 1997).

Morris, William, 'To Genuine Radicals', (1884) in Nicholas Salmon (ed.) *Contributions to Justice and Commonweal, 1883–1890* (Bristol: Thoemmes Press, 1994), pp. 47–53.

Morris, William, 'Feudal England', *Signs of Change* (1887) www.marxists.org/archive/morris/works/1888/signs/chapters/chapter3.htm [accessed 4 July 2018].

Radical America, 'Introduction', 15 (1&2), (1981): 3–5.

Radical America, 'Introduction', 14 (6), (1980): 2–5.

Rochefort, Henri, 'Radicalism in France', *The North American Review*, CXLIII (357), (1886): 151–164.

Schamis, Hector, 'Populism, Socialism, and Democratic Institutions', *Journal of Democracy*, 17, (2006): 20–34.

Schwartzmantel, John, *The Age of Ideology: Political Ideologies from the American Revolution to Postmodern Times* (New York: New York University Press, 1998).

Scriven, Tom, *Popular Virtue: Continuity and Change in Radical Moral Politics* (Manchester: Manchester University Press, 2017).

Sitrin, Maria, 'Horizontalidad and Territory in the Occupy Movements', *Tikkun*, 27 (2), (2012): 32–63.

Solnit, David, 'Introduction – The New Radicalism: Uprooting the System and Building a Better World', in David Solnit (ed.) *Globalize Liberation: How to Uproot the System and Build a Better World* (San Francisco: City Lights Books, 2004), pp. xi–xxiv.

Stavrakakis, Yannis and Giorgos Katsambekis, 'Left-Wing Populism in the European Periphery: the Case of SYRIZA', *Journal of Political Ideologies*, 19, (2014): 119–142.

Szolucha, Anna, *Real Democracy and the Occupy Movement. No Stable Ground* (London: Routledge, 2017).

The Islamic Supreme Council of America, 'Islamic Radicalism: Its Wahhabi Roots and Current Representation'. https://bit.ly/1E1YEKQ [accessed 4 July 2018].

Thomas, William, *The Philosophic Radicals: Nine Studies in Theory and Practice, 1817–41* (Oxford: Oxford University Press, 1979).

Vatter, Miguel, 'The Quarrel Between Populism and Republicanism: Machiavelli and the Antinomies of Plebeian Politics', *Contemporary Political Theory*, 11 (3), (2012): 242–263.

Venturi, Franco, *The Roots of Revolution*, trans. Francis Haskell (Chicago: University of Chicago Press, 1983 [1960]).

Webster's Dictionary 1828, 'Radical' https://bit.ly/2tSyJ8n [accessed 4 July 2018].

Zube, Kurt (ed.), *Radikaler Geist* (Berlin: Radikaler Geist, 1930).

SECTION 1

Critiques

We begin the collection with a section on critique in order to identify some of the antagonisms and oppositions that animate radical politics. Anti-oppression politics is often used as the umbrella term to describe this critique (Désil, Kaur, Kinsman: n.d.), and this section explores some of its facets. How is oppression understood by activists, and how do their critiques of domination and inequality complement and challenge one another? These are the central concerns linking chapters in this first section.

As it turned its interest in the 1990s to the sweeping changes associated with globalisation, political sociology tended to rest content with the truism that class politics and mass parties had given way to a disjointed 'politics of identity'. According to this logic, the class antagonisms rooted in material demands and/or revolutionary socialism had given way to a landscape populated by groups seeking redress for 'post-material' grievances and demanding equal institutional treatment and sociocultural recognition within capitalist democracy.

The eruption of a globally networked movement against neo-liberalism around the turn of the millennium revealed that other more significant processes had been taking place. On the one hand, movements of rural and urban workers in the global south, who mobilised against multinational corporations and neo-liberal policies, were often integrating their original forms of feminist, ecological and epistemological critiques; hence, while material and revolutionary demands were far from abandoned, they were no longer couched in traditional Marxian formulations. On the other hand, movements associated with 'post material' politics – from environmentalism to LGBT+ rights and beyond – had in fact been among the first to articulate how systemic features of capitalism, as well as discrete concentrations of corporate power, had shaped the conditions against which their protests, direct actions and campaigning were directed.

Global activist networks have consequently displayed an increased awareness of the interdependence of their struggles and the intersection among different axes of oppression (Shannon and Rogue, 2009; Jeppesen, Kruzynksi, Sarrasin and Breton, 2014). The chapters in this section clearly demonstrate the traction which these perspectives have gained, even as radicals continuing to focus on particular causes or grievances in their practical work.

In the opening chapter, a collectively written contribution, the London-based Irish diasporic group Speaking of IMELDA reflects on its direct-action campaigns for **reproductive rights** in Northern Ireland and the Republic of Ireland. Providing an overview of the group's history and explaining some of the actions the collective have undertaken, Speaking of IMELDA uses the idea of 'cutting loose' to expound a form of radical feminism that challenges gendered cultural constructions of the home state and experiments with do-it-ourselves aesthetics to develop creatively disruptive and empowering actions. Irish republican history is an important touchstone for Speaking of IMELDA's radicalism, and the discussion shows how the collective interrogate the past and its disappointments to push revolutionary initiatives in the present and for the future.

Will Boisseau offers a discussion of the **animal liberation** movement, which takes direct action to save the lives of animals while causing economic damage to the industries that exploit them. Having grown rapidly since its beginnings in the late 1960s, radical animal liberation became a significant threat to corporations and its activists were heavily repressed in the 2000s. The chapter considers the movement's principal concerns and action repertoires, before turning to the main concepts and political theories which relate to animal liberation including ecofeminism, anarchism and critical animal studies. Despite its advances and risks, animal liberation remains dogged with accusations that it represents bourgeois reformism and the preoccupations of privileged individuals. In response, the newest animal liberation activism focuses on concepts such as total liberation and the intersectionality of human, animal and Earth liberation.

In his chapter on **antifascism**, M. Testa locates its radical manifestations among activists who both reject the ballot box effort to outvote fascism and disdain state intervention, knowing that repression of fascists will invariably extend to their militant opponents. Radical antifascists' primary political space is on the viciously contested streets of their towns and cities, but while their principal concern is to physically smash fascist mobilisation, they also recognise the need to organise within their communities. Here, the task is to put forward arguments based on class rather than race which show how housing shortages, privatisation and underemployment are not the result of immigration but of vindictive austerity measures. Militant antifascism therefore involves an openness to cooperation with people whose politics may not be the same, but to whom the threat of fascism is no less dangerous.

Chris Rossdale outlines a history of **antimilitarism** and discusses the politics of a number of antimilitarist groups to demonstrate the intersectional politics of contemporary antimilitarism. Antimilitarism is analysed as a network of institutions, a body of values and a set of practices. It draws on a range of traditions: anarchist, feminist, religious, anti-imperialist and antiracist. The chapter shows how anticolonial and antiracist campaigns intersect with antimilitarist peace activism and how religiously rooted pacifism fuels nonviolent grassroots direct action. The chapter closes with two case studies – resistance to US military bases in Okinawa and the Trident Ploughshares movement against nuclear weapons – which show how the theoretical lineages identified earlier find concrete expression.

Bonnie Burstow examines **antipsychiatry**, psychiatric survivor and mad movements from an anarchist perspective and as part of an intersectional anti-oppression politics. Sensitive to the differences between these movements, the chapter explores their radicalism by (i) developing an antiauthoritarian critique of state-sanctioned professional practice and normalising discourses and (ii) rejecting reforms directed at mitigating the worst excesses of established psychiatric practice. Reflecting on the experience of antisanism activism, the chapter recommends a model of radical activism that synthesises anarchist cultural values with the adoption of strategic goals. And looking at the challenges that antipsychiatry presents to other radical movements, it links radicalism to the willingness to confront the power-relationships that emerge in the intersections of anti-oppression politics.

Leah Temper examines radical **climate justice** politics – a network of anticapitalist and anti-extractivist movements fighting for 'System change, not Climate Change'. Climate justice activism includes struggles against oil and gas extraction, coal plants and fracking, organising by the victims of floods, hurricanes and tornadoes, as well as movements fighting for food sovereignty and access to resources. Based on the understanding that those least responsible for the production of greenhouse gases are the most affected by the disruption and chaos they cause, this radical approach draws attention to the colonial and gendered dimensions of the climate crisis. Instead of the false techno-fixes poised to further exacerbate these inequalities, climate justice prompts us towards the proactive construction of a post-petroleum society and a consideration of how the economy, energy, food and transportation systems can be radically rethought and redesigned.

David Pellow focuses on the possibilities for a deepening and broadening of social justice politics within radical **environmentalism**. Based on data gathered from fieldwork, interviews, archival analysis and participant observation, he argues that while environmental movements have a long and troubled history of racism, nativism, heteropatriarchy and classism (to say nothing of misanthropy!), there are significant segments of these social formations that have invested time and energy into reimagining their work, including the very framing of the problem of the environmental crisis, along with strategies and tactics to address it. The chapter suggests new ways of defining environmental justice politics, and new ways of framing democracy and the polity itself.

In her chapter on radical **research**, Rebecca Fisher discusses the work of Corporate Watch – an independent research and publishing group which campaigns against corporate power and spreads 'information for action'. The group approaches its research with a different ethic to the one prevalent in institutional contexts – from academia and media to NGOs and think tanks. This ethic is defined by its commitment to, and position within, struggles for radical social change, and by affirming the independence that permits such an engagement. Rather than provide seemingly neutral analysis, expert advice or compromised lobbying, Corporate Watch aims to take an active, autonomous and non-vanguardist role within radical struggles.

References

Désil, J., Kaur, K. and Kinsman, G., 'Anti-Oppression Politics in Anti-Capitalist Movements', *Upping the Anti* (1) online at http://uppingtheanti.org/journal/article/01-anti-oppression-politics-in-anti-capitalist-movements/.

Jeppesen, S., Kruzynksi, A., Sarrasin, R. and Breton, É., Collective Autonomy Research Group/ CRAC, The Anarchist Commons', *Ephemera*, 14 (4), 2015.

Shannon, D. and Rogue, J., 'Refusing to Wait: Anarchism and Intersectionality' (2009) at http://anarkismo.net/article/14923.

1.1

A RADICAL FEMINIST DIASPORA

Speaking of IMELDA, Reproductive Justice and Ireland

Speaking of IMELDA

Introduction

This chapter situates the London-based, direct-action performance collective, Speaking of IMELDA, within a tradition of alternative feminist Irish diasporic activist groups in Britain who have campaigned for reproductive rights. By contextualising Irish feminist activist collectives in London from the 1970s to the present day, we argue for the political efficacy and vitality of the Irish feminist diaspora. Written collectively by members of Speaking of IMELDA, the chapter maps the actions we have undertaken to challenge the restrictions on abortion in both the Republic of Ireland and Northern Ireland. We further detail our attempts to raise awareness in Britain of the inequity experienced by Northern Irish women, due to the rigid opposition to abortion maintained by dominant political parties in Northern Ireland and the British government's failure to uphold equal access to reproductive healthcare to all UK citizens.

We frame our actions as being influenced by what we are terming a 'feminist diasporic political radicalism' – a form of radicalism that is informed by being 'cut loose' from the gendered cultural constructs of the home state, enabled by our geographical positioning outside of the island of Ireland. We further situate feminist diasporic political radicalism as being informed by the untethered freedom of 'loose women' within our collective. We theorise the idea of 'loose women' not only in terms of the looseness of our methods and aesthetics, but in how, within our actions, this sense of looseness informs the specific approaches we use to challenge oppressive cultural ideals of femininity. We argue that our actions are a messy alliance between art and politics; our loosely framed DIO (Do It Ourselves) aesthetics spill out crudely from artistic representation into the political realm where they demand a response.

This chapter traces the influence of feminist diasporic political radicalism on activist strategies. Throughout the chapter, we outline the strategies we have devised to act in solidarity with the ongoing battle for reproductive rights across the island of Ireland. First, we outline the origins of Speaking of IMELDA and situate our work in relation to the past Irish diasporic feminist activist groups that originated in Britain, in particular those focused on reproductive rights. We then explain how our work responds to the religious fundamentalism influencing legislative restrictions on reproductive rights in Northern Ireland and the Republic of Ireland. Following this, a discussion of our use of direct action and performance demonstrates the ways in which the concept of 'looseness' is central to the methods we use to subvert the constructs of femininity associated with Ireland. Finally, we outline how the positioning of the tactics deployed by Speaking of IMELDA within the intersection between culture and politics upsets the cultural hegemony of both Irish states.

Speaking of IMELDA is a collective comprised largely, although not exclusively, of Irish women living in London. Our collective is comprised of a diversity of women of all ages and from many walks of life, including those working in education, the creative arts, health, social care and activism. Our collective history of activism spans reproductive rights, antiracism, LGBTQI rights, anti-austerity movements in England and Ireland, Irish Travellers' rights, support for refugees and migrants and formerly challenging the human rights abuses by the British Army in Northern Ireland, including supporting the rights of women political prisoners during the Troubles (1968–98).

The group was initiated by women who had emigrated from Ireland since 2000 with the aim of challenging the legislative restrictions on abortion across the island of Ireland. In the Republic of Ireland, the Eighth Amendment to the Irish constitution, which equates the life of a pregnant person with that of an unborn foetus from conception, exerts a 'chilling effect' on the reproductive rights of women in Ireland (Amnesty International, 2015: 8). In the North, access to reproductive health services is also heavily restricted, due to the failure of the British state to extend the 1967 Abortion Act to Northern Ireland, alongside continued political opposition to abortion within the Northern Ireland Executive.

Speaking of IMELDA was formally established in December 2013 following a meeting at which Ann Rossiter was invited to speak about her activist history. A member of Speaking of IMELDA since that meeting, Rossiter is also a former member of Irish Women's Abortion Support Group (IWASG), a long-time abortion rights activist and the author of *Ireland's Hidden Diaspora: The Abortion Trail and the Making of a London Irish Underground 1980–2000* (2009).

Maintaining Links to the Past: Irish Feminist Diasporic Radicalism

Placing our actions in a historical context has been central to the ethos of Speaking of IMELDA. From the outset, we have sought to retrieve and activate the work of our feminist predecessors. For example, the name Imelda, a common girl's name in Ireland, recalls the work of IWASG – a group of activists who provided support to women travelling from Ireland to England for abortions between 1980 and 2000. IWASG, discussed in more depth later, used Imelda as a secret code word for abortion. This code word enabled Irish women travelling to England for abortions to keep their plans secret so as to avoid stigma and, up until 1992 when the right to travel for abortion was implemented, criminalisation. We use IMELDA as an anagram for 'Ireland Making England the Legal Destination for Abortion'. We also wear the colour red in tribute to the work of IWASG, whose members sometimes wore a red skirt, so as to be identifiable, when collecting women travelling for abortion at train stations and airport terminals. Notably, we also harness the association of red with danger and the deviant sexuality of 'loose women'. We see maintaining these links to the past as crucial to removing the long-standing barriers to progress on reproductive rights in Ireland. Such connections with past activism also make us proud and give us the commitment to continue the work.

Up to 6,000 women from the Irish region continually travel to the UK each year to access abortion services, often at considerable expense and stress. Furthermore, in 2013, the Irish Republic implemented a fourteen-year prison sentence for women who have abortions in

Ireland illegally. This has dire consequences for women who take pro-abortive medication because they cannot afford to travel or are not permitted to leave the country. We want women in the Irish region, and more widely, to have control over their own bodies and access to medical services which support their choices. In reclaiming the name IMELDA, we wish to act in solidarity with women's groups who have sought to counteract the inhumanity of state legislation in both Northern and Southern Ireland, while operating against the silencing and shaming of women who have abortions.

Irish feminist activity in Britain stretches back to the early 1880s when branches of the Ladies Land League, a proto-feminist organisation fighting against eviction and for land reform in Ireland, were established in south London (Russell, 1987). Although there were many factors and influences that differentiated the Irish and British social formations, not least Ireland's colonial position versus Britain's imperial one (Cullen Owens, 1984:103–12), interaction continued across the Irish Sea, and in Britain itself between native British women and Irish émigrés, as feminist activism evolved into a social movement in the early 1900s before the advent of First World War, Ireland's Rising against British rule in 1916 and the War of Independence, 1919–21. These interactions between first-wave feminists were notably in the areas of female suffrage and labouring women's rights (Sylvia Pankhurst being a key figure on the British side), thereby creating an early form of transnational feminism in action (Murphy, 1989). This was also visible in East London suffragette newspaper *The Women's Dreadnought* (Pankhurst, 2016), it being the first British newspaper to report on the Dublin 1916 Rising and its aftermath.

With the arrival of second-wave feminism in the late 1960s and early 1970s, an Irish diasporic feminist identity took shape within the broad parameters of the Women's Liberation Movement in Britain, and against the backdrop of three decades of the Northern Ireland 'Troubles' (1968–98). Once again, there were factors and influences differentiating Irish and British feminism. While bread-and-butter issues, such as reproductive rights, childcare, equal pay and sexuality, were common to both, Irish feminism also faced the fallout from an armed conflict in Northern Ireland including British military occupation (28,000 troops at its peak in 1972), a bombing campaign carried out mainly by the Irish Republican Army (IRA) in Northern Ireland and on the British mainland, and large-scale incarceration of men and women in Northern Irish and British jails. Following the descent into armed conflict in Northern Ireland, and coinciding with the rise of the women's movement in the western world, feminist groups, such as the Women on Ireland Collective (1973–74), the Women and Ireland Group (1976–80) and the London Armagh Coordinating Group (1980–87), were initiated mainly by Irish women around Britain. Primarily, their work involved highlighting the lives of republican women in their shattered communities in the conflict zones in Northern Ireland, drawing attention to the treatment of women political prisoners, especially the practice of strip searching as a form of sexual harassment ('Strip Searches in Armagh Jail', Women Behind the Wire, London Armagh Group, 1984) campaigning against the Prevention of Terrorism Act (1974) and for the removal of British troops (Irish Women at War: Papers from the Feminism and Ireland Workshop, 1977).

These feminist groups were open to all regardless of nationality or ethnicity. Non-Irish feminists joined with their Irish sisters in campaigning in the British movement on the various issues related to the Troubles, but their collective efforts failed to make a significant impact due to ideological differences over militant nationalism, colonialism and religion (Rossiter, 2017: 153–68). Despite international slogans of the movement like 'sisterhood is global', a lesson well learned from the experience was that unless a global sisterhood is consciously placed in its historical and political context, as it is in the notion of 'intersectionality' (the recognition of difference and the interlocking of systems of oppression), feminist solidarity is 'shaky at best' (Delmar, 1972; Mohanty, 1992: 74–92). After the Socialist Feminist Conference on Imperialism and Women's Oppression Worldwide (1980) and the mid-1980s shift towards embracing a non-unitary experience of womanhood (Wallsgrove, 1985), socialist feminism was better able to relate to the multiplicity of issues stemming from the Troubles and the Irish national question.

The Irish Women's Abortion Support Group (IWASG) 1980–2000

The formation of the IWASG (1980–2000) and the London-Irish Women's Centre (1983–2012), both exclusive to Irish women, can be viewed as a response to the marginalisation of Irish issues in the wider feminist movement and to the 'othering' and essentialising of Irish people in Britain during the Troubles. The London-Irish Women's Centre, with recognition and support from bodies such as the Greater London Council, set about articulating women's perspectives, ultimately contributing to the shaping of an 'alternative Irish community' in Britain (Rossiter, 2009: 53–74).

The London-based Irish feminists who set up the voluntary IWASG in 1980 were following a tradition of philanthropic work at ports and railway stations in Britain established in the latter half of the nineteenth century. While lay and religious welfare agencies such as the Legion of Mary (founded 1921) provided unaccompanied Irish females with practical support, emanating primarily from a desire to flag up the grave moral dangers to which women would be exposed in their new lives (Redmond, 2015: 55–76), IWASG's concern was directed specifically at pregnant women seeking a safe and legal abortion under the 1967 British Abortion Act. Such philanthropic and advocacy work has been described variously as feminist voluntarism and 'civic' or 'practice-focused' feminism (Fletcher, 2015). Importantly, it implicitly subverted the obdurate, anti-abortion stance of both Irish states in thrall to the Catholic and fundamentalist Protestant churches.

IWASG was a non-hierarchical feminist collective whose members defined themselves as lesbian, bi or straight, from Catholic or Protestant backgrounds. They had working-class, middle-class and rural origins in Northern Ireland or the Republic, or were British-born second- and third-generation Irish. The all-Irish nature of the membership, rather than being ethnically exclusive by design, was a response to abortion seekers' reports of the judgemental attitudes of their non-Irish hosts – an experience all too common during the thirty years of the Irish Troubles and the one that would be recognised by members of the Muslim community today (Casey, 2017: 213–26; Finch, 2017: 137–52), although probably not by Irish migrants of the Celtic Tiger period. The Celtic Tiger refers to the unprecedented economic boom during the 1990s, which followed the Republic of Ireland's entry into the European Economic Community in 1973 (now the European Union). During this period, wealth was generated by the provision of tax breaks to foreign, largely American, companies who set up in the Republic, alongside a disproportionate inflation in the housing market. This period of prosperity ended with the global economic crisis in 2008 and the collapse of the banks in the Irish Republic in 2010, which led to the acceptance of International Monetary Fund (IMF) and EU bailouts.

The services provided by IWASG ranged from helping to organise travel and escorting abortion seekers to and from transport hubs, to making clinic appointments, sorting out fees and providing hospitality and overnight accommodation in IWASG members' homes. In addition to fundraising and practical support, a lot of campaigning was directed at securing legal changes in Ireland and the UK. By 2000, the combined impact of the Internet, mobile phones, the widespread availability of credit and the advent of cheap airline travel eliminated the demand for help. IWASG closed down. In 2004, ESCORT, a Liverpool-based service, set up in 1988, providing escort and accommodation services (Fletcher, 2015), also ceased. However, the economic crash of 2008 impacted heavily on women with unwanted pregnancies in Northern Ireland and the Republic. The Abortion Support Network was formed in London in 2009 in response to renewed cries for help and support (ASN, 2016). Although not specifically an 'Irish' organisation, the Abortion Support Network dealing mostly with Irish clients.

The positioning of Irish feminist groups in Britain allows for a greater freedom to critique the boundaries of women's roles in Ireland. Strategically, we form a diasporic radicalism. The four current London-based voluntary groups concerned with Irish women's reproductive rights – the Abortion Support Network, Speaking of IMELDA, the London-Irish Feminist Network (founded after the London-Irish Women's Centre closed in 2012) and the London-Irish Abortion Rights Campaign (formed in 2016) – have come into existence in the third-wave feminist environment. All use social media extensively and are connected with pro-choice activists in both parts of Ireland and across the world.

Raising a Radical Diasporic Voice Against the Moral Regulation of Women in the Republic of Ireland

While Speaking of IMELDA has duly harnessed social media to heighten our message, we prioritise public interventions that are direct, loud and unapologetic. These actions have sought to radically challenge the stereotypes of the quiet and pure Irish woman so imposed by religious forces. For instance, in our first action, Speaking of IMELDA acted as dissonant voices intervening in a conference in Camden attended by Catholic clergy on the subject of faith and the Irish diaspora on International Women's Day 2014. Here, IMELDA called upon the so-called 'radical and engaged' church to take action on the silenced – but daily – reality of pregnant people travelling abroad to access reproductive healthcare (8 March 2014 action, 2014). Not only did this action make vocal a rarely spoken issue, it also infiltrated a religious space where women were able to serve an alternative role to that predetermined by church teachings – that of activists, autonomous over their own bodies and selves.

Since the formation of the Irish State in 1922, the Catholic Church has been a dominant political force in the Republic of Ireland. The interaction of church and state has not only imposed Catholic teaching on all matters of policy – from education, to social security, to health – it has also heavily infiltrated the social and cultural life of the Irish populace. This has translated into the reverence of domesticity and subservience in women, motherhood being valorised as a woman's primary sexual purpose. Female purity, as Fischer (2016) notes, became conflated with national identity. The Irish woman did not just represent herself; she was the symbol of a pure, superior and – notably – Catholic Ireland. Any deviation from this archetype was seen to tarnish not only the individual, but also to taint the idealised nation state, which had been carefully constructed by the church. As such, 'deviant' acts – particularly those concerning female sexuality – were shrouded in guilt, shame and secrecy. The Magdalene Laundries, mother and baby homes and non-consensual practices of symphysiotomy (an outdated surgical procedure whereby the pelvis is severed during childbirth that was replaced by caesarian section, which Catholic doctors revived in the Republic between the 1940s and 1980s) were emblematic of this systematic maltreatment of women (Inglis, 2005; Inglis and MacKeogh, 2012). Inglis and MacKeogh (2012) note that, despite some waning of the Church's influence, its long domination has left deep and enduring scars.

Although the country has undergone significant social and economic shifts in recent decades (for example, achieving equal marriage in 2015), restrictions on reproductive rights remain the stronghold of a patriarchal, punitive and largely Catholic state. Such ideology is enshrined in the Irish Constitution, which since 1983 has endowed the foetus with the same rights as those of the pregnant person, charging the state with the vindication of the foetus' rights. In practice, 'vindication' sanctioned, among other things, a court injunction in 1992, which forced an underage victim of rape, whose family had taken her to the UK for an abortion, to return to Ireland (known as the X-case). This court injunction was challenged on the grounds that the fourteen-year-old was suicidal as a result of the pregnancy. Although the Supreme Court ruling following the X-case asserted that suicide counted as a threat to life, this was not enacted in law until 2013 under The Protection of Life During Pregnancy Act (Houses of the Oireachtas, 2013). Notably, this Act also put in place a fourteen-year prison sentence for those who have an abortion illegally in the Republic. Despite the outlawing of interference in travel to another jurisdiction for an abortion or the provision of information about services in another state, the tentacles of the Eighth Amendment have continued to expand. In October 2012, a miscarriage was not medically assisted because of the presence of a foetal heartbeat, so risking the development of septicaemia, which resulted in the death of Savita Halappanavar. In 2014, a suicidal and clearly vulnerable asylum seeker, pregnant as a result of rape, was cajoled into agreeing to a caesarian section. Later in the same year, doctors cited the Eighth Amendment as the reason that a dead woman, who had been seventeen weeks pregnant, was kept on a life support machine until the courts ruled that the machine could be turned off (Carolan, 2014). In October 2016, the Health and Safety Executive tried – again citing the amendment – but failed, in a legal action to force a third-time mother to deliver by caesarean section.

In March 2015, Speaking of IMELDA humorously intervened in the London St. Patrick's Day Parade. This intervention into a long-established cultural event for the Irish diaspora, as well as Londoners and visitors to the city, proved a radical articulation of the presence of the issue of Ireland making England the legal destination for abortion. It also acted as a symbolic challenge to the Catholic Church and the patriarchal culture underpinning it. A twelve-foot puppet of St. Patrick, the first bishop of Ireland, garbed in green with his staff and mitre is rolled out annually in the London parade and in 2015 was greeted by a fleet of IMELDAs wearing red mitres and cloaks, as if female bishops had been permitted by the Catholic Church, and shouting 'down with Patrick-archy!' and 'stop in the name of choice!' (IMELDA disrupts the St. Patrick's Day Parade, 2015). Catholic ideologies, which seek to moralise individual choices, stretch far wider than Ireland alone. In September 2015, Pope Francis announced in a public letter that, between 8 December 2015 and 6 November 2016, absolution would be offered to women who have had abortions, so long as they expressed remorse and sought forgiveness from a priest (Kirchgaessner, 2015). The interpretation of abortion as a sin that needs to be forgiven is emblematic of Catholic ideology, where the shame lies not only in the act itself, but in failing to properly conceal it and show remorse (Inglis and MacKeogh, 2012).

IMELDA reacted to the papal comments at a 2015 nationwide pro-choice march in Dublin. Dressed as bishops once again and reading from 'the word', we sharply contradicted the Pope's language and message. Definitively counteracting the hypocrisy that cloaked the papal comments, the speech linked the statement from the Vatican to the hypocrisy of the Irish government in maintaining Ireland's abortion-free character and offering the right to travel as a substandard concession. IMELDA's pro-choice bishops drew upon Ireland's troubled history, identifying the country's lack of reproductive rights as emblematic of the systematic punishment of women, which has been a feature of the State since its conception. The speech was definitive in its proclamation: 'We do not need phoney concessions or absolution from those who have enacted such brutal misogyny against women in Ireland historically' (Solidarity Times, 2015). Here, we emphasised the autonomy vested within Irish people, acknowledging the moral agency they held over their own bodies.

These actions are particularly radical in the context of Ireland's blasphemy law. Introduced in 2009, the Defamation Act carries a penalty of up to €25,000 for anyone who 'publishes or utters blasphemous matter' in a manner intended to cause 'outrage' (Irish Statute Book, 2009). IMELDA has directly challenged this law through highlighting the hypocrisy and misogyny inherent in the Irish Church and state, both from their base in London and – importantly – at home on Irish soil. In doing so, in relation to the country's archaic abortion regime, IMELDA offers a double challenge to church and state. Embodying a dissonant voice which speaks of the oft-silenced reality of Irish abortions, we offer compassion to those who themselves have felt symbolically bound by Church and state. Similarly, in playing with the ritual emigrants return to Ireland each Christmas, we raise concerns for those forced to travel for abortions.

In 2014, we travelled by train and boat to Ireland, offering sups of choice from teapots to fellow travellers reminiscent of the housekeeper Mrs Doyle in the well-known television series *Father Ted* (A Sup of Choice for Christmas?, 2014). In Dublin, we made our arrival known by hanging a huge pair of knickers outside Dáil Éireann (Irish Assembly), carrying the message 'women are not breeding machines'. This referenced the aforementioned case of the clinically dead pregnant woman, who was being kept on life support, against her family's wishes. In 2015, we strolled around Dublin airport in our red costumes, dressed as nativity-play angels, complete with red-tinselled halos. Holding up a sign that said 'Welcome Home IMELDA', we drew attention to the fact that some of the arrivals would be returning from having an abortion abroad, with resentment rather than love in their hearts for 'the old sod'. The disruption of tradition continued with the placing of a miniature model of a Christmas angel decoration disguised as an abortion seeker with her trademark red suitcase, into the airport's Christmas crib. To ensure that the state would know that offence was in-tended, we tied tampons dipped in red ink, to simulate menstruation, to O'Connell Street's Christmas tree – a centrepiece of Dublin's festivities – and rounded off our return with a rendition of pro-choice carols under the iconic Clery's clock in collaboration with local pro-choice activists (IMELDA in collaboration with the Choicemas Carol Singers, 2015).

'We are not second-class citizens left to rot:' Challenging Restrictions on Abortion in Northern Ireland

Although it is the Catholic Church specifically which is credited with upholding cultures of shame, secrecy and repressed sexuality in Ireland, its underlying teachings mirror closely those of other Christian faiths. This is borne out in the Northern Irish context, where both Catholic and Protestant regimes conspire to keep abortion illegal (Fletcher, 2001). Indeed, the teachings of the Catholic Church in Ireland are emblematic of those of the Protestant faith in Victorian England where women were expected to adhere to a higher moral code than their male counterparts (Rowbotham, 1989; Inglis, 2005). Almost half of the population of North-ern Ireland describe themselves as Protestant, Presbyterians being the largest group, followed by Anglicans (Church of Ireland founded by Henry VIII in 1537), Methodists and small sects such as Assemblies of God and the Plymouth Brethren. This identification with Protestant-ism holds, even where significant minorities are not churchgoers and, indeed, may well be atheist or agnostic. The conflation of ethnic identity with a religious affiliation is the product of a political history stretching back to the Plantation (organised colonisation) of Ulster in the early seventeenth century and the establishment of a Protestant Ascendancy in Ireland, thanks to the victory of the Protestant King William of Orange at the Battle of the Boyne in 1690. Archaic as these events may now seem, they nonetheless set in train an enduring belief system asserting Protestantism's theological and moral superiority over Catholicism, a linking of Protestantism with Unionism (union with the British Crown and Empire), a bulwark against Catholicism, and an imperative to safeguard the union. The construction of political allegiances around religious identity has strengthened the power (paralleled in the Catholic/nationalist community) of the Protestant Churches' promotion of conservative views on social issues, particularly in relation to the family, the role of women in society, sexuality and reproductive rights. Furthermore, the Protestant Churches are integrated into the fabric of society through the clergy's involvement in secular life, whether at the social, personal or community level. As Rosemary Sales (1999, p. 141) points out, this close ethnopolitical association makes dissent a difficult prospect for many Protestants, believers and non-believers alike for fear of being seen as 'disloyal' to their community. Interestingly, opposition to abortion and gay rights has been one of the few areas of agreement between politicians and clergy across both Protestant/unionist and Catholic/nationalist communities and traditions.

Currently in Northern Ireland, abortion can only be obtained if a doctor acts 'only to save the life of the mother' or if continuing the pregnancy would result in the pregnant woman becoming a 'physical or mental wreck' (Northern Ireland Human Rights Commission, 2015). Very few people are referred to have an abortion in Northern Ireland (Jowit, 2016). Most people needing an abortion travel to England and have to pay privately as they cannot obtain it on the NHS. However, due to the fear and confusion surrounding the wording of existing abortion legislation, alongside the hostile political environment, doctors and health professionals are entirely unsure as to how they can advise people needing abortions without facing prosecution themselves for doing so. For instance, Section 58 of the 1861 Offences Against the Persons Act, on 'the offence of using drugs or instruments to procure abortion', states:

> Every woman being with child, who, with intent to procure her own miscarriage, shall unlawfully administer to herself any poison or other noxious thing, or shall unlawfully use any instrument or other means whatsoever with the like intent, and whosoever, with intent to procure the miscarriage of any woman whether she be or be not with child ... to be kept in penal servitude for life. (Offences Against the Person Act 1861, The National Archives)

The consequences of these laws were recently demonstrated, resulting in the prosecution of a young woman in Northern Ireland for taking the abortion pill in April 2016. The woman was given a three-month sentence (suspended for a year) for accessing medication that is approved by the World Health Organisation (WHO) and freely available to other women in the UK on the NHS. This woman could not afford to travel outside of Northern Ireland to access safe and legal abortion services and was reported to the police by her housemates because they felt that she was not 'remorseful' enough (McDonald, 2016). Since then, another woman who had been committed to stand trial for obtaining the abortion pill for her fifteen-year-old daughter because she could not afford to pay for a flight and private abortion won the right to contest the decision to prosecute her (Gentleman, 2016). Were she to be prosecuted, she could face life in jail if the judge has a strong anti-choice stance. It is interesting to note that abortion cases are tried as serious criminal cases similar to murder and are heard on indictment at the Crown Court. This indictment permits the judge wider discretion in sentencing, which can be anything from life in jail to a suspended sentence.

In response to the prosecution of the aforementioned woman who received the three-month suspended sentence, we created and filmed the action, *Game of Shame*. Taking the format of a game show, the *Game of Shame* demonstrated how the current law targets the most vulnerable in Northern Irish society, particularly those who cannot afford to travel to access safe and legal abortion services or those who are not permitted to travel due to their residency status. The interactions between the contestants and game show host hold a mirror up to the lack of concern for women's welfare and human rights both within the current law and the actions of those who push for increased sentencing of women. The *Game of Shame* loudly declares the right of women to have agency over their own bodies and to be fully supported in making reproductive choices without moral condemnation (*Game of Shame*, 2015). In 2016, we attended the first Rally for Choice in Belfast to stand in solidarity with activists resident in Northern Ireland. Dressed as super 'sheros', we delivered a speech praising Diana King, Colette Devlin and Kitty O'Kane, also known as the 'Derry Three' (Solidarity Times, 2016). In opposition to recent prosecutions, the 'Derry Three' handed themselves in to the police for procuring the abortion pill.

As a diasporic voice, Speaking of IMELDA also seeks to raise consciousness in Britain of the plight of Northern Irish women. In May 2014, we paid an uninvited visit to the Secretary of State for Health, Jeremy Hunt. Turning up unexpectedly to his advice surgery at a Sainsbury's supermarket in Farnham, we offered Mr Hunt advice on legislation change (Speaking of IMELDA with Jeremy Hunt, 2014). We consulted with a lawyer who informed us that a slight legislation change would at least allow women in Northern Ireland to have an abortion on the NHS in England or Scotland rather than having to pay privately. During this action, we presented Mr Hunt with bitten red apples with messages attached concerning the travesty of justice impacting on Northern Irish women. Mr Hunt stuck to the line that abortion is a devolved issue (under the control of Northern Irish Assembly and not the Westminster Parliament).

In 2015, we raised awareness of the situation faced by women in Northern Ireland at the Women of the World (WOW) Festival in London. We were not there as official participants but as Jude Kelly, the founder of WOW, asks people to be activists each year at this festival, we did not think she would mind our pop-up action. We were right: the festival staff even provided us with a microphone and amp. We performed a *Political Pageant* with entrants from England, Wales, Scotland and Northern Ireland. Entrants were judged on their access to reproductive care. Symbols from all countries adorned the entrants' costumes (Imelda Pageant 8 March, 2015). Of course, the Northern Irish entrant, wearing a necklace made of cut-out green shamrocks and red hands of Ulster, lost the political pageant. She subsequently marched around the group in a rage banging her drum (reminiscent of the Orange Marching Parades in Northern Ireland), using Virgin Mary bottles as drum sticks (a reference to Catholicism), chanting 'we are not, we are not, second class citizens left to rot'.

Reframing Femininity: Loose Methods and Loose Women

Speaking of IMELDA uses direct action and performance as an embodied method of provoking pro-choice discourse in the public realm. We aim to bring the often silenced, but very real issues impacting on women in Ireland into the public domain, thus challenging the institutional confines that maintain these silences. In our campaign video *The Quiet Woman* (2014), we challenged the valorisation of motherhood within marriage and domesticity as the primary roles for women (as enshrined in Article 41.2 of the Irish Constitution), by playfully subverting the domesticated submissiveness of a character played by Irish actress,

Maureen O'Hara, in the 1950s film *The Quiet Man* (Ford, 1952). In the video, we appear dressed in our trademark red clothing, each wearing a headscarf and sunglasses, simultaneously referencing a 50s glamour-puss, a washerwoman and a revolutionary in disguise. We then strung a washing line of knickers up in front of the Irish Embassy building in London and polished the building with the knickers, all of which were decorated with pro-choice slogans. The low-paid worker has been the valorised identity of the Irish in Britain, and in this action, we made visible the vast numbers of Irish women engaged in domestic work in Britain until the late twentieth century. The earthiness of the washerwoman, with her rolled-up sleeves, metaphorically cleaning Ireland's dirty secrets, while signalling her disgust and contempt, poses a stark challenge to the shame heaped on women who were victimised for pregnancy, poverty, sexuality and vulnerability in both Irish states. A group of IMELDA washerwomen were photographed with Panti Bliss, the iconic Irish drag artist, prior to the same-sex marriage referendum in Ireland. This act of mutual solidarity forged a new image of how 'femininity' might be reframed outside of current patriarchal norms. Indeed, our 'knicker-bombing' of the Irish Taoiseach Enda Kenny provides an apt example of our refusal to comply with patriarchal ideals of femininity. Interrupting the Taoiseach's party fundraiser at the Crown Moran Hotel in London in 2014, we landed a pair of 'knickers for choice' bearing the slogan 'Repeal the 8th Enda' on his dinner plate (Irish Taoiseach, Enda Kenny, served pro-choice knickers at fundraising dinner, 2014).

Our use of performance has been recognised as feminist Live Art practice and featured at Live Art events, for example, alongside *Are We There Yet?: Study Room Guide on Live Art and Feminism* by the Live Art Development Agency (LADA), London (LADA, 2015) and in the online exhibition, *Live Art and Feminism in the UK*, curated by LADA (2015) for the Google Cultural Institute. The subversions of domesticity and patriarchal constructions of femininity apparent within our actions are reminiscent of the aesthetics and strategies used by feminist artists such as Martha Rosler and Bobby Baker, among many others. Lois Keidan (2016, 'What Is Live Art?'), Director of the LADA, London, notes that 'Live Art is not a description of an art form or discipline, but a cultural strategy to include experimental processes and experiential practices'. She situates Live Artists as operating 'in between, and at the edges of more traditional artistic forms' (2016). Most certainly, our approach to performance is experimental and situated at the periphery of more traditional practice. We employ various methods of performance and theatre in our direct actions. For instance, in the spirit of Invisible Theatre as developed by Augusto Boal where interaction lies in improvised public action, we interjected in the London St. Patrick's Day Parade (St. Patrick's Day London, 2014) acting as women who had travelled from Ireland and asked bystanders the way to the nearest abortion clinic. Influenced by live artists, performance artists from the 1960s and the Situationists, who sought to break free of institutional confines and merge art with life, we are equally interventionist in our use of direct action. We are inspired by the aesthetics of performance-based activists, such as Pussy Riot, Sisters Uncut, Liberate Tate and the Clandestine Insurgent Rebel Clown Army. We not only perform *in* the public sphere; we actively engage *with* situations as an interventionist strategy. In turn, the actual world also intervenes and meets with our actions. Once we are in a situation, we improvise in the moment, responding to the inter-group dynamic and the inter-social dynamic with the people around us.

We use edited video of our public interventions as a means to heighten our impact, circumvent male-stream media and share our actions more widely. We equally use video as a means of sharing strategies and methods that enable those, who might not be in a position to be vocally pro-choice, to voice their dissent. For instance, *The Quiet Woman* video invites wider participation by encouraging people to decorate knickers with pro-choice slogans and hang them up in public. Our cheap and cheerful, 'loose' and 'DIO (Do It Ourselves)' aesthetics can be replicated and improvised by others.

The concept of 'looseness' has several connotations within the methods and aesthetics of Speaking of IMELDA. Our actions are loosely planned and improvised within their moment. The term 'Loose Theatre' is used by Margaretta D'Arcy (2005) to refer to her lifelong work as a 'guerrilla theatre activist'. In an article written by Speaking of IMELDA (2015) for *Contemporary Theatre Review*, we situated our activism within the lineage of D'Arcy's work, alongside the work of first-wave feminist activists in an Irish context, such as the women involved in the 1916 Rising and the Irish suffragettes. The term 'loose' is also used by Maggie B. Gale (2015) to refer to examples of 'women's protest performance'. Gale examines the 'gestural potential of women's activist bodies as occurring in public spaces in which those bodies are not socially, politically, or economically equal' (Gale, 2015: 313). Drawing on Sandra Lee Bartky's concept of the 'loose woman', Gale outlines 'the performative activism of "loose" women' as at once enabling a violation and affirmation of 'social constructions and projections of "normative" femininity' (Gale, 2015: 314).

In parodying the cultural constructions of a domesticated submissive femininity, Speaking of IMELDA, on the one hand, highlights these stereotypical ideals. On the other hand, in our loose formations, aesthetics and diversity, we simultaneously transgress and unsettle these oppressive social constructions. A loose woman has been used as a pejorative criticism – we reclaim it as free and liberatory in a similar sense to the way 'The Slut Walk' protests appropriated the derogatory labels applied to women to subvert the oppressive power of these judgements. We enjoy the association of 'loose women' and revel in subverting it to our advantage. This is evident in our Rogue Rose of Tralee action (2015) in which Speaking of IMELDA parodied the format of the annual *Rose of Tralee* pageant on the streets of Tralee, an action that ran synchronically to the main festival. The festival started in 1959 to bring Irish immigrants back to Ireland and to support tourism in the rural area of Tralee. Focused on beauty and personality, female contestants are attended by male escorts who vouch for their virtue and personality. In our version, similar to the action we performed at the WOW Festival, the winners were those who lived in countries with the best reproductive healthcare services. Ms Northern Ireland and Ms Republic of Ireland were the tragic losers, deprived of the reproductive choices available to their sisters living abroad. The action was reported by national broadsheet, the *Irish Times*, which understood Speaking of IMELDA's playful subversion of national cultural institutions that proliferate patriarchal images of women (McTiernan, 2015). On the other hand, the action also showed how national nostalgia in diasporic communities is a yearning for the past, which is often at odds with the contemporary and future needs of Irish women. As such, our 'rogue roses' not only parodied the construct of the hyper-feminine 'lovely girl', but also transcended accepted norms by speaking out about the lack of reproductive rights afforded to women across the island of Ireland (Rogue Rose of Tralee, 2015).

The extent to which women are publicly policed was made apparent a year after our action, when the Sydney Rose Brianna Parkins used her onstage interview in the 2016 pageant to call for a referendum on the repeal of the Eighth Amendment, while wearing a red dress. While her intervention was applauded by many, it was, predictably, criticised for politicising this harmless 'much-loved' ritual. Similarly, Speaking of IMELDA is often told in response to our performances that 'it is not the time or the place' to speak of abortion. While we employ humour, parody and satire in our arsenal of 'loose methods', we are also proud to be spoilsports, or killjoys to use the term as Sara Ahmed defines it in 'Living in a Feminist Life' (2010). For Ahmed, the killjoy is the one who speaks out and upsets the apparent acceptance of the status quo. She is following the advice of Audre Lorde, who warned that 'your silence will not protect you' (Lorde, 1977 paper in Sister Outsider, 2007: 41), a pertinent reminder to Irish women that the worst has already been inflicted on them and that speaking up can hardly make matters any worse. Speaking of IMEDLA are killjoys just as Pussy Riot, the Guerrilla Girls, Sisters Uncut, Black Lives Matter and Liberate Tate are. We speak up, we speak out, we break the silence and we invite others to do so too.

Writing of the Rose of Tralee Festival and the now (thankfully) defunct annual pageant, the Calor Housewife of the Year, Fintan Walsh, outlines the production of a 'homelysexuality', a domesticated, tempered femininity, which constitutes a 'female sexual accent in particular, emptied of depth, eroticism or even what might be understood as subjectivity' (Walsh, 2009: 206). Within our public performances, we aim to unsettle domesticated femininity. We do this by maintaining space for the diverse individual identities, sexualities, aesthetics and styles of group members to shine through. We purposely draw on the eclectic, intergenerational and intersectional mix of women in our group. While we wear red in our performances, members of the group self-fashion their red clothes in accordance with their own taste and style. All of our actions are devised collectively in group sessions, drawing on the expertise and, importantly, identities, of group members. Above all, Speaking of IMELDA celebrates the collectivity of women coming together.

Monuments of the Past and Future: Intervening between Politics and Culture

The collective and collaborative working practices established by Speaking of IMELDA, alongside our refusal to quietly disappear into the diasporic ether, offer a retort to the Irish state's persistent attempts to exclude women from having agency within political and cultural spheres. Describing the lack of a participative class within Irish political spheres, Michael D. Higgins responded presciently to the Finance Bill 2011 in the Oireachtas (Irish Parliament) paraphrasing the political scientist, Jürgen Habermas, 'really you can't invite people to be bound by rules and bound by decisions in which they haven't had a chance to consciously participate' (Higgins, 2011). Indicating the historical emergence of the Irish Republic in 1922 as a socialist revolutionary project as much as a project for independence from the British colonial rule, Higgins stated his disappointment between what the manifesto for Irish freedom, Poblacht na hÉireann, proclaimed and how those liberties have been upheld:

> I feel that those who wanted Ireland to be independent would have envisaged a country in which there would be far greater distribution of power, that it wouldn't just be confined to the exercise of parliamentary democracy only. There is more to political power than voting once every four or five years. There is the exercise of power in every dimension of life and if a real republic had been founded, we should have been spending decades extending and deepening political power (2011).

Further on and with specific reference to the Global Financial Crisis, Higgins declared in this, his final parliamentary speech before successfully running for the office of President, that 'an enormous price is now already being paid for the broken connection between the aspirations of the people of this planet and those who take decisions on their behalf' (2011). Indeed, since 2011, the Irish Republic has witnessed a rise in cultures of dissent, from protests against the privatisation of water and the emergence of left-wing groups such as People before Profit to the growing social movement for reproductive justice. In identifying how the state was not operating dialectically with disenchanted public spheres, Higgins confessed that administrative power was a kind of rarefied and hegemonic apparatus.

In 2014, after Higgins had become the President of Ireland, he made the first official Irish state visit to the UK. This opened an opportunity for Speaking of IMELDA to highlight how Ireland was making England the legal destination for abortion. The IMELDAs fretted about staging an intervention that would face off with the most symbolically powerful representative in Ireland. Higgins was respected in the group and had championed the reproductive rights of women in Ireland. However, in his role as the President, he could not be politically partisan. Additionally, as the symbolic head of the Irish state, the President represented national values that strategically needed to be challenged. We mapped his itinerary, dressed in our traditional red and protested outside his appointments at the Irish Embassy and a festival gala at the Royal Albert Hall in April 2014 (Irish Embassy, 8 April 2014). Inserting the unspoken arrangements on abortion into the first ever official Irish state visit to Britain felt risky at the time. The visit was seen in the Republic of Ireland as a coming of age in the relationship between the former colony and the colonising power. Speaking of IMELDA was therefore a cause of embarrassment to the Irish state and its reputation abroad and this action was largely repressed by the mainstream media but reported briefly by RTE (the Irish National Broadcaster) and the *Journal* (an online Irish newspaper). These tactics set Speaking of IMELDA up as a 'counter public' (Warner, 2002) that tackled the political administration on how Irish cultural values regarding women were reproduced. Ironically, in achieving the participative effects invoked by Higgins in his appeal for the emergence of public spheres, Higgins became the symbolic object of contestation.

Thereafter, Speaking of IMELDA began to contest cultural institutions and monuments in which we could physically trace the symbolic reproduction of androcentric attitudes and highlight how the symbolism of these institutions led to a hegemonic subjugation of women. Examples of such institutions – as explored earlier – were the *Rose of Tralee* festival for 'comely maidens' of Irish descent and the annual St. Patrick's Day Parade in London, an event heavily frequented by the Irish diaspora. Yet another was the 100-year commemoration of the 1916 Easter Rising which historically led to the emancipation of Ireland from Britain, and in which the original revolutionaries envisaged a state where women were equal. These institutions enact Irish popular culture at a liberal arm's length from the state but work to enculturate the following Irish values: the domesticated Irish female, favour for religious patriarchies whose 'moral cruelty' (Haughton and Kurdi, 2015) has punished Irish women and the Irish nation's manifesto for self-governance while forfeiting any inclusion of female participation in power. These events were intuitive interventions for Speaking of IMELDA where the cultural norms of Irish life could be publicly examined both within our country of origin (as in actions at the *Rose of Tralee Festival* and at the GPO building in Dublin) and outside it, in our adopted nation (London St. Patrick's Day celebrations, 2014, 2015, 2016). By broaching Ireland making England the legal destination for abortion as a discussion point at public cultural occasions, we demonstrate how gender is usually erased as a concern in Irish public spheres. In doing so, we conceivably critique models of public spheres as un-gendered, recognising Nancy Fraser's insights that the 'gender subtext' for Habermas' reading of public spheres is 'unthematized' (Fraser, 2013: 34).

IMELDA's interventions interrogate Irish culture and how it represents itself in terms of gender. We leverage cultural production for political ends: our cultural tactics interfere with the representational logics of mainstream institutions by aiming to create cultural shifts in popular opinion that may lead to legislative and political changes. Our work appears in popular culture where an alternative expectation for Irish society and the explicit hope for the repeal of the Eighth amendment can be shared with a broad public base. This is how we view the intersections of culture and politics, aligning ourselves with Rancière who states that a 'community of sense woven together by artistic practice is a new set of vibrations of the human community in the present; on the other hand, it is a monument that stands as a mediation or a substitute for a people to come' (Rancière, 2009: 59).

Attending to the actual monuments of the past and their capacity to mediate people to come, our Easter 2015 action focused on Poblacht na hÉireann, the manifesto of Irish freedom delivered at the General Post Office (GPO) in Dublin in 1916, the headquarters of the Easter Rising. Rearticulating the contents of the document to account for female bodily autonomy, Speaking of IMELDA performed in chains around one of the columns of the GPO, costumed in the era of 1916 (Imelda chains herself to the G.P.O., 2015). The imagery evoked the original socialist revolutionary claims for equality expressed in Poblacht na hÉireann, but the action also took the notion of the monument literally by restaging a revolutionary proclamation at the very site in which Irish national values were inaugurated 100 years earlier. Echoing Higgins' disappointment in the republic and acknowledging that monuments are an embodiment of the future to come, IMELDA aimed to show the contradictory relationship between monumentalised past hopes and present disappointments. In this way, one of IMELDA's cultural functions is to propose a realignment in the Irish Republic to its originating principle that women are embraced equally. We situate our art activism as a proposition for a 'people to come' and as a 'monument to its expectation, a monument to its absence' (Rancière, 2009: 59).

Conclusion

This chapter has demonstrated the vital role that feminist diasporic collectives such as Speaking of IMELDA play in disrupting dominant patriarchal codes – both at home and in their adopted nations. Being 'set loose', so to speak, in another jurisdiction has emboldened us with greater freedom to act as radical members of the Irish diaspora and directly expose the misogynistic norms of our home country to a new audience, in our trademark imprecise and liberated style. Acting as one of many diasporic feminist collectives in England (both throughout history and from across the globe), our actions challenge the ongoing issue of Ireland making England the legal destination for abortion, while also highlighting the broader pattern of maltreatment perpetuated against women by the Irish state. By nodding to radical diasporic networks of the past (such as the IWASG), we maintain steady traditions of diasporic activism in protesting the continued denial of bodily autonomy across the island of Ireland.

Our loose and experimental methods challenge some of the silences that surround abortion in Ireland through brazenly subverting public spaces and traditional feminine identities to make known the plight of Irish women. By intruding into areas and in forms that are traditionally unwelcome in patriarchal structures, we give voice to – and indeed embody – our dissatisfaction and broadcast the stark realities of the privileging of the unborn above the living woman to a wider populace. Our style of action is radical in its demanding of a response and forces situations to mould and engage with our interventions, in turn, enabling us to respond and adapt to the situation and drive issues forward to new terrain. We engage dissonant voices further afield through our employment of 'do it yourself' aesthetics in a manner which extends the reach of our message far beyond the boundaries of our home and adopted nations.

Although aesthetically loose, the dangerous relationship between church and state for women's autonomy is a prevailing theme in our radicalism. Our engagement with, and consistent confrontation of, religious symbolism in our performances serves to assert directly the role that both Catholic and Protestant institutions have had in policing female sexuality both North and South of the Irish border as well as internationally. Our all-island radicalism has equally brought us into direct combat with statespersons both in Ireland and the UK, and provided us with important opportunities to provoke those in positions of authority and assert the rights of people across Ireland. We recognise and welcome our place in broader channels of pro-choice and diasporic radicalism. By acting in solidarity with groups from Poland, Spain, Central America and elsewhere, as well as engaging with others fighting for bodily autonomy across Ireland and in the UK, we further the goals of radical feminist activism, by extending the struggle for reproductive rights into broader global focus and boldly asserting the power of female agency and action.

Final Note

Some advances in reproductive rights in Ireland have been made in the period between the drafting of this chapter and its publication. Following the June 2017 General Election in the UK, the Government's very narrow majority was threatened when some Conservative MPs announced that they would support an amendment to the Finance Bill by Labour MP, Stella Creasy, calling for access to NHS abortions for NI residents. The Government introduced a means-tested travel grant and access to free abortion for women travelling to Great Britain for terminations.

The law on the importation of abortion medication to NI has not changed.

Following a referendum in Ireland on 25th May, 2018, in which two thirds of the electorate voted to abolish the eighth Amendment, the right to abortion in the first twelve weeks of pregnancy, for any reason, became legal in the Irish Republic on 1st January 2019. The enabling legislation also repealed the Protection of Life During Pregnancy Act (2013).

In April 2018, Speaking of IMELDA went on a Referendum Road Trip in the South West and West of Ireland, performing alongside sixty five local activists, singers, songwriters and film makers working for repeal. Four films recording these encounters reflecting the deep and broad cultural change that was manifested in the referendum result are on our website at www.speakingofimelda.org/referendum.

References

Abortion Support Network (ASN), www.abortionsupport.org.uk/about/faqs/#4 [accessed 2 September 2016].

Ahmed, S., 'Feminist Killjoys (And Other Wilful Subjects)' in *the Scholar and Feminist Online*, published by The Barnard Center for Research on Women, 8:3 (2010), www.barnard.edu/sfonline [accessed 12 January 2017].

Amnesty International, *She Is Not a criminal: The Impact of Ireland's Abortion Law* (United Kingdom: Amnesty International, 2015).

Carolan, M., 'High Court to Rule on Case of Pregnant Woman on Friday,' *The Irish Times* (23 December 2014) www.irishtimes.com/news/crime-and-law/courts/high-court/high-court-to-rule-on-case-of-pregnant-woman-on-friday-1.2047499 [accessed 20 January 2017].

Casey, M., 'Writing as Survival', in G. Dawson, J. Dover and S. Hopkins (eds.) *The Northern Ireland Troubles in Britain: Impacts, Engagement, Legacies and Memories* (Manchester: Manchester University Press, 2017), pp. 213–226.

Cullen Owens, R., *Smashing Times: A History of the Irish Women's Suffrage Movement, 1889–1922* (Dublin: Attic Press, 1984).

D'Arcy, M., *Loose Theatre: Memoirs of a Guerrilla Theatre Activist* (Canada: Trafford Publishing & Women's Pirate Press, 2005).

Delmar, R., 'What is Feminism?', in Wandor, M. (ed.) *The Body Politic: Writings from the Women's Liberation Movement in Britain, 1969–1972* (London: Stage 1., 1972), pp. 8–33.

Finch, N., 'Policing the Irish community in Britain', in G. Dawson, J. Dover and S. Hopkins (eds.) *The Northern Ireland Troubles in Britain: Impacts, Engagements, Legacies and Memories* (Manchester: Manchester University Press, 2017), pp. 137–152.

Fischer, C., 'Gender, Nation, and the Politics of Shame: Magdalene Laundries and the Institutionalization of Feminine Transgression in Modern Ireland', *Signs: Journal of Women in Culture and Society*, 41: 4 (2016), pp. 821–843.

Fletcher, R., 'Civic Feminism and Voluntary Abortion Care: A Story of ESCORT's Contribution to Reproductive Justice', in A. Quilty, S. Kennedy and C. Conlon (eds.), *The Abortion Papers Ireland, Volume 2* (Cork: Attic, 2015), pp. 137–149.

Fletcher, R., 'Post-colonial Fragments: Representations of Abortion in Irish Law and Politics', *Journal of Law and Society*, 28:4 (2001), pp. 568–589.

Ford, J. Dir., *The Quiet Man* (1952).

Fraser, N., *Fortunes of Feminism: from State Managed Capitalism to Neoliberal Crisis* (London: Verso, 2013).

Gale, M.B., 'Resolute Presence, Fugitive Moments, and the Body in Women's Protest Performance', *Contemporary Theatre Review*, 25:3 (2015), pp. 313–326.

Gentleman, A., 'Woman Who Bought Abortion Pills for Daughter Can Challenge Prosecution' *The Guardian* (26 January 2016) www.theguardian.com/world/2017/jan/26/ulster-woman-who-bought-abortion-pills-for-daughter-can-challenge-prosecution [accessed 30 January 2017].

Haughton, M. and Kurdi, M., *Radical Contemporary Theatre Practices by Women in Ireland* (Dublin: Carysfort Press, 2015).

Higgins, Michael D., *Introduction to the Finance Bill 2011* (Dublin: House of Oireachtas, 2011) www.youtube.com/watch?v=OJJ5q1_5jX8 [accessed 20 September 2016].

Houses of the Oireachtas, 'Protection of Life during Pregnancy Act 2013' (2013) www.oireachtas.ie/viewdoc.asp?DocID=24271 [accessed 3 February 2017].

Inglis, T. and MacKeogh, C., 'The Double Bind: Women, Honour and Sexuality in Contemporary Ireland', *Media, Culture and Society*, 34:1 (2012), pp. 68–82.

Inglis, T., 'Origins and Legacies of Irish Prudery: Sexuality and Social Control in Modern Ireland', *Eire-Ireland*, 40:3–4 (2005), pp. 9–37.

Irish Statute Book, 'Defamation Act, 2009' (2009) www.irishstatutebook.ie/eli/2009/act/31/enacted/en/html [accessed 3 February 2017].

Irish Women at War: Papers from the Feminism and Ireland Workshop, London, 26 June 1977.

Jowit, J., 'Northern Ireland's Abortion Laws Remain Restrictive and Unclear', *The Guardian* (6 January 2016) www.theguardian.com/world/2016/jan/06/northern-ireland-abortion-laws-restrictive-unclear-legal-women [accessed 31 January 2017].

Keidan, L., 'What is Live Art?', *Live Art Development Agency*, Official Website www.thisisliveart.co.uk/about/what-is-live-art/ [accessed 10 September 2016].

Kirchgaessner, S., 'Pope Francis Tells Priests to Pardon Women Who Have Abortions', *The Guardian* (1 September 2015) www.theguardian.com/world/2015/sep/01/pope-francis-tells-priests-to-pardon-women-who-have-abortions [accessed 1 September 2016].

London Armagh Group, 'Strip Searches in Armagh Jail,' *Women Behind the Wire*, 2 (1984).

Lorde, A. Paper to The Modern Language Association's 'Lesbian and Literature Panel,' Chicago, Illinois (28 December 1977) published in *Sister Outsider - Essays & Speeches by Audre Lorde* (United States: 2007).

McDonald, H., 'Northern Irish Woman Given Suspended Sentence over Self-Induced Abortion', *The Guardian* (4 April 2016) www.theguardian.com/uk-news/2016/apr/04/northern-irish-woman-suspended-sentence-self-induced-abortion [accessed 30 January 2017].

McTiernan, A., 'Pro-choice Group Stage 'Rogue Rose of Tralee Pageant,' Irish Times (August 17 2015) www.irishtimes.com/news/social-affairs/pro-choice-group-stage-rogue-rose-of-tralee-pageant-1.2319646 [accessed 2 February 2017].

Mohanty, C.T., 'Feminist Encounters: Locating the Politics of Experience', in M. Barrett and A. Phillips, (eds.) *Destabilizing Theory, Contemporary Feminist Debates* (Cambridge: Polity Press, 1992), pp. 68–86.

Northern Ireland Human Rights Commission, 'Human Rights Commission Welcomes Historic Termination of Pregnancy Ruling' (30 November 2015) www.nihrc.org/news/detail/human-rights-commission-welcomes-historic-termination-of-pregnancy-ruling [accessed 20 January 2017].

Offences Against the Person Act 1861, The National Archives, www.legislation.gov.uk/ukpga/ Vict/24-25/100/crossheading/attempts-to-procure-abortion [accessed 30 January 2017].

O'Reilly, E., *Masterminds of the Right* (Dublin: Attic Press, 1992).

Pankhurst, S., 'Thoughts on Easter Week', *The Women's Dreadnought*, (13 May 2016).

Rancière, J., *The Emancipated Spectator*, trans. Gregory Elliot (London: Verso, 2009).

Redmond, J., 'Safeguarding Irish Girls: Welfare Work, Female Emigrants, and the Catholic Church, 1920s–1940s', in C.S. Brophy and C. Delay (eds.), *Women, Reform and Resistance in Ireland, 1850–1950* (Houndmills: Palgrave Macmillan, 2015) pp. 55–76.

Roberts, E., *Are We There Yet?: Study Room Guide on Live Art and Feminism* (London: Live Art Development Agency, 2015) www.thisisliveart.co.uk/publishing/are-we-there-yet-a-study-room-guide-on-live-art-and-feminism/ [accessed 12 September 2016].

Roberts, E., *Live Art and Feminism in the UK* (London: Live Art Development Agency and Google Cultural Institute, 2015) www.google.com/culturalinstitute/beta/exhibit/live-art-and-feminism-in-the-uk/1gLSx6pobvq_Ig [accessed 12 September 2016].

Rossiter, A., *Ireland's Hidden Diaspora: The Abortion Trail and the Making of a London-Irish Underground, 1980–2000* (London: Iasc Publishing, 2009).

Rossiter, A., 'Not Our Cup of Tea': Irish and British Feminist Encounters in London during the Troubles' in G. Dawson, J. Dover and S. Hopkins (eds.), *The Northern Ireland Troubles in Britain* (Manchester: Manchester University Press, 2017) pp. 153–168.

Rowbotham, J., *Good Girls Make Good Wives: Guidance for Girls in Victorian Fiction* (Oxford: Basil Blackwell, 1989).

Russell, D., 'Some Early Irish Movements in South London,' in D. Russell (ed.), *South London Record* (London: South London History Workshop, 1987), pp. 13–23.

Sales, R., (1999) 'Gender and Protestantism in Northern Ireland' in P. Shirlow and M. McGovern (eds.), *Who are 'the People?', Unionism, Protestantism and Loyalism in Northern Ireland* (London: Pluto Press, 1999) pp. 140–157.

Solidarity Times, 'IMELDA at March 4 Choice, Dublin,' (26 September 2015), www.youtube.com/ watch?v=1kF3_-f1Szg [accessed 2 February 2017].

Solidarity Times, 'Imelda at Belfast Rally4Choice,' (2 July 2016) www.youtube.com/watch?v=_ GRf7El36iE [accessed 2 February 2017].

Speaking of IMELDA, 8 March 2014 Action, Interrupting 'Dissonant Voices' Conference at Camden Irish Centre London (8 March 2014) https://www.youtube.com/watch?v=dr1z_aCKoOQ [accessed 2 February 2017].

Speaking of IMELDA, 'A Sup of Choice for Christmas?: Imelda's Festive Journey to Ireland' (20 December 2014) www.youtube.com/watch?v=cAI0R7hHmGw [accessed 2 February 2017].

Speaking of IMELDA, 'Dirty Work Still to be Done: Retrieving and Activating Feminist Acts of Resistance,' *Contemporary Theatre Review: Interventions*, May (2015) www.contemporarytheatre review.org/2015/margaretta-darcy/ [accessed 10 September 2016].

Speaking of IMELDA, 'Game of Shame,' Outside Supreme Court London, in Response to Criminalizing of Women in Northern Ireland for Taking the Abortion Pill (24 May 2016) https://youtu.be/ IjStoV3uzAk [accessed 2 February 2017].

Speaking of IMELDA, 'Imelda Chains Herself to the G.P.O.,' (6 April 2015), www.//youtu.be/ DIVS1HbOMBM [accessed 2 February 2017].

Speaking of IMELDA, 'Imelda Disrupts the St. Patrick's Day London 2015' (15 March 2015) www. youtube.com/watch?v=y9jzgPPkYW4 [accessed 2 February 2017].

Speaking of IMELDA, 'IMELDA in Collaboration with the Choicemas Carol Singers,' Homecoming 2015, Dublin Airport and Dublin City (20 December 2015), https://youtu.be/gSmWwDrWWYw [accessed 2 February 2017].

Speaking of IMELDA, 'Imelda Pageant 8 March 2015,' International Women's Day at WOW Festival in London (8 March 2015) https://youtu.be/RPawwERvXSw [accessed 2 February 2017].

Speaking of IMELDA, 'Irish Taoiseach Enda Kenny, Served Pro-choice Knickers at Fundraising Dinner' (3 October 2014) https://youtu.be/a654qvUJy [accessed 2 February 2017].

Speaking of IMELDA, 'Rogue Rose of Tralee 2015'- Speaking of Imelda in Tralee, Kerry (15 August 2015) www.youtube.com/watch?v=B_WBEmOlz7E [accessed 2 February 2017].

Speaking of IMELDA, 'Speaking of IMELDA -Irish Embassy -8 April 2014,' actions during State Visit of Irish President Michael D. Higgins, London (8 and 10 April 2014) https://youtu.be/ AqC9LVfVoTI [accessed 2 February 2017].

Speaking of IMELDA, 'St. Patrick's Day London 2014,' www.youtube.com/watch?v=sz00jyAaJyw [accessed 2 February 2017].

Speaking of IMELDA, 'Speaking of IMELDA with Jeremy Hunt May 24 2014, at Hunt's 'Advice Surgery', Sainsbury's Supermarket in Farnham (24 May 2014) https://youtu.be/mmf3c9oVQmA [accessed 2 February 2017].

Speaking of IMELDA, 'The Quiet Woman' – Campaign Video for Knickers for Choice Campaign (September 2014) https://youtu.be/cEkD_cWgxaE [accessed 2 February 2017].

Wallsgrove, R., 'Women's Liberation Movement. 1969–1985, RIP?' in *Spare Rib*, 170 (1986) p. 25.

Walsh, F., "Homelysexuality and the "Beauty" Pageant', in S. Brady and F. Walsh (eds.), *Crossroads: Performance Studies and Irish Culture* (Basingstoke: Palgrave Macmillan, 2009), pp. 196–209.

Warner, M., *Publics and Counterpublics* (New York: MIT Press, 2002).

1.2

ANIMAL LIBERATION

Will Boisseau

Moral concern about the relationship between human and non-human animals has a long history which extends to philosophers such as Pythagoras and the growth of Jainism, Buddhism and Hinduism. The first organised animal welfare societies emerged in Britain in the 1820s, including the Royal Society for the Prevention of Cruelty to Animals (RSPCA), which wanted animals to be treated 'humanely' while avoiding 'unnecessary' suffering, although the RSPCA did not campaign against vivisection or the meat industry. The radical animal liberation movement which aimed to undertake direct action to save the lives of animals while causing economic sabotage to the industries that exploited animals developed in Britain during the 1960s within the Hunt Saboteurs Association (HSA) and expanded in the mid-1970s with the formation of the Animal Liberation Front (ALF).

Since the 1970s, the animal liberation movement grew to become one of the most significant social movements in Western Europe and North America; in the early 1980s, animal liberation activists in the UK undertook 'more direct action and caused more physical and financial damage than the entire British revolutionary left put together' (Law, 1982, p. 23). The animal liberation movement inspired new generations of activists to broaden their action repertoire. Radical environmentalists such as Earth First! and the Earth Liberation Front (ELF) took 'inspiration and courage' from the 'ambitious direct action culture surrounding the ALF' (Tsolkas, 2015). New tactical advances were inspired by Stop Huntingdon Animal Cruelty (SHAC), who worked as an above-ground group, while the ALF undertook illegal direct action against the targets publicised by SHAC. It was partly the fear of these tactics spreading to other revolutionary groups that led to an international state crackdown on animal liberation activism. In America, the FBI took extensive and costly action to try and halt the rise of the ALF and ELF (Potter). In Britain, the convictions of animal liberation activists under the Serious Organised Crime and Police Act have been described by Corporate Watch (2009) as 'one of the worst injustices in the recent history of the UK's political prosecutions' (pp. 6–7). The repression, which in America included the imprisonment of a researcher for refusing to testify to a federal grand jury (Scarce, 2005), has led to a recent decline in militant forms of direct action and a rise in educational work (Starr et al., 2008, p. 267). If the animal liberation protest cycle which began in the mid-1970s with the formation of the ALF is experiencing a trough in the mid-2010s, then the growth and mainstreaming of veganism may be regarded as one unexpected residue of animal liberation activism.

Despite the advances made, and the risks undertaken, by animal liberation activists, the movement remains dogged with accusations that it represents bourgeois reformism and that animal activists are 'predominantly middle class, overwhelmingly white and privileged, insensitive to class oppression and the lack of diversity within their movements' (Best, 2014, p. 85). In response to these criticisms, new animal liberation activism focuses on concepts such as total liberation and the intersectionality of human, animal and Earth liberation.

This chapter is divided into four key sections. First, we consider the principal concerns of the movement; the second section considers the movement's action repertoire; the third section looks at the main concepts that uphold the current animal liberation movement; and the final section considers the radical political theories which relate to animal liberation including ecofeminism, anarchism and critical animal studies (CAS).

The chapter focuses on animal liberation groups who directly rescue animals from places of abuse or cause economic sabotage to companies which profit from animal abuse. The main groups we will consider are the ALF and SHAC. There are also many different animal liberation groups, for instance, those who seek to cause physical harm to animal abusers like the Animal Rights Militia (ARM), Justice Department and Animal Liberation Brigade (ALB); those who focus on a single issue such as the HSA; prisoner support groups such as Bite Back and the Animal Liberation Front Supporters' Group (ALF SG); groups who promote nonviolent direct action and open rescue such as Direct Action Everywhere (DxE); international direct action groups such as the Sea Shepherd Conservation Society and groups, connected with animal liberation, who promote veganism such as Food Not Bombs.

Before considering the movement's key concepts, the distinction between the animal liberation movement and groups associated with animal welfare and animal rights is worth noting. The animal welfare movement, connected with the RSPCA in Britain and The Humane Society of the United States in America, believes that animals should be treated humanely while avoiding unnecessary suffering, a belief in animal welfare means that animals can still be consumed as food, hunted or used in experiments but that this should not be done with gratuitous or unnecessary violence. An animal rights position, as represented by groups like People for the Ethical Treatment of Animals (PETA), states that animals should not be used instrumentally as a means to human ends under any circumstances (Singer, 1995; Regan, 2004; Francione, 2010). Finally, an animal liberation approach accepts the premise of animal rights, but focuses on the domestication of animals and has adopted tactics including direct action and the liberation of animals. Steven Best (2014) explains that while liberationists 'often rely on rights-based assumptions while upholding abolitionists' goals', they also aim to 'free animals from captivity and to attack exploiters through various means' including diverse forms of direct action and economic sabotage (p. 82).

Concerns

The animal liberation movement emerged from the hunt saboteurs' movement in Britain, and as such, the hunting of animals for fun was the first concern of the movement. The ALF widened the scope of animal liberationists to target the vivisection industry, and ultimately the ALF aimed to 'liberate animals from [all] places of abuse', including laboratories, factory farms, fur farms, circuses and pet shops, and to 'inflict economic damage to those who profit from the misery and exploitation of animals' (ALF, undated b). Soon, animal liberationists were concerned by the countless ways that animals are exploited by the 'animal-industrial complex' (Twine, 2012). The animal liberation movement has broadened its concern to the interrelation of human, animal and Earth liberation; this includes the connections between the meat industry and world hunger, and the links between the meat and dairy industries and climate change. Of course, some human issues were always embedded within the animal liberation movement, for instance, the first hunt saboteurs in Britain took pride in the class conflict with upper-class hunters involved in sabbing.

The principal concern of the HSA in Britain is disrupting hunts in order to prevent the fox, or other targeted animal, being killed. Hunt sabs act nonviolently but are prepared to use self-defence if necessary. Hunts are often disrupted by activists spraying false scent, perhaps using garlic water, calling off the hounds or otherwise distracting hunters (HSA, 1987). Activists involved in sabbing take great pride that their direct action makes an immediate and visible impact, as one activist explained: 'what you do in that day directly effects something's life, you know, quite often you'll see the animal you saved, you'll see it running away... It's still quite satisfying to know that what you did there and then saved that creature's life' (interview with hunt sab).

As we will see, it is often the experiences of activists in the field that shape the movement's political theory. In Britain, hunt sabbing has been an uncontroversial issue for the animal liberation movement; such activism involves conflicts with the police, the class enemy and the establishment. However, the issue of hunting becomes more controversial when it is carried out by indigenous communities across the world for food and sustenance. There have been fierce debates within the animal liberation movement about the hunting practices of indigenous peoples such as the Inuits and the lack of class awareness or intersectionality shown by some animal rights activists.

For many activists who have felt compelled to take part in clandestine direct action, 'there is something about vivisection that strikes a deeper chord' than other animal issues (Mann, undated). It is not just activists, but theorists as well, who believe that vivisection is somewhat unique within animal advocacy. For Gary Francione (2010), 'it is the use of animals in medical research, above all other uses, that compels us to think carefully about the moral status of animals' (p. 4). Mark Rowlands (2002) argues that the issue of animal experimentation seems unique because 'the moral case for vivisection seems much stronger than the case for animal husbandry. With animal husbandry then it is pretty clear that only trivial human interests are at stake. But with vivisection, it could be argued that the human interests involved are genuinely vital ones' (p. 126). Ultimately, Rowlands argues that humans have no vital interest in vivisection. The antivivisection movement has initiated worldwide campaigns which often focus on one company at a time which will be targeted by boycotts, petitions, blockades, home demonstrations and letter-writing campaigns until they cut their links with the vivisection industry. For instance, one global campaign has focused on Air France, which is the last major airline to transport non-human primates to animal experimentation laboratories.

Some animal liberation activists also engage in vegan outreach, which means encouraging people to adopt a vegan diet by providing sample vegan food, often at vegan festivals and fairs but also as part of wider political campaigns such as Food Not Bombs. Encouraging people to become vegan or vegetarian has always been a significant part of the animal liberation movement and since the mid-2000s (after the state crackdown on animal liberation activism in the UK, USA and Europe), activists have placed great significance on this side of their campaigning. Perhaps it is unsurprising that animal liberation activists have focused on the meat industry because far more animals are involved in the meat and dairy industry than are affected by vivisection or hunting. Eating animals is the most common relationship that most humans have with other species, and 'globally, 99 per cent of all domesticates are commodities in animal agriculture... caught in relations of human domination that involve their exploitation and oppression' (Cudworth, 2011, p. 106). Animal liberationists, and other strands of the animal advocacy spectrum, believe that they must work with urgency to protect animals, not only because approximately 70 billion farm animals are now 'produced' for food worldwide every year, but because the planet is facing the worst extinction crisis in 65 million years, and at least 10,000 species become extinct annually (Compassion in World Farming; WWF).

Animal liberationists are not solely concerned with 'animal issues'; instead, the current animal liberation movement has focused on the intersections of human, animal and Earth oppression, often using the concept of total liberation. For instance, animal liberationists highlight the damaging effect that the meat and dairy industry has upon global food distribution and the environment. Animal liberationists, and other animal activists, are concerned about a number of environmentally damaging aspects of livestock agriculture, including erosion, air and water pollution, deforestation and fresh water scarcity. The most notable connection is the contribution of the livestock sector to greenhouse gas emissions. The Intergovernmental Panel on Climate Change estimates that 'agricultural emissions account for 10–12 per cent of the global total and that by 2030 agricultural emissions are projected to grow by 36–63 per cent' (Garnett, 2010, p. 36).

Animal liberation theorist David Nibert argues that people should go vegan because at a time when half of the world's population are living in water-stressed areas, most of the fresh water of the world is being used for animal feed (Nibert, Entangled). Nibert also explains that 70% of all agricultural land on the planet is being used to produce animal products, whereas a widespread move to a non-meat and dairy system would be more efficient in combating world hunger (ibid.). Nibert also highlights that it is capitalism, rather than the meat and dairy industry alone, which is the cause of systemic food injustices. Animal liberation activists, often influenced by anarchism and other leftist philosophies, have linked animal abuse to a drive for profit and the greed that they see as inherent in the current system. Activists have used these opportunities to challenge the primacy of free market economics. Anarchist animal liberationists have also highlighted the fact that governments in Western Europe and the USA provide large subsidies to farmers to maintain the animal-industrial complex.

Actions

Before looking at the key concepts and theories behind the animal liberation movement, it is important to consider the action repertoire associated with these groups. This is significant because such actions – most notably the use of direct action – represent a core part of the movement's collective identity. David Pellow (2014) describes the use of direct action in animal and Earth liberation as 'a defining feature of their cultures of resistance – those shared understandings, ideas and knowledge that inform and support individual and collective practices of dissent' (p. 127). Alongside the use of direct action, we also consider the use of consensus decision-making, affinity groups and a non-hierarchical organisational structure. Such actions and structures link animal liberation with anarchist tactical and philosophical practices.

Direct action, which is an 'action without intermediaries, whereby an individual or a group uses their own power and resources to change reality in a desired direction' and which demands 'taking social change into one's own hands, by intervening directly in a situation rather than appealing to an external agent (typically a government) for its rectification' (Gordon, 2008, p. 17), has traditionally been associated with anarchism, and anarchists 'take great pride' in this connection (Franks, 2006, p. 115).

Direct action for animals is associated with the formation of the ALF in 1976, although such tactics were developed during the 1960s within the HSA. By 1972, members of the HSA 'decided more militant action was needed' than the nonviolent disruption of hunts, and so a small group of activists formed the Band of Mercy, who engaged in property damage in defence of animals (ALF, undated, pp. 3–4). The Band of Mercy, named after a nineteenth-century RSPCA youth group, began their campaign by 'destroying guns and sabotaging hunter's vehicles by breaking windows and slashing tyres' (ibid.). The group, including ALF founder Ronnie Lee, expanded their attention to other areas of animal abuse, and received national attention by burning seal hunting boats and expanding their arson campaign to pharmaceutical laboratories. Lee and fellow activist Cliff Goodman were arrested for this liberation and sabotage campaign, and on Lee's release from jail, the ALF was formed.

As the animal liberation movement's use of direct action grew, it came to represent more than just a tactic; instead, it became a 'process whereby activists develop decentralized and egalitarian politics based on cells, affinity groups, and consensus decision-making models' (Nocella, 2011, p. 16). The animal liberation action repertoire emerged from the mid-1970s from a process of trial and error, while individuals and groups built up confidence and trust; although Ronnie Lee and the ALF founders also possessed 'a good knowledge of the tactics of other revolutionary groups', Lee was particularly inspired by the Angry Brigade who were an urban guerrilla group responsible for a series of politically motivated bombings in Britain during the early 1970s (Mann, 2007, p. 51).

The earliest animal liberation tactics focused on directly sabotaging the apparatus used in animal abuse; this included arson against hunters' vehicles and breaking equipment in industries which profit from animal exploitation. Animal liberationists also rescued animals directly from places of abuse to free the animals where possible, or place them in safe homes when necessary. By the late 1980s, these tactics had led to the arrest and long-term imprisonment of leading ALF activists, and some in the movement felt that a relatively small number of animals were rescued for the high risks of imprisonment, and that companies could swiftly carry on without long-lasting damage to their profits. In the 1990s, campaigns were launched with the aim of closing down animal-abusing companies, such as Save the Newchurch Guinea Pigs. In 1999, the Hill Grove Cat farm was forced to close after a two-year campaign of pickets, property damage and liberations (Malle, 2002). Following this success, SHAC was formed in November 1999. SHAC set a three-year target to close down Huntingdon Life Sciences (HLS), the largest animal-testing corporation in Europe. SHAC aimed to achieve this by directly targeting investors and business partners (Crimethinc, 2006). Throughout this campaign, the SHAC model was developed:

> The idea was to focus specifically on the corporation's finances, utilizing the tactics that had closed small businesses to shut down an entire corporation. Activists set out to isolate HLS by harassing anyone involved with any corporation that did business with them. The role of SHAC as an organization was simply to distribute information about potential targets and report on actions as they occurred.
>
> *(Crimethinc, 2006)*

Animal liberationists would target these companies through office demonstrations, home demonstrations, threatening phone calls and emails. The activists 'would target companies until the point when they said they would stop working with Huntingdon', and would then move on to other targets (interview with activist). Through these actions, over 270 companies cut their links with HLS (Upton, 2011), and 'the company's share price, worth around £300 in the 1990s, fell to £1.75 in January 2001, stabilizing at 3 pence by mid-2001' (Crimethinc, 2006).

SHAC activists often participated in home demonstrations targeting people who profited from animal abuse. SHAC ran a home demonstration campaign against Andrew Baker, the principal investor in HLS. The home demonstrations provided an opportunity, like hunt sabotage, to confront the opposition in their own territory and as such exposed 'single-issue activists to the interconnections of the ruling class' (Crimethinc, 2006). Although SHAC acted as an above-ground, legal body, who promoted information on their website with the disclaimer that threatening actions should not be undertaken, SHAC activists received lengthy prison sentences and this caused the group to disband in August 2014.

Animal liberationists have made use of affinity groups. The affinity group has become an established anarchist approach, through which activists can 'avoid the necessity of coordinating action, relying instead on a small, tightly knit group [typically between 6–12 members] in which consensus is most readily available' (Cohn, 2006, p. 205). The affinity group has been regarded by animal liberationists as 'better suited to carrying off daring and decisive actions' which it would not be possible for 'the masses' to 'accomplish spontaneously' (Skirda, 2001, p. 83). This small group structure lessens 'the chances of internal hierarchies developing' and increases the likelihood of achieving consensus (Wilson and Kinna, 2012, p. 330).

Animal liberation has also been associated with consensus decision-making which is a method of decision-making which is designed to produce 'non-hierarchical and non-authoritarian' outcomes 'because everyone agrees' to decisions (in theory, at least) (Wilson and Kinna, 2012, p. 335). Meetings using consensus must be facilitated 'to ensure everyone's voice is heard' by using 'tools and procedures' to help groups 'reach decisions in a collective way' (ibid.). The use of consensus by animal liberationists connects the movement to anarchist theories and tactics, because consensus has not only 'come to be seen as a fundamental principle of anarchism', but for many anarchists, 'consensus and anarchism are all but synonymous' (ibid.).

Concepts

In this section, we consider the key concepts which shape the animal liberation movement; these ideas both help inform activism and are shaped by activist's experiences. The concepts are speciesism, total liberation, intersectionality, opposition to the state, anticapitalism and ecology.

The concept of speciesism was first used by Richard Ryder, and developed throughout the 1970s to situate animal exploitation alongside other forms of prejudice, such as racism and sexism. The concept of speciesism suggested that it was irrational to use species membership as an arbitrary cut-off for moral inclusion, when more significant characteristics, such as the ability to feel pain, cut across species divides (Ryder, 1975, 2000). As Peter Singer (1995) explained,

> Speciesism… is a prejudice or attitude of bias in favour of the interests of members of one's own species and against those of members of other species. It should be obvious that the fundamental objections to racism and sexism… apply equally to speciesism. If possessing a higher degree of intelligence does not entitle one human to use another for his or her own ends, how can it entitle humans to exploit nonhumans for the same purpose?
>
> *(p. 6)*

Speciesism remains a significant concept for the animal liberation movement; however, this is not to say that current animal liberation activists interpret the idea in exactly the same way as Ryder and Singer. In particular, many animal liberationists feel that Ryder and Singer's version of speciesism does not fully take into account intersectionality. For instance, David Pellow (2014) rejects the original use of speciesism because 'this is the kind of blanket equivalence of oppression that is unhelpful for thinking about how power functions across populations and for building coalitions' (p. 44). David Nibert (2002) agrees that the view that speciesism is simply a form of prejudice – 'a view promoted by many advocates and defenders of other animals' – 'hampers somewhat the analysis of the social structural causes of oppression of other animals' (p. 7). Animal rights theorists now often regard speciesism as a system of oppression which shares overlapping features with other forms of oppression. Nibert (2002) explains that there are three elements of mutually reinforcing mechanisms of oppression: first, economic exploitation of 'the Other'; second, iniquitous social power which is politically reflected and reproduced by the state; and finally, ideology which is emergent from and reproduces economic relations.

The concept of speciesism has effected animal liberation activism in a number of ways. As stated by Pellow and Nibert, it has caused rifts with other activist groups who do not see animal exploitation as equivalent to racism or sexism. Animal liberationists who use the concept of speciesism typically regard harm to animals as morally equivalent to harm to humans, and this widens the tactical responses that might be used to defend animals. As ALF founder Ronnie Lee (2010) argues, '[T]o say that the killer of a vivisector acted immorally, whereas the killer of a Nazi people torturer didn't, is to be guilty of speciesism. That's because it would be saying that the torture of humans merited more serious action than the torture of other animals'.

As this example makes clear, the concept of speciesism can be used to argue that violent or coercive tactics can be directed at animal abusers as legitimately as against human abusers, and this is reflected in the militant tactics of some animal liberationists.

The animal liberation movement is also informed by the concepts of total liberation and intersectionality; both concepts have been adapted from ongoing struggles. Frantz Fanon used the term total liberation to describe the intersecting struggle of colonised people and working classes against colonial oppression. The use of total liberation to describe the connections between human, animal and Earth liberation was developed by Steven Best (2014) to argue that 'human liberation is incomplete – as it would still be rooted in domination and oppression – if it does not include these other facets'. Best's theory is influenced by anarchist thinkers such as Élisée Reclus, alongside more recent social justice movements such as 'deep ecology, eco-feminism and the Environmental Justice Paradigm'. David Pellow and Hollie Nyseth Brehm (2015) believe that the concept of total liberation has emerged as a dominant social movement frame due to the combination of radical environmental and animal rights activists with 'the politics of social justice' (p. 186). According to Pellow and Nyseth Brehm, anarchism is a central component of the total liberation frame, along with anticapitalism, support for direct action and 'an ethic of justice and anti-oppression for people, nonhumans and the ecosystems' (ibid.). Total liberation is often understood as 'intersectionality in action', and involves the development of 'alternative ways of transforming social, political and economic relationships and systemic structures' (Nocella, White, Cudworth, 2015, pp. 12–13).

The concept of intersectionality relates to Kimberlé Crenshaw's (1989) approach which outlines the way that different social categories of power such as gender, race and class function in an overlapping way or rely on the same groundings such as dismissal of the 'other'. Intersectionality could theoretically show how categories such as gender, race and class overlap, or focus on how intersectionality is experienced by an individual who is oppressed in a variety of ways. Animal liberation activists often recognise that the first concept of intersectionality is pivotal to understanding multifaceted systems of domination and attempting to resist them. An understanding of intersectionality helps to explain how these various forms of oppression 'intersect and are experienced as simultaneous, as opposed to the additive model of experiencing differences' (Fitzgerald and Pellow, 2014, p. 31). As David Pellow (2014) explains, Earth and animal liberation activists believe that there are 'multiple, interlocking and reinforcing systems of inequality and domination' (pp. 10–11). This understanding of intersectionality is particularly developed by ecofeminists who explain how various forms of systemic relations influence social life in different ways. The concepts of total liberation and intersectionality are extremely important for the animal liberation movement because it has led to a practical commitment to form solidarity alliances across social justice issues.

The animal liberation movement is anticapitalist. Many animal liberation activists believe that the principle reason for animal exploitation is the drive for profit and the property status of animals under capitalism. Bob Torres (2009) argues that the hegemonic order of capitalism means that society has 'not only come to devalue our fellow humans and animals as mere laboring machines, but we also are led to believe that this is the only option for human survival and happiness' (p. 6). Torres evokes the Marxist concept of the commodity fetish to argue that capitalism has distanced customers from the products they consume to such an extent that the commodity of meat is rarely connected with the living being who was slaughtered to make the 'product' possible (p. 37).

Animal liberation activists have consistently highlighted links between the animal-industrial complex, capitalism and the state. Animal liberationists may take the anarchist view of the state as a complex array of social and political institutions which uphold internalised power relations and also have interests of its own; moreover, the state is a 'psychological phenomenon' which creates a certain 'way of thinking about the world and understanding social organisation' (Cudworth, 2007). Animal liberation activists argue that animal-exploiting industries are 'sanctioned, protected, and funded by the state' (Mann, 2007, p. 596). Indeed, this seems to be the case when one considers the large subsidies granted to agricultural industries in Europe and North America. The UK ALF Supporters' Group (2010) argued that

> [t]he British Government has made it very clear that they are the friends of animal research institutes and multinational pharmaceutical companies. This can be seen in the way they have waived the rules and regulations in planning procedures, company law and banking rules, amongst others, in the favour of these wealthy and powerful institutions.
>
> *(p. 6)*

Animal liberationists have combined their desire to end animal exploitation with wider demands for social revolution. For instance, an ALF Supporters' Group editorial in 2009 argued that

> [a]nimal rights activists are well aware of the violence, lies and injustice of the lawmakers. We have reached the state where we need revolutionary change. We have to sweep out the old order of corrupt politics and corporations whose one guiding principle is to keep their pockets full.
>
> *(p. 6)*

As we have seen, the animal liberation movement is connected to Earth liberation and the wider radical green and ecology movement and philosophy. The Earth and animal liberation movements have united partly around their shared tactical use of direct action and belief in total liberation. Earth First! activist Panagioti Tsolkas believes that the 'cross-pollination between anarchism, animal liberation and Earth First!' is partly caused by influential activists, such as Rod Coronado, who adopt these positions. Moreover, Tsolkas argues that it was 'the ambitious direct action culture surrounding the ALF' which first lent 'inspiration and courage' to radical environmentalists (2015). Animal liberationists may highlight the environmentally damaging aspects of livestock agriculture, including the contribution of the livestock sector to greenhouse gas emissions (Wirsenius et al., 2011). Animal liberationists, combining these concepts, feel that only a radical and urgent resistance to capitalism and the state, opposition to all forms of oppression and support for human, animal and Earth liberation, can save the planet from complete environmental destruction.

Theories

The animal liberation movement has been influenced by different theories and continues to feed back into the development of new radical political theories. The movement's development was partly influenced by the success of Peter Singer's *Animal Liberation*, but this is not to say that all animal liberationists would support a utilitarian position.

A growing trend of animal liberation scholar-activists is written and organised around the CAS banner. CAS emerged as an independent field of scholarship during the 2000s to provide theoretical support to the animal liberation movement. CAS scholarship is not simply interested in understanding the animal advocacy movement; instead, it also aims to promote 'a holistic social justice struggle that includes and respects nonhuman animals' (Nocella et al., 2014, p. xxvii). The key concerns of CAS are support for direct action tactics, intersectional politics, speciesism and total liberation. Many of these concerns were developed in ecofeminist writings (Twine and Taylor, 2014). In particular, Carol Adams' work *The Sexual Politics of Meat* (first published 1990) helped develop intersectional theory to include other animals. In fact, ecofeminist scholarship, particularly the works of Adams (1995) and Adams and Donovan (1995), helped shape many of the themes and concerns of CAS, particularly discussions regarding the intersectionality of oppression.

It is clear from the tactics, concerns, concepts and political cultures of the animal liberation movement that the radical political theory it most closely interrelates with is anarchism. And from the circled 'A' in the ALF symbol to the non-hierarchical affinity group structure of hunt saboteurs and the opposition to the state and capitalism of the ALF SG, we know we are witnessing an anarchist (or at least anarchistic) movement. Anarchists have traditionally been able to include all forms of oppression in one overarching critique of state capitalism and other forms of statist society, and animal liberation activists have informed the anarchist movement of the intersections of human and non-human oppression. Anarchism is highly open to intersectionality, 'if not already characterised by it', because anarchists challenge multiple forms of hierarchical domination 'around "race", ethnicity and nation; caste, class and wealth; formations of sex, sexuality and gender; colonialism, imperialism and warfare amongst others' (Cudworth, 2015, p. 93).

Anarchist animal liberationists are interested in the concept of speciesism when it is regarded as another socially constructed form of hierarchy which contributes to, and is fostered by, hierarchical ways of viewing the world. Therefore, animal liberationists – including theorist Bob Torres – have contributed to Murray Bookchin's (1991) work in seeing hierarchy (meaning the 'cultural, traditional and psychological systems of obedience and command') as more deep-rooted than the economic and political systems of class and the State (p. 4). In light of this, anarchist animal liberationists – who focus on a previously neglected form of oppression – will be at the forefront of examining how the state relates to forms of oppression that are outside capitalist relations.

Animal liberationists have seen state repression first-hand (Potter, Corporate Watch). However, anarchist animal liberationists have also been prepared to use bargaining positions created by state structures in order to bring about benefits for animals. For instance, hunt saboteurs may take police forces to court for unlawful arrest and ALF activist Barry Horne used his hunger strikes in 1997 and 1998 to force political concessions. Animal liberationists are at the forefront of tactical developments, and often feel that they have a special and urgent duty to use a diversity of tactics to alleviate the suffering of animals. Animal activists feel this duty both because of the extreme level of suffering inflicted upon animals, and because the animals themselves are unable to formulate or prohibit any tactical suggestions, and so activists are wary of excluding any tactics on the animals' behalf. Animal liberationists may believe that state structures maintain animal abuse because 'the physical, political, economic, ideological, and diversionary power of the state support and build such entangled oppressions while giving such atrocities legal and social respectability' (Nibert, 2002, pp. 184–5). However, they have also recognised that legislation acts as an important tactical means to bring about improvements as they continue to strive for more thoroughgoing revolutionary changes through direct action. Animal liberationists realise that this is a time of urgency, for the future of the planet and for the peaceful existence of humans and other animals. In this time of urgency, they continue to adopt an innovative and diverse action repertoire as they seek to liberate animals by any means necessary.

References

Adams, C. J. (1995) *Neither Man Nor Beast: Feminism and the Defence of Animals* (New York: Continuum).

Adams, C. J. and Donovan, J. (eds.) (1995) *Animals & Women: Feminist Theoretical Explorations* (Durham: Duke University Press).

ALF Supporters' Group Newsletter (April 2009).

ALF Supporters' Group Newsletter (August 2010).

Best, S. (2014) *The Politics of Total Liberation: Revolution for the 21st Century* (Basingstoke: Palgrave Macmillan).

Bookchin, M. (1991) *The Ecology of Freedom: The Emergence and Dissolution of Hierarchy* (New York: Black Rose Books).

Cohn, J. S. (2006) *Anarchism and the Crisis of Representation: Hermeneutics, Aesthetics, Politics* (Selinsgrove: Susquehanna University Press).

Corporate Watch (2009) *State Crackdown on Anti Corporate Dissent: The Animal Rights Movement* (Corporate Watch).

Crenshaw, K. (1989) 'Demarginalizing the Intersection of Race and Sex: A Black Feminist Critique of Antidiscrimination Doctrine, Feminist Theory and Antiracist Politics', *The University of Chicago Legal Forum*, Vol. 140, pp. 139–167.

Crimethinc (2006). Rolling Thunder: A Journal of Dangerous Living, No. 6. [available online, https://crimethinc.com/2008/09/01/the-shac-model-a-critical-assessment, last accessed 16/12/17].

Cudworth, E. (2007) 'Anarchism: The Politics of Anti-Statism', in. Cudworth, E. Hall, T. McGovern, J. (eds.), *The Modern State: Theories and Ideologies* (Edinburgh: Edinburgh University Press).

Cudworth, E. (2011) *Social Lives With Other Animals: Tales of Sex, Death and Love* (Basingstoke: Palgrave Macmillan).

Cudworth, E. (2015) 'Intersectionality, Species and Social Domination', in Nocella II, A. J., White, R. J. and Cudworth, E. (eds.), *Anarchism and Animal Liberation: Essays on Complementary Elements of Total Liberation* (Jefferson: McFarland).

Fitzgerald, A. J. and Pellow, D. (2014) 'Ecological Defense for Animal Liberation: A Holistic Understanding of the World' in. Nocella II, A. J., Sorenson, J., Socha, K. and Matsuoka, A. (eds.), *Defining Critical Animal Studies: An Intersectional Approach for Liberation* (New York: Peter Lang).

Franks, B. (2006) *Rebel Alliances: The Means and Ends of Contemporary British Anarchism* (Edinburgh: AK Press and Dark Star).

Francione, G. and Garner, R. (2010) *The Animal Rights Debate: Abolition or Regulation?* (New York: Columbia University Press).

Garnett, T. (2010) 'Livestock and Climate Change', in. D'Silva, J. and Webster, J. (eds.) *The Meat Crisis: Developing More Sustainable Production and Consumption* (London: Earthscan).

Gordon, U. (2008) *Anarchy Alive!: Anti-Authoritarian Politics from Practice to Theory* (London: Pluto Press).

Hunt Saboteurs Association. (1987) *New Members Pack* (Exeter: Hunt Saboteurs Association).

Law, L. (1982) *Animals* (Spectacular Times).

Lee, R. (2010) Interview, March 27th 2010 [viewed online, https://arzonetranscripts.wordpress.com/2010/03/27/ronnie-lee-interview/, last accessed 23/09/2015].

Malle, A. (ed.) (2002) *A Cat in Hell's Chance: The Story of the Campaign against Hill Grove Cat Farm* (London: Slingshot).

Mann, K. (2007) *From Dusk 'Til Dawn: An Insider's View of the Growth of the Animal Liberation Movement* (London: Puppy Pincher Press).

Nibert, D. (2002) *Animal Rights/Human Rights: Entanglements of Oppression and Liberation* (Lanham: Rowman & Littlefield).

Nocella II, A. J. (2011) 'A Dis-ability Perspective on the Stigmatization of Dissent: Critical Pedagogy, Critical Criminology, and Critical Animal Studies'. *Social Science – Dissertations*. Paper 178.

Nocella II, A. J., Sorenson, J., Socha, K. and Matsuoka, A. (eds.) (2014) *Defining Critical Animal Studies: An Intersectional Approach for Liberation* (New York: Peter Lang).

Nocella II, A. J., White, R. J. and Cudworth, E. (2015) 'Introduction: The Intersections of Critical Animal Studies and Anarchist Studies for Total Liberation', in. Nocella II, A. J., White, R. J. and Cudworth, E. (eds.), *Anarchism and Animal Liberation: Essays on Complementary Elements of Total Liberation* (Jefferson: McFarland).

Pellow, D. N. (2014) *Total Liberation: The Power and Promise of Animal Rights and the Radical Earth Movement* (Minneapolis: University of Minnesota Press).

Pellow, D. N. and Brehm, H. N. (2015) 'From the New Ecological Paradigm to Total Liberation: The Emergence of a Social Movement Frame', *The Sociological Quarterly*, Vol. 56, pp. 185–212.

Regan, T. (2004) *The Case for Animal Rights* (California: University of California Press).

Rowlands, M. (2002) *Animals Like Us* (London: Verso).

Ryder, R. D. (1975) *Victims of Science: The Use of Animals in Research* (London: Davis-Poynter).

Ryder, R. D. (2000) *Animal Revolution: Changing Attitudes towards Speciesism* (Oxford: Berg).

Scarce, R. (2005) *Contempt of Court: A Scholar's Battle for Free Speech from Behind Bars* (Maryland: AltaMira Press).

Singer, P. (1995) *Animal Liberation* (London: Pimlico).

Skirda, A. (2001) *Facing the Enemy: A History of Anarchist Organisation from Proudhon to May 1968* (Edinburgh: AK Press).

Starr, A., Fernandez, L. A., Amster, R., Wood, L. and Caro, M. J. (2008) 'The Impacts of State Surveillance on Political Assembly and Association: A Socio-legal Analysis', *Qualitative Sociology*, Vol. 31, No. 3, pp. 251–270.

Tsolkas, P. (2015) 'No System but the Ecosystem: Earth First! and Anarchism' [viewed online, http://anarchiststudies.org/2015/03/31/no-system-but-the-ecosystem-earth-first-and-anarchism-by-panagioti-tsolkas-1/, last accessed 04/06/2015].

Taylor, N. and Twine, R. (2014) 'Introduction: Locating the "critical" in Critical Animal Studies', in. Taylor, N. and Twine, R. (eds.), *The Rise of Critical Animal Studies: From the Margins to the Centre* (London: Routledge).

Twine, R. (2012) 'Revealing the "Animal-Industrial Complex" – A Concept and Method for Critical Animal Studies?', *Journal for Critical Animal Studies*, Vol. 10. No. 1, pp. 12–39.

Upton, A. (2011) 'In Testing Times: Conducting an Ethnographic Study of UK Animal Rights Protesters', Sociological Research Online, Vol. 16, No. 4, 1, 3.2, 4.1. www.socresonline.org.uk/16/4/1.html.

Wilson, M. and Kinna, R. (2012) 'Key Terms', in. Kinna. R. (ed.), *The Continuum Companion to Anarchism* (London: Continuum).

Wirsenius, S., Hedenus, F. and Mohlin, K. (2011) 'Greenhouse Gas Taxes on Animal Food Products: Rationale, Tax Scheme and Climate Mitigation Effects', *Climate Change*, Vol. 108, pp. 159–184.

WWF. (undated) 'How Many Species Are We Losing?' [viewed online, wwf.panda.org/about_our_earth/biodiversity/biodiversity/, last accessed 16/12/2015].

1.3

BASKING IN THE FIRE

Militant Antifascism as a Most Radical Gesture

M. Testa

Militant antifascists in Europe, USA and Canada have over 100 years of violent struggle to reflect on, having faced ultranationalists, fascists, Nazis, neo-Nazis and a multitude of far right groupuscules with more initials than members. Militant Antifascism is a broad and fluid movement that rejects the ballot box approach to outvote fascism; that disdains state intervention, knowing that heavy manners' legislation against fascists will invariably be used against them and whose political space is on the streets of their towns and cities which can be viciously contested by the far right.

This chapter will show how radicalism is understood by activists in contemporary antifascist organisations; it will describe the various subcultures where many radical antifascist activists come from; and it will put forward a class- not race-based explanation that the socio-economic crises in the first two decades of the twenty-first century are the result of austerity measures imposed by a rich elite government backed by a privately owned news media who have shifted the blame onto migration.

There are three distinct kinds of antifascism, by the state, by liberal or reformist groups, or via militant action and we will give a brief summation of each. The principal concern of militant antifascists is to smash fascism off the streets and physical presence, at marches, meetings, pickets, demos and other activities, and involves time, money and effort. But militant antifascism is not all so muscular: organising support in workplaces and communities, arranging benefit gigs and events to raise money for court costs, fines and petrol, as well as prisoner support, all go on in the background, and are essential to successful political activity. As is propaganda: with cheap technology and social media, militants can now maintain contact with thousands of supporters, set up live feeds at conferences or counter-demonstrations and communicate with others engaged in similar struggles across the world.

Antifascists come to a militant position by various routes, from other less aggressive antiracist organisations, left-wing groups, student or union activity, through anarchist and far left groups, through animal rights and hunt saboteur activities, and through subcultural scenes like the skinhead and punk music scenes. At time, antifascists have to cooperate with people whose politics may not be the same, but to whom the threat of fascism is no less dangerous. Finally, militants need an economic analysis of social problems and to put forward a radical class- not race-based argument.

Migrants are accused of taking up housing, unfairly claiming benefits, overwhelming healthcare and other public services, as well as 'taking our jobs', but housing shortages, benefit cuts, the privatisation of health and other public services, mass unemployment, zero-hour contracts and low wages are not because of 'immigration' as claimed by the right-wing press and far right groups, but because of vindictive politicians and their decisions to extend 'austerity measures' unnecessarily and continue to attack the living standards of the working class.

Introduction: 'There Is No Freedom without Solidarity!'

According to the news media in the UK, an alarming increase in racist crimes was recorded after Brexit and continued throughout the summer, with one attack in September 2016, being particularly horrific: a white thug racially abused then physically attacked a pregnant woman, kicking her in the stomach causing her to miscarry.

It seemed like politics in Europe and the USA were in a perpetual shift to the right, with more intolerant and insular rhetoric, blaming migration and foreigners for every economic and social problem. And it was not only politicians but media voices on TV, the web or in newspapers, that were pushing this hostility, while in many cities and towns, on the streets and in communities, there was also a rise in far right gangs, from Golden Dawn, the German AfD (Alternative for Germany) or the English Defence League (EDL) and their multiple splinter factions, attacking migrants, foreigners and political opponents.

However, in Greece, Germany and the UK, there are large groups of militant antifascists who are ready to confront the 'Euroskeptic, highly nationalist and far right parties' and kick them off the streets, a radical approach that dates back to the 1920s, when socialists, communists, syndicalists and anarchists confronted fascist mobs with equal viciousness. These antifascist militants also realised that accent and language now identified people as targets for racists, and that 'other Europeans' were viewed with as much racist hostility as those with different skin colour or obvious religious affiliation.

Militant and Other Antifascisms

This section will look at how contemporary militants continue the radical history of physical opposition to the far right, and three different approaches to 'antifascism'. First, though, it is necessary to distinguish three types of antifascism that have emerged over the last century: state antifascism, liberal or reformist antifascism, and militant antifascism. I will deal with the first two before moving on to more radical positions, then look at some radically differing antifascist conflicts.

Between 1936 and 1938, British secret services were monitoring messages sent by ships carrying munitions from Italy and Germany to General Franco's forces in Spain, having cracked the code with an early version of the Enigma machine, but this information was not passed on to the antifascist Spanish Republicans who were being hammered by the contents of the naval convoys. The conservative-led British state was monitoring fascist forces not from any innate antifascist tendency: first, they were part of a non-intervention pact with France, led by socialist leader of the Popular Front, Leon Blum, and second, they were more fearful of the spread of Soviet communism and thought that Stalin controlling the antifascist militia and army was more of a threat than Hitler or Mussolini, both of whom were supplying Franco.

This bias is evident in one detailed history of the British secret service, 1909–49, where there are no mentions of fascist leader Oswald Mosley, his British Union of Fascists (BUF) or

British fascists in general. While Hitler et al. are briefly mentioned in passing, communism, the Communist Party of Great Britain (CPGB), the Soviet Union and Spanish Republic are mentioned hundreds of times (Jeffery, 2011).

In 1936, Mosley's paramilitary blackshirts were banned from wearing political uniforms which meant that the BUF swapped blackshirts for collared ones and carried on attacking Jewish and left-wing targets as before. Then, in 1940, the British government rounded up BUF leaders under Defence Regulation 18B, fearing that a fascist fifth column could undermine the war effort at home. Mosley was jailed but later released. None of these actions were to do with the British state holding antifascist sympathies, but only a matter of self-preservation.

In the 1980s, MI5 maintained surveillance of militants: Class War who were part of Anti-Fascist Action (AFA), Socialist Workers Party (SWP) who organised the Anti-Nazi League (ANL), Militant and Youth Against Racism (YRE), and the Revolutionary Communist Party's Workers Against Racism and anti-deportation campaigns.

This indicates two things: that in the early 1980s, the radical left were focused on, and more numerous than, fascist organisations; and that state agencies were concerned by the far left much more than by the far right. After the 1979 general election brought the right-wing Margaret Thatcher to power, and, more to the point, after several years of bruising confrontations with militant antifascists, the far right National Front (NF) went from increasing their electoral respectability to collapsing into bickering groupuscules, while a nascent British National Party (BNP mark 2) and British Movement (BM) continued attacks on left-wing paper sales, bookshops, meetings, demonstrations and gigs.

The state has continued its attempts to undermine the radical left and often act as provocateurs, as exposures of undercover cops like Mark Kennedy in radical green circles showed in 2011. Just because some dirty cops have been exposed, forcing the police to apologise, it is unlikely that they have ceased their spying. The state prefers its own quietly sinister kind of 'anti-extremism' by stealth, seeking only to maintain itself. Given this kind of history, it would be self-defeating for militants to rely on any state that has continually tried to infiltrate, undermine and criminalise antifascist activities and must negate fascist provocation themselves.

Historically, liberal antifascism has fared less well: bourgeois democratic institutions have long faced the conflict between allowing fascists freedom of speech or legislating against them, emphasised by the German liberals' slogan about the Nazis before 1933: 'We are so liberal that we even grant the freedom to destroy liberty' while leading Nazi Joseph Goebbels also made his intentions perfectly clear: 'We have come to the Reichstag in order to destroy it. If democracy is stupid enough to reward us for doing this, this is the problem of democracy' (Ryan, 2001, 75). This is still a liberal conundrum, as Harris points out: 'The problem remains as to whether groups which openly abuse democracy in order to undermine it should have the same tolerance extended to them by the law, as they would deprive others of it' (Harris, 1994, 205).

For Harris, the Greeks managed to legislate by canny wording, as the 1975 Greek Constitution states 'that political parties must contribute to the untrammeled functioning of democracy' (ibid.) rather than operating to undermine it, although this has not stopped the neo-fascist Golden Dawn securing seats in parliament.

Not only are liberal antifascists reformists, but they often collude with the state in order to distance themselves from any violence. At an anti-EDL demo in Manchester, 2009, anarchists and radical socialists were extremely critical of Unite Against Fascism (UAF) for pointing out militants to police. In France, during the 2016 protests, reformist communist stewards from the CGT policed the anti-labour law demonstrations and tooled up with base-ball bats and helmets to take on the anarchists and militant black bloc. Perhaps this statement by UK anarchists clarifies the matter:

> Anti-fascism, if it's effective, is not just a problem for fascists, but a problem for the state too. While liberal anti-fascists see no problem in reinforcing the state and aim to marginalise fascism through moral arguments, militant anti-fascists have a different agenda. We don't want things to stay as they are; we want people to fight for a better society.
>
> *(Key, 2005, 32)*

For liberals, 'the essence of anti-fascism consists of struggling against fascism while supporting democracy, in other words, of struggling not for the destruction of capitalism, but to force capitalism to renounce its totalitarian form' (Barot, 2001, 2).

Anarchist antifascists, in particular, do not see fascism as an isolated problem but as an aberration caused by the failure of capitalism. Hence, they do not make demands for moderate reforms: anarchists seek the destruction of the state in order to construct a society where individual liberty coexists with communism and mutual aid.

Militant antifascism is a radical position that has to employ extreme and drastic methods to counter the far right. 'By "radical" I mean going deep down, below the obvious surface, and seeing the most basic forces at work. And by "radical" I mean making the most extreme, drastic, changes in how we look at things and what we do in action.'[1] Militants have to understand that political violence is an unfortunate though necessary form of dissuasion against opponents who are more than capable of instigating or reciprocating it.

Fascism has long fetishised violence: the physical over the intellectual; the martial over the social; the hierarchy and order of subordination; and the uniformity, weaponry and rhetoric of warriors. In the UK, the reality has frequently diverged from such idealism and far right members have been exposed as sex offenders and perpetrators of domestic violence. Militant antifascists must also engage in 'contra-legal' activity, and expect to disobey state directives, bans, dispersal orders or prevention of access during demonstrations.

The majority of militant antifascist activities are in opposition to street-level provocations when the far right mobilises with marches or demonstrations. These are organised for several reasons: to highlight or racialise an issue, i.e. immigration; to register dissent from state policy, i.e. immigration; as a show of strength to either intimidate or provoke political opponents; to generate publicity for an organisation or to gain support from voters for far right political electioneering. Unlike reformist and liberal antifascists with their slogans and party logos, many militants on counterdemonstrations, particularly anarchists, are not visibly aligned to any organisation or public figures; they are not seeking electoral respectability; they do not need favourable publicity for political programmes and are not out to capture votes: they are there to confront and prevent fascist incursions into their communities.

Antifascist Action: A Global Struggle

The AFA banner is an international one, black with a white circle in the middle showing the red and black flags of radical left solidarity, the AFA name beneath it. It was first unfurled in Germany around 1932, when the Communist Party (KPD) organised militants into physical force squads whose job was to protect workers' activities and organise 'action against high rents, evictions and confiscations', as well as pursuing a violent 'fight against the National Socialist threat in the neighbourhoods' (Rosenhaft, 2008, 54).

Since then, the design has been tattooed on militants, printed on clothing, sprayed on walls, used as a book cover design and now flies proudly above the ranks of thousands of antifascists around the world. In the history of antifascism, different levels of intensity have been required in the larger struggle against racist organisations, neo-Nazis or ultranationalists. By 2017, antifascists had been involved in protracted armed conflicts in Syria and Ukraine, as well as violent street battles in Greece and the UK. These are very different and complex situations, especially in Syria and Ukraine, where further confusion is caused by the interventions of foreign governments, rogue militias and counter-insurgents. In Syria, members of the progressive left-wing Kurdish militia are fighting against the Islamic State forces, and have been joined by militant antifascists from many other countries who have also flown the AFA flag over their positions. In the Ukraine, the armed struggle against Russian ultranationalist aggression has been difficult and deadly, but Ukrainian antifascists resisted and have flown the AFA flag over their lines also. The following section looks at these very different scales of militant engaged in the struggle against oppression in all its forms.

Syria: Fighting for Socialism, against Fascism, in the Rojava Revolution

In 2017, the fight against IS/Daesh in Syria had become an even more complex, dangerous and shifting area of conflict with combatants covertly, and not so covertly, backed by international geopolitical and military interests. Militants from around the world travelled to the Rojava region to join the People's Protection Units (YPG) organised by the left-wing Kurdish Democratic Unity Party (PYD) in the spirit of international antifascist solidarity but the Women's Protection Unit (YPJ) received more media attention. The mainstream press knows little about radical history where women and men have fought together against imperialism, patriarchy and fascism; the *sans culottes* of the French Revolution in 1789; the Spanish anarchist *Mujeres Libres*; the French *Maquis*; or revolutionaries in Cuba, Vietnam, Ireland, Nicaragua or Colombia. The images of the YPG/YPJ were also reminiscent of the Bosnian defence forces in Sarajevo (1991–95), with their AK47s, camouflage and trainers. The red and black AFA flag was raised in the Rojava by members of the International Freedom Battalion (IFB) who formed the Bob Crow Brigade, named after the UK militant trade union leader.

But are Daesh fascists? The term 'fascist' has been appropriated or misapplied to despots, crackpots and totalitarians who have little in common with twentieth-century classical fascism which is characterised by a singular leader, a managed economy, social and sexual conservatism, heavy militarisation and a convenient 'other' to blame for erosion of national morale. North Korea, Saddam's Iraq and Daesh have been called fascist despite their differences regarding power structures, expansionism and economics. North Korea is an insular nepotistic dynasty that keeps its citizens as a semi-educated urban peasantry; Saddam committed acts of genocide against Kurds, Yazidis and others, and disenfranchised Shia'ah Muslims with a brutality that also paralysed his co-religionists; Daesh have lacked a singular totemic figure like Saddam or Kim Jong-Un with any longevity; they have occupied territory through fanatical violence but have no functioning semi-state like the Afghan Taliban; and while fascist gangsters attacked opponents' printing presses to create a monopoly on information, Daesh may have elevated vicious executions into social media spectacles, but any hope of a digital monopoly is unlikely.

Fascism's economic model benefited both dictator and capitalist while enforcing an industrial class hierarchy to maintain the momentum of capital within that state and although pan-European fascism responded to capital *at that time* but did not survive beyond 1945 once the economic context had shifted. Daesh generate capital from gangsterism, extortion, illicit oil revenues and donations from certain states but wherever Daesh are based, a functioning economy and legitimate business cannot go ahead: war is chaos and disrupts imports and exports, while taxes levied on locals go towards military campaigns rather than education, health or legal structures (all of which maintain and reproduce capital and workers). The influence of Daesh may spread from North Africa to the Russian Caucasus, from Pakistan to Europe, but there is no functioning state linking these areas into a singular economy. Their influence may be wide but it is also diffuse.

Ukraine

In November 2013, when Russia annexed the Crimea in Eastern Ukraine, mass protests were organised, some reaching 800,000. These turned violent, ultimately leading to the resignation of President Victor Yanukovych who many accused of overseeing economic decline, with inadequate wages and underfunded public services. His replacement, the right-wing oligarch Petro Poroshenko, could hardly be welcomed by the left-wing activists who fought in street battles against cops and later faced intimidation from pro-government fascist gangs. In West Ukraine, there was widespread support for joining the EU, while in the mainly Russian-speaking East, militias emerged, supported by Russian forces and Russian materiel, which Putin denied. Cold War phraseology was thawed out and both the 'Western' Ukrainians and pro-Russians accused each other of being 'fascists'. And there certainly were fascists involved. On the pro-Russian side, far right mercenaries from America, Colombia and Europe were bolstering the militias, with one American calling the Ukrainian Army 'CIA backed Nazi scum' (Walker, 2015).

In Western Ukraine, organisations like Azov Battalion, Right Sector and Bandera were clearly fascist and ultranationalist, and used as militia in the armed conflict and then later as street enforcers: in Rivne, December, 2015, fascist thugs assaulted a trade union activist; in April, 2016, neo-Nazis attacked a commemoration in Odessa, while many who took part in the right-wing coup gained influence in the new government.

In early 2015, on the front lines of the contested Donbass region, Ukrainian antifascists were photographed with the AFA flag, slightly altered to read 'Anti-Imperialist Action' in reference to Putin's expansionist agenda. Activists in the UK organised support for The Anti-Fascist Committee of Ukraine to raise awareness of the complexities and ambiguities of the war. Russia organised its own Anti-Fascist Committee which, bizarrely, included Nick Griffin, former leader of the BNP, an example of how this confused and shifting political situation refused any neat binaries of left/right or fascist/antifascist.

In May, 2014, the EU offered Ukraine financial support of $15 billion to stabilise the economy although this would be contingent on 'reforms' and a deal with the International Monetary Fund. After their government took the stabilising package, the majority of Ukrainians saw living standards plummet, public spending cut, national resources privatised and the economy opened up to larger outside interests. Despite continuing social unrest, the government had little to offer but more austerity. Ukraine's exhausted economy and shaken infrastructure were now vulnerable to manipulation by outside interests, just as Greece had experienced.

Greece: 'The Future Is Uncertain'

In Athens in 2013, Pavlos Fyssas, an antifascist musician, was murdered by a member of the far right Golden Dawn party who was arrested near the site. Antifascist protests in the city turned violent, solidarity demonstrations took place in many European cities and shortly after, two members of Golden Dawn were shot and killed, with one other badly wounded. Then, in September 2013, the socialist government brought charges against the leadership of Golden Dawn in what looked like a government antifascist initiative to inhibit their growth. As is often the case, far right parties in opposition can offer simple solutions to complex economic problems that they do not have to actually act on, and that become attractive to voters and Greece was no different.

In 2009, Greece's debt crisis had reached a critical point and by 2010, general strikes, demonstrations and riots increased in number. The bailouts from the European Central Bank and the EU were contingent on successively severe austerity measures. By 2012, as the economic crisis worsened, demonstrations became more militant. Prolonged austerity measures guaranteed a bleaker future and the resignation of Prime Minister George Papandreou in 2012, and the collapse of the centrist government, saw popular support for anti-austerity parties rise. This benefited the radical left but also boosted the far right and Golden Dawn could claim 6.92% of the national vote. In the film *Burning From The Inside*, one activist said, 'Greek fascists grew stronger because of the austerity measures. Social movements suffered a defeat … and after, when ministers from Christian and Social democrats deliberately fired up a discussion on immigration' (*Burning from the Inside*, 2015).

As mass demonstrations continued to be violent, with street battles where anarchists and radicals fought against fascists and police, it was little surprise that cops would side with Golden Dawn. Police naturally tend towards authoritarianism, uniforms and violence against the left, and in the 2015 election, which saw Alexis Tsipras of the radical left-wing Syriza party became prime minister, it turned out that 50% of police officers had voted for Golden Dawn.

Not only did Tsipras have to deal with deteriorating economic conditions and mass unemployment, but the 2016 refugee crisis also hit Greece harder than most EU countries. The extensive and complicated Greek coastline, an archipelago stretching across the Mediterranean, and its proximity to the Middle East, made the country a primary destination for migrants. Despite its own dire economic forecast, Greece still took in more refugees than richer EU countries, but was clearly overwhelmed, with some places reaching crisis point.

Greek antifascists have been exemplary in solidarity with migrants stranded there, and have distributed food, clothing and household essentials, organised free language classes and held supportive meetings, demonstrations, gigs, cultural exchanges and other social events to prevent migrants becoming isolated and vulnerable. In July 2016, leftist radicals took over an empty hotel and turned it into homes for refugees. Examples like these show the kind of social organisation possible within communities, supporting the desperate, while also fighting fascists and the unwelcome attentions of the state.

UK 2017

As we have seen, antifascists are involved in highly volatile and dangerous conflicts, and as stated earlier, militant antifascism is determined by the different levels of intensity required when confronting the far right. For many militants, antifascism is a reactive force, escalated or reduced to an appropriate level in order to confront the fascist threat. However, with increasing strength, numbers and confidence, antifascists can become proactive, closing down the far right's political space and forcing them to withdraw from street confrontations.

As of 2016, despite 100 years of violent resistance, militant antifascism in the UK was relatively benign compared to Ukraine or Greece. It is remarkable that there have been so few fatalities: in 1974, Kevin Gately was killed when police attacked antifascists demonstrating against the NF and in 1979, Blair Peach was killed in a confrontation with police at an antifascist demonstration in West London. Gerry Gable, editor of Searchlight magazine, downplayed UK antifascist violence saying that 'the violence of most of these anti-fascists was for the most part a punch in the nose or a kick in the balls, whereas the Nazis were into killing or attempted murders' (Renton, 2006, 172).

Throughout 2015 and 2016, UK neo-Nazis staged several provocative demonstrations that ended in the worst violence seen for a long time. On 16 August 2015, a far right excursion into Liverpool ended up as an embarrassing disaster when the clutch of neo-Nazi groupuscules found themselves surrounded by hundreds of locals and militants, before being trapped in the train station as they were pelted with eggs, bananas and worse. A humiliating photograph of a dozen or so fascists hiding behind a steel shutter in the luggage office, their feet showing at the bottom, protected by a large amount of police was widely circulated. Other fascists caught outside police lines found themselves outmatched by mobile groups of militants. This was no ordinary antifascist demonstration with placards, paper sales and a megaphone, but a large, spontaneous and successful response by the people of Liverpool who had no intention of letting fascists march through their town.

On 30 January 2016, a far right demonstration took place in Dover that was one of the few times when the two sides engaged in prolonged and vicious fighting. Even before the demo started, there was a major clash when five coaches of antifascists and one of far right supporters stopped at the same service station on the way, leading to arrests and police preventing the coaches from carrying on to the demonstration. Despite heavy manners policing, militants and neo-Nazis battled each other throughout the day, resulting in many injuries and arrests. Members of the far right factions were filmed throwing rubble and other detritus about, most of which landed on their own supporters, causing photogenic head wounds for the mainstream media to publish and police to scrutinise. Although some neo-Nazis wore masks, many did not and were happy to perform for the cameras, which resulted in waves of arrests and harsh sentencing throughout that year: one fascist got seven years for attacking a photographer, another got four and one of the ringleaders got two and a half years. One antifascist was given four months but got out on appeal after a few weeks, while another was jailed for twelve months. Arrests continued throughout the year and saw many more fascists imprisoned.

True to the proverb 'As a dog returns to its own vomit, so fools repeat their folly', around fifty neo-Nazis returned to Liverpool on 27 February 2016, this time managing to get out of the train station before ending up surrounded by police for their own protection on the steps of St. George's Hall. There, objects and abuse flew freely as hundreds of locals and militants surrounded them. One hapless group of Polish ultranationalists tried to join the main group but were caught by militants and overwhelmed, only to fall out later with the English Nazis over their Hitler salutes. Once again, this was a spontaneous, successful reaction by locals and militants.

In April 2016, there were further confrontations and more than a dozen arrests at a Dover demonstration, where once again the far rightists were kept under heavy police protection, while antifascists, who outnumbered them at least three to one, tried to disrupt their march by blocking the route. The day turned out to be a success for the police: they brought in extra support and prevented large-scale confrontations between demonstrators; kept both sides apart from each other most of the time; and arrested some neo-Nazis over the violence in January, thus redeeming themselves after the embarrassing riot earlier that year.

On 28 May 2016, neo-Nazis organised yet another demonstration against immigration in Dover. The local Tory MP wanted to ban it and comments on the local news website appeared to support this. However, the day proved to be anticlimactic as only thirty neo-Nazis turned up, two of whom were arrested, and the rest spent most of their time surrounded by police whose high expectations of violence did not materialise. A neo-Nazi gig-organised venue over forty miles away was poorly attended. The memory of recent violence did little to endear the far right to the citizens of Dover or the truckers they were ostensibly supporting. Banning orders, bail restrictions, lack of money and bottle meant that the size of the far right demonstrations in Dover had reduced exponentially. However, this is not something antifascists can claim as a victory: although reduced numbers at both Liverpool and Dover could look like a lack of support for the far right and popular support for the left, this was a cumulative victory for the state who took decisive action via the courts and large police actions, and although antifascists could afford themselves a wee moment of *schadenfreude*, it was with the knowledge that heavy sentences for the far right will inevitably be used against the far left at some point.

Tighten Up! Antifascist Subculture

This section looks at a subculture within a subculture, considering how music has played an important role in militant antifascist politics. The various antifascisms attract many different kinds of people for many different reasons, and militant antifascism is no different. However, it is possible to identify how contemporary activists can find their way into physically opposing the far right.

People can come to militant antifascism through local, liberal antiracism groups or trade union activities; radical socialist, Trotskyite or communist fringe parties; and, in the UK particularly, from animal rights, hunt saboteur, squatter and anarchist groups. Also important are subcultural routes like the skinhead and punk music scenes. This is difficult to quantify but we can trace the historical relationship in the UK between the punk, skinhead and ska scenes, and militant antifascism.

In the UK, the black-clad anarchist style can be traced back to the stern English anarcho-pacifist collective Crass, whose radical antiwar/antistate/vegetarian agenda was propelled by buzz-cutting guitars and military drumming. Many punks were radicalised by Crass, however temporarily, while members of Crass had themselves been influenced by The Clash. After 1977, as the music began to proliferate and evolve, many on the UK punk scenes detached themselves from the initial amoral, political ambiguity of blank-faced nihilism or wearing swastikas for shock value, and began to realise that a large, aggressive fascist party, the NF, was increasing its presence on the street. Its thugs, along with neo-Nazi skinheads from the BM, were attacking punk gigs, seeing them as viable, political targets. Nazis who followed Sham 69 pretty much destroyed the band's future through violence, while others tried to break up gigs by left-wing bands. As Andy Gill from the Gang Of Four attested, 'There were physical battles with skinheads. You'd get some of them turning up at gigs and fighting with people' (Reynolds, 2009, 113).

Sex Pistols singer Johnny Rotten said about the NF, 'I deplore them. How could anyone vote for something so ridiculously inhumane?' (Birchall, 2010, 35), while many punks began to support Rock Against Racism (RAR) and the ANL, both aligned to the Trotskyite SWP. The Clash headlined one of the ANL's carnivals; RAR gigs saw reggae bands and punk bands touring under the slogan 'Black & White, Unite & Fight' and musical cross-fertilisation like feminist punks, The Slits, who mixed dub rhythms with splanky punk songs, and many other bands put an obligatory reggae tune on their records. There was genuine unity between punk and reggae musicians, while many alienated punks felt an affinity with black youth as both were visually distinctive, frequent targets of police attention and subject to fascist street hassle. RAR/ANL promoted antifascism in a diverse, positive way, with its supporters organising meetings, marches, demos, writing or selling fanzines, making badges, fly-posting, stickering, booking venues, hiring transport and hassling bands to commit.

Antifascists punks and black youth were not the only visible targets of fascist aggression: paper sales, meetings and demos by leftist organisations, including the SWP which was one of the largest and most active. The SWP began to organise squads of militants who were often associated with local football or music scenes, to defend activists from fascist marauders. Birchall writes that 'the squads were in effect the all important physical force arm of the Anti-Nazi League (ANL), launched in 1977 to counter the growing threat from the National Front.' The 'squadists' organised regionally and began taking the initiative, kicking the fascists out of gigs and engaging them at the street level. However, their increasing autonomy worried the SWP Central Committee who ordered their disbandment and expelled the main participants. Some of the squadists went on to form Red Action (RA), which was instrumental in organising AFA, expanding militant opposition to the far right throughout the UK. AFA militants had clearly learned from their time with RAR/ANL that successful, broadly supported antifascism needed a multiplatform approach: AFA organised carnivals and gigs under the Cable Street Beat logo, arranged fund raisers to pay fines and support antifascist prisoners, published magazines and other propaganda and made a programme for BBC's Open Space in 1993. The AFA network covered the entire country, with each group having its own local identity.

The anarcho-syndicalist Direct Action Movement (DAM), now known as Solidarity Federation (Solfed), supported AFA – as did Class War, which drew in some of the anarcho-punks adrift from the Crass scene, and specialised in provocations like the War On The Rich. Hann, half-jokingly, distinguished two dominant subcultures in AFA: 'anarcho/ crusty types … who we nicknamed "Smelly AFA"' and the 'more casually dressed AFA members who the Smellies nicknamed "Aftershave AFA"' (Tilzey & Hann, 2003, 144). AFA was fully operational from 1985 to the mid-1990s when the BNP, who had usurped the NF, moved from street politics to electioneering, although the AFA Fighting Talk magazine continued to be produced for several more issues.

In 2017 in the UK, Anti-Fascist Network (AFN) is a mainly anarchist initiative that developed in response to the sudden popularity of the EDL between 2009 and late 2013. Although the EDL started a painful slide into entropy following the resignation of their leader, several splinter factions emerged who were openly fascist and neo-Nazi. AFN states that they are 'non-hierarchical, will never work with the police and is not affiliated to any political party' (Anti-Fascist Network). AFN is usually at the forefront of activity in the UK, with participants also involved in other political works: Brighton AFN is linked with the Cowley Club, a radical autonomous centre that continues to host many punk gigs and fund raisers.

Stay SHARP!

The relationship between skinheads, casual racism and organised fascism is a prolonged and complex one, and, as with any other subculture, there are significant differences in beliefs, apparel and symbolism that are often only discernible to the initiated. Opinions are divided: the Redskins, an SWP punk-soul band, had stated: 'The misconception has always been that skinheads were all right wing, which they were not. If you look at the Specials audiences, the 2-Tone bands, Madness, there were a lot of skinheads, a lot of antiracist skinheads and left-wing skinheads and socialist skinheads' (Kowalski, 1986). While one neo-Nazi band member wrote: 'The [Chelsea] Shed End in the late '60s and early 70s was skinhead city, Paki-haters every one. They embraced the politics of the far right, yet listened to black music … The Skinhead Moonstomp, Harry J and the Allstars … classic reggae tunes' (Ward & Henderson, 2000, 57).

Both opinions try to bend a shared, contentious history to their individual perspectives, but at least they supply a binary of far left and far right skinheads, although the latter admits the ridiculous contradiction regarding musical choice and racism. The two definitive books on UK skinheads, Skinhead by Nick Knight (1982) and Skins by Gavin Watson (2007), both photographers, feature material from the late 1970s and early 1980s and only show a few black and mixed-race gang members.

In 1982, some New York skins started up SHARP, or Skinheads Against Racial Prejudice, to try to detach themselves from negative associations. Wearing the SHARP badge, which featured the classic warrior helmet logo from Trojan Records, was an affiliation, a statement of principle, rather than membership of a political organisation. It also served to re-emphasise the original skinhead connection with black London rude boys, ska and soul music. SHARP skins are now prevalent in the USA, Europe and the UK and other skinheads in the USA and have aligned themselves with RASH (Red and Anarchist Skinheads), or more local groups like HARM (Hoosier Anti-Racist Movement).

Neo-Nazi skins started the Blood and Honour scene, which remains clandestine due to harassment by antifascists and rejection by mainstream record companies and gig venues. 'White Power' music sounds like second-rate punk with Third Reich lyrics and a 4/4 beat. Adherents wear a semi-paramilitary style of dress at odds with the more stylish wardrobe of traditional skins. White power skinheads have tried to play down the influences of black music (ska/reggae/soul) and 'rude boy' style on the original skinheads, while some have claimed that being an antiracist skinhead is somehow contradictory, which only amplifies the reductionist views of outsider media. The UK and US punk and skinhead scenes overlap, as both favour similar music. In the UK, The Oppressed brought the SHARP idea back from a visit to the States. Original punks, The Angelic Upstarts, supported AFA in the 1980s and 1990s, and singer Mensi presented an AFA TV documentary, *Fighting Talk*. Blaggers ITA were also members of London AFA. In America, the Dead Kennedys' classic song *Nazi Punks Fuck Off!* seemed to sum it up for many punks and skins. Some punks have tried to remain apolitical and the Cockney Rejects have been subject to fascist violence because of it.

In the UK in 1979, it was 2-Tone ska that united many skinheads, punks and rude boys, in bands and in the audience: The Specials, The Beat, The Selecter fronted by Pauline Black, and the early, heavier UB40 were all multiracial bands that mixed exuberance with political comment. The 2-Tone label black-and-white graphics are iconic, and the irrepressible mix of ska, reggae and punk has been adapted and adopted by hundreds of bands around the world ever since.

A Class-Based Argument

This final section looks at how militants in the UK need to understand and put forward a class-based argument, opposed to the race-based ones of the right wing, and see how economics and populist racism become entangled and how migration is being blamed for the effects of austerity measures imposed by successive governments.

Migrants Overuse Public Resources

After the banking crisis in 2007/2008, the government bought 83% of RBS for £45bn of public money which, according to the National Audit Office, meant that the 'unprecedented'

£850bn of support for the banks was 'justified' to head off the potential damage of one or more of them going bust, and preserve people's savings and confidence in the financial system. Which means taking money from the poorest individuals who need it to survive and giving it to the richest institutions, who don't. The cost of this goes beyond quoting numbers: it has had a sustained, traumatic effect on the working class as we can see with a brief summation of UK austerity policy between 2008 and 2016. In 2008, the UK Prime Minister Gordon Brown cut £20 billion from public spending and tax cuts, and began the twenty-first century's 'Age of Austerity'. In 2010, the UK coalition government announced a £40 billion plan of increased taxes and drastic cuts affecting public services, jobs, housing, pensions and public sector wages. In 2012, the coalition announced an accumulation of £34 billion from welfare spending and increased Value Added Tax on consumer goods to 20%, all of which negatively affected the marginalised, the unemployed and the lowest paid workers. In 2013, home secretary Ian Duncan Smith said that benefits were far too generous and aimed at cutting them by £20 billion. Then, in 2014, the coalition extended the period of austerity until 2018, although this was abandoned by the Theresa May regime in July, 2016, who stated that 'we will no longer target a surplus at the end of this parliament'. While this may have been a reversal of policy, it was not a reversal of misery: the accumulated cuts to public spending of £120 billion over eight years had already impacted on the living standards of the working class.

Migrants Sell Papers!

In 2015, the mainstream press printed headlines full of suspicion and fear: on 23 July, the right-wing Daily Mail claimed that 'swarms' of migrants were desperate to get out of Calais and into the UK then two weeks after reprinted the image of a dead Syrian child washed up on a Turkish beach only to revert to their previous terminology of 'invasions' and 'floods' of immigrants who were ready to 'terrorise' us. Daily newspaper headlines from 2015 up to the Brexit referendum and beyond were frequently hysterical and matched the Leave campaign's 'Breaking Point' poster that showed long queues of migrants poised to falsely claim benefits and/or steal peoples' jobs. Panicky reports were supported by selective use of statistics. According to the Office of National Statistics, by the year ending March, 2016, 633,000 people had migrated into the UK, while 306,000 people had left it. The duration of any one person's stay will vary: some work short-term contracts or longer ones before leaving; others stay, to set up a business or start a family with a 'local' partner. Therefore, the actual make-up of the total is shifting and complex. In her 2016 conference speech, Home Secretary Amber Rudd said that she intended to make firms register 'international' workers to stop foreigners 'taking jobs British people could do'. Activists involved in the struggle against racism will have heard this rhetoric before: Labour Prime Minister Gordon Brown wanted 'British Jobs For British Workers' in 2007, and the far right BNP agreed, but with the caveat that 'When we say it, we mean it!'

Migrants Cause the Housing Crisis

In December, 2012, then home secretary Theresa May said that 'more than a third of all new housing demand in Britain was caused by immigration' and then in 2016 blamed the housing market for being 'dysfunctional' and failing working people. Chancellor of the Exchequer, Phillip Hammond, said that he would fund 15,000 new homes on unused public land and give £3 billion in 'loans to house builders to build another 25,000 homes by 2020' which was absolutely meaningless to the estimated 900,000 workers on zero-hours contracts, or the 1.4 million on minimum wage (one of the lowest in Europe) and their dependents. The government said that residents in housing associations may get the right to buy, which would further reduce public housing availability. Austerity measures were imposed to deal with the shortfall of money caused by government handouts to the banking sector, starting in 2008, and this has resulted in enormous cuts to public spending, and migrants are being blamed in the mainstream media for the effects of these economic decisions that have severely impacted on the working class in the UK. Mainstream media also maintained hostility towards migrants in the run-up to the Brexit Referendum and this populist racism helped the 'Leave' vote and data and numbers were selectively used to inflate fears of being 'swamped' or 'flooded' by migrants who have also been cited as causing a crisis in the housing market that has actually been going for some long time.

In 2015, Yannis Varoufakis, the radical Greek economist, stated that 'austerity is being used as a cover story to conduct class war' (Stone, 2015). Bank bailouts, tax breaks for multinational companies (i.e. bribes), tax cuts for the rich and individual tax dodgers mean less money for public spending. Poor wages, longer hours, underfunding and privatisation cause the NHS to be overwhelmed, not migrants. Low pay for teachers, larger class sizes and shortages of facilities and resources are due to government policy, not migrants. Local councils are strictly limited on how much they can borrow to build new social housing, while building firms are given grants to build houses for the private market. 42% of rented accommodation is substandard. This is down to government policy, not migrants.

Migrants do not impose 'sanctions' on disability benefits that lead to suicide and hardship.

Migrants did not create the need for food banks. Migrants do not pass laws that attack the poorest in society; they are often the poorest in society. All of these things are what governments do, while blaming migrants for it.

Note

1 Wayne Price, email to the author, 2017.

References

Anti-Fascist Network 'About' https://antifascistnetwork.org/about/.
Barot, Jean, *Fascism/Anti-Fascism*, London: 'In The Spirit of Emma,' 2001.
Birchall, Sean, *Beating the Fascists*, London: Freedom, 2010.
Harris, Geoffrey, *The Dark Side of Europe*, Edinburgh: University Press, 1994.
Jeffery, Keith, *MI6: The History of the Secret Intelligence Service 1909–1949*, London: Bloomsbury, 2011.
Key, Anna, *Beating Fascism: Anarchist Anti-Fascism in Theory & Practice*, London: Kate Sharpley Library, 2005.
Knight, Nick, *Skinhead*, London: Omnibus, 1982.
Kowalski, Eva, Redskins Interview, London, 1986.
Renton, Dave, *When We Touched the Sky*, Cheltenham: New Clarion, 2006.
Reynolds, Simon, *Totally Wired*, London: Faber, 2009.
Rosenhaft, Eve, *Beating the Fascists?* Cambridge: University Press, 2008.
Ryan, Nick, *Hateland*, Edinburgh: Mainstream, 2001, 75.
Stone, Joe 'Austerity is being used as a cover-story for class war against the poor', *The Independent* 25 September 2015 retrieved from www.independent.co.uk/news/uk/politics/austerity-is-being-used-as-a-cover-story-for-class-war-against-the-poor-yanis-varoufakis-says-10516247.html.
Tilzey, Steve & Dave Hann, *No Retreat*, Lytham: Milo, 2003.

Walker, Shaun, '"We are preventing a third world war": the foreigners fighting with Ukrainian rebels', *The Guardian* 24 September 2015 www.theguardian.com/world/2015/sep/24/ukraine-conflict-donbass-russia-rebels-foreigners-fighting.

Ward, Colin & Chris Henderson, *Who Wants It?* Edinburgh: Mainstream, 2000.

Watson, Gavin, *Skins*, Shropshire: Independent Music Press, 2007.

Filmography

Burning from the Inside, dir. Marsia Tzivara, 2015.

Fighting Talk, AFA for BBC2 Open Space, 1992.

1.4

THE RADICAL POLITICS OF ANTIMILITARISM

Chris Rossdale

In 1917, the anarchist Emma Goldman was arrested in New York and subsequently jailed for distributing information that told young men how they could avoid being drafted into the US army and sent across the Atlantic to fight in the First World War (Goldman 1970: 598–623). In the early 1990s in the Philippines, a coalition of NGOs, environmental groups, students, peace organisations and others, under the banner of the 'Anti-Treaty Movement', successfully pressured the Philippine Senate to refuse to ratify the Military Bases Agreement between the Philippines and the US, forcing the latter to withdraw its military personnel and close its military bases (Yeo 2012: 35–62). And in 2009, the six men and women who would later become known as the EDO Decommissioners broke into the EDO-MBM factory in Brighton and used hammers to smash as much machinery as possible, causing over £200,000 worth of damage and halting the factory's ability to supply the Israeli Air Force, which was at that point engaged in a brutal campaign of bombing raids in Gaza.

These three examples, divergent in their means and particular aims, are united by their opposition to militarism. Militarism is a social system of values and practices which promote and underpin the use of military approaches to a vast range of situations. For radicals, it is a system which provides legitimacy and energy to wars, imperialism and organised political violence. As such, opposition to militarism has been an important feature of radical politics and a key concern for radical movements for more than 150 years.

This chapter provides an introduction to the politics of antimilitarism. It is divided into four sections. In the first section, I provide a more substantive account of what militarism actually is, suggesting that it is useful to see it simultaneously (and co-constitutively) as a network of institutions, a set of values and a series of practices. In the second section, I highlight some of the political struggles in which antimilitarists are involved, outlining both major areas of focus and more specific examples. Next, I turn to look at the theoretical influences and lineages which operate within antimilitarism. Making no claims to be exhaustive, I focus on four particularly important traditions, these being anarchism, feminism, religion, and anti-imperialism and antiracism. Looking through these theoretical lenses also provides an opportunity to examine the terms of debates *amongst* antimilitarists, and I point towards some of these. In the final section, I look in more detail at two case studies. The first of these concerns the struggles of people living on the Japanese islands of Okinawa to resist the presence of US military bases on their land, and the second involves the Trident Ploughshares movement, a transnational network of activists who take direct action to oppose nuclear weapons and other militarist infrastructure. These case studies provide a closer look at the kinds of radical politics which have been discussed throughout the chapter, while also showing how the theoretical lineages identified in the third section find concrete expression and help us to better understand the radical politics of antimilitarism.

What Is Militarism?

Militarism is best understood as the system through which military values and practices are embedded within ordinary social relations, and through which societies legitimate and carry out organised political violence. From this basic starting point, there are a number of different ways in which militarism can be conceptualised, studied and resisted. Conventional accounts have tended to focus on the ways in which military establishments have exerted (undue) influence over the political sphere, or on ideological principles which link the strength of the nation to the maintenance of a strong military force (Finer 1962; Berghahn 1981; Brown and Zanardi 2013). While these dimensions of militarism are undoubtedly important, radicals are more likely to think in ways which recognise that those more visible features of militarism are underpinned by a deeper penetration of military values and practices into the social fabric (Shaw 1991: 4–28, 2013; Stavrianakis and Selby 2013: 13–14), structuring social and political lives in ways which may not immediately be apparent and which are crucial for the wider legitimation and normalisation of war, conflict and organised political violence. This more sociological understanding of militarism has a number of dimensions – here, I suggest that we can divide these into three broad and interconnected areas: militarism as a series of institutions, militarism as a system of values and militarism as a collection of practices. After introducing each in turn, I outline why it has been important for radicals to think about (and oppose) militarism on these terms.[1]

Most understandings of militarism tend to emphasise how certain institutions connected with the state, the military and arms production exert a significant degree of influence on government policy and political life. While this is perhaps most obviously the case in non-liberal states where there is a low degree of formal separation between the military and the executive, the influence of militarising institutions on state policy in apparently liberal states has been extensively documented (Johnson 2006; Singer 2008). The best-known formulation of such concerns comes from outgoing US President Dwight Eisenhower's farewell address to the nation, in which the five-star general warned his country about the malign influence of the 'military-industrial complex' which threatened to pursue its own interests at the expense of peace, security and liberty. While Eisenhower was speaking in 1961, his concerns are no less relevant today; the arms trade and private military companies continue to exert significant influence on governments around the world, and military branches of state remain powerful in both liberal and non-liberal regimes. Any critical account of militarism therefore needs to involve an understanding of how these institutions function. However, it would be limiting to view these institutions as the sole locus of militarism or to see them as discrete entities which might be limited or restrained; this would be to miss the ways in which they are embedded, draw legitimacy from and reinforce wider social structures. In E. P. Thompson's well-known formulation, 'the USA and the USSR do not *have* military-industrial complexes: they *are* such complexes' (1980).[2]

Beyond this focus on institutions, radicals concerned with militarism highlight how militarism functions as a system of values and ideas. As Alfred Vagts writes, militarism is more and sometimes less, than the love of war. It covers every system of thinking and valuing in every complex of feelings which rank military institutions and ways above the ways of civilian life, carrying military mentality and modes of acting and decision into the civilian sphere.

(1959: 17)

Most prominently, these systems of thinking and valuing concern the desirability and utility of war and organised violence. The legitimacy of militarist institutions and the policies they advocate depends on populations that believe that wars are (or can be) noble, just, natural and effective. They also depend on a much broader system of values about the nature of power, violence and humanity. For instance, Wolfi Landstreicher argues that

militarism is not just war as such. It is a social hierarchy of order givers and order takers. It is obedience, domination and submission. It is the capacity to perceive other human beings as abstractions, mere numbers, death counts. It is, at the same time, the domination of strategic considerations and efficiency for its own sake over life and the willingness to sacrifice oneself for a "Great Cause" that one has been taught to believe in.

(2009: 85)

Others have pointed out that militarism also depends on ideas about the workings of gender (in particular, the assumption that men are the natural protectors of women (Enloe 2004: 219)) and on racial prejudice and the benign or benevolent nature of imperialism (DuBois 1915; hooks 1995). These (and other) values function to legitimate and normalise the status of militarist institutions and policies while closing down space for critique.

These values and ideas cannot be imagined outside of the array of everyday social practices which sustain them (and which they, in turn, work to reproduce). These practices serve to cultivate communities and political subjects for whom militarised values and attitudes attain the status of common sense interactions with the world. The most visible forms of such practices are those which fix the status of the military in public life. These include public rituals surrounding the commemoration of war and conflict, as well as those which celebrate the ongoing role of the military as an essential component of the health of the nation. Large-scale public rituals along such lines are frequently supplemented by a more general series of injunctions to 'support the troops', whether through consuming certain products (Tidy 2015), supporting particular charities (Millar 2016) or refraining from criticising overseas military action. However, militarised practices are not confined to degrees of support for the military – indeed, there are few domains of social practice which are not militarised in certain ways. For instance, many have highlighted the ways in which education is frequently militarised – whether with respect to the kinds of citizenship values that are instilled, the forms of aspiration that are encouraged or the kinds of history that are taught (Everett et al. 2013). Others have pointed towards the militarisation of sport (Managan 2003), fitness and health (McSorley 2016), entertainment (Bourke 2014: 159–219; Gee 2014) and so on. Feminists have focused on the militarisation of familial and gender roles, which render everyday life a site for the production and normalisation of (gendered) militarised subjects (Cockburn 2012: 167). As with the discussion of values, the militarisation of these practices intersects with other social forces and struggles – and so, for example, the militarisation of citizenship runs alongside practices of nation-building, practices concerning the celebration of the military often depend heavily on social and economic classes, and the militarisation of recreation, education and fitness are highly gendered and racialised experiences.

Militarism can therefore be understood in relation to particular institutions and policies, to systems of values and ideas, and to everyday social practices. Clearly, the boundaries between these three dimensions are fluid, and it would be misguided to identify any of these areas as the root of militarism; instead, a sociological analysis of militarism recognises the ways these different aspects co-constitute to produce different forms of militarised social relations. The particular forms militarism takes are therefore highly context-specific: how militarism functions (and therefore how militarism might be resisted) change across time and place. Despite that change, opposition to militarism has been a common theme for radical movements and actors.

There are two major reasons why radicals have frequently chosen to focus their attention on militarism. The first is that it allows a systemic critique of war, conflict and organised political violence, one that refuses to rest with identifying and opposing *particular* wars or acts of violence, and which instead highlights how these particular events have their roots in wider social structures and social relations. It does this while drawing in an analysis of imperialism and racism, patriarchy, capitalism and nation statism, recognising how each of these gives particular energy and context to militarism (without militarism being reducible to any). This both sharpens a radical political analysis of how power and violence operate, and provides opportunities to link struggles together through a collective opposition to militarism. The second reason that radicals have tended to focus on militarism is that it opens spaces to link these 'big' questions of war, conflict and social structure to more intimate forms of power and domination. An important component of contemporary radical thought is the idea that we cannot exist outside of or apart from oppressive structures, and indeed that we are always to some extent complicit in their reproduction. Recognising militarism as a socially embedded phenomenon allows radicals to resist large-scale social forces while contending with the ways those same forces are present and open to challenge at an everyday level.

What Do Antimilitarists Do?

In this section, I identify a number of fronts on which antimilitarists oppose militarism. These are by no means exhaustive, but they serve to demonstrate the ways in which a focus on militarism connects together a range of issues. I show how these issues can be contested in more and less radical ways, with more radical approaches signified by their opposition to reformism, their moves to view particular aspects of militarism within their wider social and political contexts and by their conception of militarism as simultaneously a matter of institutions, values and practices.

Antimilitarists have been heavily involved in movements against war, conflict and the direct exertion of imperial power. This frequently involves opposing violence that is being inflicted on others by one's own state, as has been the case with movements against the Vietnam War within the US, against the occupation of Palestine by Israelis and against the 2003 invasion of Iraq by antimilitarists across the world. More commonly, it involves people organising to resist violence directed against their own societies, whether by domestic or international forces; prominent antimilitarist movements have organised on such terms in Palestine, India, Tibet, Iraq and in countless other places. As well as opposing particular wars and imperial relations, antimilitarists frequently target the infrastructural architecture which supports such activities. Many of the most prominent antimilitarist campaigns have focused on US (and NATO) military bases, with activists arguing that such bases (which are frequently established without the consent of local people) strengthen US military power, render the population around them vulnerable to attack and have a disastrous effect on local economic, cultural and environmental conditions. As such, antimilitarists have opposed bases in locations including Guam, Japan, Ecuador and the UK (Natividad and Kirk 2010; Cockburn and Ikeda 2012; Yeo 2012).

One of the central concerns of those involved in the sustained campaign against the US base at Greenham Common, UK (1981–2000) was the decision to station nuclear weapons at the site. Challenging the development and proliferation of nuclear weapons has been a major focus for antimilitarist struggles in the past seventy years. Activists have called attention to the ways in which nuclear proliferation radically endangers human life while allowing certain actors to dominate the international arena (Hudson 2005). Some of the key antimilitarist groups to campaign against nuclear weapons have included the Campaign for Nuclear Disarmament (CND, whose logo has become a near-universal sign of peace), Greenpeace, Friends of the Earth and the Plowshares Movement. While the antinuclear movement has receded since the end of the Cold War (when hundreds of thousands of people regularly demonstrated against nuclear proliferation), it remains an important antimilitarist focus. This focus can be articulated in more and less radical ways. For instance, the Greenham camp had a highly nuanced analysis which saw the problem of nuclear weapons as indissociable from those of racism, the nation state and patriarchal social relations, and as therefore necessitating radical political action and change (Kirk 1983; Cockburn 2012: 33–45).[3] In contrast, CND frames the issue in more straightforward terms, as a stand-alone problem which might reasonably be addressed within the prevailing political order (Hudson 2005).[4]

Another important target for antimilitarists is the international arms industry. The manufacture and sale of weapons and other military equipment is an important enabling dynamic for conflict and political violence, and states with large arms industries (such as the US, UK, Russia and China) are able to maintain their own military superiority while ensuring international influence by supplying other states (Stohl and Grillot 2009; Chew 2012; Stavrianakis 2012). One major campaign against the arms trade has been the push by a coalition of NGOs (including Amnesty International and Oxfam) to develop an Arms Trade Treaty (ATT) through the UN; such a treaty came into force in 2014, and it prohibits signatory states from selling arms to other states if there is a risk that they may be used to commit human rights abuses. While this has been hailed by some activists as a major victory (Control Arms 2013), others have argued that the treaty actually reinforces a form of 'liberal militarism', placing few new obligations on the actions of powerful states such as the UK and US while legitimating the 'humanitarian' wars they have fought in recent years (Stavrianakis 2016). Many antimilitarists have criticised the ATT on precisely such terms, and have argued that a more radical approach to the arms industry is needed. One of the most prominent groups making such a critique is the London-based Campaign Against Arms Trade (CAAT), who campaigns for total abolition of the international arms trade. CAAT works in solidarity with organisations and activists from societies under threat from British-manufactured weapons, including Palestinians, Bahrainis and Kurds, in an effort to limit British arms exports, while also working to challenge the wider legitimacy of the arms trade (Rossdale 2019).

In recent years, antimilitarists have placed increased attention on the accelerating militarisation and privatisation of policing and internal security forces. The War on Terror and accompanying expansion of state security apparatuses has involved an expansion of surveillance systems, border controls and police powers. Groups such as Stop Urban Shield in the US have opposed the militarisation of police forces, arguing that the increase in the use of tactics and equipment sourced from military contexts is leading to the (highly racialised) militarisation of communities (Stop Urban Shield 2016). In the UK, the NGO War on Want has led a campaign against G4S, the world's largest private security company, which it accuses of escalating militarisation while profiting from conflicts around the world (Chang 2014); and while the militarisation of borders is by no means a new concern, European activists working in solidarity with migrants and refugees have called attention to the intensifying militarism of Europe's borders (Akkerman 2016; Watch the Med 2016). Again, these dynamics are framed in more and less radical ways. For instance, while Stop Urban Shield situate their critique of police militarisation within the context of poverty and racism, and call for responses embedded in community empowerment and mutual aid, Amnesty USA have called on authorities 'to foster representative, accountable policing' and to ensure 'due process' (Amnesty USA 2017).

Antimilitarists have also challenged the functioning of militarist institutions by disrupting military recruitment and conscription. The latter has been one of the most persistent focuses for antimilitarists in the modern era; almost any attempt to raise armies by conscription has been met by some level of resistance (albeit with varying degrees of organisation). This has often been highly effective at weakening the military mobilisation of states, such as in South Africa during the Apartheid Era (Conway 2012) and in the US during the Vietnam War (Foley 2003). At present, anticonscription activists are particularly organised in Israel, where military service is mandatory for all non-Arabic citizens over the age of eighteen. Organisations such as New Profile work to support those who want to avoid serving, many of whom then spend time in jail (Cockburn 2012: 65–68).

Conscription is far less common in 2016, and most states rely on volunteer armies. However, antimilitarists argue that recruitment processes are often highly duplicitous, offering a rose-tinted view of life in the military, targeting young people (who are less able to make informed decisions), and focusing recruitment efforts on communities with low social mobility (Everett 2013: 61–93). Groups including Veterans for Peace (UK) work to challenge the sanitised images of life in the military put forward by militaries in an effort to hamper recruitment activities. Opposing military recruitment is often seen as an intensely radical action, insofar as it explicitly refuses the idea of the state as a virtuous protector of its citizens. Nonetheless, we can identify articulations which sit fairly neatly within liberal political frameworks, such as campaigns against the recruitment of children into militaries.[5] More radical positions, such as those adopted by Veterans for Peace, involve a wholesale opposition to military recruitment that is intended less to reform the military than to undermine or weaken it.

I argued earlier that militarism should be understood beyond its institutional configurations, and should be recognised as a socially embedded series of practices and values. Alongside their challenge to institutions, antimilitarists work to highlight, subvert and resist these less visible but nonetheless integral features of militarism. Doing so is crucial; simply opposing institutions without challenging the social relations which provide those institutions with energy and legitimacy is unlikely to lead to substantial change. For some antimilitarist organisations, undermining these values and practices takes place in tandem with their institutional focus; for instance, the antinuclear and anti-arms trade movements work hard to challenge conventional wisdom about the supposed utility of violence, and to expose the incoherence of values which equate the possession of weaponry with peace and security. Similarly, anticonscription groups such as New Profile and the End Conscription Campaign in South Africa have highlighted how the legitimacy of conscription depends on certain militarised understandings of gender and citizenship, which must themselves be challenged as part of the fight against conscription (Conway 2012).

Other antimilitarist groups place their focus more squarely on these diffuse values and practices, rather than on particular institutions. The feminist antimilitarist organisation *Women in Black* involves women around the world who hold regular public vigils, during which they dress in black and stand silently in public spaces. While their vigils might focus on particular issues (such as the Israeli occupation of Palestine, or nationalist violence in the former Yugoslavia), they have sought to relate those issues to wider questions of patriarchy, nationalism, domestic violence and so forth (Cockburn 2007). In the UK, one prominent antimilitarist campaign focuses on the militarisation of Remembrance Day, a memorial day established to commemorate soldiers who died during the First World War (and in subsequent wars). Activists have argued that the particular processes of commemoration, which include the widespread wearing of red poppies, function more to glorify both war and British imperialism than to challenge it (Basham 2016). In response, the pacifist Peace Pledge Union produces over 100,000 white poppies, which are worn in order to declare a public refusal to participate in the militarist spectacle. The question of radicalism in relation to such practices is complex. By itself, the wearing of a white poppy is not a radical act; indeed, insofar as it risks promoting a 'clean hands' attitude towards militarism and reducing militarism to a system of value statements, the wearing of white poppies risks a certain conservatism. The same might be said of public vigils. However, when mobilised alongside the kinds of institutional critique discussed earlier, these practices play an important role in the articulation of a radical antimilitarism, precisely *because* they move beyond those institutional forms and place attention on the values and practices which underpin and sustain them.

Antimilitarists also challenge militarist values and practices in more intimate and subtle ways. It is a common practice in contemporary radical politics to recognise that resisting relations of domination involves contending with the ways those forces are often present in and reproduced through spaces of resistance. Radicalism in this context means not only contending with problems 'out there', but understanding that, at least to a certain extent, resistance begins at home. This is one way of talking about prefigurative politics, the idea that radical movements should seek to embody the change for which they are fighting in the means used to achieve it. Antimilitarism has a long tradition of prefigurative politics, through which activists have sought to avoid replicating militarised practices and values as they oppose militarism. This has involved working in non-hierarchical groups, using consensus decision-making techniques, making nonviolence a central principle of organisation, and working to challenge racism, sexism and other forms of oppression (Rossdale 2015; 2019).[6] More than this, it has involved the refusal to organise in a fashion which subordinates everything to 'the Cause' – that is, to guard against militarised ways of thinking about groups, organisation and struggle. As Landstreicher argues, 'to militarize this struggle, to transform it essentially into a question of strategies and tactics, of opposing forces and numbers, is to begin to create within our struggle that which we are trying to destroy' (2009: 86). While not all antimilitarist groups have an explicitly prefigurative dimension, and while the success and failure of particular moves can be debated, it is important to recognise that antimilitarist practice involves these more subtle dimensions even as it concerns those more visible features discussed earlier.

Theoretical Lineages in Antimilitarism

The particular politics of antimilitarism have been based on and articulated through a number of different conceptual and theoretical perspectives, which have determined both what kinds of analyses and critiques of militarism have been put forward and what kinds of tactics and strategies have been developed in response. In this section, I outline four major political-philosophical traditions which have been influential within antimilitarism. While the list is by no means exhaustive, it serves to demonstrate both the breadth of perspectives on militarism as well as some of the debates amongst antimilitarists. These four traditions are anarchism, feminism, religion, and anti-imperialism and antiracism.

Anarchism is a political tradition rooted in the opposition to systematic or illegitimate forms of authority and hierarchy. Anarchists have tended to identify the nation state and capitalism as the two most entrenched and violent forms of authority and hierarchy in the contemporary world. It is on such terms that they have consistently and fiercely opposed militarism, recognising both that the nation state and capitalism are underpinned by and dependent on their ability to mobilise towards war, and that militarised social relations are coterminous with entrenched forms of hierarchy and authority (Malatesta et al. 2005: 387–9). They have also pointed out the ways in which militarism is highly destructive of human autonomy. Rudolf Rocker argues that

> Militarism is to be appraised first of all as a psychic condition. It is the renunciation of one's own thought and will, the transformation of man into a dead automaton guided and set in motion from without, carrying out blindly every command without being conscious of his own personal responsibility. In one word, militarism is the meanest and most degraded form of that slave-spirit raised to the status of a national virtue which despises all the rules of reason and is devoid of all human dignity.
>
> *(1937: 399)*

Anarchism has played an influential role in the development of antimilitarist politics, both with respect to the prevalence of analyses which link capitalism, the state and militarism together, but perhaps more substantially insofar as major principles of anarchist organising – including non-hierarchy, an aversion to representative politics and an emphasis on direct action – have become a widespread feature of antimilitarist organising principles (Rossdale 2010, 2013).[7] Part of anarchism's particular force has been the persistent critique it has made against left-wing or revolutionary projects which rely on hierarchical, authoritarian or coercive organising principles; such projects may have noble ambitions, but will end up reproducing domination (Bakunin 2005: 178). In the context of antimilitarism, such insights mean that an anarchist lens remains attentive to and wary of the dangers of leftist militarism, that is, of progressive or radical political parties and projects which mobilise militarised values, practices and forms of organisation, and which therefore help to reproduce a militarised world.

The impact of feminist thought and practice on antimilitarism has also been extensive. Feminists have identified the ways in which wars and militarism are always underpinned by patriarchal social relations, and argued that any effective opposition must account for the role of gendered power relations in legitimating and normalising militarism. The main focus for feminists has been on how militarism depends on, is constituted through and works to reproduce particular relationships between masculinity and femininity (and between different types of masculinity and types of femininity), all of these at some level institutionalising and weaponising the subordination of feminised to masculinised subjectivities. They have placed particular focus on how claims about the 'protection' of women has been central to the legitimation of all types of political violence (despite the fact that women and other marginalised gender subjects are disproportionately likely to be harmed by conflict), and on how the cultivation of militarised forms of masculinity plays a central role in the socialisation of young men around the world.[8] The recognition that war, conflict and organised political violence cannot be understood outside of the everyday social relations which sustain them has been central to the feminist understanding of militarism; feminists have perhaps gone the furthest in uncovering how militarism operates in intimate and normal spaces in ways that 'can make everyday life feel like a battlefield' (Cockburn and Ikeda 2012: 167).

Many antimilitarist groups have had explicitly feminist politics, through which they have called attention to the relationship between patriarchy, masculinity and war, and worked to support women (and men) resisting the gendered militarisation of their lives. The Greenham Common Women's Peace Camp was organised on explicitly feminist principles, with the participants' refusal to remain in their 'proper' place at home constituting a remarkable public rejection of patriarchal and militarised gender roles. New Profile, the Israeli movement which supports conscientious objectors, has an explicitly gendered analysis through which it calls attention to the patriarchal attitudes which underpin the valorisation of soldiers and soldiering (Cockburn 2012: 67–68). In 2010, War Resisters' International, who campaign for rights for conscientious objectors, published an anthology of accounts by women from Paraguay, Colombia, Turkey, Eritrea and elsewhere in which they detailed how their everyday lives – as workers, mothers, soldiers and civilians – are militarised, and declared their resistance to this militarisation (Elster and Sørensen 2010). Feminists have not stopped at challenging the relationship between the state, patriarchy and militarism, and have focused on the ways antimilitarist spaces can themselves be the site of oppressive and patriarchal gender relations, challenging the assumption 'that men in [peace movements] are somehow different from other men and therefore exempt from oppressive behaviour and sexism' (Feminism and Nonviolence Study Group 1983: 44).

Religious thought and practice has had a major influence on how antimilitarism has developed, and for many antimilitarists, it is their religious convictions which give energy and direction to their critique of and opposition to militarism, offering them moral codes which stand opposed to the use of violence and which encourage them to work towards peace and the pacific settlement of disputes. Examples of religious antimilitarism can be found in all major world religions; prominent examples include Gandhi's Hindu antimilitarism (Roy 2012: 219–30), the Khudai Khidmatgar movement's resistance to British rule in India (which was rooted in a nonviolent interpretation of Islam, Banerjee 2000: 145–66) and Catholic Worker organisations in North America and Europe (Klejment and Roberts, 1996). All of these movements have understood their religion in a manner which positions militarism as immoral, unjust and even as straightforwardly evil.

Religious antimilitarism has been closely associated with pacifism, a philosophy which maintains that violence is always illegitimate, even when used in the conduct of radical politics; this has led to some tensions across antimilitarist positions, particularly with respect to the many anti-imperialists and anarchists who have hesitated to proscribe tactics that might be used by people fighting oppression, even violence (Churchill 2007; Gelderloos 2007; Rossdale 2019: 184–96). Debates here turn on what actually constitutes the more radical position. For religious pacifists, in a world in which belief in the utility of violence underpins manifold forms of domination, refusing to use violence is an intensely radical act. As the antimilitarist Catholic priest Daniel Berrigan put it,

> One is called to live non-violently, even if the change one works for seems impossible. It may or may not be possible to turn the US around through nonviolent revolution. But one thing favours such an attempt: the total inability of violence to change anything for the better.
>
> *(1974: 52)*

For critics, an absolute insistence on nonviolence limits the range of tactics which are available to those fighting oppression, is inattentive to the dynamics of privilege which make nonviolence a viable political strategy and introduces potentially authoritarian dynamics into movements; or, to use Peter Gelderloos' well-known formulation, 'nonviolence protects the state' (2007). From this perspective, pacifism is guilty of a certain conservatism, while the idea of 'diversity of tactics' holds more radical potential.

A fourth major tradition within antimilitarism has focused on the ways militarism has been closely intertwined with the politics of imperialism and racism. Antimilitarists have argued that the development of nuclear weapons and arms export industries, and policies of foreign military intervention and occupation have been central pillars of imperial grand strategy in the twentieth and twenty-first centuries. While during the Cold War this criticism was targeted towards the USSR as much as towards the US and its allies in the West, today it is the latter group most likely to face these challenges. Antimilitarists argue that, under the guise of liberal internationalism, dominant Western powers have sought to shape the world in line with particular (neo-liberal) interests (Chomsky 2003). Beyond the focus on grand strategy as a central feature of militarism, antimilitarists concerned with racism and imperialism have highlighted the ways in which militarism is reproduced through hierarchies of race (most commonly through some form of white supremacy) (Razack 2004; Ware 2009, 2010; Thobani 2014; Inwood and Bonds 2016). As with the feminist critique of antimilitarist practices which fail to take account of gender relations, antiracist antimilitarists have challenged movements to make antiracism an integral part of their activities. As far back as 1915, W. E. B. DuBois recounts talking to a peace group: 'I appealed to the last meeting of peace societies in St. Louis, saying, "Should you not discuss racial prejudice as a prime cause of war?" The secretary was sorry but was unwilling to introduce controversial matters!' (DuBois 1915: 712). More provocatively, bell hooks argues that 'imperialism and not patriarchy is the core foundation of militarism', targeting her remarks at feminists in the US who have failed to make anti-imperialism a core component of their activities (1995: 61).

Case Studies

The diversity of theoretical influences and political foci at play in antimilitarism means that the particular nature of antimilitarism is dependent on and perhaps best understood through specific contexts. In this final section, I briefly outline two case studies of antimilitarist campaigns. For each, I identify what dimension of militarism is being opposed and highlight the different intersections of theoretical and political concerns which animate the movements involved.

My first case involves resistance to US military bases on the Japanese islands of Okinawa. Despite making up only 0.6 of the land area of Japan (and containing only around 1% of the total population), around three-quarters of the US military bases stationed in the country as part of the post-WW2 security treaty are based on the islands (Cockburn and Ikeda 2012: 152–3).[9] These bases have had a disastrous impact on local communities, who have faced high levels of crime (including sexual violence) as a result of the bases, as well as environmental destruction and pollution resulting from unexploded ordinance, depleted uranium and other hazards (ibid.: 161). The Status of Forces Agreement between the US and Japan has meant that US personnel have remained largely immune from prosecution for crimes committed, even when suspects have been identified (ibid.).

The bases have been met with fierce resistance from local populations. At present, the focal point for this resistance is the attempts to build a new base in Henoko to replace the despised airbase at Futenma. Local residents claim that this new base would have dire consequences for both the local population and the marine environment. For more than fifteen years, alongside supporters from the mainland (and some internationals), they have staged protests, sit-ins and other forms of civil disobedience. These have been successful in disrupting the development of new facilities:

> When the workmen of the Defense Facilities Administration Agency (DFAA) arrived to mount scaffolding on the coral reef, nonviolent direct action was launched, with people swimming, diving and paddling canoes in the waters of the reef, while some occupied the scaffolding. In September 2005, after ten months of confrontation, the DFAA quietly dismantled its structure and withdrew.
>
> *(ibid.: 162)*

Most of this resistance is coordinated by and carried out by local people, with some solidarity from mainland peace movements. However, Cockburn and Ikeda argue that this solidarity is limited, in a manner which can only be fully understood when understanding the colonial and racial politics of the Japanese state.

Japan invaded and occupied the island kingdom of Ryukyu in 1609, turning it into a vassal state. In 1879, the kingdom was incorporated into the Japanese state and renamed Okinawa. The state imposed educational and cultural reforms to promote Japanese (*yamoto*) identity, marginalising Ryukyuan language and culture. As Cockburn and Ikeda note, this colonisation and absorption is part of a wider history of racist domination in Japan, in which the state 'is continually represented in authoritative discourse as an "ethnically homogenous nation", in systematic delegitimation not only of Ryukyuan but of any other self-proclaimed minority identity' (ibid.: 154). They go on to cite Okinawan activists who suspect that, in order to make US military bases a non-issue in national politics and public consciousness, the Japanese state is happy to shift the burden of US bases to Okinawa. Further to this, they feel that the mainstream peace movement has allowed this move to happen, engendering a sense that 'they will cry for Iraq, but not for us' (ibid.: 165). It is therefore important to understand this case in the context of both imperial *and* colonial frames.

It is also important to recognise the gendered nature of antimilitarist resistance in Okinawa. One of the focal points for antimilitarists has been the sexual violence that local women have faced from US personnel. In 1995, three US marines abducted and raped a twelve-year-old Okinawan girl, leading to mass protests against both the immunity of US soldiers and the bases themselves. However, for feminist antimilitarists in Okinawa, the focus is not only on violence perpetrated by the US military; such exclusive attention risks obscuring the high prevalence of sexual violence carried out by Okinawan men (ibid.: 167–8). This has been something that the mainstream peace movement has been far less keen to point out, in a manner which problematically instrumentalises violence against women (which is considered important only insofar as it can be used to challenge the US). As Cockburn and Ikeda again argue, the

> masculinized discourse of the mainstream movement can have the effect of further exploiting the rape victim, making her body an object of the public gaze. Sometimes a case of rape is used to legitimate a resentful polemic against "those" men trampling on "our women", and "our Okinawan land".
>
> *(ibid.: 169)*

A feminist analysis therefore refuses the simplistic division of an antimilitarist 'us' and a militarist 'them' and reveals more complex operations of power.

My second case study is the Plowshares Movement. This movement began in 1980 when the 'Plowshares Eight' entered the General Electric plant in Pennsylvania, US, where the nose cones for nuclear warheads were manufactured: 'With hammers and blood they enacted the biblical prophecies of Isaiah (2:4) and Micah (4:3) to *"beat swords into plowshares"* by hammering on two of the nose cones and pouring blood on documents' (Laffin 2003: 1, emphasis in original). Since then, there have been over seventy-five Plowshares actions in a number of countries (most of them in the US, Northern Europe and Australasia), all of which aim 'to empower ordinary citizens to peacefully tear down the machinery of violence and to build up respect for fundamental human rights' (Zelter 2009: 21). Most have focused on doing physical damage to military equipment, and this has ranged from symbolic actions to those designed to cause the maximum possible disruption – a dynamic that was introduced after the 'Harriet-Tubman Sarah Connor Brigade Disarmament Action' cased $2.75m damage to a NAVSTAR military satellite, 'thereby challenging Plowshares and the wider disarmament movement to go beyond symbolic witness in addressing the war machine's key technologies' (Laffin 2003: 49).

Plowshares actions have targeted nuclear weapons alongside conventional military infrastructure. Activists often serve long jail terms as a result of these actions, viewing arrest, trial and even imprisonment as an integral part of challenging the system. Because the actions are often so spectacular, causing large amounts of damage and gaining widespread media attention, Plowshares actions (and their associated tactics) have been highly influential in North America and Europe over the past thirty-five years.

From a theoretical point of view, we can see two major traditions running through Plowshares. The first is the influence of anarchism; the decentralised and non-hierarchical nature of its organisation, the use of illegal direct action tactics and the general hostility to the state form all take their cue from standard anarchist organising principles. Perhaps more notable than the influence of anarchism is the importance of Christian Pacifism to the Plowshares movement's aims, principles and tactics. The founders of the movement, Daniel and Philip Berrigan, were both Catholic ministers, and saw their antimilitarism as an indissociable feature of their religion. Daniel wrote of the Plowshares Eight that, prior to the action, '[w]e passed several months in reflection and prayer and discussion: a wearying but, as we judged, absolutely crucial process' (1987: 291), and Philip claimed that '[b]eing imprisoned for one's convictions is a Christian phenomenon above all' (1970: 185). While not all of those who take part in Plowshares actions are Christians, the principles of the movement – and in particular the absolute insistence on nonviolence as a feature of antimilitarism – are heavily influenced by Christian pacifist values. This also shapes the symbols which are used in actions. For instance, while the practice of pouring blood on weapons is most obviously an attempt to call attention to their violent nature, it also 'calls Christians to remember the example of Christ, who gave his own life rather than shedding the blood of others' (Nepstad 2008: 62). Similarly, the Pit Stop Plowshares group, who in 2003 damaged equipment on a US military base in Ireland in protest against the war in Iraq, knelt praying while waiting to be arrested.

Conclusion

The understandings of militarism and antimilitarism outlined in this chapter resist the compartmentalisation of either into 'single-issue' politics. Militarism is neither an issue nor a discrete entity. Instead, we have to understand and contest militarism as series of social relations that operate across a wide range of sites and struggles, located in and reproduced through a multitude of institutions, values and practices. Resisting militarism is therefore not a particular campaign aim, but an ethos which runs through many different types of radical movement. As this chapter has made clear, this resistance is directed, negotiated and theorised in a variety of contrasting and often-interconnected ways.

Notes

1 For a fuller discussion of these points, see Rossdale (2019: 45–64).
2 C. Wright Mills makes a similar point when discussing the military power elite, who 'are now operating in a nation whose elite and whose underlying population have accepted what can only be called a military definition of reality' (1959: 198).
3 While Greenham Common was an explicitly feminist project, not all feminists supported the camp. For some, it risked *de*-radicalising the women's movement by rendering it vulnerable to co-option by the male-dominated peace movement and by reinforcing harmful stereotypes which equate women with peacemaking (Whisker 1983).
4 Notwithstanding attempts by some to drag them in more radical and anticapitalist directions (Taylor 1987).
5 For instance, see Child Soldiers International (2016).
6 While these are all common features, not all groups adhere to all of these principles. In particular, while many antimilitarist groups have an explicit commitment to nonviolent protest, others do not. This can at times lead to tensions between different groups and organisations.
7 This is not to suggest that anarchism has a monopoly on non-hierarchical organising and direct action tactics, nor that all using such tactics have been directly influenced by anarchism.
8 The literature here is substantial. The work of Cynthia Enloe has been particularly important in developing feminist accounts and critiques of militarism (2000, 2004, 2010). Also see Hutchings (2008), Higate (2003, 2012), Basham (2013), Cohn (1987) Conway (2012), as well as Rossdale (2019: 65–68) for a fuller summary.
9 For this case, I am relying heavily on the account provided by Cynthia Cockburn and Naoko Ikeda.

References

Akkerman, M., 2016. 'Border Wars: The Arms Dealers Profiting from Europe's Refugee Tragedy', Stop Wapenhandel and Transnational Institute, available from www.tni.org/files/publication-downloads/border-wars-report-web1207.pdf.
Amnesty USA, 2017. 'Police and Human Rights', available from www.amnestyusa.org/our-work/issues/military-police-and-arms/police-and-human-rights.
Bakunin, M., 2005. *Statism and Anarchy*, Cambridge: Cambridge University Press.
Banerjee, M., 2000. *The Pathan Unarmed: Opposition & Memory in the North West Frontier*, Santa Fe, NM: School of American Research Press.
Basham, V., 2013. *War, Identity and the Liberal State: Everyday Experiences of the Geopolitical in the Armed Forces*, London: Routledge.
Basham, V., 2016. 'Gender, Race, Militarism and Remembrance: The Everyday Geopolitics of the Poppy', *Gender, Place & Culture*, 23(6): 883–896.
Berghahn, V. R., 1981. *Militarism: The History of an International Debate 1861–1979*. Cambridge: Cambridge University Press.
Berrigan, D., 1974. *Lights on in the House of the Dead: A Prison Diary*, Garden City, NY: Doubleday.
Berrigan, D., 1987. *To Dwell in Peace: An Autobiography*, San Francisco, CA: Harper & Row.
Berrigan, P., 1970. *Prison Journals of a Priest Revolutionary*, New York, Chicago and San Francisco: Holt, Rinehart and Winston.
Bourke, J., 2014. *Wounding the World: How Military Violence and War-Play Invade Our Lives*, London: Virago Press.
Brown, K. and C. Zanardi, 2013. *The Chinese Military: Its Political and Economic Function*.
Chang, D., 2014. *'G4S: Securing Profits, Globalising Injustice'*, London: War on Want.
Chew, E., 2012. *Arming the Periphery: The Arms Trade in the Indian Ocean During the Age of Global Empire*, Basingstoke and New York: Palgrave.
Child Soldiers International, 2016. 'Child Recruitment', available from www.child-soldiers.org.

Chomsky, N., 2003. *Hegemony or Survival: America's Quest for Global Dominance*, New York: Metropolitan Books.

Churchill, W., 2007. *Pacifism as Pathology: Reflections on the Role of Armed Struggle in North America*, Edinburgh, Oakland and West Virginia: AK Press.

Cockburn, C., 2007. *From Where We Stand: War, Women's Activism and Feminist Analysis*, London and New York: Zed Books.

Cockburn, C., 2012. *Antimilitarism: Political and Gender Dynamics of Peace Movements*, New York and Basingstoke: Palgrave Macmillan.

Cockburn, C. and N. Ikeda, 2012. 'Seeing the Whole Picture: Anti-Militarism in Okinawa and Japan', in C. Cockburn, ed., *Anti-Militarism: Political and Gender Dynamics of Peace Movements*, Basingstoke: Palgrave, 152–179.

Cohn, C., 1987. 'Sex and Death in the Rational World of Defense Intellectuals', *Signs*, 12(4): 687–718.

Control Arms, 2013. 'States Vote Overwhelmingly for Ground-Breaking Arms Trade Treaty', controlarms.org, available from http://controlarms.org/en/news/states-vote-overwhelmingly-for-ground-breaking-arms-trade-treaty/.

Conway, D., 2012. *Masculinities, Militarisation and the End Conscription Campaign: War Resistance in Apartheid South Africa*, Manchester: Manchester University Press.

DuBois, W. E. B., 1915. 'The African Roots of War', *The Atlantic Monthly*, May.

Elster, E. and M. J. Sørensen, 2010. *Women Conscientious Objectors: An Anthology*, London: War Resisters' International.

Enloe, C., 2000. *Maneuvers: The International Politics of Militarizing Women's Lives*, Berkeley: University of California Press.

Enloe, C., 2004. *The Curious Feminist: Searching for Women in a New Age of Empire*, Berkeley, CA: University of California Press.

Enloe, C., 2010. *Nimo's War, Emma's War: Making Feminist Sense of International Politics*, Berkeley: University of California Press.

Everett, O., ed., 2013. *Sowing Seeds: The Militarisation of Youth and How to Counter It*, London: War Resisters International.

Feminism and Nonviolence Study Group (FNSG), 1983. *Piecing It Together: Feminism & Nonviolence*, pamphlet.

Finer, S. E., 1962. *The Man on Horseback*, New Brunswick, NJ: Transaction Press.

Foley, M. S., 2003. *Confronting the War Machine: Draft Resistance during the Vietnam War*, Chapel Hill: University of North Carolina Press.

Gee, D., 2014. *Spectacle, Reality, Resistance: Confronting a Culture of Militarism*, London: ForcesWatch.

Gelderloos, P., 2007. *How Nonviolence Protects the State*, Cambridge, MA: South End Press.

Goldman, E, 1970. *Living My Life (Vol. 2)*, New York: Dover Publications.

Higate, P., 2003. *Military Masculinities: Identity and the States*, Westport, CT: Praeger.

Higate, P., 2012. 'Drinking Vodka from the "Butt-Crack": Men, Masculinities and Fratriarchy in the Private Militarized Security Company', *International Feminist Journal of Politics*, 14(4): 450–469.

hooks, b., 1995. 'Feminism and Militarism: A Comment', *Women's Studies Quarterly*, 23(3/4): 58–64.

Hudson, K., 2005. *CND: Now More Than Ever – The Story of a Peace Movement*, London: Vision.

Hutchings, K., 2008. 'Making Sense of Masculinity and War', *Men and Masculinities*, 10(4): 389–404.

Inwood, J. and A. Bonds, 2016. 'Confronting White Supremacy and a Militaristic Pedagogy in the US Settler Colonial State', *Annals of the American Association of Geographers*, 106(3): 521–529.

Johnson, C., 2006. *The Sorrows of Empire: Militarism, Secrecy and the End of the Republic*, London and New York: Verso.

Kirk, G., 1983. 'Our Greenham Common: Feminism and Nonviolence', in A. Harris and Y. King, eds., *Rocking the Ship of State: Toward a Feminist Peace Politics*, London: Westview Press, 115–130.

Klejment, A. and N. L. Roberts, 1996. *American Catholic Pacifism: The Influence of Dorothy Day and the Catholic Worker Movement*, Westport, CT: Praeger.

Laffin, A., 2003. *Swords in Plowshares: A Chronology of Plowshares Disarmament Action 1980–2003*, Marion, SD: Rose Hill Books.

Landstreicher, W., 2009. *Willful Disobedience*, San Francisco: Ardent Press.

Malatesta, E., et al., 2005. 'Malatesta, The Anarchist International, and War', in D. Guérin, ed., *No Gods, No Masters: An Anthology of Anarchism*, Edinburgh and Oakland: AK Press.

Managan, J. A., ed., 2003. *The European Sports History Review, Volume 5: Militarism, Sport, Europe – War Without Weapons*, London and Portland, OR: Frank Cass.

McSorley, 2016. 'Doing Military Fitness: Physical Culture, Civilian Leisure, and Militarism', *Critical Military Studies*, 2(1–2): 103–119.

Millar, K. M., 2016. '"They Need Our Help": Non-Governmental Organizations and the Subjectifying Dynamics of the Military as a Social Cause', *Media, War and Conflict*, 9(1): 9–26.

Natividad, L. and G. Kirk, 2010. 'Fortress Guam: Resistance to US Military Mega-Buildup', *The Asia-Pacific Journal: Japan Focus*, 8(19, 1): 1–17.

Nepstad, S. E., 2008. *Religion and War Resistance in the Plowshares Movement*, Cambridge: Cambridge University Press.

Razack, S., 2004. *Dark Threats and White Knights: The Somalia Affair, Peacekeeping, and the New Imperialism*, Toronto: University of Toronto Press.

Rocker, R., 1937. *Nationalism and Culture*, Los Angeles: Rocker Publications Committee.

Rossdale, C., 2010. 'Anarchy is What Anarchists Make of it: Reclaiming the Concept of Agency in IR and Security Studies', *Millennium: Journal of International Studies*, 39(2): 483–501.

Rossdale, C., 2013. *Anarchism, Anti-Militarism and the Politics of Security*, Unpublished Doctoral Dissertation, University of Warwick.

Rossdale, C., 2015. 'Enclosing Critique: The Limits of Ontological Security', *International Political Sociology*, 9(4): 369–389.

Rossdale, C., 2019. *Resisting Militarism: Direct Action and the Politics of Subversion*, Edinburgh: Edinburgh University Press.

Roy, K., 2012. *Hinduism and the Ethics of Warfare South Asia: From Antiquity to the Present*, Cambridge: Cambridge University Press.

Shaw, M., 1991. *Post-Military Society*, Cambridge: Polity.

Shaw, M., 2013. 'Twenty-First Century Militarism: A Historical-Sociological Framework', A. Stavrianakis and J. Selby, eds., *Militarism and International Relations*, London and New York: Routledge.

Singer, P. W., 2008. *Corporate Warriors: The Rise of the Privatized Military Industry*, Ithaca, NY: Cornell University Press.

Stavrianakis, A., 2012. *Taking Aim at the Arms Trade*, London: Zed.

Stavrianakis, A., 2016. 'Legitimising Liberal Militarism: Politics, Law and War the Arms Trade Treaty', *Third World Quarterly*, 37(5): 840–865.

Stavrianakis, A. and J. Selby, 2013. 'Militarism and International Relations the 21st Century', in A. Stavrianakis and J. Selby, eds., *Militarism and International Relations*, London and New York: Routledge, 3–18.

Stohl, R. and S. Grillot, 2009. *The International Arms Trade*, Malden, MA: Polity.

Stop Urban Shield, 2016. 'Urban Shield: Abandoning Hope, Not Building Hope', available from http://stopurbanshield.org/wp-content/uploads/2016/09/US_2016_report_v2.pdf.

Taylor, R., 1987. 'The Marxist Left and the Peace Movement in Britain Since 1945', in R. Taylor and N. Young, eds., *Campaigns for Peace: British Peace Movements in the Twentieth Century*, Manchester: Manchester University Press, 162–188.

Thobani, S., 2014. 'Fighting Terror: Race, Sex, and the Monstrosity of Islam', in S. Perera and S. Razack, eds., *At the Limits of Justice: Women of Colour on Terror*, Toronto: University of Toronto Press, 57–85.

Thompson, E. P., 1980. 'Notes on Exterminism, the Last State of Civilization', *New Left Review*, I/121.

Tidy, J., 2015. 'Forces Sauces and Eggs for Soldiers: Food, Nostalgia, and the Rehabilitation of the British Military', *Critical Military Studies*, 1(3): 220–232.

Vagts, A., 1959. *A History of Militarism*, Greenwood Press.

Ware, V., 2009. 'Why Critical Whiteness Studies Needs to Think About Warfare', *Sociologisk Forskning*, 46(3): 57–64.

Ware, V., 2010. 'Whiteness in the Glare of War: Soldiers, Migrants and Citizenship', *Ethnicities*, 10(3): 313–330.

Watch the Med, 2016. 'The Sea as Frontier', watchthemed.net, available from http://watchthemed.net/index.php/page/index/1.

Whisker, ed., 1983. *Breaching the Peace: A Collection of Radical Feminist Papers*, London: Onlywomen Press.

Wright Mills, C., 1959. *The Power Elite*, New York: Oxford University Press.

Yeo, A., 2012. *Activists, Alliances, and Anti-U.S. Base Protests*, Cambridge: Cambridge University Press.

Zelter, A., 2009. 'Trident Ploughshares Support for Decommissioners', in 'If I Had A Hammer…Decommissioning the War Machine', pamphlet.

1.5

FROM 'BED-PUSH' TO BOOK ACTIVISM

Anti/Critical Psychiatry Activism

Bonnie Burstow

Introduction

Has institutional psychiatry and what it does to people (e.g. electroshocking, drugging and incarceration) ever bothered you? Were you aware that there are huge liberation movements which target it? While addressing each of the central themes in this collection (what makes the politics radical, how it is theorised and what has influenced it?), such is the purview of this chapter.

This chapter explores two highly interpenetrating movements – the antipsychiatry movement and the mad movement – with special emphasis placed on antipsychiatry (the one movement in the area consistently non-reformist in nature). While emphasis is placed on the larger network of which each of these movements forms a part – for the activists involved largely function together as a community – they are also looked at separately, for they have a different politic and, as such, have at times been theorised as separate movements (see, for example, Diamond, 2014). Mention will also be made of the psychiatric survivor movement, a phenomenon that predates the mad movement, though which largely occupies the same territory, with the designation 'mad movement', to a degree, functioning as a placeholder for 'survivor movement'.

The chapter is written from an anarchist perspective. The standpoint taken is that of an antipsychiatry activist/scholar who has been mobilising in these areas for decades. Central questions posed are: What is antipsychiatry? What is the mad movement? What makes organising against psychiatry and/or against the treatment of the mad a radical politic? What unique politics are involved? What strategies/tactics are favoured and why? What special role has the social media come to play? How important are utopian visions to this politics and why? And how are they prefigured in the activism itself?

As readers wend their way through the different strands of this activist world, they will progressively come to appreciate at once its individuality, its radicalism and its relationship to neighbouring movements (e.g. penal abolition). Important observations made and important realities which come to light are: both theoretically and practically, the movement in question is intrinsically anarchistic. That is, it at once places the state in question, challenges sanism (the prioritising of ways of thinking theorised as sane) and invites a different style of organising. Liberal politics like human rights work and lobbying for 'services' inevitably enter in, forcing activists committed to an abolitionist politic to tread a fine line. Naming is a pivotal part of the radical politic. And in the absence of a mass movement and an undisputed leadership (the latter, less common in the postmodern world), the social protest involved is necessarily decentralised, autonomous and non-hierarchical – with, paradoxically, even actions requiring tight discipline suffering when not approached accordingly.

Antipsychiatry

The term 'antipsychiatry' was initially coined in the UK by the coterie of 'mental health' professionals who coalesced around R. D. Laing (see Cooper, 1967). It referred to a more progressive approach to people's distress than what biological psychiatry offered/enforced, that theorised people's emotional problems as existential and political in nature, as opposed to biomedical, and which prioritised communication and the creation of a less alienated society. Subsequently, the term was applied to the theories of libertarian psychiatrist Thomas Szasz, who demonstrated with great precision that the concept of 'mental illness' was mere metaphor, and that it had no medical validity. Alongside Szasz were sociologists called labelling theorists, such as Goffman (1961), who traced the ways that psychiatric labels serve the interests of the professions and industries associated with them and not the people subjected to them. What began here is a war over 'mental health', repeated demonstrations of the power wielded by the system, an insistence that personal and social control is being passed off as help and an utter rejection of 'mental health' language and all it bootstraps into existence (see Szasz, 1961, 1970; Burstow, 2015a). That said, alongside these, predating both of these, and of singular importance is the psychiatric survivor liberation movement, which dates back to the nineteenth century and earlier (see Starkman, 2014, pp. 27–37; Burstow, 2015a, pp. 41–42). The figure usually associated with the start of this movement is Elizabeth Packard. An American 'patient' who had been confined by her theologian husband for years for the purportedly grievous error of rejecting the religious tenet of the total depravity of 'man', Packard, note, successfully challenged her confinement, stating:

> It has always been my fortune … to be a pioneer … therefore I am called crazy … I freely accord to … my enemies the right of opinion in believing me to be … insane … and so long as these opinions do not lead them to trespass against my *inalienable* rights, I have no right or desire to interfere with them … But since my opinion is as dear to me as those of my enemies are to them and since we have no right to do wrong, therefore, when the opinions of my enemies lead them to *kidnap* my accountability, by placing me on a level with beasts for opinion's sake merely, the law of self-defense compels me to resist.
>
> *(Packard, 1865/1974:17; emphasis in original)*

Theoretically speaking, the antipsychiatry movement today is largely founded on a combination of Szaszian and survivor movement principles. To be clear, while no one denies that people may have profound problems in living, may be even in dire need of help, what is rejected – and rejected fundamentally – is the medical model, the language and the practices surrounding it, including what is traditionally known as 'treatment'. Additionally drawing on the pivotal work of researchers like Peter Breggin (see, for example, Breggin, 1991), activists hold that not a single physical indicator has been found for a single so-called mental illness, and that treatments like the psychopharmaceutical 'medications' have been demonstrated conclusively to *create* as opposed to *redress* imbalances, moreover are modes of social control, not help; and as such, they protest at once the 'treatments' themselves and the misinformation surrounding them. Correspondingly, they object to the hegemonic depiction of survivors as dangerous. While the analysis and commitment go beyond this and amount to a total rejection of the institution, members of the movement similarly reject all involuntary confinement and all involuntary treatment – all of which is theorised as a human rights violation. They likewise have long held that there is generally wisdom in mental states currently dismissed as mad (for elucidation of this, see Chapter 9 in Burstow, 2015a).

The primary targets of the movement are psychiatrists, who wield this authoritarian power, the state which authorises their practice and the businesses, especially the psychopharmaceutical industry, that promote and benefit from it. The ultimate goals of the movement, correspondingly, are the abolition of institutional psychiatry, the widespread acceptance of difference and the creation of a more tolerant society with a 'commoning' of services – that is, voluntary services (and voluntary only) arising from and vested in the community (for elaboration, see Burstow, 2014a, b, 2015a). Subsidiary goals include eradicating poverty and achieving disability accommodation – all of which involve networking and ongoing actions with other groups

What joins antipsychiatry with the mad movement and the survivor movement are the insistence on respect for human rights, the redefinition of services as only that which is voluntary, the prioritisation of psychiatric survivors' preferences and interests, the celebrative quality of many of their actions, the realisation that those deemed mad often have special insights and the emphasis on freedom. What distinguishes it is that all antipsychiatry activists seek *the total abolition* of institutional psychiatry (and this distinction is crucial) not some just part of it and not the mere *'reform'* of the institution. This, in practice, would mean that insofar as anything vaguely resembling psychiatry continued to exist, it would have no state powers, no state funding or promotion and no authoritative 'medical' status. Additionally, while the antipsychiatry movement is composed first and foremost of survivors, unlike others in the area, this movement is not identity-based – hence, the existence of broad-based coalitions comprised survivors, radical professionals, scholars, artists and members of neighbouring movements.

To understand antipsychiatry politics, one needs to take in the pivotal rejection of reformism. All people who organise against psychiatry but who are not abolitionists are reformers. And reformers overwhelmingly want a gentler psychiatry, less use of biological 'treatments', less frequent use of force and for psychiatry to play a less dominant role in the 'mental health system'. Antipsychiatry activists by contrast totally oppose at once the use of force, the 'treatments', the tie-in with the state and the very existence of psychiatry as a 'medical specialty'.

The case against reformism – and rejecting reformism is a defining feature of current antipsychiatry – is most fully articulated in Burstow (2014e). Herein, I make the case that some things are so fundamentally wrong that they should be completely eliminated. Correspondingly, I demonstrate that far from culminating in radical social change, all the otherwise benign reforms throughout psychiatric history in the long run simply paved the way for the eventual return and the intensification of biological psychiatry, and, as such, backfired. And I conclude:

> In this as in a microscope, we can see the problem of non-foundational reform. It is not that there are no good tenets or good people involved. Indeed there are. Correspondingly, it is not that progressive psychiatrists have no role to play in the initial transformation process for again, they do. However, in refusing to take seriously both the nature

and the self-interestedness of the profession, reform (as opposed to revolution) leaves intact an inherently problematic institution, legitimates rule by 'expert', and paves the way for a return of biologism and of oppression with a vengeance.

(Burstow, 2014e)

The world's longest standing and most active antipsychiatry organisation is Coalition Against Psychiatric Assault (CAPA) in Ontario, Canada. Its mandate and an overview of its various actions may be found on its website.[1] While most organisations which challenge psychiatry have an antipsychiatry contingent, unlike CAPA, few organisations are totally antipsychiatry.

Actions typically taken by antipsychiatry activists range from exposing the profession through publications, whether it be books, blogs or survivor magazines (e.g. *Phoenix Rising* – see Psychiatric Survivor Archives of Toronto (PSAT)), to educational events, to speak-outs (see Personal Testimonies, Inquiry into Psychiatry, 2005), to petitioning the state, to spirited demonstrations (with the latter including marches, street art and theatre), to civil disobedience, including sit-ins (for details, see Diamond, 2012, pp. 199–242). In all of this, antipsychiatry activists pay special attention to language, consistently replacing institutional designations like 'mental patient' and 'medications' with non-hegemonic terms like 'psychiatric survivor' and 'psychiatric drugs' (for detailed elaboration of language, together with recommendations, see Burstow, 2014c).

While many antipsychiatry activists do their activism without the guidance of an explicit model, one model in recent years has provided appreciable guidance. It is called the attrition model, was adopted by CAPA and is explicitly modelled on the attrition model of prison abolition, which is itself predicated on the prioritisation of erosion as the means to abolition (for an articulation of the attrition model for prison abolition, see Knopp, 1976; for the initial theorisation of an attrition model for psychiatry abolition, see Burstow, 2014d). The understanding is that psychiatry, like the penal system, will not disappear overnight, but that it can be eroded over time. What is provided by this model, to be clear, are not rules but touchstones. Loosely speaking, the invitation to activists is to actively engage in only those actions or campaigns which lead in the direction of psychiatry abolition. Touchstone questions that activists are invited to ask themselves in this regard are:

1   If successful, will the actions or campaigns that we are contemplating move us closer to the long-range goal of abolition?
2   Are they likely to avoid improving or giving added legitimacy to the current system?
3   Do they avoid 'widening' psychiatry's net? (Burstow, 2014d, p. 39)

(For an informative account of how CAPA used these questions to come to a consensus on an action on which there was a disagreement, see Burstow, 2014d.)

Some final points without which readers new to the area would not understand the character of antipsychiatry activism: it is to a significant degree inherently celebrative, with people operating like a community of people who are happy to be with one another. It welcomes and accommodates difference, even when by 'normal standards', such a difference might be seen as disruptive. And the movement is intrinsically non-hierarchical, largely operating via consensus.

Antipsychiatry as a Radical Politic

If one looks at the goals of antipsychiatry, it is clear that they are intrinsically radical in that they are abolitionist and they aim at nothing less than the wholesale rejection of this system.

Beyond this, they bear a clear relationship to anarchism. Note in this regard, there is at least theoretically a total rejection of authority-over and a commitment to liberty. By the same token, there is a total rejection of such concepts as 'normal' and the hegemony involved. Correspondingly, antipsychiatry on the ground is activist and indeed anarchistic in that there are no compromise solutions – unlike with reformists. In the attrition model, for example, no action is advocated or seen as viable unless it can be demonstrated or theorised as something that would move society in the direction of psychiatry abolition.

Beyond this, what makes the politics fundamentally radical is the challenge to the state and the implicit rejection of state powers. In this regard, the incarceration and the forced treatment of survivors rest on and are 'legitimated' by two state powers – protection of the peace and what is called 'parens patriae' – a sexist notion in which the ruler is seen as the 'father' of the country. To put this simply, while protection of the peace allows for intrusion on the basis of people being deemed of danger to others, parens patriae allows for intrusion on the basis of the person being considered of danger to themselves (for details on these state powers and the use of them, see Burstow, 2015a). As an agent of the state, psychiatry is vested with precisely this power. What, in particular, makes antipsychiatry inherently radical is that it rejects this power of the state, and as such, implicitly at very least, calls the state per se into question. What makes it, beyond this, inherently anarchistic is that the activism is not predicated on reforming these powers or altering who is exercising power-over for it is *voluntary community solutions* that are being looked to – not state powers, not authoritarianism, not power-over.

Other factors that speak to the radicalism and indeed the anarchistic nature of antipsychiatry activism are: it is about freedom and equality; it is utopian – that is, it incorporates a sense of the type of society aimed at; it is prefigurative in that the treatment of members by each other realises in embryonic form the type of society which is being sought; and it includes playfulness and use of the arts – especially street art. Correspondingly, while there is room for improvement to be sure, including making greater efforts at fundamentally incorporating an antiracist analysis, there is a long history of looking at intersectional oppression, especially the intersection of mentalism, sexism and ageism.[2] Moreover, it is 'comparatively' non-hierarchical and pluralistic, and it operates via consensus. (Most of the foregoing, I would add, are attributes identified as features of the new anarchism or postanarchism by theorists like Newman, 2011, Gordon, 2008, and Kinna, 2005.)

The Mad Movement

One could reasonably date the start of the mad movement as far back as the nineteenth century, for mad politics has inevitably figured in the survivor liberation movement, with repeated attempts made throughout history to reclaim words like 'mad' and 'lunatic'.[3] That noted, if looked at more narrowly, the mad movement officially began in England in 1999, and it quickly spread – in particular throughout Europe, the Americas, Africa and to a lesser extent Australia and Asia. The largest mad organisation in the world is MindFreedom International – an organisation headquartered in the US.[4] It unites affiliate groups around the world, maintains and makes visible a roster of professional allies, and it has literally thousands of members.

The mad movement is predicated first and foremost on the rejection of sanism and a celebration and embrace of the various states of mind in which people find themselves, including those that might be conventionally seen as psychotic: all are seen as of value. As the very name MindFreedom indicates, liberation is a prominent theme. Another expression used which captures the spirit of the phenomenon is Mad Pride; and so central is this concept that the movement itself is commonly referred to as the Mad Pride movement (see, for instance, Farber, 2012). According to the UK book which in essence announced the birth of the movement (Curtis, Dellar, Leslie, and Watson, 2000), the gay liberation movement and Black Pride inspired this reclaiming and reframing. And the hallmark event is the annual Mad Pride Day, which in most locales has been extended to a whole week, so popular has the celebration become.

Mad Pride week typically includes a very full roster of activities – some artistic, some scholarly, some wildly celebratory, much of it recounting the personal history of people deemed mad – unearthing what work they did, what their contribution to society and the community around them were (for a landmark book in this area, see Reaume, 2000). Much of it also pokes fun at 'normal' and 'normals'. The choice of July 14 as the pivotal day is symbolic, coinciding as it does the storming of the Bastille – which itself signals that Mad Pride is not only a moment of culture appreciation but also a liberation movement. Symbolic of liberation likewise is the singular activity which figures in Mad Pride Weeks everywhere – the pushing of a hospital bed with a dummy in it through the streets – a now traditional event fondly referred to as the 'bed-push'. Herein, we see a symbolic act of liberation and escape from tyranny, or to put this another way, an escape from institutionalisation.

Mad Pride is seen by everyone in the movement as a moment of affirmation and liberation for the population traditionally deemed mad. Additionally, with some mad activists, though far from all, it is also seen as redemptive for society more generally. In this regard, the early advocates of Mad Pride saw Mad Pride as having a pivotal role to play in the necessary job of world transformation, with the form it would take being mockery, anger, humour, celebration and rebellion. Referring to the pieces in their own book, Curtis, Dellar, Leslie and Watson (2000: 8), for instance, write, 'These writings mock conformity, resist "normalization" and refuse to be co-opted. They rejoice in Madness from a standpoint of anger, humour, and rebellion'. The initial mandate statements issued by the leaders of the Icarus Project – a mad activist group, a support group and website collective in the US – went further, with its leaders more pointedly suggesting a special role for the mad. Indeed in the first few years of operation, leaders of the group assumed a distinctly prophetic voice, writing:

> There are so many of us out here who feel the world with thin skin and heavy hearts, who get called crazy because we are too full of fire and pain, who know that other worlds exist … A lot of us have visions about how things could be different and it's painful to keep them silent … Sometimes we get called sick and sometimes we get called sacred, but however, you label us, we are part of making this planet whole.
>
> *(Quoted from Farber, 2012, p. 20)*

The leaders of the Icarus Project are Sascha Altman DuBrul and Jacks MacNamara, and as spelt out in Farber (2012, p. 16ff.), they initially saw the mad as uniquely positioned to heal a sick world because of the special, or what DuBrul calls the 'dangerous' gifts which they possess. This represents a formidable conceptual shift from madness as a burden on the world to madness as a gift to the world. Herein, as pointed out by Farber (2012), they were influenced by figures like R. D. Laing, who depicted the world as opposed to the mad as sick, by the Old Testament prophets, who were inspired by visions which led them to rail at the conventional, also by Martin Luther King who stated in one of his sermons, 'Everyone passionately seeks to be well-adjusted … but there are some things in our world to which men of good will must be creatively maladjusted … Human salvation lies in the hands of the creatively maladjusted' (quoted from Ghaemi, 2012). While as Farber (2012) points out, the Icarus Project leaders have retreated in recent years from attributing a highly privileged place to those deemed mad, residues of this position remain nonetheless. And the week of Mad Pride is commonly dedicated at least in part to that more expansive vision, in certain instances, it taking the name 'Creative Maladjustment Week' (see cmweek.org). Herein, a unity with all other forms of 'maladjustment' is inherently being made, the idea being here that no one should be 'well-adjusted' to ableism, mentalism, classism, sexism, racism, homophobia or any of the other oppressions that characterise society. I would add that to varying degrees, the position that the mad have special insight is also commonly held by antipsychiatry activists, a survivor/activist interviewee of mine stating,

> My thoughts had roots in some kind of social consciousness . . . And I certainly don't claim that everyone who is crazy is having a fabulous spiritual experience or can necessarily be useful to others, spiritually at that time. But very many people who go crazy, or who become depressed, go through things that others would benefit from if only they could listen to what those experiences were all about.
>
> *(Shimrat, quoted from Burstow, 2015a, pp. 237–8)*

Unlike antipsychiatry adherents, members of the mad movement differ substantially among themselves with respect to their beliefs about psychiatry and what should be done about it. Some are antipsychiatry; others reject antipsychiatry and many see the overriding focus on psychiatry as mistaken. Some fundamentally critique 'psychiatric treatments'; some value the 'treatments'; some highlight research which shows that the so-called mentally ill have no chemical imbalances; still others argue that the question of whether or not there is a difference in chemistry is irrelevant. Some work within the system as peer workers or peer researchers and others reject such practices as examples of co-optation. Insofar as there is a basis of unity aside from the shared experience of being a survivor, it would be this: to some degree or other, all see mad states and mad struggles as phenomena in which to take pride; all want survivors' rights defended; all want issues of survivor poverty addressed; most disparage the untruth about the 'treatments' spread by those with power. Correspondingly, the most vocal minimally tend to deeply oppose forced treatment and involuntary confinement (for verification and a more detailed overview of both these commonalities and these differences, see Diamond, 2012).

Common events in the mad movement include: the mounting of festivals and art events, including mad theatre; the creation of mad scholarship; the identification and preservation of mad history, running support groups; lobbying and petitioning governments; mounting demonstrations; holding conferences, and in one case, and this conducted by MindFreedom International, a hunger strike (see Diamond, 2012; Burstow, 2014b).

Mad Activism as a Radical Politic

It is clear what makes Mad Pride a radical politic. Both the utter rejection of the concept 'normal' and the reframing of madness from a social burden to a gift bestowed on society are nothing short of a radical turnabout. Correspondingly, the unapologetic proclamation of mad truth in the face of psychiatric hegemony, and beyond that, in the face of a multinational pharmaceutical industry and a veritable army of professionals at work silencing that truth, and the relentless creations of blogs, websites, festivals and campaigns that speak this truth transparently constitute what philosopher Michel Foucault (1972 and 1980) aptly refers to as an insurrection of subjugated knowledge. Indeed, so utter is the turnabout in question that mad activists are celebrating those very states that those with power most construct as a malady and seek to 'cure'. More generally, mad activists are challenging authoritarian arrangements and standing up for freedom.

The politics in question, additionally, has a strong anarchist bent, indeed, and is in line with what has been called new anarchism. In this regard, besides the antiauthoritarian nature of what is happening and the insistence on equality/liberty – which is absolutely integral – the mad movement is utopian in the sense that mad activism explicitly announces that a very different world is possible. There is a rejection of the standard prioritisation of reason over emotions: activists speak now in anger, now in anguish, now in mockery, now with joy and now with humour. Pluralism in tactics, identity and belief also features in this anarchist bent. Anarchistic as well is the carnivalesque nature of many of the events, the prioritisation of culture, the frequent use of symbolic protest (as in the bed-push), the playfulness, the deployment of the arts and the emphasis on the experimental and on prefigurative politics (including the setting up of peer counselling).

I would add here that such anarchist tendencies are anything but accidental. What is relevant in this regard, although most people in the mad movement would not identify as anarchists, key leaders of the movement do. One of the two founders of the Icarus Project, Sascha DuBrul, for example (see Farber, 2012), is a self-identified anarchist as well as the founding member of a punk rock band. The cover of the book in which the mad movement made its debut is particularly telling: it features the large anarchist 'A', intersecting with the words 'Mad Pride'.

A Broader View of the Radical Activism of the Anti/Critical Psychiatry Network(s)

It would be a mistake to see either antipsychiatry or critical psychiatry groups as simply acting in isolation. Long predating the WTO protests, but nonetheless in the anarchist style which has been common in activism since this protest (for an analysis of such politics, see Gordon, 2008), groups belonging to each of these movements routinely work together in a pluralistic network. They likewise frequently work in loose coalitions with groups primarily associated with other oppressions. CAPA, for instance, commonly works in concert with parts of the feminist movement(s), correspondingly, has frequently been part of larger antipoverty campaigns, has historically networked with such groups as Ontario Coalition Against Poverty and was part of the Occupy movement/network in 2012. In this last regard, for example, as an Occupy event, CAPA mounted a demonstration called Occupy Psychiatry against the largest psychiatric facility in Ontario. This action additionally was conducted in solidarity with Boycott Normal: Occupy the American Psychiatric Association (APA).[5] Boycott Normal was, in turn, a mad movement initiative. The point is that antipsychiatry activism and groups figure as nodes within larger networks, which are themselves decentralised, weblike, shifting, non-hierarchical, antiauthoritarian and pluralistic – so typical of current radical politics.

While this way of operating has become a standard feature of the new anarchism, significantly, as already suggested, the modus operandi is not new to the groups which push back against psychiatry. Survivor and antipsychiatry groups have for decades worked together in loosely formed coalitions with groups such as prison abolitionists, feminist groups and groups that coalesce around poverty. Correspondingly, while to be clear, it is critical that greater attention be paid to intersectionality and to the integration of antiracist politics in particular, attention to the interactions of oppression has never been absent from the movement politics as historical indicators; see, for example, the antipsychiatry magazine *Phoenix Rising*'s special issues on prisons, on women and on LGBTQ jeopardy (Phoenix Rising Collective, 1980, 1981 and 1990, respectively). That said, it should be acknowledged, nonetheless, as demonstrated in Diamond (2012), that sexism, racism, ableism, heterosexism, ageism and other oppressions continue to plague this movement – and tensions linked to these oppressions inevitably play out in the politic. For example, men in the movement tend to interpret expressions of anger as inherently justified, while women often experience anger as a gender threat, and to the dissatisfaction of many of women, in such cases, the male interpretation is overwhelmingly prioritised.

More narrowly, antipsychiatry activists, people who self-identify as part of the survivor movement, people who identify as consumers, and those who call themselves mad *routinely* work together, sometimes in loose networks, sometimes in support of a specific project or action initiated by one of the groups, frequently in response to an ad hoc committee that has suddenly coalesced around an issue. In this regard, while friction can occur, and while both acknowledged and unacknowledged inequalities persist, especially those based on ability and on status, as long as the centrality of survivors is respected in meaningful ways, there is an acceptance and welcoming of all constituencies that come together to combat psychiatry. By way of example, when CAPA mounted the first conference ever held on how to organise against psychiatry – PsychOut – invitations to present were sent out to a massive number of groups and individuals both locally and internationally who touch on this area; correspondingly, despite the fact that the conference was mounted by an antipsychiatry group, all but one of the keynotes invited hailed from the mad movement.[6] Likewise, when mad scholars Brenda LeFrançois, Geoffrey Reaume and Robert Menzies decided to co-edit a book on Canadian mad scholarship, they included a large number of chapters from members of the antipsychiatry movement (see, for example, Diamond 2014; Burstow, 2014c). Similarly, when Mad Pride rolls around in Toronto, all manner of groups present, including antipsychiatry groups, in a decentralised fashion with everyone given the freedom to mount and determine their own programme and specify their own location for it.

Herein, we see the anarchist principles of co-participation, decentralisation and equality coming together. Correspondingly, in what is minimally a prefigurative fashion, we begin to see the emergence of aspects of the utopia or 'better space' that so many of us are trying to build.

Zeroing in on Radical Actions in the Critical/Antipsychiatry Network

In the interest of conveying a sense of the type of radical actions that can happen in this network, I would focus on two such actions. The first is a hunger strike put on by the mad movement MindFreedom. The second is the Day of Worldwide Protest Against Electroshock.

Initiated and overseen by the Board of MindFreedom with the intent of revealing the baselessness of psychiatry's claims, the hunger strike, called a Fast for Freedom, was a highly organised protest reminiscent of Gandhi. To the excitement of the entire network, on 15 August 2013, six American psychiatric survivors began a hunger strike, vowing to continue it until such time as they received an acceptable response from the APA. The challenge to APA was to come up with even a shred of evidence that there is a physical basis to a single 'psychiatric disorder'. In support of the hunger strikers were academics and professionals tasked with evaluating any evidence put forward by APA. Now in time, the

APA indeed responded, but as anticipated, it failed to produce anything remotely resembling evidence.[7]

That this was a radical action and reasonably successful one is clear. It was well organised, with health concerns attended to and with key players from both the survivor network and the coterie of progressive professionals integrated; and while the media coverage afforded it was limited, the reporting of it was positive. Moreover, the activism was strategic, carefully tailored to double bind APA. The point is, as the strikers knew, there is no such physical evidence, and so no matter what the APA did, it would look bad. That said, the action eventually came to an abrupt halt. After the panel of experts responded to APA's highly inadequate response – and it was indeed so judged – the action was at an end. Such a process contrasts sharply with successful historical nonviolent campaigns such as the campaign to desegregate Nashville, where one form of protest (a sit-in at a lunch-counter) was followed up by another, with the pressure for change continuing to mount over time.[8]

I would add that when I discussed the limitations of this otherwise remarkable action with one of the organisers, he informed me that he had intended follow-up but what he proposed was deemed too dangerous by the board. Which leads me to some questions:

1 How successful and ultimately how radical can a radical action be if avoidance of risk is prioritised?
2 If this action were more anarchistic and more decentralised so that other groups could pick up where this one left off, would that have been preferable to an action that could be stopped by a board decision? Or to put this differently, can what starts out as a tightly disciplined campaign necessarily controlled by one group usefully be transformed in time into a diffuse multicentred action?

The second action that I am highlighting, the Day of Worldwide Protest Against Electroshock, illustrates how well the network qua network can work and the non-hierarchical nature of what can unfold. The action was initiated by three electroshock (ECT) survivors – one in Cork, Ireland (Mary Maddock), and two in the US (Ted Chabasinksi and Debra Schwartzkopff) – two of whom identify as antipsychiatry and all of whom identify as mad. Their invitation to antipsychiatry and critical groups and individuals around the world was to join in a worldwide protest against ECT on 16 May 2015. All groups were totally free to frame their own actions as they wished. A virtual page was quickly created, containing regularly updated information on what was being planned in each city. Eager to help, Psych Rights (a legal group in Alaska) stepped up to the plate and created a page on a related website and invited people to contribute material which everyone else could use, this action resulting in a mutually created ever-expanding resource page.[9] Articles written by individual bloggers likewise appeared on the website Mad in America, encouraging people to join in (see, e.g., Chabasinski, 2015). Correspondingly, dozens of cities around the world proceeded to hold their own unique protests, some via ad hoc committees that sprang up for the purpose, some in the hands of established groups, most occurring in the streets, one in a bookstore, a few involving theatre, with examples of cities involved being: Cork, Ireland, Toronto, Canada, Montevideo, Uruguay, New York, USA, Santiago, Chile, Manchester, England, and Buenos Aires, Argentina.

The Day of Worldwide Protest Against Electroshock was not a strategic action. Nonetheless, it was an impressive one that shows how the network working in loose coalitions can orchestrate a truly global protest (not that Eurocentrism ever disappears).

The Special Role of Social Media in Anti/Critical Psychiatry Activism

As with most social movements today, social media plays a huge role in the work of these organisations and networks, has become, in short, the new face of both organising and educating in these organisations and networks. Hence the abundance of websites, blogsites, Facebook pages, YouTube postings and blog radio programmes.[10] Blogsites have proved particularly important, with the most significant of these being Mad in America.[11] This particular site fosters a huge roster of bloggers from around the world, some belonging to the mad movement, some to the antipsychiatry movement, some are survivors, some are professionals, with the site interactive, and with blogs ranging from personal stories (see Delano, 2014) to details on how to use book activism to get authors in our network read (see Burstow, 2015b).

While the use of social media is highly significant for the work of this network generally, it is absolutely essential for the very radical work of antipsychiatry for we are effectively shut out by the mainstream. In this respect, while the mainstream press, for example, will to some degree cover books that are critical psychiatry or upfront mad politics (and even then, note, coverage is very limited), not so with antipsychiatry. The reason is clear: there is a unique threat coming from antipsychiatry in that it constitutes a foundational critique of psychiatry and of the related multinational industries (from which the media, note, receives funding). Moreover, it represents a fundamental challenge to the state and its powers. And on some level, the establishment knows this, also that antipsychiatry is gaining traction (for indicators, see Burstow, 2015c). Hence the veritable freeze-out by the media.

A case in point: the largest of the anti-shock demonstrations in the Day of Worldwide Protest was in Toronto; it was an antipsychiatry demonstration for which hundreds of press were contacted. While there was some coverage of demonstrations in other cities, not a single press covered the Toronto protest, despite the fact that not only was it the largest, it promised and delivered on eye-catching spectacles like giant puppet heads. By the same token, when a press conference was held in Toronto to announce the results of groundbreaking research which substantially upheld key antipsychiatry claims, despite sustained outreach to the press, despite the involvement of University of Toronto faculty and despite obvious draws (for not only were the findings momentous, the panel included no less a person than a member of the provincial legislature), not a single member of the 'press' turned up. Not that the no-show threw us.

Having suspected as much from years of antipsychiatry activism, the anticipation of that no-show paved the way for a radical and democratising response. Activists rallied and created what we called the People's Press. Members of CAPA, in particular, turned up with cameras and with questions that they were eager to ask. The press conference happened as planned. Whereupon, the activists proceeded to mount highlights on YouTube.[12] This radical act was at once a strategic response, a democratising corrective and a prefigurative initiative, showing one way that coverage might happen in a utopia.

Herein, I would add, we find a clear indicator of the very pressing need for social media by groups who are fundamentally and uncompromisingly radical. Also an indicator of the truly radical potential of the social media.

Additional Thoughts about the Critical/Antipsychiatry Network: Why/How all Players are Needed

The mad movement is necessarily the pivotal player in the network, as is the survivor movement more broadly defined. Here is a liberation movement, and here the prioritisation of those most oppressed by sanism. To put this another way, here is the insurrection of subjugated knowledge (Foucault, 1972, 1980). That understood, insofar as substantial and long-term political change is being sought, an absolutely essential player is antipsychiatry. As can be seen by at once the rejection of reformism and the detailed attrition model, what antipsychiatry offers are clearer political directions, some way of assessing actions and a foundation that allows people to remain radical and avoid co-optation.

In this regard, as critical as cultural expression and celebration is, it is a feature which can easily be accommodated by the state even while the state continues to grow ever more oppressive. A case in point is the decision of the city of Toronto to give official recognition to Mad Pride or more markedly, the decision of the province of Ontario to fund mad movement initiatives while simultaneously working to tighten state control of those deemed mad.[13]

By the same token, the substantial co-optation of the movement is no secret (see, for example, Anonymous, in Burstow, 2015a, p. 257). Note in this regard, as discussed in Burstow (2015a) in the UK, the substantial funding of peer initiatives has resulted in both less protest and less radical protest, also with the rampant use of 'mental health' language. Significantly, the co-optation is never of those who are antipsychiatry, protection arising from the fact that the goals are clear, that both psychiatric and government languages are scrupulously avoided (for a discussion of co-optation of and through language in the survivor movement, see Burstow, 2014c) and because antipsychiatry never partners with and but rarely looks to the state for solutions.

More generally, people combatting the current system need a stronger basis of unity and a clearer direction than is currently found in the mad movement, without which 'success' cannot be easily accessed, and without which even the seemingly transparent symbols of the mad movement begin to lose meaning. One indicator of this is the slippage which has occurred with the bed-push.

As a test, about a year ago, I talked to four different mad-identified people who have enthusiastically participated in bed-pushes. All routinely enjoy the activity. However, not one actually knew what the symbol meant. By contrast, every single antipsychiatry proponent with whom I subsequently talked was clear about the meaning. Herein, we see the limitation of the celebrative and the spontaneous.

Fortunately just as psychiatry identifies antipsychiatry as the biggest threat to its dominance, progressively more members of the mad movement have come to the same conclusion. This helps to explain the recent upsurge of antipsychiatry within the mad movement, as evident by the comments on antipsychiatry articles in Mad in America (see, for example, comments in the comments section of Burstow, 2014b).

Such a shift represents the establishment's worst nightmare. And herein, I would suggest, lies the promise of an unstoppable radical politic.

Concluding Remarks: Some Implications for Radical Politics Generally

This chapter has introduced the network of people who organise against sanism and institutional psychiatry, in particular honing in on two highly important and interpenetrating movements – antipsychiatry and the mad movement. It has shed light on the nature of each and on the work of the critical/antipsychiatry network as a whole, making visible what makes the activism radical, also, what detracts from the radicality. Rather than summarising what has been stated, in ending, I would briefly touch on possible implications of the forgoing for radical politics as a whole.

With the MindFreedom hunger strike, I introduced the possibility of following up a highly focused action by a single organisation with collective and perhaps spontaneous actions by the networks as whole – a way of organising worth considering. A still more important issue that has surfaced is the significance of including more classical anarchistic elements in our protest.

In this last regard, as already noted, radical politics since the WTO protests have largely been characterised by values such as spontaneity, tentativeness of goals, celebration, the prioritisation of the cultural over the 'political' and the prefigurative over the strategic. As invaluable as the shift is, the question which has arisen in this chapter is: Do we not *also* need clear goals, clear focuses and disciplined actions? Or to put this in anarchist terms, just as we need what has been called new anarchism or postanarchism (see Kinna, 2005; Gordon, 2008; Newman, 2011), do we not also need more classical anarchism? And did not the collapse of the Occupy movement itself demonstrate this?

To be clear, what I am recommending here is that we approach the new and the classical not in the spirit of better/worse but as necessary principles/directions to hold in tension. One possibility is seeing them in a dialectical relationship, perhaps envisioning different syntheses. Another possibility is to understand them as different gears, both of which are needed in radical activism. At which point, critical questions for any given movement are: What do those gears look like in our movement? And how do we know when to shift gears?

One final observation: the very existence of the mad and the antipsychiatry movements in themselves present challenges to all other radical movements. On a simple level, Mad folk belong to all other movements and accordingly, there are times when radicals in other movements need to reconsider their politics.

An example of a mishandling which might shed light on the type of shifts needed: in a guest presentation to one of my classes, people in charge of security in Occupy Toronto discussed how they accommodated psychiatric survivors who joined their encampment. Unfortunately, their primary example of good handling was this: people at the encampment became progressively uneasy by the behaviour of a participating survivor. Whereupon, they consulted a psychiatric nurse who was one of the protestors. Correspondingly, on her advice, they got in touch with folk who, in turn, 'urged' the person in question to 'go back on their meds'.

Irrespective of whether or not cold-turkeying drugs were causing the behaviour that worried people, this action points to the problematic existence of psychiatric hegemony even within radical circles. Correspondingly, it highlights the importance of accepting differences that radicals themselves tend to pathologise, also the importance of establishing protocols whereby organisers turn to mad folk themselves for guidance on how tricky issues related to their community might be addressed – for admittedly, they can arise – as opposed to turning into 'mental health' practitioners.

Finally, a reminder that power within groups is never equal, and pre-existing power differentials and relationships do not just disappear.

Notes

1 See https://coalitionagainstpsychiatricassault.wordpress.com/.
2 Note CAPA's Mother's Day marches, one of which is described at https://coalitionagainstpsychiatricassault.wordpress.com/events/past-events/stop-shocking-our-mothers-and-grandmothers-2011/.
3 See in this regard messages still online from the 1990s group Lunatics Liberation Front at https://www.mail-archive.com/leninist-international@lists.wwpublish.com/msg01554.html.
4 See www.mindfreedom.org/.
5 For details on Occupy Psychiatry, go to CAPA website and see https://coalitionagainstpsychiatricassault.wordpress.com/events/past-events/occupy-psychiatry/.

6 See http://individual.utoronto.ca/psychout/.
7 For these and other details, see www.mindfreedom.org/kb/act/2003/mf-hunger-strike/hunger-strike-news.
8 For details, see https://en.wikipedia.org/wiki/Nashville_sit-ins.
9 See http://networkagainstpsychiatricassault.org/ElectroshockDocs.htm.
10 For an example of the latter, see www.blogtalkradio.com/talkwithtenney.
11 See www.madinamerica.com/.
12 See www.youtube.com/watch?v=pjtJvjDG4uM.
13 For one example of current new oppressive measures being considered – and this by a state which at the same time trips over itself to 'support' Mad Pride – see Bill 95 and the commentary on it, at, respectively, www.ontla.on.ca/web/bills/bills_detail.do?locale=en&BillID=3316 and www.thebarrieexaminer.com/ur/story/1050639.

References

Burstow, B. (2014a). On antipsychiatry. *The Biz O Madness Blog*. Available at http://bizomadness.blogspot.ca/2014/07/on-antipsychiatry.html (Accessed 22 March, 2016).

Burstow, B. (2014b). Antipsychiatry revisited. *Mad in America*. Available at http://bizomadness.blogspot.ca/2014/07/on-antipsychiatry.html (Accessed 22 March, 2016).

Burstow, B. (2014c). What's in a name?: Naming and the battle against psychiatry, in B. Lefrançois, R. Menzies, and G. Reaume, (eds.), *Matter Matters: A Critical Reader in Canadian Mad Studies*, 1st ed. Toronto: Canadian Scholars' Press, pp. 79–90.

Burstow, B. (2014d). The withering away of psychiatry: An attrition model for antipsychiatry, in B. Burstow, B. LeFrançois, and S. Diamond, (eds.), *Psychiatry Disrupted: Theorizing Resistance and Crafting the (R)evolution*, 1st ed. Montreal: McGill-Queen's University Press, pp. 34–51.

Burstow, B. (2014e). Liberal mental health reform: A "fail-proof" way to fail. *Mad in America*. Available at www.madinamerica.com/2014/11/liberal-mental-health-reform-fail-proof-way-fail/ (Accessed 2 April, 2016).

Burstow, B. (2015a) *Psychiatry and Business of Madness*. New York: Palgrave.

Burstow, B. (2015b). Getting our anti/critical psychiatry authors read: A case for book activism. *Mad in America*. Available at www.madinamerica.com/2015/04/getting-anticritical-psychiatry-authors-read-case-book-activism/ (Accessed 28 March, 2016).

Burstow, B. (2015c). Yes, the tide is turning against psychiatry. *Mad in America*. Available at www.madinamerica.com/2015/09/yes-the-tide-is-turning-against-psychiatry/ (Accessed 29 March, 2016).

Breggin, P. (1991). *Toxic Psychiatry*. New York: St. Martins Press.

Chabasinski, T. (2015). May 16, 2015: International protest against electroshock. *Mad in America*. Available at www.madinamerica.com/2015/03/may-16-2015-international-day-protest-shock-treatment/ (Accessed 28 March, 2016).

Cooper, D. (ed.) (1967). *Psychiatry and Antipsychiatry*. London: Paladin.

Curtis, T., Dellar, R., Leslie, E., and Watson, B., (eds.) (2000). *Mad Pride: A Celebration of Mad Culture*. London: Spare Change Books.

Delano, L. (2014). On waking up from the American dream. *Mad in America*. Available at www.madinamerica.com/2014/07/on-waking-up-from-the-american-dream/ (Accessed 28 March, 2016).

Diamond, S. (2012). *Against the Medicalization of Humanity*. Doctoral Thesis. Toronto: University of Toronto.

Diamond, S. (2014). What makes us a community? in B. Lefrançois, R. Menzies, and G. Reaume, (eds.), *Matter Matters: A Critical Reader in Canadian Mad Studies*, 1st ed. Toronto: Canadian Scholars' Press, pp. 64–77.

Farber, S. (2012). *The Spiritual Gift of Madness*. Rochester: Inner Traditions.

Foucault, M. (1972). *The Archeology of Knowledge*. New York: Harper & Row.

Foucault, M. (1980). *Power/Knowledge*. New York: Pantheon.

Ghaemi, N. (2012). Mood Swings: Martin Luther King: Depressed and creatively Maladjusted. [Blog] *Psychology Today*. Available at www.psychologytoday.com/blog/mood-swings/201201/martin-luther-king-depressed-and-creatively-maladjusted (Accessed 25 March, 2016).

Goffman, E. (1961). *Asylums: Essays on the Social Situation of Mental Patients and Other Inmates*. New York: Anchor Books.

Gordon, U. (2008). *Anarchy Alive!: Antiauthoritarian Politics from Practice to Theory*. London: Pluto Press.

Kinna, R. (2005). *Anarchism: A Beginner's Guide*. Oxford: Oneworld Publications.

Knopp, F. (1976). *Instead of Prisons*. New York: Faculty Press.

Newman, S. (2011). *The Politics of Postanarchism*. Edinburgh: Edinburgh University Press.

Packard, E. (1865/1974). *Great Disclosures of Spiritual Wickedness: An Appeal to the Government to Protect the Unalienable Rights of Married Women*. New York: Arno Press.

Personal testimonies, Inquiry into Psychiatric Assault (2005) [online]. Available at https://coalitionagains tpsychiatricassault.wordpress.com/articles/personal-narratives/ (Accessed 22 March, 2016).

Phoenix Rising Collective (1980). *Phoenix Rising*, 1:2.

Phoenix Rising Collective (1981). *Phoenix Rising*, 1:4.

Phoenix Rising Collective (1990). *Phoenix Rising*, 8:3 and 4.

PSAT: Psychiatric Survivor Archives of Toronto, n.d. [online]. Available at https://coalitionagainstpsychiatric assault.wordpress.com/articles/personal-narratives/ www.psychiatricsurvivorarchives.com/ (Accessed 22 March, 2016).

Reaume, G. (2000). *Remembrance of Patients Past*. Toronto: Oxford University Press.

Starkman, M. (2014). Mad people's history, evolving culture, and language. The movement, in B. Lefrançois, R. Menzies, and G. Reaume, (eds.), *Matter Matters: A Critical Reader in Canadian Mad Studies*, 1st ed. Toronto: Canadian Scholars' Press, pp. 27–37.

Szasz, T. (1961). *The Myth of Mental Illness*. New York: Paul B. Hoeber.

Szasz, T. (1970). *The Manufacture of Madness*. New York: Harper and Row.

1.6

RADICAL CLIMATE POLITICS

From Ogoniland to Ende Gelände

Leah Temper

In October 1990, chiefs and elders of the six Ogoni clans in the Niger Delta launched the Ogoni Bill of Rights demandinsg resource control of their natural resources, the right of the Ogoni people to self-determination and the right to protect their environment. The Ogoni Bill of Rights never once uses the term 'climate justice'; yet in many respects, the declaration may be seen as a precursor of the radical movement for climate justice in that it demands a halt to fossil fuel extraction, territorial and resource sovereignty, as well as reparations for the environmental injustices and damages inflicted (Ojo 2016). Shortly after, in 1992, the Movement for the Survival of the Ogoni People (MOSOP) decided to focus its energy on the three oil companies operating within the region: Shell, Chevron and the Nigerian National Petroleum Company. MOSOP presented the companies with an ultimatum – they demanded 10 billion dollars in damages and royalties to the Ogoni people, as well as an immediate end to the companies' violence against the Ogoni region's environment. If these demands were not met, they threatened to rally the Ogoni people in widespread popular resistance to the companies' presence. By 1993, following mass mobilisations, Shell oil pulled out of the region, leaving thousands of barrels of oil unexploited and reducing oil profits by some 200 million dollars in that year alone.

MOSOP can be seen as the first movement to successfully stem the flow of oil in their territories – to literally 'leave the oil under the soil' (Bassey 2012). The mobilisation and resistance of the movement, led by Ken Saro-Wiwa (who was executed by the Nigerian dictatorship), have served as an inspiration that continues to inform the claims, strategies and tactics of radical movements struggling to disarm the petro-economy and fossil capitalism until today (Temper et al., 2013). These movements now dot the globe, best described perhaps by the notion of 'Blockadia', described by Naomi Klein (2014) as 'a roving transnational conflict zone that is cropping up with increasing frequency and intensity wherever extractive projects are attempting to dig and drill, whether for open-pit mines, or gas fracking, or tar sands oil pipelines'.

Radical climate justice politics fights for 'System change, not Climate Change' referring to the need to overhaul the political and economic systems causing climate change. In contrast to other forms of post-political environmentalism (Swyngedouw 2010) or carbon-counting climate activism, it is a movement that calls for structural changes to the system, that is anticapitalist and anti-extractivist (Chatterton et al. 2013). It calls for energy justice and brings attention to the climate crisis as one that is racist, gendered and can only be addressed by contesting ongoing processes of colonisation, exploitation and oppression. At its core, climate justice is based on the understanding that those least responsible for the production of greenhouse gases are those who are most affected by climate disruption and chaos, and that these inequalities are being further exacerbated by the false solutions being promoted such as carbon trading and offsets, renewable projects such as mega-dams, biofuels and nuclear, geoengineering, and the green economy, including commodification of the atmosphere, land and water.

While climate justice activism has parallels with the environmental justice (EJ) movement and its history (see Pellow, this volume), climate justice distinguishes itself through the truly global nature of the cause and impacts of climate change and the scale of the response needed to combat it. This is because climate change brings to the fore the interconnectedness of our shared environment and atmosphere as never before. At the same time, similarly to the global EJ movement, it remains rooted in the specific struggles of frontline communities and serves as a connecting thread between the disparate histories of resistance of those battling environmental damage and dispossession across the planet (Martinez-Alier et al. 2016). This includes struggles against oil and gas extraction, coal plants and fracking, organising by the victims of floods, hurricanes and tornadoes, as well as movements fighting for food sovereignty and access to resources. Finally, climate justice prompts us towards the creative proactive social construction of a post-petroleum society and a consideration of how the economy, energy, food and transportation systems can be radically rethought and redesigned.

This chapter first explains the historical and theoretical roots of the movement from a global perspective. Second, it will focus on the movement's primary strategies and tactics and on the emblematic struggles that are defining radical climate politics today. In this, I focus on the following defining principles: anticapitalism, energy justice, climate debt, anti-extractivism and leaving oil in the soil, and decolonisation.

Anticapitalist

A slow and painless 'adaptation' is not possible, what is called for is a 'dramatic emissions cuts in a manner that is both redistributive (from rich to poor and North to South, and in the process male to female), and sufficiently shocking to economic structures and markets that major transformations in production and consumption are compelled.

(Bond 2008)

Radical climate justice is by definition anticapitalist and intersectional. The climate justice framework recognises that people experience climate change along lines of social and structural oppression: racism, sexism, transphobia, colonialism and class exploitation, and forces us to confront the role of capitalism and state power in driving social oppression, economic injustices and ecological devastation. Thus, a Black Lives Matter protest in Britain in September 2016 blocked London airport, arguing that 'the climate crisis is a racist crisis' because seven out of the ten countries most impacted will be in Africa, and black communities will be among the most impacted.

Radical climate justice is also informed by a metabolic understanding of the economy which acknowledges that both the impacts from extraction of fossil fuels and those related to climate change are concentrated on the most vulnerable populations and rely on ongoing processes of colonisation. This understanding is informed in part by theories from ecological economics and political ecology (Hornborg 1998). For example, concepts such as the ecological debt owed from North to South, a demand born in Latin America in 1991 and further developed by Accion Ecologica in reference to Chevron's activities in the Amazon (Martinez-Alier et al. 2014), and the theory of 'ecologically unequal exchange', draw attention to how the high material standards of developed countries are dependent on net transfers of materials and energy from the periphery to the industrial centre. At the same time, the less developed countries and regions exporting the resources experience a net increase in entropy (disorder), leading to environmental disruption and degradation, as natural resources and traditional social structures are dismembered (Hornborg 1992; Warlenius 2016).

From a metabolic perspective, environmental inequality is a result of both uneven access to the basic sources of low entropy energy – solar and terrestrial or stored energy (such as coal and oil) – as well as the uneven flows of high entropy wastes (such as carbon dioxide and other pollutants) that are discharged from the economic metabolic system and displaced onto the most vulnerable populations (Hornborg 1992). Such a socio-metabolic perspective brings to the fore how conflicts over oil extraction, coal and fossil fuels, and over sea-level rise, droughts, floods and tornadoes associated with climate chaos, are opposite sides of the same coin. Global environmental and climate justice activists increasingly bring attention to this interconnectedness between access to resources and risk, and between sources and sinks.

A radical politics of climate justice thus leads to a questioning of the basic configuration of the global socio-metabolic system. The limited capacity of the atmosphere to absorb carbon highlights the insanity of an economic system based on endless growth on a finite planet. This leads inevitably to the disavowal of an economy based on a false growth imperative and on prices that do not account for environmental costs. It also raises a question about what an alternative post-growth, post-petroleum society would look like and how to get there. This opens up potential alliances with those calling for degrowth, post-growth and *décroissance* (D'Alisa et al. 2014; Temper et al. 2013), as well as other movements aiming for a transformation of the economic system.

Payment of the Climate Debt as an Impossible Demand

> To say that we want wages for housework is to expose the fact that housework is already money for capital, that capital has made and makes money out of our cooking, smiling, fucking.
>
> *(Federici 1975)*

The climate movement has repeatedly called for the payment of the climate and ecological debt from North to South as reparations for overconsumption of environmental space, for the damages inflicted by climate chaos, and for the construction of a post-petroleum society. Climate debt is the idea that poor countries are owed various forms of reparations from rich countries for the climate crisis and, further, that nature's rights have also been violated and there is a need to pay a debt for repairing the earth.

As discussed by Bond (2010), there has been some debate over whether this demand promotes 'the financialisation of nature and the indirect reliance on markets and monetary solutions as catalysts for structural change'. In response to those who charge that demanding payment for the environmental space and services that have been stolen and appropriated from the South and from the subaltern without their permission is akin to pricing and objectifying nature, Bond (2010) argues that

> [i]f articulated fully, climate debt should cover not only the damages done by climate change but also finance the South's transcendence of extreme uneven development associated with the world economy's export-oriented operation. Payment of climate

debt damages and 'adaptation' financing - if done properly - would ideally permit (and compel) the Global South to delink from all manner of relations with the world economy that damage both the exporting economy and the climate: fossil fuel extraction, agricultural plantations and associated deforestation, export-processing zones, vast shipping operations, and foreign debt that forces further attempts to raise hard currency, which in turn reinforce the exploitative relationships that keep these countries in such poverty.

Going further, I would like to propose that this demand is akin to the feminist demand for 'wages for house-work' (Federici 1975). It is not so much a demand that can be assimilated within capitalism but instead an impossible demand that aims to undermine the ability of the capitalist system to continue appropriating environmental space for endless accumulation and therefore one that threatens the functioning and existence of the capitalist system.

Similar to Federici's argument for wages for housework (2012), the demand for payment of the Climate debt as a means of struggle aims to demystify and subvert the role performed for capitalism by extractivism, nature and the communities' ecological and reproductive labour. Just as the reproductive and caring labour of women has been invisibilised in how it serves to perpetuate capitalism, climate debt serves to highlight the ecological labour performed by nature as well as by subsistence communities that is appropriated for capitalist accumulation.

However, communities are increasingly claiming recognition for this reproductive labour and this demand can contribute towards a revolution in thinking and in social power relations. For example, when farmers' movement La Via Campesina organises around the argument, that small farmers' mode of reproduction and food sovereignty 'cools down the earth' (Martinez-Alier 2011) and when waste recyclers in Delhi claim that they are reducing the waste stream as well as carbon emissions and that they, rather than waste-to-energy plants, should be compensated for this work through the Clean Development Mechanism; such histories of struggle form part of radical climate justice politics.

By highlighting the contribution of their livelihoods and making use of 'eco-political capital', such movements are not buying into the ideology of commodifying nature to save it; they are rebelling against a capitalist system that continues to invisibilise their work and nature (Temper and Martinez-Alier 2016). Demanding payment for ecological and reproductive labour on these terms serves to threaten capital's accumulation ability, which is only possible through the exploitation, dispossession and contamination of women, nature and marginalised communities.

Against False Solutions and towards Energy Sovereignty

Radical climate politics opposes all forms of financialisation and commodification of nature and thus rejects carbon credits and mechanisms such as the UN REDD programme (Reduced Emissions from Deforestation and forest Degradation). Furthermore, radical climate politics, in contrast to a more reformist and technocratic approach, refuses to accept a shift to renewable energies as panacea for the climate crisis. This means acknowledging that a just energy future transcends a simple technological shift and entails the construction of new social systems.

Radical climate movements are increasingly engaged in the theory and praxis of energy justice, sovereignty and democracy, which focus on energy systems placed under people's common control and using technologies compatible with such control, with a radical reduction in carbon dioxide and other pollutants.

Energy sovereignty (ES) has been defined as 'the right of conscious individuals, communities and peoples to make their own decisions on energy generation, distribution and consumption in a way that is appropriate within their ecological, social, economic and cultural circumstances, provided that these do not affect others negatively' (XSE 2012). It also refers to 'political projects and visions towards a just generation, distribution and control of energy sources by organised and conscious communities, provided that these do not affect others negatively, and with respect for ecological cycles' (Del Bene et al. 2019).

At their core, energy justice and ES ask how energy can be redesigned and restructured so that everyone can access the basic energy they need. The concept of ES raises fundamental questions about the purpose and use of energy: Energy for whom? Energy for what? (Ariza-Montobbio 2015) ES calls for a reclamation of energy as 'a natural commons and the basis of life for all'. This also means decolonising the universalising understanding of *Energy* (with a capital 'E') as the abstract and uniform commercial generation of energy, and as a function of capital accumulation, and differentiating it from the incommensurable and contextually diverse uses of *energy*, with a small 'e' (Hildyard et al. 2012), able to adapt across time and space to different ecologies and human geographies.

ES emphasises technologies which challenge capitalist social relations and the ownership of the means of production. An energy transition to renewables that replicates the same patterns of expropriation of local resources is already leading to considerable conflicts across the global North and South (Avila, 2018; Del Bene et al. 2019) as land is grabbed and communities are displaced, evicted and flooded, while power continues to become concentrated. Radical climate politics thus include movements that are contesting damaging 'green technologies' as well as movements that are actively creating alternative energy futures, including the decentralisation, democratisation and municipalisation of energy, experimenting with new technologies, as well as food sovereignty, permaculture and multiple forms of energy provisioning.

De-carbonisation and Decolonisation

Radical climate justice is a de-colonial struggle that aims to disrupt and unsettle the various means of extracting energy from colonised territories and peoples, whether through slavery or through extractivism and accumulation by contamination. As the mobilisation against the Dakota Access Pipeline at Standing Rock in 2016 showed, the fight is not only about climate change, fossil fuels or water protection: it is in essence a struggle for sovereignty. This includes territorial sovereignty and food sovereignty, as well as ES and energy justice.

An indigenous struggle that inspires in its ability to unsettle us is the camp of the Unist'ot'en indigenous people in 'so-called Canada' who have been reasserting themselves on their territory. In 2010, they built a cabin directly on the GPS coordinates of the proposed route of the Pacific Trails Pipeline (PTP), which they refer to as 'the trailblazer of the prospective energy corridor that aims to traverse [our] territory'. The PTP would transport fracked shale gas 463 km from British Columbia's northern interior to a liquefaction plant and export terminal on the coast called Kitimat LNG.

Since 2009, the Unist'ot'en have been preventing trespass by industry and government interests that aim to develop projects without their consent. They have delivered eviction notices to Apache Oil, Enbridge and are currently fighting incursions by Trans-Canada's Coastal Gaslink pipeline stating that the companies are

> not permitted onto unceded lands of the Wet'suwet'en; are not permitted to place their greed ahead of Indigenous self-determination; are not permitted to destroy and exploit the lands; are not permitted to disregard the safety and health of communities; [and] are not permitted to disregard [our] Law!
>
> *(VMC 2015)*

This strategy has claimed considerable victories, with numerous divestments and projects remaining halted, not to mention how substantial support for this opposition to dirty oil helped topple the pro-gas and -pipeline government in British Columbia in 2017. The demands for self-determination made by the Unist'ot'en aim towards a structural transformation of colonial and capitalist systems of domination of nature and subjugated peoples (Bliss and Temper 2018). Such movements, in the words of Taiake Alfred (1999), are informed by 'a set of values that challenge the homogenizing force of Western Liberalism and free market capitalism; that honour the autonomy of individual conscience, non-coercive authority, and the deep interconnection between human beings and other elements of creation'.

The resistance of the Unist'ot'en does not depend on the state to grant rights to nature, but upon communities asserting their environmental responsibility through direct action. Their active spatial tactic of resistance, which regulates and physically blocks the movement of capital and commodity flows through their territory, holds both instrumental and symbolic power (Blomley 1996). It disrupts the flows of capital while creating a space for the control and practice of indigenous economic and political authorities in the face of the cultural and economic dislocation forced upon them (Temper 2019). This enables the creation of a living anticapitalist alternative, mutually informed by both an ancient system of values guiding sustainable relationships with the material world, and a transformative politics of decolonisation that seeks to revalue, reconstruct and redeploy indigenous cultural practices while deconstructing colonial and capitalist power structures (Napoleon 2013).

Ende Gelande

> There's something magical about sitting on top of an excavator and looking at the 66km² beautifully destructed landscape surrounding you, as accordion music from another silenced digger reaches your ears, with in the background a rainbow coming out of yet another halted coal-scraping monster in the distance. Almost like nature is saying 'thank you'.
>
> − *Participant in the Ende Gelände action (in CEO, 2016)*

If the proto-climate justice was born in the Niger Delta in 1990 − perhaps the most polluted and environmentally devastated place on the planet − it took some twenty-five years for activists in the world's most industrialised and richest countries to finally take up the mantle. Today, from the UK Climate Camps to the ZAD (Zone a Defendre) camp resisting airport construction in France, radical climate justice movements act as cultural laboratories experimenting with new technologies, commoning and other ways of being.

Beginning in August 2015, and again in May 2016, thousands of activists converged in Germany's Rhineland to stop the coal industry in its tracks (Buckland 2016; Rosewarme et al. 2013). In 2016, up to 4,000 activists occupied the Welzow-Süd open-pit lignite coal mine and aimed to shut down the adjacent Schwarze Pumpe coal-fired power plant in the largest global civil disobedience mobilisation against fossil fuels ever. The action was called Ende Gelände – Here and No Further.

The mine and plant, owned by the Swedish company Vatenfall, are Europe's tenth largest emitter of CO_2. One of the short-term goals of Ende Gelände was to stop the impending sale of the mining area by Vatenfall. Why, the movement questions, do the two richest countries in the world – countries that claim to be dedicated to stemming climate change and to an energy transition – need to continue to produce and burn the dirtiest fuel on the planet? Instead of selling on the dirty liabilities, the movement argued, Vatenfall could have financed a social phaseout of coal for the region and the costs of environmental reparation.

Ende Gelände was a huge success, forcing the plant to reduce its output by 20% over the forty-eight hours of the mass action, with consequences for the German electricity grid. According to John Jordan (2015),

> The protest was direct action at its best. Not a symbolic gesture that just tells a story and makes an injustice visible, but an action that targeted the very source of the problem and stopped it in its tracks. The actual stopping of CO2 emissions themselves, the fact that the lignite coal – the dirtiest type of coal in the world – was not dug out and burned that day, is what counts. Ende Gelände was a collective act of resistance that for once felt proportionate to the scale of the emergency: catastrophic climate change.

The action reignited debates in the German parliament about the sale, which eventually went through in October 2016. While Vatenfall initially expected to sell for 2–3 billion Euro, the company finally had to pay the buyer, Czech energy company EPH, 1.7 billion Euro for assuming the ecological liabilities in the region. If Germany is serious about its climate obligations, this implies that there is no future for lignite. A report by Corporate Europe Observatory (CEO 2016) suggests that EPH's strategy may thus revolve around the hope for a big payout under the Investor State Dispute Settlement that awards companies for losses due to environmental regulation in the public interest. Trade pacts that lock us into ecologically suicidal behaviour in the name of profit thus highlight the type of mechanism that ensures government inaction in the face of climate change. The strategy of Ende Gelände was, therefore, to contest both corporate power and such inaction.

The movement's motto in 2016 was 'we are the investment risk'. In 2017, Ende Gelände has set its sights on RWE, the second largest electricity producer in Germany, issuing the following ultimatum:

> Coal-based power generation is unjust. We from Ende Gelände are not prepared to accept this injustice. We fight for a climate of justice. We have made this very clear by blocking mines and power stations with the support of thousands. Because our actions in the past were not sufficient today we issue an ultimatum. Decide today to stop coal-based power-generation and close the open-cast mines and power stations! If you let this deadline pass we will take into our own hands!

Conclusion

This article has traced the birth and main principles of radical climate justice. It is a movement born in the global South, whose tactics and claims have sought to counter colonial dynamics and other forms of oppression and ecological devastation wrought by capitalism.

While climate activism in the North has often assumed a more technical and post-political approach, the urgency of the situation and the increasingly visible impacts are leading to a rise in disobedience, defiance and resistance even amongst 'civil' society. In 2013, the Sierra Club – a mainstream environmental lobbying group – committed civil disobedience for the first time in its 120-year history in a protest against the Keystone XL pipeline. Meanwhile, normal middle-class folks in America have been turned on to 'fracktivism' and eventually into climate activists once they connect the dots. Networks of resistance to the petro-economy are growing and operating along the entire chain of oil production. As Terisa Turner has written in 'Why Nigerian women are at war against Shell in Nigeria', the capitalist organisation of production and the oil market defined by the companies themselves can act as forces that unite those resident at the point of extraction and the consumers of oil. They suggest that 'When residents of oil producing communities stop production at the same time as consumers boycott oil companies by refusing to buy their products, the two groups engage in a simultaneous global "production-consumption" oil strike' (Turner and Brownhill 2004).

Remaining challenges for radical climate politics are to connect with the global working class and labour activists, transcending productive but still timid discussions of a 'just transition' (Stevis and Felli 2015). As Barca (2015) argues, this calls for the development of an 'emancipatory ecological class consciousness', as well as a redefinition of the workers' identity. Climate movements also need to connect with the struggles of indigenous communities and communities of colour fighting industrial pollution on their own terms. The atlas of EJ (www.ejatlas.org) records over 2,200 cases of EJ conflicts that form part of the same movement against environmental despoliation, degradation and dispossession (Temper et al. 2015). Carbon reductionism and a technocratic environmental approach do not resonate with such movements – yet, a new ethic of care for future generations, territory, water and all life can inform the creation of new alliances for sovereignty and eco-sufficiency.

References

Alfred, T., 1999. *Peace Power Righteousness: An Indigenous Manifesto*. Don Mills: Oxford University Press.

Ariza-Montobbio, P., 2015. Energy sovereignty: Politicising an energy transition. In Temper L., and Gilbertson T., (eds.), *Refocusing Resistance to Climate Justice: COPing in, COPing Out and Beyond Paris*, Barcelona. EJOLT report no. 23.

Avila, S., 2018. Environmental justice and the expanding geography of wind power conflicts. *Sustainability Science*, 13(3), pp. 599–616.

Barca, S., 2015. Labour and climate change. Towards an emancipatory ecological class-consciousness. Published in Temper L., and Gilbertson T., (eds.), *Refocusing Resistance to Climate Justice: COPing in, COPing Out and Beyond Paris*, EJOLT report no. 23.

Bassey, N., 2012. Leaving the oil in the soil: Communities connecting to resist oil extraction and climate change. *Development Dialogue*, 61, pp. 332–339.

Bliss, S. and Temper, L., 2018. The indigenous climate justice of the Unist'ot'en resistance. In Jacobsen, S.G., (ed.), *Climate Justice and the Economy*, 87–101. London: Routledge.

Blomley, N., 1996. 'Shut the province down': First nations blockades in British Columbia, 1984–1995.' *BC Studies: The British Columbian Quarterly*, (111), pp. 5–35.

Bond, P., 2008. The state of the global carbon trade debate. *Capitalism Nature Socialism*, *19*(4), pp. 89–106.

Bond, P., 2010. Climate debt owed to Africa: What to demand and how to collect? *African Journal of Science, Technology, Innovation and Development*, *2*(1), pp. 83–113.

Buckland, K., https://roarmag.org/essays/paris-attack-climate-justice-movements/.

CEO - Corporate Europe Observatory 2016. Ende Gelände v. Vattenfall. https://corporateeurope.org/climate-and-energy/2016/06/ende-gelaende-vs-vattenfall.

Chatterton, P., Featherstone, D., and Routledge, P., 2013. Articulating climate justice in Copenhagen: Antagonism, the commons, and solidarity. *Antipode*, *45*(3), pp. 602–620.

D'Alisa, G., Demaria, F., and Kallis, G. eds., 2014. *Degrowth: A Vocabulary for a New Era*. Routledge.

Del Bene, D., Pablo Soler, J., and Roa, T., 2019. Energy sovereignty. In Kothari, A., Salleh, A., Escobar, A., Demaria, F., and Acosta, A., (eds.), *Pluriverse: A Post-Development Dictionary*. Delhi: Authors UpFront and Tulika.

Federici, S., 1975. *Wages against Housework*. Bristol: Falling Wall Press.

Federici, S., 2012. *Revolution at Point Zero: Housework, Reproduction, and Feminist Struggle*. Oakland, CA: PM Press.

Hildyard, N., Lohman, L., and Sexton, S., 2012. *Energy Security for What? For Whom?* Sturminster Newton: The Corner House.

Hornborg, A., 1992. Machine fetishism, value, and the image of unlimited good: Towards a thermodynamics of imperialism. *Man*, *27*, pp. 1–18.

Hornborg, A., 1998. Towards an ecological theory of unequal exchange. Articulating world system theory and ecological economics. *Ecological Economics*, *25*, pp. 127–136.

Klein, N., 2014. *This Changes Everything*. New York: Simon & Schuster.

Martinez-Alier, J., 2011. The EROI of agriculture and its use by the Via Campesina. *The Journal of Peasant Studies*, *38*(1), pp. 145–160.

Martinez-Alier, J., Anguelovski, I., Bond, P., Del Bene, D., Demaria, F., Gerber, J.F., Greyl, L., Haas, W., Healy, H., Marín-Burgos, M., Ojo, G., Porto, M.F., Rijnhout, L., Rodríguez-Labajos, B., Spangenberg, J., Temper, L., Warlenius, R., and Yánez, I., 2014. Between activism and science: Grassroots concepts for sustainability coined by EJOs. *Journal of Political Ecology*, *21*, pp. 19–60.

Martinez-Alier, J., Temper, L., Del Bene, D., and Scheidel, A., 2016. Is there a global environmental justice movement? *The Journal of Peasant Studies*, *43*(3), pp. 731–755.

Napoleon, V., 2013. Thinking about indigenous legal orders. In Provost, R., and Sheppard, C., (eds.), *Dialogues on Human Rights and Legal Pluralism*, 229–245. Ius Gentium: Comparative Perspectives on Law and Justice 17. Netherlands: Springer.

Ojo, G.U., 2016. Analysis of oil wars and environmental justice in Ogoniland, Nigeria. *Multidisciplinary Journal of Research and Development Perspectives*, *5*, pp. 119–134.

Rosewarne, S., Goodman, J., and Pearse, R., 2013. *Climate Action Upsurge: The Ethnography of Climate Movement Politics*. London: Routledge.

Stevis, D. and Felli, R., 2015. Global labour unions and just transition to a green economy. *International Environmental Agreements: Politics, Law and Economics*, *15*(1), pp. 29–43.

Swyngedouw, E. 2010. Apocalypse forever? Post-political populism and the spectre of climate change. *Theory, Culture & Society*, *27*(2–3), pp. 213–232.

Temper, L. 2019. Blocking pipelines, unsettling environmental justice: From rights of nature to responsibility to territory. *Local Environment*, *24*(2), pp. 94–112.

Temper, L., del Bene, D., and Martinez-Alier, J., 2015. Mapping the frontiers and front lines of global environmental justice: The EJAtlas. *Journal of Political Ecology*, *22*, pp. 256–278.

Temper, L. and Martinez-Alier, J., 2016. Mapping ecologies of resistance. In Leah S.H. and Michael J.W. (eds.), *Grassroots Environmental Governance: Community Engagements with Industry*, 33–58. London: Routledge.

Temper, L., Yánez, I., Sharife, K., Ojo, G., Martinez-Alier, J., CANA, M.C., Cornelissen, K., Lerkelund, H., Louw, M., Martínez, E., and Minnaar, J., 2013. Towards a post-oil civilization. Yasunization and other initiatives to leave fossil fuels in the soil. *Environmental Justice Organizations, Liabilities and Trade*, (EJOLT) Report, (6).

Turner, T.E. and Brownhill, L.S., 2004. Why women are at war with Chevron: Nigerian subsistence struggles against the international oil industry. *Journal of Asian and African Studies*, *39*(1–2), pp. 63–93.

Vancouver Media Co-op 2015. Statement by Laura Holland, Wet'suwet'en Nation at the Vancouver Rally in Support of the Unist'ot'en Vancouver Media Co-Op 2015. http://vancouver.mediacoop. ca/story/statement-laura-holland-wetuweten-nation-vancouver/14735.

Warlenius, R., 2016. Linking ecological debt and ecologically unequal exchange: Stocks, flows, and unequal sink appropriation. *Journal of Political Ecology, 23*(1), pp. 364–380.

XSE (Catalan Network for Energy Sovereignty) 2012. Energy Sovereingty. Available at: http://xse. cat/wp-content/uploads/2014/03/Definiendo-la-soberanía-energética.pdf.

1.7

ECO-DEFENCE, RADICAL ENVIRONMENTALISM AND ENVIRONMENTAL JUSTICE

David Naguib Pellow

Introduction

How are radical environmental movements expanding and redefining the aim and scope of their work to link concerns for the defence and protection of non-human natures to struggles for social justice among aggrieved human populations? In other words, to what extent are activists whom we might traditionally associate with a single-issue emphasis on 'saving the earth' also integrating and reshaping those goals with greater attention to the politics of justice for people marginalised, for example, because of their gender, sexuality, racial, migration/citizenship status, ability and/or indigeneity? In this chapter, I explore the promise, tensions and possibilities for deepening and broadening of social justice politics within radical environmental movements. Based on data gathered from fieldwork, interviews, archival analysis and participant observation, I argue that while environmental movements have a long and troubled history of racism, nativism, heteropatriarchy and classism (to say nothing of misanthropy!), there are significant segments of these social formations that have invested time and energy into reimagining their work, including the very framing of the problem of the environmental crisis, along with strategies and tactics to address it. The evidence presented suggests new ways of defining environmental and environmental justice (EJ) politics and new ways of framing democracy and the polity itself.

The emergence of radical environmentalisms in the US, Britain, Australia and elsewhere in the 1980s and 1990s marked a new stage in the evolution of ecological politics. This was a moment punctuated by a discourse of radical analysis and action that we had rarely seen in environmental movements until that point. By the late 1990s and early 2000s, segments of these movements were converging around new ideas and tactics, producing a broader discourse that linked ecology, social justice and anti-oppression within groups like the Earth Liberation Front (ELF), which we also saw taking hold of and transforming groups like Earth First! (EF!), which had historically been hostile to such ideas.

What sparked the development of this kind of movement? There are many answers to that question, but the most obvious is the increase in reports of threats to planetary sustainability and ecological health. Less obvious but perhaps more important influences include a new discourse around the politics of social justice, which permeated other social movements, social change organisations and academic disciplines on university campuses beginning in the

1980s and 1990s. Concepts like *intersectionality*, and discourses and actions concerning multiple and linked oppressions and social privilege took hold in many of these spaces, and had a noticeable effect on the language and practices of social movements in the US and elsewhere, including environmental causes. The idea that we can no longer fully understand, analyse or resist a single form of oppression in isolation from other forms materialised in feminist and antiracist movements and academic circles globally, and we began seeing these ideas appear in the writings, speeches and actions of radical environmental activists who soon moved from a language of single-issue politics to multiple, interlinked issues around 'rights' and the 'liberation' of ecosystems and people. These new ideas were combined with tactics inspired by liberation movements and efforts of previous generations such as the Diggers and Levellers of Britain, slavery abolition, anarchist movements, Civil Rights, Black Power, Puerto Rican Independence, the Weather Underground, Women's Rights, Gay and Lesbian Rights, ACT UP, and the IWW.

From Europe to Australia, to Latin America and the US, radical earth liberation movements gained visibility and notoriety in recent decades, causing significant property and economic damage to timber harvesting operations, power lines, elite housing developments and ski resorts through arson, sabotage (ecotage) and vandalism. Through these actions and the discourse that supports them, activists question what they view as the violence of capitalism, state power, ecological destruction and multiple forms of oppression within human communities. And while these movements often reflect different emphases, there is a prime convergence around the discourse of *total liberation* of ecosystems, non-human species and humans (Pellow 2014). The concept of total liberation stems from a determination to understand and combat all forms of inequality and oppression. Therefore, these movements are radical because (1) they seek to get at the root of the problem of our socioecological crises; (2) they tend to be adaptive, constantly evolving, dynamic, self-critical and self-reflective, rather than fundamentalist or rigid; and (3) their goal is not to struggle with the aim of seeing their vision of the world become dominant, but to struggle against dominance itself, in whatever form that might take.

Theoretical Perspectives

Radical ecological movements have articulated the view that there are multiple, interlocking and reinforcing systems of inequality and domination that give rise to our social and ecological crises, including state power, capitalism, speciesism, dominionism, patriarchy, heterosexism, racism, classism and ableism (among others). These activists maintain that ecological crises cannot be reduced to any one or two of these systems of domination; rather, they work together to contribute to the problem. These activists articulate a vision of *total liberation*, which sees inequality as a threat to life itself – for oppressed peoples, species and ecosystems. Total liberation is a framework organised around the struggle against hierarchy and domination and is a response to global ecological and social crises. These movements organise and mobilise in favour of symbols, metaphors, language, signs, representations, practices and structures of equity and justice to do what social movements have always done: to imagine and create a better world. Only this world would be based on the idea that inequality and unfreedom in all their known manifestations should be eradicated. Total liberation draws from and extends several theories of environment–society relationships, including ecofeminism, political economy of the environment, and EJ, which I address later.

Ecofeminism's basic premise is that the exploitation of ecosystems by human beings is a reflection of exploitation among human beings. In other words, when we destroy ecosystems, ecofeminists would argue that the root of that destruction is located in the way we treat one another. In particular, ecofeminists argue that the ideology that authorises oppressions such as those based on gender, race, class, sexuality, physical abilities, etc. is the same ideology that sanctions the oppression of non-human nature (Mallory 2009; Gaard 2011). That ideology is the logic of domination, which undergirds and supports dualistic or binary thinking. Thus, ecofeminism challenges *binary* or *oppositional* thinking or *dualisms* that are often associated with traditional Western thought (Macgregor 2006). For example, we have long been taught to think of the following categories as oppositional: West versus East, European versus Other, White versus Black, male versus female, coloniser versus colonised and human versus non-human. In Western thought, these categories are traditionally thought to be opposites, discrete, fixed, homogenous and the first is superior to the second, thus reinforcing and legitimating hierarchy and domination (Mack-Canty 2004). While ecofeminist theory is inclusive of multiple categories of difference, there has been uneven attention to various categories such as race and species. Even so, the implication of ecofeminist theory's claims is that greater social equality and democracy promote ecological sustainability.

Political economy of the environment perspectives focuses on the devastating effects of capitalism on social and ecological systems locally and globally (O'Connor 1994; Faber 2008; Gould, Pellow, and Schnaiberg 2008; Foster, Clark, and York 2010). These studies reveal an ecological Marxist perspective in that when struggles over the means of production tend to favour the capitalist classes, they also produce greater ecological damage and mass social suffering. Relatedly, some social scientists have produced studies demonstrating that general measures of social and political inequalities are correlated with levels of ecological harm across societies (Downey and Strife 2010). For example, economist James Boyce finds that the level of egalitarianism in a society may be one of the strongest predictors of the general degree of environmental harm in that society. That is, societies exhibiting higher levels of economic and political inequalities are characterised by higher overall ecological harm, and the reverse is true for societies with greater egalitarian structures (Boyce 1994, 2008). This body of research is of great importance for linking concerns over social justice to ecological sustainability. Even so, much of it is rather narrowly focused on economic or political measures of inequality that fall short of capturing the complex ways in which inequality also functions across race, gender, sexuality and species.

Finally, the Environmental Justice Paradigm (EJP) is a perspective that builds on much of the conceptual orientation found in ecofeminism and political economy, focusing on specific human populations suffering directly from ecological and social violence. The EJP directs its attention to the urgent conditions that people of colour, indigenous populations, women, immigrants, the working classes and the poor confront in the form of degraded environmental conditions and threats to public health. In that regard, the EJP refuses a strictly biocentric emphasis on ecosystems (that we see in Deep Ecology, for example) and insists on centring social justice while advancing an effort to redefine environmental issues as human rights and civil rights issues. As Taylor and others have amply documented, the EJ movement emerged as a response to the mainstream environmental movement that was dominated by 'primarily White, middle-class activists who work in predominantly White, male-dominated, environmental organizations' (Taylor 2000: 551). The EJ movement and the EJP developed largely in response to that limited demographic slice of the social fabric, and featured organisations led and supported largely by working-class people, women of colour, indigenous persons and immigrants. Some ecofeminists might rightly view the EJP as paying insufficient attention to gender dynamics, since its priorities exist largely at the nexus of the politics of race and class. The EJP is also limited because it combines elements of protest and demands for change with an underlying embrace of dominant political and economic institutions. In other words, this movement generally aims to push the state and corporations to embrace some degree of EJ practice, while accepting the fundamental legitimacy and existence of those institutions (Benford 2005). Even so, the EJP recognises critical relationships between human inequality and environmental policy, and encourages dominant institutions to begin addressing these issues.

The aforementioned theoretical frameworks are among some of the most pivotal intellectual and political forces emanating from the twentieth- and early twenty-first-century ecology movements. These traditions emerged in the context of intensified industrialisation, urbanisation and globalisation in a post-Second World War world. Building on this body of sociological research and ideas from these movements, the *total liberation* framework broadens and challenges the boundaries and assumptions of these traditions to encompass a wider intersection of concerns linking social justice and ecological politics. Total liberation is a response to global ecological and social crises and is a perspective articulated and debated by activists from radical environmental movements.

Total Liberation

The total liberation frame combines important elements from other intellectual and political paradigms to chart a new course for social movements confronting our global ecological and social crises. The total liberation frame consists of an ethic of justice and anti-oppression that is inclusive of all beings and ecosystems; an embrace of direct action tactics and support for anarchism and anticapitalism. In the limited space of this short chapter, I focus only on the first two dimensions (see Pellow 2014 for a more comprehensive treatment). Most other prominent intellectual and political paradigms focused on ecological politics have stopped short of linking systems of oppression and inequality across species and have generally only called for moderate reform of political and economic institutions. In contrast, total liberation is marked by ideas, discourses and practices focused on intra-human community dynamics as well as relationships among human and non-human species and ecosystems and demands systematic transformation in social structures and societies. In what follows, I explore the possibilities and limitations of the total liberation framework, and conclude that these data and this emergent movement framework suggest a number of new directions in ecological politics that are relevant to scholars working in the fields of environmental studies, social movements, critical animal studies, and ethnic and gender studies.

Radicals

When I use the terms 'radical' versus 'mainstream', I want to avoid setting up a binary of movement types. I see environmental movements as consisting of many branches and tributaries, including radical, progressive and mainstream, and that the same individual activist, group and movement may often embrace elements of all three. But generally speaking, the following is how I characterise these approaches: radicals seek to replace the existing political and economic system with something entirely different using a range of tactics; progressives work within the system, but they demand changes within that system and employ nonviolent direct action and (sometimes) illegal tactical approaches; and mainstream groups work entirely within the current system under the belief that it can be reformed from within. For example, in the environmental movement, radicals would include EF! and the ELF; progressive groups would include Greenpeace and Friends of the Earth; and mainstream groups would include the Sierra Club and the Natural Resources Defense Council.

One Earth First!er put it to me this way:

> In biology, the radical of a seed is the germinating part of a seed. And…in Latin, it means 'root'. So I think for me, a radical analysis is to look at the root of a problem… [But] I think what's really defining as a radical is an insistence of real change.
>
> *(Interview with the author, fall 2009)*

Another veteran EF! activist and attorney spoke at length about how, for him, 'radical' also means the ability to be unconventional, self-effacing and self-critical:

> …probably the key thing that's always both attracted me to Earth First! and sustained me is the happy sense that Earth First! is not a society of 'true believers'. That, you know, we used to refer to the disparate voices of Earth First!, or even the fractious voices of Earth First. It was a place where you could scream and disagree, and where people didn't take themselves too seriously. And it was a place where people could be really self-effacing, and regularly were, which is part of, I think, the radical humility of being a radical environmentalist, and trying to recognize your place not at the apex of evolution but in the swirl. So that's why I always felt comfortable. So is Earth First radical? One thing it was to me is radically literate and self-aware [and] self-critical. Earth First! was always that.
>
> *(Interview with Hollie Nyseth Brehm of the author's research team, 30 November 2009)*

Total Liberation: Anti-oppression and Justice for Ecosystems and Humans

Environmental movements have rightly been accused of prioritising the protection of non-human animals and ecosystems over the needs of human beings, particularly women, LGBTQ folk, communities of colour, working-class populations, immigrants and indigenous peoples. While elitism and exclusion are certainly intertwined within the histories of the environmental movements (Seager 1994; Smith 2005), members of the radical wings of the movement have recently begun to grapple with issues like whiteness, racism, patriarchy, social class inequalities, homophobia, nativism and social privilege. In other words, these activists are integrating a serious social justice critique into their politics, which is a core element of the total liberation frame. Many environmental activists are learning from the difficult lessons of past (and ongoing) tensions with marginalised communities arising from offensive and insensitive campaigns, tactics, language and behaviour by environmentalists and they have decided that one of the most important approaches to movement building should be developing anti-oppression principles and practices within their ranks. EF! formalised this idea with an official Earth First! Anti-Oppression Policy, which was published in a 2007 edition of the *Earth First! Journal* and reads in part:

> The *Earth First! Journal* editorial collective recognizes that the institutional, economic, political, social and cultural dynamics of hierarchy, power and privilege that define mainstream society also permeate the radical environmental movement. These dynamics are expressed in various interlocking systems of oppression (e.g., racism, sexism, classism, heterosexism, ageism, ableism, speciesism, etc.), which prevent equal access to resources and safety, disrupt healthy communities and movement building, and severely—sometimes irreparably—harm our allies, our friends, our loved ones and ourselves. Over the years, the *Journal* has featured a growing number of articles addressing

the need to challenge these systems of oppression. This is a reflection of the editorial collective's understanding that implicit in our desire to stop the domination and exploitation of the Earth is a need to create communities that are free of oppressive social relations. We understand that failing to address oppressive behavior not only weakens our movement by alienating and further victimizing our friends and allies, it also calls into question our commitment to a better world and our qualification as a radical movement. For these reasons, the *Earth First! Journal* editorial collective has drafted this policy of active opposition to oppressive behavior of all kinds within the editorial collective, the *Journal* community and the pages of the *Journal* itself.

(Earth First! Editorial Collective 2007)

Reflecting similar sentiments, a group called the Cascadia Forest Defenders (CFD) announced in 2003 that it was withdrawing its support from the Fall Creek tree village protest camp near the Willamette National Forest's Clark Timber Sale near Eugene, Oregon. An *Earth First! Journal* article explained,

> At the heart of the issue is the fact that Fall Creek base camp participants have allowed and will continue to allow people who have a recent history of sexual violence to participate in the campaign. After a meeting was held to discuss these concerns, Fall Creek refused to adopt an anti-oppression policy and requested to separate from CFD.
>
> (Earth First! Journal *2003)*

The Fall Creek tree village was one of the most famous of its kind. It was an extraordinary network of traverses, platforms and other structures constructed by tree sitters protecting the site from timber companies in the Willamette National Forest between 1998 and 2003. Apparently, however, many activists there saw fit to reject anti-oppression principles and practices.

In yet another upheaval, in May of 2013, the *Earth First! Journal* publicly repudiated Lierre Keith and other leaders of the radical environmental group Deep Green Resistance (DGR) when it was discovered that they had made or supported statements that were degrading to transgender people. DGR and its founder Derrick Jensen have enjoyed notoriety within radical environmental communities for supporting militant resistance and calling for the dismantling of industrial civilisation in order to achieve ecological sustainability. Unfortunately, they have always suffered from a lack of analysis of intersecting oppressions, so this episode confirmed what many people had already suspected. Moreover, Aric McBay, the primary author of the book *Deep Green Resistance*, also publicly severed ties with that movement as a result. The *Earth First! Journal* decided to 'no longer print or in any way promote DGR material' in response to DGR's

> ...continued assault on trans people, with language and analysis that denies the struggles of trans-people and even goes so far as to deny the value, worth and power of their existence in radical movements, labeling trans people as somehow 'not real', or as Post-Modern manifestations of individualism.

Furthermore, the *Earth First! Journal* made a formal request that DGR leaders 'look deeper into the issues effecting trans communities' and 'create gender inclusive workshops at future DGR gatherings'. The EF!J response also quoted Aric McBay on this matter, who stated, 'I left the organization at the beginning of 2012 after a trans inclusive policy was cancelled by Derrick Jensen and Lierre Keith… transphobia–like racism and sexism and classism and homophobia–is a poison that those in power use to destroy movements and ruin lives' (Earth First! Journal Collective 2013).

In addition to these policies and practices around anti-oppression, I found that in my travels to various activist gatherings and conferences, I frequently heard the discourse of anti-oppression in casual conversations, at workshops, on panels and in the literature made available. At the EF! Round River Rendezvous (RRR) in Oregon's Umpqua National Forest, there was a trove of literature on various topics related to social justice and anti-oppression. There was a pamphlet entitled 'What is White Supremacy?' and there were many more newsletters and 'zines on the subjects of Indigenous solidarity, genocide, feminism, anarchism, the prison industrial complex and immigrant rights and justice ('What is White Supremacy?' is a 1998 essay written by the renowned Chicana activist-scholar Elizabeth 'Betita' Martinez). At that same gathering, there was a grease board featuring a schedule of workshops for the day, which included two sessions on anti-oppression, and sessions on queer and Native solidarity. I saw this kind of literature and discourse at nearly every gathering I attended during my fieldwork.

People of colour have long organised within radical environmentalist ranks. In a 'report back' from the 2008 EF! RRR, a group calling itself the People of Color Caucus wrote 'We See Color and It Fucking Matters'. The report back includes a list of grievances that seek to explain why 'Earth First! is a predominantly white movement' including 'unchecked white privilege', 'rampant cultural appropriation/fetishizing Indigenous cultures' and 'tokenization'. These are all problems for which the environmental movement and EF! have historically been notorious. What is different about this report back is that there are enough people of colour to even have a caucus, and the EF! Journal's editorial staff allowed or encouraged them to write this open letter to the movement. The People of Color Caucus offered numerous suggestions for moving EF! forward, including continuing to hold anti-oppression and antiracist workshops at the annual gatherings and insisting on a 'more open conversation and analysis of our movement's culture'. They urged readers and fellow activists 'to realize that we cannot build a strong and powerful movement to oppose environmental destruction without incorporating a deep understanding of the links between ecocide and all other forms of oppression' (People of Color Caucus 2008).

Since at least the early 1990s, gender politics has been a major theme in earth liberation movements, with concerns focused on patriarchy and sexual violence within society as well as within these activist communities. Many activists have responded creatively, with workshops focused on anti-oppression principles, while some have made efforts to integrate such principles into their campaigns and actions. Following an earlier group called the Ecofeminist Front (which began around 2003), activists launched a working group within EF! called Challenging Oppression Within (COW). A short time after that, the first Trans and Womyn's Action Camp (TWAC) was held just before the annual RRR in 2007. The TWAC is an EF!-sponsored annual gathering designed to be a safe space for LGBTQ activists who have a growing voice and presence in radical ecology movements. That first camp included workshops on tree climbing, road blockades and do-it-yourself gynaecology. As the report back from that first TWAC stated, 'In our opinion, TWAC was a step in the right direction for the Earth First! movement, which has been criticized for its lack of trans and feminist politics' (Triple 2007). Just after the 2009 TWAC, I spoke with two male EF! veterans about the movement's gender politics. One of them, Doug, told me 'This actually was originally a problem with tree sits because of the close quarters that people live in up in the tree, and the problem of oppression'. Another male EF! veteran, Dennis, agreed and recalled, 'there were issues related to our society in general when some men don't know how to treat women. We did have sexual assaults on tree sits, so that was a real concern' (author's interview with EF! veterans, July 1, 2009, Earth First! Round River Rendezvous, Umpqua National Forest, Oregon. Tree sits involve setting up long-term camp sites high up in a tree in order to prevent the cutting of [usually ancient or culturally significant] trees and forests).

Numerous activists I spoke with noted that making the links between the exploitation of ecosystems or non-human animals and humans depended upon activists recognising the role of privilege – including and especially their own – as humans, and as members of largely white, middle-class social movements. Recently, a number of activists in these movements have raised questions about the harm this privilege can do to a movement that is unable to attract a diverse range of supporters and that ignores oppression within its own ranks. Veteran EF! activist Storm Waters remembered how many activists in that movement's earlier days bristled at the call to embrace social justice politics. He recalled,

> There was a lot of people who were basically indulging in their white, upper-middle class, primarily male privilege who really didn't want to confront these issues. It was too much for them. And they were resistant to change. And I as an Earth First!er [felt] that we need to be dealing with wilderness and biodiversity issues while at the same time, confronting oppression within our circles simultaneously, or we will fail at both simultaneously.
>
> *(Interview with the author, July 2009)*

The total liberation narrative that emerges from the data I gathered on these movements draws explicitly and implicitly from ecofeminist theory, from political economy and EJ theory, and from the concept of intersectionality. The core claim here is that social justice for humans cannot be delinked from justice for non-humans. Critical legal theorist Kimberlé Crenshaw's (1994) concept of intersectionality reminds us that various forms of inequality – such as race, class, gender and sexuality – interrelate and work together to produce advantages and disadvantages for people. Earth liberation activists articulate a theory of intersectionality that expands that concept beyond the boundary of the human to include non-human species and ecosystems. They contend that the unequal relationship between human societies and ecosystems is reinforced and reflected in social inequalities among people. This suggests that they wish to articulate a much more transformative model of intersectionality that moves beyond the traditional set of categories and extends the focus on individual human beings to link entire populations across species. These ideas are not necessarily new, of course. Karl Marx recognised and decried the ways in which human labour and the earth are integrated and exploited by the same system of appropriation. In a famous passage, Marx wrote,

> All progress in capitalist agriculture is a progress in the art, not only of robbing the workers, but of robbing the soil; all progress in increasing this fertility of the soil for a given time is a progress toward ruining the more long-lasting sources of that fertility... Capitalist production, therefore, only develops the techniques and the degree of combination of the social process of production by simultaneously undermining the original sources of all wealth—the soil and the worker.
>
> *(Marx 1976: 637–8)*

Regarding the inescapable fact that humans are but one species in a larger ecological chain of being, Marx wrote,

> Man *lives* from nature, i.e., nature is his *body*, and he must maintain a continuing dia-
> logue with it if he is not to die. To say that man's physical and mental life is linked to
> nature simply means that nature is linked to itself, for man is a part of nature.
>
> *(Marx 1974: 328, emphasis in original)*

This passage reflects Marx's refusal to separate humans from nature, something that many
contemporary scholars are still struggling with, as the 'nature/culture' divide remains with
us in many quarters of the academy (Goldman and Schurman 2000). Sociologist John
Bellamy Foster writes that Marx moved beyond this conundrum early on, as embodied in
his concept of *metabolism* – the intricate, interdependent systems connecting human society
to non-human natures (Foster 2000). Today, political theorists build on that tradition and
argue that ecological movements must extend their concepts of justice and the polity itself
beyond distributional concerns among humans to include non-human nature (Schlosberg
2007; Bennett 2009).

A focus on the interconnectedness of justice for ecosystems, non-human animals and
humans stems from the belief that social and ecological inequalities have similar root causes.
Leslie James Pickering is a former spokesperson for the North American Earth Liberation
Press Office and views all forms of oppression as linked and as the root cause of our ecological crises: 'If it were not for the capitalism, racism, sexism, and imperialism that the system
perpetrates upon the world and each one of us, then there would be no clear cuts, no vivisection, no Persian Gulf War, no Nike corporation' (Pickering 2007: 2). Much of the literature
at activist gatherings my research team and I attended echoed these perspectives. For example, a 'zine we found at two of the movement functions we attended stated, 'The same values
that perpetuate sexist violence and eco-cide also perpetuate genocide, racist violence, classist
violence, destruction of the earth, and the tearing apart of indigenous peoples and cultures'
(Wemoonsarmy. N.D., an anarcha-feminist collective dedicated to envisioning and realising
a radical restructuring of society's gender and sexual dynamics).

The Cascadia Forest Alliance is a group of activists in the Pacific Northwest that embraces
total liberation. In their *Disorientation Manual*, they write:

> This battle isn't only for the earth. It's important to recognize that we must challenge
> the very mindset that allows the belief that it is an acceptable practice to exploit the
> earth for profit. It is this same mindset that empowers the domination and hierarchy
> so prevalent in our society. Our struggle isn't only for the earth but also to destroy the
> latent sexism, racism, classism, homophobia, trans phobia, and other isms and phobias
> that play into the dominant paradigm. The people who exploit the environment are
> the same people who help facilitate the exploitation of women, animals, workers, and
> the like. It is one struggle and one fight for the earth, human rights, and animal rights.
>
> *(Cascadia Forest Alliance 2003)*

Because We Must (BWM) is a collective of activists who refuse to restrict themselves to a
single movement label. The group's slogan is 'Animal, Earth, Human'. Its logo is a graphic
of a nondescript human form, an animal footprint and a leaf. This group embodies the goals
and discourse of total liberation. BWM was 'founded on the idea that all forms of oppression and, in turn, the struggles against them, are intimately connected' and that 'the white
supremacist, patriarchal, capitalist culture that dominates the planet' must be confronted
(BWM Mission Statement. Becausewemust.org. Accessed August 2011). Rylee is a part of
the BWM collective, and in a posting on BWM's website, they stated, 'I believe in total

liberation. I want to better connect ideas of human, animal, and earth liberation to create a more unified radical movement' (Rylee 2011. Becausewemust.org. Accessed October 30, 2011). As the BWM mission statement and Rylee's posting reveal, pushing the boundaries of intersectionality through a total liberation framework leads many activists to conclude that the borders that separate various social movements should be challenged as well. On this point, Jeff 'Free' Luers, a celebrated activist who spent nine years in federal prison for an ELF arson action, told us, 'Well, I don't really differentiate between movements. I think that all of our struggles are interconnected, and there are certainly different facets of struggle, but the bottom line is that we're all struggling against the same monster' (Jeff Luers interview with Hollie Nyseth Brehm of the author's research team, 7 March 2010).

Thus, for these radical ecologists, the root causes of global ecological and social crises are varied and numerous, but include the culture or mindset of domination that legitimates hierarchical relationships within humankind and between humans and non-human nature. The total liberation framework therefore extends intersectionality into the non-human realm.

Total Liberation through Direct Action

Direct action is a core component of earth liberation movement's tactical and philosophical repertoire. It is a defining feature of this movement and its cultures of resistance – those shared understandings, ideas and knowledge that inform and support individual and collective practices of dissent. There are many ways that activists approach direct action, including: mobilising ideas, knowledge, symbols and bodies to prevent or support a particular practice or policy; personal confrontation and property damage; and solidarity with other movements and oppressed peoples. These actions are variously directed at the goals of securing justice for ecosystems and people through grassroots organising. This section of the paper reveals how radical environmentalists materialised the ethic of anti-oppression and justice for all beings through direct actions.

Katuah EF! is a group of activists from East Tennessee who also work to draw links between various forms of oppression. In the 1990s, they successfully pushed the white supremacist Ku Klux Klan (KKK) to leave the area and cease open recruitment. One member of the EF! group discussed this action and how they collaborated with antiracist people of colour organisations in this effort. He recalled, 'that was a material antiracist action. And my friends that were involved in the ... predominantly African American groups [also protesting], they knew that if they needed walkie-talkies, [needed] to start a soup kitchen, [needed] bodies, whatever, that they could contact us' (author interview with Chris Irwin, October 29, 2009). The Katuah EF! antiracist work and collaboration are also significant precisely because it was led by white environmentalists in the American South – a region that is typically viewed as more openly white supremacist than anywhere else in the nation.

While the actions of Katuah EF! were public and above-ground, there are numerous direct actions by groups like the ELF that reflect an effort to link justice for people, ecosystems and non-humans that are illegal and underground. A March 2001 ELF communiqué described an illegal action at the Old Navy Outlet Center in downtown Huntington, Long Island, New York in which activists smashed several plate glass windows and a neon sign.

> ... This action served as a protest to Old Navy's owners, the Fisher family's involvement in the clear-cutting of old-growth forest in the Pacific Northwest ... Old Navy, Gap, Banana Republic care not for the species that call these forests home, care not for the

animals that comprise their leather products, and care not for their garment workers underpaid, exploited and enslaved in overseas sweatshops … We will not stop.

(*ELF communiqué, 5 March 2001*)

Banana Republic and Old Navy are subsidiaries of the Gap and have long been the subject of media reports and public concerns that many of their workers are under age (as young as ten years old), underpaid, abused and forced to labour in unsafe, sweatshop conditions in Saipan and elsewhere, and that the Mendocino Redwood Company (which is financed by the Fisher family, members of which founded and own Gap, Inc.) uses toxic herbicides to clear-cut redwood forests (see McVeigh 2007; Smithers and Ramesh 2008).

Other evidence of radical activists making the connection between anti-oppression politics and direct action abounds. The EF! Roadshow is a touring group of activists who visit many different cities around the US to build support for campaigns and to recruit activists to join the movement. During an EF! Roadshow stop in Minneapolis, the organisers offered several workshops. The Native Solidarity workshop included a discussion of the links between environmentalism and imperialism/colonialism. For example, when one of the participants asked, 'what is ecodefense?', one of the organisers – Cee – answered 'defending the earth'. Another participant answered: 'Resistance against colonization *is* ecodefense'. She also stated that 'when indigenous peoples resisted the first waves of colonization hundreds of years ago, we should recognize that as ecodefense' and 'in terms of privilege and colonization, you can't be neutral. Inaction is action in favor of colonization' (author's field notes at the Earth First! Roadshow, May 2009, Walker Church, Minneapolis, Minnesota).

In the summer of 2003, a forest defence action and tree sit began in the Willamette National Forest near Eugene, Oregon, as a protest against the Straw Devil Timber Sale. The US Forest Service was attempting to sell an ancient forest to two private logging firms and the environmental community was ramping up efforts to reverse this decision. At the time, only 5% of native forests were left standing in Oregon, so this was seen as an urgent case for forest defence. What was unique about this particular occupation and tree sit is that it was an 'all womyn action', led by a group calling itself the Ecofeminist Front who sought to highlight the links between the domination of ecosystems and women. They wrote the following statement:

…the womyn's action is dedicated to building a community that is intolerant of all forms of oppression. We are working to create a space of mutual learning and growth—a space where we can conquer not only the demons of capitalism, patriarchy and indifference that surround us but also the demons of oppression, self-loathing and fear that reside within us. The womyn's free state is a safe space where womyn can come and gain skills and perspective…. It is our belief that the oppression of womyn and the destruction of the Earth come from the same unsustainable need to dominate and control. The same people who wish to take away our autonomy also wish to take away the last of the wild beauty on Earth. As womyn, we cannot achieve liberation while the Earth is still in chains. We need oxygen, clean water and the forest to survive. We need to be able to walk around alone at night; we need our homes to be free of violence; we need a life where rape, assault and oppressive attitudes are not the norm.

(*Ecofeminist Front 2003*)

Accompanying this article in the *Earth First! Journal* was a dramatic photograph of five female activists wearing bandanas and carrying crossbows in front of a massive tree in the forest.

At the third annual TWAC gathering in 2011, activists led an action that sought to underscore their view that gender and sexual oppression are inseparable from human dominion over the forests. Participants occupied the Oregon Department of Forestry office in Molalla in solidarity with another ongoing defence action in the Elliot State Forest. The report back was colourful, dramatic, and full of flair and humour:

> Lady and trans folk, with support from our allies, occupied the office in pink fishnets, underwear, and so much sass and glitter. Three folks locked down while the queerest takeover swallowed the hallways and main front desk….People draped themselves around poles in front of the office, sissy-bounded, and temporarily stopped a logging truck, causing a road closure. Chants included 'Beavers and Divas are our natural allies' and 'We're a bunch of queer fucks, we don't want your clear cuts'. Three arrests followed suit (the arrestees are now dubbed the Rebel Bitchez) and the office remained shut down for the rest of the day.
>
> *(Lewddite Uprising 2011)*

The politics of gender and sexuality continue to provide opportunities for earth liberation activists to challenge social structures through their use of language, symbols and action.

Unresolved Tensions and Unfinished Business

Within radical environmental movement communities, even though activists are wrestling with ecological and social justice politics, such efforts are always fraught with tension and, frequently, disappointment. While many activists embrace the concept of total liberation, many others do not. With respect to social justice politics, a number of activists with strong progressive political views believe that some of their colleagues have gone too far by trying to create and enforce a 'politically correct' culture. Specifically, a number of activists feel that social justice and anti-oppression politics have dominated the movement and displaced the 'more important' goal of achieving strictly defined ecological sustainability.

Ben Rosenfeld has been an EF! supporter and legal advocate for many of the movement's most celebrated activists, including Judi Bari and Darryl Cherney. He explained that he views efforts to challenge offensive and culturally insensitive language within the movement amounts to an 'extreme political correctness and word policing that has gripped the movement or at least the people who are kind of running it, which has alienated a lot of the older folks in the movement' (Ben Rosenfeld interview with Hollie Nyseth Brehm of the author's research team, October 3, 2009). He also wrote an article in the *EF! Journal* expressing his dismay on this topic (Rosenfeld 2010).

Rosenfeld's narrative regarding the generational divide among radical environmentalists was something I heard repeatedly from the 'over 30' radical ecologist cohort. It was the subject of many conversations about the politics of gender and sexuality in the movement as well. 'Colt' is a veteran EF! activist and shared her frustrations with what she felt was an overemphasis on recognising people's differences in identity and life experiences:

> …some of the transgender orientation right now is just kind of confusing and distracting to me. Like, when I went to the Trans' and Womyn's Action Camp, I was happy that … [they] had created a safe space for people. And I like any action camp teaching activist skills as a space where they don't feel like it's too critical or too harsh or whatever. But at the same time, there were certain people in the group who would insist every time we

would sit down and talk together, everybody going through and telling us what their preferred personal pronoun was. And that got really old...So that's been kind of sticky with me. Sometimes I think it's too much emphasis.

(Colt [a pseudonym] interview with the author, 3 October 2009)

Similarly, 'Dara' worried that the focus on oppression sometimes becomes overpowering. She stated, 'The problem is that all these discussions about oppression take over instead of being a part of a larger framework around campaigns' (Dara [a pseudonym] interview with the author, Autumn 2009).

Overall, these testimonies reveal that social justice issues remain important but contentious topics of discussion and consideration within radical ecological movements. This dynamic demonstrates that issues of social privilege and difference will remain with this movement well into the future.

Conclusion

The data from my study of radical environmentalists and the emergent idea of total liberation suggest a new direction in ecological politics that is relevant to scholars working in the fields of environmental studies, social movements, critical animal studies, and ethnic and gender studies. The evidence presented suggests new ways of defining environmental and EJ politics and new ways of framing democracy and the polity itself. Specifically, if activists see the transformation of human social relations and human–nonhuman relations – through confronting all forms of hierarchy and oppression – as necessary to address our ecological crises, that reflects a perspective that calls for a broader, antiauthoritarian and multispecies approach to intersectionality and social change. Similarly, some political theorists now argue that ecological movements must extend their concepts of justice and the polity itself beyond distributional concerns among humans to include non-human nature (Schlosberg 2007; Bennett 2009).

The movements and activists considered in this chapter are radical in their views and actions because (1) they attempt to confront what they view as the root of our socioecological crises; (2) they approach their craft with an eye to maintaining an openness to change and new ideas, and an embrace of self-awareness and self-critique; and (3) their ultimate aim is to bring into existence practices and communities that reflect a commitment to equality, equity and non-hierarchical social relations.

References

Benford, Robert. 2005. 'The Half-Life of the Environmental Justice Frame: Innovation, Diffusion, and Stagnation.' Pp. 33–53 in David N. Pellow and Robert J. Brulle (Eds.), *Power, Justice and the Environment: A Critical Appraisal of the Environmental Justice Movement*. Cambridge, MA: MIT Press.

Bennett, Jane. 2009. *Vibrant Matter: A Political Ecology of Things*. Durham, NC: Duke University Press.

Boyce, James K. 1994. 'Inequality as a Cause of Environmental Degradation.' *Ecological Economics* 11: 169–78.

Boyce, James K. 2008. 'Is Inequality Bad for the Environment?' *Research in Social Problems and Public Policy* 15: 267–88.

Cascadia Forest Alliance. 2003. *Disorientation Manual*. Portland, OR: Cascadia Forest Alliance.

Crenshaw, Kimberlé. 1994. 'Mapping the Margins: Intersectionality, Identity Politics, and Violence against Women of Color.' Pp. 93–118 in Martha A. Fineman and Roxanne Mykitiuk (Eds.), *The Public Nature of Private Violence: The Discovery of Domestic Abuse*. New York: Routledge.

Downey, Liam, and Susan Strife. 2010. 'Inequality, Democracy, and Environment.' *Organization & Environment* 23, no. 2: 155–88.

Earth First! Editorial Collective. 2007. 'EF! Anti-Oppression Policy.' *Earth First! Journal* 28 (September–October): 14.

Earth First! Journal. 2003. 'CFD and Fall Creek Part Ways.' Mabon, p. 12.

Earth First! Journal Collective. 2013. 'Deep Green Transphobia.' A Statement from the *Earth First! Journal* Collective. May 15.

Ecofeminist Front. 2003. 'Moving beyond a History of Corsets and Clearcuts: Womyn's Occupation at Straw Devil Timber Sale.' *Earth First! Journal* 23, (October): 12.

Faber, Daniel. 2008. *Capitalizing on Environmental Justice: The Polluter-Industrial Complex in the Age of Globalization.* Lanham, MD: Rowman & Littlefield.

Foster, John Bellamy. 2000. *Marx's Ecology: Materialism and Nature.* New York: Monthly Review Press.

Foster, John Bellamy, Brett Clark, and Richard York. 2010. *The Ecological Rift: Capitalism's War on the Earth.* New York: Monthly Review Press.

Gaard, Greta. 2011. 'Ecofeminism Revisited: Rejecting Essentialism and Re-Placing Species in a Material Feminist Environmentalism.' *Feminist Formations* 23(2): 26–53.

Goldman, Michael, and Rachel Schurman. 2000. 'Closing the 'Great Divide': New Social Theory on Society and Nature.' *Annual Review of Sociology* 26:563–84.

Gould, Kenneth A., David N. Pellow, and Allan Schnaiberg. 2008. *The Treadmill of Production: Injustice and Unsustainability in the Global Economy.* Boulder, CO: Paradigm.

Lewddite Uprising. 2011. 'TWAC 2011 Report Back.' *Earth First! Journal* 31 (September–October): 42.

McVeigh, Karen. 2007. 'Third Death in a Year in Indian Factory That Supplies Gap.' *Guardian* (Manchester), October 14.

MacGregor, Sherilyn. 2006. *Beyond Mothering Earth: Ecological Citizenship and the Politics of Care.* Vancouver: UBC Press.

Mack-Canty, Colleen. 2004. 'Third-Wave Feminism and the Need to Reweave the Nature/Culture Duality.' *NWSA Journal* 16(3): 154–79.

Mallory, Chaone. 2009. 'Val Plumwood and Ecofeminist Solidarity: Standing with the Natural Other.' *Ethics & the Environment* 14(2): 3–21.

Martinez, Elizabeth. 1998. 'What Is White Supremacy?' Definition from the Challenging White Supremacy Workshops Conference. San Francisco.

Marx, Karl. 1974. *Early Writings.* New York: Vintage.

Marx, Karl. 1976. *Capital.* Vol. 1. New York: Vintage.

O'Connor, James. 1994. Is sustainable capitalism possible. In Martin C. (Ed.), *Is Capitalism Sustainable? Political Economy and the Politics of Ecology,* 152–175. New York: Guilford Press.

Pellow, David N. 2014. *Total Liberation: The Power and Promise of Animal Rights and the Radical Earth Movement.* Minneapolis: University of Minnesota Press.

People of Color Caucus. 2008. 'We See Color and It Fucking Matters.' *Earth First! Journal* 28, (May–June): 11.

Pickering, Leslie James. 2007. *The Earth Liberation Front: 1997–2002.* Minneapolis: Arissa Media Group.

Rosenfeld, Ben. 2010. 'Team STUFITT.' *Earth First! Journal* 30, (May–June): 5.

Rylee. 2011. 'Writer Introduction: Meet Rylee.' Becausewemust.org. Posted October 22. www.becausewemust.org/2011/10/.

Schlosberg, David. 2007. *Defining Environmental Justice: Theories, Movements, and Nature.* New York: Oxford University Press.

Seager, Joni. 1994. *Earth Follies: Coming to Feminist Terms with the Global Environmental Crisis.* New York: Routledge.

Smith, Andrea. 2005. *Conquest: Sexual Violence and American Indian Genocide.* New York: South End Press.

Smithers, Rebecca, and Randeep Ramesh. 2008. 'Charity Planning Banana Republic Protest over Employees' Plight.' *Guardian* (Manchester), March 19.

Taylor, Dorceta. 2000. 'The Rise of the Environmental Justice Paradigm: Injustice Framing and the Social Construction of Environmental Discourses.' *American Behavioral Scientist* (43)4: 508–80.

Triple C. 2007. 'EF! Trans and Wimmin's Action Camp.' *Earth First! Journal* 27, (October): 9.

1.8

'INFORMATION FOR ACTION' – RESEARCH AT CORPORATE WATCH

Rebecca Fisher

Corporate Watch aims to produce research for radical social change, to disseminate this research and to support others in producing research for similar radical objectives. This chapter aims to outline Corporate Watch's approach to research as 'information for action', some of the structures and processes we deploy to protect this approach, and how this differs from the research produced in more institutional contexts. It is important to note that our approach is neither monolithic nor static – the Corporate Watch collective includes diverse views, and this text only represents one member's perspective of Corporate Watch as it currently operates.

Since its founding in 1996, Corporate Watch has become a reliable and long-standing source of engaged, radical and rigorous research (as well as trainings and workshops). We aim to do this without sacrificing either our independence or our political principles. Rather than provide seemingly neutral analysis, expert advice or compromised lobbying, we aim to take an active, autonomous and non-vanguardist role within social struggles. Since we only speak for ourselves, we feel in a stronger position to remain faithful to this objective. At the same time, our legitimacy is, and indeed should be, limited to this, and to the fact that we are a small, unrepresentative and closed group, and not anyone's or any movement's mouthpiece. With our organisational structure, an office space and meagre wages, we can devote time and energy to tackle issues in depth – a luxury primarily afforded to research produced from more institutional contexts, such as academia or the mainstream media. Paying ourselves wages does create a difference between us and the many unpaid activists engaged in similar activities and struggles, and we don't pretend otherwise. But this is necessary to ensure that we can carry on doing this work in the long term. This organisational structure does entail constraints however – I do not wish to maintain that Corporate Watch's independence and freedom are absolute. We operate as a workers' cooperative with named directors who could bear some legal responsibility, and we receive funding from foundations to whom we must report, funding that we need in order to pay the wages that sustain us, and which means Corporate Watch can continue. Working in financially strained circumstances means that these wages are not always high enough to ensure that all co-op members can sustain themselves without taking on extra paid work outside of the co-op. It also has an impact on the diversity of the co-op in multiple ways. And as a workers' cooperative, we must act as our own employers, negotiating among ourselves our hours, wages and benefits. Due to scarce financial resources, this happens in ways which are not always as supportive as we would like (such as paying ourselves low wages). These constraints all exert a sometimes-subtle influence on how we work, the language we use and the topics we cover.

Despite this more institutional element, however, we are independent from certain institutional contexts (such as academia or the mainstream and commercial media) which so often neutralise, enclose and/or politically compromise the production of knowledge. Of course, there are always exceptions within these contexts, and certainly many who work within them make concerted and laudable efforts to overcome the institutional hurdles against producing politically engaged and radical research. We do not wish to downplay or denigrate these efforts; indeed, we frequently collaborate with other radical sites of knowledge production, and we do not wish to draw firm barriers between inside and outside of institutions. But here, I will explain briefly how we operate differently, to draw out how independent research can play a critical and engaged role in social movements, despite receiving much less fanfare, and thus visibility, legitimation and status, than more institutional research.

Why does Corporate Watch Exist?

Corporate Watch is a small, UK-based workers' cooperative, which since 1996 has produced a wide variety of investigative and analytical materials aimed at strengthening and resourcing social struggles for radical change. It grew out of the UK anti-roads movements of the late 1990s, during which there emerged a need for engaged and independent research produced from and for social struggles. It was thus part of an expanding movement experimenting with and taking direct action for different ways of living, and a resistance to capitalist encroachment into our lives, our selves and our environments. Corporate Watch took the corporation as both a mechanism and an emblem of this encroachment and proposed to analyse it and its workings. Since then, our basic aim has remained to provide 'information for action': that is, research which supports radical, anticapitalist social movements and struggles, in which we are embedded and to which we are committed. This research appears primarily in the form of written publications and online articles, but also in our workshops, trainings and events, which are often produced collaboratively. In what follows, 'writing' and 'research' serve as shorthand for our work which includes these other, often more ephemeral, outputs.

Since we are independent from any institution, we are freer to produce the kind of research we wish – rather than that deemed profitable, popular, or in line with someone else's strategy or agenda. We try to ensure that we write according to our politics and what we think is most strategic in terms of producing transformative change. Our primary criterion for choosing and evaluating our work is its potential for political and social impacts. We speak as ourselves but also *only* for ourselves, representing no other body or opinion. We do not have to conform to a particular language or discourse produced by any external institution or authority, or earn the right not to do so. We do not have to evaluate, judge or measure our work according to externally set criteria or methodologies. With no patrons, trustees, editors or publishers, we are only directly accountable to each other. We are not a charity, so the state-controlled charity commission cannot restrict how we use our funds. We apply for grant funding when we can, in order to sustain the organisation, but do not produce work we do not believe in simply because it is more likely to get funding. We also seek funding through donations and subscriptions from those who value our work. We refuse all direct state and corporate funding, while remaining vigilant about the potential for co-option by (often state and/or corporate-allied) funding bodies. This freedom isn't paid for with time spent doing work we do not wish to do, or which is not necessary for the sustainability of the organisation. However, it is paid for with a financial structure that can be precarious, leading to a concomitantly quiet voice. We do not have the clout or visibility of the well-funded NGO, mainstream newspaper, larger publishing house or prestigious academic journal. Rather than constrain ourselves within institutional structures antithetical to our wider agenda, in spite of the lavish resources they may offer, we research from within, for, and not about social movements, in the hope that this research supports and is directly engaged with the struggles against capitalism and oppression. We also try to do what we can to spread our research skills and approach, with DIY research trainings and collaborative research projects involving those taking radical political action. This all means various differences in the content, style, values and ethics of our research, which, even if theoretical in content, is directly tied to practice, indeed, that is a practice in and of itself.

The Content of our Work

Politically, Corporate Watch is resolutely anticapitalist, anti-oppression and antistate. We impose no hierarchy among these – while we tend to focus on capitalist systems of power and exploitation, we recognise that the abolition of capitalism is unthinkable without also bringing an end to other oppressive systems, such as racism and patriarchy, and that these must be tackled simultaneously. Similarly, patriarchy and other systems of oppression are reinforced by capitalist relations and systems of organising. We recognise that all of these operate in diffuse and often cultural and interpersonal ways: capitalism is inside us, as much as it is a system of economic relationships. This means that it must be confronted on multiple fronts. It also means that we must develop cultures, practices and relationships of non-capitalist sociability.

These principles guide both the content of our research and its application. We choose our topics based on a sense of what research we think is useful in combating capitalism and building alternatives. With our active, continual and long-standing position and engagement in social movements, we are well placed to spot where our research is needed, and where it can be most useful. Sometimes, the topics we are working on already have a groundswell of activist attention, which we wish to support (e.g. our migration-related research); other times, there is a groundswell of activity which we feel is being insufficiently or inadequately researched (e.g. unconventional fossil fuels); and other times, it is an area which few people are addressing but which we feel needs exploration and action (e.g. nano-technology). We also choose areas to work on based on our own personal interests (since we won't produce useful work if we are not enthused by it). This can range from investigative research into particular companies, to the web of state/corporate and other players active within a particular field, to analytical research into the wider structures of capitalist power and oppression. Our aim is to bring out the structural forces and dynamics at play within specific, concrete events or processes, to inspire and deepen action against them. These can be localised instances of corporate abrogation of power, such as the companies implementing and profiting from the brutal border regime, to more theoretical investigations, such as analysing the various mechanisms through which the financial system operates. We hope that by combining the localised with the more general, while always being attentive to the current situation, we can establish the connections between the two levels, as well as between theory and practice.

This means that we can produce work which goes further than other, compromised organisations are usually willing to. Without trustees, members or state or corporate backers, we do not have to pull our punches. NGOs typically have to tone down their materials in order to retain their 'seat at the table' within government lobbying circles (where in any case their voice is likely to be drowned out by corporate interests). Here, I speak from experience: this was precisely the reasoning I heard at the NGO where I used to work. Hence, what most differentiates us from mainstream NGOs is our outspokenness. And unlike trade unions, we do not have any particular sectors' workers' interests to protect, and so are free to take multiple angles and positions into account. Also, unlike most academics, we are free to use a directly engaged register, instead of speaking as outside, authoritative, objective analysers of a particular topic, as is the norm in academic discourse. We do not have to speak 'objectively' about our topics of study, or feign neutrality to prove our authority by adopting the voice of the detached, disinterested expert. Instead, we can admit to our many political and social biases, speaking as active participants who seek to change the issues we are researching and apply our work to this purpose.

Values

This commitment to transformative political change is difficult to maintain and push for within more mainstream, institutional contexts. Moreover, we believe that this transformative change can only come 'from below'. This is, of course, connected to our political principle of being anticapitalist, anti-oppression and antiauthoritarian, since any imposed order (i.e. from above) can only be repressive. This means that we do not believe radical change can come from petitioning governments, corporations or other institutional structures of power, since this serves to legitimate their power. Instead, we believe in the change that comes when people organise autonomously and collectively to benefit themselves, their communities and the planet. We prefer to put our energies into supporting and engaging with movements of this kind, than with those which legitimate and perpetuate the power wielded by structural forces such as the market or the state (e.g. consumer politics, liberal democracy).

Linked to this, we believe that we must experiment with creating transformative change, with new cultures and ways of living, in the here and now. In pursuing radical social change, neither the means nor the ends should be ignored, but that in fact their differences can be effaced: the means can be the ends. While we are aiming for systemic change, we do not believe that it will come through one, singular global event, like a revolution. Since power does not only operate in any one central system, but through diffuse processes, values and norms, it cannot be overthrown in one moment. Instead, we understand change as an ongoing process of destruction and creation, within society, the self and our relationships. So we must act now, and experiment, rather than wait for the revolution. We cannot design hypothetical and untested utopias in advance: to avoid replicating pre-existing oppressive power dynamics, or instituting new ones, change must emerge from and extend beyond the everyday, local struggles against oppression and exploitation, and from the experiments with other ways to organise and provide for ourselves. For how can any of us know what kind of society we will all need and want when our thinking, our very conception of what is possible, is so conditioned by and integrated within the current structures, norms and values? In addition, the 'wait for the revolution' approach requires a vanguard – an elite section of society directing and moulding social movements to bring about change – which is an approach to social change that we believe should be resisted, and which cannot be justified by any promised ends which can be quickly discarded. Change should not be created nor imposed. And that means avoiding prescribing models for ways of living, for being designed in advance these will be blind to the contingencies and particularities of the situation, and so risk, again, producing a new ruling order to replace the old.

With a view to enacting now the changes we wish to spread wider, we understand Corporate Watch as an experiment in alternative ways of organising. As a workers' co-op, we share and rotate the tasks of running the co-op and conducting the research, avoiding designated and devalued roles such as 'administrator' or 'fundraiser' and the fixed division of labour that so often creates hierarchies. We make our decisions non-hierarchically and collectively in order to avoid the hierarchical management norm with its bosses, deputies and subordinates, aiming to ensure that all voices are heard equally and in a supportive and accountable environment. This is a key element of the ethics with which we produce our research: since we have no hierarchy to move up in, there is no need to use our research to make careerist attempts at one-up-man-ship or point-scoring, and no need to precisely position oneself via self-serving critique or emulation of others. We also aim to treat our material and collaborators with responsibility and care, in a way that is aligned with our wider politics. For instance, unlike bigger organisations, we have no need or interest in the kind of self-aggrandising that can diminish or fail to acknowledge the work conducted by others, and we will always protect the anonymity of anyone who requests it.

Given that our broad aim is to produce more egalitarian and liberatory cultures, we also try to integrate these values and ethics into our relationships. The personal is political after all, and we acknowledge the need to acknowledge the power dynamics that operate within and between us. Furthermore, it is only by experimenting with new cultures and ways of living in the here and now that we can hope that they will spread and deepen. This requires active listening, trust and an openness to both challenge and change, all of which must be constantly worked at and not taken for granted. As antiauthoritarians, we are committed to actively working against all oppressive hierarchies wherever they occur – macro and micro, in society, within our own interpersonal relationships and inside ourselves. Of course, this is a never-ending experiment that will be based on 'trial and error' and constant learning, particularly since we have all been schooled under capitalism, patriarchy, racism, ableism, heteronormativity, etc. Our conscious and unconscious learned patterns of thought and behaviour make this complex and difficult.

Style/Practice

In contrast to many commercial or mainstream media outlets, we do not pretend to be neutral or impartial. We recognise that the supposed objectivity of the media, and other research organisations, is a veil to cover inherent biases and we freely acknowledge our political perspectives and principles. We are writing with an agenda – for radical, transformative change – and make no bones about this.

In our materials, we aim to make sure that our language is relatively simple, clear and well explained, basing our work on reliable and thorough investigations. We don't pretend that change, or writing to help produce change, is an easy process. It will necessarily involve radically altering the tools and structures through which we view and speak about the world, each other and our selves. This involves thinking both practically and philosophically, indeed intertwining the two. However, we try not to assume audience knowledge about the issues, concepts and terms we write about, and thus make our materials as clear and 'accessible' as possible, hopefully without being patronising or condescending. Too often, we find that research produced within institutions speaks most keenly to others within those institutions – preaching to the choir – and develops a particular and exclusionary discourse to do so. Although the processes through which this happens are certainly not reducible to the institution, nor unavoidable within it, we find being outside institutions certainly helpful in this aim.

This also includes embracing the unknown. We don't claim the authority traditionally proclaimed within institutional contexts. In part, this comes from our horizontal structure – we don't have the formally hierarchical relationships within our organisation which elsewhere encourage proclamations of, and fights for, authority and recognition. While we often write under individual names, to reflect our individual autonomy within the co-op, we also write anonymously, or in the name of the co-op, as with a lot of other research produced from within social movements. While anonymity is sometimes necessary for reasons of security, it is also helpful in moving away from the sense that knowledge is produced by individual thinkers. Such individuals are always aided and supported by others around them – no one is an island, after all. Moreover, explicitly collective knowledge production is rarely granted equal levels of prestige. For this reason, we like to stress the role of collectivity in producing knowledge. This is also connected to our recognition that we don't have the answers – only some tentative and propositional ideas among many questions. We do not wish to direct any individual, collective or movement – we are not the vanguard! Furthermore, we do not wish to prescribe what action people should take. Our research does not aim to provide explicit direction, and is written, we hope, without dogma. We realise that we and the world around us are always in flux, and what is strategic in one situation may not be applicable in another.

However, we do recognise that with our privileged position of being able to put the time and energy into this kind of research, we have accumulated knowledge and information that lend us some degree of expertise. While we wish to impart this knowledge, we do not wish to do so in a way that creates the sense that we are the experts, or that our knowledge is superior to anyone else's. Our knowledge is contingent, subjective and partial. Moreover, while we have had the luxury of time to develop particular strategies and skills, we do not wish to be seen as a service provider (an infantilising and pacifying model of working). Instead of producing research to order, we rather work with others to spread the skills needed – let's 'Do It Together'! We thus endeavour to spread the techniques of our research, and learn new ones, through our research trainings, where we have been assisting activists, campaigns, community groups and individuals in investigative research, including how to read company accounts and use of the Freedom of Information Act. The popularity of these trainings and the high level of offers of help and requests for help with research we receive show that the Do It Together model works! We hope this goes a small way towards encouraging more on-the-ground, non-institutional radical research.

Beyond the Research

We direct our material not only to those who are self-consciously engaged in organised political and social struggles, but to all those who are living with, struggling against and finding ways to confront the impacts of capitalism and oppression day to day, even without consciously thinking of themselves as 'activists'. In reaching these audiences, we rely on and support free and independent networks and alliances – such as radical bookshops and bookfairs, self-organised activists and social spaces – as well as putting all our work online for free. We collaborate frequently with other sympathetic individuals, collectives, organisations, within and without institutional contexts. And, where this is possible without compromising our message, we promote our research in more mainstream contexts such as the media. The overall objective is to support an anticapitalist and antistate culture in practice – by insisting on the validity and necessity of these non-institutionalised forms of knowledge production and practice. Our work is not produced within ivory towers, destined only to be read by other experts; nor is it produced merely for demoralising and pacifying mobilisations and 'clicktivism'. We work in areas where we think research is needed to support and strengthen radical action and change, and we target that research where we think it can make an intervention.

Successes, Challenges and Failures

Our most obvious success is remaining relevant, useful and hopefully true to our basic political goal – providing 'information for action' – established when we were formed over twenty years ago, in quite a different sociopolitical context. When we started, it was much harder to come by basic information about companies but now it's clear that our research needs to provide much more than this. We have therefore broadened out – from uncovering corporation's evasive tax structures hidden in the financial small print, to analysing the systemic forces and processes which sustain corporate power and oppression.

Trying to produce strategic work which will help to galvanise resistance can involve an impossible degree of clairvoyance – and our work does not always hit this mark (for instance, the energy behind the anti-GM movement did not signal that there would be similar amounts of energy against nanotechnology). But it is a challenge we accept, while remaining attentive to the dangers of vanguardism. Working at Corporate Watch and sharing collective responsibility for its running can be complex and stressful, particularly with stretched resources. We can too often feel as though the work involved in running and raising funds for the organisation eats into the time and energy we have for the actual research. Keeping both in the right balance is a constant challenge.

Conclusion: Different Knowledge

All in all, Corporate Watch aspires to create and promote knowledge that is produced outside the institutional context, and for rather than about radical and transformative social change. Such forms of knowledge are hard to find and hard to legitimate, in an environment where your institutional status and the discourse this requires command respect more than the 'quality' of the research (which in any case can be based on dubious criteria such as academic citations, rather than how useful it is, or what its political/social impact might be). This is a necessary result of a society in which knowledge is policed, depoliticised and defanged (e.g. by enclosure in academia or impenetrable language). We believe that knowledge is a crucial weapon in our struggles against capitalism and the state: its production is inherently political and we need to reclaim its production from those structures which serve to control and neutralise it. This is not to dismiss all research produced from within institutions – merely to indicate that there are many other sites which deserve visibility and legitimation. We believe that Corporate Watch is one such site, and in our work we seek to strengthen the non-institutional production of knowledge which supports transformative change.

Key Corporate Watch Publications and Projects

DBFO (Destroy! Burn! Fell! Obliterate!) (1995)

The first stirrings of Corporate Watch and the only publication of Corporate Watch 1.0. The DBFO booklet uncovered the companies, lobby groups and government departments behind the Design Build Finance & Operate road schemes of the mid-1990s.

Squaring Up to the Square Mile (1999)

An activist's guide book and map to the City of London and the how the finance sector works. Written in collaboration with London Reclaim the Streets in the build up to the J18 Carnival Against Capitalism, when on June 18th 1999 London's financial district was transformed into a carnival for the day, interrupting trading and causing millions of pounds of damage and questioning the divine right of capital to run the world. Corporate Watch was fingered as one of the event's organisers, leading to Corporate Watchers being hounded by the right-wing press.

What's Wrong with Supermarkets? (2002)

Still popular today, it exposes the immense power that supermarkets wield over the way we grow, buy and eat food, and how they shape our environment, health and even the way we interact socially. What's Wrong with Supermarkets helped campaigners get to grips with the reality of supermarket domination and why we must all start looking for alternatives.

Corporate Law and Structures (2004)

Can corporations ever be a force for good in the world? 'Not as they are currently structured!' says Corporate Watch. A no-punches-pulled analysis of why company law is killing the planet by ensuring that corporations are moneymaking machines for shareholders at the expense of everything and everyone else. The report shows how the law provides companies with protection originally intended for human beings while at the same time freeing them from the liabilities faced by individuals. It concludes that single-minded and legally sheltered corporations are able to prey on society and the planet while fostering an ideology that paints them as ethically concerned citizens.

CSR (Companies Spouting Rubbish) (2006)

Corporate Watch's latest heavyweight report on why, no matter how much we might love to believe otherwise, Corporate Social Responsibility is a contradiction in terms. While other organisations have criticised companies for not delivering on their CSR promises to be socially responsible, Corporate Watch's report pulls the whole mythology apart, exposing the way CSR helps companies to: dupe the public; avoid regulation; disarm critics; bolster their reputations; cosy up to governments; gain access to international summits; exploit developing country markets and continue their war on the climate. After reading it, one CSR worker contacted us to say that they quit their job!

Targeting Israeli Apartheid: A Boycott, Divestment and Sanctions Handbook (2011)

The result of in-the-field research in Palestine, Corporate Watch's first book forensically examined the Israeli economy industry in order to provide BDS campaigners with the information to target the companies – including many based in the UK – who are profiting from the occupation of Palestine. Information for action in its purest form.

Demystifying the Financial Sector: A Nuts and Bolts Guide (2012)

Despite years of economic turmoil, the workings of the financial system are bewilderingly opaque to many people (including most politicians, it seems!). With jargon deconstructed, case studies explained and many of the myths about the city and its operations debunked, this booklet was designed to give readers with little or no knowledge of the world of finance and banking an accessible overview of its workings. It was the first of a three-part 'Banking on Crisis' series, comprising a handbook, 'Making Sense of the Crisis' and a full-length report on the Eurozone crisis.

Managing Democracy, Managing Dissent (2013)

Our longest book to date, and the most difficult to summarise! MDMD was a collection of twenty essays, arguing that genuine democracy and capitalism are in fundamental contradiction, yet mutually reinforce each other: that capitalism cannot be truly democratic, but must make the *claim* to be democratic in order to survive. It explores how this paradox is sustained via propaganda, manipulation of public opinion and the co-option, marginalisation and repression of dissent. It exemplified our aim of bringing rabble-rousing ideas that are often imprisoned within academic discourse to light.

Investigating Companies: A Do-It-Yourself Handbook (2014)

Anticorporate research has become more complicated with the proliferation of information sources, but it is just as possible to do-it-yourself. Updating and expanding our previous DIY Guide, this handbook shows you how to: look into a company you've got an issue with; find and understand key pieces of information about it including reading company accounts; make Freedom of Information requests; understand company law, ownership and financing; get the most from searching the web; and find information out from the company, workers and others affected by it. It is currently our bestselling publication.

Secret filming Inside Harmondsworth Detention Centre (2015)

In 2015, Corporate Watch obtained footage filmed by a detainee of conditions within Harmondsworth Detention Centre, run by outsourcing firm Mitie. The footage revealed un-hygienic conditions within the centre that detainees were being locked in their cells for an extra two hours per night, and a Home Office staff-member admitting that the reason detainees are not allowed camera phones is because the government 'don't want the bad publicity that would entail'. We hope our exposure gave the government some well-deserved 'bad publicity'.

Underpayment of Workers in Homecare (2015–Ongoing)

Following our work on Mitie, whistleblowers within MitieHomecare came to us reporting how since they would not be paid for their travel time their wages worked came to well below the national minimum wage. Corporate Watch investigated as more and more care workers came forward with similar stories, and together we exposed systemic underpayment of staff, overall poor quality of care in the services and huge payouts to the owners, all of which is typical of privatised public services. Several care workers have since taken legal action and many have been awarded compensation.

Capitalism: What Is It and How Can We Destroy It? (2016)

Never prone to modest goals, we wrote an introduction to capitalism and asked how we might bring about its ending. We explained how capitalism operates not only as an economic system but as a culture of fear and passivity, shaping our values and desires. Although not a step-by-step guide to taking down capitalism (forthcoming!), we do hope it will give you some useful ideas.

A–Z of Green Capitalism (2016)

This clear and accessible resource explains the increasing tendency for corporations and other institutions to present their – still environmentally destructive – activities as 'green'. The A–Z format, in which key concepts, ideas and trends are explained in alphabetical order, exposes an important and relatively new development that those taking action against climate change need to get to grips with.

The UK Border Regime. A Critical Guide (2018)

This book brings together Corporate Watch's recent research on the "hostile environment" against migrants in the UK, and the companies that profit from it. It also includes a lot of new research and analysis, and looks at the history of recent migration struggles in the UK, asking what has been effective.

References

Collectivo Situationes, 'On the Researcher-Militant', http://eipcp.net/transversal/0406/colectivo situaciones/en.

Stevphen Shukaitis and David Graeber, eds. with Erika Biddle, *Constituent Imagination. Militant Investigations // Collective Theorization*. Oakland, CA: AK Press, 2007.

Team Colours Collective, 'A Collective Engaged in Militant Research to Provide Strategic Analysis for the Intervention into Everyday Life', – warmachines.info/home/main/.

SECTION 2

Solidarities

Our second section considers how activists connect struggles to develop frames of reference for anti-oppression politics, and build solidarities across intersectional movements.

The term 'solidarity' is often used to designate the attempt to find coherence and mutuality across society or subsets within it, with the evident risk of papering over significant cleavages and antagonisms (Scholz 2008; Stjernø 2009). Our understanding, conversely, refers to solidarity as a form of identification based on shared antagonisms and practices. This is most often seen within a movement where individuals are prepared to take unified action and accept compromises to support their comrades, often with the material basis of communalised resources. Yet, solidarity is also present and across movements, where those mobilising for seemingly disparate causes find ways to support one another, declaratively and/or materially (Krøvel 2010).

Coming to the fore in the latter context especially is the recurrence of concerns around asymmetric power, unexamined assumptions and behaviours associated with privilege, and the material and cultural complexities attending solidarity as conceived in the context of difference. This applies both among radicals working to remove regimes of domination from their lives, and when they act as accomplices to others' uprisings. The disproportionately white and middle-class background of many radicals concentrated in Europe and North America requires us to take our own positionality into account in supporting the mobilisation of subaltern groups and to avoiding both a saviour mentality and the condescension of revolutionary tutelage. Solidarity here is not equal: it recognises the leadership of the group which has invited it. The implications have received wide attention in settler-colonial contexts as different as Canada and Palestine, as well as in European solidarity with refugees and migrants.

The chapters in this section display a strong awareness of these asymmetries, and point towards an account of solidarity which views practices of identification through an intersectional critique, and allows us to approach solidarities from within the contingent realities of social inequality.

Narrating a history of the Canadian government's genocidal oppression of the Indigenous Nations, Pamela Palmater describes the grassroots **Indigenous struggles** organised in response. Radicalism is problematised to highlight the ways that colonisers normalise their own violence and outlaw the resistance struggles of their opponents. Indigenous peoples are radical to the extent that they organise against the settler government but are not the 'dangerous radicals' it paints them to be. The radicals are the authorities who confiscate Indigenous lands; suppress Indigenous cultures; and harass, disappear and kill Indigenous peoples. Looking at the ways that recent grass roots resistance campaigns have been organised and conducted, the chapter explains why decolonisation is the linchpin of human, environmental and social justice politics.

Maia Ramnath presents a brief history of colonisation, in order to place **decolonisation** at the heart of contemporary radical politics. Colonisation is analysed as a regime of violence linked to modernisation, capitalism, empire and racism. In terms of policy, it is felt in dispossession of land both for the exploitation of natural resources and to support Westernisation. Resistance thus links Indigenous peoples' resistance with Palestinian liberation struggles. As a radicalising framework, decolonisation exposes the structural injustices that underpin intersectional politics and the limitations of post-war decolonisation. Decolonisation remains a lived reality and undoing it involves combatting the ideological and structural forces that sustain it.

Radical **disability politics** is addressed in a roundtable discussion, in which A. J. Withers and Liat Ben-Moshe bring six prominent disability organisers in Canada and the US into conversation. This is introduced by a discussion of the tension between established disability rights frameworks and intersectional frameworks, which stress the centrality of anticapitalist, feminist and cross-disability organising, as well as the necessity of valuing interdependence and the intrinsic worth of disabled people (and everyone) outside of traditional labour economies. Within the roundtable conversation, key issues discussed are the radicalism of radical disability politics, the omissions of disability in many forms of activism, the tendency for disability organising to be single-issue and the contributions disability and a disability analysis can make to radical organising.

Claire English, Margherita Grazioli and Martina Martingnoni examine forms of **migrant solidarity** fostered by radical responses to the migration crisis. Using postcolonial theory and concepts of hybridity and difference to explore the politics of migrant solidarity activism, the authors then examine practices of Calais Migrant Solidarity, the collective established in 2009 at the end of the Calais No Border protest camp. The intersectional activism of CMS is distinguished from the border politics of charities and NGOs to underscore the radicalism of migrant solidarity and the distance between human rights and transnational discourses. Yet, the experience of CMS also shows how solidarity activism radicalises by bringing new perspectives to bear on political theory.

Claire Delisle's chapter on **prison abolitionism** focuses on the link between colonialism and punishment, looking, in particular, at the organising practices of the International Conference of Penal Abolitionism (ICOPA). Penal abolitionism is described as a theoretical, strategic and grounded position aimed at the elimination of punishment frameworks and attendant institutions (prisons, police and courts). It is also a response to the concept of criminal justice realised through the period of global 'Englishtenment'. Prison abolitionism is thus linked to a wider set of practices, techniques and institutions that dehumanise and colonise: racism and white supremacy. Exploring internal debates and tensions at ICOPA, the analysis shows how participants addressed their own colonial practices and gave those with experience of oppression and criminalisation the central role in conference organisation.

Ruth A. Deller examines the notion of **safer spaces** to highlight the everyday experience of insecurity felt by marginalised groups. Insecurity is analysed as a process of exclusion and systematic denigration, understood from the perspectives of the marginalised. The chapter explains and defends a range of policies promoted by proponents of safer spaces, notably statue-toppling, no platforming, trigger warnings and the promotion of inclusive language. It explains the theoretical underpinning with reference to feminist and postcolonial thinking. Critiques of intolerance rooted in the defence of free-speech provide a major focus for the analysis of radicalism. Against critics who are often in positions of power or enjoy considerable privileges, the chapter shows how safer spaces both equip marginalised groups to deal with insecurity and transform reality in the process. To the extent that safer spaces politics challenge existing power relationships, it is radical.

Writing for the Ontario Coalition Against Poverty (OCAP), A. J. Withers discusses its **antipoverty** organising which has won important gains for poor people. For twenty years, OCAP has organised poor communities using anticapitalist direct action. Emerging out of a province-wide coalition demanding a raise in social assistance rates during a provincial election campaign, OCAP quickly became an intergenerational, racially diverse organisation made up of primarily poor and working-class people. Focusing on the lessons learned from its experiences, the chapter discusses strengths and difficulties of poor people's organising, and the importance of addressing both individual and community needs, using disruption and resisting demobilisation.

References

Krøvel, Roy, 'Anarchism, The Zapatistas and the Global Solidarity Movement', *Global Discourse* 1(2) (2010): 20–40.
Scholz, Sally J., *Political Solidarity* (Philadelphia: Penn State University Press, 2008).
Stjernø, Steinar, *Solidary in Europe: The History of an Idea* (Cambridge: Cambridge University Press, 2009).

2.1

THE RADICAL POLITICS OF INDIGENOUS RESISTANCE AND SURVIVAL[1]

Pamela Palmater

Introduction

The most radical thing that a person can do in Canada is to be born Indigenous. Being born into any of the Mi'kmaw, Wolastoqiyik, Anishinabek or other Indigenous Nations means that we are born into Nations struggling to heal from the devastating intergenerational effects of Canada's long history of genocidal policies against Indigenous peoples. Multiple generations suffered through scalping laws, forced sterilisations, confinement to reserves, starvation and the rapes, tortures and murders of children which occurred in residential schools. Being born Indigenous means that we are born into an ongoing battle to both resist the state's ongoing assimilatory drive and survive its institutionalised racism. Modern colonisation, like historical colonisation, includes the ongoing state and corporate theft and destruction of Indigenous lands, waters and resources, as well as the violent intervention of state police and military, on behalf of powerful corporate interests, to quell both Indigenous resistance and ultimately Indigenous survival (Palmater 2017a). One of the primary ways that the Canadian state has used to control the resistance of Indigenous peoples was to criminalise every aspect of our identity, culture and subsistence, locking us into generations of abject poverty. By criminalising our efforts to survive, Canada has educated its settler populations to see Indigenous peoples as domestic terrorists. In so doing, it has created a portrait of our quest for justice and peace as one of radical politics carried out by 'rogue' Indians that are inherent 'threats to national security' (Barrera 2014a).

Since the time of contact, settler governments have viewed Indigenous peoples as less than human, as barbarians, savages, heathens and pagans (Royal Commission on Aboriginal Peoples 1996a; Paul 2006; Truth and Reconciliation Commission 2015). By being different in our appearances, languages, governance and legal systems, and spiritualities and practices, Indigenous Nations were vilified as dangerous – peoples that represented a radical and terrifying departure from European norms (Deloria 1997, 1998; Fanon 2005; Paul 2006). Indigenous identities, beliefs and worldviews were portrayed as radical by European powers as threats to settler populations under the guise of Christianity, but were in reality, for their own economic self-interests and empire-building agendas. The purposeful maligning and dehumanising of Indigenous peoples was primarily about wealth and power (Alfred 2005, 2008, 2009; Manuel 2015). Colonial governments wanted full control over Indigenous lands for settlement purposes and control over natural resources for their own wealth generation and Indigenous peoples stood in the way of that – legally, politically and physically (ibid.; Palmater 2015a).

In order to get Indigenous peoples out of the way, colonial governments enacted numerous laws, regulations and policies to separate them from their lands and resources; cultures and practices; and from one another. Any form of resistance from Indigenous peoples was treated as a crime (Manuel 2015; Palmater 2015a). It has taken many decades of research, advocacy and public commissions and inquiries to convince (some) Canadians that Canada's treatment of Indigenous peoples was wrong. However, many are still convinced that it is a shameful legacy of the past; has no connection to the problems of today; and the focus should be on moving forward (Warry 2007; Monchalin 2016: 20–22). Attempts to historicise Canada's abuses include the many political apologies offered by governments and the corresponding rhetoric around reconciliation and moving forward (Stewart 1998; Harper 2008; Duncan 2010; Selinger 2015). Yet, for Indigenous peoples, it is hard to get over something that has not stopped. Colonisation is ongoing and takes the form of impoverishing our Nations to weaken resistance, preventing us from accessing our own lands and resources, and the continued attempts to criminalise our attempts to survive as Indigenous peoples (Palmater 2017a).

Today, many acts of Indigenous resistance against the Canadian state's racist and abusive laws, policies and enforcement actions are portrayed by the state to the Canadian public as terrorism (Adese 2009; Dafnos 2014; Proulx 2014; Palmater 2017a). While Indigenous peoples have never issued any manifestos of violence or shown ill will towards Canadians, signs of Indigenous resistance on the ground are often met with heavy and sometimes lethal-armed police and/or military responses (Linden 2007; Hill 2010; Roache 2014; see also Belanger and Lackenbauer 2014). Canada has also engaged in the illegal practice of surveilling Indigenous peoples and our activities, further violating our most basic democratic rights and freedoms (Norrell 2010; Mire 2014). Following a similar pattern from the US and other G-8 countries, the federal government has used international developments related to terrorism to enact its own antiterror legislation that focuses on the pathways of resistance used by Indigenous peoples – assertions of sovereignty (our own), disruption of the economy (resource extraction), interference with infrastructure (highways, bridges and border crossings on our lands) and interference in diplomatic relations (collaboration with other Indigenous Nations in the US and South America) (Proulx 2014; Palmater 2015a). Since contact, Canada's national security agenda has deteriorated from the original partnership formalised in treaties which recognised us as military allies to treating us as domestic terrorists and enemies of the state (Palmater 2015a, 2016).

Yet, Indigenous resistance against state oppression continues and has arguably expanded, despite all the violent enforcement measures taken by the state to try to quell the resurgence of Indigenous sovereignty through criminal laws, enforcement or other suppressive tactics like targeted surveillance (Dafnos and Pasternak 2013; Diablo and Pasternak 2011). With Indigenous women leading the way, Indigenous grassroots peoples of all backgrounds – grandmothers, grandfathers, hunters, labourers, artists, lawyers and academics, together with the support of non-Indigenous allies – have come together in a massive project of decolonisation. This massive social movement involves public education, community empowerment and activism centred on our inherent right to be self-determining and the urgent need to repatriate and protect our lands and waters for the health and well-being of our future generations (Saul 2014; The Kino-nda-niimi Collective 2014; Coates 2015). Grassroots Indigenous peoples are working together with youth, elders and leaders to kick the coloniser out of our heads with a view to paving the way for a massive cultural resurgence which is land-based and focused on restoring our governments, laws, languages, cultures and identities (Alfred 2005, 2008; Simpson 2008, 2011; Coulthard 2014; McAdam 2015). It is about protecting our right to survive and thrive as Indigenous Nations and standing up for the same core human rights and freedoms afforded to settlers.

In this way, the 'radical' politics of Indigenous peoples is not radical at all – but a continued reliance on our traditional values and beliefs to revitalise our cultures and identities; reconnect with the land and ecosystems for our mutual health and well-being; and heal the wounds of colonisation by empowering and lifting our people out of the system of oppression which keeps so many of our peoples in poverty, illness and depression (Simpson 2008, 2011). Indigenous peoples have cultural obligations to honour our identities and protect our future generations from further suffering (ibid.; Palmater 2016b). We do not have a choice – survival is a basic instinct of all human beings and is not at all radical. What is radical is the state's heavy-handed legal and political responses to Indigenous resistance and survival. Despite political promises and apologies to the contrary, Canada refuses to let go of its death grip on Indigenous peoples and our lands.

Yet, there are many challenges to our unity in resistance as Indigenous peoples. Our Nations are at different stages of the decolonisation process and colonial thinking is unfortunately, but not unexpectedly, deep-rooted in our Nations. Hundreds of years of colonisation and oppression have left many Indigenous Nations socially weakened and politically divided. This resurgence in resistance, which is deeply embedded in our cultures, has sometimes been met with resistance from some of our own Indigenous leaders who act counter to the interests of the people (Carlson 2013; Scoffield 2013; Canadian Press 2014). Their ability to advocate on our behalf is sometimes compromised by the heavy-handed pressure tactics of the state which uses funding for critical social programmes as the lever to pressure leaders to support state initiatives or sign away rights. Similarly, unity in the resistance is often challenged by divisions within the activist groups themselves who want to be recognised as the leaders of the movement or who want to control the movement in some way. Even those teaching others about decolonisation can fall victim to colonial thinking in relation to power structures. Corporate colonisation is another challenge to this resistance movement, as powerful corporate interests have become deeply embedded within the state's economic and power structures (Manuel 2015; Palmater 2017a). Unfortunately, there are cases of leaders and advocates who end up 'switching sides' and working for the very corporate interests they once opposed. In this context, Indigenous resistance to state and corporate oppression is a challenge made worse by the fact that the basic survival of those in the movement has reached crisis level (Anaya 2013; Commisso 2013).

Resistance and survival in this context is daunting. Canada's current laws and enforcement mechanisms are formidable barriers to grassroots action on the ground, while real threats to Indigenous lives are not acted upon by the state. Thus, we face significant obstacles in maintaining our levels of activism and resistance as basic survival needs often take precedence. We must also find a way to address worsening socio-economic conditions, the high numbers of Indigenous women and children that are disappeared or murdered, the theft of our children into foster care at alarming rates as well as our increasing over-incarceration rates (Truth and Reconciliation Commission 2015; Palmater, Pate, and Feminist Alliance for International Action 2016). This requires that Indigenous activists and our allies must constantly adapt our political strategies, both within our Nations and externally vis-à-vis the state (White 2016). However, the new relationships created with non-Indigenous allies during the historic Idle No More social movement in 2012–13, increased access to information and critical analysis provided by activists online, and a larger network of allies connected to one another via social media mean that we have some new tools for maintaining and reinventing our political unity and advocacy even in the face of these challenges (ibid.; Pickerill 2003; Van De Donk, et al. 2004; Earl and Kimport 2011; Gerbaudo 2012).

The state criminalisation of Indigenous peoples for their actions of resistance and survival has not been adequately addressed in public discourse or settler history books. Instead, western histories tell a melancholy story of the inevitable, but accidental spread of disease, the well-intended Christianisation and education of Indigenous peoples, and the unfortunate struggles inherent in cultural difference (Royal Commission on Aboriginal Peoples 1996a). This is not historically accurate nor has it been adequately challenged in modern academic literature outside of Indigenous-focused studies. That is why this book is so important to understanding the global rise of radical politics and the quest for social justice more broadly. To this end, this chapter will provide a historical overview of the criminalisation of Indigenous peoples in Canada and highlight some of the state's genocidal policies which continue in modern forms. From this historical and legal context, the chapter will look closer at the modern evolution of Indigenous peoples' movements of resistance and survival as those who are leading the movement and their ultimate objectives. This will be followed by a brief overview of the state's radical response to collective action and its impact on Indigenous peoples. The chapter will conclude with some thoughts on what the future might hold for Indigenous resistance and survival in Canada.

State Criminalisation of Indigenous Peoples

Indigenous Nations on Turtle Island (what is now known as Canada and the US) have lived and thrived here since time immemorial. Our sovereign Nations had their own governments, laws, economies and militaries. Contrary to the settler-created fiction of one race of Indians, we were in fact Nations that were socially, politically and culturally diverse having their own languages, traditions, customs and practices. While we have been severely impacted by several hundred years of colonisation, our time ruling our territories as sovereign Nations far surpasses this dark colonial phase. In modern times, historians, anthropologists, archaeologists and politicians have all tried to limit Indigenous occupation of Turtle Island and make the argument that we are as much immigrants as the settlers are in Canada (Flanagan 2008). However, with each advance in science or discovery in archaeology, settler theories on limited Indigenous occupation in Canada and the US are discredited (Iacurci 2015; Ewen 2016; Halligan, et al. 2016). The striking similarity and consistency of Indigenous oral histories, creation stories, place names and teachings all speak of Indigenous origins on Turtle Island. Settler claims to the contrary distract the public from the fact that whether Indigenous peoples were born here or, at the very least, were here first by many millennia, we have always and continue to claim these lands in Canada as our sovereign territories (Palmater 2015b).[2] Even under colonial law, that makes Turtle Island ours, not theirs and that's why treaties were and are necessary to enable peaceful settlement and relations.

The state of Canada would not be possible were it not for the generosity, compassion and political cooperation of the Indigenous Nations on Turtle Island. Indigenous Nations in Canada were never conquered or defeated in any war (Royal Commission on Aboriginal Peoples 1996a). Canada's very sovereignty (*vis-à-vis* other states) rests entirely on the prior and ongoing sovereignty of Indigenous Nations (Palmater 2015b; St. John 2016). This is because Canada's sovereignty is an asserted one unlike the factual lived sovereignty of Indigenous peoples. In vast territories where Canada has not obtained valid surrenders of land, Canada's asserted sovereignty rests entirely on actual Indigenous sovereignty. In other words, the state of Canada could not exist without Indigenous Nations – either practically or in law (Barker 2006; St. John 2016). The state of Canada was only able to be settled through an extended treaty negotiating process (Royal Commission on Aboriginal Peoples 1996a; Palmater 2016b). The treaties signed in the Atlantic region of Canada, for example, were absolutely necessary to bring about peace and ensure the safety of new settlers. Those treaties created military allies between Britain and the Mi'kmaw Nation, promising annual supplies of ammunition to ensure our cooperation (Palmater 2016a, 2016b). Mi'kmaw treaties never surrendered sovereignty or land. Despite this, even after the peace treaties were signed, British officials enacted a proclamation which offered scalping bounties on the heads of Mi'kmaw men, women and children to try to force us off of our lands (CBC News 2000; Paul 2006, 2011). The Mi'kmaw Nation refused to surrender their lands and Britain was forced to enter into additional treaties in order to keep the peace (Palmater 2016a). Canada simply could not have carried on with the settlement project without our sovereign agreements to live together as Nations in peace.

Today, those treaty and other good faith agreements form the very basis of Canada's democratic governing system. They are foundational documents included in Canada's *Constitution Act, 1982* and are further protected in numerous international laws, declarations and conventions which Canada has since supported, signed and/or implemented (*Constitution Act 1982*; UN General Assembly 2007). Canada is not a legitimate state without the recognition, respect and implementation of those agreements. While the numerous treaties and agreements have different wording, they all boil down to three main pillars of the Nation-to-Nation relationship: mutual respect, mutual prosperity and mutual protection.

Indigenous Nations have lived up to their side of the bargain by sharing all we had with settlers, by working cooperatively with settler governments, and by defending the Crown in its international wars and military interventions as sovereign allies. The Crown has failed to live up to its side of the bargain. It has failed to respect Indigenous sovereignty and failed to share in and protect Indigenous lands and resources. Instead of protecting Indigenous peoples, as agreed to in constitutionally protected treaties, Canada continues to harm them (Alfred 2009).

From the earliest days of contact, colonial officials attempted to categorise the territory on Turtle Island as terra nullius – empty lands not claimed by any humans. They did this to dispossess Indigenous Nations of our lands and in so doing, had to treat us as non-humans in order to justify any claim that these lands were not 'claimed' by anyone (Wolfe 2006; *Tsilhqot'in Nation v. British Columbia* 2014; Manuel 2015).[3] The vilification, suppression and elimination of Indigenous identity, culture and sovereignty became the overall policy objective of colonial governments (Paul 2006; Truth and Reconciliation Commission 2015). And all of it was done 'legally', i.e. with duly passed legislation enacted by colonial governments (Isaac 1993a, 1993b; Venne 1981; Royal Commission on Aboriginal Peoples 1996a). The scalping bounties of the 1700s mentioned earlier are a good example of the legalisation of murder of Mi'kmaw men, women and children in the name of settlement and national security (Paul 2006; Palmater 2015b). It should be noted that these bounties were placed on our heads after we signed peace treaties (Cape Breton University). Our elders tell us that our refusal to give up our sovereignty and lands meant that we lost much of our population from scalping bounties (Paul 2006). National security, at that time, meant protecting colonial interests in Mi'kmaw lands, resources and trade routes – known today as economic and financial stabilities. But we resisted. We refused to surrender – despite the 'legal' bounty on our heads.

From then on, colonial governments criminalised every aspect of Indigenous identities. Early versions of the *Indian Act* outlawed our ceremonies and dances from 1884 to 1951 (Isaac 1993a, 1993b). So many Indigenous peoples had to hide their regalia and practice their dances and ceremonies in secret (Royal Commission on Aboriginal Peoples 1996a; Truth and Reconciliation Commission 2015). Criminals in our own lands according to settler laws, they knew they had to break the law to protect our cultures for future generations. After separating and subdividing Indigenous Nations into tiny and often relocated communities called 'reserves', Indigenous traditional forms of government were replaced by the *Indian Act* Chief and Council governing system (ibid.). Indigenous Nations became divided into tiny bands now referred to as First Nations in Canada (and tribes in the US).

Despite this imposition of settler law, many Indigenous Nations resisted and maintained our traditional forms of government as best they could, alongside legislated ones (Palmater 2016a). The Mi'kmaw Grand Council, for example, remains as part of the governing authority of the Mi'kmaq – despite its lack of legal recognition under the *Indian Act* (Mi'kmaq Association for Cultural Studies).

When Indigenous peoples tried officially to reject and resist these discriminatory laws, Canada used the *Indian Act* to prohibit lawyers from representing us or help us to make legal claims (Isaac 1993a, 1993b). To ensure that we could not gather in assembly with the rest of our larger Nations, our people were legally confined to small reserves and could not leave these reserves without an official pass from the Indian agent (Isaac 1993a, 1993b). These policies were enforced by Canada's national police force, the Royal Canadian Mounted Police (RCMP) despite their lack of legal authority to do so (Daschuk 2013; Williams 2015). Imprisonment of Indigenous peoples on reserve meant that our rights to gather in assembly and/or advocate on our own behalf were effectively prohibited. Similarly, any intermarriage between Indigenous women and settlers was encouraged for trade relations, but punitive to Indigenous women and their children as they lost their right to belong to and live among our communities and Nations (Palmater 2011).

Despite the protections negotiated in the treaties and other informal agreements, Indigenous peoples were often prevented from leaving reserves and engaging in traditional subsistence economies to provide for their families, communities and Nations. The 'Pass System' was instituted in the 1880s as a means of controlling Indians and preventing acts of resistance. During this time, they were forced to live on government rations which were never enough to provide for everyone on the reserve (Royal Commission on Aboriginal Peoples 1996b; Daschuk 2013). Malnourishment and ill health became rampant on reserves. Government officials appointed to control reserves, known as Indian agents, also used these rations to extort sex from young Indigenous women and girls (Razack 2002; Palmater 2017c). Police officers often looked the other way or engaged in the practice themselves (Human Rights Watch 2013; Palmater 2016c). These practices have continued over the years, where federal and provincial governments enacted numerous laws and regulations to criminalise Indigenous peoples who hunted, fished, gathered or used natural resources within our own traditional, treaty, trapping or reserve lands to sustain ourselves (*R. v. Simon* 1985; *R. v. Sioui* 1990; *R. v. Sparrow* 1990; *R. v. Van der Peet* 1996; *R. v. Marshall* 1999; *R. v. Sappier, R. v.Gray* 2006). Though our ancestors had hunted and fished since time immemorial and despite the numerous treaties which promised to protect our right to hunt and fish, we have been treated like criminals, arrested, charged and our gear seized (Palmater 2016a). The only alternative was to 'skulk around the forest' like criminals in order to feed our families (*R. v. Powley* 2001).[4] The only way to survive was to break the law, i.e. act like criminals in the minds of settlers in order to feed their families.

Many other aspects of Indigenous lives were directly or indirectly outlawed like our right to speak our own languages, engage in our cultures or be educated in our own traditional Indigenous knowledge systems by our elders. The *Indian Act* made it illegal for our peoples to refuse to send their children to residential schools (Haig-Brown 1988; Trevithick 1998; Miller 1996; Fontaine 2010; Reagan 2010; Truth and Reconciliation Commission of Canada 2012). In fact, if Indigenous children tried to run away, the RCMP would chase them and drag them back to those schools despite the horrific abuse suffered in those institutions (Royal Canadian Mounted Police 2004, 2011; Truth and Reconciliation Commission of Canada 2012). Even some of the forced sterilisations of Indigenous women and little girls were done through validly enacted legislation (Boyer 2006; Stote 2012, 2015). Just being an Indigenous person was considered a crime worthy of sterilisation or death. Although Indigenous languages were never officially outlawed, government policy was specific in its intent to 'kill the Indian in the child' (Harper 2008; Truth and Reconciliation Commission of Canada 2012). Sadly, Canada too often killed the child through various forms of torture in residential schools (known as Indian boarding schools in the US) including rape, physical and mental abuse, starvation, neglect and allowing others to medically experiment on Indigenous children (Truth and Reconciliation Commission of Canada 2012; CBC News 2013). These schools started in 1849 and the last one did not close until 1996. Given the fact that Indigenous children had a better chance of dying in residential schools than Canadian soldiers had of dying on the field in the Second World War, it should be no surprise to find that Indigenous families often broke the law to hide their children from Indian agents (Schwartz 2015; Truth and Reconciliation Commission 2015).

Although some of these laws are no longer on the books, modern laws are still used to criminalise Indigenous identity and practices today. For example, the Mohawks traditionally engaged in the growth, manufacture and trade of tobacco since long before contact (Hache 2009; Sadik 2014). Today, because their lucrative business interferes with the economic aspirations of settler corporations, their traditional activities are publicly condemned by governments and non-native businesses as 'contraband' and/or the proceeds of crime and have been made illegal (Poling 2012; Barrera 2013; Mire 2014). Standing up, as Indigenous peoples have done since time immemorial, to protect the health of their lands, waters, plants, animals and peoples has also resulted in their beatings, arrests, extended prison terms and/or deaths (Linden 2007; Patten 2013). All of this is done under duly enacted Canadian law – yet, the state fails to use its own laws to provide protection for Indigenous peoples. The crisis of thousands of murdered and disappeared Indigenous women and girls in Canada is one of the worst examples of government and law enforcement officials who consistently fail/refuse to use current laws to protect them (Committee on the Elimination of Discrimination against Women 2015).

Today, the criminalisation of Indigenous peoples has taken a drastic turn for the worse. Now, even our own poverty – caused from generations of colonisation and oppression, Canada's discriminatory laws and the theft of our lands and resources – is a reason to criminalise us. Indigenous peoples are grossly over-represented in Canada's prisons systems and the Office of the Correctional Investigator Howard Sapers has been calling this a crisis for over a decade (The Correctional Investigator Canada). Indigenous families who struggle to provide food and warm clothes for their kids have their children stolen from them and placed in foster care at rates higher than during the residential school phase (*First Nations Child and Family Caring Society of Canada v. Attorney General of Canada* 2016). In Canada, half of all children in foster care are Indigenous; yet, they only make up 4% of the Canadian population (Statistics Canada 2011, 2016). In the province of Manitoba, 90% of all children in care are

Indigenous (*Globe & Mail* 2015). Provincial officials use various laws and policies to 'legally' rob Indigenous Nations of our children which serves as a pipeline to being murdered, disappeared or exploited (Palmater 2017b).

Now, the ways in which Indigenous peoples resist inhumane and discriminatory treatment have been labelled as 'insurgent' and 'a threat to national security' (Barrera 2014a). The many ways in which Indigenous peoples and our Nations have peacefully asserted, lived and defended our sovereignty and autonomy, together with our peaceful defence of Aboriginal, treaty and inherent rights are portrayed by the state as acts of 'insurgency' (Department of National Defense Canada 2008). Under *Bill C-51* Canada's antiterrorism legislation introduced in 2014 which came into force in 2015, Indigenous public voices and communications can be criminalised (Palmater 2015a). Private conversations – one of the few ways left to support one another in social movements – can be monitored and collected as evidence of terrorist activities. Indigenous opposition and resistance to real threats to Canada, like clear-cutting of forests, strip-mining of farm lands and/or the contamination of critical waterways, can be considered threats to national security as our resistance to these destructive corporate practices may interfere with Canada's economy (ibid.; McCarthy 2015). This makes Indigenous resistance and survival efforts increasingly more dangerous: in state propaganda and laws against Indigenous peoples, we have changed from common criminals to domestic terrorists. Our metamorphosis allows the government to suspend even the most basic human rights and civil liberties to monitor, surveil and/or stop Indigenous activities. Yet, we continue to rise up in resistance despite all the risks.

Indigenous Movements of Resistance and Survival

Indigenous peoples have always tried to work in good faith with settler governments. Since contact Indigenous Nations have tried to work co-operatively with British officials through the negotiation of treaties and engaging in trade. We also tried to maintain peaceful relations with early settlers by showing them how to survive on the land in harsh winters and often inter-married with them (Royal Commission on Aboriginal Peoples 1996a). When issues did arise, Indigenous peoples often sent representatives to seek resolution with colonial officials and some, like the Haudenosaunee in 1921, even sent representatives overseas seeking an audience with the Queen's officials to resolve land disputes (Vaughan 2006; Johnson and Pritzker 2007). Throughout the historical record, one can see numerous examples of Indigenous Nations raising concerns about the various injustices that were happening and their attempts at peaceful resolution. However, once settlement took place, it did not take long for colonial governments to change their Indian policy from mutual peace and cooperation to dispossession and assimilation of Indigenous peoples (Royal Commission on Aboriginal Peoples 1996a).

Canada's Indian policy was based on two primary objectives: (1) to acquire Indigenous lands and resources and (2) to reduce financial obligations to Indians it had assumed through treaties and other agreements. The two primary methods of carrying out these objectives were assimilation and elimination (Palmater 2014; Truth and Reconciliation Commission 2015). Assimilation included the loss of 'Indian' identity through the *Indian Act's* (de)registration process (enfranchisement) and the loss of language and culture in residential schools. Canada's more insidious elimination methods included starving Indians with inadequate rations; offering bounties for Indigenous scalps; forcibly sterilising Indigenous women and girls and the many deaths in residential schools, prisons and foster care (Palmater 2014). While Canada has always denied that it engaged in any acts of genocide against Indigenous peoples, Canada's

Truth and Reconciliation Commission (TRC) which investigated the horrific abuses committed in residential schools found that throughout Canada's history, it had, in fact, committed cultural, biological and physical genocides against Indigenous peoples (Truth and Reconciliation Commission 2015). Yet, despite the significant loss of life, health and spirit, Indigenous peoples were in no way passive victims of genocide. Even the smallest of children engaged in acts of resistance in residential schools act as a testament to Indigenous strength and resilience (Truth and Reconciliation Commission 2012, 2015).

This strong will to survive and to resist the oppression and injustices committed against our peoples and Nations is what has inspired historic and modern Indigenous movements of resistance. In the early days of colonial administration, Indigenous acts of resistance included breaking the laws enacted to suppress our languages and cultures. It was not an organised movement as one might see today, but consisted of smaller, individual acts of resistance by individuals with a strong sense of identity and loyalty to their Nations. This included small children who spoke their languages in secret in residential schools; adults who hid their regalia from Indian agents and practised their ceremonies in secret; and heads of families who tried to hunt and fish without being noticed so that they could feed their families. Although these individuals were not acting in one large coordinated effort, similar acts of resistance were being carried out by individuals from other Indigenous Nations all over Canada at the same time. In this way, one could argue that Indigenous resistance is a natural reaction by sovereign peoples to the injustice of colonisation, oppression, land dispossession and violent attacks on their well-being – as opposed to an inherently political one. This is further bolstered by the fact that Indigenous resistance, while at times carried out by Indigenous political leaders, was also carried out in large part by children, elders and those not necessarily engaged at the political level vis-à-vis the state.

In modern times, Indigenous resistance has continued at the individual or localised level while at the same time taking on a more coordinated and national political dimension. After several failed attempts to organise nationally after the First and Second World Wars, the National Indian Council finally took hold in the 1961 to promote unity among all Indigenous peoples and to try to advocate nationally on shared issues like the theft of our lands and the failure to respect our treaty rights (Assembly of First Nations 2010). This organisation later became the National Indian Brotherhood which focused on First Nation issues and was one of the vehicles used to organise and respond to Canada's *1969 White Paper on Indian policy* which threatened to eliminate Indian status, Indian reserves and treaties (Government of Canada 1969). By that time, other regional advocacy organisations had also been established, including the Indian Association of Alberta (IAA), which played the lead role in responding to the *1969 White Paper*. The IAA's *Citizens Plus: The Red Paper* demanded that Indian status, reserves and treaties be protected and furthermore that First Nations should be self-governing and able to access and benefit from their own lands and resources (Indian Chiefs of Alberta 1970). Shortly thereafter, the Manitoba Indian Brotherhood penned *Wahbung: Our Tomorrows* which echoed the same sentiments found in the *Red Paper* (Manitoba Indian Brotherhood 1971). It was clear at this point that Indigenous resistance was focused on self-determination as peoples/Nations; access to/return of lands and resources; the full implementation of Indigenous rights and treaties; the protection and revitalisation of Indigenous languages and cultures; and the end of government's discriminatory laws and policies. Early Indigenous political advocacy had been fairly consistent on the core of its objectives.

While political organising was happening at the national and regional levels, Indigenous resistance movements at the community (First Nation) or Nation-based levels were also starting to gain public attention. In 1981, the Surete de Quebec (SQ) (Quebec police) conducted violent raids on the Mi'kmaw people at Listuguj to stop them from controlling their own fishery. As news spread, Indigenous peoples from other parts of Canada went to Listuguj to help. This caught the attention of the media due to the heavy law enforcement and multiple arrests which resulted in severe injuries to the Mi'kmaw people (Obomsawin 1984; National Centre for First Nations Governance 2010; Cities and Environment Unit 2013). In this case, the Mi'kmaq were asserting their right to fish and to manage the river and fishery, as aspects of both their inherent right as a sovereign Nation on unceded territory, but also as part of Mi'kmaw treaty rights to fish. These rights had long been trampled on by successive settler governments, thus inspiring the need to assert and defend them. This would not be the only time we as the Mi'kmaw Nation had to stand up to defend our rights. In 1998, the Quebec government tried to stop the Mi'kmaq from cutting timber on our own lands again at Listuguj and selling it like the many non-Indigenous lumber companies were doing (Young and Cantrick 1998). The Mi'kmaq had at all times wanted to negotiate peacefully with the Quebec government but they refused, so the traditional leaders blockaded a lumber company from logging on Mi'kmaw lands. They eventually negotiated a settlement but not until Quebec had engaged in a smear campaign calling Mi'kmaw traditional leaders 'dissidents' and implying that they were dangerous (Norris and Cherry 1998).

In 1990, the Mohawks at Kanesatake took a stand to protect their traditional territory and burial grounds from becoming a golf course by developers in the town of Oka, Quebec (York and Pindera 1991; Obomsawin 1993). Despite having made their claims over their territory since the 1800s and having filed an official land claim with the federal government, the Mayor of Oka would not reconsider the plans for the golf club and a court decision allowed the golf project to proceed. As a result, the Mohawks erected a barricade to protect their lands and when this event hit the media, Mohawks from other territories and Indigenous peoples from other First Nations went to Kahnesatake to assist. The neighbouring Mohawk community of Kahnawake blocked the Mercier bridge in solidarity. The provincial and federal governments responded swiftly and violently sending in the SQ, RCMP and the military. The blockade lasted nearly three months until a settlement was negotiated whereby the Mohawk lands would be returned to them. Equally significant was the profound effect this stand-off had on Indigenous peoples all over Canada, many of whom took pride in numerous media images of unarmed Mohawks standing up to Canada's military in defence of their lands. The high level of political solidarity coming from other Indigenous Nations in Canada was a sign that Indigenous peoples were growing increasingly impatient with decades of abuse.

However, the Mohawks are only one of many Indigenous Nations in Canada that have unresolved land claims. In 1995, the people of Kettle and Stoney Point Ojibway First Nations engaged in a peaceful information protest at Ipperwash Provincial Park – Indigenous lands that had been expropriated without their consent to build a military base (Linden 2007). What had been a peaceful protest soon turned violent when the Premier of Ontario ordered the Ontario Provincial Police (OPP) to 'get the fucking Indians out of the park' which inspired the OPP to respond in kind by plotting: 'We want to amass a fucking army. A real fucking army and do this. Do these fuckers big time' (ibid.). As a result, the OPP shot and killed an unarmed land protestor named Dudley George (Edwards 2003). The resulting inquiry into the incident found that racism against Indigenous peoples was 'widespread' and a significant problem (Linden 2007). A promise was made to return the lands wrongfully taken to First Nations, but no action on the part of government can bring back the fallen land defender.

Meanwhile in Gustafsen Lake, British Columbia (BC), the RCMP had amassed its own army against a small group of Indigenous peoples engaged in ceremonies on their unceded traditional lands (Warrior Publications 2011; Barrera 2016a). Although there was only a tiny group of Indigenous peoples, known as the Ts'Peten defenders, engaged in a sacred Sun Dance on the traditional lands of the Secwepemc Nation, Canada made history by authorising one of the largest police assaults on a civilian population in its history. Hundreds of tactical assault personnel, helicopters, armoured personnel carriers, explosive devices and thousands of rounds of ammo were used against this small group to try to force them off their traditional lands. The RCMP engaged in a 'smear campaign' against the defenders and the media were prevented from accessing the defenders to hear their side of story (Hill 2015). The violent assault on the Sun Dancers cost Canada over $5 million and resulted in numerous criminal charges. Many of these involved in this resistance were traditional or spiritual people and elders, one of whom sought asylum in the US where he remains, unable to return to Canada (Barrera 2016a). A US Federal court judge denied Canada's request for extradition of James Pitawanakwat on the grounds that his activities at Gustafsen Lake were political and exempt from extradition laws. At issue here was not only the right to engage in traditional ceremonies but to do so on their traditional lands which they had never ceded or surrendered to Canada or the province of BC.

In Esgenoopetitj, a Mi'kmaw First Nation in New Brunswick, Mi'kmaw citizens faced violent attacks, ramming of their fishing boats by law enforcement, brutal clubbings and arrests for fishing lobster in our own territory even after they had proven that their treaty right to fish was constitutionally protected at the Supreme Court of Canada (SCC) (Obomsawin 2002). In Elsipogtog, another Mi'kmaw First Nation who was engaged in an extended peaceful defence of our unceded territories against hydro-fracking were surprised one day when the RCMP swat team came out in full force to escort the hydro-fracking trucks onto Mi'kmaw lands and then violently attack and arrest the land defenders (Schwartz and Gollum 2013; Ball 2013a; Roache 2014). This was despite the fact that Mi'kmaw lands have never been ceded or surrendered under treaties. As such, we have constitutionally protected Aboriginal title to those lands and the right to decide what does and does not happen on them.

It is important to note that for all of the violent enforcements noted earlier (with the exception of Listuguj's first event in 1981), section 35 of the *Constitution Act, 1982* protecting Aboriginal and treaty rights and land title had already been enacted (*Constitution Act, 1982*).[5] This means that Aboriginal, treaty and land rights were already protected in Canada's highest law and should have been protected with as much force as was used to deny those rights. In addition, the SCC had already delivered its decision in the 1990 *Sparrow* case confirming the constitutional priority that should be afforded to Aboriginal and treaty rights, like fishing, over all other interests (*R. v. Sparrow* 1990). While the Mi'kmaq have been frequent targets of government abuse, First Nations all over Canada have been subjected to state violence, arrests and/or state takeover of their First Nations for peacefully occupying and defending their own lands, waters and resources. While there are far too many flash points to list in this chapter, a few other examples across Canada include the Unist'ot'en against pipelines in BC (Unist'ot'en; McSheffrey 2015), Algonquins of Barriere Lake against destructive logging in Quebec (Defenders of the Land; Barriere Lake Solidarity; Pasternak), Mathias Colomb Cree Nation against mining in Manitoba (Graham 2013; Small 2014), James Bay Cree against hydroelectric dams on Cree territory in Quebec (Canadian Encyclopedia), the Inuit against methylmercury contamination from hydro-dams in Newfoundland (specifically Labrador) (Brake 2017), Aamjiwnaang First Nation against massive chemical contamination in Ontario

(Shingler 2013; Amjiwnaang Solidarity), and the Mi'kmaq against gas companies polluting rivers in Nova Scotia (Luck 2016).

What is common in each of these scenarios is the localised defence of Indigenous lands, waters and/or resources from a particular corporate and/or state threat. Each involves citizens from a particular First Nation and/or larger Indigenous Nation that is facing a particular crisis. These land and water defenders include any combination of youth, men, women, elders, traditional Indigenous leaders, elected First Nation leaders and/or Indigenous and non-Indigenous allies and supporters. They come from varied backgrounds and circumstances and may never have worked together previously. While some are activists who have helped lead protests, rallies and defences previously, others have not. Some of the first to engage are usually those who are being directly impacted by development, i.e. prevented from engaging in their traditional activities like hunting and fishing, while others are concerned about the ill health effects of the contamination or pollution from various development activities. Some of the participants have strong traditional Indigenous knowledge about why land defence is necessary to protect their Nation, while others may also have a formal education and focus on the illegality of state actions on unceded lands, for example.

Although these acts of defence may develop very quickly in response to a trigger (court case, imminent threat to land/water and/or a state decision), these situations tend to develop organically after protracted periods of little or inadequate action on the part of either state officials and/or elected First Nation leaders on a particular crisis issue facing the First Nation. It is usually a combination of all of these factors that leads to the particular flash point. The number of those engaging in the protest, rally or land defence usually increases in size as the issue gains traction within the First Nation and/or when it gains attention from the media. In addition to the local group, there are individuals, organisations and allies who may also travel to join the defence or engage in acts of solidarity from afar. While they may not necessarily share the same politics, the flash point usually has a unifying effect on the group – in the sense that they often agree to set aside political differences for the sake of the specific cause. The resulting media coverage of the event creates public and political pressures on both state officials and First Nation political organisations to respond to the issue, where one or both might have been silent previously.

Although regional or more localised First Nation political organisations may support a protest from the outset, it is not uncommon in recent years to see certain national Aboriginal organisations (NAOs) either silent about the protest or making neutral comments so as not to appear adversarial towards the state – their primary funders.[6] This is a recent departure from the strong advocacy of these organisations when they were originally created. The Assembly of First Nations (AFN), for example, is a political organisation primarily funded by the federal government and represents the 633 elected First Nation Chiefs in Canada. They are an advocacy organisation and not rights holders like individual First Nations. Yet, their political influence is significant at the national level vis-à-vis the state when compared to individual First Nations and this sometimes interferes with localised issues. The AFN has faced significant and sustained criticism by First Nation elected leaders, traditional leaders, Indigenous lawyers and experts, activists and grassroots Indigenous peoples in the last fifteen years or so for its very public alignment with state governments and its failure to advocate aggressively during periods of protest, rallies or defence (Barrera 2014b). Their repeated failures to act in solidarity with individual First Nations indicates a marked departure from their past efforts and has created a substantial political rift that has resulted in some First Nation elected leaders pulling out of the AFN and calls for it to be disbanded. The AFN has fallen so far in fact, that it is not only seen as co-opted by the federal government (Lukacs 2013; Diablo 2016),[7] but government documents suggest that it has acted as state informant for the RCMP against Indigenous grassroots activists (Groves and Lukacs 2011; Lukacs 2013).

Unfortunately, the state's public defence of the AFN, while disparaging First Nation leaders who criticise the AFN's inaction, has cemented the views of many that the AFN is co-opted and cannot be relied on as part of the Indigenous resistance movement to assert and defend Indigenous sovereignty and protect our lands and waters for the future (Diablo 2013; Barrera 2016b). The state's continued oppression of Indigenous peoples and failure to recognise our rights, together with the AFN's failure to act in solidarity with the increasing number of localised First Nation protests, has forced changes in the Indigenous resistance movement. Sadly, the political transformation of the AFN from First Nation advocate to agent of the state and police informant is evidence of the ongoing impacts of colonisation and continued state abuse of power through its funding mechanisms (Tomiak 2016). Whatever the root cause of AFN's about-turn, its political betrayal is one of the primary reasons why Indigenous peoples have moved away from the organisation.

Indigenous movements like Idle No More and the Treaty Alliance are based on alliances of many First Nations coming together to support one another in both nationwide and localised resistance activities – offering alternatives to the AFN and its close relationship with state officials and law enforcement. The #NoDAPL movement out of Standing Rock Sioux Nation is unique for its combination of Indigenous Nations from Canada and the US and signifies a substantive move away from the NAOs that used to address these issues. As discussed later, Indigenous resistance movements have the changed the dynamic between Indigenous peoples and the state, and between Indigenous peoples and their own political organisations, but at the same time have also created significant solidarity across the artificial Canada–US border.

Nations Rising and Radical State Reactions

Canada's genocidal history and endless broken promises are carried forward to present day with successive governments that continue their discriminatory and lethal practices against Indigenous peoples, while engaging in a political dance of distraction. All governments (federal, provincial and territorial) of all political stripes (Liberal, Conservative and New Democrat Parties) are all equally guilty of genocide, the breach of Indigenous rights and corporate collusion in the theft and development of Indigenous lands, waters and resources. With each new federal election, there is a new party and new Prime Minister with many new promises to improve the relationship with Indigenous peoples and address long-standing issues like land claims and poverty. However, election after election, the state breaks more promises than it keeps trying always to disguise its Indian policy behind flashy acts of tokenism. With the advent of social media, Indigenous peoples have been able to inform, educate, empower, inspire and organise in ways that were not possible before. This information has allowed Indigenous peoples to rise together as Nations in solidarity to demonstrate a much stronger political force.

Conservative Prime Minister Stephen Harper was in power from 2006 until 2015 – nearly a decade of renewed oppression of Indigenous peoples; the imposition of paternalistic legislation on First Nations against their will and the public vilification of First Nation leaders (Palmater 2015c). Many labelled Harper's term as a decade of war against First Nations as he made renewed efforts to get Indigenous peoples out of the way of his aggressive resource extraction agenda and drastically cut funding to political organisations so as to circumvent our capacity to resist through usual political channels (Barrera 2015; Tomiak

2016). Under Harper's racist regime, socio-economic conditions of Indigenous peoples deteriorated, over-incarceration rates increased, the rates of Indigenous children in foster care surpassed crisis levels, and the thousands of Indigenous women and girls being murdered or disappeared were not addressed. In fact, not only did Harper deny that colonialism ever existed in Canada (Ljunggren 2009), but when pressed on the crisis of murdered and disappeared Indigenous women and girls, Harper said that it was 'not high on our radar, to be honest' (CBC News 2014). It was this blatant racist attitude by the state, the certainty that very little would ever change in Canada unless Indigenous peoples ramped up their efforts, and the failure of the AFN and others to strenuously advocate on these issues that Indigenous resistance morphed more solidly into a national grassroots movement.

Prime Minister Harper had greatly underestimated the ability of Indigenous peoples to coordinate despite ongoing funding cuts. In the minds of many, Indigenous political organisations had either stopped advocating or were co-opted by state and/or corporate funding. So, grassroots Indigenous peoples rose up en masse under our sovereign power and pushed back. Idle No More was a historic Indigenous social movement of resistance that 'started' in the summer of 2012 and maintained a very strong, public momentum for well over a year (Palmater 2012). There is really no actual start date as everything that was done during Idle No More had its origins in the long-sustained activism of Indigenous peoples and First Nations mentioned in the previous section. There were actually many Indigenous men and women conducting teach-ins and trying to empower their First Nations long before Idle No More became a social media hashtag or appeared on posters.

The movement captured the media's attention because so many grassroots people were attracted to the name and engaged in nationwide resistance activities under the banner of Idle No More – including those who were already engaged in acts of resistance or had participated in protests previously.

Idle No More was an organic grassroots movement that involved thousands of Indigenous peoples and their non-Indigenous allies all over Canada. It took many different forms including teach-ins, rallies, marches, protests, round dances, public panels and speeches, written publications, YouTube videos and social media exchanges, and extensive and sustained mainstream media coverage. While four women – Sylvia McAdam, Nina Wilson, Jessica Gordon and Sheelah Maclean – are usually credited with the movement (Caven 2013), in the very beginning, other key individuals like Tanya Kappo, Janice Makokis, Pamela Palmater and Sylvia McAdam had all communicated via emails, texts, calls and Facebook messages about ramping up teach-ins to fight back against Harper's assimilatory legislative agenda (Hasselris 2013). This much larger group all got together and started teach-ins specifically about Harper's legislation and started using the hashtag Idle No More to share videos of these teach-ins more broadly. It was actually Tanya Kappo who started the hashtag #IdleNoMore (Curtis 2012; Fong 2013).

At the same time, Art Manuel, Russ Diabo, Taiaiake Alfred, Clayton Thomas-Muller, Ellen Gabriel, Cheryl Maloney and many others continued their own panels and speaking events on urgent Indigenous issues that they had done for many years previous to Idle No More. In the beginning, several people, including Pamela Palmater and Sylvia McAdam, were used as official spokespeople for Idle No More, but this only lasted a short time (Donkin 2013). Once the movement gained attention, it very quickly and organically became a non-hierarchical movement led by each collective of grassroots individuals from all backgrounds: traditional leaders, some elected leaders, Indigenous academics, lawyers, activists, artists and anyone who chose to join. Anyone could speak to any of the issues with the media and engage in any resistance actions that had meaning for them as individuals and their own communities.

No one was at the head of the movement, nor did they control what activities took place and where. Idle No More social media groups popped up all over the country and soon activities were organised around local groups like Idle No More Toronto or Idle No More Quebec with each using their own organisers as spokespeople for different events. There was also no corporate or hierarchical structure and thus no requirement that those in the movement share the same views or politics. This was sometimes very evident when various organisers disagreed about what level of resistance should be used. For example, some thought it should only involve the sharing of culture, like round dances, while others felt strongly that blockades should be used (Ball 2013b). That was the beauty of the movement – that resistance could mean different things to different sovereign Indigenous Nations. While there were some internal differences and alleged attempts by individuals to copyright the name and control activities, for the most part, the vast majority of those involved downplayed the internal politics and focused on the life and death issues at hand. The hashtag #IdleNoMore became the slogan written on placards, stamped on T-shirts and chanted in the streets as Indigenous peoples rose in solidarity against the racist Harper government and Canada's long history of oppressing Indigenous peoples. Even today, 100 different participants in Idle No More would likely write 100 different histories of how it developed.

While the public aspect of Idle No More has faded from daily view, the work continues behind the scenes with Indigenous lawyers, activists, organisers and grassroots citizens supporting local and national efforts at resistance and social justice not just in First Nations, but in solidarity with many non-governmental organisations like women's rights, human rights, environmental, climate change and antipoverty groups. They have also worked with and in solidarity with movements like Black Lives Matter and #OccupyINAC (Democracy Now 2016). Black Lives Matter is a movement against the dehumanising of Black people and the 'virulent anti-Black racism that permeates our society' (Black Lives Matter). It was inspired by the brutal murders of Black men by police which occur all too frequently in Canada and the US. Occupy INAC refers to the series of occupations by Indigenous peoples of the government offices of Indian and Northern Affairs Canada (INAC) (Ferreira 2016). They were trying to bring awareness to the suicide epidemic in First Nations and the failure of INAC to provide adequate funding and support to help alleviate the deaths of mostly youth. In both of these movements, Idle No More members either actively participated or provided strategic support from behind the scenes. In this way, modern resistance movements are finding ways to build solidarity across issues and expand as social justice movements that involve and impact everyone.

A more recent movement, represented by the hashtag #NoDAPL, started as a localised protest which led to a historic year of resistance in the US (No DAPL). This protest originated in the Standing Rock Sioux Nation where they attempted to stop the Dakota Access Pipeline from being built on their traditional lands and potentially impacting their water sources. Although it is a movement born from the Indigenous Nations (tribes) in the US, it was as much a movement in Canada and an unprecedented number of First Nations in Canada publicly declared their political support for the Standing Rock Sioux Nation. Thousands of Indigenous peoples from both Canada and the US travelled to Standing Rock to help defend their waters. The cause gained international media attention and was captured and shared on social media by those on the ground so that the world could be witness to the reality of state and corporate oppression of Indigenous peoples and their rights. Security and/or law enforcement committed many acts of violence against men, women, youth, elders and even journalists, including attack dogs, mace, beatings and water hoses. This was accompanied by media smear campaigns by law enforcement trying to quell the rising tide of public support. The situation at Standing Rock inspired support from Hollywood actors and actresses, politicians, influential thinkers and even some commentators in mainstream media. People all over the world were engaging marches, rallies, protests, occupations and other acts of solidarity to bring international attention to the both the cause (protecting water from pipelines) but also to the violent response by state and law enforcement officials.

Despite being a movement from the US, the situation at Standing Rock also shed a light on the growing political differences between First Nations and the AFN over pipelines generally. The National Congress of American Indians (NCAI) (the US version of the AFN) came out firmly in support of Standing Rock and made public calls for action by the US government. The AFN also made a statement in support of Standing Rock, though very terse. This did not go unnoticed by Indigenous peoples in Canada who were upset that the AFN would support Standing Rock, but refused to stand in solidarity with First Nations in Canada trying to defend their lands against pipelines on the ground in the courts. The National Chief of the AFN Perry Bellegarde came to be known as 'Pipeline Perry' for his support of pipelines, oil and gas, even hosting an energy conference causing further divisions among First Nation leaders (Tasker 2016). The result of these significant political failures on behalf of the AFN and others over time was the birth of the Treaty Alliance, a formal alliance between more than 100 First Nations in Canada and Indigenous Tribes in the US against tar sands expansion and its related pipelines (Treaty Alliance Against Tar Sands Expansion).

The Treaty Alliance is not a collective of individuals, nor is it a membership-based organisation or online petition. It is a unique movement based on the ancient Indigenous tradition of forming confederacies, alliances and/or treaties between Nations (ibid.). This Treaty has only Indigenous Nations as its signatories and so far, the vast majority of them are from Canada, with BC and Manitoba having the largest number (ibid.). Some First Nations, who have already led their own protests against development on their lands, are also signatories including Standing Rock, Algonquins of Barriere Lake, Mathias Colomb Cree Nation and the Mohawks of Kahnesatake, for example. The Treaty is described as an expression of Indigenous laws specifically prohibiting pipelines, trains and tankers that are part of the Tar Sands expansion and includes prohibition of Enbridge's Northern Gateway, Kinder Morgan's Trans Mountain, Trans Canada's Keystone XL, Enbridge's Line 3 and TransCanada's Energy East pipelines. In their own words: 'The allied signatory Indigenous Nations aim to prevent a pipeline/train/tanker spill from poisoning their water and to stop the Tar Sands from increasing its output and becoming an even bigger obstacle to solving the climate crisis' (ibid.).

The Assembly of Manitoba Chiefs (AMC), which represents sixty-three First Nations in Manitoba, has adopted a similar collective approach to opposing unilateral and potentially harmful development on First Nation lands (AMC). This organisation stands out from many other organisations for their legal intervention against massive development projects in solidarity with its member Nations. The AMC recently sought leave to file judicial review of the federal government's approval of Enbridge's Line 3 pipeline (Assembly of Manitoba Chiefs 2017). It is noteworthy that the province of Manitoba contains a large number of Treaty Alliance Signatories and has a long history of Indigenous resistance at the individual and collective First Nation and Treaty level. Other organisations like the Union of British Columbia Indian Chiefs (UBCIC) also have a long history of being very active on the ground and in support of their member First Nations against unilateral development on First Nation lands (UBCIC). Their activities include petitions, marches, information sessions, protests and intervention at the court level. BC also has a large number of Treaty Alliance signatories.

In addition to the Treaty itself, there is also a Solidarity Accord that can be signed by unions, organisations and other groups specifically supporting the movement but also recognising the inherent rights of Indigenous peoples to govern and defend their lands (Treaty Alliance Against Tar Sands Expansion 2016). The common goal is to oppose tar sands expansion and to work towards a clean future. Increased public support and solidarity from non-Indigenous groups and organisations seems to be a key feature of these larger resistance movements. Their ability to help educate Canadians about important issues related to a healthy environment, addressing climate change, protecting water, human rights, equality and democratic freedoms is a core aspect of making these movements relevant to everyone and gaining support from people and organisations that did not previously support Indigenous protests.

While there are far too many First Nations and movements on the ground to cover in this chapter, it is important to note the evolution in Indigenous resistance from almost exclusively localised protests to a much more collective resistance which may involve many First Nations and allies nationally and/or in a particular region. These movements have received a great deal of support through online social networks, like the various social media tools: Facebook, Twitter, Instagram and dedicated websites, for example. However, increased coordination and strategic planning on a larger collective level has seen a corresponding increase in government surveillance – a radical state response to collective Indigenous resistance movements. State responses to Indigenous resistance movements at the localised level have always included surveillance and heavy-handed law enforcement. Many questions have been raised about the legality of state surveillance without warrants or due cause. State surveillance of Indigenous peoples includes monitoring the actions of individuals like Pamela Palmater of Idle No More (Palmater 2015a), Cindy Blackstock of the First Nation Child and Family Caring Society (Canadian Human Rights Tribunal 2013) and Clayton Thomas Muller of Defenders of the Land and 350.org (Barerra 2014c). WikiLeaks documents shared with the media further implicated Canada for spying on Mohawks with illegal wiretaps (Norrell 2010). But the problem goes much deeper than surveilling individual activists. Indigenous peoples collectively have been treated by government officials and law enforcement in ways which either directly or indirectly state or imply that we are dangerous, violent, criminals, radicals, militants, insurgents and/or terrorists.

State agents that have or are currently surveilling Indigenous Peoples and First Nation communities, in addition to Canadian Security Intelligence Services (CSIS), include (but are not limited to): INAC's Hot Spot Reporting System, RCMP Suspicious Incident Reporting, RCMP Integrated Security Unit, Integrated National Security Enforcement Team, Integrated Terrorism Assessment Centre, Canadian Forces' National Counter Intelligence Unit and the RCMP's Criminal Intelligence Aboriginal Joint Intelligence Group Reports (Palmater 2015a).

All of these groups have at some time monitored, surveilled and/or collected intelligence on First Nation leaders, organisations and individual activists in some way. It has been demonstrated that these and other federal government bodies also interfere directly/indirectly in First Nation politics and deny or reduce critical social funding in order to control First Nation leaders who do not cooperate (Pasternak 2013). Former Indigenous Affairs and Northern Development Minister Bernard Valcourt publicly declared Treaty Chiefs as 'rogues' and 'threats to national security' (Barrera 2014a). Female leaders, traditional leaders and grassroots activists were especially demonised and marginalised by the former Conservative government and right-wing-leaning media in favour of more moderate Chiefs (Adese 2009; Proulx 2014; Palmater 2015b). Government control of our Indigenous identities through law, policy, funding controls and public propaganda has maintained our identities as dangerous and subhuman savages with more modern descriptors like criminals, insurgents and terrorists. This self-serving ideology runs deep within federal and provincial

The Radical Politics

governments and public at large. The following are just a few examples of how ingrained the image of Indigenous as terrorist is in Canada's institutions.

The Department of National Defense's (DND) *Counterinsurgency Manual* lists Native Americans (like Mohawks), alongside Islamic Jihadists, Hezbollah, Tamils, Mexican Indians and North Ireland's paramilitary groups as 'insurgents' (Department of National Defense Canada 2008). The manual goes on to describe them as 'violent' and 'radical' treating them like domestic terror threats. Although DND removed the specific reference to Mohawks in the final version of its manual, the current version still lists common Indigenous political and resistance activities like: occupation, autonomy, cultural protection and political control – as acts of 'insurgency'. In other words, the core activities of Indigenous Nations asserting, living and defending their inherent human rights to be self-determining have become viewed as 'insurgent' and dangerous. It is important to note here, however, that referencing DND's list should not equate to an assumption that all other groups mentioned therein should properly be characterised as 'insurgents', as it is highly problematic for DND to presume an entire race or ethnic group, such as 'Mexican Indians', for example, as inherently dangerous.

There is no evidence to suggest that things have changed from an Indigenous struggle for justice to domestic terrorism – except in the eyes of the state (Adese 2009; Proulx 2014; Palmater 2015b). Another example which relates directly to anti-pipeline protests include the report published by Canadian Defense and Foreign Affairs Institute (CDFAI) report on *Resource Industries and Security Issues in Northern Alberta* which categorises Aboriginal-rights movements as 'violent resistance' to industrial development and lists First Nations and environmentalists as 'saboteurs', 'eco-terrorists' and 'security threats' (Flanagan 2009). It is notable that their publication specifically excluded any threats which may be posed by external threats or 'Islamic terrorists' and focused exclusively on Canadian citizens. The report also appears to blame the SCC for rendering decisions in favour of First Nations rights for creating a 'fertile field for blockades' (ibid.: 8). While the report uses a great deal of fear-based assumptions, it largely lacks an evidentiary basis for their conclusions.

Their predictions and analysis have not been borne out in reality. For example, the CDFAI report warned the government of the following 'nightmare scenario':

> A nightmare scenario from the standpoint of resource industries in northern Alberta would be a linkage between warrior societies and eco-terrorists.
>
> Members of warrior societies would brandish firearms and take public possession of geographical sites, while eco-terrorists would operate clandestinely, firebombing targets over a wide range of territory.
>
> *(ibid.: 9)*

Interestingly, it was right after this report that the massive Idle No More Movement was born – the very scenario contemplated. Instead of the nightmarish death and destruction predicted, the Idle No More movement remained a strong, but peaceful movement of unity between First Nations, environmentalists and a broad segment of Canadian society. No firearms were used, no violent threats or ultimatums were made, nor was anyone sneaking around blowing up things.

Idle No More was so massive because it was peaceful and focused on public education (The Kino-nda-niimi Collective 2014). Indigenous peoples have never advocated anything but peaceful coexistence, respect for our autonomy and the fair and just resolution of our claims.

151

The MacDonald-Laurier Institute's *Aboriginal Canada and the Natural Resource Economy* also seems to suggest that First Nation struggles may turn into a dangerous insurgency and uprising (Bland 2013). The report describes Indigenous young men as a 'warrior cohort' and makes the unsubstantiated claim that First Nations see the economy and infrastructure as vulnerable targets and further predict that 'strategic, coordinated First Nations actions against Canada's economy will occur' (ibid.: 2). Their nightmare ideations about Indigenous youth and 'armed confrontations' led them to call on governments to 'disarm' the warrior cohort. This report, like the others, supports the state's construction of an 'Indigenous terror threat' to justify unconstitutional laws to prevent any Indigenous interference with the economy (Adese 2009; Proulx 2014). It is quite clear that the state works in collusion with the extractive industry to prevent information flow to and resistance from Indigenous peoples. Radical state reactions to Indigenous resistance movements are grounded less in legitimate concerns related to national security than to economic concerns around maintaining the status quo imbalance of wealth and power.

State violation of Indigenous privacy rights through unjustified surveillance activities is compounded when Canada shares this information with third parties, like energy companies (Ismi 2013; Lukas and Groves 2013). Canada's law enforcement and intelligence agencies seem to act more like security for large corporations than serving and protecting Indigenous peoples and Canadians. In other words, the rule of law is conditional on perceptions of race and Indigenous peoples are not included in that protection (Hickman, Poitras, and Evans 1989; Royal Commission on Aboriginal Peoples 1996a; Hamilton and Sinclair 1999; Linden 2007). Canadian officials, law enforcement, corporate interests and their wide array of consultants have used these ideas to publicly vilify Indigenous peoples and engage in what appears to be illegal surveillance of our people. It seems clear that the goal of Canada's antiterrorism legislation and related surveillance activities is to quell Indigenous assertions of sovereignty, independence and legal and political jurisdiction, as well as demands for justice around treaty implementation, land claims and respect for Aboriginal rights.

Recent court cases which confirm constitutionally protected Aboriginal rights to Indigenous ownership of our lands and our right to stop resource development seem to have accelerated Canada's national security agenda. The reality is that Canada does not have a terrorism problem, nor is Canada's national security at risk – at least not from Indigenous peoples (Deen 2015). The real issue is that Canada is fearful of the growing Indigenous resistance and demands to address inequality and a failure to address long-standing claims which may act as an impediment to unfettered use and destruction of Indigenous lands, waters and natural resources (Saul 2014).

Despite all the state fear-mongering, Indigenous resistance has always been and continues to be strong but peaceful. It's the threat to Canada's extractive industries and fossil-fuel-reliant economy that is at issue here, and not any real threat to the lives of Canadians from domestic terrorism by Indigenous resistance movements. How many Canadians have been killed on Canadian soil from terrorism? Yet, how many Indigenous women and girls have been raped, murdered or gone missing in Canada – sometimes at the hands of state officials (Palmater 2016c)? Canada needs a major reality check when it comes to the clear and present danger facing the people living in Canada. That reality is that it is the state that has interfered with the economy by forcing reliance on fossil fuels, not First Nations (Walkom 2015). When all the facts are on the table, it is Indigenous peoples who have suffered violence, rape, murder and 'grave violations' of human rights at the hands of the Canadian state – not the other way around (Committee on the Elimination of Discrimination against Women 2015).

Conclusion

The only thing radical about Indigenous survival and resistance is the reaction of the state of Canada to the resilience and persistence of Indigenous peoples to live and maintain their identities. The radical politics used by state officials to dampen Indigenous resistance movements have been consistent since contact. From criminalising Indigenous customs and practices to constructing terrifying public images of Indigenous peoples, the Canadian state has done this in the name of wealth and power over stolen lands and resources. Ironically, the only way that Indigenous peoples have been able to survive has been by acting as criminals, i.e. breaking state laws to provide food for their families or maintaining important cultural practices.

The public propaganda and misinformation tactics by the state and right-wing media outlets can have devastating impacts on the work of Indigenous peoples and their allies in civil society and non-government organisations. As mentioned earlier, the targeting of Indigenous peoples includes many peaceful leaders, activists, academics and even social workers – some of whom are publicly defamed by state officials in strategic and targeted ways. The funding cuts to Indigenous advocacy organisations, increased use of law enforcement and/or litigation against Indigenous peoples, public vilification of Indigenous leaders and activists, together with increased state surveillance of Indigenous activities has multiple, overlapping effects from weakening public support and creating internal community divisions, to a reduction in organising capacity and an overall 'advocacy chill' (Eliadis 2015). In addition, some of the tactics used arguably put Indigenous activists in harms-way when the RCMP cut communications for young women activists or when media outlets publish personal information about Indigenous activists, as Sun Media did when they posted a Google map of where I lived on television.

Yet, there persist many Indigenous individuals who, despite state intimidation, continue to research, investigate, publish, educate and inform others on what is happening on Indigenous territories and how to act in resistance. Dr Taiaiake Alfred is a Mohawk academic whose publications are followed by several generations of young Indigenous activists and whose work acts as a guidepost to the best ways to decolonise and resist ongoing state oppression. Others like Russ Diabo, a Mohawk political strategist, advisor and author, focus on the political aspect of the relation between Indigenous peoples and the state publishing the First Nations Strategic Bulletin to keep First Nations up to date on critical political developments and information to help decode state misinformation. Arthur Manuel from the Secwepemc Nation was an activist and leader his whole life who left us with his life lessons in his book *Unsettling Canada: A National Wake-Up Call* (Manuel 2015). Clayton Thomas Muller, a Cree, travels the world trying to build solidarity in action to resist destructive extractive practices and development on Indigenous lands.

Indigenous women are just as active. Cheryl Maloney, an Indigenous leader and activist, has taken her resistance to the ground to protect lands and waters and recently won a battle over Alton Gas. Sharon McIvor has sued Canada in court and won, and now pursues gender equality for Indigenous women at the international level. Marie Battiste is a strong academic who works tirelessly to help educate and decolonise young Indigenous and non-Indigenous students. Sylvia McAdam, Tanya Kappo, Janice Makokis and other Indigenous women helped lead and sustain the Idle No More movement and now work behind the scenes with First Nations. Dr Cindy Blackstock continues her battle against state discrimination and the theft of Indigenous children into foster care, as have the many families of murdered and missing Indigenous women and girls.

The common denominator in Indigenous resistance is the focus on sovereignty, justice and well-being for all who live on Indigenous territories and a refusal to rely on either the state or state- compromised First Nation organisations, like the AFN, to come up with solutions. The Indigenous resistance movement is not just critical of state tactics, but also Indigenous organisations that are co-opted by state funding and political pressures – a strong signal that Indigenous resistance movements have adapted. They know that it is not the political terminology that is important – sovereignty, nationhood, peoplehood or self-determination. What matters is asserting, living and defending Indigenous independence and social justice on Indigenous territories that is the most important theoretical and practical aspect of Indigenous resistance to ongoing colonisation and oppression.

There is nothing radical about Indigenous peoples wanting to live in relative safety and well- being and to enjoy and protect their territories from irreparable harm. The only thing radical about Indigenous resistance movements is the state's radical reactions to the rise of larger collective movements. Indigenous peoples are not trying to organise a political coup, they are not trying to sabotage critical social infrastructure, nor are they trying to hurt anyone for religious reasons or any of the reasons real terrorists use to justify their attacks on innocent civilians. In fact, Indigenous peoples are the last people on Turtle Island who would want to hurt the lands, waters, plants, animals or other people living on Indigenous territories. Many signed sacred treaties with the newcomers to protect one another and that is exactly what Indigenous peoples are doing in their advocacy.

We also know from the Truth and Reconciliation Commission Report that Canada, far from embracing Indigenous peoples, has committed cultural, physical and biological genocides against them. In so doing, the state has jeopardised the lives of all Canadians, and indeed the planet, by choosing wealth over health and ignoring the responsibility we all have for human and environmental justice. The least radical thing the state could do is recognise and support Indigenous peoples to govern themselves and their territories so that we may all have a future.

Notes

1 This chapter is dedicated to Indigenous warriors like Donald Marshall Jr., Arthur Manuel, Dudley George and all our Indigenous brothers and sisters whose short lives were dedicated to defending our Nations and our lands.

2 While some Indigenous scholars object to the use of the English word 'sovereignty' because of its various political and legal interpretations, the concept can also be described as nationhood, peoplehood or self-determination. For discussion on problems with the word 'sovereignty', see Alfred (2006) and Barker (2006).

3 The doctrine of terra nullius (that no one owned the land prior to European assertion of sovereignty) never applied in Canada, as confirmed by the *Royal Proclamation* (1763), R.S.C. 1985, App. II, No. 1.

4 *R. v. Powley*, [2001] 2 C.N.L.R. 291 at para. 37 trial judge: 'If the Métis exercise their Aboriginal rights without the benefit of a licence, they are not only putting themselves at risk of legislative sanctions but they are forced to *skulk through the forests like criminals* as opposed to hunters exercising their constitutional rights...' (emphasis added).

5 Section 35(1) 'The existing aboriginal and treaty rights of the aboriginal peoples of Canada are hereby recognized and affirmed'.

6 National Aboriginal organizations (NAOs) include the Assembly of First Nations (AFN) representing 633 First Nation chiefs, Congress of Aboriginal Peoples (CAP) representing Indigenous peoples living off-reserve, Inuit Tapiriit Kanatami (ITK) representing Inuit in northern Canada, Metis National Council (MNC) representing the Metis Nation and Native Women's Association of Canada (NWAC) representing Indigenous women often excluded from the previous male-dominated organisations.

7 Martin Lukacs, 'Assembly of First Nations, RCMP co-operated on response to mass protests in 2007' (February 27, 2013), online: <https://martinlukacs.ca/2013/02/27/investigative-article-about-afn-collaboration-with-rcmp/> [*AFN RCMP*] cites Russ Diabo, an Indigenous policy analyst who used to work for the AFN: 'These exchanges with police are more evidence that the federal government thoroughly co-opted the Assembly of First Nations under Phil Fontaine'. Russ Diabo, 'Federal Justice Minister is Selling Decades Old Termination Plan as a New 'Reconciliation' Framework for First Nations' (July 22, 2016) issue 7, winter 2017 the volcano, online: <http://thevolcano.org/2016/07/22/federal-justice-minister-is-selling-decades-old-termination-plan-as-a-new-reconciliation-framework-for-first-nations-by-russ-diablo/> [Russ 2016].

References

Adese, J., 'Constructing the Aboriginal Terrorist: Depictions of Aboriginal Protests, the Caledonia Reclamation, and Canadian Neoliberalism', in Vardalos, et al., (eds.), *Engaging Terror: A Critical and Interdisciplinary Approach* (Boca Raton: Brown Walker Press, 2009), pp. 275–85.

Alfred, T., *Wasase: Indigenous Pathways of Action and Freedom* (Toronto: University of Toronto Press, 2005).

Alfred, T. ''Sovereignty' – An Inappropriate Concept', in R. Maak and C. Andersen (eds.), *The Indigenous Experience: Global Perspectives* (Toronto: Canadian Scholars Press, 2006), p. 322.

Alfred, T., *Peace, Power and Righteousness: An Indigenous Manifesto*, 2nd ed. (Toronto: University of Oxford Press, 2008).

Alfred, T., 'Colonialism and State Dependency', *Journal of Aboriginal Health*, 5 (2009): 42–60.

Amjiwnaang Solidarity, 'Aamjiwnaang Solidarity Against Chemical Valley', https://aamjiwnaangsolidarity.com/.

An Act to Enact the Security of Canada Information Sharing Act and the Secure Air Travel Act, to amend the Criminal Code, the Canadian Security Intelligence Service Act and the Immigration and Refugee Protection Act and to make related and consequential amendments to other Acts (2015) R.S.C. c-51.

Anaya, J., *Statement upon Conclusion of the Visit to Canada* (Geneva: United Nations Special Rapporteur on the Rights of Indigenous Peoples, 2013): http://unsr.jamesanaya.org/statements/statement-upon-conclusion-of-the-visit-to-canada.

Assembly of First Nations, 'Our Story', (Ottawa: AFN, 2010): www.afn/our-story.

Assembly of Manitoba Chiefs, 'Assembly of Manitoba Chiefs Files Application for Leave to File Judicial Review with the Federal Court of Appeal to Challenge the Approval of the Enbridge Line 3 Replacement Project', (Winnipeg: AMC, 2017): www.manitobachiefs.com/grand-chief-speaks-to-university-of-manitoba-students/.

Assembly of Manitoba Chiefs, 'Assembly of Manitoba Chiefs: Empowering our Nations', www.manitobachiefs.com/.

Ball, D., 'Elsipogtog Anti-fracking Blockade Spurs over 50 Protests in Support', *Windspeaker*, 31:8 (2013a): www.ammsa.com/publications/windspeaker/rcmp-crackdown-elsipogtog-anti-fracking-blockade-spurs-over-50-protests-sup.

Ball, D., 'Cross-Canada Indigenous Blockades Highlight Idle No More Tactics' Tensions', *Indian Country Today* (2013b): https://indiancountrymedianetwork.com/news/first-nations/cross-canada-indigenous-blockades-highlight-idle-no-more-tactics-tensions/.

Barker, J., *Sovereignty Matters: Locations of Contestation and Possibility in Indigenous Struggles for Self-Determination* (Lincoln: University of Nebraska Press, 2006).

Barrera, J., 'RCMP Pressured Canada Revenue Agency to Not License Mohawk Tobacco Firms: Court Docs', *APTN* (2013): http://aptn.ca/news/2013/03/13/rcmp-pressured-canada-revenue-agency-to-not-license-mohawk-tobacco-firms- court-docs/.

Barrera, J., 'Valcourt Attacks Confederacy of Nations, Calls Chiefs 'Rogue' and Threats to National Security', *APTN* (2014a): http://aptnnews.ca/2014/05/16/valcourt-attacks-confederacy-nations-calls-chiefs-rogue-threats-national-securit/.

Barrera, J., 'Chiefs Plotting Revival of Dormant 'Confederacy of Nations' to Stop FN Education Bill', *APTN* (2014b): http://aptnnews.ca/2014/05/02/chiefs-plotting-revival-dormant-confederacy-nations-stop-fn-education-bill/.

Barrera, J., 'Former Idle No More Organizer Unfazed RCMP Have Him under surveillance', *APTN* (2014c): http://aptn.ca/news/2014/10/21/former-idle-organizer-unfazed-rcmp-surveillance/.

Barrera, J. 'Aboriginal Organizations Hit with $60 Million Worth of Cuts, Inuit Faced Steepest Reduction: AFN Analysis', *APTN* (2015): http://aptnnews.ca/2015/01/13/aboriginal-organizations-hit-60-million-worth-cuts-inuit-faced-steepest- reduction-afn-analysis/.

Barrera, J., 'Gustafsen Lake Warrior Granted Political Asylum in US Wants Return Home to Canada', *APTN* (2016a): http://aptnnews.ca/2016/01/15/gustafsen-lake-warrior-granted-political-asylum-in-us-wants-return-home-to-canada/.

Barrera, J. 'AFN National Chief Bellegarde Facing Summer of Political Turmoil', *APTN* (2016b): http://aptnnews.ca/2016/06/24/afn-national-chief-bellegarde-facing-summer-of-political-turmoil/.

Barriere Lake Solidarity, 'Frequently Asked Questions', www.barrierelakesolidarity.org/2008/03/resources.html.

Belanger, Y. D. and W. Lackenbrauer (eds.), *Blockades or Breakthroughs?: Aboriginal Peoples Confront the Canadian State* (Montreal: McGill-Queen's University Press, 2014).

Black Lives Matter, 'About Black Lives Matter Network', http://blacklivesmatter.com/about/.

Bland, D., *Canada and the First Nations: Cooperation or Conflict?* (Ottawa: MacDonald-Laurier Institute, 2013).

Boyer, Y., 'Discussion Paper in Aboriginal Health: Legal Issues, No. 4 First Nations, Métis, and Inuit Women's Health' (Ottawa: National Aboriginal Health Organization, 2006).

Brake, J. 'Land Protectors Face Criminal Charges for Defending Water, Food, Culture', *The Independent* (2017): http://theindependent.ca/2017/03/18/land-protectors-face-criminal-charges-for-defending-water-food-culture/.

Canadian Encyclopedia, 'James Bay Project', www.thecanadianencyclopedia.ca/en/article/james-bay-project/.

Canadian Human Rights Tribunal between First Nations Child and Family Caring Society of Canada and Assembly of First Nations and Canadian Human Rights Commission and Attorney General of Canada, *First Nations Child and Family Caring Society Written Submissions on Section 14.1 Retaliation Allegations* (2013) (File No. T-1340-7008).

Canadian Press, 'Chiefs Vow to Do 'Whatever It Takes' to Scrap Aboriginal Education Bill', *CBC News* (2014): www.cbc.ca/news/indigenous/chiefs-vow-to-do-whatever-it-takes-to-scrap-aboriginal-education-bill- 1.2624438.

Canadian Press, 'Shawn Atleo, First Nations National Chief, Resigns Amid Education Debate', *Huffington Post* (2014): www.huffingtonpost.ca/2014/05/02/shawn-atleo-resigns-first-nations-chief_n_5255294.html.

Cape Breton University, Mi'kmaq Resource Centre, 'Treaties', www.cbu.ca/mrc/treaties#.VR-shdPnF9zg>. Treaties of 1725–26, 1749, 1752, and 1760–61.

Carlson, K. B., 'Dissidents Seize on Atleo's Illness, Chiefs Calls for Non-confidence Vote', *National Post* (2013): http://news.nationalpost.com/news/canada/they-would-have-a-heck-of-a-time-ousting-him-dissidents-seize-on- atleos-illness-chiefs-call-for-non-confidence-vote.

Caven, F., *Being Idle No More: The Women Behind the Movement* (Cambridge, MA: Magazine, March 2013): www.culturalsurvival.org/publications/cultural-survival-quarterly/being-idle-no-more-women-behind-movement.

CBC News, 'Two Hundred Year-Old Scalp Law Still on Books in Nova Scotia' (2000): www.cbc.ca/news/canada/two-hundred-year-old-scalp-law- still-on-books-in-nova-scotia-1.230906.

CBC News, 'Full Text of Peter Mansbridge's Interview with Stephen Harper' (2014): www.cbc.ca/news/politics/full-text-of-peter-mansbridge-s-interview-with-stephen-harper-1.2876934.

Cities and Environment Unit, *Listuguj Comprehensive Community Plan: Draft #1* (Listuguj, QC: Listuguj, 2013).

Coates, K., *#IdleNoMore and the Remaking of Canada* (Regina: University of Regina Press, 2015).

Commisso, C., 'Canada Faces a Crisis on Aboriginal Reserves: UN Investigator', *CTV News* (2013): www.ctvnews.ca/canada/canada-faces-a-crisis-on-aboriginal-reserves-un-investigator-1.1497612.

Committee on the Elimination of Discrimination against Women, 'Report of the Inquiry Concerning Canada of the Committee of the Elimination of Discrimination against Women under Article 8 of the Optional Protocol to the Convention on the Elimination of All Forms of Discrimination against Women' (2015).

Coulthard, G., *Red Skin, White Masks: Rejecting the Colonial Politics of Recognition* (Minnesota: University of Minnesota Press, 2014).

Curtis, C., 'We Believe Our Future Is at Stake: Idle No More Movement Founder Tanya Kappo Says', *National Post* (2012): http://news.nationalpost.com/news/canada/we-believe-our-future-is-at-stake-idle-no-more-movement-founder-tanya-kappo-says.

Dafnos, T., 'Social Movements and Critical Resistance: Policing Colonial Capitalist Order', in Deborah Brock, et al., eds., *Criminalization, Representation, Regulation: Thinking Differently About Crime* (Toronto: University of Toronto Press, 2014), pp. 385–418.

Dafnos, T. and S. Pasternak, 'The Criminalization of Aboriginal Protests in Recent History and the Implications for Sovereignty Summer', *For the Defence: Criminal Lawyers' Association Newsletter*, 34:3 (2013): 15–23.

Daschuk, J., *Clearing the Plains: Disease, Politics of Starvation, and the Loss of Aboriginal Life* (Regina: University of Regina Press, 2013).

Deen, T., 'Top UN Official says 'Global War on Terror' is Laying Waste to Human Rights', *Common Dreams* (2015): www.commondreams.org/news/2015/02/06/top-un-official-says-global-war-terror-laying-waste-human-rights.

Defenders of the Land, 'Barriere Lake: Resisting Assimilation, Dispossession, and Genocide', www.defendersoftheland.org/node/55.

Deloria, V., *Custer Died for Your Sins: An Indian Manifesto* (Oklahoma: University of Oklahoma Press, 1988).

Deloria, V., *Red Earth, White Lies: Native Americans and the Myth of Scientific Fact* (Golden, CO: Fulcrum Publishing, 1997).

Democracy Now, 'Occupied Canada: Indigenous & Black Lives Matter Activists Unite to Protest Violence & Neglect', *Democracy Now* (2016): www.democracynow.org/2016/5/20/occupied_canada_indigenous_black_lives_matter.

Department of National Defense Canada, 'Counter-Insurgency Operations Manual' (Ottawa: Canadian Department of National Defence, 2008): https://file.wikileaks.org/file/canadian-coin-operations- manual.pdf.

Diabo, R., 'Idling Some More', *The Media Co-op* (2013): www.mediacoop.ca/story/idling-some-more/19150

Diabo, R. and S. Pasternak, 'Harper Government Prepares for First Nations 'Unrest'', *First Nations Strategic Bulletin* 9 (2011): 1–5.

Donkin, K., 'Idle No More: The Rise of Pam Palmater', *Toronto Star* (2013): www.thestar.com/news/weekend/2013/01/19/idle_no_more_the_rise_of_pam_palmater.html.

Duncan, J., 'Apology for the Inuit High Arctic Relocation' (Ottawa: Government of Canada, 2010).

Earl, J., and K. Kimport, *Digitally Enabled Social Change: Activism in the Internet Age* (Cambridge, MA: The MIT Press, 2011).

Edwards, P., *One Dead Indian: The Premier, the Police, and the Ipperwash Crisis* (Toronto: McClelland & Stewart, 2003).

Eliadis, P., 'Dismantling Democracy: Stifling Debate and Dissent in Civil Society and Indigenous Peoples', in T. Healy, S. Trew (eds.), *The Harper-Record 2008–2015* (Ottawa: Canadian Centre for Policy Alternatives, 2015), pp. 37–73.

Ewen, A., 'New Research Sinks Bering Strait Land Bridge Theory' (New York: Indian Country Media Network, 2016): https://indiancountrymedianetwork.com/history/genealogy/new-research-sinks-bering-strait-land-bridge-theory/.

Faculty of Science, University of Copenhagen, 'Textbook Story of How Humans Populated America is 'Biologically Unviable', Study Finds' (Copenhagen: University of Copenhagen, 2016): www.science.ku.dk/english/press/news/2016/textbook-story-of-how-humans-populated-america-is-biologically-unviable-study-finds/.

Fanon, F., *The Wretched of the Earth* (New York: Grove Press, 2005).

Ferreira, V., 'Aboriginal Protestors Occupy Federal Offices across Canada, Demanding Trudeau Visit Attawapiskat', *National Post* (2016): http://news.nationalpost.com/toronto/idle-no-more-protesters-occupy-federal-office-building-in-toronto-to-demand-action-for-attawapiskat.

First Nations Child and Family Caring Society of Canada v. Attorney General of Canada, (Minister of Indian Affairs and Northern Development, 2016).

Flanagan, T., *First Nations? Second Thoughts*, 2nd ed., (Montreal: McGill-Queen's University Press, 2008).

Flanagan, T., *Resource Industries and Security Issues in Northern Alberta* (Calgary: Canadian Defence and Foreign Affairs Institute, 2009).

Fong, P., 'Idle No More: Tanya Kappo Has First Epiphany as a Native in Derelict Residential School', *Toronto Star* (2013): www.thestar.com/news/canada/2013/01/11/tanya_kappo_had_first_epiphany_as_a_native_in_derelict_ residential_school.html.

Fontaine, T., *Broken Circle: The Dark Legacy of Indian Residential Schools: A Memoir* (Victoria: Heritage House Publishing, 2010).

Gerbaudo, P., *Tweets and Streets: Social Media and Contemporary Activism* (London: Pluto Press, 2012).

Globe and Mail, 'Why are Manitoba Foster Kids Still Living in Hotels' (2015): www.theglobeandmail. com/globe-debate/editorials/why-are-manitoba-foster-kids-still-living-in- hotels/article23586104/.

Government of Canada, *Statement of the Government of Canada on Indian Policy 1969* (Ottawa: Government of Canada, 1969).

Graham, I., 'Manto Sipi Chief Supports Mathias Colomb Cree Nation in Letter to Premier', *Thompson Citizen* (2013): www.thompsoncitizen.net/news/nickel-belt/manto-sipi-chief-supports-mathias-colomb-cree-nation-in-letter-to-premier-1.1360551.

Groves, T. and M. Lukacs. 'Mounties Spied on Native Protest Groups', *Toronto Star* (2011): https:// martinlukacs.ca/2011/12/11/mounties-spied-on-indigenous- communities-in-land-struggle/.

Hache, T., 'Commercial Tobacco in First Nations & Inuit Communities' (2009): www.nsraadnf.ca/ cms/file/files/pdf/Commercial_Tobacco_in_First_Nations_and_Inuit_Communities.pdf.

Haig-Brown, C., *Resistance and Renewal: Surviving the Indian Residential School* (Vancouver: Arsenal Pulp Press, 1988).

Halligan, J., et al., 'Pre-Clovis Occupation 14,550 Years Ago at the Page- Ladson Site, Florida, and the Peopling of the Americas', *Science Advances*, 2:5 (2016): http://advances.sciencemag.org/content/ advances/2/5/e1600375.full.pdf.

Hamilton, A. and M. Sinclair, 'Report of the Aboriginal Justice Inquiry of Manitoba', *Aboriginal Justice Inquiry* (Manitoba: Province of Manitoba: 1999).

Harper, S., *Statement of Apology to Former Students of Indian Residential Schools* (Ottawa: Government of Canada, 2008).

Hasselris, K., 'Rise Up! Idle No More's Pam Palmater', *Herizons* (2013): www.herizons.ca/node/536.

Hickman, T., L. Poitras, and G. Evans, *Report of the Royal Commission on the Donald Marshall Jr., Prosecution* (Halifax: Province of Nova Scotia, 1989).

Hill, G., *500 Years of Indigenous Resistance* (Oakland, CA: PM Press, 2010).

Hill, G., 'Gustafsen Lake Standoff: In 5 Minutes' (2015): www.youtube.com/watch?v=PynWtpqgyJ8.

Human Rights Watch, 'Those Who Take Us Away: Abusive Policing and Failures in Protection of Indigenous Women and Girls in Northern British Columbia' (2013): www.hrw.org/sites/default/ files/reports/canada0213webwcover_0.pdf.

Iacurci, J., 'Scientists Disprove 'Ice Bridge' Theory of Human Migration', *Nature World News* (2015): www.natureworldnews.com/articles/14376/20150428/scientists-disprove-ice-bridge-theory-of-human- migration.htm.

Indian Chiefs of Alberta, *Citizens Plus* (Edmonton: Indian Association of Alberta, 1970).

Isaac, T., *Native Law Centre, Pre-1868 Legislation Concerning Indians: A Selected and Indexed Collection* (Saskatoon: Native Law Centre, 1993a).

Isaac, T., *The Indian Act and Amendments 1970–1993: An Indexed Collection* (Saskatoon: Native Law Centre, 1993b).

Ismi, A. 'Massive Secret Surveillance in Canada', *Canadian Centre for Policy Alternatives* (2013): www. policyalternatives.ca/publications/monitor/massive-secret-surveillance-canada.

Johnson, B. and B. Pritzker (eds.), *Encyclopedia of American Indian History* (Santa Barbara: ABC-CLIO, 2007).

Linden, S. B., 'Report of the Ipperwash Inquiry' (Ottawa: Government of Ontario, 2007), part 2, chap.2, 'Primer on Aboriginal Occupations', www.attorneygeneral.jus.gov.on.ca/inquiries/ipperwash/report/ vol_2/pdf/E_Vol_2_CH02.pdf.

Ljunggren, D., 'Every G20 Nation Wants to be Canada, Insists PM' (Pittsburgh: Reuters, 2009): www.reuters.com/article/columns-us-g20-canada-advantages-idUSTRE58P05Z20090926.

Luck, S., 'Alton Gas Protestors to Conduct Their Own Shubenacadie River Research', *CBC News* (2016): www.cbc.ca/news/canada/nova-scotia/alton-gas-shubenacadie-river-protest-dfo-fisheries-altagas-sipekne-katik-1.3755170.

Lukacs, M., 'Assembly of First Nations, RCMP Co-operated on Response to Mass Protests in 2007' (2013): https://martinlukacs.ca/2013/02/27/investigative-article-about-afn-collaboration-with-rcmp/.

Lukas, M. and T. Groves, 'Canadian Spies Met with Energy Firms, Documents Reveal', *The Guardian* (2013): www.niagara-news.com/index.php/mobile-editorial-opinion/3378-gamble-on-canadian-oil- sands-not-paying-out.

Manitoba Indian Brotherhood, *Wahbung: Our Tomorrows* (Winnipeg: Manitoba Indian Brotherhood, 1971).

Manuel, A., *Unsettling Canada: A National Wake-Up Call* (Toronto: Between the Lines, 2015).

McAdam, S., *Nationhood Interrupted: Revitalizing nehiyaw Legal Systems* (Saskatoon: Purich Publishing, 2015).

McCarthy, S., 'Anti-petroleum' Movement a Growing Security Threat to Canada, RCMP say', *Globe and Mail* (2015): www.theglobeandmail.com/news/politics/anti-petroleum-movement-a-growing-security-threat-to-canada-rcmp-say/article23019252/.

McSheffrey, E., 'What You Need to Know about the Unist'ot'en-pipeline Stand-off', *Vancouver Observer* (2015): www.vancouverobserver.com/news/what-you-need-know-about-unistoten-pipeline-standoff.

Mi'kmaq Association for Cultural Studies, 'Grand Council – Sante' Mawio'mi', http://mikmaqhistorymonth.com/treaty-day/grand-council-members/.

Miller, J. R., *Shingwauk's Vision: A History of Native Residential Schools* (Toronto: University of Toronto Press, 1996).

Mire, M., 'The RCMP is Spending Nearly $100 Million to Spy on the Mohawk's Black Market Tobacco Trade', *Vice* (2014): www.vice.com/en_ca/read/the-rcmp-is-spending-nearly-100-million-to-spy-on-the-mohawks-black-market-tobacco-trade.

Monchalin, L., *The Colonial Problem: An Indigenous Perspective on Crime and Injustice in Canada* (Toronto: University of Toronto Press, 2016).

National Centre for First Nations Governance. 'Making First Nation Law: The Kistuguj Mi'gmaq Fishery' (Vancouver: NCFNG & NNI, 2010).

NoDAPL, 'NoDAPL', www.nodapl.life/.

Norrell, B., 'Wikileaks: Canada's Unauthorized Wiretaps of Mohawks' (2010): http://bsnorrell.blogspot.ca/2010/08/wikileaks-canadas-unauthorized-wiretaps.html.

Norris, A. and P. Cherry, 'Dissidents Claim Victory in Bitter Dispute over Logging Rights', *Montreal Gazette* (1998).

NOW Toronto. 'Idle No More: Is This Just the beginning' (2013): https://nowtoronto.com/news/idle-no-more-is-this-just-the-beginning/.

Obomsawin, A., *Incident at Restigouche* (Ottawa: National Film Board of Canada, 1984).

Obomsawin, A., *Kahnehsatake: 270 Years of Resistance* (Ottawa: National Film Board, 1993).

Obomsawin, A., *Is the Crown at War with Us?* (Ottawa: National Film Board of Canada, 2002).

Ophardt, J., 'Gamble on Canadian Oil Sands Not Paying Out', *Niagara News* (2015): www.niagara-news.com/index.php/mobile-editorial-opinion/3378-gamble-on-canadian-oil-sands- not-paying-out.

Palmater, P., *Beyond Blood: Rethinking Indigenous Identity* (Saskatoon: Purich Publishing, 2011).

Palmater, P., 'Why We Are Idle No More', *Ottawa Citizen* (2012).

Palmater, P., 'Idle No More: What Do We Want and Where Are We Headed?' *Rabble* (2013): http://rabble.ca/blogs/bloggers/pamela-palmater/2013/01/what-idle-no-more-movement-really.

Palmater, P., 'Genocide, Indian Policy and the Legislated Elimination of Indians in Canada', *Aboriginal Policy Studies Journal* 3:3 (2014): 27–54.

Palmater, P. 'Presentation to Standing Committee on Public Safety and National Security re *Bill C-51- An Act to Enact the Security of Canada Information Sharing Act and the Secure Air Travel Act, to Amend the Criminal Code, the Canadian Security Intelligence Service Act and the Immigration and Refugee Protection Act and to Make Related and Consequential Amendments to Other Acts*' (invited expert submission/testimony entered into evidence March 24, 2015a).

Palmater, P., *Indigenous Nationhood: Empowering Grassroots Citizens* (Winnipeg: Fernwood Publishing, 2015b).

Palmater, P., 'Harper's 10 Year War on First Nations' (Toronto: The Harper Decade, 16 July 2015c).

Palmater, P., 'Presentation to Parliamentary Standing Committee on International Trade re Trans-Pacific Partnership Agreement (TPP) and Its Impacts on Indigenous Rights in Canada' (invited expert testimony entered into evidence 14 June 2016a).

Palmater, P., 'My Tribe, My Heirs and Their Heirs Forever: Living Mi'kmaw Treaty', in M. Battiste (ed.), *Living Treaties: Narrating Mi'kmaw Treaty Relations* (Cape Breton: Cape Breton University Press, 2016b).

Palmater, P., 'Shining Light on the Dark Places: Addressing Police Racism and Sexualized Violence against Indigenous Women and Girls in the National Inquiry', *Canadian Journal of Women and the Law* 28:2 (2016c): 253–84.

Palmater, P., 'Death by Poverty: The Lethal Impacts of Colonialism', in W. Antony, J. Antony and L. Samuelson, (eds.), *Power and Resistance* 6th ed., (Winnipeg: Fernwood Publishing, 2017a).

Palmater, P., 'From Foster Care to Missing or Murdered: Canada's Other Tragic Pipeline', *Maclean's* (2017b): www.macleans.ca/news/canada/from-foster-care-to-missing-or-murdered-canadas-other-tragic-pipeline/.

Palmater, P., 'Sexualized Genocide', *Working It Out Together* (2017c): http://workingitouttogether. com/content/canadas-legacy-of-sexualized-genocide- mmiwg/.

Palmater, P., K. Pate and Feminist Alliance for International Action, 'Reply to Issues 2, 3, 16 & 18: Indigenous Women and Women in Detention: Report to the Committee on the Elimination of Discrimination against Women on the Occasion of the Committee's Eighth and Ninth Periodic Review of Canada' (Toronto: Ryerson Chair in Indigenous Governance, Feminist Alliance for International Action, Canadian Association of Elizabeth Fry Societies, October 2016).

Pasternak, S., *On Jurisdiction and Settler Colonialism: The Algonquins of Barriere Lake against the Federal Land Claims Policy* (Toronto: University of Toronto PhD Thesis, 2013).

Pasternak, S., 'Barriere Lake sues Aboriginal Affairs and Third Party Managers', (2015): www. shiripasternak.com/barriere-lake-sues- aboriginal-affairs-and-third-party-managers/#more.

Patten, M., 'Elsipogtog First Nation Sees Violence as RCMP Moves to End Protest', *Huffington Post* (2013): www.huffingtonpost.ca/2013/10/17/elsipogtog-photos-rcmp-protest-violence_n_ 4114506.html.

Paul Tasker, J., 'Trudeau Narrowly Avoids Walkout during Speech of First Nations Chiefs', *CBC News* (2016): www.cbc.ca/news/politics/afn-meeting-bellegard-downie-trudeau-1.3882476.

Paul, D., *We Were Not the Savages: Collision between European and Native American Civilizations*, 3rd ed. (Halifax: Fernwood Publishing, 2006).

Paul D., 'The Hidden History of the Americas: The Destruction and Depopulation of the Indigenous Civilizations of the Americas by European Invaders', *Settler Colonial Studies* 1:2 (2011): 167–81.

Pickerill, J., *Cyberprotest: Environmental activism online* (Manchester: Manchester University Press, 2003).

Poling, J., *Smoke Signals: The Native Takeback of North America's Tobacco Industry* (Toronto: Dundurn Press, 2012).

Proulx, C., 'Colonizing Surveillance: Canada Constructs an Indigenous Terror Threat', *Anthropologica* 56:1 (2014): 83.

R. v. Marshall, [1999] 3 S.C.R. 456 [*Marshall 1*].

R. v. Marshall, [1999] 3 S.C.R. 533 [*Marshall 2*].

R. v. Powley, [2001].

R. v. Sappier, R. v. Gray, [2006] 2 S.C.R. 686.

R. v. Simon, [1985] 2 S.C.R. 387.

R. v. Sioui [1990] 1 S.C.R. 102, *R. v. Sparrow*, [1990] 1.

R. v. Van der Peet, [1996].

Radia, A., 'First Nations Activist Calls for the Impeachment of AFN Chief Shawn Atleo over Education Bill', *Yahoo News* (2014): https://ca.news.yahoo.com/blogs/canada-politics/first-nations-activist-calls-impeachment-afn-chief-shawn-194543972.html.

Razack, S., 'Gendered Racial Violence and Spatialized Justice: The Murder of Pamela George', in S. Razack, (ed.), *Race, Space, and the Law: Unmapping White Settler Society* (Toronto: Between the Lines, 2002), pp. 121–157.

Reagan, P., *Unsettling the Settler Within: Indian Residential Schools, Truth Telling and Reconciliation in Canada* (Vancouver: UBC Press, 2010).

Roache, T., 'Hundreds of Complaints Filed against RCMP after Elsipogtog Fracking Blockade' *APTN* (2014): http://aptnnews.ca/2014/10/16/hundreds-complaints-filed-rcmp-elsipogtog-fracking-blockade/.

Royal Canadian Mounted Police, 'RCMP apology', (2004): www.rcmp-grc.gc.ca/aboriginal-autochtone/ apo-reg-eng.htm.

Royal Canadian Mounted Police, 'The Role of the Royal Canadian Mounted Police during the Indian Residential School System', (2011): www.rcmp-grc.gc.ca/aboriginal-autochtone/irs-spi-eng.htm.

Royal Commission on Aboriginal Peoples, 'Report of the Royal Commission on Aboriginal Peoples' vols.1–5, (Ottawa: Minister of Supply and Services, 1996a).

Royal Commission on Aboriginal Peoples, 'Highlights from the Report of the Royal Commission on Aboriginal Peoples,' (Ottawa: Minister of Supply and Services Canada, 1996b) at 'Policies of Domination and Control'.

S.C.R. 1075 [*Sparrow*].

Sadik, T., 'Traditional Use of Tobacco among Indigenous Peoples of North America: Literature Review' (2014): http://cottfn.com/wp-content/uploads/2015/11/TUT-Literature-Review.pdf.

Saul, J.R., *The Comeback: How Aboriginals are Reclaiming Power and Influence* (Toronto: Penguin Random House, 2014).

Schwartz, D., 'Truth and Reconciliation Commission: By the Numbers', *CBC News* (2015): www.cbc.ca/news/indigenous/truth-and-reconciliation-commission-by-the-numbers-1.3096185.

Schwartz, D. and M. Gollum., 'N.B. Fracking Protests and the Fight for Aboriginal Rights', *CBC News* (2013): www.cbc.ca/news/canada/n-b-fracking-protests-and-the-fight-for-aboriginal-rights-1.2126515.

Scoffield, H., 'National Chief Shawn Atleo Takes Sick Leave Amidst Idle No More political crisis', *National Post* (2013): http://news.nationalpost.com/news/canada/national-chief-shawn-atleo-takes-sick-leave-amidst-idle-no-more-political-crisis.

Selinger, G., 'Apology to First Nations, Metis and Inuit Survivors of the Sixties Scoop', (Winnipeg: Province of Manitoba, 2015).

Shingler, B., 'Sarnia Area First Nation Facing Health Problem from Exposure to Pollutants', *Toronto Star* (2013): www.thestar.com/news/canada/2013/11/24/sarnia_area_first_nation_facing_health_problems_from_ex posure_to_pollutants.html.

Simpson, L. (ed.), *Lighting the Eighth Fire: The Liberation, Resurgence and Protection of Indigenous Nations* (Winnipeg: ARP Books, 2008).

Simpson, L., *Dancing on Our Turtle's Back: Stories of Nishnaabeg Re-creation, Resurgence, and a New Emergence* (Winnipeg: ARP Books, 2011).

Small, R. and J. Jefferson, 'Hudbay Minerals: Confronting a Corporate Criminal', *Alternatives Journal* (2014): www.alternativesjournal.ca/community/blogs/aj-special-delivery/hudbay-minerals-confronting-corporate-criminal.

St. John, M., *Colonization Road* (Toronto: Decolonization Road Productions, 2016).

Stand with Standing Rock, 'Stand with Standing Rock', http://standwithstandingrock.net/.

Statistics Canada, 'National Household Survey 2011: Aboriginal Peoples in Canada: First Nations People, Metis and Inuit' (Ottawa: Statistics Canada, 2011): www12.statcan.gc.ca/nhs-enm/2011/as-sa/99-011-x/99-011-x2011001-eng.pdf.

Statistics Canada, 'Living Arrangements of Aboriginal Children Aged 14 and Under' (Ottawa: Statistics Canada, 2016): www.statcan.gc.ca/pub/75-006-x/2016001/article/14547- eng.pdf.

Stewart, J., 'Address by the Honourable Jane Stewart Minister of Indian Affairs and Northern Development on the Occasion of the Unveiling of Gathering Strength – Canada's Aboriginal Action Plan' (Ottawa: Government of Canada, 1998).

Stote, K., 'The Coercive Sterilization of Aboriginal Women in Canada' (2012) vol. 36, no.3, *American Indian Culture and Research Journal*, i. 117–50.

Stote, K., *An Act of Genocide: Colonialism and the Sterilization of Aboriginal Women* (Halifax: Fernwood Publishing, 2015).

The Canadian Encyclopedia, 'Assembly of First Nations' (2015): www.thecanadianencyclopedia.ca/en/article/assembly-of-first-nations/.

The Constitution Act, 1982, Being Schedule B to the *Canada Act 1982* (UK), 1982, c 11.

The Correctional Investigator Canada, 'Annual Report of the Office of the Correctional Investigator' (Ottawa: Her Majesty the Queen in Right of Canada, 1998–2011).

The Kino-nda-niimi Collective (ed.), *The Winter We Danced: Voices from the Past, the Future, and the Idle No More Movement* (Winnipeg: ARP Press, 2014).

Tomiak, J., 'Navigating the Contradictions of the Shadow State: The Assembly of First Nations, State Funding, and the Scales of Indigenous Resistance', *Studies in Political Economy* 97:3 (2016): 217–33.

Treaty Alliance against Tar Sands Expansion, 'Solidarity Accord' (2016): www.treatyalliance.org/wp-content/uploads/2016/11/TAATSE-SolidarityAccord-EN-R03-20161101- OL.pdf.

Treaty Alliance against Tar Sands Expansion, 'Treaty Alliance against Tar Sands Expansion' www.treatyalliance.org/.

Trevithick, S., 'Native Residential Schooling in Canada: A Review of Literature' *Canadian Journal of Native Studies*, 18 (1998): 49–86.

Truth and Reconciliation Commission of Canada, 'They Came for the Children' (Winnipeg: The Truth and Reconciliation Commission, 2012).

Truth and Reconciliation Commission, 'Report of the Truth and Reconciliation Commission' (Ottawa: Truth and Reconciliation Commission of Canada, 2015).

Tsilhqot'in Nation v. British Columbia. (2014).

UN General Assembly, *United Nations Declaration on the Rights of Indigenous Peoples: Resolution/Adopted by the General Assembly*, (2007), A/RES/61/295.

Union of British Columbia Indian Chiefs, 'Union of British Colombia Indian Chiefs: Working towards the Recognition, Implementation and Exercise of Our Inherent Indigenous Title, Rights and Treaty Rights' www.ubcic.bc.ca/.

Unist'ot'en, 'Unist'ot'en Camp', http://unistoten.camp/.

Van De Donk, W., et al., (eds.), *Cyberprotest: New Media, Citizens and Social Movements* (Abingdon: Routledge, 2004).

Vaughan, A., *Transatlantic Encounters: American Indians in Britain, 1500–1776* (New York: Columbia University, 2006).

Venne, S., *Native Law Centre, Indian Acts and Amendments 1868–1975: An Indexed Collection* (Saskatoon: Native Law Centre, 1981).

Walkom, T., 'Terror Fixation Draws Attention from Failing Economy', *Toronto Star* (2015): www.thestar.com/news/canada/2015/03/06/terror-fixation-draws-attention-from-failing-economy-walkom.html.

Warrior Publications, 'Ts'Peten, 1995' (2011): https://warriorpublications.wordpress.com/2011/02/12/tspeten-1995/.

Warry, W., *Ending Denial: Understanding Aboriginal Issues* (Toronto: University of Toronto Press, 2007).

White, M., *The End of Protest: A New Playbook for Revolution* (Toronto: Knopf Canada, 2016).

Williams, A., *The Pass System* (Toronto: Tamarack Productions, 2015).

Wolfe, P., 'Settler Colonialism and the Elimination of the Native', *Journal of Genocide Research* 8:4 (2006): 387–409.

York, G. and L. Pindera, *People of the Pines: The Warriors and the Legacy of Oka* (New York: Little Brown, 1991).

Young, J. and B. Cantrick. 'Micmac Natives Fight for Land Rights in Quebec', *The Militant* 62:31 (1998), (September 7, 1998): www.themilitant.com/1998/6231/6231_17.html.

2.2

ON DECOLONISATION[1]

Maia Ramnath

In the 2016 version of the film *The Magnificent Seven*,[2] a cutthroat land speculator addresses a gathering of hardscrabble local farmers in a frontier church. Contemptuously, he contrasts the meaning of land as he sees it and as they see it, confident in his ability to impose his will. To them, it is what they live, suffer and die for, the numinous focus of all their love, hope and obsession. To him too, it is an obsession, but only in the form of its fungibility, transferred into quantifiable packets of value in gold, which in accordance with the American theology, he notes cynically, has further equivalent currency exchanges along a chain of signification linking capitalism, progress and democracy as transcendent ideal. Thus, to obstruct the extraction of resources and real estate surplus value is tantamount to opposing divine will itself. The conflict to control the land is a contest of gods.

While clearly the townspeople are the intended sharers of viewer sympathies in this scenario, the contest is not such an easy binary. Here is the self-determined local community of rugged individualists versus a ruthless and insatiable corporate behemoth. But it's not really their land either to invest with sweat, blood, spiritual identifications and desired futurities. Despite the legitimation of claim implied by the inclusion of an indigenous member among the band of seven renegades who come together to defend the community (and a Mexican, and a Korean, along with three whites including a southern veteran of the Confederacy, all under the leadership of a Black man, recruited and supplemented by a rebellious woman), nevertheless they are settlers. This neo-Western is an apt microcosm of an American mythology wherein even the most virtuous and multi-ethnically layered version of egalitarian yeoman freedom was premised upon an originary dispossession.

What Is Radical about Decolonisation

If the language of decolonisation seems ubiquitous in recent years within the social movement landscape, this is as it should be, given that the historical foundations of the societies in which these movements dwell were built upon originary acts of violence – making literal the blood sacrifices of legend buried beneath the walls of various castles and edifices, like Tintagel or the Taj Mahal.

Some of the most crucial sites of antisystemic resistance in the world today are anti- or decolonial, although not always framed this way. In fact, to frame them this way is precisely what further radicalises them. Take, for example, the issue of environment and climate change, growing in urgency: opposition to fossil fuel extraction and transport – oil, tar sands, fracked gas, coal or uranium mining, nuclear waste – is in many cases located simultaneously at the front lines of battles for indigenous sovereignty within a centuries-old geography of resource expropriation, land claims and water rights. A decolonial perspective such as that provided by the presence of indigenous groups at global climate summits, or voiced in North America by organisations like Indigenous Environmental Network and Idle No More whose spokespeople identify a five-hundred-year continuity of anticapitalist, anti-imperialist resistance, is what adds the deeper levels of racial and economic justice to environmental concerns, demanding fundamental changes in the global economic and political structures.[3]

Or take the question of Palestine, urgent as ever in the past half-century: to identify this as an anticolonial struggle, although commonplace throughout the global south, turns upside down the way it is conventionally portrayed in the dominant western discourse. The erasure of an analysis cognisant of settlement – as an act of initial assault that instituted a system of long-term structural violence, asymmetrical power relations and systematic dispossession of land, resources, culture, livelihood and even geographic nomenclature – magically renders aggression into defence, protecting civilised innocents from irrationally irreconcilable hostiles.

I'll return later to the parallels and relationships between these two cases, which are among the most pressing sites of decolonisation visible in the world right now, and which connect the newest and oldest manifestations of US imperial power projection. But first, without getting mired in self-referentiality, decolonisation does call for explicit positioning of one's intellectual and activist pursuits in relation to colonial past history and present implications. So I should begin by acknowledging my location: this was written on Lenape and Lakota land, on, respectively, the eastern seaboard and north central plains of Turtle Island; by an author with immigrant origins in South Asia one generation ago and northern Europe four generations ago, employed until recently at a nineteenth-century land-grant university with intimate ties to the military, while also engaged in on-the-ground organising on multiple fronts with anticolonial goals, aspiring always towards more consistently decolonial methods.

That means that from this specific location, at the crosshatching of several layers of the colonial grid, my reference points tend to be oriented towards the particular aspects in which I am most embedded, at the risk of neglecting others. It's also clear that there are sometimes conflicts and contradictions between these aspects, and that given the complexity and multiplicity of colonial histories, observations made pertinent to one context may be problematic for another. Nevertheless, I can only speak from where I am standing. Looking through a decolonial lens from this vantage point, this is what I see.

Among certain circles – namely anyone from a community previously colonised and racialised – the concept of decolonisation has been self-evident for decades. But for the mainstreaming of the language, to the point where it too may require some decolonisation to restore it to meaningful effectiveness, at least part of the blame on this continent may belong to Occupy Wall Street.

The spread of this viral brand of 2011–12 (itself a spin-off of the viral brand of the Arab Spring uprisings, combined with the inspiration of anticapitalist insurgencies in Greece and Spain, and earlier encampments confronting neo-liberal austerities in the US) activated a counter-tendency from among its own internal critics, who took issue with the implications of its rhetoric. If to 'occupy' something was being used to mean taking back public space from the clutches of miniscule plutocratic elite, reappropriating common goods from the logic of capitalism, then the concept of occupation was the wrong one. To many Native Americans/First Nations peoples, radical people of colour, Palestinians or anyone else with an awareness of colonial history, or of the neocolonialism of today's global economy, the word 'occupation' invoked military incursion, subjugation and dispossession. If the intended meaning was restoration and liberation, why not speak of decolonising, rather than occupying? Furthermore, calls to 'occupy everything', or even to 'reclaim the commons', evoked a righteous sense of entitlement to claim territory, while failing to recognise that these claims too were appropriative.[4] Thus, this radical movement was far less decolonial than it could have been and should have been. In any case, the 'decolonise' language, beyond the ebb of 'occupy', has since proliferated into wide familiarity.

There is a legitimate reason for the ubiquity of 'decolonisation', because colonisation does underlie every aspect of the modern industrial capitalist world as we know it. Colonialism has left its marks on culture, economy, politics, psychology, pedagogy, knowledge systems, race relations, carceral regimes, industrial production and modern state formation, working through all the modes of hard and soft power. Yet, we should be wary of evacuating meaning from the term if over-applied to everything. Colonisation and decolonisation are rooted in historical specificities, not theoretical concepts, and cannot be abstracted into all-purpose metaphor. Eve Tuck and K. Wayne Yang insist upon this point as well in their influential article calling out the appropriation of the term to use for any social justice, antiracist, alternative education, urban gentrification or anticapitalist initiative, as *substitute* for (and convenient evasion of) addressing colonial realities (2012: 1–40). There are valuable structural analogies to colonisation in many of these cases, but the distinction does need to be made or we risk yet again erasing the material reality of the colonised.

The approach to any of these issues and structures may be radicalised by thinking of them as components of decolonisation, in order to illuminate their multiple complex *connections* to the historical processes by which, for example, colonies were used as laboratories for testing new weapons and techniques of surveillance, discipline, biopower, policing and counter-insurgency, which were then circulated among other colonies and finally reimported to become the standard in the metropole itself. Or by which conquerors have typically employed rape as a tool for subjugation, and education as a mode of cultural genocide.

By contrast, to detach such issues from colonial history deradicalises them. Efforts focusing on issues like gentrification, the prison–industrial complex, sexual violence or racial justice *only* function as decolonial – that is, actively contribute to undoing past and present effects of colonial systems, consciously subverting the behaviours, assumptions and structural complicities that reproduce racial hierarchy, cultural hegemony and structural inequity – if activists and scholars explicitly recognise their own efforts as embedded in the same analytical and causal field as these systems. Therefore, adding an awareness of history and its structural, epistemic and psychological impacts to any issue is required in order to render them into components of decolonisation, rather than merely colonial appropriations of the language of decolonisation.

Likewise, decolonisation as a concept itself has to be historicised to retain its radical character as an actual rather than a theoretical process. And, a decolonial framework *as* a radicalising framework for analysis and strategy is by definition a deeply historical framework. In some ways, applying a decolonial lens is much the same as applying a historical, which is to say a deeply contextual, which is to say a critical, which is to say a quintessentially radical lens: it goes to the root of the generative structures of contemporary realities.

Decolonial history is a reclamation of the past, of memory and record, which literally overthrows the master('s) narrative of the present. Colonialism needed to rewrite the past in order to legitimate itself by erasing the very memory of the conquered, or by painting them as destined for natural extinction, unworthy of progressive futurity (whether by virtue of alleged savagery or alleged decadence).

Furthermore, modern world history, as I understand it, is inseparable from colonial history – which means that it is also inseparable from the history of anticolonial struggles for emancipation and self-determination. Walter Mignolo and other associated Latin American scholars in fact argue that modernity and coloniality should be understood as virtual synonyms, as the obscrued and illumined sides of the same coin.[5] In order to further explain why decolonisation adds a radicalising dimension to many issues, then it is necessary to recount some history.

The growth of capitalism and the Industrial Revolution would have been impossible without the joint transformation of land, human bodies and labour into commodities. For a *primarily* anticolonial (as opposed to a *primarily* anticapitalist) analysis (or in other words, an analysis such as those based in a perspective rooted in colonised regions, and such as those articulated by Asian and African leftists throughout the twentieth century), dispossession rather than proletarianisation was the key ignition point for industrial capitalist modernity – which is to say, emphasising the extraction of surplus from the expropriation of land rather than the exploitation of labour. Of course, both were necessary components of an integrated system.

The initial globality that we know as modernity was the result of the unprecedented economic integration of Eastern and Western Hemispheres. Access to 'New World' resources gave Europe the advantage it had previously lacked to dominate the Afro-Eurasian ecumene – a dramatic upset by a previously marginal backwater of the 'Old World' (these being obviously colonial designations). British industrialisation was built upon the steam-driven machinery of mass-produced textiles, which devoured not just cheap coal but cheap raw cotton. This was procured through a multi-continental complex of enslaved and dehumanised African labour working on American land seized by genocidal expropriation from dehumanised prior inhabitants, for monocrop plantation production.[6]

Along with geographer David Harvey (and drawing upon earlier critical thinkers like Rosa Luxemburg or C. L. R. James), we refer to this catalyst for capitalism as accumulation by dispossession rather than primitive accumulation, to indicate that it was not an originary singularity limited to the primordial past, but a process required again and again to bridge the system's inevitable metabolic rifts and resolve its crises through expansion. Thus, anticolonial primary resistance – fighting back against initial invasion and military occupation, defending land and sovereignty against coercive settlement, dispossession and resource expropriation at the new profit-frontiers of cash crops, ores, minerals, water, strategic topography, labour – is still underway to this day; a truly postcolonial era does not yet exist.

What Are the Principle Concerns of the Movements Involved with Decolonisation

Decolonisation requires resisting new appropriations of common goods, territory and resources, countering each new suction of wealth outward and upward towards remote concentration, skirmishing along a moving frontier line of extraction which in many cases, not coincidentally, matches the barrier of racialised difference. Structural and discursive location in relation to this line of coloniality – akin to the 'colour line', namely the racial divide as the primary contradiction identified by W. E. B. Du Bois in *The Souls of Black Folk* as 'the problem of the Twentieth Century', and by A. Sivanandan (as immortalised by Asian Dub Foundation) as synonymous with 'the power line ... the poverty line' – is the crucial point differentiating such expropriations from the structurally similar enclosures described by British Marxist historians that turned European land-based agrarian communities into a landless industrial waged labour force, removed from their extra-capitalist means of subsistence.

But decolonisation also requires more than that. Damages sown long ago have sustained time-release effects. The racially structured modes of social engineering and control that were used to justify settlement claims and mask surplus extraction mechanisms have left their stamp on the global economic disparities and dependencies that distinguish the mutually constituted 'developed' and 'developing' worlds (i.e. the colonising global north and colonised global south), on global food systems and commodity chains, on the vectors of warfare, on the trajectories of migrants and refugees, and on the discrimination met by these diasporic communities upon arrival. Every dysfunctional racial dynamic we now live with is rooted in this history. (Not to mention our addictions to sugar, coffee, tea, chocolate, tobacco, opiates and fossil fuels.)

The antithesis to colonisation, with its multiple historical emanations – at different times from different centres by different logics with different goals in different places (Cooper and Stoler, 1997; Cooper, 2005) – is not a single moment or single event, but rather a multilayered, intersectional process of unravelling a totalising system and its entrenched effects. The process exists contemporaneously at every phase of its life cycle somewhere in the world.

The layers include

- resisting new frontiers of colonisation;
- countering the persistent structures put in place by prior colonisation;
- healing the lingering effects of colonial damage and trauma to communities and individuals;
- revising the national autobiographies of colonial states; challenging their historical blind spots and self-delusions;
- restoring the dynamism of subjugated, damaged or near-obliterated cultures, languages and knowledge bases.

Beyond anticolonial resistance then, decolonisation is also a more complex and sustained task requiring the undoing of institutions, dismantling of structures, intervening in the narratives and imagery of cultural representation. Since colonisation was carried out upon lands, resource bases, bodies, minds, practices and discourses, all of these may become grounds of decolonial action.

Restoration does not mean a nostalgic attempt to turn back the clock towards a cleaner, purer moment before the destruction began, fixed into ahistorical stasis (which is how vigorous colonisers often like to portray those supposedly slated for obsolescence). But it does entail – as Glenn Coulthard, Leanne Simpson, Taiaiake Alfred and other indigenous intellectuals emphasise – reweaving the torn fabric of interrelationship among individuals, community (human and non-human) and place, grounded in the immanent spiritual ecology of indigenous lifeways and practices (Alfred, 2009; Corntassel, 2012).

Decolonial restoration generates new growth on the apparently defoliated branches of alternative social forms, intellectual and cultural traditions rooted in principles very different from those of a colonial (imperial, capitalist, extractive, patriarchal, racial-supremacist) regime, although they may also find resonances and alliances with non-dominant elements suppressed or eliminated from within the regime's own body. To revitalise subjugated knowledge is not a choice between new ways and old ways, statically defined, but of alternate ways that have both old and new existence as they continually unfold across a long time span. Since colonisation artificially truncated the unfoldment of one of them, decolonisation would entail mending the cut, allowing the unfoldment to resume in new contexts and conditions.

So where do we see these efforts manifesting today? Even more important than a history of colonisation is the contrapuntal history of decolonisation, taking into account the interference patterns (convergent amplifications, frictions or collisions) among its subsequent layers and differently located aspects.

Dane Kennedy periodises this history into several major waves of decolonisation, of which the first took place in the late eighteenth- to early nineteenth-century Caribbean and South America, with the Haitian and Bolivarian revolutions. We are overlooking here the settler revolt of the slaveholding North American colonists for more autonomy from the British mother country; their grievances, framed as 'anticolonial' resistance to tyranny and taxation without representation, included chafing against restrictions on the 'freedom' to expand settlement further westwards into indigenous lands. The resultant fledgling independent creole republic almost immediately moved towards incremental takeover of the territorial claims of the French and Spanish empires, and recolonised its southern neighbours by staking out a sphere of influence to enforce their own prerogatives of exploitation, intervention, intensive resource extraction and plantation production against rivals. From this point onwards, the US was the dominant imperial power in the Americas.

Back in Europe, the high-imperial scramble for colonies on all remaining Asian, African and Oceanic territories from the late nineteenth into the early twentieth century set off an inter-imperial collision course to the First World War, the effects of which dismantled the Ottoman and Austro-Hungarian empires only to reassign their Near Eastern/Middle Eastern/West Asian territories to Britain and France. The war and its aftermath catalysed self-determination struggles around the world including in India, Egypt, China and Ireland, which intensified transnational solidarities among Asian and African 'oppressed peoples' including pan-African, pan-Islamic, pan-Asian and pan-Arab formations, often framed in relation to the Communist International and/or the League Against Imperialism.

The Second World War was the death blow for the modern empires, unleashing the next few major waves of global decolonisation. From the 1940s to the 1990s, decolonisation mainly referred to the post-war spate of African and Asian national liberation struggles resulting in the twenty-nine newly independent nation states constituent of the Bandung Afro-Asian ideal and the framework of Non-Aligned or Third World solidarity.[7] Even now, most scholarship on colonial and decolonial histories, postcolonial theory and literature takes these formations as the assumed reference point.

As the remaining European empires were dismantled, the turbulent front line of decolonisation (i.e. the track of the death throes of imperial rule) migrated from South Asia to Southeast Asia and North Africa, then Sub-Saharan Africa. Meanwhile, radical wings of black diasporic liberation struggles within the global north identified themselves with African decolonisation, while radical wings of white leftist struggles pledged antiracist and anti-imperialist solidarities with Algeria, Vietnam, Cuba and Maoist China. By the early 1970s in the US, the Black Panthers, American Indian Movement (AIM), Movimiento Estudiantil Chicano de Aztlan (MEChA),[8] Puerto Rican Young Lords and Asian-American I Wor Kuen had all crystallised as militantly anticolonial formations.

However, a couple of neocolonial counterforces were also on the rise. For one thing, it seems clear in retrospect that translating Third World decolonisation into nation state building was a disastrous mistake. The former colonial regimes' governmental infrastructures and administrative, legal, judicial, military and security apparatuses, taken over largely intact by the new postcolonial countries, did not provide a fitting vehicle for the emancipatory impulse that had generated the various forms of far more ambitiously transformative movements. Furthermore, many of these new states had inherited not just colonial apparatuses but colonial boundaries, mapped contingently by the limits of conquest, or arbitrarily in the name of 'efficient' administration. These were often based upon presumptions of ethnic exclusivity, despite the fact that the boundaries did not necessarily match up with different ethnies' homeplaces, cutting across their lived geographies so that groups such as the Kurds, the Pashtun or the Rohingya became minorities in multiple states. Sometimes, it prohibited previously existing nomadism or coexistence. The resulting partitions led to much bloody misery and sectarian violence.

The postcolonial nation states have since perpetrated much quite familiar colonial behaviour upon their own borderlands and internal tribal populations: from disenfranchisement and marginalisation combined with expropriation of land and resources (minerals, fossil fuels, lumber, etc.) for capital accumulation, up to occupation by hostile forces granted special powers with violent impunity in a legalised permanent state of exception (see, for example, Khalil, 2015; Chakravati, 2010, 2012; Ross, 2014). Such have been the narratives of Manipur, Mizoram, Assam, Nagaland, Kashmir, the putative Khalistan and other regions in relation to the Indian state; Bangladesh (formerly East Pakistan) and Baluchistan to the (West) Pakistani state; Mindanao to the Filipino state; the Shan states to Burma; West Papua and East Timor to Indonesia; and West Sahara to Morocco.

In short, the post-war waves of Third World decolonisation, though partially emancipatory, failed to complete the mission, or even betrayed it. The transition to statehood was ultimately not just deradicalising but counter-revolutionary, perpetuating the same oppressive functions that those structures had been designed to do under colonial rule, now under new management. This is why such a transition to independence might have been considered anti-imperial but not truly decolonising.[9] To continue the work of decolonisation today requires confronting the consequences of these states' actions and the reactionary ideologies that were also generated by the anticolonial dialectic.

Secondly, while the European empires in Asia and Africa were in retreat, US imperial ambition surged forward, driven by the quest for economic, ideological, military and political dominance around the globe, but above all by the strategic imperative to secure access to oil in the Middle East. Control of fossil fuel sources and transport routes was defined as essential to national security (and robust consumer capitalism). And in this, the US found it convenient to build up an ally in the modern ethno-religious nationalist movement of Zionism, which the decolonising Afro-Asian solidarity discourse viewed since 1948 as not only an instrument of American interests, but an explicitly European colonising project that aimed to supercede a civilisationally 'backward' West Asian population.[10] The horrific victimisation of one people, the Jews of Europe, they argued, should not logically have provided the justification for oppression of another, the Arabs of Palestine.

This sets up the context for linking these two most salient fronts of decolonisation today: Palestine and indigenous North America. These are major foci for current radicalism both because they are the flashpoints of crucial contemporary conflicts, and because they require us to dig a layer deeper – that is, more radical, in terms of the depth of critical questioning and the degree of fundamental epistemic and structural change required.[11] Contemplating this level of decolonisation generates a very necessary discomfort of fundamentally unsettling everything about how we live and what we know.

A striking and very specific continuity of logic, methodology and legitimating mythology bind the US and Israel, even deeper than the dovetailing of their political and strategic interests. Activists and intellectuals are increasingly noting the parallels between Zionism and the American national project. Countering the oldest and newest settler states brings together the deepest and the highest, the most entrenched and the most urgent, the first and the final frontiers of decolonial thought and action, juxtaposing the original scars with the rawest wounds.

In recent years, indigenous North American activists and intellectuals along with other committed activist-scholars of colonialism/postcolonialism have participated in delegations to Palestine, and returned to speak powerfully on the parallels between these struggles against settler colonisation. In the fall of 2016, the Palestinian flag could be seen snapping in the fierce North Dakota prairie wind along the row of indigenous nations' and tribes' banners that formed the spine of the Oceti Sakowin water protectors' encampment at the Standing Rock Sioux reservation. Palestinian and Palestine solidarity groups had mobilised regular caravans there from various parts of the country, expressing their recognition of that struggle for sovereignty, land and water rights, as deeply akin to their own.

Both settler projects proceeded through a comparable pattern of violence, land acquisition whether by dubious purchase or by direct military occupation followed by the metastasis of fortified squatting, ethnic cleansing, mass transfer or segregation and incarceration of populations, repeated violations of treaties and international law, collective punishment, security regimes restricting physical movement enforced by barriers, checkpoints, aerial surveillance and heavily militarised policing. Stephen Salaita quotes historian Ari Shavit on 'the difference between US and Israeli massacres. "About 100 years"' (Salaita, 2016: 20).

In both the American and Israeli colonial regimes, European settlers, taking land from prior inhabitants, justified their actions through rhetorics that have melded the teleological inevitability of modern progress with a divinely sanctioned messianic mandate, a self-fulfilling prophecy by which settlers strive by acts of genocidal violence and displacement to make the facts on the ground accord with the myth of *terra nullius* – the empty land awaiting its righteous, predestined inhabitants.

The two locations complete a circle. Iberian conquest in the Western Hemisphere was explicitly projected as a continuation of the Crusades, cloaking a quest for gold as god's mission against the savage, whether Arab or Amerindian. It was no accident that the Christian reconquest of Moorish Spain coincided with Columbus's initial predatory landfall in the Caribbean. Subsequent British and French conquest justified itself through a different primary logic: enlightenment rationalism declared land unclaimed for capitalist production as waste, and therefore up for grabs by whoever demonstrated ownership by 'improving' it, rendering it 'productive' of surplus value, while at the same time invoking Biblical Christian imagery equating claims to the New World with claims to the Promised Land (not to mention a Protestant interpretation of material affluence as the outward sign of morality and godliness).

Here are interwoven two versions of the utopian impulse: the most sophisticated modern technological paradise and the most pure and virtuous enclave for the end of times. Zionism too contains both logics: a right-wing religious mission to reclaim god-given land for a chosen people, and a left-liberal civilising mission to render land maximally productive, technologised, surplus-generating. Twentieth-century Revisionist Zionism drew explicitly on upon the precedent of nineteenth-century US conquest and policy of removal of natives as model and justification for its own goals.[12] And for the past half-century the US military habitually refers to the land it invades, facing stubborn resistance in hostile territory from Vietnam to Iraq and Afghanistan, as 'Indian Country' to evoke its nineteenth-century wars of conquest.

Perhaps the main difference between the American and Israeli settler narratives is the claim to primordial nativity; the latter case cites a connection lost through millennia of exile, versus the former's claim to a Manifest Destiny unprecedented yet triumphantly fore-ordained as a historical culmination. Nevertheless whether looking to past or future, both proclaim the similarly exceptional status of serving as a beacon of enlightenment unto the nations, whether in theological or secular terms. Such exceptionalism, which absolves perpetrators of the originary acts of violence required to clear the space for such a wonderful thing to be unfurled, also necessitates a continual effort of erasure whereby, shorn of context, resistance to structural violence can be portrayed as aggression, and settler state terrorism as defence.

I believe that this is why the frequently encountered 'PEP (Progressive Except Palestine)' syndrome is so recalcitrant in the US: because indicting Israel in this way hits too close to home. Logically, it requires questioning America's own foundational self-image and legitimating narrative. This cannot be borne, and so must not be seen. This is the epistemic event horizon, the ultimate limitation on what may be spoken or even thought. But for decolonisation in both places to occur, unmasking this shared myth is essential.

How Is the Politics of Decolonisation Theorised and What, If Any, Influences Are Active in Decolonisation Movements?

It is perhaps less important to *theorise* the politics of decolonisation than to enact and manifest them through the practices of history, literature, art and pedagogy. There is always a relationship between scholarship and activism in decolonisation, because colonisation was carried out on an epistemic as well as physical ground. Theory and practice are impossible to separate in this context.

Educational institutions have historically been used as an important mechanism of subjugation, assimilation and discipline. The field of anthropology has a notorious record of treating cultural artefacts and bodies, living and dead, as dehumanised objects of scientific study, while at the same time, domination of the narrative (through ideological apparatuses ranging from archives to policies to pedagogy to popular media) has been deployed towards erasure of the past and naturalisation of an unjust present order. Colonial regimes seek control of what is allowed to enter into the field of perception and cognition; hence for those subjected to the threat of physical and/or cultural genocide, the significance of asserting visible presence in both art and protest, manifesting existence as resistance. However, it should be stressed that battles on the discursive level are not a substitute for structural change, albeit a necessary but insufficient component.

Given its location and orientation, academic postcolonial theory is not always the best source of *effectively* decolonial thinking in action, although a decolonial intellectual tradition does overlap with a canonical list of the politically engaged precursors, current practitioners or interlocutors of 'postcolonial' criticism, such as Frantz Fanon, Amilcar Cabral, Aimé Cesaire, Leopold Sedar Senghor, Kwame Nkrumah, Albert Memmi, Achille Mbembe, Edward Said, Ngugi wa Thiong'o and Stuart Hall. Decolonial thinking is also theorised/practiced under the banners of Africana critical theory, liberation theology and liberation philosophy, cultural studies (Birmingham and Inter-Asian), South Asian and Latin American subaltern studies, Women of Colour/Third World feminism, ethnic studies and indigenous critical theory.[13]

But true criticality of theory means precisely its radicalism, its committedness to praxis and intentionality towards social change. The bridging of scholarship and activism that characterises it then also requires redefining what counts as valid work within the confining definitions of the conventional academy. This is not always feasible, as academic institutions grow more corporatised and neo-liberalised, and ever more tied to the military-industrial-research complex.[14] The key thing for aspiring decolonial scholars who attempt to wear both hats to remember is that ultimately the work they do in the academy has to be oriented towards movements, rather than the other way around. They must remain clear on which goals and interests they are serving, and to whom their work is accountable, accessible and relevant.

The journal *Decolonisation: Indigeneity, Education and Society* is a good example of an intellectual production geared towards contributing to actual decolonisation, as opposed to making it an abstract object of study.[15] Other examples: there has been a good deal of overlap in academic boycott-divestment-sanctions (BDS) mobilisation with participation in art and activism initiatives like the Gulf Labor Artist Coalition (http://gulflabor.org/) and Decolonize This Place project based in New York City (http://decolonizethisplace.org/), which link neocolonialism in the global economy, imperialism, analyses of settler colonialism linking indigenous struggles, Palestine, black liberation, migrant South Asian labour in the Persian Gulf, the economic and cultural colonialism implicit in art and media representation. Many of those involved played key roles in foregrounding the issues in political and academic discourses, notably the controversial stand taken by the Asian American and American Studies Associations in support of the Palestinian BDS movement.[16]

Meanwhile, much decolonial thinking, on-the-ground analysis, critique, strategising, movement-based reportage, tactical discussion and creative expression emerge directly from journals and websites, zines and pamphlets, Facebook and YouTube videos, addressing the sites of conflict, resistance and decolonisation that are unfolding in real time.[17]

Let me return for a moment to the observation that addressing settler regimes today is the next step for decolonial thought and action. Just as the addition of an anticolonial analysis in general can radicalise the approach to other issues, an analysis of settler colonialism, in particular, challenges already anticolonial writing and organising even further by pushing it towards greater accountability for the very material and epistemic ground on which it stands. Even other modes of social justice and critical theory/praxis can remain complicit with settler-colonial structures when they hold back from this step.

For example, incorporating this analysis complicates the ways in which racial justice and immigrant rights are spoken of in the US Radical claims for racial justice that transcend liberal claims for civil rights demand recognition of the history of enslavement and its successor forms of systemic white supremacy, through carceral discipline, political and economic exclusion, segregation, etc. But as Coulthard, Jodi Byrd, Kevin Bruyneel and others point out, in a settler state, even these claims can still be framed within the bounds of democratic inclusion in, and recognition by, a settler state, the establishment of which existentially underlies the very condition of possibility for all later claims on rights and equity within it (Bruyneel, 2007; Byrd, 2011; Coulthard, 2014).

Even an important strand of radical black liberation struggle, which has understood itself at least since the 1920s as tied to an African diasporic network of global decolonisation, and since the 1960s as one among other Third World national liberation struggles, has the potential for settler complicity. The '40 acres' promise of Emancipation, quite reasonably justified purely on the basis of the (Lockean or Marxian) labour theory of value, or the aspirational establishment of New Afrika in the 'black belt' states of the old south, on the same grounds, would still require expropriation from indigenous residents unless based upon a new dispensation of mutual alliance.[18] The sophisticated historical and intersectional circulating among the current Black Lives Matter, BDS and indigenous sovereignty movements suggests reason for hope.

Furthermore, each new stream of non-white, marginalised arrivants (Byrd's term), even those whose journeys have ultimately resulted from colonisation of their own places of origin, must negotiate the meanings and requirements of their positionality within the coloniser/colonised grid: whether to aim for assimilation into the settler/white supremacist structure and its social imaginary, identifying with its hegemonic aspirations, or to attempt to oppose, subvert, disrupt, challenge and dismantle it. Despite having been impelled by colonial history into diaspora – whether as refugees or political convicts, by enslavement or indenture, or put into motion by the dizzying neocolonial imbalances in global wealth concentration – they are also placed, upon arrival, into various possible complicities with settlement.

There are other frictions or disconnects among different strands of radical (decolonial?) theory/praxis, such as those between postcolonial theory and indigenous critical theory, between postcolonial theory and leftist anti-imperialism, or between leftist anti-imperialism and indigenous critical theory, though for different reasons.

One of the objections some indigenous critical theory has to some postcolonial theory is the latter's rejection of essentialism and emphasis on hybridity and strict social construction as emancipatory concepts. Yet, these too can be used in disempowering and re-subjugating ways, pointed out. As Coulthard, Arif Dirlik and others point out, no concept is implicitly emancipatory in all contexts, and that an essentialism of the powerful may be different from an essentialism of powerless – meaning perhaps something like Gayatri Spivak's 'strategic' version, appropriate to those still enmeshed in struggle against an existential threat as opposed to dealing with its aftershocks.[19]

However, it may also be noticed that sometimes, once the tables have turned, the powerful continue to identify themselves as the powerless; or at least to claim the moral standing of victimhood when they are actually in the position of dominant aggressor. Zionism and Hindutva (far right-wing Hindu nationalism, in many ways its cognate) are cases in point. To take the convoluted case of Indian nationalism, in both domestic and diasporic forms, Hindutva aspires to equate itself to the aforementioned American/Zionist mould, and at the same time to claim the (debatable) mantle of indigenous, place-based spiritual identification with land, touting restoration of one (dubious) interpretation of Sanskritic tradition as revitalising a lost precolonial culture, while at the same time linking this identification to fascistic and xenophobic exclusivity and hyper-developmentalist ambition. Meanwhile, the emphatically rationalist South Asian left tends to be suspicious of postcolonial/subaltern theory for its scepticism towards enlightenment rationalism and scientific positivism, along with its valorisation of pre-industrial lifeways and modes of production.[20]

Throughout the nineteenth and twentieth centuries, the European-based left despite its emancipatory agenda also contributed to colonisation (and ecological destruction) through its emphasis on progress and industrial development. Today's international left faces an existentially inescapable need to envision a social future beyond the context of industrial modernity (albeit perhaps highly technological). Here again, the implication is that indigenous critical theory/praxis has the capacity to further radicalise left anticolonial thinking in ways imperative for the twenty-first century. A banner at a recent oil pipeline blockade equated a future of indigenous sovereignty with a future of ecological sustainability. The implicit message, angled towards an aerial drone's-eye view, was that given a North American decolonisation, the alternative ethos and subjugated knowledge base in question happen to be ones that could potentially save us all.

Even so, colonial behaviours are insidious, as the bearers of such messages also point out: the fact that some subjugated knowledge does contain skills, concepts and philosophies containing possible keys to planetary and human survival reveals the importance of reflexive vigilance at all levels lest we assume the right to expropriate or extract such knowledge without asking or giving due credit, rather than letting the deployment, and sharing and teaching of knowledge be guided by those from whom it originates and who have long guarded it.[21]

Today, a global neocolonial system layered upon the ongoing effects of older colonial systems reveals many sites of intervention: every point of surplus extraction, every point of racial control, is a potential point of resistance and decolonisation. How each one of us is implicated in the histories and contexts in which decolonisation occurs depends on our location, but we *are* all implicated. Contributing to decolonisation calls for an analysis of each location and its particular accountabilities. For those based in settler regimes, decolonisation taken to its logical conclusion could begin with the honouring of existing treaty terms, proceed through the granting of reparations and ultimately lead to the full restoration of land, self-determination and sovereignty in that geographical space.

Is This Possible?

Can What's Been Broken Be Fixed?

Is the destruction of environments and cultures, the loss of languages and knowledge, irrevocable? Not so long as there is anyone still fighting back, or still practising and reproducing lifeways. People will always defend themselves against conquest and dispossession unless totally annihilated – physically and culturally, existentially and epistemologically. But how many generations would it take to reverse centuries of cumulative immiseration, impoverishment and imbalance in the global distribution of wealth, power and well-being?

Given all the plausible ways the world could end – by climate catastrophe, pandemic or war, nuclear or otherwise – the immediate future needs to be concerned with decolonisation. This requires not just resistance but also recreation: of lost or erased names of people and places on maps (since in some places, using the wrong map, or the wrong name, or the wrong language, can be seen as an act of treason or a provocation to violence); of relationship to place, entailing different kinds of relations among human and non-human beings; of non-capitalist, non-fossil-fuel-intensive, non-resource-extractive ways of living.

Decolonising climate justice means foregrounding indigenous sovereignty concerns in all deliberations. Decolonising racial justice and immigrant/migrant politics means acknowledging the settler framework of the state within which such claims are made and arrivals absorbed or shut out. Decolonising the framework of world peace means recognising American and Israeli occupations in West Asia as culpable for instigating and exacerbating geopolitical conflict.

Decolonisation would unsettle the foundation of the dominant institutions and episteme of the world most of us live in most of the time. With its embeddedness in history, it carries by definition a deep awareness of the past. But it carries by definition an equally far-reaching awareness of futurity, in that its means are prefigurative and its ends dynamically revitalising.

Notes

1 Parts of this piece are adapted and expanded from my article in *STRIKE! Magazine* (2016). It also builds further upon writings contributed to anthologies edited by Carl Levy and Saul Newman, *The Anarchist Imagination* (Routledge, 2015); and Raymond Craib and Barry Maxwell, *No Gods, No Masters, No Peripheries* (PM Press, 2015).

2 *The Magnificent Seven* (2016), directed by Antoine Fuqua, written by Nick Pizzolatto and Richard Wenk, produced by Village Roadshow for MGM and Columbia Pictures.
3 www.ienearth.org/ www.idlenomore.ca/.
4 In fall 2016, I cringed to hear a couple of white activists who had recently visited the by then world-famous water protectors' encampment at the Standing Rock Sioux reservation in North Dakota reflecting delightedly how much it 'reminded them of Occupy Wall Street!' – as if OWS had not itself been an echo of centuries-old camping techniques, participatory deliberative practices, collective modes of existence and pseudo-tribal cultural forms.
    For a collection of documents related to these debates within the OWS movement, see Amy Schrager Lang and Daniel Lang/Levitsky, eds., *Dreaming in Public: Building the Occupy Movement* (New Internationalist Publications, 2012).
5 This premise builds on the fact that colonisation in Central and South America predated the more conventional periodisation of the modern era that takes more enlightenment-based traits as a starting point, therefore obscuring and distorting an understanding of colonialism, modernity, logics of resistance and the conclusions of postcolonial theory. See, for example, Mabel Moraña, Enrique Dussel and Carlos Jauregui, eds., *Coloniality At Large* (Duke University Press, 2008); Walter Mignolo, *The Darker Side of Western Modernity: Global Futures, Decolonial Options* (Duke University Press, 2011).
6 This is comprehensively laid out by Sven Beckert, *Empire of Cotton* (Vintage, 2014); Lisa Lowe, *The Intimacies of Four Continents* (Duke University Press, 2015). On New World slavery and the development of capitalism, see the work of Edward Baptist, Robin Blackburn and Eric Williams.
7 Initially fronted most prominently by a cluster of Third World state leaders of international stature: Jawaharlal Nehru (India), Sukarno (Indonesia), Gamal Abdel Nasser (Egypt), and Kwame Nkrumah (Ghana).
8 Aztlan was the name for the pre-Colombian Mexican/Aztecan civilisation including the portions of the US annexed from Mexico in the war of 1848. Chicanos claim indigeneity to the southwestern quarter of what's now the US.
9 The same may be true of tribal governments: leadership and law enforcement structures put in place by the federal government under the Indian Reorganization Act of 1934 are not always recognised as legitimate by all tribal members, who in some cases view them as corrupt and self-serving, complicit with colonial regime and/or extractive industries, or prioritising the interests of state and capital over the interests of sovereignty and community. Again, the point is that achieving an independent government is not necessarily the same thing as decolonisation.
10 This included the Jewish population who *were* actually indigenous to the region: the ethnic/cultural divide *within* Israel between Ashkenazi and Mizrahi communities mirrors the European/Arab fault line.
11 In fact [in 'Decolonisation is not a metaphor' pp], Tuck and Yang define decolonisation in strictest terms *only* as the dismantling of settler colonial structures, noncommensurate with other forms of anticolonial struggle. They stress that repatriation of land and sovereignty to indigenous inhabitants is related but not identical to anti-imperial conflicts elsewhere, such as those with regard to military occupations, administrative, extractive or labour colonies. I would argue that it is not that such things are in no way decolonial. They are to a degree, even if insufficiently and incompletely so: they may do necessary service in undoing more superficial strata of colonisation even if not penetrating as far as the base layer of settlement.
12 Salaita has extensively catalogued the rhetorical parallels in *The Holy Land in Transit* (Syracuse University Press, 2006) and *Inter/Nationalism*. See in the latter, in particular, his comparison of the rhetoric of Andrew Jackson and Vladimir Jabotinsky, pp. 71–102.
13 Such as historians Robert Young, Pransenjit Duara, Antoinette Burton, Catherine Hall, Ranajit Guha, Sumit Sarkar, Tanika Sarkar, Patrick Wolfe, Mahmood Mamdani; political-historical-cultural theorists Reiland Rabaka, Cedric Robinson, Aijaz Ahmad, Eqbal Ahmad, Ania Loomba, Paul Gilroy … and so many more.
14 On decolonising the academy, pedagogy and research, see (among a large literature) Linda Tuhiwai Smith, *Decolonising Methodologies* (Zed Books, 2012); Sara Ahmed, *On Being Included* (Duke University Press, 2012); Piya Chatterjee and Sunaina Maira, *The Imperial University* (University of Minnesota Press, 2014); Stevphen Shukaitis, David Graeber and Erica Biddle, eds., *Constituent Imagination: Militant Researches, Collective Theorization* (AK Press, 2007); bell hooks, *Teaching to Transgress* (Routledge, 1994).

15 http://decolonization.org/index.php/des. Established in 2012, its editorial staff and board include many significant indigenous and decolonial scholar-activists. Editor Eric Ritskes explains its mission at https://intercontinentalcry.org/what-is-decolonization-and-why-does-it-matter. Accessed 16/4/17.

16 Strong voices in these efforts have included J. Kehaulani-Kauanui, Dean Saranillio, Sunaina Maira, Robin D.G. Kelley, Angela Davis, Stephen Salaita, Andrew Ross, Jasbir Puar, Vijay Prashad, Rashid Khalidi and Leena Dallasheh. In addition to their extensive bodies of scholarship and frequent public addresses, some of the concerns, connections and arguments of the above-mentioned projects are laid out in the pamphlet 'Palestine Boycott Beyond' by the collective Tidal: Occupy Theory, Occupy Strategy. http://decolonizethisplace.org/zines/161104_Palestine_BLM_Boycott_Arts_Zine_PrinterSpreads.pdf; and in materials viewable at http://artistsspace.org/exhibitions/decolonizethisplace; http://decolonizethisplace.org, and http://gulflabor.org. Accessed 16/4/17.

17 Two acutely practical critiques/proposals for decolonial activist practice: 'Accomplices Not Allies' Version 2: 5/02/2014, www.indigenousaction.org/accomplices-not-allies-abolishing-the-ally-industrial-complex; Liza Minno-Bloom and Berkley Carnine, 'Towards Decolonisation and Settler Responsibility: Reflections on a Decade of Indigenous Solidarity Organizing'. *Counterpunch*, October 3, 2016. www.counterpunch.org/2016/10/03/towards-decolonization-and-settler-responsibility-reflections-on-a-decade-of-indigenous-solidarity-organizing. Accessed 16/4/17. See also Waziyatawin Angela Wilson and Michael Yellow Bird, eds., *For Indigenous Eyes Only: A Decolonisation Handbook* (School for Advanced Research Press, 2005).

18 African and indigenous interactions in American history are complex, ranging from slaveholding by the Cherokee to widespread absorption of runaway slaves by the Seminole, and intermarriage in many communities not uncommon though largely invisibilised until recently. For illumination of some of these variations, see the work of Barbara Krauthamer and Tiya Miles.

19 This refers to Spivak's famous line from the 1988 essay 'Can the Subaltern Speak?' on the strategic essentialism of the subaltern, utilising identity categories of oppression as the tactical, contextual basis of solidarity in order to counteract the relevant structures of oppression, but without endorsing an ahistorical, intrinsic essence.

20 It is indisputable that science has been used as a tool of colonisation in the past; it is equally indisputable that science can be used as a bulwark against the racism, xenophobia and climate change denial by which colonisation is furthered in the present. Here is another iteration of the point that no concept or epistemology is either implicitly emancipatory or inevitably oppressive in all contexts.

21 See the educational resources available at www.nodaplsolidarity.net. Accessed 13/3/17. This site is now defunct, but many of the same resources can be found in the Standing Rock Syllabus compiled by the NYC Stands with Standing Rock Collective, 2016. https://nycstandswithstandingrock.files.wordpress.com/2016/10/standingrocksyllabus7.pdf. Accessed 16/4/17.

References

Ahmed, Sara. *On Being Included* (Duke University Press, 2012).

Alfred, Taiaiake. *Peace, Power, Righteousness* (Oxford University Press, 2009).

Beckert, Sven. *Empire of Cotton* (Vintage, 2014).

Bruyneel, Kevin. *The Third Space of Sovereignty: The Postcolonial Politics of U.S.-Indigenous Relations* (University of Minnesota Press, 2007).

Byrd, Jodi. *The Transit of Empire: Indigenous Critiques of Colonialism* (University of Minnesota Press, 2011).

Chatterjee, Piya and Sunaina Maira. *The Imperial University* (University of Minnesota Press, 2014).

Cooper, Frederick and Ann Laura Stoler, introduction to *Tensions of Empire* (University of California Press, 1997).

Cooper, Frederick. *Colonialism in Question* (University of California Press, 2005).

Corntassel, Jeff. 'Re-envisioning Resurgence: Indigenous Pathways to De-colonisation and Sustainable Self-Determination'. *Decolonisation* 1:1, (2012), pp. 86–101.

Coulthard, Glen. *Red Skin White Masks* (University of Minnesota Press, 2014).

Indigenous Action Media. 'Accomplices Not Allies.' 2014. www.indigenousaction.org/accomplices-not-allies-abolishing-the-ally-industrial-complex.

Kennedy, Dane. *Decolonization: A Very Short Introduction* (Oxford University Press, 2016).

Khalil, Tasneem. *Jallad: Death Squads in South Asia* (Pluto Press, 2015).

Lang, Amy Schrager and Daniel Lang/Levitsky, eds., *Dreaming in Public: Building the Occupy Movement* (New Internationalist Publications, 2012).

Lowe, Lisa. *The Intimacies of Four Continents* (Duke University Press, 2015).

Mignolo, Walter. *The Darker Side of Western Modernity: Global Futures, Decolonial Options* (Duke University Press, 2011).

Minno-Bloom, Liza and Berkley Carnine. 'Towards Decolonisation and Settler Responsibility: Reflections on a Decade of Indigenous Solidarity Organizing'. *Counterpunch*, October 3, 2016. www. counterpunch.org/2016/10/03/towards-decolonization-and-settler-responsibility-reflections-on-a-decade-of-indigenous-solidarity-organizing.

Moraña, Mabel, Enrique Dussel and Carlos Jauregui, eds., *Coloniality At Large* (Duke University Press, 2008).

NYC Stands with Standing Rock Collective. 'Standing Rock Syllabus'. 2016. https://nycstandswith-standingrock.files.wordpress.com/2016/10/standingrocksyllabus7.pf.

Ramnath, Maia, 'An Anarchist Guide to Decolonisation', *Strike!* 15, March 2016.

Ross, Alexander Reid ed., *Grabbing Back: Essays Against the Global Land Grab* (AK Press, 2014).

Salaita, Stephen. *Inter/Nationalism: Decolonising Native America and Palestine* (University of Minnesota Press, 2016).

Smith, Linda Tuhiwai. *Decolonising Methodologies* (Zed Books, 2012).

TIDAL. 'Palestine Boycott Beyond.' http://decolonizethisplace.org/zines/161104_Palestine_BLM_Boycott_Arts_Zine_PrinterSpreads.pdf.

Tuck, Eve and K. Wayne Yang, 'Decolonisation is Not a Metaphor'. *Decolonisation: Indigeneity, Education & Society*, 1:1 (2012), pp. 1–40.

Waziyatawin and Michael Yellow Bird, eds., *For Indigenous Eyes Only: A Decolonisation Handbook* (School for Advanced Research Press, 2005).

2.3

RADICAL DISABILITY POLITICS

A. J. Withers and Liat Ben-Moshe (eds) with Lydia X. Z. Brown,
Loree Erickson, Rachel da Silva Gorman, Talila A. Lewis,
Lateef McLeod and Mia Mingus

Introduction

A.J. and Liat: Like all radical politics, disability politics are always in flux as social contexts shift. Unlike many strands of radical politics, however, disability issues have often been ignored or marginalised within (other) radical theory; and, disability oppression has, at times, been repeated or reinforced by many radical theories and praxis. There are many complex reasons for this, including ableism/disablism on the left as well as the tendency towards liberalism (and with it), white supremacy, patriarchy, heterosexism and cissism within mainstream disability organising. It is because of the diversity of thought about and approaches to disability that, as editors, we felt it would be most useful to demonstrate that diversity. When we were approached by the Handbook editors, therefore, we decided to showcase the voices of a variety of radical disability/social justice activists (or activist/scholars) residing in the US and Canada in a conversation rather than provide our own partial assessment of where these politics are at.

Before getting to the roundtable conversation, which took place in the spring of 2017, we want to provide some context regarding the history of radical disability politics and some of the ongoing debates within and between disabled communities. While there are many sites of contention within radical disability politics, we will focus here on disagreements around language, who can or is considered to be disabled and what the suggested paths to liberation might be.

Radical disability theory (emerging from and then influencing social movements) is often understood as emerging in the 1970s from the lived experience of disabled people in the Global North. It was a shift in thought that diverged from, at least to some degree, the hegemonic views of disability as tragic, individual and part of the medical domain. This hegemonic understanding is commonly called the individual model (Oliver 1996) or the medical model (Elliott and Dreer 2007; Withers 2012).

The 'radical' frameworks emerging at that time include the social model and the rights model of disability. The social model was primarily developed by physically disabled white Marxists, many of whom were living in nursing homes and other residential institutions. They theorised impairment (the physical condition that differs from the norm) as being separate from disability (the physical/access and social barriers imposed on impaired people)

(Oliver 1996; Thomas 2004). In the US, around the same time, the rights model was developed by groups of primarily physically disabled white people. Understanding disabled people as a minority group, as influenced by strands of civil rights movements, the disability rights framework emphasises social inclusion and legislative protections against discrimination (Fleischer and Zames 2001; Jaeger and Bowman 2005). This framework also birthed the independent living movement (DeJong 1979). Both models (social and rights) were later applied, with differing success, onto people who were psychiatrised or labelled as intellectually disabled.

For their time, both models marked radical paradigm shifts in some important ways. However, they have been thoroughly critiqued for imposing their model of physical disability on other groups (Beresford 2004; Nabbali 2009), being patriarchal (Morris 1992; O'Toole 2004) and maintaining white supremacy (Bell 2006; Ferri 2010). The disability rights model also critiques disabled people's lack of access to capitalism rather than capitalism itself. Rights frameworks in general can be described as assimilationist rather than radical (radical in the sense of transforming the root causes of oppression).

Other less discussed frameworks take a much deeper intersectional and transformative approach to understandings and organising around disability. Frames of thought and activism (such as disability justice, Berne 2015; or radical disability theory, Withers 2012)[1] stress the centrality of anticapitalist, intersectional and cross-disability organising and the necessity of valuing interdependence and the intrinsic value of disabled people (and everyone) outside of market labour economies. These frameworks also call for community-based, organic (rather than universal) accessibility, calling them 'collective access' (Berne 2015), 'access intimacy' (Mingus 2016) and 'radical access' (Withers 2012).[2] Community-based accessibility, however, is about meeting the needs of community members in intersectional ways. This includes, for example, creating 'safer spaces' that combat oppression, ensuring financial access, having child care, having active listeners, etc.

These transformative approaches also describe the social construction of disability (although what has been termed 'the radical model' stresses the significance of this much more). These intersectional radical frameworks call for people who are directly affected by particular injustices in intersecting ways (mostly people of colour, gender non-conforming people and those disabled and otherwise marginalised) to frame the demands and be the leadership.

Within all these approaches of disability organising and theory, there is no consensus with respect to a number of basic issues, as evident in the roundtable conversation later. These issues include how to call/name ourselves and our oppression. The terms 'disabled people', 'non-disabled people' and 'disablism' are preferred by those who emphasise the social model of disability (Oliver 1996) and are the dominant terms used in the UK (with, at times, the exception of 'people with learning difficulties'). Those who emphasise rights and inclusion tend to use 'people with disabilities', 'able-bodied' and 'ableism'. These are used in the US, which has a tradition based in the disability rights model (Goodley 2010). Those advocating for the use of 'people first language' (as in 'people with disabilities') do so because they want to emphasise personhood over disability status (Enns 1999), especially in relation to people with intellectual disabilities (referred to in the UK as people with learning differences), who aren't often counted as equal citizens/persons.

Proponents of 'disabled people' terminology argue that 'people first language' unnecessarily separates disability from the people who embody it (Sinclair 2013). They also critique the terms 'able-bodied' and 'ableism' for confusing ability (function or capacity) with disability (a socially imposed label) (Oliver 1996). Some also critique the term 'able-bodied' because it is physical disability-centric while, at the same time, erasing the actual capacities and capabilities of disabled people's bodies (Withers 2012). Some scholars, however, differentiate between ableism and disablism. 'Ableism' through this view is the imagined ideal of 'the perfect, species-typical and therefore essential and fully human' that we are all measured against (Campbell 2008: 44) and not only the oppression that disabled people experience. Crip is also a term that is used by some, especially those with physical disabilities or mobility impairments who are a part of disability culture. The term comes from the derogatory name 'cripple' but had been reclaimed to indicate a sense of community and pride in disability identity (Kafer 2013). Some also use 'crip' in a similar way to queer, as a systemic way of critiquing and resisting normativity (McRuer 2006). It is therefore a self-identification (and a form of critique as in the verb 'cripping') that is distinguishable from mainstream disability identities and rights (Sandahl 2003).

Who falls under the disability umbrella is also a site of contestation within radical disability theory and politics. Deaf (Lane 2008), trans (e.g. Withers 2013) and psychiatric consumer/survivor/ex-patients/mad people (Beresford 2000), to name a few, have all had a contentious relation to the category of disability. In the roundtable below, we use 'disabled' expansively to also refer to Deaf, mad and other communities and identifications.

Within radical disability organising and theory, there has been an important shift away from the single-issue politics of the 1970s towards intersectional organising. A number of the authors in the roundtable talk about the necessity of this because, as Fellows and Razack describe it, 'systems of oppression come into existence in and through one another' (1997: 335). Furthermore, as a number of the authors discuss, disability isn't a discrete identity; disabled people are also people of colour, queer people, women, trans-people and poor people. Single-issue organising misses this intersectional component, as the contributors reflect in regards to incarceration and institutionalisation, for example (for more on disability and incarceration writ large, see Ben-Moshe, Chapman and Carey 2014).

The mainstream disability rights movement/s is often nationally focused, if not a part of nation-building projects – legitimising the state as a just entity as certain disabled people are brought into the fold of full citizenship (Withers, 2012; Spade, 2015). However, a focus on disability justice also calls on radical activists to work transnationally (Gorman 2013). Disability organising should not simply stop at national borders, especially if we perceive a rights framework as insufficient. There are many reasons to work transnationally, including the reality that poverty and war are the dominant causes of disability globally (Erevelles 2011; Puar 2017). Both of these are fed or led by colonial and imperial programmes of the Global North. In addition, a decolonial framework that connects with Indigenous struggles would also critique the legitimacy of nation states (such as Canada and the US) to grant rights as a continuation of settler colonialism.

All of the roundtable contributors agree that social justice movements need to meaningfully include disability and this inclusion will make radical organising more meaningful and relevant. Lydia Brown argues that some radical politics use disability as 'a prop' and ableism within movements, including 'patterns of abuse, erasure, and gaslighting', is violence. In response to this exclusion, Loree Erickson calls for the recognition of disability 'as a necessary and generative part of our lives, movements and social organization. It opens up vital alternative ways of living and being'. Lateef McLeod calls on movements to recognise that 'we can all contribute to the ultimate goal of liberation'; this, according to Mia Mingus, '*necessarily* change[s] our work and our goals'. There are, however, different (although not mutually exclusive) approaches to end the oppression of disabled people. Talila Lewis calls for 'advocacy framework that cuts across identities and across movements' in relation to state violence, while Rachel Gorman argues that it is 'material change' that is needed.

There are many active debates around language, identity and paths to liberation. Rather than being a weakness, we hope that the below discussion demonstrates the vibrancy and utility of intersectional and variant disability politics. Radical disability politics, although often in flux and sometimes contested, can have significant contributions to make to broader radical organising and radical thought.

What is (or what could be) so 'radical' about disability, disability politics and/or disability organising (or Deaf culture/ neurodiversity/ madness/ crip or other related locations)? How can disability be utilised as a radical political position and for what purposes? How does it play out in your life, in your organising/activism?

Loree: When we recognise disability outside dominant frameworks not as a deficit, but as a necessary and generative part of our lives, movements and social organisation – vital alternative ways of living and being are opened. Radical disability politics and practices allow us to interrupt violent and damaging ideologies about bodies, difference, vulnerability and power. Interdependence, as an example, a way of being and caring with and for each other that operates from the belief that we all have needs, we all need each other and we can all provide care, centres and celebrates difference and needs in a way that interrupts the individualism, isolation, and normalisation so key to the operation of oppressive logics. Individualism, isolation and normalisation join together to ensure that we remain disconnected from ourselves and each other. One of the most insidious ways movements are undermined is through the propagation of cultures of undesirability which create policies, environments, structures and ideologies that tell marginalised people that we are disposable unless we are consumable (e.g. rehabilitative and prison labour, medical and social work professions). These cultures of undesirability manifest everywhere from immigration and reproductive policies to who is deemed sexy. We are told that we are 'less than' and/or 'too much' to encourage us to turn away from the very things about us that are different from the dominant culture and hold the most potential for doing things differently.

Mia: Radical disability politics are inherently radical because it asserts that disability and disabled people are important in our work for liberation. In an incredibly able-bodied supremacist and ableist society, challenging the deeply entrenched belief that disability and disabled people are not disposable, tragic and ugly burdens is radical – including within our movements for social justice. Social justice movements do not take place in a vacuum and many of our movements continue to support and actively perpetuate ableist notions and practices. No matter who you are working with, you are working with disabled people and/ or you are working with people who will become disabled. Disabled people are one of the largest oppressed groups on the planet and we are part of every single community; the potential for mass mobilisation is profound.

Even within radical politics, disability continues to push the envelope and challenge us in our thinking of what justice and liberation mean; what leadership means and what kinds of bodies and minds get to be understood and respected as leaders; what political 'work' is and how to reimagine 'work' and 'labour' that is not rooted in capitalism and ableism; and what 'healing' and 'sustainability' mean outside of able-bodied supremacy.

Radical disability political organising is liberatory, not only because of its political content, but even in the pragmatic and concrete work of simply bringing, for example, queer and trans-disabled people of colour together to organise. The cross-disability work it takes to navigate ableism and access to simply get disabled people in a room together is both a practice in resistance and resilience. It is both resisting against the world we don't want and simultaneously creating the world we long for. In a world that not only segregates disabled people from society at large, but also intentionally divides people with different kinds of disabilities, the work to build disabled organising and community is nothing short of revolutionary. To me, this is one of the most profound aspects of radical disability politics: it requires that we not only fight against the dangerous systems in place (e.g. white supremacy, misogyny, colonisation), but that we also have to – quite literally – build anew because the world we live in was never built for disabled people. The work it takes for disabled people to simply create home is a study in creativity and building alternatives.

I think the political knowledge being put forth by radical disability political work is cutting edge and gives us a political perspective that is deeply unique and that has so much to offer to our broader work for liberation. Much of this knowledge is coming directly out of disabled people's everyday lived experiences and survival. The work to fight ableism has implications for *everyone*, not only disabled people. The places where disability cuts across and is at times indistinguishable from age, gender, race, mortality, class, trauma or sexuality are ripe for cross-movement building work and has the potential to deepen and expand our understanding of oppression and violence like never before. How can we live in such a violent and traumatising world and *not* talk about disability and ableism?

Rachel: In many ways, the concept of 'disability' – as it is mobilised through law, state policy, education, workplaces and social services – marks the limit of inclusion. For example, when dealing with the law, people who are declared 'mentally incompetent' cannot make decisions about things that affect them, including the right to refuse potentially harmful and violent treatment. In education, students who are found to have 'an exceptionality' can be segregated for all or part of the day. Educational streaming, which is based on the premise of dis/ability (although it closely mirrors class and race inequality), determines whether a student can go on to further and higher education, and whether they can access work opportunities after graduating. So from the perspective of policy equity and formal rights, a radical political position would take disability as a start point, as it is often the mechanism of formal disqualification. At the same time, people who look or act in ways that are different from social norms may experience exclusion in family and community contexts. So a radical reimagining of family and community could start from the perspective of disability.

If we talk about embodied experiences of social inequality and social violence – for example, settler colonialism, racism, poverty, precarious work and gender-based violence – we find that one of the ways that people live in inequality is through differential outcomes in health and well-being (including access to healthcare itself). So if we are talking about any kind of radical politics, we are talking about people's embodied experience of inequality, and we may also be talking about disability and disablement.

Finally, disability discrimination through medicalisation and medical violence is a particular way in which disabled people and/or people labelled with disability experience violence through unnecessary, and/or coerced medical treatment. Reimagining healthcare and social services from a disability-positive perspective would be quite radical, and it would get us closer to having services that more people would find helpful and supportive and healing.

Talila: For myriad reasons, Black people, Indigenous and Native nations, people living with little or no income, womxn and LGBTransQI people are all disproportionately represented in the class of disability. And so, the state's systematic targeting of these communities means that disabled people are being targeted – more specifically, multiply marginalised disabled people are being targeted.

Too many move through politics, advocacy, life without acknowledging that it is impossible to address the perennial crisis of state violence without addressing society's systematic failure to provide equal access to education, resources, healthcare and justice to people with disabilities and people who are deaf. Indeed, the structural and systemic state violence perpetuated against communities of colour and educationally and economically disenfranchised communities has always been deeply rooted in *at least*, race, class *and* disability. As such, ending this violence has always required not only an understanding of disability and disability-based oppressions, but also a keen understanding of how disability exists and arises in, and interacts with marginalised individuals and communities. More to the point, ending this violence has always demanded that we understand how race-, class- and disability-based oppressions interact with one another; and precisely how seamlessly each is interwoven into social, political, economic and legal mores and codes – written and unwritten.

For example, many have begun important discussions about the grave harms our 'education' and criminal legal systems visit upon many marginalised communities. However, there is very little attention devoted to the injustices visited upon people with disabilities and deaf people by the same systems. And it is a very rare treasure to witness political or advocacy conversations about disabled or deaf people whose bodies are home to multiple marginalities. And yet, people with disabilities are particularly susceptible to unjust encounters with and in our education and criminal legal systems.

As an educator and attorney, I am horrified and heartbroken by just how little educational institutions, 'law enforcement,' lawyers, judges and carceral administrators understand about disability and care about disabled people.

Education institutions define education for some students as 'special' – cementing very early on, that fundamentally flawed understanding of education, disability and humanity: that such a thing as 'normal' exists. This enshrines ableism, audism and sanism into the very fabric of society and into the hearts and minds of the youngest among us. Similarly, our legal institutions profess to seek and mete out 'justice', but no marginalised or multiply marginalised community has *ever* experienced justice therein.

Radical disability politics means naming that justice demands that we abandon education and legal systems as we know them.

Lydia: Disability is about the body, perhaps more directly and explicitly than other categories of identity or experience. It's possible to theorise gender while attempting to work away from the body, for example, but you can't do that with disability. You cannot engage disability without confronting the body – the frail, vulnerable, traumatised, precarious, neurodivergent, unpredictable, unruly, unstable, incoherent or noncompliant body. (I discuss the 'body', but I mean a 'bodymind'. Mind and body are not separate. As an autistic person navigating anxiety and trauma, folks talk about my kind of disability as mental, meaning non-physical, but autism, anxiety and trauma are woven into my physicality and embodiment. I only avoid using the word 'bodymind' because it feels too academic.) Disabled, neurodivergent, mad folks are in every community and movement. Whether explicitly and intentionally political or not, our survival in a world literally out to kill us – particularly disabled folks targeted by multiple oppressions – is resistance and political.

We can't talk about any oppression – like racism, transmisogyny, classism and adultism – without addressing ableism. Ableism is both dependent on and necessary for every other form of oppression to exist. Attending to disability is radical because it allows us to grapple with our own and others' bodies in all their complexities. That means rethinking whose (and what types of) labour we consider valuable versus lesser, disposable and forgettable; whose performance of radicalness is praised versus inadequate or insufficient, whose traumas we centre versus dismiss or erase; whose bodily narratives we consider acceptable versus whose we consider threatening and undermining.

Lack of access, isolation and stigma – that is violence. Speaking out against state violence while ignoring the role ableism plays in its justification – that is violence. Recreating traumatising patterns of abuse, erasure and gaslighting (denying someone's experiences) in activism, community organising and social change movements (spaces supposedly committed to social justice) – that is violence. All of these violent patterns are tied to ableism, and depend on marginalising people targeted by multiple forms of oppression. White supremacy, rape culture and replication of capitalist hierarchies in organising all thrive on ableism. Silencing and marginalising people who can't access college don't know critical theory vocabulary, can't navigate toxic social dynamics and struggle to participate – these patterns depend on ableism. (I say that as someone who experiences many privileges while also experiencing many oppressions.)

We cannot do justice by anyone without working towards disability justice – there is no reproductive, economic, racial or transgender justice; no dismantling white supremacy or settler colonialism; without disability justice.

Lateef: Disability politics should be incorporated in the radical politics framework because the liberation of disabled people calls for the dismantling of the capitalist system. The reason why we need the abolishment of capitalism is because it forces people to conform to an able-bodied model to enter the workforce, to which some people with disabilities cannot do. This creates a divide between the disability community and the rest of the populace who are stigmatised for not being a worker in this economy. Specifically being someone with cerebral palsy, I have seen how our system of capitalism has relegated me to a marginalised position. As a black man who does not speak orally and communicates with an AAC (Augmentative and Alternative Communication) device, I have been read as less competent and autonomous than I actually am many times.

In the last few years, I have networked with other disability justice activists in the artist collective, Sins Invalid, in developing a disability justice platform. We are trying to develop an anticapitalist philosophy that centres on the experiences of LGBTQIA people of colour with disabilities. In our collective intersectionality, we hope to address a pathway for liberation for our communities. This is the same work that I also try to pursue in my graduate programme. My main reason for entering my graduate programme at California Institute for Integral Studies in the Anthropology and the Social Change Department is to find ways to challenge and hopefully dismantle systems of oppression such as white supremacy, patriarchy, sexism, homophobia and ableism that we face in this country. I feel fortunate to be dedicated to do this work in a department that is dedicated to an anticapitalist critique of society and the liberation of marginalised people in society. It is my aim to centre people with disabilities in my study and to start to devise ways in which we can incorporate disability justice in our cultural practices.

In what ways can non-disability-specific struggles for liberation from oppression be informed by a radical disability politics? What about vice versa – what are some affinities and also tensions or omissions between disability politics/culture/activism and other forms of activism or political movements?

Loree: Just as we cannot peel apart the layers of who we are and the multiple and contradictory meanings assigned to those differences and ways of being, we also cannot and should not organise without attention to our complex personhood (Gordon 1996). The ways that structural inequality targets us are always acting in concert. As Eli Clare (1999; 2003) so elegantly captures in much of his work, we rarely know what exactly it is that the gawkers are gawking at. How many of us have witnessed or felt the breaking apart that occurs with single-issue politics? Audre Lorde (1984) reminds us that we do not live single-issue lives; therefore, we must organise in a way that recognises our multiplicity and the interlocking nature of structural inequality. One only needs to look at the harm and violence inherent to the Prison Industrial Complex and the overrepresentation of disabled people, Black, Indigenous, people of colour, poor people and sex workers, which many in this roundtable have spoken to, to recognise that white supremacy, colonialism, disablism and capitalism are powerfully interconnected systems.

We can also look at what happens when disabled organisations organise from a rights-based approach and work towards integration, without transformation. We see organisations that specifically target the experience of incarceration within a given institution, for example, nursing homes or psychiatric wards (sites that absolutely need dismantling), without challenging institutional thinking and carceral logics that support the current flow of power. People are moved from one oppressive institution to another. We can also see what happens when mainstream disability rights organisations ignore the operation of white supremacy, erasing the experiences and expertise of racialised disabled people and simply achieve conditional improvements for those with relative privilege. Or, when antipoverty organising does not recognise the connections between inaccessibility, job discrimination and compulsory able-bodiedness in the life-crushing capitalist ideology of productivity above all else. Disability, rather than limiting our movements, adds necessary texture and complexity. Radical disability organising recognises that all of our liberation is connected and keeps us, and our movements, messy and whole – moving together.

Mia: I think many of our movements are grappling with this very question. Especially as more and more disabled people disclose their disabilities and as more and more activists and organisers become disabled or embrace their disabilities, they have always had, but never felt comfortable enough to claim. Disabled people are already in social justice movements and often we have learned to individualise and depoliticise our disabled identities and experiences because of how effective ableism continues to be. Because the stigma around disability is so incredibly intense, many people who are disabled do not identify as disabled. This is especially true for those of us who have multiple oppressed identities because it can be impossible to identify as disabled when your survival depends on you denying it.

As the radical disability political community grows and more and more disabled people of multiple oppressed identities refuse to leave our disabilities at the door, our political movements will be forced to contend with their histories of exclusion, stigma and avoidance. To me, it is vital that politically disabled people, not only descriptively disabled people, be at the centre of this shift to be informed by radical disability politics.

It is important to remember that many movements may already be doing 'radical disability work', but not calling it as such and are more well versed in 'justice' than 'disability'. Work with poor communities and/or addressing domestic violence within immigrant communities and/or prison abolition work are already very much at the intersection of radical disability politics, given that poverty, violence, trauma and prisons are key sites in not only *how* people become disabled, but also where so many disabled people are located. So, for many of these movements what is lacking is a strong analysis and understanding of disability, ableism and able-bodied supremacy, as well as the practice of access and access intimacy.

I think about the example of healing justice work and how there is a growing number of healers within that work who understand that there is no liberatory healing work without a deep and historical understanding of how healing, cure and health have been used as weapons against so many of our communities, including disabled communities, and how ableism is a key part of the intersectional core of this.

In much of the cross-movement and cross-community works I have been part of, there are so many similarities that different communities and movements share that can bring us together. The work of interdependence, for example, has been crucial to, not only disability, but also building queer chosen family or kinship networks for poor and/or immigrant and/ or communities of colour to survive and has informed our organising.

I think one of the main tensions in all of this is the need for practice. Even though disabled people are everywhere, disability is so segregated and individualised that many people either don't have experience with disabled people or are with the diversity of disability experiences out there; or they also may not understand their experiences as 'disabled experiences' because of how absolute the stigma surrounding disability is and how oblivious their able-bodied privilege makes them.

Lateef: Black liberation can definitely be informed by a radical disability politics. Organisations like Black Lives Matter can definitely implement a disability justice framework in their practices. Especially because a good portion of state violence and murder against people of colour are committed on people with disabilities. Emmitt Thrower, working with my friend, Leroy Moore, has documented this several times and has even wrote a documentary about the matter entitled *Where Is Hope: The Art of Murder* (2015). To fully address this attack on our community, organisations like Black Lives Matter need to have people with disabilities in their membership and leadership to fully advocate for the victims. See, for example, the statement from the Harriet Tubman Collective regarding 'The Vision for Black Lives' platform statement and its omission and dismissal of disability (Harriet Tubman Collective, 2016). Likewise, there should be more networking and collaboration between disability organisations and people of colour organisations to deal with the state oppression that we experience. An example of this is when I was a part of a Sins Invalid's disability justice tutorial presented to the Brown Boi Project, which is a social justice organisation dedicated to politicising and organising LGBTQIA people of colour in the Bay Area with their headquarters located in Oakland. That built a good working relationship between the organisations with the Brown Boi Project learning strategies of how to organise in the disability community.

There still needs to be more education about how the disability identity is a politicised identity in African American community. Many people see disability as an individual problem and not connected to a larger historical struggle. If people can make the connection of how black people with disabilities contributed to the black liberation struggle in the past, it can make a stronger argument about how temporarily able-bodied people and people who have disabilities can come together in the African American community to work for all of our liberation. However, from my perspective, this can only come about if African Americans in the social justice arena get rid of some of their fear and ignorance around people with disabilities and disability issues. As with all communities under capitalism, there is some shame and uneasiness fellowship with people who do not easily pair up to the ableist image of what a 'typical' human is pictured to be. Only with honest dialogue within our community can resolve these rifts and fears and work together for the liberation that we all need to acquire.

Talila: Important and necessary conversations on race and justice cannot be fully had without disability justice at their centre. People of colour with disabilities are hardest hit by the overlapping structural inequality that exists within all of our institutions. We, therefore, cannot avoid the fact that our communities experience common and overlapping oppressions that require an advocacy framework that cuts across identities and across movements.

Common and interrelated struggles and liberation goals are just two of the reasons why marginalised communities should be in constant communication and solidarity. For instance, state-imposed and sanctioned violence including forced familial separation, enslavement, genocide, mass incarceration, institutionalisation, theft of resources and criminalisation of existence is not new to marginalised communities in the US. Moreover, each of these communities has been engaged in near-constant struggle against oppressive and violent systems. As such, Black, Latinx, Indigenous, LGBTransQI and Disabled communities, among others, should be strategising and mobilising together because each community has unique perspectives and contributions to continue to make to the freedom struggle.

Mia's depiction of communities unknowingly being already deep in the trenches of radical disability justice work is so apt. Take mass incarceration, for instance. Disabled people and advocates/attorneys have long since battled otherising, criminalisation and violence that invite institutionalisation, forced labour, forced sterilisation and medical procedures, and abuse of disabled people in 'institutions'. So too have other disenfranchised communities been long engaged in this same struggle – under the guise of 'prison abolition' – where we find yet another brand of 'institution' swallowing up whole communities of disabled people, committing all manner of violence against them, and creating disabilities in non-disabled individuals en masse. It bears noting that these individuals are disproportionately people of colour and otherwise marginalised individuals.

So much of most marginalised communities' historic and present work regarding deinstitutionalisation, justice and healing already is steeped in the creation of innovative and transformative policies and practices. Often however, some of the staunchest race, trans, economic, immigration justice advocates unintentionally further disability-based oppressions because of their failure to understand what I term 'critical intersectionality' and to foreground disability justice.

This brings me to why it is so important to approach our advocacy in a more holistic way – to understand disability justice as quintessential to reproductive, economic, racial and transgender justice, as Lydia noted. We will never dismantle any oppressive institutions if advocates, community builders and others who are in struggle do not name, analyse and dismantle ableism. Ableism undergirds, depends upon and reifies every other oppression. So, we will never deconstruct *white supremacist capitalist cisheteropatriarchal imperialism* if we are not constantly working to unpack our own privileges around ableism, audism and other disability-based oppressions. Ironically, those who attempt to dismantle oppressive systems without acknowledging and unpacking these disability-centric privileges are contributing to violence and oppression within their own communities and society writ large.

We must create disability solidarity within every movement, such that disability rights organisations are working to advance intersectional justice, and non-disability rights civil rights organisations are showing up for disability justice. Policy-wise, the same is true. When will we see disability-positive and race-responsive education and legal policies? When will education institutions engage in trauma-informed practices that centre the whole humanity of our youth? When will we see actual innocence legislation that is disability-responsive, requiring automatic review or overturning of convictions of Deaf or disabled individuals who had absolutely no access to police, legal counsel or the court?

Until we can say *now* to these and many similar questions, we will continue to see shameful injustice within education and criminal legal systems; and violence, poverty and mass incarceration will continue to live here.

Lydia: As Mia Mingus discussed earlier, movements and work tackling disability already exist, whether or not they're using the language of disability justice. But, as Talila Lewis reminds us, we desperately need our movements to be cross-identity and cross-community, because those of us at the intersections (particularly Black, Brown, Latinx, Indigenous or People of Colour; Queer, Trans, Asexual or Intersex disabled and deaf folks) are most targeted by interpersonal and state violence.

I often notice (usually non-disabled) folks in policy work talking about the crisis of mass incarceration impacting folks with psychosocial disabilities/mental illnesses. After noting disproportionate representation, they'll insist that because prisons aren't the right place, we need to build psychiatric treatment facilities – completely missing the connection: institutionalisation is incarceration. Psychiatric institutions and prisons exist for surveillance and control, and engender the same violence.

Similarly, with increased reporting of mass shootings, and the usual rhetoric about 'mentally unstable' perpetrators (especially when they are white and non-Muslim, making it impossible to Other them directly through white supremacy or Islamoracism), even people on the left often blame gun violence on mental disability, neurodivergence or madness. They take an issue about violence and impunity for similar acts (like police gun violence against Black, Latinx and Indigenous disabled and deaf folks), and blame disability for it. Ableism uses disability as a convenient tool for othering – ableism says that if we fix the 'pathology', we excise the problem without having to grapple with racism, misogyny or police.

In reproductive justice, disability should be central, but is usually only a prop. If the narrative is that pregnant people need abortion access in case of disabled foetuses; that the tragedy of the Zika virus and Flint, Michigan's lead-poisoned water lies in the possibility of causing new disabilities; that disabled people are incapable of sexual consent, but neither capable of desire nor of being desired; that disabled people are automatically unfit to parent; that it's better to be dead than disabled … then we are failing. Reproductive justice must mean disability *justice*, honouring our bodies as they are and not mourning or fearing the shadows of undesirable, disposable bodies.

As Loree mentions, it is equally imperative for disability movements to examine how we fail. I am often the only person of colour in a disability-related event, and that's a problem. I'm a fairly class-privileged, college-educated, light-complexioned East Asian from a nearly all-white family. None of that makes me a less genuine person of colour, but it does mean that white supremacy considers me more palatable, less scary and closer to whiteness – which makes white people eager to tokenise me for those reasons. This reality is, however, only part of a much broader white supremacy problem.

When resourced disability organisations (usually white-led) discuss police violence, they focus on stories of white people like Robert Ethan Saylor or Kayden Clark while ignoring or only mentioning disabled or deaf Black, Brown, Latinx, Indigenous or other People of Colour killed by police. I often only notice discussion of race, disability and other identities of folks like Tanisha Anderson, Korryn Gaines, Alfred Olango, Natasha McKenna, Kajieme Powell, Tawon Boyd, John Williams, Terence Crutcher, Chieu Di Thi Vo, Mohammad Usman Chaudhry, Reginald Thomas, Michael Cho or Stephon Watts (and many others) when among other disabled and deaf people of colour. And despite my relative privilege, I am still threatened when I dare speak in the face of erasure. This violence informs my work constantly.

We as disabled folks can and should talk about how every social movement erases disability and ableism, but we have to clean our own house too. Disability justice means we have to hold ourselves accountable – liberation happens when we all get free.

Rachel: I don't know about radical disability politics per se, but having disability in my life – in my own life, and in the lives of people in my close community – has taught me a lot about resilience and long-term thinking. From my own involvement in liberation struggles in the North American context, I see that we think only in the short term, and immediate, and that we haven't been able to sustain communities in struggle over the long term. Part of the consequence of that is that we are missing even the most short-term history – we don't build on what happened twenty, ten or even five years ago.

People in my life who I met in disability organising eighteen years ago are still in my life – and while we are more or less dejected about the state of the world and disability politics, we have learned a lot from each other about long-term strategies for individual and collective survival. We have also learned that symbolic rights are no substitute for material change – state disability supports are far too low. From loved ones who have been accessing these supports over the long term, I have learned that the stress is cumulative – the stress of not quite making ends meet, the stress of constant administrative harassment and the stress of random programme cuts all have real impacts on people's long-term health.

If we are going to make radical change in the Canadian context, broader non-Indigenous social movements have to learn how to be in it for the long haul. Many Indigenous and Black organisers, and organisers in many national contexts in Africa, Asia and Latin America know this already.

How does/can disability (again, writ large, including Deaf culture/neurodiversity/madness/ crip, etc.) affect the goals but also the *form* of radical politics? How does the presence or absence of disability from radical policies transform the ways we organise, strategise and push for liberation?

Lateef: Disability can redirect our radical politics focus to where we fight and advocate for a society where all our identities are fully accepted. Radical politics will not advocate for the lives of people with disabilities until people with disabilities get involved with radical politics. We as radical scholars with disabilities have to direct the conversation among our colleagues on imagining the society where people with disabilities can prosper. Our able-bodied colleagues will not work on our liberation without us, only we can develop the way to our freedom.

There has been a disturbing trend where temporarily abled people decide policies for people who have disabilities without talking to us to find out what we want. This follows the culture troupe that is still prevalent in society that people who have disabilities are incompetent and needs a temporarily able-bodied person to do most things for us. We do not need able-bodied saviours to rescue us from our situations, but allies that can work with us to accomplish the goals for our community. We need to refuse and dismantle these cultural tropes and develop policies to change society to one where our bodies and contributions are valued properly. We need temporarily able-bodied people to see that the liberation of people with disabilities is in their best interest as well. So we have to work for liberation together, which means that all the ways that we organise and strategise for our liberation must be accessible and fully welcoming to those of us with disabilities. What I mean is that not all of us can go in the street and protest, but we can all contribute to the ultimate goal of liberation in other ways.

Talila: In arguing for solidarity, many people like to note that 'disability is the only protected class that everyone will join at some point in life'. While this is true, it misunderstands the foundational underpinning of collective liberation – namely that you need not identify with an oppressed community to fight to dismantle systems that impose violence against them; and that all of our liberation is inextricably linked to the next person's. We all have a vested interest in ensuring equal and adequate protections for all people *not* because we are like them or because our unborn child may be like them. We have an interest in dismantling oppressions and systems of oppression because we exist.

I push back on the notion that the inclusion of disability is something 'radical'. It should not be considered radical to assert that we should consider disability in all things – all actions, all systems, all reforms, all dismantling. The fact that this framework is considered 'radical' illustrates precisely how radical (i.e. extensive, total, far-reaching, complete, exhaustive, etc.)

ableism is in our society. So central is ableism that the very assertion of the need to dismantle ableism often is met with untold vitriol – even within 'social justice' and 'deaf/disability rights' spaces. Several of the authors have made mention of this phenomenon.

All the contributors discuss dreaming, reimagining and reclaiming. These are part and parcel of radical politics and disability justice. That is why this conversation is so important.

Disability justice allows us to re-envision the world – to remind people that like race, class and crime, disability is a social construct. Disability justice reminds all of us that there never has been and never will be a 'normal'. Disability justice allows us to define education and justice; decriminalise disability; disarm the police; divert all people away from jails, prisons, institutions; deinstitutionalise those who are presently trapped in the violent, unforgiving clutch of our institutions because society failed to provide meaningful support in the first instance. Disability justice is deliverance, healing, love, liberation. Justice.

Lydia: Toxic 'call-out' culture (as the call-out tactic is so often co-opted and misused by people with privilege and power) and privileged, fragile critiques of more marginal-ised people's rightful anger (leading to silencing and further outcasting); the hierarchy of activism replicated from capitalism; and activist burnout and suicides – these are disability problems. Addressing disability and ableism means addressing classism, racism and (trans) misogyny. We've got to do the hard work to make space for harsh, emotional call-outs – especially, as Ashleigh Shackelford (2016) reminds us, by those often prevented from express-ing themselves – *and* practice compassionate accountability that rejects instant disposability (which also has its most pernicious effects on the most marginalised, as Porpentine reminds us) and punitive criminal justice mentality (Heartscape 2015). We've got to affirm devalued, erased and minimised labour, and recognise that our labour, whatever it is, is necessary, radical and militant – just as being in the streets, testifying at a hearing, presenting at a conference or leading an organisation (Anderson et al. 2014). As my friend Mikael Lee con-stantly reminds us, crip survival from bed is also resistance.

We've got to resist the binary of abused/abuser, and recognise that we all have capacity to harm. We're all learning and growing. Forgetting or not knowing doesn't excuse harm but shouldn't necessarily mean further isolation and disposability either. We've got to recognise all contributions and multiple tactics as vital. This means not attacking the person who found solace and empowerment the first time they discovered academic words that matched their life experiences, but no longer privileging their language and access over the work done by folks who've never had the privilege of formal education either. It means being careful to recognise who our movements and communities welcome and who those same movements and communities exclude, because it's always a question of access. Centring disability is critical to sustaining our movements and addressing our own systemic problems, just as anti-ableism is necessary to end all oppression. Talila has it precisely – refusing to address ableism is complicity in oppression.

Mia: There is no liberation without disabled people. There is no collective justice if it does not take into account the needs and realities of people with disabilities. I don't know how a disability analysis could *not* inform a radical politic. As someone who was disabled since I was an infant and never was able-bodied, I have supported countless people who be-come disabled as adults. Disability changes their lives – how could it not? So too, this is true for radical politics. The literal presence (either in person or skyping someone into a meeting) of disability and disabled people *necessarily* change our work and our goals because disabled people are constantly navigating a world that does not want us to be part of it. The presence of disability forces able-bodied people to confront their own internalised ableism whether it is fears about mortality and dependence, or ugliness and undesirability, or unproductiveness and pace, or simply need and interdependence. And this is true on both an individual and collective level for communities, movements, countries and entire regions of the world. Organisers would need to rethink their protests and make them more accessible, change their goals to better reflect 'all queer people' or 'all women', create conference schedules and spaces that allow for many different kinds of bodies, energy levels and learning styles.

A true integration of radical disability politics requires us to move slower and to create more accessible language and to not turn away from the complex, often very challenging, reality of disability within an ableist world. It is not a coincidence that just as disabled people have been (and continue to be) denied access to the public sphere (e.g. employment, education, community), we have also been denied access to political movements and communities. If radical communities are serious about their commitment to a radical disability politic, then they must be committed to the cultural, interpersonal and systemic changes needed to fight and end ableism. As with any solidarity work, it requires a full commitment not only in words, but in deeds as well, and not only when it is convenient. This, of course, changes, not only your goals, but who you are as well because any true solidarity is simply another word for love.

Rachel: One striking and enduring absence of disability in radical organising, including disability organising, is the absence of people labelled with intellectual disability. Often, parents of labelled people stand in for people labelled with intellectual disability – even when they are adults – both in Canada and internationally. Even with the recent emergence of the neurodiversity movement, the focus has been on arguing that people labelled with autism do not have an intellectual disability. If disability movements centred people labelled with intellectual disability, we might finally be able to take on the legal and social domination of people who have been declared incompetent – including children, people labelled with certain mental health conditions and people labelled with intellectual disabilities. We would also have the opportunity to imagine more meaningful relations of community interdependence, and to reimagine deinstitutionalisation so that it includes people living in group homes, and half-way and rooming houses, as well as psychiatric and long-term care facilities, and prisons.

Loree: A key component to radical politics is disruption of the status quo, of the taken for granted organisation of things that benefits those with relative power and privilege. Disability is disruptive. It forces us to rethink everything and to keep revisiting and rethinking because bodies and needs are always changing. As Mia discussed earlier, disability changes us, radicalism changes us. One really important and powerful change that disability can offer, particularly when politicised, is the opportunity to listen to our bodies and centre our needs. Dominant ideologies all push us towards ignoring or covering over the very things about us that make us different from the status quo. Needs not recognised as typical are seen as limitations and tragedies rather than as possibilities.

As someone who has a body that needs other bodies to help me get out of bed, go to the bathroom, organise my glittery things, eat and so much more has changed me and how I think about care, bodies and needs. Also as someone who because of various structural limitations (inadequate state funding, homophobia, etc.) has gotten my care needs met through a collective of people from the various communities which I am a part of I am reminded on a daily basis of how powerfully connected community building and care are and how necessary it is to build relationship building and needs into the justice work we are doing.

Needs are actually quite central to most organising, after all the goal of most organising is to envision and bring into being a world where all of our collective needs are met. And yet, outside disability organising and theorising needs are rarely explicitly acknowledged or discussed. One of the most useful gifts radical disability organising offers is practice and skill in thinking about and incorporating needs and care into everything we do. A thread running through many of the contributions is the overwhelming presence of isolation, silencing and divisiveness in our movements. We need to build into our organising care and relationship building. This can include changing the pace of our organising so that we make sure to build in time and resources for self and collective care so that our movements are sustainable as well as devoting resources to creating immersive accessibility that leaves no one behind. Radical accessibility is crucial to creating movements where we move together.

Notes

1 While these are the·published texts, both frames emerged out of ongoing, collective activism in the US and Canada that began years earlier and cannot be attributed to a single author.
2 Universal accessibility, coming from universal design, creates a design standard for environments and products that can be used by all people to the greatest extent possible (North Carolina State University College of Design; see Hamraie (2017) for elaboration and critiques).

References

Anderson, P., K. U. Barrett, E. Dixon, R. Garrido, E. Kane, B. Nancherla, D. Narichania, S. Narasimhan, A. Rabiyah, and M. Richart, '26 ways to be in the struggle beyond the streets', *Tikkun*, December, 2014, accessed July 3, 2017, www.tikkun.org/tikkundaily/2014/12/18/26-ways-to-be-in-the-struggle-for-liberation-beyond-the-streets/.

Bell, C., 'Introducing white disability studies: A modest proposal', in L. J. Davis (ed.), *The Disability Studies Reader* (New York: Routledge, 2nd ed., 2006), 275–282.

Ben-Moshe, L., C. Chapman, and A. C. Carey, (eds.), *Disability Incarcerated: Imprisonment and Disability in the United States and Canada* (New York: Palgrave Macmillan, 2014).

Beresford, P., 'Madness, distress, research and a social model', in C. Barnes and G. Mercer, (eds.), *Implementing the Social Model of Disability: Theory and Research* (Leeds: The Disability Press, 2004), 208–222.

Beresford, P., 'What have madness and psychiatric system survivors got to do with disability and disability studies?', *Disability & Society* 15:1 (2000), 167–172.

Berne, P., 'Disability justice – a working draft', *Sins Invalid* (2015). Retrieved June 15, 2017, sinsinvalid.org/blog/disability-justice-a-working-draft-by-patty-berne.

Campbell, F. A. K., 'Exploring internalized ableism using critical race theory', *Disability & Society* 23:2 (2008), 151–162.

Clare, E., *Exile and Pride: Disability Queerness and Liberation.* (Cambridge, MA: South End Press, 1999.)

Clare, E., 'Gawking, gaping, staring', *GLQ: A Journal of Lesbian and Gay Studies* 9:1–2 (2003), 257–261.

DeJong, G., 'Independent living: From social movement to analytic paradigm', *Archives of Physical Medicine and Rehabilitation* 60:10 (1979), 435–446.

Elliott, T.R. and Dreer, L., 'Disability', in: S. Ayers, A. Baum, C. McManus, S. Newman, K. Wallston, J. Weinman, and R. West (eds.), *Cambridge Handbook of Psychology, Health and Medicine* (Cambridge: Cambridge University Press, 2007), 80–84.

Enns, R., *A Voice Unheard: The Latimer Case and People with Disabilities.* (Black Point: Fernwood, 1999).

Erevelles, N., *Disability and Difference in Global Contexts: Enabling a Transformative Body Politic* (New York: Palgrave Macmillan, 2011).

Fellows, M. L. and S. Razack, 'The race to innocence: Confronting hierarchical relations among women', *Journal of Gender, Race and Justice* 1 (1997), 335–352.

Ferri, B. A., 'A dialogue we've yet to have: Race and disability studies', in C. Dudley-Marling and A. Gurn (eds.), *The Myth of the Normal Curve* (New York: Peter Lang, 2010), 139–150.

Fleischer, D.Z. and F. Zames, *Disability Rights Movement: From Charity to Confrontation* (Philadelphia: Temple University Press, 2001).

Goodley, D., *Disability Studies: An Interdisciplinary Introduction.* (Los Angeles: SAGE, 2010).

Gordon, A., *Ghostly Matters: Haunting and the Sociological Imagination.* (Minneapolis: University of Minnesota Press, 1996).

Gorman, R., 'Mad nation?: Thinking through race, class and mad identity politics', in B.A. LeFrançois, R. Menzies, and G. Reaume (eds.), *Mad Matters: A Critical Reader in Canadian Mad Studies* (Toronto: Canadian Scholars' Press, 2013), 269–280.

Hamraie, A., *Building Access: Universal Design and the Politics of Disability* (Winnipeg: University of Minnesota Press, 2017).

The Harriet Tubman Collective, 'Disability solidarity: Completing the 'vision for Black lives'', 2016, retrieved June 15, 2017 from: harriettubmancollective.tumblr.com/post/150072319030/htcvision4blacklives.

Heartscape, P. C., 'Hot allostatic load', *The New Inquiry* (11 May 2015) retrieved May 12, 2017 from: thenewinquiry.com/essays/hot-allostatic-load/.

Jaeger, P.T. and C. A. Bowman, *Understanding Disability: Inclusion, Access, Diversity, and Civil Rights* (Westpoint, CT: Praeger, 2005).

Kafer, A., *Feminist, Queer, Crip.* (Bloomington: Indiana University Press, 2013).

Lane, H., 'Do Deaf people have a disability', in H. L. Bauman (ed.), *Open Your Eyes: Deaf Studies Talking* (Minneapolis: University of Minnesota Press, 2008), 277–292.

Lorde, A., *Sister Outsider* (Berkeley: The Crossing Press, 1984).

McRuer, R., *Crip Theory: Cultural Signs of Queerness and Disability* (New York: NYU Press, 2006).

Mingus, M., *Leaving Evidence* (2016). Accessed September 28, 2017, leavingevidence.wordpress.com.

Morris, J., 'Personal and political: A feminist perspective on researching physical disability', *Disability, Handicap & Society* 7:2 (1992), 157–166.

Nabbali, E. M., 'A 'mad' critique of the social model of disability', *The International Journal of Diversity in Organizations, Communities and Nations* 9:4 (2009): 1–12.

Oliver, M., *Understanding Disability: From Theory to Practice* (New York: St. Martin's Press, 1996).

O'Toole, C. J., 'The sexist inheritance of the disability movement', in B. G. Smith and B. Hutchison (eds.), *Gendering Disability* (New Brunswick: Rutgers University Press, 2004), 294–300.

Puar, J. K., *The Right to Maim: Debility, Capacity, Disability* (Dhuram: Duke University Press, 2017).

Sandahl, C., 'Queering the crip or cripping the queer?: Intersections of queer and crip identities in solo autobiographical performance', *GLQ: A Journal of Lesbian and Gay Studies* 9:1 (2003), 25–56.

Shackelford, A., ''Call out culture' and effectiveness: On accountability, dragging your faves, and transformative growth', *Wear Your Voice* (April 28 2016) Retrieved June 5, 2017 wearyourvoicemag.com/more/politics/call-culture-effectiveness-accountability-dragging-faves-transformative-growth.

Sinclair, J., 'Why I dislike 'person first' language', *Autonomy, the Critical Journal of Interdisciplinary Autism Studies* 1:2 (2013), n.p.

Spade, D., *Normal Life: Administrative Violence, Critical Trans Politics, and the Limits of Law* (Dhuram: Duke University Press, 2015).

Thomas, C., 'Disability and impairment', in J. Swain, S. French, C. Barnes, and C. Thomas (eds.), *Disabling Barriers, Enabling Environments*, (London: SAGE, 2nd ed., 2004), 21–27.

Where is Hope - The Art of Murder. [Film]. E.H. Thrower. dir. (New York: Wabi Sabi Productions Inc., 2015).

Withers, A. J., *Disability Politics and Theory* (Black Point: Fernwood, 2012).

Withers, A. J., 'Disabling trans: political implications and possibilities of constructions of trans as a disability' (Masters major research paper, York University, 2013), retrieved August 17, 2017 from stillmyrevolution.files.wordpress.com/2015/05/withers-fully-completed-mrp-doccument.pdf.

2.4

MIGRANT SOLIDARITY IN POSTCOLONIAL EUROPE

Challenging Borders, Creating Mobile Commons

Claire English, Margherita Grazioli and Martina Martignoni

Introduction

Today, migration is one of the main concerns of global politics: social inequality, war and climate change are producing everyday people with the need (or the will) to move; globalisation and associated forms of communication have created the space for imagining a smaller and nearer world, where moving and migrating can and must be possible for everybody. Yet, the richest countries of the world are 'protecting' their borders, impeding freedom of movement of those who, coming from poorer countries, want to enter. In recent years, Europe and its (fluctuating) borders have come under particular scrutiny because of the intensity of the flux of migrants forced to travel through 'illegal' and unsafe routes. Can migrant solidarity as it is currently organised confront these issues, as part of a radical politics? How can migrant solidarity activism inform political theory? In this chapter, we will explore some possible answers to these questions.

Various forms of activism have proliferated in response to the levels of poverty and conflict at the borders of Europe and in favour of the right to move freely between nation states. Activists have devised various kinds of support for people on the move: camping together at the borders; providing food, shelter and protection from hostile forces; appealing to European institutions to let people move freely; 'illegally' crossing the borders alongside migrants; engaging in various forms of collective organising; making European peoples aware of migrants' situation through videos, articles, pictures, public speeches, theatre, art and many other forms of resistance.[1] Activists who support freedom of movement are heterogeneous and come from different political traditions – from anarchism to Catholicism; also, struggles around borders are multiplying and shifting, frequently because of the intrinsic mobility of the conflict. This makes it impossible to speak of one movement or one struggle around migration(s) in Europe. To the extent that it has the power to put in tension any ideological attitude to politics and to force activists to rethink what a political act is, the question of migrant politics is surely a peculiar one – as we will discuss in this chapter. This is, in our view, the radical impact of migration on activism and politics, and it is the starting point for our research about what the radical politics of migrant solidarity can look like.

The chapter begins by looking at some of the theoretical influences that underscore radical migrant solidarity projects: the origins and foci of postcolonial theory; an approach to migrations as autonomous and questions regarding difference and hybridity. We then look at an example, Calais Migrant Solidarity, and the tensions that emerge within these kinds of organising spaces. One tension concerns the limits of solidarity and what sets the work of transnational migrant solidarity collectives apart from the work of the charitable border-workers; another is the question of what kind of politics activists want to enact when engaging in solidarity practices with migrants: 'anticipatory politics' and the 'mobile commons' will be introduced here as possible answers to this tension. Finally, we introduce elements for thinking beyond solidarity and towards a political theory of migrants' everyday practices. In particular, critiquing human rights and citizenship discourses, we look instead for an entry point for a radical theory of solidarity as an everyday practice and existential modality.

Migrations in Postcoloniality

Migrant solidarity projects as a set of experiments in social relations are just one of many similar attempts to re-express the activist organisational form as one that can incorporate strategies militating against the legacies of colonialism and subsequent issues of racism and power imbalances. Transnational migrant solidarity organisations represent many different people from many different backgrounds and identities – these groups create a certain kind of uneven space in which to organise collectively. The following sections will look at the theories that underpin the possibility for solidarity between different subjectivities when trying to create, maintain or defend the political space for mobility together.

The potential radicality and impact of migrant solidarity theories and practices cannot be fully comprehended today without considering that the geographical and historical spaces claiming ownerships of these forms of politics – those from European nations, in particular – are strongly influenced by postcoloniality. This is a complex term with a number of dimensions: first, it refers to the importance of the colonial period and its legacies in building the western world, both materially and perceptually. Second, it describes the fundamental role that anticolonial struggles – and anti-Apartheid and antiracist struggles – play in exploding the inequalities of colonial and racist systems and, in doing so, in opening up global perspectives on history and the present from places that have been labelled as 'peripheral'. Third, postcoloniality highlights the contemporary postcolonial composition of the former metropoles – the geographical spaces of the coloniser countries, in opposition to the colonies themselves – and therefore the active role of migrants in creating them.

Postcoloniality can be defined as the reproduction and diffusion of a 'protean space', peculiar to colonial societies, inside the former metropolitan space (Fanon, 1961): a heterogeneous social space characterised by the coexistence on the same territory of different ways of production, different work regimes and different historical temporalities. The global diffusion and the eruption of this heterogeneous space, typical of colonial spaces, both inside and outside the western world, allows us to define our present as *postcolonial* (Mezzadra, 2008). We can also imagine the postcolonial as the implosion of geographical, historical and political distances inside the same space. Elements once distant and separate collapse into the same time-space; this creates heterogeneity and so challenges the boundaries of (supposed) homogenous nation states.

The movement of people across borders is at the centre of this transformation. The heterogeneity stemming from migrations poses challenges to politics and in particular to radical politics, inviting questions about the ways that difference should be understood and organised and how different subjects come to act and struggle together. The issues posed by postcolonial time – the movement of people across borders and the creation of heterogeneity – define the very radicality of politics around migrations, in particular autonomous politics involving migrants and non-migrants. But how do migrant solidarity activists interpret this distinction and how, in particular, do they understand migrants' subjectivities and the role of migrations inside social movements? The next section describes the theoretical approach to migrations based on and nurtured by activists' experience.

Autonomy of Migration

Migrant solidarity involves, among many other activities, facilitating the crossing of borders, investigating safe 'illegal' routes, the creation of transnational networks, and the constant and daily work of defying migration policies that attempt to curtail mobility. Crossing boundaries entails moving them, which means both reshaping the forms of control through borders and moving borders to create more differentiations inside a space. Borders today, and especially the borders of the European Union and the US, have to be thought of, first of all, as crossed borders, as a relation between the autonomous mobility of people and state control. Their nature is defined by the crossing of mobile people who, violating them, or crossing them 'illegally', continuously move and reshape borders. Borders are, by definition, porous and because of that they are responsive to the migrations of people (Papadopoulos et al., 2008: 162). In fact, one can say that borders are shaped by this response to the autonomous movements of people and then reordered and reshaped as migratory flows vary in intensity and routes change in geographical location or mode of transport. Borders, therefore, have to be thought as flexible tools because they change 'making a world rather than dividing an already-made world' (Mezzadra and Neilson, 2013: 59).

People migrating through the 'Balkan route' in the summer of 2015 illustrated this process. Powerful images clearly showed thousands of people walking from Budapest to Vienna on the highway actively defying – and reconstructing – the border (and its controls) in their way. Migrant solidarity strengthens the autonomous capacity of people on the move, by materially helping people sustain themselves by their self-organisation. The achievement and the reproduction of the objective work through infrastructures of support are used and combined to foster mobility (Larkin, 2013; Papadopoulos and Tsianos, 2013; Papadopoulos, 2014): cars, mobile phones, information on alternative routes, food, clothes, shelters, etc. Ventimiglia, Calais and many other cities and villages across Europe have also witnessed the organisation of groups creating the mechanisms to facilitate the movement of 'undocumented' people. These political actions of solidarity between migrants and non-migrants have the power to create autonomous transnational networks as well as to push governments to answer and change policies designed to control the flux of migrants. These answers are not uncontestable or unproblematic but still show how self-organised movements of people across borders are capable of reshaping – even if only partially and temporarily – the debate around migrations. Challenging national borders and migration policies through autonomous movement is therefore the first radical point of migrant solidarity practices.

For scholars and activists of migration, the autonomy of migration is intrinsic in the movement of people. This approach looks at migrants as a multifarious composition that does not simply react to the control and power confronting it, but operates as an autonomous creator and self-organiser (Bishop, 2012). It recognises that migrations are often self-organised by migrants, their families and communities and not by institutions (Rodriguez, 1996), and that they force central institutions of the nation state such as the border and citizenship to be reshaped themselves (Moulier Boutang, 1998; Karakayali and Tsianos, 2005; Papadopoulos and Tsianos, 2007; Papadopoulos et al., 2008; Mezzadra, 2011; Papadopoulos and Tsianos,

2013; Martignoni and Papadopoulos, 2014). An autonomous perspective on mobility attempts to see migration not simply as a response to political and economic necessities but as a constituent force in the formation of polity and social life. It rejects understanding migration as a mere response to economic and social malaise (e.g. Jessop and Sum, 2006). The autonomy of migration approach foregrounds the idea that migration is not primarily a movement occurring within the spaces for action and voice defined by institutional governance. It rather means that the mobility itself becomes an inherently political statement of presence, and a social movement that subsequently forces constituted power to reorganise itself. The autonomy of migration thesis highlights the social and subjective aspects of mobility before control. Migration is autonomous, meaning that it has the capacity to develop its own logics, its own motivation and its own trajectories that control comes later to respond to, not the other way round (Transit Migration Forschungsgruppe, 2006). This does not, of course, mean that mobility operates independently of control. Very often, it is subjected to it and succumbs to violent state or private interventions that attempt to tame it.

And yet, migration(s) from this viewpoint are no longer seen as a phenomenon to be treated exclusively from a humanitarian viewpoint or as a social problem. Migrants are continuously showing that what they want above all is to be free to determine their own future and that the first 'human right' (see below for a critique and contextualisation of this concept) that should be respected is freedom of movement. This can be seen in various ways: at the border between Italy and France, where migrants refused to apply for asylum in Italy and instead crossed the border to either move again or settle down and build their future (see Papadopoulos and Tsianos, 2013). And it can be seen in the camps themselves where offers of blankets, shoes and cold weather shelters were rejected as insufficient to achieve what migrants really need – mobility and open borders (this refusal will be explored further in the case study about Calais). Migrants remain suspicious of humanitarian organisations and charities, especially those linked to the state, because (as was noted in the recent example of homelessness charities being complicit in rough sleeper deportations)[2], they can be the kind of organisation whose objectives rely upon locking them inside the tangles of the European migration system.

The aim of migrant solidarity activists, unlike the charities, is to foster freedom of mobility not inspired by a humanitarian spirit, but as a profoundly political movement, a constituent movement able to defy postcolonial disparities and racisms, and national sovereignty itself. In order to achieve this goal, activists have long worked on the need to create new forms of organisation able to represent heterogeneity and to reinvent organisational forms emerging from western social movements' heritage.

Hybridity and Difference in Migrant Solidarity Practices

The radical stance of migrant solidarity practices resides in the need and practical effort to build forms of organising that take heterogeneity, difference and mobility into consideration. Migrant solidarity practices downplay geographical stability, social similarity or even homogeneity, and are at odds with radical political experiments in which shared time-space and a shared social, identity or economic belonging are the basis for a collective action. What is difference and how encounters among differences actually work are two active discussions inside postcolonial studies. The key concept, and the one that has fuelled these debates in recent years, is hybridity. For Homi Bhabha (1994), hybridity is conceived as the encounter between two social groups with different cultural traditions and potentials of power and as a special kind of negotiation and translation that takes place in a third space of enunciation

(2009: xiii). Hybridity is the moment that cannot be translated in terms of the discourse of 'cultural difference'; it is the disjuncture that 'makes it possible for discursive authority to be renegotiated, despite the asymmetrical relations of power' (2009: xi). Bhabha describes these spaces as occurring in the midst of the encounter between the colonised subject and the coloniser where 'the incalculable colonised subject – half acquiescent, half oppositional, always untrustworthy' (Bhabha, 1994: 48) – produces an unresolvable problem: the formation of a space where there can be neither the decisive victory of one over the other, nor a combination of the two but a third entity. Bhabha and Robert Young (1995) focus on the term 'hybridity' to describe the processes of cultural displacement of the postmodern subject, of which the migrant could be said to be a paradigmatic figure.

At the same time, it has been claimed that this concept, theorised in order to critique a dialectical and binary structure of power, risks neglecting the fact that power is no longer organised in a symmetrical way. Hybridity should therefore be read not only as a 'liberating' movement but also as a 'symptom' of the establishment of a new form of domination in contemporary globalised capitalism (Hardt and Negri, 2000: 137–59). Inside this economic and political landscape, power has assumed the productivity of differences. In other words, we need to be aware that, unlike the colonial power that needed to code hybridity in binarism (orientalism) (Frenkel and Shenhav, 2006), contemporary forms of domination do not have this imperative. Although only apparently and anyway always contained within a codification, there has been a shift from differences as something to be repressed to differences as something to be exposed and valorised. The 'weapon' of hybridity against power, then, would be a weak one, or at worst, it could even reinforce a power that has completely assumed the productivity of differences or 'normalise subjectivities in transnational and post-colonial conditions by including them in shuddering multicultural societies' (Papadopoulos et al., 2008: 141).

The politics of difference and feminisms, in particular, have also raised the problem of conceptualising difference, as it is a concept that oscillates between the possibility of defining freedom, distinctiveness and power and the risk of defining categories, essentialising belongings and restricting freedom (e.g. Weedon, 1999). Difference is a concept that can be employed in various ways and is highly determined by the political use we put it to. It can be argued that the explosion of modernist binarisms has been replaced by a multiplication of borders, based on a myriad of differences and intersections that are often functional to capital (Mezzadra and Neilson, 2013). Yet, if the modernist paradigm based on sharp binarisms in which differences were placed has been replaced by a rhetoric of hybridity and multiculturalism, it remains the case that the western world is continuously experiencing tensions and conflicts around the impact of those binarisms – just think of the riots and protests in the US against institutional racism and violence (Swaine, 2015) or the conflicts around Europe and Islamophobia.

What shall we do with differences then? One option is to dismiss their relevance in order to think about alternative and contesting forms of life. Postcolonial studies have shown this by observing centrality of differences in history – and of historical difference – and by questioning western colonialist and capitalist homogenisations of lives, production, space and time. Ignoring such insights would be an error. We need, therefore, to embrace this relevance, understand how power today embraces it as well and move towards an attempt to think differences inside alternative forms of organising that disrupt the functioning of power. We need to question how radical politics around migrations can be 'postcolonial' as an adjective, in a way that entails a demand for equality in conditions of inequality. This demand is not that those excluded, marginalised or exploited are extended the same rights and obligations as dominant 'races' and classes. It is a demand for a re-articulation of the body politic which transforms the conditions in which lives are lived, and the terms on which subjects recognise each other and themselves (Devenney, 2007).

Migrants, as autonomous actors of our present, are makers of new routes, solidarities, spaces and organisations. The encounter of differences – thanks to migrations today – opens the possibility of rethinking political struggle and organisation. It is an occasion for a struggle that is not only a gesture of solidarity towards someone who has less rights, but a fight for a common horizon – although not homogeneous – that is to say the construction of a new model of social life regarding everyone. This is what the politics of migrant solidarity and migrant solidarity activists are experimenting with. The next section, drawing on an activist ethnography of Calais Migrant Solidarity (CMS)[3] (see English, 2015), will look at the work of transnational migrant solidarity collectives and particularly at what sets it apart from the work of the more charitable border-workers (Rumsford, 2009).

Navigating 'Charity' and 'Solidarity' in Migrant Solidarity

CMS is an activist collective that was established at the end of the Calais No Border protest camp in 2009.[4] Some of the solidarity work it does could be considered charitable, and there are ongoing arguments about how to locate the project alongside critiques of the big society[5] and its model citizens. The list of activities currently being carried out includes: free English classes, free basic legal advice, workshops running through the questions the UK Border Agency may ask during the asylum application process, sleeping in front of the squats and encampments (often referred to as the 'jungles') to prevent immigration raids; organising demonstrations, producing myth-busting leaflets about what the International Organisation of Migration (IOM) may actually provide to those agreeing to 'voluntarily' return to their countries of origin rather than attempting to cross the Channel, and organising large-scale meal provision when the charities take a summer hiatus. There are also informal activities, such as buying ingredients to cook together with the migrants in the 'jungles' when invited to do so. The group is constantly revising what is 'too charitable' to be considered solidarity work and the tensions around this issue will be explored later. It is not the purpose of this chapter to outline unilaterally what makes something charitable or political or an act of solidarity, but to flag the navigation of these concerns as a major consideration when making collective decisions about the priorities of migrant solidarity projects.

There are ongoing issues in CMS in finding ways to balance the so-called 'political' work with the desire to co-create spaces for collectivised forms of social reproduction together with migrants and local Calaisians. When British and European activists provide free English classes and legal advice, is this solidarity (an act arising from shared interests in accordance with radical migrant solidarity theory), or a benevolent charitable act (using one's own power and influence to help the disempowered who cannot help themselves)? The argument for free language provision is that if it is possible to create a space where everyone learns something (language exchange, for example, allows activists to learn rudimentary Arabic or any number of other languages), then perhaps it is an environment where we gain the skills to thrive and endure together rather than simply administering assistance. Some knowledge of both the English language and basic knowledge of immigration procedures are arguably necessary if not in Calais, then certainly upon arrival in the United Kingdom – a point reiterated by the migrants themselves – but, of course, language exchange classes and legal information workshops alone do not construct the structures necessary to live in a borderless world, especially when one language is that of the colonial global north and one is not.

There are a number of overlapping projects run by CMS activists and the charities in Calais, especially food provision, when the charities are on a summer break, and the distribution of shoes and clothing donated to the group. It is by undertaking these more 'charitable' acts that it becomes clear that even when both kinds of organisations work at full capacity, the needs of irregular migrants in Calais can never be met. These humanitarian projects cannot provide a solution to the problems people face at the border in Calais or elsewhere, as will be explained later in the third section of this chapter on human rights and migrant justice. At the end of the Calais No Border Camp in 2009, a solidarity activist asked if the migrants would like the makeshift bathroom facilities left in the camping area or donations of sleeping bags. The firm answer given by one young Afghan man was that they did not need bathrooms or blankets they needed the activists to open the border![6] This response begs questions about the potential of this kind of 'political' solidarity work to change the social fabric of society, challenge cultures of racism and break down the possibility of migrant destitution in Calais. It also invites reflection on the kind of charitable acts that are required in the meantime practically to sustain migrant communities and contribute to a process of transformation at the same time.

Living in Anticipation

The space – material and conceptual – that is inhabited voluntarily by activists and forcibly by migrants becomes central in the reflection on the kind of politics that are created and carried on. It is important to think about the kinds of spaces transnational migrant solidarity collectives create and what structures can be designed to enable a more collective, democratic and equitable space in which to organise and reproduce ourselves. Who does the work to make these spaces enjoyable? What role do migrants play in these spaces? Who feels comfortable and safe and is it ever the case that one person's comfort provokes another's alienation?

Those invested in cultivating alternative organisational structures and those that rely upon hierarchies and externally imposed rules and controls, including anarchist and activist groupings such as CMS, stress the need to craft a prefigurative[7] or an 'anticipatory' model of organising (Brown, 2011: 201), that is, one that could contribute to a more equitable and democratic post-capitalist system. Prefiguration also involves the idea that a particular solidaristic ethos will emerge from the alternative structures and spaces that activists organise: organising in this way will develop and promote non-hierarchical cultures (Brown, 2011: 202). The hope is that individuals would take more responsibility for their own actions, social positioning or privileges and transform society both on a collective and individual basis.

CMS aims to create spaces where people coalesce around desire to constitute non-capitalist, egalitarian and solidaristic forms of political, social and economic organisations alongside others. As such, it fits what Jenny Pickerill and Paul Chatterton refer to as an 'experiment in social autonomy, like social centres, convergence spaces and intentional communities', constructed through active resistance and the creation of alternatives (Pickerill and Chatterton, 2006: 730). During the No Border Camp in Calais in 2010, many experiments in living together were carried out. In an interview about the Calais No Border Camp with Joe Rigby, a migrant solidarity activist and scholar said:

> There are less geographical borders, which also need to be challenged and broken down, very intimate borders you carry round inside your head. In this I think the camp had more success … But not all borders are physical, and it is really the confluence of

physical and social borders which people suffer from. In the camp some of the social borders which accompany physical ones were actively broken down. Some meetings and discussions were held in four or five languages, and discussions, exchanges and encounters occurred which disrupted the rhythms of everyday lives and the habituses of the activist, the citizen and the undocumented. In facilitating this, the camp helped undermine assumptions and preconceptions about different kinds of difference.

(Rigby, 2012)

The CMS collective often fails to 'hold on to' its organising spaces, due to constant police harassment.[8] As a result of their vulnerability to demolition, these collective experiments cannot make spaces feel sustainable and fail to attract larger numbers of participants. This is evident when examining the 'social spatial forms of enclosure' (Gordon, 2010), like the jungles, the No Borders Office, the squats, food distribution centre. What does it mean when the ability to build and sustain spaces to reproduce each other constantly risks having their 'assets stripped'? (Woods, 2009: 769). One answer is to look to the 'imperceptible politics' of the mobile commons (Tsianos, Papadopoulos and Stephenson, 2008) and at the solidarity work associated with it that is both non-normatively 'political' and caring.

Imperceptible politics describes a politics that we are not trained to perceive as 'proper' because they do not appeal to and they cannot be accommodated in the existing system of political representation and of citizenship. These politics use the status of invisibility in which often migrants are constrained to reinforce practices of solidarity, of knowledge sharing, of networking and of care, creating a 'mobile commons' (Tsianos et al., 2012: 450) that have the power to change the very conditions of existence for the participating actors, as well as exerting a transformative power upon sovereignty. The shared organising spaces in Calais can be considered as part of an 'imperceptible politics'. Glimpses can be seen in the stories that are told when cooking together, in the connections that are made on one side of the border and then another and in the emotions that come forth when meeting old friends in new places.

In Calais, shared organising spaces must be rejuvenating and reconstituting in order to continue to nourish and encourage the involvement of those participating in these struggles. This means caring for each other, thinking about what is possible together, theorising individual and collective experiences of vulnerability and what we can learn from them (Institute of Precarious Consciousness, 2014), and undertaking discussion and action so that a new kind of sustainable activist subjectivity can come into being, one that is reflective about the ways activist praxis is influenced by the postcolonial context in which this work is done. Calais is one example of borderland where mobile commons are nurtured and anticipatory politics imagined. The many borderlands existing today – not necessarily located at the border of states – are the spaces in which radical politics of migrant solidarity are experienced. What can we learn from them and what kind of political theory can be drawn?

Critical Solidarity: Moving towards a Political Theory

From the previous sections, we can draw two important points for sketching a political theory of radical practices of solidarity towards (and more importantly, with!) migrants, so as to help understanding the contemporary character of migration, and the rationale underpinning autonomous practices of solidarity in camps as Calais and other borderlands. First is the way in which borderlands become the sites not only for contesting and resisting contemporary migration regimes, but also for inventing new forms of existence in the interplay of autonomy and coercion inside which mobile commons are developed (Mezzadra and Neilson, 2013; Papadopoulos and Tsianos, 2013). Second, and following from this, is the potential for new forms of existence to emerge from the imperceptible politics that underpin autonomous organisational practices and the infrastructures devised to survive borders. On the one side, borders have not simply a coercive power but a subjectivating power. On the other side, the power of the border is contested by the generative potential of grassroots solidarity practices that produce autonomous geographies even within a coercive and violent, yet porous mobility regime (Pickerill and Chatterton, 2006; Vasudevan, 2015).

In order to provide the coordinates for structuring the theoretical framework of a radical theory of solidarity practices, we propose a genealogical concatenation of concepts and spatial perspectives, starting from the seemingly more blurred one: the border and postcolonial locations in which solidarity work is undertaken, first of all, as symbols of contemporary battlefields around freedom of movement. Second, as sites where we can observe on a daily basis the entanglement of autonomy and coercion generating organisational forms, alternative forms of life in common, networks political strategies and tactics aiming at fostering settlement, mobility and more in general guaranteeing dignity also to people on the move (Linebaugh, 2008; Papadopoulos and Tsianos, 2013). These forms of life not only recast justice as a politics of matter (Stephenson and Papadopoulos, 2006), but also contest the very fundamentals of national sovereignty with their irreducible creativity in circumventing borders proliferating far beyond national frontiers (Mezzadra and Neilson, 2013).

The second passage of the genealogical concatenation addresses the contrast between the situated experience of people challenging the borders and the universal grid through which their experience is often conflated, as well as depoliticised: human rights. A critical analysis of the fictionality of human rights will be proposed, vis-à-vis their attachment to the figure of the citizen as the legitimate bearer thereof. The tensions between charitable activities and solidaristic activities experimented in the Calais site will be used as empirical evidence. The third and last passage will then address the paramount political subject expressing the relationship between space and sovereignty, which is the citizen. Again, citizenship will be critically deconstructed in relationship to the materiality of human and social rights in a neo-liberal, post-welfare context where the dichotomy migrant/citizen does not suffice any longer to account for the forms of intersectional, hybrid marginality experienced by the seemingly more diverse subjects. The conclusion will address the relevance of using the situated perspective of the border as a standpoint for questioning the theoretical and political validities of the categories usually deployed in order to interpret social turmoil relating to mobility. The scope, ultimately, is to contribute to the reflection upon autonomous forms of solidarity, and increase the effectiveness of their material deployment as tools for fostering mobility, settlement and overall social justice.

As for the issue of borders, autonomy of migration scholars (see the earlier section) has widely debated the profound mutation of the materiality of the border in its globalised articulations. Borders, nowadays, are not only epitomised by the wall, the detention camp or even the borderline separating two sovereign territories (Nail, 2012), as in Calais and Ventimiglia, even though these are all still extremely relevant for the violence they deploy. Rather, the role of borders is to institutionalise uncertainty and precarity in the guise of enforcing the constant threat of being deported. They ensure subjugation to exploitation, segregation and social marginality (De Genova, 2012). The proliferation of borders – beyond nation state – in other words, is symptomatic of the establishment of a complex mass of control devices, supranational entities and differentials points of entry that shape social reproduction. Furthermore, they criss-cross the likewise multifarious lines of subjectivation characterising individual and collective experience beyond nationality and race: ethnicity, gender, migratory status, class and cultural background, skill levels and so on. An example drawn from the borderlands of Calais and Ventimiglia could be the rhetoric aimed at secluding Syrian 'authentic refugees', supposedly more well-educated, highly skilled and moderate in terms of religion from the migrants of other nationalities, depicted in public discourses as less skilled, more needy, less worthy of being granted safe mobility and overall less 'civilised' and qualified for 'integration'.

In a nutshell, borders are nowadays a mixture of differential regimes and locations (Sassen, 2015), aimed at attuning the movements of people to capitalist speed of flows and need for labour (Papadopoulos and Tsianos, 2013). They are designed by nation states as well as supranational entities (Castles and Miller, 2009; Mezzadra and Neilson, 2011), and are generative of subjectivation processes, wherefore they establish 'a specified stabilized circulation of desired social and economic effects: profit, property, racial division' (Nail, 2012). That is to say, ultimately, that borders are biopolitical devices turning the body of the migrant into the carrier of bordering enforcement, punishment and exploitation (Sassen, 2015). Yet, the role of the border is neither univocal nor uncontested. No Borders and Anti-Raids campaigning in the so-called 'receiving' countries produce practices of resistance and solidarity in eluding control and aiding migrants with differential migratory statuses (from asylum seekers to undocumented people) to juggle the grey areas of the system.

Indeed, as stressed in the previous sections, bordering devices are also the sites where unprecedented forms of kinship, assemblages of subjectivities, organisational practices arise, at the crossroads of the complicated interplay between subjection and subjectivation characterising the so-called 'fabric of migration' (Mezzadra, 2015). These practices and forms of life show to what extent migrants' autonomy exceeds migration management, designed according to capitalist just-in-time and to-the-point imperatives for highly mobile, yet controllable and selectable workforce (Moulier Boutang, 1998, 2012; Mitropoulos, 2007; Papadopoulos et al., 2008; Andrijasevic, 2009; Anderson, 2010; Mezzadra and Neilson, 2011).

It is crucial to problematise and rethink solidarity in either its solely political or charitable understanding, and to re-conceptualise it from the perspective of grassroots solidarity practices stemming from the complex interplay of autonomous and coercion influencing mobility in the contemporary porous and diffused borders regime. Indeed, when it comes down to migrants and solidarity, the privileged perspectives are either the 'charitable' one, imprinted by the supposedly universal paradigm of human rights (Sassen, 2015), or, the one conflating migrants' autonomy with a sort of automatism in struggling against marginalisation (Papadopoulos and Tsianos, 2013) and for 'integration' into the supposedly homogeneous space of the nation and the citizen. The proposal here is to start from what is not pure, from those imperceptible, non-conventional, affective politics of mobile commons, embedded in the everyday practices that aim at enhancing mobility and settlement, producing space through alternative organisational practices and challenging the mixed spatial and temporal constituencies of borders and cities as well (Sassen, 2015). Indeed, autonomous practices of solidarity, as the experiences of the jungle of Calais and the camp of Ventimiglia show, challenge borders, readapt pre-existing spatialities and create new forms of existence that recast social justice as politics of matter in everydayness (Papadopoulos, 2014; Vasudevan, 2015), beyond the limits imposed by the institutional practice of solidarity, mostly limited to charitable acts exerted within the frame of stated governmentality, and then hidden beyond the veil of human rights.

The next section will question the abstractness of solidarity when it is read through the lens of supposedly universal human rights. It will instead harness the theoretical elements outlined in the previous sections for proposing a radical theory of solidarity encompassing situated, affective and intersectional practices and existential modalities challenging the pro-liferation of borders in everyday life.

From Universal to Situated: Solidarity and Everydayness

The idea that all people have human rights is the umbrella under which the vast majority of institutional and grassroots claims of solidarity towards migrants, refugees and asylum seek-ers has usually been extended. Indeed, they are generally supposed to be universal, whereas human beings are supposed to be the enfranchised subjects thereof, and thus disembodied of national, racial, ethnic, gendered, cultural, religious distinctions. Yet, as many authors have pointed out, the universality of human rights is merely fictional. On the other hand, the tensions and conflicts connected to migration display that human rights are not natural features of each human being, whereas they are factually appointed to citizens, and dispensed by nation states and international bodies to the members of the international community they have designed (see Stephenson and Papadopoulos, 2006; Sassen, 2015).

Thus, first and foremost, contextualising solidarity through the vast array of quotidian organisational practices claiming social justice instead of human rights helps to overcome the impasse caused by the reference to the latter. Indeed, contemporaneity shows the paradox of the political abuse of the notion of liberty, that is supposed to be universal, yet overlaps with citizenship and legal statuses provided solely by liberal democracies. As our temporality is benchmarked by states of exception to democratic cornerstones in the name of the war on terrorism, defence of national identities against 'migrant invasion' and transfer of personal freedoms in the name of securitisation, it becomes even more apparent that the deployment of human rights is the pivotal form of exertion of sovereign power, as they are inherently bound to the fictional, unitary figure of the national citizen (Agamben, 1995).

Moreover, it is necessary to question the mobilisation of human rights in its flattening of universally intelligible categories away from subjective experiences that are inherently bound to their situatedness, and from embodied practices of solidarity that stem in response to intersectional regimes of subjectification and control (de Certeau, 1984; Stephenson and Papadopoulos 2006; Papadopoulos and Tsianos, 2013). Additionally, decoupling autonomous practices of solidarity from the spectrum of human rights also encompasses problematising the value of citizenship as the only enticing horizon for people on the move, as despite the connec-tions to various entitlements to settling and moving freely, it may not always be the best option.

When it comes to the nation state, it is relevant to note that the definition of its prerog-atives and conditions of co-optation has been the core of the theoretical speculation upon modernity, as well as the space for pinpointing the spaces of political legitimacy. Thence, its perspective has so far been the unquestioned lens for analysing the overall movements of politics (Cuppini, 2015). Consequently, the citizen has been conflated with the utmost polit-ical subject of modernity, enfranchised with rights, voice and agency, shaping the dichotomy citizen/alien in the first place. In fact, when it comes to migration, this certainty also reso-nates in the academic milieu, where formalised forms of organising (i.e. NGOs, parochial structures, recognised political collective and so on) created by native social practitioners, volunteers and activists tend to be privileged in the analysis. This effaces more impercep-tible ways of creating commons, devised by subjects who are often mobile and irreducible to reductionist paradigms and official forms of organising due to their status, professional position, gender, ethnicity, cultural background, habits and so on. Finally, this often implies delegating the voice and agency of migrants to legitimised actors or native activists, mostly in the name of their status.

This irreducibility to flattening categories corresponds to the hybridity we have addressed in the previous sections of this chapter as the result of the existential modalities, autonomous infrastructures and alternative politics arising from organisational practices devised in order to foster settlement and mobility. Indeed, different types of mobile commons (Papadopoulos and Tsianos, 2013) – from camping on a borderline like Calais and Ventimiglia to housing squats inhabited by both native and migrant dwellers spreading in Southern Europe – show how subjectivities and binary categories get subverted in everydayness. Indeed, they produce *mestizo* identities and new assemblages of subjectivities in relation to situated spatial and temporal arrangements (see Haraway, 1991; Anzaldúa, 2007). By the same token, the autonomous organisational practices stemming from these hybrid assemblages cannot be separated from the time and space in which they operate (de Certeau, 1984). These practices produce autonomous geographies (see Vasudevan, 2015) that unearth two prerequisites of the foundational myth of the nation state: the supposedly fixed assemblage of territory and homogeneous community; sedentariness as one of the bedrocks of social cooperation, whereas the borders designed in official maps are the outcome of the state's violent effort to efface and curtail movements as well as social unrest (Deleuze and Guattari, 2005).

Not only are borders proliferating and becoming more porous, they are also being challenged by mobility. Within a complex border regime where norms are established with the sole purpose of curtailing freedom of movement according to capitalist requirements, it is necessary to be clear that it is not acceptable to use humanitarian organisations and principles as a shield for arbitrarily dividing migrants as 'good' from 'bad'. This tension is epitomised in the case of Calais' so-called jungle, where the European Union, the United Kingdom and France and a plurality of mixed actors (from NGOs to parochial associations and autonomous No Borders network) exerted converging and diverging actions that questioned the materiality and governance of the border, as well as the symbolic figures it presupposes. Indeed, what is at stake in the Calais conflict, as well as in other European borderlands (from Ventimiglia to Idomeni) is the possibility of trespassing the border and enjoying the same freedom of movement that is appointed to EU countries' citizens as members of a supranational and multinational entity that is constantly shaken by political turmoil questioning its role and legitimacy. Nowadays, the right to mobility is regulated on a supranational scale (especially in terms of free trade and circulation of goods in the EU case), but is also autonomously practised by migrants through thick, yet ephemeral networks of solidarity. Finally, both migration management and solidaristic activities operate not only through coalescing around national identities, but according to intersectional lines of differential inclusion/exclusion (i.e. ethnicity, gender, class, cultural and educational background, religion, sexual orientation and so on). Therefore, there is the conceptual necessity to frame the materiality of mobile commons beyond citizenship, as Papadopoulos and Tsianos (2013) themselves suggest.

Following Papadopoulos and Tsianos (2013), we think this is not the case. We propose a theoretical framework for radical practices of solidarity that assumes the mobilisation of borders as the starting point for overcoming the analytical grids provided by nation states' subjective figures. Secondly, we propose autonomous practices that foster settlement and mobility as the analytical lens for problematising the subjective assemblages involved in juggling proliferating, porous and mobile borders. First of all, our proposals entail discerning the situated, intersectional conditions of marginality equating migrant and native dwellers in unprecedented ways. Secondly, we propose to put under theoretical scrutiny the unprecedented ontological forms, and alternative assemblages of social reproduction, stemming from the autonomous practice of intersectional solidarity. Indeed, they cannot be conflated with marginality insofar as they create new subjective figures that question the inner workings of citizenship, human, civil and social rights.

Indeed, the current post-welfare crisis and austerity context contradict the conceptualisation of social citizenship as a progressive appointment of rights and possibilities of escalating the ladder for those constructed as citizens on the grounds of their availability to sustain a social pact based on 'fair' capitalist inequality (see Marshall and Bottomore, 1992; Gibson-Graham, 2006). By the same token, those who are excluded from this status or incapable/unavailable to fulfil expectations of capitalist social reproduction and exploit their full labour force as the plurality of their human qualities are either silenced in the public discourse or conflated with the dichotomy marginality-criminalisation. This is even more prominent in a post-Fordist and post-welfare context, where mobile commons as practices enhancing mobility and settlement get entangled with autonomous, prefigurative politics designed on a daily basis in order to survive neo-liberal governmental arrangements (Mitropoulos, 2013; Vasudevan, 2015). One example is the widespread phenomenon of squatting enacted by refugees and migrants with differential status together with homeless Italian citizens in the metropolis of Rome, and how it gets articulated within the public discourse (Grazioli, 2017).

Hence, urban movements aiming at recasting right to the city and social justice (see Lefebvre, 1996; Purcell, 2002; Merrifield, 2011) find themselves confronted with forms of subjectivation and, above all, life in common (e.g. housing squats) that they experiment as they are confronted with the double necessity of coping with compelling material deprivation, and doing it outside of the residual, and increasingly inaccessible, social welfare framework.

As neo-liberal rationale erodes state primacy in distributing and managing resources, nation states become increasingly incapable of reabsorbing social conflict through either political representativeness or the use of welfare state for reconciling social unrest through the promises of equalising at least the most unbearable injustices produced by the capitalist exploitation and extraction of surplus by the overall social cooperation (see Marshall and Bottomore, 1992). The fact that these forms of solidarity, life in common and grassroots resistance to neo-liberal hostility (see Avallone and Torre, 2016), realised by migrants and native citizens out of unprecedented conditions of proximity in marginalisation, do not produce generalised revolts should come as no surprise for those analysing them without conflating migrants' and natives' experiences of material deprivation, pauperisation and exclusion with the sole category of class. Also, the fact that migrants do not emerge as a new revolutionary *avant-garde* does not undermine the political relevance of the ways in which they create networks of solidarity capable of supporting their autonomous forms of life settlement and mobility.

On the contrary, these tensions and critical points shed light upon the partiality of the analytical grids that scholars and activists usually deploy for analysing the turmoil occurring on multiple sites and multifarious borderlands; first and foremost, the idea of the 'citizen' as the bearer of rights appointed for exerting agency, voice and politicity in contraposition to the disembodied 'migrant' as sheer voiceless, powerless, impolitical bare life. In a nutshell, seemingly marginal practices of solidarities exerted by subaltern subjects shall not be discarded as ephemeral, and then neglectable. Contrariwise, they can constitute the privileged perspective for critically addressing the frame of citizenship and rights, and supporting the effort of elaborating a theoretical framework capable of reading through the multiplicity of autonomous practices invented on a daily basis for sustaining freedom of movement vis-à-vis an increasingly pervasive border regime.

Conclusion

A radical theory of migrant solidarity affirms the importance of imperceptible politics and encounters occurring in everydayness among migrants and between migrants and non-migrant activists. These are practices that help migrants to move across the borders defying control and assist their settlement despite the many difficulties caused by their migration status. Often, these politics are 'imperceptible' because they do not claim rights or appeal to the state or humanitarian organisations, but they act autonomously and in the everyday. This radical form of solidarity, we claim, wanting to create new forms of existence, moves beyond (and in some occasions against) forms of solidarity informed by the values of human rights and citizenship – that are clearly shown to be inconsistently useful in the postcolonial conditions created by migrations.

The postcolonial condition is the context in which we are working to understand the contemporary heterogeneity of forms of existence, rights and levels of citizenship cohabitating the same space. These multilayered spatialities and temporalities constitute the battlefield where the resistance against the contemporary border regimes occurs. Migrants are active subjects of these struggles as well as of radical solidarity practices that are often initiated by migrants themselves. Conceptualising migrant solidarity entails considering heterogeneity and difference as cornerstones for deploying effective organisational practices and crafting genuine political alliances, as interpolated by intersectional politics and theories of difference.

Through the example of the work of CMS, this theoretical stance has been 'tested'. In particular, the description of the infrastructures created inside the camp has allowed us to explore the tensions between solidarity understood as autonomous organising or charitable support. The materiality of political solidarity as a set of practices challenging and transforming the contemporary border regime and social fabric has thus been framed as anticipatory politics. The latter have been conceived as the experimentation of organisational, political and existential modalities coalescing around the necessity of resistance, and the desire to create alternative ontological forms at the same time. Often though, as happened in Calais most recently in 2016 after yet another eviction of the camp, the material assets and infrastructures of anticipatory politics get stripped by the state, showing once again that the legacy of these projects can only be in their fostering of a culture of shared social reproduction and mutual aid rather than in any ability to maintain material infrastructures. We looked at the imperceptible politics of mobile commons that sets the conditions for moments of excess (The Free Association, 2011) and new ontological forms building solidarity as non-normatively political and caring.

In conclusion, how does migrant solidarity operate as both a political theory and a form of radical politics? Autonomous practices of migrant solidarity can be generative of cooperative forms of life and organisation that foster collective settlement and mobility, in contrast with the compelling individualist and competitive rationale of capitalist governmental arrangements (De Angelis and Harvie, 2014). Grasping their deployment, though, requires a continuous exercise of open-mindedness and confrontation with complex time and space arrangements in order to grasp the innumerable, uncoordinated, yet cooperative actions contributing to its continuous theorisation and enaction (Papadopoulos and Tsianos, 2013). A radical theory of solidarity indeed is the one capable of mapping the autonomous geographies produced by migrants' agency and voice, encompassing the plurality and hybridity of everyday practices ignored by universal, generalising theories and fixed understandings of borders and subjectivity. This work is an invaluable opportunity for scholars, activists and social practitioners to analyse spontaneous and innovative forms of post-capitalist social reproduction and cooperation, capable of transforming relationships and practices (Cooper, 1986; Gibson-Graham, 2006; Heyman et al., 2014) that allow for an imagining of migrant solidarity beyond contemporary capitalist infrastructures and towards a freedom of movement for all.

Notes

1 See examples at www.calaismigrantsolidarity.wordpress.com.
2 Full story available here: www.politics.co.uk/news/2016/09/15/homeless-charities-complicit-in-rough-sleeper-deportations.
3 Calais Migrant Solidarity is a direct action-focused group initiated to show solidarity with migrants intending to move to the UK, 'legally' or otherwise, and in principle it does not do humanitarian/charitable work, though in practice this is often disputed (www.calaismigrantsolidarity.wordpress.com).
4 Since this time, the British and French governments, often in coalition, have dismantled the jungles, at times via seemingly mundane everyday acts such as spraying all the tents with pepper spray so that they are uncomfortable to sleep in and have to be thrown away, other times in more explosive and performative ways with bulldozers, destroying the full village infrastructures of mosques, churches, stores, libraries and hairdressers. But the jungles are always rebuilt, just as the movement of people keeps on coming (calaismigrantsolidarity.wordpress.com).
5 According to Walker and Corbett (2013), 'The "Big Society" draws on a mix of conservative communitarianism and libertarian paternalism. Together, they constitute a long-term vision of integrating the free market with a theory of social solidarity based on hierarchy and voluntarism'. The Tory government initiative encourages citizens' volunteers to run services that they believe are worthwhile, allowing the state to withdraw from providing basic services such as libraries and elder care allowing 'market efficiency' to decide which public services continue to run.
6 More about the No Border Camp in 2009 can be found in this interview with Joe Rigby (https://libcom.org/library/interview-no-borders-calais).
7 Pickerill and Chatterton (2006:738) summarise prefigurative politics in the phrase 'be the change you want to see', and see change as possible through an accumulation of small changes, providing much-needed sense of hope. Part of this is the belief in 'doing it yourself' (see McKay, 1998) or creating workable alternatives outside the state. Many examples have flourished embracing ecological direct action, free parties and the rave scene, squatting and social centres, and open-source software and independent media. Resources are creatively reused, skills shared and popular or participatory education techniques deployed, aiming to develop a critical consciousness, political and media literacy and clear ethical judgements (Freire, 1979 in Pickerill and Chatterton 2006).
8 calaismigrantsolidarity.wordpress.org.

References

Agamben, G., *Homo Sacer. Il Potere Sovrano e La Nuda Vita* (Torino: Giulio Einaudi Editore, 1995).
Anderson, B., 'Migration, Immigration, Controls and the Fashioning of Precarious Workers', *Work Employment Society*, 24:2 (2010), 300–317.
Andrijasevic, R., 'Sex on the Move: Gender, Subjectivity and Differential Inclusion', *Subjectivity*, 29:1 (2009), 389–406.
Anzaldúa, G., *Borderlands/ La Frontera. The New Mestiza* (San Francisco: Aunt Lute Books, 2007).
Avallone, G. and Torre, S., 'Dalla Città Ostile Alla Città Bene Comune. I Migranti Di Fronte Alla Crisi Dell'Abitare', *Archivio Di Studi Urbani E Regionali*, 115:1 (2016), 51–74.
Bhabha, H., *The Location of Culture* (London: Routledge, 1994).
Bhabha, H., 'In the Cave of Making: Thoughts on Third Space', in K. Ikas and G. Wagner (eds.), *Communicating in the Third Space* (London: Routledge, 2009), pp. ix–xiv.
Bishop, H., 'The Worlds That Migrants Are Making: The Politics of Care and Transnational Mobility' (PhD Dissertation, Cardiff University, 2012).
Brown, G., 'Mutinous Eruptions: Autonomous Spaces of Radical Queer Activism', *Environment and Planning*, A:39 (2007), 2685–2698.
Brown, G., 'Amateurism and Anarchism in the Creation of Autonomous Queer Spaces', in J. Heckert and R. Cleminson (eds.), *Anarchism & Sexuality: Ethics, Relationships and Power* (Oxon: Routledge, 2011), pp. 200–224.
Castles, S. and Miller, M.J., *The Age of Migration. International Population Movements in the Modern World* (Basingstoke: Palgrave McMillan, 2009).

Calais Migrant Solidarity. 'Who We Are.' 2015, from https://calaismigrantsolidarity.wordpress.com/who-are-we-?/مونېر-څوک-یو-؟-ما-کی-هستیم-؟-

Chatterton, P. and J. Pickerill, 'Everyday Activism and Transitions Towards Post-Capitalist Worlds', *Transactions of the Institute of British Geographers*, 35:4 (2010), 475–490.

Cooper, R., 'Organization/Disorganization', *Social Science Information*, 25:2 (1986), 299–335.

Cuppini, N., 'Verso una Teoria Politica della Città Globalizzata', *Scienza & Politica*, XXVII:53 (2015), 247–262.

De Angelis, M. and D. Harvie, 'The Commons', in M. Parker, G. Cheney, V. Fournier, and C. Land, (eds.), *The Routledge Companion to Alternative Organization* (London/New York: Routledge, 2014), pp. 280–294.

de Certeau, M., *The Practice of Everyday Life* (Berkeley: The University of California Press, 1984).

De Genova, N., 'The Deportation Regime. Sovereignty, Space and the Freedom of Movement', in N. De Genova and N. Peutz (eds.), *The Deportation Regime. Sovereignty, Space and the Freedom of Movement* (Durham/London: Duke University Press, 2012), pp. 33–65.

Deleuze, G. and F. Guattari. *A Thousand Plateaus: Capitalism and Schizophrenia* (London/New York: Bloomsbury Academic, 1987/2005 ed.).

Devenney, M., 'Thinking the Postcolonial as Political', *Borderlands*, 6 (2007), www.borderlands.net.au/vol6no2_2007/devenney_postcolonial.htm [accessed: 26/10/2012].

English, C., 'Bordering on Reproducing the State: Migrant Solidarity Collectives and Constructions of the Other in Safer Space', in S. Price and R. Sanz-Sabido (eds.), *Contemporary Protest and the Legacy of Dissent* (London: Rowman and Littlefield, 2015), pp. 171–189.

Fanon, F., *Les Damnés De La Terre* (Paris: Maspero, 1961).

The Free Association, *Moments of Excess: Movements, Protest and Everyday Life* (Oakland: PM Press, 2011).

Frenkel, M. and Y. Shenhav, 'From Binarism Back to Hybridity: A Postcolonial Reading of Management and Organization Studies', *Organization Studies*, 27:6 (2006), 855–876.

Gibson-Graham, J.K., *A Postcapitalist Politics* (Kindle Edition edn. Minneapolis, MN: University of Minnesota Press, 2006).

Gordon, A., *Commoning, Piracy, Running Away and Other Incidents in the Life of Living Otherwise*, The AV Festival. Feral Trade Café, Newcastle UK, (2010). available: www.averygordon.net/writing-utopian-escape/commoning-piracy-running-away/.

Grazioli, M., 'From Citizens to *Citadins*? Rethinking Right to the City Inside Housing Squats in Rome, Italy', *Citizenship Studies*, 21 (2017): 393–408.

Haraway, D., *Simians, Cyborgs and Women: The Reinvention of Nature* (London: Routledge, 1991).

Hardt, M. and A. Negri, *Empire* (Cambridge, MA: Harvard University Press, 2000).

Heyman, J., N. Fischer, and J. Loucky, 'Immigrants and Immigration', in M. Parker, G. Cheney, V. Fournier and C. Land. (eds.), *The Routledge Companion to Alternative Organization* (London/New York: Routledge, 2014), pp. 135–150.

Institute for Precarious Consciousness 'We are all Very Anxious: Six Theses on Anxiety and Why It is Effectively Preventing Militancy, and One Possible Strategy for Overcoming It.' 14 April 2014, from www.weareplanc.org/we-are-all-very-anxious/#.U0vKdVdMiSr.

Jessop, B. and N.-L. Sum, *Beyond the Regulation Approach: Putting Capitalist Economies in their Place* (Chelthenham: Edward Elgar, 2006).

Karakayali, S. and V. Tsianos, 'Mapping the Order of New Migration. Undokumentierte Arbeit Und Die Autonomie Der Migration', *Peripherie*, 97–98 (2005), 35–64.

Larkin, B., 'The Politics and Poetics of Infrastructure', *Annual Review of Anthropology*, 42 (2013), 327–343.

Lefebvre, H., *Writing On Cities* (Oxford/Malden, MA: Blackwell Publishers, 1996).

Linebaugh, P., *The Magna Carta Manifesto: Liberties and Commons for All* (Berkeley: University of California Press, 2008).

Marshall, T.H. and T. Bottomore, *Citizenship and Social Class* (London: Pluto, 1992).

Martignoni, M. and D. Papadopoulos, 'Genealogies of Autonomous Mobility', in E. F. Isin, and P. Nyers, (eds.), *Routledge Handbook of Global Citizenship Studies* (London: Routledge, 2014), pp. 38–48.

McKay, G., *DiY Culture: Party & Protest in Nineties Britain* (London: Verso, 1998).

Merrifield, A., 'The Right to the City and Beyond', *City*, 15:3–4 (2011), 473–481.

Mezzadra, S., *La Condizione Postcoloniale* (Verona: Ombrecorte, 2008).

Mezzadra, S., 'The Gaze of Autonomy. Capitalism, Migration and Social Struggles', *The Contested Politics of Mobility: Borderzones and Irregularity* (London: Routledge, 2011), pp. 121–142.

Mezzadra, S. 'The Proliferation of Borders and the Right to Escape' in Y. Jansen, R. Celikates and J. de Bloois (eds.), *The Irregularization of Migration in Contemporary Europe. Detention, Deportation, Drowning* (London-New York: Rowman & Littlefield, 2015), pp. 121–135.

Mezzadra, S. and B. Neilson, 'Borderscapes of Differential Inclusion. Subjectivity on the Threshold of Justice Effects', in É. Balibar, S. Mezzadra and R. Samaddar (eds.), *The Borders of Justice* (Philadelphia: Temple University Press, 2011), pp. 181–200.

Mezzadra, S. and B. Neilson, *Border as Method, Or, the Multiplication of Labor* (Durham/London: Duke University Press, 2013).

Moulier Boutang, Y., *De l'esclavage au Salariat: Economie Historique du Salariat Bridé* (Paris: Presses universitaires de France, 1998).

Moulier Boutang, Y., *Cognitive Capitalism* (Cambridge: Polity Press, 2012).

Mitropoulos, A., 'Autonomy, Recognition, Movement', in S. Shukaitis, S. Graeber and E. Biddle (eds.), *Constituent Imagination. Militant Investigations, Collective Theorization* (Oakland: AK Press, 2007), pp. 127–137.

Mitropoulos, A., *Contract and Contagion: From Biopolitics to Oikonomia* (Brooklyn, NY: Minor Compositions, 2013).

Nail, T., 'Violence at the Borders: Nomadic Solidarity and Non-Status Migrant Resistance', *Radical Philosophy Review*, 15:1 (2012), 241–257.

Papadopoulos, D., 'Generation M. Matter, Makers, Microbiomes: Compost for Gaia', *Teknokultura*, 11:3 (2014), 637–645.

Papadopoulos, D., N. Stephenson, et al., *Escape Routes: Control and Subversion in the Twenty First Century* (London: Pluto Press, 2008).

Papadopoulos, D. and V. Tsianos, 'The Autonomy of Migration: The Animals of Undocumented Mobility', in A. Hickey-Moody, and P. Malins, (eds.), *Deleuzian Encounters: Studies in Contemporary Social Issues* (Basingstoke: Palgrave Macmillan, 2007), pp. 223–235.

Papadopoulos, D. and V. Tsianos, 'After Citizenship: Autonomy of Migration, Organisational Ontology and Mobile Commons', *Citizenship Studies*, 17 (2013), 2178–2196.

Pickerill, J. and P. Chatterton, 'Notes Towards Autonomous Geographies: Creation, Resistance and Self-management as Survival Tactics', *Progress in Human Geography*, 30:6 (2006), 730–746.

Purcell, M., 'Excavating Lefebvre: The Right to the City and Its Urban Politics of the Inhabitant', *GeoJournal*, 58 (2002), 99–108.

Rigby, J., Interview with No Borders in Calais, Libcom, 2012, from https://libcom.org/library/interview-no-borders-calais.

Rodriguez, N., 'The Battle for the Border: Notes on Autonomous Migration, Transnational Communities, and the State', *Social Justice*, 23:3 (1996), 21.

Rumsford, C., *Citizens and Borderwork in Contemporary Europe* (London: Routledge, 2009).

Sassen, S., 'Old Borders and New Bordering Capabilities: Cities as Frontiers Zones', *Scienza & Politica*, XXVII: 53 (2015), 295–306.

Stephenson, N., and D. Papadopoulos, *Analysing Everyday Experience. Social Research and Political Change* (Basingstoke & New York: Palgrave Macmillan, 2006).

Swaine, J., 'Baltimore Freddie Gray Protests Turn Violent as Police and Crowds Clash', *The Guardian*, 26th April 2015.

Transit Migration Forschungsgruppe (ed.), *Turbulente Rander. Neue Perspektiven auf Migration an den Grenzen Europas* (Bielefeld: Transcript, 2006).

Tsianos, V., D. Papadopoulos, et al., 'This Is Class War from Above and They Are Winning It: What Is to Be Done?', *Rethinking Marxism*, 24:3 (2012), 448–457.

Vasudevan, A., 'The Autonomous City: Towards a Critical Geography of Occupation', *Progress in Human Geography*, 39:3 (2015), 316–337.

Weedon, C., *Feminism, Theory and the Politics of Difference* (Oxford: Blackwell Publishers, 1999).

Woods, C., 'Les Misérables of New Orleans: Trap Economics and the Asset Stripping Blues, Part 1', *American Quarterly*, 61:3 (2009), 769–796.

Young, R., *Colonial Desire: Hybridity in Theory, Culture, and Race* (London: Routledge, 1995).

2.5

PENAL ABOLITION ORGANISING

Can New Courses Be Charted
by Troubling Privilege?[1]

Claire Delisle

Introduction

Penal abolitionism is a radical stance and its project is an ambitious one given the ubiquity of punishment frameworks in place the world over. Its success depends on effectively communicating the perniciousness of criminal justice processes and practices; expanding abolitionist conceptualisations of alternative responses to harm; organising resistance to punishment through antiprison, antipolice and anti-criminal justice system campaigns. Communicative strategies devised in the organising of such campaigns are both drawn from, and inspire, scholarly and activist analyses. The goals are to show the injustice resultant from criminal justice processes and practices and to highlight the merits of community, solidarity and an understanding of power and oppression in working towards safety and security. Within scholarly analyses, there remain blind spots in the treatment of certain issues related to ending punishment, such as what to do with 'the dangerous few' and the abstract notion of community (Carrier and Piché, 2015, para. 5). Another occlusion that is common among some is the connection between colonialism and punishment. At the International Conference on Penal Abolition (ICOPA), this occlusion is a source of frustration for some participants. It affects discussion within ICOPA where unacknowledged white privilege stands in the way of grasping the extent to which our societies still function within a well-entrenched colonialist paradigm, and how such a paradigm still colours our collective organising discourses and practices. If penal abolition is grounded in respect, community, solidarity and equality, abolitionists must prefigure these principles in their activism and scholarship, and in the spaces they create for the purpose of sharing and learning from other abolitionists, their practices and their intellectual work.

This chapter presents the racism/privilege dynamic among the scholars, activists and survivors of state or social harm who are invested in prefiguring, theorising and practising abolitionism at ICOPA. First, penal abolitionism is presented as an alternative to the punishment framework and highlights some of the work done by abolitionist theorists. Then, some of the historical highlights of ICOPA are explored in order to showcase the long-standing tension about race within the entity. I expose the current internal debate about the role colonialism plays as an important analytical frame to theorise punishment and about the necessity of examining racism and white privilege in interactions at the conference. I draw upon contemporary social movement scholarship, in particular, as it relates to the World Social Forum (WSF) (Juris, 2008; Conway, 2013) which has opened up critically reflexive conversations about stubborn hegemonic epistemologies and practices at work in social movements, and the merit of creating intentional space, at the risk of losing openness (Juris, 2008). I briefly discuss the benefits of focusing on privilege as well as oppression. Finally, I explore mechanisms aimed at dislodging language and action that hinder discernment of oppression and privilege, thereby initiating a praxis where grassroots groups feel ownership in respect of the direction of the conversations and actions within ICOPA, which stand to open up the possibility of creating a truly radical space. I propose avenues that may work in favour of charting new courses that multiply opportunities to abolish laws, practices, techniques and institutions of dehumanisation.

And I present how ICOPA 17 upended traditional conference elaboration by placing colonialism front and centre, and calling directly on participants to consider its legacy.

Integrating counterbalances to traditional organisation and knowledge-sharing can foster relationship, allyship, solidarity and motivation for struggle, a practice especially central for such a project. This can only happen when grassroots groups play a central role in the conference, thus enabling their voices and agency to contribute to crafting new understandings, solidarities and ways forward to dismantle the punishment framework *in toto*. Those emanating from the grass roots are most apt to have suffered oppression and criminalisation, and are thus well-placed to provide experiential knowledge that contributes, in an important way, to our understanding of the inherent problems with the punishment framework.

Penal Abolitionism

Criminal justice is a paradigm that came into being during the enlightenment (Agozino, 2003), initially as a response to 'demonic judicial processes' (13) characterised by public torture and execution (Foucault, 1987). Rational application of the law and the principle of equality were introduced by Cesare Beccaria in 1764 in his Treatise on Crime and Punishment. So absurd and dangerous did this appear to his detractors that the book was banned for 200 years (Agozino, op. cit., 13). In western liberal democracies, criminal justice systems are still based on this axiom. Justice is considered to have been rendered when the 'offender' is held to account by serving a sentence (jail, prison, community work, probation, etc.); and that justice exists when all people are treated in the same way. Conventional analyses typically occlude the macro-sociological dimensions of disproportionately criminalising persons who come from marginalised groups in regards class, race, gender identity and ability, among others.

Penal abolitionism is a theoretical, strategic and grounded position aimed at the elimination of punishment frameworks, penal systems and their component parts including the police, courts and corrections. It has been amply demonstrated by empirical and theoretical research that on moral, pragmatic and strategic grounds, punishment for the transgression of laws or for perpetuating harm against fellow humans does not hold the promise of satisfactorily resolving conflict, protecting communities or stemming violence (see, for example, Mathiesen, 1996; Christie, 2001; Golash, 2005). Moreover, the magnitude of state and corporate violence, which is but rarely prosecuted, is considered to be far greater than street 'crime' (see, for example, Tombs, in Hillyard et al., 2004; Ward, 2004).

Several scholars have written extensively on why penal abolitionism is necessary. For instance, Thomas Mathiesen (1996) tackled the punishment framework in terms of the illogical 'balance of scales' notion of justice (108–40) wherein he demonstrates how attaining justice through punishment is logically not viable because one cannot make an equivalence between the degree of suffering incurred by the harm and the degree of suffering incurred by the punishment (see also Golash, 2005). He also suggests that the concept of deterrence is based on a fallacy. Deterrence is based on rational choice theory, but he shows that perpetrators of harm do not engage in cost–benefit analysis when on the cusp of committing harm (55–84).

Other scholars have focused on the relationship of punishment to colonialism. In Counter-Colonial Criminology, Biko Agozino (2003) makes the point that the roots of the criminal justice system are intimately connected to enlightenment principles and to colonialism:

> It was at the height of the slave trade that classicism emerged to challenge the arbitrary nature of punishment in medieval Europe, but this insight was not extended to enslaved Africans who were arbitrarily victimised… However, it was not until the height of colonialism in Africa and Asia that Europe discovered the new 'science' of criminology as a tool to aid the control of the Other.
>
> *(15)*

Acclaimed activist and abolitionist, Angela Davis (2000), examines the link between slavery and the penitentiary. Drawing on Hirsch (1992), she argues that the prison has similarities with the Slave Codes (Davis, 2000, 20). In fact, the prison industrial complex in the US is a continuation of slavery (see also Wacquant, 2000). Saleh-Hanna (2008, 2015) shows further the connection between colonialism, patriarchy, slavery and the criminal justice system.

Saleh-Hanna (2008) says penal abolitionism 'recognize[s] that societies have existed and were able to function without penal sanctions in the past, and thus contemporary society, though mentally and structurally reliant on the penal system, is capable of functioning without such a violent system' (458). She offers a 'penal abolitionist dictionary' (459) wherein she dispels certain myths and sets the record straight about what the concept entails. For instance, under 'responsibility', she says the abolitionist notion of the term entails that '… all persons who partake in violent, harmful behaviours should accept direct responsibility for their actions in non-violent, non-harmful ways' (461); unlike in the current system, where perpetrators are put behind bars, and where '… the penal system claims ownership of their actions and takes responsibility for their lives' (ibid.).

In subsequent writing, Saleh-Hanna (2015) explores Black feminist hauntology. In her interpretation of Toni Morrison's Beloved (1987), a novel about Fugitive Slave Laws in nineteenth-century US, she discusses penal colonialism and proposes a 'metamorphic liberation' of colonised and enslaved bodies:

> what I present is an exorcizing framework that, to start, names the structurally abusive nature of colonial race relations and the colonizing praxis of punishment that forms its power… Black Feminist Hauntology can be applied to lands, systems, histories and circumstances that, like European colonialism and chattel slavery, extend far beyond the borders of [the United States].
>
> *(para. 6)*

Beyond abolitionist scholarship, antipenal and antiprison movements around the world mount campaigns and devise strategies for abolition. No New SF Jail Coalition in the San Francisco (2017) area in the US is one local movement that successfully blocked the construction of a new jail and continues to fight against incarceration (No New SF Jail). The Oakland chapter of the US abolitionist organisation, Critical Resistance, has created 'an initiative to engage Oakland residents in building community power and wellbeing without relying on cops' (Critical Resistance, 2017). In Spain, an entrenched anarchist struggle in prison continues to flourish (Solar, 2016). Other countries also have active antiprison and antipenal movements (see, for instance, WIPAN which is now the Women's Justice Network, and JusticeAction in Australia; Empty Cages Collective in Britain).

The International Conference on Penal Abolition (ICOPA)

The only global and exclusively penal abolitionist gathering is ICOPA. The organisation meets in a different location usually every two years with the aim of learning from different struggles taking place on the ground; to help consolidate struggle in the jurisdiction where the conference is held; to provide a space to hear from survivors of state or social harm; to develop and further abolitionist theory; and to strategise penal abolition more broadly (see actionicopa.org). The three-day conference features plenaries, panels, art exhibits and performances, workshops and film screenings. It provides a space for the dissemination of prisoner writing, and usually organises a rally or march to protest a local case of injustice featuring the penal system.

ICOPA is organised by the local members. Typically, a person proposes their locale as the next site, and if the plenary agrees, they begin to organise locally with help from past ICOPA organisers. Some members have been attending ICOPAs for decades. Others are new and unfamiliar to it. There is a mix of academics (students and professors), activists, ex-prisoners, survivors of state or social harm and those close to the criminalised. There is overlap among these categories, some participants belonging to more than one group. It is worth noting that the academic contingent is preponderant, and often plays a central role in the conference's organisation and presentations.

Qualitative intersubjective analysis undertaken before during and after the fifteenth edition of ICOPA revealed the following concerns: decision-making and governance in an entity with no formal structures in a context where academics have more resources; tension around the emphasis on a critique of colonialism as a central plank in abolitionist thought and around racism and white privilege within ICOPA. These two considerations are related. The question of 'voice', and which type of participant has more or less attention from others in ICOPA, is the one that has been raised at plenaries and during interviews (Delisle et al., 2015). There is also the question of abolitionist purity, where those who favour reform measures to ameliorate criminal justice systems are viewed with suspicion (ibid.).

Some participants have called for a greater emphasis on the legacies of colonialism in abolitionist analysis that engender and perpetuate unearned privilege, oppression and the consequent criminalisation of certain groups; others conclude that such a colonialist analysis does not address the totality of abolitionist concerns. While a broad understanding of colonialism can explain the motivation and practice of controlling undesirable 'others', this line of inquiry is occluded for some who do not make the connections between colonialism and all forms of oppression. Plenary and informal conversations at several ICOPAs reveal this tension. Furthermore, there have been calls to undertake a process of conscientisation (Freire, 1972) in order that participants with prized statuses become more aware of others' oppressions, the effects of these and of their own privilege; grassroots groups (especially groups made up largely of working-class people of colour and Indigenous people) find meaning in taking part in ICOPA; subjugated voices (who more often are, or have been, criminalised) be emboldened and heard; unconscious and privileged zealousness be kept in check, in order to build prefigurative relations of solidarity and struggle among penal aboli-tionists internationally (Delisle et al., 2015).

Known as a conference-movement (Piché and Larsen 2010), ICOPA held its foundational conference in 1983. The brainchild of Canadian Quaker and abolitionist, Ruth Morris, and Dutch legal scholar, Louk Hulsman, it was conceived of as a space where abolitionist principles could thrive by bringing together scholars and activists to share, strategise and learn from each other. At the 1985 conference, held in Amsterdam, Canadian abolitionist Claire Culhane asked where the prisoners were. How, she asked, could there be a prison abolition conference without hearing first-hand from prisoners and ex-prisoners? (Delisle et al., 2015, Interview, July 11) So, when the conference was staged in Montreal in 1987, organisers ensured that prisoners' voices were central. Prisoners attended, having obtained 'Unescorted Temporary Absences' from their penal institution, or their writings were read out by others. Former prisoners were also in attendance. As a result of this conference, the primacy of prisoners' voices was translated into the creation of a peer-reviewed scholarly publication, the *Journal of Prisoners on Prisons*, which still thrives as a prized resource for antipenal scholars and activists alike. Contributions to this publication are made exclusively by prisoners or former prisoners in keeping with its goals: to provide scholars and other readers with a prisoner's viewpoint on incarceration rather than re-lying on scholarly or correctional perspectives. The critical publication provides its readership with on-the-ground critiques of punishment, by those targeted by state violence.

Questions about racism, patriarchy, (cis)heteronormativity, ableism and class have figured in ICOPA plenaries for a considerable number of years, though the focus here is primarily on the question of racism. During the 2000 meeting in Toronto, a debate surfaced about the lack of representation of people of colour within the group. While Indigenous people were present, people of colour were not well represented. Angela Davis (2000) states that '... the racial homogeneity of ICOPA, and the related failure to incorporate an analysis of race into the theoretical framework of their version of abolitionism, is a major weakness' (214). Dylan Rodriguez (2000) goes further: '... I found that the political vision of ICOPA was extraordinarily limited, especially considering its professed commitment to a more radical abolitionist analysis and program. This undoubtedly had a lot to do with the underlying racism of the organisation itself...' (ibid.). It was said that organisers had failed to solicit input and participation from major Canadian abolition groups made up mostly of people of colour. One participant noted, 'people were comfortable talking about how racist the system was, but not able to confront the fact that ICOPA was dominantly a white space' (Delisle et al., 2015, interview July 14a). While the representation of people of colour was lacking, there were a number of indigenous participants. This Indigenous participation is presented contra the notion that racism exists in ICOPA.

In 2008, at ICOPA XII, a conversation took place at the closing plenary dealing with race, gender, sexual preference and (dis)ableism. This led to the adoption of guiding princi-ples that included the timidly phrased goal of reaching 'the widest number of activist groups, people who experience discrimination, youth and recipients of the carceral, and encourage their participation as organizers, keynote speakers and presenters' (Creating a scandal, 2008). In the ICOPA 14[2] report, penalism is referred to as a construction based on 'the legacy of slavery and colonization' (ICOPA XIV (sic) Report, 2012). At ICOPAs 15 and 16, held on Algonquin territory (Ottawa) in 2014 and Quito, Ecuador in 2016, respectively, final ple-naries once more focused on racism and white privilege within the entity. The organisation that funds ICOPA reiterated their desire to see a fundamental change in the number of people of colour fully participating at the conference. They asserted that the disbursement of monies for the conference would hitherto be dependent on efforts at decolonising ICOPA (Statements by representatives of the Prisonless Society at ICOPA 14 and 16 final plenaries). Some participants see the fact that ICOPA is a predominantly white space not as a manifestation or indication of any inherently racist approach.

The staging of ICOPAs remains unproblematised with typically resource-heavy white academics in charge of their organisation. There are several reasons for this including the practicality of obtaining institutional space at little or no cost.[3] Salient questions about oppressive practices and unattended privilege have mobilised discussions, but have – to a certain extent – fallen on deaf ears. This is sometimes because oppressed groups '… are likely to have a heightened consciousness of their oppression, whereas those privileged by prized statuses often remain blithely unaware of them' (Pease, 2010, 19). Where such consciousness does exist among the privileged, there remains an inability to mobilise the participation of local grassroots groups at the organising level. If ICOPA is to be the nerve centre for penal abolitionists worldwide, it must find appropriate and effective ways to address this ongoing concern, in order to remain relevant.

ICOPA 17, held in New Bedford, Massachusetts, in July 2017, addressed the racism/privilege dynamic in no uncertain terms: the title of the conference was 'Abolition and its Ghosts: Historic Memory and Ongoing Struggles Against Colonialism and Slavery'. Intent on centring the conference on the impacts of colonial conquest, the programme called on participants to 'reflect upon and work towards articulating the veto power position that white supremacy holds at each point of the process required to birth and institute the repressive economic, cultural and gendering bodies of the criminal justice system' (Saleh-Hanna, 2017). The programme introduction continues: '… White supremacy, heteropatriarchy and Europe's imperialist economies … are issues that have plagued abolitionist thought and organizing from its very inception' (ibid.). It continues: 'We encourage you to begin the process of facing these ghosts so that you can begin to understand the impact they have had on our relationships to each other and to this movement' (ibid.). Grassroots groups – made up mostly of people of colour – played a central role in organising the conference. Intentional space (see below) can be orchestrated by groups who are traditionally more formal, or privileged, as a self-conscious way to provide a central space to grassroots groups of colour. In the case of ICOPA 17, the intentional space was fought for by people of colour and grass roots themselves.

The World Social Forum

As a confluence of worldwide social movements, the WSF is an international gathering of activists opposed to neo-liberal globalisation (Juris, 2008, 355). It began in Porto Alegre, Brazil in 2001 and has produced several editions, mostly in the global south, although the 2016 edition took place in Montreal. Concurrently, there have been regional manifestations of the WSF in different jurisdictions. Jai Sen (2007) characterises the WSF as a '… manifestation of world civil politics' (506), an '"open space"' for the '"incubation"' of movements' (507), 'not just a sidewalk, but a whole avenue, a boulevard' (512), and a 'global commons' (ibid.). While being an open and non-directed space, there are nonetheless power struggles, in part, because it is difficult for people (especially people from the global North) to let go of hegemonic structures of power and practices (Conway, 2013).

The WSF began in response to current neo-liberal agendas exemplified by international finance and trade organisations like the IMF, the World Bank, the WTO and the World Economic Forum (Conway, 2013, 1; 6). Conceived as an open space, that is, non-deliberative (9), the only prerequisite for participation is an opposition to neo-liberalism (ibid.). It gathers together social movements and individuals engaged in resistance to many forms of injustice (for instance in regards gender, race, class, ecology and others) and meets once a year. Examining some of the debates and conceptualisations of the WSF opens up a line of questioning that can be helpful when considering the power dynamics in ICOPA. A robust literature has developed which focuses on the workings of the forum itself. Among the critiques of the WSF is the notion of hegemonic epistemologies. Since the writings about the WSF are largely authored by white men of the global north, given their intellectual culture, a blindness to other forms of knowledge and praxis is evident (20). Open space and a massive number of diverse participants notwithstanding, Conway (2013) declares: '... the movements of the WSF are encountering each other on a historically unequal playing field constituted by the coloniality of power' (24).

Likewise in ICOPA, its roots, heritage and culture emanate from white, academic, often male portions of the global north, and this results in a reticence to not only adopt a colonial reading of punishment, but a stubborn resistance to considering interactions among ICOPA participants as rooted in the colonial mindset.

Intentional Space

One strategy for troubling unacknowledged privilege in the US Regional WSF event in 2007 in Atlanta is the creation of 'intentional space' (Juris, 2008). In order to rectify the lopsided white, resource-heavy and middle-class participation in some radical movements (i.e. WSFs, Occupy), the stewards of the US Social Forum (USSF), Grassroots Global Justice (GGJ), targeted grassroots working-class groups with a majority of people of colour in their ranks, for the initial organising call for the forum (359). The object was to ensure that grassroots movements made up of oppressed groups played a central part and wanted to participate. Intentional space *a contrario* open space can be seen as restricting certain 'hegemonic' voices. Such an intentional space was seen as necessary because, as one USSF participant put it:

> Having a nonhierarchical or horizontal collective structure doesn't mean just having an open circle for everyone to come in... It means having very intentional, deliberate structures... If we just have an open space, our internalized privileges or oppressions or entitlements come out.
>
> *(USSF participant, Juris, 2008)*

So creating this type of intentional space upends the 'highly institutionalized politics' of traditional movements (labour, non-profit organisations), and the more 'personalized' politics seen among middle-class activists (360). In addition, Juris argues, '... the communities that are most directly affected by prevailing structures of exploitation and inequality are viewed as the principal agents of social change' (ibid.).

Such a preferential scheme of organising can appear to limit openness. Indeed, some may invoke questions of fairness in such an approach. However, such a response points to the inability to consider that hegemonic power relations actually require intentional moves to disrupt privilege and to purposefully organise events and spaces aimed at equalising the playing field.

Oppression and Privilege

Mullaly (2002) proposes that the strategies to eradicate oppression are embedded in anti-oppression practice, which can be used at personal, cultural and institutional levels. He suggests that new social movements are one avenue for challenging such relations of domination. Problematically, however, none of his remedies involve addressing privilege (Pease, 2010, 169). For Pease (2010), it stands to reason that complementary strategies for addressing the reproduction of privilege include a necessary step in the process of abolishing domination, whether it be racial, class, patriarchal, (cis)heteronormative or ableist. One way is to challenge the normalisation of privilege; increasing awareness of people's privileges stands to alter this dynamic (170–1). Looking at social practices and determining which of these contribute to oppression is a start. Once acknowledged, the work of taking responsibility for one's own contribution to the oppressive situation becomes a possibility.

One such strategy incorporates the development of a 'pedagogy of the privileged' (Curry-Stevens, 2004, 2007 in Pease, 2010, 172). Inspired by Freire's (1972) Pedagogy of the Oppressed, Curry-Stevens offers a series of steps that may assist in developing an awareness of one's privilege, to looking at the structural dynamics in play, locating one's self in the spectrum, gaining an understanding of the benefits that accrue to the privileged and knowing the role one plays in contributing to the oppression of others (172).

Responses to privilege can occur in different ways. Sometimes, people avoid participating in a space where those with prized statuses ignore their role in oppression, or are defensive about their status, which is seen, for instance, in the remark 'I'm not racist'. In other cases, people from oppressed groups, once again, are put in the role of having to educate the privileged on oppression and privilege (hooks, 1988). This may involve calling out the unacknowledged privilege in a group or session. Often, it results in discomfort, frustration and anger among the people who have prized statuses but do not grasp the unearned benefits accrued to these statuses.

Avenues for Change

Anti-oppression and Pedagogy of Privilege Workshops

Potential avenues to dislodge the inequality rut in which entities such as ICOPA find themselves include establishing systematic workshops on anti-oppression and privilege, and decolonisation, in the conference programme; instituting 'intentional spaces' (see Juris, 2008) to promote grassroots involvement and overcome marginalisation within ICOPA; and that past and new organisers who work together towards the next edition be committed to ensuring the primacy of these considerations. The format of the opening plenary of ICOPA should be shortened in order to make room for an oppression-privilege workshop. This workshop can also integrate a decolonisation component. Regular acknowledgement of Indigenous territory (depending on the location) at the beginning of each plenary and each session is a helpful way to instil awareness of the harms done by colonisation. In addition, purposeful workshops such as 'The Blanket Exercise'[4] can be powerful reminders of the legacy of colonialist projects.

Traditionally, one of the opening keynote speakers is tasked with explaining ICOPA to the people assembled at the plenary and reminding participants of past ICOPA highlights. Addressing the tensions in ICOPA during this presentation would go a long way towards contextualising a number of debates. During the unfolding of the conference, delegates can continue to speak to issues and refer to the learning that took place during the plenary and/or the workshop, and this can contribute to further understanding the privilege/oppression dynamic.

Intentional Space

ICOPA 15 participants were surveyed for their reactions to the conference. Among the responses, some concerned the oppression/privilege axis and the need for intentional spaces for participants. Participants wanted exclusive space to receive support from peers if triggered by others' oppressive statements in the sessions or plenary, for instance, a space dedicated to people of colour, or to women. And some also signalled the need to have intentional spaces that were dedicated to coordinating support and solutions for the loved ones and allies of people currently incarcerated.

Intentional space in the sense in which it is used by Juris (2008) is different. But extrapolating from the survey, it points to the need for such intentionality. Subjugating the prominent voices in favour of a purposeful measure to give up openness so that individuals and groups, who are part of oppressed communities, take charge of the event's organisation and have a preponderant role in the conference presentations is one way to address the hegemonic structures of power. This would not be new in ICOPA since organisers have traditionally selected abolitionist presentations over proposals that contain a more reformist tone (see Delisle et al., 2015), thereby limiting the openness of the space based on theoretical considerations. Doing the same in regards to prioritising proposals from grassroots groups composed of people of colour may predispose the event to new and different ways to understand organising. It means that traditional ways of undertaking the tasks involved in bringing an international gathering together may change. It may mean giving preference to speakers, panel organisers and presenters who emanate from the oppressed groups to the detriment of mainly white, mainly privileged participants.

'ICOPA 17 was antipodal to regular conference organizing. The conference was organized by working class grassroots and academic people of colour and their allies, who called for holding an ICOPA on the traditional lands of the Wampanoag nation (now New Bedford, Massachusetts)' (Saleh-Hanna, 2017). By constructing the conference around the theme of colonialism and enslavement, it forced a reckoning with white supremacy, privilege and consequent occlusions of the workings of criminal (in)justice systems. The programme states: 'Tying our theme to historic memory and histories of enslavement and colonial conquest, disallows us from engaging with penal abolition in manners that deny or minimize the foundational properties of the problem at hand' (ibid.).

Conclusion

As with other social movement spaces, ICOPA is straddling traditional ways of converging with calls for new prefigurative practices that take into account subjugated voices in a meaningful way. Such new practices, it is hoped, will have repercussions not only for advancing abolitionist campaigns, but also on the ways in which penal abolitionism is theorised. Purposeful strategies of this kind can positively affect the overall tenor of conversations within the conference, abolitionist theory and abolitionist practice. The impacts of such strategies aim for a more robust engagement with others, in a space that is respectful and understanding of difference, a generosity of spirit and a heightened level of trust among participants. Such praxis opens up the possibility of deepening abolitionist thought, and collectively creating new forms of argumentation.

A guarantor of making ICOPA truly radical lies in a commitment to forego 'leading' tendencies by those with prized statuses, in favour of embracing a commitment to let others do the driving, others for whom oppression is a very real struggle they combat on an ongoing basis. This opens up the possibility of ICOPA becoming a radical space founded on solidarity and prefigurative politics that can lead to creative breakthroughs in theory and strategy geared towards abolishing penal systems. Can ICOPA craft a radical space dedicated to finding language and action that confront key areas of dissension? Can ICOPA chart new courses that multiply opportunities to abolish laws, practices, techniques and institutions of dehumanisation?

Radicalism and social movement organising confront and resist unfair power differentials in society. As such, a central feature of such activity involves an understanding of how power works, both at the social and societal levels. It thus makes sense that if groups do not adequately check power and privilege in their interactions, they risk reproducing the same injustice that they fight to abolish. Addressing these issues should be an ongoing and normal part of collective action. These questions reflect some of the concerns of ICOPA participants, go to the heart of prefiguring a radical abolitionist stance and provide a direction for deepening theoretical considerations about radical organising, and abolitionist strategy.

Notes

1 This chapter is based on a qualitative collaborative research project. I wish to thank Maria Basualdo, Adina Ilea, Andrea Hughes and Justin Piché for participating in this project. Thanks also to Ruth Kinna for the astute comments in the elaboration of this work.
2 A motion was adopted at ICOPA XII to change the numbering of conferences from Roman to Arabic as the latter was considered more accessible to a greater number of people.
3 The only funds attached to ICOPA are usually dedicated to ensuring that those with lived experience of criminalisation are able to attend the conference, and are therefore reserved for their travel and lodging. Academics are affiliated to universities where space can be obtained at little or no cost.
4 The Blanket Exercise was conceived by a Canadian organisation, Kairos, in which workshop participants stand on blankets, while a facilitator narrates the history of land-grabbing and the institution of the Reserve system for Indigenous people in Canada. The folding of blankets into smaller entities, while participants crowd onto ever-smaller blankets provides a powerful visual for the unjust and harmful effects of relegating Indigenous peoples to ever smaller and inhospitable portions of land.

References

Agozino, B. (2003). *Counter-Colonial Criminology: A Critique of Imperialist Reason*. London: Pluto Press.
Beccaria, C. (1764). Translation of Di Dellitti e Delle Pene. N.p.: Lorenzo da Ponte Italian Library series.
Carrier, N. and Piché, J. (2015). 'Blind Spots of Abolitionist Thought in Academia: On Longstanding and Emerging Challenges', Champ Pénal/Penal Field, XII, Abolitionnisme. http://champpenal. revues.org/9162. Last retrieved 27 May 2017.
Christie, N. (2001). *Crime Control as Industry: Towards Gulags Western Style*, 3rd ed. London: Routledge.
Conway, J. (2013). *Edges of Global Justice: The World Social Forum and its 'Others'*. London: Routledge.
Critical Resistance. http://criticalresistance.org/chapters/cr-oakland/the-oakland-power-projects/. Last retrieved 27 May 2017.
Curry-Stevens, A. (2007). 'New Forms of Transformative Education: Pedagogy for the Privileged', Journal of Transformative Education, 5, 33–58.
Davis A. and Rodriguez D. (2000). 'The Challenge of Prison Abolition: A Conversation', History is a Weapon www.historyisaweapon.com/defcon1/davisinterview.html. Last retrieved 23 August 2014.
Delisle, C., Basualdo, M., Ilea, A., and Hughes. A. (2015). 'The International Conference on Penal Abolition (ICOPA): Exploring Dynamics and Controversies as Observed at ICOPA 15 on Algonquin Territory' in Penal Field / Champ pénal, XII, Abolitionnisme. https://champpenal.revues. org/9146. Last retrieved 10 May 2015.
Empty Cages Collective: Organising & Action Against the Prison Industrial Complex. www.prisonabolition. org/. Last retrieved 24 June 2017.
Foucault, M. and Sheridan, A. (transl.). (1977). Discipline and Punish: The Birth of the Prison. New York: Vintage books.

Freire, P. and Bergman Ramos M. (transl.) (1972). The Pedagogy of the Oppressed. New York, NY: Herder & Herder.

Golash, D. (2005). *The Case Against Punishment: Retribution, Crime Prevention, and the Law.* New York: New York University Press.

Hillyard, P., Pantazis, C., and Tombs, S., (2004). Beyond Criminology: Taking Harm Seriously. Blackpoint, NS: Fernwood Publishing.

Hirsh, A. J. (1992). *The Rise of the Penitentiary: Prisons and Punishment in Early America.* New Haven and London: Yale University Press, 84.

hooks, b. (1988). *Talking Back: Thinking Feminist, Thinking Black.* Toronto: Between the Lines.

International Conference on Penal Abolition (ICOPA) XII (2008). *Creating a Scandal: Prison Abolition and the Policy Agenda*, Program. London: Howard League. http://actionicopa.org/items/83-ICOPA%2012_program.pdf

International Conference on Penal Abolition (ICOPA). www.actionicopa.org. Last retrieved 27 May 2017.

Journal of Prisoners on Prisons. www.jpp.org. Last retrieved 2 March 2016.

Juris, J. (2008). 'Spaces of Intentionality: Race, Class and Horizontality at the United States Social Forum'. Mobilisation: An International Journal, 13(4), 353–371.

Mathiesen, T. (1996). *Prison on Trial*, 3rd ed. Winchester, UK: Waterside Press.

Mathiesen, T. (2006). Prison on Trial, 3rd English ed. Winchester, UK: Waterford Press.

Morrison, T. (1987). *Beloved.* New York: Alfred A. Knopf.

Mullaly, B. (2002). *Challenging Oppression: A Critical Social Work Approach.* Don Mills, Ontario: Oxford University Press.

No New SF Jail. https://nonewsfjail.wordpress.com. Last retrieved 27 May 2017.

Pease, R. (2010). *Undoing Privilege: Unearned Advantage in a Divided World.* London: Zed Books.

Piché, J. and Larsen, M. (2010). 'The Moving Targets of Penal Abolitionism: ICOPA, Past, Present and Future', Contemporary Justice Review: Issues in Criminal, Social, and Restorative Justice, 13(4), 391–410.

Saleh-Hanna, V. (2008). Colonial Systems of Control: Criminal Justice in Nigeria. Ottawa: University of Ottawa Press.

Saleh-Hanna, V. (2015). 'Black Feminist Hauntology: Rememory the Ghosts of Abolition', Champs pénal / Penal Field, Abolitionnisme - Abolitionism, XII.

Saleh-Hanna, V. (2017). 'The 17th International Conference on Penal Abolition: Abolition and its Ghosts', Conference Programme. https://icopa17.wordpress.com/conference-program/. Last retrieved 2 September 2017.

Sen, J. (2007). 'The World Social Forum as an emergent learning process', Futures, 39, 505–522.

Solar, F. (2016). 'Nothing Is Over: On the Need to Accept the Fullness of Our Choices', in, 325. https://325.nostate.net/2016/06/07/letter-from-imprisoned-anarchist-comrade-francisco-solar-nothing-is-over-spain/. Last retrieved 27 May 2017.

Tombs, S. (2004). 'Workplace Injury and Death: Social Harm and the Illusions of Law' in, Hillyard, P., Pantazis, C., and Tombs, S. (eds.), Beyond Criminology: Taking Harm Seriously. Blackpoint, NS: Fernwood Publishing, 156–177.

Wacquant, L. (2003). Deadly Symbiosis: Race and the Rise of Neoliberal Penalty. Oxford: Oxford Blackwell Publishers.

Ward, A. (2004). 'State Harms', in, Hillyard, P., Pantazis, C., and Tombs, S. (eds.), Beyond Criminology: Taking Harm Seriously. Blackpoint, NS: Fernwood Publishing, 84–100.

World Social Forum 2016, Montreal, 9–14 August, 2016. https://fsm2016.org/en/. Last retrieved 14 July 2016.

2.6

SAFER SPACES

Ruth A. Deller

Introduction

In this chapter, I explore the notions of 'safer spaces' – places where people from different marginalised groups can gather, speak and be resourced in safety. Safer spaces can be physical, but they are also cultural – framed by a series of boundaries, principles and practices designed to support members of the group(s) needing the safer space. I explore here some of the motivations and underlying principles of safer spaces, and the roles they can play in radical politics. This chapter focuses predominantly on examples relating to gender, sex, ethnicity, health and dis/ability although the cultivation of safer spaces can also include practices such as creating equality and diversity policies; providing appropriate dietary options for vegetarians, vegans, members of different faith groups and those with food allergies or other medical conditions; health and safety policies that ensure the physical safety of events and organisations, and ethics policies that ensure appropriate research and professional conduct in a variety of contexts. I explore a number of ways safer spaces operate in different contexts such as education, healthcare and political groups and consider their implications as spaces of resistance, mobilisation and care – as well as media debates over safer spaces and political activism.

I also reflect on the outcomes of four workshops (two in the UK, two in the USA) with academics, educators and activists discussing issues of social justice and safe spaces and sharing experiences of implementing different strategies. The number of attendants at each workshop varied; in the smallest events, in the UK, there were around twenty participants and in the largest, in the USA, around fifty, and in the other two events approximately thirty to forty participants. A range of ethnic, gender and sexual identities were present in all four events, although the majority lived in Western countries (some as immigrants from places including India, Pakistan and Singapore). The ages of participants varied from 18 to 60.[1]

In the last few years, issues relating to 'safe spaces' have dominated newspaper headlines around the world – as ideas and practices well established in political movements have increasingly spread to workplaces, educational establishments and Internet groups. The phenomenon of safer spaces and different aspects associated with these, such as trigger warnings (TWs) and practices of inclusivity (e.g. gender-neutral language, diversity policies) have garnered coverage and debate in both traditional and newer media outlets.[2]

While media coverage of safe spaces often portrays them as a recent trend, practices of creating safe (or rather, *safer*, as no environment can necessarily be completely safe) spaces are not new to those involved in radical politics. Challenging dominant discourses and power structures through activities such as 'no platforming', implementing TWs, establishing boundaries around meetings, privileging minority voices and creating protected physical spaces have long been part of the ethos and praxis of feminist, queer and other radical groups.

At the heart of creating safer spaces is the acknowledgement that, while the world is not truly 'safe' for anyone, it is more dangerous for some than others. Gender, ethnicity, sexuality, age, class, dis/ability and many other factors contribute to the status or privilege different individuals have within any society as well as their personal safety. The types of danger vary, but can include violence, verbal abuse, bullying, exclusion, discrimination, harm to property, inequality of access to services, resources or justice, emotional trauma and even death. Harm may result from encounters between individuals, or it may be embedded within institutionalised practices and customs that favour some groups over others. It is worth noting here that within many of the debates around harm and safety, the concept of 'offence' regularly recurs. Critics of safer-space practices often perceive 'offence' as distinct from 'harm'; yet, it is often difficult to distinguish between the two in practice. For example, when racist slurs are used against others, it is often difficult to draw a clear line between 'hurt' and 'offence' in that person's affective response. In this article, I will, therefore, focus more on notions of 'harm' or 'hurt', except when discussing examples that specifically reference 'offence' – while acknowledging that this area is far from clear-cut.

Safer-space practice is about understanding and prioritising the needs of the most at-risk – not as a way of sealing them off from the realities of life, but as a way of resourcing, equipping and supporting people to meet those realities. It is about challenging and transforming those realities. The direct action group Sisters Uncut explain: 'Sisters Uncut aims to create a respectful, compassionate and kind space… When we come together to organise in a respectful and considerate way, we are creating the change we want to see in the world' (Sisters Uncut 2016). To give another example, Black Lives Matter states:

> We are committed to collectively, lovingly and courageously working vigorously for freedom and justice for Black people and, by extension all people. As we forge our path, we intentionally build and nurture a beloved community that is bonded together through a beautiful struggle that is restorative, not depleting.
>
> *(Black Lives Matter 2017)*

In many countries, we could argue that there have been a number of positive improvements for members of groups that have historically been marginalised: the legalisation of same-sex marriage; increased visibility and acceptance of trans and non-binary individuals; heightened awareness of a range of mental and physical health problems; public examples of 'calling out' behaviour that could be seen as racist, sexist, homophobic and so on. Media, education, healthcare and politics have all been shaped by equality politics in radical ways over the last 100 years and there is increasing recognition of the ways in which dominant groups have marginalised and oppressed non-dominant groups. We could certainly argue that many countries are now legally, politically and culturally safer spaces for those who have historically suffered systemic oppression.

Sadly, of course, despite these changes, there are still many ways in which even the most liberal societies remain unequal and unsafe as others in this collection discuss. Some improvement in these areas does not mean all battles have been won. The Black Lives Matter movement emerged during Obama's presidency. As a response to the killing of (often young) black men at the hands of white police, the movement is a stark reminder that the reality for many black Americans is one in which they – and even Obama himself – are still subject to systemic racism. As Morgan notes,

> An exemplary black man was elected into the highest office in the nation - twice - and not only was he subjected to the harshest, most racially-charged criticism himself, but the day-to-day lives of black and brown people improved very little… When people are already dying en masse, it is belittling to argue that it's better than it was. If 1892 was the most violent year of lynchings in the United States -161 black people that we know of were murdered - then what good does it do to tell black youth that things are better if 258 black people were killed by police in 2016? The comparative lens doesn't hold.
>
> *(Morgan 2017)*

Contemporary radical movements explicitly draw attention to the continuing insecurity felt particularly in minority communities. Black Lives Matter says:

> We are broadening the conversation around state violence to include all of the ways in which Black people are intentionally left powerless at the hands of the state. We are talking about the ways in which Black lives are deprived of our basic human rights and dignity.
>
> *(Black Lives Matter 2017)*

The Women's March reiterates the point:

> We must create a society in which women - including Black women, Native women, poor women, immigrant women, disabled women, Muslim women, lesbian, queer and trans women - are free and able to care for and nurture their families, however they are formed, in safe and healthy environments free from structural impediments.
>
> *(Women's March 2017)*

Activists seek to carve out safer space at multiple levels – from the macro level of large-scale campaigns and interventions that bring societal change, to the micro level of cultivating localised safer spaces within small communities. Many of the examples discussed in this chapter are small-scale – individual educators and their students; activist bloggers; sexual health centres. Others are networked groups campaigning to affect changes across multiple locations, such as Rhodes Must Fall (RMF), an international movement calling for the decolonisation of university campuses – including the removal of colonial iconography.

What I present here is not so much a 'how-to', but a reflection on the complexities and challenges of creating safer spaces, both in terms of the practical implications and the implications for challenging power and privilege. I focus here both on physical and cultural forms of safer space, recognising that different contexts require different strategies.

Safer Spaces and Physical Environments

In this section, I explore a range of ways that physical environments can be created or modified as forms of safer space.[3] Physical forms of safer space may include modifications to existing spaces to make them safer for a range of users; providing resources and spaces solely for the use of one group (e.g. rooms, events, transport, festivals, hostels, addiction support meetings, therapy centres). Other forms of physical safer space may include neighbourhoods, cities or even countries that, while not necessarily 'exclusive' to one particular group, offer freedom, sanctuary and a sense of community – e.g. districts that have high concentrations of immigrant or LGBTQ+ residents and businesses (see Kenney 2001; Hanhardt 2013), or the idea of 'cities of sanctuary' (Darling 2010; Squire 2011) that welcome refugees.

Although we might often think of safer spaces as being *distinct* spaces set aside for the use of particular groups (and I will discuss such spaces later in this section), activists and campaigners have a long history of highlighting that the built environment is often unsafe for members of marginalised communities, and have sought to effect change. While there is a growing awareness of the need to make buildings accessible for people with disabilities (although there is still a long way to go here), physical environments and public spaces also have gendered and racialised components that may not present the same physical barriers as, say a set of steps would pose to a wheelchair user, but offer symbolic barriers instead.

For example, public toilets pose a number of issues when we think about safe and inclusive spaces. Traditionally, public toilets have segregated people along binary gender lines with traditional 'male' and 'female' designations. Accessible toilets, commonly marked out with the wheelchair symbol, on the other hand, serve to de-gender people with disabilities as well as reinforcing the idea that all people who might need such a facility use wheelchairs.

The binary-gendering of public toilets poses challenges for non-binary individuals who either have to choose a gender identity for the purposes of relieving themselves or use the disabled facility when they are not disabled – something not always possible, as in the case of disabled toilets requiring a Radar key or similar to enter, nor desirable as it may prevent a disabled person from using it. Gender-neutral toilets are slowly becoming more commonplace (see Sanghani 2015), although there are often cultural and practical reasons why these are hard to implement everywhere.

However, even for those who identify as male or female, public toilets can prove challenging. In the USA, for example, there were a number of headlines in 2016 generated by the idea of 'bathroom bills', such as North Carolina's Public Facilities Privacy and Security Act which requires individuals to use the toilets for the sex assigned on their birth certificate, which means transpeople who have not had their birth certificate altered (and in some states, this is only possible following full reassignment surgery) have to use the toilet of the sex on their birth certificate, rather than the gender they identify as – thus meaning transwomen have to use men's toilets and vice versa. Furthermore, if users do not carry their birth certificates, there is the chance people could be refused use of the bathroom even if they have the 'correct' genitals if they don't look sufficiently 'male' or 'female'. These bills often use the idea of 'safety' as a justification:

> The federal government's mandate requiring Texas public schools to provide students access to restrooms, showers, and dressing rooms based on an individual student's internal sense of gender is alarming and could potentially lead to boys and girls showering

together... children receiving an education in Texas public schools and open-enrollment charter schools are entitled to a safe and secure learning environment, including when using intimate facilities.

(*Texas Senate Bill 6, cited in Ura and Murphy 2017*)

The North Carolina act specifically removed 'gender' as a basis for safeguarding individuals, replacing it with 'biological sex', and claiming that the bathroom policy was not discriminatory because of this:

It is the public policy of this State to protect and safeguard the right and opportunity of all individuals within the State to enjoy fully and equally... places of public accommodation free of discrimination because of race, religion, color, national origin, or biological sex, provided that designating multiple or single occupancy bathrooms or changing facilities according to biological sex, as defined in G.S. 143–760(a)(1), (3), and (5), shall not be deemed to constitute discrimination.

(*General Assembly of North Carolina 2016: 5*)

Despite the rhetoric of 'safety' as a rationale for these bills, many commentators note that there is little-to-no risk to cisgendered users from transindividuals using the bathroom aligning with their gender identity. For example, 'CNN reached out to 20 law enforcement agencies in states with antidiscrimination policies covering gender identity. None who answered reported any bathroom assaults after the policies took effect' (Grinberg and Stewart 2017). The symbolic denial of transpeople's experience in these bills acts as a form of harm in numerous ways. In research conducted with trans and non-binary individuals, Herman (2013) identified instances of bullying, verbal and physical assault, stress, social exclusion and even urinary and kidney problems linked to their experiences of using toilets.

The problems of space are not confined to toilets, however. Faces and bodies represented in posters, banners and signs also play a role in signifying who is, and is not included in a community – and architecture and artworks likewise have a role to play in creating the culture of physical environments, from steps inaccessible by wheelchair users to statues celebrating only old white men, the way space is constructed both symbolically and practically reinforces and normalises forms of injustice and discrimination.

Several student-led movements have recently highlighted racial inequalities on university campuses. For example, the campaign I, Too, Am Harvard and its equivalents at other universities, including Oxford, featured photographs from students from different minority ethnic groups holding cards detailing some of the racist comments they had encountered from others on campus. These students articulated how they found the public spaces of the universities exclusionary and unsafe: 'Our voices often go unheard on this campus, our experiences are devalued, our presence is questioned – this project is our way of speaking back, of claiming this campus, of standing up to say: We are here. This place is ours' (I, Too, Am Harvard 2014); 'Students in their daily encounters at Oxford are made to feel different and Othered from the Oxford community' (I, Too, Am Oxford 2014).

Another high-profile campaign, RMF, is an international movement calling for the decolonisation of university campuses – including the removal of colonial iconography, such as statues of Cecil Rhodes.[4] The two most publicised campaigns of RMF were its calls to topple statues of Rhodes in Cape Town and Oxford. The former was successful, with the statue removed in April 2015, while (at the time of writing) the statue in Oxford remains. As with 'I, Too, Am…', RMF highlighted systemic issues within universities that were compounded by the presence of iconography such as the Rhodes statues in public spaces on campus, reinforcing a sense for black and minority ethnic students and staff that this space was not one in which they were safe or welcome. Its aims included:

> Tackling the plague of colonial iconography (in the form of statues, plaques and paintings) that seeks to whitewash and distort history… Reforming the Euro-centric curriculum … Addressing the underrepresentation and lack of welfare provision for Black and minority ethnic (BME) amongst Oxford's academic staff and students. RMFO is about more than a statue. However, we believe that statues and symbols matter; they are a means through which communities express their values. The normalised glorification of a man who for so many is a symbol of their historical oppression is a tacit admission that – as it stands – Oxford does not consider their history to be important.
>
> *(RMF Oxford 2015)*

Movements like RMF have, at their heart, an agenda to highlight the way practices of marginalisation, discrimination and oppression are embedded into everyday life through the physical environment, and that which may seem 'normal' and 'everyday' often represents systemic inequalities. The responses to the movement from Oxford's chancellor and vice chancellor (who are both white) demonstrated a lack of willingness to engage with the issues raised, instead criticising the students and, ironically, claiming that students were stifling debate, while themselves refusing to debate the situation. For example, on Radio 4's *Today* show, the Chancellor, Chris Patten, said that, perhaps, the students who did not approve of the statue 'should think about being educated elsewhere' and argued: 'People have to face up to facts in history which they don't like and talk about them and debate them' (cited in Gayle and Khomami 2016), while vice chancellor Louise Richardson wanted students to 'appreciate the value of engaging with ideas they find objectionable … without forgetting the traditions that bind us to our forebears' (cited in Oxford University 2016).

'Freedom of speech' was cited as a reason for keeping the statue; yet, statues do not speak. Other arguments cited the need to understand and respect history rather than erase it; yet, such arguments have been thin on the ground when statues of Lenin, Hitler, Sadaam Hussein and even Jimmy Savile have been removed from public spaces around the world. Indeed, the toppling of statues is an act imbued with symbolism, and politicians and media have often celebrated the act as symbolising change. As Rao observes,

> It has been fascinating to watch pillars of the British establishment deride RMFO's demand for the removal of the Rhodes statue as an impingement on freedom of thought, when in fact the British state and media have, in other contexts, treated the toppling of statues as synonymous with the embrace of freedom … statues are never merely symbolic, which is also to say that there is nothing mere about symbolism.
>
> *(Rao 2016)*

This long history of statue-toppling as a symbolic act is precisely why it has formed a core part of RMF's call to action – something largely ignored by the movement's critics.

As with many such arguments about 'pampered' students, the disregard for RMF's grievances and protests appears to be the alternative of 'free' speech. By characterising student protest thus, those in power appear, instead, to be trying to silence debate and thus avoid looking at the continued legacy of systemic privilege and oppression. RMFO spoke out against this hypocrisy:

> The new Vice-Chancellor, Louise Richardson, when asked about Rhodes Must Fall in May 2016 responded by talking about 'cosseted' students and the need for free speech, forgetting the fact that Rhodes Must Fall has always aimed to start a debate about colonisation, slavery and historical injustice at Oxford. It is the University that has tried to shut down this debate. It is the University that has wanted to create a safe space – to commemorate and thus valorise colonialism and slavery.
>
> *(RMFO 2016)*

While I have thus far discussed attempts to make public spaces safer, there are examples of activist groups carving out specific spaces to gather, be they online groups, or dedicated rooms and buildings. Such congregating allows strategic visibility for marginalised communities, as Kenney notes, '[v]isibility, in the context of gay and lesbian activism, has been at the centre of collective attempts to confront the risk … Place works as both a physical and social site of resistance and as a manifestation of shared meaning in specific contexts and communities' (2001: 15).

In the same vein, forms of activism such as public protests, marches, vigils and rallies are often about creating temporal safer spaces in often unsafe public arenas. Through mobilising large numbers of people to gather with a common agenda, marches and other gatherings attempt to reclaim space for those often marginalised by it. Chan (2004) notes that, for example, the long-running women's march Reclaim The Night 'creates a space for women only, where they feel strengthened by the sense of richness and connectedness with other women. Women can have a sense of claiming the spaces which they have once thought of as fearful such as walking the streets alone at night' (p20. See also: Bhavnani and Coulson 1986; Hanhardt 2008).

Physical safe space can allow marginalised individuals to group together, both for mobilisation to collective action and for collective care (Kenney 2001). It can provide sanctuary and protection for victims of violence or respite and care for people experiencing a mental health crisis. It provides those struggling with addictions a place to share their experiences and support one another's recovery. In many varied ways, physical safe space offers a place of refuge, retreat and regrouping. Successful safer spaces enable users to live more effectively in the wider world. For example, Garcia et al.'s (2015) work highlights how safer spaces for black men who have sex with men, including specific spaces for those with HIV, give users a sense of community while empowering them to live and thrive when social and bureaucratic infrastructures fail them. Likewise, LGBTQ+ young people studied by Richard Barry (2000) used their safer spaces as ways of exploring and owning their identities and questioning the power and norms of the wider world, drawing strength from each other.

Contrary to much of the criticism of safer spaces as places to 'hide from ideas' (Berg, 2015), safer spaces are not meant to be separate from the world around them; rather, they offer space to return to and go from. Those who use safer spaces are usually fully aware of, and engaged in, the so-called 'real world'. It is the exposure to 'real world' prejudice, hatred, violence, abuse and damage that makes safer spaces important as a way of tending to the wounds caused by living day-to-day in that world.

In addition to the examples outlined in this chapter, there are many other issues surrounding the physical safety of spaces. At one of the workshops we ran in the USA, a university lecturer spoke about her fear for her physical safety and that of her colleagues and students now that guns were to be allowed on campus (and, of course, both advocates and opponents of guns use the rhetoric of safety and security to justify their position). As a Brit to whom such a threat is entirely alien, I do not feel able to comment on how to stay safe in such a context, although Firmin DeBrabander's *Do Guns Make Us Free?* (2015) is an interesting discussion of the issue from an American perspective.[5]

Whether through carving out rooms or venues for groups together, mobilising in public for a march or calling for the gender, racial and ability inequalities in spaces to be addressed, physical safer spaces can play an important role in supporting activists, mobilising the marginalised and, ultimately, securing changes to make all spaces safer for those who use them.

Setting the Boundaries of Safer Spaces

When it comes to safer-space practice, boundary setting is a crucial component, whether we are talking about physical safer spaces such as specialist rooms, or more conceptual safer spaces, such as online communities or activist groups. Establishing who can and cannot 'come in', and why, and agreeing what is and is not acceptable within the space contribute to helping it feel safe for members.

In the workshops on safer spaces, one challenge many people spoke of was how to set boundaries around safe space that were protective of those who needed the space without being hostile or unnecessarily exclusionary. Different groups adopted different strategies, from focusing on participant identification – e.g. queer spaces with a policy of 'if you identify as queer, you're welcome' (and similar for women-only spaces), to specific boundary-marking practices such as listing codes of conduct outside the entrance to venues and expecting entrants to abide by them. Many groups used identifiers such as flags and graphics to symbolise the groups a space was designed for. Likewise, in online communities, boundary creation occurred through practices such as users agreeing to terms and conditions, clearly worded mission statements and, again, visual signifiers such as flags and icons.

Of course, while boundary creation serves ideally to protect members of a community, it can sometimes be perceived as hostile or discriminatory, such as in the case of women/ womyn-only spaces that exclude transwomen, the most famous example being the now defunct Michigan Womyn's Festival, which had a 'womyn-born-womyn' policy – meaning those assigned female at birth. When it comes to enacting boundaries and process of inclusion/exclusion, what is always at stake is power and identity. Excluding transwomen serves to misgender them, and reinforces their status as marginalised outsiders. Cisgender women thus exercise their power and privilege by excluding transwomen, which perhaps runs counter to a sense of sisterhood or female solidarity.

In a similar vein, there have been numerous examples of feminist and queer spaces often perpetuating other forms of 'othering' and exclusion through the dominance of white and able-bodied individuals (Simons 1979; Lloyd 2001; Poynter and Washington 2005). Even at one of the workshops we ran, where we thought we had established a culture of inclusivity which gave everyone a chance to speak, we encountered the challenges of intersecting identities. A middle-aged white cisgender gay man clashed with two younger contributors (one female and Asian; the other white and non-binary – their sexual orientations were not disclosed). While their disagreement was merely on how to enact cultures of safer space, drawing on their own experiences, they felt that he was using the power accorded to him by his ethnicity, age and gender to speak over them and they became hostile towards him. He, then, responded out of hurt, calling attention to his membership of a minority community

(Irish Travellers) that had long suffered abuse on both an ethnic and class-based level and that he, as a middle-aged gay man, had also suffered prejudices for this identity in ways that he perceived younger queer people might not. Although we, as facilitators, attempted to mitigate the tension by allowing each of them to speak, the younger participants left the session early and one of my colleagues spent significant time after the session talking with the man concerned. This incident reminded us that, often, people's experiences of discrimination and hurt are never far from the surface, even in seemingly 'safe' environments.

Cultures of Safer Spaces

Regardless of whether we are referring to a physically bounded space or not, safer spaces are about developing a culture in which members feel safe to belong, to speak, to gather, to heal and to build from. All the decolonised campuses and gender-neutral toilets in the world mean little if they are not accompanied by practices of inclusivity, respect and care.

Practices adopted in safer spaces vary according to context, but almost always involve creating a set of guidelines or code of practice outlining the values of the space and the expectations of users. These, ideally, should be created by members of the group – although in larger institutions such as schools or hospitals, this may be harder to achieve en masse and may operate more at local levels (although campaigning for policy change is a huge part of the work of radical politics).

Groups differ significantly in how they establish and practice their boundaries. For some in the workshops, such as a young queer activist group, and an addiction recovery group, these codes are pinned on walls, visibly reinforcing the formally presented boundaries and values. Some of the teachers we spoke to asked their students to set the culture of lessons at the start of the academic year – although varied in practice as to what extent this was formalised into a set of guidelines, code of conduct or similar.

However, there is more to creating and enacting cultures of safer space than writing guidelines and policies. There are several practices groups can engage in to try and create this safety. Some of these may be about applying legal or institutional regulations such as having equality and diversity policies or complying with human rights legislation. But there are also smaller actions, often on a local level, that can be adopted. No platforming, the adoption of inclusive language and TWs are three examples discussed below.

No Platforming

One such action is the process of 'no-platforming' – a concept that has made headlines in the 2010s as a result of the complaints that high-profile figures including writers Julie Bindel and Milo Yiannopoulo, Australian second-wave feminist thinker Germaine Greer and UK rights activist Peter Tatchell have been no-platformed and barred from speaking at events, most notably at universities (Morris 2015, Sterne and Spargo 2015). No platforming is a process whereby groups or individuals are denied permission to speak in certain groups or venues. The National Union of Students (NUS), for example, has a no-platform policy against extremist groups such as the British National Party and Hizb ut-tahrir (NUS 2017).

There is a lot of misunderstanding about no platforming and speakers have sometimes claimed that they have been 'no platformed' when in fact no policy exists. For example, the oft-repeated claim that the NUS has an official no-platform policy against Julie Bindel, because she 'is vile', is inaccurate (Lewis 2015). While individual university unions or groups within the NUS have separate no-platforming policies, the NUS as a whole has only no-platformed *organisations*.

The safety issues with which no platforming is associated are also sometimes lost in public debates. A 2015 Cardiff University students' petition to stop Germaine Greer giving a guest lecture due to her antitransgender views (among other things, Greer has said that transgender women are not women (see McMahon 2015)) was all-too-often presented as a 'campaign to silence her' (Morris 2015) rather than a legitimate criticism of her views on transpeople. The event was not cancelled, although others have been. An event on 'free speech' featuring Julie Bindel and Milo Yiannopoulos at Manchester Students' Union (Sterne and Spargo 2015) was stopped because the Union felt that their 'views could incite hatred against both transpeople and women who have experienced sexual violence' and breach the safe space policy (Manchester Students' Union 2015).

Criticisms of these protests almost always refer to the importance of 'freedom of speech'. *Spiked* Deputy Editor Tom Slater calls no platforming 'a palpable threat to the founding principles of the academy, and, by connection, democratic society' (2016). However, one of the fundamental problems with the deification of 'free speech' is that speech is rarely, if ever, free. Structural inequalities continue to promote certain voices over others and therefore an alleged 'freedom' inevitably means that the loudest voices tend to be those with certain privileges. Tatchell, Greer, Bindel and Yianoppolous all have access to a range of platforms via the status conferred on them by their celebrity (as well as age, ethnicity, career background and other factors); academics have status conferred on them by their roles and qualifications and, of course, male, white, middle-aged cisgender and heterosexual voices remain the loudest in many contexts. As Ahmed puts it,

> Whenever people keep being given a platform to say they have no platform, or whenever people speak endlessly about being silenced, you not only have a performative contradiction; you are witnessing a mechanism of power. I often describe diversity work as mechanical work. We know a lot about the mechanisms of power when we try to transform the norms embedded in a situation.
>
> *(Ahmed 2015)*

Arguments about 'freedom of speech' need to also acknowledge the structural inequalities and systemic injustices and abuses that facilitate the need for 'safer spaces' in the first place. Often, such valorisation of freedom of speech merely legitimises the rights of racists, homophobes and others to perpetuate prejudicial ideologies by presenting them merely as part of a 'debate' – and campaigners seeking to challenge this prejudice through protest, no platforming or other forms of creating safe space are often characterised as bullying or unreasonable. Such discourse only serves to further disempower those voices:

> Transphobia and anti-trans statements should not be treated as just another viewpoint that we should be free to express at a happy diversity table … When you have dialogue or debate with those who wish to eliminate you from the conversation (because they do not recognise what is necessary for your survival or because they don't even think your existence is possible), then dialogue and debate becomes another technique of elimination. A refusal to have some dialogues and some debates can thus be a key tactic for survival. The presentation of trans activists as a lobby and as bullies rather than as minorities who are constantly being called upon to defend their right to exist is a mechanism of power.
>
> *(Ahmed 2015)*

Inclusive Language

Part of the issue of 'freedom of speech', apart from the views being aired and those doing the speaking, represents the problematic power structures of language itself. Making languages 'safer' by encouraging the use of inclusive terms and by identifying and 'calling out' slurs and discriminatory language has long been a part of radical politics. As language expresses how we perceive the world around us and communicate with one another, it is a powerful tool for members of radical political movements. The transformation of language often takes place when changes of practice adopted by small groups are disseminated into the wider world through repetition, media and other communicative practices (see Cameron 1990; McKenzie-Mohr 2014).

What happens to language once it becomes more widely spread is never certain: 'Once new vocabulary takes hold beyond its movement – which is, after all, the intention – it is taken up and activated by those with varying goals and interests and it is often reshaped as it is used more widely' (Devault 2014: 24). Changes in practice that become helpful to marginalised groups, such as the adoption of gender-neutral phrases, or the removal from everyday language of racist slurs – to name just two examples – still operate within existing social relations. Thus, there is no real control over how the initial disruption and transformation will be used – it may not achieve its original aims.

It is also important to remember the varying social and cultural contexts in which language has played a part and the contestations that result from deliberate disruptions. In recent years, the phrase 'person (or people) of colour' (POC) has become increasingly widespread as a catch-all term for people from a range of ethnic backgrounds. In the USA, this term has become widely adopted in radical politics, first spread online before becoming commonplace in the media and other cultural outlets. In the UK, there has been a mixed response to the term. Indeed, in the latter part of the twentieth century, a lot of work was done in public discourse to alter the language used to talk about ethnicity. The term 'coloured' was denounced for its insensitive othering and the homogenisation of different minority ethnicities under an unhelpful blanket term. In its place, it became much more commonplace to refer to somebody as 'black', 'white', 'Asian' or 'mixed-race' (although these categories, too, are highly reductive and imprecise as well as excluding a range of identities that do not fit neatly into them). Other terms emerged in public discourse to deal with diversity: 'ethnic minorities' and, more recently 'BAME (Black, Asian and Minority Ethnic)'. Certainly, in discourse produced by UK businesses, large organisations and governments, these terms are far more prevalent than 'POC' or its variants. We could make a similar point about the use of 'handicapped'. In the USA, this is used in everyday life to refer to people with disabilities; yet, it is deemed offensive in the UK. So we must be mindful that when we are using language that is seen to be inclusive or acceptable in one culture, it may not always travel well.

Trigger warnings

The third of the most frequently debated aspects of safer spaces in recent years has been the phenomenon of 'trigger warnings' or 'content notes' – a system of providing warnings for content that might be deemed 'triggering' in different ways. The process of 'triggering' refers to something that might enact a response in trauma sufferers, such as panic attacks, flashbacks or other unwanted symptoms, although its critics tend to characterise the term as also encompassing hurt, offence or anger (Halberstam 2014; Lukianoff and Haidt 2015).

TWs are commonplace on many parts of the Internet, including blogs, Tumblr, feminist and LGBTQ+ sites and fan fiction archives, where content may be prefigured with a list of TWs (e.g. for rape, violence, racist slurs). Content can also be tagged in some platforms, such as Instagram, Twitter or Tumblr allowing users either to actively search out that content or blacklist it (e.g. tags such as #edchat which deal with conversations around eating disorders).

Not all online environments use TWs, of course. However, many outlets offer other clues as to the content of their articles. *Jezebel*, for example, does not use TWs, but 'our headlines and intro text are meant to clearly convey where the content of each post is heading' (Jessica Coen in Moore, 2014). The reason TWs have become part of a wider media debate, however, is primarily due to stories about their use (or lack of) in education.

The use of TWs has been criticised for infantalising students, giving them an excuse to avoid complicated subjects: much of this criticism refers specifically to using TWs for literature or art (even though 'trigger warnings' are widely accepted when applied to film, TV and video games, suggesting a perception of 'harm' that is different when applied to 'high' culture as opposed to 'popular' culture).

In the safer-space workshops, there was a range of practice in this area. One queer activism group used signs in venues detailing both their inclusion policy and 'warnings' for the kind of topics that would be discussed at their events (in a similar way to warnings for strobe lighting in concert venues). A blogger listed TWs before their posts and always provided a 'more' button so that users had to actively click through to read the article rather than coming across potentially triggering content. One psychology lecturer told students at the start of term when they would be discussing topics such as rape, mental health, etc., so that students could be prepared and were told that if the issue was 'live' for them, they had freedom to either not attend that week or leave if needed. A film studies tutor offered statements in module handbooks about which films on the module contained sensitive or potentially upsetting material. A secondary school teacher did not use TWs but did set parameters with their class on how students would treat each other and handle talking about difficult issues at the start of the academic year.

Participants discussed the complexity of personal triggers – at one event, a wall of post-its revealed dozens of potential triggers from the obvious ones such as rape to perhaps more unusual ones including seeing people eat meat. There were discussions about potential options – databases of TWs that users could look up before reading a book or attending an event; only providing warnings for common triggers such as rape/sexual assault, racism or mental health issues; giving informal warnings but without labelling them as a 'trigger warning' per se.

Others do not have a specific policy themselves, but allow students or group members to create their own position on warnings: 'I've never required student writers to use trigger warnings, but I've kept the space open for them to respect the requests of their classmates … a sizable number were very excited to have the conversation, something they reported had been mocked by other creative writing professors' (Lawlor in Milks 2014).

Of course, what is really at stake when it comes to establishing safer-space culture is not whether or not TWs are adopted – or any other specific practice. The issue is about to what extent communities and groups are inclusive, which almost always relates to the way power operates within such groups. For groups to be truly radical, they need to create a culture that celebrates, includes and listens to the most marginalised members of that group and that ultimately prioritises *people* over principles.

Safer Spaces in an Unsafe World

As I have discussed, there is a lot of hostility to 'safer space' practices. However, asking people to simply accept that 'life is triggering' and criticising those who 'take offence', protest against injustice or challenge oppressive and discriminatory aspects of culture simply seeks to undermine their voices and agency. Such rhetoric only serves to reinforce a message of conforming to the status quo and accepting the inequalities of life. As Liv Little, editor-in-chief of online magazine *gal-dem*, puts it,

> I don't get what they want to happen. Do they want people to be quiet and suck it up? Do they want people to have breakdowns and be really unhappy and accept a political system that doesn't represent them?… A lot of offensive stuff is happening. Why should people not be offended? People are offended but they're using that feeling of being offended to bring about change. Things are so dire sometimes that it's necessary. If I want to carve out a safe space, why shouldn't I?'
>
> *(In Nicholson 2016)*

Arguments made against safe spaces all too often delegitimise the voices of the people that need those spaces. Asking people to simply 'grow up' and 'get over themselves' reduces their experience to something that is trivial, childish or inconsequential. Often those who use the argument of free speech do not understand that speech is rarely free – and that platforms and power are not available equally to all. Many of those clamouring for safer spaces are simply searching for a space in which they can be seen and heard. When their experiences, sensitivities, traumas and identities are not only questioned, but rejected, their voices become harder and harder to hear. Wrongly accused by the power of controlling the parameters of communication, they become (or remain) controlled, subdued and disempowered.

Those seeking 'safer space' are often dismissed as demanding, oversensitive or 'special snowflakes' (Nicholson 2016) afraid of life. However, as Roxanne Gay points out, those who make these criticisms often are those 'who are able to take safety for granted' (2015). Of course, the irony is that critics of such practices often act even more offended and hurt, such as the famous example of President Donald Trump complaining on Twitter after Mike Pence was booed during a performance of *Hamilton* that 'The Theater must always be a safe and special place. The cast of Hamilton was very rude last night to a very good man, Mike Pence. Apologize!' (Trump, cited in Nagesh 2016).

This example may demonstrate that emotions run high on both 'sides' of these debates. At one workshop focused specifically on higher education and safer spaces, I was in a peer group discussing the Germaine Greer Cardiff example mentioned earlier in this chapter. This peer group comprised a mixture of genders, ages and races, but we all shared the view that we would be uncomfortable with inviting Greer to speak on topics relating to gender and sexual identity, particularly where it was likely to make a significant number of the students feel uncomfortable. We thought that it would be wise to consult with students first and either to not invite Greer at all, or to ensure her position was countered. To us, it seemed a similar situation to inviting Nick Griffin (the former British National Party leader) to a debate on immigration or race.

However, the moderator of the session – a woman whose political and academic life had coincided largely with the second-wave feminist movement – became quite agitated and upset when talking to us about the situation and our perspective on it. She did not agree that students' opinions should be taken into account here because of a combination of the importance of the issues at hand and the status of Greer. Interestingly, she had not been this strident when it came to discussing TWs, sexism or other aspects of safer spaces earlier in the session – it was clearly this particular debate that struck a raw nerve for her. For this woman, a lot was at stake emotionally. Reflecting on it later, it seemed to me like much of this emotion came from the fear that the battles won by the second feminist movement and the influence of Greer and her contemporaries at that time could be lost or forgotten amidst the controversy around Greer's more recent statements around transidentity.

This example illustrated starkly to me that what is at stake is not a matter of intellectual debate. Were that the case, both second-wave feminists and student protesters would no doubt realise that they share a desire to challenge the idea of binary gender norms and essentialist ideas about masculinity and femininity – and may well mutually conclude that it is possible to do this while also supporting the rights and experiences of trans and non-binary individuals. But it is not about that – is about the *affective experience* of power, access and inclusion. The students in Cardiff protested Greer because her statements deny the existence of transpeople and affording her a platform gives her power and could be seen to reinforce her views. For my colleague, the issue was also exclusion – protests against Greer were felt as a rejection of her generation of activists.

Just as in the example of the clash between the middle-aged gay man and the younger female and non-binary individuals mentioned earlier in the chapter, both 'sides' bring with them a plethora of felt experiences of hurt, inequality and struggle. Both groups have wrestled with powerlessness – and when they perceive a threat to what little power they do have, this causes an affective response. Indeed, this is true of most situations discussed in this chapter. Those who seek to retain statues of Cecil Rhodes at Oxford are as motivated by affect as the members of RMF: there may be affective ties to the past, perhaps, or maybe to architectural aesthetics. But the biggest issue at stake here is, of course, power. When activists attempt to claim safe space for themselves, be that through taking over a room, marching through a city or calling for a statue to be removed, they are threatening the status of those in power – and the powerful will have an emotional response.

Safer spaces, as with most aspects of radical politics, cannot be discussed merely as a matter of intellectual reasoning – these things matter to people because they have an impact on our physical, emotional and mental well-being and are often embedded within the cultural, legal and societal frameworks that govern all our lives. Without understanding each other's lived experience, we cannot meaningfully effect change. As Paulo Freire puts it:

> revolutionary leaders commit many errors and miscalculations by not taking into account something so real as the people's view of the world: a view which explicitly and implicitly contains their concerns, their doubts, their hopes, their way of seeing the leaders, their perceptions of themselves and of the oppressors, their religious beliefs (almost always syncretic), their fatalism, their rebellious reactions.
>
> *(2000: 182)*

I am not saying that people's hurts and fears justify their behaviours and attitudes. However, it is only through remembering both our humanity and that of the people or groups we may be in dispute with that we can ever possibly hope to achieve change. Let us take heed of Freire's reminder that, in order for our struggles to have meaning:

> the oppressed must not, in seeking to regain their humanity, becoming turn oppressors of the oppressors, but rather restorers of the humanity of both ... Who are better

prepared than the oppressed to understand the terrible significance of an oppressive society?... Who can better understand the necessity of liberation?

(2000: 45)

Even within radical groups, there can be dissent and members can hurt one another. The history of feminism, for example, is littered with heartbreaking examples of racism and transphobia. No safer-space policy is perfect. We will cause distress – what matters is our commitment to one another and to changing our practices and attitudes where necessary. Truitt argues that the term 'accountable space' may sometimes be more helpful:

> Accountability means being responsible to oneself and each other for our own words. It means entering a space with good intentions but understanding that we all screw up and need to accept responsibility for our mistakes. It means being open to being called out. It means acknowledging when others are triggered and when we feel pain and working to learn and grow from this experience. And it requires something incredibly difficult, a trust in those we share a space with that their intentions are good, that they mean well just like we do, that we are all in a process of learning and growing and that making mistakes is part of how this happens.
>
> *(Truitt 2009)*

To create a truly radical politics means caring for one another – and it also means looking after ourselves. The work of social justice can be emotionally and physically draining and we will inevitably get knocked and bruised along the way. Therefore, we must remember Lorde's assertion that 'Caring for myself is not self-indulgence, it is self-preservation, and that is an act of political warfare' (1988: 131). Keeping ourselves safe will help strengthen us to protect, and advocate for, others. Meg-John Barker, in a helpful comic dedicated to self-care, lists mantras we should speak to ourselves, including:

- Looking after myself means that I survive in a world that doesn't want people like me to survive.
- Caring for myself demonstrates that people like me are valuable even if we are being treated as though we were disposable.
- Self-care gives me the energy to resist (2017: 4).

Ultimately, to create a truly safe space is to become skilled at radical care, radical kindness and radical love – of oneself, of one another and of the world which we live in: 'And this fight, because of the purpose given it by the oppressed, will actually constitute an act of love opposing the lovelessness which lies at the heart of the oppressors' violence' (Freire 2000:45).

What is really at stake here, of course, is the cultivation of communities that are inclusive and supportive – that equip people to fight for their place in the wider world, to seek justice and enact change. Things like TWs, no platforming and diversity policies are merely mechanisms that can be utilised within communities to enact their principles in practice. Inevitably, we will cause one another harm in some way, whether intentional or not. As Harris helpfully reminds us, 'There's virtually no way to create a room of two people that doesn't include the reproduction of some unequal power relation, but there's also no way to engage in politics by yourself' (2015). Creating a supportive culture is far more important than which techniques are utilised in that creation. What is central is that everyone wants to feel that they matter; that they can be heard; that they can have some power to impact the world around them.

Notes

1 None of these events were recorded onto audio or video and so I discuss these examples by referring to things that were discussed in the sessions and to notes made by myself, my co-organisers and participants themselves during each event (for example, there were a number of exercises in which participants wrote things on post-its or flip charts), but I am unable to provide verbatim quotes from individuals.

2 It is worth noting that the issues around safer spaces are not only debated differently in different outlets (as one might expect, given the age and political leanings of different audiences), but that media coverage also differs according to country. In addition, this is not an issue we can easily frame in terms of left/right or liberal/conservative. For example, in the USA, much of the antagonistic discourse comes from right leaning movements, including the so-called 'alt right', whilst in the UK, both left- and right-wing commenters have been notably critical of some safer-space practices.

3 Of course, whilst there is insufficient room in this chapter to cover this area, environmental concern and practices to conserve the planet represent another form of enacting safer space.

4 As this volume went to press, in August 2017, the issue of statues in public spaces made the news once more. Following the decision to remove a statue of Confederate army general Robert E Lee from a park in Charlottesville, Virginia, a protest against the decision by a group of far right activists calling themselves 'Unite the Right' made news worldwide as a protestor drove a vehicle into a group of antifascist demonstrators, killing thirty-two-year-old Heather Heyer and injuring nineteen others.

5 It is also worth noting that practices ostensibly designed to make spaces safe from violence, such as security checking for weapons and explosives, have all too often been used as excuses for racial profiling, discrimination and unlawful arrests, violence and even killings – as the Black Lives Matter movement (among others) emphasises. As Hanhardt puts it, 'The increased attention paid to security has revealed the disparate understandings of threat held among those considered representative of and those marginal to the national body politic' (2008: 62).

References

Ahmed, Sara, 'You Are Oppressing Us!', *Feminist Killjoys* (2015) https://feministkilljoys.com/2015/02/15/you-are-oppressing-us/.

Barker, Meg John, 'Hell Yeah Self-Care', *Rewriting the Rules* (2017) http://rewriting-the-rules.com/wp-content/uploads/2017/02/HellYeahSelfCare.pdf.

Barry, Richard, 'Sheltered "Children": The Self-Creation of a Safe Space by Gay, Lesbian, and Bisexual Students'. In Lois Weis and Michelle Fine (eds.), *Construction Sites: Excavating Race, Class, and Gender among Urban Youth* (New York: Teachers College Press, 2000), 84–99.

Berg, Chris, 'When Safe Spaces Become an Attack on Ideas', *ABC News* (17 November 2015) www.abc.net.au/news/2015-11-17/berg-when-safe-spaces-become-an-attack-on-ideas/6946534.

Bhavnani, Kum-Kum and Margaret Coulson, 'Transforming Socialist-Feminism: The Challenge of Racism', *Feminist Review*, 23 (1986), 81–92.

Black Lives Matter 'Guiding Principles', *BLM website* (2017) http://blacklivesmatter.com/guiding-principles/.

Cameron, Deborah (ed.), *The Feminist Critique of Language: A Reader.* (London: Routledge, 1990).

Chan, Beatrice, 'Reclaim the Night', *Social Movements in Action Conference Papers.* (New South Wales and Sydney: Research Initiative in International Activism, 2004), 20–23.

Darling, Jonathan, 'A City of Sanctuary: The Relational Re-imagining of Sheffield's Asylum Politics', *Transactions of the Institute of British Geographers*, 35: 1 (2010), 125–140.

DeBrabander, Firmin, *Do Guns Make Us Free? Democracy and the Armed Society.* (New Haven, CT: Yale University Press, 2015).

Devault, Marjorie L, 'Language and Stories in Motion'. In Suzanne McKenzie-Mohr and Michelle N Lafrance (eds.), *Women Voicing Resistance* (London: Routledge, 2014), 16–28.

Freire, Paulo, *Pedagogy of the Oppressed*, 30th anniversary edition. (London: Bloomsbury, 2000).

Garcia, Jonathan et al., '"You're Really Gonna Kick Us All Out?" Sustaining Safe Spaces for Community-Based HIV Prevention and Control among Black Men Who Have Sex with Men', *PLoS ONE* 10: 10 (2015) doi:10.1371/journal.pone.0141326.

Gay, Roxanne, 'The Seduction of Safety, on Campus and Beyond', *New York Times* (15 November 2015) www.nytimes.com/2015/11/15/opinion/sunday/the-seduction-of-safety-on-campus-and-beyond.html.

General Assembly of North Carolina, 'Public Facilities Privacy & Security Act', *North Carolina General Assembly* (2016) www.ncleg.net/Sessions/2015E2/Bills/House/PDF/H2v0.pdf.

Grinberg, Emanuella and Stewart, Danni, '3 Myths That Shape the Transgender Bathroom Debate', *CNN* (8 March 2017) http://edition.cnn.com/2017/03/07/health/transgender-bathroom-law-facts-myths/index.html.

Halberstam, Jack, 'You Are Triggering Me: The Neo Liberal Rhetoric of Harm, Danger and Trauma', *Bully Bloggers* (5 July 2014) https://bullybloggers.wordpress.com/2014/07/05/you-are-triggering-me-the-neo-liberal-rhetoric-of-harm-danger-and-trauma/.

Hanhardt, Christina B., 'Butterflies, Whistles, and Fists: Gay Safe Streets Patrols and the New Gay Ghetto, 1976–1981', *Radical History Review* 100 (2008), 61–85.

Hanhardt, Christina B, *Safe Space: Gay Neighborhood History and the Politics of Violence.* (Durham: Duke University Press, 2013).

Harris, Malcolm, 'What's a 'Safe Space'? A Look at the Phrase's 50-Year History', *Fusion* (2015) http://fusion.net/story/231089/safe-space-history/.

Herman, Jody L., 'Gendered Restrooms and Minority Stress: The Public Regulation of Gender and Its Impact on Transgender People's Lives', *Journal of Public Management and Social Policy* 19: 1 (2013), 65–80.

I, Too Am Harvard (2014) http://itooamharvard.tumblr.com/.

I, Too Am Oxford (2014) http://itooamoxford.tumblr.com/.

Kenney, Moira R., *Mapping Gay LA* (Philadelphia: Temple, 2001).

Lewis, Helen, 'What the Row over Banning Germaine Greer Is Really About', *New Scientist* (27 October 2015), www.newstatesman.com/politics/feminism/2015/10/what-row-over-banning-germaine-greer-really-about.

Lloyd, Margaret, 'The Politics of Disability and Feminism: Discord or Synthesis?', *Sociology* 35: 3 (August 2001), 715–728.

Lorde, Audre, *A Burst of Light: Essays* (New York: Firebrand, 1988).

Lukianoff, Greg and Haidt, Jonathan 'The Coddling of the American Mind' *The Atlantic* (September 2015) www.theatlantic.com/magazine/archive/2015/09/the-coddling-of-the-american-mind/399356/.

Manchester Students' Union 'UPDATED Statement from the Students' Union 05.10.2015' *MSU Website* (5 October 2015) http://manchesterstudentsunion.com/articles/updated-statement-from-the-students-union-05-10-2015.

McKenzie-Mohr, Suzanne, 'Counter-Storying Rape'. In Suzanne McKenzie-Mohr and Michelle N Lafrance (eds.), *Women Voicing Resistance* (London: Routledge, 2014), 64–83.

McMahon, Alle, 'Germaine Greer Defends Views on Transgender Issues Amid Calls for Cancellation of Feminism Lecture', *ABC News* (25 October 2015) www.abc.net.au/news/2015-10-25/germaine-greer-defends-views-on-transgender-issues/6883132.

Milks, Megan, 'On Trigger Warnings: A Roundtable', *Entropy* (14 April 2014) https://entropymag.org/on-trigger-warnings-part-i-in-the-creative-writing-classroom/.

Morgan, Danielle Fuentes, 'Obama and Black Lives Matter: An epilogue', *Al Jazeera* (27 January 2017) www.aljazeera.com/indepth/opinion/2017/01/obama-black-lives-matter-epilogue-170126073428660.html.

Moore, Tracy, 'We Don't Have to Use Trigger Warnings, But We Can Learn From Them', *Jezebel* (20 May 2014) https://jezebel.com/we-dont-have-to-use-trigger-warnings-but-we-can-learn-1578653191.

Morris, Stephen, 'Germaine Greer gives University Lecture Despite Campaign to Silence Her', *The Guardian* (18 November 2015) www.theguardian.com/books/2015/nov/18/transgender-activists-protest-germaine-greer-lecture-cardiff-university.

Nagesh, Ashitha, 'Special Snowflake Donald Trump Demands 'Safe Spaces' After People Boo Mike Pence', *Metro* (19 November 2016) http://metro.co.uk/2016/11/19/special-snowflake-donald-trump-demands-safe-spaces-after-people-boo-mike-pence-6269311/.

Nicholson, Rebecca, '"Poor Little Snowflake": The Defining Insult of 2016', *The Guardian* (28 Nov 2016) www.theguardian.com/science/2016/nov/28/snowflake-insult-disdain-young-people.

NUS, 'NUS' no-platform policy', *NUS* (13 February 2017) www.nusconnect.org.uk/resources/nus-no-platform-policy-f22f.

Oxford University, 'New Oxford Vice-Chancellor Calls for 'Agile' University at the Forefront of Global Change', *Oxford University website* (12 January 2016) www.ox.ac.uk/news/2016-01-12-new-oxford-vice-chancellor-calls-agile-university-forefront-global-change.

Poynter, Kerry John and Washington, Jamie, 'Multiple Identities: Creating Community on Campus for LGBT Students', *New Directions for Student Services* 111 (Autumn 2005), 41–47.

Rao, Rahul, 'On Statues'. *The Disorder of Things* (2 April 2016) https://thedisorderofthings.com/2016/04/02/on-statues/.

Rhodes Must Fall Oxford, 'Update', *RMFO Facebook*, (2 December 2016) www.facebook.com/RhodesMustFallOxford/posts/1830215297249169.

Rhodes Must Fall Oxford, 'Our Aim', *RMFO Website* (2015) https://rmfoxford.wordpress.com/about/.

Sanghani, Radikha, 'Why the UK Should Ditch Male and Female Toilets for 'Gender-Neutral' Loos', *The Telegraph* (14 December 2015) www.telegraph.co.uk/women/life/why-the-uk-should-ditch-male-and-female-toilets-for-gender-neutr/.

Simons, Margaret A, 'Racism and Feminism: A Schism in the Sisterhood', *Feminist Studies* 5: 2 (Summer 1979), 384–401.

Sisters Uncut, 'Safer Spaces Policy', *Sisters Uncut* (2016) www.sistersuncut.org/saferspaces/.

Slater, Tom, 'The Tyranny of Safe Spaces', *Spiked* (15 January 2016) www.spiked-online.com/newsite/article/the-tyranny-of-safe-spaces/17933#.WL7ho9LyiW9.

Squire, Vicki, 'From Community Cohesion to Mobile Solidarities: The City of Sanctuary Network and the Strangers into Citizens Campaign', *Political Studies* 59: 2 (2011), 290–307.

Sterne, Jenny and Spargo, Charlie, 'Update: Yiannopoulos Also Banned from Censorship Event', *The Mancunion* (7 October 2015) http://mancunion.com/2015/10/07/update-yiannopoulos-also-banned-from-censorship-event/.

Truitt, Jos, 'There Are No Safe Spaces', *Feministing* (12 August 2009) http://feministing.com/2009/08/12/there-are-no-safe-spaces/.

Ura, Alexa and Murphy, Ryan, 'Here's What the Texas Bathroom Bill Means in Plain English', *Texas Tribune* (9 June 2017) https://apps.texastribune.org/texas-bathroom-bill-annotated/.

Women's March, 'Global Unity Principles', *Women's March* (2017) https://womensmarchglobal.org/about/unity-principles/.

2.7

FIGHTING TO WIN

Radical Antipoverty Organising

A. J. Withers for the Ontario Coalition Against Poverty (OCAP)

Introduction

The rich are consolidating global wealth. The world's richest 1% owns half of global wealth and the richest 10% owns 88% of global wealth. At the same time, the poorest 50% of the world's population owns below 1% of global wealth (Credit Suisse AG Research Institute 2015). But, even in the context of neo-liberal globalisation, poor people have made important gains. In South Africa, the Western Cape Anti-Eviction Campaign has prevented hundreds, if not thousands, of evictions in Cape Town (van Erdewijk and Dubel 2012). In Québec, Canada, over 1,000 Algerians gained immigration status through a specialised process that was fought for by the Action Committee for Non-Status Algerians and No One is Illegal (Lowry and Nyers 2003). Brazil's Landless Worker's Movement (MST) has won 7.5 million hectares of land for poor people (Friends of the MST, n.d.). A coalition of, largely, working-class people of colour in New York City won oversight of the police and the legal prohibition of racial profiling (DRUM, 2013).

Radical antipoverty organising is hard work and involves fighting an uphill battle; nevertheless, it has and can continue to win important gains for poor people and is an integral part of the global struggle for social justice. In this chapter, I will discuss some of the strengths and difficulties of poor people's organising, primarily focusing on the lessons learned from the Ontario Coalition Against Poverty (OCAP). Using OCAP as an example, I will discuss the importance of addressing both individual and community needs, using disruption and resisting demobilisation.

For twenty-five years, OCAP has organised poor communities using anticapitalist direct action in Ontario, Canada. OCAP emerged out of a province-wide coalition demanding a raise in social assistance rates during a provincial election campaign. At a protest, John Clarke, who would go on to become an OCAP founder, called the sitting Premier the 'poverty premier' which stuck and helped swing the election (McCuaig 1990) in favour of a supposedly social democratic party. The New Democratic Party (NDP) government enacted a series of austerity measures which were profoundly detrimental to poor communities. While much of the Left failed to take action against the NDP government, believing this was the best that could be done, OCAP became a scrappy group unafraid to take direct action to improve the lives of poor people. OCAP quickly became a Toronto-based organisation rather than a province-wide coalition. OCAP is an intergenerational, racially diverse (although majority white) organisation made up of primarily poor and working-class people.

What Is Radical Antipoverty Organising?

A variety of organisations use the term 'antipoverty' to describe the work they do. The World Bank (2016), for example, says 'our dream is a world free of poverty' even though it inflicts poverty and misery around the world, particularly in the Global South (Klein 2007; Bateman 2010). There is nothing radical about this kind of 'antipoverty' work. Radical means 'from the root' – fighting poverty at its root causes. Indeed, there is nothing antipoverty about this work. Anticapitalist theory is fundamental to radical poor people's organising because capitalism both creates and relies on poverty. Dixon (2014) argues: 'capitalism is a system of social relations based on dispossession, exploitation, and alienation for the benefit of a small minority' (67). Capitalism creates poverty and exploits workers. Consequently, groups actually working to eliminate poverty must also be anticapitalist.

Anticapitalist theory, however, has often been reductive – holding that the elimination of capitalism is the fundamental or only change needed to end oppression. Opposing capitalism but upholding and/or supporting white supremacy, patriarchy, disablism, heterosexism, cissism or other forms of oppression is not radical. Radical antipoverty organising emerges out of the understanding that oppressions are interlocked. Fellows and Razack (1997) write that this 'means that the systems of oppression come into existence in and through one another' (335). They argue that sexism and racism enable class exploitation; I would also add that disablism, heterosexism and cissism are interlocked with and enable class exploitation. While eliminating the capitalist system is essential for eliminating poverty, it will not eliminate the suffering of the groups of people who are currently poor. Other forms of oppression must also be eliminated. It will also not fully eliminate the relations that create oppression. Bannerji (1995) observes that oppression, like capitalism, is the result of social and economic relations between people. It is only by ending these particular relations that they can be eliminated.

Because oppressions are interlocked and relational, radical antipoverty organising often involves organising around issues that might not usually be considered antipoverty work. For instance, the OCAP often does anticolonial, migrant justice, antipolice brutality, antiviolence against women, antiwar and disability justice organising. This is also why Piven and Cloward (1979), whose influential book *Poor People's Movements: Why they Succeed, How they Fail* I will be discussing extensively for its contribution to antipoverty theory and practice, dedicated a chapter to the Civil Rights Movement, although its primary issue was race rather than class. The concepts of interlocking and relational oppression help frame contemporary poor people's movements and the work that they do in areas that are not typically considered antipoverty organising.

Of course, poor people do not generally join organisations with a pre-existing radical analysis of oppression or capitalism (and developing anti-oppression politics is a lifelong venture). There can be significant tensions between diverse groups of poor people. One OCAP organiser explains this attitude: 'So if you are poor and you're white it's not the government's fault that you're poor, it is that working class white people have their jobs stolen by immigrants' (Henaway in Fortier, 2005, p. 97). In addition to migrant bashing, non-Indigenous people often blame Indigenous people for their poverty because they perceive Indigenous people to be receiving 'extra' resources (Acharya and Scott 2016). However, some poor people benefit from the oppression of others. While Indigenous people aren't the cause of non-Indigenous people's poverty in settler states, non-Indigenous people are complicit in the injustices inflicted on Indigenous people, including poverty. Franz Fanon (2004/1968) demonstrates how the working class in colonial states have an interest in maintaining colonialism, rather than in aligning themselves with Third World workers. Colonial relations benefit people who are a part of the colonising group, including those most disadvantaged in that group. In settler states like Canada, settlers benefit not only from the exploitation of resources and labour in colonised states but also from the very land and water used to sustain their existence.

Developing class consciousness among poor people who have settler, immigration and/or racial privilege helps enable them to see their poverty as a result of capitalist social relations rather than other poor people. It is necessary to shift the blame from migrants, Indigenous people and other scapegoated groups who are also exploited and oppressed by these relations. Because of the injustices of colonialism and the subjugation of colonised people, an anticolonial/decolonial politic is necessary for antipoverty organising in colonising states to truly be radical.

Furthermore, it is with a broad community base that movements have strong foundations to withstand decline or attack in to push ruling relations into concessions. Our work is also based on the idea that OCAP organisers are a part of the communities in which we organise – primarily as poor people, but also as neighbours and workers. We aren't outsiders and we know we are no better than the people we are organising with. We do not think we know best what someone needs but we do acknowledge that we have particular kinds of skills and knowledge that are an asset. Most of our organisers and members are or have been on social assistance or low wage workers and we have an intimate understanding of how the system works and the impact it has on people. The people who we are organising with are not our 'clients'; they are people with whom we are united in struggle.

Furthermore, radical antipoverty work links local struggles to broader global justice movements. OCAP believes: 'While continuing the colonization and genocide of Indigenous people here, Canada plays an imperial role on an international scale. It is integral that our organisation chooses to support resistance to imperialism in Afghanistan, Palestine and across the world' (Clarke, 2010). In addition to OCAP's organising work within antiwar and anti-imperialism struggles in Toronto, OCAP has organised 'reciprocal solidarity' (Fortier 2005: 52) demonstrations in support of disabled activists fighting institutional abuses in Greece, tenants in New Orleans and South Africa, tent city residents in Japan, workers in South Korea and Sri Lanka, and poor and disabled people in the UK and Palestine. When OCAP was facing intense repression and criminalisation, solidarity actions to support us were held by groups in Brazil, South Africa, South Korea, Japan, the US and UK.

Finally, radical movements fight to win.[1] Social movements, including antipoverty organising, are vehicles for change. If they have no intention to bring about meaningful change, there is no reason for them to exist. Indeed, symbolic organising that simply works to register dissent can impede the change that it purportedly advocates. In OCAP, 'the extraordinary durability of notions such as token protest and sedate accommodation have proven to be a massive obstacle for us' (Clarke 2003, p. 501). There are long-standing critiques of symbolic protest or what Ryan (1998) calls protesting as 'a form of catharsis', that alleviates protestors from their guilt 'without posing a threat' (139). An example is when a group of artists pieced together a scarf they hoped would wrap around a square Toronto block to 'raise awareness' about homelessness. They got to feel very good about themselves but no change would come of it. Some antiwar protests also fall into this category: people passively march through the streets with no intention to make change but to feel better about themselves for having 'done something'. Drawing on and supporting Churchill's (1998/1986) *Pacifism as Pathology*, Ryan continues: 'clearly the state allows us to engage in these actions because they're harmless or, worse, because they reinforce the popular myth of Canadian democracy' (140). Reinforcing this myth is not benign. It works to legitimise and uphold ruling relations.[2]

Sometimes, however, what would be considered a symbolic protest in some circumstances is not in others. OCAP and other organisations who oppose symbolic protest for its own sake may sometimes use symbolic protest strategically as part of a larger campaign that is designed to win real gains.

The OCAP Organising Model

The 'OCAP model' combines mass mobilising with direct action casework as our way of hooking the collective and individual, the systemic and specific, into one another. Mass mobilising is the organisation of campaigns to win our collective demands. These campaigns are generally longer term struggles (from a few months to years) and primarily focused on increasing social assistance rates and shelter (including increased emergency shelter beds and for homeless people as well as decent, affordable, accessible housing). This model evolved out of work being done by the London (Ontario) Union of Unemployed Workers which developed ways to respond to the treatments of poor people by, primarily, social assistance. One of the Union's founders, John Clarke, was also a founder of OCAP. The model was also influenced by Wal Hannington's (1936) organising accounts in the UK. After OCAP was established, members found *Poor People's Movements* by Piven and Cloward (1979) to be a helpful resource. It focuses on historical poor people's movements, particularly during the Great Depression and welfare rights and civil rights organising in the 1960s. This work helped solidify OCAP's theoretical understandings of poor people's organising and commitment to coupling direct action casework with mass mobilising.

While the campaigns have shifted over the years, they generally prioritise issues of income and shelter. OCAP believes that we can't simply fight for sweeping social change, including our demands of at least a 55% increase in social assistance and housing for all and ultimately the overthrow of capitalism and oppression, without dealing with poor people's immediate needs. At the same time, only dealing with someone's immediate needs, like a welfare benefit or unreturned damage deposit, doesn't do anything to change the systems that keep poor people down. The way that we fight for people's immediate individual needs is through direct action casework. I will primarily focus on our direct action casework in this section and discuss mass mobilising in the next.

The success of direct action casework, like all of our work, relies on the strategy of disruption. Poor people's organising has particular limitations because we have so few resources and so little individual power. There are a number of barriers to organising poor people. John Clarke (1992) writes 'oppression never fails to leave its mark on its victims' (216) and this impacts all aspects of poor people's lives, including organising. Organising can be difficult with any group of people but with poor people, the lack of resources, access to elites and exclusion from the political process intensify this difficulty. All of these barriers are related to the social and economic marginalisation of poor people and result in poor people not having 'normal' mechanisms to affect change. Consequently, poor people have to take 'non-normative collective action' (Piven and Cloward 1991, also see 1979).

Because of our lack of resources and individual power, Alinsky (1971) argues, 'Have-Nots must build power from their own flesh and blood' (127). Piven and Cloward (1979) maintain that collective disruption is the only way that poor people can win concessions from ruling relations precisely because of their social status. It is through the collective refusal to cooperate with institutional life that poor people's power can be enacted. Or as an ally of OCAP said: 'unionized workers can assert their strength by not being where their employer wants them to be, but the poor can only have power by being where they're not supposed to be' (in Clarke 2010, p. n.p.). Piven argues that 'poor people's cooperation tends to be kept in place by rules' rather than with economic power in an employer-employee relationship (Miller and Piven 2012). Social assistance rules, tenancy rules, immigration rules and criminal rules all work to regulate poor people and it is in breaking these rules that poor people can make material gains. Poor people's power is generated, then, through collective disruption.

Disruption has been the cornerstone of OCAP's strategy and tactics and, I would argue, this is necessary for any antipoverty organising that hopes to be effective. Disruption can take any number of forms. For OCAP, it has included the crashing of fancy governing party fundraisers or press events – making speeches about the injustices the government is perpetuating, putting forward our demands and, often, taking some food for ourselves. Because food, and the lack of it, is so significant to poor people's lives, we have disrupted normal grocery store operations by protesting outside, bringing the tills to a halt and stealing food. We have occupied government offices, city council, political party headquarters, the Provincial Cabinet Office and Minister's offices, refusing to allow business-as-usual to take place. We even shut down the tenancy tribunal – throwing a wrench in the government's eviction machine for a day.

In the early 2000s, we engaged in a campaign of economic disruption designed to target the corporate backers of the Conservative government that had viciously attacked poor people – including the criminalisation of panhandling and cutting social assistance rates by 22%. By that point, hundreds of thousands of people, mostly workers, had marched in the streets against this government to no effect. Our logic was that if the Premier would not be responsive to the people, we would attack the businesses that supported him and make it too expensive to keep him in power. Along with groups across the province, we organised a week of economic disruption around Ontario. The night before OCAP's action in Toronto, which involved a large snake march through the financial district, the Premier resigned.

In 2004, OCAP launched a campaign for full entitlement of social assistance benefits. We sought to disrupt the system by using it against itself and strategically seeking 'non-reformist reforms' (Gorz 1987). We gave people information about what they were entitled to and backed them up with direct action casework or mass demonstrations as needed. Quickly, we focused on the Special Diet benefit which gave people with health-related dietary needs extra money for food. Our aim was to force a raise in social assistance rates by creating a crisis in the system. We successfully created a crisis and multiple moves on the part of both the municipal and provincial governments to curb or eliminate the benefit were defeated through mass organising. Through a variety of procedural changes between 2005 and 2011, the government was able to limit how and for what people got the Special Diet; nevertheless, the campaign won hundreds of millions of dollars for people on social assistance – a win that is still paying out. Today, more than 100,000 people get some Special Diet money than did before we began the campaign, totalling an increase of about $200 million a year.

Disruption as a tactic and a strategy cannot be divorced from the context that it is to be used in. Strategic and appropriate organisational responses to local context are necessary for poor people's organisation's legitimacy, relevance and success. Context also informs what groups can achieve. Piven and Cloward (1979) argue 'what was won must be judged by what was possible' (p. xiii). In a world in which social programmes are under attack and privatisation is rampant, keeping something (like the Special Diet) or diminishing the severity of a cut can be an important victory. In a different social context, however, that significant win could be a sign of ineffectual organising.

Social movements, including poor people's movements, sometimes appear to explode out of nowhere – this is very much about the context being organised in. Piven and Cloward (1979) argue that movements spontaneously emerge. However, I would argue this understanding of movements as spontaneous works to make organising less effective. I adopt the view that spontaneity is, rather, 'properly understood as a rupture' (Thorburn et al. 2012, n.p.). While there are moments when movements erupt, triggered by some form of social breakdown, movements are sustained by organising. Indeed, 'most struggles', Choudry (2015) argues, 'emerge from the hard work of organising, incremental learning, lineages of earlier movements, and efforts to organise together' (9). Indeed, community rootedness is not particularly important if one thinks that movements emerge spontaneously. However, in rejecting the idea that movements emerge in out of spontaneous vacuums, based on the historical and material evidence, organising and organisations become necessary and community rootedness is essential to both.

To be clear, while our model is amazing and it works a lot of the time, it is not a magic bullet; it works for us but won't necessarily work for other radical antipoverty organising. While we have a basic framework, our organising adapts and evolves. Imposing a stagnant and romanticised model is not a good organising strategy. While there are many lessons that can be gleaned from our twenty-five years, the OCAP model of organising cannot be applied like a cookie cutter.

Other organisations have worked to build on the OCAP model in ways that are appropriate to their own communities. Groups including No One Is Illegal, a migrant justice group in a number of cities in Canada, and the London (England) Coalition Against Poverty (LCAP) and Sudbury (Canada) Coalition Against Poverty (S-CAP) went on to develop their own forms of casework. Their models were largely based on our work but designed to be responsive to and appropriate for the communities in which they work while also doing mass mobilising. Both No One Is Illegal and Sudbury Coalition Against Poverty chose to use the term support work rather than casework (Kinsman, forthcoming; Walia 2013). Gary Kinsman (forthcoming), a founder of S-CAP, reports that they chose the term 'support work' in order to avoid 'the clinical sound of "case" work'. Montreal's Committee for Non-Status Algerians and No One Is Illegal had a profound victory, as I mentioned earlier. Immigration status was won for over 1,000 non-status Algerians through a mass regularisation campaign (Lowry and Nyers 2003). This went on to influence OCAP's mass casework actions around the Special Diet and our thinking about group casework rather than individual casework. This, I would argue, is evidence of the very real and active strategic conversation that happens between allied groups within the movement. This strategic conversation has worked to strengthen casework in several cities, making not only each organisation stronger but social justice movements more effective. In other words, while OCAP has an organising model, we adjust and adapt it based on the social and political contexts we find ourselves in.

Direct action casework bypasses formal legal appeal mechanisms.[3] We refuse to work through (often incredibly slow) official channels that are designed to keep poor people in line. Instead, we use collective disruption to force the system to capitulate to us quickly. What seem like rigid and unmovable bureaucratic structures to individual poor people can become flexible and accommodating when groups of poor people collectively demand. In OCAP, we reject passivity; we refuse to be submissive. Action is essential for us for a number of reasons, not in the least because it is the only way that change can ever truly be won. Furthermore, poor people are taught to be meek, to accept our lot; we refuse this role in OCAP and view it as a purposeful construction in order to maintain the status quo.

Sometime around 1999, welfare bureaucrats in Toronto initiated a simple policy shift. From that point onwards, if OCAP brought a case forward, it was dealt with as quickly and as quietly as possible. If our demand could be legally granted, it was. Almost overnight, we went from welfare case actions being a relatively routine event in OCAP to them being relatively rare (from what we estimate was a few times a month to a few times a year). We soon saw a similar pattern with the Ontario Disability Support Program – the disability social assistance programme. This shift was a clear response to our success as an organisation: social assistance bureaucrats did not want OCAP in their offices, they did not want business-as-usual to be disrupted, they did not want other people on social assistance to learn what we do and they certainly did not want people on social assistance to witness our victories. This shift also fundamentally changed the way that most social assistance casework happens in OCAP. Now, in most situations, we simply need to write a letter or make a phone call in order to win what the person needs. The threat of disruptive action remains present and ensures we can win a case much more quickly than it would take a legal clinic or agency.

The change in the approach to OCAP casework is an excellent example of how state concessions are granted in order to demobilise resistance deemed to pose a threat. Poor people's organising can pose threats to government credibility – negatively impacting their electoral prospects. But poor people can do more than threaten a particular ruling party; we can overthrow the ruling class. From the government's perspective, putting out small fires is far simpler than letting them burn – building into a movement strong enough to topple the system.

Bureaucratic attempts to demobilise us by changing how they dealt with letters from OCAP were an important indication of the organisation's success but it also worked to demobilise our casework programme (as it was intended to do). Direct action caseworkers were, in some ways, turned into bureaucratic agents: into letter writers rather than protest organisers. With the exception of flashpoints around the Special Diet and Housing Stabilization Fund, we have been able to almost always win our social assistance cases without having to engage in direct action. It makes casework fast and effective but it also means that some people we work with simply see us as a social service organisation working *for* them rather than as part of a political struggle and as working *with* them. For the most part, poor people have been taught by the complex bureaucracy of the social assistance system (and housing and labour and immigration, etc.) that they do not possess the skills to navigate appeals and complaints on their own. Poor people have been taught to either give up or passively accept expert assistance. Many people are confused by OCAP's active resistance because it is outside of their realm of experience.

It is our radical analysis coupled with the use of disruption that makes our casework different from a social service agency and it is what makes it effective. Disruption manifests in a lot of different ways – from shutting down a welfare office until our demands are met to picketing a business that withheld wages. The possibility for disruption is a basic principle of OCAP's casework: we only take on cases when there is a possibility that direct action and/or disruption can be used. If the person we are working with does not want to use protest tactics or if the only possible route for the case is through formal legal channels, it is not the case for us. This is not to deny the injustice but we recognise that we have limited resources and focus on cases that we can hook individual struggles into our ongoing collective ones.

The second key principle is that the case must actually be 'winnable'. This is because we refuse to take on cases simply for their symbolic drama or to register our dissent. OCAP fights to win – and that includes casework. Here, the distinction between what is winnable through individual direct action casework and what is winnable through broader organising is important. When taking on the government, direct action casework has proven to be highly effective when policies have been unjustly applied. However, changing the policy itself needs longer-term, larger-scale organising and mass mobilising. An example of an unjustly applied policy is the denial of welfare to someone who is entitled to it while an unjust policy is the one which says that people without immigration status cannot get welfare. Both struggles are winnable but the first can be won through direct action casework focused on that individual, while the second requires mass mobilising.

We also practice non-duplication: if there is a funded service that would do the same thing we would do, we send people there. We have very limited resources and have never collected a dime of government funding. If a legal clinic or agency is doing the same thing, we need to conserve our resources (and if it is just paper pushing, chances are they would do it better than us). This principle is also directly related to the disruption principle. However, legal clinics and agencies do not use direct action, so if there is a possibility we would, we do not necessarily see it as a duplication.

Another key principle of our casework, and the one we haven't really written about elsewhere, is trust. It is equally important that we trust the people who come to us and that they trust us. Direct action casework is impossible without the trust of the communities we work with because people will simply refuse to reach out to us – we will have no casework to do. People need to trust that we will fight to win to respect them and their boundaries and to be honest about what we are doing, why and what our capabilities are. With respect to us trusting the people who come to us, it seems basic: we believe someone unless we have a good reason not to. Poor people, especially people on welfare, are often depicted as liars, as lazy and as fraudulent. At OCAP, we know that welfare puts people in the position of having to lie (about income, about who they are living with, etc.) or starve. There is nothing inherently honourable about choosing to go hungry over lying to an unjust system. We know that even if someone has lied to social assistance, that doesn't make them untrustworthy. For some people, simply hearing the words 'I believe you' from an OCAP member is the first act of political solidarity they ever experience. We make a political choice to believe the word of poor people.

That said, while trust is a good starting place, things can sometimes get messy. Sometimes, we take on cases without having the whole story – cases we would not otherwise have taken on. Most of the time, this happens because the person did not understand everything that had happened, not because of dishonesty. We also take on cases when people are really upset, and rightly so, but they are unable to always give us all of the information. When we have a good reason to be unsure about what we are told or when the person does not know themselves, our response is not to send a letter threatening to do an action. We request information. Once we have all the files, we go from there.

The last key principle of our casework is that it has to be something that can further our political aims. While OCAP wants all poor people's lives to be better, we are a political organisation not a charity. On any given day, someone calls the office asking for our help with something that may be incredibly important but is in no way connected to our campaigns. For instance, someone called us because he was upset that the provincial government was changing the way tires were being recycled and it meant that he would lose his income because of it. While we were sympathetic to him, this change was not linked to any of the campaigns that we work on. Issues like that simply do not make sense for us to take on. If we just took on every case that came to us, we would actually end up being less politically effective because we would be spread too thin.

Poorly executed direct action casework fails to be strategic about these capacity and campaign issues. It can lead to an organisation co-opting itself, turning itself into a bureaucratic service agency that has abandoned its own politics in practice, if not in principle. It can lead to feelings of hopelessness. It has the real risk of leading to hunger, homelessness and/or deportation if done poorly.[4] People doing direct action casework also have to know and be able to handle the reality that, even if done well, it can still lead to hunger, homelessness and/or deportation – we simply can't prevent all of the violence of poverty through casework. Systems are unjust – sometimes we lose. Direct action casework is not something you can pick up for a summer or be flaky about; it requires commitment and follow through.

That said, at its best, casework can strengthen, legitimise and ground an organisation. It works as a form of research: people bring us their problems and that flags changes in the system that need to be fought. What we learn through our casework can help inform and guide our existing campaigns and point us in the direction of new ones we need to develop. Direct action casework builds hope in poor communities – hope in resistance and in our collective power. Direct action casework can result in relatively easy wins that can empower and embolden people. A direct action casework win is an effective educational tool – both about the injustices of the system and that victory is possible with collective action.

Winning to Fight: Demobilisation and the Struggle against Pacification

Ironically, winning what you are fighting for, including partial victories, can have negative consequences for movements, organisations and organising. This can be especially damaging for organisations caught unprepared to manage their own successes. OCAP has learned the necessity of working strategically, not only for victory but also beyond it in order to continue to build struggle.

Victories, according to Piven and Cloward, are won by forcing ruling relations to concede something. These concessions are designed to 'channel the energies and angers of the protestors into more legitimate and less disruptive forms of political behavior' (1979, 30). Consequently, concessions are won only when movements threaten elites and are 'shaped as much by elite ideas and interests as by movement demands' (1979, 17 n17). For instance, as part of a coalition, OCAP won 24-hour drop-in centres for women and transpeople in 2015 – an important victory. The City, however, used those spaces as a pressure valve for the full shelter system which gave them the opportunity to further resist opening new shelter beds. This strategy can be effective. Here, winning the very thing we are fighting for can help reduce or diminish struggle. Thompson (2014) observes: 'compromise and consent can both pacify and embolden' (513) and one cannot necessarily anticipate which it will be.

Importantly, the appearance of winning can have similar demobilising effects to winning itself. Greene (2006) argues, 'simply altering the nature of the problem, by taking action to reduce the visibility and urgency of the grievance, may be as effective in dampening the prospects for the emergence of more sustained forms of mobilization than if the authorities took substantive remedial action' (53). Partial or smokescreen victories allow the soothing of public opinion and quietening of protest by ruling relations without enacting meaningful change. If the relevant authorities provide the appearance of addressing the problem in a serious and satisfactory manner, meaningful concessions may be sidestepped.

We have experienced how this demobilisation happens first-hand in OCAP. For example, OCAP fought for more and better shelter beds for years and was successful in winning a City Council resolution capping shelter occupancy at 90% to prevent overcrowding, the opening of warming centres, 24-hour drop-ins for women and transpeople and a number of new shelter beds (Ontario Coalition Against Poverty 2013) – all of which are significant victories. However, the City has never implemented the 90% cap on shelter occupancy, delayed opening the drop-ins and attempted to eliminate the warming centres. Furthermore, even with the shelter beds OCAP fought for and was able to win, 1,000 shelter beds were cut from the system between 2000 and 2015 (Lesley Wood, pers. comm.). As concessions are won by poor people because they pose a threat to ruling relations, having effectively disrupted them, there will always be a pushback against poor people's gains.

Successes can also lead to the overwhelming of organisations and the depletion of organisational resources. This upswing can then make it difficult to maintain the organising work and organisation. For example, during the Special Diet campaign, OCAP was overwhelmed with over 100 phone calls in a day by people trying to get access to the benefit (Palmer and Heroux 2016). Significant wins can lead to strains within the organisation or community if organisations are unprepared to handle them.

Achieving success can also lead to demobilisation through divisiveness. Rameau (2008) argues that it can reveal 'the problems associated with lacking political unity' (69). It is in trying to decide how to move forward after a success that underlying political differences emerge, making ongoing strategising and organising difficult. Dixon (2014) argues that planning strategically rather than organising in continual crisis can help radical groups ensure long-term and sustained organising. This could also help organisations navigate the inevitable ebbs and flows of movement activity. However, Dixon also recognises that this is particularly difficult with organising in communities that are often, if not always, in crisis. Poverty is a crisis. So, grounded radical antipoverty organising will, at least sometimes, have to respond to crisis and from crises.

Another potential demobiliser is the individualisation of a collective struggle which can work to depoliticise an issue and to demobilise a movement. For example, OCAP worked hard to maintain collective solidarity through our Special Diet campaign. Our tactic of holding group clinics helped build a sense of shared struggle among very diverse groups of poor people. However, even strong solidarity could not overcome the fact that, at the end of the day, individuals had individual special diet forms to be filled out and there was individual amount of money allotted to each person. While our campaign won hundreds of millions of dollars for poor people, it was not successful in forcing the government to raise everyone's social assistance collectively. When the Province imposed restrictions on the Special Diet to curtail our successes, this tension grew significantly. Organising cannot always prevent the state from attempting to individualise an issue but organisations can anticipate this and build contingencies and solidarities in order to keep individualisation from demobilising a struggle.

Individualisation can be thought of as a form of (attempted) co-optation of individuals; co-optation can also target organisations and campaigns. As discussed earlier, Piven and Cloward (1979) warn against the creation of poor people's organisations because they view the co-optation of organisations as inevitable. They argue that organisations will become obsessed with maintaining themselves and abandon their original principles and aims. While it is definitely a danger, co-optation is not inevitable (also see Gamson 1975; Kinsman 1992; Scott and Wood 2004; Rameau 2008). However, the form is not the problem. Indeed, organisations play the necessary roles of building and maintaining connections, consciousness raising and mobilisation. For example, OCAP has organised for twenty-five years without being co-opted or corrupted and is steadfastly anticapitalist and direct actionist.

We have, however, witnessed the widespread suppression of dissent or critique of government practices among agencies that work with poor people. These groups, including drop-in centres, shelters, food centres and healthcare facilities, used to routinely speak out against government policies that were hurting poor people. These agencies would frequently do outreach, provide meals and bring delegations to and provide speakers for protests. Now, the support that we have is off the books – sometimes, meals or meeting space is provided but it often can't be made public that this was the case. There are a lot of reasons for this but, at its core, it is rooted in the way that the government administers funds. Organisations have become more business-like, social work has become professionalised (replacing many workers who were rooted in the communities served with middle-class social workers) and agencies have diminished their political activity out of the fear that they would lose their funding – although this hasn't actually been the case.[5] We think this is evidence of how elite funding, either through the state or foundations, is used to demobilise resistance. INCITE! Women of Color Against Violence (2007) put out an anthology called *The Revolution Will Not Be Funded* arguing that support from the rich (largely through foundations) works to co-opt radical organising. For poor people's organisations, the issue of funding is particularly significant because of the lack of resources in poor communities. OCAP has never taken government funds and has severed ties with or been cut off by our funders rather than tame our tactics or demands (for more on this, see Coulter 2012).

The final demobilising tool I want to address is repression. OCAP has faced mass arrest, the criminalisation of protest and persecution of our leadership. The purpose of this repression was to suppress and/or destroy the movement we were building. However, it was unsuccessful. OCAP's Gaetan Heroux attributed our ability to withstand repression and public vilification to the fact that 'the base was too strong, the roots are too deep' (quoted in Thompson 2004, p. 96). We were able to turn the state's own repression against it, mobilising more public and vocal support than we had had before. This is why, writing about OCAP, Greene (2006) notes that repression can create political opportunities for mobilisation.

There are cycles of protest that deeply impact organising and mobilisation (see Tarrow 1994). OCAP has endured through the rise and decline of upsurges in mobilising and dissent. Organising is exciting and comparatively easy during periods of widespread activity and much more difficult when it recedes. Resisting demobilisation and remaining active when it is occurring are both necessary in order to quickly respond to crises and/or upswings in movement activity.

Conclusion

Antipoverty organising work is slow, it is tedious and it is difficult. Even when we win, we must struggle to get our victories implemented and ensure that we do not allow ourselves to be demobilised. OCAP's organising model couples mass mobilising and direct action casework and works to help guide our organisation and continue to be relevant to poor communities. Disruption allows people who have little political power as individuals to force concessions and build collective strength and defiance. While difficult, when we successfully build power through collective action, winning is possible. The state of emergency our communities find themselves in makes winning urgently and absolutely essential.

Notes

1 This is OCAP's primary organising slogan.
2 Dorothy Smith's (2002) concepts of ruling relations are those that 'coordinate people's activities across and beyond local sites of everyday experience' (45).
3 This is not to be confused with legal application mechanisms. For instance, with respect to social assistance, people have to make applications for benefits but, if denied, we do not follow the established legal pathways.
4 OCAP used to do immigration casework. However, with the emergence of No One Is Illegal, a direct action migrant justice organisation, we stopped doing this kind of casework.

5 One exception to this is when the Canadian Arab Federation's funding for English as a second language instruction for newcomers was cut. This was done, by a racist federal government after the group had been (unjustly) accused of supporting terrorism (The Canadian Press, 2016).

References

Acharya, Y. and M. Scott, 'Migration and poverty', *Talking About Social Justice: OCAP Speakers' Series*. (Toronto: April 21, 2016).

Alinsky, S., *Rules for Radicals: A Practical Primer for Realistic Radicals*. (New York: Random House, 1971).

Bannerji, H., *Thinking Through: Essays on Feminism, Marxism and Anti-racism*. (Toronto: Women's Press, 1995).

Bateman, M., *Why Doesn't Microfinance Work?: The Destructive Rise of Local Neoliberalism*. (New York: Zed Books, 2010).

Choudry, A., *Learning Activism: The Intellectual Life of Contemporary Social Movements*. (Toronto: University of Toronto Press, 2015).

Churchill, W., *Pacifism as Pathology: Reflections on the Role of Armed Struggle in North America*. (Winnipeg: Arbeiter Ring Publishing, 1998).

Clarke, J., 'OCAP marks its first twenty years', *The Bullet*, 432 (2010).

Clarke, J., 'Social movements: The struggle intensifies', In C. Leys and M. Margurite (eds.) *Culture and Social Change: Social Movements in Québec and Ontario* (Montreal: Black Rose Books, 1992), 213–224.

Clarke, J., 'Social resistance and the disturbing of the peace', *Osgoode Hall Law Journal*, 41 (2003), 491–503.

Coulter, K., 'Solidarity in deed: Poor people's organizations, unions, and the politics of antipoverty work in Ontario', *Anthropology of Work Review*, 33:2 (2012), 101–112.

Credit Suisse AG Research Institute, *Global Wealth Report 2015* (Zurich: Credit Suisse AG Research Institute, 2015).

Dixon, C., *Another Politics: Talking Across Today's Transformative Movements*. (Oakland: University of California Press, 2014).

DRUM, 'NYC's historic win for landmark civil rights legislation is decades in the making. DRUM', (23 August 2013), retrieved 16 October 2017, www.drumnyc.org/1644/.

Fanon, F., *The Wretched of the Earth*. (New York: Grove Press, 2004).

Fellows, M.L. and Razack, S., 'The race to innocence: Confronting hierarchical relations among women', *Journal of Gender and Race Justice*, 1 (1997), 335–352.

Fortier, C., '"Regent Park is our Fallujah": Constructing an activist praxis within local contestations of war and globalization in Toronto' (Master's thesis, University of Toronto, 2005).

Friends of the MST. n.d. "What Is the MST?" n.d. http://www.mstbrazil.org/content/what-mst.

Gamson, W., *Strategy of Social Protest*. (Homewood: The Dorsey Press, 1975).

Gorz, A., 'Strategy for labor', in S. Larson, and B. Nissen (eds.), *Theories of the Labor Movement*. (Detroit: Wayne State University Press, 1987), 100–116.

Greene, J.S., 'Visibility, urgency, and protest: Anti-poverty Activism in Neo-liberal Times', (PhD dissertation, Queen's University, 2006).

Hannington, W., *Unemployed Struggles, 1919–1936: My Life and Struggles Amongst the Unemployed*. (London: Lawrence and Wishar, 1936).

INCITE! Women of Color Against Violence (Ed.), *The Revolution Will Not be Funded: Beyond the Non-profit Industrial Complex*. (Cambridge: South End Press, 2007).

Kinsman, G., 'Managing AIDS Organizing: "Consultation", "Partnership", and the National AIDS Strategy,' in W.K. Carroll (ed.), *Organizing Dissent: Contemporary Social Movements in Theory and Practice: Studies in the Politics of Counter-Hegemony*, (Toronto: Garamond Press, 1992), 215–233.

Kinsman, G., 'Direct action as political activist ethnography: Activist research in the Sudbury Coalition Against Poverty', in I. Hussey and L. Bisaillon, (eds.), *Political Activist Ethnography: Studies in the Social Relations of Struggle*, (forthcoming).

Klein, N., *The Shock Doctrine: The Rise of Disaster Capitalism*. (New York: Metropolitan Books, 2007).

Lowry, M. and P. Nyers, 'Roundtable report "No One Is Illegal": The fight for refugee and migrant rights in Canada', *Refuge: Canada's Journal on Refugees*, 21:3 (2003), 66–72.

McCuaig, K., 'Social movements crucial factor in Ontario election', *Canadian Dimension*, 24 (1990), 8–9.

Miller, R.J. and F.F. Piven, 'Poor peoples' movements and the power to disrupt: An interview with Frances Fox Piven', *Journal of Poverty*, 16:3 (2012), 363–373.

Ontario Coalition Against Poverty, 2013. 'Update on Toronto shelters campaign: City Council votes to open beds for homeless!' (5 April, 2013), retrieved 9 February, 2016, www.ocap.ca/node/1073.

Palmer, B.D and G. Heroux, *Toronto's Poor: A Rebellious History.* (Toronto: Between The Lines, 2016).

Piven, F.F. and R.A. Cloward, 'Collective protest: A critique of resource mobilization theory', *International Journal of Politics, Culture and Society*, 4:4 (1991), 435–458.

Piven, F.F. and R.A. Cloward, *Poor People's Movements: Why they Succeed, How they Fail*, (New York: Vintage Books, 1979).

Rameau, M., *Take Back the Land: Land, Gentrification and the Umoja Village Shantytown.* (Miami: Nia Press, 2008).

Ryan, M., 'On Ward Churchill's "pacifism as pathology": Toward a consistent revolutionary practice,' in W. Churchill and M. Ryan (eds.), *Pacifism as Pathology: Reflections on the Role of Armed Struggle in North America.* (Winnipeg: Arbeiter Ring Publishing, 1998), 131–165.

Scott, M. and L. Wood, 'Beyond radical social work: Casework for change', *New Socialist*, 45, (2004), n.p., http://newsocialist.org/old_mag/magazine/45/article18.html

Tarrow, S.G., *Power in Movement: Social Movements, Collective Action and Politics.* (New York: Cambridge University Press, 1994).

Thompson, D.A., 'Direct action, subsidiarity and the counterhegemonic: Three case studies of antipoverty activism in twentieth century Canada', (Masters thesis, University of Victoria, 2004).

Thompson, D.A., 'Working-class anguish and revolutionary indignation: The making of radical and socialist unemployment movements in Canada, 1875–1928', (PhD dissertation, Queen's University, 2014).

Thorburn, E., A. Naylor, and R. Letson, 'Notes on spontaneity and organization', *Upping the Anti*, 14 (2012), n.p., http://uppingtheanti.org/journal/article/14-editorial/

van Erdewijk, and I. Dubel, 'Substantive gender mainstreaming and the missing middle: A view from Dutch development agencies', *Gender and Development*, 20:3 (2012), 491–504.

Walia, H., *Undoing Border Imperialism.* (Oakland: AK Press/Institute for Anarchist Studies, 2013).

World Bank, 'Poverty overview' Retrieved: 14 Oct., 2016, www.worldbank.org/en/topic/poverty/overview.

SECTION 3

Repertoires

This section focuses on a number of actions and tactics which activists deploy. While obviously covering only a very few examples, the selection attempts to convey the sheer variety of radicals' transgressive and transformative repertoire.

To pick up one of the themes explored in the introduction, direct action is a unifying theme for this section – a 'Do-It-Yourself/Do-It-Ourselves' mode of politics where activists take social change into their own hands, intervening directly in a situation and seek to either disrupt an injustice or create alternatives using their own power and capacities. This is opposed to indirect means which appeal to (and thus legitimate) an external authority to act on one's behalf.

While the term itself is much older, its recent prominence can be explained largely with reference to the rift that emerged during the alter-global protest wave between radical groups and trade unions, NGOs and political parties (de Cleyre 1912; Carter 1983; Franks 2003; Graeber 2009). Here, radicals' preference for direct action was intimately related to their rejection of top-down organisation, lobbying and programmes to seize state power in favour of anti-hierarchical and anticapitalist practices such as decentralised organisation and decision-making by consensus. Also linked to direct action is the idea of prefigurative politics – the insistence that the means activists use should demonstrate, in embryonic form, the type of society they wish to create. Hence, the effort to identify and counteract regimes of domination and discrimination (e.g. patriarchy, racism, homophobia and ableism) in activists' own lives and interactions, as well as in their repertoires of action. Dynamics of mainstreaming and co-optation have meant that some of these efforts, in their broken transmission to later cycles of contention, have become detached from their radical roots and now appear in disfigured forms such as language policing. Yet, their importance on the radical, direct-action end of the political spectrum, where they are clearly associated with agendas for anti-hierarchical social transformation, has not diminished.

In his chapter on international **nonviolent accompaniment**, Patrick Coy examines action which aims to secure increased political space for local experiments in radical politics. By providing international observers to walk alongside local activists under threat, accompaniment seeks to deter potential aggressors, preserve grassroots agency and empower local activists. The complicated intersections between international accompaniment and radical politics are examined, pointing out both the benefits and the pitfalls that can occur between local actors and international observers.

Public **performance interventions** to reclaim space are at the focus of Mel Evans's chapter. It examines actions which radically reclaim and revivify public spaces to create new potentials for dissent, transformation and structural change. In these actions, artists and activists disrupt social norms to tackle massive corporate and government structures head on. Using examples big and small, coordinated and spontaneous, the chapter picks out of personal experience moments where the scope of the possible has broadened and lengthened, whether set in the street, protest camps, corporate spaces and museums and galleries. In each case, opening access to public space is an important site for collective action and building community around key social issues.

Aurora Trujillo and Matthew Wilson examine radical **bicycle politics** which bring an antiauthoritarian, anticapitalist and ecologically committed approach to cycling and transportation. Presenting the diversity of such political expression, the chapter argues that the bicycle has frequently played a role in radical (and not so radical) social movements. However, while old and new radical political struggles have often considered the bicycle as an intrinsically valuable object, it could be argued that its role has fluctuated along two axes. The one tracks whether the movement focuses on mobility-related political aims such as promoting cycling or opposing motor traffic in their own right, or whether it uses the bicycle as a symbolic and/or practical tool to further non-mobility-related political aims, such as feminism or environmentalism. The other axis is structurally focused and examines how overt and encompassing the politics of the movement is.

Francis Dupuis-Déri's chapter is dedicated to **black blocs** – a tactical formation in which masked militants in black form part of a larger protest, sometimes fighting police and/or damaging corporate property. Tracing the history of black blocs from the German Autonomen in the 1980s through the alterglobalisation movements of the 2000s to recent years' post-economic-crash mobilisations, the chapter explains the bloc's aesthetics, tactics and composition. Using the critique of violence to problematise the meaning of radicalism, the chapter probes the gap between practice and theory to show the limits of black bloc revolutionary action and explores how it nevertheless advances an idea of radicalising practice through collective, autonomous organisation.

Jeff Shantz examines the radical **online activism** which has challenged state and corporate governance structures and sought alternatives based on openness, sharing, collaboration and self-determination. Practices including hacking, whistleblowing and denial of service attacks show novel tactical reach and anonymity. However, much of online activism has direct antecedents in familiar activist repertoires. The collective, material practices of activist groups working online, including TAO.ca and riseup.net, are based on radical perspectives such as anarchism and feminism. While cyber activists have sought to realise its liberatory potential, the Internet has proven to be a site of struggle, exposed to state and corporate enclosure, surveillance and repression.

Josep Lobera and Diego Parejo consider significant innovations that have recently linked radicalism to **electoral politics**. The development of radical left political parties (Syriza in Greece) or the emergence of new political parties (Podemos in Spain or M5S in Italy) has transformed perspectives on the traditional role of the radical left in government. Furthermore, these parties have brought new social demands to the electoral field, thus becoming their contested representatives within the institutions. The chapter argues that the window of opportunity for the emergence of such new actors was opened not only by the economic crisis, but also by the preceding political crisis of representative disaffection. Against the exclusionary politics emerging in European populist movements, the emergence of inclusive social protest movements and electoral parties has allowed for the dispute about the social construction of 'the people' to avoid displacement towards a cultural struggle associated with exclusive populism.

Michael Loadenthal looks at underground **insurrectionary cells** which carry out direct, unmediated attacks on the state and capital. Based on an ethic of informality, clandestinity and temporality, cells exist in secret only as long as deemed necessary for a particular action. Unlike social movement organisations and above-ground campaigns, the cells that populate the insurrectionary milieu are not something to 'belong to' but something to 'act through', a momentary assemblage of like-minded individuals united for a particular attack by voluntary association and through shared affinity. This chapter explores how the cell model, the communiqué and the adoptable moniker allow for the creation of a globally dispersed, decentralised, open-involvement movement united against capitalism, the state and those who would seek to control it.

Sandra Jeppesen introduces four **radical media** practices: DIY media create communities of practice; community media anchor social movement analyses; protest media mobilise using the snowball effect and global media develop international solidarity. These practices create radical products and processes, empowering media-makers by amplifying systemically silenced voices in horizontal organisations. Illustrated with contemporary global examples, five radical media genres – print, audio, image, video and online – are mapped to four dimensions of media practice – movements, representations, structures and digital networks. Debates within media movements are critically analysed, including the contradictions of social media, and the challenges of sustainable funding.

In an interview Ramsey Kanaan tells how he came to set up AK and PM press, interweaving his personal story with a frank analysis of the decline of radical **publishing** since the 1960s. Kanaan's view is that this decline reflects a deeper malaise in anarchist activism. Distinguishing the anarchist movement from the anarchist milieu, he argues that anarchist ideas have animated radical politics for at least the last forty years but that anarchists have failed to construct robust institutions. Drawing on his experiences in AK press to illustrate the political shifts within anarchism and, in particular, the rise of identity politics, he explains how PM confronts the pressures of commercial production as an anarchist worker's cooperative and continues in its efforts to construct viable, enduring anarchist institutions.

References

Carter, A. 1983, *Direct Action*. Housmans/Peace News, London 1983.

De Cleyre, V., 'Direct Action' [1912], online at Anarchy Archives http://dwardmac.pitzer.edu/Anarchist_Archives/bright/cleyre/direct.html.

Franks, B. 2003, 'The Direct Action Ethic: From 59 Upwards', *Anarchist Studies*, vol. 11, no. 1, p. 15.

Graeber, D. 2009, *Direct Action: An Ethnography*. AK Press, Edinburgh and Oakland.

3.1

THE INTERSECTIONS OF INTERNATIONAL NONVIOLENT ACCOMPANIMENT AND RADICAL LOCAL POLITICS

Patrick G. Coy

Introduction

Accompaniment was a part of human history long before humans started writing down their experiences and stories. Eons ago, when members of a clan or a tribe visited contested spaces like watering holes or wells, or when they undertook journeys along travel corridors thought to be uncommonly dangerous, they would often be accompanied by others whose added presence was thought to provide an additional modicum of security. Both historically and today, nonviolent protective accompaniment takes many forms; its tactical repertoire is bounded only by the limits of human imagination and ingenuity.

For example, when exiled political activists and human rights defenders return to their homeland to test political openings and to take up organising again against oppressive governments, they may be accompanied on the trip by high-profile international dignitaries, whose presence may deter or at least internationalise any violent attacks. Such was the case for Kim Dae Jung returning to South Korea in 1985. Whenever self-exiled indigenous rights activist Rigoberta Menchu ventured to return to Guatemala in mid-1980s, she was usually accompanied by volunteer nonviolent accompaniers from the non-governmental organisation, Peace Brigades International. Tonight when a woman student on a university campus in South Africa or Serbia or Spain is walking home late at night, she may first place a call to a free service for volunteer escorts to walk alongside her – often just fellow students who care enough to lend their body and their time – increasing both her perceived and even her real safety.

These examples of accompaniment are structured, deliberate, organised in step-by-step fashion in advance, often with elaborate preparations to ensure that they are more likely to provide the intended protections. But accompaniment initiatives also pop up instantaneously in response to new threats and novel dangers.

The week in November of 2016 in which Donald Trump was elected US President after running a particularly divisive campaign, some immigrants and minority citizens were feeling threatened and were being openly harassed, even on their daily commutes in the New York City subway system. Kayla Santosuosso, deputy director of the Arab American Association of New York, was asked on Facebook if she could find someone to accompany a

Muslim woman who was repeatedly being hassled on her way to and from school each day. So Santosuosso made a Facebook post and created a Google docs sign-up form to pair people up by NYC neighbourhoods and their commuting patterns. Within four days, over 6,000 people signed up to be impromptu volunteer accompaniers for Muslims, people of colour, LGBTQ folks and others feeling threatened during their daily commutes on public transportation in New York City. This sort of community-based, impromptu response to threats and danger is yet another face of accompaniment (Phillips 2016).

Radical politics is many things to many people. One thing most can agree on is that at its core, radical politics is marked by the notion that responsibly minded citizens ought not to wait for the local government, the national state or the international community to do the proper thing and promote and protect human rights. Instead, it is up to individual citizens to step into the breach on the local, national and international level and provide what is needed to facilitate the creation of environments with more justice, more security and more equality. Accompaniment rests on this very notion of direct and meaningful action, a notion that is also central to radical politics. There are two complimentary tracks that run parallel to each other in this shared approach. One is based on a profound respect for the agency of the individual citizen; the other is tied tightly to a critique of state sovereignty in human affairs. Together, they imbue both accompaniment and radical politics with significant power against the excesses of states and their unfortunately concomitant violations of human dignity and rights.

Another way to understand accompaniment is to see it as a device or a tactic that local nonviolent political activists may choose to use to expand their capacities and their effectiveness. Sometimes, those providing accompaniment come from within the community itself. In these cases, the accompaniers may be elders, clergy, mothers and grandmothers, faculty, veterans, former gang members or all sorts of other kinds of community leaders who use their position or authority in the local community to advantage and protect others who are under threat of violence. Relying on local resources like this may occasion significant capacity and empowerment possibilities.

Other times and often out of political necessity, the accompaniers come to the community from the outside; their outsider status changes the political dynamics and the balances of power. In those ways, it also impacts the calculations of would-be repressors, thereby benefiting and increasing the security of those local activists who have opted to receive accompaniment. The internationals or outsiders may be able to offer more or at least different kinds of protection and security than locals can presently create for themselves and their colleagues and neighbours. The dynamics of deterrence change.

While 'transnational accompaniment' is the more accurate term (Eguren 2009), the tactic is generally known as international accompaniment and will be used here. The tactic of international nonviolent protective accompaniment as it is now commonly practised in many contested political spaces across the globe was largely pioneered in Central America in the early 1980s by Peace Brigades International.

The Dynamics of International Nonviolent Accompaniment

Much of the Latin American region at that time was governed by oppressive military dictatorships infamous for their disregard for the rule of law and basic human rights. Safe political space was hard to come by, dramatically restricting the kind of political work local citizens could do without severe reprisal. These activists, long repressed by their own governments for engaging in local organising, community development, identity politics and other kinds of political change efforts, discovered that they could often change the local political equation to their advantage by requesting and receiving accompaniment from international non-governmental organisations.

International protective accompaniment relies, in part, on the Observer Effect for its presumed efficacy. The Observer Effect is the well-established principle that most of the time most people modify, and especially moderate, their behaviour when they know they are being observed. We know this to be true in our everyday lives in a variety of our personal, routinised social settings, but it is also true in highly charged political spaces, sometimes even especially so.

For example, when local activists in Guatemala and in El Salvador asked for and received accompaniment from Peace Brigade International in the 1980s, they discovered that the presence of international outsiders changed the behaviour of police and military and other potential repressors towards their own populace. These local activists found that with international accompaniment, they could do more and different kinds of political work without suffering the overt persecution to which they had been accustomed, including harassment, illegal detention and torture, disappearance and even death (Coy 1993; Mahony & Eguren 1997). The political landscape shifted; the boundaries of safe civil space were expanded through accompaniment. But it isn't just the political landscape that changes.

Equally important, the empowerment individual local activists experience also changes the cognitive landscape as the self-understandings of individuals and even collective identities of communities are altered. This, in turn, serves to embolden still others to reclaim their political and economic agency in novel ways.

What does international accompaniment actually look like on the ground? A useful way to understand international protective accompaniment is to first compare it to the more well-known human rights promotion work of Amnesty International and Human Rights Watch (Hopgood 2007; Becker 2013).

Amnesty International, in particular, forged a new model in the 1960s by using targeted letter-writing campaigns to 'name and shame' governments and their officials responsible for violating the human rights of their own citizens. Here, the coordinated advocacy letter campaigns and the actual letters themselves symbolically represented the international community of conscience and its concern for threatened local activists. The targeted nature of this tactic, directed as it usually was at top-level decision makers in governments, militaries, police and prisons, delivered impactful responses. It worked, in part precisely because of whom it tried to influence. But that was also in some ways its Achilles heel.

First, governments learned how to adjust their repressive tactics and stymied the effectiveness of the letter-writing tactic in the 1980s and 1990s by taking fewer political prisoners or no longer openly assassinating opponents. They turned instead towards simply 'disappearing' civil society activists, creating plausible deniability and thereby more easily deflecting the pressure.

Second, the reliance on letters and written communication to promote and protect human rights is predicated on putting pressure on repressive systems' top leaders – those who either make the decisions or give the orders. But political repression and violence usually pass through and rely on a lengthy chain of command. The order to intimidate, to pillage, to rape or to kill passes downwards through many levels. Yet, it must eventually be put into actual operation at the level of the individual perpetrator. Someone must do the deed.

What international protective accompaniment did was it expanded international human rights advocacy by putting actual bodies, i.e. uniformed international observers, into contested political spaces where local activists and their communities were reclaiming agency through acts of radical politics. It complimented the top-level work by targeting the entire chain of command, down to the level of the perpetrator of violent repression (Mahony 2006).

In this model of accompaniment, international observers 'armed' with foreign passports, cell phones, cameras, uniforms and membership in a recognised international non-governmental organisation quite literally walk alongside local activists targeted for persecution by state and parastate groups due to their political and human rights work. They also open up dialogue with lower level and mid-level police, military and government officials, explaining the work of international accompaniment, attempting to multiply the observer effect in a cross-cutting manner up and down and across the entire chain of command. In these ways, international accompaniment changes the considerations and consequences would-be perpetrators face even while it expands the political space available to local activists who are under threat for their work.

For example, the community organisers associated with the Negombo United People's Organisation (NUPO) in Sri Lanka who worked in the midst of extreme levels of political violence during the ethnic conflict there often used PBI accompaniment to send two messages: one to potential attackers, and one to local community members fearful to organise themselves politically. When organising meetings were being held held at the NUPO offices for various community groups, PBI observers would be present, sitting outside on the porch. As one of the NUPO staffers put it:

> When PBI is here with us, it decreases our fear and the fear of the people who come to the center with the groups we animate. The violence here has gotten inside people; it does not just operate on the outside, just kill the body. It also operates on the inside through fear and kills the spirit of the people. But we see that we are not alone in our struggle, and that helps us overcome that fear...The people see that this work is important and that others care about it.
>
> *(Coy 1997: 98)*

The Goals of Accompaniment

International nonviolent protective accompaniment has at least four goals. First, it is meant to deter possible repression. The international observers are trained in communication skills, nonviolent intervention and de-escalation tactics and they are backed up by broad international advocacy networks willing to apply citizen-based, economic, diplomatic and political pressures of various sorts should the deterrence on the ground fail. Seeking to establish and maintain the deterrence effect, the observers maintain regular communication with local police, military, government officials and other possible sources of political repression, explaining their presence and their work on behalf of human rights promotion and protection in the local context. They also explain, in advance, the political, economic and social pressures they help bring to bear against repressors should deterrence fail and human rights violations occur. Effective deterrence always relies on the clear communication of costs and consequences, in advance, for proscribed behaviours by repressors (Mahony & Eguren 1997; Coy 2001).

Second, the presence of international accompaniers walking alongside risk-taking local activists provides much-needed moral and psychological support; it facilitates citizens being able to overcome the debilitating fear and political paralysis that repressive governments and

259

other human rights violators rely so much upon to deny political agency and to maintain the repressive status quo.

For example, during the ethnic conflict in Sri Lanka, the 1994 Parliamentary elections were critically important for increased prospects of eventual peace; unfortunately, widespread election violence was predicted. Nonetheless, or in part because of the predicted election violence, local Sri Lankan human rights defenders wanted to field Sri Lankan election observers for the Parliamentary elections. This had two goals: (1) to ensure as free and as fair of an election as possible; (2) to rebuild citizen trust in and ownership of democratic processes. This was no easy task given that the elections were occurring in the midst of a long-running ethnic conflict, rampant corruption and widespread human rights violations by the government and by rebel groups. Recruitment of local election observers – a key tool in rebuilding a citizen-based democracy – was badly hampered by a pervasive fear factor.

When citizens have experienced past trauma due to their political activities, the trauma tentacles may be far-reaching. This not only effectively constrains and restricts what an individual citizen is willing to do, but it hamstrings the development of civil society. In this case, Sri Lankan election observers were fearful of even entering police stations to make their reports of balloting law abuses, due to past trauma associated with the police. As Freddie Gamage, secretary of the Coalition of Human Rights Organisations, put it to me: 'We think of the police station as a place where people should not go ... Most people still have the fear mentality about the police station because that is the place where people are condemned' (Coy 1995: 10). Consequently, to combat this fear psychosis while still empowering civil society, two grassroots Sri Lankan NGOs asked three International NGOs to provide internationals to accompany their local, Sri Lankan election observers. This changed the costs/benefit calculation facing the domestic monitors, and yet maintained Sri Lankan control over the election monitoring. Gunaratna Konara, the brave secretary of the Monaragala Human Rights Organisation who, like Gamage, had personally experienced governmental repression, had no doubt as to the empowering effect of accompaniment: 'The (election) monitoring would not have been possible without the international escorts. Their presence made us unafraid to go where we otherwise would not have gone' (Coy, 1995: 11).

Third, international accompaniment strengthens the political networks so needed to effectively resist the excesses of state-based politics. The rich and thick connections that grow between localised grassroots initiatives and supportive internationals strengthen the connective fibres that when woven together through accompaniment create an international community of conscience that serves as an antidote to liberal, state-based paradigms. A mutually beneficial relation develops as internationals learn from the locals they are privileged to walk alongside. There may be no better example of this dynamic than the Zapatistas in Mexico and their profound influence on counter-globalisation networking.

Fourth, and equally important, when the international accompaniers eventually return to their home countries, they bring with them new understandings about meaningful political engagement and the need for risk-taking (Griffin-Nolan 1991). Many are personally transformed by the experience and become organisers for human rights, justice and peace in their home communities and beyond. They also help build bridges, connecting their home community and its policymakers with the local organisations they served through accompaniment. In these ways, they not only strengthen the international community of conscience while serving as accompaniers but also expand it once they return home (Mahoney 2004). The work of International Solidarity Movement and other accompaniment organisations on the ground in Palestine demonstrates this point particularly well.

Today, at least thirty-five organisations provide international accompaniment services on request from local activists under threat in a wide variety of contexts. Some of the more prominent and experienced organisations include Peace Brigades International, Witness for Peace, Nonviolent Peaceforce, Christian Peacemaker Teams, International Solidarity Movement and FOR Peace Presence. Since 1990 alone, these and other organisations have collectively fielded accompaniment teams on six continents and in thirty-five different countries (Janzen 2015). While these organisations share many values and approaches to accompaniment, they also exhibit notable differences in terms of how partisan or non-partisan they are, the degrees of interventionism they will engage in and their adherence to local laws (for a comparative analysis, see Coy 2012).

Agency, Accompaniment and Zones of Peace

A key dimension in radical politics is the claiming and maintenance of agency, both on the level of the individual and on that of the local community. Agency is defined as being able to make one's own choices about how to order one's social, political and economic affairs. Notably, this includes being somewhat free of the confining restrictions of choices that are associated with social structures. Put more simply, agency has to do first with having control over one's own actions; and second, agency also means being able to take an additional step by having some reasonable chance of influencing the outcomes produced by one's choices (Hancock 2016). Put even more simply, agency means being able to choose, and having those choices matter. Agency applies not only to individuals, but also to the small collectives and local communities of which they are a part. Understood thusly, agency is obviously a critical dimension to meaningful lived experiments in radical politics. In fact, we can't have the latter without the former.

A good example of how the agency inherent in radical politics operates and intersects with accompaniment is in the creation of local Zones of Peace (ZoPs). In recent decades, violent, armed conflicts have increasingly become intra-state civil wars, with various sorts of insurgents challenging the state even while also challenging each other (Mazzei 2017). One result of this trend towards intra-state violent conflict is the fluid nature of contested spaces inside a country as the state and challenging groups vie for territories, for taxation powers, for the ability to exploit natural and material resources, for control of both legal and illegal commerce, e.g. drug production and trade, and for various kinds of political and economic loyalties from the citizenry. The violence experienced in such settings by local citizens can be sobering.

Communities are forced off of ancestral homelands, kidnappings, illegal detentions, torture, political disappearances, and assassination are all used by governments and paramilitaries and drug cartels to force locals into compliance. Sexual violence is used as a tool of terror, and forced recruitment into a conflict party are all too common aspects of many civil wars. In addition, corruption and forced, ad hoc taxation schemes levelled on the local population by multiple parties to the conflict add debilitating economic insult to serious physical injury.

Yet amidst the doom and gloom is hope and promise that is born of local agency and the practice of home-grown radical politics. The predictable panoply of difficulties that being caught in the cross hairs of violent interstate conflicts creates for local communities have resulted in the flowering of locally declared and locally managed ZoPs in many countries, some with long-running civil conflicts, including Colombia, Philippines, El Salvador, Aceh, the former Yugoslavia and elsewhere.

ZoPs are frequently conceptualised as being of two sorts: top-down, UN-declared and administered ones; and grassroots-based, horizontally declared and administered ones where local citizens create and maintain the Zone. In both instances, a primary purpose of the ZoP is to create a territorial island of safety and security in a sea of violence. Here, we are only interested in ZoPs of the second sort: the organic, localised versions marked by citizen agency to control the present and future environment within which people are trying to live without being victimised by the surrounding political violence. These ZoPs include not only demarcated physical spaces but they are also social sanctuaries (Mitchell & Hancock 2007). The most robust models cultivate a sense of safe social space within which community members work collectively together to create their own political and economic realities, and futures. There are many hundreds of these ZoP operating in dozens of countries around the world (Hancock & Iyer 2007).

These sorts of ZoP include saying a clear and 'reactive no' in the form of a community-wide renunciation of any participation whatsoever in the civil conflict. But they also often include a ringing and 'proactive yes' said to the creation of alternative, community-controlled political institutions and economic ventures. The proactive yes reinforces the reactive no; indeed, it makes the reactive no feasible and meaningful in new and different ways. In the Indian struggle for independence from Great Britain, Gandhi termed this proactive yes the 'constructive programme'. He saw it as even more important than the reactive no, than direct nonviolent resistance and civil disobedience. As he put it: 'The constructive programme is the truthful and non-violent way of winning Poorna Swaraj [complete independence]. Its wholesale fulfilment is complete Independence…Civil disobedience, mass or individual is an aid to the constructive effort' (Gandhi 1945: iii).

Combined, the constructive, proactive yes and the negative, reactive no give the ZoP viability and longer-term sustainability as an experiment in radical politics in a social and political environment otherwise marked by the deep uncertainties that always travel with civil wars.

One such ZoP is the Peace Community of San Jose de Apartado, which was founded in 1997 in the region of Uraba in the department or province of Antioquia in north-western Colombia. Until its historic 2016 peace agreement, Columbia was wracked by the oldest armed conflict in the Western Hemisphere, with 40+ years of civil war.

The Peace Community of San Jose de Apartado was founded by villagers in the region who were caught up at various times in the many cross-currents of the violent conflicts raging between the Colombian government, right-wing paramilitaries and leftist insurgents. These villagers had both the good and the bad fortune to live in a region known not only for its lucrative banana plantations and export-focused cash cropping, but the one that also has immense strategic significance situated as it is in extreme north-western Colombia where South America meets Central America. A region marked by territorial competitions between militarised parties, arms smugglers and drug runners, it was a flashpoint in Columbia's decades long civil war. Warring factions vied not only for control of the physical region and its associated economies, but for the cooperation, support and even loyalty of the local populace. Life became intolerable.

While many families and communities were assassinated when they refused to relinquish their land, or left the region under threat and became part of the massive numbers of internally displaced persons in Columbia, the founders of the Peace Community of San Jose de Apartado decided to 'stay put' on their land (Masullo 2015). In 1997, when right-wing paramilitaries informed about 500 people from a cluster of villages that they had three days to vacate their land or be killed, they banded together in an act of nonviolent non-cooperation. The original group of 500 were joined over time by another 1,000 from the region.

They refused to be cowed or to cooperate; they declined to fight even while they rejected flight. Instead, in an expression of radical politics, these villagers reclaimed their agency. They declared themselves as wholly neutral non-participants in the conflicts, and exerted control over their own territory by organising themselves in an alternative political and geographic order where all weapons born by all parties were completely disallowed. They rejected victimhood and reclaimed autonomy.

They declared themselves non-combatant civilians, publicly committed themselves and the community to nonviolence, refused all cooperation with any armed group – notably including both the police and the Columbian army – and organised themselves politically and economically along lines of mutual respect, dialogue, small-scale economic self-sufficiency and sustainable resource use, and even consensus decision-making (Chiari 2009; Gray 2012; Mitchell & Rojas 2012).

All of that is a tall order. But equally notable is that in laying local claim and control to these many arenas of life and space and resources and politics, this and other similar ZoPs are also challenging the ultimate value of the state: its very sovereignty (Brown 2016). Viewed in this way, a ZoP like this is one of the many faces of radical politics.

But managing to do this while navigating through a sea of militarised violence means it is radical politics supreme. Indeed, the residents of the Peace Community of San Jose de Apartado see the fact that they have successfully resisted various violent actors and been able to maintain control over their land by using nonviolent action alone as their greatest achievement (Zebechi, quoted in Gray 2012). Others apparently agree: the American Friends Service Committee, a past recipient of the Nobel Peace Prize, nominated the community for the Nobel Peace Prize in 2007.

Nonetheless, the Peace Community's declarations as a ZoP have been frequently violated – by both the government and by paramilitaries. While forced displacement, murders and disappearances declined notably from 1997 to 2009 in San Jose de Apartado, other forms of political violence continued, including threats, arbitrary detentions, blockades, harassment and theft (Valenzuela, cited in Mitchell & Rojas 2012).

To mitigate these and related pressures while at the same time maintaining their agency and their radical experiment in politics, the Peace Community of San Jose de Apartado turned to international protective accompaniment by Peace Brigades International and to the Fellowship of Reconciliation's Peace Presence accompaniment programme. This is an excellent example of how local communities engaged in radical politics, including maintaining control of their land and their lives, can increase their security and effectiveness by leveraging the extra power provided by international accompaniers. Over time, this increased daily ability to exercise fundamental human rights, due in part to transnational accompaniment, also contributes to the strengthening of civil society and institutionalises democratic practices and even democracy itself in organic ways (Henderson 2009).

Accompaniment and Radical Politics Intersections

One understanding of radical politics may argue that introducing international accompaniment into a community's ZoP or into other similar situations where civil society ventures are under threat compromises the radical nature of the local political experiment. Similarly, many applications of international accompaniment have often relied on putting into the field accompaniers from the north and the west; in so doing, they have at least engaged if not relied upon the dynamics of privilege that frequently accrue to such accompaniers. Even though those dynamics of privilege are exploited in order to expand safe political space for local activists, they still may serve to solidify rather than dismantle those same systems of privilege and hierarchy (Coy 1993; Boothe & Smithey 2007). The problems here are obvious and not insignificant. The good news is that this pattern, which was prominent while international nonviolent accompaniment developed in its early decades of the 1980s and 1980s, has always been heavily critiqued from within (Coy 2012). As a result, reliance on and even engagement with privilege has been moderated by many organisations like Nonviolent Peaceforce and Peace Brigades International and it continues to be subject to critical analysis within many international groups doing accompaniment and solidarity work (Hackl 2016).

In addition, there are positive developmental aspects that must also be considered with regard to the busy intersection of international accompaniment and local radical politics. First, international accompanier organisations do not take over or gain control or even unduly influence local political action. Local citizens engaged in political action remain the decision makers; they retain their agency. Of course, there have been isolated exceptions to this principled pattern (Dudouet 2009), but they are the exceptions that prove the general rule.

Second, accompaniment organisations embrace an ethic of empowerment. They assiduously avoid creating dependencies; most even refuse to provide material or humanitarian aid, for example (Julian & Schweitzer 2015). Indeed, most accompaniers see that they are not just there to provide protection for local citizens; they recognise that another of their primary tasks is supporting local ownership of all aspects of political life, including locally controlled problem-solving initiatives of various sorts designed to address the causes of the conflict and violence (Furnari 2015).

Third, while international accompaniment at times exploits the dynamics of the state-based international system to deter, and to name and shame and pressure human rights violators when its deterrence may fail, accompaniment is nonetheless carried out by civil society-based international non-governmental organisations. Perhaps even more important is the fact that both formal and informal grassroots solidarity networks are often intimately involved in accompaniment as well. The independent, mutually supportive relationships that are developed across state lines with local citizenry contribute to building a civil society that can serve as an antidote to statism while contributing to local expressions of radical politics.

Fourth, mutually supportive relationships between local civil society and solidarity networks and international accompaniment organisations add stature and credibility to grassroots experiments in radical politics (Eguren 2009). On the one hand, that increased stature may reduce future risks from governmental authorities (Martin 2009). On the other hand, it may also inspire in civil society bystanders who have not yet found their political voice or claimed their social place to create still more varied expressions of local agency and radical politics. Examples of this abound and include rich expressions of solidarity, like Jewish Israeli citizens taking up activism on behalf of the citizens of Palestine or white Americans taking to the streets with Black Lives Matter to both protest and document police violence against the black community.

Fifth, many of the international non-governmental organisations that provide accompaniment operate on modifications of a consensus decision-making model (Coy 2003). Consensus decision-making aims for horizontalism that will erode hierarchies and weaken structures of privilege. That is why, for example, consensus became a central pillar in the radical experiment that was the Occupy movement in 2011 (Szolucha 2013). In this way, accompaniment organisations using and modelling consensus decision-making are contributing to the larger experiments in radical politics.

Finally, the dynamic relationships that develop between the international non-governmental accompaniment organisations and the local expressions of radical politics are also a counter weight to the hegemonic nation state system; indeed, they challenge that hegemony and create additional political openings for still other kinds of resistance (Maney, Woehrle & Coy 2005). In these many ways, while accompaniment is a complicated, compromised and incomplete expression of radical politics, it is most often an important and much-needed complimentary expression of radical politics.

References

Becker, J. 2013, *Campaigning for Justice: Human Rights Advocacy in Practice*. Stanford University Press, Stanford, CA.

Boothe, I. & Smithey, L.A. 2007, 'Privilege, Empowerment, and Nonviolent Intervention', *Peace and Change*, vol. 32, no. 1, pp. 39–61.

Brown, C. 2016, 'Supporting a Radical Peace: Reflections on the Peace Community of San Jose de Apartado', *Journal of Peacebuilding & Development*, vol. 11, no. 1, pp. 70–74.

Chiari, R. April 20, 2009, San José de Apartado: Colombian Peace Community Stands Up for Humanity. Available from: http://upsidedownworld.org/archives/colombia/san-jose-apartado-colombian-peace-community-stands-up-for-humanity/.

Coy, P. 2011, 'The Privilege Problematic in International Nonviolent Accompaniment's Early Decades', *Journal of Religion, Conflict, and Peace*, vol. 4, no. 2. [Online] at www.religionconflictpeace.org/volume-4-issue-2-spring-2011/privilege-problematic-international-nonviolent-accompaniment%E2%80%99s-early

Coy, P. 1994, 'Going Where We Otherwise Would Not Have Gone: Accompaniment and Election Monitoring in Sri Lanka', *Fellowship*, vol. 61, no. 5, pp. 10–12.

Coy, P.G. 2012, 'Nonpartisanship, Interventionism and Legality in Accompaniment: Comparative Analyses of Peace Brigades International, Christian Peacemaker Teams, and the International Solidarity Movement', *International Journal of Human Rights,* vol. 16, no. 7, pp. 963–981.

Coy, P.G. 2003, 'Negotiating Danger and Safety Under the Gun: Consensus Decision Making on Peace Brigades International Teams' in *Consensus Decision-Making, Northern Ireland, and Indigenous Movements, Research in Social Movements, Conflicts and Change*, Vol. 24, ed. P.G. Coy, Elsevier Science/JAI Press, Oxford, pp. 85–122.

Coy, P.G. 2001, 'Shared Risks and Research Dilemmas on a Peace Brigades International Team in Sri Lanka', *Journal of Contemporary Ethnography*, vol. 30, no. 5, pp. 575–606.

Coy, P.G. 1997, 'Cooperative Accompaniment by Peace Brigades International in Sri Lanka' in *Transnational Social Movements and Global Politics: Solidarity Beyond the State*, eds. J. Smith, C. Chatfield & R. Pagnucco, Syracuse University Press, Syracuse, NY, pp. 81–100.

Coy, P.G. 1993, 'Protective Accompaniment: How Peace Brigades International Secures Political Space and Human Rights Nonviolently' in *Nonviolence: Social and Psychological Issues*, ed. V.K. Kool, University Press of America, Latham, MD, pp. 235–244.

Dudouet, V. 2009, 'Cross-Border Nonviolent Advocacy during the Second Palestinian Intifada: The International Solidarity Movement' in *People Power: Unarmed Resistance and Global Solidarity*, ed. H. Clark, Pluto Press, London, pp. 125–135.

Eguren, L.E. 2009, 'Developing Strategy for Accompaniment' in *People Power: Unarmed Resistance and Global Solidarity*, ed. H. Clark, Pluto Press, London, pp. 98–107.

Furnari, E. 2015, 'Relationships Are Critical for Peacekeeping', *Peace Review,* vol. 27, no. 1, pp. 25–30.

Gandhi, M.K. 1945, *Constructive Programme: Its Meaning and Place.* Navajivan Trust, Ahmedabad, India, revised edition.

Gray, V.J. 2012, 'Nonviolence and Sustainable Resource Use with External Support: A Survival Strategy in Rural Colombia', *Latin American Perspectives*, vol. 39, no. 1, pp. 43–114.

Griffin-Nolan, E. 1991, *Witness for Peace: A Story of Resistance*. Westminster/John Knox Press, Louisville.

Hackl, A. 2016, 'An Orchestra of Civil Resistance: Privilege, Diversity, and Identification Among Cross-Border Activists in a Palestinian Village', *Peace & Change*, vol. 41, no. 2, pp. 167–193.

Hancock, L.E. 2016, 'Agency & Peacebuilding: The Promise of Local Zones of Peace', *Peacebuilding*, pp. 1–15.

Hancock, L.E. & Iyer, P. 2007, 'The Nature, Structure, and Variety of Peace Zones' in *Zones of Peace*, eds. L.E. Hancock & C. Mitchell, Kumarian Press, Bloomfield, CT, pp. 29–50.

Henderson, V.L. 2009, 'Citizenship in the Line of Fire: Protective Accompaniment, Proxy Citizenship, and Pathways for Transnational Solidarity in Guatemala', *Annals of the Association of American Geographers*, vol. 99, no. 5, pp. 969–976.

Hopgood, S. 2013, *Keepers of the Flame: Understanding Amnesty International*. Cornell University Press, Ithaca, NY.

Janzen, R. 2014, 'Shifting Practices of Peace: What is the Current State of Unarmed Civilian Peacekeeping', *Peace Studies Journal*, vol. 7, no. 3, pp. 46–60.

Julian, R. & Schweitzer, C. 2015, 'The Origins and Development of Unarmed Civilian Peacekeeping', *Peace Review*, vol. 27, no. 1, pp. 1–8.

Mahony, L. 2006, 'Proactive Presence', Field Strategies For Civilian Protection. Geneva: Henry Dunant Centre for Humanitarian Dialogue. [Online] at www.hdcentre.org/publications/[10.9.2008].

Mahony, L. 2004, *'Side by Side', Protecting and Encouraging Threatened Activists with Unarmed International Accompaniment*. The Center for Victims of Torture, Minneapolis.

Maney, G.M., Woehrle, L.M. & Coy, P.G. 2005, 'Harnessing and Challenging Hegemony: The U.S. Peace Movement after 9/11', *Sociological Perspectives*, vol. 38, no. 3, pp. 357–381.

Martin, B. 2009, *People Power: Unarmed Resistance and Global Solidarity*, ed. H. Clark, Pluto Press, London, pp. 93–97.

Masullo, J. 2015, *The Power of Staying Put: Nonviolent Resistance against Armed Groups in Colombia*. International Center on Nonviolent Conflict, Washington, DC.

Mazzei, J. (ed.) 2017, *Non-state Actors Violent Actors and Social Movement Organizations: Influence, Adaptation and Change*, Vol. 41, Research in Social Movements, Conflicts and Change edn., Emerald Group Publishing, Bingley, UK.

Mitchell, C. & Hancock, L.E. 2007, 'Local Zones of Peace and a Theory of Sanctuary' in *Zones of Peace*, eds. L.E. Hancock & C. Mitchell, Kumarian Press, Bloomfield, CT, pp. 189–221.

Mitchell, C. & Rojas, C. 2012, 'Against the Stream: Columbian Zones of Peace under Democractic Security' in *Local Peacebuilding and National Peace: Interaction between Grassroots and Elite Processes*, eds. C. Mitchell & L.E. Hancock, Continuum, London, pp. 39–68.

Phillips, K. 2106. 'After Trump's Win, Some Minorities Feel Unsafe: Now, Thousands Want to Protect Them.' *Washington Post*. November 14. Available from: www.washingtonpost.com/news/inspired-life/wp/2016/11/14/after-trumps-win-some-minorities-feel-unsafe-now-thousands-want-to-protect-them/?utm_term=.1a0a55d2a332.

Szolucha, A. 2013, 'Learning Consensus Decision Making in Occupy: Uncertainty, Responsibility, Commitment', *Research in Social Movements, Conflicts and Change*, vol. 36, pp. 205–234.

3.2

MAKING SPACES OUR OWN

Performance Interventions to Disrupt, Revive and Reclaim Public Spaces

Mel Evans

Fighting for Territory

Wherever we go, corporations follow us: on the street, in our homes, in public spaces like sports events and galleries. There's no looking away. Via advertising, multitudes of consumer products and their repetitive, zombielike shopfront visual presence on every street, these several hundred brands owned by a remarkably short list of corporations are everywhere we turn in post-industrial cities and towns. They're always *there*. Invading our thoughts, persuading our desires and desperately attempting to convince us that 'they are an essential part of our daily lives' (Klein, 2000), and that without them, our whole world would collapse. And yet, so much of what we do among these spaces is not remotely reliant on the looming figures that haunt them: when we grow food and prepare it, teach and learn, make and share, even buy and sell. The corporate takeover of public life is omnipresent but not omnipotent.

When we pick a fight with a corporation, we seek them out too: in their headquarters, their high street shopfronts, and where they sponsor public events and institutions. Any physical or visual presence in urban public life becomes a stage for questioning and challenging the corporation's wider set of activities anywhere in the world. The office desks and sales checkouts become the frontline of everything corporations say and do, the border between us and them, and which therefore serves as a site for our battles.

In cityscapes that are rapidly being gentrified and redeveloped, where every patch of gravelly land and square foot of dusty floorboard is sold to the highest bidder, visual artists, theatre-makers, performance artists and musicians alike increasingly struggle to find spaces to make and share creative work. To make art in a time characterised by the corporate takeover of public life is to embrace nomadism and its artistic lexicon: site-specific, promenade, installation, digital content; whatever it takes to make work without anywhere to make it.

These three ingredients make for a dynamic mix: corporates seeking evermore exposure and ways to build brand identity; artists thrown out on the street and activists looking for opportunities to undermine corporate power and engage the public in social issues. In this cat-and-mouse game, artists and activists have found ways to destabilise the corporate entity in its public form, and in doing so, grasp at a new method of making spaces public. By engaging audiences onsite and online in the sharing of performance and protest against corporate misdemeanours, a functioning commons is being reclaimed.

Whose Space?

The idea encompassed in the title of 'the commons' dates back to pre-enclosure England, when land for common agricultural or festive use formed a centre point to social life. It is a practice of land use which is continued by Indigenous Peoples in the Americas, despite ongoing resistance to colonialism and the refusal to recognise land rights by settler colonial states such as Brazil (see the Munduruku) and the USA (see the Standing Rock Sioux). Shared space in which to gather remains desirable the world over, hidden as it is in raucous gatherings of young people in shopping centres, wistful hoverings of adults of all ages in galleries and museums, on park benches and train platforms. Even during commuter claustrophobia, the introverted among us still long to share space, to be together. The notion of public space denotes this messier conflation of different powers, actors and messages. It is a dynamic concept constantly being shaped to suit different agendas. Where Jurgen Habermas' (1962) construction of the 'public sphere' has been rightly critiqued as exclusive and elitist – because Habermas focuses solely on the influence of upper middle classes on politics and social life – ideas around the uses of public space especially but not exclusively in urban environments remain important. Their significance has, in contrast, evolved to be immensely more accessible to diverse participants in community organising, political resistance and social movements than Habermas' original notion claimed.

For social geographer Doreen Massey (2007), places are temporary sites that hold continually changing representations of historical moments – a contested territory which is permanently shifting rather than antagonistically fixed. In this understanding, the role of critical intervention becomes necessarily short-lived with as much historical weight as the given site's more physically permanent structures. Once something has happened in a space, it will forever haunt it. Massey warns to be 'wary of certain forms of localism'; yet, she argues that '"place" would seem to have real and, maybe ironically in this age of globalisation, even increasing potential as a locus of political responsibility and an arena for political engagement' (Massey 2007: 208–9). Massey's assertion offers an important entry point to reframing public space for political artists and activists.

Corporate presence in public space by way of premises, purchases or advertising can feel pervasive. For decades, the roadside billboard has been a favourite opportunity for social comment or corporate critique, needing only the simple tool of paint in a pressurised aerosol container and a catchy few words to bring about transformation. Graffiti is one strategy to challenge the visual dominance of the billboard in public space, but parodying the entire visual language of advertising steps beyond this to deconstruct the broader logic and methods of consumer capitalism. Barbara Kruger's art and writing (2010) explores the interaction between corporate messaging and peoples' thoughts and ideas via public space. She undermines the advertisers' techniques through parody. For Kruger, the public visual space is a contested territory in which political philosophy can be fought and the ideas that inform our thoughts, feelings and ways of life can be questioned, shaped or transformed. Kruger's work calls for a thorough and critical approach to aesthetics from artists and activists working in the public realm.

Theatre and performance are important art practices shaping our understandings and interventions in the scenes of everyday life. Theatre historian Marvin Carlson (1989) writes, 'the late Middle Ages and early Renaissance constitute the major historical period when theatre existed as an important part of urban life without any specific architectural element being devoted to its exclusive use'. While current black box theatres and proscenium arch stages contain performance within a limited boundary, there was once a time when the drama unfolded fluidly within everyday contexts – not dissimilar to street performance or fringe theatre. This older, alternative potential for participation in performances in public spaces offers an opportunity to use public performance to disrupt ordinary social roles.

The political convergence or action camp offers more permanent revolutions in the use of public space when located in public settings. In 'Protest Camps', Anna Feigenbaum, Fabian Frenzel and Patrick McCurdy (2013) explore the historical development of camps since the 1960s onwards and the political applications of setting up camps in carefully chosen sites. Camps combine the countercultural with the everyday. For however long they last – days, weeks, months or sometimes years – they provide a parallel universe structured by mainstream culture and its critique. Taking over space and living together in it necessarily spark exploration of alternatives, even though camps operate within the limitations of current forms of social organisation.

So how do we radically reclaim and revivify public spaces to create new potentials for dissent, transformation and structural change? How have artists and activists disrupted social norms to tackle massive corporate and government structures head on? And how do these practices offer scope to enliven politics, increase public engagement and push for wider cultural shifts around social justice issues? Using examples big and small, coordinated and spontaneous, I will pick out from personal experience moments where the scope of the possible has broadened and lengthened, set in *the street, protest camps, corporate spaces* and *museums and galleries*. In each, the open access public space will emerge as an important site for collectivity and building community around key social issues.

The following stories are windows into a much wider world of shape-shifting and creative confrontation that seeks to refresh the normal boundaries of protest and public life to light fireworks for alternative thinking and doing. Each relate to the analyses of public space, art, performance and protest as described by Massey, Kruger, Carlson and Feigenbaum, Frenzel and McCurdy.

In the Street

Visual artist Barbara Kruger says her 'cut and paste' artistic practice was shaped by her early experiences as a designer at a women's magazine, and calls her time in the editing room as 'the biggest influence on my work'. Carol Squiers examines the relationship between Kruger's early career and her later work as an artist and concludes, 'She began to pose questions about the construction of everyday life and the social mechanisms of consumption, seduction, and control, which flowed as much from her experiences in fashion and lifestyle publishing as they did from the critical theory she read'. This blending of content and form in her source material was also to prove a rich vein of critical artistic process when she combined critical ideas with the imagery of fashion advertising. Squiers continues, 'The young woman who hadn't imagined herself as an artist took her experience at shaping fashion's upbeat enticements and turned it to her own artistic ends: to challenge, lampoon, and subvert the protocols of power' (Squiers 2010: 232). As Squiers describes it, Kruger turned the tools of advertising and used it to parody the internal logic of consumer capitalism, adhering to the form in order to fully expose it. Her stark white statements on bright lipstick red solid backgrounds shout out their bold claims in direct address to or implication of the audience, and are at once thoughtful, suggestive and confronting, for example 'I shop therefore I am', 'Your body is a battleground' and 'In violence we forget who we are'. This is no ordinary advert in the path of the passersby.

Kruger's artworks installed on billboards, bus stops and buildings interrupt the otherwise closed text of urban street advertising. This kind of intervention reframes everything around it and much of what the audience goes on to view that day and beyond. Exposing the key features of advertising as a form enables the viewer to deconstruct everything else on display around her. In 2007 on the shopping streets of Glasgow, some friends and I set out to use performance techniques of parody to do something similar to Kruger's disruptive un-advertising.

It's midday on a busy Saturday afternoon on Buchanan Street in Glasgow, the most central and most upmarket pedestrianised high street in the place that prides itself in being known as the UK's second shopping city, however that is determined. The city centre is hilly and Buchanan Street descends gently offering stunning views of the hills lying eastwards above the hats and heads of the shoppers as they jostle past bagpipe players, chuggers and each other – it's 2007, before the financial crises and the austerity cuts, and everyone's merrily consuming capitalism. Me, Beth and Tilly have a dare on: it's sort of performance art, sort of direct action, but mainly it's a dare. We've walked past the mannequins in the shops hundreds of times, rolled our eyes at their pale skin and pointy breasts, touting clothes that look good until you try them on. We've queried their impact on young women's sense of self, but we've never thought of the mannequins as equally trapped in the social structure; we've never interacted with them before. The dare is can you get in there with them, and how long can you stay? Beth goes first. She slips into the display area having grabbed a t-shirt from the rack on her way in. She moves slowly, she's trained in physical theatre and mime, and quickly at her simple movements a few young girls gather to giggle at something that they instinctively know is naughty and subversive. Beth chats for a little with her mannequin friend and gets a good five minutes performance time in before security catch up and send her on her way. She gives them a surprised look of 'Oh am I not supposed to be here?' and the gathered girl gang uproars in laughter. I'm next and I opt for a frozen revolutionary stance in a smart women's clothing store's khaki and denim shop window. Security are on to me fast – turns out all the shops on the street share radio channels and our antics have been passed down the chain – but it's tricky for the guy when, as a mannequin, I simply don't respond to his request for me to leave. I can't hear him. I'm made of plastic. He continues his monologue arms folded across his chest, almost frozen and now part of the scene himself until I activate and smiling, slip right back out of the shop. We carry on with our experiments until we're shunned from all doors with grinning faces of bemused guards who got our descriptions and our game. And so it is that we switch streets, find Ann Summers, the dare steps up a notch and Tilly and I find ourselves competing to see who can hold a freeze going down on a mannequin on Sauchiehall Street in Glasgow. Can't be the first time it has happened?

Our dare played with gender roles, corporate space, consumerism and body image, and was all built around a transgression that uprooted the sense of what could or could not happen for passersby, how things might or might not be in these worlds that we daily co-create. We disrupted the sense that nothing can change, and that corporate control over our minds and bodies was something we could playfully fight. By setting up a parody of femininity in parallel to its normative construction, we were able to reveal a wider critical dimension, and undermine the policing of gender roles via consumer capitalist stages in public life.

Protest Camps

In Doreen Massey's analysis, place can be 'one base, among many others, for collectivity'. This succinctly provides the foundation for art and protest that takes the activity of dissent beyond narrowly scripted marches and rallies and into new territories where co-creation and collaboration are necessary and centred – where the forming and practising of community are fundamental. In this understanding, coming together in sites of antagonism or political significance gives way to active democracy where it is incumbent on the participants to make the event, thereby engendering a public life that is elsewhere narrower and more tightly scripted in normative politics and cultures.

Climate Camp was both physical and imaginary; both practical and prefigurative; both politically effective and politically inspiring. It happened annually from 2006 to 2010 inclusive, and in each instance bore the same trademarks: a week-long site occupation of land on or next to a current or planned piece of fossil fuel infrastructure in which people lived in an ecologically sustainable way, organised non-hierarchically by consensus, shared talks and workshops to understand and consider the social politics of the environment, and planned direct action on the root causes of climate change.

From coal power stations, to the planned third runway at Heathrow, the financial district of London to RBS headquarters in Edinburgh, the camp sprung up, confronted security and police, and created a welcoming, lively space of action, discussion and social change. Each day at Climate Camp was packed: a neighbourhood meeting at 9 a.m., with participants who live in your region of the country, making links and feeding in thoughts and ideas for the main meeting at 9.30 a.m. – where if you're a spokesperson for your neighbourhood you head straight to, shape consensus decisions, bring back info for the noticeboard. From there, a workshop on class war and climate change or DIY renewable energy, to an action planning session, and don't forget you signed up to chop carrots for lunch. By the evening, you've made several new friends for life, soaked up some sun and felt the possibility of connection with kith and kin seep back into your bones through your bare feet on the grass which one week later will have been tidied to the last fag butt, when all that remains of your taste of utopia is a mass of newspaper cut-outs of headlines proclaiming hippies have landed but content wise finally forced to bring climate change and fossil fuel corporations into the main stories.

Alongside the full swathe of campaigning tactics utilised by aligned groups, the camp saw huge successes: the shelving of government plans for a raft of coal plants, starting with the initial target Kingsnorth; the halting – for some years – of Heathrow expansion plans and eventually the phasing out of fossil fuel finance by RBS. The example of Climate Camp was tightly mirroring its predecessor Horizone, the action planning camp in Stirling, Scotland set up to target the G8 summit in Gleneagles in 2005. This camp was, of course, itself shaped by numerous protest camp influences from Reclaim the Streets to Greenham Common Women's Peace Camp. Climate Camp later provided practical resources for Occupy London Stock Exchange when various groups joined to set it up in response to the global call to action by Occupy Wall Street in 2011.

The genealogy of camps is laid out beautifully in 'Protest Camps' by Anna Feigenbaum, Fabian Frenzel and Patrick McCurdy (2013). In part, they lay the purpose of these endeavours in social movements as founded in an attempt to resolve the problems of the present day with a steer towards a radical or utopian alternative: 'Protest camps are not simply mirror images of a social order devoid of any relationship to the here and now. Indeed in protest camps the tensions between antagonistic demands for a new beginning meet with the practical requirements of making things work in the present' (2013: 220–1). This analysis speaks to the application of the form by Climate Camp, both in its practice of radical horizontal organising and tangible alternative renewable energy as visions for the future practised in the here and now. This experimentation with visionary possibilities is vital to reclaiming spaces for a public conversation around what our collective future might look like, and stepping into practices of creating those futures more broadly and more often.

Mel Evans

Corporate Spaces

Privately owned public spaces are casually encroaching on the public urban environment in cities with significant financial centres like London and New York. Accessible to all but tightly monitored to police unacceptable entrants, dress, assembly or behaviours, these locales are strict in both dull minimalist aesthetics and heavy-handed social conditioning. These spaces are drafted by a different social script than many others, with a narrower set of costumes, movements and participants expected to appear on the stage.

In his analysis of street performance in Medieval towns, Marvin Carlson describes 'a situation allowing those producing a performance to place it in whatever locale seemed most suitable meant that theatre could use to its own advantage the already existing connotations of other spaces both in themselves and in their placement in the city'. The built-up environment was understood as its own stage already: areas were used freely for public performance and sites provided context understood by all involved. A familiarity with performance in public space invited participation by all on the street, rather than the automatic audience formation commonly emerging around street performances today. This potential performance dialogue with the cityscape and the participation in performances by its inhabitants was denied by the ascent of royal power, however. Royal authority within cities form the later Middle Ages onwards asserted a different dynamic in public space: one of performance and audience, wherein the public witnessed the royals' power. Carlson notes, 'the city was no longer available as stage primarily for the separate scenes of citizens' dramas but became rather the scene for the display of princely power, at which citizens were present by sufferance – as spectators only' (Carlson 1989).

The princely power now finds itself replaced by other objects of fetish and command. Where Carlson noted the flexibility of the Middle Ages street for public performance lost to royal authority, the new power's control over the public realm occurs by the advertising industry's infiltration of our imaginations explored by artist Barbara Kruger. Present-day areas owned by corporations extend this corporate influence to architectural and extralegal limitations commanded through ownership. Beyond the lures of the shopping malls, areas in London such as Canary Wharf, More London beside City Hall and Exchange Square in the financial district all apply stricter regulations of corporate control of streets, pathways and otherwise presumed areas of 'public' space.

In 2013 with Platform,[1] I wrote and produced a piece of immersive site-specific theatre made for the financial district of London, titled 'Oil City'. For two weeks as part of the 2 Degrees arts and climate change festival, three performances took place daily in which audiences of ten, invited to follow the UBS bank's dress code (BBC news, 2004), joined three actors in a live investigation into the connections between the banks surrounding Liverpool Street Station and finance for the expansion of the tar sands in Canada. The financial district was reframed as theatrical stage, deconstructing the power and authority of its financiers as they went about their daily business while on the same walkways, benches and bland corporate art centred social spaces the group of interlopers critiqued the impacts of the banks' operations far beyond their shiny glass walls. The piece turned the theatricality of power in the financial sector against it, undermining the normalised authority of the big banks by revealing its inner workings. Theatre critic Lyn Gardner described the experience: 'It operates intriguingly at the point where fact and fiction meet … It's also a reminder that art and activism are close cousins: together, they can make connections' (Gardner, 2013). In this case, the work followed a somewhat medieval performance strategy by using the existing context as a not only suitable site but indeed the subject of the performance. In doing so, the corporate space was made more public by inviting members of the public into critical dialogue with this place that, through the financial crisis, debt and controversial and destructive project finance around the world, affects every aspect of lives.

Oil company headquarters are a favoured and necessary target of coordinated dissent around the globe. These smart clean offices are an aesthetic world away from the grime and pollution of oil extraction, transport and refineries. Therefore, attempting the evoke this distant cognitive dissonance in the physical space of the HQ has radical potential: it brings all who interact with the place, be they staff, visitors or passersby, into more visceral sense of what company they are in fact keeping. These corporate spaces located in capital cities' central business districts offer an important site for performance and protest that aims to bring public attention to the real-world impacts made by soft taps on computer keyboards at desks cleaned daily within the insulated walls of the buildings.

In 2007 during Climate Camp Heathrow, a group of seven climate justice activists closed BP HQ in St James Square London for a day. Two of us had dressed in suits and chained ourselves to a doorway to block it. From a pool of oily molasses, we wailed like two birds caught in an oil spill and two businesswomen cornered by our own consciences. In 2010, Climate Camp was held at RBS HQ in Edinburgh for a week of stand offs and a daily disruption of business as usual. It is Shell's monumental headquarters on the Southbank in London that have received the most frequent and ardent statements of dissent to the companies' activities in Nigeria – by Platform, Social Action and others, in the Canadian tar sands, by the UK Tar Sands Network and the Indigenous Environmental Network, and the Arctic, by Greenpeace. Consecutive creative interruptions here by Greenpeace evoked the distant Arctic through art, in the form of an enormous double decker bus-sized polar bear marionette, the part-bear, part-ship creature known as Aurora, who vigilantly eyed staff in the first and second floor offices in 2015 as the company attempted to drill for oil in the Arctic. Her presence there followed a month of daily recitals of a 'Requiem for Arctic Ice' performed by numerous musicians including Charlotte Church, who sang Dinah Washington and Max Richter's arrangement of Clyde Otis's 'This Bitter Earth' and Richter's own 'On the Nature of Daylight' (Greenpeace and Charlotte Church, 2015). After the two-month occupation of the place and the imaginations of all who frequent it, and following a tidal wave of global resistance that ranged from rig climbing to bridge blockades in the Pacific, Shell halted its drilling and withdrew its plans from the table.

The confrontation between what is public and what is corporate that can take place in both corporate-owned spaces and corporate headquarters brings the impact of multinational corporations to come into scrutiny. These spaces become a stage on which the public interest can be conjured or represented and as such a practice of creating public space emerges.

Museums and Galleries

Cultural institutions are a physical manifestation of a microcosm of the histories we are told and the ways we frame and contain our nevertheless shifting cultures. Conservation of artefacts and art objects, by definition, fixes periods of time in box frames and glass containers. And yet, a conversation is going on in these spaces already in which dissent clearly has a role: what are our ethics, how do they differ to those who came before us, what defines this age? Any intervention that could be called protest makes a contribution to that conversation at the same time as it objects to the content on display be that exhibits or corporate logos.

From 2010 to 2016, Liberate Tate made unsanctioned live art inside Tate galleries with a central strategic objective of ending BP sponsorship of the institution (which it achieved in 2016), and a set of broader aims of questioning the ethics of the art museum, exploring its potential as a site of public engagement and debate, and highlighting the various harmful impacts of the international oil industry from ecological damage to environmental racism. In one performance, *Time Piece*, in 2015, we stayed in the Tate Modern Turbine Hall overnight as part of a twenty-five-hour durational performance exploring concepts of time, from that of geological time and the anthropocene, all the way to gallery-opening hours. From a bibliography of publications on oil, art and climate change, we transcribed texts in willow charcoal in a rising tide up the slope of the gallery. Books included Rachel Carson's 'Silent Spring', Vandana Shiva's 'Earth Democracy' and Ursula Le Guin's 'The Dispossessed'. The performance lasted its intended duration when the police and management concluded to refrain from removing us from the building after we assembled our compost toilet in defiance of their shutting off access to the gallery toilets. By the second high tide on the River Thames adjacent to the gallery, which marked the end of the performance, the floor was awash with delicate patterns of words written by over a hundred performers, engaging the interaction of thousands of visitors and millions of people online. A community was built – both inside and outside the institution, through links with the Public and Commercial Services union representing gallery floor staff as much as artists through online platforms – and this community shifted the wider attitude and encouraged the board of Trustees to change.

Over the course of the campaign, the art collective made over sixteen such performance interventions, and inspired various groups in the UK, Norway, the Netherlands and North America whose interventions and campaigns saw other victories, such as Statoil losing sponsorship contracts with music festivals in Norway. The global movement for institutional liberation has grown and diversified in its aims and practices over the years 2015–17. An important example in this powerful movement is Decolonize This Place, an artist and protest organising space from which an action at the American Museum of Natural History in New York was designed as a collaboration between NYC Stands With Standing Rock and the New York chapter of Black Lives Matter. Inside the museum, the groups gathered around 250 people who took part in an alternative tour, critically reframing the racist content on display in the museum's exhibits. The tour was followed by a ceremony outside to cover a racist statue at the museum's main entrance. In a call for its removal, the participants chanted, 'Respect. Remove. Rename' (Gonzalez, 2016). The action signified a global challenge to all involved in confrontations with gallery and museum ethics to directly connect this work with a process of decolonisation of these institutions whose collections and histories are so deeply connected to the stolen riches of colonialism, imperialism, the cultural theft of slavery and the contemporary narratives that normalise white supremacy.

In both examples, the museum or gallery emerges as a particularly interesting site for protest activity because of its distinct differences to the street and corporate physical structures – and to the cordoned-off spaces belonging to activist communities be they social centres or protest camps. Within cultural institutions, visitors and staff enter a liminal space: not one which is in flux with the transitory mixed messages of the street; not a hyper-controlled and aesthetically two-dimensional binary corporate space; not a 'safe', limited, intra-community echo chamber over which activists hold complete jurisdiction, but a carefully curated yet necessarily contested space in which rapid readings and critical visual analysis spark off on the cue of the opening sliding doors. The public gallery becomes a space in which live questioning of social structures can be made possible, and in depth.

Conclusion

Public space has been politicised and instrumentalised in processes of cultural, social and political changes in various ways over centuries and decades. In today's politics of fear and polarisation, methods that bring people together and, in so-doing, build trust, resilience and solidarity are evermore important. At this time, all methods are vital, and the techniques we use to remake and reframe these spaces will be necessarily more and more creative. The reasons to make spaces public are: to hothouse ideas and relationships in the protest, demonstration or camp, to disrupt the corporate conformity of the street, to prick the status quo of elite corridors of power and to revive dissent within the public cultural institution.

This is the ultimate potential of disruptive, creative, critical intervention: to invite us each to transgress the rules of public space, and in doing so to open out radical political possibilities. When we transgress together, new communities are built that can shift the politics and ideas in the wider culture. For artists, the challenge is to change spaces not simply seek out a place to make art in. For artists and activists alike, it is surely better to be out on the street than cocooned in an echo chamber. Without spaces of our own, we are fruitfully forced into contact, connection and perhaps confrontation with the world, the environment, the public, corporations – and that's exactly where we should be.

Note

1 Platform is an interdisciplinary organisation working between the arts, research, education and campaigning. Much of the work is based around the organisation's articulation of the Carbon Web, and the branches of supporting infrastructure that support and maintain the international oil industry's profitable operations. I worked in the organisation from 2008 to 2014 and remain an active part of its network. www.platformlondon.org.

References

Carlson, Marvin. 1989. *Places of Performance: The Semiotics of Theatre Architecture*. London: Cornell University Press.

Climate Camp. 2006–2011. [online] Available at: facebook.com/climatecamp or see descriptions documented by the British Science Association. [online] Available at: collectivememory.british-scienceassociation.org/memory/camp-for-climate-action. Accessed 29 January 2017.

Decolonize This Place. 2016. [online] Available at: http://decolonizethisplace.org/. Accessed 29 January 2017.

Feigenbaum, Anna, Fabian Frenzel, and McCurdy Patrick. 2013. *Protest Camps*. London: Zed.

Gardner, Lyn. 2013. *Oil City: Review* [online] Available at: www.theguardian.com/stage/2013/jun/20/oil-city-review. Accessed 29 January 2017.

Gonzalez, Catherine. 2016. *Respect, Rename, Remove!*. [online] Available at: https://bitchmedia.org/article/respect-rename-remove/activist-anti-columbus-day-tour-aims-decolonize-history-museum. Accessed 29 January 2017.

Greenpeace and Charlotte Church. 2015. *Requiem for Arctic Ice*. [online] Available at: www.youtube.com/watch?v=2EMAhrnFGBQ. Accessed 8 October 2017.

Habermas, Jürgen. 1962. 'The Structural Transformation of the Public Sphere: An Inquiry into a Category of Bourgeois Society' translated by Thomas Burger with the assistance of Frederick Lawrence. Cambridge, MA: MIT Press 1989.

Klein, Naomi. 2000. *No Logo*. Toronto: Vintage Canada.

Kruger, Barbara. 2010. *Remote Control: Power, Cultures and the World of Appearances*. Cambridge, MA: MIT Press.

Liberate Tate. 2010-present. [online] Available at: liberatetate.org.uk/performances/time-piece/bibliography. Accessed 29 January 2017.

Massey, Doreen. 2007. *World City*. Cambridge: Polity.

Squiers, Carol in Kruger, Barbara. 2010. *Remote Control: Power, Cultures and the World of Appearances*. Cambridge, MA: MIT Press.

3.3

RADICAL BICYCLE POLITICS

Confronting Car Culture and Capitalism as Root Causes of Mobility Injustice[1]

Aurora Trujillo and Matthew Wilson

After more than a decade of cycling being their primary form of transport, and having been involved for as many years in both the radical and mainstream cycling worlds, one of us has been forced to walk instead of cycle.

> I have parked my loyal bike. My mental health is suffering and I need a less stressful mode of transport, at least for a while. The extreme attention that is needed to cycle in a city like London and the adrenaline rush and stress that it provokes is not tolerable or beneficial for me at the moment.

This is not an exceptional situation. Cycling is too stressful and scary for many people in the UK to even try. 'I'd love to cycle', a lot of people say, 'but I'm too scared'; and understandably so. Compared to many activities, cycling is, *statistically*, relatively safe. But, as Dave Horton has argued, this statistical reality misses the crucial point that it is not simply the number of incidents that ought to concern us; what also matters is how it *feels* to cycle. And the truth is, under the UK's current traffic conditions, cycling often feels dangerous, threatening and unsettling (Horton 2007; Pooley et al. 2013). Recent studies on the frequency and impact of incidents that do not result in the injury or death of cyclists but which do constitute 'near misses' show that the often severe emotional consequences of these incidents deeply affect how cyclists experience their journeys and their likeliness to continue cycling (Aldred 2016).

Inevitably Political: A Double-Axe Approach

Bicycle *politics* is about much more than bicycles and cycling. It is about the wider cultural, political and economic value systems, as well as the material conditions, that cycling and bicycles are situated in; it is about interrogating whether cycling is facilitated or prevented by those systems and conditions and/or whether and how its promotion can be used to move towards and shape new ones. No mode of transport is simply a *mode* of transport. Mobility is deeply political. As Ivan Illich said, 'Tell me how fast you travel and I'll tell you who you are' (Illich 1974). Our mobility needs, how these needs are created in the first place, by whom and for whom, and how we meet them, are not value-free questions that planners and engineers can find neutral, technological solutions to. These are value-laden questions about which kind of society we[2] want to live in, how we want to organise our lives, in the interest and empowerment of whom, according to which values and in pursuit of which relationships (cultural and economic) (Simmie 1974; Hayden 1981; MacGregor 1995; Thomas 2000). Do we want a society in which a great majority of people find cycling too intimidating to even try, or one in which everyone who wishes can enjoy the many benefits of cycling, including improved mental health? Do we want a world in which commuting for hours every week is normalised or one in which that time can be used in more fulfilling ways? A world in which children cannot play outdoors for fear of being run over, a world in which people are encouraged to stay at home to avoid high levels of pollution on the streets?[3] Or a world in which our streets are places to hang out and live, rather than mere corridors for motor traffic or places to consume? Should the contribution of the car industry to the British economy trump social equality and ecological needs? The list goes on.

Radical bicycle politics is about approaching the questions and challenges that bicycle politics poses from an antiauthoritarian, anticapitalist, anti-oppression, ecologically committed approach, one which also embraces a diversity of tactics to bring change. This, we assume, is what broadly characterises radical politics.

With this in mind, the following chapter presents a diversity of expressions of contemporary radical bicycle politics, mostly focusing on the UK. As we will see, the bicycle has frequently played a role in radical (and not so radical) social movements. However, while old and new radical political struggles have often considered the bicycle as an intrinsically valuable object, it could be argued that its role has fluctuated along two axes or spectrums.

One of the axes tracks whether the movement focuses on mobility-related political aims such as promoting cycling or opposing motor traffic in their own right, or whether it uses the bicycle as a symbolic and/or practical tool to further non-mobility-related political aims, such as feminism or environmentalism. The other axis is structurally focused and examines how overt and encompassing the politics of the movement is.

These axes cross each other forming multiple combinations. In reality, movements are messy and often various aspects are present at different points in time in diverse and unpredictable ways. The axes work, however, as an analytical framework.

The chapter will use this basic framework to explain a diversity of contemporary and historical expressions of bicycle politics: older expressions of radial politics, such as the Situationists, Provos and early socialist and feminist movements; DIY bike workshops and not-for-profit bike businesses, as spaces where alternative forms of economics, and anti-oppression politics, are problematised and practised; the evolution of the Critical Mass (CM) movement as a way to reclaim public space; global climate biketivism, where the bike is used as a protest tool in grassroots environmental, direct action movements; the anti-roads protests of the 1990s, as the clearest anti-car movement in the UK's recent history; grassroots direct action cycling campaigning, which coexists with more mainstream cycling advocacy, creating an intersection of radical and reformist politics.

Some questions we will ask using the proposed double-axe approach are: How engaged are DIY bike workshops in mobility politics? How overtly antiauthoritarian and anticapitalist is Critical Mass as a movement? Is it possible and desirable to create a more politicised and explicitly anti-car cycling movement? Did the anti-roads movement of the 1990s have a wider mobility politics?

In order to contextualise the different expressions of radical bicycle politics explained in the chapter, we provide in the next section a brief analysis of the wider cultural, political and economic value systems and of the material conditions that define the current state of mobility in which cycling sits. It is a situation characterised by unequal power relations between different actors and visions of mobility and society. This will help us ground the use of the analytical framework just exposed.

Cars[4] versus People: The Traffic Power Structure

The easiest way to begin thinking about cycling in a critical and political way is to understand that there is a clear hierarchy at play when it comes to transport policy (and, indeed, any related policy areas, such as urban planning). The car sits comfortably and unchallenged at the top of this hierarchy; it is enough to step outside our homes – especially if we live in urban environments – to notice this. Cars are like the air they so relentlessly pollute; we are surrounded by them to the point that we have grown entirely accustomed to them (Sheller and Urry 2000; Vigar 2002; Urry 2004). Often, we barely register their existence. At certain times, though, for example, when we experience near misses on our bikes, when a loved one is killed in a car crash, or when wheelchair users, blind and deaf people tell us how they cannot move around freely, we are starkly reminded of the impacts that a world built around the car brings. Even then, we often rationalise these as tragic but unavoidable circumstances or dangers. Having been normalised, the negative consequences of car culture are unlikely to be seen by those experiencing them first-hand as a *political* wrong. Walking, cycling and public transport, that is, people that choose or need to use those transport systems, are at the bottom of the pile, pushed literally and metaphorically to the margins of our streets. As Planka.nu succinctly put it, 'the traffic power structure determines not only the relationship between car and bus but also between human being and human being' (Planka.nu 2016, 6). Recognition of this fundamental inequality should lie at the core of any notion of radical bicycle politics.

This state of affairs, however, is not accidental, but the result of a gradual intensification of the role of the car in meeting (and creating!) our mobility needs (Horton and Jones 2015). The car was adopted and sustained as the dominant mode of transport overland by a series of social, political, cultural, economic and infrastructural systems, values and assumptions. This is what we call *car culture* (Gorz 1980; Ward 1991; Wolf 1996; Riechmann 2004, 2005; Horton 2006a, 2006b; Paterson 2007). This domination is particularly noticeable in towns and cities, although rural areas too have been dramatically reshaped, physically and culturally, in response to car ownership. Capital and associated powers, such as liberal states, are what brought the car to this position and what allow it to remain unquestioned, despite the incredibly damaging impacts that it is having on our lives and the planet (Engler and Mugyenyi 2011, Planka.nu 2016), and the social injustices and inequalities that it is creating (Sustrans, n.d.).

When people do consider the negative impacts of motor traffic, the most obvious issue is that of climate change, perhaps followed by broader, vaguer notions of environmental destruction and pollution.[5] But there are other impacts that are too often forgotten, if they are considered at all, and that seem to remain (at least politically) invisible to us. Even the issue of pollution, despite recent focus in the mainstream arena of organisations such as Clean Air and Greenpeace (Jones 2017),[6] and direct action groups such as Stop Killing Londoners, is poorly understood by many, and vastly under-acknowledged on a cultural level; think, for example, of how present and powerful the discourse around cigarettes is, and then consider that exposure to nitrogen dioxide (NO_2) is estimated to have killed 23,500 people in the UK alone each year; and small particulate matter pollution (PM2.5) caused the equivalent of 29,000 deaths in the UK. The biggest source of NO_2 and PM2.5 are diesel engines (Campaign for Better Transport 2014). The same engines are subjected to the emissions scandal in 2015 (Corporate Europe Observatory 2016).

More directly, 1,732 people died on UK roads in 2015 (Department for Transport 2015). That is, 4.7 people a day. Serious injuries from Road Traffic Accidents stretch into the tens of thousands every year, with 22,137 people seriously injured and 186,209 casualties of all severities (Department for Transport 2015). Road injury is within the ten leading causes of death in the world according to the World Health Organisation; 1.3 million people died as a result of road traffic incidents in 2012, more than from cancer, for example.

The question of space is another much under-discussed problem; of course, it is impossible to separate entirely the infrastructure needed for cars from that needed for other forms of transport, but it is equally not so hard to see, when we think of the vast road networks and car parks that criss-cross the entire 'civilised' planet, that we have given over far too much of that planet to the automobile.

Other, even less tangible, consequences stem from our car-centric culture. We hear ever-increasing concerns that we have lost a sense of community in our neighbourhoods; that, for example, our streets are no longer safe, that we no longer know our neighbours and so on (Appleyard et al. 1981). Yet rarely is the role that cars play in fragmenting the very fabric of our lives explicitly acknowledged. Children no longer play on the streets; they feel unsafe, and unpleasant, noisy and polluted places to be, so the idea of simply hanging out on them, of chatting with our neighbours, becomes less possible and desirable. Add to this the increasing dispersal of social amenities – for example, the local shop being closed and replaced with the out-of-town supermarket (facilitated by car-centric society) and we have a world of atomised individuals, stepping from one privatised box into another. Far from broadening our world, the car has in some respects closed it off (Whitelegg 1997; Sloman 2006; Paterson 2007).

These issues are compounded further when we consider questions of inequality. It's a cruel paradox that those unable to afford a car are often the worst affected by them. For instance, nearly all households with above-average income have a car but half of low-income households do not (Department for Transport 2011), and it ought not surprise us that when it comes to town planning, it is the poorer areas that are far more likely to find themselves in the middle of large and busy road networks. Certain residential areas have become little less than rat runs, with traffic, and even motorways, literally ripping their way through once-closed communities. Poorer people are thus forced to endure the effects of heavy traffic – or else they are forcibly relocated to make way for more roads (see Furness 2010, 59–60, for an account of one striking example of this).

Despite this devastation, many of us have come to accept the inevitability, the normalisation, of cars; again, like air, it is hard to imagine a life without them. We may actually come to believe in their necessity, their desirability even. However, this state of affairs – what we refer to here as car culture – is neither inevitable, nor, we would argue, desirable. The car's position at the top of the transport hierarchy does not just lead to inequalities, it actively *excludes* other ways of travelling; and it also actively shapes the way we *think* about travelling, and why and where we travel. It has, in other words, restructured our world, physically and mentally, in ways that are extremely damaging and exclusive. And, having done so, it has made itself almost indispensable.

Why so much talk of cars in an article about bicycles? Well, because contemporary bicycle politics, when focusing on mobility politics, is, in essence, a tug of war with car culture. In the same way that one cannot talk about workers' rights without referring to the bosses, or slavery without acknowledging white privilege, we would argue that one cannot talk about bicycle politics without acknowledging the role of motor traffic. Like so much else in this world of ours, the car is a dream come true for a select few; for others, including those who have no choice but to drive, it is a living nightmare. And, like real nightmares, it appears to be one we are facing with our eyes kept firmly shut. Whilst the car offers *certain* people a viable and even desirable way to travel, it should come as no surprise that the *transport* hierarchy reflects other *social* hierarchies; groups that are in one way or another socially marginalised very often find this marginalisation continue on the road. And, let us not get enticed by the narratives of green capitalism (Corporate Watch 2016). It is questionable whether 'green' cars and driverless cars will achieve pollution- free (Paterson 2007) and incident-free cars. But even if this was achieved, the other problems associated with the car still remain.

When we look at the impacts of car culture through the lens of power structures, we realise how their dominance is not only the dominance of a certain mode of transport or technology over another, but the dominance of the wealthy over the poor, the obsession for economic 'progress' over planetary survival, the dominance of those who can access and choose to drive over those who wish or need to cycle or walk and, more importantly, be full and equal participants in the shared space that our streets could be, rather than the corridors for motor traffic that they have become. In short, car culture is the dominance of one political, economic and ethical approach to life over many others. How *radical* different approaches to bicycle politics are hinges on which political, economic and ethical approach they are based on and which view of the world they are striving for.

Expressions of Radical Bicycle Politics

With the aforementioned in mind, we now present the main expressions of contemporary radical bicycle politics and analyse their political approaches and intricacies using the double-axis framework introduced earlier.

A Potted History up to the 1990s

Historically, the bicycle has frequently played a role in radical politics. In Europe, much of the socialist and feminist movement of the late nineteenth and early twentieth centuries embraced the bicycle as a symbolic and practical tool to further their campaigns (Horton 2006a). The bicycle provided a unique opportunity for autonomous mobility, allowing women and the working classes to travel greater distances to find work, for example. It also allowed many people previously stuck in inside cities to access the countryside, often for the first time. Escape from the slums, however fleeting, came to symbolise a better, socialist world to come. For feminists, the bicycle was, once again, a literal and metaphorical tool through which women could enhance their all-too-limited freedom; as with the working classes, women used the bike to travel independently, but the bicycle also had unexpected consequences with regard to clothing. Women were expected to adhere to a strict dress code, which required the wearing of skirts or dresses. Suddenly, they had an excuse for wearing other clothing, opening up an avenue to reclaim their right to their own choices. For both socialists and feminists, cycling mostly played the role of advancing other political values, such as freedom, autonomy and independence.[7] Regarding the first axes, then, these movements used cycling as a tool to advance non-mobility-related aims. This may have been because car culture was in its infancy then, and while being seen negatively by many, the car posed nothing like the problems it does today; so the additional component of contemporary radical bike politics, namely, its engagement with mobility from a political perspective and its *opposition* to car culture, was simply not as relevant. Regarding the second axes, these movements offered a very structured and overt kind of politics: socialism and feminism, and used the bike as a symbol and a tool to elaborate on them.

The bicycle re-emerged in numerous post-war countercultural movements, such as the Autonomen, the Provos, the Situationists and a number of other European anarchist movements in the 1950s, 1960s and 1970s. By this time, the car was already occupying a much more dominant role in daily life, so unlike previous movements, these countercultural engagements with the bicycle were often framed within an explicitly anti-car discourse. The Situationists saw the car as a prime symbol of capitalism, a 'pre-eminent consumer commodity' that lay at the forefront of the subjugation of daily life (Furness 2010). The Provos made similar charges. But they also went on to develop numerous tactics which are still used by activists today; perhaps most famously, these Dutch anarchists created a project whereby old, refurbished bikes would be painted white, and left out in the street for people to use. The idea was simple: you could *use* the bike, as and how you wanted, but you could not *own* it – when you parked it at the end of your ride, it was to be left for someone else to use themselves. This scheme, which has been replicated in cities around the world, had two clear agendas. First, to provide more bikes for people to use and, second, to challenge traditional notions of *use* and *ownership* and to develop a new cultural logic to replace capitalist values (Kempton 2007).

Not surprisingly, encouraging people to reject conventional notions of possession did not sit well with the state or the corporate world, and the White Bike project was made illegal, demonstrating very clearly what the Provos already knew – that the supposedly *free* market quickly turns to state power when people use it to their own advantage.

Unlike many earlier socialists and feminists, who tended to look to the state as a means by which a better society could be created, and who therefore focused their politics on the mobilisation of people to join and vote for certain parties, the Provos drew on libertarian socialist and anarchist ideas and adopted and developed a culture of *prefigurative* tactics, encouraging and helping people in the creation of new ways of living *within*, but against, the dominant system. Whether contemporary radicals are aware or not of the existence of these Dutch anarchists, much of what radicals do today in terms of prefiguration stems from these early pioneers of prefiguration.

Regarding the two axes then, these movements had an explicit mobility-related politics, as well as a structured and overtly anticapitalist and antistate politics.

DIY Bike Workshops[8]

DIY bike workshops have occupied a prominent place in the radical political landscape since at least the 1990s (Carlsson 2008). Due to the broader political outlook of those involved, these projects differ from conventional bike shops in numerous ways. Often growing out of broader anticapitalist and anarchist movements, these bike spaces follow a prefigurative approach, whereby workshops are run according to values, principles and behaviours which those involved would ultimately like to see in the world at large. As such, they tend to either be volunteer-led or established as non-hierarchical, not-for-profit social enterprises or workers' co-ops, and many will provide their services for free, for donations, or at a low cost.

Additionally, many of them have an ecological motivation and will therefore try to reduce their consumption levels, placing a high value on reusing and recycling, going to great lengths to salvage bits from bikes that normal bike shops would simply throw away and replace with new parts. Many of them share a fundamental recognition that cycling, in and of itself, has the potential to become one more component of the capitalist way of life. Bikes, and all the related paraphernalia which comes with them, are becoming big business, and, following the standard narrative of mainstream markets, they tend to be either overpriced and therefore inaccessible to many, or of such low quality that they quickly become broken and unserviceable. And while offering many benefits once they are made, their initial production also come with a high price tag in terms of their environmental and social costs. For radical bike workshops then, the promotion of cycling comes with serious provisos, whereby the entire lifespan of the bike, and not simply its use as a mode of transport, is considered to be hugely important.

Bike workshops also form networks of mutual support and knowledge creation and exchange. In the UK, this is called 'Community Bikes', a network of radical bike projects that aims to meet at least once a year to exchange practical knowledge and reflect on their own development, progression and viability (almost always in question), as well as exploring their relationship to the wider cultural, political and economic contexts. Two examples of interesting initiatives that have come out of this network over the years are Common Wheel and Bespoked Fringe 2017. Common Wheel was an attempt to form a more structured association of bike projects that could form a 'buying group' to bargain with the big cycling trade companies, which are responsible for the distribution of bike parts. The fact that these companies hold immense power and that radical bike workshops are competing with mainstream bike workshops which have more resources and hence more bargaining power means that radical bike workshops end up paying more for the parts they need, or are even unable to access many of them, putting them at a considerable disadvantage. The idea was that by associating with each other, their combined bargaining power would increase and workshops with more resources could also support those starting out (in a similar vein to the Radical Routes co-ops network). As well as an economic incentive, there was also an environmental one, as radical bike workshops cannot choose certain more environmentally friendly options from a market that does not offer them in the first place. Common Wheel aimed to encourage, or even create, more environmentally sound production methods. With regard to the Bespoked Fringe 2017 and in the words of one of the instigators

> Bespoked is a public show where boutique frame builders gather to display their bikes to try and sell more of them to posh white men. I'd love if we could show the mainstream UK bike public and media that there is another side to cycling […] I would like you to display to the public your freak bikes, your earn-a-bikes initiatives, the shit bikes that keep people moving. I want us to show our attitudes of self-empowerment through tools, our outreach work with marginalised groups, our women and gender variant workshops.
>
> *(Email communication, Community Bikes list)*

As well as throwing down a challenge to capitalist economics then, radical bike shops also place considerable emphasis on empowering those who use radical bike workshops; rather than simply fixing peoples' bike, and charging them for the service, bike workshops will usually try to encourage people to learn those skills themselves, while offering the necessary guidance, and providing information and advice. This project is an integral part of the commitment to challenge the systematic and engrained power dynamics and oppression at play in society. Many of these organisations make genuine efforts to question and change this dynamics, including those that have traditionally been unwelcome in these spaces, and providing a respite from the oppression people experience as women, non-binary, queer, People of Colour and as a result of mental or physical problems.

While bike workshops are facilitating cycling and hence, in one respect, engaging with mobility politics, they do not generally engage with the full range of this politics; their main activities are not overtly addressed at questioning the current transport system or questioning car culture. In that sense, their politics is not strictly mobility-related when we are talking about the first axis. On the second axis, their politics is quite comprehensive and has a focus on anticapitalism and anti-oppression.

Critical Mass

Perhaps the most famous and far-reaching example of bike activism is CM (Carlsson 2002). CM bike rides began in San Francisco in 1992, and have since spread all over the world; Masses now regularly take place on the last Friday of the month in hundreds of cities. Following the cultural logic of many other forms of radical politics, CM is a network of global autonomous groups situated, united by little more than the name and, to a greater or lesser extent, a shared ethos. Even within a ride there can be multiple views around what the precise aims of the Mass are, or how it should be realised. Unifying riders, though, is the view that cyclists ought to be free to ride without the dangers usually associated with busy roads, and the safety-in-numbers of a Mass provides a temporary bubble where cyclists can, often for the only time, experience what it might be like to live in a world not so dominated by cars. For some riders, this is as much as can be hoped for, and demands or expectations are limited to a desire to *share* the roads with cars; for others, Masses represent a more radical vision of entirely, or almost, car-free cities. Either way, Masses undoubtedly, if only temporarily, turn the tables on cars, often forcing drivers to give way while cyclists take the dominant role.

While the rhetoric suggesting that CMs are unorganised and spontaneous events is rarely, if ever, true, the logic behind such a claim is fundamental to the underlying philosophy of Masses. Cars bring chaos to our cities on a daily basis; yet, this is entirely normalised, and whilst drivers and the media might express frustration that this occurs, their response is almost always to simply demand still more infrastructure for cars. The notion that car driving is a disruptive activity, in and of itself, is rarely even considered. CMs often need to be organised in the current transport climate but the reality they briefly create, where cyclists are so predominant that they have the power to force cars to take a back seat, is the one which, under different conditions, could well be the norm. Indeed, in cities such as London, this is in fact happening; at times, cyclists merge into genuinely spontaneous Masses, and the result is precisely what CMs aim to achieve – the validation, and normalisation, of mass cycling.

Responses to Masses, from car drivers and the authorities, vary considerably, but it is worth noting briefly a classic position taken, which has ironically helped Massers define their philosophy in a beautifully succinct way. Like other forms of protests, Masses are often accused of disrupting traffic, and at times this reasoning is taken to its unjust but sadly inevitable conclusion, with Massers being forced off the road and even arrested. The response from the CM network is simple: we are not *disrupting* traffic, we *are* traffic!

CM has a clear mobility-related political aim in relation to the first axis, as its aim is disrupting the traffic power structure to open up space for cyclists, temporarily, but also with the hope of this becoming the norm. On the second axis, their wider politics are complex and unclear, differing from Mass to Mass and from individual to individual. However, following social media groups, such as London CM Facebook page, it is clear that anarchist and anticapitalist politics, or even less radical forms of politics, are not central, and that, for the most part, the main focus of the movement is that of celebrating cycling in opposition to car culture, rather than questioning wider political issues.

The UK's Anti-roads Protest Movement of the 1990s

The 1990s saw the biggest opposition to road infrastructure and hence to cars in the history of the UK (McKay 1996; Welsh and McLeish 1996; Wall 1999). Groups such as Earth First!, Reclaim the Streets and many individuals and communities created the biggest direct action campaign the UK has seen in decades, and can justifiably claim at least part of the credit for stopping some of the most important schemes proposed by Margaret Thatcher's government's 'Roads for prosperity' programme and eventually shelf the entire project, as three quarters of the plans never got off the drawing board (Campaign for Better Transport 2012). As with most radical politics, the anti-roads movement was a diverse network of activists, with no overarching power structure, and hence no dominant political discourse beyond the immediate opposition to the building of certain new roads; even here, it was not always clear whether it was all new roads, or only certain projects, which were being rejected. However, groups such as Reclaim the Streets and many individuals associated with Earth First! were unapologetically anti-car and saw the fight against roads (and the car) as a wider attack on capitalism as a system. Recollections from that time by those involved include messages such as 'In the rejection of mobility for its own sake there is an implied rejection of the whole restlessness of capitalist modernity' and 'Claremont was not merely an attempt to influence transport policy, narrowly conceived. Many of those involved are expressing a much deeper social and cultural critique'. In the same recollection of events, this anti-roads protester states 'less striking, yet more insidious, the time has now come to declare war on a more fundamental enemy: the car' (Welsh and McLeish 1996). In that sense, the most radical versions of the anti-roads movement had clear mobility-related aims in terms of the first axis and, despite its diversity, a clearly anticapitalist and anti-establishment aim in relation to the second axis. Whilst Earth First!, for instance, has retained its love of bikes and a shared understanding that car driving and road building should be opposed, it has focused on other equally problematic and destructive aspects of contemporary society and capitalism, such as fossil fuels extraction and forms of extreme energy production. Sadly, the Coalition Government's new road building project announced in 2012, did not meet the same opposition, even though it is as far-reaching as the one proposed in the 1990s (Campaign for Better Transport 2012).

Climate Biketivism

Biketivism is the idea and practice of using bikes as tools for activism. This usually translates into group bike rides to show the distance that can be travelled on a bike and to use the rides as platforms from which to engage people and communities in discussions about radical solutions to the multiple crises we currently face; as a form of solidarity with different front-line communities nationally and internationally; as well as to strengthen the relationships of those within the bike ride, often to form affinity groups that may take action later on. Bikes are also being used as tools for protest and direct action, literally to serve as barriers in confrontations with the police or to form blockades.

There is a long history of using long bike rides to draw attention to wider political causes. This has historical roots in movements including the nineteenth- and twentieth-century socialist movements mentioned earlier. Two members of the Clarion Cycling Club,[9] for instance, cycled from Glasgow to Barcelona in 1938. 'Their aim was to collect money from sympathisers with the Spanish Republican Government, and with the money to buy food for the women and children of Spain. They hoped to raise about £70; in fact they raised over £300' (Warren 2008). Seventy years later, in 2008, another ride was organised to commemorate this ride (ibid.). In the 2000s, the G8 Bike Ride, a group of sixty riders travelled from London to Gleneagles (Scotland) where social movements gathered to oppose the G8 in 2005 (G8 Bike Ride). Their mission was to combine the excitement of cycling with activist commitment: 'not only is this the most environmentally sound way of getting there, but it should be great fun and will provide excellent opportunities to network, show support for various campaigns along the way, and to make plans for action on arrival' (ibid.). That ride gave birth to Bicycology. Active between 2006 and 2010, Bicycology ran workshops and activities during three tours around the UK and one static week of events. The group aimed to demonstrate the possibilities of using bikes in unusual and challenging ways and to engage people in issues such as climate change, car culture, even capitalism and anarchism. Bicycology also travelled to the Climate Camps and took an active role in them over the years it was active. A recent reincarnation of these past versions of biketivism is Time to Cycle: 'Time to Cycle mobilises to take action on climate crisis. We ride to raise awareness of these issues, to share knowledge, and to build solidarity. We welcome everyone whose integrity drives them to face the upcoming climate catastrophe and to take action to avert it' (Time to Cycle). Time to Cycle was part of the climate mobilisations against COP21 in Paris, and has subsequently organised rides to Ende Gelande in Germany. Reclaim the Power camp actions and a ride to support le ZAD in France (Time to Cycle/Past Rides). Other examples of UK biketivism include the Ride to Mayo in Ireland in 2010 to oppose an oil pipeline, and recent mobilisations against Heathrow airport expansion by Reclaim the Power. Often, these bike rides have converged and merged with other international bike rides, as was the case of a Spanish contingent joining the Ride to Mayo and the confluence of rides from different parts of Europe in the case of the Time to Cycle ride to the Paris climate talks.

With regard to the axes, each instance of biketivism has engaged with transport politics in different ways and to different extents, with Bicycology expressing a clear anti-car politics, and Time to Cycle focusing more on wider climate goals. In terms of the second axes, all have had an overtly radical approach to politics.

Transport and Cycling Campaigning: Lacking a Radical Approach

It is interesting that at the time of writing (2017), transport and cycling campaigning in the UK is mostly the terrain of less politicised, reformist groups. Mainstream cycle campaigning is encapsulated in national organisations such as the Cycling UK and Sustrans, though local groups also play a key role. The London Cycling Campaign (LCC) is the most prominent of these and the largest city-cycling organisation in the world. Other large key organisations campaigning on wider transport issues include: Campaign for Better Transport, Road Peace or Living Streets campaign on wider transport issues.

All of the aforementioned share a view of a world with fewer cars and more provision for cyclists. Most of them challenge the car to some extent and some of them even speak about equality issues, such as Sustrans' Transport Poverty study mentioned earlier. In that sense, they clearly engage with mobility politics in respect of the first axis. However, they do so from a clearly liberal and reformist perspective, which does not fundamentally challenge the political status quo, and which at best is very timid in relation to the wider political implications of mobility policies. What characterises these organisations in terms of the second axis is their reformist politics, and their willingness to work closely with the state. Often taking the role of government advisory or policy implementation bodies, these groups, unsurprisingly, end up forming close working and financial relationships with government departments. It is clear that being so intertwined with decision makers, often relying heavily on state funding, seriously compromises their independence and capacity to engage in transformative politics. They also have little hesitation in forming alliances with business, big or small, and generally see the commercial success of the capitalist cycling industry as a positive advance for the advocacy of cycling.

Mainstream cycling campaigning either lacks an analysis of the powerful forces at play behind governments' decisions, such as the car, oil and media industries, or chooses not to engage with that analysis because it is seen as 'too political'. Of course, this type of campaigning necessarily rubs against car culture; however, as liberal reformist organisations, the aim appears to be the incorporation of cycling into the world as is, rather than questioning the deeper roots of the problematic politics of transport and cycling. Such a strategy revolves around the view that what is needed is to convince the government and the general population that there are better solutions for the majority of our transport needs than car driving – whether by rational argumentation or by showing popular support via campaign endorsement strategies.

Alongside these organisations, we find groups, mainly in London, such as Stop Killing Cyclists who have a more radical stance. Stop Killing Cyclists is a grassroots group with a direct action approach and which was born out of the frustration of what was perceived as a too soft approach by mainstream organisations such as LCC. Their manifesto reads: 'this campaign intends to build a **peaceful** but more radical approach to fighting for safer infrastructure for all of the city's road users, though with a focus on cycling, within a framework that drives the message home to those who really need to hear it' (Stop Killing Cyclists). Their self-proclaimed radical approach mostly refers to their tactics and form of organisation, as well as the urgency of their demand on government. However, little is mentioned about wider political and economic factors and the role that cars and car culture play in the current transport system in cities such as London (The Ecologist 2014). Like mainstream transport and cycling campaigns, this more radical approach falls into the mobility politics first axis and into a liberal, reformist approach on the second, even if their *tactics* – of direct action – are more commonly associated with political radical movements.

Conclusion

As we have seen, radical bicycle politics is fragmented and diverse. Different groups and collectives focus on different aims and represent different angles of a more general radical political aspiration. Using the double-axis framework, we have been able to analyse the different levels of engagement of the movements with mobility politics on the one hand and radical politics on the other. We would like to highlight the moments when movements have been able to combine a genuine engagement in radical mobility politics, with an overt opposition to the car and making the connections to wider radical politics. This was the approach of the Situationists, Provos and Autonomen in the early twentieth century, the anti-roads movement, Earth First! and Reclaim the Streets in the 1990s and of some biketivism initiatives such as The G8 Bike Ride and Bicycology in the 2000s. Equally valuable is the work of DIY bike workshops, CM or other forms of biketivism. They all have played their role in advancing radical politics more generally and different aspects of a radical approach to mobility, such as an alternative to the capitalist cycling industry and the incredibly important role of challenging privilege in order to build a truly equal and inclusive movement and society, as well as demonstrating that the bike is a viable alternative to the car and a very useful tool to oppose a wide range of injustices. However, given the mobility context introduced earlier in the chapter and the realisation that most outright mobility politics is undertaken by mainstream groups or the ones which do not overtly engage with radical politics, it seems important to question whether radicals should focus on those aspects and engage with past strategies and targets.

We believe that a crucial part of a radical cycling movement must be to try to present a counter-narrative to that of the car industry and car culture. When radically imagining alternatives to car-based societies, we need to keep in mind a number of very important things; first, that the rise of the car was not due to its inherent appeal but the result of a deliberate and deep collusion of industry and government (Planka.nu 2016); second, that people who might argue for the car's continuing role in our lives are likely to be those least affected by such a decision (and that, conversely, those without access to, and/or who are more directly affected by cars, are rarely given a voice); and, finally, that to imagine a car-free world is to imagine a world that is radically altered in multiple ways, with changes being made both to the physical landscape, as well as to our cultural expectations, demands and desires.

However, whatever we may imagine of a future world, there are also questions of how we get there or how we even begin to move in the right direction. But this question poses us bigger questions about how social change happens and what tools and strategies, as well as which targets, radicals should focus on. Which tactics should be used? Direct action? How would this be articulated in this specific case? Is there a place for reformist politics? What is the place of prefigurative and system change politics? These are all questions that movements are constantly struggling with, and which are sadly beyond the scope of this chapter to answer. What is undoubtedly clear is that transport and, therefore, cycling are deeply political matters, and hence cannot be left unchallenged. They are not marginal or neutral, technical problems, but the ones in which the forces of capital, the power of the status quo and the marginalisation of those who fall out of it, as well as other issues of social and economic importance are playing very clear and crucial roles and hence must be, in one way or other, engaged with.

At the very least, we would argue that the radical (and indeed the not-so-radical) bike movement ought to be more clear about what the root of the problem is, and more vocal both about the multiple negative impacts of the car, and about the positive alternatives that might arise if a drastic reduction in car use were to happen. The prevalence of attention given to neo-liberal solutions such as 'green' cars (now so-called ultra-low-emission vehicles) and taxation, specifically when addressing the pollution problem, demonstrates the extent to which a significant number of problems caused or heightened by the car are still woefully misunderstood, missed or seen as too complex to be tackled without disrupting the ideology and politics of the current system. However, as we have seen, mass car driving, no matter what fuel is used, can never be green or socially just.

Part of making this leap would be to challenge the interlinked *ideologies* of the motorcar (Gorz 1980) and capitalism and the *material realities* they give rise to. As we have seen, the cultural silence we find in relation to the car's destruction is not accidental, but there is also a great deal of noise being made too – about the freedom to drive, and the war on the motorist. Attacking car culture is presented as a direct attack on personal freedom, and despite the obvious counterargument – that people driving is an attack on others' freedom – all too many cycle advocates, and radicals more generally, appear to have been silenced by this grotesque ideological manoeuvre. It is grotesque not only because the freedom of the car driver relies on the dismantling of others' freedoms, but also because it implies that the majority people who do drive do so willingly. Without a deeper understanding of how multiple interrelated phenomena would also radically alter in the event of a serious curtailment of car use, it is no wonder that people imagine losing the car in such a negative way. We may not know how to get there or how exactly the world we want to build might look, but we should not shy away from and be crystal clear about the values and material, social and economic premises of the world we want to get to – and of the extreme, unjustifiable and high costs of the car-centric and capitalist world we currently inhabit.

Notes

1 We would like to thank Dave Horton for his input and comments on draft versions of this article.
2 Using words such as 'our' and 'we' is complex and should be unpacked in the light of wider and crucial issues of intersectionality, oppression, equality, inclusivity and participation, which sadly we don't have space to discuss here, but 'our' and 'we' should include everyone's rights and not just of those whose needs are promoted by the status quo or with current power to affect decisions.
3 Cities such as London often reach levels of pollution so high that it is advisable for vulnerable people to stay at home or not do much exercise. See Transport for London's daily's pollution monitoring and advice here: https://tfl.gov.uk/corporate/about-tfl/air-quality-advice?intcmp=41599 and the pollution crisis declared by Sadiq Khan in London in January 2017 www.independent. co.uk/news/uk/home-news/london-toxic-air-alert-pollution-mayor-sadiq-khan-public-health-emergency-latest-a7532941.html.
4 We will use cars, motor traffic and car culture interchangeably. It is important to highlight that when we suggest cars, motor traffic and car culture should be challenged; we do not mean all cars and motor traffic should be completely abolished, but rather that the system by which this mode of transport dominates to the point of exclusion of any other ought to be radically altered. The number of cars and motor traffics that could be sustained in an alternative transport system is obviously a debatable question but we would argue that this number should be reduced massively.
5 Transport accounted for 23% of the UK's greenhouse emissions in 2014 (Department of Energy and Climate Change) and Surface transport was the second source of greenhouses emissions in that same year behind energy supply (Committee on Climate Change).
6 See, for instance, http://cleanair.london/ and www.greenpeace.org.uk/tags/clean-air-now.
7 Of course, this was also true of the car, but the relative affordability of the bicycle meant its benefits were experienced by significantly greater numbers.
8 There are too many DIY bike workshops and projects to list here. It is easy to locate most of them with a quick online search.
9 Named after the socialist newspaper, *The Clarion*, these were socialist cycling clubs who promoted cycling whilst also using their cycling trips to distribute socialist propaganda.

References

Aldred, R. (2016) Cycling Near Misses: Their Frequency, Impact, and Prevention, in *Transportation Research Part A: Policy and Practice*, 90, pp. 69–83.
Appleyard, D., Gearson, M.S. and Lintell, M. (1981) *Livable Streets* (Berkeley: University of California Press).
Campaign for Better Transport (2012) *Going Backwards: The New Roads Programme* http://bettertransport. org.uk/sites/default/files/research-files/Roads_to_Nowhere_October2012_web_spreads_0.pdf.
Campaign for Better Transport (2014) www.bettertransport.org.uk/media/archive/2014/05.
Carlsson, C. (ed.) (2002) *Critical Mass: Bicycling's Defiant Celebration* (Oakland, CA: AK Press).
Carlsson, C. (2008) *Nowtopia: How Pirate Programmers, Outlaw Bicyclists, and Vacant Gardeners are Inventing the Future Today!* (Oakland, CA: AK Press).
Corporate Europe Observatory, 'Dieselgate Report Slams Commission and National Governments for Maladministration', 16 December, 2016 https://corporateeurope.org/power-lobbies/2016/12/dieselgate-report-slams-commission-and-national-governments-maladministration.
Corporate Watch (2016) *A to Z to Green Capitalism* (London: Corporate Watch).
Department for Transport, (2011). National Travel Survey www.gov.uk/government/statistics/national-travel-survey-2011.

Department for Transport (2015) 'Reported Road Casualties in Great Britain: Main Results' www. gov.uk/government/statistics/reported-road-casualties-in-great-britain-main-results-2015.

Engler, Y. and Mugyenyi, B. (2011) *Cars and Capitalism: On the Road to Economic, Social and Ecological Decay* (Nova Scotia, Canada: Fernwood Publishing Company).

Furness, Z. (2010) *One Less Car: Bicycling and the Politics of Automobility* (Philadelphia, PA: Temple University Press).

Gorz, A. (1980) 'The Social Ideology of the Motorcar', in Gorz, André (ed.), *Ecology as Politics* (Boston: South End Press).

Hayden, D. (1981) *The Grand Domestic Revolution* (Baskerville: The Colonial Cooperative Press).

Horton, D. (2006a) 'Environmentalism and the Bicycle' *Environmental Politics* 15 (1): 41–58.

Horton, D. (2006b) 'Social Movements and the Bicycle' (Unpublished Article).

Horton, D. (2007) 'Fear of Cycling', in Dave Horton, Paul Rosen and Peter Cox (eds.), *Cycling and Society*, pp. 133–52, Aldershot: Ashgate.

Horton, D. and Jones, T (2015): Rhetoric & Reality: Understanding the English Cycling Situation, in Peter Cox (ed.), *Cycling Cultures*, pp. 63–77 (Chester: University of Chester Press).

Illich, I. (1974) *Energy and Equity* (London: Calder and Boyas).

Jones, Anna (2017) 'Kids Need Clean Air', Greenpeace, www.greenpeace.org.uk/tag/clean-air-now/

Kempton, R. (2007) *Provo: Amsterdam's Anarchist Revolt* (New York: Autonomedia).

McCarthy, D. (2014) Stop Killing Cyclists – the Birth of a Movement, in *Ecologist, the Journal for the Post-Industrial Age* https://theecologist.org/2014/jan/15/stop-killing-cyclists-birth-movement.

MacGregor, S. (1995) 'Deconstructing the Man Made City: Feminist Critiques of Planning Thought and Action' in Eichler, M. (ed.) *Change of Plans: Towards a non-sexist sustainable City*, pp. 25–50 (Toronto: Garamond Press).

McKay, G. (1996): *Senseless Acts of Beauty: Cultures of Resistence Since the Sixties* (London: Verso)

Paterson, M. (2007) *Automobile Politics: Ecology and Cultural Political Economy* (Cambridge: Cambridge University Press).

Planka.nu (2016) The traffic Power Structure (Oakland: Planka.nu Collective).

Pooley, C., Jones, T., Tight, M., Horton, D., Scheldeman, G., Mullen, C., Jopson, A., and Strano, E. (2013) *Promoting Walking and Cycling: New Perspectives on Sustainable Travel* (Bristol: Policy Press).

Riechmann, J. (2004) *Gente que no quiere viajar a Marte: ensayos sobre ecología, ética y autolimitación* (Madrid: Libros La Catarata).

Riechmann, J. (2005) *Un mundo vulnerable: ensayos sobre ecología, ética y tecnociencia* (Madrid: Libros La Catarata).

Sheller, M. & Urry, J. (2000): The City & the Car, in *International Journal of Urban & Regional Research*, (24), pp. 737–757, (Wiley-Blackwell).

Simmie, J. M. (1974) *Citizens in Conflict: the Sociology of Town Planning* (London: Hutchison Educational).

Sloman, L. (2006) *Car Sick: Solutions for a Car-addicted Culture* (Totnes: Greenbooks).

Sustrans, (n.d.) *Locked Out: Transport Poverty in England*, http://www.sustrans.org.uk/lockedout

Thomas, H. (2000) *Race and Planning: The UK Experience* (London: UCL Press).

Urry, J. (2004), The 'System' of Automobility, *Theory, Culture & Society*, 21 (4–5), pp. 25–39, (Sage).

Vigar, G. (2002) *The Politics of Mobility*. (London: Spon).

Wall, D. (1999) *Earth First! and the Anti-Roads Movement: Radical Environmentalism and Comparative Social Movements* (London and New York: Routledge).

Ward, C. (1991) *Freedom to Go: After the Motor Age* (London: Freedom Press).

Warren, Alan. (2008). 'Socialists, Cycling and Sunny Spain', https://1938glasgow2barcelona2008. wordpress.com/

Welsh, I. and McLeish, P. (1996) The European Road to Nowhere: Anarchism and Direct Action against the UK Roads Programme, *Anarchist Studies*, 4 (1): 27–44.

Whitelegg, J. (1997) *Critical Mass: Transport, Environment and Society in the Twenty-first Century* (Northampton: Pluto Press).

Wolf, W. (1996) *Car Mania: A Critical History of Transport* (Chicago: Pluto Press).

Groups and Organisations

Bicycology, www.bicycology.org.uk/

Campaign for Better Transport www.bettertransport.org.uk/

Carbusters, http://carbusters.org/

Community Bikes, UK (no public facing website)
Cycling UK, www.cyclinguk.org/
G8 Bike Ride, www.g8bikeride.org.uk/
Living Streets, www.livingstreets.org.uk/
London Cycling Campaign, https://lcc.org.uk/
Radical Routes, www.radicalroutes.org.uk/
Reclaim the Power, https://reclaimthepower.org.uk/aviation-flashmob-critical-mass/
Road Peace, www.road-peace.org.uk/
Stop Killing Cyclists, http://stopkillingcyclists.org/
Stop Killing Londoners, www.stopkillinglondoners.org.uk/
Sustrans, www.sustrans.org.uk
Time to Cycle, www.timetocycle.org/
World Free Car Network, www.worldcarfree.net/

3.4

BLACK BLOCS

A Complex Case of Radicalism

Francis Dupuis-Déri[1]

Introduction

The Black Bloc is a street tactic consisting of individuals masking their faces and wearing black clothes in order to form a homogeneous group to express a radical presence within a protest. There is no consensus about the legitimacy, relevance or effectiveness of such a tactic. Nevertheless, it is advocated by radical activists from different but related networks: anarchists and other anticapitalists, ecologists, antipolice activists, feminists and queers (who also advocate the Pink Bloc). By 'blocking up', an individual publicly expresses her or his radical political identity, while simultaneously dissolving as individual into the mass to create a collective political actor. One Black Bloc participant described the tactic succinctly, saying, '[t]he Black Bloc is our banner' (Shantz 2011: 52). 'Blocking up' simultaneously gives participants a sense of being invisible and anonymous within the group, and of being extremely visible (even too visible sometimes, when alone facing the police).

Most of the time, Black Blocs walk peacefully in mass demonstrations, holding banners bearing anticapitalist and antiauthoritarian slogans, waving black (or red and black) anarchist flags and chanting radical slogans, such as 'A! Anti! Antipitalista!' or 'No Justice, No Peace! Fuck the Police!' But Black Blocs are also infamous for smashing the windows of banks and multinational capitalist businesses (Gap, McDonald's, Nike, Starbucks, etc.). And yet despite the claims of many politicians, police officers, journalists and even social movement spokespeople, these actions cannot be considered blind violence. Rather, the target is the message.

Black Blocs may clash with the police, either to show antagonism or to protect the demonstration from police violence. Blackblockers have been known to lob tear gas canisters back at the police and to provide first aid to injured protesters. During the 2012 Maple Spring movement in Québec, a female protester wrote on Facebook:

> I didn't hear anyone thank the members of *the Black Bloc and the other radicals* who had the courage to put themselves between the police and the population… THANK YOU… I refuse to condemn you… I hope you won't have to intervene again. I would like for your presence to be unnecessary… But you are actually the last defensive wall for people trying to exercise their democratic rights.

(Emphasis added)

While this is rare, a Black Bloc may also take action by itself, without any mass protest; for instance, they may participate in antigentrification hit-and-run actions against expensive new stores in formerly affordable neighbourhoods.

The relationship between the Black Bloc and radicalism is complex and often paradoxical. There is a dialectical tension within the Black Bloc, by which I mean a fundamental opposition between a thesis (being radical) and an antithesis (not being radical) within the same phenomenon of the Black Bloc. It all depends on who is speaking about whom, and on your understanding of the meanings and practices surrounding 'radicalism' and 'violence'.

Indeed, there are different constructions of radicalism, being framed in terms of types of actions, political identity and aspiration, organisation, etc. As we shall see, critics of Black Bloc-style organisation simplistically suggest that blackblockers are too 'violent' and therefore too 'radical', while blackblockers themselves may claim to be radical because they resort to violence, or to be radical although their actions are not violent, or to be respectable common folks resorting to legitimate political force, or to be legitimate because their violence is not violence, but rather symbolic deeds and artistic performativity. With regard to violence, you can consider the Black Bloc radical or not, depending on your understanding of what violence is, and also depending on how you compare Black Bloc actions to other expressions of political violence today and throughout history. A person's tendency to classify Black Bloc tactics as radical or not also depends on their chosen definition of political legitimacy, on whether they interact with allies or competitors ('friends' or 'foes') in social movements, and on many other things besides.

Most of the time, however, the Black Bloc is experienced by its actors as the embodiment of an individual and collective public expression of political radicalism, voiced against oppressive systems including but not limited to capitalism, the state and the police. To be part of a Black Bloc is, in itself, a subjective experience that fuels its participants with feelings of radicalism. It might be somewhat addictive: once tasted, it draws participants back for more. It might therefore lead to cynicism with regard to peaceful demonstrators in particular and day-to-day activists in general. And yet, many politicians, police officers, journalists, academics and liberal and dogmatic nonviolent activists share the view that the Black Bloc is the embodiment of autonomous radical irrational outrage and consequently deserves to be neutralised.

A Brief History

Black Blocs first made an appearance during the Cold War in West Berlin, around 1980, in protests by the Autonomen (i.e. anticapitalist and antifascist squatters) (Katsiaficas 2006; Rahmani 2009). Black Blocs still take to the streets in Germany for various events, including anticapitalist May 1st protests and antifascist demonstrations. The tactic spread across national borders in the 1990s through the anarcho-punk music scene and through radical activist networks such as the Anti-Racist Action (ARA) groups in North America.

The tactic has been very influential in the 'alterglobalisation' movement of recent counter-summit mobilisations, including those in Seattle (1999), Washington and Prague (2000), Québec and Genoa (2001), Cancun (2003), Scotland (2005) and Toronto (2010). Around 2000, the tactic was at the centre of a furious debate opposing 'fluffy vs. spiky' (i.e. 'nonviolent' vs. 'violent') activists, in a reiteration of a similar debate in the Autonomen movement in the 1980s between the hippies or 'Müslis' (in reference to the healthy cereal) and the punks or 'Mollis' (in reference to Molotov cocktails) (Katsiaficas 2006: 91).

During the meetings between the International Monetary Fund (IMF) and the World Bank (WB) in Prague in September 2000, activists divided the city into colour zones in an attempt to reduce tension and foster solidarity between factions using various tactics. There was one zone for each 'bloc': the Black Bloc, the Pink and Silver Bloc and the White Overalls or Tute Bianche. Although she participated in the Pink and Silver Blocs dressed as a giant fairy, one activist from the Tactical Frivolity Collective made it clear that her tactical choice should not be seen as a rejection of the Black Bloc. 'What is violence anyway when the State is like killing people every day, man. And the people in the World Bank eat Third World babies for breakfast, so if they get bricked then hey, that's their fault' (Evans 2003: 293).

In the same spirit, the Montréal-based Anti-Capitalist Convergence (Convergence des luttes anticapitalistes – CLAC) developed the principle of 'respect for a diversity of tactics' a few months later, in April 2001, during the Quebec City mobilisation against the Free Trade Agreement of the Americas (FTAA) Summit. According to this principle, activists should respect each other's goals, choices, desires, hopes and fears, and should express solidarity instead of publicly condemning those who choose other forms of collective action. This 'respect for a diversity of tactics' principle was proposed as a way to bring people from diverse backgrounds and advocating different tactics together into a united (although antiauthoritarian and heterogenous) radical anticapitalist movement. CLAC's main goal was to open a safe space for practising Black Bloc tactics in a context where so many activists saw such tactics as 'violent' and therefore as problematic with regard to both the security and the legitimacy of the movement in the eyes of the public. Many such activists think that in order to be effective, they must look respectable for the mainstream media and cultivate approval in public opinion.

Because of its attention-grabbing and spectacular 'violent' deeds, the Black Bloc became an icon of the alterglobalisation movement, or at least of its street demonstrations and its radical elements. Black Blocs were on the streets for the anti-austerity protests in Greece in 2010, the anti-cuts movement in London, the Indignados movement in Spain and the international Occupy movement in 2011. They subsequently took action in the students' strike in Québec 2012 and for various similar causes in 2013 in Brazil, Egypt, Tunisia and Turkey. In some countries, blackblockers are known as the 'hooded ones' (*koukoulofori* in Greece; *encapuchados* in Latin America).

The Black Bloc has become an icon of the young anarchist rioter, not only within the activist milieu, but for the mainstream media as well. Characters wearing black masks and hoodies are seen rioting in various music videos (two examples are the songs *Mosh* by Eminem and *Indi Groove* by Chinese Man). While the German Autonomen in the 1980 wore black leather jackets as their collective symbol and uniform, many of today's blackblockers wear cotton hoodies. This countercultural statement mixing post-punk and post-grunge symbols translates into a form of cultural and political identities born out of adherence to Black Bloc tactics. Indeed, the black hoodie is now associated with political radicalism, as noted by Laura Portwood-Stacer, New York City feminist and author of *Lifestyle Politics and Radical Activism*,

> The symbolic cachet of the Black Bloc look transcends the time, place and bodies of actual Black Bloc protests. Dressing on an everyday basis as if one is ready for such an event is a way of indicating a kind of militant preparedness to fight - if only metaphorically or ideologically - when the need arises. The symbolism is all the more powerful when one's subcultural peers are well dressed similarly on a daily basis, with the conscious or unconscious message being something like, 'together, we'll be ready for the revolution when it comes'.

> *(Portwood-Stacer 2013: 54)*

Being ready for a revolution, or more probably a riot, is clearly a priority for blackblockers. They seem to be hoping for a riot, as two anarchists of the Calisse Brigade explained with a poetic touch when protesting at the G8 Summit in Germany, in 2007:

> Similar to love, a riot can sometimes take us by surprise when we think we are not prepared, but if we have an open disposition, a riot, like love, will allow us to seize opportunities and situations. It would be futile to say that we can prepare a riot, though we can at least prepare *for* riots: do what it takes to help ignite the fire.
>
> *(Calisse Brigade 2007)*

Black Bloc tactics have such a strong aesthetic that they may quite easily be co-opted by other groups for their own aims, or even 'hijacked' by extreme-right radicals such as the neo-Nazi German activists who call themselves 'autonomous-nationalists' or 'anti-antifascist action groups'. Since the early 2000s, these groups have organised Black Blocs in nationalist street demonstrations, in which they wear dark glasses and hoodies and carry banners.

A more interesting example, politically speaking, of the appropriation of the Black Bloc aesthetic was the decision of the women-only feminist collective Les Sorcières (the Witches), to organise a Black Bloc in 2015 not for a street protest, but as an anonymous bloc walking into the Montréal Anarchist Bookfair. Their aim was to protest against the tolerance for sexual predators within the anarchist milieu. In their literature, Les Sorcières explained,

> [w]e are coming masked today for the same reasons we mask ourselves in street protests: for our safety. As survivors of aggression and their allies, we don't feel safe and we don't want to be recognised in our own milieu. It is scary that we need to protect ourselves here for fear of retaliation, the same way we protect ourselves from the police?[2]

This action echoes T-Bone Kneegrabber's comments, who explained,

> [y]ou can easily round up 500 black clad anarchists to fuck shit up at a frat house where rapists live, but someone points a finger at a 'progressive' man and all of a sudden there's a process; all of a sudden she [the survivor] is being divisive... We, as 'anarchists,' hold a society (that we do not have faith in) to a higher standard than we hold our friends to!... Just because a man identifies as *radical*, does not make him an angel.
>
> *(Kneegrabber 2002: 38–39, emphasis added)*

Black Bloc and Diversity

Black Blocs have been the target of criticism for being a boys' club: an exclusively white, middle-class, young male tactic, thereby embodying classism, sexism, racism and ableism. In practice, different Black Blocs have had various levels of success in making themselves inclusive to people of colour, women and queer people. This inclusivity is often dependent on the cause for which the Bloc is demonstrating, the country or even the city. For instance, Black Blocs in Rio de Janeiro and Sao Paulo are very different with regard to the proportion of participants who are women, people of colour and poor youth from the favelas. With regard to women's participation in Black Blocs in North America, there appear to be more women participants now than there were in 2000 (according to my own observation), not only as street medics or scouts (both important tasks that often go disregarded), but also in women-only Black Blocs on the front line of street protests.

After the G20 Summit in Toronto, in 2010, Harsha Walia from the Vancouver collective No One Is Illegal released the text *10 Points on the Black Bloc*, in which she deals with the issue of exclusion, including sexism, racism and ableism:

> I don't personally engage in black block tactics, but as a long-time community organizer and as a woman of colour, I stand in full and firm support of diversity of tactics and in solidarity with those who are facing police repression during this time. [...] While I cannot speak for the personal motivations and intentions of those who engage in black block tactics, I think the distance that I have from those tactics is somewhat useful in this debate, because there is this idea that only those who engage in black block actions support black block tactics. This is an attempt to marginalize and isolate our comrades which I hope my presence here will counter. [...]. One of the criticisms of the black block tactic is that it's undertaken by predominantly white males and therefore is inherently oppressive to women of colour and Indigenous women in particular. As a woman of colour with a myriad of precarious systemic barriers including precarious legal status and health – and I can only speak for myself – but I can say that the black block tactic does not in itself oppress me or render me more vulnerable in protest. So I'd appreciate it if other white men did not make such pronouncements on my behalf.
>
> *(Walia 2010: 3)*

On one occasion in Montréal, in November 2016, an old woman in a wheelchair passed by a face-to-face deadlock opposing about fifty police officers and as many blackblockers protesting in front of a theatre against a rock-metal band uttering anti-Semitic comments. On the spot, the woman accused the blackblockers of being a group of thugs bringing chaos into her neighbourhood. After a few female blackblockers explained the situation to her, she decided to join the Black Bloc, masking her face with her black scarf, asking for a black flag and chanting slogans with the bloc: 'No fascists in my neighbourhood'.

According to Krystalline Kraus, who participated in a Black Bloc around 2001,

> 'Blocking up' to become the Black Bloc is the great equaliser. With everyone looking the same - everyone's hair tucked away, our faces obscured by masks, I'm nothing less and nothing more than one entity moving with the whole. Everyone is capable of the same. And the politics of 'nice girls don't throw stones' is suspended, and I'm free to act outside of the traditional 'serve tea, not Molotov cocktails' rules.
>
> *(Kraus 2002)*

Such an understanding of the subversive potential of anonymity within the bloc leads some adherents to conclude that the Black Bloc is a place where gender identities are radically erased, suggesting, as did A. K. Thompson in 2008 that 'you can't do gender in a riot'. As an example of Black Bloc practices that are inclusive of people of different genders and orientations, during the anti-G20 protests in Pittsburgh in 2009, blackblockers walked down the streets chanting: 'We're here! We're queer! We're anarchists, we'll fuck you up!' (Avery-Natale 2010).

And yet, the Black Bloc is not a perfect milieu with regard to radical principles such as liberty, equality, solidarity, diversity and inclusion. For instance, Krystalline Kraus laments that '[with] machismo still running the streets – especially during a riot – what women have to say often gets lost in the tear gas fog' (Kraus 2002). A self-identified anarchist and queer woman who has been involved in several black blocs (mainly in Canada), underlines differences between the behaviours and approaches of men and women in a Black Bloc:

> We [the women] talk more and generally leave more room for living the moment. There are fewer preconceptions of what we aim to accomplish and more discussion of how to go about it. We stick together and there's much more communication when the decision is being made in the street. Men are more individualistic. They don't feel obliged to come back to the group and can take off without warning. It's 'My top priority is me!' I call them 'lone wolves', whereas women form wolf packs.
>
> *(interview with the author)*

Black Bloc and Radicalism: Violence and Terrorism

The Black Bloc has been called radical because it is 'violent'; some sources in the French media even say that it is nothing other than pure violence or 'ultra-violence'. According to such a frame of thought, practice and action is the embodiment of political identity, and therefore violent action embodies and expresses radicalism. For example, a few weeks before the 2002 G8 Summit in Kananaskis, the Canadian Security Intelligence Service (CSIS) made explicit reference to *'radical Black Block* elements that disrupted previous international summits' (in Fernandez 2008: 158, emphasis added).

Even blackblockers and their allies equate radicalism and violence, and therefore associate the Black Bloc with radicalism because of its deeds. For example, with regard to the 'anti-cuts' protests in London in March 2011, one blackblocker explained:

> We had no idea of the numbers before the event on Saturday, and no idea it would be *so radical in its actions*. The black bloc idea spread like a ripple through the march. As people saw others in black, they changed into black themselves. Some marchers even left the protest to buy black clothing.
>
> *(Moss 2011, emphasis added)*

Such a definition conflating radicalism with violence is commonly shared by the media, official authorities, security pundits and even activists. Such confusion is also at the core of the public discourse about radicalisation and the perceived threat of what is referred to as Islamist 'terrorism'.[3] For instance, the new Center for the Prevention of Radicalization Leading to Violence, in Montréal, Québec, provides this definition of radicalisation on its website: 'a process whereby people adopt an extremist belief system – *including the intent to use, encourage or facilitate violence* – in order to promote an ideology, a political project or a cause as a means of social transformation' (emphasis added).[4] Although this organisation was created to focus mainly on Islamism and would-be jihadists in the global context of the 'war against terrorism', its chair publicly explained that it also has, as a mandate, to monitor and prevent extreme-right and extreme-left radicalisation, including anarchists (Scali 2015; Teisceira-Lessard and Normandin 2016). On February 2019, the organisation launched a video on its website entitled 'To understand the process of radicalisation toward extreme-left'. It tells the fictional story of 'Jérémy', a 'vulnerable' young student who joined a mysterious anarchist group, Radar. With his new friends, he ends up burning down a bank automated teller machine. By the end of the video, the narrator explains off camera: 'Without realising it, Jérémy slowly radicalized itself toward violence … Be pro-active, and communicate with us in absolute confidentiality if you are concerned about some one'.

According to the Canadian Center for the Prevention of Radicalization Leading to Violence, a process of radicalisation implies a 'belief in the use of *violent means* to promote a cause' and 'the merging of ideology and *violent action*' (emphasis added). Radicalisation is not necessarily opposed to liberal or republican democracy, since 'most of the progress in democratic societies has been the result of a certain form of radicalization' (a reference to Martin Luther King and Gandhi, famous and beloved radicals). The institution's website goes on to state that '[r]adical viewpoints only become a problem when they approve of, or encourage, the *use of violence* or other forms of extremist behavior, *including terrorism*' (emphasis added). Such an understanding of radicalism recalls the 'theory of extremes' proposed by the Federal Office for the Protection of the Constitution, in West Germany, which monitored the Autonomen and believed that both the extreme left and the extreme right were threats to liberal democracy (Fourment 2014).

In the mainstream media, blackblockers have regularly been compared to and even confused with Islamist terrorists, because they both target symbols of capitalism (the World Trade Centre for Osama bin Laden's jihadists; bank windows for the Black Bloc), or perhaps because blackblockers as well as militiamen of the Islamic State wear black clothes and masks. Even within the academic field, some experts view blackblockers as similar to other 'terrorists', Islamists, in particular. For instance, political scientist José Pedro Zuquete wrote an article entitled 'Men in Black: Dynamics, Violence, and Lone Wolf Potential', which was published in *Terrorism and Political Violence*, a journal that has labelled itself 'essential reading for all academics, decision makers, and security specialists concerned with understanding political violence' (Terrorism and Political Violence, 2017). The author's aim is to describe the 'autoradicalization process' of a hypothetical lone wolf blackblocker and to analyse the process of becoming a leftist terrorist.

It is true that many young men may be driven to participate in Black Blocs when they see the exhilarating direct-action tactics used by these groups (the 'cool factor' of being involved in a Black Bloc). The aesthetisation of the Black Bloc's actions as spectacular gestures may also explain why young men want to be part of the movement (portrayals of Black Block actions have been called 'riot porn'). And yet, Zuquete admits that the beauty of an ideology that divides the world into friends and foes is not enough to attract people to the Black Bloc, not to mention convert them into 'terrorists'. What is necessary is an 'emancipatory vision of violence, in which violence is *the* solution for individual despair'. The author goes on to observe that '[u]sually there is a psychological factor at work in the form of a disturbance or traumatic experience that compels one to embark on a lone wolf action or campaign. […] In any case, the political becomes personal. These dynamics make prediction a very unreliable affair' (Zuquete 2014: 104–5).

Such comments echo those of long-time activist Micheal Albert in the aftermath of Seattle in 1999, and those of French scholar Marc Lazar after the actions of the 'cortège de tête'[5] in France during the Spring 2016 mobilisation against Labour Law reforms. Albert's analysis of the Weather Underground in the US and Lazar's study of the Italian Red Brigade both warn about the risks associated with blackblockers going underground and resorting to deadly 'terrorism' (Albert 2001; Lazar 2016).

These confusing analyses of radicalism and its relationship with violence raise the question: What is the extent of the Black Bloc's violence, anyway? First, no armed struggle has emerged after almost forty years of Black Bloc actions. While it is true that in the past, anarchists attempted and perpetrated deadly attacks on many heads of state and were involved in revolutionary armed struggles (Russian, Spanish, Chinese, Cuban, etc.), these examples of anarchist activism all involved far more violence than any actions of our modern Black Bloc, and used far more deadly weapons than the stones, clubs, empty bottles and slingshots that are used today (along with the occasional firework and petrol bomb). Today, the most violent (and therefore most radical?) anarchists are a group of anonymous Italian activists mailing bombs (the group has yet to cause a casualty), along with a group of Greek militants of the Conspiracy of Cells of Fire who are standing trial for shooting a businessman in the legs with a gun. With Greek activists calling for armed struggle from their prison cells, these anarchists can be considered more violent (and arguably more radical) than any Black Bloc on the street. Although one may ask if today's anarchists should resort to armed struggle, it is obvious that contemporary anarchism is a nonviolent, or at least non-lethal movement, especially if compared to its own history, and to other contemporary social movements (anti-Islam, anti-abortion and the so-called 'involuntary celibates' for instance).

Indeed, the Black Bloc's so-called violence is much closer to nonviolent civil disobedience – blocking, sabotage, etc. – than it is to any 'armed revolutionary' movement, never mind the deadly mass violence of many nation state governments, which have perpetrated such acts as colonialism and genocide, extermination camps, 'total wars', carpet and atomic bombing of cities, drone strikes, and police brutality. In comparison to the history of almost any nation state on the planet, the Black Bloc's deeds barely register on the scale of political violence. Indeed, Brazilian scholar Pablo Ortellado argues that in the context of the US in the 1990s and 2000s, Black Bloc tactics fit, from a theoretical point of view, within the tradition of civil nonviolent disobedience. These tactics are all about committing transgressive actions while avoiding causing pain to any living being (with the exception of well-armed and well-armoured cops), in order to draw the attention of the public, the media and the police, which often react in ways that are symptomatic of systemic violence (Ortellado 2014: 284–6).

Although radicalisation is often conflated with violence even by academic specialists of social movements (Tarrow 1989), sociologist Marcos Ancelovici is right to raise doubts about such an association. In reference to trade union mobilisations, Ancelovici states

> Such an assumption is problematic because the public significance of a given mode of action is historically, politically, and institutionally situated. It becomes meaningful and thereby exists socially insofar as it is inserted into a hierarchy of symbolic structures in terms of which it is - together with all the acts to which it is related and contrasted - produced, perceived, and interpreted. A barricade, picketing, the occupation of a factory, or a sit-in, will not have the same meaning and significance in all places at all times.
>
> *(Ancelovici 2011: 133)*

Following Ancelovici's line of thought, it might be said that an open debate about the extent of Black Bloc radicalisation might help us better understand the contemporary symbolic and material power relationship between progressive and conservative and reactionary forces. If the Black Bloc has anything to tell us about this power relationship, it is that the capacity for collective action by today's 'radicals' who wish to confront the system face-to-face is limited to rioting for a few hours.

Black Blocs disrupt the status quo by making trouble in the streets and are viewed in the media as militant rebels, often stealing the media show at events such as collective legal actions and the official ceremonies in international summits. And yet with the exception of these types of symbolic disturbance, Black Bloc actions do not disrupt the system or its institutions (except for potentially increasing road traffic for a few hours and interrupting the business of a few banks and corporations). Thus, if radicalism in tactics translates to radicalism in political ambition, the Black Blocs are not truly very radical, considering the gap between their claims of smashing the state or capitalism, and their actual deeds.

Nevertheless, Tammy Kovich, who participated in a Toronto-based Black Bloc in 2010, stated that peaceful mass demonstrations are also quite useless:

The pacifist position is accepted without question, while advocates of more aggressive tactics are put on the defensive. We need to turn the debate on its head - given the severity of the situation we face, in light of the pervasive nature of the systems of domination and oppression that we oppose, and acknowledging the pressing need for an intensification or our struggle, we need to begin asking ourselves if *non-violence* can be justified.

(Kovich 2011a: 136)

The Black Bloc is what extreme-left radicalism looks like today when compared to pacifist activism. And yet, neither group can claim to achieve much with regard to disrupting the global state and capitalist system.

Downplaying Radicalism

Some blackblockers try to downplay their so-called radicalism by presenting themselves as good and reasonable citizens in order to negate the perception that they are a bunch of irrational young troublemakers with no political ideas or principles, moved only by the desire to smash things for the sake of smashing them. Indeed, many people have claimed that blackblockers are irrational thugs and mentally unhinged troublemakers. For instance, after the 2001 G8 Summit, an anonymous resident of Genoa stated that the 'vandals and radicals' had 'no specific target in view but simply wanted to destroy things' (Blanc 2001). Others claimed that blackblockers are 'criminal anarchists'. According to these critics, blackblockers are apolitical actors or parasites who 'hijack' legitimate protests, as was claimed by detective Kory Flowers of the Greensboro Police Department in North Carolina in an article entitled 'Understanding the Black Bloc', published in the online web-journal *Police: The Law Enforcement Magazine*.

By claiming to be good and reasonable citizens, blackblockers seek to wrong-foot their critics in mainstream social movements, such as American liberal intellectual Chris Hedges who described the Black Bloc as a 'cancer' during the Occupy mobilisation. And he is not alone; many people think that blackblockers are the cells of a cancerous tumour undermining the legitimacy and force of a movement. It has even been suggested by well-known opinion leaders from major social movements that they be excluded or neutralised by 'peace police' activists, or by the police itself. Pierre Jasmin, former chair of Artists for Peace (Québec), stated that the police 'should have the right to search, arrest, file and detain during the time of the protest ... protesters from the Black Bloc fringe' (Jasmin 2013: 624). From an even more extreme 'antiradicalism' perspective, a few days after the 1999 Seattle protest, United People's Ole Fjord Larsen suggested, in reference to the hypothetical upcoming protests, that

> [t]he coordinating group of the participating organizations must to an even higher degree [...] prepare the demonstrators for knocking down and turning over to the police any unwanted hooligans. Even if a hooligan should be killed, it would be very little loss as compared with the daily rate of 20,000 dead children due to corporate rule.
>
> *(Larsen 1999)*

In an attempt to defuse these criticisms,[6] blackblockers regularly publish manifestos, communiqués and letters claiming that

> [m]ost folks ... who have used Black Bloc tactics have day jobs working for nonprofits. Some are schoolteachers, labor organisers, or students. Some don't have full-time jobs, but instead spend most of their time working for change in their communities. They start urban

garden projects and bike libraries; they cook food for Food Not Bombs and other groups. These are thinking and caring folks who, if they did not have *radical* political and social agendas, would be compared with nuns, monks, and others who live their lives in service.

(Black 2001, emphasis added)

In their communiqué 'Who Is the Black Bloc? Where Is the Black Bloc?', the Italian Autonomous University Collective claimed, in 2010, that 'the faces behind the scarves ... are the same faces that pay your rent for derelict houses; the faces you look at when asking to sign work contracts of 500 euros a month ... They are the faces that submit dissertation proposals and who you force to mention your boring texts ... they make your cappuccino with froth ... They are the ones whose life-blood is being sapped by precariousness, whose lives are shit, and they are tired of putting up with it' (Autonomous University Collective 2011: 130).

During the 2012 Maple Spring movement in Québec, an activist group whose name translates to 'Anarchists Among Many' published a *'Manifeste du Carré noir'* (Black Square Manifesto), with this opening assertion: 'We are women and men. We are students. We are workers. We are unemployed. We are angry. [...] We do not infiltrate demonstrations, we help organize them, we bring them to life' (Des anarchistes parmi d'autres 2012). Moreover, Black Bloc communiqués and manifestos often state that smashing a window is not a violent deed, since there is no pain at stake. In other words, violence is only about living beings.

Another way to dispute the claim that blackblockers are too radical is to think about their actions not in terms of 'violence', but of performance art. Artist Marc James Léger and scholars Maxime Boidy and Jeffrey Juris suggest that what matters are the 'symbolic-expressive' aspects of such performative violence, which 'produc[es] concrete messages challenging global capitalism and the state' and 'generate[s] *radical identities*' (Jeffrey Juris, emphasis added).

Radicalisation of the Debate about Capitalism and Democracy

Some scholars recall that in its deepest meaning, the word *radicalism* refers to 'a political analysis focusing on the root of an issue' (Dufour et al. 2012). According to my interview with a Quebecois woman who had participated in several Black Blocs, '[w]e are in a period when there is no possibility of a revolution', and so '[w]e do what we can to *radicalize* the debate and to reach people so a more *radical* politicization can come about' (emphasis added). According to Swiss political philosopher Nicolas Tavaglione, 'Black Blocs are the best political philosophers of our times', because though their actions, they ask society to make a 'choice as old as Europe: freedom or security' (Tavaglione 2003: 4).

Like other forms of political action, the Black Bloc is also radical in the way it is organised and structured. With regard to the 'prefigurative characteristics' of the Bloc, Tammy Kovich comments:

> It is absolutely true that smashing a window does not begin to approximate the acts required to create a new society; however, there is more to a black bloc than the smashing of windows. The bloc, as a pulsing body on the street, is organized horizontally. Decisions are made on the ground by all participants ... The picture of the bloc from the outside is very different from the reality and experience on the inside; the ethos of the black bloc is one of solidarity and collective care ... Crucial to the project of creating a new society is creating new ways of being, interacting and organizing with each other.

(Kovich 2011b: 17–18)

We might then surmise that the Black Bloc is radical, since 'radicalism may be measured in terms of level of autonomy and difference with regard to traditional spaces of political involvement' (Sarrasin et al. 2012: 142). In light of this, it is important to recall the Black Bloc's origins in the 1980s among the Autonomen in Germany, for whom political autonomy meant non-collaboration with official institutions (state bodies, political parties, labour unions, media, universities, etc.), as well as individual and collective autonomies in the decision-making process (Katsiaficas). In terms of autonomy, inner organisation and the decision-making process, Black Blocs are approximately as radical as other so-called 'prefigurative' experiences including Pink Blocs, autonomous activist collectives, revolutionary gardening and food collectives, self-managed working or housing coops (autonomous media, etc.), squats, etc.

Notes

1 The author wishes to acknowledge the financial support of the Observatoire sur les profilages (CRSH) and the translator Ellen Warkentin, who helped him with regard to the English language.
2 To watch a video about the action: https://www.youtube.com/watch?v=G8Qk4S9oAH4&feature=youtu.be;toreadtheirflyer"Agresseur-e-sdehors!":http://www.lessorcieres.org/agresseur-e-s%20dehors.pdf.
3 I use the words 'terrorism' and 'terrorists' in quotes because they are ideologically loaded terms. Indeed, it is extremely rare to find a reference in the mainstream media of Europe or North America about State terrorism (drone strike, carpet bombing, torture, etc.), and it seems really difficult for the mainstream media to label mass murders perpetrated by white males against racialised women as terrorism (Butler 2015). See Mélissa Blais (2014) and Mélissa Blais et al. (2010) for an analysis of the public discourse about the December 6, 1989 'Montreal Massacre', in which a man shot to death fourteen women at École polytechnique, claiming that he hates feminists.
4 https://info-radical.org/en/search/
5 The 'cortège de tête' was a group of approximately 1,000 people walking at the head of the trade union's mass demonstration. My estimate, for the June 14 protest, was that there were perhaps 300 well-organised blackblockers and another approximately 300 people who were not wearing black but who were equipped with defensive kits to deal with tear gas (scarves, goggles, water, etc.). The rest of the *cortège* walked in solidarity with this bloc. The 'cortège de tête' did not disband, despite several violent charges by police riot squads. This mass of people offered a safer space for blackblockers to use their tactics of choice (i.e. painting graffiti, smashing windows, attacking the police, etc.).
6 It might also be an attempt to enlarge the definition of the radical collective subject, following the tradition of the autonomia movement in Italia and Germany: it is no more only the 'proletariat', since it also encompasses the unemployed, the student, the woman working at home, etc. (thanks to the anonymous woman who raised this issue during the conference 'The Subversion of Politics', at Université du Québec à Montréal, April 7, 2017).

References

Albert, M. 'On trashing and movement building' (2001) [www.zmag.org/on_trashing.htm].
Ancelovici, M. 'The hot autumn of 2010 and the transformation of labour contention in France' *French Politics, Culture and Society* 29(3) (2011): 121–140.
Autonomous University Collective, 'Who is the black bloc? Where is the black bloc?', C. Solomon and T. Palmieri (eds.), *Springtime: The New Student Rebellions* (London: Verso, 2011, 130–131).
Avery-Natale, E. 'We're here! We're queer! We're anarchists': the nature of identification and subjectivity among Black Blocs,' *Anarchist Developments in Cultural Studies* 1 (2010).
Black, M. 'Letter from inside the black bloc' (2001) (Web).
Blais, M. *'I Hate Feminists!' December 6, 1989 and its Aftermath* (Halifax: Fernwood Press, 2014).
Blais, M. & als. *Retour sur un attentat antiféministe: École polytechnique de Montréal, 6 décembre 1989* (Montreal: Remue-ménage, 2010).
Blanc, S. 'Gênes achève le G8 complètement groggy' (Agence France Press — AFP, July 22, 2001).
Butler, A. 'Shooters of color are called 'terrorists' and 'thugs': Why are' white shooters called 'mentally ill'?' *Washington Post*, June 18, 2015 (Web).

Calisse Brigade, 'A. Anti. Anti-capitalista!' (2007) (Web).

Centre de prevention de la radicalisation menant à la violence 'Comprendre le processus de radicalisation vers l'extrémisme de gauche' (February 2019) [www.youtube.com/watch?v=lw89mqimZIc&-feature=youtu.be].

Des anarchistes parmi d'autres 'Manifeste du Carré noir' (Centre des medias alternatifs du Québec [CMAQ], March 2012) (Web).

Dufour, P., Hayes, G. and Ollitrault, S. 'Présentation: radicalités et radicalisations — la fabrication d'une nouvelle 'norme' politique?', *Lien social et politiques*, 68 (2012).

Evans, K. 'It's got to be silver and pink: On the road with tactical frivolity', Notes from nowhere (ed.) *We are Everywhere* (London-New York: Verso, 2003) 293.

Fernandez, L. *Policing Dissent* (New Brunswick, NJ: Rutgers University Press, 2008).

Fourment, E. Cagoule noire et ongles roses: Féminismes et rapports de genre dans la gauche radicale de Göttingen (master thesis, Institut d'Etudes Politiques de Paris, 2014).

Jasmin, P., *Commission special d'examen des événements du printemps 2012* (Québec: Gouvernement du Québec, October 22, 2013).

Katsiaficas, G. *The Subversion of Politics: European Autonomous Social Movements and the Decolinization of Everyday Life* (Oakland-Edinburgh: AK Press, 2006).

Kneegrabber, T-Bone 'Real feminists don't get raped and other fairy tales,' *The Peak* (special issue: 'Sexual Assault in Activist Communities,' 2002).

Kovich, T., 'Marching with the Black Bloc—'Violence' and movement building', T. Malleson and D. Wachsmuth (ed.), *Whose Streets? The Toronto G20 and the Challenges of Summit Protest* (Toronto: Between the Lines, 2011a, 157–164).

Kovich, T., 'The Black Bloc and the New society,' *Upping the Anti* 10 (2011b).

Kraus, K. 'Sisters in struggle,' *rabble.ca* (June 21st, 2002) (Web).

Larsen, O.F. 'Future planning after Seattle' (December 12, 1999) [www.mail-archive.com/futurework@dijkstra.uwaterloo.ca/msg05369.html].

Lazar, M. 'L'ultragauche est engage dans une logique de 'confrontation avec l'État'', *Le Monde* (June 20, 2016) (Web).

Moss, S. 'Black Bloc: 'Only actions count now', *The Guardian* (March 31 2011) (Web).

Ortellado, P. 'Posfacio: O Black Bloc e a violência', Esther Solano, Bruno Paes Manso, Willian Novaes (ed.), *Mascarados: A Verdadeira Historia Dos Adeptos Da Tatica Black Bloc* (Sâo Paulo, Geração, 2014, 284–286) (thanks to Denis Valliquette for the translation).

Portwood-Stacer, L. *Lifestyle Politics and Radical Activism* (New York-London: Bloomsbury, 2013).

Rahmani, S. 'Macht kaput was euch kaput macht: on the history and the meaning of the Balck Block,' *Politics and Culture*, 4 (Nov. 9, 2009). Web.

Sarrasin, R., Kruzynski, A., Jeppesen, S. and Breton, É. 'Radicaliser l'action collective: portrait de l'option libertaire au Québec', *Lien social et politiques*, 68 (2012): 141–166.

Scali, D., 'Prévenir la radicalisation,' *Journal de Montréal* (July 18, 2015). [www.journaldemontreal.com/2015/07/18/prevenir-la-radicalisation].

Shantz, J. *Active Anarchy: Political Practice in Contemporary Movements* (Lanham, MD: Lexington Books, 2011).

Tarrow, S., *Democracy and Disorder: Protest and Politics in Italy, 1965–1975* (Oxford: Oxford University Press, 1989).

Tavaglione, N. 'Qui a peur de l'homme noir?', *Le Courrier* (Geneva) (June 11, 2003) 4.

Teisceira-Lessard, P. and Normandin, P.-A., 'Le Centre de prévention de la radicalisation s'intéresse aux groupes d'extrême gauche,' *La Presse* (May 31st, 2016) [www.lapresse.ca/actualites/justice-et-affaires-criminelles/affaires-criminelles/201605/30/01-4986786-le-centre-de-prevention-de-la-radicalisation-sinteresse-aux-groupes-dextreme-gauche.php].

Thompson, A.K. 'You can't do gender in a riot: violence and post-representational politics' *Berkeley Journal of Sociology*, 52 (2008): 24–49.

Walia, H. *10 Points on the Black Bloc*, (2010) [https://theanarchistlibrary.org/library/harsha-walia-10-points-on-the-black-bloc].

Zuquete, J.P., 'Men in Black: Dynamics, violence, and Lone Wolf potential', *Terrorism and Political Violence*, 26 (2014): 95–109.

3.5

ONLINE ACTIVISM

Jeff Shantz

Radical activists have pursued visions of political autonomy, sovereignty and community in online practice. They have used it to challenge state and corporate governance structures and sought alternative social relations (based on openness and self-determination). Very early on, anarchist perspectives became a key framework for online actors and provided crucial guidance for the development of cyberspace – both for those who envisioned the Internet and those who participated in it. Indeed, although this has been under-examined and under-theorised, it could be said that the development of the Internet and the place of anarchist ideas within early debates around it played a large part in revitalising anarchist ideas in the last decade of the twentieth century. Arguably, this happened alongside or even before the alternative globalisation movements which broke through to public consciousness following the Seattle blockades in 1999.

Through the Internet, online activists created spaces of inter/action that could thrive beyond the realm of traditional powers, particularly nation states. Of course, the Internet has proven to be a realm of struggle, like any other in state capitalist contexts, and corporations and states have moved quickly to enclose the online (imagined) commons through various mechanisms of surveillance, control and repression, advertising (ideology) and monetarisation. This has led some commentators to speak of struggles over cyberspace as new enclosures, hearkening to the struggles over the natural commons that marked early capitalist development. Despite the early hopes, radical activism has never been certain nor even likely in cyberspace. Yet, it continues to thrive in diverse ways.

Online Activist Organisations

Early intersections and networks of hacker activists converged around the Chaos Computer Club (CCC). The CCC was founded early on in the digital age, in 1981. It is one of the most durable and influential community organisations addressing especially the security and privacy aspects of contemporary technologies, particularly in the German-speaking world. CCC is Europe's largest association of hackers, with an estimated 5,500 members. It is organised in a decentralised manner, with twenty-five so-called Erfakreisen (regional hackerspaces) and many more smaller groupings, the 'Chaostreffs'. The many physical hackerspaces in and around Germany share a common bond with the CCC through commitment to their stated hacker ethics, as discussed later. This distinguishes them from those who crack systems to steal information for personal gain or pleasure or to damage for purposes of competitive advantage.

CCC has been active in developing and disseminating analyses of a range of both technical and social issues. Their overarching focus has been on surveillance, privacy, freedom of information, hacktivism and data security. Towards this end, they produce occasional publications on specific themes and issues. In terms of activism, the CCC organises real-world campaigns and special events, as well as active lobbying. Their technical work involves anonymising services and communication infrastructure. Their hacker congress, an original one still held on an old school face-to-face conference basis, is quite large and well attended. The CCC has hosted this annual Chaos Communication Congress since 1984 and still edits its publication *Die Datenschleuder*. Many of the women hackers who participated in the CyberFeminist International (meetings held in Rotterdam) were from the CCC. The CyberFeminist International targeted both patriarchal structures of oppression and exploitation of labour within the cyber industries and cybernetic capitalism, and the marginalisation of women within hacking movements and cultures. Women in the CyberFeminist International focused very much on issues of production and reproduction within hacking spaces and prioritised the organisation of work (recognising unequal distributions of labour within hacking and alternative media spaces).

The oldest autonomous service provider in Europe is the ECN (European Counter Network – ecn.org). The ECN provides free email accounts, mailing lists and websites to organisations, activists and movements that are explicitly involved in a range of social struggles, including around issues of human rights, freedom of speech and information freedom in Italy and Europe. Years before sites such as YouTube and Vimeo were created, ECN pioneered a platform called NGV at which people could upload and share video of relevance to social justice struggles. Notably, especially in a context of growing far right movements in Europe and beyond, the ECN has espoused an explicitly antifascist politics and prioritised work with antifascist and anti-Nazi movements across Europe. Beyond technical services and support, the ECN provides physical space and material resources to political and social organising centres.

In the North American context, one of the early influential online activist groups was TAO Communications, formed in Toronto, Ontario in 1996. Sometimes sourced in eastern philosophical underpinnings 'tao k'o tao fei chang tao', and shifting explanations of its name as an acronym play on words (The Amazing Orangutans, Tasty Apples and Oranges), TAO was from the start an explicitly anarchist grouping (even 'The Anarchy Organisation') which sought to build real-world organising spaces as well as provide online resources and skills. TAO was explicitly syndicalist in its orientation, understanding its members as tech workers in a tech economy, which they sought to confront and abolish. TAO eventually formed a job shop of the Industrial Workers of the World ('Communication and Computer Workers, Industrial Union 560') as an expression of their commitment to workers' control and abolition of wage slavery. TAO provided labour as a gift to militant antipoverty organisations like the Ontario Coalition Against Poverty, and its members were instrumental in the formation of anti-borders and migrant defence movements in Canada. A TAO worker seeded the 'No One Is Illegal' meme within North American organising after attending a Next Five Minutes conference in Amsterdam where members of the Berlin-based 'Kein Mensch Ist Illegal' and Paris-based 'Sans Papiers' movements simultaneously gathered with many international hacktivists. Through initial outreach via old print mailing lists and zine networks, the online publication of A-Infos was established through TAO, and continues publishing news 'by, for and about anarchists' in twelve languages at ainfos.ca. An early adopter of the Debian flavour of linux, TAO served as an incubator and seedbed for other radical online groupings, many of which have gone on to outlive the originals. One such offshoot is Resist.ca, which has provided web and email resources for a variety of anarchist and non-authoritarian activist groups and individuals, particularly on the West Coast of North America. After a re-organisation in 2003, the Toronto TAO collective reformed under the OAT acronym, 'Organizing for Autonomous Telecommunications'.

Another active group, and the one that formed alongside TAO, is the Mayfirst/People Link. Mayfirst/People Link began life as NYC TAO, similarly to Resist.ca which was once TAO Vancouver. MayFirst/People Link (mayfirst.org) identifies as a politically progressive, member-run and -controlled organisation that works to redefine the concept of 'Internet Service Provider' in a collective and collaborative way. This is, like TAO, an attempt to break down the division between producers and users/consumers, aiming to make use and/or service provision mutually educational. Emphasis is placed on knowledge and skill sharing. May First/People Link's formal members are organisers and activists. In their model of organising, they have collectively chosen to elect a Leadership Committee to maintain operations between meetings and to give some continuity to organisational practices. They organise internally as a cooperative among active members. These active members pay dues, buy equipment and then share the organisational equipment for websites, email, email lists and other active Internet purposes. Mayfirst/People Link was targeted by US federal authorities for a server seizure in 2012.

Perhaps the most active and widespread organisation in the North American context today is Riseup Networks (riseup.net). Riseup provides online communication tools for people and groups working explicitly on liberatory social change, with more than six million users, operating over 14,000 mailing lists and running on servers which are not in the cloud, but employ full disk encryption and are fully secured under their control, and regularly publish a 'canary statement' regarding their refusal to cooperate with subpoenas or search warrants. With a strong set of political principles, Riseup also consistently defends its users from surveillance through its 'zero knowledge', 'no logs, no masters' policies, which includes personally encrypted email storage and full disk encryption. They don't require a phone number nor home address to sign up, but rely on an invite code system in order to use Riseup services; so, if you lose your password and your recovery code, you're out of luck. The emphasis is on providing resources that will be used in actions supporting liberation movements and actions against exploitation and oppression. Riseup seeks to create democratic alternatives to corporate resources and practices self-determination within its collective network by controlling their own secure means of communications. They also provide regular security updates to users and actively work to produce new, secure infrastructures, such as their VPN services.

Anonymous

Arguably, the most famous and impactful example of online radical activism, certainly in popular culture, is Anonymous. With their Guy Fawkes masks and cryptic videos, these hacktivists have forged a striking image and reputation. The name Anonymous refers to a decentred, loose affinity group of online activists and hackers. Their decentred structure means that they are largely formless and structureless in reality and practice, not only in image. As communications scholar Gabriella Coleman suggests, 'Anonymous is a little bit hard to define, because it's a collective name that anyone around the world can take' (quoted in Early Edition 2015). Anonymous activists share primarily an action orientation and an identity. They express important shared narrative practices, and symbolism. They hold up a banner that can be adopted by diverse users as needs and circumstances arise (Shantz and Tomblin 2014). By their very nature as an anonymous grouping that seeks privacy and to avoid surveillance, their members are largely unknown, nameless and unidentifiable.

Anonymous activists carry out their activism through a mix of what might be viewed as newer and older tactics, from denial of service attacks and hacks to whistleblowing or public shaming. In DDOS (distributed denial of service) attacks, overwhelming traffic is directed to a specific website, causing the server to shut down and leading to economic damage. Whistleblowing has included circulating confidential documents and information, such as the anarchist Jeremy Hammond, who is currently serving prison time for his involvement in Anonymous' 2012 hack of the private intelligence firm Stratfor and then releasing the information, which included states' collaboration to criminalise dissent, via WikiLeaks (Shantz and Tomblin 2014). More recently, Anonymous has turned to doxxing – the exposure of offending individuals' identity by publicly releasing their names and private information such as phone numbers or home addresses.

Coleman notes that Anonymous initially gained notoriety for Internet pranks 'for the lulz' and established themselves early with 'Project Chanology', a series of protests and disruptions targeting the Church of Scientology. Since 2008, they have turned to direct action and political campaigns, projects and interventions that are more serious in intent and design. Among the issues Anonymous has prioritised are censorship, surveillance and free speech. Since the emergence of Black Lives Matter, Anonymous has actively supported community movements opposing police violence. 'Operation Ferguson' provided resources for protesters speaking out and mobilising against the racist practices of the Ferguson police force, responsible for killing unarmed teenager Michael Brown in August 2014. Anonymous has also worked to dox officers involved in the killing of civilians and to counter police misinformation aimed at blaming the victims.

In one particularly significant and effective action, Anonymous took responsibility for shutting down the websites of the Canadian Security and Intelligence Service (CSIS), the Canadian government's spy agency. This was done as an appeal for Canadians to oppose Bill C-51, a particularly repressive piece of legislation that became law as the Anti-Terror Act of 2015. The Act contains provisions that give CSIS investigative powers, allow for pre-emptive arrest and enable the criminalisation of the so-called bad thoughts alone (that is, media posts that the state interprets as supporting or promoting acts that the state views as terrorist, rather than actual commission of terrorist actions), as well as economic activity such as strikes, boycotts or blockades. The Act also extends the scope for repressing protests, particularly against energy projects in Canada. The DDOS attack was brief lasting only a few hours.

While primarily viewed as an online phenomenon, Anonymous activism also occurs in the material world, as in the case of Indigenous activist James McIntyre against the British Columbia government's plan to build the Site C dam. With the RCMP killing of James McIntyre in 2016, Anonymous announced that McIntyre was the fourth of its members to be killed by security forces around the world in four years.

Anarchy in Cyberspace

Early crypto-anarchy theorist Peter Ludlow suggests that anarchism became such a central topic of interest in cyberspace in part because the widespread availability of certain technologies renders certain anarchist ideas not only possible but perhaps inevitable. As he argues, 'cryptography and related technologies like anonymous remailers and electronic cash may undermine the concentrations of power that we are currently familiar with (nation states, for example), thus allowing us to take on substantially more individual responsibility' (2001: xvii). This also relates to the emergence of new, possibly utopian, governance structures, as 'the Internet provides the opportunity for utopias to emerge in various remote corners of cyberspace'. The public Internet continues to develop through a convergence of accessible technologies and anarchic self-directed practices.

Yet, these self-governing practices are perhaps more ambiguous than is generally recognised. While some certainly create opportunities and possibilities for opposition to state and corporate modes of regulation and control, others play into and reinforce neo-liberal forms of governance and obedience. The refusal of corporate and state interaction, and exploitation is accompanied by new forms of exploitation and spreading commercialisation, and the development of commercial subjectivities among Internet 'users'.

New technologies and resources can carve out space for activities beyond the control of nation states and corporations. The Internet facilitates the spread and connectivity of virtual communities, which in some sense anarchism has always been. That is, there is no anarchist homeland or hereditary anarchism. Anarchism, like other voluntary groupings, consists of intentional networks though they have historically been face-to-face, more integral. The Internet has grown through the spread of virtual communities and reinforces the types of arrangements anarchism, as for other subaltern or subterranean groupings, has always comprised.

From the early days of the Internet, commentators have espoused the affinity between the Net and anarchism. These commentators and many practitioners saw the Net as a form of actual anarchy in action due especially to the apparent absence of an external, imposed authority and the self-direction, autonomy and liberty expressed in Net practices.

Even as the authorities have made their impositions felt more really and forcefully (in commercialisation, monetisation, subpoenas, surveillance and the end of net neutrality in the US), for many the real, true form of the Internet remains anarchy. And many are willing to fight for the Net as a space of anarchy and to oppose the authoritarian interlopers.

In the early days of the Internet, many believed that anarchist principles of autonomy and resistance to hierarchy and centralised authority were embedded in the horizontal and decentralised protocols of its basic design. With the rise of the 'walled gardens' of Facebook, and the concentration of network control into fewer and more centralised platforms such as Amazon and Google however, the increasingly forceful push of corporate control has enmeshed even nation states into relinquishing their supposed 'net neutrality' and revealing their subservience to the demands of capital. At this time, it's not an easy struggle for those who are pushing for a radical redecentralisation of the Internet and they do so often outside and against the waves of mainstream users, creating community mesh networks, open-source-encrypted virtual private networks to tunnel and hide traffic, and other methods to provide anonymity, like the TOR onion layer. They are developing currencies, social contracts and new relationships built on the blockchain, an encrypted, distributed ledger system that is causing many to rethink the possibilities of a resurgence in resistance to centralised banking authorities. While many are willing to fight for these distributed protocols, the main interests driving the growth of cryptocurrencies are not oriented towards international solidarity, but rather the wealthy hiding their money in tax havens, delinking labour from organisation and building intensified platforms for exploitation and narco-trafficking.

Collective Organising Online

The notion of 'online organising' may invoke caricatures of anarchism as an individual mode of rebellion showing little commitment or accountability to others. To be sure, identities like Anonymous, floating signifiers that can be claimed by anyone who wishes to do so are emblematic of this form of action (to which could be added clicktivism or twitter activism).

It would be a mistake, however, to limit the extent of online radical organisation to individualised (ephemeral, temporary, immaterial, distant, etc.) forms of virtual action. From the beginning of radicals' involvement in cyberspace (which dates back to the very emergence of the public Internet itself), they have pursued collective actions through material organisation. This has included material (real) world, old school, organising on a face-to-face basis in actual immediate contexts, often in rather traditional forms such as affinity groups, activist collectives, workers' cooperatives and so on. And it has taken place in physical organising spaces (in clubs, community centres, anarchist infoshops, etc.). Online resources and networks become tools (or weapons) depending on context.

Very quickly given the nature of the Internet, collectives and groupings in dispersed locales found each other, connected and federated online. The forms of organisation within the federations may have been largely ethereal and online but this is not the entire story. Radical collectives online often, and more of than is generally supposed, regularly held, and hold, gatherings and conventions in which members of diverse collectives have travelled to a specific locale to meet, socialise, strategise and develop their shared organisational capacities.

For years, TAO rented an office in a mid-century office building in downtown Toronto, right in the heart of the emerging new technology and media district. Few could have guessed that a thriving anarchist collective held regular meetings in a historic building situated midway between CityTV and the Canadian Broadcasting Corporation (CBC) headquarters. Meetings were held at least once a week with a half-dozen, or more, members regularly in attendance. The space was also something of a meeting space and organising centre for local anarchists as well as people involved in campus organising, antipoverty movements, and union organising.

TAO's online work was always viewed as part of broader, and deeply rooted, community organising. As such, TAO workers provided labour and technical education and insight to numerous local community and workplace movement groups. They also provided logistical support and communications infrastructure for larger mobilisations and actions, including civil disobedience, protests and demonstrations, eviction defence for tenants, housing squats, occupations, anti-deportation defence and other direct actions. TAO also lent equipment to groups organising their own actions, often lower income groups who could not have otherwise afforded it. TAO also provided equipment and training to anarchist spaces like the Anarchist Free Space and Free Skool which could not have accessed such material and knowledge otherwise.

The supposedly ephemeral realm of online organising has given rise to very real, and relatively durable, movement infrastructures. These have in many cases outlived the collectives that produced them in the first place. Many of these infrastructures are now into their second decades, having lasted as long as the public Internet itself and become essential components of anticapitalist and antistatist projects. These infrastructures have provided resources and connectivity for, in some cases, literally millions of people across several continents. Many have given rise to multiple original projects, from activist archives and discussion fora to newsletters, hacking groups and more.

Process

It is less often remarked that the format of online discussion is in many ways anathema to preferred anarchist processes of deliberation and debate. Anarchists generally prefer face-to-face discussion and consensus processes of decision-making. The Internet, on the contrary, is, by definition, not face-to-face (not physically anyway) and discussion often tends towards monologue and assertion rather than constructive dialogue and consensus.

All of the acknowledged problems of online discussion are perhaps magnified in relation to anarchist organising practices. Among these problems are the lack of nuance in online discussion and the fact that moods do not come across well over the Internet. At their best, anarchists are particularly attuned to the well-being of participants and go out of their way to facilitate participation and create conditions conducive to active involvement by all. This includes paying attention to inclusive language, and practices of respectful, active listening. It also involves awareness of privilege among speakers (gender, racialisation, linguistic, economic, etc.). These are more difficult to pursue online. Meanings can be easily misinterpreted; moods can be misread or missed completely. Humour is culturally and site-specific and may not travel well. Anger can flare and the so-called flame wars can erupt without warning. Empathy does not come readily.

Worker cooperatives and (progressive, ethical, etc.) hackteams have also been developing many new forms of collaborative groupware and 'teamwork' apps which try to address this. Again, Riseup Labs has been instrumental in releasing open-source software, like Crabgrass, which fosters collaborativity and productive sharing capacity. Distributed, decentralised social media is the goal of projects like GNU Social, Mastodon and Diaspora... these seek to 'treat censorship as damage and route around it' while avoiding the 'gated communities' exclusion of Facebook proprietary protocols. While corporate solutions like Slack and Wire offer secure real-time chat and file sharing, one might also refer to LOOMIO: one of the Occupy comms groups out of Wellington, New Zealand, in fact formed a worker cooperative to develop and distribute their group decision-making software when they wanted to translate the four basic hand signals of consensus to online organising. They wanted a tool to assist in turning the open-ended meetings of larger, physical, assemblies into proposals that could be carried out in practice. An aim is transparency and horizontal decision-making through real, vital consensus-building processes.

Cyber anarchist collectives like TAO, as part of their organising practice, consciously work to overcome, or at least address and reduce, the gender division of online practices and the dominance of technical activities by males. This includes opening to transfolks and transhumanists. Over the past two decades, important horizontalist critiques and inclusive tactical communications' work has been developed in women-led and/or trans-identified hackspaces, for example, CyberFeminist International in 1998 in Rotterdam (gathered prior and alongside one of the historic Next Five Minutes gatherings in Amsterdam) and the Old Boys Network (women-identified critics of nettime discussion list), Studio XX in Montreal and looser networks or smaller collectives. Many of the makerspaces have also had intense and transformative struggles over male domination in the tech sector.

The AnarchaFeminist Hackerhive out of Noisebridge in San Francisco and the many strong women out of the CCC can be mentioned here. As a small minority of the free software hacker community, women have constantly had to organise together to fight to establish and defend such spaces for further inclusivity and training. There was also much discussion about toxic masculinity and rape culture within the free software movement after the accusations against Jacob Appelbaum in 2017.

Collectives have sought gender parity and collectives like TAO have had equal or greater involvement by women-identified members relative to men in their collectives. And women have been active in all regards, whether ideological production, online presence, programming, hacktivism, media work, writing and publishing, space maintenance or meeting facilitation.

Hacker Ethics

Hacker ethics refer to core values stressed within hacker cultures and communities. Key principles include access, freedom of information, collective collaboration and making positive contributions to social life. These ethics are geared towards guiding practices of sharing of information as a positive social value with benefits to communal development.

The formal term of 'hacker ethics' is believed to have been coined by Steven Levy in his book *Hackers: Heroes of the Computer Revolution* (2001). Early hackers at the Massachusetts Institute of Technology (MIT), in the Tech Model Railroad Club, espoused key values and practices that would form a basis of hacker ethics.

Key aspects of hacker ethics identified by Levy are: sharing; openness; decentralisation; free access to computers and social improvement, including democratisation. This is a strong distrust of authority. There is a critique of economic, political and social bureaucracies that tend to impede or restrict information for their own purposes (Levy 2001).

Access is the key in people gaining skills and experiences. Free exchange of information allows for greater creativity and improvement or rethinking of practices and systems.

Richard Stallman, whom Levy has referred to as a 'true hacker', developed the free software movement with others who pursued hacker ethics in their practice. Free software advocates assert especially the hands on imperative in pursuing free and open software. In their view, this is crucial in allowing access to source code used to create software, allowing it to be further understood, shared and worked on. This can allow for greater accessibility to information, and to learning, participatory practices and democratic decision-making.

The hands-on initiative in hacking has resonance with anarchist and punk notions of do-it-yourself (DIY). For hackers, getting your own hands on things, taking them apart and seeing first-hand how they work, increases understanding, contributes to demystification and increases possibilities for creativity.

Where there is a restriction on information and access, the hacker ethics advocate and justify opening it up, removing restrictions and getting your hands on it. They stress that they are not seeking to harm users. They distinguish themselves from those who crack systems to steal for personal gain or to trash or damage for the sake of personal gain or pleasure. This distinguishes them from corporate spies, identity thieves or government operatives. Now, there is a discussion of encouraging White Hat hacking and discouraging Black Hat hacking.

The hacker ethics also stress community and collaboration. In early hacking, there were real-world, geographically based communities where collaboration took place in person, as in the labs at MIT and the University of California at Berkeley, for example (Levy 2001). That, and the need for it, has lessened with the widened availability of the Internet. Developments are still collaborative, of course.

Stallman asserts hacker ethics as community ethics more broadly, a sense of right and wrong guiding hacker practice. Key in this is sharing knowledge with those who can benefit from it (Stallman 1996). It is about getting people the needed resources that would otherwise go to waste or be squandered (Stallman 2002). Stallman notes that hacking itself does not imply certain ethics (one cannot assume hackers are acting for good or community betterment, for example), but hacking does often encourage thinking about ethical issues in acting (Stallman 2002).

Finnish philosopher Pekka Himanen proposes as hacker ethics on lines of communitarianism. He emphasises enthusiastic and creative sharing of skills with a community of common purpose. He stresses intrinsic motivations (recognition, inner drives and purposes, personal satisfaction, etc.) rather than the extrinsic motivations of capitalism (pay, wealth, avoidance of punishment, etc.). Social hacking is based on care for the other (as in vegetarianism) and sharing, rather than the proprietarian systems of private capital. One's work is shared as part of collective efforts towards collective social advancement (Himanen 2001).

Surveillance Capitalism

Surveillance capitalism relies on maximised user involvement to generate and monitor data. Philosopher Byung-chul Han poses Big Data as a new perfection of Bentham's Panopticon. Searches and clicks are stoned, observed and recorded. Big Data records thoughts and desires in a way Bentham's Panopticon did not (Han 2017, 62). It manages not only to watch over human behaviour but to subject it to psychopolitical steering (Han 2017, 55). It is an efficient form of control. It is suggested that it allows for data totalitarianism. State and market merge in data mining and elections. Data are purchased and micro targeting deployed to influence voters. This is psychopolitics driven by data (Han 2017, 62).

Social media, which many view as an important activist tool, is a key part of this. Social media has been a financial boon for capital (in ads and sales, for example). It has also allowed law enforcement the collection and organisation of large quantities of data. It innovates possibilities for surveillance, tracking and control of specific populations. And, in a way distinct from disciplinary surveillance, people are encouraged to give up their information freely and voluntarily. Social media blends surveillance with self-expression and social networking, pleasure and self-motivation.

Self-measurement and self-monitoring are deployed to enhance performance (Han 2017, 60). Today's subject is 'an entrepreneur of the self', and it practices self-exploitation and self-surveillance (Han 2017, 61). In Han's dire terms, 'The auto-exploiting subject carries around its own labor camp; here, it is perpetrator and victim at one and the same time' (2017, 61). Big Data can access desires we did not even know we had. It can make them known and develop a psychopolitics around them. These unconscious desires can be rendered exploitable. Big Data is Big Business. It is a commercial practice. It is the merging of the market and the surveillance state (Han 2017, 65).

In a contested Anonymous communique in 2011, one that generated much debate, a call was put forward for the destruction of Facebook. It raised concerns about questionable aspects of social media, especially surveillance prospects. At that time, Facebook had at least 800 million users. Facebook, Twitter and Google have all been subjects of Federal Trade Commission complaints over their mishandling of users' information (Tucker 2013, 293). Data mining has been used by police and intelligence agencies. Post-secondary institutions have used social media to surveil student activists and faculty critics. Social media posts have been used by Rightwingers to target critical faculty and some have lost their jobs on that basis.

Tucker identifies four crucial problems with social media. (1) Information is not secure. It is controlled by corporations which sell it to other corporations and share it with governments. (2) The amount of information and possibilities and its analysis are massive. (3) User profiles are, what he terms, self-generated intelligence dossiers. (4) Social media extends and accelerates the mapping of social networks (2013: 290–1).

FBI surveillance of Myspace led to charges against environmental activists Eric McDavid, Zachary Jenson and Lauren Weiner. The infamous 2006 case *US vs. Eric McDavid et al.* showed that the government monitored the accounts of Jenson and Weiner in tracking radical environmental activism and support for such activism. The government used information from this surveillance to portray them publicly as 'eco-terrorists'. Myspace pages, blog posts, comments and friend lists were used as evidence by the government (Tucker 2013). Weiner infamously agreed to cooperate with the state and testify against her co-defendants. McDavid was sentenced to about twenty years in prison in part on the basis of evidence on Jenson's Myspace page. McDavid did not even have a page of his own.

The case of Aaron Barr shows another example of state-corporate surveillance. Barr, the CEO of HB Gary Federal, used social media sites to map networks of hackers with a plan to expose and name Anonymous activists. He created fake Facebook and Twitter accounts to 'friend' people he viewed as connected. When Anonymous hacked his computer system and blew the lid off his plan, it came out that HB Gary Federal was contracted with the US government as well as with the Chamber of Commerce (to target unions) (Tucker 2013, 302).

There are also issues of censorship and ideological framing. Facebook and Google have created systems of surveillance and censorship in which they collaborate with state agencies. Machines are trained to collaborate with intelligence agencies of the US government. Content can be flagged and blocked before it is even posted. These are not announced and are unknown to users unlike open systems of censorship.

In light of the developing panopticon of surveillance capitalism, some activists call for the abandonment of social media as run by the main social media companies. While recognising some communications' opportunities of social media, it is suggested that the costs are too high.

Beyond Novelty

As the Internet becomes more and more a sphere of commercial and state activities, it becomes a crucial realm for antistatist and anticapitalist organisers. There is no question, and has not been for some time, that the Internet is a central sphere of capitalist development and state surveillance as well as of human social interaction, one of historic consequences.

The Internet has gone from being a means of human engagement, a tool, to a form or, an expression of, human engagement itself. The medium is more than the message. It has transcended being mere medium almost entirely. It is now social relation.

From the beginning, while many saw, hopefully, a sphere of unfettered human activity, interaction and freedom, anarchists saw the Internet as a crucial site of social struggle – even before this was sensed by most media analysts and certainly by the public at large, but that it would be crucial to recognise the human social organisation in new forms of that struggle. It is in this sense that the old adage which TAO activists maintained, and expressed publicly in various venues, makes even more sense today: that the Internet does not exist. (With the Riseup corollary, 'no logs, no masters' which carries the hope of zero-knowledge network provision with secure, encrypted 'perfect forward' secrecy, to establish shared, distributed, defended movement resources.)

Too much popular discussion, and academic analysis alike, has tended to focus on the supposed novelty of online activism. Whether the focus is on Anonymous or earlier manifestations of hacking or WikiLeaks or denial of service attacks (DDOS), the emphasis has been overwhelmingly on novelty. While there are, to be sure, novel aspects of online activism (particularly in the reach of tactics, means of hiding identities that might otherwise be criminalised, etc.), much of online activism has direct antecedents in fairly familiar activist repertoires. Anonymous and hacking have antecedents in forms of sabotage. WikiLeaks extends and innovates practices of whistleblowing, Denial of service actions represent forms of civil disobedience such as sit-ins or blockades.

Connectivity

What is perhaps most notable and new about the Internet is the reach it has given to radical organisers and ideas. It has provided an unprecedented means for the dissemination, promotion and, significantly, explanation of diverse radical ideas and projects. It has also opened access, even to long-time radical activists, to heretofore hidden, obscured, inaccessible, forgotten activist histories, documents and ideological products (essays, newspapers, zines, speeches, etc.). It has also opened important channels for communication and alliance building. The Internet has provided a means for bringing together previously far-flung radical individuals and collectives in ways that allow for acknowledgement, support, solidarity and concerted actions.

It is hard to overestimate the role of the Internet in the late twentieth-century revival of radical activism, and particularly anarchism, in North America especially. It seems clear though that much of the development of radical activism over the last twenty years is owed to online organising of various sorts. This is so even at the level of communication alone. Prior to the spread of the Internet, in the period of the 1980s for example, communication with radicals in other areas was confined to information read in limited numbers of small magazines, journals and zines as well as through correspondence with their publishers and authors. The other source of communication came through occasional meetings with travellers from other areas. Even these latter opportunities were limited if one was not living in areas where there was an existing social space where folks from afar could land, connect with and meet local activists. In the absence of free spaces, bookshops or infoshops, isolation could be stark, leaving even local radicals unknown to each other.

References

Coleman, Gabriella. 2014. *Hacker, Hoaxer, Whistleblower, Spy: The Many Faces of Anonymous*. London: Verso.

Early Edition. 2015. 'Anonymous: What Is It and How Serious Are Its Threats?' *CBC News*. July 21. www.cbc.ca/news/canada/british-columbia/anonymous-what-is-it-and-how-serious-are-its-threats-1.3160906.

Han, Byung-chul. 2017. *Psychopolitics*. London: Verso.

Himanen, Pekka. 2001. *The Hacker Ethic and the Spirit of the Information Age*. New York: Penguin.

Levy, Steven. 2001. *Hackers: Heroes of the Computer Revolution*. New York: Penguin.

Ludlow, Peter. 2001. *Crypto Anarchy, Cyberstates, and Pirate Utopia*. Cambridge, MA: MIT Press.

Shantz, Jeff and Jordon Tomblin. 2014. *Cyber Disobedience: Re://Presenting Online Anarchy*. London: Zero Books.

Stallman, Richard. 1996. 'MEME 2.04' memex.org/meme2–04.html.

Stallman, Richard. 2002. 'The Hacker Community and Ethics.' www.gnu.org/philosophy/rms-hack.htmi.

Tucker, Evan. 2013. 'Who Needs the NSA When We Have Facebook?' In *Life During Wartime: Resisting Counterinsurgency*, Kristian Williams, Will Munger, and Lara Messersmith-Glavin (eds.). Oakland: AK Press, 289–312.

3.6

STREETS AND INSTITUTIONS?

The Electoral Extension of Social Movements and Its Tensions

Josep Lobera and Diego Parejo

In recent years, radical forms of political innovation have appeared in the electoral field, most intensely in Southern Europe. These include the creation of new parties, influence over traditional parties and new forms of political articulation. These activities have distinctive roles in different countries, but similarities can also be analysed.

The financial crisis that erupted in the US aggravated existing political crises and disaffection. As Zamora-Kapoor and Coller (2014) point out, the increasingly weakened role of the State, combined with its subordination to the demands of the European Union's austerity policy, led to unpredictable consequences.

In this context, the development of radical left political parties (Syriza in Greece) or the emergence of new political parties (Podemos in Spain or M5S in Italy) has transformed perspectives on the traditional role of the radical left in government (Olsen et al. 2010). Furthermore, these parties have brought new social demands to the electoral field, thus becoming their legitimate (or illegitimate) representatives within the institutions.

We will address two hypotheses in this study. The first is that the window of opportunity that has opened for the emergence of new political actors in the electoral field is not only marked by the economic crisis, but also by the political crisis of representative disaffection that was developing before it (Lobera 2015, 2019). This disaffection was motivated by a dominant bipartisanism in Greece and Spain (Rodríguez 2013, 2016; Iglesias 2015a, 2015b; Katsourides 2016).

Our second hypothesis presents the existence of an *inclusive* populist model. Against the exclusionary politics emerging in European populist movements – UKIP, Front National, Vox, Golden Dawn, etc. (Mudde 2015) – the emergence of inclusive social protest movements has allowed for the dispute about the social construction of the 'people' to avoid displacement towards a cultural struggle associated with exclusive populism (Mudde and Rovira-Kaltwasser 2013; Žižek 2016[1]).

This chapter is divided into three parts: in the first, we analyse the distinct types of radical political innovation that have emerged, and the sociopolitical context that has favoured them. In the second, we analyse the political changes that have occurred in Spain and Greece, as the maximum exponents of the dynamics examined in this chapter. Finally, we analyse the characteristics of new parties, specifically Syriza and Podemos, based on three dimensions (materialist, political and symbolic). The emergence of these new parties is connected to previous theoretical frames.

Radical Innovations in the Electoral Field: The Electoral Extension of Protests

Despite responding to different political and social contexts, the last decade's protest cycles in diverse world regions have some common characteristics. Their dynamism and organisation respond to an 'emerging model' of social movements, called by different authors 'network social movements' (Castells 2012: 213), 'on-line multitudes' (Sampedro 2005), 'network-system' (Sánchez-Cedillo 2011) or 'network-movement' (Monterde 2013: 294). The growth of political dissatisfaction in contemporary democracies, aggravated by the economic crisis in some regions – especially in Southern Europe – resulted in an increase in 'orphan voters' who were more willing to identify with new social movements (Lobera 2019).

In this context of double crisis (political and economic), new types of protest movements emerged that were not based in strong pre-existing organisations, but rather in a process of decentralised, social media-based, 'swarm' style self-organisations: #SidiBouzid in Tunisia, #15M in Spain, #aganaktismenoi in Greece and #OccupyWallStreet in US in 2011; #YoSoy132 in Mexico in 2012; #PasseLivre in Brazil and #OccupyGezi in Turkey in 2013. These years were characterised by very high levels of social mobilisation. Despite their many differences of cultural and economic contexts, all these movements certainly have points in common. They are part of a new cycle of contention where engagement and conflict are directed towards neo-liberal economics, liberal democracy and the institutions that promote them (Hughes 2011; Flesher Fominaya 2017). Nevertheless, not all of these mobilisations had the same electoral impact and, of course, not all of them resulted in the emergence of new political parties with significant influence in the electoral field, as in Spain and Greece.[2]

These movements succeeded in developing a collective identity and sharing connective frameworks. They could be qualified as *reflexive*, which is to say that they possessed a significant power of persuasion in public opinion, as well as a capacity to raise normative controversy around previously unquestioned issues (Melucci 1989; Laraña 1999). Thus, they acted as 'agencies of collective significance', spreading new ideas in society (Snow and Benford 1988; Gusfield 1994). These centred on traditional political parties' inability to represent the will of the citizens and respond to the grave economic crisis that affected their countries. This would be of paramount importance for the subsequent changes in political systems, since these mobilisations were not *one* movement, but rather acted as a sounding board, giving form to a new 'consensual dissent' shared by millions in their countries (Sampedro and Lobera 2014).

On the one hand, these movements performed a cultural task by building and advancing new repertoires of protest and cultural practices. On the other hand, they performed an instrumental task, managing to popularise core demands such as institutional transparency against corruption and government responsiveness, as well as more democracy and socio-economic justice. The power of these 'reflexive organizations' (Gusfield 1994) lies not in their organisational potential, but also in their capacity to persuade citizens of the veracity of their mobilisation and to get support for the solutions they promote (Laraña 2009).

The 'reflexive convulsion' that these movements produce is not electorally inert, but rather has sensible impacts in the electoral field. Protest can be interpreted as a non-institutionalised form of political impact (Kaase 2007: 789). Thus, it is not surprising that a protest movement can – and that part of it desires to – extend itself towards the field of political representation. This extension can be multifaceted, from influence in the regeneration of existing parties, through the active promotion of voting patterns, to the creation of new political formations (Lobera 2015).

This electoral extension, however, does not resolve the tensions among the participants of the protest movements themselves. Although the protesters agree on the objective of influencing institutional politics, they have different opinions on how to actualise that goal. The drivers of the 2011 mobilisations mistrusted the classical parties and demanded non-party participation, in Greece as much as in Spain. As Vogiatzoglou points out for the Greek case: 'the party and organizations' members were obliged to refrain from openly referring to their political identity. This characteristic gradually changed in time, as the movement became more and more politicized' (2017: 110). In the Spanish case, several activist sectors expressed their fear of the co-optation of the movement (Calvo and Álvarez 2015), as well as being trapped within the margins of what is simply considered to be electoral (Rodríguez 2016).

Changing in the Voting Patterns in Greece and Spain

One of the principle concerns of these movements is to have an effective impact on institutional policy while simultaneously generating changes in public opinion through the development of new frame alignment processes. The data show that protest movements in Spain and Greece have been successful, both in their extent and intensity at the moment of mobilisation. However, in the cases that we have analysed, success in the street does not usually reflect immediately in the electoral contest (Lobera and Rogero 2017).

In 2011, the 15M movement in Spain boosted a pre-existing electoral boycott campaign called *No Les Votes* ('Don't Vote for Them').[3] *No Les Votes* began during the municipal and regional elections on 22 May 2011. Aside from in the Autonomous Community of Madrid, where the protests had a measurable effect on public opinion surveys and in the electoral result, the electoral repercussions were minor. The movement carried on into the general elections in November, where the effect was most pronounced among left and centre-left voters. This dispersed the vote to alternative parties and buried PSOE, which had not received so few votes since the Transition (Bosco 2013:21).

In Greece, the signing of the Memorandum by Yorgos Papandreu is considered to be 'the final blow to PASOK's socialist character' and the beginning of a period of social contestation. This included twenty-seven general strikes (Katsourides 2016: 95) against the structural adjustment plan entrusted to Greece by the Troika (Central European Bank, European Commission and the International Monetary Fund). Following Syriza's spectacular ascension in the 2012 elections, the formation of a coalition between PASOK and New Democracy (ND) to instate the European Memorandum represented a solidification of the cleavage between pro/anti-memorandum camps (Katsourides 2016:96) and between old/new parties (Tsakatika 2016). These strengthening relationships displaced, as they did in Spain, the cleavage between the left and right. Additionally, several Greek analysts affirm the key role of Syriza's turn to a populist discourse.

Tables 3.6.1 and 3.6.2 show the electoral results in Spain and Greece, respectively. In these, we can observe the strong increase in support for the radical left in Greece and a surge in support for a Spanish alternative populist party in the 2014 European Parliament elections (Pavía et al. 2016). The effect of electoral dissatisfaction was observed to be asymmetrical in left-right terms, with greater effects seen in social democratic parties (Keating and

Table 3.6.1 Results in Spanish elections

	General election 2008	Support for the 15M arguments. June 2011	Autonomic and local election 2011	General election 2011	Support for the protesters' arguments. October 2012	European parliament election 2014	General election 2015	General election 2016
Popular Party (PP)	39.9% 154 seats	58%	37.5%	44.6% 186 seats	61%	26%	28.7% 123 seats	33% 137 seats
Socialist Party (PSOE)	43.8% 169 seats	88%	27.7%	28.7% 110 seats	88%	23%	22% 90 seats	22.6% 85 seats
Podemos	–	–	–	–	–	7.9%	20.7% 69 seats	–
United Left (IU)	3.7% 2 seats	90.9%	6.3%	6.9% 11 seats	94.7%	10%	3.6% 2 seats	–
Ciudadanos	1.1%	–	–	–	–	3.1%	13.9% 40 seats	13%
UPyD	1.19% 1 seats	68.8%	2%	4.7% 5 seats	81.1%	6.5%	–	–
UNIDOS PODEMOS (Podemos+IU)	–	–	–	–	–	–	–	21.1% 71 seats

Source: Compiled by the authors using data from the Spanish Ministry of Interior at http://www.infoelectoral.mir.es/

Table 3.6.2 Results in Greek elections

	General election 2009	General election May 2012	General election June 2012	Local election 2014	European parliament election 2014	General election January 2015	General election September 2015
ND	33.5% 91 seats	18.9% 108 seats	29.7% 129 seats	26.3%	22.71%	27.8% 76 seats	28.1% 75 seats
PASOK	43.9% 160 seats	13.2% 41 seats	12.3% 33 seats	16.2%	–	4.7% 13 seats	6.3% (PASOK-DIMAR) 17 seats
KKE	7.5% 21 seats	8.5% 26 seats	4.5% 12 seats	8.8%	6.09%	5.5% 15 seats	5.6% 15 seats
LAOS	5.6% 15 seats	2.9% 0 seats	–	–	–	–	–
SYRIZA	4.6% 13 seats	16.8% 52 seats	26.9% 71 seats	17.7%	25.58%	36.3% 149 seats	35.5% 145 seats
TO POTAMI	–	–	–	–	6.6%	6% 17 seats	4.1% 11 seats
ANEL	–	10.6% 33 seats	7.5% 20 seats	3.2%	3.46%	4.8% 13 seats	3.7% 10 seats
XA	–	7.0% 21 seats	6.9% 18 seats	8.1%	9.4%	6.7% 17 seats	7.0% 18 seats
DIMAR	–	6.1% 19 seats	6.2% 17 seats	3.8%	–	–	–

Source: Compiled by the authors using data from the Hellenistic Ministry of Interior at http://www.ypes.gr/en/Elections/

McCrone 2013; Lobera and Ferrándiz 2013). In this context, these parties are not generally seen as 'parastatal agents' (Van Biezen and Poguntke 2014: 214) or as a sufficient and effective option for solving the problems citizens face. This aspect is most significant in the case of Greece. The signing of the European memorandum and the coalition with the ND sent PASOK's share of votes plummeting from 43.9% in 2009 to 4.7% in the January 2015 elections, in which Syriza triumphed.

A New Electoral Space: The Populist Hypothesis

McAdam and Tarrow (2011) propose an analytical framework of electoral contest, focusing on processes that show a reciprocal relationship between social movements and elections. This specifically regards social movements that amplify protests during the election period and social movements that strategically use elections to gain political power. Sociologist Emmanuel Rodríguez argues for a significant connection between social movements in Latin America and the development of populist governments, ignited through strong social movements or picking up their slack when these weakened (2013: 299). However, there is more to the 'populist moment', understood as the rapid convulsion of the electoral field, than the collective action of social movements. Studies on populism, with specific intensity and focus on Latin America (De la Torre 2010; Mudde and Rovira-Kaltwasser 2013; Stavrakakis et al. 2016), note the development of charismatic leaderships where civil society has already retroceded. Such charismatic leadership is present in both Syriza and Podemos (Stavrakakis 2015;

Katsambekis 2016), as well as in related municipal political parties in Madrid and Barcelona such as Ahora Madrid, with Manuela Carmena, and Barcelona En Comú, with Ada Colau.

There exists a time frame coming after the break from the cycle of protests and the creation of new frameworks for reflexive movements to oppose traditional parties, a 'populist moment'. In that moment, the emergence of charismatic leaderships allows for the development of a new electoral option that would bring in, at least apparently, the main proposals developed during the protest cycle. This rapid growth has occurred in Spain, Greece and Italy, in different ways, and it is not exempt from organisational and ideological problems.

The characterisation of the new emerging parties in the 'populist moment' has not been evident. At the beginning, the 'antisystemic' category or 'radical left' category was adopted. The former has often been applied to parties that challenged established party systems (Sartori 1976; Keren 2000). Even Iglesias used this category several times to describe his own organisation (Iglesias 2015b, 38–39). However, the 'antisystemic' concept cannot be applied rigorously to these new parties – the main objection being that they do not oppose electoral democracy itself.

Rather, they are populist alternatives in the sense used by Laclau (2005), who states that social antagonism has returned to politics in a context where the right and left compete for the concept of 'the people' (Errejón and Mouffe 2015). This competition is divided between two perspectives, exclusionary and inclusionary. Podemos and Syriza adopted the latter (Katsambekis 2016), steering away from an exclusionary perspective based on cultural fundamentalism (Stolcke 1999), which seeks to build the idea of 'the people' around an organic community that excludes the migrant (Errejón and Mouffe 2015: 98). Thus, left-wing populism in Europe 'emphasizes egalitarianism and inclusivity rather than the openly exclusivist anti-immigrant or anti-foreigner concerns of right-populism (i.e. its concern is the *demos* not the *ethnos*)' (March 2012: 122).

Unlike Podemos, whose roots can be traced back to the 15M movement, Syriza was essentially a collection of mostly radical leftist groups that came together in early 2000, but gained popularity after Greece plummeted into debt (Katsambekis 2016). As discussed earlier, the party turned to inclusive populism, not for moral reasons, but for economic and political ones. As Katsambekis explains, to Syriza the populist category 'the people' is a pluralist concept: 'the people' are the working class, the middle class, the LGBT movement, young people, feminist movements and so on. Podemos shares this inclusionary approach and its leaders have repeatedly stated it. For example, Pablo Iglesias states: 'these immigrant workers, no one has the right to call you foreigners in Spain' (Iglesias 2015b: 184).

In Greece, the increased popularity of an extreme right party has prevented the total displacement of the 'left-right' cleavage by the 'people-elites' one (Katsourides 2016: 96). Voters who support Golden Dawn (GD) in Greece have high levels of disaffection not only with politics but also with democracy. They also openly support the use of violence (Lamprianou and Ellinas 2016), particularly against immigrants (Dinas et al. 2016).

Conversely, Podemos enjoyed an undisputed space to construct the concept of 'the people' during its early years in Spain (Errejón and Mouffe 2015; Iglesias 2015a, 2015b). In her dialogue with Errejón, Chantal Mouffe questioned whether this discourse could work as easily in other countries. She argued that if Podemos's leaders were to confront Marine Le Pen, they could not simply say 'we are the people' (Errejón and Mouffe 2015: 99), since the Front National has already appealed to 'the people' in its discourse. Indeed, after the rise of the independence movement in Catalonia, there have been a *patriotization* of the political discourse in Spain. Particularly since 2017, traditional (PP) and new parties (Ciudadanos and Vox) have moved to the center of their political discourse the concept of the Spanish *pueblo*, used from a nationalistic perspective.

Similarities and Dissimilarities between Podemos and Syriza

The dots linking Syriza with Podemos seem fairly obvious in their early years. Both parties shared discourse and political practice, led the movement of the new European left and shared the stage in rallies. We can identify three dimensions (material, political and symbolic) in the demands of both organisations: eliminate austerity politics, end the 'bipartisan' system and preserve citizens' dignity (Katsourides 2016:101).

Material Dimension

Both Syriza and Podemos support the restructuring of external debt, advocate for progressive state intervention in the economy and support tax reform and anti-austerity measures.

Syriza seeks to raise income taxes on yearly earnings over 500,000 euros, secularise Greece (ending special favours to the Church), cut military spending and military operations, create a mandatory minimum wage, nationalise banks and fund initiatives free child meals and housing for the homeless. It also wants to restructure the national debt so that bailout money from the European Union would be used to fund some of their social welfare initiatives.

Initially, the Podemos economic platform included 'a basic universal wage for all citizens' (instead, there will be more state aid to those in poverty), the nationalisation of 'strategic sectors of the economy', the lowering of the retirement age to sixty (instead, it will drop from sixty-seven back to sixty-five) and the cancellation of the Spanish state's debt (now the party is in favour of renegotiation, a cue most likely taken from Syriza). These ideas no longer appear in the Podemos platform.

Instead, after the 2014 European Parliamentary elections, its platform included progressive taxation, the establishment of a public bank, the repeal of the Popular Party's labour reform, a thirty-five-hour week and a tax on selling and buying operations on the stock exchange. Many of the proposals would be funded by ending rampant tax evasion and the establishment of a level of taxation similar to the average rate in the EU.

Electoral tactics have led both parties to a certain deradicalisation of many of their proposals, adapting them to a contested electoral space. During the 2016 electoral campaign, Podemos claimed to be a Social Democratic party. These electoral tactics have led to ideological tensions within the organisations, overlapping with leadership tensions.

Political Dimension

Both parties focus their political dimension on ending bipartisanism and giving 'the people' more of a voice, tapping into public discontent with how democracy functions.[4] Even if their supporters are mainly leftists, they focus on the political discontent with traditional parties rather than on classic left-wing ideological questions.

Syriza was a bottom-up 'social movement', made up of many left-wing parties (Katsambekis 2016; Katsourides 2016). It brought together several different identities such as feminists, anticapitalists and especially those concerned about the environment. At the beginning, its identity was mostly about being radical and against the establishment-European elite.

Conversely, Podemos was created 'top-down' – in opposition to the 15M spirit of horizontality and popular assemblies. It thus went beyond *movimentismo* and its motto 'There are no shortcuts', linked to the Italian workerist tradition. The Podemos hypothesis claimed that the electoral field can also be a space for the articulation and construction of new political identities. Their leaders and activists strategically use social media and television to disseminate their political discourse. Iglesias himself defends this strategy, arguing that people do not participate in political parties in Spain, but they would affiliate with TV channels (2015a, 2015b).

Symbolic Dimension

Syriza appealed to Greeks by simple empathy for the recuperation of their dignity, which they felt had been robbed by the intense economic crisis and, by extension, by the European Union (Stavrakakis 2015). Syriza links symbolically with the National Liberation Front (EAM for its acronym in Greek) and to particular events that occurred during the resistance period against fascism. As an example of this, the presence of a resistance hero, Manolis Glezos, in some Syriza meetings can be interpreted as a clear appeal to dignity against austerity imposed by present-day Germany (Katsambekis 2016; Tsakatika 2016). We can find similar past references to dignity in speeches by Pablo Iglesias and others on the night of 20 December 2015, after the general election results.

The Greek people were promised to be Syriza's first priority, even in the international arena. This makes the party even more appealing, and people identified with it in a way some may call charismatic (Stravakakis 2015: 277–80). Syriza represented a voice and inspired hope that had been missing at a time when many Greeks were feeling powerless. It appealed to their humanity and common goals of reclaiming dignity and being more independent from the European Union. This position, as that of Podemos, is not so much about Euroscepticism as about questioning the pillars on which the European Union is founded. As della Porta *et al.* (2017: 230) point out, 'the issue was not the country's participation in the EU, but the EU itself, a *social* versus a *neoliberal* Europe'.

Podemos puts more emphasis on moral discourse: 'unjust laws', 'indecent elites' and 'decent people' (Iglesias 2015b: 179). 'The people' is identified in moral and socio-economic terms, because 'the people is diverse' (Iglesias 2015b), while 'the caste' is used for corrupt politicians and businessmen. The slogan 'We are not antisystem, the system is anti us' perfectly sums up the symbolic approach taken by Podemos: a corrupt minority that uses great economic and political power to subdue the decent majority, the people.

Tensions and Transformations

The populist moment is a moment of exceptionality, a window of opportunity to extend protest to the electoral field over a new, consensual form of dissent. However, in this populist hypothesis, a separation with the original social movements takes place, as well as a certain deactivation of the movement based on tactical electoral reasons – a deactivation going beyond the cycle of the protests. There is, then, an intrinsic tension in this populist moment, between activism in the streets and its institutional extension, between the logics of collective action and populist action.

Core activists in 15M and the Greeks Indignants promoted new ways of organising and 'doing' politics and democracy. They have often been linked to the autonomist workerist tradition and anarchist movements (Rodríguez 2013, 2016; Monge 2017), which proposes that a strong civil society can subvert social relations and transform them on the margins of the state. In fact, the populist hypothesis proposes the change of political institutions from within by playing in the electoral field with new tactics and taking advantage of the framework of the new social movements to reach cross-sectional majorities.[5] This leads to a greater level of ambiguity and a lack of explicit radicalism in the electoral proposals, in order to adapt them to a 'rapid and effective electoral warfare machinery', as Errejón describes it.[6]

Chantal Mouffe (2013) reduces this tension through her concept of 'agonistic politics', where antagonism itself is reduced: from the 'other as an enemy' to the 'other as an adversary' that can be respected. This point of balance becomes a knot of tensions, however, when internal power dynamics come into play within the organisations themselves. Both Syriza and Podemos experienced extraordinarily rapid electoral and organisational growth. This growth has not always occurred in a harmonious way, causing leadership rivalries at all organisational levels. These rivalries often leverage the tension between street and institution in the struggle for internal power.

Positions thus are established within the parties: those closer to the street are more radical in their approach to confrontation; while others who are closer to electoral tactics utilise seemingly more cross-sectional approaches among potential voters. Narratives are developed to justify these internal rivalries and power struggles: 'they are not with the streets, they are sold to institutionalization'; 'they are not pragmatic, they will never win in the electoral field with such explicit radical proposals'. These narratives are continually used to strengthen or conquer positions within these very young organisations.

These main narratives tend to binary frames, allowing various groups in conflict within the party to be recognised ('us' and 'them', 'the ones closer to street, to the essence of the movements', 'the ones closer to pragmatism, to the electoral victory'). They create at least two political 'families' within the party, two 'imagined communities' (Anderson 1983: 15) in the sense that most of their supporters will never meet or even hear of each other, yet recognise themselves as a part of the matrix of belonging. At the same time, these two narratives generate distrust of the 'others', the inner 'enemy'. The development of these narratives of 'streets or institutions' generates tension among the participants and, therefore, reinforces leadership positions. Leaders in both subgroups identify these two predominant narratives and employ them in their discourses to legitimise their actions and their leadership within the party.

The resolution of the 'street-institution' tension is complicated. First, because it fulfils functions in the struggle for leadership in these rapidly growing organisations. Second, because populism is fundamentally reactive, contrary to radical emancipatory praxis which is proactive (Žižek 2009: 61). Podemos and Syriza have already faced internal crises that have shaken the formations and still cannot be considered concluded. In the case of Podemos, the Second Citizen Assembly of Vistalegre (February 2017) consolidated the leadership of Pablo Iglesias over Íñigo Errejón. The narrative of 'more street' came out stronger in this case. The party proposed 'a chain of transmission' between the institution and the street, 'democratizing and integrating, meeting again with social movements and becoming a mobilizing agent'.

In the case of Syriza, despite having revalidated the government after the elections of September 2015, the referendum on the EU memorandum caused the party to split, with Popular Unity emerging from the Eurosceptic wing of the party (Tsakatika 2016). Shortly after, Syriza's youth wing also broke with the party as a result of the acceptance of the third memorandum (Syriza Youth Central Committee 2015).

Over the past year and a half, the Tsipras administration has been heavily contested in the streets for its austerity policies. It has faced three general strikes and lost a significant amount of its electoral support – down to 16% and surpassed by ND (25%). As of 2017, Alexis Tsipras's approval ratings as the prime minister are at an extraordinary low of 12%.[7] The populist tension in Greece is flowing into a fragmentation of the inclusive populist movement, potentially weakening its advantage over exclusivist options like GD, which could reach 8% in an election.

In addition to this, we can observe two risks frequently associated with the use of the concept of populism. First, as Jacques Rancière (2014: 120) suggests, the use of this term by the traditional parties is aimed at discrediting its political rivals. In this context, the term 'populist' is associated with 'demagogue'. Second, as Stavrakakis (2015) points out, there is a risk of including under the same label divergent policy options, such as GD and Syriza, and pervert in this way the analysis of left-wing, egalitarian and inclusive populist movements.

The question remains: streets or institutions? In the Spanish case, alternative routes out of this dilemma have been opened in the form of Popular Unity Candidacies (PUC). With the important but not hegemonic participation of Podemos, these candidacies were constituted for the local and regional elections of May 2015, obtaining triumphs in the main Spanish cities. They were constituted out of social movements linked to 15M, and to campaigns to protect public health, education and civil rights. They took the form of an 'instrumental party' establishing open primary processes for the election of candidates, being more participative and horizontal than Podemos during those same electoral campaigns. The PUC continued to carry the intrinsic tension between streets and institutions of the populist moment; nevertheless, during their early years in the main Spanish town halls, this tension was slightly less strong because they were perceived to be more closely related to social movements than Podemos and Syriza. Finally, in the last years of their first term, the street-institution tension has strongly affected some of these PUC, articulating internal conflicts around these narratives. This was particularly the case of Ahora Madrid, where the leader (Manuela Carmena) advocated "more institutionalization" in an internal process with multiple fractures.

Each specific national context generates a specific context of mobilisation. In the case of the new parties, moreover, the specific moment in its development stage is determinant for its analysis. The exceptionality of the populist moment makes the landscape of all these parties susceptible to change rapidly. Speeches and strategies are subject to abrupt changes in the conjuncture of communication and political organisation. In this context, the intrinsic tension between the forces of institutionalisation and the forces of mobilisation will be a central element in the analysis of the evolution of these parties in the near future.

Notes

1 In this sense, Zizek's approach concludes that before the absence of leftist mobilisation, the class struggle was displaced by a struggle that placed exclusion and culture as its centre (2016: 67).
2 It is important to note that a certain transnational diffusion of these social movements did take place (Castells 2012; Voulgarelis 2012; Tejerina et al. 2013; Flesher Fominaya 2014; Romanos 2016; Díez 2017). This transnational diffusion 'was not only ideational' in relation to the agency component of the collective action frames; it also 'included forms of action such as occupying the main square of the city with the aim of achieving a certain permanence' (Romanos 2016: 114).
3 *No Les Votes* ('Do not vote them') was a 'grassroots anti-campaign' aimed at the main parties (*PP*, *PSOE* and *Convergència i Unió*) which at the same time called for people to vote for alternative parties.
4 In Spain, in June 2011, 70% did not feel their interests represented by any political party and 83% considered that who really command in the world are no longer the states but 'the markets' (Lobera y Ferrándiz 2013:51–52).
5 The doctoral thesis of Pablo Iglesias (2008) was an appeal to an autonomist movement to being able to renew itself and open up new opportunities for social change. Later, Iglesias (2015b) himself acknowledged that the development of Podemos implies a revision of his own thesis (2015b).
6 Público, 23/10/2014, available at: www.publico.es/actualidad/construir-maquinaria-guerra-electoral.html.
7 See survey results in http://greece.greekreporter.com/2017/02/01/new-poll-shows-new-democracy-10-2-ahead-of-syriza/.

References

Anderson, B. (1983). *Imagined Communities: Reflections on the Origin and Spread of Nationalism*. London: Verso.

Bosco, A. (2013). The Long Adiós: The PSOE and the End of the Zapatero Era. In: B. Field and A. Botti (Eds.), *Politics and Society in Contemporary Spain*. New York: Palgrave Macmillan US, 21–39.

Calvo, K. and Álvarez, I. (2015). Limitations and Exclusions in the Institutionalization of Indignation: From 15-M to Podemos. *Revista Española de Sociología*, 24: 115–122.

Castells, M. (2012). *Networks of Outrage and Hope: Social Movements in the Internet Age*. Cambridge: Polity.

De la Torre, C. (2010). *Populist Seduction in Latin America*. Athens: Ohio University Press.

Della Porta, D., Kouki, H. and Fernández J. (2017). Left's Love and Hate for Europe: Syriza, Podemos and Critical Visions of Europe During the Crisis. In: M. Caiani, S. Guerra (eds.), *Euroscepticism, Democracy and the Media*. Palgrave Studies in European Political Sociology.

Díez, R. (2017). The 'Indignados' in Space and Time: Transnational Networks and Historical Roots. *Global Society*, 31(1): 43–64.

Dinas, E., Georgiadou, V., Konstantinidis, I., and Rori, L. (2016). From Dusk to Dawn: Local Party Organization and Party Success of Right-Wing Extremism. *Party Politics*, 22(1): 80–92.

Errejón, I. and Mouffe, C. (2015). *Construir pueblo. Hegemonía y radicalización de la democracia*. Barcelona: Icaria.

Flesher Fominaya, C. (2014) *Social Movements and Globalization*. New York: Palgrave.

Flesher Fominaya, C. (2017). European Anti-austerity and Pro-democracy Protests in the Wake of the Global Financial Crisis. *Social Movement Studies*, 16(1): 1–20.

Gusfield, J. (1994). The Reflexivity of Social Movements: Collective Behavior and Mass Society Revisited. In: L. Enrique, H. Johnston and J.R. Gusfield (eds.), *New Social Movements: From Ideology to Identity*. Philadelphia: Temple University Press, 58–78.

Hughes, N. (2011). Young People Took to the Streets and All of a Sudden All of the Political Parties Got Old': The 15M Movement in Spain. *Social Movement Studies*, 10(4): 407–413.

Iglesias, P. (2015a). Understanding Podemos. *New Left Review*, 93: 7–22.

Iglesias, P. (2015b). *Una nueva transición: materiales del año del cambio*. Madrid: Akal.

Kaase, M. (2007). Perspectives on Political Participation. In: J. D. Russell and H. D. Klingemann (eds.), *The Oxford Handbook of Political Behaviour*, New York: Oxford University Press, 783–796.

Katsambekis, G. (2016), Radical Left Populism in Contemporary Greece: Syriza's Trajectory from Minoritarian Opposition to Power. *Constellations*, 23: 391–403. DOI:10.1111/1467–8675.12234.

Katsourides, Y. (2016). *Radical Left Parties in Government: The Cases of SYRIZA and AKEL*. London: Springer.

Keating, M. and McCrone, D. (Ed.). (2013). *Crisis of Social Democracy in Europe*. Edinburgh: Edinburgh University Press.

Keren, M. (2000). Political Perfectionism and the 'Anti-system' Party, *Party Politics*, 6(1): 107–116.

Laclau, E. (2005). *On Populist Reason*. New York: Verso Books.

Lamprianou, I. and Ellinas, A. (2016). Institutional Grievances and Right-Wing Extremism: Voting for Golden Dawn in Greece, *South European Society and Politics*, DOI: 10.1080/13608746.2016.1207302.

Laraña, E. (1999). *La construcción de los movimientos sociales*, Alianza Editorial: Madrid.

Laraña, E. (2009). Is Still Spain a Statist Society? A Research Perspective on Organizations, Reflexivity and Collective Action. Working Paper, Institute for the Study of Social Change.

Lobera, J. (2015). From Movements to Political Parties. The Electoral Crystallization of Protest. *Revista Española de Sociología*, 24: 97–105.

Lobera, J. (2019). 'Anti-austerity Movements in Europe.' In: C. Flesher Fominaya and R. Feenstra (eds.), *Routledge Handbook European Social Movements*, London: Routledge.

Lobera, J. and Ferrándiz, J.P. (2013). El peso de la desconfianza política en la dinámica electoral en España. In: I. Crespo (ed.), *Partidos, medios y electores en proceso de cambio: las elecciones generales españolas de 2011*. Valencia: Tirant Humanidades, 33–57.

Lobera, J. and Rogero, J. (2017). Measurement of the electoral crystallization of a social movement: from indignation to vote. *Empiria*, 38: 151–176.

March, L. (2012). *Radical lLeft pParties in Europe*. London: Routledge.

McAdam, D. and Tarrow, S. (2011). Movimientos sociales, elecciones y política contenciosa: construyendo puentes conceptuales. In: MJ. Funes (ed.) *A propósito de Tilly. Conflicto, poder y acción colectiva*. Madrid: Centro de Investigaciones Sociológicas, 161–178.

Melucci, A. (1989): *Nomads of the Present*. Philadelphia, PA: Temple University Press.

Monge, C. (2017). *15M. Un movimiento político para democratizar la sociedad*. Zaragoza: Prensas de la Universidad de Zaragoza.

Monterde, A. (2013). Las mutaciones del movimiento red 15-M. In: E. Serrano, A. Calleja-López, A. Monterde and J. Toret (eds.), *15Mp2p. Una mirada transdisciplinar del 15M*. Barcelona: UOC, 294–301.

Mouffe, C. (2013). *Agonistics: Thinking the World Politically*. London and New York: Verso Books.

Mudde, C., and Rovira-Kaltwasser, C. (2013). Exclusionary vs. Inclusionary Populism: Comparing Contemporary Europe and Latin America. *Government and Opposition*, 48(02), 147–174.

Mudde, C. (2015). Populist Radical Right Parties in Europe Today. In: J. Abromeit, Y. Norman, G. Marotta, and B.M. Chesterton (eds.), *Transformations of Populism in Europe and the Americas*. London: Bloomsbury Academic, 295–307.

Olsen, J., Koss, M. and Hough, D. (Eds.). (2010). *Left Parties in National Governments*. London: Palgrave Macmillan.

Pavía, J.M., Bodoque, A., and Martin, J. (2016). The Birth of a New Party: Podemos, a Hurricane in the Spanish Crisis of Trust. *Open Journal of Social Sciences*, 4: 67–86.

Rancière, J. (2014). El inhallable populismo. In: Badiou, A. et al. (eds.), *¿Qué es un pueblo?* Buenos Aires: Eterna Cadencia Editora.

Rodríguez, E. (2013). *Hipótesis Democracia. Quince tesis para la revolución anunciada*. Madrid: Traficantes de sueños.

Rodríguez, E. (2016). *La política en el ocaso de la clase media. El ciclo 15M-Podemos*. Madrid: Traficantes de Sueños.

Romanos, E. (2016). From Tahrir to Puerta del Sol to Wall Street: The Transnational Diffusion of Social Movements in Comparative Perspective. *Revista Española de Investigaciones Sociológicas (REIS)*, 154(1): 103–133.

Sánchez-Cedillo, R. (2011). El 15M como insurrección del cuerpo-maquina. Universidad Nómada. Noviembre 2011. Retrieved from: http://bit.ly/2oPGiY0.

Sampedro, V. (Ed.) (2005). *13M: Multitudes online*. Madrid: La Catarata.

Sampedro, V. and Lobera, J. (2014). The Spanish 15-M Movement: A Consensual Dissent? *Journal of Spanish Cultural Studies*, 15(1–2): 61–80.

Sartori, G. (1976). *Parties and Party Systems. A Framework for Analysis*. Cambridge: Cambridge University Press.

Snow, D.A. and Benford, R.D. (1988). Ideology, Frame Ressonance and Participant Mobilization. In: Klandermans et al. (eds.), *International Social Movement Research*, vol. 1, Greenwich: JAI Press.

Stavrakakis, Y. (2015). Populism in Power: Syriza's Challenge to Europe. *Juncture*, 21: 273–280.

Stavrakakis, Y., Kioupkiolis, A., Katsambekis, G., Nikisianis, N., and Siomos, T. (2016). Contemporary Left-Wing Populism in Latin America: Leadership, Horizontalism, and Postdemocracy in Chávez's Venezuela. *Latin American Politics and Society*, 58: 51–76.

Stolcke, V. (1999). New Rhetorics of Exclusion in Europe. *International Social Science Journal*, 51(159): 25–35.

Syriza Youth Central Committee (2015). Why We Broke With Syriza. *Jacobin Magazine*. Retrieved from: www.jacobinmag.com/2015/09/tsipras-greece-snap-elections-syriza-youth/.

Tejerina, B. et al. (2013). From Indignation to Occupation: A New Wave of Global Mobilization. *Current Sociology*, 61(4): 377–392.

Tsakatika, M. (2016). SYRIZA's Electoral Rise in Greece: Protest, Trust and the Art of Political Manipulation. *South European Society and Politics*, 21(4): 1–22.

Van Biezen, I. and Poguntke, T. (2014). The Decline of Membership-Based Politics. *Party Politics*, 20(2): 205–216.

Voulgarelis, A. (2012). Nights in Syntagma Square. In: A. Schiffrin and E. Kircher-Allen, (eds.), *From Cairo to Wall Street*. New York: The New Press, 168–173.

Zamora-Kapoor, A. and Coller, X. (2014). The Effects of the Crisis: Why Southern Europe? *American Behavioral Scientist*, 58(12): 1511–1516.

Žižek, S. (2009). *First As Tragedy, Then As Farce*. London: Verso Books.

Žižek, S. (2016). *Against the Double Blackmail: Refugees, Terror and Other Troubles with the Neighbours*. London: Penguin UK.

3.7

CELLS, COMMUNIQUÉS AND MONIKERS

The Insurrectionary Networks of Antistate Attack

Michael Loadenthal

Introduction

Spanning over a century, the insurrectionary spirit of anarchism has been on the forefront of direct, unmediated attacks on the state and capital. Insurrectionary praxis is based on an ethic of informality, clandestinity and temporality, and as a result, its cells exist in secret only as long as deemed necessary for a particular action. Unlike social movement *organisations* and above-ground campaigns, the cells that populate the insurrectionary milieu are not something to 'belong to' but something to 'act through'; a momentary assemblage of like-minded individuals united for a particular attack by voluntary association and through shared affinity. While the modern cell networks gained visibly in Europe around the millennium, their rapid replication has led to similarly styled formations in dozens of countries from the Americas to Asia.

This franchised replication is aided by the use of adoptable monikers – static labels used to associate an attack with others, and to ideologically tag them as insurrectionary. Oftentimes, these are acronyms whose names communicate the politics of the attackers, such as the Informal Anarchist Federation (FAI), Conspiracy of Cells of Fire (CCF), International Revolutionary Front (IRF) as well as older, not explicitly insurrectionary monikers such as the Animal Liberation Front (ALF) and Earth Liberation Front (ELF). The use of moniker-linked attacks, which form into a campaign of sorts, is a distinctive feature of the insurrectionary cells. For example, in June 2013, a Greek cell of the FAI bombed a vehicle belonging to a prison director overseeing the incarceration of comrades. This attack marked 'act one' of the Phoenix Project, and would be followed by thirteen additional attacks, spanning eight countries over a twelve-month period. The Phoenix Project highlights the strength of the adoptable moniker, as through its usage, an arson targeting an Indonesian hotel and the sabotage of Italian fuel pumps can be united into a shared, global effort, and not understood as disparate acts of lone wolves. This chapter will explore how the insurrectionary anarchist networks utilise the cell model, the communiqué and the adoptable moniker to allow for the creation of a globally dispersed, decentralised, open involvement movement united in its rejection of capitalism, the state and those who would seek to control it.

The Informal Anarchist Federation

Though a variety of direct attack networks, monikers and individual cells have emerged since the postmillennial reinvigoration of the urban guerrilla, the strategy and momentum of direct, antistate attack was carried forth most notably by the Informal Anarchist Federation [*Federazione Anarchica Informale*]. The FAI has been linked to attacks dating as early as 1999, but its current, internationalised, adoptable moniker form emerged around 2004 in the Italian city of Bologna. In 1999, the network sent mail bombs to the Greek embassy in Rome, a tourism office in Madrid and a branch of Citibank in Barcelona (Hanrahan 2013). Subsequently, pre-2003 FAI bombs targeted newspapers, churches, courts, police, prisons and other targets located in Western Europe, largely in Spain and Italy.

In describing one's enrolment with the FAI, convicted militant Alfredo Cospito states:

> One becomes part of FAI-IRF only at the very moment he/she acts and strikes claiming as FAI, then everyone returns to their own projects, their own individual perspective, within a black international that includes a variety of practices, all aggressive and violent.
>
> *(Cospito 2014)*

The FAI, like other adoptable monikers, is united by an aesthetic, and a broad set of ethics. The individual cells form, carry out attacks and announce these strikes widely through communiqués and intra-movement publications, which, as opposed to communiqués, are intended outwards to circulate amongst the movement's networks. In exploring the history of the FAI, one can note the informality of the network, as well as its proclivity for unmediated, direct forms of confrontation carried out through clandestinely organised strikes on state and corporate targets.

In the final days of 2003 (29 December), as part of the FAI's 'Operation Santa Claus', two letter bombs were mailed to Europol – a Europe-wide police data centre – headquartered in The Hague, and to the head of the European Central Bank, Jean-Claude Trichet. Technicians defused the Europol bomb, and German police discovered the IED sent to Trichet in the bank's mail room. Both bombs were postmarked in Bologna. One day prior, a third mail bomb exploded at the Bologna home of Romano Prodi, the heard of the European Commission, and former Italian Prime Minister (1996–98, 2006–8). According to FAI communiqués, this was the third bomb to target Prodi that week (BBC 2003b). Two previous explosions occurred in trash receptacles, and the third IED, the one delivered with the mail, was assembled inside of a book and addressed to Prodi's wife. The book bomb, according to Prodi, '[produced] a big flame but without an explosion' (BBC 2003a).

The next day, a fourth letter bomb was mailed, this time to the headquarters of Eurojust, a European policing agency. The IED did not explode and according to officials was the work of the same network (BBC 2003c). Additional IEDs, also originating in Bologna, were sent to the president and vice president of the European People's Party, as well as to Gary Titley, a British Labour Member of the European Parliament. Titley called the bombings an 'attack on democracy... [likely] from an Italian anarchist group' (BBC 2004). In response to the six mailed IEDs, the Italian city of Bologna halted the delivery of parcels from the region to EU institutions (BBC 2003d).

The FAI (2003) explained their motivation in a communiqué entitled 'Open Letter to the Anarchist and Anti-Authoritarian Movement'. This document serves to announce the FAI to the world, to begin to develop its methodology for attack and to communicate with sympathetic allies in the producing of future attacks. According to some historical accounts (Cospito 2014), the letter is a signpost marking the real emergence of the FAI global network. In the text, the network claims responsibility for the attacks, calling their targets the 'repressive apparatus that plays the democratic farce and that will bring the main characters and institutions to the new European order' (FAI 2003). The attackers quantify their enemy as 'the various police departments … a prison system … bureaucrats and politicians', proclaiming:

> Attack and destroy the responsible for repression and exploitation!
> Attack and destroy prisons, banks, courts and police stations!
> Revolt is contagious and can be reproduced!
> Social war against capital and the State!
>
> *(FAI 2003)*

The FAI describes their network as 'a federation formed either by groups of action or by single individuals, in order to go beyond the limits implied in single projects and to experiment the real potentialities of informal organization' (2003, 3). The communiqué goes on to describe the network's interpretation of 'informal', 'anarchist' and 'federation' and discusses strategy, organisation and other questions of practicality.

Following the Bologna-based bombing campaign, the FAI expanded, forming components such as the 'Armed Cells for International Solidarity Brigade' which continued to mail explosives (2 April 2004, 10–11 December 2004), the 'Metropolitan Cells' which detonated IEDs in Milan (29 October 2004) and numerous joint formations, such as the FAI/'July 20 Brigade', and the FAI/'Crafts and Fire Cooperative', which detonated IEDs targeting police and prisons (3 March 2005). These cells operated in the Italian cities of Bologna, Genoa, Rome and Milan, and were responsible for at least sixteen explosive attacks, with security sources estimating the network's composition to be 50–250 individuals (Marone 2014). According to pro-FAI movement historians, between December 2003 and December 2006, the network carried out '7 revolutionary campaigns … [and] 30 incendiary and explosive attacks on things and people' (Anonymous 2006). These bombs targeted courts, police buildings and individual officials such as Mayors and corporate directors.

Years later, the FAI would prove to be long-lasting, sending additional parcel bombs including:

- 15 December 2009: Director of Centre for Identification and Expulsion, an immigration detention centre, in Gradisca d'Isonzo, Italy.
- 16 December 2009: Bocconi University in Milan. c. 28 March 2010: Headquarters of the Northern League, a right-wing political party in Milan. The device injured a postal worker.
- 23 December 2010: Embassy of Greece in Paris.
- 23 December 2010: Embassies of Chile and Switzerland in Rome. These devices injured two.
- 30 March 2011: Nuclear company Swissnuclear in Olten, Switzerland. This device injured two.
- 31 March 2011: Barracks of Italian paratroopers deploying to Afghanistan located in Livorno, Italy. This attack injured one soldier severely.
- 7 December 2011: The Chief Executive of Deutsche Bank. The device was intercepted in Frankfurt.

- c. 9 December 2011: Josef Ackermann, director of Equitalia state tax collection agency in Rome. This attack seriously injured Ackerman.
- 9 April 2013: La Stampa newspaper in Turin, Italy.
- 10 April 2013: Europol offices in Brescia, Italy.

Of its scores of attacks, the most infamous is likely that which occurred on 7 May 2012. On this date, a cell of the FAI was responsible for the non-fatal shooting (i.e. 'kneecapping')[1] of Roberto Adinolfi, the fifty-six-year-old chief executive of Ansaldo Nucleare, an Italian nuclear company affiliated with defence/aerospace firm Finmeccanica. The masked attackers fired three times, shooting Adinolfi in the knees from atop a motorcycle, as the target left his Genoa home. The shooting of Adinolfi was claimed via a four-page communiqué – as the 'Olga Nucleus'[2] (2012) cell of the FAI-IRF – received on 11 May 2012 by an Italian newspaper. A year after the shooting, the FAI named the attack as part of 'Operation Hunt the Spy' (Hornby and Rossi 2013) linking it to the 2013 bombings of La Stampa and Europol. The three attacks were rhetorically linked in the communiqué, noting:

> [Europol] provides the forces of order with equipment such as microchips, micro-cameras and other technological wickedness...[and] 'La Stampa' [is] always ready to corroborate the frame-ups of the carabinieri [Italian military police] and police, especially when they strike those who are at war against the state.
>
> *(FAI/IRF Damiano Bolano Cell 2013)*

In September 2012, two male individuals, thirty-five-year-old Nicola Gai, and forty-six-year-old Alfredo Cospito, were arrested in Turin and linked to the crime via surveillance footage, wiretaps and textual analysis of the communiqué. The two individuals were convicted and imprisoned for a combined sentence of twenty years. Their sentence was assigned a *'finalità di terrorismo'* [purpose of terrorism] condition due to the antistate politics of the shooting.

With similar regularity to its IEDs, FAI cells have used timed improvised *incendiary* devices (IIDs) such as the ones that ignited under the cars of the Lord Mayor of Bristol, Geoff Gollop, and Tory Councillor Kevin Quartley (7 November 2011), claimed by the FAI's 'Class Terror' (2011) cell. Despite being conservative functionaries within the British state, the two men expressed shock that they were targeted. Lord Gollop stated, 'I am at a total loss why anyone would want to do this. I have got absolutely no idea what the motive could possibly be' (The Bristol Post 2011). Councillor Quartley expressed similar sentiments stating, 'I've got no idea why this has happened' (The Bristol Post 2011).

While the FAI was established in Italy, like other moniker-based networks, it was quickly exported as an internationalist model. In June 2012, police arrested eight individuals in Italy, one in Switzerland, and one in Germany, all accused of affiliation with the FAI/IRF. In at least one case, an Italian judge issuing warrants charged the accused with 'subversion, terrorist conspiracy and international terrorism' (Hooper 2012). State officials noted presumed links between the arrested FAI members and the Greek CCF. As the imprisoned members of the Greek network stated in their letter to the Italian FAI, 'The Informal Anarchist Federation travels over borders and cities, carrying with it the momentum of a lasting anarchist insurrection' (Ekonomidou et al. 2012). By 2014, cells of the FAI had claimed attacks in a variety of countries beyond Italy including Argentina, Bolivia, Chile, Greece, Indonesia, Mexico, the Netherlands, Peru, Russia, Spain, the UK and the US. Also, while the FAI name would be combined in endless combinations with the CCF, IRF and others, it was also regularly used in conjunction with the ALF/ELF monikers, such as an attack in Moscow (around 21 February 2012) where a group ignited two IIDs to burn cellular phone towers in an area popular with hunters.

Around September 2011, two Italian FAI nodes operating since 2004 – the 'Artisans Cooperative of Fire and Similar (occasionally spectacular)' cell and the '20th July Brigade' – released a lengthy statement entitled, 'Do Not Say That We Are Few' (2011). In this document – termed a 'contribution to discussing communication, organization and armed struggle at the dawn of a new era' (2011) – the authors claim responsibility for several mail bombs, express solidarity with the CCF and discuss an international campaign of insur-rectionary direct action. The anonymous authors speak of the deterritorialisation of their network, writing:

> Many things have happened since we launched the proposal for an 'Informal Anarchist Federation'. Today, thanks to the sisters and brothers of the 'Conspiracy of Cells of Fire', who have re-launched it, the 'FAI/International Revolutionary Front', the 'FAI/Global Network', the 'International Network of Action and Solidarity', the 'Informal Anar-chist Federation–Global Network' has become reality with their one thousand names. A reality that needs to grow up especially now through the instrument of informal organization on a worldly level and thanks to a federation of action groups. Dozens and dozens of cells, nuclei, movements, individual comrades, united by a clear and strong horizontal and widespread pact of mutual aid, wage war on the existent in a chaotic and destructive way.
>
> *(FAI-IRF Artisans Cooperative of Fire and Similar (occasionally spectacular)*
> *and FAI-IRF 20th July Brigade 2011)*

Following this, the statement details the names and national locations of thirty-six cells spread across nine countries: Italy (12 cells), Mexico (9), Greece (8), Chile (2) and 1 each in Indonesia, Russia, Peru, the Netherlands and England.

Succeeding the shooting of Adinolfi, and in response to repeated attacks targeting Equitalia – the Italian tax collection agency – the Italian Ministry of the Interior reas-signed 18,000 officers to 'security detail' (Delaney 2012) and carried out a series of police raids, arresting eight, and serving warrants to already imprisoned (and infamous) anarchist militants Gabriel Pombo Da Silva[3] and Marco Camenisch.[4] Since its emergence, there have been at least nine individuals (Loadenthal 2015, 465–7, 2017) arrested in connection to FAI attacks, though in general the network has been resistant to disruption. Because the FAI's attacks have tended to avoid injury, the network's actions have been consistently 'underes-timated' (Marone 2014) by both police and academics. In a report to the Italian parliament by the Ministry of the Interior, the FAI is described as the 'most dangerous form of domestic non-jihadist terrorism in the country' (Marone 2014); yet, Muslim non-state actors still re-ceive far more 'focused intensity' (Winfield and Gatopoulos 2010) from police. Nonetheless, according to Europol, 'attacks by far-left and anarchist militant groups jumped 43 percent in 2009 [compared to 2008]', and have doubled since 2007 (Winfield and Gatopoulos 2010).

The Phoenix Project

The global insurrectionary networks are organised through a decentralised model drawn from the larger anarchist praxis. The roles played by antiauthoritarian, horizontalist poli-tics in the moulding of leftist networks have been the subject of much scholarship. Gordon

(2008, 14–15) described the generalised anarchist milieu as 'network of informal interactions between a plurality of individuals, groups and/or organisations...on the basis of a shared collective identity', viewing this 'movement's architecture' as 'a decentralised global network of communication, coordination and mutual support among countless autonomous nodes of social struggle, overwhelmingly lacking formal membership or fixed boundaries'. Such a description is applicable to the insurrectionary milieu, which can be understood as a subset or derivative of the larger anarchist tendency. For the insurrectionists, international campaigns of attack are coordinated through a diverse, virtual exchange of ideas played out via the texts of communiqués and claims of responsibility.

To accurately portray this organisational tendency through a modern insurrectionary example, we can examine the 2013–2015 Phoenix Project. The campaign began on 7 June 2013, when a cell identifying with the CCF-FAI/IRF moniker claimed responsibility for a bomb attack in Athens. The targeted vehicle belonged to Maria Stefi, the director of the prison where members of the CCF were being held. The cell was quick to claim the attack 'as a display of genuine solidarity with our ten imprisoned brothers and sisters' (CCF-FAI/IRF, Consciousness Gangs-FAI/IRF, and Sole-Baleno Cell 2013). Interestingly, the IED disrupted a period of inactivity for the CCF, as the authors write:

> After almost two years of silence throughout the Greek territory, the CCF returns. Maintaining a common front with the...FAI cells ('Antifascist Front', 'Unscathed Cell of Vengeance', 'Lone Wolf Cell', etc.)...we support and strengthen the international conspiracy of the Informal Anarchist Federation/International Revolutionary Front.
> *(CCF-FAI/IRF, Consciousness Gangs-FAI/IRF, and Sole-Baleno Cell 2013)*

The re-emergence of the CCF moniker and the reinvigoration of this network were portrayed as the rising of the phoenix. The attackers called the bombing part of the Phoenix Project implying that the incident was not a single occurrence.

Less than two weeks later, the 'International Conspiracy for Revenge/FAI' (2013a) claimed responsibly for the second Phoenix Project attack – the bombing of a car belonging to a 'hated prison guard in Argos, Greece'. A few days later, in what the attackers called 'Phoenix Project –Act Two', the third in a series of attacks in Greece occurred, similarly targeting the vehicle of a prison worker. Around 22 June 2013, the 'FAI-International Conspiracy for Revenge' (2013b) – the same moniker which claimed the second Phoenix attack – blew up the car of a prison guard whom they accuse of abuse, intimidation and bullying, writing that 'the enemies of freedom have names and addresses'. The communiqué addresses the issue of prison abuse and uses the text to further expand on the internationalist network, stating:

> The new anarchist urban guerrilla is not a means of struggle, it is our existence itself. All the rest which does not promote the continuous anarchist insurrection is ideological cowardice.
>
> FAI (Informal Anarchist Federation) in cooperation with the Conspiracy of Cells of Fire aims to create a diffuse network of direct action cell in the Greek territory which will strike where the enemy does not expect it. Small autonomous flexible armed cells watch, collect info, sometimes cooperate sometimes not and choose the moment of sudden attack. Only in the attack is there life. We are anarchists of action, chaotic, nihilist, egoists, godless, we are the carriers of the black flags of anarcho-nihilism.
> *(International Conspiracy for Revenge/FAI 2013b)*

A few days after this communiqué was issued, expanding on and articulating the networked reality of the FAI, the Phoenix Project internationalised.

On 26 June 2013, insurrectionists in Jakarta, Indonesia carried out an arson attack targeting the Sheraton Hotel. The arsonists labelled their attack 'Phoenix Project – Part 3' and noted that they acted as '[their] decision to respond to the call from our Greek comrades' (International Conspiracy for Revenge/FAI-IRF and Anger Unit 2013). In their closing remarks, the authors encourage further continuation of the campaign writing 'Let's make the Phoenix project as an international project for revenge!' signing the communiqué the 'Anger Unit of the International Conspiracy for Revenge/FAI-IRF' (2013), once again utilising that shared moniker and adding a new service unit. After the attack in Jakarta, at least thirteen more attacks would occur, totalling seventeen Phoenix Project attacks (in nine countries: Greece, Italy, Germany, England, Czech Republic, Russia, Chile, Mexico and Indonesia) as of 3 January 2016 (Loadenthal 2015, 475–7; Anarchist Arson Attack Cell 'Fire and Consciousness' FAI-IRF 2016). Following one such attack, the authors summarise the intent of the campaign writing:

> Project Phoenix is a punch in the gut. A punch in the gut because the new anarchist urban guerrilla is here and tears down the desires of all these worms to terminate our actions. Old groups are activated and new are created, with the promise to give life to the nightmares of authority and its subjects.
>
> *(Commando Mauricio Morales/FAI-IRF 2013)*

From the brief history of the Phoenix Project, one can see the deployment of adoptable network monikers to claim cell-level responsibility for attacks while simultaneously demonstrating coordination and ideological affinity within larger movement-level initiatives. We see monikers deterritorialise, adapt, grow and change. From one initial challenge and call to action, cells around the world attack, and in doing so, develop a decentralised campaign of sorts.

Borrowing from the work of anthropologist Jeff Juris, Gordon points out that anarchist networks most often do not seek traditional social movement 'recruitment' but instead the reproduction of networks through a 'horizontal expansion and enhanced "connectivity"' (ibid.). In describing the structuring and strategy of the global network of attack, the authors describe these horizontally connected networks and state:

> We coordinate our attacks through the FAI/IRF international network…FAI/IRF is an international conspiracy of anarchists of praxis…It gets rid of the smell of mold that has settled in anarchy seen at amphitheaters, and fills the air with the smell of gunpowder, black anarchy, nighttime, explosions, gunshots, sabotages. This explains why the International Revolutionary Front of FAI and Conspiracy is on top of the anarchist dangers list as cited in recent Europol reports.
>
> Diffusion and informal organizing within the new anarchy into autonomous cells of direct action are what really scare the police of the whole world. Therefore, the State and the enemies of anarchy do not easily forget the anarchist militants who are held captive under their prisons' authority.
>
> *(CCF-FAI/IRF, Consciousness Gangs-FAI/IRF, and Sole-Baleno Cell 2013)*

This has been the method, which originated in Italy, and rapidly spread to Greece, Mexico and nearly thirty additional countries. More than two and a half years after the initiation of the Phoenix Project, combatant cells were still carrying the model forward. In a communiqué issued in April 2015, the authors state that their IID attack targeting an office of Microsoft was carried out as a 'contribution to the comrades of Czech FAI/IRF suggestion, who burned a police car and suggested the creation of an international action project named "Let's Destroy Repression", modelled on the "Phoenix" Project' (Combative Anarchy, FAI-IRF 2015). A few days later, yet another Phoenix Project-linked attack was claimed, this time the arson of a meat company's office in Chile.

The Ethics of Insurrectionary Attack

Clandestine insurrectionary cell networks like the FAI are not unified by any manner of codified system of association, but rather demonstrate affinity by carrying our similarly styled attacks, and framing these actions through recurrent themes. In trying to best describe what an insurrectionary cell is, one can review the attackers' claims of responsibility – often termed a communiqué – to try and excavate these thematic tropes. Though a great deal of diversity exists *within* the networks, the insurrectionary ethical worldview can be usefully understood in terms of eight themes: the promotion of *attack* as a strategy, advocating 'social war' to engage in generalised contestation, a rejection of identity politics in favour of a form of radical intersectionality, a rejection of managed dissent through the vehicle of the Left, a rejection of reformism and democratic politicking, a promotion of illegality, a keen awareness of impending ecological crisis and the negative effects of technology and industrial civilisation, and finally, the embracing of an individualist, ego-driven spirit of wildness.

According to the most recurrent thread of insurrectionary agreement, what defines the tendency is its promotion of *attack* as both a strategy and an ethic. In a 2009 essay, pro-insurrectionary proponents write:

> Our [insurrectionary anarchist] subculture has come to emphasize the attack. We are compelled to act immediately, despite the sheer impoverishment of our revolutionary context. We cannot wait until the 'right moment,' the progression of capital is too rapid to spare even one more second. To the quiet satisfaction of our most intelligent enemies, the ethos of attack has come to imply a neglect of a developed long-term strategy. We of course understand that every recruiting center, police station, and real-estate development needs to be razed as soon as possible.
>
> *(Til it Breaks collective 2009, 17)*

According to advocates, the forces of domination must be confronted through a direct attack that is immediate, continuous and spontaneous. An individual only learns how to act through experimentation, and thus anyone is capable of acting in furtherance of greater freedom through the deployment of easily reproducible tactics targeting whatever available localised manifestation of the enemy. Second, the wider conflict with the state and capital takes the form of a social war, which seeks to create points of rupture in the sociopolitical order through exacerbating existing tensions, dissatisfactions and sites of alienation in society which are produced by power and control. Third, in locating the enemy one must move beyond identity-based politics and seek a more all-encompassing idea of intersectionality wherein the goal is confrontation with 'The Totality' and total liberation (A Gang of Criminal Quees 2008). This understanding is based on a rejection of domination, not specific systems of oppression such as sexism, racism or homophobia.

Therefore, the battles of the non-heterosexual and those of the non-white are inextricably linked as they both resist top-down power.

Fourth, forms of protest and contestation must be unmanaged, temporary and outside of the Left's traditional conceptions of social movements. This rejection of representation, mediation and ritual must be recognised in all aspects of praxis. The prized model for insurrection is thus the fostering of informal, temporary collectives of individuals, allied through friendship and ties of affinity. Fifth, the insurrectionary vision for social change rejects reformist measures and Western liberal notions of democratic participation. Reformists are seen as the enemies of radical social transformation, despite being commonly portrayed as allies in resistance. Sixth, insurrection is inherently illegal, and embraces a heritage of anarchist illegalism and criminality including expropriation, assassination and the rejection of civil engagement. Seventh, the influence of the ecological crisis is apparent in the insurrectionary agenda, along with primitivist critiques of domestication and technology. Finally, the insurrectionary milieu seeks to be constituted by individualists, acting in their own right, informed by a sense of wild egoism. The notion of 'the wild' runs throughout this understanding and evokes an untamed, pre-capitalist worldview.

Taken as a collection of values, these components constitute a basis for insurrectionary affinity. They are gleaned from thousands of brief texts, authored at the level of the cell, typically following some transgressive act of antisocial, antistate and/or anticapitalist attack. The insurrectionary actor speaks via the mechanism of the communiqué, and utilises the space created by a temporary disruption to the status quo. In doing so, the actor further develops the political analysis of the wider milieu, and creates another page in the fluid, amorphous, canon. The *community* of insurrectionary networks meets at these points of ideological, rhetorical and strategic affinities, and it is constituted and reproduced on the basis of this affiliation.

Full-Time Professional (Revolutionaries) versus Part-Timers

One additional distinguishing characteristic of insurrectionary networks, and the cultural realities they promote, is the notion of a non-professional, un-specialised, full-time revolutionary. This notion is distinctive from older Marxist-Leninist forms of vanguardism, as well as from the strategic vision advocated by classical proponents of guerrilla warfare such as Che Guevara, Régis Debray and Mao Tse-Tung. This contends that from the proletarian masses, a vanguard cadre emerges, and it is this cadre that organises the masses and leads it in combat with the state. To borrow language from the 1970s-era, American, militant, vanguard known as the Weather Underground Organization (WUO), this would involve a 'cadre organization' facilitating an 'active mass base' movement as a 'division of the International Liberation Army' (Ashley et al. 1970, 88, 90).

In this model, the participant leaves their civilian life behind, and through paramilitary preparations, becomes a soldier in a Marxist army. For Leninists, 'The vanguard elite are... not just a theoretical category to explain the development of political strategies, but a specific grouping of special individuals who must be identified and trained distinctly from the broad mass of the population' (Franks 2010, 106). The vanguard-cadre model with a unified, central organisation was furthered by urban guerrilla movements such as the WUO – described as a self-styled revolutionary vanguard (Kroes 1974, 87) – who spoke of the 'revolutionary youth movement' *requiring* a cadre organization ... toward the creation of a unified revolutionary *party*' (Ashley et al. 1970, 88–9 [emphasis added]). This form of centralisation and professionalisation aimed at militants' full immersion which separated the activist from the militant, and the revolutionary from the guerrilla.

This facilitated organising of the masses via an intentionally constructed minority is an essential difference between the Leninist-styled fighting organisations of the 1960s–70s and the insurrectionary networks of today. Lenin assumed that the suffering proletariat already possessed a readiness to revolt and that the role of the vanguard was not to incite, but to organise these masses for revolution. Therefore, under Lenin's logic, all of the proletariat were potential 'full-timers' but only the vanguard had reached the required level of consciousness to become mobilised. This is different from the insurrectionary understanding, which posits that the masses do *not* possess a pre-eminent analysis of alienation and domination and that it is the role of the underground to display the possibility for revolution through political violence. While Lenin presumed that those under the yoke of capitalism would be radicalised by their position, the insurrectionaries argue that systems of control and coercion obscure this oppression and disincentivise the oppressed to organise and strike.

The urban–rural divide further exaggerates this binary – fully immersed militant versus part-time activists – as difficulties arise when urban-based movements attempt to build, maintain and conceal large memberships, a task more suited to rural organisations. One member of the Italian Red Brigades described this twenty-four-hour guerrilla immersion as 'a hidden life at all times'... [an] 'all-absorbing and highly demanding' (Orsini 2011, 48). Within this strategic organisation, some movements stratified their combatants (Wolf 1981, 21) into 'regulars' – full-time militants who lived underground – and 'irregulars' (Meade 1990, 51; Orsini 2011, 50–51), who appeared to live normal lives in the world of legality. Furthermore, for professionalised units like the RB, militants existed apart from the larger community, their family and other unaffiliated individuals. The brigadists were to live separate from their immediate family, children and those not in the fight in an ultimate act of isolationist self-denial that even restricted sexual contact (Orsini 2011, 51) to the coordination *by the Brigade's* technocrats. In a study on radicalisation authored by the Asymmetric Warfare Group of the US Army (2010, 49), the authors report that 'anarchy ideologues' (i.e. anarchist-identifying revolutionary activists) are specifically prone to severe breaks with pre-existing social networks after dedicating themselves to a lifestyle of revolt, noting that this shift 'represents a complete break with society, requiring an underground existence'.

For the vanguardist, highly organised networks of armed cadres, one's desires were subordinated to the struggle, their joy traded for duty and sacrifice. For those embedded in professionalised vanguardist models, this self-denial is all-encompassing, intentionally segregating and non-negotiable. One Italian fascist militant, the 'political and military mind of the Movimento Politico Ordine Nuovo (MPON)' (Orsini 2011, 263) spoke of this experience as a professional, underground utiliser of revolutionary violence:

> You have to break contact with all those you had left behind: friends, family, boyfriend or girlfriend....[emotional ties] had to be eliminated or removed. Because when you're being hunted, when you live underground, you can't allow them. You can't allow yourself anything.
>
> *(Orsini 2011, 264)*

This modus operandi of self-denial, martyrdom and a sense of obligatory duty is abandoned in the neo-insurrectionary model. Additionally, at the level of organisation, contemporary attackers abandon the two-tiered taxonomy – separating 'full time militants', also known as 'professional revolutionaries', from those who lived 'normal lives'. As imprisoned members of the CCF explained in their self-reflective publication, 'The Sun Still Rises':

> The CCF, instead, proposes informal organization of tightly-knit groups of friends in which specialization is levelled by generalization of skills and knowledge, and in which daily life and intimate relationships are not separated from the practice of revolt. This is the revolutionary as diffuse guerrilla and the guerrilla as insurrectionist.
>
> *(Tsakalos et al. 2012, 2)*

This logic is repeated by the authors of *The Coming Insurrection* who speak of 'what is political in friendship', rejecting the 'neutral idea of friendship understood as a pure affection with no consequences' (TIC 2007, 98). Here, the social ties of friendship are a powerful unifying force; more powerful than the membership lists and donor records of the NGO or grass-roots movement.

The modern insurrectionary movement can be thought of as engaging in an anti-authoritarian form of warfare. The goal of these neo-guerrillas is not to *lead* the masses or direct the antistate war through a vanguard, but those burning banks and slashing tyres function with the hopes that their 'propaganda of the deed' will demonstrate not only an anarcho-praxis, but also the feasibility of attacking an enemy as stoic and rigid as the modern neo-liberal state. This strategy exposes an often-critiqued aspect of insurrectionary theory typically represented as 'steps towards the revolution', and mockingly expressed in a variety of forms such as:

1   Break a window, light a fire, detonate a bomb....
2   Write a communiqué
3   Circulate your communiqué
4   ?????? [insert unknown series of steps here]
5   Live the insurrection![5]

This recurring critique, delivered in the form of a snarky message board comment or out-right joke, is formulaic: it contains an element of insurrectionary tactics (e.g. break a window, light a fire, glue a lock), the production of a communiqué, and ends in insurrection. Quite obviously, this approach skips over the quite necessary period where isolated attack leads to a system-level response and the victory against the state. This is an often-maligned breakdown in the insurrectionary strategy which stands in stark contrast to Marxist (e.g. Guevarian, Debrayian) programmes which are predictive in their understandings of the steps from at-tack to revolution. Instead of offering such a *strategy*, insurrectionary theory coalesces more closely around a shared set of *tactics*. In their discussion of militant social movements, the anonymous authors of CrimethInc. write 'different formats for confrontation [i.e. tactics] encode different power relations and forms of social change within them' (CrimethInc. Ex-Workers' Collective 2014). This is precisely why insurrectionists base their tactical array around their shared organisational ethics, most notably informality, spontaneity and direct (non-mediated) interactions with power. Therefore, one can understand the insurrectionary approach as a collection of tactics more than a central strategy; yet, all is informed by a jointly constituted and globally shared set of ethics.

Thus while insurrectionary action can be seen as the production of a *focal point* for antisocial, antistate and anticapitalist resistance, it rejects the centrism, hierarchy and leadership-reliance embedded in Guevarist methods. It also abandons artificial separation between an underground and above-ground life and the self-sacrificial, militarised ethos of duty and 'giving one's self' to the revolution, in favour of a struggle grounded in the joy of an antisocial, confrontational attacker. An imprisoned member of the CCF writes,

> The urban guerrilla of another time was one of hierarchy, martyrdom, and leninism. It claimed to be the vanguard of the coming revolution, while always maintaining a patronizing view toward others which inevitably led toward fantasies of centralized power. The new guerrilla avoids these pitfalls...[for] the Conspiracy of Cells of Fire, self sacrifice is rejected, along with orthodoxy and hierarchy in all its forms...What we see is the implementation of insurrectionary anarchist methodology within the context of guerrilla warfare. While criticisms of armed struggle, militarism, and guerrilla warfare are central aspects of insurrectionary anarchist critique, these have thus far been a response to the Marxist-Leninist guerrilla warfare of the 60's and 70's, with its authoritarian communist rhetoric and joyless, sacrificial practices. What shows its masked face now is something more horrible: an insurrectionist guerrilla with contempt for all leaders and vanguards, whose revolt is as inextricably linked with the joy of life as it is with the urgency of our situation.
>
> *(Tsakalos et al. 2012, 2)*

Here, we see that members identifying with the CCF moniker align themselves squarely with this new insurrectionary tendency, one that rejects the 'authoritarian communist [and] joyless sacrificial practices' of bygone urban guerrillas. This is not to say that the model ignores the risk of capture, imprisonment and death faced by those acting against the state. While this cannot be denied when clandestine actors are building explosive devices and confronting police, the aim is to *avoid* sacrificial acts that may lead to capture and instead focus on damaging the target while avoiding the repression of the state. For the insurrectionists, there is no utility in martyrdom, as it removes an individual from the arena of struggle.

Conclusion

The insurrectionary cell, as both a structural and strategic formation of clandestine political networks, is both novel and aged. It should be understood as emanating from centuries of militant political contestation on the part of anarchists advocating propaganda of the deed and has taken a remarkably modern formulation with the popularisation of digital communities. For moniker-based networks such as the FAI, their international campaign of attack against the state and capital would not have been possible before the age of the Internet. This is not to say that insurrectionary politics and underground networks could not exist – as they clearly could and have – but rather that the methods the FAI has grown into are decidedly modern.

The campaign of the Phoenix Project provides insight into a series of strikes, coordinated through these digital networks, and linked through a shared moniker. In this case, an insurrectionary cell in Greece attacked the car of a prison director, followed by another attack in Greece two weeks later. In this second attack, the car of a prison guard was attacked. Following the second attack, it took less than four days for the next strike, proving for the FAI the viability of their campaign. On 26 June 2013, only nineteen days after the campaign was announced, allies of the Grecian cell in Indonesia set fire to a Western hotel chain, and claimed the arson in the name of those who stuck against the prison officials. At least thirteen additional attacks, all claimed by self-described cells of the FAI, and all in the name of the Phoenix, followed the Indonesian arson targeting the Sheraton. This series of sixteen attacks demonstrates the modern insurrectionary praxis and approach: carry out your own attacks through clandestine, self-organised, informal cells, and follow this up with a communiqué, distributed online, which explains your reasoning. Within this communiqué, urge readers to continue the struggle by attacking as well. The wider ethics of informality, illegality, voluntary association, and a rejection of social movements and institutionalised politics in favour of unmediated attacks, distinguishes insurrectionary cell networks from all other forms of contentious politics and clandestine networks. They are decentralised, non-hierarchical and do not require outside support from a state sponsor or quasi-state bureaucracy.

Finally, it is important to remember the function – broadly speaking – of political violence. Political violence, including terrorism, militant protest, industrial sabotage, armed expropriations, etc., all belong to a continuum of methods of social change. At one end are passive methods such as withdrawing one's consent, followed by illegal pacifist means such as nonviolent civil disobedience. Towards the middle are traditional methods of change such as electoral politics, sanctioned demonstrations and letter writing which ultimately rely on the institutionalised violence of the state. Finally, on the end opposite pacifist means are those methods of sociopolitical contestation described as militant or terroristic. These include the use of arson, explosives and other means to harm one's opponent, create spectacle and bring attention to one's critique and analysis. In this manner, all political violence – but especially that which creates fantastical images and interruptions to the daily functioning of society – is a form of politics. As philosophers debate whether warfare is a form of politics, or politics is a form of war, insurrectionary cells continue to take matters into their own hands and engage in direct combat with the state regardless of the odds. Therefore, the practical function of insurrectionary networks must be understood to play two distinct roles: the first to financially, politically and spiritually disrupt, oppose and damage the forces of the state, capitalism, etc., and the second, to force the state and the wider populace to interrupt their lives for a moment, and consider the revolutionary analysis offered by their fiery communiqués.

Notes

1 The use of 'kneecapping' (*gambizzazioni* in Italian) was common among the RB active in 1970–80s Italy.
2 The 'Olga' namesake is a tribute to Olga Ikonomidou, an imprisoned member of the CCF network in Greece.
3 Gabriel Pombo Da Silva is an anarchist militant who was involved in revolutionary bank expropriations since age fifteen. After being imprisoned in Spain, he escaped in 2004. While trying to flee to Germany, he was discovered at a border crossing and exchanged fire with security forces. No one was injured in the shooting but Da Silva was arrested and convicted of attempted murder and kidnapping. He is currently serving thirteen years.
4 Marco Camenisch is an anarchist militant currently imprisoned for murder. Camenisch was involved in radical environmental movements prior to his arrest and had served time for industrial sabotage and other actions targeting power stations. After being arrested in 1980 for sabotaging a Swiss power station, he was sentenced to ten years in prison. In 1981, he escaped along with five other prisoners. During the escape, a prison guard was shot and killed and a second injured. From 1981 to 1991, Camenisch went underground, and on 5 November 1991, Italian security forces arrested him. Upon capture, Camenisch opened fire wounding one soldier, and was shot and injured in the process. In 1992, he was sentenced to twelve years for the shooting and the sabotage, serving nine years in solitary confinement. In 2002, he was extradited to Switzerland, and in 2004, sentenced to seventeen years in prison for the alleged killing of a Swiss border guard in 1989.
5 A nod to this style of prescriptive strategy can be seen in the Invisible Committee's recommendations for strategy as outlined in their four stages: 'Get going!', 'Find each other', 'Get organized' and 'Insurrection' corresponding to Chapters 10, 11, 12, and 13, respectively.

References

A Gang of Criminal Queers. 2008. Towards the Queerest Insurrection, Milwaukee, WI, Online edition, http://zinelibrary.info/files/QueerestImposed.pdf

Anarchist Arson Attack Cell 'Fire and Consciousness' FAI-IRF. 2016. 'Phoenix Project – Incendiary Attack against a Security Company by FAI-IRF.' Insurrection News. https://insurrectionnewsworldwide.com/2016/01/10/chile-phoenix-project-incendiary-attack-against-isp-security-by-fai-irf/.

Anonymous. 2006. 'Four Years......Dec. 2006.' In *Escalation: Some Texts Concerning the Informal Anarchist Federation (FAI) and the Insurrectionist Project*, Online, 4–9. 325.nostate.net. http://325.nostate.net/library/escalation1.pdf.

Ashley, Karin, Bill Ayers, Bernardine Dohrn, John Jacobs, Jeff Jones, Gerry Long, Howie Machtinger, et al. 1970. 'You Don't Need A Weatherman to Know Which Way the Wind Blows.' In *Weatherman*, edited by Harold Jacobs, 51–90. San Francisco, CA: Ramparts Press, Inc. (originally in New Left Notes).

BBC. 2003a. 'Prodi Survives Parcel Bomb Attack.' *BBC*, December 28, Online edition, sec. Europe. http://news.bbc.co.uk/2/hi/europe/3351697.stm.

———. 2003b. 'Letter Bombs Sent to EU Figures.' *BBC*, December 29, Online edition, sec. Europe. http://news.bbc.co.uk/2/hi/europe/3355521.stm.

———. 2003c. 'New Letter Bomb Reaches EU Target.' *BBC*, December 30, Online edition, sec. Europe. http://news.bbc.co.uk/2/hi/europe/3357063.stm.

———. 2003d. 'Bologna Mail Blocked after Bombs.' *BBC*, December 31, Online edition, sec. Europe. http://news.bbc.co.uk/2/hi/europe/3359281.stm.

———. 2004. 'Letter Bomb Explodes at MEP's Office.' *BBC*, January 5, Online edition, sec. Manchester. http://news.bbc.co.uk/2/hi/uk_news/england/manchester/3370213.stm.

CCF-FAI/IRF, Consciousness Gangs-FAI/IRF, and Sole-Baleno Cell. 2013. 'Responsibility Claim for Explosive Attack on Vehicle of the Koridallos Prisons Director, in the District of Dafni.' Translated by contra-info. Athens Indymedia (republished by 325.nostate.net). http://325.nostate.net/?p=8080.

Class Terror/FAI. 2011. 'Attacks against Vehicles of Lord Mayor & Tory Councillor in Bristol.' UK Indymedia (republished by 325.nostate.net). http://325.nostate.net/?p=3517.

Combative Anarchy, FAI-IRF. 2015. 'Incendiary Attack against the Central Offices of Microsoft by 'Combative Anarchy – FAI/IRF.'' Translated by Inter Arma. Inter Arma (republished by 325.nostate.net). http://325.nostate.net/?p=15815.

Commando Mauricio Morales/FAI-IRF. 2013. ''Commando Mauricio Morales / FAI-IRF' Takes Responsibility for the Sending of a Parcelbomb to Dimitris Horianopoulos, Scumbag Former Commander of the Anti-Terrorist Division.' Translated by boubourAs. Act for Freedom Now! (republished by 325.nostate.net). http://325.nostate.net/?p=8334.

Cospito, Alfredo. 2014. Interview by CCF – Imprisoned Members Cell with Alfredo Cospito (Greece, Italy) Interview by CCF - Imprisoned Members Cell. Online. Translated by Nihil Admirari. http://325.nostate.net/?p=13394.

CrimethInc. Ex-Workers' Collective. 2014. 'The Ukrainian Revolution & the Future of Social Movements.' CrimethInc. Ex-Workers' Collective. www.crimethinc.com/texts/ux/ukraine.html.

Delaney, Sarah. 2012. 'Fearing Anarchist Attacks, Italy Tightens Security.' *LA Times Blogs*. May 17. http://latimesblogs.latimes.com/world_now/2012/05/fearing-anarchist-attacks-italy-tightens-security.html.

Ekonomidou, Olga, Giorgos Polidoros, Gerasimos Tsakalos, Panagiotis Argirou, Christos Tsakalos, Damiano Bolano, Michalis Nikolopoulos, Giorgos Nikolopoulos, Haris Hadjimihelakis, and Theofilos Mavropoulos. 2012. 'CCF-Bullets of Words for the Bullets of the FAI/FRI.' Translated by contra-info. Athens Indymedia (republished by contra-info). http://en.contrainfo.espiv.net/2012/05/14/greece-ccf-bullets-of-words-for-the-bullets-of-faifri/.

FAI. 2003. 'Open Letter to the Anarchist and Anti-Authoritarian Movement.' In *Escalation: Some Texts Concerning the Informal Anarchist Federation (FAI) and the Insurrectionist Project*, 3–4. Bologna, IT: 325.nostate.net. http://325.nostate.net/library/escalation1.pdf.

FAI-IRF Artisans Cooperative of Fire and Similar (Occasionally Spectacular), and FAI-IRF 20th July Brigade. 2011. 'Do Not Say That We Are Few - Statement from the Italian FAI.' 325.nostate.net. http://325.nostate.net/?p=3015.

FAI/IRF Damiano Bolano Cell. 2013. ''Damiano Bolano' FAI/FRI Cell Claim the Parcel Bombs Sent to the Daily La Stampa of Turin and the Private Investigation Agency Europol of Brescia.' Translated by 325.nostate.net. 325.nostate.net. http://325.nostate.net/?p=7697.

Franks, Benjamin. 2010. 'Vanguards and Paternalism.' In *New Perspectives on Anarchism*, edited by Nathan J. Jun and Wahl Shane, 99–120. Lanham, MD: Lexington Books.

Gordon, Uri. 2008. *Anarchy Alive! Anti-Authoritarian Politics from Practice to Theory*. Ann Arbor, MI: Pluto Press.

Hanrahan, Jake. 2013. 'Meet the Nihilist-Anarchist Network Bringing Chaos to a Town Near You.' *VICE*. February 13. www.vice.com/read/the-fai-are-the-worlds-true-anarchists.

Hooper, John. 2012. 'Italian Police Arrest Leftwing Terror Suspects.' *The Guardian*, June 13, Online edition, sec. World news. www.theguardian.com/world/2012/jun/13/italian-police-arrest-terror-suspects.

Hornby, Catherine, and Sara Rossi. 2013. 'Anarchists Claim Parcel Bombs Sent to Italy Newspaper and Agency.' *Reuters*, April 12, Online edition, sec. World News. http://mobile.reuters.com/article/worldNews/idUSBRE93B0M120130412?feedType=RSS&feedName=worldNews.

International Conspiracy for Revenge/FAI. 2013a. 'Explosion Destroys the Personal Car of a Prison Guard – ICR / FAI Take Responsibility as Part of Phoenix Project.' Athens Indymedia (republished by 325.nostate.net). http://325.nostate.net/?p=8149.

———. 2013b. 'International Conspiracy for Revenge / FAI Take Responsibility for Blowing up the Vehicle of Argiris Gelbouras, Navplio Prison Screw.' Translated by boubourAs. Act for Freedom Now! (republished by 325.nostate.net). http://325.nostate.net/?p=8174.

International Conspiracy for Revenge/FAI-IRF, and Anger Unit. 2013. 'Anger Unit / ICR-FAI-IRF Burn down the Third Floor of Former Sheraton Hotel, 'The Media Hotel and Tower.'' 325.nostate.net. http://325.nostate.net/?p=8227.

Kroes, Rob. 1974. 'Violence in America: Spontaneity and Strategy.' In *Urban Guerrilla: Studies on the Theory, Strategy and Practice of Political Violence in Modern Societies*, edited by Johan Niezing, Proceedings of the 1st International Working Conference on Violence and Non-violent Action in Industrialized Societies, 4:81–93. Brussels, BE: Rotterdam University Press/Polemological Centre of the Free University of Brussels.

Loadenthal, Michael. 2015. 'The Politics of the Attack: A Discourse of Insurrectionary Communiqués.' PhD dissertation, Fairfax, VA: School for Conflict Analysis and Resolution, George Mason University.

Loadenthal, Michael. 2017. *The Politics of Attack: Communiqués and Insurrectionary Violence*. Manchester: Manchester University Press.

Marone, Francesco. 2014. 'A Profile of the Informal Anarchist Federation in Italy.' Combating Terrorism Center at West Point. www.ctc.usma.edu/posts/a-profile-of-the-informal-anarchist-federation-in-italy.

Meade, Robert C. 1990. *The Red Brigades: The Story of Italian Terrorism*. New York, NY: St. Martin's Press.

Olga Cell: FAI/IRF. 2012. 'Italy: Claim of Responsibility for the Armed Attack against Roberto Adinolfi of Ansaldo Nuclear (Corrected).' culmine.noblogs.org via waronsociety.noblogs.org/. http://waronsociety.noblogs.org/?p=4610.

Orsini, Alessandro. 2011. *Anatomy of the Red Brigades: The Religious Mind-Set of Modern Terrorists*. Ithaca, NY: Cornell University Press.

The Bristol Post. 2011. 'Bristol Councillors' Cars Torched in Late-Night Arson Attacks.' *The Bristol Post*, November 8, Online edition, sec. News. www.bristolpost.co.uk/Bristol-councillors-cars-torched-late-night-arson/story-13787504-detail/story.html.

TIC. 2007. *The Coming Insurrection*. Intervention Series 1. Los Angeles, CA: Semiotext(e).

Til it Breaks Collective. 2009. 'Strategic Social War.' *Til It Breaks*. (Denver, CO), October.

Tsakalos, Gerasimos, Olga Economidou, Haris Hatzimichelakis, Christos Tsakalos, Giorgos Nikolopoulos, Michalis Nikolopoulos, Damiano Bolano, Panayiotis Argyrou, and Giorgos Polydoras. 2012. 'The Sun Still Rises.' Untorelli Press. http://destroybristol.files.wordpress.com/2012/02/ccf_0.pdf.

U.S. Army Asymmetric Warfare Group. 2010. 'Radicalization: Relevant Psychological and Sociological Concepts.' The Johns Hopkins University Applied Physics Labratory (republished by Public Intelligence). http://info.publicintelligence.net/USArmy-RadicalizationConcepts.pdf.

Winfield, Nicole, and Derek Gatopoulos. 2010. 'European Anarchists Grow More Violent, Coordinated.' *The Huffington Post*, December 28, Online edition. www.huffingtonpost.com/2010/12/29/european-anarchists-grow-_n_802277.html.

Wolf, John B. 1981. *Fear of Fear: A Survey of Terrorist Operations and Controls in Open Societies*. New York, NY: Plenum Press.

3.8

RADICAL MEDIA

Sandra Jeppesen

Introduction

Radical media are central to the promotion of radical political ideas and actions, including developing and sharing radical analysis and discourses including the representation of marginalised or silenced voices, on the one hand, and by mobilising and reporting on contentious social protests and other direct actions, on the other. Radical media activists are thus key to the propagation of radical social movements, engaging in media and other activism from positions rooted within movements with whom they share social habitus, alternative values, organising practices and political vision. While some scholars suggest that radical media is a niche form of media with a small audience-reach limited to those already active in radical social movements, Jeppesen et al. (2014) have found that radical alternative media have several different objectives, the first two related to propagating ideas, and the second two related to mobilising actions.

Discourses

First, radical media makers often create small-scale or Do It Yourself (DIY) media projects such as zines or flyers which are shared among small groups primarily with the objective to create safe(r) spaces, scenes and communities of practices. Second, in creating community media with an anchor point, a media project can generate radical political analysis to influence or radicalise a broader related movement, e.g. an anarchist-feminist collective whose radio programme influences the mainstream feminist movement.

Actions

Third, protest media that are oriented towards mobilising the public to participate in mass movements or mobilisations can use the snowball effect, producing and sharing media virally to reach a wide audience. Fourth, global media strategies are used in multi-linguistic or visual forms that can support the development of international solidarity movements. This range of strategies, from small and local to large and global, demonstrates how radical media are not one thing, but rather radical media practices develop out of and respond to everyday needs within radical political social movements.

Given these four objectives, Chris Atton (2002) has found alternative media focus on two specific dimensions of media production: product and process. The product is the media output or content, from print and radio to video and online media, whereas the process is the way in which media producers organise themselves and structure their projects. Both product and process or structure challenge hegemonic or dominant media constructs and power.

Product

Content in radical media products is oriented towards radical social transformation, on multiple issues from austerity and capitalism to gender, sexuality, feminism, antiracism, colonialism, disability, LGBTQ+ liberation, climate justice, border issues, police brutality and more, including ways in which many of these will play a role in any given issue. The content is distinct from alt-right news in that it is oriented towards social justice, and from fake news in that it is oriented towards the truth.

Process

The process is the way media production projects are organised, how decisions are made and ways in which alternative values are put into practice. There is a strong influence of social anarchism and autonomous Marxism in radical media, shaping media practices that include horizontal structures, power-sharing, task rotation, skill sharing, mentorship, anti-oppression practices and consensus decision-making. This contributes to social justice through the empowerment of participation in at least two ways: first, by developing a voice for the voiceless, and second, through horizontal organisational and ownership practices, establishing counter-power processes crucial to radical politics, which are discussed elsewhere in this book.

Controlling the means of production of representation (process) and the representations themselves (products), radical media shifts the sphere of the possible. Producing new and innovative visual, textual, aural and digital discourses to challenge dominant regimes of truth, radical media activists are simultaneously developing alternative value-based equitable relationships in practice. Moreover, directly challenging structures of domination, they create alternatively and sometimes experimentally structured media and arts production groups, networks, formats, platforms, work methods, outputs and institutions. Furthermore, in advocating for revolutionary social transformation with a counter-power strategy, media activists express opposition to power structures but they also build media networks that challenge 'the very survival of the power structure' (Downing, 2001, xi). This is key to understanding the revolutionary aims of radical media – it is not directed towards creating new content or democratising media through increased participation, which are liberal political goals, but towards challenging the very survival of dominant media structures, and thereby reclaiming media power.

Given this basic understanding of the objectives of radical media, it is important to understand four key dimensions of contemporary radical social movement media repertoires of communication: being rooted within radical social movements that attack the dominant power structures in society; organising in experimental anticapitalist forms that challenge dominant media structures; developing radically transformative discursive and representational forms; and engaging in translocal and transmedia mobilisation networks to reclaim digital media power.

This chapter maps out five key media genres – print, audio, image, video and online – considering how they are reconceived by radical media practitioners. It critically analyses

Table 3.8.1 Key analytical dimensions of radical media by genre

	Social movements	Representations	Structures	Digital networks
Print	Autonomous journalism	Radical discursive formations	Anticapitalist editorial collectives	Open editorial platforms
Audio	Community radio mobilisations	Voices of 'the voiceless'	Pirate radio hordes	Radical podcasts
Image	Activist art, posters	Radical image formations, comix	Radical community art spaces	Culture jamming, memes
Video	Livestreaming protest	Radical activist documentaries	Video activist collectives	Sousveillance
Online	Connective action	Transmedia mobilisations	Translocal mobilisations	Technopolitics

Source: Table devised and complied by the author.

how each radical media genre engages the four key dimensions outlined earlier: social movement participation, anticapitalist organisational forms, transformative discursive representations and reclaiming digital networks (see Table 3.8.1). It then considers emergent debates, focusing on unresolved challenges, contradictions and tensions.

Print

Autonomous Journalism

Radical movements have long published autonomous journalism in independent newspapers, pamphlets and flyers, to develop and disseminate analysis around specific issues, mobilise and cover activist campaigns and protests, and otherwise participate in social movements. Autonomous journalists report on and support social movements, playing the role of activist and journalist simultaneously. They write articles providing critical analysis of movement issues, produce media content to support mobilisations and engage in direct actions as well as direct-action reporting from the perspective of protesters. Globally, there are many independent radical newspapers and magazines that might be considered autonomous journalism. *The Bristol Cable* in Bristol, UK is an autonomous newspaper that reports on local community issues, focusing on housing, racism, austerity, poverty and more. In Canada, *Briarpatch* is a long-running radical political magazine that reports from a radical left perspective with an emphasis on collective organising. *Indigenous Rising Media* is an anticolonial news site that reports on social movement actions of the Indigenous Environmental Network, focusing on Indigenous mobilisation against resource extraction on treaty lands, demonstrating links between climate justice, colonisation and land rights.[1] Self-reporting allows activists to tell the truth about their movements and communities from an insider perspective. In intentionally reporting from an overt subject position, they disrupt the claim that journalism is objective, challenging the closed, top-down power structures of dominant or mainstream media systems. There are also important models of solidarity journalism based on the principle of foregrounding the voices of those affected, with allies in positions of relative privilege making space for those in marginalised or silenced communities to produce media (Jeppesen, 2016), and respecting the leadership of local communities (Sunkel & Girvan, 1973).

Multi-issue Radical Discursive Formations

Reporting from within radical social movements and marginalised communities, media activists generate new discursive formations through developing alternative media frames, or ways of thinking about and discussing issues. Mainstream media perpetuates a discursive regime of truth, repeating and entrenching the dominant or accepted way of thinking about issues, whereas radical media challenges these regimes of truth by revealing their assumptions, and providing a range of alternative perspectives from the viewpoint of people with different experiences and social locations within society that often are not interviewed or do not have access to representation in mainstream media. This includes reporting on multiple issues, and revealing ways in which they are connected and related to each other, helping to develop common ground among many groups who can act in solidarity once they see how their issues and therefore their achievement of liberation are linked. For example, *Brand* is an anarchist magazine produced in Stockholm, Sweden, since 1898 on radical political movements covering many different issues related to social class, oppression and liberation, promoting pacifism, reproductive rights and free love in a historical context, and more recently in 2000 writing about riots and other direct actions. Covering each of the issues mentioned here has led to writers from *Brand* magazine being charged with criminal offenses. This criminalisation of autonomous journalists reveals how crucial the construction of antiauthoritarian discourses is in challenging unjust laws and illegitimate power.

Intersectional Anticapitalist Editorial Collectives

Radical media reject the editorial structures typically found in journalism or news organisations, with a top-down hierarchical structure. Mainstream media ownership models are shaped by corporate convergence and vertical integration, meaning that a few corporations control various forms of media – from telecommunications, cell phones, satellites and ISPs to newspapers, TV stations, radio stations and online platforms. Not only does this limit the viewing choices and thus global democratic debate on issues, it is also organised in top-down structures that will influence media content. Counter to this, radical media organise in often much smaller local editorial collectives where decision-making is shared among all members, writing is done collaboratively engaging strategies such as peer skill sharing and mentorship for new writers, and administrative tasks may be rotated or shared among participants. For example, zines, or small self-produced magazines, were printed and widely distributed, along with their music, by the Riot Grrrl movement from the 1990s. These zines were created by small groups of Riot Grrrls working together on designing, writing, copying and distributing them. Riot Grrrls were explicitly anticapitalist and feminist in their content and organisational styles. However, these kinds of small-scale productions can often not offer any pay for the labour required to produce them, as they reject capitalist advertising or profit motives. In Barcelona, XNet addresses the unpaid labour challenge by generating funds to liberate media activists by providing them with a full year of sustainable income. Not constrained by the capitalist labour market, the 'liberated' media activist is then free to support radical media and social movement projects. Horizontal organising structures can challenge structures of oppression and power in mainstream media; however, they have also been critiqued for not offering enough checks and balances against informal power hierarchies, or providing enough structure for accountability and responsibility to be transparent.

Open Editorial Platforms

While most online mainstream news platforms offer some form of audience interactivity such as commenting, reposting or sharing content previously produced by paid professional journalists, autonomous journalism platforms operate somewhat differently. Content is produced voluntarily by unpaid unprofessional or semi-professional writers and journalists who may not know each other or the people maintaining the platform, but who nonetheless share political and social values as well as radical social movement objectives. Platforms are designed according to open editorial principles, so that anyone can post an article that they have written that they feel is appropriate to the platform. Often, there is no moderator, or only modest moderation to remove hate speech. One of the earliest such open editorial platforms that has been well documented is Indymedia, which came into existence in late 1999 to support and report on the Seattle anti-WTO activist mobilisations which included counter-summits, trainings and multi-day street protests. Indymedia was one of the first websites to provide live updates from protesters in the streets, and as such they were able to contradict and challenge the mainstream regime of truth regarding the mobilisations, which was largely sensationalist and inaccurate. Indymedia is still in existence in some global locations, such as Indymedia Athens which has been reporting on the Indignados of Greece movement from an anarchist perspective. But in other locations, it has fallen dormant, or been modified to take other shapes, such as the Media Co-op in Canada which is a multi-stakeholder cooperative originally with four chapters across Canada, and a national editorial collective that produces and distributes the *Dominion* magazine as well. Open editorial platforms struggle with issues such as hostile alt-right articles and trolling, particularly feminist news being trolled by aggressively misogynist comments, and anticolonial antiracist news trolled by racist anti-Indigenous comments. The tension remains unresolved in terms of how to create an open editorial policy without censorship, and how to deal with hateful trolling which is a pressing question for this genre of radical media.

Audio

Community Radio Mobilisations

Radio broadcasts are considered easier to produce than either print media, which requires writing and literacy skills, or video, which requires expensive equipment and editing skills. Non-corporate, not-for-profit radio stations, including community and campus radio, have historically been used by communities to further local aims, mobilise political actions and build community. For Clemencia Rodriquez (2001), access for community members to produce citizens' media allows them to engage in civic action, challenging neocolonial capitalist power structures. Building on her work, Bailey, Cammaerts and Carpentier (2007) propose four key dimensions to radical community media: they serve a community, function as an alternative to mainstream media, forge links with civil society and civic action from grassroots movements to policy change, and work as a partially visible rhizome. For example, in Colombia, community radio has been used to develop political consciousness, mobilising people to take action in their communities, engage in networking opportunities with neighbours through in-person interactions at the radio station, revealing the radical political functions of community radio beyond broadcasting (Murillo, 2003). Similarly, Radio Alice, which operated in Bologna in fascist Italy in the 1970s, brought people into the nearby radio station to broadcast public debates and promote civic action contesting fascism in Italy.

'Radio Alice actively challenged listener passivity and encouraged its audience members to become engaged in direct speech on the airwaves through relaying live call-ins aimed at unleashing strategic reports from the barricades, along with the unfiltered rage of protesters in the streets and the poetic laughter of the insurgent imagination in flight' (Langlois, Sakolsky & van der Zon, 2010, 6). In this sense, community radio functions as a public square to broadcast and amplify community conversations geared towards organising direct action and broadcasting from the scene of that action, directly challenging both media and state power. Due to transgressive content, community radio often faces repression by the state. Radio Alice, for example, was shut down and many activists arrested, charged with sedition (6).

Voice of the Voiceless

In terms of its function in generating transformative discursive representations, community, campus and other types of non-profit radio stations serve as the 'voice of the voiceless'. Communities that have been silenced, misrepresented, stereotyped or otherwise rendered voiceless by the regime of truth in a city, town or region can use broadcast radio stations to foster local voices, develop local skills in radio programming and production, and nurture leadership capacities. Speaking their own truth, communities create alternative discourses through conversations that they have together, and radio serves to amplify those conversations. For example, Radio Bubble, in Athens, Greece, broadcasting from its own café, served as a key organising hub during the 2011 anti-austerity protests, challenging the dominant discourse of the mainstream media about the inevitability of financial bailouts, and providing alternative economic discourses such as cooperative social economies, and mobilising people to take action against austerity measures (radiobubble.gr). While in Brazil, the MST or landless rural workers movement, active since the 1970s, has used local radio stations broadcasting from schools, their movement has also built to transmit important information not just about the movement to build consciousness around land use issues, but also to provide information regarding local seed distribution, road closures and other infrastructural or logistical information pertinent to the everyday life of their communities (Sartoretto). As Arundhati Roy indicates in the epigraph to this chapter, voicelessness is not natural or inevitable, but political and intentional on the side of the powerful who attempt to control discourse. Non-profit radio provides a space where people can quite literally speak together, combing to voice on the radio about what is happening in their communities, and develop the capacities to make change.

Pirate Radio

Pirate radio famously made an appearance in the cult classic, *American Graffiti*, where a DJ known as Wolfman Jack broadcasts music and aphorisms illegally from an unknown location. Where broadcast licences are not available, controlled by the state or prohibitively expensive, people have turned to pirate radio, broadcasting using home-made transmitters that can fit into a small tin, and thus can easily be transported to protests, located in a moving vehicle such as a car or bike, or hidden and moved to evade authorities. Pirate radio is an 'unlicensed form of radio broadcasting that relies on the airwaves for transmission' (Langlois, Sakolsky & van der Zon, 2010, 3) that embraces 'the radical imagination and the practice of direct action' (4), evading regulation, administration and sanctions by providing an entirely autonomous alternative. Its small size, easy construction and portability make it particularly appealing to activists wanting to set up temporary communications' alternatives. Pirate radio was particularly prevalent in the UK in the 1960s and 1970s, where activists set

346

up longer-term offshore radio stations on boats as an underground method of transmission, with programming ranging from radical political movement discourses to transgressive music genres. In the alterglobalisation movement in the 1990s and early 2000s, we saw evidence of 'the nomadic radio pirate strategically broadcasting the location and movements of the police to global justice activists during the heat of confrontation in the streets [that] engages in direct action by occupying the airwaves' (Langlois, Sakolsky & van der Zon, 2010, 4). While this tactic is now also used by livestreaming protest, discussed below, pirate radio has the advantage of still being viable if the state blocks or throttles the Internet during protests.

Podcasts

Today podcasts, or radio-like audio programmes streamed over the Internet, have emerged as a hybrid media form where people can easily record and upload interviews or other types of programming for a global audience. A noted podcast engaged in decolonising media on the east coast of Turtle Island (Canada) is Pjilasi Mi'kma'ki or Welcome to Mi'kma'ki, a bilingual Mi'kmaq and English podcast produced by a Mi'kmaq woman among communities engaged in anti-fracking activism in Elsipogtog.[2] The podcast covers issues such as the Sixties Scoop (the removal by the Canadian government of thousands of Indigenous children from their homes in the 1960s to be placed and raised in the homes of white people), title and treaty rights, the art and cultural relevance of baskets, and Indigenous governance models. By self-producing this knowledge from a position rooted within the community, deeper knowledge can be produced and shared with a broader audience. The use of the Mi'kmaq language develops trust and comfort levels among the interviewees, and recentres Indigenous experiences and voices largely absent in mainstream media. The Sixties Scoop podcast, for example, was picked up by various regional and national media, and the issue has now gained traction in the public sphere. As part of the radical media repertoire of communication, this particular podcast is rooted within social movement organising, exploring cutting-edge forms through its integral use of two languages and original soundscapes. Moreover, it generates new discursive and cognitive frames for understanding the deeply damaging impact of colonisation on children removed from their homes, thereby furthering anticolonial movements and decolonising media. Like pirate radio, podcasts operate as temporary autonomous media zones, carving out their own discursive political spaces outside the regulatory frameworks of TV and radio broadcast, transgressing national borders, and challenging media dominance by commercial radio.

Image

Activist art Posters

Posters put up in public spaces are used to promote radical ideas, mobilise social movement actions and as an outlet for creative expression. Challenging the capitalist logic of the art world and the utilitarian logic of some political organising, artist collectives and cooperatives produces art with social messages, as well as organising their artistic production in more liberatory, horizontal forms. Image-based systems produced by activists challenge the dominant image systems of mainstream media, with respect to social class, race, gender, sexuality, beauty myths and more. They are also used to both inform and mobilise activists to participate in political protests or events such as anarchist bookfairs. While this traditional mode of mobilisation often serves as the public face and aesthetic of social movements, it has not always been respected by radical activists and non-political artists alike. Activists often question the importance of art, labelling it an elite capitalist pursuit, while artists often critique political art for being too dogmatic. As Josh MacPhee and Erik Reuland, members of the Just Seeds Artists' Cooperative, explain, 'as anarchists, we have seen our politics denigrated by other artists; as artists, we have had our cultural production attacked as frivolous by activists' (2007, 3).[3] Just Seeds has produced a series of posters, for example, called 'Celebrating People's History' that depicts social movement struggles from the past and present. These posters produce alternative histories or histories from below through images that challenge dominant discourses on political issues.

Comic Journalism

Comic journalism is an art form frequently used by media activists to mobilise transformative discursive visual and textual representations. It subverts the expectations of comics by creating political and historical content, while also subverting the expectation that politics should be represented in formal texts. Joe Sacco, who first came to public attention with his critically acclaimed political graphic novel, *Palestine* (1997), has pioneered the form, building on the work of the underground comics scene (Worden, 2015). Culture jamming and political comic artists transform radical discourses into visual representations that combine print images with text to challenge hegemonic discourses and framing of issues. The comics collective, Dotterbolaget, is a radical queer transfeminist network of comic and graphic novel artists in Sweden (Dotterbolaget n.d.) that supports opportunities for their members to engage in creative cultural labour. A Dotterbolaget member, an indigenous woman from Chile living in Sweden, has engaged with members of the local immigrant community in her town to generate testimonials of their experiences around sexual violence, which were then sketched out as a comic with three versions of text in English, Swedish and Spanish. This comic challenges the silence, stigma, self-blame and victim blaming in experiences of sexual abuse, while integrating images and text, making it easy to read across cultures and literacy levels. Moreover, it engages new cognitive and discursive practices rooted in social movements engaged in intersectional politics considering sexual violence and sex work as often-racialised gender oppression in the context of social class, race, immigration and colonial relations.

Arts Collectives and Spaces

Radical political artists tend to organise themselves into collectives and arts spaces that reject not just the commercial imperative of artistic production but also the enforced isolation, and the concept of the lone genius artist, embracing instead practices of collaboration and resource sharing. In the US, for example, there is 'a growing community of radical artists [that includes] The Drawing Resistance traveling art show, the Beehive Collective poster project, the Celebrate People's History poster project and the Street Art Workers' (Stern 2007, 105). Many articulate the tension of wanting to make art against capitalism and having to survive in a capitalist economy. Courtney Daily, for example, would prefer to 'give things away or trade' (as cited in Stern, 2007, 106); Swoon says, 'I hate the idea of what I am making being narrowed down to its value as an object for investment or sale' (as cited in Stern, 2007, 106); Josh MacPhee argues that 'art should be affordable to people that are interested in it' (as cited in Stern, 2007, 106); and Chris Stain says that 'art becomes soulless and loses its value when produced for commercial purposes' (as cited in Stern, 2007, 106). Artist collectives challenge the individualist ideology of consumer capitalism by working cooperatively to produce artwork, sharing resources and eschewing the gallery system of elitist hegemonic art production and consecration. In Canada, the Ste-Emilie Skillshare is an example of a community arts space that was opened up by a small collective of antiracist queer and trans antiauthoritarian activists in Montreal to provide space for antiracist organisers to make art in support of social movements (Jeppesen et al., 2016). Serving as both a safe space and a creative workshop, artist collectives radicalise ownership forms and organisational structures of studios and the gallery system. Moreover, they attempt to find ways to share their work for free, through barter and gift economies, or by exhibiting it for free in public spaces.

Culture Jamming and Memes

According to Leah Lievrouw, culture jamming is one of five activist genres covered in her book, *Alternative and Activist New Media* (2011). It operates in the social domain of popular culture, particularly targeting corporate advertising, and takes the form of appropriated images and text that subvert the designer's original meaning with the objective of humorous cultural critique. Mark Dery refers to culture jamming as hoaxes that jam the empire of signs, and includes 'media hacking, information warfare, terror-art, and guerrilla semiotics' (1993) in the mix. Guerrilla semiotics is a term first coined by Umberto Eco (1987) to describe fighting back against dominant culture at the level of decoding signs and signifiers. Culture jamming has its roots even further back, as Lievrouw argues that 'what makes culture jamming distinctive as a genre of alternative/activist new media is that it "mines" mainstream culture to reveal and criticise its fundamental inequities, hypocrisies, and absurdities, very much in the tradition of Dada and the Situationists'. Memes are a very specific form of culture jamming that reference a whole host of cultural signifiers turning them towards a re-coded message, or what Jonah Peretti calls 'micromedia' (2001). While culture jamming has 'a degree of subversive power' (Lievrouw, 2011), it is open to reappropriation by mainstream media, and subject to 'the fragmentation and rapid turnover of ideas, images, and discourse' (Lievrouw, 2011). *Adbusters* magazine, the Billboard Liberation Front and the Surveillance Camera Players, who culture jammed magazine ads, billboards and surveillance cameras, respectively, remain classic examples of this form of radical media.

Video

Livestreaming Protest

'Video is increasingly used to communicate dissent' (Widgington, 2005, 107). Livestreaming of protests has become a mainstay in the radical repertoire of communication. Reporting and providing live commentary, video activists use technologies to document protest from the street, where the live-streamer is also participating in the protest. The livestream broadcast is thus not just a media tactic but also a protest tactic – a protest media tactic. Like the Mi'kmaq podcast, being rooted in the movement fosters authenticity and trust, closing the distance between the reporter and the reported. Ferguson Black Lives Matter (BLM) livestreamed the 2014 protests against the police shooting death of black teenager Michael Brown by a white police officer. Livestream activists, such as hip-hop artist and Clemson communications professor Chenjerai Kumanyika, participated in the demonstrations, livestreaming footage as protests unfolded. While livestreaming protest, activists maintain a constant video uplink, interact with audience members on the livestream channel and post the livestream link on social media using hybrid media forms to garner a wider audience. Kumanyika's livestream of the 2014 BLM Ferguson protests generated over twenty-thousand views (UMassAmherst, 2015; Kumanyika, 2015, 2016a, 2016b). This is a quintessential example of rooted reporting from within a social movement. Engaging a team of media activists in multiple locations, it reconfigures experimental technologies to propagate counter-hegemonic antiracist public discourses, reframes issues of anti-Black police brutality from the perspective of those directly affected and recentres marginalised or silenced voices largely absent from mainstream media. It also encourages viewers to participate in the action, by joining the protest, posting the link on social media or contributing live comments.

Activist Documentaries

Like livestream footage, activist documentaries provide alternative image-based narratives on issues that contest the current political and discursive regimes. Documentary has 'always claimed a particular place for itself in the process of media citizenship' (Dovey, 2014), providing space for civic engagement through the creating of more authentic image systems. Shifting towards the digital media ecology, digital documentaries generate greater participatory frameworks that 'constitute dynamic, mobile, generative experiences' for audience members as they 'can be linked to, liked, forward, promoted, posted' (Dovey, 2014). Moreover, 'The online documentary is contingent, mutable, dynamic: its meanings generated through the user's interactions with it' (2014). Our Planet TV, for example, in Tokyo, Japan, has been producing documentaries since 2001.[4] Their mandate is to produce documentaries that distribute information 'from the citizen's own standpoint' (About Us). They worked with director Oguma Eiji on the documentary film *Tell the Prime Minister* (2015) that provided an inside look at the antinuclear movement after the Fukushima reactor meltdown caused by the 2011 Tohoku earthquake and tsunami. This film innovatively integrated crowdsourced digital footage found online, including footage by videographers from OurPlanetTV, to create a collaborative grassroots documentary. The post-Fukushima antinuclear movement included a diverse array of social groups: 'These included farmers and fisher folk confronting radioactive contamination, housewives alert to the radioactive contamination of foodstuffs and the special risk to infants and children, intellectuals critical of nuclear power in an earthquake-prone nation, and other social groups' (Eiji, 2016). The diversity of perspectives in the crowdsourced-footage documentary benefits from shifts towards participatory, collaborative production. Traditional political documentary producers and collaborative crowdsourced footage such as *Tell the Prime Minister* can reframe dominant discursive regimes by circulating images and voices from global social struggles.

Video Activist Collectives

'It's important to note that an activist video is not by definition a documentary film that tries to capture a slice of reality by following real people through real events' (Widgington, 2005, 112), as formats, styles, contributors, objectives and organising structures vary greatly. Many video activist collectives organise themselves horizontally. Integrated into grassroots non-hierarchical social movements, video activists engage in similar organising strategies and structures. 'Video activism reaches beyond video making. It also delves into the process of organizing by forming collective structures to assist in the production and distribution of activist videos' (Widgington, 2005, 105). At video activist film screenings, such as those organised by *Cinema Politica*, 'the largest volunteer-run, community and campus-based documentary-screening network in the world', the format of the screening challenges the film industry's capitalist logic. Entry is free or by donation; activist groups table outside the cinema with flyers, posters, zines, books, patches and other media; and participants appearing in the film may be present at the screening as they themselves are activists there to discuss how people can support their movement. Video activist collectives thus challenge the mainstream capitalist logic of the film industry, organising as anticapitalists; producing social change through more socially just image systems and changing social relationships from the ground up by bridging the distance between who appears in films, who participates in social movements and who has access to representation. Closing this gap is a direct challenge to Guy Debord's 'society of the spectacle' where images seen on-screen are critically analysed as distant mind-numbing representations of constructed desires impossible to reach, thus crushing the viewer's capacity for desire and even life itself.

Sousveillance

Radical activists have long used photography and video activism to document direct actions, using footage of arrests to exonerate activists in court. Citizens also use video cameras to document police violence, starting with the controversial case of Rodney King, a taxi driver whose beating by four LAPD officers in 1991was filmed by a community member in a nearby building, forwarded to a news station and shown worldwide. One of the earliest cases of police *sousveillance* by bystanders, the video nonetheless was insufficient to convict the officers. With the advent of ubiquitous cell phone cameras, media activists have been using reverse surveillance or *sousveillance* to hold the police accountable for their actions (Abu-Laban, 2015; Stole, Williams, Mitchell & Pandell, 2016), reversing the act of putting citizens under surveillance by turning the eye of the camera on the powerful. The police shooting of Alton Sterling on July 5, 2016 followed by the police shooting of Philando Castile on July 6, 2016 were both livestreamed to social media. The people close to the victims were powerless to prevent the death, but documented unfolding events, images which generated media power and mobilised widespread protests (Stole et al., 2016).[5] Functioning in the digital domain, *sousveillance* reclaims the storytelling function of mass media by distributing a direct account of events, circumventing not just the editorial gatekeeping and framing function of mainstream journalism but also bypassing police spokesperson structures that can hide actions behind the blue line, the so-called brotherhood of police unions and internal self-investigation. *Sousveillance* has also been used by a group at Goldsmiths University in London, UK to show wrongdoing by those in positions of power in the case of the 'left to die' boat – a refugee ship in the Mediterranean 'in which sixty-three migrants lost their lives while drifting for fourteen days within the NATO maritime surveillance area' (Forensic Architecture, 2012; Heller, n.d.). A data justice research team was able to use this surveillance data to implicate NATO and other ships in the area. 'The Forensic Oceanography report turned the knowledge generated through surveillance means into evidence of responsibility for the crime of nonassistance' (Forensic Architecture, 2012). Forensically analysed state surveillance data were used to charge the state with wrongdoing in sixty-three refugee deaths.

Online

Connective Action

New affordances of participatory culture in the era of digitisation include affiliation, expression, collaborative problem-solving and circulations (Jenkins, 2006). These lend themselves as well to social movement mobilisations that can be participated in by millions of people who do not know each other, have a language in common and will never be at the same event. Nonetheless, the mobilisation frames and political demands and actions will be synchronised and coordinated through participatory culture. Bennett and Segerberg have found that the pre-network-society logic of collective action has been supplanted by what they call the logic of connection action (2012). Their study of the Indignados or 15M movement in Spain was based on a rejection of political parties, unions and other powerful groups, and a turn towards 'the richly layered digital and interpersonal communication networks centering around the media hub of *Democracia real YA!*' (Bennett & Segerberg, 2012, 741) and the on-the-ground organising of protest camps in the squares, what Paolo Gerbaudo calls the hybrid strategy of 'tweets and the streets' (2012). Eschewing collective action frames, these new digital protest networks instead provide 'interactive digital media and easy-to-personalize action themes' (742) such as the Indignados or 'indignant ones' of the 15M movement, or 'We are the 99%' of the Occupy movement. These connective action frames are then powerfully mobilised through social media distribution, and some groups in Spain such as XNet were able to both establish an emotional or affective connection for participants, and to hack the algorithms of Facebook and Twitter to create trending topics on these two and other social media platforms. Further digital opportunities include website organisations, event notices, distribution networks and reposted links, among others (753). These online strategies provide not just media networks but participatory structures for communicative action that are peer to peer and face to face rather than top-down and authoritarian.

Transmedia Mobilisations

The theory and practices of connective action take it as given that activists will have recourse to and be engaged in producing a multiplicity of media genres, types and styles. These can be both analogue and digital, and they can be produced by anyone in the movement, and shared hand to hand in person or peer to peer online. This multiplicity of media, Costanza-Chock notes, is transmediated: 'Transmedia mobilization involves engaging the social base of the movement in participatory media making practices across multiple platforms… produc[ing] multimodal movement narratives that reach and involve diverse audiences' (Costanza-Chock, 2011, 113). Transmedia mobilisations create, share, remix, repost, comment and redistribute all genres of media, 'strengthening movement identity formation and outcomes' (113). For example, photocopied anarchafeminist zines may be scanned and uploaded to an activist blog or website as a downloadable PDF, and then shared via Facebook, linked via Twitter, images can be shared on Instagram, etc. The Occupy movement is an excellent example of how this works: 'Media practices within Occupy are marked by extensive offline, analogue, poster and print based, and "low-tech" forms of media production, in parallel with cutting-edge technology development and use (autonomous wireless networks, hackathons, creation of new tools and platforms). In many cases, Occupy activists make and circulate media elements across platforms (including analogue media forms and channels)' (Costanza-Chock, 2012, 378). Transmedia mobilisations are a form of intensifying collective intelligence where the discursive shifts and new knowledge produced in total are much greater than the sum of the parts. As activists at distributed geographical locations engage with each other's multimodal media repertoires of contention and communication, global movements benefit from and contribute to the collective shift in the dominant regime of truth.

Translocal 'Banner' Mobilisations

This global collective shift is also reflected in what Uri Gordon calls 'banner' movements, or movements organising under the same banner (Gordon, 2008, 12–15) where activists 'may be on the other side of the world, but they do not require a club, a party, or a shared ideological frame to make the connection' (Bennett & Segerberg, 2012, 753). The exchange of ideas, movement frames, analysis, political demands and action repertoires results in what I am calling translocal mobilisations, defined as a local social movement action that is part of a global mobilisation using recognisably similar repertoires of contention and communication, and shifting them to suit their specific local situation. SlutWalk is an example of a feminist translocal mobilisation that first emerged in Toronto, Canada in 2011 after a police officer told women at York University that to combat rape they should 'avoid dressing like sluts' (Carr, 2013, 24). Toronto activists organised the first SlutWalk against rape culture – defined as the predominance of social attitudes and behaviours that normalise sexual harassment, abuse and rape – with subsequent SlutWalks in over fifty cities. For example, in Delhi, India, to protest targeted rapes of call centre workers, educated women or women who go out at night, as well as other issues such as female infanticide and honour killings, activists organised a SlutWalk campaign demanding that women have the right to safety and respect. However, protesters were encouraged to dress 'normally', dropping the locally controversial emphasis on the so-called slutty clothing (Carr, 2013, 26). Similarly in London, UK, a group called 'Hijabs, Hoodies & Hotpants' joined a breakaway march within the SlutWalk protest, with participants emphasising that rape 'has absolutely nothing to do with what you wear, and loads of women that are covered head to toe get raped' (Lim & Fanghanel, 2013, 9). The banner of SlutWalk thus spreads as a translocal mobilisation, with critiques of global rape culture translated into locally powerful messages and movements. Structurally, nobody owns SlutWalk; rather, many groups have taken up this banner to mobilise on their own terms in ways that have challenged not just global rape culture but also the dominance of Western liberal feminism.

Technopolitics

Technopolitics can be defined as 'a complex blend of technological knowledge and digital expertise used for radical political purposes with the technology itself seen as a site of contestation' (Treré et al., 2017, 413). Technopolitics emphasises antiauthoritarian or anarchist horizontal social processes utilised within the free culture, open source and hacker movements, while extending radical activist technological practices engaged by programmers, social media platform users and other so-called freedom technologists (Postill, 2016). While some technopolitics activists focus on hacking the Facebook, Twitter and other algorithms, others emphasise movement ownership of ICTs including social movement websites. The Spanish Indignados are well known for their technopolitics practices (Toret et al., 2013). They used collaborative authoring strategies, where online document sharing enabled activists to co-author documents without being co-present to develop analysis, discuss policy and more, attributing new knowledge and ideas to the movement, thus challenging the enclosure of knowledge by sharing it for free and not claiming individual authorship, ownership or copyright, rejecting the notion of activist superstars or intellectuals and instead focusing on collective intelligence. Some groups participating in the Indignados also used Titan pads to take minutes at general assemblies, providing publicly accessible documentation of collective decision-making. Most importantly, activists have long asserted the importance of movement ownership of digital media platforms; building on this, technopolitical strategies emphasise ownership models of websites, blogs and platforms, so their work does not profit capitalist media conglomerates. 'By creating independent communication infrastructure, activists seek to contribute to the efforts of contemporary progressive social movements to shape the world according to principles of justice, equality, and participation' (Milan, 2013, 2). This ownership model usually also means that the radical media outlet or platform will be organised in an intersectional anticapitalist way, against hierarchies, with consensus decision-making, task rotation, skill and resource sharing, and often a great deal of unpaid communicative labour, disavowing the economic imperatives of mainstream media.

Conclusion: Radical Media Contradictions and Challenges

The Contradiction of Social Media

The Benefit of Participation

Social media platforms, such as Facebook, Instagram, SnapChat and Twitter, facilitate interactive media content production and distribution among millions of users worldwide. They offer a sense of empowerment through participatory interaction, and have been touted as key to the success of movements such as the Arab Spring being dubbed the 'Twitter Revolution' by some. For example, in the Greek Indignados or Aganaktismenoi movement, the original call to occupy Syntagma Square in Athens went out in a Facebook post, and one of the main sites of mobilisation and debate was the Facebook page of the Indignados of Syntagma Square.

The Exploitation of Capitalist Ownership

Based on Antonio Negri's concept of the social factory, media activists understand digital media 'as a form of free labour exploited and appropriated for capital accumulation by corporations, brands and advertising' (Dovey, 2014). For example, when users post content on Facebook, they assign its copyright to Facebook, while generating personal metadata through the social reward system of Likes, which is mined, aggregated and sold to advertisers (Cohen, 2013). Facebook generated $17.1 billion in ad revenue in 2015, and in 2016, it made $5.2 billion in the first quarter (Seetharaman, 2016), 80% from mobile ads (Kokalitcheva, 2015).[6] Thus, social media activists directly generate profits for social media corporations, without receiving any payment for this work. Moreover, they are directly supporting a capitalist political economy of social media through their movement work against capitalism. Social media labour has a gendered and racialised dimension, as women, queer and trans, and people of colour turn increasingly to social media as their voices are excluded from mainstream media; however, their work risks being appropriated for the profit of white males (Jeppesen et al., forthcoming).

The Threat of Police Surveillance

Social media users are vulnerable to police surveillance, as dialogues, debates, action plans and personal locations are publicly available on platforms, and have been scraped by the police to trace and prosecute activists. 'The dangers posed by public discussions, organisations, and networks being observed, monitored, archived and censored by corporate enterprises have serious implications for cyber activism and for social movement organizing online'

(Flesher Fominaya & Gillan, 2017, 389). Sometimes, this plays a role in predictive policing, informing decisions to pre-emptively arrest protest organisers before mass convergences. Social media data can also be invoked in court cases against activists.

The Success of Algorithm Hacking

Technopolitics activists in the Spanish Indignados discovered how the Facebook and Twitter algorithms worked, developing and sharing coordinated plans to collectively exploit or 'ride the algorithm', so that their posts and reposts would go viral. These practices were skill-shared horizontally, making them available beyond the small sphere of tech-savvy activists (Toret et al., 2013; Treré et al., 2017).

The Challenge of Sustainable Funding

Radicalising Resource Strategies

Rejecting most forms of advertising, radical media projects need to develop resources through nontraditional sources and practices. Using digital platforms, some turn to crowd-funding, with specific guidelines to ensure funding is consistent with the political content of their media. Other media collectives will engage in ethical advertising, partnering with groups they share values with. Yet, others will engage in resource sharing with like-minded groups, tabling at each other's events, sharing offices or mentoring new activists in media production, horizontal processes and anti-oppression practices.

Disavowing the Economic

Pierre Bourdieu (1993) argues that avant-garde producers will often disavow the economic imperative of cultural production, preferring to produce for an engaged audience who are also producers, and eschewing the need to make money from their work. In radical media, this disavowal has two implications: first, the media producer must have an outside means of economic support, and second, there are non-capitalist avenues for producing, distributing and valuing media. Not legitimated by mainstream journalist organisations, radical media is self-legitimating, dependent on a *produser* audience, a radical political community that generates and consumes content.

Paid vs. Unpaid Labour

Disavowing the economic means some radical media projects consider media production a labour of love, rather than paid employment. Strike, for example, an alternative journalism project in London, UK that produces both a website and a newspaper, do not pay people for media work, as they believe people should write for strictly political reasons. Other projects, such as the Bristol Cable, a radical newspaper produced in Bristol, UK, believe that it is important to pay alternative journalists; they generate funds through monthly sustainer donations as small as £1–2 and are continuously increasing the number of hours per week they can pay employees for. Some projects incorporate anti-oppression or decolonisation politics into their decisions regarding who should be paid for media labour. For example, Ricochet Media in Canada, an online news source, ran a successful Indigenous Reporting crowdfunding campaign as a decolonising media practice.

The Controversy of Grants

Some alternative media producers can sometimes gain access to public or private grants to fund their projects on a temporary basis. These grants are controversial for several reasons. Media activists who are antistate might question the legitimacy of the state as a funder for their work, as it may limit their capacity to critique the state, or in other words, their political media content would have to be toned down or they might risk losing their funding. Media activists with critiques of corporate or private funding schemes might similarly question the ethics of the funder and their potential demand to censor or control editorial output or organisational structures. For example, Indymedia was at one point offered a substantial grant from the Ford Foundation; however, the international network came to consensus to reject the funding as they had serious critiques of the ethics and politics of Ford (Lievrouw, 2011). On the other hand, some media projects find that grants are an excellent way to access short-term funding for specific initiatives, and moreover they may believe that taxpayers should fund alternative media organisations. For example, Ricochet Media in Canada was successfully able to access funds from the City of Vancouver to report on homelessness in the city. Some media activists find grants very difficult to access, and have experienced racialised and/or gendered biases in the selection process and outcomes (Jeppesen et al., 2018).

Conclusion

What emerges in this brief sketch of the five genres of radical media and their approaches to social movements, representations, structures and digital networks is a complex series of critiques of the current media ecology undertaken through radicalising and perhaps even revolutionising media production practices. Rather than orienting themselves towards the economic imperative of mainstream media, radical alternative media do not just focus on generating alternative representations in content. They contravene and call into question the so-called objectivity of representation touted by the mainstream, support social movement representations, develop organisational structures focused on self-determination and horizontalism, and engage in participatory digital networks from grassroots power-sharing perspectives. The VOID Network in Athens, Greece offers an excellent example of this. In existence for more than thirty years now, they operate with the objective of generating excellent cultural outputs that can effectively showcase the talents within their community. They do this through organising massive cultural events such as hip-hop or techno shows with thousands of participants, and by developing community-owned and -run infrastructure, such as squatted theatre spaces, thereby developing social or sharing economies that are community rather than profit-oriented and generating prefigurative explorations of the possible or 'an image from the future'.

Notes

1 http://indigenousrising.org/.
2 https://pjilasimikmaki.wordpress.com/.
3 justseeds.org.
4 ourplanet-tv.org.
5 cinemapolitica.org.
6 statistia.com.

References

Abu-Laban, Y. (2015). Gendering Surveillance Studies: The Empirical and Normative Promise of Feminist Methodology. *Surveillance & Society* 13(1): 44–56.

Atton, C. (2002). *Alternative Media*. London: Sage.

Bailey, O., Cammaerts, B. & Carpentier, N. (2007). *Understanding Alternative Media*. New York: Open University Press.

Bennett, L. & Segerberg, A. (2012). The Logic of Connective Action: Digital Media and the Personalization of Contentious Politics. *Information, Communication & Society* 15(5): 739–768.

Bourdieu, P. (1993). *The Field of Cultural Production*. New York: Columbia UP.

Carr, J.L. (2013). The SlutWalk Movement: A Study in Transnational Feminist Activism. *Journal of Feminist Scholarship* 4 (Spring): 24–38.

Cohen, N.S. (2013). Commodifying Free Labour Online: Social Media, Audiences, and Advertising. In M. P. McAllister & E. West (Eds.), *The Routledge Companion to Advertising and Promotional Culture*. London: Routledge, pp. 177–191.

Costanza-Chock, S. (2011). *Se ve, se siente: Transmedia mobilization in the Los Angeles immigrant rights movement*. Dissertation, USC.

Costanza-Chock, S. (2012). Mic Check! Media Cultures and the Occupy Movement. *Social Movement Studies* 11(3–4): 375–385.

Dotterbolaget (nd). www.dotterbolaget.com/ [Accessed June 22, 2017].

Dovey, J. (2014). Documentary Ecosystems: Collaboration and Exploitation. In K. Nash, C. Hight & C. Summerhayes (eds.), *New Documentary Ecologies: Emerging Platforms, Practices and Discourses*. New York: Palgrave Macmillan, pp. 11–32.

Downing, J. (1984) 2001. *Radical Media*. London: Sage.

Eiji, Oguma (2016). A New Wave Against the Rock: New Social Movements in Japan since the Fukushima Nuclear Meltdown. Translated by Alexander Brown. http://apjjf.org/2016/13/Oguma.html [Accessed Nov 6, 2017].

Flesher Fominaya, C. & Gillan, K. (2017). Navigating the Technology-Media-Movements Complex. *Social Movement Studies* 16(4): 383–402.

Forensic Architecture (2012). The Left-To-Die Boat. www.forensic-architecture.org/case/left-die-boat/ [Accessed November 7, 2017].

Gerbaudo, P. (2012). *Tweet and the Streets: Social Media & Contemporary Activism*. London: Pluto Press.

Gordon, U. 2008. *Anarchy Alive!: Anti-Authoritarian Politics from Practice to Theory*. London: Pluto Press.

Heller, C. Liquid Traces: The Left-To-Die Boat Case. https://vimeo.com/89790770.

Heller, C., Pezzani, L. & Situ Studio (nd). Report on the 'Left-To-Die Boat'. London: Forensic Architecture.

Jenkins, H. 2006. *Convergence Culture: Where Old and New Media Collide*. New York and London: NYU Press.

Jeppesen, S., Kruzynski, A., Lakoff, A. & Sarrasin, R. (2014). Grassroots Autonomous Media Practices: A Diversity of Tactics. *Journal of Media Practice* 15(1): 21–38.

Jeppesen, S. (2016). 'Direct-Action Journalism: Resilience in Grassroots Autonomous Media', *Journal of Applied Journalism & Media Studies* 5(3): 383–403.

Jeppesen, S. & Petrick, K. 2018. Toward An Intersectional Political Economy of Autonomous Media Resources. *Interface: A Journal for and About Social Movements* 10(1–2): 8–37.

Kokalitcheva, K. (2015). Mobile is Facebook's Cash Cow. July 29, 2015. *Fortune* http://fortune.com/2015/07/29/facebook-mobile-ad-revenue/ [Accessed August 18, 2016].

Kumanyika, C. (2015). Vocal Color in Public Radio. http://transom.org/2015/chenjerai-kumanyika/ [Accessed June 22, 2017].

——— (2016a). Policing and the 'War on Black Bodies'. *College Literature: A Journal of Critical Literary Studies* 43(1): 252–258.

——— (2016b). Learn How to Livestream at Social Justice Events. Media Activism Research Conference. www.youtube.com/watch?v=oxRr-aEmDvI.

Langlois, A., Sakolsky, R. & van der Zon, M. (2010). *Islands of Resistance: Pirate Radio in Canada*. Vancouver: New Star Books.

Lievrouw, L. 2011. *Alternative and Activist New Media*. Polity.

Lim, J. & Fanghanel, A. (2013). 'Hijabs, Hoodies and Hotpants': Negotiating the 'Slut' in SlutWalk. *Geoforum* 48: 207–215.

Milan, S. (2013). *Social Movements and Their Technologies: Wiring Social Change*. Springer.

Murillo, M. (2003). Community Radio in Colombia: Civil Conflict, Popular Media and the Construction of a Public Sphere. *Journal of Radio Studies* 10 (1): 120–140.

Postill, J. (2013). *Spain's Indignados and the Mediated Aesthetics of Nonviolence*. Melbourne: RMIT University.

Seetharaman, D. (2016). Facebook Revenue Soars on Ad Growth. *The Wall Street Journal*. April 28, 2016. www.wsj.com/articles/facebook-revenue-soars-on-ad-growth-1461787856 [Accessed August 12, 2016].

Stern, M. (2007). Subversive Multiples: A Conversation between Contemporary Printmakers. In J. MacPheee & E. Reuland (eds.), *Realizing the Impossible: Art against Authority*. Oakland: AK Press, pp. 105–199.

Stole, B., Williams, B., Mitchell, M. & Pandell, L. (2016). The Power of Livestreaming in America. *WIRED* December issue. www.wired.com/2016/11/black-lives-matter-social-media-witnesses-three-days-of-police-brutality/ [Accessed November 7, 2017].

Sunkel, O. & Girvan, C. (1973). Transnational Capitalism and National Disintegration in Latin America. *Social and Economic Studies* 22(1): 132–176.

Toret, J., Calleja, A., Datanalysis, M, Marin Miro, O., Aragon, P., Aguilera, M. & Lumbreras, A. (2013). *Tecnopolitica: la potencia de las multitudes conectadas. El Sistema red 15M, un nuevo paradigma de la politica distribuida*. Internet Interdisciplinary Institute Working Paper Series, Universitat Oberta de Catalunya.

Treré E., Jeppesen S. & Mattoni A. (2017). Comparing Digital Protest Media Imaginaries: Anti-austerity Movements in Greece, Italy & Spain. *Triple C: Communication, Capitalism & Critique* 15(2): 406–424.

UMassAmherst (2015). All Voices Matter: Real Talk about Diversity in Public Radio with Chenjerai Kumanyika. www.honors.umass.edu/event/all-voices-matter-real-talk-about-diversity-public-radio-chenjerai-kumanyika [Accessed June 20, 2017].

Widgington, D. (2005). Screening the Revolution Faqs about Video Activism. In A. Langlois & F. Dubois (eds.), *Autonomous Media*. Montreal: Cumulus Press, pp. 103–122.

Worden, D. (2015). (Ed). *The Comics of Joe Sacco: Journalism in a Visual World*. Jackson: University Press of Mississippi.

3.9

ANARCHIST PUBLISHING

An Interview with Ramsey Kanaan

Ramsey Kanaan

The interviews were conducted on August 23 and September 11 2017.

Part 1. The Publishing Landscape c. 1960 to the Present Day

RUTH KINNA: How did you get involved in publishing?

RAMSEY KANAAN: In 1979 I discovered punk rock and politics. That politics was anarchism. What drew me to punk rock and anarchism was very similar. I had a fairly nuanced view of what anarchism was by the time I was 13. I could not only define myself as an anarchist but I was also aware that I was an anarchist as opposed to a Labour party supporter or Marxist. I did not come from a political family except that from being a toddler onwards I grew up in a house full of books and I was always encouraged to read. While I decided I was an anarchist I hadn't read anything about anarchism as such, but I had read a wide variety of literature. By the time I was 13, I had read many of the classics of literature: Orwell's *1984* and *Animal Farm*, Camus, Aldous Huxley. I'm assuming it was my interpretation of that canon of classic literature that gave me my definition of anarchism and demarcated me from other left and right groups.

Punk rock was the first form of music that I actively listened to. Punk rock was a weird mix of being mainstream and not mainstream. All the bands were all on *Top of the Pops*.[1] I grew up watching the mainstream bands: UK Subs, The Damned, The Clash, Crass. And they were also all on Radio 1,[2] albeit John Peel.[3] Britain was unusual because punk rock also had a national music press: *New Musical Express*, *Sounds*, *Melody Maker*. They covered even the more radical underground stuff.

The important thing is that punk had this whole DIY, so-called do-it-yourself thing. This is actually an incredible individualist misnomer, because it's not doing it yourself, it's quite the opposite: it's actually doing it in concert with others. DIY meant doing one's own concerts, media, the rebirth of the fanzine, underground literature; putting out your own records. I was an active part of that very politicised subculture.

Looking back on it, the politics of anarcho-punk, the politics of Crass[4] had little to do with anarchism. It was an angry, very articulate militant liberalism – meaning they were very big on single issues. Crass pretty much popularised CND but the issues that they took were middle class issues: they were vegetarian, they were against war. Their concept of anarchism was woolly, at best, and their interactions with the anarchists at that time were minimal and mutually hostile. But Crass were a gateway drug.

My first encounter with anarchist literature was on a CND march in 1979. It was a copy of *Xtra!*, a very inflammatory, incendiary publication, explicitly anarchist with an anarchist politics, what you'd now call a direct action politics. I bought it because it was sold by punk rockers: whatever the problematic of those subcultures, they were gateway drugs to me.

Because I was in a band, I was involved in these underground distribution and dissemination networks. We produced our own music and more important for me, in terms of publishing, literature. We were being interviewed by fanzines and very early on I asked for copies to sell. In 1980–81, I became the guy who walked around with a poly bag selling fanzines. Purely by chance I was in London at a Crass concert with my poly bag and I saw some guys from Housmans[5] tabling the event. It seemed like a better way of selling literature than the plastic bag so I began pestering them with my questions. From then on, I went down to London every school holiday and hung out at Housmans.

Housmans really was, for me personally and for the wider anarchist milieu the linchpin. It's difficult to overstate its importance. It was the hub for the dissemination for radical literature in the UK. Not only did they have two full floors of radical literature, they were a major distributor. They imported radical books from the States. They were the distributor for Black Rose, Black and Red.[6] They disseminated *Society of the Spectacle* in the UK.[7] Not only did they have physical space and distribution, they also did publishing. A lot of it was Tolstoyan, peace activist literature but several of the individuals who worked at Housmans did publishing of their own. These guys were doing all the things I had ever fantasised or dreamed about or hadn't yet imagined was possible. In a very real sense they mentored me in the ways of distribution and publishing. And they enabled me. The first things I published as AK Press were co-publications with some of these people.[8] If it hadn't been for Housmans, AK wouldn't have existed. Nothing ever happens in a vacuum.

RKI: Can you tell me about the publishing environment?

RKA: This was all happening in the early 80s at the tail end of the 60s when there was something like 52 or 54 self-identified radical bookstores in the UK. These were booksellers with brick and mortar store fronts. In the early 80s Edinburgh had a generic radical bookstore called The First of May,[9] it had a women's bookstore and it had an antinuclear bookstore. This was replicated in major and minor cities all over the UK. Today in the UK, there are maybe six such self-identified radical bookstores left.

Radical literature, in fact, any and all literature, rises and falls with social movements. If you look at history, the first great outpouring of literature, both radical and reactionary, was the English Revolution. Not only did the English civil war produce the Digger tracts and the Leveller tracts it also produced a whole range of writing in reaction to that, Royalist tracts. The next great outpouring of literature was around the French Revolution. At that time Tom Paine's *Common Sense* sold 100,000 copies in the UK alone. That's in a population of about 6 million, the vast majority of whom were illiterate. That's astounding. It would be astounding today. Edmund Burke was equally a bestseller. The same is true in France. The period before and after the Revolution produced in a massive outpouring of literature. In the late nineteenth/early twentieth century, [Peter] Kropotkin's best-selling pamphlet, *An Appeal to the Young*, also sold over 100,000 copies.

The last great upsurge of social movements was the 60s. The 50-odd UK bookstores that existed in the 1980s were the end result of the massive social movements of the 60s and the 70s. These engendered the radical literature they sold. Before there was a women's movement, there wasn't women's literature. It didn't exist conceptually or physically or any other way. Before there was gay liberation there wasn't any gay literature. The concept didn't exist. Not only did the movements of the 60s and 70s create all these ideas, they also created a literature and then, typically, they had to create the means or the wherewithal to disseminate them. There was a growth of independent publishing and then the growth of independent distributors and the growth of these, in effect, movement bookstores. Ever since then, social movements and the left in general have been in decline. During our lifetime, all of our active lives, it has been fighting these defensive, rearguard actions, trying to hang on to the gains made by these social movements.

RKI: How have things changed since you started?

RKA: Publishing, of any stripe, is never commercially viable. It's always subsidised by someone – universities, the state or wealthy individuals. Newspaper publishers, of the left or the right, put up their money to publish. Publishing was always known as the gentlemen's profession because it was always subsidised by rich gentlemen, irrespective of their political persuasions. Whatever publishers did – whether it was for the Left Book Club[10] or Paine or whatever – they published for the cause. The cause could be self-advancement or social justice but publishing meant that you put up the dough.

There were three stages to the mortal wound to media in general and publishing in particular. First, in the 80s, most famously with Rupert Murdoch, big corporations started buying up publishing houses. These venerable institutions used to be independent publishing houses and hence used to subsidising it. Partly because of that, partly because it's not commercially viable it was always very badly paid – hence a lot of women were always involved in publishing. So in the 80s when the big bastards moved in and started buying up everything the first thing they did was send in the accountants and then they suddenly realised that it's actually not commercially viable. The concentration in publishing was typical: mergers and acquisitions are never expansions, they're always contractions. People get laid off. The first big blow to publishing in the 80s was that, with the concentration of many independent publishers to a few big ones, everyone was laid off, including the authors.

The old logic of publishing was that you were investing in the ideas, you were investing in an author. You hoped that the authors would break out on their third novel, hence you'd build their career, their reputation. All that went out the window. If authors were selling a couple of thousand books a year that's wasn't making the publishers any money, they cancelled the contract and put the books out of print. That was an attack on the way things had been done previously, for 100 years.

Second, the same thing happened in terms of distribution and dissemination: it was the rise of the chain bookstores. In America, it was Barnes and Noble and Borders, and in the UK, it was Waterstones. They not only opened up on the high street opposite the old bookstores, they also aggressively discounted books and, to get the customer base, initially did the things that independent bookstores used to do because it was popular at the time. So in the 80s, Waterstones would be full of Gandhi biographies because the film had just come out. Stuff that you could previously only get at Housmans or wherever was suddenly available on your high street. You could get your gay literature, you could get your feminist literature. You could buy Marge Piercy, Ursula le Guin. Of course, as soon as all the independents had gone, Waterstones stopped carrying this stuff. So there was an attack on the supply side.

Third, publishing is based on the rise and fall of literacy. Understandably, across the world and throughout history, radical movements have always placed a great prize on literacy – translating the Bible from Latin to make it available to everyone or taking control of the printing press to disseminate propaganda. The reason that radical ideas are fucked at the moment and the media in general is completely fucked is because the lack of social movements, the constraints put on these different forms of subsidies and the fall in adult literacy. This fall is both in real terms, in literal terms, because of education, teaching and so forth (the average person that goes to prison has the reading age of an eight year old), and also in behavioural terms. The fact is that people no longer read.

The idea that Amazon killed the book trade is not true. The rise of the Internet was the final nail, though it was already walking wounded by then. The average age of people consuming media keeps rising. If you were in America 10–15 years ago the average age of someone who listened to the radio, read a book, subscribed to a magazine, was fifty-five. That's the average age. The typical age is actually much higher. The problem is not just that people are not reading anymore, but they're not listening either – people don't listen to music anymore. In the year 2000 before downloading became ubiquitous, when CDs were still king and hundreds of millions of CDs were sold every year in America, CD sales were outstripped by video games. More people were consuming video games than there were listening to music, of any genre, whether Beethoven or Crass. The average person under forty was doing neither, nor listening to the radio. They were playing video games. This has only got worse. In America, figures for total book sales in the last ten years (meaning in all formats, e-books and hardcopy), have fallen in every single category, every category of fiction, whether its romance, science fiction, literature and every non-fiction category: academic, trade, general. It's fallen every year for the last ten years. So when I say people are not reading, I mean that in a literal sense. And this is at the same time that, with the digital age, there's more stuff than ever before. There's millions of books being published every year and less and less of it being consumed.

RKI: How have these changes affected what you do?

RKA: Over the last thirty-five years, during the period when all these disasters have happened in the industry, PM[11] sales have pretty much remained the same. When I first started publishing in the early 80s the average print run of an AK Press book was somewhere between 2000–4000 copies. That is still the case today. The difference is how we are able to sell them.

In one sense publishing is easy and it's become easier with the advancement of technologies – the desktop publishing revolution and then going digital made things easier. If you're willing to take the time, energy and effort it's not difficult to produce something that's really good. The role of the publisher and the challenges of a publisher are twofold: one is to find the good stuff – the curatorial role; and once found, to make it as good as it can be. The other is dissemination. How do you get the good stuff out there? The answer is a social movement. That means finding venues. In the days when there were still record stores we were very successful in selling our literature in there. We've been very active in tabling at rock concerts – Housmans were doing it long before I was – we went on tour with bands, attending bookfairs.

RKI: Some people would say that the anarchist movement is healthier now than it has been since the sixties. You seem to be suggesting that this is misleading?

RKA: Anarchism since the 60s has been the only game in town for young people. The mainstream left, the parliamentary left, the extraparliamentary-Leninist left has basically been irrelevant. Crass boasted that they kick-started or revitalised CND. And I think that's not an empty boast. Punk rock in the 80s energised and politicised a generation – my generation – but that has continued and anarchism has been the only game in town for the last forty years. Compare the London Radical Bookfair, which was a pretty quiet affair in 2017, to the Anarchist Bookfair and it's probably ten times the size in terms of attendees and two or three times the size in terms of people tabling at the venue.[12] And the same is true in America. But the problem that anarchism has faced since the Second World War is its inability to actually organise and to institutionalise.

In terms of radical publishing, the 60s had these institutions. It had its independent distributors, its independent publishers, its independent bookstores. Virtually all of them have gone. So the fact that anarchism is the only game in town has actually been despite anybody's effort. When we publish, when we are able to disseminate that strikes a chord. When we organise a bookfair people come to it and when we attempt to organise and when we do actually organise, it's wildly successful. Whether it's the sales of *Class War*,[13] whether it's the Anti-poll tax movement, whether it's the J20.[14] When anarchists actually organise it usually big and it's usually pretty damn successful, as opposed to when the rest of the left tries to organise.

My crowning achievement is boring persistence. AK and now PM have succeeded because I'm willing to do it, able to do it and still doing it. But I can't think of many other institutions, if a publishing house is an institution. We on the left are still trundling along with institutions that were built decades before, typically by members of the Communist Party or the Quakers. Housmans only exists because the Quakers bought the building 100 years ago. Anarchists have had successes but we've built very little.

RKI: What should anarchists be doing?

RKA: Any student of anarchist history will tell you that the Spanish Revolution and the Spanish anarchists were successful only because they spent forty years organising and building institutions – Ferrerian radical education, building the union structures, the neighbourhood organisations – so on, at all levels.[15] Whether it's building your publishing houses, your means, your wherewithal to do anything comes through slow, patient building of institutions and structures.

The reason that the SWP in the UK or the ISO[16] in America gets thousands of recruits every year – even if they leave after nine months – is because they have the structures, typically on university campuses. People who are interested in radical stuff can gravitate towards them. If you're interested in anarchism, what do you do? Where do you go? How d'you find out about it? I found out about it because I was a voracious reader and my entry into politics was through punk.

One of the bizarre things about punk rock it that it remains that gateway drug into politics. People who were not born when Crass had already broken up (1984) are discovering radical politics through that gateway. But there's only so much you can do not collectively, and that's the fundamental problem of anarchism.

In the 60s and 70s the mainstream was really into anarchism. But the mainstream is interested in anything that we sell. At lot of what we call anarchist classics were originally published by big publishers *Anarchy in Action* by Colin Ward, *The Floodgates of Anarchy*, *Blood in My Eye* by George Jackson, Abbie Hoffman. These were published by big publishers. Insofar as anarchism is popular again, sure *The Guardian* will feature anarchists as columnists, sure David Graeber is lauded as the great man. I think that's great that David Graeber can write for *The Guardian*. I wish there were more sane voices in the mainstream. But let's be honest. The only reason they're there is because anarchism is flavour of the month.

RKI: So the problem is not the lack of anarchists, but the failure to build lasting institutions?

RKA: The first thing I did when I came to America was organise an anarchist bookfair. The San Francisco anarchist bookfairs rapidly became the world leader because there were already loads of anarchists here. It became the single biggest bookfair in the Bay Area. It dwarfed mainstream ones. It was a focal point – because the milieu already existed. This vibrant milieu has never been a movement. It has produced certain great things, it has coalesced sometimes. But it has never undertaken any serious organising except for the short-term situational change.

The Anti-poll tax movement didn't just come from nowhere in the 80s. It came out of ten years of organising having some structures in place. Anarchism had three national organisations in the UK: Direct Action Movement, Anarchist Federation[17] and Class War, which was at the time a federation, membership organisation. We had anarchist groups in most places. So when we started in Edinburgh we appealed to our comrades and it did spread like wildfire because it could spread. There were organisational structures, even if it was only two guys in each town. Occupy also came on the back of anarchist and anarchist inflected organising in the mid-90s which had a high point in Seattle. It was the beneficiary of these decades of organising.

The milieu has completely failed to build any sort of institutions on any level or scale or lasting import. It's pathetic how little anarchists have done. It's sad. There are a few individuals who are able and willing to do certain things. Without them, there's nothing there. The milieu would remain. Interested individuals will remain. Other than these sometimes spectacular successes, which are situational – Seattle, the poll tax movement, J20 – or whether it's certain individuals putting in the effort to organise a bookfair we're talking realistically about a handful of people. Without them, what you're left with is the situation the anarchist movement's always been in: there'll always been the occasional writer published by the mainstream like Colin Ward or Paul Goodman.[18] There'll always be the occasional incredibly dedicated individuals – the Albert Meltzers and Stuart Christies – who are battering on in the wilderness, trying.[19] But that's been the history of anarchism when it's not actually a mass movement. And a mass movement only comes through building these institutional structures: the trade union, the lasting physical spaces. There are the odd oases but the fact that we can name them shows that we're talking about a handful of people and an even smaller number of actual institutions. These things rise or fall on a tiny handful of people. That's a sad thing. That's not to champion the individual. It's not a great man view of history, it's the reality of what we're dealing with. And we're dealing with that because there is no wider movement, as opposed to the milieu, or the infrastructures to act and engender that wider movement. It's the classic chicken and egg situation.

Part II: Anarchist Publishing

RUTH KINNA: How is PM organised?

RAMSEY KANAAN: The people who started PM press eight or nine years ago all came out of AK Press and our experiences there explains how we choose to organise PM as we do.

RKI: How was AK organised?

RKA: AK was set up as a workers' cooperative, which is a legal entity in the UK and it doesn't exist in America. Being a co-op in the UK means that you have a legal structure and a framework but we tried to be more principled in the way we organised. There were three 'rules', ingrained in our bye-laws (which themselves have nothing – necessarily – to do with being a co-op, or not)

One was 'one-person-one-vote'. At the time, in 1990, the current so-called anarchist obsession with consensus didn't exist, certainly not in the UK (why it's suddenly become a tenet of anarchism is beyond comprehension as far as I'm concerned). In terms of direct democracy, the principle was one-person-one-vote.

The second principle was that everyone was paid the same. So working within the strictures and confines of capitalism there was an attempt to recognise that everyone's labour was of equal value and to practice the idea of each according to needs.

The third was that there are no owners. We had shares, because that's part of being a co-op in the UK. But we were a self-managed workplace. In 1994, when we decided to set up a sister organisation in the US, we set up as a regular corporation and also had to issue shares. When you joined AK press, you were given a share, and when you left you had to give up that share. That was how we protected the integrity of AK press as a political project, ensure that it couldn't be taken over and that no one was able to buy up all the shares.

RKI: How well did the principles work in practice?

RKA: Those principles are fantastically important, but they don't help you deal with the nitty-gritty of cooperation; and there were certain issues that came up through the process of working which we had to deal with and which affected our organisation.

Some stemmed from the attempt to work as a self-managed political project within the strictures of capitalism – coping with the economic imperative. AK and also PM press are run as commercial ventures. We are purely commercial, capitalist organisations, in that banal sense. And that brings in a whole bunch of pressures and tensions – because much of what we actually publish and distribute is not commercially viable. It means that there's always a balancing act between trying to do stuff that is more commercially viable and the more political material. Typically, perhaps understandably, the more commercially viable stuff is less 'radical'. AK Press's best-selling books were those that would appeal to a more mainstream audience. That doesn't mean that their content is worthless, but effectively it means that they're dealing with more liberal democratic issues and concerns. There's almost a direct inverse relation between sales and politics, and particularly anarchist politics. Anarchist primers sell very well but a book on a more specialist theme won't sell. One of the books we published early on, the first ever translation of Nestor Makhno's writings, didn't sell.[20] We printed 2000 copies in the early 1990s, and when I left AK 10–15 years later, we hadn't sold the run. No one is interested in one of the most famous anarchists, not even in the movement let alone in the outside world. No one actually cares about Makhno or wants to read Makhno. So there's always that problem, that tension.

The commercial imperative creates other problems, too. Part of it is that if you're not paying the living wage then there's a high turnover and it's virtually impossible to recruit anyone. People with marketable skills can get better paid elsewhere. So you're reliant either on young people who are enthusiastic but don't have any skills so to speak, and typically don't have the most sophisticated politics (because they're young and none of us is born perfectly formed); or you're reliant on forms of internal subsidy or self-exploitation: working long hours, or you have a partner who's much better paid, or you have a lucky rent situation. That's not a really a strong framework on which to build an organisation which can survive the ups and downs of boom and bust capitalism, let alone support the long-term work and effort required to build a movement.

RKI: How were these pressures felt internally in AK?

RKA: Internally, there was a whole set of pressures that arose partly in reaction to the external circumstances. One person one vote is fine in theory but in practice it raises a lot of red flags.

The most obvious is how you weigh or gauge knowledge, experience or interest. Some folks don't even care what they're voting on. The reality was felt in AK's management.

RKI: Can you give me an example?

RKA: When I left, AK was eleven people in America; in terms of small radical projects, it was a big organisation; too big to have every person vote on every aspect of your business: you don't want eleven people bickering over what's the best cover design for a particular book – you don't have time. So there was always some specialisation, a division of labour. The Michael Albert Parecon job-rotation was never part of AK because it was not considered to be practical.[21] We took a more bluntly Fordist model and we each had different responsibilities in the production line, producing and distributing books.

The collective was involved in all the broader decisions: can we afford to hire someone? can we afford a wage-rise? do we want to have a wage-rise or pay for health care (which in America you have to pay for)? What books are we going to publish and what books are we going to distribute? Those were the collective decisions and they affected the overall health and wellbeing of the organisation.

In my time (things might have changed since) we developed a system which was to have two readers for each manuscript. Those readers would report to the wider collective on the book's merits using three criteria: political content (is it worth us doing, is it important?), the quality of the manuscript (is it well written, will it take us a lot of effort to polish this rough diamond into a jewel?), commercial potential (is this something we can sell?). These three criteria are weighed against each other: we might have the most important collection of anarchist poetry in the world, but if we can't sell it, because we can't sell poetry, it might not be right for us; or we might think that something that has no commercial value is so vitally important that we'll do it anyway, or it'll take us a hell of a lot of work, but that work is worth it.

Each reader would give a report and that might take ten minutes each. So on the basis of a twenty-minute report to the wider collective everyone, including the two readers, would vote on whether to do the book or not. These votes would be based on virtually no discussion and, in the case of the other nine votes, virtually no knowledge other than the recommendations of the two readers. What would often happen was that the readers were really gung-ho on it and they just would be outvoted. That raised the question about how you weigh interest, aptitude, experience?

RKI: Would you say that the editorial decisions were the major cause of tensions?

RKA: There was another dynamic that grew up within AK. That arose because the majority of people who ended up working at AK had very little experience. They weren't necessarily young, though that was often the case, but they had very little experience of the book trade or how publishing and distribution works. This spawned a majority culture which was that everyone was able to do everything and that experience or knowledge doesn't really matter. In parallel to this, the second majority culture that grew up was about identity politics. This played out in AK as a commitment to build a 'healthy collective'. This became the primary goal of the political project and it meant that we had to have a diverse collective.

In practice it meant that we would no longer hire self-identified heterosexual white males. We had one young woman who said that she thought anarchism was stupid at the interview, but she was still hired on AK's majority vote because she was a queer woman of colour and that was important for the health and diversity of the collective. The fact that she said that she thought anarchism was stupid didn't make any difference. It was irrelevant.

RKI: How did all these experiences of organising in AK affect the structure of PM?

RKA: PM came from the minority faction in AK. That faction was made up of the three longest-serving, most experienced folks. I'm not saying we were the best, or that we were necessarily right. But there's only so long that you can be outvoted before it's time to move on.

What we learned was that one of the many tensions and problems of the self-managed workplace is about self-management. If you don't have a hierarchical structure, you have to decide how to self-manage. You have to think about how you deal with discipline: how do you deal with someone who doesn't do what they're told (meaning, what has collectively been agreed on)? What do you do when someone comes in late every day and is late for a collective meeting?

When this happened at AK, our initial response was to use the daily collective meeting and in the case of one particular member, for each of us to say, in turn, that we no longer wished to work with that person. That's not a good way of dealing with issues of management or discipline. And as a result of that we instituted a more formal, codified structure which basically just replicated what the rest of the capitalist world was doing: two written warnings and you get fired. This became part of the rules of AK's governance.

Having struggled with all this for decades, when we started PM, we retained the one-person-one vote and the rule that everyone was paid the same but, crucially for us, the decision we took away from the experience at AK was that we were only going to work with people that we knew.

In terms of ownership, we pay no dividends on shares but there are two owners with five shares each. Part of the PM culture is that we have virtually no meetings: we're all spread out across the world. We talk individually and sometimes collectively, but there are no collective meetings and that's by design as well as by the accident of distribution. It means that the coordination is overseen by two of us and we take some of the smaller decisions or decide when to take these to the larger group.

We're totally transparent. Not only is everyone paid the same but the data bases, invoices and everything we do is all in the cloud. Everyone has access in real time from wherever they are in the world. If people wish to check things out for themselves, if people wish to be involved in certain things, they have the same means as anyone else. There's no group decision about whether to pay a wage rise when it's clear from the financial figures (that are open to everyone) that we can't afford it. But when we can in principle think about wage rises, there is a big discussion. We have talked about whether to pay higher wages or pay for health care.

People are involved in the editorial decisions as much as they want to be and that will depend on their particular interests, desires, areas of knowledge or expertise. But two of us are the linchpins and we do most of the editorial acquisitions. There's a lot of back and forth between us and with the other people in PM, particularly when we're not sure about projects or when we need special advice. But in the end, we're the linchpins.

We use the same criteria adopted in AK to decide what to publish. However, those decisions are more diversified and much more informal and they don't necessarily involve the entire group. In terms of politics, PM is modelled like an affinity group rather than a consensus group.

RKI: It seems from the website that PM seeks to foster close relationships with authors, is that a conscious policy?

RKA: Yes, and for two reasons: political and commercial. The political is that while we have to sell products to pay our wages and pay our rents, the products actually mean something to us. So we have a vested interest in selling as many of those products as possible. We're not just looking for the next bestseller. In mainstream publishing, resources are always directed to the next bestseller. We wish we had more bestsellers but because we also have another criterion: when we publish something we think it's worth putting out into the world and we want as much of that world as realistically possible to interact with that product. We have a political reason for putting extra effort into authors and we have a commercial reason because, with the collapse of regular way of selling books, these other ways of selling books are pretty important. It's not that we want to make the author work harder for us, because that's easier for us. We want the author, ideally, to collaborate with us to make it better for everyone. And we try and involve the authors as much as they want to be. We want to encourage and enable our authors to get to get out into the wider world so we help with setting up events, coach authors how to speak in public and so forth.

RKI: PM promotes itself as a publisher of radical, Marxist and anarchist literature. How do you understand those terms and their relationship to each other?

RKA: 'Radical' is a horrendous term. It means nothing. It's like 'revolutionary' or 'intersectionalism'. Nevertheless, it projects an image. AK was an explicitly anarchist publisher. In terms of getting anarchism out to a wider world, we felt in PM that that was too limiting or off-putting in terms of public perceptions. Second, in terms of what was actually published by AK or PM, the vision was considerably broader than just anarchism. Personally, too, my influences are far wider. As far as mainstream perceptions were concerned, PM was trying to have a bit of truth in advertising. Combining anarchism, Marxism and radical is a way of being all encompassing and non-sectarian.

RKI: What's the ambition of PM press?

RKA: Since there's not a strong, vibrant anarchist movement, what we're doing is keeping the flame alive, trying to shape as best we can, trying to interact as best we can. That's all we can do. We can't have a movement if we operate in a vacuum of amnesia. We'll spin our wheels forever and go nowhere. There's a difference between activism and actually building movements.

RKI: Which books would you take to a desert island?

RKA: E.P. Thompson's *The Making of the English Working Class*. I must have read that book cover to cover about six times. Feminism had a huge influence on me as a kid, even though in retrospect some of it seems quite reactionary or liberal: nevertheless, reading *The Women's Room* by Marylin French, *The Second Sex* by Simone de Beaviour, probably more important and better, reading the novels of Marge Piercy and Ursula le Guin had a profound impact. Reading the anarchist classics – Kropotkin, Malatesta, Goldman – was like common sense, they confirmed what I was already thinking. Reading feminist literature really got my brain going, as opposed to just nodding. Then in my later teens reading Murray Bookchin and Noam Chomsky really got me going and at the same time reading socialists: reading all the prefaces to Bernard Shaw's works (the preface to *Androcles and the Lion* was the best take down of Christianity I'd ever read). Of the more contemporary authors, probably my favourite writer after E.P. Thompson is Maurice Brinton, another ex-Trot who remained until his dying day viciously antianarchist. But *The Bolsheviks and Workers' Control* is probably the best book I've read on the Leninist coup and the Russian Revolution.

Taking a holistic view, I think anarchism is really good in much of its tactics, strategies, theories; the role of the individual and collective action. A lot of the Marxist stuff is good on different kinds of organisation and more importantly, economics, where anarchism's always been a bit weak. Also Marxists, unless you're Colin Ward, have been much better at using that Marxist prism to analyse other aspects of society. There is a Marxist view on literature, numerous views, in fact; and that's very rare in anarchism. Emma Goldman wrote about theatre, there were various anarchist in the 60s that wrote about crime and punishment; Colin Ward is a shining beacon, looking all over the map. But often the Marxists are much better at looking at daily life, lived reality through that Marxist lens.

Notes

1 *Top of the Pops* was a weekly chart music programme which ran on the BBC between 1964 and 2006.
2 Radio 1 was established in 1967 as part of a reorganisation prompted by the success of pirate radio and it targeted a youth audience with playlists largely dependent on national record sales.
3 John Peel (1939–2004) was a broadcaster whose nightly programme on the BBC was celebrated for its eclecticism and unorthodoxy.
4 See the Facebook page maintained on behalf of ex-members of the band www.facebook.com/pg/crass/about/?ref=page_internal [last access 6 December 2017].
5 Housmans is a radical book shop in London, www.housmans.com/ [last access 6 December 2017].
6 Black Rose Books was set up in 1970 http://blackrosebooks.net/ Black and Red started in 1968 www.blackandred.org/pages/about.html [last access 6 December 2017].
7 Guy Debord, *Society of the Spectacle*, trans. Greg Adargo (Black and Red 1977 [1967]) online at www.marxists.org/reference/archive/debord/society.htm [last access 6 December 2017].
8 AK Press was founded in 1987 by Ramsey Kanaan. www.akpress.org/ [last access 6 December 2017].
9 First of May was a bookstore and meeting place. For a recollection, see http://eotdt.org/index.php/the-word-bank/297-the-first-of-may-bookshop [last access 6 December 2017].
10 Left Book Club was set up to promote socialism in 1936 by Victor Gollancz. A new Left Book Club was established in 2015 www.leftbookclub.com/history/ [last access 6 December 2017].
11 PM Press founded at the end of 2007 and publishing in Oakland, California http://pmpress.org/content/index.php?topic=about [last access 6 December 2017].
12 London Radical Bookfair is organised by the Alliance of Radical Booksellers www.radicalbook-sellers.co.uk/?page_id=245; the London Anarchist Bookfair has been running since 1981 http://anarchistbookfair.org.uk/ [last access 6 December 2017].
13 *Class War* is the newspaper of the UK anarchist group Class War, first published in 1983 http://anarchistbookfair.org.uk/ [last access 6 December 2017].
14 For the Anti-Poll Tax Movement, see the article at Libcom https://libcom.org/history/1989-1990-opposition-poll-tax. For J20, see www.disruptj20.org/about/ [last access 6 December 2017].
15 Francisco Ferrer was an educationalist and anarchist, executed in 1909. For Ferrer's account of the Modern School, see *The Origins and Ideas of the Modern School*, trans. Joseph McCabe online at https://theanarchistlibrary.org/library/francisco-ferrer-the-origin-and-ideals-of-the-modern-school [last access 6 December 2017].
16 The SWP is the Socialist Workers Party www.swp.org.uk/. The ISO is the International Socialist Organisation http://www.internationalsocialist.org/ [last access 6 December 2017].
17 For a history of the Direct Action Movement, see Kate Sharpley Library www.katesharpleylibrary.net/x69qfd. For Anarchist Federation, see www.afed.org.uk/ [last access 6 December 2017].
18 For Colin Ward (1924–2010), see Stuart White, 'The Incremental Anarchist' in *Radical Philosophy*, 161 www.radicalphilosophy.com/obituary/colin-ward-1924%E2%80%932010 and Paul Goodman, (1911–72) Robert Graham, 'The Emergence of New Anarchism' www.radicalphilosophy.com/obituary/colin-ward-1924%E2%80%932010 [last access 6 December 2017].
19 For Meltzer, see Stuart Christie 'Albert Meltzer, anarchist' Kate Sharpley Library, www.radical-philosophy.com/obituary/colin-ward-1924%E2%80%932010. For Stuart Christie, see the entry in Matthew Wilson and Ruth Kinna 'Key Terms', in Kinna (ed.) *Bloomsbury Companion to Anarchism* (Bloomsbury, 2014).
20 Nestor Makhno, *The Struggle Against the State and Other Essays* (Edinburgh & Oakland: AK Press, 1996).
21 On Parecon, see Znet www.akpress.org/struggleagainstthestateandotheressays.html [last access 6 December 2017].

SECTION 4

Transformations

In this final section, we consider some of the ideas and visions that animate radical activism. What kinds of alternatives are radicals aiming to advance? And how have these been honed over time?

To be sure, radicals today are more reluctant than ever to suggest detailed programmes and blueprints for what should replace class society, hierarchical government and intersecting regimes of domination. Unlike utopian socialists (and Soviet planners), radicals have tended to privilege repeated, concrete experiences of social struggle in which the tension between aspirations and experience is continuously worked out, and to emphasise the necessarily emergent and unexpected qualities of any social arrangements that would emerge through an unconstrained process of self-organisation (Davis and Kinna, 2014). This explains the tendency to view 'revolution' as a present-day process and potential dimension of every-day life not as a one-off event; the emphasis on the imperfect and experimental nature of alternative-building (however sustained and collective) and the widespread endorsement of pluralism, heterogeneity and iconoclasm in the production of alternatives.

This section, then, offers critical accounts of several major sites at which radicals have been experimenting with alternatives in practice. Between them, the chapters portray to the richness and diversity of such initiatives, and the divergent perspectives that have come to interact in their production. They also seek to interrogate the connections or disconnections between such initiatives and more thoroughgoing social transformation, and between their local dimensions and the often-global dimensions of the structures against which they posit themselves.

Peter Seyferth provides an overview of historical and contemporary Marxist and anarchist thinking about **work and its abolition**. Comparing different approaches within Marxist and anarchist traditions, Seyferth shows that work is an essential component of exploitation and/or domination, not an aspect of social relations corrupted by power relations that can be somehow improved or transformed. Explaining the lack of mass anti-work movements, the chapter finds the possibilities for revolutionary change in the complementarity of Marxist policy-led reforms and anarchist direct action.

Emily Charkin and Judith Suissa develop a radical conception of **education** based on an overview of historical and contemporary experiments. This involves a commitment to critique dominant norms, practices, values and institutions of existing society and to offer alternatives. Radicals have sometimes pioneered learning practices designed to confront power relationships between learners and instructors, but the radicalism of alternative education lies in the recognition that education is not a neutral tool or technique for learning but a moralising instrument. Education is part of a process of socialisation that sustains types of social relations. It is radical, then, to the extent that it is transformative of the exploitative relationships that prevail. Radical educators offer alternatives which challenge existing power relationships and encourage other modes of living.

In his chapter on the politics of **dumpstered food**, Sean Parson explores the ability of Food Not Bombs, an anarchist homeless food organisation that serves vegetarian dumpstered food for free for all who are hungry, to 'decommodify food'. The chapter begins with a historical and theoretical exploration of the commodification of food before engaging with the concept of the ex-commodity. Food Not Bombs formed out of antinuclear and antimilitarist movements but grew into a network of groups whose free meals became identified with anticapitalist protest. The chapter examines how FNB groups use the ex-commodity as part of a broader politics of decommodifying food and undermining the capitalist food system.

Focusing on left-libertarian social centres in Italy, Luca Lapolla's discussion of **urban community activism** presents social centres as a concrete radical alternative to mainstream society. It illustrates how they serve as contexts for applying left-libertarian principles such as direct democracy, self-management and mutual aid and combining them with a strong anticapitalist critique. The chapter examines the generational changes in social centres, which reduced the presence of theory in practice, and highlights the importance of place and memory in the lifespans and politics of social centres.

Jim Donaghey resents an analysis of anarchism and **popular music** to examine radical culture. Rejecting approaches that identify radicalism with particular aesthetics or formats and showing how radical tropes, ideas and themes are reproduced through mass marketing, the chapter defines radicalism with reference to alternative anticorporate, grassroots production and distribution systems. Do-It-Yourself ethics provides the model for radical cultural production. Yet, radicalism also involves recognising the impossibility of detaching radical from mainstream culture and the diversity of radical subcultures. Building 'cultures of resistance' through networking and solidarity is essential part of transformative cultural practice. And the aim is not to construct a new dominant culture but to support new relationships of non-domination across subcultural groups.

In an interview Jim Thomas considers what a radical politics of **technology** would look like that could link disparate struggles against specific applications like GM crops, geoengineering and nuclear power. Essential features of such a politics include: a rejection of 'techno-fix' approaches to problems such as hunger or climate change, which leave social and economic structures unquestioned; a critique of how new technologies promote corporate concentration and power, including across disparate industries now linked by platforms like genetics or nanotechnology; and leadership by indigenous and peasant movements from the global south, whose own knowledge and technologies are often far more conducive to social equality, local autonomy and genuine ecological sustainability.

Lisa Trocchia-Baḷḳīts examines a decentralised, leaderless **local food** movement in Athens, Georgia to analyse the revolutionary potential of alternative food production. Radicalism is defined in terms of transformative potential: the power to introduce practices that challenge existing patterns of consumption and the cultures of production that sustain them. An important part of the food movement is 'entrepreneurial'. Its modest aim is to provide consumers with ethically sourced alternatives to the food manufactured through agribusiness. The genuinely radical part of the movement creates a new social ecology by constructing community networks that are horizontal, autonomous and based on mutual aid and complex reciprocity. This radical food movement fosters cooperative social relationships that are essential to social change.

Bürge Abiral's chapter looks at the promises and limitations of **Permaculture** – an approach to systems design widely applicable to sustainable food production, shelter construction and resilient communities and economies. The chapter argues that the truly radical promise of Permaculture may be undercut both by the flexibility it provides for practice, and by the need for educational and economic capital for its application. The case study of the Permaculture community in Turkey demonstrates that while tied to social movements, its radical ethics may remain in the background. In such situations, Permaculture activism may become a matter of proving its viability as a cultivation technique in rural compounds, or of lifestyle activism in urban centres.

Alexandre Christoyannopoulos and Anthony Fiscella provide a critical overview of the concepts of 'religion' and 'radicalism' to develop an anticolonial conception of **'religious radicalism'**. Focusing on Indigenous anticolonial traditions, nonviolent antimilitarist and egalitarian Christian groups, and the activity of marginalised groups seeking to organise new ways of living, the chapter links radicalism to the rejection of dominant orders, the adoption of cooperative, solidaristic values and practices and the commitment to life stories that acknowledge superhuman forces. Noting the intersections across apparently religious and non-religious radicals involved in contemporary movements, the authors question the usefulness of the construction of religion to discuss radicalism and recommend the adoption of an alternative grammar that facilitates intercultural exchange, learning and dialogue.

Narrating a history of European squatter movements from the 1970s using movement materials, Bart van der Steen finds the radicalism of **squatting** in the subcultures it fosters. Squatters advanced a radical critique of representation; class domination and inequalities of wealth, power and knowledge. Squatters were centrally involved in resisting technocratic urban gentrification projects and in antinuclear and antiglobalisation struggles. As a practice, squatting reflected a wider commitment to direct action, adopted to disrupt existing political regimes. The chapter describes how squatters negotiated internal conflicts to deal with everyday transgressions but also to confront power asymmetries based on class, race and gender. Plotting the emergence of the movements from the student politics and guerrilla activism of the 1970s, it also examines contested debates about the conception of politics and the ways that shifts in global politics have rebounded in squatter movements.

Finally, Laurence Cox considers **activist sustainability** – the challenging question of how people – especially people who lack power, wealth and/or cultural privilege – can become and remain active and radical political subjects. The chapter discusses issues that appear in a range of practical dimensions including legal support and prisoner solidarity, alternative livelihoods, challenges to discrimination and hate speech, informal economic support and international solidarity. In its broadest sense, sustainable activism is a process that involves participants remaking themselves and their relationships to one another, as they remake the world around them.

Reference

Davis, Laurence and Ruth Kinna (eds.). *Anarchism and Utopianism* (Manchester: Manchester University press, 2014).

4.1

ANTI-WORK

A Stab in the Heart of Capitalism

Peter Seyferth

Rejection of the work regime is neither ubiquitous amongst nor confined to radicals. But those that radically turn against work argue that it is a relationship of exploitation, submission and alienation that has to be abolished. Indeed, there is a long history of worker resistance against drudgery, starting from Luddite sabotage, later tamed by unions, nowadays appearing more silent as absenteeism. There are two complementary radical frameworks of anti-work. On the one hand, neo-Marxists criticise work ideology and demand a universal basic income (UBI) from the state. On the other hand, anarchists reject the state and focus on direct resistance action against work.

One of the core elements of modern domination is work. Without work, capitalism and, arguably, the state would be impossible. Anti-work radicals argue and struggle for the abolition of work, which is, in their view, a precondition for freedom from domination. Work is a praxis and a power machine that acts on intersecting social identities, as Fineman (2012: 3) has observed: 'Today, pecking orders of who does what kind of work remain in all parts of globe, heavily influenced by social class, education, wealth, gender, race, age, or ethnicity'. Alongside the paid jobs that appear in the Gross National Product and are often held by privileged people (mostly skilled, white, healthy males), there are several other kinds of work that are even more frustrating, dangerous and demeaning while yielding less resources (or none at all) and thus have to be done by underprivileged people: domestic labour, voluntary work, black economy (13). Although each of these activities could theoretically be done due to its intrinsical value – if the respective worker happens to attribute such a value to the activity – most work is regarded as means for some external good: as a necessary evil.

Ethical attitudes towards work vary wildly from appreciation to rejection (5), so to motivate people to work, work has to meet the needs of people (10–12). Since many jobs fail to do so, there have to be mechanisms to force people to work. The easiest way is to deprive those that do not work from what they need and want, be it food and shelter or status, power and dignity – although even those that do work often lack many of these essential goods. If one must work to survive, one can and will easily be exploited. Emancipatory radicals deal with the (at least potential) evils of work in quite different ways: some aim at improvements within the sphere of work; others strive for the abolition of work itself. The better-work/ anti-work cleavage cuts across the usual dividing lines of radical traditions. In the following, I will first show the ambiguity of nineteenth- and early twentieth-century radical thinkers towards work. Second, I will sketch the transformation of work regimes in the second half of the twentieth century and assess worker's everyday resistance to it. Third, I will present the theories of several anti-work neo-Marxists. Finally, I will highlight central points of anarchist anti-work agitation. My aim is to shed light on the differences of anti-work radicalisms while making plausible why one might want to abolish work.

Radical but Ambiguous Stances Over Work in the Nineteenth and Early Twentieth Centuries

The most widely known critic of capitalism, Karl Marx, stated in his early manuscripts of 1844 that the oppression of workers is not just a case of economic exploitation, but also of human estrangement. On the one hand, the worker is alienated from the product of his work (it does not belong to him but to the capitalist). But on the other hand, 'estrangement is manifested not only in the result but in the act of production, within the producing activity, itself'. Thus,

> labor is *external* to the worker, i.e., it does not belong to his intrinsic nature; that in his work, therefore, he does not affirm himself but denies himself, does not feel content but unhappy, does not develop freely his physical and mental energy but mortifies his body and ruins his mind.

> *(Marx, 2009: 30)*

Work seems to be a vile thing. One might expect Marx, being an infamous radical, to reject work altogether. But Marx's theoretical attitude is quite ambiguous. In the third volume of his *Capital* (posthumously published in 1894), he indeed seems to contrast freedom with work: 'the realm of freedom actually begins only where labour which is determined by necessity and mundane considerations ceases'. Too bad that this is impossible, for Marx. People will have to work 'in all social formations and under all possible modes of production', including communism; there always remains 'a realm of necessity. Beyond it begins that development of human energy which is an end in itself, the true realm of freedom, which, however, can blossom forth only with this realm of necessity as its basis'. The best thing to hope for is thus a 'shortening of the working-day', made possible by increased productivity (Marx, 2010: 571). Consequently, Marx's most successful followers (Leninists and Social Democrats) sought to appear not only worker-friendly, but also work-friendly. They adhered to a strict work ethic and imposed it on their subjects whenever they took state power. The culmination of this was the Stakhanovite movement that tried to maximise production without cutting working hours from 1935 onwards, but already in 1879 August Bebel (1904: 275) was quite clear on this point: 'So soon as society is in possession of all the means of production, *the duty to work, on the part of all able to work, without distinction of sex, becomes the organic law of socialized society*'.

It is plausible to attribute Marxism's fondness of forced labour not only to its inherently authoritarian utopian vision (where coerced work is one tool of the dictatorship of the party), but also to its official rejection of bourgeois lifestyle and social stratification. Indeed, the ruling classes of all times showed a distinct odium for work. This attitude may have been stronger with the nobility in antiquity and the Middle Ages than with the robber barons and misers of capitalism, but the unequal distribution of productive and leisured activity is similar.

An example of the aristocratic devaluation of work can be found in Friedrich Nietzsche's thought, especially from 1878 to 1882. For him, dirty work is a true vice that interferes with the desire for autonomy because it accustoms workers to repetitive petty goals that are easy to achieve. Insofar as it does so, work polices and subdues. Individuals become overwrought and their spiritlessness impedes cogitation. Thusly, idle time is experienced as boredom by workers; idleness is suitable only for artists and thinkers who need it for their creative work. Consequently, Nietzsche demands a robust division of humanity into two species: many 'slaves' with menial jobs, and a few freemen with aesthetic duties that do not occupy more than one-third of a day.[1]

This kind of attitude was not uncommon amongst anti-egalitarians. No wonder, then, that Bebel (1904: 275) cried: 'The silly claim that the Socialist does not wish to work, that he seeks to abolish work, is a matchless absurdity, which fits our adversaries alone. Non-workers, idlers, exist in capitalist society *only*'. Similar ideas appear in Paul Lafargue's famous 1880 essay *The Right to be Lazy*. The capitalist class appears to be 'settled down into absolute laziness and demoralized by enforced enjoyment'. Unsurprisingly, '[t]he sight of the miserable conditions of life resignedly accepted by the working class and the sight of the organic degradation engendered by the depraved passion for work increased its aversion for all compulsory labor and all restrictions of its pleasures' (Lafargue, 2010: 14). Like Nietzsche, Lafargue relies on ancient Greek and Roman thinkers (5, 21–22). But unlike Nietzsche, Lafargue was a socialist, and unlike Bebel, he harshly criticised the notion that 'the proletariat, betraying its instincts, despising its historic mission, has let itself be perverted by the dogma of work' (5). He contrasted the 'noble savage' that does not yet know work with Europe's workers, 'our miserable slaves of machines', and identified work as 'the cause of all intellectual degeneracy, of all organic deformity' (4). In the end, Lafargue demanded that the proletariat 'must return to its natural instincts, it must proclaim the Rights of Laziness' (10), which in practice, means: 'It must accustom itself to working but three hours a day, reserving the rest of the day and night for leisure and feasting' (11). This would be made possible by technological progress. In a similar vein, Bertrand Russell, in his 1932 article *In Praise of Idleness*, speculated on the emancipatory possibilities of Taylorism (Frederick Taylor's highly compartmentalised and deskilled division of labour which imposed strict factory discipline and was vividly exemplified in the Tramp's experience on the assembly line in Charlie Chaplin's 1936 classic, *Modern Times*): 'If at the end of the war the scientific organization which had been created in order to liberate men for fighting and munition work had been preserved, and the hours of work had been cut down to four, all would have been well' (1932: 554). All this is not far from Marx's claim that with automation, the realm of necessity could be reduced – without completely abolishing work.

What about those socialists that valued freedom over parties and discipline? The anarchists, too, have had ambiguous attitudes towards work. Like most other socialists of his time, Peter Kropotkin embraced technological progress and shorter working hours, e.g. in many articles published from 1886 to 1890. But to this question of efficiency, he adds the question of everyday joyous experience. Factories are needed (and possible) that are 'so well managed that it would be a real pleasure to work in them, if the work, be it well understood, were not to last more than four or five hours a day, and if every one had the possibility of varying it according to his tastes' (Kropotkin, 1907: 144–5). Work has to be agreeable, and this includes housework, because 'a revolution, intoxicated with the beautiful words Liberty, Equality, Solidarity would not be a revolution if it maintained slavery at home. Half humanity subjected to the slavery of the hearth would still have to rebel against the other half' (154–5). Therefore, Kropotkin attacks the division of labour by gender and/or skill differences and calls for the abandonment of 'any system of wages' (212). To be entitled to the products one needs, it should be irrelevant how long or how qualified one has worked before; otherwise, a dividing line between new classes would be erected (205, 207, 210–13). The principle of distribution should not be wealth or work, but need; the work necessary for the satisfaction of needs should be minimised and as varied as possible (223). Using Adam Smith's example of the smith that is 'sentenced for life to the making of heads of nails', Kropotkin illustrated the frustration, emptiness and disempowerment such divided work imposed on workers (232–3). His alternative vision entailed all people freely working half a day, spending the other half in artistic or scientific activities and retiring at the age of forty (Kropotkin, 1998: 187). This stands in stark opposition to Marx's or Russell's ideas.[2] It must not be misunderstood as appreciation of idleness, though: Kropotkin (1907: 197–199) was sure that people hated and tried to avoid work only when it stifles them; to suppress this cause of laziness through the revolutionary restructuring of work in a meaningful and rewarding way would end idleness without the need to punish sluggards.

Sadly, this emancipatory strategy towards necessary work and its avoidance has not always been followed by anarchist activists. Take as an example the CNT/FAI industrial policy during the Spanish Civil War 1936–39. Spain seemed to be an underdeveloped country to many Spanish anarcho-syndicalists who, consequently, glorified work as emancipatory and actively promoted industrialisation, as Michael Seidman (1991: 42) has observed. One of the CNT leaders, wartime Minister of the Economy Diego Abad de Santillán, 'noted approvingly that Taylorization had eliminated the "unproductive movements of the individual" and had increased "his productivity"' (45); he 'underlined the necessity of eliminating "parasitism" and of providing work for all. Work would be both a right and a duty in revolutionary society, and he approved the old saying, Those who do not work, do not eat' (46). This is quite the opposite of Kropotkin's anti-Taylorist strategy; but in the civil war situation, a productive military industry seemed to be essential. 'The new elite of union militants employed both old and new techniques of coercion to make workers labor harder and produce more' (96). This led to manifold forms of resistance against work: absenteeism, fake illnesses, lateness, strikes, theft, sabotage, slowdowns, indiscipline and indifference (8). The CNT reacted with harsh punishments; their Minister of Justice, Juan García Oliver, even initiated 'concentration camps' with forced labour which were lauded by CNT militants as 'progressive' because they replaced torture and were designed to change the prisoner's soul and values in a productivist way (99). But the workers themselves did not stop to resist work. Seidman speculates that 'the way to eliminate resistance is not by workers' control of the means of production but rather by the abolition of wage labor itself' (17).

Transformation of Work and Silent Resistance to Work

So both Marxists and anarchists have a critical view of capitalism but are ambiguous about one of capitalism's core features: work. At least, this was the case in the late nineteenth and early twentieth centuries. But work has changed since then, hasn't it? The 'scientific management' of Frederick Taylor, initially adopted to increase productivity through decreasing worker's shirking, has evolved into a largely automated and computerised industry – but a process of deskilling is still in force, stripping workers (even in the tertiary sector) of pride and dignity (Fineman, 2012: 56–57). Workers react to this by inventing their own work practices, sometimes by informal self-organisation (including punishing too productive co-workers), and sometimes just by bitter humour (58–59). Attempts by managers to use workers' resistant tactics for profit optimisation – imposed 'fun', job 'enrichment' or forced 'empowerment' (59–62) – rarely have emancipatory outcomes. 'For example, having stripped out layers of supervision to save costs, empowerment can appear as an excuse by management to intensify work, pushing more work and responsibility onto relatively fewer people, often for no extra reward' (62). In spite of the health risks of long working hours, some workers adopt a 'presenteeism' – constant presence – for fear that not constantly being seen at the workplace risks career or job security (63–64). Others choose the opposite strategy: downshifting, i.e. switching to jobs that demand and pay less. This is 'a radical response to the emptiness that some people feel as they chase ever more goods and services' (66), but it suits only those with a certain level of wealth. If working less is involuntary, it is called 'underemployment' and often results in demoralisation, stress and illness (106). Similarly, unemployment does not free the worker from the necessity to work, only from the possibility. It is very widespread today and it serves as a threat to job holders. Today, you do not want a job because you like the job – you want it because joblessness is made highly inimical to good life. And nonetheless, people flee work in astonishing numbers, entailing much research on absenteeism. According to an official report, sickness absences cost the UK economy £15 billion in lost output, £9 billion in financial costs for the employers and £13 billion for the state – every year (Black and Frost, 2011: 14). This is the result of the 140 million working days lost per year in the UK. 'This equates to 2.2 per cent of all working time, or 4.9 days for each worker each year, and is broadly comparable to many other developed countries (the United States, France, Germany and the Netherlands have similar rates)' (19). This report 'is premised on the fact that work is good for health in most cases', at least when work is 'good' (18). Let's put aside the incredibleness of this 'fact' for a moment and consider how these many sickness absences can be explained. One might think, after all, that if there was something wrong with the workplace, workers could use regular methods of industrial action to improve the situation without questioning the work regime as such. But a meta-analysis of eighty-two workplace ethnographies (covering 160 years in Britain and the US) showed that strikes occurred in approximately 21% of the cases, while absenteeism occurred in 45% of the cases (work avoidance at the workplace: 57%; social sabotage: 43%; playing dumb: 27%; theft: 20%) (Roscigno and Hodson, 2004: 22). While collective resistance (i.e. striking) is positively correlated with the presence of conflict and unions at the workplace (unions without conflict actually lessen the likelihood of strike action), individualised resistance like absenteeism does not have these requirements and can be used by workers in many circumstances (29, 31, 34). Because 'collective and more individualized forms of resistance are not mutually exclusive in terms of their emergence or the factors that drive them' (33), absenteeism is an obvious and commonplace tactic of class struggle that opens the door for anti-work action.

Absenteeism is notoriously difficult to study because it is a 'mildly deviant behavior', so people will not always tell the truth to researchers (Johns, 2003: 159); for statistical analyses, 'there are simply far too many intervening factors (known and unknown)' (Hoxsey, 2010: 553). All findings cited below should therefore be read with caution – not least because their normative stance is to get as many people to work as much as possible. Shi and Skuterud (2015: 403) have shown that a rising recreational quality of the weather increases short-term sickness absence. Since good weather does not make people sick, it is plausible to assume that skipping workers can think of better things to do than work. By taking a sickie, workers express their preference for less hours of work (Livanos and Zangelidis, 2013: 494); it is their 'labor-leisure choice' (Lusinyan and Bonato, 2007: 477), made in a direct action rather than by pleading to superiors. It has to be noted, though, that this direct action happens in the framework of labour laws and often results in salary continuation, so it is not a valid indicator for deliberate anarchist attitudes. Although not enough attention has yet been given 'to the *meaning* and *role* of absenteeism from the *absentee's* perspective', it can be said that there is at least 'a modest link between absenteeism and job satisfaction' (Hackett, 1989: 246). Workers often dislike their job and thus try to avoid it.

Why do so many people hate their jobs? Unfair payment can be a reason: job satisfaction is the highest when the workers are neither underpaid nor overpaid – but absenteeism is the lowest when the workers are overpaid (because that makes them compensate the guilt they feel through working more) (Sauer and Valet, 2013: 145–6). If the managerial goal is not workers' satisfaction, but their attendance, an 'unequal wage structure can be efficient to some degree' because '[a]bsenteeism is negatively correlated with absolute wages, relative wages, and hierarchical levels' (Pfeifer, 2010: 59). Logically, not all can be paid relatively better or ranked higher, and to increase absolute wages for all amounts to inflation. Dissatisfaction with the job can sometimes be compensated with job involvement: Wegge et al. (2007: 81) found that absenteeism is high only when both job satisfaction and job involvement are low; van Yperen and Hagedoorn (1996: 370–1) showed that if, contrariwise, job involvement is high, workers' intent to leave is low – that holds especially for deprived workers whose payment violates equity norms. It remains somewhat unclear which working conditions can increase job satisfaction or job involvement. Beblo and Ortlieb (2012: 89) pointed to 'lack of autonomy' and 'work-related relationship with colleagues and superiors' as factors for increased absenteeism. But for many jobs, it would be principally impossible to improve on these factors, as anti-work thinkers emphasise. Many pro-work researchers therefore count on repressive measures. An intolerant group absence norm leads to a lower intent to report sick (van Yperen and Hagedoorn, 1996: 370–1); consequently, work groups should have enforcement mechanisms for attendance (Johns, 2003: 175). As Lusinyan and Bonato (2007: 477) lament: 'With imperfect monitoring, the decision about sick leave is ultimately left to workers, and moral hazard arises'. Lechmann and Schnabel (2014: 386–7) have observed that self-employed workers are less often absent because they monitor themselves (so no principal-agent problems apply) and they do not have the same protection as employees. Lusinyan and Bonato (2007: 478–81, 492, 496, 502) identify full employment, generous unemployment insurance, employment protection and sickness benefits – as well as too long working hours – as causes of absenteeism.

Contemporary empirical research has not yet found definitive reasons for the work defiance that impedes capitalism's profiting. But it has shown the difficulties of making work 'good', the non-profitability of workers' legal protection and the tendency to turn to repressive methods of practically forcing workers into their place, the workplace. Since at least the 1980s, radically undogmatic Marxist and anarchist thinkers have turned against the streams of productivism in their respective traditions, formulated harsh critiques of work and sketched anti-work theories and practices. Let us now turn to them.

Neo-Marxist Anti-work

André Gorz stands at the vanguard of contemporary neo-Marxist anti-work thought. He analysed the transformation of work regimes in developed countries and argued that the neo-liberal order has already abolished work on a massive scale, but in a way that is exploitative and dominating, forcing everyone to fight each other for vanishing employment. In contrast to the productivist tradition of orthodox Marxism, he claims that '[i]t is not this abolition we should object to, but its claiming to perpetuate that same work, the norms, dignity and availability of which it is abolishing, as an obligation, as a norm, and as the irreplaceable foundation of the rights and dignity of all' (Gorz, 1999: 1). Taylorism/Fordism had to totally repress the self-organisation, ingenuity and creativity of the workers because it understood them as sources of rebellion; the new regime of Toyotism/Post-Fordism treats these as 'a resource to be developed and exploited' (30). Hence, everyone is forced to sell their personality, to commodify their selves. One has to show a particular state of mind, a willing disposition: 'eagerness' (43). The professionalisation of pleasant and attentive attitudes ultimately poisons the arts of living because now even a nice smile falls under the suspicion of hypocrisy: it could be the 'commercial smile' or 'standardized, superficial bonhomie' of salespersons (70–71). Gorz's criticism points not just to a hollow lifestyle, but to a profoundly political struggle for power because 'the unfettered power capital has assumed over labour, society and everyone's lives depends precisely on "work" – not the work you do, but the work you are made to do – retaining its centrality in everyone's lives and minds' (53, see also 58). So, capitalism has an 'ideological hold on people's minds' by refusing income from activities that are not ordered and paid for by others, and thereby persuading people of the '*imperative need to work*' (72).

Other neo-Marxist thinkers like Nick Srnicek and Alex Williams or Michael Hirsch build on and expand Gorz's critique. Typically, they emphasise the odd effects of high productivity. This should make classic demands of the left achievable (provided that distribution will be changed by reform or revolution), but it, in fact, worsens the workers' plight by increasing the threat of unemployment. The liberal notion of 'freedom of contract' has become an absurdity as neo-liberal state policies have transformed welfare to workfare – basic social rights have been supplanted by compulsory work (Srnicek and Williams, 2015: 1–2, 93, 100–104; Hirsch, 2016: 10, 14, 40, 76). Hirsch exposes contemporary work society to be a Platonic order. In his *Republic*, Plato (1991: 111 [433a]) claims that in the just state, 'each one must practice one of the functions in the city, that one for which his nature made him naturally most fit. [...] justice is the minding of one's own business and not being a busybody'. This is precisely the opposite of Gorz's (1999: 73) alternative to the wage-based society: 'multi-active life'. But according to Hirsch, today's developed countries follow the Platonic idea: everyone has to have a work position they identify with. The economic existence and social status of the individual depends on a lifelong full-time job. Since there are not enough such jobs, the Platonic order makes individuals accept economically meaningless occupations, sometimes by threat of a debasing exclusion, and sometimes by sheer force. On the one hand, this is necessary to reproduce the hierarchy of classes, professions and genders. On the other hand, this work does not add value to the economy (Hirsch, 2016: 16–17, 20, 46, 59–66, 74). So, it is purely ideological: a cultural hegemony upheld by an alliance of capital, unions, social democracy, state apparatus, media and academy. Progressives should re-enter the fight over the definition of reality, over what we take for granted. Hirsch theorises the hegemony of work with Pierre Bourdieu's notion of 'symbolic violence' (22, 27–29, 68–69, 104, 177); Srnicek and Williams stick to Antonio Gramsci's older but similar concept of 'hegemony' for their analysis. 'The fact that so many people find it impossible to imagine a meaningful life outside of work demonstrates the extent to which the work ethic has infected our minds' (Srnicek and Williams, 2015: 124). This has an almost religious quality: 'The central ideological support for the work ethic is that remuneration be tied to suffering' (125). They concentrate on the genesis of neo-liberalism's hegemony, from the Mount Pelerin Society through networks and ideological infrastructures to palpable policies and politicians – and propound a similar counter-hegemonic strategy to eventually arrive at a world without work (52–67).

The neo-Marxists discussed here approve of imagining future alternatives to work society, but do not give many details. Gorz (1999: 77, 78) aims at 'the multi-activity-based society' where 'everybody will engage in a range of different activities and modes of membership of the society'. Srnicek and Williams (2015: 85–86) want a 'post-work world' that is 'not a world of idleness; rather, it is a world in which people are no longer bound to their jobs, but free to create their own lives'. Hirsch's (2016: 251, 43) 'utopia of an egalitarian and variegated society' promises 'an equal freedom *of*, *in*, and *to* work. Ultimately, it is about free access to and equal recognition of all forms of work'.[3] However, the neo-Marxists rather focus on transformative strategies, especially the role of the state in the counter-hegemonic emancipation from work. Since this is a fight about the definition of reality and since the state (as a 'bank of symbolic capital') produces and enforces categories of thought, it is crucial how the state understands its function, argues Hirsch (27–32). In the case of the creation of jobs being perceived as the state's mission, the state is made undemocratic; in the other case, if the mission is to eliminate useless work, a lot of reforms are obviously necessary: wealth, working hours and skills have to be redistributed justly; social security, individual freedom and democratic sovereignty have to be provided without force. From this follows voluntary social self-organisation (9, 11, 103, 105). Similarly, Gorz (1999: 100, 21) has already advocated the state to create free space and thus the possibility of independent activity, financed by some sort of Tobin tax that presupposes the state's willingness to overpower financial capital. And Srnicek and Williams (2015: 108) demand 'non-reformist reforms' that push capitalism beyond its acceptable parameters; such reforms would be, for example, more state investment, research devoted to technologies that replace workers, higher minimum wages, support for labour movements, reduction of working hours, etc. (112–14). These neo-Marxists agree on one central state policy to be the key for emancipation: a UBI. It is a means 'to free them [the recipients] from the constraints of the labour market. The basic social income must enable them to refuse work and reject "inhuman" working conditions' (Gorz, 1999: 83). Its significance 'lies in the way it overturns the asymmetry of power that currently exists between labour and capital' because with it, workers 'have the option to choose whether to take a job or not [...] A UBI therefore unbinds the coercive aspects of wage labour, partially decommodifies labour, and thus transforms the political relationship between labour and capital' (Srnicek and Williams, 2015: 120). It saves the workers from blackmail by the state and capital, grants more autonomy regarding time and lifestyle, enables activities that make sense but are not profitable, changes power relations between employers and employees, and ultimately quits the Platonic order (Hirsch, 2016: 101, 111–17). Alas, the UBI is a tool that could serve the capitalists as well (and has been demanded by neo-liberals), as all four neo-Marxists hasten to concede. If it is set below the breadline, its recipients are still forced to accept all kinds of jobs – then it is just a subsidy for capitalists who offer jobs no one would do without compulsion (Gorz, 1999: 82; Srnicek and William, 2015: 119; Hirsch, 2016: 102). It remains unclear how this danger could be averted; one may only guess that the neo-Marxists assume that the government that fulfils their demands will withstand all well-funded lobbying activities and elections from then onwards.

This is where the neo-Marxists most obviously deviate from anarchists. Although they appreciate the absenteeism and even rebelliousness of workers who hate work and ennoble the surplus population with titles like 'revolutionary subject' or 'vanguard', it is ultimately the state, preferably represented by left-wing populist politicians, that has to set things right (Gorz, 1999: 40, 63–64, 79, 110; Srnicek and Williams, 2015: 47, 114, 156–60; Hirsch, 2016: 230–1, 243–4). Srnicek and Williams (2015: 11, 22–23, 26–29, 32, 35) explicitly position themselves against the 'contemporary anarchist-tinged politics' of the contemporary left. This tendency of 'horizontalism' or 'folk politics' as exemplified by Michael Bakunin and Peter Kropotkin in the past and by small anarchist movements analysed by Uri Gordon today face a barrage of Srnicek's and Williams's criticism: it is too exclusive, too small, too harmless – in their view 'evidence shows that hierarchical organisations are crucial in defending movements against the state' (33). But, from an anarchist perspective, the fault of classical Marxism is that these hierarchical organisations tend to become wielders of state power themselves; this is why, so many neo-Marxists are quite critical of taking power nowadays. Following Gorz, who, in passing, mentions some Proudhonists and Paul Goodman but ultimately claims the indispensability of the state (1999: 84, 110), Hirsch (2016: 227) argues for a 'radically anarchic position of individual autonomy' without actually embracing anarchism. Almost like Kropotkin, he demands to politically abolish the divisions of work (both in the paid and unpaid spheres), the cause of most forms of social and gender hierarchies (240). For him, criticism of the work society is only emancipatory if it is also a radical criticism of domination (247). All this is typical for anti-work anarchists, but for Hirsch, the state must not be destroyed, but appropriated in a radical democratic way (251).

Some neo-Marxist anti-work arguments are wholeheartedly hostile to the state, notably the Krisis group's *Manifesto against Labour* (1999). Here, the state is seen as a derivative of labour; a state-controlled UBI is thus rejected; generally, 'the opponents of labour don't want to take the control centres of power, but want to switch them off' (Krisis, 1999). The Krisis group developed its theory on the grounds that 'Marxism itself was not sufficiently radical in its critique' (Trenkle, 2001). Krisis dismisses the classical class struggle of unions and parties whom it perceives to be part of the 'labour camp' (i.e. those that fight *for* work). On the one hand, Krisis (1999) promises that '[m]arket and state, institutions (once) alienated from human society, will be replaced by a graded system of councils, from town district level to the global level, where associations of free individuals will decide about the flow of resources in letting prevail sensual, social, and ecological reason'. For *Wildcat*, a syndicalist circular with tendencies towards communism, this is a sign of Krisis's individualist anarchism (H., 1999). On the other hand, for Krisis (1999), '[o]nly an explicitly formulated critique of labour along with a corresponding theoretical debate could bring about a new public awareness; the latter being the indispensable prerequisite for the constitution of a social movement that puts labour critique into practice'. This is a sign of Krisis's Leninism, and its supposed intellectual superiority over the masses who lack the proper consciousness, according to *Wildcat*'s anonymous author (H., 1999).

Anarchist Leninism seems to be a contradiction in terms. Let's have a look at those enemies of work that actually self-identify as anarchists to shed some light on the differences between anti-productivist neo-Marxists and anti-productivist anarchists.

Anarchist Anti-work

The two most obvious differences between the neo-Marxists and the anarchists are the latter's rejection of hierarchical organisations (like the state) and their focus not on theory but on resistant action. Surely, anarchists develop theories, too. But by consciously devaluating even their own theories, they shun the dogmatic scholasticism they see in Marxism. From this follows a multiplicity of anarchisms that are to some extent internally contradictory. Anti-productivism is notably strong in the primitivist and insurrectionist currents of anarchism, which are also notoriously hostile to academic theory. John Zerzan (1999: 133) stresses that 'our many compromises and accommodations with a grisly world are the real field of our effort to break free, more so than merely stating our ideas'. In this field, Marx has failed totally, both personally (with his 'ruling-class mentality' bringing misery to his family; 138, 133) and politically (with the 'gradualist, collaborationist, and highly statist' nature of his demands, essentially accepting the misery of capitalist development; 135). Zerzan's main point of criticism of work, capitalism and civilisation itself is the alienation inherent in them. Alienation is also a central term of Marxist theory. But 'Marx's overriding concern with externalities – principally economic crises, of course – was a trademark of his practical as well as theoretical approach; it obviously reflects his slight regard for the subjectivity of the majority of people, for their potential autonomy, imagination, and strength' (138).

So, Zerzan focuses his own observations of work precisely on these bottom-up resistance practices that are typically devoid of theory. In a series of articles published from 1974 to 1986, he tells the story of unruly struggles against industrialism. From the mid-eighteenth century onwards, artisanal freedom is pressurised by the rising capitalist factory system. Against this, '[a]bsenteeism, as well as turnover, [...] was part of the syndrome of striving to maintain a maximum of personal liberty' (100). The height of this resistance was 'the wide-spread revolutionary movement' of the machine breaking Luddites (105) that was almost anarchist: 'the Luddites organized themselves locally and even federally, including workers from all trades, with an amazing, spontaneous coordination. Eschewing an alienating structure, their organization was neither formal nor permanent. Their revolt tradition was without a center', although it 'was not a completely egalitarian movement' (109). Zerzan draws a sharp contrast between, on the one hand, machine breakers, rioters and insurrectionaries 'who mounted the most extreme forms of opposition' (117) and, on the other hand, the labour movement organised in parties and unions. The latter helped shape the factory model of society (that itself reproduced the prison model), fulfilling the factory owners' wish for 'a more subdued populace' (118, 129). Hereby, 'the union became the effective agency for suppressing workers' direct action against speed-up or other grievances' (181). By reducing class struggle to wage bargaining, the unions separate the workers from autonomous control over the working conditions. Because they are mainly interested in member fees and often strive to control the workers by 'closed shop' arrangements (so that, just like the bosses, union officials can fire unruly workers), unions are actually instruments of domination and not the right place to start fighting. Zerzan is sure most people feel deep inside that 'the falseness of trading away one's life in order to purchase things is a transparently barren death-trip' (233). He cites a great many examples of disenchantment, withdrawal and resistance to work: absenteeism, turnover, employee theft, illness, drinking, drug-taking, suicide, stress, job burn-out, misuse of on-the-job time, sabotage (208, 213, 217, 219, 222, 223, 228, 231–2, 245, 246, 248, 256, 258). But Zerzan's criticism goes much farther. Disenchantment, withdrawal and resistance also turn against everyday life: declining civic virtue, increasing shoplifting, an immense prison population, tax cheating, child arson, insomnia, emotional disability, loneliness, depression, anorexia, bulimia, gambling, refusal of literacy – an intentional aversion to the whole of modern life (217, 246, 247, 257–8). 'The possibility that the impoverishment of daily life might even render work relatively satisfying, due to the vacuum of substance elsewhere, is rendered unlikely by technology's progressive degradation of work. There is no area of authenticity, no place to hide, and no one can miss this commonplace' (257).

Zerzan was himself a union official in the 1960s. His turn away from organised leftism and towards a broader anti-work and even anticivilisation attitudes was inspired by anarcho-primitivist Fredy Perlman's (1983: 37) conviction that '[l]abor is always forced labor' and that the Stone Age was some kind of Garden of Eden; it was civilisation that turned 'the Garden into a forced-labor camp' (258). Zerzan (1994: 16) adopted this view that 'life before domestication/agriculture was in fact largely one of leisure, intimacy with nature, sensual wisdom, sexual equality, and health. This was our human nature, for a couple of million years, prior to enslavement by priests, kings, and bosses'. The enslavement has taken the form of division of labour, which is deeply alienating. 'The relative wholeness of pre-civilized life was first and foremost an absence of the narrowing, confining separation of people into differentiated roles and functions'. This social stratification has been a central idea of 'key ideologues of civilization' since Plato (147). But the division goes even deeper – its initiation coincides with the 'dissolution of the original unity between humanity and nature' (Zerzan, 1999: 37). This split makes humans into alienated beings that have to use abstract symbols (time, language, number, art, etc.) instead of directly interacting with their environment. It was the implementation of agriculture that brought this estrangement to humanity. Agriculture is 'the end of life as mainly sensuous activity, the embodiment and generator of separated life. Artificiality and work have steadily increased since its inception and are known as culture: in domesticating animals and plants man necessarily domesticated himself' (73). Before the neolithic revolution, work was inexistent. Since then, life quality deteriorated as repression and alienation increased, especially in the course of industrialisation. Because the '[d]ivision of labor embodies, as an implicit purpose, the control and domination of the work process and those tied to it' (118), it has to be overcome. For Zerzan, this does not only entail the abolition of work, but of all alienation and thus of civilisation itself.

It remains somewhat unclear how this may actually be done. Bob Black (1991), in his 1986 essay *The Abolition of Work*, proposes a 'ludic revolution' that creates 'a new way of life based on play'. In the 1980s, Black (1992: 11) learned of 'the idea of zerowork. I'd already been brought close to it by such writers as Fourier, Morris and Kropotkin when I discovered John Zerzan's studies of work refusal'. Like Perlman and Zerzan, Black (1991) is convinced that 'work is forced labor, that is, compulsory production', which is 'the source of nearly all the misery in the world'. Work degrades workers by discipline ('surveillance, rotework, imposed work tempos, production quotas, punching-in and out, etc.'), and makes them dumb and habituated to hierarchy, even in their free time (which is 'mostly devoted to getting ready for work, going to work, returning from work, and recovering from work'). Work, in the end, is deadly – it is 'mass murder or genocide. Directly or indirectly, work will kill most of the people who read these words'. Black attributes most deaths by cars, industrial pollution, alcohol, drugs, cancer and heart disease to work, because '[e]ven if you aren't killed or crippled while actually working, you very well might be while going to work, coming from work, looking for work, or trying to forget about work'.[4] Work steals workers most of their time, even if nothing valuable is produced in working time. Actually, 'most work serves the unproductive purposes of commerce or social control'. Therefore, useless and pernicious work has to be cut down massively. Insofar as work serves useful purposes, it has to be transformed into 'a pleasing variety of game-like and craft-like pastimes, indistinguishable from other pleasurable pastimes except that they happen to yield useful end-products'. Black takes inspiration from Charles Fourier. Most necessary and useful activities are attractive to many people – at least from time to time, as long as they are done without compulsion but in enjoyable circumstances. This also evokes William Morris's utopia of work turned into artisanal handicraft (in his *News from Nowhere*).[5] Black agrees with Zerzan that technology does not save labour: 'When productive technology went from hunter-gathering to agriculture and on to industry, work increased while skills and self-determination diminished'. But Black does not want to do away with all technology. Contrary to the neo-Marxists cited earlier, he agrees with Morris that technology should play just a small role in this transformation. Yet, Black's quite optimistic outlook has a different flavour from Morris's: 'An optimal sexual encounter is the paradigm of productive play. The participants potentiate each other's pleasures, nobody keeps score, and everybody wins. The more you give, the more you get. In the ludic life, the best of sex will diffuse into the better part of daily life. Generalized play leads to the libidinization of life. Sex, in turn, can become less urgent and desperate, more playful'.

A series of anti-work articles written by the insurrectionalist anarchist Alfredo M. Bonanno (1987–1995) are much bleaker and more militant. He distances himself from most other anti-work activists and theorists, asserting he does 'not feel any nostalgia for lost professionalism', being 'even less interested in elaborating libertarian alternatives to grim factory work or intellectual labour', and going so far as to decry 'the abolition of work or its reduction to the minimum required for a meaningful happy life' (Bonanno, 2009: 6). Not even the substitution of work with play satisfies Bonanno, because 'none of that escapes the essential rules of work seen in terms of the global organization of control' (8). Traditional anti-work strategies have mostly been recuperated by capitalism, so they 'have now become normal procedures for capital itself' (9). Like Zerzan, Bonanno decries alienation (14) while deeming Marxist ideas useless (27) and criticising the unions for their participation in business decisions, whereby they abandon more militant activism and essentially pursue 'complete social pacification' (45). Even self-managed co-ops are too peaceful and impotent and therefore not revolutionary enough (17, 38). 'So we see that work cannot be abolished progressively: we need to approach the problem in a destructive manner' (8). Bonanno mainly discusses two strategies: sabotage and bank robbery. They are destructive, but not even they suffice: sabotage cannot destroy the worker identity, and robbery can become a full-time job – in Bonanno's experience (as a convicted robber talking to other prison inmates), the crucial problem is to know what to do with all the money (10–11). So, 'the essential part of any project to destroy work is creativity taken to the maximum possible degree' (10). Bonanno calls this 'projectuality' ('progettualità') – having a 'project in terms of life', or rather inventing this project 'by reflecting upon what one wants to do with one's life and finding the necessary means to realise it, without working' (11). Wolfi Landstreicher (2003) explains 'projectuality' as a prefigurative autonomous direct action that is explicitly aggressive, an 'active refusal of alienated existence' and 'the reappropriation of life'. Referring to Bonanno, Landstreicher gives a definition: 'anarchist projectuality is the practical recognition in one's life that anarchy is not just an aim for the distant future, an ideal that we hope to experience in a far away utopia. Much more essentially, it is a way of confronting life and struggle, a way that puts us at odds with the world as it is. [...] When we make the choice to cease to be a cog, when we make the choice to break the machine rather than continuing to adjust it, passivity ceases and projectuality begins'.

Arguably, the publications of the CrimethInc. ex-worker's collective combine such a projectuality with Black's ludic revolution. CrimethInc. positions itself at the post-left end of the anarchists' spectrum. The root of the collective is anarcho-punk (notably the band Catharsis). According to Thompson (2004: 109), CrimethInc. 'began as Brian D[ingledine]'s personal zine, *Inside Front*, and began operating as a collective only in 1996'. In *Inside Front*, personal accounts of travelling and dropping out are prevalent. Dingledine (1996) explains why he refuses to work: 'When I don't work for them, they don't get to use my labor to perpetuate the status quo. When I don't receive an income from them, I don't have capital to give back to them for them to use to perpetuate the status quo. And most of all, my time and energy are mine to be used to fight against them, rather than to support present conditions'. Similarly, the later CrimethInc. collective asserts that because it is the combined labour and consumption of all workers and employees that powers the system, resistance cannot be a part-time hobby of people who work full-time to maintain it (CrimethInc., 2004: 8). The revolutionary purpose is not just quitting jobs, but 'deserting and ultimately destroying the class system itself. [...] a universal rejection of all possible positions within the social order, in order to create classless communities'. So, CrimethInc.'s class struggle is a struggle against class as such (9). Consequently, '[w]e shouldn't base our solidarity on shared attributes or social positions, but on a shared refusal of our roles in the economy' (CrimethInc., 2011: 250). Instead of dropping out, it would sometimes be better to use the resources of your position for revolutionary purposes and interrupt the system in your position until they fire you (349). 'Not working is only half the battle, and not the important half, at that. The real question is what you do instead. [...] You only discover what interests you by engaging with the world, and in capitalist society, employment and consumption can seem like the only ways to engage. As you cut down on these, replace them immediately with new projects, with the things you dreamed of doing when you didn't have a moment free' (CrimethInc., 2005: 582). This could be volunteering in community groups (or inventing them), making a project out of enjoying oneself, learning, exploring, following ideas – and being happily and proudly unemployed, so as to radicalise the community one comes from (582–3; cf. CrimethInc., 2004: 9). The CrimethInc. collective criticises (neo)-Marxism for making radicals try to look like the mainstream, so as to influence it in revolutionary ways; dropping out, by contrast, creates many alternative ways of life, thereby challenging the dominant order (CrimethInc., 2006: 13).

To have energy to fight the system, one needs food, shelter and other resources, of course. CrimethInc.'s most popular strategy for non-symbolic assaults on the system and no-work sustenance at the same time is theft from corporations. Shoplifting (as well as dumpster diving and squatting) not only rescues resources, it also gives the feeling of freedom and power; it is an attack on consumerism, and it is better than boycotting, because it directly harms the corporations (CrimethInc., 2001: 237–9; cf. Dingledine, 1996). But stealing individually without revolting will not interrupt the status quo – so stealing should be part of building community (CrimethInc., 2011: 276, 278). The hope is that fighting and stealing and living determinedly and desirously might be infectious, so others join in to reclaim the resources of the society, ultimately leading to transformation (CrimethInc., 2001: 256). The collective invites the reader: 'Join us in making the "revolution" a *game*; a game played for the highest stakes of all, but a joyous, carefree game nonetheless!' (192) This sounds quite hedonistic, but at least in later publications, CrimethInc. does not demand that everything is fun or easy; fighting work is hard work (CrimethInc., 2011: 38). And in spite of the individualistic – often even Stirnerite – flavour of much CrimethInc. literature, the struggle against work is one that requires massive support networks and connections between disparate social circles. These should not be organisations with homogenous membership, but coalitions of solidarity between anticapitalist people of all walks of life (CrimethInc., 2004: 9).

The basic unit of direct action is the affinity group: 'the affinity group/cluster/spokescouncil model is simply another incarnation of the communes and workers' councils that formed the backbone of earlier successful (however short-lived) anarchist revolutions' (CrimethInc., 2005: 31). One can experiment with many formats: 'a self-defense league, a thieves' ring, a secret society for revolutionary consciousness' (CrimethInc., 2011: 347), 'a labor union of the unemployed' or, more generally, 'local infrastructures for distributing things people need' (CrimethInc., 2005: 584, 580; cf. 2004: 9; 2001: 78, 165, 253, 255). 'It might be that "dropping out" and "mobilizing the working class" are not opposite revolutionary strategies, after all – so long as dropout communities stay humble and connected to other sectors of society, they can contribute to a feedback loop of revolutionary ambition and tactics' (CrimethInc., 2006: 18).

Like Zerzan, the CrimethInc. collective attacks factories and unions (CrimethInc., 2011: 91–97). The evils of modern society alienate people from each other and the environment and so make life dull, meaningless and vile. Meaning and pleasure are crippled by cultural restraints that therefore have to be fought (CrimethInc., 2001: 155). But the collective appends that the ennui and disorientation of the middle and upper class point to a poverty inherent of the western lifestyle as such; today's problems cannot be reduced to class conflict alone (81). Work is a chief obstacle for the best possible economic security, which is 'being part of a long-term community in which people looked out for each other, a community based on mutual assistance rather than financial incentives' (CrimethInc., 2011: 34). Earning money is very costly: one has to become efficient and compliant, until 'following orders becomes an unconscious reflex' (CrimethInc., 2004: 8). Morally, work is disastrous because the economic system makes responsibility too expensive – most injustices have been carried out by employees (CrimethInc., 2011: 35); economically, 'work makes people poor' (25); and psychologically, 'instead of enabling people to achieve happiness, work fosters the worst kind of self-denial [...] we become commodities' (31; cf. CrimethInc., 2004: 9).

CrimethInc.'s criticism of work does not ground on high theory, because '[t]he idea that you need *a complete understanding of the economy* to come to any conclusions about it just serves to silence people' (CrimethInc., 2011: 41). So, the collective drafts a simple model of the economy that categorises the many positions of people in regard to work, all of which have reasons to despise and fight work: capitalists, exploited, excluded (42). 'So we all, rich and poor, must band together to transform our situation' (CrimethInc., 2001: 81), and '[t]his will take different forms for different individuals, according to the classes they are escaping and the details of their lives' (CrimethInc., 2004: 9). Of course, that is too simplistic. But 'the point isn't to be *right*, but to be *dangerous*' (CrimethInc., 2011: 349).

Conclusion

At the anti-work end of the radical spectrum, there are notable differences between neo-Marxists and anarchists. The former rely on the state and its power to redistribute wealth and organise necessary work. To prevail upon state authorities to carry out anti-work policies (like a UBI), anti-work neo-Marxists try to change hegemonic public opinion through theoretical leadership. The anarchists, on the other hand, rely on the direct actions of individuals and small groups to build networks among themselves without ossifying into formal organisations; the state is deeply mistrusted. Therefore, anarchist anti-work literature is much more likely to be inflammatory and action-oriented than focused on theoretical coherency. Politically, there is the possibility of dividing a strong anti-work movement (should such a one come into existence – at the moment, the resistance is mostly acted out by isolated individuals and groups and without revolutionary consequences) by granting the neo-Marxists some reforms while making the anarchists appear as mindless, extremist hooligans. But the two strands of radicalism offer complementary not contradictory strategies. And most points of criticism against work (alienation, exploitation, violence, degradation, submission, etc.) are at the core of both Marxist and anarchist anti-work radicalism. Coalition-building should be possible, even if serious reservations remain valid.

Ursula McTaggart (2009: 35) makes 'the scandalous suggestion that socialists should be open to working with, speaking with, and taking seriously the positions of anarcho-primitivists', including Bob Black (36); and even, the outspokenly anti-anarchist neo-Marxists Srnicek and Williams (2015: 163) are open to coalesce with horizontalist (i.e. anarchist) groups when they assert: 'The divisions between spontaneous uprisings and organisational longevity, short-term desires and long-term strategy, have split what should be a broadly consistent project for building a post-work world'. The anarchists, having negative experiences with Marxists and in danger yet again of being used as cannon fodder for what is ultimately another state project, are much more reluctant. But they also build pragmatic coalitions. Although the Anarchist Federation (2015a), for example, ultimately seeks to abolish work (3) and is highly critical of unions that 'become a layer of management with the main task of controlling our ability to take collective direct action' (26), it nonetheless advocates mainly workplace strategies typical of the classical (if militant) worker movement. Many anarchists have joined the Industrial Workers of the World (IWW), including David Graeber (2013) who lambasts 'bullshit jobs'. The IWW (2017) emphasise that they are neither anarchist nor non-anarchist, but 'open to all workers'. The IWW is a union that – not through petition but through direct action – aims at legislation that significantly cuts the work week (IWW, 2013). This is, expectedly, regarding the constituency, reformist, but at least the Anarchist Federation (2015b) can grudgingly live with that.

Anti-work is radical because it aims at the *radix*, the root of exploitation and domination in capitalism. This is what differentiates anti-work from industrial action: it is not just a fight for better exploitation (higher wages for the workers) and for a more humane domination (safer workplaces and friendlier bosses), but for the abolition of work as such. Anti-work is a political and cultural struggle. As a political struggle, it tries to wrest power from the superiors – this can become a dirty fight with violence (burning factories, using state authority) and compromise. But as a cultural struggle, it tries to build up new awareness and new practices – and this can be a beautiful act that inspires revolutionary association and facilitates free creativity.

Notes

1 Nietzsche's thoughts on work are unsystematically scattered throughout the aphorisms of his middle creative period. Here, I compiled what I found in *Menschliches, Allzumenschliches, Morgenröthe* and *Die fröhliche Wissenschaft* (1999a: 231–2, 234, 299, 312–13, 346, 623–4; 1999b: 173, 329, 408, 556).

2 Obviously, the famous description of life under communism in Marx's and Engels's *The German Ideology* ('in communist society, where nobody has one exclusive sphere of activity but each can become accomplished in any branch he wishes, society regulates the general production and thus makes it possible for me to do one thing today and another tomorrow, to hunt in the morning, fish in the afternoon, rear cattle in the evening, criticise after dinner, just as I have a mind, without ever becoming hunter, fisherman, herdsman or critic'. Marx and Engels, 2000: 12) has some similarities to Kropotkin's mixture of fields, factories and workshops (and, in fact, leisure). But while for Kropotkin (1998: 197), this vision is 'already possible, already realisable' because the technologies exist and just have to be decentralized (and, of course, expropriated), Marx and Engels prefer a centralization of politics and production that makes the 'withering away' of the state very unlikely and a non-dominating industrial management virtually impossible. The difference is thus that Kropotkin depicts a concrete, immediate goal, whereas Marx and Engels speculate about a far-future magical land they do not really believe in.

3 At the moment, Hirsch's book is available in German language only. Therefore, all English-language citations are translations by me.

4 Most of Black's description fits paid work and domestic labour alike, even if it only refers to the former. Domestic workers may not have to commute as much, but they, too, are in danger of being killed in traffic accidents (while going to the mall or the kindergarten) and often use dangerous substances to forget about their plight. An additional danger for them is abuse by brutal spouses.

5 Here is not the space to discuss the role of work in anarchist (or, in Morris's case, libertarian socialist) utopias. Suffice it to say that it is expectedly as ambiguous as anarchism's (and generally, socialism's) attitude towards work. In Morris's *News from Nowhere* (1890), technology has only a minor role in production; industrialism has yielded to a pastoral agriculture and an artisanal work that is as fulfilling as art or play. In Ursula K. Le Guin's first utopia, *The Dispossessed* (1974), the anarcho-syndicalist planet Anarres is so barren that industrialist productivism seems to be inevitable; consequently, the struggle for efficiency in the management of work engenders a bureaucracy that seriously endangers freedom. But in Le Guin's second utopia, *Always Coming Home* (1985), technology has almost been abandoned by the future Stone-Age people Kesh; they do not like to work and are so lazy that they just eat with spoons – they do not want to clean more cutlery. And in Chris Carlsson's *After the Deluge* (2004), a full system of voluntary work that maintains a gift economy and frees (almost) everyone from unwanted drudgery or (work-related) alienation is described.

References

Anarchist Federation (2015a) *Work*, [Pamphlet and Online], Available: https://afed.org.uk/wp-content/uploads/2015/09/WORK-online-version.pdf [3 Nov 2016].

Anarchist Federation (2015b) 'The working class needs who?' *AFED* Homepage, [Online], Available: https://afed.org.uk/the-working-class-needs-who/ [25 Jan 2017].

Bebel, A. (1904) *Woman Under Socialism*. New York: New York Labor News Company.

Beblo, M. and Ortlieb, R. (2012) 'Absent from work? The impact of household and work conditions in Germany', *Feminist Economics*, vol. 18, no. 1, pp. 73–97.

Black, B. (1991) *The Abolition of Work*, [Online], Available: http://inspiracy.com/black/abolition/abolitionofwork.html [4 Jan 2017].

Black. B. (1992) *Friendly Fire*. Brooklyn, NY: Autonomedia.

Black, D. C. and Frost, D. (2011) *Health at Work – an Independent Review of Sickness Absence*, [Online], Available: www.gov.uk/government/uploads/system/uploads/attachment_data/file/181060/health-at-work.pdf [11 Nov 2016].

Bonanno, A. M. (2009) *Let's Destroy Work, Let's Destroy the Economy*, [Online], Available: https://theanarchistlibrary.org/library/alfredo-m-bonanno-let-s-destroy-work-let-s-destroy-the-economy.pdf [10 Dec 2016].

CrimethInc. (2001) *Days of War, Nights of Love: Crimethink for Beginners*. Atlanta, GA: CrimethInc. Free Press.

CrimethInc. (2004) 'Déclassé war: Dropouts cutting class (exiting the economy as a strategy for reclaiming your life and saving the world)', *Harbinger*, no. 5, pp. 8–9, [Online], Available: https://libcom.org/files/harbinger-5.pdf [21 Jan 2017].

CrimethInc. (2005) *Recipes for Disaster. An Anarchist Cookbook*. Olympia, WA: CrimethInc. Workers' Collective.

CrimethInc. (2006) 'Dropping out', *Rolling Thunder*, no. 2, pp. 10–19.

CrimethInc. (2011) *Work. Capitalism. Economics. Resistance*. Salem, OR: CrimethInc. Far East.

D[ingledine], B. (1996) 'How I spent my permanent vacation', *Inside Front*, [Online], Available: https://crimethinc.com/1996/01/01/how-i-spent-my-permanent-vacation [21 Jan 2017].

Fineman, S. (2012) *Work. A Very Short Introduction*. Oxford: Oxford University Press.

Gorz, A. (1999) *Reclaiming Work: Beyond the Wage-Based Society*. Cambridge: Polity Press.

Graeber, D. (2013) 'The modern phenomenon of nonsense jobs', *The Sydney Morning Herald*, [Online], Available: www.smh.com.au/action/printArticle?id=4709791 [29 Nov 2016].

H. (1999) 'Kritik am Manifest gegen die Arbeit', *Wildcat-Zirkular*, no. 54, pp. 43–54, [Online], Available: www.wildcat-www.de/zirkular/54/z54kritk.htm [26 Dec 2016].

Hackett, R. D. (1989) 'Work attitudes and employee absenteeism: A synthesis of the literature', *Journal of Occupational Psychology*, vol. 62, pp. 236–248.

Hirsch, M. (2016) *Die Überwindung der Arbeitsgesellschaft. Eine politische Philosophie der Arbeit*. Wiesbaden: Springer VS.

Hoxsey, D. (2010) 'Are happy employees healthy employees? Researching the effects of employee engagement on absenteeism', *Canadian Public Administration/Administration Publique du Canada*, vol. 53, no. 4, pp. 551–571.

IWW (2013) 'Arguments for a four-hour day', *Beyond Resistance*, [Online], Available: https://beyondresistance.wordpress.com/2013/03/23/iww-arguments-for-a-four-hour-day/ [29 Dec 2015].

IWW (2017) 'The IWW stance on political parties and anarchism', *IWW Official Website*, [Online], Available: iww.org/about/political_parties_and_anarchism [29 Mar 2017].

Johns, G. (2003) 'How methodological diversity has improved our understanding of absenteeism from work', *Human Resource Management Review*, vol. 13, pp. 157–184.

Krisis (1999) *Manifesto against Labour*, [Online], Available: www.krisis.org/1999/manifesto-against-labour/ [22 Aug 2016].

Kropotkin, P. (1907) *The Conquest of Bread*. New York/London: G.P. Putnam's Sons.

Kropotkin, P. (1998) *Fields, Factories and Workshops Tomorrow*. London: Freedom Press.

Lafargue, P. (2010) *The Right to Be Lazy*, [Online], Available: https://theanarchistlibrary.org/library/paul-lafargue-the-right-to-be-lazy.pdf [5 Nov 2016].

Landstreicher. W. (2003) 'On Projectuality', *Willful Disobedience*, vol. 4, no. 1, [Online], Available: www.reocities.com/kk_abacus/vb/wd4-1words.html [08 Jan 2017].

Lechmann, D. S. J. and Schnabel, C. (2014) 'Absence from work of the self-employed: a comparison with paid employees', *Kyklos*, vol. 67, no. 3, pp. 368–390.

Livanos, I. and Zangelidis, A. (2013) 'Unemployment, labor market flexibility, and absenteeism: a pan-European study', *Industrial Relations*, vol. 52, no. 2, pp. 492–515.

Lusinyan, L. and Bonato, L. (2007) 'Work absence in Europe', *IMF Staff Papers*, vol. 54, no. 3, pp. 475–538.

Marx, K. (2009) *Economic & Philosophic Manuscripts of 1844*, [Online], Available: www.marxists.org/archive/marx/works/download/pdf/Economic-Philosophic-Manuscripts-1844.pdf [4 Nov 2016].

Marx, K. (2010) *Capital. A Critique of Political Economy. Volume III*, [Online], Available: www.marxists.org/archive/marx/works/download/pdf/Capital-Volume-III.pdf [4 Nov 2016].

Marx, K. and Engels, F. (2000) *A Critique of the German Ideology*, [Online], Available: www.marxists.org/archive/marx/works/download/Marx_The_German_Ideology.pdf [6 Nov 2016].

McTaggart, U. (2009) 'Can we build socialist-anarchist alliances? Revolution meets apocalypse', *Against the Current*, no. 141, pp. 35–37.

Nietzsche, F. (1999a) *Menschliches, Allzumenschliches. KSA 2*, Munich/Berlin/New York: dtv/Walter de Gruyter.

Nietzsche, F. (1999b) *Morgenröthe. Idyllen aus Messina. Die fröhliche Wissenschaft. KSA 3*, Munich/Berlin/New York: dtv/Walter de Gruyter.

Perlman, F. (1983) *Against His-story, against Leviathan!*. Detroit, MI: Black & Red.

Pfeifer, C. (2010) 'Impact of wages and job levels on worker absenteeism', *International Journal of Manpower*, vol. 31, no. 1, pp. 59–72.

Plato (1991) *The Republic of Plato*, 2nd edition. Translated with notes and an interpretive essay by Allan Bloom, New York: BasicBooks.

Roscigno, V. J. and Hodson, R. (2004) 'The organizational and social foundations of worker resistance', *American Sociological Review*, vol. 69, no. 1, pp. 14–39.

Russell, B. (1932) 'In praise of idleness', *Harper's Monthly Magazine*, no. 165, pp. 552–559.

Sauer, C. and Valet, P. (2013) 'Less is sometimes more: Consequences of overpayment on job satisfaction and absenteeism', *Social Justice Research*, vol. 26, pp. 132–150.

Seidman, M. (1991) *Workers Against Work. Labor in Paris and Barcelona during the Popular Fronts*. Berkeley/Los Angeles/Oxford: University of California Press.

Shi, J. and Skuterud, M. (2015) 'Gone fishing! Reported sickness absenteeism and the weather', *Economic Inquiry*, vol. 53, no. 1, pp. 388–405.

Srnicek, N. and Williams, A. (2015) *Inventing the Future. Postcapitalism and a World Without Work*. London/New York: Verso.

Thompson, S. (2004) *Punk Productions. Unfinished Business*. Albany, NY: State University of New York Press.

Trenkle, N. (2003) *Presenting the Krisis Group's Manifesto against Labor*, [Online], Available: https://libcom.org/library/presenting-krisis-groups-manifesto-against-labor-norbert-trenkle [26 Dec 2016].

van Yperen, N. W. and Hagedoorn, M. (1996) 'Intent to leave and absenteeism as reactions to perceived inequity: The role of psychological and social constraints', *Journal of Occupational and Organizational Psychology*, vol. 69, pp. 367–372.

Wegge, J., Schmidt, K.-H., Parkes, C. and van Dick, R. (2007) '"Taking a sickie": Job satisfaction and job involvement as interactive predictors of absenteeism in a public organization', *Journal of Occupational and Organizational Psychology*, vol. 80, pp. 77–89.

Zerzan, J. (1999) *Elements of Refusal*, 2nd edition. Columbia, MO: C.A.L. Press/Paleo Editions.

Zerzan, J. (1994) *Future Primitive and Other Essays*. Brooklyn, NY/Columbia, MO: Autonomedia/Anarchy: A Journal of Desire Armed.

4.2

RADICAL EDUCATION

Emily Charkin and Judith Suissa

Introduction – 'Politicising' Education

In March 2003, it was widely reported in the British media that hundreds of school students had missed classes to take part in the mass rallies taking place across the country against the US-led invasion of Iraq. Head teachers and education policy officials interviewed in the press were quoted as condemning the students' actions, with some head teachers locking the gates of their schools after they had discovered students leaving the premises during break-time. The deputy head of Fortismere School, a state comprehensive in North London, where sixty pupils were found to have left school to attend the rally in central London, was quoted as saying that he was 'horrified by the pupils' actions' and that 'It is irresponsible and dangerous to do this. The organisers are sixth-formers but many of the children who have gone with them are younger. They should be in school' (BBC, 2003).

These comments would have been anathema to the radical educators we will consider in this chapter. While there are significant differences and even tensions between the variants of radical educational practice that we discuss, what they share – and what makes them, we argue, 'radical' – is both the *conceptual starting point* from which education, as a social process, is always, in some sense, 'political' and the *utopian impulse* to challenge and improve upon dominant social and political values through the creation of educational alternatives. Indeed, as Brian Simon (1972) notes, the radical tradition in education sees educational change as a key aspect of radical social change.

It is both challenging and urgent to defend this politically substantive notion of radical education in the contemporary context.[1] As Michael Fielding and Peter Moss, contemporary advocates of radical education within the state school system, have argued, we are living under a 'dictatorship of no alternatives' and a climate in which 'the political and ethical have been drained out of public discourse on education and schools' (Fielding and Moss, 2011: 1, 21). This nihilism is manifested in policy debates which are dominated by technical questions about 'what works' and ignore moral questions about 'what matters'.

Even those who are critical of the current schooling system tend to forget that the near-ubiquitous model of universal state-funded compulsory schooling and the wider political structures within which it is constituted are a relatively recent and contested invention from the second half of the nineteenth century. We have forgotten what Quentin Skinner calls the 'battles behind the apparent certainties' and are 'bewitched' (Skinner, 2002: 6) by our current educational arrangements. This chapter explores some of what Skinner would call the 'different possible worlds' revealed by radical educational ideas and practices (ibid.).

Radical education is not only neglected but sometimes demonised in an era in which teachers and schools across Europe and America are under pressure to join a 'fight against radicalisation' under the banner of fighting global terrorism, an 'anti-radicalisation' agenda that, as Mayssoun Sukarieh and Stuart Tannock have forcefully argued, is part and parcel of the neo-liberal ideology dominating the provision, content and control of schooling in many Western schools, and that is 'leading to the abandonment and undermining of the radical tradition in education at precisely the time it is needed most' (Sukarieh and Tannock, 2016: 3).

This chapter, therefore, seeks to defend an account of radical education which embodies a set of political commitments to substantive values such as freedom, equality and justice, and that regards social institutions, amongst them schools, as subject to constant questioning, challenges and deep-rooted change in the interests of bringing about a more just, less oppressive form of social and political life. This account does not imply a simplistic notion of education as a means to bring about political ends, but rather reflects the point that, as Richard Johnson notes, 'in the political-radical mainstream, politics and education went together in a complicated web of means-ends relationships' (Johnson, 1979: 97).

In the following discussion, we aim to uncover and interrogate some of the ways in which radical education practices from the past and present continue to challenge some fundamental ideas about education, politics and social change.

Many of our examples are small, experimental schools and communities set up outside of and, often, in antithesis to the values and approaches of the state system. However, we recognise that in certain times and places radicalism has also played out within the state system. This can occur both at the level of innovation within individual institutions and in wider campaigns. Examples are the struggle for universal free schooling in a historical context in which education was often the preserve of a privileged elite, or the comprehensive movement in England in the 1960s, which, as Brian Simon has argued, was originally a 'grass roots movement in Britain, the first schools being established in the late 1940s or early 1950s by certain advanced local authorities in opposition to government policy and advice … a hard and difficult process, disturbing deeply engrained vested interests, and for some, quite traumatic' (Simon, 2005: 147). The radicalism of these initiatives in their historical contexts can easily be forgotten as they are co-opted to more conservative and authoritarian agendas and as the notion of 'public' behind a commitment to public educational provision has, in many Western capitalist states, been eroded.

Many of our examples are drawn from the past, partly because it is more possible to identify what is radical with historical perspective and partly as a reflection of the hostility of the current context to radical educational practices. However, we also recognise contemporary examples of educational spaces where radical practices of alterity and resistance persist – in spite of – or perhaps partly, as a result of – difficult times.

What is Radical Education?

The aforementioned discussion suggests some important distinctions that will help to clarify when it makes sense to describe particular educational practices as 'radical'. One such useful distinction is that between pedagogy and education. As Robin Alexander notes, commenting on Brian Simon's seminal 1981 paper 'Why No Pedagogy in England?' (Simon, 1981), the word 'pedagogy' 'still does not enjoy widespread currency in England' (Alexander, 2004: 9).

In contrast to its usage in the continental European tradition, where the term 'brings together within one concept the act of teaching and the body of knowledge, argument and evidence in which it is embedded and by which particular classroom practices are justified' (Alexander, 2004: 10), when used in English, 'pedagogy' has a fairly narrow meaning, 'to equate with the practice of teaching' (ibid.).

'Education', on the other hand, is a far broader and, critically, an inherently evaluative term, encompassing ideas about value and worth, at least in the analytic sense developed in Richard Peters' classic account (Peters, 1966), according to which, unlike the case with related terms such as 'learning', 'training' or 'instruction', it would be conceptually incoherent to say that someone had been educated but had not changed for the better. This analytic distinction is useful as it enables us to clarify why it makes sense to consider certain *educational* projects radical, in keeping with a broad definition of radicalism whereby, as Paul McLaughlin puts it, drawing on Zygmunt Bauman, 'To be radical is to seek (practically or theoretically) to uncover and uproot the roots, foundations or origins of a problem or a project' (McLaughlin, 2012: 19). On this view, to educate someone is necessarily to act with a certain intention, oriented towards bringing about a desired state of affairs; whereas pedagogy, understood as a set of teaching practices, cannot on its own, without this intentional context, be construed as 'radical'.

Thus, the radicalism of the tradition of Critical Pedagogy associated most famously with Paulo Freire consists, in spite of its name, not in a particular set of classroom techniques and practices. Rather, it is the underlying commitment to challenging oppressive structures and relationships, and the belief that coming to a consciousness of oppression through educational encounters can and will lead to a commitment to ending it, which makes Critical Pedagogy radical. Indeed, while Freire's work reflects the insight that there is no such thing as a politically neutral educational process, contemporary theorists and practitioners of critical pedagogy have repeatedly warned against the danger of reducing Critical Pedagogy to a technique or a method rather than seeing it as an ongoing political and moral project (see Giroux, 2013).

The aforementioned analysis can help to understand how it is that in certain times and places, pedagogical practices, for example participatory styles of teaching, student-led project-based learning or peer assessment, may be labelled 'radical' without being truly radical in the political sense. Likewise, focusing on the pedagogical approaches and practices that often characterise experimental, alternative forms of education may allow us to lose sight of the political outlook and motivation behind these alternatives, and thus of what made them radical.

In the contemporary context, we can find examples of innovative pedagogical practices that are often promoted as 'radical' new ways of 'improving learning' in their departure from traditional institutional schooling and classroom pedagogy, such as Ken Robinson's endorsement of the 'flipped classroom' pioneered by online Massive Open Online Course (MOOC) provider the Khan Academy, or Sugata Mitra's proposals for getting rid of traditional classrooms and teachers and replacing them with a 'School in the Cloud'.[2] However, these examples are not radical in the wider political sense in which we explore the term in this chapter.

The flip side of this argument is that many radical educational movements may adopt, perhaps surprisingly, traditional pedagogical methods and practices. It is an empirical question beyond the scope of this chapter whether or not the commitment to radical social and political changes is enhanced or impeded by particular pedagogical relationships and practices. However, it is certainly the case that many radical educational movements have at times used pedagogical practices that on the surface seem fairly conservative. For example, Rebecca Tarlau documents in her studies of the Landless People's movement in Brazil how, as part of their endeavour to radically change public education in pursuit of a radically different social world, activists and educators within the movement occasionally use pedagogical practices, such as 'strict discipline, mandatory work schedules and celebrations of socialist struggles', which many would regard as morally questionable (Tarlau, 2015: 26). Similarly, in Summerhill School, one of the most famous radical educational experiments (see below), while children are free to choose whether or not to attend lessons, the lessons take the form of fairly traditional teaching of standard curriculum subjects.

We suggest, therefore, that the 'radical' nature of radical educational experiments consists in their underlying commitment to both critiquing the dominant norms, practices, values and institutions of existing society, and in positing an alternative. The associated pedagogical practices may or may not be a well-thought-out element of this alternative. As we explore later, these tensions between pedagogy and political commitment, between means and ends, and between the posited ideal society and the current social institutions, in which its conditions are created, are reflected in the variety of educational experiments that constitute the broad tradition of radical education.

Anarchist Education

Educational experiments within the anarchist tradition offer an important challenge to unexamined assumptions about the role of the state in education and, perhaps, the clearest examples of how education in schools and communities can be part of a wider vision for social and economic changes.

In a time when the role of the state in education is taken for granted, we need to remind ourselves of a radical tradition that dissented from the idea of mass state provision of education from its earliest days. William Godwin, the early anarchist theorist who wrote of 'the evils of national education' in his 1793 text 'Enquiry Concerning Political Justice', argued that

> The project of national education ought uniformly to be discouraged on account of its obvious alliance with national government. [...] Before we put so powerful a machine under the direction of so ambiguous an agent, it behoves us to consider well what it is that we do. Government will not fail to employ it, to strengthen its hands, and perpetuate its institutions [...]
>
> *(Godwin, in Marshall, 1986: 147)*

This position, while most closely associated with the anarchists, was also held by J.S. Mill, the forefather of modern liberal theory, who vehemently opposed the idea of universal state education, on the grounds that it was 'a mere contrivance for molding people to be exactly like one another' (Mill, 1991 [1859]: 117).

In the late nineteenth and early twentieth centuries, this critique of state schooling and of the state itself – at least the capitalist, hierarchical, militaristic state – translated into the setting up of anarchist schools and communities, most of which were established by educators and activists affiliated with the movement of social anarchism, the strand of anarchist theory and practice associated with early socialist thinkers such as Pierre-Joseph Proudhon, Michael Bakunin and Peter Kropotkin, who emphasised the values of fraternity, equality and mutual aid. As historical accounts of these early anarchist schools make clear (see Avrich, 2006; Smith, 1983), they were generally set up as part of anarchist communities. The work of the school was an integral element of the daily life of the community, whether through participation in the self-governing structures and activities of self-sufficient farming communities such as Stelton, New Jersey, founded in 1915 (see Avrich, 2006: 241–311) or through serving as community centres for political activism, adult education and cultural events, such as The New York Ferrer School, founded in 1911 (see Avrich, 2006: 75–121).

The rejection of the idea of a neutral education as both conceptually incoherent and politically dangerous – a position that, as we argued earlier, is a central feature of radical education – was forcefully articulated by Franciso Ferrer, the founder of the Escuela Moderna in Barcelona, perhaps the most famous and influential of the anarchist schools (Avrich, 2006). In 1904, Ferrer declared in the school's prospectus:

> Neutrality in the school can be nothing but hypocrisy ... We should not, in the school, hide the fact that we would awaken in the children a desire for a society of men truly free and truly equal, a society without violence, without hierarchies, and without privilege of any sort.
>
> *(Ferrer, 1909: 6)*

These anarchist schools also allow us to explore and problematise the distinction between education and pedagogy discussed earlier. It appears that most anarchist schools were characterised by innovative pedagogical practices such as learning-by-doing, student-led learning, a rejection of traditional student-teacher relationships and the absence of corporal punishment. These practices were often shared with other libertarian and progressive educational experiments, as we discuss later. However, the impetus behind the adoption of these practices was not a commitment to libertarian or progressive pedagogy per se, but a political opposition to the unequally structured, hierarchical capitalist state and the institutional form of education designed to mould children to fit into and sustain it. One could argue that, in their rejection of the idea of neutrality in education and their adoption of a substantive curriculum, where children were explicitly taught about the evils of capitalism, militarism and religious dogma, and encouraged to value solidarity, internationalism and mutual aid, these early anarchist schools were far from libertarian or child-centred, at least in the sense associated with early progressive thinkers such as Rousseau. In fact, Rousseau's romantic view of the child was ridiculed by social anarchist thinkers like Bakunin (Suissa, 2006: 10, 28), not out of any hostility towards child-centred educational practices, but because he rejected the social ontology behind Rousseau's position, which assumed a pre-social human nature rather than the contextual account of human nature developed by the social anarchists (see Morland, 1997).

One could argue that it is precisely the insistence that human society is 'the real starting point of all human civilization and the only medium in which the personality and liberty of man can really be born and grow' (Bakunin, in Morris 1993: 87–88) that explains the anarchists' support for forms of education that, rather than emphasising the absolute freedom of the child, emphasise the substantive moral and political values underlying the school as a microcosm of an alternative society.

The early anarchist schools, such as Sebastien Faure's La Ruche and Ferrer's Escuela Moderna, were committed to the principle of integral education, so that children not only studied academic subjects but also learned crafts and practical skills – both in the school workshop and garden, and in visits to factories and laboratories (see Suissa, 2006: 80; Avrich, 2006). These aspects of anarchist education were clearly similar to the wider progressive movement's emphasis on 'learning by doing', a notion most famously associated with the work of John Dewey (see Dewey, 1916, 1938). Yet rather than being promoted to provide a more effective form of learning, their rationale was an explicitly political one. As Kropotkin and Bakunin argued, the goal was to 'raise manual labour to the place of honour it ought to occupy in society' and thereby to challenge what they viewed as the pernicious division between 'brain work' and 'manual work', which reflected the structural inequalities inherent in the capitalist state (Kropotkin in Ward, 1974: 180). An example of how these political ideas ran through the curriculum, pedagogy and organisation of these anarchist schools is given by Robert Louzon (quoted in Smith, 1983: 42) who describes a lesson in arithmetic based on children's experience of work in a foundry, where the children were given information about the number of employees, their status and their earnings, and then asked to work out the answers to questions about their yearly average and difference.

These schools were animated by a vision of a society free of the oppressive structures and institutions of the present. They, therefore, treated the children as the prospective creators and inhabitants of such a society. Ferrer wrote:

> Having practised the coeducation of boys and girls, of rich and poor – having, that is to say, started from the principle of solidarity and equality – we are not prepared to create a new inequality. Hence in the Modern School there will be no rewards and no punishments; there will be no examinations to puff up some children with the flattering title of 'excellent' to give others the vulgar title of 'good', and make others unhappy with a consciousness of incapacity and failure.
>
> *(Ferrer, 1913: 55)*

Here, we see how the rejection of examinations and rewards stems not from an enthusiasm for a particular pedagogical approach as being more effective at bringing about learning; nor from any reliance on empirical evidence or psychological theories, but from an avowed commitment to a substantive set of moral and social values that, the social anarchists believed, could and would underpin and sustain the self-governing libertarian socialist society of the future. The school was to embody a microcosm of this society, explicitly challenging the underlying values of the current state and offering an alternative through its ethos and daily life.

Although the anarchist society hoped for by these educators has not yet arrived, Paul Avrich's research on ex-pupils of anarchist schools in America in the twentieth century does suggest that 'the great majority appear to have carried away a strong co-operative and libertarian ethic, a spirit of mutual aid and individual sovereignty which has remained with them throughout their adult years' (Avrich, 2006: 385). There are also ongoing anarchist educational experiments with a similar orientation – in schools, universities, home education groups, adult education and in wider social movements. For example, the Paideia school in Spain describes how it 'is first and foremost a political project; an intervention in capitalist society with the ambition of contributing to its radical overthrow'.[3] Similarly, the Free Skool Santa Cruz, part of a network of explicitly Anarchist free schools across North America and Canada, describes itself as 'a grassroots educational project beyond institutional control', stating 'We see Free Skool as a direct challenge to dominant institutions and hierarchical relationships'.[4]

In the current climate, the explicit target of the anarchist critique reflected in these experiments is often less the state and its control of educational institutions, and more the pervasive language and ideology of neo-liberalism and corporate interests that have increasingly come to characterise the governance and content of education. For example, the recent Antiuniversity Now project, started in London in 2015, continues the radical educational positions embodied in the work of the anarchist theorists and practitioners discussed earlier, in their commitment to 'challenge academic and class hierarchy through an open invitation to teach and learn any subject, in any form, anywhere'.[5]

Free Schools in Britain and America

The anarchist educational movement has been closely connected to a wider libertarian and progressive movement in education which, in the twentieth century, spawned numerous small, private schools, including the relatively long-lived Summerhill in the Suffolk countryside in the UK, founded in 1921. Summerhill is perhaps the school most likely to come to people's minds as an example of a 'radical' educational experiment. However, Summerhill and other private schools like it sit somewhat uncomfortably with the radical tradition that regards 'fundamental social change as a core goal of education' (Sukarieh and Tannock, 2016: 6) since they do not espouse an explicit political agenda, and charge fees which are prohibitive for some families.

Summerhill's founder, A.S. Neill, avoided any overt political or moral messages in Summerhill's materials and teaching, out of a conviction that 'If left to himself without adult suggestion of any kind, [the child] will develop as far as he is capable of developing' (Neill, in Lamb, 1992: 9). One could therefore see Neill as subscribing to the view, rejected by the social anarchists, that there can be such a thing as an education that is politically neutral, and of endorsing a Rousseauian view of a benign, pre-social human nature. However, one could also read his insistence on freedom as the only desirable and legitimate form of education or upbringing as itself a political statement. In other words, Neill can be seen as taking an implicit political position, both in his implementation of democratic practices in the day-to-day governance and running of the school community, and in his insistence that 'children must determine their own values, in culture as in morality' (Hemmings, 1972: 35). In today's political climate, Neill's insistence that real democracy requires individuals to be granted the freedom to make their own decisions about their lives, that this kind of freedom has to be experienced from childhood in order to be realised and that it is the absence or indeed denial of such genuine freedom to individuals that is responsible for all manner of social ills can indeed seem politically radical.

A similar perspective is echoed in the statements by the staff and founders of Sudbury Valley School, founded in 1968 in Massachusetts, USA. Although Sudbury Valley, unlike Summerhill, is not a boarding school, its creators see it as a community of children and adults where the emphasis is on providing an environment in which children can 'develop the ability to direct their own lives, be accountable for their actions, set priorities, allocate resources, deal with complex ethical issues, and work with others in a vibrant community'.[6] Thus while not advocating a substantive curriculum, and possibly, as we suggested earlier, being less overtly motivated than early anarchist educators and Critical Pedagogues by the view of education as a central aspect of radical political change, educators within the free school movement are nevertheless committed to a participatory view of democracy and individual liberty. They thus offer a radical challenge to the liberal democratic ideas arguably reflected in and reinforced by dominant forms of state schooling. Like Neill, Sudbury's founders believe that

> The only way to accustom children to democracy is to practice it [...] To take people you've been pushing around for twelve years in the authoritarian environment of traditional school, and sit them down for fifty minutes of talking about this being a free country, and what freedom is about, and what their rights are, is laughable.[7]

Summerhill has also been an inspiration for many other experimental private schools in the twentieth century. In particular, during the Second World War, a number of schools were set up not only as an attempt to provide an alternative education but as a kind of political response to the horrors of the War. John Aitkenhead, founder of Kilquhanity in Scotland in 1940, describes how in its early years, teachers were drawn to Kilquhanity as a 'moral crusade' embodied in an 'international school promoting the arts and eschewing violence' (Aitkenhead, 1990: 8). In the same year, Kenneth Barnes set up Wennington School in Yorkshire based on a manifesto which positioned the school as part of the 'foundations of a changed and just society within the scope of the common people...' (Barnes, 1980: 3) and a stated aim to achieve a 'classless society' (Barnes, 1936).

Later in the twentieth century, the Free School Movement in Britain and the USA in the 1960s and 1970s also connected educational experiment to social change. Political radicals, such as Paul Goodman (1911–1972) and Ivan Illich (1926–2002), argued for the 'disestablishment' of schools as part of a wider critique of the 'schooled' society (Illich, 1971). They argued for non-institutional alternatives which would 'serve personal, creative and autonomous interaction' such as 'learning networks', 'mini-schools', 'store-front schools', 'co-operative work schemes' and home education. Goodman also argued for an environmental view of education based on 'incidental' learning rather than pedagogy (Goodman, 1970: 1). Therefore, he argued for wider societal reform since he claimed that contemporary society was 'deficient in worth-while goals that could make growing up possible' (Goodman, 1957: 12).

First Street School (1964–66) is a good example of a 'mini-school' developed within this climate as an explicit attempt to put radical ideas into practice in a deprived area of New York. It was funded by private donations so that 'in practice we were a public school, open to whoever in the neighbourhood cared to come' (Dennison, 1969: 29). In the journal *Anarchy*, Dennison, who was a teacher at the school, positioned the school as an antidote to the 'dehumanization of the public school system' (Dennison, 1967: 70) with voluntary attendance and a pedagogy based on 'reality of encounter' and the primacy of relationships not of 'teachers' and 'pupils' but adults and children and children and children (Dennison, 1967: 74). He describes in some detail the ways in which these relationships were prioritised, for example, the curriculum at First Street School was 'talk, talk, talk', eroding the usual boundaries between teachers and pupils such that they were involved with the realities of each other's lives.

Dennison also positioned the school as a small but practical attempt to challenge wider inequalities and injustices:

> Against all that is shoddy and violent and treacherous and emotionally impoverished in American life, we might propose conventions which were rational and straightforward, rich both in feeling and thought and which treated individuals with a respect we do little more at present than proclaim from our public rostrums.
>
> *(Dennison, 1969: 7)*

As with many radical educational experiments, it was short-lived. The school had to close after two years due to lack of funding. However, Dennison argued that the school 'made a great difference in the lives of some few children' (Dennison, 1969: 30) – and also with the parents who, in 'banding together' to support the school, developed 'new relations' and 'to some small extent, turned the neighbourhood in the direction of community' (Dennison, 1969: 268–9).

The contemporary situation for free schools is a mixed picture. On the one hand, these kinds of small-scale experiments continue to emerge – albeit sometimes under-the-radar as part of a growing home education scene. On the other hand, such schools tend to position themselves as part of an 'alternative education' movement, emphasising a more holistic, child-centred view than that seen as characterising mainstream state schooling, rather than as part of a radical political movement. These 'alternative' schools thus include Montessori and Rudolph Steiner Schools. Meanwhile, the term 'free schools' has been hijacked by the current UK Conservative government as a term for its new policy to fund schools initiated by parents and communities and funded by central government and businesses. We have argued elsewhere that there is nothing 'free' about the 'free schools' which have so far been supported and opened under this policy (Charkin, 2011). In fact, they tend to reinforce the existing purposes and values of mainstream schooling, an inevitable consequence, perhaps, of the application and approval process for such schools, which rests entirely with the central government.

Radical Education at Home and in Communities

In the contemporary context, perhaps the most significant and controversial challenge to state hegemony in education is the increasing numbers of home-educating families, in countries where home education is legal such as the UK, USA and Australia. In the UK, numbers are estimated at between 50,000 and 150,000 and in the USA, around 2 million (Kraftl, 2015: 8). Numbers are hard to estimate because home-educated children are, to an extent, under-the-radar of state monitoring – part of the motivation for some home-educating families who value this freedom from state control. From a numbers' point of view, in the current context, home education represents a far greater challenge to the status quo than democratic, free or anarchist schools.

Motivation for home education is extremely varied – including families who opt to home-educate in order to fast-track their children academically or to raise their children with particular religious values – and can seem anything but radical. However, in many cases, it can be understood as a contemporary expression of the kinds of radical educational and political ideas expressed in the small, free schools of the 1960s and 1970s described earlier – with an emphasis on higher levels of freedom and control over their own lives for the children and their families. Helen Lees, Editor of the journal *Other Education*, has argued that home education is the 'greatest anarchist style "people power" scenario relating to education that there is' and that 'it is perhaps politically and socially structurally close to the philosophical underpinning of anarchist education without outwardly declaring anarchist politics' (Lees, 2014: 25). Lees' interviews with home-educating families suggest that while most parents do not have an explicit political agenda, nevertheless, 'it takes a certain frame of mind to go against the grain, to not do what everybody else does' (Lees, 2014: 98). John Holt, a champion of home education in America in the 1970s, connected home education to social change by arguing in the first ever edition of *Growing Without Schooling*, a newsletter for home-educating families, that 'we are putting into practice a nickel-and-dime theory about social change, which is that important and lasting change always comes slowly, and only when people change their lives, not just their political beliefs or parties' (Holt, 1977: 1).

Home education has been criticised by some advocates of radical education, as part of a wider undermining of the school 'as a unique and vital public institution' and an 'invaluable site of encounter, exchange and relationships between citizens' (Fielding and Moss, 2011: 88–89). However, home-educating families can have an explicit commitment to their role as active citizens in the community and public sphere which underpins and works alongside their decision to home-educate. The experience of self-organisation can be empowering and lead to a kind of radicalisation in more political spheres, as Peter Kraftl has described in his book on the *Geographies of Alternative Education*. British home educators gathered together to lobby parliament about threats to home educators' freedoms through the Badman Review in 2009 (Kraftl, 2015: 110). They also take part in political action relating to wider issues such as refugee camps and environmental issues. Kraftl found that political beliefs 'bubble under' the practices of alternative education and that there is often an 'implicit influence of anarchist thinking upon the smallness of scale and interpersonal relations that are key to many alternative learning spaces' (Kraftl, 2015: 111–13). Even those families without an explicit political agenda can tend to be closely connected to their local community (outside of the school) because local libraries, swimming pools, parks and community spaces act as important alternatives to school in their weekly routines (Sheffer, 2008, 231).

The practice of home education can also lead to a kind of grassroots collaboration between families as they actively create spaces to meet their needs. In some ways, these groups represent a radical alternative to top-down, state provision of children's education and care. For example, in the UK, home-educating communities have created groups and spaces such as the three-days-a-week 'home education annex' called A Place to Grow in Stroud (Lucas, 2015); the Self Managed Learning College in Brighton; and The Otherwise Club in London, a community group for home-educating families (Safran in Webster, 2008).[8] These places are shaped by the social and educational needs of the families and children who attend and are characterised by high levels of parental involvement, mixed age groups, freedom from state inspection, democratic or 'community' meetings, children setting their own projects and goals, and use of domestic or community spaces.

Ian Cunningham, who founded the Self Managed Learning College, explicitly positions its work as part of a tradition inspired by primitive hunter-gatherer anarchies and Kropotkin's *Mutual Aid*. He argues that 'democratic education needs to be based on the more natural processes of living that we humans need rather than how democracy has evolved at the macro political level...it is not about replicating nation state processes and structures. It has to be emancipatory and liberatory' (Cunningham, 2011: 1). In practice, the children and adults are part of non-hierarchical learning groups and a regular morning meeting. He contrasts the values embodied in these structures of the learning centre with a more individualistic direction of travel in wider society, exemplified by 'fashionable' classes such as 'mindfulness' (Cunningham, 2016).

Home education, as reflected in government ambivalence and/or hostility in some countries, represents a growing challenge to the hegemony of state provision and control. While we acknowledge the tensions posed by home education around issues to do with parents' rights and the rights and interests of children (see Reich, 2002), we would argue for regarding the practice as potentially 'radical' in the sense that it can represent a challenge to dominant social and political structures and institutions.

Radical Education within the State

The anarchist, small-scale free schools and home education groups described earlier all position themselves very clearly outside of the state and often claim that they could not survive within it. However, neither the mere fact of their removal from state control nor their rejection of the curriculum or pedagogical practices that characterise state schooling renders educational alternatives 'radical'. For example, the independent school sector in England comprises many institutions which, while free to experiment with a range of pedagogical approaches and innovative curricular design, do nothing to challenge and, it could be argued, even reinforce the hegemonic ideology of the capitalist state. And the American radical educator Jonathan Kozol argued in the 1970s that even supposedly progressive schools operating outside of the state sector were a 'dangerous and disheartening phenomenon' which ignored or even reinforced inequalities and structures of oppression (Kozol, 1972: 10).

Whether or not radical education, as part of a broader goal for radical social change, requires a total disengagement from the institutional form of (state) public education is an open question, and one which is, in fact, reflected in the tensions and shifts within some radical social movements themselves. Thus, Rebecca Tarlau has documented how the Landless People's Movement (MST) in Brazil underwent a shift in their position in the late 1990s when, having initially invested their educational energies into setting up informal, popular education projects as an alternative to the public school system, they 'began to realize that transforming public schools was necessary for the movement's social and political goals'. As Tarlau points out, the activism of the MST within public schooling in Brazil, through teacher training programmes for example, not only led to changes in curricula and pedagogical practice that enabled the inclusion of children from marginalised communities into the public school system, thus meeting some of their political demands for recognition, but also shifted the debate about the very nature of public education in society (Tarlau, 2015: 6).

The history of radical education in Britain contains significant examples of radical ideas and practice *within* the state sector, such as Braehead (1957–68), St-George's-in-the-East (1945–55), Prestolee (1919–52), Risinghill (1960–65) and Stantonbury (1974–). In these examples, the daily life of the school constituted an attempt to challenge the dominant social values of competitiveness, hierarchies and individualism and to enact a more participatory, democratic and collegial form of social interaction. In practice, these schools went against the practices of mainstream schooling and the expectations of parents and teachers by avoiding corporal punishment and competition. Instead, they sought, as Bloom, head teacher of St George's put it, the making of a 'consciously democratic community' (Bloom, 1948: 120–1) in which the children would learn to 'live creatively not for themselves alone, but also for their community' (Bloom, 1949: 170).

The head teachers at these schools saw their work as part of a wider campaign for social change. As Mackenzie, head of Braehead (1957–68) and Summerhill Academy (1969–74), secondary schools in Scotland, wrote: 'if you are going to create a new society, it is in the schools that you must begin' (Mackenzie, 1970: 14). He argued that 'it is the task of the Left, in education as in politics, to win freedom in the battle against the authoritarians' (Mackenzie, 1977). Bloom's wider aim was for children and adults to experience and practice 'just relationships with persons' (1952: 142, 136) and O'Neill in Prestolee sought to create a space in which 'pupils otherwise destined for a life in manufacturing, were encouraged to see beyond their immediate horizons' (quoted in Burke and Dudek, 2010: 204).

These historical examples demonstrate, as Bloom argued at the time, that working within the state has its 'limitations' but that 'progressive education is possible' (Bloom, 1949: 170). Even today, Michael Fielding argues that these historical examples, albeit few and far between, allow the radical movement to 'contest the dictatorship of no alternatives' (2011: 1) and 'insist on the practical possibility of another reality, of living life as it might be' (2011: 2–3).

In short, to the extent that radical educational practices are integral to radically different visions of what society can look like, it is possible – although arguably more and more difficult within the current instrumental, competitive and centrally controlled schooling regime that characterises most capitalist states – to enact such radical practices even within schools provided by and controlled by the state. This is because, as John Yandell and Adam Unwin put it in their book, 'despite the best efforts of neo-liberalism, classrooms – all classrooms – remain extraordinarily complex places [and] places where work gets done, where transformations happen' (Unwin and Yandell, 2016: 137–8).

Many radical educators working within the state education system, especially in the field of social justice education and antiracist education, identify with the Freirian tradition of Critical Pedagogy which, understood as a political project rather than a set of classroom practices (see above), has clear affinities with the radical movements discussed earlier. Although Freire's original educational practice and theory was developed not within schools but with adults in community settings outside the school system (Freire, 1970), the theory and practice of critical pedagogy, developed both by Freire himself and by theorists and educators who brought his work into a North American and European context, have been hugely influential as part of a movement of radical education that is often most prominent within the public school system. Proponents such as Henry Giroux and Joe Kincheloe have argued for defending the radical democratic potential of schools and for teachers' role as 'transformative intellectuals' (Giroux, 1988; Kincheloe, 2004) challenging, through their work in classrooms, the hegemonic values and discourses of contemporary capitalist society.

The Future of Radical Education?

Our account of radical education has emphasised the common underpinning view that radical social change is both desirable and possible, and that educational processes are never neutral. The critical and utopian flavour of the type of experiments in alternative educational provision that we have described briefly here is captured in Paulo Freire's remark that '[p]rophetic thought, which is also utopian, implies *denouncing* how we are living and *announcing* how we could live. It is, for this very reason, a hope-filled form of thought' (Freire, 2004, 105). Possibilities for such denouncing and announcing, and the gradual political transformations that they open up, can happen, as our discussion has illustrated, in all sorts of pedagogical practices, spaces and relationships.

To the extent that critical teachers in inner-city schools, social movement activists, youth workers, home-schooling communities and practitioners in democratic schools and learning centres are all engaged in creating pedagogical spaces in which to question, challenge and critique dominant ideas about individual flourishing, social institutions and political systems, and to explore possibilities of creating something better in the interests of human freedom, equality and dignity, they should be recognised and supported as part of an important and long tradition of radical education.

In an era of universal state schooling, radical educational experiments and projects have been characterised by a set of inescapable tensions: between the demand for equal access to knowledge and education and the critique of state control of educational provision and dominant conceptions of knowledge; between the demand for greater democratic participation and strengthening of local democratic control of education, and the enthusiasm for small, private experiments in democratic education outside the state sector; between the commitment to the values of individual autonomy and freedom and the promotion of a substantive curriculum; and the related tension between a rejection of all forms of domination and an espousal of a form of pedagogical authority between adults and children.

Our discussion of historical and contemporary examples of radical education has explored the ways radical educators embodied and navigated some of these tensions, problematising the assumption that there can be such thing as neutral educational provision. Above all, these examples remind us how educational experiences and processes reflect political ideas about what society is and what it could be.

Notes

1 Most of the examples we discuss here are taken from a Western context. We are aware of the limitations of this perspective, but our analysis is largely based on the historical and political contexts of Western models of universal state education, and our examples reflect this context.
2 www.khanacademy.org/, accessed on 31st October 2016, www.theschoolinthecloud.org/, accessed on 31st October 2016.
3 http://autonomies.org/ru/2015/03/anarchy-in-the-school-escuela-libre-paideia/, accessed on 31st October 2016.
4 see http://santacruz.freeskool.org/content/list-other-free-skools-north-america, accessed on 31st October 2016, http://santacruz.freeskool.org/content/about-free-skool-santa-cruz, accessed on 31st October 2016.
5 http://antiuniversity.org/, accessed on 31st October 2016.
6 from www.sudval.org/essays/082016.shtml.
7 www.sudval.org/essays/082016.shtml, accessed on 31st October 2016.
8 http://college.selfmanagedlearning.org/.

References

Aitkenhead, John, *Kilquhanity's Jubilee, Reflections and Creations, 1940–1990*, C. Cameron (ed.) (London: Blackrose Press, 1990).
Alexander, Robin, 'Still no pedagogy? Principle, pragmatism and compliance in primary education', *Cambridge Journal of Education*, 34:1 (2004), 7–33.
Avrich, Paul, *The Modern School Movement; Anarchism and Education in the United States* (Oakland: AK Press, 2006).
Barnes, Kenneth and Barnes, Frances, *Proposal for a New School* (Surrey: S.C. Jennings and Sons Ltd, 1936).
Barnes, Kenneth, *Energy Unbound – The Story of Wennington School* (York: William Sessions Ltd., 1980).
BBC News, 'Pupils walk out over war', Wednesday 5 March, 2003. http://news.bbc.co.uk/1/hi/england/2821871.stm (last accessed 27.9.16).
Bloom, Alex, 'Notes on a school community', *New Era*, 29:6 (1948), 120–121.
Bloom, Alex, 'Compete or co-operate', *New Era*, 30:8 (1949), 170–172.
Bloom, Alex, 'Learning through living', M.A. Pink (ed.) *Moral Foundations of Citizenship* (London: University of London Press, 1952).
Burke, Catherine and Dudek, Mark, 'Experiences of learning within a twentieth-century radical experiment in education: Prestolee School, 1919–1952', *Oxford Review of Education*, 36:2 (2010), 203–218.
Charkin, Emily, 'For a real free school, look to post-war Peckham', *The Guardian* (30th August 2011) at www.theguardian.com/commentisfree/2011/aug/30/free-school-peckham-education (last accessed on 24 October 2016).
Cunningham, Ian, 'Democratic education – some notes towards defining the term', Conference Paper for International Democratic Education Conference, Israel, July 2011.
Cunningham, Ian, Talk at 'Libertarian education: Marginal experiment or instrument of social change?' given on 18 April in the May Day Rooms, London.
Dennison, George, 'The First Street School', *Anarchy*, 73 (March 1967), 70–80.
Dennison, George, *The Lives of Children* (New York: Random House, 1969).
Dewey, John, *Experience and Education* (New York: Kappa Delta Pi, 1938).
Dewey, John, *Democracy and Education: An Introduction to the Philosophy of Education* (New York: MacMillan, 1916).
Ferrer y Guardia, Francisco, 'The rational education of children', *The Modern School* (New York: Mother Earth Publishing Association, 1909).
Ferrer y Guardia, Francisco, *The Origins and Ideals of the Modern School* (London: Watts, 1913).
Fielding, Michael and Moss, Peter, *Radical Education and the Common School: A Democratic Alternative* (London: Routledge, 2011).
Freire, Paulo, *Pedagogy of the Oppressed* (New York: Herder and Herder, 1970).
Giroux, Henry, 'The necessity of critical pedagogy in dark times', *Global Education Magazine* (6 February 2013) www.truth-out.org/news/item/14331-a-critical-interview-with-henry-giroux

Giroux, Henry, Teachers as Intellectuals: Toward a Critical Pedagogy of Learning (Westport: Bergin and Garvey, 1988).

Goodman, Paul, *Growing Up Absurd* (New York: Vintage Books, 1957).

Goodman, Paul, 'The Present Moment in Education', *Anarchy*, 107: 10/1 (1970), 1–16.

Hemmings, Ray, *Fifty Years of Freedom: Study of the Development of the Ideas of A.S.Neill* (London: George Allen and Unwin, 1972)

Holt, John, Growing Without Schooling, 1: 1 (1977).

Illich, Ivan, *Deschooling Society* (New York: Harper and Row, 1971).

Johnson, Richard, 'Really useful knowledge', J. Clarke et al. (eds.) *Working Class Culture* (London: Hutchinson, 1979).

Kincheloe, Joe L., *Critical Pedagogy* (New York: Peter Lang, 2004).

Kozol, Jonathan, *Free Schools* (Boston, MA: Houghton Mifflin, 1972).

Kraftl, Peter, *Geographies of Alternative Education* (Bristol: Policy Press, 2015).

Kropotkin, Peter, *Fields, Factories and Workshops Tomorrow*, C. Ward (ed.) (London: Freedom Press, 1974 [1901]).

Lamb, Albert, (ed.) *The New Summerhill* (London: Penguin, 1992).

Lees, Helen, *Education Without Schools: Discovering Alternatives* (Bristol: Policy Press, 2014).

Lucas, Hussein, *A Place To Grow* (2015) at www.libed.org.uk/index.php/articles/508-a-place-to-grow (last accessed on 21.09.2016).

Mackenzie, R. F. *State School* (London: Penguin, 1970).

Mackenzie, R.F. 'Letter to the Editor' in *Kilquhanity Broadsheet*, (6th April, 1977), number 31.

Marshall, Peter (ed.), *The Anarchist Writings of William Godwin* (London: Freedom Press, 1986).

McLaughlin, Paul, *Radicalism: A Philosophical Study* (Hampshire: Palgrave Macmillan, 2012).

Mill, John Stuart, *On Liberty and Other Essays* (Oxford: Oxford University Press, 1991 [1859]).

Morland, David, *Demanding the Impossible? Human Nature and Politics in Nineteenth Century Social Anarchism* (London: Cassell, 1997).

Morris, Brian, *Bakunin: The Philosophy of Freedom* (Montreal: Black Rose Books, 1993).

Peters, Richard Stanley, *Ethics and Education* (London: George Allen and Unwin, 1966).

Reich, Rob, 'Testing the boundaries of parental authority over education: the case of homeschooling', S. Macedo and Y. Tamir (eds.), *Political and Moral Education, NOMOS XLIII* (New York: New York University Press, 2002).

Safran, Leslie, 'The otherwise club: an invitational learning community', *Personalised Learning: Taking Choice Seriously*, M. Webster (ed.), (Shrewsbury: Educational Heretics Press, 2008).

Sheffer, Susannah, 'Doing something very different', M. Hern (ed.), *Everywhere All the Time* (Oakland: AK Press, 2008).

Simon, Brian, 'Can education change society?', G. McCulloch (ed.), *The RoutledgeFalmer Reader in History of Education* (Oxon: Routledge, 2005).

Simon, Brian, 'Why no Pedagogy in England?', B. Simon and W. Taylor (eds.), *Education in the Eighties* (London: Batsford, 1981).

Simon, Brian (ed.), *The Radical Tradition in Education in Britain* (London: Lawrence & Wishart Ltd, 1972).

Skinner, Quentin, *Visions of Politics* (Cambridge: Cambridge University Press, 2002).

Smith, Michael, *The Libertarians and Education* (London: George Allen and Unwin, 1983).

Suissa, Judith, *Anarchism and Education: A Philosophical Perspective* (Oxon: Routledge, 2006).

Sukarieh, Mayssoun and Tannock, Stuart, 'The deradicalisation of education: terror, youth and the assault on learning', *Race and Class*, 57: 4 (2016), 22–38.

Tarlau, Rebecca, 'How do new critical pedagogies develop? Educational innovation, social change, and landless workers in Brazil 2019, *Teachers College Record*, 117 (2015), 1–36.

Unwin, Adam and Yandell, John, *NoNonsense Rethinking Education: Whose Knowledge is it Anyway?* (London: New Internationalist, 2016).

4.3

THE POLITICS OF DUMPSTERED SOUP

Food Not Bombs and the Limits of Decommodifying Food

Sean Parson

Most people that I have met have a knee jerk reaction to dumpstered food.[1] In graduate school, I regularly dumpstered food – for both political and survival reasons – and whenever I told a colleague that I had done so, they expressed disgust. From their perspective, the food, by being thrown away, had transformed from food to waste. In effect, they defined food as acceptable based entirely on where the food was procured: food that was purchased was good and healthy (especially if it was from the organic grocery store), while dumpstered food (even the dumpster from that same organic food store they loved) was tainted. Undergirding their logic around food was the ideology of contemporary consumer capitalism, and clearly the more money food cost, the better it is.

Alex Barnard in his book *Freegans: Diving into the Wealth of Food Waste in America* refers to the thrown away produce gleaned from dumpsters as ex-*commodities* (Barnard, 2016). This idea of ex-commodity, which will be discussed in more detail later, helps understand the intense reaction from the public to the eating of dumpstered food. To Barnard, 'the hysterical response most people have to the idea of eating ex-commodified food – fears that are far quite removed from the real risks involved – illustrate how, under advanced capitalism, we have come to equate all "waste" with "pollution"' (Barnard, 2016: 21). The idea of disgust being linked to waste goes much deeper though, as Silvia Federici showed in her discussion on the role that manners played in the development of capitalism. She wrote: 'Many practices began to appearing daily life to signal the deep transformation occurring...The body began to inspire fear and repugnance' (Federici, 2014: 153). During the period, the politics of bodily practices – eating, procreating and excretion – became unseemly and, somehow, unnatural. Chad Lavin in *Eating Anxiety* expands on this notion highlighting that we, in society, produce ideological apparatus that regulate our relationship to food and also help us define the political values and assumptions we make about the world (Lavin, 2013). The ideas of waste and disgust are socially constructed terms that cannot be viewed outside of the context of social power and ideology. Likewise, the resistance to these social norms and policies emerges from and is embedded within the same network of meaning.

In this chapter, I am going to engage with the politics of dumpstered food while exploring the ability of Food Not Bombs, an anarchist homeless food organisation that serves vegetarian dumpstered food for free for all who are hungry, to 'decommodify food'. This chapter begins with a historical and theoretical exploration of the commodification of food before engaging with the concept of the ex-commodity. Following that, I will provide an overview of Food Not Bombs and then examine the ways that the network of group uses the ex-commodity as part of a broader politics of decommodifying food undermining the capitalist food system.

The Commodification of Food

Radical environmentalist and eco-anarchists have, historically, focused intensively on the process of farming around 10,000 years ago. In the common eco-anarchist reading of this process, which they borrow heavily from Rousseau (1992), the development of agriculture began a process of centralisation that was essential for the development of the state. Agriculture, in effect, shifted traditional gatherer-hunter and village societies into sedentary-state structures around hierarchies, inequalities and domination. For instance, Rousseau famously wrote, in his essay *Discourse on Inequality*, that

> The first person who, having enclosed a plot of land, took it into his head to say this is mine and found people simple enough to believe him was the true founder of civil society. What crimes, wars, murders, what miseries and horrors would the human race have been spared, had some one pulled up the stakes or filled in the ditch and cried out to his fellow men: 'Do not listen to this imposter. You are lost if you forget that the fruits of the earth belong to all and the earth to no one!'
>
> *(Rousseau & Cress, 1992)*

Agriculture, here, is linked with property and led to the end of natural equality and the development of social inequality. We damned ourselves when we planted that first fenced in field. But Rousseau is not alone. Anarchist Murray Bookchin in *The Ecology of Freedom* argued that with agriculture emerged domination and from there increasing social divisions of labour led to the rise of priestly and military classes (Bookchin, 2005). In effect, the state emerged from the inequality developed by the agricultural revolution. Similarly, to the chagrin of Bookchin, Anarcho-primitivist John Zerzan also critiques agriculture, and the process of plant domestication (as well as the earlier development of representational thought) as being a big shift in human society, a shift that has led to lead to ecological, social and political collapse (Zerzan, 1999, 2012). If eco-anarchists are correct, then focusing on the process of farming and food production provides valuable insights into the dehumanising and destructive aspects of contemporary society.

A commodity, according to Karl Marx, is any product that has both exchange and use value. By use value, Marx merely meant that a product provides a certain level of joy and happiness for the person who consumes or uses it. By exchange value, he means that the product can be traded for a certain number of other goods. This second form, the exchange value, is the most important aspect of the capitalist economy, and cannot exist without the development of a market system. Throughout human history, not all products were commodities as there were times when goods were not traded or sold at high numbers. According to David Graeber, the primary economic relation between humans prior to the development of hierarchal state structures was the gift economy. In a gift economy, people trade and exchange and share goods as gifts, not as bartered objects (Graeber, 2011). In many ways, this early gift economy resembled aspects of Marx's famous mantra for communism 'from each according to ability to each according to need'. This early system of shared goods developed close-knit societies and limited social and economic hierarchies. To Marx, and most radical thinkers, the early communisms of humans needed to be destroyed and broken in order to allow the development of markets, commodities and with it the accumulation of capital and wealth.

Agriculture led to a boom in human population globally, and concentrated people within certain areas. The growth in a dense human population and the hierarchies that developed between farmers, owners and skilled labourers was central to the production of the earliest civilizations. Describing this history, Fredy Perlman gives a mythopoetic account of the state-Leviathan, the mythical monster of biblical and Hobbesian imagination. To Perlman, these sedentary and hierarchal war machines conquered the hunter-gatherer and nomadic peoples in the region developing larger and larger civilizational structures. In this way, both war and agriculture were linked in the first instances of massive colonisation (Perlman, 2010). But even though food was an essential aspect of the developing state system, it was not yet a commodity because farmers often produced their own food, often being required to give up a percentage of what they grew as a tribute to the master. Since a large percentage of people at that time were involved in food production, this meant that most people produced their own food needs via a subsistence process, and often traded and shared excess food in a gift or barter system. At the core of these earlier food regimes were farmers producing food for their own need, or for the food's use value, and not for the exchange value. The development of a food regime based primarily on exchange value only developed with the rise of capitalism in the seventeenth and eighteenth centuries. As feudalism in Europe died and commons were enclosed, a massive influx of new labour filled the cities and laboured in the growing factory economy. In a dance between population growth, scientific discovery and economic need, over time production was mechanised and industrialised in the city and lagging slowly behind the urban industrialisation was agricultural and food production.

Since the development of industrial capitalism, there are a handful of different food regimes that the core western capitalist nations have passed through, from the early slave labour system of the early North and South American economy to the neo-liberal food regime that we currently exist within (McMichael, 2009; Pritchard, Dixon, Hull, & Choithani, 2016). Each of these regimes expresses a period in which there was a stable connection and relationship between capital, labour and food production. Each followed, or mirrored, the overall trend of capitalist development. The most massive transitions in food economy and politics happened during the Second World War in the US, when centralised development and planning were essential to maintain the food production needed to feed soldiers during the war. The result was full industrialisation of the food system: the seed production, the watering and maintaining of crops, the production and raising of animals, the harvesting of crops and the slaughter of animals, and the production networks (Fitzgerald, 2003). From this moment onwards, nearly every aspect of contemporary food production was structured to maximise efficiency and exchange value and with that the concentration of food production into large corporate hand. The result is that factory farming dominates the poultry (72%), egg (42%) and pork (55%) markets and four large corporations control over 75% of the global grain market. The massive economic power of corporate industrialised food production has shaped the global production of food, even at the local level as smaller or local farms are primarily linked to a larger global commodity market that structures and constrains their own behaviour, which is why local food, farmers' markets and niche ethical markets have become some of the only means for small local farms to compete. These niches are not a critique of the commodity form of food but are, instead, a symptom of it.

If eco-anarchists are correct and that the production of food played a central role in the development of sedentary societies, and with it the state and, later, capitalism, then contemporary radical activists and thinkers need to engage with the current food regime and work to undermine the logic of capitalist food production. The next few sections are attempts to do just that, while focusing on the food political project of Food Not Bombs.

The Ex-commodity and Decommodified Food

Alex Barnard referred to the food dumpstered by Freegans, a person who attempts to limit the negative impact of their food consumption by procuring most of their food from dumpsters or urban foraging, and Food Not Bombs activists as ex-commodities. To Barnard, this produce and canned food are ex-commodities because they tend to be otherwise healthy and safe food products that are thrown away for a range of reasons – from fruits and vegetables with unsightly blemishes, to food being past its premature 'sell by date', to a loop hole in the tax plan that allows stores to get tax credits for food waste. What this means is that the food that is often grabbed from the dumpsters hidden behind grocery stores throughout the country is, for the most part, no different from the commodified food inside the store (Barnard, 2016: 13–14). The commodified food in the store was created due to its exchange value (the amount that a product makes in exchange for another) and not its use value (how much value people get out of consuming or using the good) in order to maximise the capitalists' profits. As Barnard highlights, Marx in *Capital vol.1* argued that capitalism is a ruthless efficient system that attempts to squeeze as much surplus labour out of the workers and the machines at their disposal by cutting wasted time and standardising the process. But as Marx in *Capital vol. 3* started to realise, as capitalism increases its efficiency and cuts wages, there becomes a crisis of overproduction as more is produced than can be consumed. This is, generally the problem that currently exists within modern capitalism.

The throwing away of food, for Barnard, becomes one of ways that modern food production keeps the price of food elevated enough to make a profit. In a sense, the donation of some food allows for the creation of an artificial exchange value that allows for increased capitalist profits. In addition to just throwing away food, agricultural corporations have used changes in law to commodify donation food and recuperate profit while keeping prices elevated. The tax code changes and federal Good Samaritan laws passed during the 1970s allowed corporations to donate unused food for tax breaks (Poppendieck, 1999). Corporate food producers benefited from surplus food stocks as a result, because it allowed them to construct a new economic market to be formed around the disposal of food. The massive food bank storage centres, distribution networks and transportation systems that have emerged in the wake of the legislation make this evident. These networks, as examined by George Henderson, are essential by-products of capitalism's need to develop an exchange value for discarded food – allowing wealth accumulation to exist even with their waste. The problem is that

> ...individual firms or enterprises—lets say, food producers and sellers—accumulate a surplus of commodities that cannot be gotten rid of through normal channels of commodification without devaluing a portion of their remaining commodities...With the rise of food banking since the 1980s, a so-called secondary market has arisen through which food producers and sellers can recoup some value from the devalued surplus by selling it off at a discount to food bankers.
>
> *(Henderson, 2004: 491–2)*

Thus, by finding a financially viable alternative to their waste food, capitalists can keep their 'marketable food' at inflated prices. In effect, food producers constructed a new market to dump their surplus products. This expanded network, especially with the increased federal funding to support it, acted as a backdoor profit-making process for large agricultural and food-producing corporations.

Modern food capitalism keeps prices elevated through, in part, a two-pronged approach of disposing of and donating food. This process is an intentional plan to offset the crisis of overproduction that currently exists within the food system. Throwing the food away allows for them to keep an artificial scarcity and the donation allows them to receive tax breaks and credits, and therefore recuperate additional economic gain out of a small subset of the food they plan to dispose. If, on the contrary, all wasted food was provided for free to those who are hungry, so argues the actions of Food Not Bombs make, the entire logic of the commodity food market would be put into crises leading to the potential to shift food from, rhetorically and morally, being a commodity to being a right. How do they do this? In my experience working with many Food Not Bombs chapters, most of the chapters engage in the following process: a few days before the weekly meal service, activists with the local chapter organise either bike brigades to dumpster produce from local grocery stores and bakers or send people to local groceries to grab donations. The food is usually stored at a central meeting place – often an activist's house but sometimes a community centre – where, on the day the meal is going to happen, activists meet up, democratically decide which vegetarian dishes are going to be made and then cook them together. Following that, activists transport the food to a local park by either bike or car, and set up a free picnic where hungry people line up to grab food, and eat with the activists.

When it comes to food politics, the dumpstering project of Food Not Bombs can be seen as an attempt to radically decommodify the entire food system by providing an alternative narrative, and practice, of democratically and freely produced and distributed food. This network, as the next section will show, attempts to undermine the commodity logic of food by providing 'ex-commodities' for free to all those who are hungry. By turning what capitalism calls waste into health and nutritious food, Food Not Bombs, attempts to alter the relationship people have with food – moving that relationship away from market relationships.

Not Feeding the Revolution? A Short History of Food Not Bombs

Food Not Bombs formed out of the antinuclear movement of the 1980s and linked hunger, the violence of structural poverty, with the bloated military budget and militaristic culture in the US. The group, which started in Boston, developed and grew into a network or organisations throughout the 1980s and 1990s, partially due to increased media presence, and the development of a radical and large chapter in San Francisco, who regularly conflicted with the City of San Francisco from 1988 to 1995. During this period, which spanned two mayoral administrations, over 1,000 activists were cited or arrested for distributing food without a permit, violating a court injunction or resisting arrest. The media attention helped the network develop and grow and by the end of the decade, Food Not Bombs had around 400 chapters throughout the world.

It was also during the 1990s that Food Not Bombs networked its politics beyond the antinuclear and peace movements to the broader anarchist and social justice movement. During this time, Food Not Bombs meals became commonplace at protests in the US. In North America, Food Not Bombs chapters worked together in 1999 to coordinate food services for the WTO protest in Seattle, and the iconic image of a clenched fist holding a carrot has been seen in nearly every major left-wing protest since, including the massive protests opposing the wars in Afghanistan and Iraq and the public occupations of parks during the Occupy movement. The wide-ranging roots of resistance that Food Not Bombs has watered have been referred to by Richard Day as typifying the politics of 'groundless solidarity' (Day, 2005).

During the 1990s, Food Not Bombs also became associated with contemporary anarchism, and is now one of the most recognisable anarchist groups in the world. While originally the group was not explicitly anarchist, these tendencies thrived during their early years partially because of the influence and importance of anarchist principles within the antinuclear movement out of which they developed (Epstein, 1991). The San Francisco chapter, which had large numbers of anarchist organisers, as well as strong connections with the underground punk scene in the Bay area, helped develop this connection. Chris Crass, a San Francisco Food Not Bombs organiser from 1993 to 2000, most succinctly highlighted the connection between them and anarchism in his short but influential article 'Non-Violence and Anarchism':

> Anarchism is movement for a society in which the violence of racism, sexism, homophobia, capitalism, and coercion are removed from our daily lives. Anarchism is the belief in a world without war and economic poverty. Anarchism is a philosophy and movement working to build cooperative, egalitarian human relationships and social structures that promote mutual aid, radical democratic control of political and economic decisions, and ecological sustainability. So how does this apply directly to FNB?
>
> *(Crass, 1995)*

In answering the latter question, Crass argues that the principles of Food Not Bombs (nonviolence, animal rights, consensus and direct action) are all explicitly anarchist principles. He asserts that even though anarchism is often misunderstood in public debates, the group should explicitly view itself as part of this wider movement. This article was widely circulated and has become influential in Food Not Bombs and anarchist circles.

In embracing nonviolence, Food Not Bombs has constantly contrasted their politics with the institutional and structural violence of neo-liberalism and austerity politics. As co-founders, Keith McHenry and C.T. Butler stated

> Globally, we continue to spend more time and resources developing, using, and threatening to use weapons of massive human and planetary destruction than on nurturing and celebrating life. By spending this money on bombs instead of food, our government perpetuates and exacerbates poverty's violence by not providing food for everyone in need.
>
> *(Bulter & McHenry, 1992: 72)*

As this quote shows, Food Not Bombs understands poverty as a form of structural violence. While the violence of poverty is not as spectacular as bombs and bullets, it is just as horrific in its impact. Thus, poverty, hunger and gentrification are seen as topics that any nonviolent movement must confront.

Our current food and economic system does not just perpetuate violence against humans, the commodification of food causes enormous violence to non-human animals and the natural world. As David Nibert (2002) persuasively shows, our current economic and social system has institutionalised violence against non-humans, following the logic of violence that occurs with all oppressive relationships, naturalises and justifies this repression. To Nibert and others within the animal rights community, non-humans experience extreme violence in nearly all aspects of their lives – from the forcible separation of children and mothers to the horrific treatment they receive during their lives, to their eventual slaughter. Food Not Bombs, by typically serving only vegan or vegetarian food, is taking a strong stance against the violence needed to ensure that meat, dairy and eggs arrive on our plates.

Food Not Bombs and the Act of Food Resistance

The last section on Food Not Bombs' history and the aforementioned description combined highlight both the strengths and weaknesses of the Food Not Bombs project when it comes to the goal of confronting the capitalist food system. Food Not Bombs provides a radically unique food relief and homeless support programme, one that actively engages in, at least, four incredible important practices. First, Food Not Bombs actively works to undermine the distinction between volunteer and client that is central to most charity organisations by sharing food, having many homeless activists involved in the group and setting up a more communal space. Second, they emphasise democratic practice, and view cooking and serving food as a collective and social process. Third, it is the way that they use as few purchased foods as possible, trying to make everything out of 'ex-commodified' food both to lower costs and to provide a powerful form of 'propaganda by the deed'. Fourth, activists with Food Not Bombs work to cook only vegetarian meals (with the exception, in my experience, of the salmon not bombs chapter organised in Fairbanks, Alaska during the Occupy protests, which was also a decolonial response to both western veganism and anarchism) for both health concerns – vegan food is less likely to go bad in a hot dumpster – and for political reasons – as the production of meat, dairy and eggs requires a large amount of violence. In effect, Food Not Bombs provides a democratic, solidaristic, supportive service that exemplifies the vision of mutual aid. Finally, Food Not Bombs queers the line between the public and private spheres by providing free public meals (as well as working to defend public encampments) in public space. As Kathleen Arnold (2004) and Leonard Feldman (2006) both noted, the private/public divide is essential to the logic of the liberal political subject. Food Not Bombs defends the homeless, who, due to their status, have to engage in private behaviour – eating, sleeping, drinking, intimate relationships, urinating and defecating – in public spaces – parks or sidewalks.

That said, there are serious limitations to their approach taken by Food Not Bombs when it comes to confronting the reality of the commodified food system. First off, and most clearly, the scale and scope of commodity food are too large for any form of localised grassroots politics to threaten it. The food system is now a global corporate network that has been expanded and defended through the process of neo-liberal economic globalisation. There has also been a process of recuperation in which larger agricultural corporations have purchased and hidden their involvement in 'niche' food markets such as vegan foods, natural and organic foods, and the like (see Alkon & Agyeman, 2011; Alkon, 2012; Patel, 2012). In many instances, when it comes to exploitation of animals and labour, local and non-corporate farms have had to borrow and use the industrial process used by their larger cousins, meaning that even some local food production is not necessarily better in practice. This is why Ryan Gunderson correctly argues that local food movements, ethical consumerism and other attempts at alternative food networks are limited in their ability to enact the change they wish to see (Gunderson, 2014). At best, Gunderson argues, local experiments in alternative food distribution systems – like Food Not Bombs – provide a symbolic boon, showing that alternatives to capitalist food distribution are, in fact, possible. However,

> small-scale alternative food projects, creation of niche markets, and the adjustment of some individual consumptive habits are certainly not enough to create an ecologically sustainable and socially just food system. For sustainable food production to free itself from alternative status and to become the norm, a total restructuring of our current social formation may be needed due to the constraints of capitalism outlined above.
>
> *(Gunderson, 2014)*

In a similar way, Food Not Bombs provides a symbolic example of an alternative institution but much like the commune movement, and other attempts at alternative institutions, the impact tends to be relatively localised.

Secondly, there is a core tension within Food Not Bombs between providing as much food for free as it can and confrontation and conflicts with dominant institutions. Often times, these two desires are mutually exclusive, as direct conflicts with the state limit the effectiveness and ability of local chapters to provide food, but not always. For instance, during the height of the conflict between Food Not Bombs and San Francisco, the chapter was still providing free meals twice daily – an amount which, since the conflicts ended, it has not been able to emulate. More times than not though Food Not Bombs chapters attempt to limit their conflict with the state and engage in what Olin Wright calls interstitial politics. Interstitial politics looks to build resistance institutions within the cracks of the dominant order effectively building a new world in the shell of the old. At its best, the interstitial approach allows for institutions and counter, dual power structures, to develop but more is needed for social transformation; there is a need for conflict with the dominant institutions, what Wright calls ruptural (Wright, 2010). The balance between Interstitial and ruptural is a constant problem for local Food Not Bombs chapters and often, the conflicts that do emerge are not the result of Food Not Bombs actions but government crackdowns.

Third, the political project of Food Not Bombs can best be seen as part of what Don Mitchell and Nik Heynon call 'geographies of survival'. Geographies of survival are complex, and sometimes illegal, practices that the poor need to survive. This can include dumpstering, squatting, petty theft, public encampments, foraging, recycling, public transit loitering, etc. (Mitchell & Heynen, 2009). For many urban homeless residents, Food Not Bombs is another spot in a large archipelago of survival that they often traverse on a daily basis. Unlike many of the other islands in this archipelago, Food Not Bombs is openly political, providing critiques of local politics, capitalism and militarism. What is less known is how well the groups' political values and messages lead to a process of empowering and radicalising of homeless residents. In my own experience, many of the people who come to meals, while generally enjoying the meal, conversation and politics of the local chapter, do not leave with radically different political views then when they first came nor are they more likely to become political organisers or agitators. If the politics of Food Not Bombs does not radicalise and organise the homeless what do they do?

According to a homeless San Francisco critique of Food Not Bombs in the 1990s, Geoffrey McDonald

> This is supposed to be empowering. In truth, the relationship of homeless individuals to the group is parasitic. It could hardly be otherwise: for the homeless, life is a desperate

scramble to stay alive. While there is nothing radicalising about their misery, for FNB activists, identification with the plight of the homeless is a source of righteousness.

(McDonald, n.d.-a)

This critique, that Food Not Bombs actions satiate the desires of middle-class activists to appear altruistic by feeding the homeless, is in my estimation too harsh (as many Food Not Bombs activists are homeless or formerly homeless).Yet it prompts an important and provocative question: do the actions of Food Not Bombs constitute a radical critique of capital via the process of decommodification or is this work part of an ethical politics, similar to the 'bourgeois socialism' Marx and Engels critiqued in the *Communist Manifesto*?

Finally, one can critique the priority that Food Not Bombs gives to the process of distribution over production. By focusing on taking ex-commodities and distributing them through a gift economy, Food Not Bombs attempts to undermine the entire logic of 'food as commodity' by showing that it can be distributed for free, and that via waste alone, capitalism provides enough to feed the hungry. But if we think of the capitalist food system as largely dependent on the exploitation of labour – throughout the process – is expropriating the waste a logic process to undermine this system? Once again, Food Not Bombs critic Geoffrey McDonald writes that while it is true that a massive amount of food goes to waste

> … The problem of hunger in the United States--like that of homelessness--is not reducible to distribution of the surplus; it is a logical consequence of the profit system itself. Food that cannot be sold at a profit is a loss for the capitalist, whether large-scale or small. The real surplus that capitalism generates is in labor, that is, in people who are unable to sell themselves to the rich and thus can't purchase the means of survival. The homeless, as Peter Marcuse put it, are 'the surplus of the surplus.'

(McDonald, n.d.-b)

In essence, his critique is that Food Not Bombs confronts the capitalist food industry by taking the ex-commodity and using that as a weapon to undermine the logic of the commodity form more generally, but this is a limited approach since the structure of capitalist economies is founded on the exploitation and maintenance of a surplus of labour in the process of production and that homelessness is a by-product of this system. In effect, to McDonald, if you want to end homelessness, you have to end the exploitation of workers in the process of production, a strongly Marxist and anarchist response.

McDonald's critique is somewhat valid but takes Food Not Bombs as an isolated group and not an intended larger network of radical organising around labour, distribution, housing, etc. To round out the view of McDonald Kropotkin's perspectives on poverty, capitalism and revolutionary politics in 'From Expropriation' balances out the critique in place. In this piece, Kropotkin states that the core of capitalism is poverty, as poverty is essential to creating the needed surplus labour to fill the factories and enrich the owners of capital. In discussing this, he wrote that 'when there is no longer any destitute there will no longer be any rich to exploit them' and that when poverty is addressed that 'No one will volunteer for the enrichment of your Rothschilds' (Kropotkin in McKay, 2014: 518). Of course though, Kropotkin was not arguing that poverty could be addressed simply by revolutionising and providing the free distribution of services, though expropriation of bread for distribution will be essential to the revolutionary case, but also by the worker and community expropriation of industry and housing as well. To Kropotkin, distribution and production both are essential in the maintenance of capitalism and, if anything, the interconnected nature of capitalism means that

> all is interdependent in a civilized society; it is impossible to reform any one thing with altering the whole. On that day when we strike against private property, under any one of its forms, territorial or industrial, we shall be obliged to attack all its manifestations. The very success of the revolution will demand it.
>
> *(Kropotkin in McKay, 2014: 520)*

In effect, both Kropotkin and McDonald are arguing slightly different, though I think interconnected points. Both of them are exploring the root causes of capitalism and theorising the location of struggle and action. With McDonald, he views homelessness as an essential and related product of capitalism – in that capitalism keeps a surplus population for labouring and a pressure valve – while Kropotkin is exploring the process that forces the poor, the destitute and workers in general to sell their blood and sweat to capitalist producers. In this regard, both are correct – homelessness is a result of capitalist economic need and people are embedded in the capitalist system because there are no other accessible means for people to garner the goods and services that they need to survive. The lesson from both McDonald and Kroptokin is that the focus on any single issue will not be enough, what we need is not a revolutionising of the system of food distribution, but a revolutionising of the entire food economy – production, transportation, distribution. This is also though a critique of McDonald, as the focus on production is also not enough.

Conclusion

Food Not Bombs and its public meals provide an important and essential role in the radical political movement and in the geographies of survival that the homeless and poor rely on. The network provides a radical urban food relief and homeless rights organisation that does not turn ex-commodities into health meals while also confronting and struggling against state's attempts to criminalise and harass the poor and homeless. That said, there are limitations to what they, as a network, can do via the process of decommodification of food to actually confront the capitalist food system. At best, their dumpstered meals provide an essential institutional support that can nourish and inspire resistance and solidarity, while at their worst, the process can be a self-aggrandising process of middle-class, mostly white punks showing their bona fides. On average though, the networks' actions are somewhere in the middle – between feeding the revolution and stroking the ego – and we can see the meals as a form of propaganda by the deed, showing that an alternative way of gleaning and serving food exists and providing grassroots and practical skills in decentralised and democratic institution building. Of course, expecting one group (or network of groups) to create the revolution by distributing soup made out of distressed produce is holding them up to an impossible standard.

Capitalism has, echoing the sentiments of Guy Debord, found ways to recuperate resistance into a stable and continual system of capitalist growth. Local, organic, free-range, vegan. All are fully incorporated in the leviathan of Agro-food. As such, there is no silver bullet type solution but instead a variety of different techniques and approaches are needed to attack and confront at a multitude of locations and with a range of differing tactics. A focus on just Food Not Bombs and their attempt to turn ex-commodities (distressed food) into a meal and provide it free as part of a gift economy shows some of the strengths and weaknesses of radical attempts to alter food distribution networks and the attempts of resisting the food commodity by undermining the logic of food as a commercial product. Learning the limitations of one approach provides insight into what other forms or organisations and groups are needed to compliment an overall strategy. While goliath was taken down with only one rock, to destroy capitalism, we will need mountains of them, or maybe in this instance a mountain of dumpstered bagels.

Note

1   A dumpster is large trash receptacle. The British terms are skip and skipping.

References

Alkon, A. H. (2012). *Black, white, and green: farmers markets, race, and the green economy.* Athens: University of Georgia Press.

Alkon, A. H., & Agyeman, J. (Eds.). (2011). *Cultivating food justice: race, class, and sustainability.* Cambridge, MA: MIT Press.

Arnold, K. R. (2004). *Homelessness, citizenship, and identity: the uncanniness of late modernity.* Albany: State University of New York Press.

Barnard, A. V. (2016). *Freegans: diving into the wealth of food waste in America.* Minneapolis: University of Minnesota Press.

Bookchin, M. (2005). *The ecology of freedom: the emergence and dissolution of hierarchy.* Oakland, CA: AK Press.

Butler, C.T.L., & McHenry, K. (1992). *Food not bombs: how to feed the hungry and build community.* Tucson: See Sharp Press.

Crass, C. (1995). Towards a non-violent society: a position paper on anarchism, social change and Food Not Bombs. *The Anarchist Library.* http://bit.ly/2nea9vF.

Day, R. J. F. (2005). *Gramsci is dead: anarchist currents in the newest social movements.* London; Ann Arbor, MI : Toronto: Pluto Press.

Epstein, B. L. (1991). *Political protest and cultural revolution: nonviolent direct action in the 1970s and 1980s.* Berkeley: University of California Press.

Federici, S. (2014). *Caliban and the witch* (2nd ed). New York, NY: Autonomedia.

Feldman, L. C. (2006). *Citizens without shelter: homelessness, democracy, and political exclusion.* Ithaca: Cornell University Press.

Fitzgerald, D. (2003). *Every farm a factory.* New Haven, CT: Yale University Press.

Graeber, D. (2011). *Debt: the first 5,000 years.* Brooklyn, NY: Melville House.

Gunderson, R. (2014). Problems with the defetishization thesis: ethical consumerism, alternative food systems, and commodity fetishism. *Agriculture and Human Values, 31*(1), 109–117.

Henderson, G. (2004). 'Free' food, the local production of worth, and the circuit of decommodification: a value theory of the surplus. *Environment and Planning D: Society and Space, 22*(4), 485–512.

Kropotkin, P. A. (2014). *Direct struggle against capital: a Peter Kropotkin anthology.* Ed. I. McKay. Edinburgh: AK Press.

Lavin, C. (2013). *Eating anxiety: the perils of food politics.* Minneapolis: University of Minnesota Press.

McDonald, G. (n.d.-a). A CHARITY OPERATION, TOO. Retrieved May 30, 2017, from www.foundsf.org/index.php?title=A_CHARITY_OPERATION,_TOO.

McDonald, G. (n.d.-b). SURPLUSES and DISTRIBUTION. Retrieved May 30, 2017, from www.foundsf.org/index.php?title=SURPLUSES_and_DISTRIBUTION.

McMichael, P. (2009). A food regime genealogy. *The Journal of Peasant Studies, 36*(1), 139–169.

Mitchell, D., & Heynen, N. (2009). The geography of survival and the right to the city: speculations on surveillance, legal innovation, and the criminalization of intervention. *Urban Geography, 30*(6), 611–632.

Nibert, D. A. (2002). *Animal rights/human rights: entanglements of oppression and liberation.* Lanham, MD: Rowman & Littlefield.

Patel, R. (2012). *Stuffed and starved: the hidden battle for the world food system* (2nd ed). Brooklyn, NY: Melville House Pub.

Perlman, F. (2010). *Against his-story, against Leviathan!: an essay*. Detroit, MI: Black & Red.

Poppendieck, J. (1999). *Sweet charity?: emergency food and the end of entitlement*. New York, NY: Penguin.

Pritchard, B., Dixon, J., Hull, E., & Choithani, C. (2016). 'Stepping back and moving in': the role of the state in the contemporary food regime. *The Journal of Peasant Studies, 43*(3), 693–710.

Rousseau, J.-J., & Cress, D. A. (1992). *Discourse on the origin of inequality*. Indianapolis: Hackett Pub. Co.

Wright, E. O. (2010). *Envisioning real utopias*. London ; New York: Verso.

Zerzan, J. (1999). *Elements of refusal* (2nd, ed). Columbia, MO: C.A.L. Press/Paleo Editions.

Zerzan, J. (2012). *Future primitive revisited*. Port Townsend; Minneapolis: Feral House Consortium Book.

4.4

SOCIAL CENTRES AS RADICAL SOCIAL LABORATORIES

Luca Lapolla

Introduction

Can social centres be the sociopolitical counterpart of workplace-based syndicalist organisations aiming at 'forming the structure of the new society within the shell of the old' (Industrial Workers of the World 1905)?[1] If syndicalism searches for alternatives to capitalism as the dominant socio-economic system, can social centres be radical social laboratories in which activists and citizens experimentally implement alternative solutions to organise society? In this chapter, I will try to answer these questions by drawing mostly on interviews with people involved in British and Italian social centres between the 1970s and today. I will investigate case studies from the British cities of Bristol and London, and the Italian cities of Bari and Milan. The reason for this time frame is that it is only during the 1970s that the modern concept of a social centre took shape, although sometimes under different names. Moreover, I have decided to focus on Britain and Italy because social centres developed along different lines in each country, reflecting different sociopolitical contexts. By analysing the radical aspects of social centres, their relation with the wider radical world and some of the problems that affect them, I aim to present modern social centres as 'radical social laboratories'.

What Is a Social Centre?

The term 'social centre' has been used to identify different experiences in different times. Here, I will focus on modern-day social centres – those that emerged as a by-product of the countercultures and subcultures of the 1960s and 1970s. Such are the experiences that Stuart Hodkingson and Paul Chatterton described as 'turn[ing] unused or condemned public buildings and factories into self-organised cultural and political gathering spaces for the provision of radical social services, protest-planning and experimentation with independent cultural production' (Hodkinson and Chatterton 2006:306). In addition to this, I will here illustrate how social centres embodied – more or less consciously, and with clear limitations – concrete Left-libertarian alternatives to our contemporary society based on principles such as profit, authority and individualism.

Yet, the same term was used to identify places that diverged greatly from these definitions in late nineteenth-century Britain and US, as well as in 1950s Italy, when the term first appeared. Then, social centres were an instrument in the hands of the ruling class to maintain class and social tensions under control. Italian *centri sociali* (social centres) originally denoted community centres run by municipal authorities (Mudu 2013:63; Ibba 1995). Similarly, in Britain, social centres were clubs, classes and institutes, whose function was to help 'young men and women … be so full of healthy and useful effort that there shall be no room for what is unworthy and mean' (Hogg 1892:9–14). In America, both Progressives and reformist socialists backed social centres, which were mostly urban schools that in the evening became recreational, social and civic spaces (Weston 1905; Perry 1912; Curtis 1913:80). Progressives – like presidents Theodore Roosevelt and Wilson – used them to achieve 'a socially efficient society' by helping children and adults 'make the right use of their [leisure] time', and 'Americanising' newly arrived migrants (Stevens 1972:18–25). The socialists, on the other hand, aimed at entertaining and educating all citizens (Jozwiak 2003:13). For them, social centres had a normative role comparable to that of early nineteenth-century Sunday schools aiming to 'render [the children of the poor] honest, obedient, courteous, industrious, submissive, and orderly' (Thompson 1963:401). Like Sunday schools, social centres participated in the training of new docile generations of citizens and workers. This is confirmed by a St Louis librarian reporting on a group of anarchists frequenting the local social centre:

> [T]he brand of anarchism that they profess has grown perceptibly milder since they have met in the library. It is getting to be literary, academic, philosophic. Nourished in a saloon, with a little injudicious repression, it might perhaps have borne fruit of bombs and dynamite.
>
> *(Stevens 1972:24)*

This does not mean that there was no radical version of 'mainstream' social centres at the time. Both in Britain and in Italy, in the nineteenth century, appeared radical spaces for socialising and organising political action, such as anarchist clubs (Moses 2016), radical workers' clubs, mutual-aid societies (Woodcock 1962:447; Marshall 1993:489) and *case del popolo* (People's Houses) (Degl'Innocenti 1984; De Michelis 1986). Spaces that were real reference points to local workers and radicals. Besides carrying out a pragmatic function and hosting recreational activities, these spaces became 'hubs of lively political participation and debates' (Editorial Staff 1989:8). Although the latter examples used various denominations, their spirit and actions characterise them as precursors of contemporary social centres, whereas nineteenth-century social centres were certainly not. Hence, for my analysis on 'radical social laboratories', I will consider spaces that, rather than simply using the expression 'social centres', promoted the experimentation of radical solutions to overcome the capitalist/neo-liberal society.

What Is Radical about Social Centres?

In 2007, Saul Newman reflected on a redefinition for 'radical politics' to suit the contemporary age of 'post-politics', in which 'the global neo-liberal consensus is shared by the parliamentary Right and Left alike (an ideological distinction that has become, at the formal level, largely meaningless)'. A global scenario aggravated by the resurgence of the Far Right, the appearance of religious fundamentalism and the 'violent reassertion of the authoritarian state under the dubious pretext of "security"'. Within this context, Newman identified the emergence of a new radical politics focused on 'a non Statist, anti-institutional form of politics that rejects traditional modes of party representation, eschews Marxist economism, and yet remains faithful to the ideals of unconditional liberty and equality' (Newman 2007:3, 17).

Can we apply Newman's definition to social centres? Social centres vary greatly depending on factors such as political affiliation and organisational modes, which renders it extremely difficult to generalise (Dines 1999; Bregman 2001). From informal chats with people involved in the social centres' movement, the legal status of a space is often a decisive sign of its 'radicality'. Lucy Finchett-Maddock seems to adhere to this categorisation, as she defines squatted centres as 'practice-based communities', and the rented/owned spaces as 'counter-institutions' that 'ease the pressure on those in power by providing voluntary social services' (Finchett-Maddock 2008:21, 30). Certainly, occupying abandoned buildings is a radical act, as it is a form of direct action that defies the institutions.[2] Yet, I will highlight how also rented/owned social centres can be radical, according to Newman's definition.

Squatting Communities

Squatting was widespread in 1970s Britain and Italy. In mid-1970s London, 40,000–50,000 people were squatting – often taking over whole streets and neighbourhoods, which behaved like 'decentralised urban self-managed communit[ies]' (Coates 2012:295). The Italian squatting movement was the only one in Europe, with the Dutch, to keep pace with the British, as masses of students and southern workers moved to the industrialised cities of centre-north Italy (Gimson 1980:216–18).

Throughout the 1970s, intensely squatted areas fulfilled the function of spaces to socialise and radicalise. A former squatter and old anarchist militant who asked to be named as Stroppy Old Git highlighted that such areas

> functioned as social centres, with loads of things going on, according to people's interests. All sort of stuff happened in squatted streets, like Huntley street. It depended on who was there. Including just hanging out, street parties. Who would need to set up a social centre in those days? And it wasn't just for squatters. ... The need for social centres only really arose when people [became] more scattered and you [didn't] have focal points with squatted blocks or squatted streets, or intensely squatted areas.
>
> *(Stroppy Old Git 2016)*

Freedom from rent – continued Stroppy Old Git – and thus from a stable job to pay the rent meant that squatters could use their time differently. He, for one, became involved in 'lots of things which are anarchist in their whole politics', such as the Advisory Service for Squatters, the revolutionary libertarian group Big Flame and later the radical environmental group Earth First! and the direct action collective Reclaim the Streets (RTS). Squatters had also time to organise and defend their own interests as a movement, he added, because they attended the meetings of council housing committees – whereas, he concluded, 'all that died away ... I think the squatters' movement lost its capacity to ... leave muddy footprints in the corridors of power' (Stroppy Old Git 2016).

Occupied Social Centres

The first self-defined social centres appeared around the same period in the suburbs of Italian metropoles, where post-1968 disillusioned youths – mostly underpaid temporary workers, but also unemployed people and students – suffered from the absence of spaces to socialise. Nanni Balestrini and Primo Moroni reported the experience of Vincenzo from Limbiate, in the Milanese hinterland. There, to overcome the 'problem of free time' (perceived as a time for 'boredom and alienation'), young people gathered on the benches near the local train station, since the local cafes 'kicked us out because [they saw us as] long-haired, drug addicts, and especially because we didn't consume much'. Day after day, they met to talk and spend time together, until they grew in number and started desiring 'something more' because – they thought – 'we're too young to accept to rot here'. Hence, they discussed those issues together, and set up the *circoli del proletariato giovanile* (proletarian youth clubs), which fostered the creation of *centri sociali* (social centres) by occupying abandoned buildings such as houses and factories as a form of direct action (Balestrini and Moroni 1997:509–18).[3]

Social centres spread in Italy. By the end of 1977, they numbered around fifty in Milan alone, with up to 7,000 people participating in their self-managed activities (Ginsborg 1990:382). In those years, squatting had become an increasingly popular answer to the housing problem, especially in the industrialised cities of central-northern Italy. In 1976, a group of Milanese anarchists combined the two issues – housing and social spaces – and occupied two buildings in the Ticinese district, an area that Pino – one of the anarchist occupiers – described as dangerous, with old overcrowded flats lacking water or heating, and external shared toilets (Pino 2015). Antonio M., a member of the anarchist group *Bandiera Nera* (Black Flag), explained that their aim was both to provide housing for destitute families and to give local anarchist groups a place to meet (Editorial Staff 1976a).

One collective, formed mostly of young anarchist workers and southern squatting families, managed both occupations – Conchetta and Torricelli – which hosted two social centres, a 'barter shop', a housing committee, a libertarian students' and workers' committee, and a healthcare workers' committee. The latter contributed to the refoundation of the historical anarchist syndicate *Unione Sindacale Italiana* (USI) (Editorial Staff 1976b; Pino 2015). The proximity with radical activists contributed to the politicisation of the working-class squatters, who endorsed the adoption of libertarian principles to regulate their communal life. More recently, the social centre of Conchetta – refounded as Cox18 – also demonstrated its influence over the neighbourhood, as its activists taught direct action tactics to local residents, who lamented the high volume of traffic and pollution. Together, they organised meetings and blocked via Conchetta (Cox 18, Archivio Primo Moroni, and Calusca City Lights 2010:47–64).

Rented Social Centres

Similar results, however, were achieved by a non-squatted precursor of social centres – the *comitato di quartiere San Pasquale* (CdQ, San Pasquale neighbourhood committee). In 1973, local residents had rented a street-level venue in the working-class area of San Pasquale in Bari. It started as a self-managed after-school club, but a group of young anarcho-communists joined in 1974 because they considered its 'contents and methods objectively libertarian', although it remained non-confrontational and limited to single-issue campaigns (Organizzazione Rivoluzionaria Anarchica n.d.). An activist, Nicola Laucelli, described it as 'like a present-day social centre, but well-rooted in the neighbourhood' (Laucelli 2009). Like current social centres, they promoted events, such as concerts, theatre shows and film clubs – all with a strong political focus ('about [working-class] daily problems'), as they aimed to radicalise the neighbourhood (Comitato di quartiere San Pasquale 1976).

They engaged in counter-information and conscientiousness-raising activities among the local residents, including explaining changes in housing laws (Organizzazione Anarchica Pugliese 1974b; see also Comitati di quartiere rioni San Pasquale e San Marcello 1978). Activists Pina Buttiglione and Luciano Sepe remembered that local women 'believed that a civil wedding wasn't valid', and practised illegal 'abortion [as] the normal contraceptive' (Sepe 2009; Buttiglione

2010). Therefore, they provided information on their bulletins, promoted a petition to legalise abortion, opened a free clinic for women and organised weekly women-only meetings to 'discuss their problems' (Comitato di quartiere San Pasquale 1976). The neighbourhood participated in the CdQ's activities and, as in the case of Cox18, went through a process of radicalisation. Some residents started frequenting the meetings of the anarchist group, and many took part in the occupation and transformation of an abandoned villa into a kindergarten (Caggese 2009; Laucelli 2009; Sepe 2009). The experience of San Pasquale was so successful that residents of the neighbouring San Marcello district opened a twinned CdQ (Comitato di quartiere San Marcello n.d.; Nucleo Promotore "Comitato di quartiere rione San Marcello" 1977).

Social Centres as Radical Hubs

Depending on the interests/competences of the activists, and on needs of the local community, social centres developed a range of social and cultural activities. Bristol-based Kebele evolved from a squatted house into a space with a vegan café, a bike workshop, an allotment, a service of radical information and publications, different forms of art, and numerous events and meetings with speakers and artists (Kebele collective n.d.). Whereas, the Barese Fucine Meridionali hosted debates, punk concerts, alternative theatre experiences, film clubs and other initiatives that attracted 'a multitude of people' (Arcangelo 2015).

In addition to this, a social centre also works as 'a hub, a base, or a centre for the wider alternative community to socialise, organise activities, discuss, debate, argue, get pissed, watch films … a living example of [radical] politics in action' (Tim 2015). As the activist Gennaro confirmed, Fucine was the 'base … but all the [political] initiatives were in the city' (Gennaro 2015). Social centres contribute to the wider political scene by 'provid[ing] a sense of something alternative that is happening and ongoing' (Tim 2015). Like a catalyst, they attract other radicals, who contribute to the further radicalisation of an area, as in the case of the London-based Ex-Grand Banks. One of its founders, Alessio Lunghi, stated that its opening drew activists and squatters who occupied other places in the Kentish Town area – 'so, at a point we had four spaces' (Lunghi 2016).

As Cox18 and CdQ San Pasquale have demonstrated, one last radical and probably most significant contribution of social centres is the politicisation of local communities. To achieve this, activists use social and cultural events to attract 'ordinary people' and introduce them to practices that embody libertarian principles like self-organisation, anti-hierarchy, direct action, anticapitalism (Lunghi 2007). Thus, the Ex-Grand Banks attracted many local pupils, who – proudly affirmed Alessio – could have otherwise entered local gangs – and 'some are still active, socially and politically' (Lunghi 2016). However, events and activities are necessary but not often sufficient. The squatting community of Claremont Road in East London radicalised many among both squatters and local residents, as they all united with long-term campaigners and anarchist activists against the construction of the M11 link road. Living side by side and experiencing the repressive face of the state helped residents overcome their prejudices against squatters/activists, who could also share their analyses and tactics with the residents (Carolyn 2016).

Despite the defeat of the No-M11 campaign, that experience created a network of radicals, who kept working together on this and other issues. For instance, they revitalised the RTS network by drawing on their Claremont road experience, which united joyful street parties and the nonviolent struggle to reclaim urban spaces for the people rather than for the cars or other infrastructures of capitalism. Such a combination of direct action and communitarian fun was successful, and the network became a national phenomenon that peaked with a 10,000-people street party that paralysed the City of London during the global carnival against capital on 18 June 1999 (Carolyn 2016).

Squatting/occupying can appear as a radical act in itself, but the experience of centres like CdQ San Pasquale proves that rented/owned spaces can be just as radical. In fact, squatting/occupying can even be reactionary, as in the case of the neo-fascist Italian organisation CasaPound – famous for squatting houses and occupying social centres 'for the exclusive use of citizens of Italian nationality' (Di Tullio 2006; Ferrari 2011; Vereni 2015:153). More indicative of the radical character of a space is the ability to enact radical politics as a part of its everyday life. The social centres I presented earlier embodied Newman's definition of radical politics by creating spaces that aim to challenge the state and its institutions. They are examples of alternative societies based on the principles of self-management, equality, direct action and direct democracy. Besides providing social and cultural services to (usually) deprived areas, social centres can function as a gateway for people into radical politics. Moreover, they can become hubs for activists to meet and organise political activities, and – even after their demise – activists can draw on those experiences to develop new movements.

How Is the Social Centres Movement Theorised and Influenced?

For both personal and academic reasons, I have had the chance to speak to people involved in current and previous experiences of social centres. What emerged from such conversations is that social centres' activists privilege practice over theory. Nevertheless, their actions are influenced by contemporary events and by the theoretical debates developed within the wider radical scene. In this section, I want to explore some of these relationships and their effects on the social centres' movement.

1970s: Between Spontaneism and Radical Theories

The subcultures and countercultures of the 1960s and 1970s – sets of alternative values that reject and aim at replacing the hegemonic ones – had a fundamental role in the development of social centres (Yinger 1960). Unsatisfied with parliamentary politics, masses of young people embraced – more or less consciously – the anarchist principles of direct action, self-management, equality and prefiguration.[4] British squatting communities embodied such principles, although people squatted for diverse reasons. Many were simply homeless people in need of shelter ('working-class and under-educated ... without shock-absorbers'), while others were political activists (mostly from radical 'groupuscules'). The latter, like Ron Bailey and Jim Radford, aimed to be an example to follow, and sometimes managed to politicise others (Walter 1969). There were also middle-class students and 'highly-educated artist dropouts' who – according to former squatter Josefine Speyer – often considered themselves anarchists. Yet, they spent a lot of time talking of 'music, art, philosophy, but no politics. You just saw [politics] as a load of crap' (Speyer 2016). Overall, British squatters formed communities that anticipated social centres' themes, such as direct action and self-management. Overall, besides a minority of so-called politicos, squatters often adopted a pragmatic approach that eschewed political theorisations.

The influence of countercultures was strong in Italy too, although there, the young students and workers involved in the emerging phenomenon of social centres were generally more politicised, as Italy, in general, presented a higher level of political activism. From the late 1960s, the confrontation between radicals and state/reactionary forces had transformed violence into an integral element of the political discourse (Ginsborg 1990:379–83). Throughout the 1970s, the *Autonomia* (autonomous movement) developed which united Workers' Autonomy, Metropolitan Indians and women's movements (Katsiaficas 2006:17–27).[5] Their shared trademark was the 'refusal of work' – hence, the adoption of tactics that included sabotage, absenteeism and self-reductions (Bianchi and Caminiti 2007:51–52). Squats and social centres were often hubs for radical groups, free radio stations and alternative publications, which helped autonomist tactics and principles take root within the social centres' movement (Gimson 1980:216–18).

Another influential movement for Italian social centre activists was anarchism, which former squatter Erri recognised as 'an important reference point' (Erri 2015). As in the case of Conchetta, anarchists promoted the practice of squatting and opening social centres (Editorial Staff 1971). I interviewed some of those anarchists and noticed that – unlike the British self-proclaimed anarchist squatters – their direct actions often came from theoretical reflections following the rediscovery of classic anarchist authors. The anarcho-communists of CdQ San Pasquale became involved in neighbourhood committees – as well as in the students' movement and workers' unions – because they aimed to apply platformism and Malatesta's 'gradualism' (Dadà 1984:137; Lapolla 2011:85–148).[6] Therefore, they used CdQs as a strategy to 'help proletarians raise their consciousness' and connect them 'with the class movement [and] the broader anti-capitalist struggle' (Organizzazione Anarchica Pugliese 1974a:14–15). Both *autonomi* and anarchists demonstrated a clear interest in theoretical reflections. However, little remained of such a theoretical preparation when, at the end of the 1970s, a wave of repression hit the radical movement.

Punx: Regenerating Social Centres

In the early 1980s, most Italian social centres were either closed by the authorities or faced *Riflusso* (ebb), as most activists quit any political engagement and often sought escape in hard drugs – while a minority joined the armed struggle (Bianchi and Caminiti 2007:41–60). The few surviving social centres turned into places for partying and heroin consumption (Editorial Staff 1989:9). A different type of ebb hit Britain too, as Thatcherism alienated a generation of angry and non-conformist youths. Punk music and its mottoes ('do it yourself', 'no future', 'against all authority') seemed to address perfectly the rage and rebellion of that generation that had lost all hope in transforming mainstream society. The punk movement started spreading in Britain around 1975, while it was only in 1977–79 that the first self-declared punks appeared in the streets of big Italian cities like Milan, where becoming a punk symbolised a reaction to social homogenisation, invasive police control, suburban council estate ghettos, heroin and criminality (Consorzio Aaster et al. 1996:109).

Punks filled the void left by the ebb by opening *Centri Sociali Occupati Autogestiti* (CSOAs, Self-managed Occupied Social Centres). This second generation of social centres started in central-northern Italy, as punks escaped suburban ghettos in search of places to meet, rehearse and play their music. They evolved into gateways to activism for disillusioned young people, as punk music treated themes such as self-management, antimilitarism and antifascism. Moreover, CSOAs helped regenerate the phenomenon of social centres by spreading the concepts of self-production and Do-It-Yourself material, like cassettes and fanzines (Editorial Staff 1989:10–11). Such material facilitated the circulation of ideas within the movement, and social centres became places generating grassroots culture, DIY politics and unconventional lifestyles (Philopat 2006:111).

Punks also helped broaden the focus of radical politics by supporting themes like ecology and antispeciesism. The punk movement was heterogeneous, with symbols spanning both anarchist circle-As and nazi swastikas. Many punks had a 'spontaneous libertarian spirit', which favoured a collaboration with anarchists. Several punks openly embraced anarchism and started calling themselves 'punx' to distinguish themselves from the rest of the movement (Consorzio Aaster et al. 1996:112,113). Exemplary is the case of the Virus – the first punk social centre – which opened in Milan in 1981, near the anarchist squats and social centres of Correggio, Conchetta and Torricelli (Mosca 2012). Punks and anarchists co-organised anti-heroin concerts at Conchetta, and numerous punx participated in the early 1980s mass-protests against nuclear missiles at the newly opened NATO base of Comiso, in Sicily (Pino 2015). Then, in 1988, the ex-Virus punx – evicted in 1984 – even refounded Conchetta as CSOA Cox18 together with activists involved in grassroots syndicalism and in the radical bookshop Calusca. The arrival of punks ended the period of semi-inactivity that Conchetta had experienced after most squatters moved out, having accepted the offer of council flats (Cox 18, Archivio Primo Moroni, and Calusca City Lights 2010:26; Cox 18 n.d.).

In Britain too, punks had an enormous influence on the social centres' movement. In fact, they contributed to its foundation together with squatters and radical activists, although social centres were then called Autonomy Clubs. Among the first were the Autonomy Centre in Wapping (1982–83), Centro Iberico in West London (1982) and the 1 in 12 Club in Bradford. The 1 in 12 was founded in 1981, and still exists today as 'a group of people who work together to promote certain political ideals and social change; [and] a members social club' (Bradford 1 in 12 Club Constitution n.d.). Their political action has focused on unemployment, antifascism and animal liberation, and they periodically host live music, book fairs, fanzine conventions, discussion groups, films, debates and political workshops (Hodkinson and Chatterton 2006). Like in Italy, such spaces facilitated the politicisation of punks and squatters – although in a less structured way compared to those of the 1970s – and influenced the wider radical movement with new themes. As the former squatter and punk Bibi confirmed, 'It was almost uncool to take [politics] seriously or think about it, but at the same time everyone was very political. We all used to go to protests about everything, from gay rights and animal rights to the anti-Poll Tax' (Bibi 2014).[7]

The Influence of Global, National and Local Contexts on CSOAs and Infoshops

In the 1990s, the British and Italian experiences of social centres diverged further, as the wider radical scenes focused on different issues. Britain went through a new surge in activism, especially against the road and airport expansion programme, and the Criminal Justice Act of 1994. The Act gave the police new stop-and-search powers and introduced 'criminal sanctions against travellers, ravers, festival-goers, public assemblies and political protests', thus affecting mostly youths and radicals (McKay 1998:61). What emerged was a new generation of activists that blended radical environmentalism with anarchist direct action and the 'party and protest' attitude of rave culture. People inspired by the Earth First! movement and by Hakim Bey's concept of Temporary Autonomous Zones (TAZs) led to the occupation of rural and urban areas threatened by road expansion, and revitalised the RTS network.[8] At the same time, Italian social centres experienced a new expanding phase after a national wave of protests by students, who used CSOAs as meeting and organisational spaces, and even as 'social enterprises' (spaces with an economic dimension to provide social services). However, radical ecology, the so-called new rurality and the defence of the commons spread in Italy only from the early 2000s, together with the peak of the antiglobalisation protests (Membretti and Mudu 2013:76–81).

In the early 1990s, British radical environmentalists opposed the building of roads they deemed 'non-necessary' and spoiling the rural landscape – beginning with the M3 extension in Twyford Down, Hampshire, in 1991–92. Later, they integrated environmentalism with the issues of 'housing, pollution and use of "community" space'. The turning point was the 'No M11-Link' campaign in 1993–95, when the area of Claremont road in East London faced the demolition of houses and green areas for the construction of a link road (McKay 1998:102; see also Wakefield and Grrrt 1995). Claremont road evolved into a squatting community with plenty of spaces to socialise, create art and engage in political activism, like a squat café offering cheap and usually vegan food.

Squat cafes and infoshops became a common sight in the British cities with a lively squatting scene such as London and Bristol. Besides serving food, squat cafes worked as social centres, since they also hosted DIY cultural events and represented a 'living example of anarchist politics' (Hodkinson and Chatterton 2006:306–7). Similarly, infoshops fulfilled the role of social centres, as they provided radical activists with useful information and meeting spaces (Solidarity Federation 2016). Kebele, in Bristol, started as a squatted building in 1995, but when the initial anarchist squatters – also involved in RTS – realised that the building had a 'far greater [potential] than just providing a place to live', they opened both a squat café and an infoshop (Barry 2015).

Like in Britain, anticapitalism became increasingly central to the politics of Italian social centres, which increased in number – especially in the northern cities (Mudu 2013:71–75).[9] What is peculiar of the Italian context is that the expansion of CSOAs was fuelled by a national student movement – the so-called Pantera. In 1989–90, the Pantera protests and occupations against the education reform politicised thousands of students, who later continued their radicalisation process swelling the ranks of the social centres' movement. CSOAs also became more antagonistic, as right-wing parties gained momentum. The collapse of the Eastern European bloc and the nationwide political scandal *Tangentopoli* (Bribesville) had caused the disappearance of Italy's historical parties.[10] This prepared the way for the growth of Silvio Berlusconi's populist party, the racist Northern League and the neo-fascist National Alliance (Sassoon 1997:186). Within this new political context, journalists and politicians likened social centres to terrorist hideouts, and repression followed. Many CSOAs were threatened with evictions, but activists usually took to the streets to resist such attempts.

CSOA activists became involved in heated debates on the opportunity of entering into agreements with municipalities or landlords by agreeing to be relocated or to pay a rent to avoid evictions, which is what up to half of social centres did in 1998 (Mudu 2013:70; Cox 18, Archivio Primo Moroni, and Calusca City Lights 2010:xxiii). In a climate of both expansion and repression, social centres' activists also debated various ways to unite and redirect the movement, such as the need for a national coordinating organism. They also rediscovered the importance of moments of collective theoretical reflection, as the movement's principal reference points remained anarchism and *Autonomia*, with the addition of the Mexican Zapatista movement. The latter became particularly influential with its combination of traditional Left-libertarian themes – like self-management and anticapitalism – with alterglobalisation (Wu Ming 2001).

Zapatismo represented the beginning of the shift, among 1990s radical activists, towards a politicised but more composite identity. Most of the activists I have met and interviewed had difficulties in defining their own political identity, but I noticed that post-1990s social centres' activists tended to reject classifications *tout-court*. They perceived old political definitions as 'outdated'. According to Gennaro, the Bari-based CSOA Fucine Meridionali openly aimed to be 'a common house for all movements'. Thanks to their composite political identity – he continued – that Fucine became a regional radical catalyst and maintained positive relations with social centres across the country (Gennaro 2015).

With the global spreading of the alterglobalisation movement in the early 2000s, social centres perfected their role as organisational hubs for the wider radical movement. In fact, the opposition to capitalist globalisation and its symbols reinforced the movement by creating or strengthening activist networks, even though state repression hit once again. The London-based anarchist collective Wombles (2001–06) launched in Britain the first self-defined social centres 'based on experiences from around Europe and especially Italy', since they considered squat cafes and autonomy clubs to be self-segregating spaces for radicals (L. 2007). It was at the Prague mobilisation against the IMF and World Bank in 2000 that Alessio Lunghi and other Wombles first made contact with Italians involved in CSOAs. They later visited several social centres in Italy, which inspired the creation of spaces like the Ex-Grand Banks in 2004.

Both global and national phenomena had direct repercussions on the discussions and actions of social centres. Fucine, for instance, shaped its politics around the Zapatist discourse on alterglobalisation, but also emerging national issues like immigration, anti-prohibition and precarity. Yet, equally influential were themes at a local level, such as the presence of abandoned and dangerous places in town, including a former asbestos factory in the heart of Bari. To this, Fucine's activists reacted with a series of 'flash-occupations' to draw media and citizen attention to the problem (Arcangelo 2015). The same happened at Kebele, whose creation and development were the result of a combination of forces at different levels – from the emergence of the transnational alterglobalisation movement to the British anti-roads movement, but also local elements like the radical reputation of a place and the presence of local radical networks. As Tim confirmed, Kebele benefited from the existence of a radical milieu in Bristol because of the city's broader image as a 'radical place', which attracted many activists. In addition, other local radical projects – like an anarchist mixed-gendered football club – created a mutually supportive environment (Tim 2015). Such experiences demonstrate that theoretical debates – like that on TAZ or alterglobalisation – play an important role in the delineation of social centres' politics. Also important are other radical experiences, whose example, support and memory can inspire and influence social centres.

The Problems of Social Centres

When I interviewed the Barese former-activist Arcangelo, he declared that one of the reasons behind the foundation of CSOA Fucine Meridionali in 1994 was the creation of 'a model for the alternative society we wanted' (Arcangelo 2015). As we have seen in the previous section, there are many different factors favouring the foundation and development of a social centre, whereas others can hinder this process. In this last section, I will identify and analyse some of the principal problems social centres have faced as this will explain why many social centres – such as Fucine – failed to become that model of alternative society.

Repression

Among the external factors preventing social centres from succeeding is the hostility of authorities, who – to quote the activist Carolyn – often send 'undercover police to spy on the movement and to try and repress it' (Carolyn 2016). In particular, what she referred to was the recent case of undercover agents who infiltrated the British radical green movement (Jones and Wilson 2015) – a practice so widespread that activists usually refused my interviews or treated me with distrust, and often asked me to use pseudonyms because they stated: 'we need to protect ourselves from infiltrators, telltales [and] journalists' (Francesco and Ruggiero 2014). An understandable paranoia that I observed when, during an assembly at the Barese CSOA Ex-Caserma Liberata, some activists explained to me that the 'tense atmosphere' I had noticed was due to their recent discovery that the police had tapped them. They claimed receiving a full transcript from a previous activist-only meeting. This fear can also negatively influence a social centre by creating an 'under siege' feeling, and leading the activists to turn in on themselves.

Another classic tool of repression is eviction. One solution, when possible, is that of entering into agreements with the owner of the premises – usually either people or firms or local/national authorities. This is, for instance, what allowed Kebele to be a radical hub in Bristol for over twenty years, as Kebele's activists formed a housing cooperative that purchased the building in 1998 (Kebele collective n.d.). However, this is not always possible or convenient, as the 1977 Greater London Council (GLC) amnesty shows. When the majority of the 7,000 London-based squatters in over 1,859 GLC properties accepted to be rehoused or regularised, the entire radical movement suffered a setback (Wates and Wolmar 1980:89). The radical network of communities fractured, and the time squatters dedicated to activism diminished now that they needed jobs to pay their rents (Stroppy Old Git 2014).

Other squatters – like those in Freston road, Notting Hill – wanted to remain in an area and with people they felt attached to. To defend their community, Freston road squatters declared independence from Great Britain as the Free Independent Republic of Frestonia (Wates and Wolmar 1980:91–94). Former Frestonian Shelley Assiter admitted it 'was a publicity stunt ... because otherwise we were not being heard'. An action that attracted television crews and changed mainstream society's view of squatters, who – in Shelley's opinion – used to be seen as 'the lowest of the lowest'. As a consequence, they managed to remain in the area and to participate in the renovation project. According to Shelley, this victory – together with the absence of a common room – led to a more individualistic attitude and a decrease in their participation (Assiter 2016).

(Self)-Segregation

For a social centre to become a successful model for an alternative society, decisive is also the type of relationship it establishes with its neighbourhood and the city. It must function as a 'port of call' for non-activists rather than as a ghetto for subcultures and militants, as feared by the Wombles collective. Yet, the relation between activists and 'ordinary people' has often been problematic because of subcultural, political, cultural, ethnic and class-based reasons.

Gennaro lamented that, in mid-1990s Bari, Fucine's relation with 'the surrounding houses was awful ... they threw at us bottles full of frozen water! ... Many saw us as aliens – weirdos with green hair and dogs' (Gennaro 2015). It was surely unhelpful – as Arcangelo declared – 'to host gigs every weekend [with that] huge and constant hustle and bustle' (Arcangelo 2015). Twenty years later, in 2015, Barese citizens showed little enthusiasm for another CSOA: Ex-Caserma Liberata. Rather than hostility towards an exuberant subculture, many local residents distanced themselves on political grounds. A man with an interest in local politics told me that, after experiencing a strong excitement for the 'recovery of this beautiful space', he distanced himself from the CSOA because of a 'muddled' organisational process, and an internal 'closed group' of activists functioning as the real decisional organism (Frank 2015). One of Ex-Caserma's activists also said that people complained for their consensus-based decision method, which they called time-wasting, and she admitted that another local resident told her: 'I wish you'd never occupied [Ex-Caserma]!' (Carmen and Tony 2015).[11]

Less-politicised or 'ordinary' people often feel uneasy about the very idea of walking into a social centre, especially if it is squatted/occupied. They can be discouraged from crossing a threshold that is both physical and psychological, as walls with political murals and doors kept locked to avoid evictions are charged with 'symbolic meanings, defining areas of authorities' (Samson 1992:26). A way to overcome this barrier is organising initiatives to attract the local residents. The Barese CSOA Villa Roth offered in 2011–14 a social vegetable garden, a library, football matches for children, acoustic concerts and experimental theatre shows (Dossier Villa Roth Occupata 2014). This time, the neighbourhood welcomed the social centre, but when the CSOA was evicted in 2014, none of them joined the demonstrations or showed active solidarity. According to activist Carmen, local residents saw Villa Roth as 'a community centre ... a provider of services'. In other words, the social centre had failed to politicise them (Carmen and Tony 2015). Equally problematic can be the more cultured and politicised frequenters – usually students or white-collar workers – who behave like 'rule-breakers by night and "integrated" by day', and intend social centres as 'places of cultured and socialising entertainment' (Consorzio Aaster et al. 1996:137).

Kebele's activists lamented a similar situation, although in this case the barrier was ethnic/cultural. The Bristol-based social centre is in the multi-ethnic area of Easton, but activist Barry acknowledged that there are 'more white people that come to Kebele than I would like' (Barry 2015). The only exception, said Tim, is the bike workshop on Wednesdays, when there are mostly 'Somali and Afro-Caribbean and Asian kids ... [who] can't afford a new bike'. The participation of the local non-white population is limited to the occasional 'consumption' of the space, with no political involvement. In Tim's opinion, this reflects the wider anarchist/radical movement in Britain that 'is largely white ... [despite the] refugees and asylum seekers solidarity, and antifascist/antiracist work' (Tim 2015). This does not mean that ethnic minorities are not radical, but simply that they probably have different priorities and perceive a predominantly white space as an obstacle.

Another obstacle to the active participation of local residents can be class. For example, CdQ San Pasquale's activists claimed that many residents frequented the space, but they admitted: 'people consider the committee as an organisation to go to in order to have their problems solved' because they were accustomed to delegating (Comitato di quartiere San Pasquale 1976; Sepe 2009). The political participation of San Pasquale residents was often limited to single issues. Former CdQ militant Gennaro Gadaleta Caldarola admitted this happened because mostly middle-class activists and largely working-class residents lived two different realities: 'We were young and full of ideas, but we weren't inside the reality people lived in' (Gadaleta Caldarola 2010). In Pina Buttiglione's opinion, this situation alienated the working class, who had 'fewer cultural instruments to understand these ideas, and ... urgent needs to satisfy instead' (Buttiglione 2010).

Internal Issues

A challenge to the role of social centres as models for a radical society can also come from their internal composition. In particular, politics, class and (sub)culture have often been problematic for the cohesion of the collectives managing social centres. Ex-squatter Tom Osborn believed that squatting produces a classless society, as squatters leave their old social position behind by learning from each other (Osborn 1980:186). However, Stroppy Old Git remarked that class division is still evident between people in need of accommodation and those he called 'middle-class arty-farty wankers' (Stroppy Old Git 2016). Class-based division is present in social centres too, as Arcangelo mentioned a fracture between the components of

CSOA Fucine Meridionali – the politicised and the 'lumpenproletariat': 'Individuals on the edge between legality and illegality, with a difficult background, even with prison experience'. As the two components could not overcome this fracture, Fucine did not survive the following split. A lesson Arcangelo learned the hard way, as he said: 'Today I'd avoid the fracture. Nobody realised what we were going to lose ... We were defeated' (Arcangelo 2015).

In 2010, the activists that opened the CSOA Ex-Mercato Occupato in Bari replicated Fucine's mistake when, as Carmen explained, a 'class-based split' emerged between squatters ('coming from the street, less-educated') and activists (educated middle-class students) over the commitment towards the management of the space (Carmen and Tony 2015). This example introduces two related issues that can also endanger the survival of social centres: the loss of radical memory and activists dropping out of active politics. Authoritarian repression – like arresting activists and evicting social centres – certainly hinders the transmission of knowledge between generations of activists by closing the gateways to radical activism. But so does the dropping-out of experienced activists, due to either their falling back to mainstream society, or 'burnout'.

Arcangelo experienced both. After months of heated arguments with the other occupants, he and other activists started a political organisation – Red66 – but they brought Fucine's tensions with them, and soon individualism took hold of Red66 activists. Tired of that environment, Arcangelo first fled to Germany to experience the techno-rave movement, and then – back in Bari – he opened a radical publishing house and bookshop. Now in his forties, with a full-time job and a family, he justified his lack of involvement in current social centres because 'if you have an evening off, you must decide: "Shall I go to the assembly or stay with my son?"' (Arcangelo 2015).

Conclusion

I opened this chapter asking if social centres could be radical social laboratories, in which activists and citizens experiment and implement alternative solutions to organise society. To answer this question, I have first reflected on the meaning of social centres and of radical politics. Then, I explored some key radical elements of social centres, such as their role as a hub for activists and a gateway into political activism for 'ordinary citizens'. I illustrated the relation of mutual influence between theory and practice – as social centres' activists interact with the wider radical movement on multiple levels – and highlighted some common characteristics holding social centres back. In addition, by focusing on case studies from Britain and Italy, I also showed the effect of the spatial context – with local, national and global dimensions all affecting the development of the social centre. Despite the differences, though, what emerged from this analysis is that radical social centres share an active commitment: they all experiment with alternative socio-economic relations centred around principles like self-management, direct action and equality. They can thus be seen as 'radical social laboratories'. Yet, to successfully propagate such experiments on a larger scale, they need to develop a cohesive but open and flexible collective; enter a mutually supportive network of radical experiences; involve and politicise new generations and local residents by adapting to their needs – when suitable – without becoming a provider of social services; and, most importantly, be resilient.

Notes

1 '[S]yndicalism is explicitly anticapitalist, antilandlordist, and antistatist, and envisages the union structures as the building blocks of a self-managed, stateless, socialist order' (Schmidt and van der Walt 2009: 22).

2   Direct action: 'action which … *realises the end desired*, so far as this lies within one's power', as opposed to 'delegating others' (David Wieck in: Ward 1996:12).
3   I refer to 'occupying' as a generic term for taking possession of a property without permission, and 'squatting' for residential occupations.
4   Prefiguration: when 'the means are consistent with the ends' (Franks 2006:17, 97–100).
5   Workers' Autonomy believed in 'raising the level of struggle within the state apparatus', while Metropolitan Indians were Situationist-like creatives who dressed as native Americans.
6   The so-called Platform was a 1926 document by Russian anarchist exiles, which distinguished between 'specific organisation' (the political group) and 'mass organisation', such as neighbourhood committees and student associations, in which anarchist militants could cooperate with working-class people 'to realise … the social revolution' (Convegno Nazionale dei Lavoratori Anarchici 1973). Malatesta's 'gradualism' stated: '[s]ince one cannot convert all the people at once …, it is necessary to find a way to realise as much anarchy as possible amidst people who are not anarchist' (Malatesta 1982).
7   The Poll Tax was a flat-rate tax on every adult, without reference to their income or resources. It was introduced in Britain between 1989 and 1990 by the Thatcher conservative government, and replaced by the Council Tax in 1993 after mass opposition and riots.
8   TAZs are the embodiment of a never-ending indirect guerrilla against the State: a collective liberates an area, then dissolves before the State can crush it and reappears somewhere or sometime else (Bey 1993:14).
9   To this contributed the social conservativeness of the South, youth migration towards more prestigious northern universities, and the presence of organised crime exercising a direct control over the territory.
10 Tangentopoli unearthed a deep-rooted situation of political corruption, and was followed by a nationwide judicial investigation that led to a series of incarcerations and suicides of politicians from all major parties and businessmen. Following the fall of the Eastern communist regimes, the old Italian Communist Party lost its traditional influence trying to restructure itself as an up-with-the-times social-democratic party.
11 Decisions by consensus require 'non-adversarial and patient discussion, valuing everyone's voice and concerns', as everybody involved in the decisional process has veto power (Gordon 2008:70).

References

Arcangelo, Interview on Fucine Meridionali. February 2, 2015.
Assiter, Shelley, Interview on Frestonia. February 25, 2016.
Balestrini, Nanni, and Primo Moroni, *L'orda d'oro : 1968–1977 : la grande ondata rivoluzionaria e creativa, politica ed esistenziale*. Nuova ed. (Milano: Feltrinelli, 1997).
Barry, Interview on Kebele. April 28, 2015.
Bey, Hakim, T.A.Z. *Zone Temporaneamente Autonome*. (Milano: Shake Edizioni, 1993).
Bianchi, Sergio, and Lanfranco Caminiti, eds., Gli Autonomi. Volume 1. (Roma: DeriveApprodi, 2007).
Bibi, Interview on Squatting in London. November 4, 2014.
Bradford 1 in 12 Club. Constitution (n.d.). www.1in12.com/our-constitution.html, accessed May 25, 2016.
Bregman, Adam, *Italy's Social Centers*. Los Angeles Indymedia, July 2001. http://la.indymedia.org/news/2001/07/8690.php, accessed October 6, 2016.
Buttiglione, Pina. Interview on OAP-ORA. July 6, 2010.
Caggese, Salvatore, Interview on OAP-ORA. November 15, 2009.
Carmen, and Tony, Interview on Bari Social Centres. February 1, 2015.
Carolyn, Interview on Squatting in London. March 3/10, 2016.
Coates, Chris, *Communes Britannica*. (London: Diggers and Dreamers Publications, 2012).
Comitati di quartiere rioni San Pasquale e San Marcello, Bollettino Interno: Edilizia. Franco Salomone (1978).
Comitato di quartiere San Marcello, Bollettino Interno. (n.d.)
Comitato di quartiere San Pasquale Bollettino Interno Del Comitato Di Quartiere San Pasquale, (1976)
Consorzio Aaster, Centro Sociale Cox 18, Centro Sociale Leoncavallo, and Primo Moroni, *Centri Sociali: Geografie Del Desiderio*. (Shake Edizioni Underground, 1996).

Convegno Nazionale dei Lavoratori Anarchici. I CNLA Bulletin. (1973).

Cox 18, 'Cox18: La Storia'. *Cox18Stream* (n.d.). http://cox18stream.noblogs.org/la-storia/. Accessed May 3, 2014.

Cox 18, Archivio Primo Moroni, and Calusca City Lights. *Storia Di Un'autogestione.* (Milano: Colibrì, 2010).

Curtis, Henry S., The Rural Social Center. *American Journal of Sociology* 19(1): 79–90 (1913).

Dadà, Adriana, *L'anarchismo in Italia: Tra Movimento E Partito. Storia E Documenti Dell'anarchismo Italiano* (Milano: Teti, 1984).

De Michelis, Marco, *Case Del Popolo* (Venice: Marsilio, 1986).

Degl'Innocenti, Maurizio, ed., *Le Case Del Popolo in Europa: Dalle Origini Alla Seconda Guerra Mondiale.* (Florence: Sansoni, 1984).

Di Tullio, Domenico, *Centri Sociali Di Destra: Occupazioni E Culture Non Conformi* (Roma: Castelvecchi, 2006).

Dines, Nick, 'Centri Sociali: Occupazioni Autogestite a Napoli Negli Anni Novanta'. *Quaderni Di Sociologia* 43(21): 90–111 (1999).

Editorial Staff, 'La Lotta per La Casa'. *A-Rivista Anarchica*, February 1971. www.arivista.org/?nr=001&pag=1_11.htm.

Editorial Staff, 'La Casa È Di Chi L'abita'. *A-Rivista Anarchica*, July 1976a. www.arivista.org/?nr=050&pag=50_03.htm, accessed April 12, 2014.

Editorial Staff, 'Occupazioni Di Case E Scambio Libero'. *A-Rivista Anarchica*, October 1976b. www.arivista.org/?nr=051&pag=51_01.htm, accessed April 12, 2014.

Editorial Staff, 'Dossier Centri Sociali'. *A-Rivista Anarchica*, 1989: 8–23.

Erri. Interview on Milanese Libertarian Communities. January 27, 2015.

Ferrari, Saverio, Cuore Nero E Dintorni. A-Rivista Anarchica, 2011. www.arivista.org/index.php?nr=364&pag=40.htm&key=casa%20pound, accessed October 12, 2016.

Finchett-Maddock, Lucy, An Anarchist's Wetherspoons or Virtuous Resistance? Social Centres as MacIntyre's Vision of Practice-Based Communities. *Philosophy of Management* 7(1): 21–32 (2008).

Francesco, and Ruggiero. Interview on Ex-Caserma Liberata. August 17, 2014.

Frank, Interview on Ex-Caserma Liberata. January 2, 2015.

Franks, Benjamin, *Rebel Alliances.* (Edinburgh: AK Press, 2006).

Gadaleta Caldarola, Gennaro, Interview on OAP-ORA. July 11, 2010.

Gennaro, Interview on Fucine Meridionali and Ex-Caserma Liberata. January 31, 2015.

Gimson, Mark, Everybody's Doing It. In *Squatting: The Real Story*, eds. Nick Wates and Christian Wolmar (London: Bay Leaf, 1980), 206–219.

Ginsborg, Paul, *A History of Contemporary Italy : Society and Politics, 1943–1988* (London: Penguin, 1990).

Gordon, Uri, *Anarchy Alive!* (London: Pluto, 2008).

Hodkinson, Stuart, and Paul Chatterton, Autonomy in the City? Reflections on the Social Centres Movement in the UK. *City* 10(3): 305–314 (2006).

Hogg, Quintin, ed., *The Social Centres of London: Being a Comprehensive Guide to the Social Educational, Recreative and Religious Institutes, and Clubs of the Metropolis.* (London: Polytechnic Reception Bureau, 1892).

Ibba, Alberto, *Leoncavallo 1975–1995: Venti Anni Di Storia Autogestita* (Genova: Costa & Nolan, 1995).

Industrial Workers of the World. Preamble to the Constitution of the Industrial Workers of the World (1905); www.iww.org/culture/official/preamble.shtml, accessed January 29, 2016.

Jones, Lisa, and Kate Wilson. 'Relationships with Undercover Officers Wreck Lives. The Lies Must Stop'. *The Guardian*, July 28, 2015. www.theguardian.com/commentisfree/2015/jul/28/relationships-undercover-officers-lies-mark-kennedy-police, accessed October 29, 2015.

Jozwiak, Elizabeth, 'Socialism, Free Speech, and Social Centers in Milwaukee'. *The Wisconsin Magazine of History* 86(3): 10–21 (2003).

Katsiaficas, George, *The Subversion of Politics* (Oakland: AK Press, 2006).

Kebele collective, Our Story. *Kebele Community Co-Op* (N.d.). https://network23.org/kebele2/ourstory/, accessed May 26, 2016.

Lapolla, Luca, *Gli anarchici di piazza Umberto. La sinistra libertaria a Bari negli anni Settanta* (Fano: Alternativa Libertaria, 2011).

Laucelli, Nicola. Interview on OAP-ORA. November 10, 2009.

Lunghi, Alessio, 'The Spring of Social Centres'. In *What's This Place?* (Leeds: Footprints Workers Co-operative, 2007): 33–34.

Lunghi, Alessio, Interview on Social Centres in London. February 27, 2016.

Malatesta, Errico, 'Il Possibilismo Anarchico'. In *Rivoluzione E Lotta Quotidiana*. Torino: Edizioni Antistato, 1982). www.intratext.com/ixt/ITA2048/_P1U.HTM#$1W, accessed June 18, 2015.

Marshall, Peter, *Demanding the Impossible: A History of Anarchism* (London: Fontana, 1993).

McKay, George, *DiY Culture. Party & Protest in Nineties Britain* (London: Verso, 1998).

Membretti, Andrea, and Pierpaolo Mudu, 'Where Global Meets Local: Italian Social Centres and the Alterglobalisation Movement'. In *Understanding European Movements*, eds. Cristina Flesher Fominaya and Laurence Cox (London: Routledge, 2013): 76–81.

Mosca, Simone, Philopat E Il Punk Di via Correggio. *La Repubblica.it*. September 8, 2012. http://ricerca.repubblica.it/repubblica/archivio/repubblica/2012/08/09/philopat-il-punk-di-via-correggio.html, accessed December 6, 2014.

Moses, Jonathan. *The Texture of Politics: London's Anarchist Clubs, 1884–1914*. 2016. https://www.ribaj.com/intelligence/the-texture-of-politics-london-s-anarchists-clubs-1882-1914

Mudu, Pierpaolo, Resisting and Challenging Neoliberalism: The Development of Italian Social Centers. In *Squatting in Europe: Radical Spaces, Urban Struggles*, ed. Squatting Europe Kollective (New York: Minor Compositions, 2013): 61–88.

Newman, Saul, Poststructuralism and the Future of Radical Politics. *SubStance* 36(2): 3–19 (2007).

Nucleo Promotore, "Comitato di quartiere rione San Marcello". Untitled (1977).

Organizzazione Anarchica Pugliese, Lotta Di Classe Nel Quartiere (1974a).

Organizzazione Anarchica Pugliese, Bollettino Interno 2 - Lotta Di Classe Nel Quartiere. (1974b).

Organizzazione Rivoluzionaria Anarchica, Dibattito Politico 1 - I Consigli Di Quartiere. (N.d).

Osborn, Tom, Outpost of a New Culture. In *Squatting: The Real Story*, eds. Nick Wates and Christian Wolmar. (London: Bay Leaf, 1980): 186–191.

Perry, Clarence Arthur, A Survey of the Social-Center Movement. *The Elementary School Teacher* 13(3): 124–133 (1912).

Philopat, Marco, ed. *Lumi Di Punk*. (Milano: Agenzia X, 2006).

Pino, Interview on Milan social centres. January 27, 2015.

Samson, Ross, Knowledge, Constraint, and Power in Inaction: The Defenseless Medieval Wall. *Historical Archaeology* 26(3): 26–44 (1992).

Sassoon, Donald, *Contemporary Italy. Economy Society and Politics since 1945*. Second edition. (London, New York: Longman, 1997).

Schmidt, Michael, and van der Walt, Lucien, *Black Flame*. (Oakland: AK Press, 2009).

Sepe, Luciano, Interview on OAP-ORA. November 20, 2009.

Solidarity Federation, 'Social Centres in the UK', *Organise!* 2016.

Speyer, Josefine, Interview on Frestonia. February 9, 2016.

Stevens, Edward W. 'Social Centers, Politics, and Social Efficiency in the Progressive Era'. *History of Education Quarterly* 12(1): 16–33 (1972).

Stroppy Old Git, Interview on Squatting in London. September 12, 2014.

Stroppy Old Git, Interview on Squatting in London. March 5, 2016.

Thompson, Edward Palmer, *The Making of the English Working Class* (London: Gollancz, 1963).

Tim, Interview on Kebele. March 8, 2015.

Vereni, Piero, Addomesticare Il Welfare Dal Basso. Prospettive E Paradossi Delle Occupazioni Abitative Romane. *Meridiana* 83: 147–169 (2015).

Villa Roth Occupata, Dossier (2014). Bari: Villa Roth Social Centre.

Wakefield, Stacy, and Grrrt, eds., *Not for Rent*. (Amsterdam, Seattle: Evil Twin, 1995).

Walter, Nicolas, 'The New Squatters'. *Anarchy*, August 1969: 225–229.

Ward, Colin, *Anarchy in Action*. (London: Freedom Press, 1996).

Wates, Nick, and Christian Wolmar, eds. *Squatting. The Real Story* (London: Bay Leaf, 1980).

Weston, Olive E. The Public School as a Social Center. *The Elementary School Teacher* 6(2): 108–116 (1905).

Woodcock, George. *Anarchism: A History of Libertarian Ideas and Movements*. (New York: Meridian, 1962).

Wu Ming, 'Tute Bianche: The Practical Side of Myth Making'. *Catastrophic Times* (Wu Ming Foundation, 2001). www.wumingfoundation.com/english/giap/giapdigest11.html, accessed October 17, 2016.

Yinger, J. Milton. 'Contraculture and Subculture'. *American Sociological Review* 25(5): 625–635 (1960).

4.5

DANCES WITH AGITATORS

What Is 'Anarchist Music'?

Jim Donaghey

Introduction

Robin Ballinger argues that '[m]usic is neither transcendental nor trivial, but inhibits a site where hegemonic processes are contested' (in Sakolsky and Ho (eds.), 1995: 14) – in other words, music *matters*. However, music (and culture more widely) is often viewed as being of minor importance within social movements, as something coincidental rather than fundamental. Consideration of anarchism and music contributes to an understanding of the complex relationships between culture and radical politics more widely, while challenging those narrow conceptions of radicalism that fail to take cultural aspects into account. This chapter points to the core role of culture (and music) in social movements, and the recognition of this importance across a wide spectrum of anarchist perspectives. The chapter then considers evaluations of 'anarchist music', identifying the aspects which are too easily recuperated by the State and capital (such as aesthetics and lyrics), and highlighting those aspects which contain *radical transformative potential* (such as Do-It-Yourself or DIY production processes – though this is necessarily marginal in character and scope). A transformation is not a fixed entity; it only operates in relation to an a priori situation. Evaluation of 'anarchist music' in terms of transformation is therefore alive to shifting contexts, and does not impose a particular set of criteria – yet, it still usefully problematises any claim of a particular music as being 'anarchist'. However, no form of music (in terms of its aesthetic or production process) is entirely immune to co-optation, and it is argued here that music's radical transformative potential is most fully realised, and most resilient, when engaged within a culture of resistance.

Culture

At the dances I was one of the most untiring and gayest. One evening ... a young boy took me aside. With a grave face, as if he were about to announce the death of a dear comrade, he whispered to me that it did not behoove an agitator to dance. Certainly not with such reckless abandon, anyway. It was undignified for one who was on the way to become a force in the anarchist movement. My frivolity would only hurt the Cause.

I grew furious at the impudent interference of the boy. I told him to mind his own business ... I did not believe that a Cause which stood for a beautiful ideal, for anarchism, for release and freedom from convention and prejudice, should demand the denial of life and joy ... If it meant that, I did not want it. 'I want freedom, the right to self-expression, everybody's right to beautiful, radiant things' ... I would live my beautiful ideal.

(Goldman, 1934: 56)

The aforementioned quotation from Emma Goldman[1] is often expressed in condensed form as: 'If I can't dance, it's not my revolution', and highlights an oft-repeated tension in the anarchist movement around cultural expression. For the purposes of this chapter, Goldman and the young comrade represent two poles of this dispute: the chastising young comrade represents those who insist on a 'serious', materialist anarchism based on a reductive economistic philosophy; and Goldman represents anarchisms which *also* embrace the 'non-material' aspects of society, such as revolutionary agency[2] and culture. 'Culture' is a broad term, understood in different ways depending on its context – theatre, literature, art, sport, dancing and music are denoted in a narrow use of the term, but 'culture' understood in a wider sense may also express the sum of human (or other animal) social activity, from tool usage and forms of language, to how societies organise themselves. Rudolf Rocker[3] discusses culture in this wider understanding, arguing that 'a culture ... is in its innermost essence anarchistic' (1937: 353). He argues that culture 'has grown organically' and 'knows no subterfuge', while 'States create no culture'; so therefore, culture and the State are 'in the deepest sense, irreconcilable opposites' (Rocker, 1937: 283, 81). Rocker understands culture as developing in a bottom-up, popular manner. He was writing in the early 1930s in a period when mass culture was only just beginning to appear, and while it is possible to point to cultures which fit with Rocker's understanding, the trajectory of the twentieth century throws up a litany of cultures which are in no sense anarchistic. Rocker does identify this in his distinction between 'nationalism' and 'culture', but later critiques, such as those of Antonio Gramsci[4] or the Situationists,[5] recognise more explicitly that culture is manipulated and even generated by the State and capitalist institutions in a top-down manner to influence society in ways that they find beneficial – encouraging national pride, obedience to authority and insatiable consumerism, for example. This recognition of culture as a potentially oppressive force is expressed by numerous anarchist writers and groups. For example, Murray Bookchin[6] (1995: 52) writes that '[c]apitalism swirls around us – not only materially but *culturally*' – the logics and behaviours of capitalism are engrained in society beyond the level of economic transaction. Class War[7] identify mass culture as oppressive and as operating to preserve the State by stopping 'those at the bottom from revolting':

for advanced capitalism to work effectively, the workforce has to identify and agree with the aims and values of the capitalists ... modern capitalism and the State have to fill people's minds with the 'right' ideas, and deny the validity of those ideas that question the status-quo.

(Class War Federation, 1992: 52–53)

Most contemporary anarchists recognise this potentially oppressive manifestation of culture, but culture is not solely a tool of the State and capital. As Harold Barclay (1997: 36) points out: 'a culture is only manifest through the individual behaviour of its participants and in no culture are those participants clones. In every system there is variation in terms of behaviour and interpretation of behaviour. And this situation provides then the opportunity for conflict'. So while culture can be oppressive, and it often is, the terrain of culture is not closed-off from struggle. This 'culture war' is recognised as being of key importance by many anarchists (though it is important to add, *not by all*). Reclaim the Streets! co-founder John Jordan argues (in McKay (ed.), 1998: 130) that 'cultural values ... are at the centre of the global ecological and social problems ... If the problem is one of values – a cultural problem – it therefore requires a cultural response'. CrimethInc.[8] follow a similar tack: 're-sisting capitalism isn't just an economic matter but also a cultural one, involving a shift in values and practices' (CrimethInc. Ex-Workers Collective, 2011: 323). The mass culture engendered by capitalism and the State is otherwise termed as 'hegemonic' or 'mainstream', and outside of this, there are 'subcultures' and 'countercultures' which embody different values and practices, though often with significant overlap with the dominant mass culture. Anarchists, according to Laura Portwood-Stacer (2013: 7), 'can only be understood ... as *both* subculture and movement'. Indeed, this aspect of Portwood-Stacer's analysis of the contemporary anarchist movement in the US readily applies to historical anarchist movements as well. Chris Ealham (2005: 35) points to 'a specifically anarchist counter-culture ... in the *barris* [of Barcelona]' in the years preceding the social revolution and Civil War in Spain (1936–39). He writes that the

> CNT[9] was just one element in Barcelona's growing proletarian public sphere, an alternative grassroots social infrastructure comprising newspapers, cultural associations and social clubs. The other key institution was the *ateneu* (atheneum), a popular cultural and social centre ... [which] organised a wide choice of leisure activities, such as theatre, choral and musical groups.
>
> *(Ealham, 2005: 41)*

Through this,

> the CNT was able to influence an *oppositional working-class culture* and help to mould a relatively autonomous proletarian world view during a time when, elsewhere in Europe, the advent of new forms of mass culture, such as football and music halls, was beginning to erode and dilute socialist consciousness.
>
> *(Ealham, 2005: 43)*

Albert Meltzer[10] identifies the same cultural emphasis and engagement 'in the life of the local community' by syndicalist unions in Italy, Germany and Argentina (2002: 8). Ealham, using Situationist and Gramscian terminologies, understands this oppositional culture as 'a kind of counter-spectacle with its own values, ideas, rituals, organisations and practices ... a counter-hegemonic project' (2005: 43). Today, the term most often used by anarchists to describe this strategy is 'culture of resistance'.

But this understanding of anarchists as 'cultural activists' (Sakolsky and Ho (eds.), 1995: 9) is, for some, contentious, with cultural resistance 'often seen as a retreat from more direct, "effective" forms of political confrontation' (Portwood-Stacer, 2013: 8). As avant-garde anarchist violinist Norman Nawrocki puts it,

> too many anarchists tend to downplay if not denigrate the role of 'culture' in our fight for a new world, and thus, refuse to give active support or credence to those who try to develop and practice through self-expression a new anarchist aesthetic – musical

or otherwise. 'Where's the struggle?' hardcore, culturally-challenged anarchoids often protest, as Emma Goldman screeches, kicks off her dancing shoes and rolls over in her grave.

(in O'Guérin (ed.), 2012: 62)

These 'hardcore, culturally-challenged anarchoids' do not understand culture as part of the struggle, which is conceived as being fought solely on the grounds of economics or 'Politics'. 'Politics' is understood in various ways depending on its context – in some senses, *everything* is political in its effect on society, but Wilhelm Reich warns specifically against '[t]he fetish of "politics"' understood as 'diplomatic exchanges between the representatives of great and minor powers which decide the fate of humanity' (which might otherwise be termed 'capital P Politics' or 'politicking'). Reich argues that 'politics' is alienating for the 'political layman [*sic*]' who 'rightly says that he [*sic*] doesn't understand anything about it' (1973: 44). Reich's solution is 'to cut through the inextricable knot of bourgeois politics, by ceasing to imitate it and opposing it with the basic principle of revolutionary politics ... to democratise and simplify politics and make it accessible to everyone' (1973: 48). This simplification and democratisation entails the politicisation of 'private life, fairs, dance-halls, cinemas, markets, bedrooms, hostels, betting shops! Revolutionary energy lies in everyday life!' (1973: 73). This foreshadows the feminist slogan 'the personal is political' which dissolves the boundary between the domestic and the public spheres – but crucially here, it also emphasises the *cultural* aspects of revolutionary struggle (dance halls and cinemas), eschewing the narrow understanding of 'politics' for a much broader and encompassing definition. The contemporary US anarchist movement (and indeed those elsewhere) provides an example of this broader, culturally inclusive understanding, where, in Portwood-Stacer's (2013: 7–8) analysis, 'culture and politics are co-constitutive; to resist one is to resist the other', and likewise, Uri Gordon (2008: 4) describes contemporary anarchism as a *'political culture'*. Murray Bookchin too, even in the midst of his anti-lifestylist polemic (1995: 9 f.n.), identifies the 'anarchic counterculture during the early part of the hectic 1960s [as] often intensely political'.

The writers and groups referenced in discussion of culture thus far come from a wide spectrum of diverging anarchist perspectives and traditions,[11] but coalesce in (loose) agreement in terms of the seriousness with which culture (in its 'narrow' definition) ought to be taken by anarchists. Those anarchists who reject culture entirely are a minor fringe in the movement, and generally speaking their objection to 'culture' boils down to a personal distaste for a particular aesthetic, while they, of course, still engage in cultural activities at a practical level.

So culture is crucial, even while it is contentious, and consideration of culture and music is essential in understanding any social movement.

Music

Focusing closely on 'anarchist music' allows an examination of the tensions and complexities which surround the wider relationships between anarchism and culture. Petesy Burns, an anarchist punk musician (in O'Guérin (ed.), 2012: 50), argues that the 'combination' of anarchism and music 'can be a potent force for change'. This 'force for change', this *radical transformative potential*, is a fruitful framework in consideration of anarchism and music – an evaluation of music can be made in terms of its social impact, or the potential thereof.

Perhaps the most directly transformative aspect of music is its ability to inspire and radicalise. Nawrocki celebrates this potential:

this magical musical moment was a turning point in their life and marked a renewal of commitment, a blossoming of consciousness, a pivotal psychic insight that reaffirmed their anarchist convictions and practice. Thanks to the music, one more pair of arms for the barricades, one more match for the fire, one more point of resistance on the map towards freedom.

(In O'Guérin (ed.), 2012: 65)

Wilhelm Reich,[12] writing in the 1930s, pointed to the same potential, recognising '[f]olk song and dancing as a spur to revolutionary feeling' (1973: 58). Reich argued that the emotive power of music could be instrumentalised for revolutionary ends:

> everywhere where the bearers of the coming revolution live their lives; by means of good folk music, a folk dance, folk-songs utilisable by the revolution, already anticapitalist in themselves, appropriate to the feelings of the oppressed, they can create, disseminate and plant in peoples' feelings that atmosphere which is bitterly necessary for us to make the broadest of masses sympathetic to the revolution.

(Reich, 1973: 58)

Crucially, Reich considers folk music (taken to mean popular music written, performed and enjoyed by ordinary people on a peer-to-peer level, rather than the narrow generic descriptor it occupies now) to be *'already* anticapitalist', and inherently so. Reich does not explain what it is about folk music that is necessarily anticapitalist – but possible elements could be some particular lyrical content, non-capitalist production processes, inclusive and democratic norms of performance, or even the aesthetic form of the music. Robb Johnson, a contemporary anarchist folk musician, argues that some music forms engender an anarchistic aesthetic, pointing to 'the radical element to creativity' in 1930s jazz or 1960s pop wherein *'the very form itself* is the revolutionary agent' even when 'typified by primarily a–Political content' (in O'Guérin (ed.), 2012: 55). Here, the actual musical arrangement, the sound and feel of the music, is identified as the transformative aspect, and avant-garde and experimental musicians engaged with anarchism would make a similar case in terms of radical aesthetics. The breaking-down of the barrier between audience and performer is a core ideal in genres and scenes such as punk and hip-hop, and also folk, jazz and many avant-garde music forms. This is a further example of an aesthetic anarchistic musical impetus in its radical democratisation of music performance.

However, evaluation of 'anarchist music' in terms of aesthetic or performance is not entirely convincing. The aforementioned examples cover a widely diverse range of musical styles and performance approaches,[13] and while they contain elements which are arguably *anarchistic*, it is difficult to assert that any aesthetic is *inherently* or *exclusively* anarchist, or that their anarchistic elements result in any radical transformative potential. Nawrocki agrees that '[t]here is certainly music that inspires anarchist thoughts, inclinations, and the desire for full and total, absolute and unrestrained social evolution here and now', but, pointing to the experience of anarchist punk band Propagandhi, 'this same music can also fuel unthinking drunken frat boys' (in O'Guérin (ed.), 2012: 63). The anarchist intent behind a musical aesthetic does not prevent it from being misinterpreted in ways that are completely antithetical to anarchism. And in a similar logic, no aesthetic is immune from capital co-optation. The influence of capitalist production will be discussed in more detail later, but in terms of aesthetic, consider the blast beats and demonic roarings of grindcore/extreme metal band Napalm Death. Their deliberately abrasive aesthetic developed in the anarcho-punk and

DIY UK Hardcore scene of the late 1980s, but despite their decidedly counter-normative sound, they have released music with the major corporate label Sony Music Entertainment through imprints such as Columbia, Relativity and Century Media. Even clearly expressed oppositionalism through lyrics is open to (perhaps wilful) misinterpretation, as, for example, when former Tory Prime Minister (and Eton alumni) David Cameron announced that The Jam's 'The Eton Rifles' (1979) was one of his favourite songs (Radio 4, 2008). The Jam's Paul Weller was duly horrified, shaking his head with disbelief and asking: 'Which part of it didn't he get? It wasn't intended as a fucking jolly drinking song for the cadet corps' (in Wilson, 2008). Johnny Marr of The Smiths was similarly appalled when Cameron expressed affection for his band, publicly stating on social media: 'David Cameron, stop saying that you like The Smiths, no you don't. I forbid you to like it' (Marr, 2010). But, as Marr's humorous tweet reveals of course, no amount of protest by the artist can prevent such warped interpretations of the original intent of the music – the music's radicalism can be completely demolished in the subjective process of interpretation by the listener.

To be clear, there is no aesthetic prescription for anarchist music; any attempt to define it solely on the basis of sound or style is fruitless. Any aesthetic that is identified as 'anarchist' is immediately undercut by non-anarchist manifestations of that same aesthetic – but in an even more fundamental sense, it *shouldn't* be possible to identify an anarchist aesthetic. The musical forms, genres and scenes associated with anarchism are myriad,[14] which is to be expected since anarchism itself is highly amorphous and ill-defined. As Boff Whalley of anarchist band Chumbawamba puts it, '[r]adical and libertarian music, *by its nature*, can't be defined musically' (in O'Guérin (ed.), 2012: 81).

This is not to say that aesthetic considerations are irrelevant in discussion of 'anarchist music', but the theme of 'radical transformation' emerges as a more useful evaluative tool. Three main evaluations of 'anarchist music' will be made here: (1) music which espouses anarchist ideals, perhaps even without the intention of doing so, but which is produced and distributed within mainstream/capitalist cultural frameworks; (2) music which is produced and distributed through alternative, non-capitalist and anticapitalist networks (DIY) whether or not it is explicitly anarchist or espouses anarchist ideals; and (3) music which emanates from within the anarchist movement itself, promotes or supports anarchism explicitly and forms part of an anarchist culture of resistance. These evaluations are not intended as some kind of 'anarchy test' or a set of qualifying criteria, but to help develop an understanding of the relationships between anarchism and music, and as a result, the wider relationships between anarchism and culture.

Accidentally Anarchist Music

In an opposing corollary to David Cameron's subjective appropriation of the Jam and the Smiths, Nawrocki (in O'Guérin (ed.), 2012: 61) asks whether 'occasional musical "accidents", unintentionally anarchist in spirit or content, but perceived as such by listeners, count as "anarchist music"?' For example, the core anarchist tenet of freedom is a repeated trope in many genres of music. Even in the most vapidly banal lyrical use of 'freedom', with no anarchist intent whatsoever, there is nothing to prevent listeners attaching an anarchistic interpretation – a lack of didactic content allows scope for any number of interpretations. Even specifically, radical/transformative themes such as revolution, provide fodder for banal lyrics.

For example, the 1999 UK Number One single 'Because We Want To' (*Honey To The B*, (Innocent, Virgin [EMI], 1999)), by short-lived pop sensation Billie, contains references to revolution, freedom and self-empowerment. Taken at face value, there are clearly radical elements to the lyrics here – they could even be reasonably interpreted as anarchistic. While Billie's call to revolution was not heeded on a society-wide level (and, to be sure, there was no real revolutionary intent behind the track), it is impossible to rule out at least *some* grain of radical transformative potential. Capitalism is, in many senses, a totalising system, seeking to monetise all aspects of society – but it is not total. Even though the lyrics have been essentially voided of their substantive content, merely to posture as 'edgy' in pursuit of record sales, there remains the possibility that someone hearing Billie's 'revolutionary' lyrics might take them entirely seriously, despite their decidedly *un*revolutionary context.

In any case, as Ballinger points out, '[u]nderstanding the politics of music from a text-based analysis is particularly problematic' (in Sakolksy and Ho (eds), 1995: 17). The scope for interpretation is just too subjective to be analysed with any usefulness, especially in the banal lyrics of most commercially oriented music. Ballinger (in Sakolksy and Ho (eds), 1995: 17) asks an insightful question in this regard: 'what might "protest lyrics" be in social contexts where the very language of struggle has been co-opted?' In the case of Billie's 'revolutionary' verse, co-optation is clearly at work. 'Because We Want To' was distributed via celebrity millionaire Richard Branson's label Virgin, which was owned by EMI, and subsequently absorbed into Universal Music Group (one of the remaining 'Big Three' corporate music industry behemoths). So, the production processes behind Billie's 'revolution' are in no sense revolutionary, because no matter what the 'accidental' potential for transformation within the lyrical content (minimal though it is), Universal Music Group makes a profit – corporate capitalism is the ultimate beneficiary. This seriously problematises any transformative claim made of 'accidentally' anarchist music, but corporate influence has an even more direct impact in terms of copyright infringement claims made against content uploaded to the Internet. Gil Scott Heron said that the revolution would not be televised ('The Revolution Will Not Be Televised' (Flying Dutchman, 1971)),[15] and it seems that it won't be streamed online either – a version of The Beatles song 'Revolution' uploaded to YouTube is replaced with the message: 'This video contains content from UMG_MK,[16] who has blocked it in your country on copyright grounds' (appended in a much smaller font with, 'Sorry about that').[17] Universal Music Group profits from The Beatles' 'Revolution' (2008) just as it profits from Billie's, and it *actively* curtails the free[18] sharing of these songs through an ideology of private property rights and an opposition to free access to resources – the interests and activities of Universal Music Group are clearly antithetical to anarchism.

The lyrical allusion to 'revolution' by Billie and the Beatles does not by any sensible measure equate them with 'anarchist music' – but there should be no expectation for this to be the case, and neither Billie nor the Beatles make any claim otherwise. The point is that, even while music which 'accidentally' conjures up broadly anarchistic themes *could* be interpreted as potentially transformative, this is seriously problematised, and often completely undermined, by the production processes behind these songs, which is very often inimical to anarchism. Songs explicitly referencing anarchy or anarchism carry more expectation in this regard – their lyrical invocation is far more particular, but again, this is far from straightforward. Consider, for example, the song titled 'Anarcho-Syndicalism' (*Oakland's Tight – Hella Tight* (Round Whirled Records, 2010)) by Carne Cruda, a 'Post-Latin' ska outfit from Oakland, California. It is almost entirely instrumental, except for a reverb-laden voice sample (which sounds like Noam Chomsky) repeating the phrase 'anarcho-syndicalism'. Carne Cruda's website describes the band's members as a 'roster of Capitalism-smashers' who find that 'playing booty-shaking Latin and Caribbean music is far superior to working for The Man' (www.carnecruda.com/about-us), but these instances of radical rhetoric are fairly anomalous against the background of frivolous lyrical tropes, such as their current single 'I Love You More Than Tacos' (Round Whirled Records, 2016). Again, basing analysis on the lyrical expression of a band is not a decisively insightful approach, but while the band is on a small independent label, they also happily promote their music on Apple's iTunes, and there is no evidence of any further connection to anarchism or anticapitalist production practices or distribution networks. So even though Carne Cruda explicitly references a relatively niche anarchist strategy, in this context 'anarcho-syndicalism' is just a curio with an aurally pleasing arrangement of syllables, and the radical transformative potential does not tangibly exceed that of Billie's 'Because We Want To'.

Perhaps the best-known lyrical use of 'anarchy' is the Sex Pistols' 1976 single 'Anarchy in the UK' (EMI, 1976), and indeed, punk is amongst the musical genres with the widest and deepest connections to anarchism. However, even here, the expression of anarchism is decidedly vague – in the opening lines of the first verse, the pronunciation of 'anarchist' is mangled to rhyme with 'anti-christ', and the closing lines identify the task of an 'anarchist' as 'Get Pissed, Destroy'. The musical impetus of constructing rhymes is, for most musicians, a more important concern than providing an accurate portrayal of a political philosophy (and there is no expectation that it should be otherwise), but in terms of production and distribution, the single version of 'Anarchy in the UK' was released on major label EMI, and the album version (on Never Mind the Bollocks, Here's the Sex Pistols (Virgin, 1977)) was released on Virgin, both now subsumed under Universal Music Group. It would be easy to write off the Sex Pistols' 'anarchy' as just empty posturing, engineered by manager Malcolm McLaren to sell more trousers from his overpriced Kings Road shop and ultimately profiting the corporate music industry, but it had an undeniably substantial impact, and was an important influence behind the explosion of DIY punk bands, including many which were (and are) explicitly anarchist. Penny Rimbaud, co-founder of anarcho-punk progenitors Crass, exemplifies this:

> I first heard the Sex Pistols 'Anarchy in the UK' [with Steve Ignorant] … and although we both felt that the Pistols probably didn't mean it, to us it was a battle cry. When Johnny Rotten proclaimed that there was 'no future', we saw it as a challenge. We both knew that there was a future if we were prepared to fight for it. It was our world and it had been stolen from us. We set out to demand it back.
>
> *(Rimbaud, 1998: 216)*

Despite remaining firmly within mainstream, corporate production practices, the Sex Pistols' 'accidentally' radical transformative potential was realised in the subsequent development of a fiercely politically committed anarchist punk underground, which has spread globally and thrives to this day. While 'anarchist music' that is produced and distributed through non-anarchist production processes is still deeply problematic, the fact that it contains at least some radical transformative potential cannot be ignored – and this applies to Billie, the Beatles and Carne Cruda, as well as the Sex Pistols. As Steven Taylor argues (and as the example of the Sex Pistols appears to confirm): 'the commodification of an original artefact may dilute the impact of the pure product, but it doesn't render it meaningless. Given wide distribution, a particular commodity may inform and influence the mass culture' (2003: 13). Taylor's comment is arguably even more salient in the case of bands and musicians who emerged from DIY and anarchist-engaged music scenes, but 'sold out' to major labels and corporate production processes. 'Anarchist bands' such as Chumbawamba (who signed to EMI in 1997) or Against Me! (who signed to Warner Music Group imprint, Sire, in

2005, having previously signed to Fat Wreck Chords, which was distributed by Sony BMG, in 2003) can reasonably be argued to have 'diluted their impact' as a result of 'selling out', but any new fans acquired in their foray into the corporate music industry are also likely to encounter their previous DIY output as a result, and with it an exposure to the DIY anarchist music scene from which these 'sellouts' emerged. They act as a form of gateway from mainstream commercial culture into alternative, underground culture – and this relationship highlights a key point: cultures of resistance stand in opposition to mainstream capitalist culture but they are not isolated from it.

However, this is not to say that underground and DIY cultural communities are grateful to sellouts for bringing increased exposure to their music scenes – far from it. Todd Taylor of *Razorcake* zine writes that 'every artist from Hole to Rage Against The Machine who said they were going to bring the machine down from the inside ... lied or [was] delusional. The machine has paid them well and they've since shut their fuckin' mouths about toppling the industry' (in *Razorcake* #39, quoted in Dunn, 2012: 234). Sandra Jeppesen also recognises engagement with the corporate music industry as fatal to music's radical transformative potential, arguing that the influence of 'corporate production or control ... be[ing] co-opted or recuperated by the mainstream ... takes the powerful message out of punk (or anarchism, protest, hip-hop etc.) and sells it back to people, emptied of its former meaning' (2011: 29). The perceived sell-outs by 'anarchist bands' such as Chumbawamba and Against Me! were met with repercussions from the DIY community. Chumbawamba member Boff Whalley writes that

> The history of anti-Chumbawamba rhetoric from self-described anarchists would fill half my house ... Sell outs! How dare you claim to be anarchists and yet participate in the consumerist commodification of art! There's even an EP[19] of songs available about the band featuring songs with choruses of 'Chumbawamba, you're shit!'
>
> *(In O'Guérin, 2012: 80)*

Against Me! signed to major label imprint Sire records in 2005, but it was signing to Fat Wreck in 2003 (from the independent label No Idea) that sparked the fiercest reaction. According to Against Me!'s singer, Laura-Jane, *MaximumRockNRoll* columnist Bill Florio called on the band's fans to:

> come to the shows and pour bleach on our T-shirts and merch – just this insane ranting and raving in his columns, saying that we were the fucking devil ... While we were playing, [someone went] out and slashed our tyres. They weren't even trying to hide it that they did it. They were just like, 'Yeah, we fucking slashed your tires [*sic*], you fucking sellouts'.
>
> *(Nguyen, 2007)*

Whatever the arguments around the degree to which these bands 'sold out', or the imagined consequences of doing so, the visceral reaction from their former DIY music communities makes a clear point – sellouts are not tolerated. DIY represents an alternative economy, organised along ethics and values distinct from the mainstream corporate/capitalist industry, and as Alan O'Connor notes,

> If successful bands simply leave this underground for the major labels the autonomy of the entire field is weakened. Imagine if these bands instead used their popularity to

strengthen independent labels and their distributors, independent promoters and community space, zines and the whole punk underground.

(O'Connor, 2008: 24)

The 'alternative economy' represented by DIY is damaged when participants sell out – which explains why 'selling out' is viewed so negatively, despite the potential to take their radical message to a wider audience.

So, in terms of 'accidentally' anarchist music, it is impossible to write off at least a degree of radical transformative potential. This is seriously problematised by the underlying non-anarchist production processes and distribution networks – this point is made starkly in the case of 'anarchist musicians' who sell out, where the impact of music that actually *has* anarchist intent behind it is diminished and undermined by mainstream capitalist production.

DIY (Do It Yourself)

The issues around selling out demonstrate that production and distribution are key concerns in any analysis of the radical transformative potential of 'anarchist music'. Tim Yohannan (1945–98), founder and long-time editor of influential DIY punk zine *MaximumRockNRoll*, argued that '[i]n the long run … what's important about punk is not the lyrics, what people say, but what *they do*' (interviewed by Turner, in Sakolsky and Ho (eds.), 1995: 181), Kevin Dunn quotes Walter Benjamin[20] to make a similar point:

> What matters … is the exemplary character of production, which is able, first, to induce other producers to produce, and, second, to put an improved apparatus at their disposal. And this apparatus is better, the more consumers it is able to turn into producers – that is, readers or spectators into collaborators.
>
> *(Benjamin, 1934: 777, in Dunn, 2012: 234)*

Dunn (2012: 234) therefore argues that '*being* DIY and independent is far more effective than *talking* about being DIY and independent. It is a form of cultural production that can turn passive consumers into producers in their own right'. So DIY is transformative in its capacity to expand the field of DIY production, at the expense of mainstream capitalist production.

DIY ethics and production are recognised as transformative by anarchists too, and this extends far beyond the realm of music production. As anarchist historian George Woodcock (1912–95) put it, '"Do-it-yourself" is … the essence of anarchist action, and the more people apply it on every level, in education, in the workplace, in the family, the more ineffective restrictive structures will become and the more dependence will be replaced by individual and collective self-reliance' (Woodcock, 1986: 421). More DIY production means less corporate capitalist production and less State control, and in this respect, DIY is oppositional and radically transformative.

Bound up with the contention around culture and anarchism discussed earlier, DIY is often associated with 'lifestylist' anarchisms. This is an oversimplified and sectarian view, and an emphasis on DIY in fact extends across the spectrum of anarchist political perspectives. Among those who might be identified as 'lifestylist', George McKay (1998: 14) argues that 'DiY's most consistent historical and theoretical antecedents lie in anarchist thought and practice', while Portwood-Stacer (2013: 31) notes: 'The DIY principle can be, and is, applied to almost everything anarchists consume'. DIY is also reflected in the anarchist mutualism/co-operativism advocated by the likes of Pierre-Joseph Proudhon,[21] or, more recently, Colin

Ward,[22] and Sean Martin-Iverson identifies 'autonomous "Do-It-Yourself" forms of cultural production [as] a *prefigurative* politics of praxis, as workers struggling against the imposition of work' (Martin-Iverson, 2014: 10). DIY extends beyond typically 'lifestylist' perspectives to also find expression in anarchisms which are at the furthest remove from 'lifestylism', for example in anarcho-syndicalist and labour union strategies. Jack Kirkpatrick describes the Industrial Workers of the World[23] as a 'scrappy little *DIY* union' (in Ness (ed.), 2014: 246) and Geoffrey Ostergaard (1963) describes the anarcho-syndicalist implementation of direct action as a 'grass-roots, *do-it-yourself* kind of action' (in Ward, 1987: 141).

So, DIY clearly has a grounding in anarchism and this extends across the spectrum of anarchist political perspectives, but, as in the previous section, it is informative to analyse DIY music forms in terms of their radical transformative potential, or even the extent to which they embody an *already achieved* radical transformation.

Invoking a classic revolutionary socialist demand, CrimethInc. (2006: 3) exhort their readers to 'seiz[e] all the means of production you can get your hands on', but CrimethInc. elsewhere (2008: 113) challenge the materialist assumptions behind this demand by asserting that '*culture* is the ultimate means of production, the one that produces human life itself … it can be seized and shared like any other!' In terms of seizing the means of production and distribution of music, DIY practitioners have achieved *some* success. Ballinger argues that '[d]evelopments in music technology and mass communications have … facilitated networks of alternative music like rap and punk, and create the potential for a transnational oppositional culture' (in Sakolsky and Ho (eds.), 1995: 19). CrimethInc., who themselves emerged from the anarchist punk scene, argue that this oppositional culture extends into production as well: 'Underground punk bands released their own records and established their own venues, *setting up an alternative economy* based on "do-it-yourself" networks and anticapitalist values' (2011: 325). These 'anticapitalist' values are chiefly expressed (and are evaluable) in two related ways. Firstly, DIY music producers are concerned with minimising price (and often eschew profit entirely) – these DIY 'business' ventures are 'a failure in commercial terms' (Thompson, 2004: 150). Charging too much money for DIY-produced commodities or events invites an accusation of 'selling out' just as much as actual engagement with corporate industry. Secondly, DIY production is viewed as 'a passion rather than a job' (O'Connor, 2008: 80) which establishes a 'challenge to alienated labour' (Martin-Iverson, draft c. 2014: 11), which Martin-Iverson marks as an 'especially' important aspect to being genuinely DIY (draft c. 2014: 10). The concept of 'alienated labour' comes from Marxist theory, and argues that a core aspect of capitalism is the separation of the producer from the products of their labour. This is related to profit, since if a DIY producer is not making money, they are unable to pay others to produce on their behalf, and they are unable to 'take a cut' or cream off the profit, as would be the case in the 'normal' terms of economic exploitation in capitalist production. So, DIY practice means that the producers themselves engage in unalienated labour and are directly connected to their product, and, further, means that DIY producers cannot *employ* alienated labour.

In punk, and other DIY music scenes, these non-capitalist production practices are recognised as being explicitly oppositional and *anti*capitalist. As Thompson notes, 'the corporate music industry stands in for the whole of capitalism, for it is when they confront the major labels' business practices, music, and bands that punks best understand themselves as opposed to capitalism' (2004: 4). Through these anticapitalist modes of production and distribution (by minimising or eschewing profit, and rejecting alienated labour), and by establishing their own networks of commodity exchange, DIY music forms represent a form of 'anarchy in action'. Thompson points to the prefigurative aspect of DIY punk, in which he identifies 'the seeds of a society in which collectives own the means of production and produce for non-commercial ends' (2004: 78), or to quote the preamble of the Industrial Workers of the World (IWW), they are 'forming the new society within the shell of the old' (Brown, 1990: 19).

However, this DIY production remains largely at the level of representation – it is not easy to sidestep the totalising influence of capitalist social relations, and this limits the successes of DIY production. The independent networks and alternative economies created through DIY music production and distribution are not isolated from the wider capitalist economy. Despite the fringe successes of DIY networks, the means of production and distribution are still in capitalist hands, producing for profit rather than to meet social needs. To evade this would mean either producing no commodities whatsoever (as might be observed in folk music's emphasis on direct communication and non-commercialism), or seizing *all* means of production, in a way that penetrates vertically downwards through the economy – for music production, this would include the oil rigs which extract the raw materials for vinyl records and plastic CDs and tapes, the oil refineries, the delivery trucks (and then also the raw materials and factories to build the delivery trucks) and so on up (and across) the production chain until an entirely 'vertically integrated' DIY economy could be realised, independent from capitalist production.

Because DIY networks are inescapably connected to capitalist production, DIY producers cannot evade the alienated labour carried in the overhead costs of their 'punk businesses', despite attempts to distance themselves from profit. Even if a DIY producer keeps prices to an absolute minimum, making zero profit, with no price markup whatsoever, they are still passing on the alienated (exploited) labour contained in the price of everything sourced from the non-DIY economy. The vinyl for records, the sound system for a gig, the paper for advertising material, the delivery companies, the computer manufacturers and Internet providers – these are all (at present) non-DIY, and all entail alienated labour and profit. If DIY producers were to sell commodities at a loss or give them away for free, this *still* would not fully negate the profit of non-DIY producers and the alienated labour they employ, since the loss would inevitably have to be paid for by the DIY producer themselves, which in all likelihood would be money from a 'day job' engaged in alienated labour. The taint of capitalist production can be passed on, but not eliminated.

The marginality of DIY's successes in taking over the means of production means that, as A. K. Thompson notes: 'DIY ethics must come to terms with the fact that – at present – it primarily represents people's *intention* to become direct producers. In truth, most of what actually gets "produced" remains representational in character' (2010: 22). Stacy Thompson concurs that 'the economic practices of [DIY punk do not] … fully succeed, if success means a complete, if local or temporary, overthrow of the capitalist mode of production' (2004: 81–82). Fredy Perlman[24] writes that the kind of anticapitalist production represented by DIY: 'can *only* [be done] marginally; men's [sic] appropriation and use of the materials and tools available to them can only take place after the overthrow of the capitalist form of activity' (2002: 11). Hubert Lagardelle,[25] from a revolutionary-syndicalist perspective, recognises the essential weakness of economic resistance which remains at the margins of capitalism: 'it is only by seizing the instruments of labour, by making itself the *exclusive* owner of the factories, workshops, etc., that [the working class] will assure its emancipation' (2011: n.p.). A recognition of DIY's limitations is not to say that DIY is not worthwhile or transformative – it prefiguratively points to alternative economies, and to some degree embodies this alternative, while providing a material infrastructure for cultures of resistance, as will be discussed later.

However, more than simply being limited in its opposition to capitalism, it has been argued that DIY production practices in fact bolster capitalism. William K. Carroll and Matthew Greeno (in Fisher (ed.), 2013: 123) write that rather than challenging capitalism, DIY music subcultures merely supply more markets and consumers: 'Each subculture and identity group offers a niche market to corporate capital. As market principles invade culture they absorb and commodify the voices of subjugated groups within the chain of production and consumption'. Martin-Iverson points to the pervasiveness of capitalist social relations in the Indonesian punk scene, arguing that '[w]ith the growing commercialisation of the scene, punk autonomy has been harnessed to a neoliberal, entrepreneurial independence which reproduces precariousness and class exploitation within the scene' (draft c. 2014: 6). DIY, especially when it fails to eschew profit and alienated labour, reproduces capitalist social relations – these producers *become capitalists*. As CrimethInc. (2011: 88) put it: 'like the magnate in miniature ... [they] ha[ve] to internalise the logic of the market, taking its pressures and values to heart'. Tom Frank (in Sakolsky and Ho (eds.), 1995: 111) argues that 'rebel ideology ... has fuelled business culture ever since the 1960s ... [a] long, silly parade of "countercultural" entrepreneurship'. So, it is possible for DIY to be co-opted into a neo-liberal capitalist framework, especially in the subjectivity of small-scale entrepreneurs. In this view, an apparently anarchistic production practice is no more immune from capitalist co-optation than the anarchistic aesthetics discussed earlier. But, in the final evaluation, Martin-Iverson (draft c. 2014: 10) argues that 'DIY production is a form of anarchist prefigurative politics, aimed at the *active production of alternative social values* rather than simply making demands or expressing opposition'. Despite its limitations and vulnerabilities, DIY is essentially radical and transformative. McKay (1998: 27) is insightful when he comments: 'maybe we should be talking less of Do it Yourself than Do it *Ourselves*'. This shift from individualised to cooperative production is key to resisting capitalist co-optation and expanding the field of DIY production.

So, 'accidentally' anarchist music was argued to be seriously problematised by its underlying production processes – but even production practices like DIY, which are understood as anarchistic, are limited and an evaluation of DIY as 'anarchist music' is not straightforward. As suggested earlier, DIY production and anarchistic aesthetics are most clearly evaluable as 'anarchist music' when tied to anarchist political philosophy, and this is observable in anarchist cultures of resistance.

Cultures of Resistance

Examples of music forms which emanate from the anarchist movement include: the samba bands and drum corps that feature at protests; the sound systems that thump late into the night at squat parties or are loaded onto specially welded bikes for Critical Mass rides; gigs and records which raise funds for anarchist causes such as prisoner support, Food Not Bombs, and specific anarchist campaigns, groups and unions; music events which provide the social setting for activists to meet, relax, talk and (of course) dance. Echoing the Emma Goldman quote near the start of the chapter, Earth First! and IWW organiser Judi Bari (1949–97) argued that, 'as an individual, music enriches your life. So, if a movement is going to go anywhere, there has to be some joy in it. It has to be something people want to do' (interviewed by Sakolsky in Sakolsky and Ho (eds.), 1995: 173). But music is more than just the backing-track to the anarchist movement; it is the vibrant cultural glue that holds the movement together. As Bari puts it, 'a movement that's held together with music is way stronger, it's going to survive a lot more, inspire people a lot more' (interviewed by Sakolsky in Sakolsky and Ho (eds.), 1995: 173). This isn't to say that a musical or cultural focus replaces the multifaceted aspects of struggle for social transformation – but it does augment them. Music is an important part of *cultures of resistance* – and taking 'culture' in its narrow interpretation, as discussed earlier, it can be argued that many music forms are themselves a form of resistance culture.

However, there is a sense that culture is *not* 'political' (and certainly not 'Politics' or politicking) – this is at the root of dismissals of culture by some anarchists, but is also recognised by those attuned to culture's radically transformative role. Discussing DIY and culturally active groups in *Anarchy in Action*, Colin Ward points out that

> None of them fits into the framework of conventional politics. In fact, they don't speak the same language as political parties. They talk in the language of anarchism and they insist on anarchist principles of organisation, which they have learned not only from political theory but from their own experience.
>
> *(Ward, 1996 [1973]: 137–8)*

As Steven Duncombe (1997: 175) puts it, 'the politics of culture never announce themselves as political ... the politics expressed within and through culture become part of us, get under our skin, and become part of our "common sense"'. This 'unannounced' aspect is key to the radical transformative potential in cultures of resistance – the transformation of 'common sense' arguably has a more fundamental impact in society than shifts in mere 'politics' or 'economics'. Class War makes this very point: 'We believe that our ideas must become part of peoples everyday lives, not just a reaction to a hostile economic, social or political environment' (*Class War*, c. 1991: n.p.).

The building of cultures of resistance is expressly argued as a core strategy by numerous writers and activist groups from a range of anarchist perspectives. But as CrimethInc. (2011: 323) warn, 'culture can appear "different" and even oppositional without actually challenging capitalism at all'; so, *resistance* stands as a crucial and defining aspect of anarchist cultural activity and organising. These cultures are 'resisting' against the dominant culture (or intersecting cultures) of bourgeois capitalism, patriarchy, racism, heterosexism, statism, nationalism (etc. *ad nauseam*). This widely ranging resistance is evident specifically within music as well, for example CamBagMag's songbook *Four Chord Revolution. Songs of Protest. Sing n Fling with chord diagrams* (1987) covers a whole range of issues including squatting, solidarity with South African and Namibian prisoners, Nicaragua, apartheid, the Diggers, anti-Thatcher, asbestos, anticops, anti-McDonald's, and is accompanied by information and links to numerous anarchist groups and campaigns, including *Black Flag*, Class War, Nicaragua Solidarity Campaign, Direct Action [probably indicating the Direct Action Movement], West Midlands Hunt Saboteurs and Anarchist Communist Federation. Class War are explicit about this oppositional aspect of cultural resistance: 'Capitalists dominate and control most forms of cultural production ... and recreate popular cultural activities infected with THEIR ideology. Because of this an essential part of revolutionary politics is to develop a revolutionary culture of resistance' (*Class War* no. 47, c. 1991: n.p.). And, for Class War, this opposition must be unerringly confrontational and uncompromising – cultures of resistance must make 'demands that the ruling class cannot even contemplate, let alone fulfil' (Class War Federation, 1992: 76). Similarly to Reich's identification of an *already* anticapitalist folk music tradition, Class War views it as 'essential to promote and strengthen the working class culture that *already exists*' (Class War Federation, 1992: 76), and again, a similar argument is made by Bookchin (1995: 21), who celebrates 'the rich *culture* that was created by revolutionaries over the past centuries, indeed by ordinary working people'.

Ballinger points to these same oppositional, resistant and culturally constructive aspects in music specifically, asserting that 'oppositional music practices not only act as a form of resistance against domination, but generate social relationships and experience which can form the basis of a new cultural sensibility and, in fact, are involved in *the struggle for a new culture*' (in Sakolsky and Ho (eds.), 1995: 14).

An oft-cited example of music in the anarchist movement is found in the IWW.[26] Daniel O'Guérin (2012: 3–4) discusses the IWW's 'tradition of folk songs and poems that aroused solidarity among workers in struggle or kept their stories alive around the camp fire'. Bari identifies this instrumental aspect of music, describing it as 'a really good organising tool. It gives the whole thing a kind of spirit; it really fuels the movement in a lot of ways' (interviewed by Sakolsky in Sakolsky and Ho (eds.), 1995: 173). In this vein, Class War sought to instrumentalise music in their 'Rock Against The Rich' gigs and tours of the late 1980s and mid-2010s. Their rationale was based on a belief that rock music could 'be a force in bringing people together for organised resistance' (*Class War* c. 1988: n.p.). So in addition to individual enjoyment and social cohesion, music also plays a practical role in cultures of resistance. These cultures serve as a bedrock from which more specifically focused resistance movements can spring. As CrimethInc. (2009: 74) argue, 'A sustainable space that nurtures long-term communities of resistance can ultimately contribute more to militant struggle than the sort of impatient insurrectionism that starts with confrontation rather than building to it'. As discussed earlier in the chapter, the CNT in Barcelona in the early 1900s provides a historical example of this function of resistance cultures.

However, anarchist cultures of resistance are distinct from Gramscian or autonomous Marxist counter-hegemonic projects, because the point is not to replace the dominant culture (or cultures) with a *new* dominant culture. As CrimethInc. (2006: 17) put it, 'radicals should never conflate offering paths to liberation with promoting their own subcultures. It should never appear that, like those who speak of converting the masses, our goal is to assimilate everyone else'. Portwood-Stacer (2013: 63) quotes Adam Tinnell, who in an 'anarchist fashion' blog argues that

> With such a diverse politic as anarchism, being interpreted and enacted in thousands of different cultures around the world, not to mention the contributions of anarcha-feminism and queer anarchism, it's totally unacceptable to let one or two subcultures dominate the look and the feel of this movement.
>
> *(Tinnell, 2009)*

However, while music and culture are *necessary* aspects of radically transformative or revolutionary struggle, and may in some respects be prior to other forms of struggle, this is not to say they are pre-eminent or sufficient in isolation. As Nawrocki puts it (in O'Guérin (ed.), 2012: 67), 'rock 'n roll, anarcho or not, just isn't revolution. We always saw our daily work, our cultural contribution, as only a small part of the equation'. Cultures of resistance cease to be effectively oppositional when they become 'anarcho-ghettos' into which activists recede. As in the discussion of DIY, earlier, an attachment to anarchist political philosophy is essential in maintaining the resistant and radically transformative aspects of cultures of resistance.

Conclusion

In writing this chapter on 'anarchist music', there was a temptation to proffer a list of music forms which 'qualify' as anarchist. However, any such list would have been severely skewed by my own aesthetic preferences, and by the music forms to which I have been exposed. I am in no position (and nor is anyone) to prescribe what music people should enjoy making or listening to.

Rather, this chapter has sought to explore possible frames of evaluation behind the complex question: 'what is anarchist music?' The key interrogation here has been the potential for, or realisation of, *radical transformation*. This interrogation of radical transformative potential has been applied to 'anarchist music' in terms of 'anarchist' aesthetics, 'anarchist' lyrics, 'anarchist' DIY production practices and 'anarchist' cultures of resistance. This has not been to present a static definition of what constitutes 'anarchist music', but to present an evaluation which teases out some of the key issues in the relationship between anarchism and music, and between anarchism and culture more widely.

It is hoped that this chapter might influence the reader's own evaluation of 'anarchist music' in terms of music consumption *and* music-making – but for an immersive and engaged evaluation, the surest approach is to Do It Yourself.

Notes

1 Emma Goldman (1869–1940) was an anarchist activist famous for her fiery orations. Much of her activist 'career' was in the US, but she was also a first-hand witness of the aftermath of the Bolshevik Revolution in Russia in 1917 and the Spanish Revolution in 1936. Her writings have been influential in the anarchist and feminist movements. A useful introductory text is *Anarchism and Other Essays* (London: Active Distribution, Zagreb: Što čitaš, 2014 [1910]), which includes a brief autobiography and includes several key writings – available free at: https://theanarchistlibrary.org/library/emma-goldman-anarchism-and-other-essays [accessed 22 October 2016].

2 Revolutionary agency refers to the idea that social change must occur concurrently with a change in the mindsets of the individuals that make up that society. See, for example, the writings of Gustav Landauer (1870–1919), such as *Revolution and Other Writings: a Political Reader* ed. and trans. Gabriel Kuhn, (Oakland: PM Press, 2010), available free at: https://libcom.org/files/Landauer_Revolution_and_Other_Writings.pdf [accessed 22 October 2016].

3 Rudolf Rocker (1873–1958) was an anarchist writer and activist. Forced to leave Germany in the 1930s because of the rise of Nazism, he was involved in organising Yiddish-speaking tailors in the East End of London, and eventually made his way to the US. Among his most popular writings is *Anarcho-syndicalism* (London: Pluto Press, 1989 [1938]), available free at: https://libcom.org/files/Rocker%20-%20Anarcho-Syndicalism%20Theory%20and%20Practice.pdf [accessed 22 October 2016].

4 Antonio Gramsci (1891–1937) was a Marxist and founder of the Communist Party of Italy. An excellent introduction to his key concepts can be found in Roger Simon, *Gramsci's Political Thought: an introduction* 3rd edn. (London: Lawrence & Wishart, 2015).

5 See especially Guy Debord, *Society of the Spectacle* (New York: Zone Books, 1994) [1967], available free at: www.antiworld.se/project/references/texts/The_Society%20_Of%20_The%20_Spectacle.pdf [accessed 22 October 2016].

6 Murray Bookchin (1921–2006) was an anarchist writer based in the US. His early work developed key contemporary themes such as 'social ecology' but late in his life, he moved away from anarchism to espouse ideas under the rubric of 'libertarian municipalism' (see *Social Ecology and Communalism* (Edinburgh: AK Press, 2007)), which has found contemporary resonance with revolutionary groups in the Kurdish region of Rojava (see Abdullah Öcalan, *Democratic Confederalism* (Cologne: International Initiative, 2011), Can Cemgil and Clemens Hoffmann, 'The "Rojava Revolution" in Syrian Kurdistan: A Model of Development for the Middle East?' *IDS Bulletin*, 47:3 (2016), 53–76, and Yagmur Savran, 'The Rojava Revolution and British Solidarity', *Anarchist Studies*, 24:1 (2016), 7–12).

7 The Class War Federation is an anarchist activist group that formed in the UK in 1986, though the *Class War* newspaper was first published in 1982 as a way to expose politicised punks to class-struggle anarchism. Their most recent incarnation is the Class War Party, which fielded candidates (albeit subversively) in the 2015 UK General Election. See: www.classwarparty.org.uk/ [accessed 22 October 2016].

8 The CrimethInc. Ex-Workers' collective is a loose collection of anarchist activists, writers and propagandists, primarily based in the US, which emerged from the punk scene in the 1990s.

9 *Confederación Nacional del Trabajo* or National Confederation of Labour, a prominent anarcho-syndicalist union founded in 1910, which, though banned by Franco during the Fascist dictatorship, remains active. See: www.cnt.es/ [accessed 22 October 2016].

10 Albert Meltzer (1920–96) was an anarchist activist in Britain, and co-founder of *Black Flag* newspaper and the Kate Sharpley library and publisher.

11 For example, Bookchin is notorious for his anti-lifestylist polemic, and Meltzer and Class War have also been outspoken against lifestylism, while Portwood-Stacer defends 'lifestyle activism' and CrimethInc. are frequently identified by detractors as lifestylists – yet in terms of culture, there is broad agreement (even if they would be wont to admit the similarity).

12 Wilhelm Reich (1897–1957) was born in Austria, but moved to the US to escape Nazism, and was a pioneering psychoanalyst, especially in the field of sexual liberation. He also wrote on political themes from a Freudian–Marxist perspective.

13 For more on some of the numerous manifestations of anarchist culture, see: Jesse Cohn, *Underground Passages: Anarchist Resistance Culture, 1848–2011*, (Edinburgh: AK Press, 2014).

14 To aid the reader's own exploration of 'anarchist music', some music forms commonly associated with anarchism include: folk, hip-hop, punk, hardcore, ska, reggae, Oi!, grindcore, death metal, dance musics (such as grime, dub-step, rave and techno), jazz, avant-garde/classical, pop, samba, Greek rebetiko, Mexican corridos, Krautrock.

15 Latterly distributed by RCA and currently owned and distributed by Sony Music Entertainment.

16 The UK arm of Universal Music Group, based in Milton Keynes (MK).

17 www.youtube.com/watch?v=KrkwgTBrW78.

18 In the case of YouTube, 'free' content is paid for with reams of advertising – effectively selling your attention to corporate companies.

19 The record in question is titled *Bare Faced Hypocrisy Sells Records/The Anti-Chumbawamba EP* (Ruptured Ambitions, Propa Git, 1998).

20 Walter Benjamin (1892–1940) was associated with the Frankfurt School philosophers, who took an unorthodox approach to Marxism, and were especially concerned with cultural issues. Benjamin died while trying to escape the Nazis.

21 Pierre-Joseph Proudhon (1809–1865) was the first self-described anarchist political philosopher.

22 Colin Ward (1924–2010) emphasised the already existing anarchy observable in activities such as squatting and many other aspects of life which are organised away from the interference of the State or corporate capitalism. See: Colin Ward, *Anarchy in Action* (London: Freedom Press 1996 [1973]), available free at: https://libcom.org/files/Ward_-_Anarchy_in_Action_3.pdf [accessed 24 October 2016].

23 The Industrial Workers of the World (IWW or 'Wobblies') is a union founded in the US in 1905, which has many commonalities with anarcho-syndicalism, and counts many anarchists as members. See: https://www.iww.org/ [accessed 24 October 2016].

24 Fredy Perlman (1934–85) was an author, lecturer and IWW member. While he did not describe himself as an anarchist, his writings have been influential in anarchist circles, especially *Against His-story, Against Leviathan* (1983), available free at: https://theanarchistlibrary.org/library/fredy-perlman-against-his-story-against-leviathan [accessed 24 October 2016].

25 Hubert Lagardelle (1874–1958) was an early proponent of revolutionary-syndicalism, which was a forerunner of what is now known as anarcho-syndicalism. However, he later became a fascist sympathiser and took a post in the Vichy government in France during the Second World War.

26 A digital transfer of a 1954 record of IWW songs is available free at: https://archive.org/details/SongsOfTheWobblies [accessed 24 October 2016].

References

Ballinger, Robin 'Sounds of Resistance', in Ron Sakolsky and Fred Wei-Han Ho (eds.), *Sounding Off! Music as Subversion/Resistance/Revolution* (New York: Autonomedia, 1995), 13–26.

Barclay, Harold *Culture and Anarchism* (London: Freedom Press, 1997).

Benjamin, Walter 'The Author as Producer', trans. John Heckman, *New Left Review*, 1:62, (1970) [1934], 83–96.

Bookchin, Murray *Social Anarchism or Lifestyle Anarchism. An Unbridgeable Chasm* (Edinburgh: AK Press, 1995).

Bookchin, Murray *Social Ecology and Communalism* (Edinburgh: AK Press, 2007).

Brown, Tom *Syndicalism* (London: Phoenix Press, 1990).

Burns, Petesy 'The Social Space', in Daniel O'Guérin (ed.), *Arena Three: Anarchism in Music* (Hastings: ChristieBooks, 2012), 44–51.

CamBagMag *Four Chord Revolution. Songs of Protest. Sing n Fling with Chord Diagrams* (Balsall Heath, c. 1987).

Carne Cruda 'About Us', www.carnecruda.com/about-us [accessed 26 October 2016].

Carroll, William K. and Matthew Greeno, 'Neoliberal Hegemony and the Organization of Consent', in Rebecca Fisher (ed.), *Managing Democracy, Managing Dissent. Capitalism, Democracy and the Organisation of Consent* (London: Corporate Watch, 2013), 121–135.

Cemgil, Can and Clemens Hoffmann, 'The "Rojava Revolution" in Syrian Kurdistan: A Model of Development for the Middle East?' *IDS Bulletin*, 47:3 (2016), 53–76.

Class War, (c. 1988), not numbered, not dated, n.p.

Class War, 47 (c. 1991), not dated. n.p.

Class War Federation, *Unfinished Business… the Politics of Class War* (Edinburgh: AK Press, 1992).

Class War Party website, www.classwarparty.org.uk/ [accessed 22 October 2016].

Cohn, Jesse *Underground Passages: Anarchist Resistance Culture, 1848–2011* (Edinburgh: AK Press, 2014.

Confederación Nacional del Trabajo website, www.cnt.es/ [accessed 22 October 2016].

CrimethInc. Ex-Workers' Collective, *Rolling Thunder: An Anarchist Journal of Dangerous Living*, 2 (winter 2006).

CrimethInc. Ex-Workers' Collective, *Expect Resistance. A Field Manual* (Salem, Oregon: CrimethInc., 2008).

CrimethInc. Ex-Workers' Collective, *Rolling Thunder: An Anarchist Journal of Dangerous Living*, 7 (spring 2009).

CrimethInc. Ex-Workers' Collective, *Work* (Salem, OR: CrimethInc., 2011).

Debord, Guy *Society of the Spectacle* (New York: Zone Books, 1994 [first published 1967]).

Duncombe, Steven *Notes from the Underground: Zines and the Politics of Alternative Culture* (London: Verso, 1997).

Dunn, Kevin '"If It Ain't Cheap, It Ain't Punk": Walter Benjamin's Progressive Cultural Production and DIY Punk Record Labels', *Journal of Popular Music Studies*, 24:2 (2012), 217–37.

Ealham, Chris *Class, Culture and Conflict in Barcelona 1898–1937* (London: Routledge, 2005).

Frank, Tom 'Alternative to What?', in Ron Sakolsky and Fred Wei-Han Ho (eds.), *Sounding Off! Music as Subversion/Resistance/Revolution* (New York: Autonomedia, 1995), 109–119.

Goldman, Emma *Living My Life* (New York: Knopf, 1934).

Goldman, Emma *Anarchism and Other Essays* (London: Active Distribution, Zagreb: Što čitaš, 2014 [first published 1910]).

Gordon, Uri *Anarchy Alive! Anti-Authoritarian Politics from Practice to Theory* (London: Pluto Press, 2008).

Industrial Workers of the World website, www.iww.org/ [accessed 24 October 2016].

Johnson, Robb 'What I Do', in Daniel O'Guérin (ed.), *Arena Three: Anarchism in Music* (Hastings: ChristieBooks, 2012), 52–59.

Jordan, John 'The Art of Necessity: The Subversive Imagination of Anti-road Protest and Reclaim the Streets', in George McKay (ed.), *DIY Culture. Party & Protest in Nineties Britain* (London: Verso, 1998), 129–151.

Jeppesen, Sandra 'The DIY Post-Punk Post-Situationist Politics of CrimethInc', *Anarchist Studies*, 19:1 (2011), 139–143.

Kirkpatrick, Jack 'The IWW Cleaners Branch Union in the United Kingdom', in Immanuel Ness (ed.), *New Forms of Worker Organization: The Syndicalist and Autonomist Restoration of Class-Struggle Unionism* (Oakland: PM Press, 2014), 233–257.

Lagardelle, Hubert *Syndicalism*, posted by Alias Recluse, (14 September 2011) [written between 1902 and 1909], www.libcom.org/library/syndicalism-hubert-lagardelle [accessed 26 October 2016].

Landauer, Gustav *Revolution and Other Writings: a Political Reader* ed. and trans. Gabriel Kuhn (Oakland: PM Press, 2010).

Marr, Johnny Twitter Feed, 1 December 2010, www.twitter.com/johnny_marr/status/10237162679177216? lang=en-gb [accessed 6 February 2017].

Martin-Iverson, Sean '*Anak punk* and *kaum pekerja*: Indonesian Punk and Class Recomposition in Urban Indonesia', (draft version c. 2014).

McKay, George 'DiY Culture: Notes Towards an Intro', in George McKay (ed.), *DIY Culture. Party & Protest in Nineties Britain* (London: Verso, 1998), 1–53.

Meltzer, Albert *First Flight. The Origins of Anarcho-Syndicalism in Britain* (London: Kate Sharpley Library, 2002 [first published 1991]).

Nawrocki, Norman 'From Rhythm Activism to Bakunin's Bum: Reflections of an Unrepentant Anarchist Violinist on "anarchist music"', in Daniel O'Guérin (ed.), *Arena Three: Anarchism in Music* (Hastings: ChristieBooks, 2012), 60–70.

Nguyen, Tuyet 'Punk Sell Out? Against Me! Would Rather Make a Statement than Starve', *CleveScene* website, (9 May 2007), www.clevescene.com/cleveland/punk-sell-out/Content?oid=1498514 [accessed 29 January 2016].

O'Connor, Alan *Punk Record Labels and the Struggle for Autonomy: The Emergence of DIY* (Plymouth: Lexington Books, 2008).

O'Guérin, Daniel (Back2front zine), 'What's in (A) Song? An Introduction to Libertarian Music', in Daniel O'Guérin (ed.), *Arena Three: Anarchism in Music* (Hastings: ChristieBooks, 2012), 3–22.

Öcalan, Abdullah *Democratic Confederalism* (Cologne: International Initiative, 2011).

Ostergaard, Geoffrey 'The Relevance of Syndicalism', *Anarchy*, 28, (June 1963).

Perlman, Fredy *The Reproduction of Daily Life* (Detroit: Black & Red, 2002 [reprint of 1969 *Kalamazoo* issue]).

Perlman, Fredy *Against His-story, Against Leviathan* (Detriot: Black and Red, 1983).

Portwood-Stacer, Laura *Lifestyle Politics and Radical Activism* (New York/London: Bloomsbury, 2013).

Radio 4 'The Jam Generation', 4 March 2008, www.bbc.co.uk/programmes/b0093348 [accessed 6 February 2017].

Rimbaud, Penny *Shibboleth: My Revolting Life* (Edinburgh: AK Press, 1998).

Reich, Wilhelm *What is Class Consciousness* (London: Socialist Reproduction, 1973 [first published 1934]).

Rocker, Rudolf *Nationalism and Culture* trans. Ray E. Chase (St. Paul, Minnesota: Michael E. Coughlin, 1978 [first published 1937]).

Rocker, Rudolf *Anarcho-Syndicalism* (London: Pluto Press, 1989 [first published 1938]).

Sakolsky, Ron "Timber!: An Interview with Judi Bari (7 November 1994)', in Ron Sakolsky and Fred Wei-Han Ho (eds.), *Sounding Off! Music as Subversion/Resistance/Revolution* (New York: Autonomedia, 1995), 173–179.

Savran, Yagmur 'The Rojava Revolution and British Solidarity', *Anarchist Studies*, 24:1 (2016), 7–12.

Simon, Roger *Gramsci's Political Thought: An Introduction* 3rd edn. (London: Lawrence & Wishart, 2015).

Taylor, Steven *False Prophet. Fieldnotes from the Punk Underground* (Middletown CT: Wesleyan University Press, 2003).

The Beatles, 'Revolution', Accompanied with Still Images Uploaded to YouTube by SkiMwal Ker4mtHehilLs 14 March 2008 – www.youtube.com/watch?v=KrkwgTBrW78 [accessed 26 October 2016].

Thompson, A. K. *Black Bloc White Riot. Anti-Globalization and the Genealogy of Dissent* (Oakland: AK Press, 2010).

Thompson, Stacy *Punk Productions. Unfinished Business* (Albany: State University of New York Press, 2004).

Tinnell, Adam *The Boulevardier* 2009 http://boulevardier4eva.wordpress.com/ [not accessed – private WordPress site]

Turner Scott M. X., 'Maximising Rock and Roll: An Interview with Tim Yohannon [*sic*]', in Ron Sakolsky and Fred Wei-Han Ho (eds.), *Sounding Off! Music as Subversion/Resistance/Revolution* (New York: Autonomedia, 1995), 180–194.

Ward, Colin *Anarchy in Action* (London: Freedom Press, 1996 [first published 1973]).

Ward, Colin (ed.) *A Decade of Anarchy 1961–1970: Selections from the Monthly Journal Anarchy* (London: Freedom Press, 1987).

Whalley, Boff 'Anarchism and Music: Theory and Practice', in Daniel O'Guérin (ed.), *Arena Three: Anarchism in music* (Hastings: ChristieBooks, 2012), 77–82.

Wilson, John 'Chasing the Blues Away', *New Statesman*, 15 May 2008, www.newstatesman.com/music/2008/05/paul-weller-jam-album-song [accessed 6 February 2017].

Woodcock, George *Anarchism: A History of Libertarian Ideas and Movements* 2nd edn. (Harmondsworth: Penguin Books, 1986).

Discography

Billie, 'Because We Want To', *Honey To The B* (Innocent, Virgin, 1999).

Carne Cruda, 'Anarcho-Syndicalism', *Oakland's Tight – Hella Tight* (Round Whirled Records, 2010).

Carne Cruda, 'I Love You More Than Tacos', (Round Whirled Records, 2016).

Gil Scott Heron, 'The Revolution Will Not Be Televised', (Flying Dutchman, 1971).

Sex Pistols, 'Anarchy in the UK', (EMI, 1976).

Sex Pistols, *Never Mind the Bollocks, Here's the Sex Pistols* (Virgin, 1977).

The Jam, 'The Eton Rifles', *Setting Sons* (Polydor, 1979).

Various, *Bare Faced Hypocrisy Sells Records/The Anti-Chumbawamba EP* (Ruptured Ambitions, Propa Git, 1998).

4.6

TECHNO-POLITICS

An Interview with Jim Thomas, ETC Group

Jim Thomas/ETC Group

URI GORDON: Would you like to start by describing some of the groups or movements that organise around a radical politics of technology?

JIM THOMAS: I think I would start by saying that there is not yet a radical technology politics movement, and that it is incipient in other movements. It's interesting to look at the fragmented ways in which radical movements, and civil society movements more broadly, grapple with technology. I think it is less helpful to talk about a movement as such, and better to think of it in terms of radical technology politics as they feature in various struggles. So, for example, on the one hand, there are questions around openness – open source, open technology, whether it's about hacker movements, including biohackers, or the maker movement and so on. Those struggles are sometimes disconnected from those who take on questions of technological power and control as it affects questions around risk and precaution. There is clearly theorised work about technology more generally that has come out of movements against GM crops, industrial agriculture, toxic chemicals and nuclear power. Then, there's the movement against militarism and military technology. And then, there is a whole indigenous critique of how technology is used as a colonial, imperial force. And finally, of course, critique of technology features in more broadly anticapitalist, anticorporate struggles and in climate justice and environmental justice discourse.

A lot of these things don't connect very well, it's important to say. Much of civil society does not have a very obvious place to start, or even any set of obvious questions towards technology that are broadly socialised. There is a lot of good theoretical, including radical theoretical, work that is not effectively shared between movements. What we commonly see are very site-specific fights on specific technologies and sometimes specific technology platforms, where an existing movement goes up against the technological machine. For example, isolated fights over fracking, GM crops, mobile phones and vaccinations, where often a technological critique is created in isolation and in partial ways. What is only beginning now is the attempt to link across all these technological fights to find the common drivers, common opponents and common agendas.

Part of what I think will make this clearer is the 'convergence agenda' that elites are pushing very hard on. The World Economic Forum calls it the 'fourth industrial revolution'; for years, it has been called 'converging technologies'. Artificial intelligence and automation trends are bringing that convergence to the fore. The captains of capital are now the heads of technology firms, that is increasingly obvious, and they are increasingly seeing technology as the way to move forward the interests of capital, even more so than trade agreements or rewriting governance laws – since technology can bypass a lot of that.

UG: Does this have to do with the convergence of biological, computer and materials technologies?

JT: Well the idea of converging technologies that has become traditionalised in the last decade is that of the convergence of nanotechnology, biotechnology, information technology and neural technologies. That gets configured in different ways, whether GRAIN – Genetics, Robotics, Artificial Intelligence and Nano, or BANG – Bits, Atoms, Neurons and Genes. The World Economic Forum titles it as the 'fourth industrial revolution' and it is becoming really obvious in the current AI bubble how there is a lot of excitement about flexible manufacturing and robotics, which is taking off in a big way. In fact, talking about convergence in this way misses the fact that it's a convergence of corporate sectors and economics as much as of technological platforms. At the same time, you're moving decision-making into technological solutions, apps basically. 'Don't worry be 'appy'. There is an app for everything and in governance terms, you can shrink engagement including democratic engagement in decision-making and say 'we will just deploy one technological app after another', all of which have to be made and developed researched and tested and produced for money.

So a very important discussion that needs to take place in civil society and social movements is the one around the so-called solutions. Evgeny Morozov has done some great work around 'solutionism' and it applies to the techno-driven language which many NGOs unthinkingly use in this respect. The interesting thing about him is that he comes from that 'open world', 'digital society' agenda, and in his book *To Save Everything Click Here*, he poked at the idea that we can turn all social problems into solvable, engineerable solutions. This idea that comes from Silicon Valley that everything can be reduced to a solution gives the idea that the challenges we face are kind of glorified maths problems.

UG: Meaning they're technical and managerial rather than social and political?

JT: Right – and the implication is if we can find the technical engineering solution it can be resolved, and we can move on. Of course, what we are facing are not math problems, what we are facing are situations which are historical, cultural, social that are about power inequities. The way you address that is through political action and people having to engage with each other – but all of that is swept aside when the answer becomes a technological solution. Climate change has been turned into a technical maths problem about CO_2 in the air and the solution is that we have to install solar panels and we have to take out carbon dioxide. But climate change is nothing like that, climate change is really about our civilisation and how we have inequitably shared resources over time while deliberately arranging everything around a fuel source that enables monopoly. But instead we are told that it is an inefficiency problem as long as we can technologically and financially solve it.

UG: So what would be an alternative perspective? Thinking of agriculture, for example.

JT: Certainly, peasant movements like the Landless Workers' Movement (MST) and Via Campesina are encouraging a move towards agroecology and agroecological systems, which is recognising that indigenous technology already has answers. These sort of complex diverse technological systems we would call wide-tech - rather than hi-tech.

UG: 'Technology' in the sense of land management practices that have existed for centuries?

JT: Yes. Often technology is captured by popular imagination, especially in the global North, as exogenous technology that comes from elsewhere and is given to you from on high. But every civilisation is innovating from below at all times. Innovation is one of those words that have been captured and hijacked for a very specific narrow technoscience, but it is also what farmers and indigenous people do all the time. One of the tasks we find ourselves doing at the ETC Group is trying to point to indigenous innovations as innovation, as science and technology, and agroecology is a perfect example. But of course, it is always going to be local and diverse. We always talk about '3D innovation': diverse, decentralised and democratic. Those are the innovation systems that really exist and really deliver, including peasant agriculture and agroecology.

While agribusiness and agritechnology companies are saying that they are moving to 'precision agriculture' or 'climate smart agriculture' based on further hi-tech intervention, the response from peasant and food sovereignty movements is that we already have agroecology – it exists, we can show it, it's all over the place. And if your concern is about climate change, it already is low carbon. If your concern is about hunger, it's already feeding people. If your concern is about the impact on nutrients, it's already cycling nutrients. However you cut it, this diverse decentralised set of technologies and approaches is meeting every one of these needs.

UG: And how does this conflict between opposing agendas manifest in practice?

JT: It goes all ways. On the one hand, there's direct action like landless peasants from MST and Via Campesina trying to close GM tree plantations in Brazil and turn them into agroecology centres, and there are other direct confrontations with corporate projects and technologies. On the other hand, there's the effort to try to get this language into institutional settings. So now the concept of agroecology, for example, is beginning to appear in discussions and documents from the UN Food and Agriculture Organisation, the Committee on World Food Security and the International Panel of Experts on Food Systems. It's an interesting contrast to the way the mainstream climate movement has gone, which was to demand renewables, meaning a set of technological solutions that is not socially grounded in the same way agroecology is. Agroecology is really a set of social technologies.

UG: Do movements in the global South link these critiques of exogenous technologies to colonialism?

JT: What gets linked clearly is the new high technology, the technosciences. GM crops and GM tech are very closely linked to colonialism because they come with monoculture projects that are taking land away, with systems where the seed is no longer controlled by peasants but large companies. This is not only through patents on seeds or plant breeder's rights, but also simply that seeds brought in through industrial agriculture are not adapted to diverse small farmer ecology. They are high-input seeds that are designed to be part of a monocultural operation. Certainly, GM seeds were designed for monoculture, originally with the American prairies in mind so that Monsanto, Dupont, Syngenta and so forth could sell them to large industrial operations. A herbicide-resistant GM crop implies a large growing area where herbicide is sprayed, and was developed for monoculture corn or soy or cotton. It can't be co-planted with other crops that don't resist this herbicide and it only makes sense in a high-input system where you're using one crop. The same for GM crops that produce their own pesticide, where the assumption is that you want 'clean' fields – once again, you're talking about a monocultural system since this crop is going to kill all the biodiversity around it.

Here, one of the most interesting fights surrounds climate smart agriculture, or 'climate ready' traits. So you have crops being developed where the stories from the biotech and agribusiness companies are that we are making crops to feed the world, be able to resist floods or deal with drought or more saline soils because of desertification, and therefore we are providing for expanded food production in the South, and they are looking at the South particularly. The reality is what they are doing is allowing monoculture crops to move onto land where monoculture crops couldn't go before. Monoculture crops didn't do very well on saline soil, and monoculture crops didn't do very well in drought systems, on the so-called marginal land. That is where peasant and agroecological systems still held sway. In effect, the best land has already been taken for plantation agriculture but on marginal land, it's harder to one-size-fits-all agriculture; you need to have seeds which are more locally adapted and systems which support the soil in other ways. All of this is done by peasant agriculture and not done very well by industrial agriculture. So from the peasant point of view, climate-ready crops and so-called climate-smart agriculture are about adapting industrial agriculture crops to take over more of their land. So it's a technology that enables further land grabs from peasants and indigenous people, a colonial and imperial behaviour and does nothing for the systems that are in place. But to the North, it's sold as 'here is how we are helping create more food for the world' – although these monoculture commodities are not what feeds the world.

UG: It strikes me that a critique of technology which emphasises power inequalities, encroachments and colonialism is quite different from techno-critiques based on precaution, hazard and risk.

JT: I think, in part, this is a difference between North and South responses; we just talked about GM technology but with other technologies too. We see that very clearly surrounding geoengineering – meaning deliberate and large-scale technological intervention in the functioning of earth systems. The South sees it as a power play about control, and especially military control, while the North sees geoengineering as a technical risk that could go wrong if something unexpected happens. Of course, both things are true and it's an interesting interplay between what happens if it works the way it's supposed to – which creates a colonial power play – and what happens if it doesn't work the way it's supposed to – where you still probably have a colonial power play going on but also unexpected physical things too.

Geoengineering has always been a potential weapon; there is a long history of weather warfare and military weather modification. A lot of political leverage comes with being able to credibly say that by making a specific intervention in a climate system, you can get a predictable output somewhere else. So, for example, if by putting sulphates in Northern latitudes around Iceland you can ensure greater or lesser monsoons around Sub-Saharan Africa, that gives you serious regional power and that should be chilling. But more importantly, I think it is about derailing the climate agenda. Any real joined-up action around climate change involves changing industrial systems and infrastructures. When this agenda began to rise, the first response of the fossil fuel industry was denial, and that worked for a certain period of time but not really anymore. So the second response is to put forward a false technical solution that supposedly allows us to maintain high emissions and avoid real change. I think it's here that geoengineering is the big distraction. Whether it works or not doesn't matter – it's how you change the agenda by putting it forward. We see this again and again in these big promethean techno-fix narratives and to their credit the climate justice movement has been leading in pointing out the phenomena of 'false solutions'.

It's similar with GM crops. Looking back twenty years, Monsanto said they were going to have hundreds of different GM varieties and be a massive part of the food system. None of that has happened and really, because of such massive resistance, they ended up releasing relatively little. On the other hand, it was a huge success because in the process they bought out lots of seed companies and concentrated them, so Monsanto is now one of six companies that controls chemical, agrochemical and seeds technologies right across the food chain. In that sense, the GM technology was hugely successful regardless of whether or not it really made it into agriculture. And we're now looking at three further mergers: Monsanto-Bayer, Dow-DuPont and Syngenta-ChemChina, all structured around the next set of technological developments, data-driven precision agriculture or 'digital farming', so corporate concentration is becoming even more extreme.

UG: So let's talk about alternatives to corporate concentration. Do you see any hope in the idea that an open-source ethos could be applied not only to software but to more material technologies?

JT: I don't regard the various maker, biohacker and open-source movements as particularly radical. If you go back to the 1850s, there was a massive growing movement of chemistry hackers in Western Europe, young people who were trying to develop synthetic chemistry in their own homes, equivalent to garage inventors. For example, you had people like William Perkins, in the UK, who came up with the chemical version of the colour indigo. And that really rolled back the patent movement, particularly in Germany, so you could say there was an anti-monopoly, grassroots, bottom-up movement that seemed to be doing successfully what the current open-source hardware movements want to do. Yet once they worked out the core technologies through this open and free approach, then capital reasserted itself and those people set up what were to become BASF, Bayer and what ultimately became IG Farben, the most highly concentrated company in the beginning of the twentieth century.

Every new technology platform needs a period of openness and freedom to work out what it is about, work out what its killer apps are and how it will function in a capitalist system. You also see that with the Internet. Apple was part of a home brew computer club. I find it similar with biohackers, this growing movement using biotech in an open-sourced way with all the genetic parts being accessible, sharable, not patented and so forth. There are biohackers with very strong anticorporate sentiments and often a well-theorised understanding of the problems of monopoly, but much of this movement is ultimately driven by privileged individuals arguing for greater freedom to operate – wanting to master the technology and then be able to set up start-ups. For capital, that's great. You need that time of openness, but once you sort out the basic technologies, then capital moves in and closes everything down again.

UG: Would you say the same thing about the free software movement?

JT: Yes, because I see a unidimensional movement that doesn't engage well with an actual material politics of technology, in the way that Ivan Illich talked about it, understanding that technologies have social relations built into them, that there are elite technologies, undemocratic technologies that are inherently authoritarian. The hacker ethos says everything can be made democratic as long as you hand it to enough people and that's just not true. The underlying politics of the technology itself will reassert themselves and that understanding is just missing in the free software movement as I observe it – there's no critique of computers per se.

Something like 3D printing is also a really good example. Whoever is going to benefit most from 3D printing on a large scale is whoever controls the data, and to control data you need to have large data processing and storage capabilities. Those are capital and energy-intensive, so it is always going to be an advantage for corporations and ecological ramifications. It feels to me like that excitement in the 1960s that we were all going to control our TV stations through community television. Well you can set up your community television or Indymedia sites but the Internet or TV as a whole is not going to be controlled by Indymedia. On balance, it is going to be a corporate-controlled environment moving forward the interest of capital. You have these small sites where communities feel that they are using it for themselves but overall the direction of that technology is towards capital. The excitement about biohacking and 3D printing and blockchains and so on certainly doesn't come from peasant or workers' movements in the South.

Southern movements often very clearly articulate that they want technology that is driven by their own indigenous and traditional knowledge systems. A small but really good example was when it was found that genetically modified corn had contaminated the centre of origin in Mexico, and traditional peasant communities were very concerned about this contamination. The question was what to do about it, and you had sympathetic scientists from the North saying that DIY genetic labs could be set up where corn could be tested for contamination. The communities discussed this and said no, because that was moving to a technology system that was not based on indigenous knowledge – it required external expertise about genetics, external capital to keep the labs going, so the political economy of that solution did not fit with their own knowledge and ways of doing things. In the end, the communities said, instead let's work out the traditional way to protect maze systems: we are going to look more closely at the cobs of maze, which look familiar and unfamiliar, and make sure we save them the way they always were.

UG: Does this kind of technological assessment help move from specific struggles towards a broader movement around the politics of technology?

JT: I think so. Technology assessment as such has been around for many years; some governments have technology assessment bodies connected to their parliaments, many of which have been defunded but some are coming back. Now, we have been involved with many civil society groups to try and create regional technology assessment networks, what we call TAPs – Technology Assessment Platforms where a range of different groups come together to track what the emerging technologies are, what technologies matter across different issues and then put them through a social, economic, cultural and risk assessment together. But this is coming from people's knowledge and drawing on experiments in participatory technology assessment like citizens' juries or community knowledge exchanges. For the ETC Group, that is really important, building up the practice of social movements to assess technologies in a broad and multi-criteria way. This kind of participation helps move towards a view of technology as an object of political engagement.

UG: What other actors apart from peasant movements offer a radical critique of technology and technology practices?

JT: The disability rights movement has an extremely good critique of technology because they are consistently excluded from technology, whether it is just getting on buses or the Internet, they have a very good sense of how building a technological infrastructure implicitly includes or excludes certain kinds of people. The disability rights actions around things like access really go to the core of how technology engages, chooses and pushes forward structures of power. With workers' rights, there are also interesting developments. The traditional labour movement has engaged with technology on the level of risk, but now there is bound to be more engagement because of how flexible robotics, automation and AI are taking off. Where previously you had robots, in the car industry, for example, they'd do a single operation. With flexible robotics, tasks are reprogrammable and a whole factory can potentially change its manufacturing from one day to the other depending on the data it's given. So again, this is an opening for workers to engage with technology politics on a deeper level.

So going back to where we started, currently you have skirmishes over specific technologies: GMOs, nuclear, fracking, mobile phones or whatever. They get so far in a technological critique and then go back to the specifics of their own issue. But with newly emerging technologies, movements are often better able to cross-pollinate and connect to other fights and other critiques. When everything is coming into being, it's an open space politically; there is a lot to fight for and there is a lot of ground to gain. This is the space where you can articulate struggles in terms of technological power as such, and begin to push back on those broader terms.

4.7

THE REVOLUTION UNDER THE TABLE

On the Social Ecology of the Local Food Movement in the US

Lisa Trocchia-Baļķīts

Since the first decades of the twentieth century, the US began investing in food production strategies that would enable it to feed a growing and increasingly urban domestic population, as well as its allies in Europe during two world wars. Since that time, it has established a reputation as 'the world's "residual supplier" of agricultural commodities, the one place to turn to in emergencies' (Rosenfeld 1974, 19). The deeply resonant belief among its citizens that 'America feeds the world' empowers a tenacious grand narrative. Constructed in the post-WWII rhetoric that framed the US as the most powerful nation on earth, for many, the task of providing food for the world continues to stir up a sense of moral pride in capability.

This narrative conjures values of benevolence and responsibility that overlook its origins in a calculated political and paternalistic approach to humanitarianism intentionally allied with strategies for economic dominance (Fousek 2000, 68). The 'feed the world' narrative fails to recognise that nearly half of the largest crop raised in the US, corn, goes to the production of fuel, not food, and that the type of food exported to the rest of the world does not address adequate nutritional needs (Charles 2013, 2:12; 3:27). Further complicating the psychology behind the persistence of the grand narrative is the current reality that over forty-two million people in the US live in food-insecure households (Feeding America 2015). Still, the idea that American farmers have the moral responsibility to feed the world animates a form of patriotism that takes pride in dominating global agricultural markets and justifies pushing production methods towards higher and higher yields.

In practical terms, this kind of growth in the agricultural sector has been achieved at the expense of smallholder diversified farms, by exploiting homogeneity in both plants and animals (a requirement to realise the benefits of economies of scale), and through the use of cheap labour, energy-intensive systems, petrochemicals and genetic manipulation.

The 'feed the world' grand narrative plays to the contemporary agricultural policies of the US, which have matured within the framework of neo-liberal ideologies and under the formidable influence of corporate control of the structures of food production, aggregation, processing, transportation, distribution, marketing and consumption – otherwise known as the industrial food system. Because the US maintains a position of significant economic and political influence around the world, which includes shaping global liberalisation through the agricultural policies of the International Monetary Fund (IMF) and the World Bank (The Thistle 2000), the industrial food systems model has become globally dominant.

Enter the counternarrative: there is now a shift in consciousness arising from the grass roots in countries around the world. In response to a growing awareness that the industrial food system is inextricably linked to global environmental, economic, political and social systems, citizens are resisting the inherent lack of ecological sustainability, economic equity and social justice found within the dominant food systems model. This resistance, which I refer to here as 'the local food movement', is remarkably powerful precisely because it is de-centralised, yet focused. In this leaderless movement (Latham 2016), resistance is created by a common understanding of global food systems issues, often shared through self-organised networks of communication and exchange, but notably shaped by the culture of place.

In many countries, including the US, extraordinary and culturally unique examples of the local food movement are manifesting in significant ways. As a diverse and place-based project, the local food movement is manifesting as farmworker solidarity, as attention to food resiliency and preservation of biodiversity through seed saving, as the nurturing of heritage animal breeds and organic and/or permaculture food production, and as policies and approaches that address hunger and poor nutrition, equal access to food, and global fair trade arrangements. While these are necessary and positive developments and without doubt relevant to my thesis, providing a detailed analysis of these very visible and material outcomes is not my primary focus. Here, my intent is to take a closer look at the framing and infrastructure of the local food movement in the US, and, in particular, to cast a critical eye over the widely popular idea of a 'food revolution' in a cultural context.

Talk of a 'food revolution' is commonplace in the US. Following a campaign championed by British chef and restaurateur, Jamie Oliver, one now finds Hollywood celebrities, American non-profit organisations, philanthropic foundations, food writers, chefs and elected government officials actively encouraging a food revolution. There are food revolution public conferences, cookbooks, websites, songs and at least one major university campus which actively promotes 'food revolution day'.[1] Even Walmart, the world's largest retailer (Gensler 2016), donated one million dollars to the Wisconsin-based urban agriculture organisation, Growing Power, for their work supporting a 'Good Food Revolution' (Milwaukee Business Journal 2011). Throughout history, the call for revolution has been issued from the fringes of society; yet, it seems obvious today, in the US, that advocating for a food revolution is not considered to be particularly radical. Recognising that the local food movement in the US is also situated well within a capitalist structure (at least in terms of a revolution being defined as the replacement of an established order), it begs an equally obvious question: is it at all revolutionary?

As I move through this subject, I consider the ways the local food movement has set a table with what appears to be delicious alternatives to the products of the industrial food system, but it has also clearly laid out the food revolution with consumerism in mind. In conversation with individuals who are actually creating food systems alternatives (in this case, food producers regarded as leaders in the local food movement), I demonstrate how systemic problems are beginning to reveal the limitations of basing change on a recipe sourced from the capitalist power cookbook. To this end, I am compelled to take a look under the table, to discover what of revolution might be found in the oddments. I suggest that it is in the unnoticed spaces where one can find indicators of a more radical revolution in process. It is here where the overlooked social structures that are more horizontal than hierarchical, and more cooperative than competitive point to significant shifts in how people relate to one another. Excavating beneath the table reveals unexpressed diverse economies and pericapitalist associations performing within the dominant economic structure. The implication is that what can be gleaned from underneath the food on the table may, in fact, constitute the most exciting and promising potential for resistance to the corporate-controlled industrial food system, as well as transformative social change.

To begin, it is helpful to examine how the local food movement in the US is framed. The rhetoric and initiatives that define it support entrepreneurs and enterprise solutions, the creation of direct markets, the building of strong regional food economies, local wealth creation and growth, increased food security and, of course, more consumer choice. 'Buy Local!' is the battle cry of the revolution and the mantra, 'Vote with Your Fork', is meant to connect citizen-eaters with the sense of enacting democracy. From a communications perspective, this language brings into focus the extent to which a 'market-as-movement' strategy (Pollan 2006) has manifested. Furthermore, this type of framing is provocative enough to prompt questions regarding co-option strategies by the dominant paradigm in maintaining hegemony. While I feel that an expansive discussion on this point is just beyond the scope of my purpose here, relevant are ideas that examine where power resides inside the social ecology of a food system, and how liberated social and economic spaces may differ from those on which specific ideologies have been imposed. Within a capitalist-based local food movement-as-alternative, such as in the US, the potential for revolutionary change – which might arguably be realised through the free association of people and the recognition of the value in diverse economies (Gibson-Graham 2008, 5) – is mitigated and de-incentivised by an alternative food system structure embedded within commodified re-alations (Hinrich 2000, 301). The difficult irony to accept for many – perhaps even heresy to a few – is to suggest that the language and conceptual frame of such a revolution acts at cross-purposes to its goals. The counternarrative used to define the movement represents a cultural construction that continues to support the dominant economic system, one that is impossible to disentangle from the very systems of oppression associated with the most negative impacts of the industrial food system model. In this sense, and in simple terms, I characterise the alternatives offered on the table of the local food movement in the US as a 'revolution' located in the privilege of capital.

That said, I feel compelled to note that if the local food movement is simply a sprout growing from capitalist roots, it does not negate the good that has come from it. There are many examples of capital transformed into successful programmes that educate the public about food and nutrition, and, in very real ways, improve the environment, the quality of life in targeted communities and the health and well-being of animals consumed as food. My focus here, however, in deconstructing the idea of an American food revolution, is not to dispute or chronicle the material outcomes of the local food movement; rather, it is to consider a context in which an entrepreneurial-based model for food system's change can affect transformative social change. It is with this in mind that I examine the potential of considering a social ecology of the local food movement in the US and suggest that the most radical revolution may actually be emerging from under the local food table. I explore the idea that the truly revolutionary aspect of a new food systems consciousness is not simply the availability of products representing socially just and environmentally sound alternatives to those produced by the industrial system, but a consciousness that transforms pure consumption into a moral element of understanding the transformative power of community and citizenry. I offer that within the local food movement, it is the social ecology itself – the cooperative relationships and the diverse economic structures formed by networks of citizens – that remains under-valued and under-theorised in food systems scholarship as an important site of radical social change.

Within a local food paradigm, the emergent self-organised social networks between food producers and citizens perform as critical spaces for cooperation and resistance in a country where there is no strong association with socialism, and where there is robust persuasion for activities that privilege individualism, profit and competition. In the pages ahead, I provide examples of self-organised local food praxis from my research in Athens, Ohio, where the 'ground truth' of the revolution looks like solidarity networks, cooperation, horizontal organisational structures, complex reciprocity, autonomous zones, radical earth care, bioregionalism and mutual aid. These activities and behaviours are demonstrated not only in and among the Appalachian foothills of southeastern Ohio; the social ecology of the local food movement in the US is dense and interconnected nationally through purpose and people. To illustrate this point, I share other parallel activities found around the country that are emerging from self-organised local food networks.

To explore this topic in its richness, I believe it is helpful to imagine the social ecology of the local food movement in the US as a complex adaptive system. Situating the social within theories normally reserved for the activities of molecules and atoms in a quantum physics context is actually not so far afield. Systems in a complexity paradigm are considered to have many independent entities interacting with each other in many ways and on many scales. In the abundance of these interactions, the system as a whole performs 'spontaneous self-organization' innovating and adapting to challenges (Waldrop 1992, 11). In this paradigm, all actions that emerge from local experience have value for their generative ability to co-create change on the macro level. Characterising the social ecology of food as a living concern – in this case, by suggesting that it is a socio-environmental ecology of decentralised networks – complex links are revealed between the social relationships embedded in cultural, economic and political ideological systems. This, in turn, illustrates associations between what it is people eat as a factor determining the future of the planet, vis-à-vis extracted fossil fuels and mined minerals; energy use; biodiversity; and the subsequent quality of air, soil and water as commons.

Within these networks, motivated by the desire to change the food system, individuals tend to cooperate in activities that strengthen the local food community. From a networked, community-based perspective, exploring innovations and adapting to disruption at each step create iterations of change that are enabled and facilitated at the most basic level through cooperation, solidarity and mutual aid. Because the idea of supporting 'local' over global and industrial is central to the movement, these networks also begin to function at differing scales, reanimating ideals of bioregionalism, or a 'socio-geographic space' (Kloppenburg et al. 1996, 37). It is through the social relationships within community-based local food systems that a bioregional praxis is radically reordering and reclaiming geographies and culture, challenging labels, straight lines and artificial, politically expedient borders. In this way, social networks are prefiguring new ways of honouring and protecting the complexity and interdependencies between biotic and abiotic communities – that is to say, the living and non-living parts of an ecosystem. As 'systems thinking' within the local food movement becomes the baseline strategy for moving away from segmented industrialised processes, a self-organised, socially co-created bioregional dynamic becomes a critical indicator of important changes in values and identity. Cultivating bioregionalism is, as authors McGinnis, House and Jordan write, a form of creating an 'ecology of shared identity'. They describe it as 'a *practice* performed by a community that extends its identity to biospheric life as manifested by particular places; a human community which begins to define itself through its continuity with and immersion in ecologial systems' (McGinnis, House, and Jordan 1999, 212.)

When considered collectively, on a national scale, the types of prefiguration I discuss suggest my central (and provocative) question: if the social ecology of the local food movement is modelling an environmental consciousness, cooperation, solidarity and diverse economies, is the local food revolution actually building capacity for radical transformative social change?

The well-polished wooden bar between us is made from a plank of local, sustainably harvested poplar. It's a long, curvilinear slab, the topplaned smooth to reveal beautiful shades of deep brown and gold. Art Oestrike, owner of Jackie-O's Tap Room, Jackie O's Pub and Brewery, and Jackie O's Barrel Ridge Farm (the businesses all named to honour his late mother, Jackie, but with an obvious nod to the celebrity association), invites me to sit on one side of this handcrafted bar at the Tap Room. He remains standing on the other. Technically, we are doing an interview at 8:30 in the morning, but Art is multitasking between his iPhone, checking cash register receipts, chatting with staff, keeping a watchful eye on an electrical project initiated in the back of the room and brewing coffee. Finally, placing all of his attention on pouring the dark, locally roasted, fair-trade, shade-grown organic coffee into a tall Jackie O's pint glass, he stops to talk ... but not for long.

Art Oestrike owns businesses located in Athens, Ohio, home to one of the most successful and long-standing local food economies in the US (Kellogg n.d.; Meter 2011; Ackerman-Leist 2013). He is representative of a brave new wave of serious business people – food producers and entrepreneurs – deeply committed to the idea of 'local'. Art explains to me how he understands the craft beer market in this country as being locally driven and how he considers the business model he employs as 'walking the walk'. He portrays this as what makes Jackie O's a national leader in the local food/craft beer movements. He describes ten years of sourcing locally and defines this as buying close to home, and from local farmers, when possible. Aside from owning a farm from which he is able to source food for his restaurant, he cultivates relationships with area food producers to fill the gaps. Malted barley is not available locally yet (he has a plan!), nor are there hops on the scale he requires, although he does purchase from local growers what he can. He says, 'If we can buy something within twenty miles, we tend to do it. If not there, it's within 300 miles, and if not there, it's a North American product. And if it's not there, I'd rather go to Europe than elsewhere'.[2]

Art's practices for 'buying local' raise a critical issue primary to any discussion of a local food revolution. What precisely is local? Interestingly, the definition of local is widely contested within the movement itself and variously defined across the country. Art's businesses are located within the smallest local food initiative in the US, known as the Athens 30 Mile Meal.™ The concept of a thirty-mile meal originated as a branding-initiative intended to market culinary and agri-tourism along with 'local foods earning opportunities for farmers, food producers, food markets, food events, and local food enterprises' (The 30 Mile Meal 2010). Within this intentionally constructed foodshed, citizens are able to obtain an ample variety of locally grown and produced foods, everything needed for a balanced, if not gourmet, meal. This includes everything from grains and flours, beans and nuts, to vegetables, meats, cheeses, breads and pastries; from fermented and wild-harvested foods, eggs and milk products, to craft beers, wines and distilled spirits. For the people living within the Athens 30-mile foodshed – which just happens to be located outside of densely populated urban areas and in one of the most biodiverse ecoregions on the planet (World Wildlife Fund 2016) – a narrow definition of what is local makes sense. In other parts of the country, there are radius configurations that extend well into the hundreds of miles; however, studies show that most consumers consider local food to be grown within 100 miles of their homes (DeWeerdt 2009).

Certainly, there has always been a strong sense of local and regional food in the US. As a country of immigrants, food and foodways reflect many cultural influences, as well as agricultural responses to local climates and specific geographies. The wines of the Napa Valley in California, cheeses from Vermont and Wisconsin, Maryland crab cakes, chillies from

New Mexico and Virginia ham are just some examples of regional foods that are celebrated and considered to be local specialties. As such, they also represent a significant foundation for regional tourism. The difference with the local food movement is that it is not one food or several that constitute the identity and economy of a region; rather, the goal is to develop a more complete food system.

The local food movement is focused on creating infrastructure for the production and distribution of a wide variety of foods. While the foods may still reflect local cultural preferences, be sustainably wild-harvested, or the product of working creatively with land and weather limitations, the idea is to 're-localise' community-based systems that were lost to the industrialisation process. This attempt is one of creating regional food security and of local wealth creation. For example, very few communities in the US have locally run grain mills or meat-processing facilities. These have long been in the control of large food corporations and removed from any community context. The local food movement engages in building new infrastructure, creating direct markets for farmers and food producers so that options to bypass the corporate structure are multiplied. This keeps money circulating locally, establishing strong community-based local economies. A local food system liberates citizens from their dependence on large corporate food entities, making communities more food-secure and autonomous. When farmers have direct relationships with citizens and local businesses, and access to local mills and processing facilities, it opens the way for a more sustainable, agroecological approach to farming. The objective is to free farmers from corporate contracts and the expectation of super-high yields, which are only made possible by monocropping and the use of genetically modified seeds, chemical herbicides, pesticides and fertilisers. For animal farmers, local markets and infrastructure mean opportunities to raise and process heritage livestock breeds, free of the growth hormones and antibiotics, and to engage in pasture-based, or free-range, practices. In these ways, the local food movement encourages personal relationships and systems of food production, processing, distribution and consumption that centre on communities. It is in this context that the 'miles from home' construct emerged. The 'mileage' variances in defining what is local can be accounted for by obvious environmental differences in a nation as large as the US. There is no 'one size fits all'.

The popularity of a mileage-based definition of local gained traction as the case was made for how shorter supply chains begin to address environmental concerns over the amount of fossil fuels used to get food from its source to the dinner plate. Studies at the Leopold Center for Sustainable Agriculture revealed that food, as part of the industrial system in the US, travels an average of about 1,500 miles (2,400 km) to reach the consumer (Pirog et al. 2001,14). These data serve as a powerful conceptual tool for illustrating how industrialised systems of production and distribution are contributing to CO_2 emissions. As well, the vast distances between 'farm gate-to-dinner plate' have been established as factors that impact taste and nutrition (Frith 2007, 3).

Despite ongoing discussions regarding the definition and parameters of local, for the purposes of exploring what holds revolutionary promise in the local food movement in the US, I suggest that the simple act of asserting alternative geographies in this process is the most salient. Emplacing an ecological, sociocultural consciousness within a temporal and spatial awareness is a creative process inspiring new ways to consider inhabiting one's 'life-place' (Thayer 2003, 3). Bioregionalism, as a grassroots initiative, supports relationships and codifies systems that are outside government-established boundaries. This is a revolutionary act, and one that is manifesting a new set of values. For example, the Athens 30-mile bioregion unifies and defines an area that includes seven counties and two states. This type of bioregional framework holds the potential for citizens to actively challenge economic and political forms of governance and organisation that limit the protection and allocation of resources to arbitrary frameworks determined by the state.

I see Warren near the dairy case at the supermarket in Athens. He is cheerful and energetic, stocking the shelves with yogurt, milk and heavy whipping cream. This is not the usual place one might encounter the owner and CEO of a successful food business, but Warren Taylor, owner of Snowville Creamery, is cut from different cloth. I get a generous hug and although I have known Warren for many years, his pro-fuse enthusiasm is in no way reserved for close friends only. I haven't seen Warren in at least six months, but he tells me immediately, without prompting, almost as if we were picking up a conversation we had been engaged in a few minutes ago that local food producers are 'up against the wall'. He characterises large retailers as having 'predatory monopolies' which keep sustainable local food enterprises from being economically viable. He says, 'Here's what no one is talking about: We are all working our tails off, and nobody is making any money'.[3] Warren is an organiser and an activist and he has convinced a group of local food producers to get together to talk about the topic nobody wants to address. They have met only once so far and he invites me to come to the next meeting.

In the enthusiasm to support a local food revolution, the economic problems faced by food producers rarely rise above a level of media density saturated with positive examples of entrepreneurship. Perhaps attributable to the propensity for Americans to valorise the entre-preneur, to cast the capitalist system as accessible to all, to tout hard work and innovation as the means to realise economic success, the media highlight stories that emphasise the 'up-side' of the local food movement. In many cases, the success stories are perpetuated by the same producers who find that they fall short of making a living wage, of securing affordable medical benefits for themselves and their employees after a decade or more of depending on local direct markets, growing food using sustainable and organic practices, or owning a community-based food business.

In many ways, it is understandable why farmers are complicit in perpetuating stories the media like to tell. Maintaining a strong positive counternarrative is a critical part of construct-ing the space for possibility and an essential piece in building support for consumer-dependent change. Reinforcing success within an established socio-economic metric is a vital part of what it takes to influence food policy, as well as to secure financial support from foundations and lending institutions. For those farmers and food producers heavily invested in the local food movement, maintaining a story line that communicates 'this can work' is critical. This is true to the degree that across the US, many of the players in the local food movement are reluctant to identify that, in fact, there is an elephant sitting on the local food table. The elephant has always been there and it is easier to grow accustomed to it, to look past it, than to admit that the success of the entrepreneurial-based local food movement in the US is one bound by the bottom-line profit and unending growth constraints of capitalism. To look the elephant in the eye is to admit that the construct for creating a sustainable alternative food system is ultimately at odds with the values that animate it.

However, it is the context of promoting the local food revolution and championing 'en-tre*manure*ship' that the successes of a strong local food economy continue to be celebrated in the media, with communities like Athens, Ohio featured as the vanguard. Athens is the county seat of a rural area in the southeastern portion of the state, culturally and geograph-ically part of the federally designated Central Appalachian region (Appalachian Regional Commission, n.d.). In a region where generational poverty looms large, an intentional sustainable community development strategy has been cooperatively supported for over forty years. The concept is to provide entrepreneurial opportunities through an asset-based focus on direct marketing for farmers and on creating the infrastructure for the produc-tion and marketing of value-added local food products. With one of the first 'kitchen incubator' facilities in the country, Athens created a model for building a cooperative local food economy now emulated by other communities around the country. At present, there are over 200 such incubators that help to reduce the obstacles to food entrepreneurship in thirty-nine states, just over half being in urban areas, and the others in suburban and rural areas (Wodka 2016, 4).

In *Sustainable Planet: Solutions for the Twenty-First Century*, Mark Ritchie calls Athens 'one of the most exciting and dynamic local food systems in the country' (Ritchie 2002, 96), and the region's food economy has been characterised as 'a national model of sustainable community development' (Olson 2002). The Athens Farmers Market, operating year-round with over 100 vendors and contributing an estimated $3 million dollars annually into the local economy,[4] is cited as one of the top ten farmers' markets in the nation (Thomas 2006). Athens, a community of just under 25,000, was profiled in the well-respected Utne Reader magazine, as one of three places in the world engaged in 'some of the brightest ideas in the local food movement' (Olson 2002). An Athens couple, Michelle Ajamian and Brandon Jaeger, were included in the same magazine in 2010 as part of the feature, '25 Visionaries Changing Your World' for their regional food systems infrastructure work developing Shag-bark Seed and Mill (Olson 2010). Ken Meter, one of the most experienced food systems analysts in the US, commented that 'Athens sets the tone', referring to the strategy of building cooperative community-based food business clusters, and stated that this is 'the best vehicle for rebuilding the American economy' (Meter, 110).

Accolades such as these occupy prime space atop the table of the local food revolution. These are the success narratives meant for public consumption. These are the stories that inspire and encourage localised alternatives to the industrialised food system. Yet, does a strong local or regional food economy equate to a revolution (and a sustainable alternative) when success and failure remain bound within the precarity of capitalism? No matter how local the kale one eats, how much love and sunshine chickens enjoy, how organic the fields are where farmworkers spend their days, if the business of offering local, just, environmentally restorative food is not one that can compete successfully in a growth market, it will fail. It is, as Murray Bookchin characterises it, 'the brutally competitive imperative of grow or die' (Bookchin 2007, 20). Sooner or later, the local farmer or food producer will be faced with the pressures of growth in order to remain viable. They will run up against what Warren Taylor describes as 'predatory monopolies', the rapacious and impenetrable food systems fortresses constructed by concentrated transnational corporate interests. Warren talks about retail giants, such as Kroger and Walmart,[5] and the tightly controlled distribution networks that allow them to put a full gallon of milk on hundreds of grocery stores' shelves around the state of Ohio for only ten cents per unit. He rightly questions how it is possible for local food producers to remain competitive in this environment. His company, Snowville Creamery, as an independent producer, is forced to deliver their product themselves, limiting how many stores they can reach. The cost of this added expense – necessary if Snowville is to sell any milk at all to Ohioans – must be passed to consumers at nearly a dollar added to only a half-gallon of milk.[6]

By any stretch, this isn't a fair playing field. I can extend the illustration of limitations faced by local food producers to include how corporate control limits consumer access to nutritious food if a comparison of the products themselves is considered. Snowville Creamery milk is produced by pasture-based, grass-grazing methods and by cows with 100% A2/A2 genetics.[7] The cows are never exposed to GMO feeds or forage and they are not treated with rbST (bovine growth hormones). The milk is not homogenised (the cream naturally rises to the top) and it is 'pasteurized at the lowest legal temperatures, resulting in milk that tastes sweet, clean, and delicious' (Snowville Creamery 2016). This type of product stands in stark contrast to the type of milk produced by cows on 'factory farm' confinement lots; yet because of the monopolies controlling production and distribution, many consumers will never have the opportunity to see Snowville products on the shelves of their local grocery. Of those who do, economic realities will determine who is able to pay more per gallon for the privilege of taking a half a gallon home.

The idea that consumers are given more choices through direct markets is a talking point for the local food movement. But, at the end of the day, the biggest corporate food systems players determine what a consumer can choose – not to mention the limits of choice based on one's food budget. Given these realities, it seems hard to argue that the food revolution in the US, in its present configuration, is anything more than a parallel business track – a new market for privileged consumers – and ultimately limited and controlled by large corporate food monopolies.

My analysis, after nearly twenty years of local food systems work, goes back to (or begins with) the elephant sitting on the local food table – a metaphor, of course, for the incredible weight the dominant economic structure has on the movement. Because the elephant has been there since the beginning, even the alternative economies of the local food movement (emergent, promising and innovative pericapitalist mechanisms), by the necessity of attaching themselves to the behemoth, are mostly invisible within its shadow. The elephant refuses to acknowledge that these alternative economies are present, much less, credible. The local food movement is reluctant to acknowledge the elephant, so the notion of diverse economic structures as viable mechanisms for change is also dismissed. While a particular value system may have constructed the local foods' table, and can rightly claim satisfaction in many of the good offerings laid upon it, the weight of the elephant has created a precarious balance. It cannot, however, be asked to get up and leave. To do so would tip the table tip over completely.

Would such an act qualify as the real food revolution? Does the local food movement need to push over America's dinner table to create space for a new food system? There have long been arguments that revolution rises from the ashes of destruction. However, as I have mentioned, I am more inclined towards complexity theories that suggest change is continuous, emergent and co-created. If the food system is to be considered as a complex adaptive system, then there are new ways to understand how change happens. In a complex system, if the table remains upright and accessible, and the elephant continues to be a dominant presence on top, then it is necessarily part of that system. The elephant is, itself, contributing to the proliferation of independent interactions taking place within the system that move it away from dominance and into balance.

Along the rim of the table, beneath where the elephant sits, is where creativity and innovation 'are forever nibbling away at the edges of the status quo, and where even the most entrenched old guard will eventually be overthrown' (Waldrof 1992, 12). This is known, by complexity theorists, as 'the edge of chaos', a zone where the complexity of interactions engages the forces of inertia and mayhem in adaptive responses. Change in a complex adaptive system happens here, at the edge of chaos. As M. Mitchell Waldrop writes,

> The edge of chaos is where centuries of slavery and segregation suddenly gave way to the civil rights movement of the 1950s and 1960s; where seventy years of Soviet communism suddenly gave way to political turmoil and ferment; where eons of evolutionary stability suddenly give way to wholesale species transformations.
>
> *(Waldrop 1992, 12)*

Many would argue that the local food movement is emerging from within a post-capitalist construct, which is to suggest that the current capitalist system has now crossed the apex of its arc of dominance. If change in the system is conceived of as a function of complexity, then it is at the edge of chaos where interactions between a new local food movement and the old industrialised system will build more synergistic and horizontal structures. The emergent pericapitalist phenomena found at the edges of the local food movement represent examples of what J. K. Gibson-Graham describe as a 'queering of economic identity' by establishing infrastructure that acts to disrupt capitalism's relatively unchallenged ideological density (Gibson-Graham 2001, 264).

Values are very clearly at the forefront of the local food movement. The very act of problematising the industrial food system is an expression of the values not present within it. To articulate how a neo-liberal agenda creates globalised and corporate-controlled food systems is to reaffirm the values that are being oppressed as a result. By characterising the local food movement as a decentralised complex adaptive system, the range of interests expressed by its affinity groups, concerns such as food justice, food sovereignty, food safety, food politics, environmental restoration and resiliency, animal health and welfare, reach into all sectors of society. In its simplest form, the work of these affinity groups emanates from experience-based value-expressions regarding human life, dignity, culture and community. Present in local food system activity is the attempt to validate cooperation, diversity, kindness and the necessity of being good stewards of the planet and to all living things.

In the matter of the food we eat, where it comes from, where we eat it and the relationships between those with whom it is (or isn't) shared, food values are performative on multiple levels. Food engages with 'multisensorial embodied ways of knowing in human interaction' (Pink 2015, 18). As such, food constructs a sense of home, community, culture and morality. Shared values about food among people are what holds the deepest promise for radical and transformative changes and I posit that it is within the social ecology of the local food movement that values are resonating in their interconnectivity. In this roiling, radical solidarity is emergent.

Sitting here, amid the bodies engaging with local food, I am compelled to attend to the affective, what I intuit as an environment that summons a deep solidarity of purpose. I feel authenticity and a sense of place and community in the forward-leaning postures of those reading the corkboard by the door. It is tacked with colourfully askew papers announcing local food and health-related activities – workshops, movies, lectures – as well as a flyer from a farm selling Community Supported Agriculture (CSA) shares, noting that it now accepts government food benefit cards issued to low-income households. There are posters explaining the local time exchange (alternative currency) initiative, an appeal to reduce energy consumption with a number to call for free compact fluorescent light bulbs, and information on protests being planned against fracking on nearby National Forest land. As the door opens and closes, the papers flutter like prayer flags dispersing and intermingling this atmosphere of shared values in the air.

Tucked back in from a busy street, the Village Bakery feels vibrant, not because of the commerce taking place, which is brisk, but because of the interactions between people and the emotional space this creates just inside the door. I notice open smiles, eye contact and soft, light touches between hands exchanging currency. There are interactions between young and old. The space between bodies is close enough to feel an amplification of curiosity and anticipation about what will be eaten. I taste community in my own food. This is what a local food network feels like. There is a din of animated conversation punctuated with laughter, and I notice more often than not, as people come and go, the door is held for those who are passing in spontaneous acts of kindness. In this space, there are more hugs than handshakes.

In this witness, I reflect on my discussions with the food producers in this same community. When I ask them, each and every one – without dropping a beat – says that they absolutely support each other when it comes to purchasing what they need, even if they know they could get that good or service for much cheaper through a national distributor or a large corporate entity. Across the board, they recount the ways they cooperate with each other. In any other business context, these 'others' would be the competition. I marvel at that. Will this strategy be the doing-in of the local food movement, or will it be the radical human element that makes it all work? I question them about how this does work, in terms of market-share pressures and making a profit. Not one of them deviates from the sentiment expressed by Art Oestrike when he told me. 'It's just the right thing to do'.[8]

The values of the local food movement create a solidarity of purpose. Solidarity, however, for all we hear of it, remains a slippery concept. Heckscher and McCarthy describe solidarity as 'a rather neglected academic topic' in that there is 'little understanding based on how it is created or how it has changed' (Heckscher and McCarthy 2014, 628). Perhaps as an illustration, they submit a decidedly non-academic definition of solidarity as, 'what you are supposed to do when your community engages in collective action' (Heckscher and McCarthy 2014, 629). In a community context, then, solidarity may arise from deep feelings and as 'not fully brokered', as Judith Butler describes it. Perhaps this is a consequence of complexity, where 'ethical questions are invariably implicated in social and economic ones' (Butler 2015, 23, 152).

Nonetheless, I believe that there is a deeply affective component to local food systems solidarity. It makes me think of the definition that comes from the Sandinistas (members of the former Sandinista National Liberation Front in Nicaragua): 'Solidarity is the tenderness of the people' (Power and Charlip 2009, 3). Although what is carried out in the name of solidarity can certainly range from empathy to violence, the Sandinista definition captures the sense that solidarity is action expanding from a set of moral principles. Rebecca Todd Peters describes solidarity as an ethic that offers 'a moral foundation for building a new set of economic, political, and social relations that respond to the very real needs of a planet in crisis...' (Peters 2014, 99).

If, in fact, as Heckscher and McCarthy suggest, 'the main source of solidarity is in daily social relations' (Heckscher and McCarthy 2014, 629), what could be more everyday than food? In fact, it may be in nurturing solidarity through our everyday food encounters – within and between bioregions, and from the values that have come to constitute the local food movement – that a kind of clarity necessary to differentiate 'superficial change from structural change' will emerge (Holt-Gimenez and Wang 2011, 95).

If the local food movement in the US is cultivating social ideals that create solidarity, if this solidarity continues to support the praxis of cooperation, mutual aid and self-organising, if it is creating new social and economic identities, if it is facilitating more inclusive and resilient relationships between people and the natural world, then I believe local food networks can be considered radical in the US. It is conceivable, in this context, that these local networks (socially woven webs of solidarity praxis which now cover the nation) represent 'a non-centralized, growing rejection of the current state and capitalism' (Born 2013), and perhaps might even be characterised as 'a slow motion general strike' (Holland 2011). It is my theory that just under the table, across urban and rural lines, the social ecology of the local food movement is forming autonomous social structures based on 'solidarity and co-ordinated action rather than on contractual and commoditized relationships' (Lockie 2012), and in this, building revolution.

In Athens, Ohio, like many other communities across the US, there are examples of how community-based citizen food networks are facilitating valuable structures that push against normative practices. To begin, it is worth mentioning that not all structures holding radical space perform outside the mechanisms of market capitalism. It is important to emphasise that capitalism is not a monolithic or segregated economic form. Capitalist and non-capitalist modes 'interact in pericapitalist spaces', and in terms of an embodied food revolution, it may be most helpful to consider in a strategic context the spaces where capitalism depends to some degree upon non-capitalist elements (Tsing 2015, 65).

Consider the local farmers' market, clearly an extension of market capitalism and a site some might regard rather benignly in terms of revolution. While there are a number of valid reasons why most farmers in the US are not accumulating wealth from farmers' markets (expanding on them here will take us too far from the point of mentioning this example), the theory of facilitating direct markets – that is to say, supporting opportunities for one-to-one relationships between farmers, food producers and citizens – creates opportunities for farmers to escape from the economic exploitation of 'middleman' distributors and retailers. As well, direct markets create spaces that eliminate the oppressive arrangements of contract farming. These contractual arrangements with corporations, which in many cases are the only viable option for farmers of livestock, dictate everything from what breed of animal the farmer must raise, what types of structures must be constructed to house the animals, to the schedules for administering hormones and antibiotics. Contracts establish what brand of feed must be used and in what amounts, the conditions under which the animals are raised, how long the animals will live and most importantly, how much money the farmer will be paid for assuming nearly all the risk. Contract farming is most common in large-scale animal production scenarios, but they act to reduce farmers to employees, subtracting the wisdom and value of generations of embodied farming knowledge from their identities. The same might be said of commodity farming. This type of agriculture demands large-scale monocrop production requiring farmers to incur heavy debt and a devotion to corporate-prescribed protocols that include genetically engineered seeds and the use of petrochemicals to remain viable in the market. In this sense, structures such as farmers' markets that support direct relationships between farmers and consumers are at least a start at dismantling corporate hegemony. They offer farmers a path, in partnership with citizens, to reclaim their autonomy with the promise of establishing more ecological harmony in agricultural production.

The direct relationships nurtured at farmers' markets are also social opportunities to cultivate meaningful relationships with, if not respect for, those who may otherwise circulate outside one's everyday social sphere. The feeling of 'knowing your farmer'[9] does more than provide a sense of food security in communities. The affective results of inclusive relationships based on trust create a very functional form of solidarity.

In the US, there are certainly other expressions of solidarity networks that work within traditional market structures. Very much alive within these activities are principles of self-organising, mutual aid, cooperation and voluntary non-hierarchical associations. For example, there are food buying clubs that apply the purchase power of citizen cooperatives to either bypass the markups and choice restrictions of dealing with retailers, or to collectively support local or regional food producers. In Athens, there are several 'buying clubs' that have been in existence for decades. They are self-organised by groups of individuals, usually neighbours or friends, who place orders with a regional food distributor to get products that are either unavailable from local retailers or food producers, or are only available regionally at retail prices higher than through a distributor. In several cases, buying clubs are organised around the purchase of produce from a local produce auction, which directly supports local farmers. Participation in these buying clubs is horizontal in nature, usually free to join and without monetary compensation for leadership roles. Through a consensus process, participants agree on who will take orders, where the shipments will arrive and in the case of bulk items, participants cooperate on how these will be divided.

The notion of horizontalism, or 'horizontalidad', a concept that emerged in Argentina in 2001,[10] as a response to the collapse of the monetary system is a form of solidarity present in the CSA movement. CSAs are a type of buying club that allows citizens to self-organise cooperatively in economic support of specific farmers and food producers. Throughout the country, this is a popular means for providing local food businesses (anything from small organic farms to mills and distilleries) with much needed and difficult to obtain capital, enabling them to work outside of the debt structures and restrictions of traditional financial institutions. Mutualism, as a value of local food networks, is demonstrated by the willingness of citizens to pay 'up-front' for food products they will receive later. The upfront cash infusion becomes capital for the business to invest in production. This is remarkable because there are no guarantees in this scheme. Crops can fail, leaving the citizen-investor with no return whatsoever. I suggest that this type of behaviour is an exemplar of 'the tenderness of the people', a sort of alien logic to status quo values that stress individualism and gain from exploitation. CSAs are an exercise in empathy (should the crop fail), trust and cooperation. This is the profound kind of solidarity that emanates from the belief that co-creating a vibrant community with a strong local food infrastructure is simply the right thing to do.

Community is nothing, if not a natural form of caring for each other. Natural caring has been described as 'the human condition that we, consciously or unconsciously, perceive as "good"' (Noddings 2013, 5). Much has been written about community gardens in this context – the emotional, social and health benefits people get from their associations with this type of activity (Alaimo et al. 2016), has inspired their proliferation across the country.[11] Community gardens are spaces where people come together, many times across age, gender, race and class divides, and often times in the shared effort to hold green space in urban areas. These experiences lead to the formation of relationships of trust that stem from acts of cooperatively working in a shared space. At a very basic level, what happens in these gardens creates informal social networks that add depth and density to the capacity of the local food movement.

One expression of community gardeners building social capacity in Athens began with searching for a way to avoid wasting the 'extra' vegetables they grew. Gardeners organised a project, cooperating with a local non-profit organisation, which established ways to make it easy for community and home gardeners across the city to donate their produce to food-insecure families. The project became extremely popular and eventually grew into a bioregional effort that includes a presence at local farmers' markets and produce auctions. Not only can community and home gardeners contribute fresh produce, they can contribute money to buy food at an 'after the market' rate. This gives farmers a viable option for the 'left over' items they did not sell at market and would not otherwise be able to sell at full retail price. As well, it is an easy donation for shoppers at the markets who are encouraged to buy two and donate one. In 2015, this project, now known as the Donation Station, provided nearly 90,000 lbs. of fresh produce to the charitable food system, augmenting the shelf-stable and highly processed foodstuffs received by the food-insecure in the region through food banks and pantries.[12]

Outside of these more mainstream activities of the local food movement, there are examples of how strong social networks use diversity and technology as an asset, building capacity for a non-monetary, cooperative society based on the right to food for all citizens. In Athens, as in communities in California, Vermont and elsewhere, there have been self-organised and crowd-sourced maps created and made publicly available that list food-producing trees and plants located on public property. In most cases, the fruit is usually not used and is available for free to anyone for the picking. The use of social media in these efforts is a network-weaving endeavour, linking individuals locally, as well as across the country who are interested in food democracy, food security and food justice issues.

Activism is central to these types of local food networks. The praxis of activist networks can push against the law, as well. Just this side of legal, many citizens have come together to find loopholes that will allow them to express their rights to food sovereignty. In many states in the US, the sale of products such as raw milk, or certain fermented products, is against the law. Citizens who maintain these foods should be allowed for nutritional, medical or even cultural reasons, and form underground trade and barter networks, so that no money is exchanged, and therefore, no laws are broken. There are also 'herd share' initiatives that are structured like CSAs, but take advantage of provisions in the law that allow the owners of dairy livestock to consume the milk that comes from that animal. With a herd share, a farmer sells 'shares' of a goat, or a cow, and in return, all the 'owners' are legally permitted to consume the raw milk that comes from it. In many cases, citizens 'sell' items like contraband raw milk or cheeses openly at farmers' markets or other such events, but they are clearly (and clearly deceptively) marked as 'pet food' or 'not for human consumption' (Godoy 2011).

Disrupting the ability of the government to regulate the kind of food communities are legally permitted to consume has also created instances within the local food movement where the laws have been successfully challenged. In 2015, claims of food sovereignty and community rights resulted in the passing of a 'Local Food and Community Self-Governance Ordinance' by an overwhelming margin in Bingham, Maine. Bingham is at least the sixteenth town in that state to pass such an ordinance.[13] This type of open defiance of federal law, accomplished through a democratic process by citizens who advocate for alternatives in the food system, is a powerful expression of solidarity. It highlights the agency of an empowered citizenry to resist government policies created, in many cases, to satisfy the pervasive lobby of dominant 'Big Ag' and corporate food systems interests. If the potential for revolution is to insist on participatory democracy, then it can be found here, and facilitated by the self-organised networks of citizens engaged in local foods' praxis.

I find it interesting that in Athens, in many ways, the political expression of the local food movement is beginning to manifest through the election of government officials who are also local food producers. The current mayor of the City of Athens (a former member of the area food policy council and a farmer raising specialty crops for local breweries and restaurants), as well as a county commissioner (a goat-farmer, wild foods entrepreneur and specialty local food producer) have managed on a political level to champion economic development issues that serve the interests of all, but very definitely support the growth of a local food economy. Beyond this, and because of the influence and visibility these individuals have in these particular positions, they are also taking leadership roles on energy and environmental issues that ultimately relate to the capacity for farmers to produce food sustainably. Because these are elected officials, I understand this to be an example of the ways social capital, earned by virtue of enacting the values of the local food movement, can be spent in other sectors of society.

A profound example of this comes from the account of a protest action in Athens County in 2014. I suggest that this event highlights the most significant argument for the generative and performative capacity of local food movement social networks to create radical, transformative change. Opposed to the issuance of permits that allow for storing the toxic fluid wastes from the process of fracking for shale gas in an open pit facility, eight individuals (who were part of a larger protest) engaged in a nonviolent direct action at the site and were arrested. These eight were also high-profile participants in the local food economy – business owners, food workers, farmers and food producers. 'The Athens 8', as they became known, were strongly supported by the community for their actions, which brought widespread media attention to the issue of the health and environmental risks associated with the process of fracking. Their activism to safeguard community health and well-being, and specifically, to protect the water and the natural ecology of the region was a performance of solidarity with the values held in common by the environmental and local food movements. They successfully raised public awareness of an environmental issue through the goodwill and trust they had earned as farmers and food producers.

This example illustrates the fluidity of boundaries. It demonstrates how food issues intersect with political, environmental and economic issues in a very social context. As such, it constitutes the radical potential in the social ecology of the local food movement – what I hold to be the capacity for transformative social change emergent in these interconnected webs of relationships. The values of the local food movement that embody justice, equality and environmental restoration and protection are weaving webs of solidarity based in the affirmation that democracy must be participatory and that democracy must prevail over the interests of corporations. These social networks are finding power in unity, cooperation, self-organising, mutual aid, in non-hierarchical voluntary associations, and in relationships that foster complex reciprocity. I suggest that in the ground-truth of these actions, the praxis of these values, in the structural, under-the-table happenings in the local food movement in the US, one finds the radical 'politics of effective togetherness' (Thrift 2008, 22). And here, there is revolution.

Notes

1 As part of a sustainability initiative focused on education and awareness, Stanford University participates in the Jamie Oliver Food Foundation's Food Revolution Day. http://rde.stanford.edu/dining/education-awareness.
2 Art Oestrike in a personal conversation with the author, June 2016, Athens, Ohio.
3 Warren Taylor in a personal conversation with the author, September 2016, Athens, Ohio.
4 Leslie Schaller, Director of Programming at the Appalachian Center for Economic Networks, in a personal conversation with the author. October 24, 2013.
5 Kroger is the second largest retailer in the US and Walmart, the largest retailer in the world. Wahba, Phil. 2016. '5 Surprising Things You Don't Know About Kroger'. Fortune. (June). Accessed 11/5/16. www.fortune.com/2016/06/22-kroger-fortune500/.
6 Warren Taylor in a personal email correspondence with the author, September 29, 2016.
7 Information sourced from the Snowville Creamery website, and supported by scientific studies, suggests that the original form of casein protein found in dairy milk was A-2 beta-casein. Most commercial milk production comes from cows with A-1 beta-casein, a genetic mutation. Preliminary studies suggest that milk with A-1 beta-casein (which contains a peptide called BCM7) may be linked to Type 1 diabetes as well as negative effects to the central nervous system and cardiovascular system. A-1 beta-casein may also be responsible for symptoms of milk intolerance. www.snowvillecreamery.com/health.html.
8 Art Oestrike in a personal conversation with the author, June 2016, Athens, Ohio.
9 'Know Your Farmer, Know Your Food' is an initiative of the U.S. Department of Agriculture in support of local and regional food economies. www.usda.gov/wps/portal/usda/usdahome?navid=KYF_COMPASS.
10 Marina Sitrin has written extensively on the concept of horizontalidad, stating that 'Horizontalidad is a social relationship that implies, as it sounds, a flat plane upon which to communicate'. www.marinasitrin.com/?page_id=108.
11 The American Community Gardening Association estimates that there are 18,000 community gardens throughout the US and Canada. www.communitygarden.org/resources/faq/.
12 The Donation Station is a project of the non-profit organisation, Community Food Initiatives. In 2015, 86,991 lbs. of produce and local food products were distributed to food pantries and agencies in Appalachian Ohio. www.communityfoodinitiatives.org/donation-station.

13 'Sixteenth Main Town Passes Food Sovereignty Ordinance'. Farm-to-Consumer.org. July 10, 2011. www.farmtoconsumer.org/blog/2015/07/10/sixteeth-maine-town-passes-food-sovereignty-ordinance/.

References

Ackerman-Leist, Philip. 2013. *Rebuilding the Foodshed: How to Create Local, Sustainable, and Secure Food Systems*. White River Junction, Vermont: Chelsea Green.

Alaimo, Katherine, Alyssa W. Beavers, Caroline Crawford, Elizabeth Hodges Snyder, and Jill S. Litt. 2016. 'Amplifying Health Through Community Gardens: A Framework for Advancing Multi-component, Behaviorally Based Neighborhood Interventions.' *Current Environmental Health Reports* 3(3): 302–312. doi: 10.1007/s40572-016-0105-0.

Appalachian Regional Commission. n.d. 'Counties of Appalachia.' Accessed 12 November 2016. www.arc.gov/counties.

Bookchin, Murray. 2007. What is Social Ecology? In *Social Ecology and Communalism*. Oakland, CA: AK Press, pp. 19–52.

Born, Branden. 2013. 'A Research Agenda for Food System Transformation through Autonomous Community-Based Food Projects.' *Journal of Agriculture, Food Systems, and Community Development* 3(4): 213–217. doi: 10.5304/jafscd.2013.034.026.

Butler, Judith. 2015. *Notes Toward a Performative Theory of Assembly*. Cambridge: Harvard University Press.

Charles, Dan. 2013. 'America's Farmers Say They Feed the World, But Do They?' Broadcast on *Morning Edition*, National Public Radio. 17 March 2013. Accessed 3 February 2017. www.npr.org/sections/thesalt/2013/09/17/221376803/american-farmers-say-they-feed-the-world-but-do-they.

DeWeerdt, Sarah. 2008. 'Is Local Food Better?' *Worldwatch Magazine* 22(3). May/June. Accessed 29 October 2016. www.worldwatch.org/node/6064.

Feeding America. 2017. "Poverty and Hunger in America." Accessed 3 February 2017. www.feeding america.org/hunger-in-america/impact-of-hunger-and-poverty/.

Fousek, John. 2000. *To Lead the Free World: American Nationalism and the Culture Roots of the Cold War*. Chapel Hill: University of North Carolina Press.

Frith, Kathleen. 2007. 'Is Local More Nutritious?' White Paper. Boston: Harvard School of Public Health. Accessed 12 November 2016. www.chgeharvard.org/resource/local-more-nutritious.

Gibson-Graham. J.K. 2001. *Postcolonial Queer*. Albany: State University of New York Press.

Gibson-Graham, J.K. 2008. Diverse Economies: Performative Practices for 'Other Worlds." *Progress in Human Geography* 32(5): 613–632. doi: 10.1177/0309132508090821.

Godoy, Maria. 2011. 'A Legal Loophole for Raw Milk Lovers: Call it "Pet Food."' *National Public Radio*. The Salt: What's on Your Plate? Accessed 3 November 2016. www.npr.org/selections/thesalt/2011/10/13/141249172/a-legal-loophole-for-raw-milk-lovers-call-it-pet-food.

Hinrichs, C. Claire. 2000. 'Embeddedness and Local Food Systems: Notes on Two Types of Direct Agricultural Market.' *Journal of Rural Studies* 16(2): 295–303.

Holland, E.W. 2011. *Nomad Citizenship: Free-Market Communism and the Slow Motion General Strike*. Minneapolis: University of Minnesota Press.

Holt-Gimenez, Eric and Yi Wang. 2011. 'Reform of Transformation? The Pivotal Role of Food Justice in the U.S. Food Movement.' *Race/Ethnicity: Multidisciplinary Global Contexts* 5(1): 88–102.

Heckscher, Charles and John McCarthy. 2014. 'Transient Solidarities: Commitment and Collective Action in Post-Industrial Societies.' *British Journal of Industrial Relations* 52(4): 627–657. doi: 10.1111/bjir.12084.

Kellogg, W.K. n.d. 'Food For Thought: Community-Based Food Systems Enterprises: Issues for the 21st Century Food System.' Accessed 15 April 2016. www.wkkf.org/~/media/3909FEC-5250149C7B271018A65AE8B22.ashx.

Kloppenburg, J., Hendrickson, J. and Stevenson, G.W. 1996. 'Coming in to the Foodshed.' *Agriculture and Human Values* 13, 33–42. www.cias.wisc.edu/wp-content/uploads/2008/07/comingin1.pdf.

Latham, Jonathan. 2016. 'Why the Food Movement is Unstoppable.' *Counterpunch* 21 September. Accessed 24 October 2016. www.counterpunch.org/2016/09/21/food-liberation-why-the-food-movement-is-unstoppable/.

Lockie, Steward. 2012. 'Responsibility and Agency within Alternative Food Networks: Assembling the 'Citizen Consumer.' *Agriculture and Human Values* 26(3): 193–201. doi: 10.1007/s10460-008-9155-8.

McGinnis, Michael Vincent, Freeman House and William Jordan III. 1999. 'Bioregional Restoration: Re-establishing an Ecology of Shared Identity.' In *Bioregionalism*, edited by Michael Vincent McGinnis. London: Routledge, 212 pp.

Meter, Ken. 2011. 'Ohio's Food Systems – Farms at the Heart of It All.' *Crossroads Resource Center.* Accessed 13 November 2013. http://uac.utoledo.edu/Publications/ohfood.pdf.

Milwaukee Business Journal. 2011. 'Wal-Mart to Donate $1M to Growing Power.' September 6. Accessed 24 October 2016. http://bizjournals.com/milwaukee/news/2011/09/06/walmart-to-donate-1m-to-growing-power.html.

Noddings, Nel. 2013. *Caring: A Relational Approach to Ethics and Moral Education.* Berkeley: University of California Press.

Olson, Karen. 2002. 'How Local Food Can Enrich a Community.' *Utne Reader.* May/June. Accessed 12 November 2013. www.utne.com/environment/homegrown.aspx#axzz2g10VcU2L.

———. 2010. '25 Visionaries Who Are Changing Your World.' *Utne Reader.* November/December. Accessed 15 May 2012. www.utne.com/Politics/25-visionaries-changing-your-world-2010.aspx.

Peters, Rebecca Todd. 2014. *Solidarity Ethics: Transformation in a Globalized World.* Minneapolis, MN: Fortress Press.

Pink, Sarah. 2015. *Doing Sensory Ethnography.* London: Sage.

Pirog, Rich, Timothy Van Pelt, Kamyar Enshayan, and Ellen Cook. 2001. 'Food, Fuel, and Freeways: An Iowa Perspective on How Far Food Travels, Fuel Usage, and Greenhouse Gas Emissions.' *Leopold Center Pubs and Papers.* Paper 3. http://lib.dr.iastate.edu/leopold_pubspapers/3.

Pollan, Michael. 2006. 'Voting with Your Fork.' *New York Times.* Accessed 20 October 2016. http://pollan.blogs.nytimes.com/2006/05/07/voting-with-your-fork/.

Power, Margaret and Julie A. Charlip. 2009. 'Introduction: On Solidarity.' *Latin American Perspectives* 36(6): 3–9. www.jstor.org/stable/i20684680.

Ritchie, Mark. 2002. 'Be A Local Hero: Strengthening our Communities, Health and Environment by Eating Local.' In *Sustainable Planet: Solutions for the Twenty-first Century*, edited by Juliet B. Schor and Betsy Taylor. Boston: Beacon Press.

Rosenfeld, Stephen S. 1974. "The Politics of Food." *Foreign Policy* 14: 17–29.

Snowville Creamery. 2016 'What Makes Our Milk Different?' Accessed 5 November 2016. www.snowvillecreamery.com/about.html.

Thayer, Jr. Robert L. 2003. *Life Place: Bioregional Thought and Practice.* Berkeley: University of California Press.

The 30 Mile Meal. 2010. 'Why the 30 Mile Meal Project Matters.' Accessed 24 October 2016. http://30milemeal.wordpress.com.

The Thistle. 2000. "The IMF and the World Bank: Puppets of the Neoliberal Onslaught." *The Thistle Alternative News Collective*, a publication of the Massachusetts Institute of Technology 13(2). Accessed 2 February 2017. www.mit.edu/~thistle/v13/2/imf.html.

Thomas, Mary-Powel. 2006. 'The Ripe Stuff.' In *Audubon Magazine.* March. Accessed 15 May 2012. http://archive.audubonmagazine.org/features0603/market.html.

Thrift, Nigel. 2008. *Non-Representational Theory: Space, Politics, Affect.* New York: Routledge.

Tsing, Anna Lowenhaupt. 2015. *The Mushroom at the End of the World.* Princeton: Princeton University Press.

Waldrop, M. Mitchell. 1992. *Complexity: The Emerging Science at the Edge and Order of Chaos.* New York, NY: Simon & Schuster.

Wodka, Adam. 2016. 'U.S. Kitchen Incubators: An Industry Update.' *American Communities Trust, Econsult Solutions, and Urbane Development.* March. Accessed 30 October 2016. www.actimpact.org/wp-content/uploads/2016/03/U.S.-Kitchen-Incubators-An-Industry-Update_Final.pdf.

World Wildlife Fund. 2016. 'Appalachian Mixed Mesophytic Forests.' Description Biological Distinctiveness. Accessed 12 November 2016. www.worldwildlife.org/ecoregions/na0402.

4.8

PERMACULTURE AND ECOLOGICAL LIFESTYLE

A Restricted Radicalism?[1]

Bürge Abiral

'So you're working on permaculture? I thought it was a middle class thing!' exclaimed a fellow scholar in a conference I attended at the University of York in 2014. I had given a presentation that same day on permaculture, an ecological design system and a philosophy of action used and promoted to create sustainable livelihoods. My talk focused on the life-style and anti-consumption strategies employed by permaculturists in Turkey. The comment came out almost depreciatively, as if permaculture as 'a middle class thing' could have little connection to the title of our conference, 'Resources of Resistance: Production, Consumption, Transformation'.

In fact, my colleague had a valid point, albeit one that I had not necessarily dismissed in my talk. As a term newly entering the vocabulary of urbanites, permaculture was little known in Turkey when I started my Master's research in 2014, except among educated people from middle and upper-middle classes. Over the one and a half year in which I conducted my research, many people I interacted with in my daily life inquired about the topic of my thesis. Most often, they had no idea what permaculture is. Otherwise, several people who were already acquainted with permaculture told me that they had seen the term in a café in Cihangir, an upscale neighbourhood in Istanbul that became gentrified starting in the 1990s. They were referring to a hipster-style café which hosts the books published by Sinek Sekiz, an ecologically oriented publishing house that printed Bill Mollison's *Introduction to Permaculture* in Turkish (Mollison 2012). This random acquaintance with permaculture among urbanites I interacted with indicated the relative visibility of permaculture in alternative yet stylish spaces in Istanbul, and conversely its possible invisibility in others.

Two years later, I presented another chapter from my MA thesis, this time on apocalypticism and hope in permaculture circles, at the annual meeting of the American Anthropological Association. I mentioned in my talk that permaculture appealed especially to middle- and upper-middle-class circles in Turkey and emphasised the privileged positions of those who identify as permaculturists. After the panel, an anthropologist working in the highly politicised Dersim region in Turkey approached me to share an ethnographic instance from her field site. In a meeting of revolutionaries, permaculture had been discussed and people had come to the conclusion that she conveyed to me: 'Permaculture is actually revolutionary!' Her criticism of my talk implied that my assertion of permaculture's middle-class appeal would dismiss its revolutionary potential.

I start with these different perceptions of permaculture, as people from various walks of life relayed to me in conversations, not simply because they show the differential under-standings that permaculture conveys at large – at least in Turkey and in the UK – but also because they point to a theoretical conundrum: how to establish the radicalness of perma-culture? Is it simply a middle-class movement that remains limited in its reach and scope and does not concern itself with the plight of farmers, or is it a 'revolution disguised as organic farming', or 'as gardening' as some suggest, carrying the promise of larger societal change (Babbs 2012; Alexander 2016)? What prospect does it hold, if at all, as a global movement in our contemporary moment in which the world's agriculture is highly privatised and industrialised?

Permaculture is an all-encompassing approach to systems design which recognises the interrelatedness of different spheres of life, and which deals not only with sustainable food production, but also with self-sustaining shelters, self-sufficient communities and resil-ient economies. A holy book for permaculturists, Bill Mollison's *Permaculture: A Designer's Manual* outlines in detail the ethical, social and ecological groundwork for all things re-lated to permaculture, from landscape design to methods for organising community and building resilience. In the very first pages, Mollison sets the tone of the book as a call to action. He writes,

> The world can no longer sustain the damage caused by modern agriculture, monocul-tural forestry, and thoughtless settlement design, and in the near future we will see the end of wasted energy, or the end of civilization as we know it, due to human-caused pollution and climate change.
>
> *(Mollison 2002, i)*

Surely, these words sound quite radical. The call that Mollison made years ago found fol-lowers worldwide, and today permaculture is a global movement of people who imagine a future of degrowth and a reversal of the capitalist and consumerist world order. Yet, the local articulations of this movement vary. In Turkey, for instance, being a permaculturist, in addition to giving courses and spreading permaculture as a worldview, often remains limited to lifestyle activism and anti-consumption strategies.

Within the existing literature, permaculture is often discussed uncritically, as unproblem-atically radical (for a very early exception, see Furze 1992). In their introduction to the edited collection titled *Environmental Anthropology Engaging Ecotopia: Bioregionalism, Permaculture, and Ecovillages*, anthropologists Joshua Lockyer and James Veteto (2013) describe these three movements as ecotopian (ecologically utopian) for positing 'imaginative responses and viable alternatives' (1) to current socio-economic and environmental injustices, and oppose them, albeit implicitly, to the politics of protest, which they seem to find ineffective and seek to 'move beyond' (6). Indeed, permaculture suggests 'an alternative paradigm of development' (Veteto and Lockyer 2013, 96) which challenges many assumptions about human-nature relationships and which proposes local solutions to global problems. Yet, closer analytical scrutiny needs to be given to the model of social change proposed by permaculture, one that 'emphasizes individual personal responsibility and voluntary action [with] a relative lack of interest in influencing policy or large institutions' (Ferguson and Lovell 2014, 266).

The observations that I started with demonstrate, in other words, the two ways in which permaculture is discussed in public and academic discourses. On the one hand, some people see it as a novel and radical project, yet fail to criticise its limits and shortcomings. On the other, it is dismissed as a 'middle class thing' that carries no potential for change. In this chapter, I seek to find a middle ground that critically assesses permaculture's radicalness without dismissing its promise. By the term 'radical', I use the dictionary definition of 'going to the root or origin' of a problem. Of course, this usage entails an ability to promote positive societal transformation, a structural change at the macro level. In discussing permaculture, however, it may be useful to distinguish between its theoretical promise and its practical application. At first glance, the theory of permaculture presents a radical critique of the neo-liberal world order. Yet, theory also informs practice; while the techniques that permaculture introduces may help people become self-sufficient in food production, and show substantial promise for food sovereignty and food security against the monopoly of transnational capital, they also allow for ample flexibility. As a result, while permaculturists' aspirations are radical – as they wish to enact substantial change in the world at a large scale – the effects of their actions remain restricted. Even though permaculture provides a radical critique of the current agro-food system and capitalist world order, it does not transform into structural change.

In this chapter, I focus on two factors that I identify as limiting the radicalness of permaculture: the flexibility that permacultural theory provides for practice, and the need for educational and economic capital for the practical application of permaculture, which keeps it rather restricted to middle and upper-middle classes in many countries. I begin with a detailed description of permaculture and of its conceptualisation of social change, and describe the process of becoming a 'certified' permaculturist. Then, I zoom in on the permaculture community in Turkey, as a case study which demonstrates that even though permaculture has radical proposals with regard to organising as communities at the grass roots, these may remain in the background. In a country like Turkey, permaculture activism becomes a matter of proving the viability of the cultivation technique in rural compounds, or of lifestyle activism in urban centres. I then turn to the literature on lifestyle activism to discuss how lifestyle becomes a space of action and what promise it holds in permaculture. I conclude with considerations of permaculture experiments elsewhere in the world, emphasising permaculture's potential, one that currently remains unrealised for larger social change.

Permaculture Worldwide: The Why and the How

Permaculture is an ethical landscape design approach introduced in the 1970s by Bill Mollison and David Holmgren in Australia, in order to provide an alternative integrated system of livelihood that cares not solely for humans, but for all beings. In the words of Mollison,

> Permaculture (permanent agriculture) is the conscious design and maintenance of agriculturally productive ecosystems which have the diversity, stability, and resilience of natural ecosystems. It is the harmonious integration of landscape and people providing their food, energy, shelter, and other material and non-material needs in a sustainable way. Without permanent agriculture there is no possibility of a stable social order.
>
> *(Mollison 2002, ix)*

Developed as a reaction to the destructive effects of the hegemonic global economic order and industrialised agriculture which have been destroying the soil and local/indigenous knowledge(s), and threatening independent food systems, permaculture originates from the counterculture movements of the 1960s and 1970s (Lockyer and Veteto 2013). According to David Holmgren, 'permaculture was one of the environmental alternatives which emerged from the first great wave of modern environmental awareness, following the Club of Rome report in 1972 and the oil shocks of 1973 and 1975' (2002, xvii). In their review of the literature on permaculture, Ferguson and Lovell characterise it as 'an alternative agroecology movement', and describe how the design system relates to the movement and the ethical principles: 'Permaculture is (1) an international and regional movement that disseminates and practices (2) a design system and (3) a best practice framework. The design system and best practice framework are contextualised by (4) the worldview that is carried by the movement' (2014, 255). In other words, the term permaculture connotes all at the same time a movement, a design system, a practical framework and a worldview. The decentralised structure of the movement makes it grow in both formal and informal networks.

The permaculture movement maintains close relations with the ecovillages' movement (Lockyer and Veteto 2013), with several ecovillages adopting the principles of permaculture (Dawson 2006; Burke and Arjona 2013). It has also given rise to other movements. In 2004, for instance, permaculture designer Rob Hopkins initiated the Transition Town Movement in the United Kingdom and founded the Transition Network in 2006 in order to encourage communities to become self-sufficient to buffer the effects of peak oil and climate change (Neal 2013). Other design systems such as holistic management, initiated by Allan Savory (Savory and Butterfield 1999; 2016), resemble permaculture, as do other movements such as those around voluntary simplicity (Maniates 2002b), Slow Food (Leitch 2000; Andrews 2008), Slow City (Pink 2008) and off-grid living (Rosen 2010; Vannini and Taggart 2015), to name a few.

Mollison's official life narrative as it appears in the first few pages of *A Designer's Manual* is often relayed in permaculture courses to give a sense of his multilayered background and character. The 'father' of permaculture was born in 1928 in a small fishing village in Tasmania, Australia. He worked in various professions during his lifetime, including as a baker, wilderness researcher, fisherman, environmental psychologist and biologist. In 1954, he worked as a wildlife manager and conducted fieldwork and long-term observations of various plants and animals. In 1974, he developed the concept of permaculture with his student David Holmgren and devoted his life to further improving and spreading the design system after leaving the university once and for all in 1978. He then started to give permaculture courses all over the world. Mollison and Holmgren together devised an education system by which to spread permaculture and developed the curriculum of the Permaculture Design Course (PDC). They also established the Permaculture Research Institute (PRI) in Australia, the main institution of permaculture, which was later also established in other countries through formal affiliation, including in Turkey.

In his *A Designer's Manual*, Mollison suggests that permaculture, as an ethical practice, combines modern and indigenous knowledge and wisdom, and highlights how social change would occur through the coming together of individual and collective actions. He emphasises the need to take action in the present to recover what is lost, and suggests permaculture practice as the way out of ecological crisis. The book outlines the three basic principles permaculture is based on: 'care of the Earth, care of people, and setting limits to population and consumption' (Mollison 2002, 2). Over time, the highly contested last principle came to be articulated variously as the distribution and return of surplus, or 'fair share'. Mollison's ethical codes are complemented by twelve design principles outlining key approaches towards designing sustainable landscapes with low external input: 'Observe and Interact', 'Capture and Store Energy', 'Obtain a Yield', 'Apply Self-regulation and Accept Feedback', 'Use and Value Renewable Resources and Services', 'Produce No Waste', 'Design from Patterns to Details', 'Integrate Rather Than Segregate', 'Use Small and Slow Solutions', 'Use and Value Diversity', 'Use Edges and Value the Marginal' and 'Creatively Use and Respond' (Holmgren 2002, viii).

The idea of imitating natural processes runs deep in permaculture design. Observing ecosystems, interacting with them, evaluating any feedback and then acting in accordance with natural processes is the key. Practitioners who will design a landscape are usually advised to observe the area for a year, and only then create their design plan. Yet, this recommendation is rarely followed, as it would take a lot of time and other resources to engage in such detailed observation. As Mollison acknowledges, 'Nothing we can observe is regular, partly because we ourselves are imperfect observers' (2002, 71). What he proposes is then a general understanding of natural patterns as flexible ground rules to follow. While these basic guidelines would pertain to any physical design of space, permaculture also involves the organisation of communities. This is what some people call 'social permaculture' or 'social design'. Even though Veteto and Lockyer define permaculture as 'an ecotopian methodology' (2013, 11), the worldview that is propagated through permaculture accompanies the design system. Permaculture then provides 'a conceptual framework for the evaluation and adoption of practices, rather than a bundle of techniques' (Ferguson and Lovell 2014, 264).

Mollison's famous aphorism 'Though the problems of the world are increasingly complex, the solutions remain embarrassingly simple' – often rephrased as 'The problem is the solution' – points to the belief that 'the solutions to environmental and social crises [are] both simple and known' (Ferguson and Lovell 2014, 266). The last chapter of *A Designer's Manual*, named 'Strategies for an Alternative Nation' (or as in the table of contents, 'The Strategies of An Alternative *Global* Nation'), also known as 'Chapter 14' among permaculturists, outlines the blueprint for building a global permaculture network which, while existing within the capitalist economy, would strive to remain as independent from it as possible by establishing food sovereignty and self-sufficiency in all kinds of production. Mollison suggests a plethora of strategies to devise alternative systems of invisible structures – 'the intangible elements necessary for the healthy functioning of a system' (Brock n.d.) – from bioregional organisation and local consumption, to the creation of local currencies and alternative banks. In the chapter, Mollison suggests an alternative definition of 'nation' as 'a people subscribing to a common ethic' (2002, 508; emphasis removed), thus implicitly suggesting the erasure of national borders and nation states through the establishment of morally connected self-sufficient communities. Yet, one need not necessarily start an ecovillage to practise permaculture. The design system can be applied in diverse settings; for instance, a family can grow food in their balcony or garden using permaculture principles and reduce their dependence on outside consumption. This flexibility allows practitioners to start small and do whatever they can with the resources available at their disposal.

In his *Manual*, Mollison places special emphasis on personal responsibility for Earth repair. He writes, 'Although this book is about design, it is also about values and ethics, and above all about a sense of personal responsibility' (2002, 1). He thus suggests a move away from traditional forms of engaging in politics towards the reclamation of individual and communal responsibilities for self-empowerment and change:

> The tragic reality is that very few sustainable systems are designed or applied by those who hold power, and the reason for this is obvious and simple: to let people arrange their own food, energy, and shelter is to lose economic and political control over them. We should cease to look to power structures, hierarchical systems, or governments to help us, and devise ways to help ourselves.
>
> *(2002, 506)*

Mollison suggests a move away from the politics of protest and traditional forms of organising to instead take the future of Earth repair in one's own hands. Preaching cooperation and creativity, he envisions permaculture practice as having the potential to appeal to a wide range of people regardless of their religious beliefs and political affiliations, as long as they subscribe to the ethical principles of care. When it comes to practise, however, this conceptualisation of social change as available to everyone and possible at all costs does not necessarily recognise the structural obstacles that may prevent people from participating in the movement. Differently put, the theoretical and methodological flexibility put forth by Mollison disables permaculture and many of its practitioners from recognising different forms of structural violence that need to be addressed.

The Process of Becoming a Permaculturist

The flexible and seemingly decentralised structure of the permaculture movement is regulated through a centralised system of expertise recognition, managed through the PRIs worldwide and the PDC. The PDC is a seventy-two-hour official training that covers a set curriculum summarising the gist of *A Designer's Manual*, almost always taken with a fee. Prospective permaculturists are inundated with novel information during this intense course and learn the details of what it means to design a landscape. Usually, PDCs take place in a rural compound and last between 10 and 14 days, allowing the participants to experience communal and ecological living situations, both of which are important aspects of permaculture. As such, they act as rites of passages and provide a real conversion experience, a transition in a person's life from a passive to an active state whereby she is trained to think and act permaculturally. At times, however, classes are offered in cities, and the training is spread to seven weekends. Online classes are also available. PDCs end with a practical project for which participants design a space according to permaculture principles.

When a student graduates from the PDC, she receives a Permaculture Design Certificate, which certifies her expertise and gives her the legal licence to use the term 'permaculture' in her designs. Practitioners have estimated that there were between 100,000 and 150,000 PDC graduates worldwide in 2011 (Tortorello 2011). This licencing system is not uncontested within the permaculture community, as for some it represents a capitalist logic of ownership. Yet, most permaculturists would defend the need for certification and patenting in order to prevent people from using the name of permaculture for purposes that would oppose its ethical principles, i.e. full-blown capitalist enterprises or profit-making courses.

While the PDC constitutes the first step to become a permaculture practitioner, there are further formally recognised training opportunities, such as internships in permaculture farms. One of the most popular internships takes place in Zaytuna Farms, famous instructor Geoff Lawton's farm in Australia, where permaculturists learn to practise the different aspects of permaculture, including taking care of animals, growing food forests and community-building, for around three and a half months, again for a considerable sum of money. Smaller, more specialised courses are also offered post-PDC, such as rainwater harvesting, detailed compost methods and disaster relief. Overall, even if courses were free, permaculture disseminates through educational activities which require a penchant for learning in classroom settings as much as on land, and the acquisition of further knowledge through a self-initiated learning process with books and videos. These means may not be accessible to many, as they require free time, literacy and access to technology. What I describe here is, of course, a generalised version of the learning process, and may vary from one setting to another. In the case that anthropologist Abigail Conrad (2014) explores, for instance, some farmers in Malawi apply permaculture to their fields without necessarily receiving formal training, as they acquire knowledge mostly through observation and social learning. Therefore, the process I describe here may be most relevant for those who have no prior farming knowledge.

Ultimately, a practitioner may go through the Teacher Training Course offered by the PRI and build a professional profile (see https://permacultureglobal.org/users). This profile system encompasses the formal trainings one has gone through, almost replicating the formality of the mainstream educational system. Some PDC teachers are affiliated with the official PRIs; others work independently. While these trainings are recognised to reflect a practitioner's stages of expertise, the permaculture community commonly acknowledges the significance of on-site practice. Internships are significant for that reason. Some permaculturists go on to establish their own farms and start practising permaculture on their own land. Some also work as permaculture consultants, advising others in their farms.

The Case in Turkey

As part of permaculture's worldwide proliferation, Turkey has seen its spread, even if on a modest scale, in both urban and rural areas. The country's first encounter with permaculture was in 1990, when permaculture instructor Max Lindegger gave a PDC in Hocamköy, a rural ecological initiative in central Anatolia. Hocamköy did not live to last, and permaculture remained rather dormant until 2009 when several people simultaneously set out to organise workshops and courses on the topic, training others to become permaculturists. That same year, Marmariç Ecological Life Association, a non-governmental organisation and ecovillage initiative in an abandoned village near Izmir, decided to implement permaculture in its compound and started a project supported by the UN Global Environmental Facility's Small Grants Programme (Marmariç Ekolojik Yaşam Derneği 2011). In 2011, the permaculturists at Marmariç officially established the Permaculture Research Institute of Turkey. As the number of practitioners increased with time through PDCs, some went on to become instructors; therefore, the total number of courses and workshops offered in Turkey has been increasing almost exponentially for the past several years. The Gezi protests, which erupted in 2013 against the demolition of a public park in Istanbul and the oppressive power of the governing Justice and Development Party, also became a turning point for permaculture's visibility. As protestors engaged in solidarity and urban gardening experiments during the occupation of the park, the term 'permaculture' became more widely known.

In Turkey as elsewhere, many stages of the official permaculture training require economic resources and free time. In the summer of 2017, a fourteen-day PDC at the Permaculture Institute of Turkey costs 2,900 Turkish Liras (about 600 GBP) – almost double the gross monthly minimum wage. Many permaculturists stress that scholarships are available and that some people have access to the PDC for free for that reason; yet, criticisms against the high pricing of this course abound. There have been efforts to decrease and waive this fee, among them a municipally subsidised free PDC organised in Bursa in 2015 by instructor Taner Aksel.

Currently, the most commonly known farms that identify themselves as permaculture initiatives are Marmariç, Kızıltepe and Aksel's Belentepe. These initiatives are chiefly intended to prove permaculture's efficacy as a cultivation technique, and serve as spaces for hosting PDCs, other courses and internships. Unfortunately, there is not much communication or interaction between settler permaculturists and small-scale farmers, limiting the spread of permaculture to people whose profession is farming. Interviews with permaculturists living in the countryside reveal that farmers in their locality often perceive them with suspicion, criticise their curious approach and do not see permaculture as a feasible alternative to conventional farming. Permaculturists, however, believe that once they prove permaculture's viability, especially to the extent of making some financial profit, farmers may join them.[2]

Of course, settling on land, whether to set up a permaculture farm or to grow a small garden in a village, requires considerable initial capital. Those who for financial or other reasons do not switch to a rural lifestyle come together in cities. In Istanbul, Permablitz served as a gathering hub for permaculturists and those who were interested in learning about the design system between 2012 and 2013. Based on a counterpart model in Australia, Permablitz involved a day in which people gathered together to design someone's garden, usually one of the participants. These gatherings were a way for recent PDC graduates to practise their knowledge, and for new volunteers to get engaged with permaculture. They also served as a recruitment ground for future permaculturists, as many volunteers later went on to take the PDC. Permablitz was succeeded by another urban initiative, the Istanbul Permaculture Collective. This initiative organises courses and workshops in diverse practical skills including composting, beekeeping, soap- and cheese-making, and ecological healthy cooking.

The majority of permaculturists in Turkey are working-age adults who already possess educational and economic capital. The younger ones are likely to rely on their parents' capital to engage in permaculture, from the stage of attending courses and workshops to, if they do so, buying land and settling on it. That most permaculturists in Turkey are from middle and upper-middle classes is surely related to the political and economic developments in the recent history of the country. Turkey experienced several military interventions over the last fifty years; the 1980 coup d'état most severely interrupted political opposition and paved the way for a neo-liberal economy. These developments have often been associated with a subsequent depoliticisation of youth and public discourse. It is true that state violence and fear increased the stakes for political participation after the 1980 coup, but more accurately, it was people from a certain class background that were, in the words of sociologist Demet Lüküslü, 'socialised in a largely unopposed system of neo-liberalism' (2005, 34). Being integrated into a rising consumer society, they remained sceptical even towards the limited available means of political participation. Middle and upper-middle classes, instead of aspiring for political change, were now moved by aspirations of upward mobility, consumption and personal happiness.

If the permaculture movement in Turkey has thus far failed to cross class lines and to extend from the middle and upper-middle strata to economically underprivileged sections of society, especially peasants, it also has not been successful in crossing ethnic lines, and to cooperate with other social and political movements, especially the Kurdish movement.[3] Contrary to my initial expectations, some of my permaculturist interlocutors grew up in previously 'revolutionary' families, and had themselves been involved in leftist organising, yet later quit their respective organisation or group. Still, the majority fell under the category of 'depoliticised' in their university years, meaning that they had little to do with politics as such. Therefore, permaculturists' current lack of engagement with other forms of organising in Turkey derives either from previous involvement with and disillusionment about leftist politics, or from lack of familiarity with other forms of organising. The latter stance also involves a mistrust and bias not only against the left, but also about politics in general. In a context in which most channels of involvement in grassroots politics were either closed or deemed inappropriate or futile, permaculture made sense as a way of acting in the world. This is because its special emphasis on individualised actions leading to collective change fit well with the dominant neo-liberal paradigm in Turkey whereby youth developed an alternative understanding of political participation that accentuated individual choices (see Neyzi 2001; Lüküslü 2005). In this context, the flexibility of permaculture allows people to establish lifestyle as a space of action due to structural constraints. I now take a closer look at such lifestyle activism.

Lifestyle as a Space of Action

At the time of my fieldwork, several of my interlocutors had already transitioned to a rural lifestyle, which to a great extent requires radical changes in one's comfort level and consumption habits. Almost all countryside-based 'permies' grow a small portion of their own food, procure the rest from other local and preferably sustainable producers, and engage in permaculture experiments in their land to serve as models to others. Some live with other people, also experimenting with communal living situations, while others experience rural life with their significant others or by themselves, all the while keeping in close contact with other back-to-the-landers in their area.

For permaculturally trained urbanites, however, moving to a village may not be an option right away for reasons including lack of economic capital and lack of community with whom to start a permaculture initiative. If one has a garden, which is quite exceptional in a metropolis like Istanbul, one can always design it according to permaculture principles, and start to grow one's own good in the city. If not, even a small balcony may suffice. If growing tomatoes and peppers in one's balcony is not that convenient, there are always simpler plants and herbs such as basil, mint and parsley, which can be easily grown in small pots in the kitchen. As one permaculturist put it during a presentation at an environmental gathering,

> We're in the city, we consume, but what's important is to change our options a little bit more, I mean, even if you can't do anything, start little by little or start to grow things, your tomato, your pepper, I don't know, your parsley, if you grow only parsley, then you won't be buying *that* from the supermarket, *at the least*.

This reasoning echoes permaculture's emphasis on starting small within the possible range available to a person. A permaculturist can also raise earthworms in a tub or aquarium, to will turn her leftover food into compost. These little red worms (*eisenia fetida*) reproduce quickly and are so popular in the permaculture community that during get-togethers, permies jokingly compete over whose worms are the most numerous and the healthiest.

Myriad other ways in which permaculturists who live in Istanbul can *do something* revolve around consumption. They can bake their own bread or ferment their own yogurt, kefir and pickles instead of buying them. On a more collective level, they can participate in exchange and barter networks such as Zumbara, a time bank where people exchange services on the basis of time instead of money, and Eşya Kütüphanesi (Library of Stuff), a platform where participants borrow and lend their goods, including electronics, clothes and musical instruments. A permaculturist in Istanbul can always acquire her clothes from the barter markets. Even when buying produce, there are organic markets or consumer cooperatives that directly buy from the producer. These have also been proliferating in Turkey, bringing together concerned urbanites and farmers who produce food without using agrochemicals. This direct exchange whereby small-scale farmers receive the worth of their labour,[4] some believe, may encourage other farmers to produce ecologically, if not permaculturally.

At times, these small actions can turn into bigger campaigns. For instance, the Slow Food chapter in Turkey started in 2010 as an organised consumer campaign against the sale of bluefish under 24 centimetres. Fish caught and sold under this size have not yet produced offspring, thus increasing the threat of extinction in Istanbul's waters. The campaign co-incided with another campaign by Greenpeace Mediterranean that drew attention to the catch of small fish in general. Slow Food activists thus created an influential lobby for policy change and petitioned the authorities. While the campaign proved effective in bringing civil society actors together and pushing for change, the new regulation increased the catch length from 14 centimetres to only 19, still not adequate to allow for the fish to reproduce. Even so, together with the Greenpeace campaign, Slow Food pointed to the potential impact of consumer movements on supply and production. This action perspective is epitomised in the word 'prosumer', a combination of 'producer' and 'consumer', coined by futurist author Alvin Toffler in 1980 and co-opted by the Slow Food movement (Toffler 1980). Its counterpart in Turkish is 'türetici', a combination of 'tüketici' and 'üretici'. The idea behind the word itself is often articulated when permaculturists link their consumption practices to their possible effects on the production of market goods, energy and so forth.

Sociologist Mike Featherstone (1987, 55) argues that lifestyle connotes 'individuality, self-expression, and stylistic self-consciousness'. Accordingly, 'one's body, clothes, speech, leisure pastimes, eating and drinking preferences, home, car, choice of holidays, etc., are to be regarded as indicators of the individuality of taste and sense of style of the owner/consumer'. This 'reflexive project of the self', as described by sociologist Anthony Giddens (1991, 5), is intricately tied to one's consumption choice and everyday habits. Scholars in various fields, including sociology, environmental studies and marketing, have conducted research on the relationship between alternative consumption practices related to lifestyle choices and their political repercussions through concepts like green consumption (Czarnezki 2011), political consumerism (Micheletti 2003; Micheletti and Stolle 2008) and commodity activism (Banet-Weiser and Mukherjee 2012). These analyses mostly focus on the US or European countries, where alternative consumption and green living practices have been spreading since the 1970s (Maniates 2002a), along with awareness of environmental problems. Some scholars almost uncritically acclaim such lifestyle practices and their potential to bring about cultural, social and political changes (see, e.g., Czarnezki 2011). Others, however, harshly criticise individual acts of green consumption for laying responsibility on individuals and ignoring the structurally produced and enhanced economic and political causes of environmental problems (Maniates 2002a; Schutz 2009a; Schutz 2009b; Maniates 2012). An early critic of this trend was Murray Bookchin, who, despite his earlier emphasis on holistic and non-instrumental approaches to radicalism (1979), became a harsh critic of 'lifestyle anarchism', arguing that 'If 'simple living' and militant recycling are the main solutions to the environmental crisis, the crisis will certainly continue and intensify' (Bookchin 1989, 22; see also Bookchin 1995).

According to Maniates, several factors contributed to the mass individualisation of responsibility to free the world from environmental ills, including the rising conservatism in the US in the 1980s and the then-president Ronald Reagan's 'doctrine of personal responsibility, corporate initiative, and limited government' (2002, 53). While these political and economic developments are partially responsible for the spread of individualised solutions, Maniates also blames the appropriate technology movements of the 1970s, for they redirected responsibility from governments to individuals, while also convincing governments and corporations to invest in technological advances to 'save the world'. According to media and communication scholar Tania Lewis, a 'growing cynicism regarding political will in relation to environmental issues at a state and federal level' is also a possible reason for which people turn to green practices (2015, 2).

While these criticisms unquestionably raise valid points, few studies take on an ethnographic lens and focus on the motivations of people who deliberately engage in alternative consumption patterns. Communication scholar Laura Portwood-Stacer's (2013) study of anarchists in the US is one of the few exceptions, in its attempt to understand the meanings and practices associated with lifestyle by scrutinising consumption patterns, personal style and practices of sexual nonconformity. Through her close encounter with anarchist groups, Portwood-Stacer offers a nuanced analysis that goes beyond the either/or divide. Discussing the kinds of meanings associated with lifestyle changes and emphasising that anarchists combine lifestyle with other political strategies, instead of giving up on the latter, she argues that 'the strategic deployment of lifestyle tactics pursued by radical activists is not the same as the a-strategic preoccupation with the self encouraged by neoliberal ideology' (6). Giving a detailed account of the different lifestyle strategies that US anarchists employ, Portwood-Stacer argues that while some strategies serve for 'personal gratification', others confirm one's 'moral rectitude', while others work to enhance 'social communication'. While some are used towards 'activist intervention', some become 'identificatory performance'. All in all, Portwood-Stacer shows that lifestyle tactics are not always necessarily about inducing change, but they may, in some instances, serve that end, and they always serve one or several of these other purposes.

The recognition of the very similar context in Turkey, which I have described in the previous section, does not therefore mean that lifestyle strategies are simply a capitalist co-optation of dissent, and that permaculturists are merely serving neo-liberal ideology. Such an approach would not only refuse to acknowledge the subjectivities of permaculturists who strongly strive to live ethically and thus influence others for larger change, but would also ignore the specific interruptions they manage to make into neo-liberal discourses. Critiques of lifestyle activism, for instance, often do not make an analytical distinction between the greening of consumption and a significant reduction in consumption. In other words, they criticise the turn of consumers to green or fair trade products, as Maniates (2002a, 58) puts it, 'feeling bad and guilty about far-off mega-environmental destruction, and then traveling down to the corner store to find a "green" product whose purchase will somehow empower somebody, somewhere, to do good'. All the permaculturists I interacted with, however, are well aware of the dangers of green capitalism and constantly criticise it. Instead of buying into these marketing strategies which do more harm than good, they significantly reduce their consumption and seek out alternative consumption routes. While many permaculturists who live in cities would also mostly buy organic, they acknowledge that organic agriculture bears its own problems. As a design system that values diversity, permaculture positions itself against all types of monocultural agriculture, whether organic or not.

Criticisms of lifestyle activism also work to create binaries between the personal and the collective, the individual and the institutional, and constantly articulate these as dichotomous categories. Permaculturists, however, strive to forge links between the two, by, for instance, organising collective events and appealing to municipalities for local change. There is a constant recognition that the success of lifestyle activism overall depends on the collective, that is, on other people's actions. If everyone engages in these types of ecologically aware actions, then the world might change; they constantly repeat. While the assumption that everyone may engage in these actions sounds at first naïve, this statement also recognises its own failure. On the one hand, then, there is a strong desire to change the world through one's own actions, while, on the other, many permies recognise the difficulty, if not the impossibility, of doing so.

While lifestyle activism in and of itself may not enable structural change, it can provide a ground on which to build collectivities at moments of opportunity. For instance, when protestors occupied Gezi Park in 2013, some immediately established a vegetable garden at one corner of the park. The few groups that engage in community gardens and sustainable food production in the city, some of which are permaculturists, thus made a statement that linked the reclaiming of public space to sovereignty over food production. Permaculturists' existing networks and experience also served to organise people, both during the occupation of the park and in its aftermath. For example, there were calls to avoid shopping malls during the protests, as it was a mall that was planned in place of the park. As one of the permaculturists put it, 'People kept saying, "Don't go to malls." [My friend] and I thought, "Ok, you keep telling them not to go to the malls," all the time something based on *not doing*, alright, but *what are they gonna do?* That's what we need to tell them 'cause they don't know any alternatives'. This speaker was active in organising barter markets as part of the neighbourhood forums that became prominent after the police brutally ended the occupation of the park. In these forums, alternative economy experiments proliferated. In addition, permaculture activists have been influential in revitalising several urban gardens in Istanbul, and thus reclaiming public space after the Gezi protests. These examples suggest that permaculture organising around lifestyle and consumption can provide possible resources in times of otherwise unexpected political events. If permaculture does not right away change social practice, it prepares a basis for future engagements when opportunities arise. It carries the potential to transform into politically effective action under the right circumstances. This contingency, however, also means that permaculture may never materialise into larger change, a condition which is openly recognised by many permaculturists.

Conclusion

'[Permaculture] came into the picture [in Turkey] as a very petit bourgeois thing, (…) I'm a little disappointed 'cause it works in fact a bit like a hobby gardening thing here', told me one of the permaculturists I interviewed. In this view, gardening was not working as a revolution in Turkey, as it was supposed to be, but as a 'petty bourgeois' 'hobby'. The disillusionment expressed by the permaculturist only arises because he had seen something inherently radical and revolutionary in permaculture. Thus, his statement simultaneously points to permaculture's radical potential *and* its failure. However, the recognition of this failure does not prevent permaculturists from constantly asserting permaculture's potential. The utterer of this sentence is one of the people who do not give up emphasising permaculture's necessity in the world today. Many of the permaculturists in Turkey often refer to examples elsewhere in the world to justify permaculture's feasibility and potential success, including the crisis-induced rise of solidarity economies in Greece (see Rakopolous 2014); Geoff Lawton's 'Greening the Desert' project in Jordan whereby a particularly dry and saline landscape was transformed into a productive one (see 'Greening the Desert' 2007); and the rise of urban agriculture in Cuba. Oftentimes, these references may be misleading, however. As scholars point out, while coming out of necessity, urban agriculture has been a state-sponsored project in Cuba, incorporated into a patriotic revolutionary discourse, and did not even potentially challenge the status quo (Premat 2009; Gold 2014).

Even though permaculturists in Turkey believe that adoption of permaculture by more people, especially by farmers, would be one step towards larger change, research in Malawi shows that permaculture adoption by a number of peasants as a cultivation technique did not necessarily lead to a structural change in the agro-food system in the country (Conrad 2014).

Instead, permaculture adoption, when compared to conventional farming, creates a buffer against malnutrition and food insecurity in Malawi, but does not completely solve these issues. Together with a positive effect on the nutrition and health for farmers overall, it improves farmers' adaptive capacity to climatic and economic vulnerabilities, yet with effects remaining limited to the household level.

Critics blame permaculture for being focused on individual solutions. It is accurate that Mollison's recommended path for social change starts at the individual, and such view does not always recognise the structural obstacles that may prevent people from participating in the permaculture movement, such as lack of capital or free time for learning (Furze 1992). Conrad (2014, 85), too, writes, 'I suggest that the methods that many permaculturalists promote are neo-liberal because of the emphasis on individual action and responsibility'. Throughout this chapter, I tried to complicate the suggestion that permaculture is neo-liberal. The methods put forth by permaculture texts are not neo-liberal in and of themselves, as there is much emphasis on prefigurative and collective grassroots organising and action as delineated in *A Designer's Manual*. However, these methods are by default interpreted and put into action in a neo-liberal context, such as in the post-coup Turkey, with individual solutions taking precedent. This incongruity largely arises from the methodological flexibility inherent in permacultural theory. Together with the problematic of unequal access through paid courses and workshops, permaculture's radicalism thus remains limited, and only exists as a potential. The task ahead then, as Furze (1994, 154) insightfully writes, should be 'to ensure [that] the potential is realised'.

Notes

1 I would like to thank Hira Doğrul and Uri Gordon for their insightful comments on the chapter.
2 It is important to mention here that it takes up to several years to set up a landscape completely according to permaculture principles. According to some permaculturists in Turkey, this temporal lag is one of the reasons why they have not been able to prove permaculture's viability to other farmers in their locality. The claim that permaculture can be commercially profitable because of the low input it requires may be challenged by Conrad's (2014) study of farmers in Malawi: while farmers who switched to permaculture became mostly self-sufficient, thus independent of the market, permaculture practice mostly provided for their household needs, and did not necessarily bring any commercial gain.
3 This seems to be not much different from the situation in the US where the permaculture movement is predominantly white (Ferguson 2014). Even though I have heard bits and pieces about possible cooperation between permaculturists and the Kurdish movement, there is no collaboration to date.
4 Farmers often receive more profit in direct exchange with customers than what they receive after selling their produce to wholesale commissioners.

References

Alexander, Samuel. 2016. 'A Revolution Disguised as Organic Gardening: in Memory of Bill Mollison' *The Conversation US*, September 28. Accessed on December 11, 2017, at https://theconversation.com/a-revolution-disguised-as-organic-gardening-in-memory-of-bill-mollison-66137.

Andrews, Geoff. 2008. *The Slow Food Story*. London: Pluto Press.

Babbs, Helen. 2012. 'Diary of a Window Box Garden: The Permaculture Prescription' *The Guardian*, April 13. Accessed on December 1, 2017, at www.theguardian.com/lifeandstyle/gardening-blog/2012/apr/13/diary-window-box-garden-permaculture.

Banet-Weiser, Sarah, and Roopali Mukherjee. 2012. Introduction: Commodity Activism in Neoliberal Times. In *Commodity Activism: Cultural Resistance in Neoliberal Times*, edited by R. Mukherjee and S. Banet-Weiser. New York: New York University Press.

Bookchin, Murray. 1979. Post-Scarcity Anarchism. In *Contemporary Anarchism*, edited by T. M. Perlin. New Brunswick, NJ: Transaction. First published in 1971.

Bookchin, Murray.1989. Death of a Small Planet. *The Progressive*. August, p. 22.

Bookchin, Murray. 1995. *Social Anarchism or Lifestyle Anarchism: An Unbridgeable Chasm*. San Francisco, CA: AK Press.

Brock, Adam. N.d. Invisible Structures. www.peoplepattern.org/about/invisible-structures/, accessed May 15, 2015.

Burke, Brian J., and Beatriz Arjona. 2013. Creating Alternative Political Ecologies through the Construction of Ecovillages and Ecovillagers in Colombia. In *Environmental Anthropology Engaging Ecotopia: Bioregionalism, Permaculture, and Ecovillages*, edited by J. Lockyer and J. R. Veteto. New York: Berghahn Books.

Conrad, Abigail. 2014. *'We Are Farmers': Agriculture, Food Security, and Adaptive Capacity among Permaculture and Conventional Farmers in Central Malawi*. PhD Dissertation, American University.

Czarnezki, Jason, 2011. *Everyday Environmentalism: Law, Nature, & Individual Behavior*. Washington, DC: Environmental Law Institute Press.

Dawson, Jonathan. 2006. *Ecovillages: New Frontiers for Sustainability*. White River Junction, VT: Schumacher Society by Chelsea Green Pub. Co.

Featherstone, Mike. 1987. Lifestyle and Consumer Culture. *Theory, Culture and Society* 4 (1): 54–70.

Ferguson, Rafter Sass. 2014. Critical Questions for Permaculture. *Permaculture Activist*, August: 3–8.

Ferguson, Rafter Sass, and Sarah Taylor Lovell. 2014. Permaculture for Agroecology: Design, Movement, Practice, and Worldview. A Review. *Agronomy for Sustainable Development* 34 (2): 251–274.

Furze, Brian. 1992. Ecologically Sustainable Rural Development and the Difficulty of Social Change. *Environmental Values* 1 (2): 141–155.

Giddens, Anthony 1991. *Modernity and Self-Identity: Self and Society in the Late Modern Age*. Stanford, CA: Stanford University Press.

Gold, Marina. 2014. Peasant, Patriot, Environmentalist: Sustainable Development Discourse in Havana. *Bulletin of Latin American Research* 33 (4): 405–418.

'Greening the Desert'. 2007. Permaculture Research Institute blog post. Accessed on November 29, 2017 at https://permaculturenews.org/2007/03/01/greening-the-desert-now-on-youtube/.

Holmgren, David. 2002. *Permaculture: Principles & Pathways Beyond Sustainability*. Hepburn, Vic: Holmgren Design Services.

Leitch, Alison. 2000. The Social Life of Lardo. *The Asia Pacific Journal of Anthropology* 1 (1): 103–118.

Lewis, Tania. 2015. 'One City Block at a Time': Researching and Cultivating Green Transformations. *International Journal of Cultural Studies* 18 (3): 347–363, first published online on January 16, 2014.

Lockyer, Joshua, and James R. Veteto. 2013. *Environmental Anthropology Engaging Ecotopia: Bioregionalism, Permaculture, and Ecovillages*. New York: Berghahn Books.

Lüküslü, Demet G. 2005. 'Constructors and Constructed: Youth as a Political Actor in Modernising Turkey'. In *Revisiting Youth Political Participation: Challenges for Research and Democratic Practice in Europe*, edited by J. Forbig. Strasbourg: Council of Europe Publishing.

Maniates, Michael. 2002a. Individualization: Plant a Tree, Buy a Bike, Save the World?, In *Confronting Consumption*, edited by T Princen et al. Cambridge, MA: MIT Press.

Maniates, Michael. 2002b. In Search of Consumptive Resistance: The Voluntary Simplicity Movement. In *Confronting Consumption*, edited by T. Princen et al. Cambridge, MA: MIT Press.

Maniates, Michael. 2012. Everyday Possibilities. *Global Environmental Politics* 12 (1): 121–125.

Marmariç Ekolojik Yaşam Derneği. 2011. *Permakültür El Kitabı ve Marmariç Örneği*. http://permaculture turkey.org/wp-content/uploads/permakultur_el_kitabi.pdf, accessed July 21, 2014.

Micheletti, Michele. 2003. *Political Virtue and Shopping: Individuals, Consumerism, and Collective Action*. New York: Palgrave.

Micheletti, Michele, and Dietlind Stolle. 2008. Fashioning Social Justice through Political Consumerism, Capitalism, and the Internet. *Cultural Studies* 22 (5): 749–769.

Mollison, Bill. 2002. *Permaculture: A Designer's Manual*. Australia: Tagari Publications.

Mollison, Bill. 2012. *Permakültüre Giriş*. Translated by Egemen Özkan. Istanbul: Sinek Sekiz Yayınevi.

Neal, Sarah. 2013. Transition Culture: Politics, Localities and Ruralities. *Journal of Rural Studies* 32: 60–69.

Neyzi, Leyla. 2001. 'Object or Subject? The Paradox of 'youth' in Turkey. *International Journal of Middle East Studies* 33: 411–432.

Pink Sarah. 2008. Sense and Sustainability: The Case of the Slow City Movement. *Local Environment* 13 (2): 95–106.

Portwood-Stacer, Laura. 2013. *Lifestyle Politics and Radical Activism*. London: Bloomsbury Academic.

Premat, Adriana. 2009. State Power, Private Plots and the Greening of Havana's Urban Agriculture Movement. *City & Society* 21(1): 28–57.

Rakopolous, Theodoros. 2014. The Crisis Seen from Below, Within, and Against: From Solidarity Economy to Food Distribution Cooperatives in Greece. *Dialectical Anthropology* 38 (2): 189–207.

Rosen, Nick. 2010. *Off the Grid: Inside the Movement for More Space, Less Government, and True Independence in Modern America*. New York: Penguin Books.

Savory, Allan, and Jody Butterfield. 1999. *Holistic Management: A New Framework for Decision Making*. Washington, DC: Island Press.

Savory, Allan, and Jody Butterfield. 2016. *Holistic Management: A Commonsense Revolution to Restore Our Environment*. Washington, DC: Island Press.

Schutz, Aaron. 2009a. Self-Delusion and The Lie of Lifestyle Activism'. *OpenLeft*, 26 April. www.openleft.com/diary/13032/selfdelusion-and-the-lie-of-lifestyle-politics-core-dilemmas-of-community-organizing, accessed June 5, 2014.

Schutz, Aaron. 2009b. The Distortions of Lifestyle Politics. *OpenLeft*, 24 July. www.openleft.com/diary/14295/part-ii-the-distortions-of-lifestyle-politics-core-dilemmas-of-community-organizing, accessed June 5, 2014.

Toffler, Alvin. 1980. *The Third Wave*. New York: William Morrow.

Tortorello, Michael. 2011. The Permaculture Movements Grows From Underground. *New York Times*, July 27. www.nytimes.com/2011/07/28/garden/permaculture-emerges-from-the-underground.html?pagewanted=all&_r=0, accessed on April 28th, 2015.

Vannini, Phillip, and Jonathan Taggart. 2015. *Off the Grid: Re-assembling Domestic Life*. New York: Routledge.

Veteto, James R., and Joshua Lockyer. 2013. Environmental Anthropology Engaging Permaculture: Moving Theory and Practice toward Sustainability. In *Environmental Anthropology Engaging Ecotopia: Bioregionalism, Permaculture, and Ecovillages*, edited by J. Lockyer and J. Veteto. New York: Berghahn Books.

4.9

'RELIGIOUS' RADICALISM

Alexandre Christoyannopoulos and Anthony T. Fiscella

Introduction

As long as there has existed hierarchy and domination, the oppressed have engaged in resistance and sustained egalitarian relationships in the face of such domination. However, what qualifies as 'radical' resistance, as 'religious' relationships or as 'religious radicalism' depends on the perspective of the observer. For instance, 'religious radicalism' might describe either a 'radicalism' in the sense of an extreme position (on any number of issues) which also has 'religious' attributes, or a 'religious' claim which also happens to come across as 'radical' (in the sense of more extreme, more deeply passionate and committed than common examples). Indeed, the semantic coverage of both 'religious' and 'radical' overlaps where both can be taken to mean a certain kind of zeal or passionate commitment.[1]

Turning to etymology does not narrow and sharpen the focus a great deal either: 'radical' points to the roots (Latin *radicalis* and *radix* = roots); hence, a 'radical movement' could be taken to refer to a movement that seeks to change something at its root rather than merely superficially; and 'religion' is often considered to refer to something that socially binds people together (Latin *religare* = to bind together) as opposed to something that atomises social groups into individuals each out for their own self-centred gain. Taken together, this would seem to point to 'religious radicalism' as referring to a deep-rooted commitment to something which binds people together. However, etymology can be interpreted in different directions too. For instance, 'religion' could be read as pointing to a binding obligation with God. The etymology of 'religion' is also quite contested: some argue that it derives from *re-legere* = to read again. Clearly, therefore, 'religion' and 'radicalism' are both slippery terms.

It is therefore not surprising that studies ostensibly addressing 'religious radicalism' have focused on very different kinds of examples depending on the inclination of the scholar. For instance, some scholars have focused on US-based movements such as Christian Identity, neo-Nordic pagans, Children of Noah and the Anti-Cult Movement (Kaplan 1997), as well as on Islamists in the Middle East such as the Taliban, Hezbollah and Hamas (Berman 2009); some have posited 'religious radicals' in contrast to 'religious conservatives' and 'religious liberals' in a US context (Dreger and Adkins 1991); others speak of a 'radical conservative socialist' Buddhism in Thailand (Zöllner 2014) and others still have discussed examples of 'religious radical' individuals and groups that are largely antiracist, anticapitalist and/ or broadly aligned with anarchist critiques of dominant orders (McKanan 2011, Raboteau 2016).

Partly due to limited space and partly mindful of the types of radicalism discussed in this volume, this chapter focuses on the latter among the aforementioned categories: groups which can be described as both 'religious' and 'radical' in the sense of anti-oppression and anti-hierarchical, and which have presented fundamental challenges to dominant social orders (Christoyannopoulos 2009, Wiley 2014). This includes fairly predictable examples such as Christian or Muslim 'radicals', but not to be overlooked are also Indigenous, communal and so-called 'primitive' cultures that pose challenges to the dominant order. That such Indigenous traditions and philosophies often contain a 'religious' element is both a factor in their frequent neglect and a reason why they deserve a central role in discussions of 'religious radicalism'. Clearly, however, discussions of 'religious radicalism' could justifiably be expanded to include a broader variety of fairly different 'radical' and 'religious' phenomena. Here, we contribute to such discussions with only a small selection.

One of the aims of this chapter, therefore, after providing a critical overview of the concepts of 'religion' and 'radicalism' and in particular after settling on a broader understanding of 'religion', is to present a number of examples of what might be characterised as 'religious radicals' that stand in opposition to hierarchy and oppression. Three types of examples are considered: Indigenous traditions which stand as radical alternatives to colonial orders (e.g. Tonga, BaMbuti, Lakota); nonviolent currents *within* dominant regimes that challenge central pillars of those regimes such as the military, property or hierarchy (e.g. Catholic Workers, Plowshares and liberation theologians); and marginalised people in the process of negotiating alternative life-organising stories within nation state contexts (e.g. the Zapatistas, the MOVE Organization and Womanists). In presenting these examples, our second aim is to inform reflections on the following questions: what is radical about these groups of 'religious radicals'; what are their principal concerns; how are their views and activism theorised; and what, if any, influences are active in the movements under discussion?

Underlying our presentation of these examples is an argument that what is most interesting with these groups and their ideas is not whether or not they qualify as 'religious' or even 'radical', but the degree to which their visions, practices and holistic worldviews contest dominant orders with principles of egalitarianism, nonviolence and inclusive diversity. That is, arguably the most 'radical' examples put forward a way of seeing and being in the world which provides an alternative to dominant orders which can be described as ontological, deep-rooted and total.

Problematising Definitions

The implication behind the title of this chapter is that there is a subset of 'radicalism' which is appropriately labelled 'religious'. It seems pertinent to start by unpacking some of the problems with some of the assumptions that underlie such a label – assumptions that arguably are widespread among many of the likely readers of this book. In exploring these assumptions, we seek to open up the landscape by putting forward a perspective premised on a number of arguments which are often overlooked in mainstream social and political science. Given our limited space, we cannot resolve all the issues that this gives rise to here, but at least we can give a taster to angles of analysis which are likely to be unfamiliar to many Western commentators.

There are at least four claims which our limited discussion of definitions hopes to substantiate to some extent. It is worth spelling them out at the outset to clarify our main positions. First, there is an anti-'religious' bias in Western leftist thinking which stems partly from an ideological framing (or at any rate a simplistic categorisation) of 'religion'. Second, this bias was co-constituted, both historically and philosophically, in tandem with European colonialism. Third, closer attention to much of what was excluded in the process uncovers countless examples of 'religious radicalism', indeed a long history of resistance to colonialism, oppression and hierarchy. Fourth, Western categories and assumptions about 'religion' therefore need unpacking, especially by 'radicals' opposed to colonial and neocolonial hierarchies and institutions.

'Religion'

The term 'religion' is particularly problematic. This is in large part because of the assumption, arguably implicit in some of our own use of the aforementioned term, that there exists something called 'religion' as distinct from 'politics', 'law', 'science' or 'culture'. This is a distorting lens in a vast majority of cases. Not only is such an assumption unique to European languages, but it was not a common assumption even in Europe prior to the 1700s (Cavanaugh 2009, Dubuisson 1998/2003, Fitzgerald 2007, Josephson 2012, McCutcheon 2003). The now widespread notion that there is a sphere of life that can be identified as 'religion' and separated from other spheres of life is a product of the modern, colonial European mindset: both colonialism and this framing of 'religion' as a separate sphere occurred in the same era, for overlapping purposes and due to interlinking causes. Fitzgerald goes even further when he writes that '[t]he ideology of religious studies', that is, as a separate sphere of study, 'defines both modernity and colonial consciousness', a consciousness which he explains is then reproduced each time we frame our analysis through its terminology (2007: 26).

Although scholars and laypersons outside of religious studies often use the term 'religion' as if there were some self-evident meaning, there is no consensus among religious studies scholars (nor legal scholars, for that matter) on how to define it or even which traditions and groups might be considered 'religious'. Depending on the scholar or study, anything from football clubs to Buddhist meditation, from Star Wars fans to Labour Party activism may or may not be regarded as 'religious'. Besides, the exact definition and limits of 'politics' have also evaded scholarly consensus (is it based on power, conflict-resolution, distribution of resources, territorial sovereignty, appointment of decision makers and/or organising public values?). Yet, the casual assumption that 'politics' and 'religion' are clearly definable and best kept separate is entrenched both in the mainstream public discourse and among many academics.

Furthermore, it is commonly accepted by scholars that 'most people in the world are religious' (Graham and Haidt 2010; Johnson 2012; Randal and Argyle 2005).[2] If one were to follow this line of thinking, assume that 'radicals' are fairly evenly spread across the planet, and furthermore assume that 'radicalism' does not preclude 'religiosity', then it would follow that many, if not most, 'radicals' would also likely be 'religious'. Without consensus on how 'religion' is defined, this admittedly does not tell us much, except perhaps that '*anti*-religious' leftists would be mistaken to expect all leftists to be 'non-religious' or all 'religion' to be right-wing or reactionary. There is, after all, a degree of prejudice and bias against people who identify as 'religious' (or seem to do so) in some leftist contexts. Prejudice need not be accurate to be real and to lead to concrete bias. Just as Islamophobia can result in violence against Sikhs who are mistaken for Muslims, 'anti-religious' prejudice can lead to bias against persons and traditions regardless of whether or not they are 'religious' and regardless of whether the category of 'religion' is useful.

History is more complex than prejudice tends to allow. Syndicalist militias killed priests and nuns during the Spanish Civil War due to the Church's collaboration with fascists and elites; yet, a few decades prior, Father Hagerty, a Catholic priest and revolutionary communist, wrote the preamble to the Industrial Workers of the World. Hagerty was far from a solitary example of Christians fiercely advocating social justice and equality: Gerard Winstanley and the Levellers in 1600s England rooted their opposition to state and capital in Bible-based understandings of justice; the German Peasant rebellions of the 1520s (including the communist preacher Thomas Müntzer) and the Münster commune of the 1530s were both led by Christian revolutionaries; and radical insurrectionists Nat Turner and John Brown were both guided by their Christian faith, as was Harriet Tubman. Other more recent examples include Quakers and Unitarian Universalists such as Florence Beaumont, Alice Herz and Norman Morrison who self-immolated in opposition to the US war against Vietnam, and contemporary Christian anarchists such as the Jesus Radicals, a mainly US-based community coordinated through an eponymous website. Many armed anticolonialist movements across the Muslim world were led by supposedly quietist Sufis. Prominent social movement leaders of the twentieth century, such as Zeinab al-Ghazali, Malcolm X and Mohandas Gandhi, were rooted in faith communities of active resistance. Across the world today, people in faith communities are leading struggles against colonial orders, corporate power and state persecution. Not only does stereotyping 'religion' tend erroneously to position the so-called 'believers' on the 'right/authoritarian' end of the ideological landscape, but it conceptually ignores all non-state cultures, traditions and philosophies outside this landscape. We wanted to avoid the same tendencies furthermore narrowing the parameters of scholarship on 'radicalism'.

Critics have argued that many European anarchists, in other words even those who are among the more receptive to non-state cultures, also have this blind spot, not noticing the 'religion' in those they feel affinity for, and instead locating it elsewhere. In other words, even anarchists can struggle to think outside the dominant framing of 'religion' inherited from colonialism and the Enlightenment, obsessing instead about one particular kind of 'religion' they want to passionately oppose (see, for instance, Lagalisse 2011). Among many European anarchists, the Enlightenment as a philosophical starting point and set of assumptions about 'civilisation' has been taken for granted despite the underlying colonial relations that facilitated developments such as 'rationality' and 'freedom' (Fiscella 2015). Furthermore, their very conception of 'religion' (see, for example, Bakunin's *God and the State* which took statist variants of Protestantism and Roman Catholicism as prototypical of 'religion') has been conceptually rooted in worldviews constructed by white colonialist-era philosophers. That is why political scientist Cedric Robinson, for example, criticised European anarchists for not actually envisioning a new society but merely 'rearranging the ideas of that bourgeois society' (Robinson 1980: 215).[3] As H. L. T. Quan, political theorist and filmmaker, put it, 'despite its claim of heresy, anarchism in the West remains faithful and obedient to the ontologies and life-worlds that gave birth to it' (2013: 125).

In contrast to European anarchist thought, Robinson pointed to non-European examples of anarchist praxis. One example of such praxis might be Rastafarians who advocate 'radical freedom and liberty of the individual' on the one hand and 'a strong sense of collectivism, communalism and community [and] anti-capitalist, anti-materialist ethos' on the other (Barnett 2002: 54). Robinson himself specifically cited the stateless Tonga as a case of non-European anarchist praxis. To follow the Tongan example, according to Robinson, would imply the dismantling of political authority and replacing it with systems of interconnectedness, inclusivity, mythology, kinships, brotherhoods and sisterhoods and 'perhaps, with an authority which identified order and responsibility in terms of the indivisibility of things' (1980: 200). Yet typically, that which has been translated into European languages as 'religion' (and as a consequence been dismissed or overlooked by anti-religious critics) has encompassed for Indigenous peoples the entirety of life – including governance and social relations in general. As Native American studies scholar Jack Forbes wrote,

> The life of Native American peoples revolves around the concept of sacredness, beauty, power and relatedness of *all forms* of existence. In short, the ethics or moral values of Native people are part and parcel of their cosmology or total world view. Most Native languages have no word for 'religion' and it may be true that a word for religion is never needed until a people no longer have it. ... Religion is, in reality, living. Our religion is not what we profess, or what we say, or what we proclaim; our religion is what we do, what we desire, what we seek, what we dream about, what we fantasize, what we think – all of these things – twenty-four hours a day. *One's religion, then, is one's life, not merely the ideal life but the life as it is actually lived.* Religion is not prayer, it is not a church, it is not theistic, it is not atheistic, it has little to do with what white people call 'religion'. It is our every act. If we tromp on a bug, that is our religion; if we experiment on living animals, that is our religion; if we cheat at cards, that is our religion; if we dream of being famous, that is our religion ... the massive federal center for experimentation with animals on Staten Island is a church, the Pentagon and CIA complexes near Washington, DC, are churches, etc. Many people often pretend that they can escape from the consequences of their own acts, but Native philosophy teaches differently.
>
> *(2008 [1979]: 15–16, italics in original)*

In order to reconcile such a broad-ended and anticolonialist approach to defining 'religion' with the academic quest for a precise and coherent use of terms, we conceive of 'religion' in this broad sense as subsumed under the category of 'life-organising stories' – all partial and holistic narratives as well as cognitive frameworks that are used to orient individuals and groups in relation to the world and one another. This would include everything from Catholic meditation to Buddhist sacraments, but also anything from academic rituals to electoral procedures, from astrophysics to children's fairy tales. This broader understanding of the 'religious' therefore opens up the landscape of 'religious radicalism' to examples we will be considering further later.

Three important points here are worth noting. First, what is interesting is not whether or not a story is falsifiable but the ways in which any given story helps people organise and orient themselves (and their stories) in relation to one another. That is, the claim of 'scientific' stories versus 'superstitious' stories obscures the more interesting dynamics of how interrelated stories sustain certain social orders. Second, the claim that a story is 'religious' does not provide much explanatory power about life choices. In other words, it may be easy to divide people into categories of 'religious' and 'non-religious' or 'Muslim' versus 'Buddhist' but the labels do not necessarily tell us anything at all. For example, French-Lebanese author Amin Maalouf wrote: 'You could read a dozen large tomes on the history of Islam from its very beginning and you still wouldn't understand what's going on in Algeria. But read 30 pages on colonization and decolonization and then you'll understand quite a lot' (2001: 66). Third, similarly, even within stories purportedly based, for example, on the teachings of Jesus or the Buddha, we learn little by characterising them as 'religious' or 'non-religious', but we learn more by examining whether a given set of stories have been crafted, edited and developed by elites and imperial interests or by grassroots actors who tied those stories to simpler lifestyles both different from and in opposition to domination and oppression. Subsequently, rather than asking whether or not certain life-organising stories are 'religious' or not, we can ask if they are connecting people to one another and to all living beings and the ecosystems we share or if they lead to and are built upon traditions of division and domination.

While this understanding of 'religion' is broad, it provides a base for subcategories and greater specificity that, unlike typical understandings of 'religion', can be truly 'universal' precisely because all cultures can relate to the idea of stories that provide central reference points for orienting individuals within that culture. The lines of distinction do not fall between 'faith' and 'fact' or 'secular' and 'spiritual' but along various genres of stories: 'short stories' that address only one or two aspects of life, 'anthologies' that bind together various narratives with themes, 'terror stories' that cultivate fear and distrust, 'news stories' that inform about social developments, 'authoritative stories' that expect compliance with a dominant narrative, and so on. In any case, rather than propose a stable and final definition of 'religion' or 'life organising stories', this chapter primarily aims to provide examples of groups and ideas that often get less detailed coverage partly because of broader assumptions shared across wider 'European' societies about the significance of such 'religious' groups.

'Radical'

The word 'radical' also raises difficulties. Depending on the context and assumptions of the reader, the term might evoke any number of prototypical images: a person of colour, a white person, a male, a female, a genderqueer, an Islamist, a Communist, a peace activist, an armed militant, etc. In other words, our thinking about 'radicalism' is shaped by socially conditioned factors and assumptions that lead us to privilege certain types of actors over others for earning the label: 'radical'. As prominent academic voices are not representative of the population at large, the dynamics of skewed individual perspectives within academia can exclude a large number of people from the very dialogue about what might constitute social change or justice and how they ought to be strived for. In the examples we selected below, we tried to include frequently excluded voices, but we inevitably were forced to leave out many too.

The *Journal for the Study of Radicalism* might be a reasonably representative starting point for a definition given that it draws together scholars specialising in radicalism. Its approach is 'to loosely define "radical" as distinguished from "reformers", to mean groups who seek revolutionary alternatives to hegemonic social and political institutions, and who use violent or non-violent means to resist authority and to bring about change'.[4] This definition might sound consistent with both common conceptions and the etymological source of 'radical'; yet, it belies the fact that some of the earliest uses of 'radical' in a political sense referred to 'radical reformists', whereas today 'radical' and 'reformist' are typically considered to be opposites. Nor does radical necessarily imply anti-elitism or revolutionary inclination. For example, Noam Chomsky and others have used the term 'radical' to refer to corporate capitalism and its ravaging effects on democracy and social order.[5] Hence, an important question could be: radical in relation to what? After all, the 'hegemonic social and political institutions' and 'authority' that radicals oppose will change according to context.[6] In many cases, these changes are rooted in basic needs and responses to oppression rather than overarching theories or academic literature.

Examples of 'Religious Radicalism'

Having now discussed some of the difficulties inherent in using terms such as 'radicalism' and especially 'religious', we can now provide a variety of examples that might qualify as 'religious radicals' in the sense of life-organising stories which stand in marked contrast to dominant social orders, and in the process begin to reflect on their main concerns and the way in which they think about their radicalism. Of course, thousands of groups could have potentially been considered. The limited space means only a small selection could be listed. They were selected according to two main criteria: first, they might justifiably be considered 'radical' in that their ideas and practices seem to present serious epistemic and/or structural challenges to the functioning of domination and colonial/capitalist-oriented societies; and second, they might justifiably be considered 'religious' in the broad approach outlined by Forbes: that is, their life-organising stories and social practices are interwoven with all major aspects of life including governance, the nature of existence, relationships to animals and earth, conflict resolution, ethics and so on. Groups and ideas were also selected according to taste: that is, we, the authors, find these groups interesting and worthy of discussion.

Indigenous Traditions

Many Indigenous societies include those cultures, traditions or social contexts whose very existence, paradigms and lifestyles function as examples of powerful 'radical' alternatives to dominant orders including coercive governance and competitive individualism. Centring 'radical' social change upon Indigenous peoples simultaneously decentres all colonialist-based models from nation states to anarchist theory, from banking to *Das Kapital*. That they are suffused by life-organising stories and cultures that position them in larger cosmologies and holistic worldviews integrated into their daily life is what would qualify them as 'religious' according to Forbes. If nothing else, the very question of land and ownership of the wild which is central to colonialism requires the annihilation or assimilation of Indigenous peoples and their claims to the land. Indigenous people power implies, therefore, a core threat to social orders built upon the legacy of colonialism.

Common principles among Indigenous communities include building small-scale societies based on mutual aid, shared obligations, minimal technology and violence, and maximum harmony with surrounding ecosystems. Turnbull observes in his research on the BaMbuti in the Congo: 'Pygmies dislike and avoid personal authority, though they are by no means devoid of a sense of responsibility. It is rather that they think of responsibility as communal' (1968: 125). According to Turnbull, their faith was in the forest and in one another. Conflicts tended to be resolved with a minimal amount of violence. Indeed, they had minimal technology, minimal depletion of resources, minimal bureaucracy, minimal hierarchy and minimal destruction. Their simple living and harmony with their environment can be found in other Indigenous peoples. For example, Kate Luckie of the Wintu Nation in the 1920s is recorded to have said:

> When we build houses, we make little holes. When we burn grass for grasshoppers, we don't ruin things. We shake down acorns and pine nuts. We don't chop down trees. We only use dead wood. But the White people plow up the ground, pull up the trees, kill everything. The tree says, 'Don't. I am sore. Don't hurt me.' But they chop it down and cut it up. The spirit of the land hates them ... Everywhere the White man has touched, it is sore.
>
> *(Forbes 2008: 14)*

While Indigenous peoples anywhere present a particular challenge to nation states at the very core of their legitimacy and territorial claims, the Indigenous peoples of the US pose a particularly strong challenge to dominant orders precisely because the pillars of dominant orders in economic, political, cultural and military terms are located therein. In other words, the proximity of Indigenous peoples in the US to the core pillars of global power marks out their 'radicalism' as particularly 'radical' in their context. Furthermore, their struggles against domination did not start in the eighteenth or nineteenth century but have been going on for far longer, and this endurance grants deeper roots to their legitimacy and to the threat they pose to the dominant order (Dunbar-Ortiz 2014). Hence, if there is a radical challenge posed to imperial domination by Indigenous peoples, the existence, claims and traditions of Native Americans pose a greater threat than, for example, the Saami in northern Scandinavia or even the Natives of the Basque region. This means that colonial orders have a greater interest in obscuring, obstructing and attacking their gains – even at the level of recognition and acknowledgement (formal and informal). Russell Means, a co-organiser of the American Indian Movement, has pointed out that the very identity of Indigenous peoples (he refers to 'American Indians') is rooted in the European creation of such terms and that to speak accurately and indigenously, one would only be able to say Oglala, Brulé, Diné, Miccosukee, etc. Thus, it takes great effort to *not* become Europeanised for this and other reasons. Yet once language is Europeanised, the lens through which one sees and through which discourse takes place similarly becomes Europeanised. Indigenous paradigms become eradicated in 'indoctrination mills' (Means' term for 'schools'). Subsequently, leftist 'radicalism' is hardly a solution: 'Revolutionary Marxism is committed to even further perpetuation and perfection of the very industrial process which is destroying us all. … Industrialization is fine and necessary. How do they know this? Faith. Science will find a way' (Means 1991: 76–78).

Much could also be said about the way in which much European science, anthropology in particular, imposed a colonial understanding of entire Indigenous cultures which is fragmented. The label 'religion' was then imposed on specific aspects fragmented out of what was a total and interconnected way of life. Indigenous studies scholar Kim Tallbear, for instance, remarked that the Dakota word that has been translated as 'spirituality' or 'religion' actually means 'in relation'.[7] To be in relation with land, animals and people is a very direct phenomenon that does not necessarily imply a mystery God, belief in an afterlife, an immaterial 'soul' or some future salvation (and even if it did, the point is that 'religion' for these cultures puts relationships at the core, irrespective of specific theological beliefs). It does imply a certain stewardship and care for the relations that one maintains in life and relations that people are dependent upon. Significantly, it implies that there is no such thing as an isolated individual. Rather, each person is part of a web of relations, an interdependency with others from which one's personal identity cannot be disentangled.

Theoretically, the most recent development is a growing recognition within academia for the long-standing relevance of decolonial perspectives. From the popularity of Frantz Fanon's analysis of racism and violence as essential pillars of colonialism to Linda Tuhiwai Smith's description of how 'scientific research is implicated in the worst excesses of colonialism', institutions based on white academia have become increasingly critiqued from within (1999: 1). As Walter Mignolo has observed, the role of 'religion' is central to the cosmology of colonialism: 'The history of knowledge-making in modern Western history from the Renaissance on will have, then, theology and philosophy-science as the two cosmological frames, competing with each other at one level, but collaborating with each other when the matter is to disqualify forms of knowledge beyond these two frames' (2009: 164).

While some scholars have emphasised that decolonialisation therefore begins in the mind (hooks 1994, Waziyatawin and Yellow Bird 2012), others have insisted on the centrality of land claims and Indigenous sovereignty (Tuck and Yang 2012). In either case, these are fundamental challenges to core tenets of colonial orders (even within social justice movements such as Occupy or environmental movements which tend to conceptually 'occupy' Natives out of existence).[8]

Nonviolent Alternatives within Dominant Orders

History is full of radical social change developing from people organising nonviolently from within nation states or imperial societies. Within Muslim contexts, one might mention Heba Raouf Ezzat's theoretical blend of anarchism, social democracy and Islamic civic organisation, Ali Shariati's call for a classless society in Iran, or the weaponless 'peace army' of the Khudai Khidmatgars ('servants of God') led by Abdul Ghaffar Khan in India. Within other traditions, one can mention: Thich Nhat Hahn and Engaged Buddhism; Starhawk and other pagan activists in the global justice movement; Gandhi's Sardovaya Movement; magick traditions and genderqueering through Genesis Breyer P-Orridge and others; and activists within Transcendentalist and Theosophical circles such as Henry David Thoreau (who popularised the idea of civil disobedience) and Annie Besant (socialist, feminist and anticolonialist activist). However, the focus here will be on those who have applied a very different approach to the teachings of Jesus than those who used those same teachings to enslave, conquer and colonise.

There are many examples of such radical offshoots emerging from within Christian contexts. From the celibate Shakers led by Mother Lee to the single mother Frances Ellen Watkins Harper – simultaneously Unitarian and African Methodist Episcopal – who organised against white domination and patriarchy in nineteenth-century US, to the earliest Christians who refused military service and shared their belongings, current-day Christian communists such as the Bruderhof, who share their wealth among themselves, and neo-monastics such as Shane Claiborne who choose lives of simplicity and communal living while working for social justice in poor neighbourhoods, there is a long legacy of radical Christianity that nonviolently challenges interpretations of scripture that wed church power to the power of states and ruling classes (Bradstock 2002). Our focus here is on three such radical currents, all still active today: the Catholic Workers, Plowshares and liberation theologies.

The Catholic Worker movement was co-founded in 1933 by Dorothy Day and Peter Maurin. Their radical vision was to produce a cheap newspaper for ordinary people that would provide radically antimilitaristic and anticapitalist news and establish communes in the city as well as the countryside. The urban communes or houses of hospitality would welcome the poor and homeless into their walls for food and shelter. The rural communes would provide alternatives to industrialised society as well as grow the food to be provided to their fellows in the city. Inspired by Kropotkin, Tolstoy, the Industrial Workers of the World and the gospel of Jesus Christ, Dorothy Day set about to do what she could to resist what she described as 'this filthy rotten system' (Riegle 2012: 142). Yet, resistance was only one part of the Catholic Worker praxis. As Peter Maurin pointed out, their mission was to help create a world in which 'it's easier to be good' (ibid.). Today, there are more than 190 Catholic Worker communes across the world run by Catholics and non-Catholics. They continue to take part in antimilitaristic and anticapitalist campaigns as well as prefigure communities of mutual aid and hospitality to the destitute (including refugees).

Closely associated with the Catholic Worker movement is the Plowshare movement that gained notoriety in 1980 and continues today with the specific aim of doing direct nonviolent actions against the military industrial complex. Its roots go back to the late 1960s. In particular, on 17 May 1968, nine Catholic activists broke into government offices in Catonsville, Maryland, removing hundreds of draft files, and then burning them with homemade napalm (saving all of those young men from being drafted for the war). They included the Berrigan brothers, who would later be involved in the first 'Plowshares' action proper: on 9 September 1980, with a group of six others, they trespassed onto a nuclear missile facility in King of

Prussia, Pennsylvania, where they damaged nuclear cones ('turned them into plowshares' as prophesied in the Bible) and poured blood onto various documents. There have been over seventy Plowshare actions since then. These actions have always rooted their radical opposition to the military machine in Biblical tropes, both in their theorisation of their action and in the symbolism chosen in those particular actions.

One of the most popular and widespread radical movements in Christian contexts is that of liberation theologies which, depending on your proclivity, could be traced back to Moses, Jesus Christ, Bartolomé de las Casas, the Medellín Conference of Latin American Bishops in 1968 or Chimbote, Peru earlier that same year (Gutiérrez 1988: xviii). Alternately, Gustavo Gutiérrez wrote in *A Theology of Liberation* in 1971 that liberation theologies take their root in the unjust death of countless poor and oppressed throughout history. The Second Vatican Council (1962–65) with its modernising directives, emphasis on communal equality and support for local autonomy certainly helped facilitate the popularisation and spread of liberation theologies throughout the world. In particular, base ecclesial communities such as the many that sprouted up in Brazil became local tools for lay people to interpret scripture out from their own needs and the 'preferential option for the poor' (a phrase originating among liberation theologians and repeated by Popes John Paul II and Francis). In such contexts, 'sin', for example, is interpreted as social injustice and 'a breach of friendship with God and others' (Gutiérrez 1988: 24). Rather than theorising theology 'from an armchair', liberation theologies expressed new ways of *doing* theology. In general, liberation theologies tend to be not so much theory as outgrowths of solidarity and active commitment to people who are poor and marginalised (Rowland 1999: 4). Yet, written documents have played an important role as well. In 1965, Dom Hélder Camara, a bishop from Rio de Janeiro, organised a group document signed by 15 bishops from Asia, Africa and Latin America during the end of Vatican II that described 'the people of the Third World' as 'the proletariat of today's humanity' and insisted that 'the gospel demands the first, radical revolution' wherein 'wealth must be shared by all' (Smith 1991: 16). Many liberation theologians such as Camara and José Miranda equated Christianity with 'true' socialism and communism – meaning antiracist, antisexist, antiauthoritarian systems of sharing the wealth. As Gutiérrez put it,

> [t]o support the social revolution means to abolish the present status quo and to attempt to replace it with a qualitatively different one, ... not only better living conditions, a radical change of structures, a social revolution; [but] much more: the continuous creation, never ending, of a new way to be human, a *permanent cultural revolution*.
>
> (Emphasis in original 1988: 31, 21)

Marginalised People Organising New Stories

A third type of example concerns a few select groups and individuals who are drawn from marginalised peoples struggling to retain autonomy within nation states and/or create viable alternatives. Some of them may seem 'radical' in the spirit of Malcolm X who declared, 'I believe in a religion that believes in freedom. Any time I have to accept a religion that won't let me fight a battle for my people, I say to hell with that religion' (1970: 142). Some may not seem 'radical' in a full revolutionary sense; yet by articulating their own voice, they implicitly threaten the status quo which has consistently relegated them to the margins.

For example, Vine Deloria, Jr was a Native American whose father and grandfather were both Episcopalian preachers and he himself acquired degrees in law, political science and theology. At the same time, he was tremendously critical of racism and colonial dominance as well as the entire epistemological paradigm upon which European nation states and capitalism are constructed. In Deloria's words,

> The people who maintain the structures of science, religion, and politics have one thing in common that they don't share with the rest of society. They are responsible for creating a technical language, incomprehensible to the rest of us, whereby we cede to them our right and responsibility to think. They in turn formulate a beautiful set of lies that lull us to sleep and allow us to forget about our troubles, eventually depriving us of all rights, including, increasingly, the right to live in a livable world.
>
> *(Jensen 2008: 249)*

Similarly, one might mention any number of long-standing cultures such as Bedouin or Berbers in North Africa who have maintained relatively technologically advanced societies without prisons, police, and who apply mediation and councils of elders rather than courts and governments to provide social order (see Barclay 1982). One might also see Jewish people who have historically been excluded from dominant cultures. Amnon Shapira, doctor of Bible Studies, has argued that anarchism remains embedded in Jewish scripture in a number of ways – whether in the way Jewish communities were originally egalitarian and non-centralised, in the critique of how power corrupts, in the preference for kingship of God rather than human rule, and so on.[9] Indeed, there is hardly a shortage of historically radical Jews from Emma Goldman and Martin Buber to Noam Chomsky and Gustav Landauer. More recently, Michael Lerner of the Jewish social justice journal *Tikkun* has made radical calls such as for the 'elimination of national boundaries and all restrictions on immigration' and 'a non-violent revolution' including a 'Global Marshall Plan' requiring the wealthiest twenty countries to donate 1%–2% of their annual GDP for the next thirty years to end global poverty (Lerner 2015: 19).

Three examples of 'new stories' that we shall consider in a little more depth are the Zapatistas, the MOVE Organization and Womanist authors. The Zapatista National Liberation Army (EZLN) appeared before the world on January 1, 1994 when they made a spectacular insurrection in the Mexican state of Chiapas. This was the same day that the North American Free Trade Agreement (NAFTA) had come into effect. And just as NAFTA had been many years in the making so too had the Zapatistas been training for years albeit hidden from public view. They had been not only training militarily but also democratically. They routinely held democratic referendums with local people in Chiapas in order to be guided by their will as to when and how an insurrection ought to take place. When people determined that the time was right, they struck and caught the Mexican state off guard. The Zapatistas then soon put down their weapons, emphasising that a military showdown was not their aim. Their aims, instead, were (and remain) peaceful autonomy for Indigenous peoples and justice for all marginalised and poor people in the region. They see themselves as part of a global struggle against neo-liberal policies, the influence of corporate power, authoritarian party politics and rampant racism towards Indigenous peoples, and they want to do this from the bottom-up. As one-time spokesman Subcomandante Marcos said,

> We do not struggle to take power, we struggle for democracy, liberty, and justice. [...] It is not our arms which make us radical; it is the new political practice which we propose and in which we are immersed with thousands of men and women in Mexico and the world: the construction of a political practice which does not seek the taking of power but the organization of society.
>
> *(Flood 2001)*

Despite poverty and continual harassment by the Mexican state and paramilitaries, certain regions in Chiapas have remained under Zapatista control, and have managed to flourish through their own system of direct democracy.

Most accounts of the Zapatistas do not tend to discuss their 'religious' aspects. This can, in part, be ascribed to an 'anti-religion' attitude among much of the Zapatista supporters in Northern European-based cultures such as the US and Canada. For example, Lagalisse (2011) documented a speaking tour of two Zapatistas in which the more 'religious' woman speaker was gradually marginalised by organisers and audiences, while the more 'secular' male was given centre stage. Indeed, there has been much lost in translation as supporters and critics from dominant cultures looked on at evolving movements in the South, and wrote their stories in European language. Yet, the approach of the Zapatistas is reminiscent of a quote by Mujeres Creando in Bolivia who stated, 'I've said it [before] and I'll say it again that we're not anarchists by Bakunin or the CNT, but rather by our grandmothers, and that's a beautiful school of anarchism' (Lasky 2008: 18). This approach is not rooted in European theory but in Indigenous terrain and tradition. It does not exclude Europeans, but it does not privilege them either. Moreover, with Chiapas hosting Protestants, Catholics, Mayan traditionalists and (more recently) Muslims in ways that constitute 'a multifaceted complex of competing and overlapping cults' that often include women in prominent roles (Gossen [1999] 2013: 184), describing Zapatista life-organising stories and practices is not easy. In a famous quote, Subcomandante Marcos explained his 'true' identity as follows:

> Marcos is gay in San Francisco, black in South America, an Asian in Europe, a Chicano in San Ysidro, an anarchist in Spain, a Palestinian in Israel, a Mayan Indian in the streets of San Cristobal, a Jew in Germany, a Gypsy in Poland, a Mohawk in Quebec, a pacifist in Bosnia, a single woman on the Metro at 10 p.m., a peasant without land, a gang member in the slums, an unemployed worker, an unhappy student, and, of course, a Zapatista in the mountains.
>
> *(Lasky 2008: 8)*

It is characteristic of this approach that Subcomandante Marcos stated his age as '518' – the number of years it had been since the beginning of European interference in the Americas. In sum, the Zapatistas managed to fuse European-based socialist activism with indigenous perspectives on direct democracy and grassroots organising.

Another example of a 'radical' new life-organising story is the MOVE Organization. In this case, a mixed ethnic group of urbanites espoused a lifestyle and belief that bore strong similarities to those of many Indigenous peoples with a critical view of technology, the state, economics and dominant conceptions of 'religion'. MOVE was founded in Philadelphia by John Africa in the early 1970s with the aim of educating people on the evils of the 'system' by which they meant the entire technological complex and all that has made it possible. MOVE members also see violence against any creature (including bugs) as violence against one's self. They were the first group in the US to combine earth liberation and animal liberation philosophies as well as the first US group to hold an animal liberation protest (in 1974, prior to the 1975 publication of *Animal Liberation* by Peter Singer or the 1976 formation of the *Animal Liberation Front*). They were violently repressed by city authorities in 1985 when Philadelphia police infamously dropped a bomb on MOVE's row home, burning down an entire city block and killing eleven people in the process.

John Africa taught that the only legitimate government was the government of self and that all ideologies and administrations – whether liberal, communist, capitalist, fascist or socialist – were all hallucinations. States were depicted as gang leaders who terrorised people across the planet and MOVE's mission was to enlighten people to this and dismantle both industry and external forms of government. True law, according to MOVE, was 'natural law' – provided by nature – equally applicable to all people (such as the need to breathe or drink) and eternal as opposed to laws made by humans that are constantly subject to change. Their 'religion', MOVE members will say, is simply life. 'Mama Nature' herself was God and when each of us supposedly dies, the actual process is simply one of cycling back to earth.

One person who has spoken out on behalf of MOVE and against the violent actions of the police is the author, Alice Walker. Walker is also the person who, in 1983, coined the term 'womanism' in reference to black feminism that has some key distinctions from white feminism. Layli Phillips explained the new approach in *The Womanist Reader*:

> Womanism is a social change perspective rooted in Black women's and other women of color's everyday experiences and everyday methods of problem solving in everyday spaces extended to the problem of ending all forms of oppression for all people, restoring the balance between people and the environment/nature, and reconciling human life with the spiritual dimension.
>
> *(Phillips 2006: xx)*

The 'spiritual dimension' that she has articulated also happened to be very much in line with the type of philosophy articulated by John Africa. Walker has written: 'I seem to have spent all of my life rebelling against the church or other people's interpretations of what religion is – the truth is probably that I don't believe there is a God, although I would like to believe it. Certainly I don't believe there is a God beyond nature. The world is God. Man is God. So is a leaf or a snake' (cited in Pinn 2012: 125–6).

This is reminiscent both of John Africa's statement that 'God is as common as dirt'[10] and Buddhist statements about the Buddha being found in ordinary places – even dung. Both Walker and MOVE speak of a single God in the feminine form. Both regard this single God as the essence of all existence as manifested in what most people call 'nature' unsullied by technology and human interventions. Both of them tie this commitment to active resistance to imperial orders and their subsequent pillars of colonialism, racism, capitalism, industrialism and militarism.

Reflecting on 'Religious Radicalism'

Having now evoked a broad variety of examples of 'religious radicalism', we can return to some of the core issues upon which each chapter in this book was invited to reflect. With regard to the questions outlined in the beginning, the first section noted that the term 'radical' is not unproblematic and varies according to context and observer. However, a distinction between 'radicalism' and 'reformism' has been echoed here to refer to those who are more committed to significant and holistic change of society.

Indigenous cultures and their way of life have been characterised as 'radical' here insofar as they threaten the dominant order by the very alternative they present to it and by continuing to survive parallel to it. This includes entire societies whose traditions are testimony to the possibility of life without prisons, police, militaries or bureaucracies. Their languages and traditions carry codes, values and paradigms that bring them in inevitable and fundamental conflict with the many facets of the dominant way of life. They could be seen as 'religious' because they could be subject to 'anti-religious' bias through their use of terms such 'God' or

'Great Spirit', their acceptance of revelation as a form of knowledge, and/or the holistic and interwoven character of their life-organising stories. The question here is not whether they are 'religious' or not but how 'anti-religious' bias, because of both its prejudiced conception of 'religion' and its shared origins with colonialism, has often resulted in them being omitted from 'typical studies of radicalism'. They are premised upon life-organising stories which colonial and anti-religious mindsets have a tendency to dismiss too quickly.

The other examples cited earlier have been regarded as 'radical' due to their deliberate point of departure from dominant cultures, a contestation relative to their original positionality. Moreover, because their contestation is egalitarian, anti-domination and anti-hierarchical, they are on the left of the usual political spectrum, despite being 'religious'. For instance, with those nonviolent groups who based their actions on the teachings of Jesus, what is 'radical' is their contestation of two major pillars of the dominant right-wing order: private property and organised violence. They are 'religious' in the sense that they too are subject to 'anti-religious' bias in the context of 'radicalism' due to their use of terms such as 'God', their dependency upon scriptures such as Gospels and their collaboration with or membership in institutions identified as 'religious' by themselves or others. These and the other examples considered earlier nevertheless all exemplify 'religious radicalism' by raising the voices of marginalised peoples up against dominating, hierarchical and anti-egalitarian orders even as they are forced to negotiate their lives within nation states and dominant cultures.

With regard to the second question (what are the principal concerns of those movements?), given how varied a set of examples of 'religious radicals' we considered (and there are, of course, many, many more), any set of principal concerns will remain quite broad and vague about the specifics: they tend to emphasise cooperation rather than competition, egalitarianism rather than hierarchy, sharing rather than hoarding, gender and ethnic equality rather than patriarchy and white supremacy, and nonviolence rather than militarism. They also share a determination to either directly (by confronting) or indirectly (by prefiguring alternatives) oppose the existing order which is perceived as unjust, violent, inauthentic and in tragic disharmony with global ecology. Finally, they are all committed to raising their own marginalised voices and/or the voices of marginalised peoples with whom they are in solidarity.

As for the third question (how their politics is theorised), the theorisation of the politics of the activism of each of those groups varies significantly from group to group. Yet in all cases, there is some reference point to life-organising stories based on principles which in their eyes are larger than human-based constructs. Whether those ideas are presented as God, Life or Earth, the stories are broader than mere anthropocentric concerns. 'Theorisation' here consists in large part in the affirmation and protection of these alternatives in the suffocating cacophony, repression, discrimination and indoctrination of dominant cultures. Yet, the lack of formal academic theory is also one common trait of this type of 'radicalism'. Emphasis on 'theory' can result in a shift of power towards academic scholars and the elitist language of academia. Rather than submit to the primacy of written word as a predecessor to action and societal change, many of these examples prioritise direct action. As John Africa of MOVE stated, 'Application don't need no conversation' (Africa 1994: 1). Similarly, liberation theologians have long argued that theory is subordinate to action and that the first act for a committed theologian is not to theorise about God or politics but to take an active stand on the side of the oppressed. Still, in terms of the Catholic Workers, Plowshares and liberation theologians, 'theorisation' of their activism is articulated in relation to their interpretations of the teachings of Jesus as decidedly peaceful, antiwar, antistate and communistic.

Womanists, in turn, took their theory directly from their experience of being excluded by dominant white feminist and male antiracist discourses.

It might be worth comparing the answers to these three questions with those of 'radicals' who would neither typically describe themselves, nor typically be described, as 'religious'. The concerns for injustice, materialism, individualism, ecology, property and state violence, to name a few, are concerns that intersect across 'religious' and 'non-religious' radicals. Whether categorised as 'religious' or not, radical communities tend to construct moral frameworks that challenge the roots of hegemonic violence and injustice by resisting the practical and theoretical premises upon which that order is founded. To distinguish between radicals here as 'religious' or not remains a problematic act which carries with it a significant dose of colonialist thinking. We do not mean to resolve this difficulty here, but merely to reiterate it and be respectful of its implications.

At the same time, those life-organising stories that might be characterised as 'religious' and 'radical' do tend to have certain general characteristics that are relevant for radical struggle. First, they tend to conceive of relational and holistic systems wherein struggle for justice is part of larger commitments and traditions. Second, they tend to utilise concepts of sacredness that transcend economic calculations – particularly in relation to the commons which provide opportunities for people and animals to fulfil their needs (water, land, air, food, etc.). Third, they often engage some sort of semiotic marker such as 'Creator', 'Life' and/or 'God' which seems to both facilitate holistic thinking, evoke appreciation for the sacred, manage long-term intergenerational goals and connect each person to cosmological and social narratives that bind their broader identities of animal and human communities, earth and the entirety of existence. Notably, in relation to radical struggles, these ultimate markers or signs of fundamental dedication indicate a loyalty to social and/or existential orders that are distinct from and more important than any possible loyalty to a state (and often they are antithetical to the state).

Thus, 'religious' radicals can be described as aligning themselves with various life-organising stories that remain critical of dominant orders. They tend to display a sense of obligation to try to address this and they may demonstrate a willingness to commit significant sacrifices to that end. Again, though, much the same could be said of non-'religious' radicals too. Perhaps, then, instead of classifying particular groups as 'religious' and often paying less attention to them as a result, all 'radicals' might consider borrowing from the grammar of 'religious' radicals, working together on common concerns, and learning patiently from each other and on an equal footing about each other's life-organising stories and cultures.

Conclusion

This chapter has argued that dominant approaches to 'radicalism' are so embedded within dominant orders that what often qualifies as prototypical for 'radical' risks ignoring the 'radicality' of Indigenous stateless societies and egalitarian cultures upon whose backs and land dominant orders have generally been constructed, as well as others who might be dismissed as 'religious' without questioning problems inherent in the very concept of 'religion'. This chapter has therefore conceived of 'radicalism' by focusing on these oft-excluded cases and placing Indigenous cultures at the core of what it means to be 'radical'.

This chapter has also argued that 'religion' is a particularly problematic category especially when posed as mutually exclusive in relation to 'politics', an act which removes entire sets of life-organising stories and cultures from conversations about governance, power and popular decision-making. Nor does the dichotomy between 'religious' and 'non-religious' radicals necessarily tell us much about whom we are talking about. Indeed, there are as many differences *between* so-called 'religious' and 'non-religious' radicals as there are *among* members of each category. Rather than determine who is or is not a 'religious radical', this chapter has aimed to provide several possible examples to broaden the topic, and has queried the very terms 'radical' and especially 'religious' in order to expand the spectrum of discussion. After all, including formerly excluded people might be precisely what should be expected from a 'radical' approach to research about 'religious radicalism'.

Notes

1 This sense of 'radical religion' as 'true believer' seems to underlie the conception applied by Jeffrey Kaplan when he has written about the topic (2016: 11).
2 There is also some empirical support for this assumption. According to the 2012 Global Index of Religiosity and Atheism by WIN-Gallup International, 59% of the world self-identify as 'religious', 23% as 'not religious' and 13% as 'atheists'. By 2015, the numbers had actually risen with 63% self-identifying as religious, 22% self-identified as not religious and 11% as atheist. See Win-Gallup International, www.wingia.com/web/files/news/14/file/14.pdf (2012), respectively, www.wingia.com/web/files/news/290/file/290.pdf (2015). Another prominent survey source, Pew Research Center, stated in a 2010 study: 'Worldwide, more than eight-in-ten people identify with a religious group.' See Pew Forum www.pewforum.org/2012/12/18/global-religious-landscape-exec/.
3 Until Quan (2013), Robinson's discussion of anarchism (1980) had been ignored by anarchist scholars and activists.
4 *The Journal for the Study of Radicalism*, http://msupress.org/journals/jsr/ Accessed 15 October 2015.
5 See, for example, some of Chomsky's recent statements published on *Alternet*, 5 March 2013 or 5 December 2015.
6 Although we wrote this chapter about 'religious radicalism' because we have previously written about Christian anarchism (Christoyannopoulos 2010, 2016) and Islamic anarchism (Fiscella 2009, 2014), respectively, we decided however not to focus on our previous material (e.g. Tolstoy, taqwacore) and open up for a broader discussion about how 'radicalism' is conceived.
7 Quote taken from Kim Tallbear's presentation on 21 March 2016 at Undisciplined Environments, the International Conference of the European Network of Political Ecology in Stockholm.
8 Occupy Oakland is particularly interesting in this regard in that there were more Natives involved in it than in many other Occupy sites, and Occupy Oakland was also a site where Natives were critical of the name 'Occupy'. See, for example, Queena Kim, 'The Campaign to "Decolonize" Oakland: Native Americans Say "Occupy" Terminology Is Offensive,' *Truthout*, 28 December 2011 www.truth-out.org/news/item/5786:the-campaign-to-decolonize-oakland-native-americans-say-occupy-terminology-is-offensive.
9 Drawn from Shapira's English translation of his work in Hebrew entitled *Religious Jewish Anarchism (Or: Does the Jewish Religion Sanctify State Rule?)* 2013.
10 John Africa, 'On the MOVE: Quotes from JOHN AFRICA.' *FIRST DAY* 15, p. 2.

References

Africa, Delbert. '"Application Don't Need No Conversation."' *FIRST DAY* 3, [n.d. est. 1994]: 1–2.
Barclay, Harold. *People Without Government: An Anthropology of Anarchism*. London: Kahn & Averill and Cienfuegos Press, 1982.
Barnett, Michael. 'Rastafari Dialectism: The Epistemological Individualism and Collectivism of Rastafari.' *Caribbean Quarterly* 48, no. 4 (2002): 54–61.
Berman, Eli. *Radical, Religious, and Violent: The New Economics of Terrorism*. Cambridge and London: MIT Press, 2009.
Bradstock, Andrew and Christopher Rowland (Eds.) *Radical Christian Writings: A Reader*. Oxford: Blackwell, 2002.
Cavanaugh, William T. *The Myth of Religious Violence: Secular Ideology and the Roots of Modern Conflict*. New York, NY: Oxford University Press, 2009.

Christoyannopoulos, Alexandre (ed.). *Religious Anarchism: New Perspectives.* Newcastle upon Tyne: Cambridge Scholars Publishing, 2009.

Christoyannopoulos, Alexandre. *Christian Anarchism: A Political Commentary on the Gospel (Abridged edition).* Exeter: Imprint Academic, 2011.

Christoyannopoulos, Alexandre. 'Leo Tolstoy's Anticlericalism in Its Context and Beyond: A Case against Churches and Clerics, Religious and Secular.' *Religions* 7, no. 59 (2016): 1–20.

Dreger, Ralph Mason, and Susan A. Adkins. 'A Restandardization of a Brief Scale of Religious Orthodoxy, Religious Humanism, and Religious Radicalism.' *The International Journal for the Psychology of Religion* 1, no. 3 (1991): 173–181.

Dubuisson, Daniel. *The Western Construction of Religion: Myths, Knowledge, and Ideology.* William Sayers (Trans.) Baltimore, MD and London: The John Hopkins University Press, 1998/2003.

Dunbar-Ortiz, Roxanne. *An Indigenous Peoples' History of the United States.* Boston, MA: Beacon Press, 2014.

Fiscella, Anthony T. 'Imagining an Islamic Anarchism: A New Field of Study is Ploughed.' In *Religious Anarchism: New Perspectives.* Edited by Alexandre Christoyannopoulos, 280–317. Newcastle upon Tyne: Cambridge Scholars Publishing, 2009.

Fiscella, Anthony T. *Varieties of Islamic Anarchism: A Brief Introduction.* Alpine Anarchist Productions, 2014.

Fiscella, Anthony T. *Universal Burdens: Stories of (Un)Freedom from the Unitarian Universalist Association, The MOVE Organization, and Taqwacore.* Ph.D. Thesis, Lund University, 2015.

Fitzgerald, Timothy. *Discourse on Civility and Barbarity: A Critical History of Religion and Related Categories.* Oxford and New York: Oxford University Press, 2007.

Flood, Andrew. *Why Are the Zapatistas Different?* Feb. 2001, PDF edition http://zap.to/chiapas.

Forbes, Jack D. *Columbus and Other Cannibals* [revised edition]. New York: Seven Stories Press, [1979] 2008.

Gossen, Gary. *Telling Maya Tales: Tzotzil Identities in Modern Mexico.* New York: Routledge, [1999] 2013.

Graham, Jesse and Jonathan Haidt, 'Beyond Beliefs: Religions Bind Individuals Into Moral Communities.' *Personality and Social Psychology Review* 14, no. 1 (2010): 140–150.

Gutiérrez, Gustavo. *A Theology of Liberation: History, Politics, and Salvation.* Translated by Sister Caridad Inda and John Eagleson. London: SCM Press, LTD, [1973] 1988.

hooks, bell. 'Love as the Practice of Freedom.' In *Outlaw Culture: Resisting Representations*, edited by bell hooks, 243–250. New York and London: Routledge, 1994.

Jensen, Derrick. *How Shall I Live My Life? On Liberating the Earth from Civilization.* Oakland, CA: PM Press, 2008.

Johnson, Dominic. 'What Are Atheists For? Hypotheses on the Functions of Non-belief in the Evolution of Religion.' *Religion, Brain & Behavior* 2, no. 1 (2012): 48–99.

Josephson, Jason Ānanda. *The Invention of Religion in Japan.* Chicago: University of Chicago Press, 2012.

Kaplan, Jeffrey. *Radical Religion in America: Millenarian Movements from the Far Right to the Children of Noah.* Syracuse: Syracuse University Press, 1997.

Kaplan, Jeffrey. *Radical Religion and Violence: Theory and Case Studies.* London and New York: Routledge, 2016.

Lagalisse, Erica Michelle. '"Marginalizing Magdalena": Intersections of Gender and the Secular in Anarchoindigenist Solidarity Activism.' *Signs* 36, no. 3 (2011): 653–678.

Lasky, Jacqueline. 'Indigenism, Anarchism, Feminism: An Emerging Framework for Exploring Post-Imperial Futures.' *Affinities* 5, no. 1 (2011): 3–36.

Lerner, Michael. 'It's Time to Get Serious About Saving the Planet from Destruction.' *Tikkun* 30, no. 2 (2015): 18–20.

Maalouf, Amin. *In the Name of Identity: Violence and the Need to Belong.* Translated by Barbara Bray. New York: Arcade Publishing, 2001.

McKanan, Dan. *Prophetic Encounters: Religion and the American Radical Tradition.* Boston, MA: Beacon Press, 2011.

McCutcheon, Russell T. *The Discipline of Religion: Structure, Meaning, Rhetoric.* London and New York: Routledge, 2003.

Means, Russell. 'Fighting Words for the Future of the Earth.' In *Questioning Technology*, edited by John Zerzan and Alice Carnes, 71–82. Philadelphia, PA and Gabriola Island, BC: New Society Publishers, 1991.

Mignolo, Walter D. 'Epistemic Disobedience, Independent Thought and Decolonial Freedom.' *Theory, Culture & Society* 26, no. 7–8 (2009): 159–181.

Phillips, Layli. *The Womanist Reader.* New York, NY. Routledge, Taylor & Francis, 2006.

Pinn, Anthony B. *The End of God-Talk: An African American Humanist Theology.* New York and Oxford: Oxford University Press, 2012.

Quan, H.L.T. 'Emancipatory Social Inquiry: Democratic Anarchism and the Robinsonian Method.' *African Identities* 11, no. 2 (2013): 117–132.

Raboteau, Albert J. *American Prophets: Seven Religious Radicals and Their Struggle for Social and Political Justice.* Princeton and Oxford: Princeton University Press, 2016.

Randal, Patte and Nick Argyle. '"Spiritual Emergency"–a Useful Explanatory Model? A Literature Review and Discussion Paper.' *Spirituality Special Interest Group Publications Archive* (2005).

Riegle, Rosalie G. (ed.). *Doing Time for Peace: Resistance, Family, and Community.* Nashville: Vanderbilt University Press, 2012.

Robinson, Cedric. *The Terms of Order: Political Science and the Myth of Leadership.* Albany: State University of New York Press, 1980.

Rowland, Christopher (ed.). *The Cambridge Companion to Liberation Theology.* Cambridge: Cambridge University Press, 1999.

Smith, Christian. *The Emergence of Liberation Theology: Radical Religion and Social Movement Theory.* Chicago and London: University of Chicago Press, 1991.

Smith, Linda Tuhiwai. *Decolonizing Methodologies: Research and Indigenous Peoples.* London and New York: Zed Books, 1999.

Tuck, Eve and K. Wayne Yang. 'Decolonization is Not a Metaphor.' *Decolonization: Indigeneity, Education & Society* 1, no. 1 (2012):1–40.

Turnbull, Colin M. *The Forest People.* New York and London: Simon & Schuster, 1968.

Waziyatawin and Michael Yellow Bird. *For Indigenous Minds Only: A Decolonization Handbook.* Santa Fe, NM: SAR Press, 2012.

Wiley, Anthony Terrance. *Angelic Troublemakers: Religion and Anarchism in America.* New York and New Delhi: Bloomsbury, 2014.

X, Malcolm. *By Any Means Necessary.* Edited by George Breitman. New York: Pathfinder Press, 1970.

Zöllner, Hans-Bernd. 'Radical Conservative Socialism: Buddhadasa Bhikkhu's Vision of a Perfect World Society and its Implication for Thailand's Political Culture.' *Politics, Religion & Ideology* 15, no. 2 (2014): 244–263.

4.10

HOW POLITICAL IS A POLITICAL SUBCULTURE?

The Paradoxical Place of Politics within the Squatter Movement

Bart van der Steen

Introduction

The squatters' movement emerged in Western Europe in the early 1970s and traces its roots to the student and youth revolts of the late 1960s.[1] The combination of a massive housing shortage and large swaths of vacant houses in many of the larger cities of Western Europe led radical youths to try and solve the former problem with the occupation of the latter. From the mid-1970s onwards, squatting also spread to smaller cities and even provincial towns. In the 1990s, squatting spread to former communist states in Eastern Europe.[2]

From the beginning, squatters were a colourful mixture of political activists and youths from alternative scenes. Some of those involved saw squatting mainly as a political means to raise awareness of issues such as the housing shortage and the destruction of historical sites. The political horizon of most political activists was more encompassing, however. It was based on anarchist ideals which were at the forefront of anticapitalist, ecological, antimilitarist and feminist activism. Other squatters saw squatting as a practical means to solve individual housing problems and to provide cultural space. For them, squatting was a means to overcome homelessness, but also to create spaces for alternative music, art and socialising. As a result, squatting acquired a distinct subcultural character in which do-it-yourself-attitudes fuelled an urge to experiment and move beyond mainstream culture. A third group did not make a strong distinction between politics and subculture and felt attracted to both.

Radical politics, alternative culture and practical action against homelessness thus came together and even merged within the squatter movement. They made up three different currents within the movement, although there was a large degree of overlap. The same goes for the identities of those involved. Some squatters were mainly (or even mostly) interested in anticapitalist direct action, while others were in it 'purely' for the parties or the shelter that squats provided. Mostly, however, squatters were sympathetic to all three goals, albeit in varying degrees. Still, these differing goals and identities could lead to strife or even (physical) conflict, for example, when subcultural attitudes infringed on political norms. Conceptually, the overlap raises the question what squatters truly form: a political movement, a subcultural scene, both or something entirely different? Answering this question has implications for the concepts, sources and methods we use when researching (the history of) squatters.

In this chapter, I claim that there is a political squatter movement, even though the role of politics within squatting is contested. Because this movement organises informally, focuses on direct activism and merges politics and subculture, it should not be researched in a traditional way. Research on squatter politics has little to gain from a focus on communiqués, political statements and conference reports. Instead, I argue, research should take into account the above-mentioned characteristics of the movement and focus on the way politics take shape within squats and squatter groups; how they are developed, practised and communicated and how squatters experience political activity. This chapter explains why such a focus is preferable over more traditional political history approaches and offers hints as to how such a research can be conducted.

The squatter movement has left its mark on many European cities and even on European culture. Squatter activists played an important role in struggles against technocratic urban renewal in the 1970s and 1980s, in protests against nuclear energy and nuclear weapons in the 1980s, in the antiglobalisation movement of the 1990s and the antiwar and anti-austerity movements since 2001 and 2008, respectively. Underground music and lifestyle currents such as punk and techno house trace their origins to the squatter movement. In many cities, boroughs with a strong squatter presence have become tourist hotspots – Kreuzberg in Berlin and Christiania in Copenhagen are only two of the best-known examples.[3]

The subcultural nature of squatter politics has become a distinguishing feature of the movement. In the squatter movement, radical politics and subculture merge. Some claim that this feature explains the movement's enduring existence. Others, however, identify it as a source of weakness. According to the latter, the subcultural element has impeded the movement's political strength. Since the movement mainly organises youths, the turnover is high and movement learning processes are continuously disrupted. Furthermore, since many are attracted to the movement's subcultural elements, a large part of the movement is either uninterested in or even hostile to political theory (Geronimo 1992; Ziere 1992; Hillenkamp 1995; Duist 1986; Ruyter 1986a and 1986b; Schwarzmeier 2001). The place of politics within the movement is thus contested. At the same time, there is a distinct kind of squatter politics, with a specific political programme, organisational culture and action repertoire.[4]

Squatter politics can best be characterised by its radicalism. First of all, political squatters are radical in their political analysis in the sense that they focus on the root cause of social and political conflicts, which is that society sustains a high degree of inequality when it comes to wealth, power and knowledge. At the same time, squatter politics is radical in the sense that it denounces traditional ways of political representation, dialogue or compromise. Instead, it focuses on direct action as a way to subvert political routines. Finally, the movement is radical in that it criticises internal power relations and aims to demolish inner movement hierarchies. Over time, the movement has grown to become increasingly aware of class, race and gender inequalities within the movement, although this does not necessarily mean that it has been capable of dealing with them in a generally satisfactory way. Rather, it is the negotiating between radical ideals and coarse realities that cause debates or conflicts. Reconstructing these conflicts offers a way to analyse the social and political outlooks of squatter activists and inner movement dynamics – more so than its often more general political statements.

Next to arguing for a distinct research method, this chapter investigates the politics and political philosophy that drives squatting and explains the paradoxical place of politics within the movement. In doing so, it focuses mainly on the overtly political currents within the movement. The difference between 'squatting' and 'political squatting' is made explicit in Germany, where one can distinguish between squatters and autonomists, the latter being more explicitly political. In other countries, such as Denmark and the Netherlands, such a subdivision is rarely made in wording, although it exists in practice (Steen 2014a, 3).

The first part of the chapter uncovers the origins and development of squatter politics and reconstructs the movement's struggles to balance its political and subcultural parts. The second part investigates how this double nature has influenced the inner life of the squatter movement. To do so, it focuses on moments in which politics and subculture clashed within squatted places and social centres.

A Movement Focused on Practice

Researching the politics and ideology of a social movement such as the squatter movement poses specific challenges. It is very different from researching a political party. In the latter case, one can base oneself on the texts of leading party intellectuals, party manifestoes and electoral programmes to reconstruct the party's ideology and its behaviours. The squatter movement does not have a national organisation or governing body, and no regular conferences where programmes or manifestoes are passed – it even lacks clearly visible leading intellectuals, since programmatic texts are generally published anonymously or signed collectively by a group (Katsiaficas 2006).

Some have deemed autonomist Marxism, or *operaismo*, the guiding philosophy of the squatter movement, and have identified Tony Negri as one of its leading philosophers (Kraatz 1986; Balestrini and Moroni 2002; Wright 2002; Turchetto 2007). Although autonomist Marxism has a certain influence on parts of the squatter movement, it would be an exaggeration to equate squatting with autonomist Marxism. Within the squatter movement, interest in Marxism and labour struggles has generally been marginal.

Rather, it has been accepted generally within the movement that squatting is first of all a practice. Moving into a building or organising the collective occupation of a larger construction first of all requires practical knowledge: how to get in, how to keep unwanted people out, how to isolate the roof, how to fix the plumbing, etc. Even political interventions and campaigns, such as protests against urban renewal projects, or the construction of a road or nuclear power plant, can be framed as thoroughly practical: the organisation of blockades, demonstrations and acts of sabotage all are foremost dependent on practical and organisational skills. This, next to the previously mentioned subcultural nature of the movement, has led many observers and even squatters to state that there are no political ideals driving the movement.

This attitude can be illustrated by the squatter handbook. In many countries where squatters are active, squatter handbooks are circulated. These texts rarely dwell long on the motivations to squat and focus instead on the *how*. Guides provide thoroughly practical information about squatting and securing a building (Lucy Finchett-Maddock 2014, 221–2; Geronimo 2014, xvi–xvii).

The fact, however, that the act of squatting needs little or no explanation, that it can be adopted by various groups and that it spreads easily does not mean that there is no politics behind it. Rather, these politics are often implicitly acknowledged or assumed to be well-known. The politics of the squatter movement can be abstracted from its practices, by looking (i) at the historical development and roots of the movement, (ii) the way in which the squatter movement delineates itself from other movements and (iii) the way in which major controversies are played out within the movement.[5]

512

The primary source material for this analysis has been gathered mainly from squatting and autonomist activism in (West) Germany and the Netherlands in the 1980s. The discussion also draws on secondary literature about the movement in other European countries.[6]

The Crystallisation of a Political Movement

The squatter movement has multiple points of origin. In the late 1960s and early 1970s, radical activists in the Netherlands and West Germany lamented the conservative and oppressive political culture and claimed autonomous spaces to experiment with new ways of life and living together, free from the taboos, prejudices and often violent repression of alternative lifestyles in mainstream society. The Vietnam War and other anticolonial struggles, next to debates about the connections of ruling politicians, government and business officials to the Nazi era provided a global and national framework in which oppositional, critical and non-conformist behaviour became linked to radical oppositional politics (Schildt and Siegfried 2006; Reichhardt and Siegfried 2010).

In the Netherlands, squatters soon started to focus their political attention on protests against urban renewal projects that aimed at levelling historical boroughs and on international solidarity with what was then referred to as the Third World (Duivenvoorden 2000; Kadir 2014). In West Germany, some groups were inspired by wildcat strike movements in Italy and made attempts to organise unskilled labourers and migrant workers. In places such as Frankfurt and Hamburg, these groups were also involved in squatting campaigns (Frombeloff 1993; Ebbinghaus 2003, 2007; Arps 2011).

The squatters' movement emerged in the wake of the decline of the student movement and was heavily influenced by this development. As the student movement declined, some of the radicals within it redirected their energies to the rediscovery of pre-World War radical currents in Western Marxism. Soon however, the stereotype of the radical intellectual emerged. This described the person who wrote cryptic texts while refraining from practical activism – a negative image of the radical that had a lasting influence on the squatter movement.[7]

Others focused their energies on building up neo-Leninist parties, often of a Maoist inclination. Although nowadays generally forgotten, these parties attracted hundreds of activists in the Netherlands and even thousands in Western Germany. It is estimated that in the 1970s between 100,000 and 150,000 people in Western Germany were for a longer or shorter time involved in a Maoist party or related organisation. By 1980, most of these projects had faltered, but not without thoroughly traumatising a number of highly vocal veterans, who lamented the strict party discipline, the fetishising of 'the worker' and a party culture that tended to make members' personal needs subservient to that of the party organisation.[8]

A third group that grew out of the student movement strove to avoid the twin trap of intellectualism and party politics, and aimed to strike a real blow at capitalist power. These anti-imperialists formed armed underground groups that sought to undermine corporate and state power through kidnappings, bank robberies, bomb attacks and even executions. The most infamous became the Red Army Faction in West Germany and the Red Brigades in Italy, although similar groups were formed in almost all Western European states. As their actions became more violent and murderous, popular support for them decreased, thus initiating a vicious cycle of evermore violent and unpopular armed attacks (Aust 2008; Kraushaar 2008).

While the three main heirs of the student movement pinned their hopes on abstract knowledge, the party/proletariat or the Third World, the radical feminist movement emphasised the need to *live* political ideals as a way to avoid alienation.[9] According to this view, politics had to be tangible, concrete and direct. Consciousness-raising – through theatrical and mediatised actions and internal group discussions – became key, as did the commitment to give everyone involved a voice. Horizontal forms of organisation, in small local groups, were adopted as standard. In creating a network of women's houses, bars and book stores, the feminist movement laid out an organisational model that the squatters' movement would also soon adopt (Notz 2004; Melzer 2012, 2017).

Finally, the squatters were influenced by the massive and at times radical forms of protest against the construction of a series of nuclear power plants in Western Germany in the 1970s and 1980s. Hundreds of thousands of protestors were mobilised by campaigns against nuclear installations in Brokdorf, Gorleben and Whyl and elsewhere. These protests included both peaceful actions and gatherings, and militant demonstrations, sabotage actions and the occupation of building sites. Political parties and trade unions tried to keep the protests peaceful and under their control, but they were only partly successful. To squatters, these protests showed that there was potential and support for radical activism and that the position of traditional left or liberal left organisations was weak. Squatters soon positioned themselves as the militant wing of the antinuclear movement (Grauwacke 2003; Geronimo 2012).

The 1970s thus witnessed the evolution of the squatter movement into a new kind of radical movement. As their political profile crystallised, especially in opposition to other groups and parties, their political horizon also broadened. Next to squatting and the struggle for autonomous spaces and the protection of historical sites, the squatter programme expanded to include international solidarity, ecology and feminism. The movement developed a strong aversion to party politics, became committed to the feminist ideal of living politics, horizontal organisation and direct action. Its strategy focused on radical protest against both corporate and government actors and included militant demonstrations, occupations and acts of sabotage. Although militant demonstrations could give way to riots and sabotage actions could result in property damage, the movement generally refrained from targeted violence against individuals, thus drawing a clear line between itself and the armed urban guerrilla groups like the RAF.

Autonomist Squatting in the 1980s

The first wave of squatting reached its height by the mid-1970s. By the end of the decade, however, the movement was on the rise again. In 1979, for example, cautious attempts were made at squatting in Amsterdam and West Berlin. In 1980 and 1981, respectively, eviction attempts by the police led to days of rioting in both cities. In the following months, squatting spread rapidly throughout both cities and the rest of the country – a development which was accompanied by more police interventions and resulting riots (Bodenschatz 1983). In 1981, Amsterdam counted more than 206 squatted houses, while West Berlin counted 165 squats (Raad 1982, 14; Grauwacke 2003, 40). The willingness of the squatters to defend their squats with force and confront the police head-on impressed contemporaries (Mak 1980; Wetenschappelijke Raad 1980; Hofland 1981; Jugendwerk 1981; Enquete-Kommission 1983). Images of militant squatters, wearing leather jackets, balaclavas and motor helmets, appeared in the newspapers and soon became a staple of European protest culture. The militant squatter movement also became known as the autonomist movement and was especially strong in West Germany, the Netherlands and Denmark.

The renewed militancy was, in part, the result of the coming together of squatting and punk. While squatters provided space for punk concerts, practice rooms and gathering places, the punks provided the squatter movement with a militant aesthetic and attitude. Thus, the music historians Goossens and Vedder mention how 'the sandals and Afghan jackets were replaced by Mohawks, army boots and black leather jackets'. According to them, 'it may go a bit too far to state that punk was responsible for the hardening of the squatters movement ... But at the same time it is remarkable that the militant squatter manifested itself after the punk and squatter movement had formed an alliance' (Goossens and Vedder 1996). As dozens of new houses were squatted, thousands flocked into the squatter movement. Not all of them were motivated by radical politics, but politics did play an important role in the movement. For many, entering the squatters' movement was the beginning of a political learning process. One veteran activist remembered how his group adopted the name 'autonomist' because 'we could not really choose between communism and anarchism and it seemed a good compromise to call ourselves simply "autonomist"' (Schulz 2010).

Through informal meetings and public gatherings, the movement's media – consisting of dozens of magazines and pamphlets – and (inter)national contacts, ideas and experiences were exchanged. The text that comes closest to a foundational document was the text 'Anarchie als Minimalforderung'. This appeared in the magazine *radikal* and was the result of a meeting between West-German and Italian radicals (Anarchie 1981). The text specified that the autonomist movement was not to fight in the name of others, as the Maoists had done, but only for itself. It further laid out that the movement was not to articulate any political demands that could be fulfilled by those in government, since this would result in co-optation by the government. It however did not say much about forms of organisation, political goals or action repertoires. By this time, these were considered to be well-known.

While some autonomist squatters were driven by classical anarchist ideals, these were certainly not shared by all. Classical anarchism, as articulated by Bakunin and Proudhon, was deemed old-fashioned, tame and too intellectual. The attitude was summed up by an autonomist in the late 1990s, who stated: 'They (anarchists) are scared of us because we do the kinds of things they only talk about' (Katsiaficas 2006). At the same time, other political ideologies, such as anti-imperialism, have not become dominant either. Although there is a political ideal that drives squatting, it is often left implicit.

The Paradoxes of Implicit Rules

In practice, libertarian ideals form the heart of the movement's politics and philosophy, as it sets out to confront and attack all forms of political, economic and cultural inequalities. It aims to do so in a confrontational way, not by working for compromise but by principled acts of protest and/or resistance. These ends are achieved by organising in local, horizontal groups. Interregional coordination takes shape via networks of groups. The movement's repertoire ranges from traditional political means such as picketing to radical forms of action such as militant demonstrations and sabotage actions. The same libertarian ideals guide the internal life of the movement. Squatters set out to replace the hierarchies, taboos and violence that shape personal contacts in mainstream society by more egalitarian, caring and honest ways of living together (Jeugd en Samenleving 1981; Marge 1986).

These ideals tie the movement together, but certainly do not ensure a life without conflicts, since neither politics nor living together is ever without conflict. When it came to politics in the 1980s, the main conflicts revolved around informal hierarchies and militancy. Although the movement adhered to horizontal forms of organisation, many groups and even cities knew informal leaders. The adversity towards formal ways of organisation made the hierarchies within the groups all the more unclear. The debates about hierarchy became even more intense when groups or individuals pleaded or opted for controversial (militant) forms of action. With hindsight, it is clear that the autonomist movement had a clearly defined action repertoire, but throughout the 1980s, there was a fear – both amongst observers and activists – that some may cross the line, going over to armed struggle.[10] Here too, the lack of any clearly defined rules was one of the causes of continuous debate – although it must be said that the movement also drew strength from its seemingly 'limitless' action repertoire; had it clearly defined its repertoire from the outset, it would not have been as threatening to the authorities. Finally, the practice of confronting the authorities in a militant way led to criticism because it stimulated some to assume macho or all too masculine attitudes (Haunss 2004, 131–90; Op den Camp 2013).

Within squats and social centres, the ideal of creating free spaces clashed with practical problems that resulted precisely from this absence of rules. Many squatted places went through an initial phase in which 'all' were welcome, 'everything' was possible and 'everyone' tolerated each other. Soon, however, rules were agreed upon with regard to bills, chores and behaviour. In many cases, this process developed relatively smoothly and peacefully. Some even claim that they were truly socialised within the movement. Thus goes the story of Henk Borst, a difficult young man, who had spent most of his youth in boarding schools. After his return to Amsterdam in 1980, he spent his days on the streets, sleeping with his parents, with friends or in squats. 'It was the riots that attracted me', he stated later, 'I was not political at all'. His drug use and resulting behaviour, 'stealing and ego-tripping', led to conflicts and even fights with other squatters. Even so, he would later claim that the squatter movement 'saved' him. Here, he learned the skills of a construction worker and was introduced to social skills he had not picked up earlier: 'The squatters accepted you, even when you were a petty thief. There were more like me, I was not the only one' (Poppe and Rottenberg 2000, 84–89).[11]

However, not all experiences were as positive. As the movement evolved, norms grew stricter and tolerance for antisocial behaviour diminished. Transgressive behaviour did not only include drug abuse, stealing, ego-tripping and physical assault, but could also lead to sexual violence against women. In June 1984, a woman was molested and raped in the squatted Hafenstrasse in Hamburg. The other squatters responded with violence against the perpetrators, not knowing what else to do. The tragedy led to intense debates among the West-German radical left, but the squatters of the Hafenstrasse mainly felt 'horror' and 'powerlessness' (Amantine 2011; Borgstede 2013; Küllmer 2013). In 2013, one squatter stated: 'Up to now it has not been dealt with properly, neither publicly nor internally' (Küllmer 2013, 76). In Amsterdam, in the early 1980s, the Wyers squat evolved into a venue that during the weekend 'would sometimes attract eight hundred people'. Jaap Draaisma was a squatter who would later remember how heroin users and pushers claimed a floor and 'completely uncontrollable individuals would come directly from the train station to Wyers'. After a woman was molested and raped within the building, the squatters took matters more firmly into their own hands. Draaisma: 'We were forced to organise evermore. A security team was formed. We then disbanded the heroine-club and rehoused the junkies in other collectives; others were evicted and housed elsewhere. It was heartbreaking' (Poppe and Rottenberg 2000, 14–21).

In both cases, the main traumas were caused by the fact that women were molested within squats – places that were supposed to be free of the oppressive and violent behaviour associated with mainstream society. The traumas were however intensified by the fact that squatters had up to that point not imagined this possibility, or reflected on how to deal with these kinds of transgression. In practice, the movement responded by increasing social control and exclusion of those who did not conform to the norms within squats. In 1986, two veteran Amsterdam activists remarked that the number of 'internal evictions' far outnumbered the number of 'official evictions' (Lovink and Spek 1986). In other words, people who caused trouble were removed from squats – by the squatters themselves. This situation was however only rarely reflected on. These developments also came at a time where the squatter movement's expansion had ended and its claim to space was diminishing. In Amsterdam, it was very easy to get or get into a squat in 1980/1981. Thus, one squatter remembers: 'I took the cargo tricycle, moved my stuff and I lived there'. When another squatter went to Amsterdam in 1983, looking for a place to live, he found out that all squats were full or closed to strangers (Wietsma 1982, 20–22; Luchteling, 1997).

Autonomism and Its Discontents

By the end of the 1980s, the autonomist movement had grown more aware of the position of women within the squatter movement and within squatted social centres. In the 1990s, several groups advocated a politics to combat sexual violence within the movement, by making the names of accused perpetrators public and demanding that other groups exclude the accused from their networks. This strategy was controversial and did not become a standard practice within the movement (Haunss 2004, 149–69). On the other hand, social control within social centres did increase and focused on preventing assaults on women. Occasionally, jokes are cracked about the strictness of social centres, which is especially ironic given the fact that the squatter movement emerged with one of its goals being to overcome the overly restrictive and prudish nature of mainstream society (Biskamp 2017). The rules are however testimony to the movement's commitment to feminist politics.

From the late 1980s to the early 1990s, another debate within the movement focused on the organisational structure of the movement, with critics lamenting the movement's focus on campaigns and actions and its neglect for concerted attempts to move towards a more developed political theory or permanent organisation. In Germany, West-Berlin autonomist activists established just such an organisation under the name Fels (Für eine linke Strömung – for a left current), while autonomist antifascists also tried to set up a nationwide organisation (Geronimo 1992, 1997; Fels 2011). While Fels remained active until 2015, the nationwide antifascist organisation disbanded in 2001. Overall, the autonomist squatter movement viewed the attempts to form nationwide permanent organisations with interest, but did not support them *en masse*.

A major point of division within the German movement since 9/11 has been the question of how to relate to the military conflicts in the Middle East. Traditionally, the autonomist movement had been critical of Israel and the US and supportive of Palestine and its allies. After the terrorist attacks of 9/11, a significant part of the German radical left grew critical of traditional anti-imperialism, and instead pleaded for support of Israel and the US in their struggle against Islamic fundamentalism. These debates had a lasting impact on the German autonomist movement, but went by relatively unnoticed in other countries (Mohr and Haunss 2004; Ogman 2013).

The main focus of the autonomist movement in the 1990s became antifascism, which included both counterdemonstrations and blockades of marches by extreme right groups, but also more general activism for radical left causes (Birchall 2010; Hann 2013; Testa 2015; Copsey 2016). Antifascism became especially important in Germany, both amongst autonomists and anti-German activists, even though they underpinned their antifascist activism in a different way. From the late 1990s onwards, the autonomist movement has played an important role in mobilisations against international summits of the G8, the IMF and the European

Union (Grauwacke 2003, 203–38; Rilling 2008). While the autonomist movement's main strength was in Northern Europe in the 1980s, the movement now has an especially strong presence in the Southern Europe (Schwarz 2010; Dalakoglou and Vradis 2011; Harvey 2012; Mason 2012, 2013; Cattaneo and Tudela 2014; Kritidis 2014).

Politics in Movement

In 1995, when autonomist activists organised a conference in Berlin, the left liberal *Tageszeitung* asked: 'How long will the autonomists remain?' (Rada 1995) Around the same time, the social scientist Ruud Koopmans predicted that the autonomists would stick around, but argued that they had lost their role as politically significant actors (Koopmans 1995, 210–14). Ten years later, however, the autonomists played an important role in the antiglobalisation movement. Currently, they play a leading role in anti-austerity protests in Greece, Spain and Italy. Historically, the significance of the movement cannot be denied. Apart from the political and cultural impacts mentioned in the introduction, it has been estimated that in the Netherlands alone, 50,000 people at one time or another lived in a squat between 1965 and 1999. The city of Amsterdam acquired 200 squats during this era, thus legalising them and adding them to the social housing stock (Pruijt 2004; Duivenvoorden 2000, 323).

The autonomist squatter movement is driven by a specific political philosophy, but it is often underdeveloped and remains implicit. To reconstruct, analyse and discuss its political philosophy, it is therefore more useful to focus on the development of the movement and the way in which it delineated itself from other actors. The advantage of such a method over focusing on political statements and pamphlets is that it provides a more nuanced, detailed and historically contextualised image of the movement's political outlook.

An even more promising way of examining squatter politics is to focus on the activities of the movement and the specific conflicts and controversies it confronted. Through the reconstructions of controversies, it becomes clear which political opinions and attitudes were generally accepted and which were more controversial. By focusing in detail on how conflicts over social or political issues within squats or within the squatter movement played out, one can move beyond mere political statements and assess what specific statements or decisions meant in practice.

The digitation of newspapers and other sources makes it ever easier to research social movements from home or from the office. The history of squatting in Berlin and a number of other European cities has been visualised in digital maps that allow for browsing both over time and space in the city.[12] Social movement researchers have, however, warned against an excessive focus on newspaper and mainstream media in researching social movements (Eilders 2001; Haumann 2005; Zelizer 2008). Many squatter and autonomist movement publications have not been digitised, and many individual experiences and recollections have not yet been documented.[13] Focusing on these sources will produce an insider view of the movement and give voice to those who were involved in it. Such an approach from below seems fitting for a movement that traditionally rejected officialdom and formal organisation.

Notes

1 I would like to thank Knud Andresen, Albertine Bloemendal, Ruth Kinna and Irina Pulyakhina for their valuable comments on an earlier draft of this text.
2 This chapter focuses on squatting in Europe, and more specifically on squatting in (West) Germany and the Netherlands. For a European survey and guide to the main literature, I refer to: Steen 2014a and 2014b. See also Katsiaficas (2006) and Pruijt (2012).

Already before the fall of communism, there were attempts made at squatting, albeit often in a less public or overtly political way than in Western Europe. See for this Grasshoff (2011).

3 On squatting and tourism, see Owens (2008) and Blechschmidt (2007). Strongly related to these developments are debates between squatting and gentrification. For this, see Holm (2010); Häussermann (2002); Kuhn (2014).

4 Classic histories that are sympathetic to the movement are Katsiaficas (2006) and Geronimo (2012).

5 Those who are interested in a more traditional approach towards political history can rely, for example, on position papers, conference texts and documentations. See, for example, Anarchie (1981); *Arbeitsergebnisse* (1987); *Drei zu Eins* (1993); *Autonomie-Kongress* (1997); Wantok (2011).

6 Throughout the text, references are included as advice for further reading. Next to the references in endnote 2, this text relies on the following studies.

For Germany: Anders (2010); Haunss (2008); Manns and Treusch (1987).

For the Netherlands: Duivenvoorden (2000); Kadir (2014); Owens (2009); Adilkno (1994).

7 This sentiment was among other articulated by the popular Hamburg punk band Slime in their song 'linke Spießer', which appeared on their album *Alle gegen Alle* (1983). There it went: 'Always critical and political / Marx and Lenin on the bedside table / But you've got something against clashes / And you happily make room for the police. ... And when we become aggressive / You are all suddenly conservative'.

In German, the lyrics are: 'Immer kritisch und politisch / Marx und Lenin auf dem Nachttisch / Doch ihr habt was gegen Rabatz / Und macht den Bullen gerne Platz ... Und werden wir mal aggressiv /Seid ihr auf einmal konservativ'. See also: Ryser (2013).

8 On Maoism in Western Germany and the Netherlands: Kühn (2005); Koenen (2001); Baum (2010); Beekers (2005); Verbij (2005).

For contemporary reflections by party veterans, see *Wir warn die stärkste* (1977); Schlögel et al. (1981); Zomeren (1994).

9 This concept was summarised in the slogan 'the personal is political' and in many ways precursor to the prefigurative politics propagated by Occupy activists. See Graeber (2009).

10 Only in Frankfurt on 2 November 1987 did a demonstration end in a deadly shooting of police officers by an autonomous activist. In the wake of this tragic and unique action, the local autonomous scene was not only repressed but also faced disintegration as many activists no longer identified with the movement. For a discussion of the shooting and its aftermath, see Geronimo (2012).

11 Jan-Henrik Friedrichs has reconstructed how squatters in Zurich during the 1980s tried to develop new and less repressive ways of dealing with drug addicts within the movement, which set them apart from squatters in other cities, who often tried to exclude drug abusers. See Friedrichs (2016).

12 These maps can be found under http://berlin-besetzt.de and https://maps.squat.net/en/cities. See also: Aquilera (2016).

13 A number of personal recollections and interview books have been published. See among other: *Stand der Bewegung* (1995); Langer (2004); Poppe and Rottenberg (2000); Wietsma (1982); Adilkno (1994); *De stad was* (1998); Luchteling (1997).

References

Adilkno, *Cracking the Movement: Squatting Beyond the Media* (New York: Autonomedia, 1994).

Amantine, *Gender und Häuserkampf* (Münster: Unrast, 2011).

'Anarchie als Minimalforderung', *Radikal* 97 (September 1981).

Anders, F., 'Wohnraum, Freiraum, Widerstand: Die Formierung der Autonomen in den Konflikten um Hausbesetzungen Anfang der achtziger Jahre' in D. Siegfried and S. Reichardt (eds.), *Das Alternative Milieu: Antibürgerlicher Lebensstil und linke Politik in der Bundesrepublik Deutschland und Europa, 1968–1983* (Göttingen: Wallstein, 2010), 473–498.

Aquilera, T. et al., 'Mapping the Movement: Producing maps of squatted social centres in Western Europe' (2016) via: www.trespass.network/?p=231&lang=en.

Arbeitsergebnisse der Libertären Tage '87 (Frankfurt am Main, 1987).

Arps, J.O., *Frühschicht: Linke Fabrikintervention in den 70er Jahren* (Berlin: Assoziation A, 2011).

Aust, S., *Der Baader Meinhof Komplex* (Hamburg: Hoffmann und Campe, 2008).

Autonomie-Kongress der Undogmatischen Linken Bewegungen: Standpunkte, Provokationen, Thesen (Münster: Unrast, 1997).

Balestrini N. and P. Moroni, *Die goldene Horde: Arbeiterautonomie, Jugendrevolte und bewaffneter Kampf in Italien* (Berlin: Assoziation A, 2002).

Baum, F., 'Grosse bizarre Kulturrevolution', *Tageszeitung* (27 July 2010).

Beekers, W., *Mao in de polder: Een historisch-sociologische benadering van het Nederlandse maoïsme 1964–1978* (MA thesis 2005).

Birchall, S., *Beating the Fascists: The Untold Story of Anti-Fascist Action* (London: Freedom Press, 2010).

Biskamp, F., 'Kein Herrenwitz', *Konkret* (January 2017), 15.

Blechschmidt, A., 'Die Rote Flora im Hamburger Alltag. Stör- oder Standortfaktor?' in P. Birke and C. Holmsted Larsen (eds.), *Besetze deine Stadt! Bz din by! Häuserkämpfe und Stadtentwicklung in Kopenhagen* (Hamburg: Assoziation A, 2007), 190–198.

Bodenschatz, H. et al., *Schluß mit der Zerstörung? Stadterneuerung und städtische Opposition in West-Berlin, Amsterdam und London* (Giessen: Anabas, 1983).

Borgstede, S., 'Der Kampf um das Gemeinsame: St. Paul Hafenstrasse' in S. Borgstede et al. (eds.), *Häuserkampf II. Wir wollen alles. Hausbesetzungen in Hamburg* (Laika Verlag: Hamburg, 2013), 105–149.

Cattaneo, C. and E. Tudela, '¡El Carrer Es Nostre! The Autonomous Movement in Barcelona, 1980–2012' in B. van der Steen (ed.), *The City Is Ours: Squatting and Autonomous Movements in Europe from the 1970s to the Present* (Oakland: PM Press, 2014), 95–129.

Copsey, N., 'Crossing Borders: Anti-Fascist Action (UK) and Transnational Anti-Fascist Militancy in the 1990s', *Contemporary European History* 25:4 (2016), 707–727.

Dalakoglou D. and A. Vradis (eds.), *Revolt and Crisis in Greece: Between a Present Yet to Pass and a Future Still to Come* (London: AK Press, 2011).

De stad was van ons: 28 vraaggesprekken met krakers en kraaksters (Amsterdam: Snotneus, 1998).

Der Stand der Bewegung: 18 Gespräche über linksradikale Politik. Lesebuch zum Autonomie-Kongress Ostern 1995 (Berlin, 1995).

Drei zu Eins: Texte zu den Themen Patriarchat, Rassismus und Internationalismus (Berlin: ID-Archiv, 1993).

Duist, T. van, *De bloem der natie in Amsterdam: Kraken, subcultuur en het probleem van de openbare orde* (Leiden: COMT, 1986).

Duivenvoorden, E., *Een voet tussen de deur: Geschiedenis van de Nederlandse kraakbeweging, 1964–1999* (Amsterdam: Arbeiderspers, 2000).

Ebbinghaus, A., 'Die "andere" Arbeiterbewegung: Operaistische Strömungen in den 1970er Jahren' in A. Klönne et al. (eds.), *Fluchtpunkte: Das soziale Gedächtnis der Arbeiterbewegung* (Hamburg: VSA, 2003), 240–249.

Ebbinghaus, A., 'Was bleibt vom Operaismus?' in M. van der Linden and C. Lieber (eds.), *Kontroversen über den Zustand der Welt. Weltmarkt, Arbeitsformen, Hegemoniezyklen* (Hamburg: VSA, 2007), 45–62.

Eilders, C., 'Die Darstellung von Protesten in ausgewählten deutschen Tageszeitungen' in D. Rucht, (ed.) *Protest in der Bundesrepublik: Strukturen und Entwicklungen* (Frankfurt am Main: Campus, 2001), 275–311.

Enquete-Kommission des Deutschen Bundestages, *Jugendprotest im demokratischen Staat* (Bonn: Bundeszentrale für politische Bildung, 1983).

Fels, *Die Heinz Schenk Debatte: Texte zur Kritik an den Autonomen. Organisierungsdebatte. Gründung der Gruppe 'Für eine linke Strömung'* (Berlin: Fels, 2011).

Finchett-Maddock, L., 'Squatting in London: Squatters' Rights and Legal Movement(s)' in B. van der Steen et al. (eds.), *The City Is Ours: Squatting and Autonomous Movements in Europe from the 1970s to the Present* (Oakland: PM Press, 2014), 207–231.

Friedrichs, J.H., 'Freiräume? Geschlechterkonstruktionen und –konflikte in der westdeutschen Hausbesetzerbewegung der 1980er Jahre' in S. Lehmann et al (eds.), *Neue Muster, alte Maschen? Interdisziplinäre Perspektiven auf die Verschränkungen von Raum und Geschlecht* (Bielefeld: transcript, 2015), 181–205.

Friedrichs, J.H., 'Revolt or Transgression? Squatted Houses and Meeting Places of the Heroin Scene in Zurich and Berlin as Spaces of Transgressive Youth' in K. Andresen and B. van der Steen (eds.), *A European Youth Revolt: European Perspectives on Youth Protest and Social Movements in the 1980s* (Basingstoke: Palgrave 2016), 81–94.

Frombeloff (ed.), *… und es begann die Zeit der Autonomie. Politische Texte von Karl Heinz Roth* (Hamburg: VLA, 1993).

Geronimo et al., *Feuer und Flamme 2: Kritiken, Reflexionen und Anmerkungen zur Lage der Autonomen* (Berlin: ID-Archiv, 1992).

Geronimo, *Glut und Asche: Reflexionen zur Politik der autonomen Bewegung* (Münster: Unrast, 1997).

Geronimo, *Fire and Flames: A History of the German Autonomist Movement* (Oakland: PM Press, 2012).

Geronimo, 'Redistribute the Grid!' in B. van der Steen et al. (eds.), *The City Is Ours: Squatting and Autonomous Movements in Europe from the 1970s to the Present* (Oakland: PM Press, 2014), xiii–xix.

Goossens J. and J. Vedder, *Het gejuich was massaal: Punk in Nederland, 1976–1982* (Amsterdam: Mets, 1996).

Graeber, D., *Direct Action: An Ethnography* (Oakland: AK Press, 2009).

Grasshoff, U., Schwarzwohnen: Die Unterwanderung der staatlichen Wohnraumlenkung in der DDR (V&R Unipress: Göttingen, 2011).

Grauwacke, A.G., *Autonome in Bewegung: Aus den ersten 23 Jahre* (Berlin: Assoziation A, 2003).

Haumann, S., 'Hausbesetzungen 1980–1982 in Hilden: Möglichkeiten der Mikroforschung für die Protestgeschichte', *Mitteilungsblatt des Instituts für soziale Bewegungen* 34 (2005), 155–171.

Hann, D., *Physical Resistance: A Hundred Years of Anti-Fascism* (Ropley: Zero, 2013).

Harvey, D., *Rebel Cities: From the Right to the City to the Urban Revolution* (London: Verso, 2012).

Haunss, S., *Identität in Bewegung: Prozesse kollektiver Identität bei den Autonomen und in der Schwulenbewegung* (Wiesbaden: VS Verlag für Sozialwissenschaften, 2004).

Haunss, S., 'Antiimperialismus und Autonomie: Linksradikalismus seit der Studentenbewegung' in R. Roth and D. Rucht (eds.), *Die Sozialen Bewegungen in Deutschland seit 1945: Ein Handbuch* (Frankfurt am Main: Campus, 2008), 447–473.

Häussermann, H., et al., *Stadterneuerung in der Berliner Republik: Modernisierung in Berlin-Prenzlauer Berg* (Opladen: Leske + Budrich, 2002).

Hillenkamp, S., 'Die Autonomen: Zwischen Kultureller Wirklichkeit und Politischer Wirksamkeit', *Forschungsjournal Neue Soziale Bewegungen* 8:2 (1995), 54–66.

Holm, A., *Wir bleiben alle! Gentrifizierung, Städtische Konflikte um Aufwertung und Verdrängung* (Münster: Unrast, 2010).

Hofland, H.J.A., *De stadsoorlog. Amsterdam '80* (Alphen aan den Rijn: Sijthoff, 1981).

Jeugd en Samenleving 11:2 (1981).

Jugendwerk der Deutsche Shell, *Jugend '81: Lebensentwürfe, Alltagskulturen, Zukunftsbilder* (Hamburg: Jugendwerk der Deutsche Shell, 1981).

Kadir, N., 'Myth and Reality in the Amsterdam Squatters' Movement, 1975–2012' in B. van der Steen (ed.), *The City Is Ours: Squatting and Autonomous Movements in Europe from the 1970s to the Present* (Oakland: PM Press, 2014), 21–61.

Katsiaficas, G., *The Subversion of Politics: European Autonomous Movements and the Decolonization of Everyday Life* (Oakland: AK Press, 2006).

Koenen, G., *Das rote Jahrzehnt. Unsere kleine deutsche Kulturrevolution, 1967–1977* (Cologne: Kiepenheuer & Witsch, 2001).

Koopmans, R., *Democracy from Below: New Social Movements and the Political System in West Germany* (Boulder: Westview Press, 1995), 210–214.

Kraatz, B., 'Der Traum vom Paradies. Über die Stadtindianer und Autonomia in Italien' in M. Haller (ed.), *Aussteigen oder Rebellieren: Jugendliche gegen Staat und Gesellschaft* (Reinbek bei Hamburg: Rowohlt, 1986), 35–47.

Kraushaar, W. (eds.), *Die RAF und der linke Terrorismus* (Hamburg: Hamburger Edition, 2008).

Kritidis, G., 'The Rise and Crisis of the Anarchist and Libertarian Movement in Greece, 1973–2012' in B. van der Steen (ed.), *The City Is Ours: Squatting and Autonomous Movements in Europe from the 1970s to the Present* (Oakland: PM Press, 2014), 63–93.

Kühn, A., *Stalins Enkel, Maos Söhne: Die Lebenswelt der K-Gruppen in der Bundesrepublik der 70er Jahre* (Frankfurt am Main: Campus, 2005).

Küllmer, H., 'Zusammen leben, zusammen kämpfen' in S. Borgstede et al. (eds.), *Häuserkampf II. Wir wollen alles. Hausbesetzungen in Hamburg* (Hamburg: Laika Verlag, 2013), 75–89.

Langer, B. *Operation 1653: Stay rude, stay rebel* (Berlin: Plättners, 2004).

Lovink, G. and J. van de Spek, 'Buikdansen op de barrikade', *Marge* 10:1 (1986), 22–29.

Luchteling, V., *Axie! Herinneringen uit de Amsterdamse kraakbeweging* (Amsterdam: Arbeiderspers, 1997).

Mak, G., 'De rek is eruit', *De Groene Amsterdammer* (6 March 1980).

Manns, H. and W.S. Treusch, '"Hau Weg die Scheiße": Autonomer Widerstand in der Bundesrepublik', *Vorgänge* 26:1 (1987), 65–74.

Marge 10:1 (1986).

Mason, P., *Why It's Kicking Off Everywhere* (London: Verso, 2012).

Mason, P. *Why It's Still Kicking Off Everywhere* (London: Verso, 2013).

Melzer, P., '"Women of Peace' We Are Not". Feminist Militants in the West German Autonomen and the Women's Movement', *German Studies Review* 40:2 (2017), 313–332.

Melzer, P., '"Frauen gegen Imperialismus und Patriarchat zerschlagen den Herrschaftsapparat". Autonome Frauen, feministischer Protest und Gewalt in Westdeutschland' in H. Balz and J.H. Friedrichs (eds.), *'All we Ever Wanted…' Eine Kulturgeschichte europäischer Protestbewegungen der 1980er Jahre* (Berlin: Dietz, 2012), 157–177.

Mohr, M. and S. Haunss, 'Die Autonomen und die anti-deutsche Frage. Oder: "Deutschland muss…"' in G. Hanloser (ed.), *'Sie warn die Antideutschesten der deutschen Linken': Zu Geschichte, Kritik und Zukunft antideutscher Politik* (Münster: Unrast, 2004), 65–86.

Notz, G., 'Die autonomen Frauenbewegungen der Siebziger Jahre: Entstehungsgeschichte, Organisationsformen, politische Konzepte', *Archiv für Sozialgeschichte* 44 (2004), 123–148.

Ogman, R., *Against the Nation: Anti-national Politics in Germany* (Porsgrunn: New Compass Press, 2013).

Op den Camp, R., *Achter elke succesvolle kraker, staat een sterke kraakster: Een representatie van de vrouwelijke kraker in de Amsterdamse kraakbeweging, 1967–1985* (MA thesis 2013).

Owens, L., 'From Tourists to Anti-tourists to Tourist Attractions: The Transformation of the Amsterdam Squatters' Movement', *Social Movement Studies* 7 (2008), 43–59.

Owens, L., *Cracking under Pressure: Narrating the Decline of the Amsterdam Squatters' Movement* (Amsterdam: Amsterdam University Press, 2009).

Poppe, I. and S. Rottenberg, *De kraakgeneratie. 18 portretten van krakers uit de lichting 1955–1965* (Amsterdam: De Balie, 2000).

Pruijt, H., 'The Impact of Citizens' Protest on City Planning in Amsterdam' in L. Deben et al. (eds.), *Cultural Heritage and the Future of the Historic Inner City of Amsterdam* (Amsterdam: Aksant, 2004), 228–244.

Pruijt, H., 'The Logic of Urban Squatting', *International Journal of Urban and Regional Research* 37:1 (2012), 19–45.

Raad, J.W. van der, *Kraken in Amsterdam* (Amsterdam: Roelof Keller Stichting, 1982).

Rada, U., 'Wie lange wird es die Autonomen noch geben?', *Tageszeitung* (18 April 1995).

Reichhardt S. and D. Siegfried, *Das Alternative Milieu: Antibürgerlicher Lebensstil und linke Politik in der Bundesrepublik Deutschland und Europa 1968–1983* (Göttingen: Wallstein, 2010).

Rilling, R. (ed.), *Eine Frage der Gewalt: Antworten von links* (Berlin: Dietz, 2008).

Ruyter, D. de, 'Het onbehagen in de subcultuur', *Marge* 10:1 (1986a), 12–16.

Ruyter, D. de, *Een baksteen als bewustzijn: De geweldskultuur van de kraakbeweging* (Den Bosch: Marge, 1986b).

Ryser, D., *Slime: Deutschland muss sterben* (Munich: Heyne, 2013).

Schildt A. and D. Siegfried (eds.), *Between Marx and Coca-Cola: Youth Cultures in Changing European Societies, 1960–1980* (New York: Berghahn, 2006).

Schlögel K. et al., *Partei kaputt: Das Scheitern der KPD und die Krise der Linken* (Berlin: Olle & Wolter, 1981).

Schulz, J., 'Zapfenstreich am Schwarzen Dienstag', *Jungle World* (6 May 2010).

Schwarz, A.G. et al., *We Are an Image from the Future: The Greek Revolt of December 2008* (Oakland: PM Press, 2010).

Schwarzmeier, J., *Die Autonomen zwischen Subkultur und sozialer Bewegung* (Norderstedt, 2001).

Steen, B. van der et al., 'Squatting and Autonomous Action in Europe, 1980–2012' in B. van der Steen et al. (eds.), *The City Is Ours: Squatting and Autonomous Movements in Europe from the 1970s to the Present* (Oakland: PM Press, 2014a), 1–19.

Steen, B. van der, 'De papieren van de revolte: De kraakbeweging en haar geschiedschrijving', *Tijdschrift voor Stadsgeschiedenis* 9:2 (2014b), 166–181.

Testa, M., *Militant Anti-Fascism: A Hundred Years of Resistance* (New York: AK Press, 2015).

Turchetto, M., 'From "mass worker" to 'empire'. The Disconcerting Trajectory of Italian Operaismo' in J. Bidet and S. Kouvelakis (eds.), *Critical Companion to Contemporary Marxism* (Leiden: Brill, 2007), 285–308.

Verbij, A., *Tien Rode Jaren: Links Radicalisme in Nederland, 1970–1980* (Amsterdam: Ambo, 2005).

Wantok, A.G. (eds.), *Perspektiven autonomer Politik* (Münster: Unrast, 2011).

Wetenschappelijke Raad voor het Regeringsbeleid, *Democratie en geweld: Probleemanalyse naar aanleiding van de gebeurtenissen in Amsterdam op 30 april 1980* (Den Haag: Staatsuitgeverij, 1980).

Wietsma, A. et al., *Als je leven je lief is: Vraaggesprekken met krakers en kraaksters* (Amsterdam: Lont, 1982), 20–22.

Wir warn die stärkste der Partein... Erfahrungsberichte aus d. Welt d. K-Gruppen (Berlin: Rotbuch, 1977).

Wright, S., *Storming Heaven: Class Composition and Struggle in Italian Autonomist Marxism* (London: Pluto, 2002).

Zelizer, B., 'Why Memory's Work on Journalism Does Not Reflect Journalism's Work on Memory', *Memory Studies* 1:1 (2008), 79–87.

Ziere, P., '"Laat het duidelijk zijn: neem helm, stok en molotovs mee!" De ontwikkeling van de kraakbeweging tot radicale beweging' in J.W. Duivendak et al. (eds.), *Tussen verbeelding en macht: 25 jaar nieuwe sociale bewegingen in Nederland* (Amsterdam: Sua, 1992), 141–160.

Zomeren, K. van, *Een jaar in scherven* (Amsterdam: Arbeiderspers, 1994).

4.11

SUSTAINABLE ACTIVISM

Laurence Cox

Introduction: Sustainable Activism as a Radical Concern

Human beings struggle to survive, not only physically as 'bare life' but as beings with a 'wealth of needs', in search of dignity and who want to be happy. Not in every society, but certainly in societies which are based on the economic exploitation of human labour in many forms, on unequal power relations grounded in the physical coercion and exercise of authority against weaker groups, and on cultural hierarchies which position many people as subaltern, the struggle to survive as a fully human subject is also a struggle against existing social relationships.

It is sometimes said that under these circumstances, survival is itself a radical act. If this was automatically true, radical movements would be far stronger than they are: in practice, people often struggle to cope at the expense of those closest to them, or at the expense of other subaltern groups; they can enter into all sorts of clientelistic and collaborative relationships. They can direct their aggression not at those who are exploiting, oppressing or stigmatising them but into domestic violence, addictions, fundamentalist religion, racism, misogyny and many other attempts to cope, or to survive, at other people's expense. It is partly because these forms of (misplaced) struggle to survive are so widespread, and so 'obvious' in our kinds of societies, that sustainable activism – not only seeing beyond these, but acting beyond these and doing so consistently – is an impressive and fragile achievement.

In this chapter, I want to make a smaller claim: that *sustainable activism* is a radical achievement. To become, and remain, a member of a community or social movement whose struggle actively challenges dominant relations of power, economics and culture is radical in the sense of durable participation in the attempt to transform these relationships.[1]

I want to go further and suggest that sustainable activism in this sense is far *more* radical than the simple production and consumption of radical *opinions*, whether on social media or in academic papers. Opinion politics can simply reproduce existing social relationships if it not carried out as part of the classic radical tasks of agitating (attempting to convince the unconvinced, which starts by communicating with them and not only within one's own opinion community); educating (discussing with others who are already engaged in struggle and attempting to develop their movements) and organising (which should need no explanation).

'Radical' has no meaning if it is not tied to *action* of some kind; and the attempt to *sustain* agency is of equal importance to attempts to *develop* and *widen* it.

What Is Sustainable Activism?

From one point of view, sustainable activism can be defined simply as the attempt to become, and remain, effectively involved in collective political agency. We can start with Geoff Eley's observation that democracy, in the sense of

> free, universal, secret, adult and universal suffrage; the classic civil freedoms of speech, conscience, assembly, association, and the press; and freedom from arrest without trial ... was achieved nowhere in the world during the nineteenth century and arrived in only four states before 1914 – New Zealand (1893), Australia (1903), Finland (1906), and Norway (1913).
>
> *(2002: 3)*

As will be fairly obvious, virtually no states *before* this period were democratic in anything remotely approaching this sense; and we might reasonably ask how far 'the classic civil freedoms' can really be said to be available in countries like the present-day UK or US, let alone Mexico, Turkey or India. It is, of course, true that state power was shaped very differently in pre-capitalist societies, and we can identify moderate degrees of self-government on the part of, say, Russian peasant communities or various social groups in medieval India; however, these were typically structured by high degrees of traditional action and often included strong internal power relations tied to gender, ethnic and religious membership, age and marital status, economic position and so on.

In other words, within the class societies that have dominated the world for the past several thousand years, it has been an exceptional situation when most people have had any significant say in the main decisions that affected them. Of course on the margins of these societies, there have been significant stateless societies; some self-governing communities of pirates, deserters and the like; and some revolutionary situations. The struggle to become, and remain, a political agent in this context has thus historically been a huge challenge, if by agency we mean something more than clientelism, acts of violence on behalf of the powerful and wealthy, and so on. It is only within living memory that fascist dictatorships have been (provisionally) beaten; that most of the globe has ceased to be divided up among a handful of empires; or that (most) state socialisms have collapsed. Eley's very minimal definition of formal democracy is thus a rare flower.

Within these formally democratic contexts, however, political agency outside the narrow boundaries defined here – including much or most social movement activity – has routinely been treated as threatening (and has in some cases actually been so) to dominant power relations, the economic structures they defend and the cultural hierarchies erected around them. Active attempts to assert democratic participation, from the Chartists through to popular resistance against fracking, and from the struggle against domestic violence to the self-assertion of indigenous communities, consistently meet with a high degree of opposition in all three dimensions.

State repression (formal and informal) needs no introduction to anyone involved in radical movements and those which employ confrontational strategies. The economic price paid, whether in terms of dismissal or unemployment, the financial costs of prioritising movement activities or the simple costs of maintaining movements, can be very high. Those who identify with existing cultural routines and 'normality' may also take opportunities to attack those who question them, in forms ranging from violence to exclusion.

Since most people – particularly those in communities in struggle and many of those motivated to take part in radical movements – lack the economic, power and cultural privilege to deflect such attacks painlessly, their ability to keep going and sustain their activism is regularly put in question. These costs are often targeted not only at activists but also at their families, towards whom they may have all sorts of different (financial, care, parenting, etc.) responsibilities; and they undermine activists' ability to sustain their networks and support one another. In some contexts, all of this can lead activists to a more or less conscious strategy of putting those who are seen as having least to lose, those who can most easily absorb such costs or those who are believed least likely to be attacked in the most visible positions (most dramatically in international solidarity contexts where Northern volunteers cannot be targeted in the ways that are routine for local activists). There is something to be said for each strategy, but also familiar downsides in terms of the internal politics of class, gender, ethnicity and so on.

While the phrase itself is only used in some traditions, sustainable activism in the sense used here is a major concern for most movements and communities in struggle. Newcomers have to be enabled to overcome these hurdles; existing participants have to be supported; networks and communities have to be defended; knowledge and connections have to be protected and extended; movement presence in different areas of society has to be fought for; and learning and generational transmission has to be worked on. These can be thought about in terms of legal support and prisoner solidarity, economic networking or creating alternative ways of making a living, challenging various forms of discrimination and hate speech, celebrating movement struggles in ways that make the hardships of the present meaningful, informal support to families under pressure, international solidarity and many other ways.

Movements that do not work on making activism sustainable (whatever language they use) will not last. They will run out of participants, fold under pressure or turn into something more compatible with dominant social relationships – a publication, a lifestyle, an academic niche and so on. This does not always mean that they think about sustainability consciously: they may have arrived at viable solutions some time back and have found a way of transmitting those across generations. Nonetheless, the work still needs to be done.

... and Prefiguration?

Many radical movements and communities engage in a greater or lesser degree of prefiguration. Put more historically, it is not always possible to maintain a sharp disjuncture between who we are, how we act now and the world we hope to see without wider political, military or employment structures that support this kind of compartmentalisation. It is a backhanded tribute to the relative success of social movements at creating new kinds of state, or inserting themselves within effective ones, that prefiguration has become a stronger demand in recent decades and scepticism towards instrumental strategies has grown.

The experience of winning universal suffrage and welfare states, legal battles for citizenship or against discrimination, national independence and ethno-religious states, conflicts over language and consumption and the like are widely experienced as ambiguous successes in terms of popular power. In most cases, the populations that benefit from these – and that often inherited them as the gains of previous struggles – do value these gains, at least for themselves (and even despite the platforms of parties they may vote for). *But* the credibility of the armed vanguard, the radical lawyer, the political party, the NGO, the religious crusade or the campaign to change cultural symbolism is eroded as much by its external success as by its opponents.

When there were few if any of these experiences to look back on, it could be reasonably believed (for example) that getting the vote, changing how people spoke, writing new laws, winning national independence, enshrining religious values in the constitution, educating people and so on would change *everything*. We now know from long historical experience that it is not that easy; these struggles win something, but not as much as is promised, and often more for leaders than for grassroots activists, let alone the wider constituency they mobilise.

In this sense, the belief that the future will justify all the sacrifices of the present has become harder to sustain credibly, at least within social movements from below.[2] Communities and movements fighting for more *equal* economic, political and cultural relationships are now more likely to want to see some link between how we organise now and the alternatives we are struggling for. Sustainable activism, then, in the sense of movements and communities which do not treat their participants as ultimately expendable, has become a more explicit focus in internally democratic movements than in forms of organisation modelled on military or religious structures.

Sustainable Activism in Different Movement Contexts[3]

Activist sustainability means very different things in different contexts, because the dimensions which are difficult to achieve vary hugely. In previous work, I have identified three aspects of this difference: social inequality and the situation of different movements' core participants; institutionalisation and how different movements interface with the structures of everyday life; and how movement cultures sit within the wider society.

Social Inequality

What dimensions of personal sustainability matter most to different participants in different times, places and social contexts? This is above all a question of social inequality and of how individuals are located within their local social order.

Everyday Survival

This covers the issues that people need to cover in order simply to keep going in terms of their everyday social situation. It includes people's health, physical and mental energy and vulnerabilities; how much they are physically and socially dependent on other people, along with their caring and workplace responsibilities to other people. More generally, it includes how far their living and working situation, family and personal networks support participation in movements or make it difficult to maintain. For most people most of the time, these are fundamental – and by definition nobody can *sustainably* ignore them. But depending on who one is, different issues will stand out as problematic.

Movement-Relevant Resources

By this, I mean the things that people need to manage in order to be able practically to engage in movement activity. People have to manage time and money pressures and the other ways in which class, gender, race and so on make it easier or harder to engage in movement activities. Access to the different means of communication, transport, practical organisation and so on is unevenly distributed in unequal societies, while in different contexts, there are also different expectations around public activities, and the cognitive and political tools involved may be more or less easily available. It is certainly possible to create new kinds of movement participation and contest the social order in creative ways that work better for people in different situations; or put another way, people will always work with what they have. At the same time, 'they do not do so just as they please', but in a world not of their own making where participation in politics is very uneven and often very limited. Hence, movements often have to strike a difficult balance, consciously or otherwise, between enabling participation (for example, through education and training programmes) and having an immediate impact on wider power relations (with people who are already familiar with the activities involved).

Emotional Sustainability

People can have their everyday life more or less under control and have the resources they need to engage in social movements, without doing so – or without being able to handle doing so emotionally. In some political traditions and supportive movement cultures, as well as some class, ethnic or religious cultures, there are established, socially supported ways of being in the world that make it relatively easy on a personal level to 'be an activist'. There are, of course, many different ways into the skills and supports for emotional self-management, handling one's own mental health and dealing with violence and conflict. At its most basic, few people find conflict entirely easy, and a stable emotional relationship to conflict is an important aspect of activist sustainability.

Movements and Everyday Life

Different movements interface with everyday life and social routines in different ways. Put another way, someone's movement participation can be primarily a job, an identity, a part of their everyday culture or a dimension of their working life; and these different situations affect individual activists but also shape movements insofar as most movements have a centre of gravity in one or other of these (perhaps a characteristic of a truly powerful movement is its presence across multiple dimensions). Each of these brings up different issues in relation to activist sustainability:

Workplace-Based Movements

Peasant and labour struggles are naturally workplace-based, while other types of activism (e.g. some aspects of resistance to fascism) can also be centred here. In workplaces, the key issues for sustainability obviously include conflict with managers and landowners, relations with other workers (e.g. solidarity vs scabbing), workplace 'custom and practice', whether people value the job they do or see it simply as a means to earn money and so on. Even something as simple as knowing how to picket and respond to pickets can be a source of stress, or conversely routinised and well-understood all round.

Community-Based Movements

Some movements naturally tend to organise within people's residential or social communities – working-class community organising, GLBTQI activism and many ethnic or religious movements, for example. Some of the particular sustainability challenges here come from the situation of the community as a whole (coping with poverty, oppression, cultural stigma and so on), while others come from *other* forms of organising within the community (e.g. religious, gang, business).

Professional or Full-Time Activism

In some kinds of movement situation (parties, unions, media, NGOs and so on), many or most activists are employed *by* movement organisations. The challenge is then how to make sure that the stress involved in keeping the organisational show on the road (shaping conflicts into particular institutional routines) and dealing with everything else that arrives in the door of highly visible organisations does not take over from the wider motivations for action. When activism is professionalised, workplace issues and tensions take on a very particular character, and there can be strong tendencies towards internal (self-)exploitation.

'Leisure' Activism

Finally, some kinds of movements take place outside where most of their participants work and live, in the social space otherwise occupied by leisure activities. Obviously enough, this sort of activism sits awkwardly in relation to everything else that might be going on in people's lives, so that isolation, guilt and burnout can become particular problems.

These different situations represent different forms of institutionalisation (or lack of it). Institutionalisation, together with routinisation and social normalisation, has effects on many other aspects of sustainability. The sort of work involved, the routine risks and conflicts encountered, the most common emotional and mental health challenges, and what individuals (or other activists) are good at dealing with and responding to and what is unsupported vary hugely between these different kinds of setting.

Movement Activism in the Wider Society

The history of different movements, and the state of struggle in different societies at different times, means that participants can find themselves more or less at odds with the world around them. *As activists*, they may be more or less supported in the rest of their lives, facing ongoing conflict with family and friends, workmates and neighbours, school or religious community. In fact, their own activist biography is likely to be shaped by how the movement 'sits' within the wider society:

Long-Standing Movement Cultures

In some cases, movements have not only lasted for generations but they are widely represented within a wider culture and large sections of the community can be expected to get involved at times. Some activists may be more or less literally born into movement families, while for others there are well-understood and easily managed ways of joining movements, learning and finding mutual support. Either way, such situations are particularly likely to offer viable emotional repertoires (not to mention community rituals, biographies and so on) that support movement participation. Some ethnonationalist or radical left cultures may approximate this, such as republicanism in some parts of Northern Ireland or the Italian left for much of the post-war period.

Supportive Classes or Cultures

A slightly weaker case is where most people in a given class or culture are not themselves active but there is nonetheless general support for those who do get involved in movements, so that it is a fairly well-understood, and moderately unproblematic, role to adopt. This has been the case for some radical religious groups like the Quakers, some US black communities and some parts of the European working class in the twentieth century.

Moments of Generational Transformation

The big waves of movement mobilisation, such as that at the end of the 1960s and early 1970s, bring what can feel like a whole generation of young people into movements, marking a break from their parents as well as from pre-existing institutions, even those nominally in the same movement. For this first generation, their participation involves a far more radical shift in relation to who they have been brought up to be, something which may not be so evident in later generations. Examples might include feminist and GLBTQI activists in this period, who often had to rediscover their movements' prehistory because of the *lack* of available connections at the time. Over time, these situations tend to become easier to live with, if only because of the large numbers of other people struggling with – and discussing – the same kinds of tension.

Newly Formed, or Fundamentally Marginal, Movements

Lastly, where movement participation involves a break not only with one's family and wider cultures but also with one's peers, producing a sustainable movement culture essentially amounts to the challenge of producing a new counterculture. Such movements can struggle to institutionalise themselves and become subcultural in the sense of largely consisting of young adults, meaning that they have failed to solve the problem of how to live with movement participation in later life. Along with this, the intensity of the cultural tensions is often hard to sustain emotionally. Much animal rights activism seems to follow this pattern, with older (let alone second-generation) activism being rare. In other cases, such as Deaf or trans activism, the nature of the issue itself may make a breach with one's culture of origin particularly likely but entail a much longer-term involvement, and often the construction of activist personas and narratives within the movement geared to this kind of transformation.

It is obviously hugely important in terms of the sustainability of activism whether it is a family expectation, one respected (or at least familiar) choice among others, a breach with older generations or a standing reproach to one's whole culture. This dimension overlaps with wider issues of 'habitus', in Bourdieu's (1977) terminology. What sorts of emotional repertoires and expectations go along with activism in different local, classed or ethnic cultures? What kinds of activist roles and personas are recognised? Is political participation understood by others as a statement of morality, of personality or of career? How do people live with particular kinds of situations (martyrdom, unemployment, fame, family conflict)?

Reflections

These different dimensions are obviously interconnected in any practical situation: the social situation that movement participants find themselves in shapes the kinds of organisation they prioritise, while the longer history of movement success or failure (or at least institutionalisation) shapes how other people within their social world relate to them. However, these dimensions vary so widely as between different movements that most general statements about activist sustainability fall quite far of the mark.

Understandably, most activist writing (and most research geared to an individual movement) focuses on the aspects of sustainability that are most challenging for participants (or would-be participants) in that particular movement, and treats these as defining sustainability in general, without seeing the dimensions which are relatively unproblematic for its members (or more exactly which can be handled by existing routines, whether these belong to the wider culture or to the movement). Of course, as the discussion of how activism relates to the wider society suggests, different movements also operate with a greater or lesser degree of cultural radicalism, and a greater or lesser acceptance of conventional kinds of interpersonal and collective relationships. These things, in turn, impact greatly on activist sustainability, when everyday culture is intolerable on a personal level (a GLTBQI person in a homophobic culture, for example) or when activists' emotional stability depends on 'not rocking the boat' in their own social world.

These point to a wider problem: in a world shaped by oppression, exploitation and stigmatisation, activists' personal lives can be very squeezed for many reasons, and they often have to make movements work for themselves to some extent, even if only in the sense that much of their human contact, friendships or relationships happen there. In other cases, a movement may be thoroughly interwoven with everyday care and reproduction; it might offer employment possibilities (or indeed lead to being blacklisted). The challenge, in other words, is how to make the movement live and work in people's lives but without this means becoming an end in itself.

Much academic and activist analysis takes for granted the ways in which participation in a given movement sits easily within the existing world – professionalisation, cultural conservatism, in-group behaviour, reliance on dominant forms of power internally – and highlights what is problematic for group members. It is important, particularly from a radical perspective in which we do not take the simple existence of movements as an end in itself, to remain wary of this and ask after the shadow side – while recognising that for movements to survive at all, they may not be able to afford to resist and transform *all* social relations at once. This is particularly true when their participants are poor, relatively powerless, culturally stigmatised, physically vulnerable or otherwise struggling to cope with everyday life, let alone movements. Conversely, it is no critique of the most demanding approaches to activism to say that they may be more accessible to those who have the resources to engage in them. We do know from history, and some present-day examples like Chiapas or Rojava, that this is not an absolute, and movements of the most oppressed can at times be the most radical on these dimensions too – when they are truly mass movements.

Our Common Activist Heritage

The first part of this chapter presented activist sustainability as an important dimension both of surviving as a decent human being in an unjust society, and especially of the ongoing struggle for meaningful democratic participation. The second section showed just how much is involved in these achievements, but also argued that – depending on movement participants' social situations, how movements are institutionalised and how participation sits within the wider culture – activists will experience different patterns of what threatens sustainability, so that there is no easy checklist of 'sustainability issues' that works across all movements and all times and places.

However since any given movement experiences a concrete set of problems in relation to activist sustainability, activists develop situation-specific ways of thinking about these problems, as well as strategies to resolve these particular issues. Without any pretence of exhaustiveness, I want to explore a few relatively common approaches. I relate each to one or more concrete movements, not because any individual approach is the sole property of the movements mentioned (or because everyone in the movement in question subscribes to that approach) but simply because no strategy for activist sustainability really makes sense *outside* of a concrete movement context.

Still, in the wider picture, each of these approaches represents important aspects of human flourishing (or, more darkly, how these are attacked in our societies). Radical movements, then, should treat all of these as our common heritage, as well as thinking about what is specific to other people's struggles as well as (a harder challenge) to our own.

Challenging the System

Movements and ideologies which focus on the bigger picture – Marxists and anarchists, feminists and GLTBQI activists, anticolonial and radical black liberation approaches, etc. – often point to the extent to which it is structural features of contemporary society that get in the way of activist sustainability. This is a centrally important point – the very reasons we struggle are also among the things which make the struggle hard – and it can be easily missed in approaches which place all the responsibility for sustainability on movements' own internal organisations and require added efforts from activists.

At the same time, this approach is sometimes used to dismiss concerns with sustainability as mere self-indulgence, with the added implication that they express a sheltered life or the luxury of privilege. This is a familiar sound from the leaderships of organisations structured around a very high activist turnover – recruiting, using and losing participants 'for the greater good of the organisation' – which are therefore threatened by any attention given to the actual experience of membership. It is also familiar from advocates of a macho, 'just do it' approach to movements, for whom these are implicitly feminine or weak concerns that get in the way of 'real' (high-octane) activism. This position is, of course, in turn, the privilege of those who are not struggling with the effects of trauma, for example.

There is also a more privileged and at times more liberal version of this refusal to look inwards: as various forms of feminism, Marxism, gay studies, Black studies, etc., have entered the academy or the media, they have often become individualised and professionalised. In their own lives, their advocates have relatively high rewards compared to most of those on whose behalf they speak, but often lack the time and energy to respond to the needs of other participants other than financially. The logic of both media and academic activism, too, is often towards a relentless emphasis on structure and the avoidance of serious discussion of, or engagement with, popular agency and its discontents.

Of course, there are also honourable exceptions in all of these camps. However, a serious recognition of just how deep-seated and damaging are the structures we are up against should logically also entail thinking seriously about the challenges of developing and sustaining movements for the long haul under these circumstances, not refusing to think about the problem. Structural constraints will indeed constantly erode our individual and collective capacity, and it is indeed an illusion to think that we can achieve ideal movement-internal relationships this side of a massive change in social power; however, we will not get there if we do not pay attention to supporting each other.

Conversely, what those with a shorter historical memory often forget is *just how transformative* large-scale collective action is, including in terms of sustainability. Oppressed people who become political agents find themselves recovering a sense of pride and dignity, of power and voice in the wider society; they transform themselves and each other in the process of making another world and find a sense of real possibility absent in previously trapped lives. What can be hard to achieve in a small group over years can sometimes be achieved in mass struggle in 'weeks where decades happen' (Lenin).

Survival-Oriented Solidarity

In disadvantaged communities, there is often no real dividing line between the everyday forms of mutual aid that people rely on to get through the week or to get through hard times, and activist solidarity. This underpins one of the strengths of mobilisation in such contexts: people are mobilised in families, in streets or neighbourhoods, in workplaces, in churches, in ethnic groups – the same social relationships that they are tied into for everyday survival. Conversely, these relationships tend to be what determines movement involvement, and powerful forms of internal clientelism can develop under patriarchal or 'notable' leadership, prioritising the interests of the latter. When internal power relationships are less hierarchical and more participative, such community-based struggles can be both radical and very hard to defeat, precisely because of the centrality of sustainability to their organising relationships.

In these situations, activist sustainability consists first and foremost of everyday survival: person-to-person or collectively organised financial help for individuals; sharing food and goods; 'caring labour' in all its many forms; listening and emotional support; advocacy to help people deal with powerful institutions; and practical support around life crises such as sickness, bereavement, unwanted pregnancy, unemployment, eviction or imprisonment. Well-organised community activism often goes beyond this to organise training and education that supports people to become political subjects, from literacy and voter registration to media training and assistance in setting up formally registered organisations. As Nilsen (2010) has observed, these strategies are often successful at lower levels of the political system (becoming citizens) and ineffective at higher levels (substantive change in power relationships). They often follow a logic of brokerage whereby community members are encouraged to engage with formal institutions along approved lines – lines which have worked for professional activists and upwardly mobile activist families, but which are less effective at resolving large-scale structural inequality.

However to note the potential pitfalls around, this form of sustainability in no way changes the historical fact that very large numbers of people – majorities in many societies – find themselves forced to depend on self-organised mechanisms of mutual aid. The real question, then, is not whether this is a good thing but how best to organise it. Nor is it any surprise that activism in such contexts is geared around an extension of these relationships – 'activist mothering' in Nancy Naples' (1998) neat phrase, whereby the black and Latina community activists she studied on the US East Coast extended their own care work both to the wider community and more specifically to the younger women activists they mentored.

Coping with Criminalisation

The legal and prison systems are explicitly designed as repressive apparatuses, intended to punish those who challenge the state, including those who resist what they see as unjust laws. In earlier periods, liberals, democrats, nationalists, suffragettes, anarchists and socialists all found themselves at the sharp end of the same monarchical, authoritarian or colonial regimes; in parliamentary democracies, at least this experience had been comfortably relegated to origin myths by the first four of these, until the recent authoritarian turns in majority world countries from Turkey to India.

For today's radicals, however, the experience of state repression remains a live one, whether challenging the institutions of neo-liberalism, resisting wars, fighting for animal rights, resisting biopolitical attacks on women's and GLTBQI bodies, challenging police killings or defending the earth. Many of our best people still find themselves going through the courts and prisons. This process is hugely challenging for the individuals targeted, in many different ways, and movements which regularly encounter legal repression usually develop more or less effective legal and prisoner support structures, designed to support the individual through what is intended as an isolating and dehumanising experience.

But the costs of repression are not only felt by the individual: in movements where the police only stand limited chances of actually securing convictions on substantial charges, they can raise the costs of activism substantially by campaigns of low-level harassment (arrest without charge, repeated trials on minor offences or constant deferral of trial dates) as well as through surveillance (sowing distrust and forcing activists to spend time on countermeasures). All of this is felt by the targets' family and friends, and in some contexts, their neighbours or workmates can be mobilised against them.

This is more or less consciously theorised in different contexts: often, movements build successful counternarratives which valorise the victims of repression and use visible cases of injustice as a source of outrage, mobilisation and radicalisation. When handled well, this can force the state to back off; when handled badly, it can lock movements into an emotional dynamic of intensifying conflict which simultaneously isolates them from the wider population, and provide police and security forces with a permanently available justification for increased funding and sharpened legislation. This was one of the main internal criticisms of European and North American urban guerrilla movements in the 1970s and 1980s, reviving an older left critique of conspiratorial organisation.

Direct Action and Coping with Trauma

Partly because of this, many radical movements have repositioned their activism on a terrain which limits the scope for state repression within normal legislation and enables them to seek support from a much wider population. This is the case, for example, for much ecological direct action and more radical traditions within alterglobalisation and anti-austerity activism in the global North. The state, in turn, has often (not always) readjusted its focus, with an increased attention, in particular, to forms of non-lethal violence and intimidation in the physical confrontations that often characterise these forms of activism (such as summit protests or protest encampments). It is hard for activists to effectively prevent, or even gain retrospective satisfaction for, beatings, pepper-sprayings, sexual assault, kettlings, spying of various kinds, even in extreme cases such as the UK undercover policemen who had long-term relationships and in some cases children with activists – and hard for legal successes in these areas to prevent repeat performances, except where the police and security services have also suffered a substantial loss of public legitimacy in the process.

Consequently – and because these movements have recruited widely, often among young people with no previous background in movements – activists have had to work hard at recognising, learning about and responding to trauma, in particular. Often interacting with the many other forms of psychological damage inflicted by oppressive social relationships, trauma and PTSD can have sharp and sudden effects on activists' capacity to engage in movements, or to do so productively and in ways that are not damaging to others. Activist trauma support groups, networks and resources have thus become an important feature of many movement contexts.

Psychological

At a less extreme scale, burnout and other mental health issues such as depression, isolation or addiction are widely experienced in some social movement contexts (as in our societies more generally). In the nature of things, radical movements involve a huge personal effort against very powerful opponents, with limited chances of success and often few immediate rewards. This situation is not a happy one psychologically unless it is managed effectively, for example, with a supportive movement culture which notices real effects on the world, develops enjoyable relationships between participants and a strongly positive sense of the value of the movement and its activity, and it is unsurprising that participation takes its toll.

By their nature, too, movements appear to some people suffering with mental health issues as a place where they may be able to make friends, have an effect on the world and express the things that are important to them – or, in less constructive ways, 'act out' their mental health issues, from aggression through paranoia to personal aggrandisement. Most movements do not seek to police their boundaries tightly, and for obvious reasons activists rarely want to exclude people for behaving in ways different from the mainstream norm. However, this does not mean that movement participants are necessarily always equipped to recognise and respond to mental health issues.

Thus as far back as the 1970s, women's and GLTBQI movements have worked on various aspects of mental health, both in a problem-solving approach, aiming to rework existing forms of therapy and counselling for participants, and in a constructive approach, aiming to create new ways of living well, group rituals and alternative identities (Ernst and Goodison, 1993). Here, the 'consciousness-raising' approach, Paolo Freire's reworking of the normally transformative effects of the collective self-expression of subaltern groups into a form of adult education, became radicalised and generalised: movement participation became simultaneously a space for rethinking one's self in relation to others. This model has been highly influential in subsequent movements, in a wide variety of different forms, and has been adopted far beyond activist contexts.

Prefigurative Approaches

Ecological and radical-spiritual activism too often seeks to remake activist subjects within the process of mobilisation, in ways that go beyond the purely political. 'Cultural radicalism', in Epstein's (1991) neat analysis, is a particularly precarious project because of the attempt to remake its own psychological and interpersonal basis, in a sense to rebuild the boat while sailing in it. As many readers will know from their own experience, there is huge transformative potential in certain kinds of activism, and it is entirely possible both to challenge power relations radically and to unpick one's inner allegiance to those relationships. Usually, this is best done in a relatively trusting but high-intensity small-group context, such as a camp or occupation, where time and depth of relationships permit a collective remaking of selves and rethinking of interactions.

From the movement point of view, a decisive question may be how much collective preparation – for the pressures of conflict and in terms of prefiguring a different way of being – the group has engaged in before this kind of confrontation, and how much time is available for subsequent processing. A shared religious basis can often provide this kind of support in advance, while once the group is thoroughly formed, it is not uncommon for members to create institutions (intentional communities, social centres, political or publishing projects) intended to make it possible to continue the new way of being with one another while simultaneously challenging wider social relationships.

Of course, the pressures are often great: we are often drawn to cultural radicalism because of our own disjunctures with existing social relationships, something which in our society often exacts a high psychological toll, or may arise from underlying trauma, etc. Confrontation with powerful others, and small-group dynamics, can also make such situations highly unstable; for example, successful *long-term* intentional communities are the exception rather than the rule, and are often based either on religious commitments, sexual and family relationships or successful economic projects.

Prefiguration thus logically draws on the particular tools of such contexts. Practices such as meditation, service to others, vegetarianism and other forms of food politics, artistic creativity and ritual can all be organised in ways that place the group or community at the centre while infusing its movement activities with deep personal meaning. They can also enable the ritualisation of confrontational activities: as forms of asceticism, as performance art or as displays of mutual commitment. Sustainability in these contexts, however, is a particularly fragile achievement, which often has to be invented again to work for each specific context, while people who fall out of the group can struggle to sustain the transformed sense of themselves in a world which does not treat them that way.

Cultural Survival

Finally, indigenous communities, in particular, can often find themselves in situations where the struggle to sustain themselves *as indigenous* and *as communities* is put in peril by the forces they are fighting against, and where movement mobilisation can offer a way of revitalising and restating cultural ideals which have often come under heavy attack from other societies and may also need reworking for a new situation. This is one reason why indigenous groups have often been such effective opponents of extractivist projects (drilling, mining, logging, etc.): if the project goes ahead, and the wider processes it symbolises continue, their young people are at risk of becoming migrant labourers, losing their language, abandoning their traditional economic activities and cultural practices, etc.: in other words, ceasing to be active members of the community. The alternative to resistance, in other words, is often to accept becoming a racially despised shanty-town population – though Zibechi's (2010) remarkable ethnography of El Alto shows just how much is actually preserved in such situations, including for radical struggles.

Such situations often pit different agendas for sustainability against one another: among Native Americans, for example, conservatives and cultural radicals may both assert the value of tradition and culture but with very different inflections. Gender and sexuality can pit patriarchal customs against young people's struggles for self-assertion and acceptance. Well-meaning organisers who want to bring mainstream education, technology and emotional practices may wind up undermining more creative attempts to assert local rationalities.

Put another way, indigenous communities are characterised in the modern world by their coexistence with more powerful societies, economies, states and cultures, and the viability of different strategies for sustainability often depends on how much agency the community is capable of asserting under these circumstances.

Nonetheless, it is clear that there is an extraordinary political and personal strength available when communities are capable, even partly, of standing outside dominant social relationships, an experience that is well worth reflecting on for other movements, even though the situation cannot be replicated.

Conclusion

In the very broadest sense, activist sustainability represents the challenging question of how people lacking power, wealth or cultural privilege can become and remain active and radical political subjects. Those who highlight the need for structural resolutions of this problem are not wrong in saying that some of these problems can never be fully resolved within existing social forms. The chicken-and-egg problem, though, is that it is precisely such movements that are needed to overthrow existing social forms, so that sustainability and democratic participation are always likely to be a work in progress until movements have overthrown class society, patriarchy and the racialised world order. That process will, as I think this argument makes clear but we can also see from the experience of successful revolutions, involve participants remaking themselves and their relationships to one another as they remake the world around them.

In the meantime, activist sustainability is a wheel that will continually be reinvented, or more exactly a challenge that will always be rediscovered as part of the necessary learning process of movement participation. We will always be scrambling to keep up with the challenges we meet in this area, starting from the very real problem of recognising and naming the difficulties. In the process, hopefully, we can come to treat ourselves and each other less in line with mainstream social and cultural relations and with more radical forms of relationship and emotion – solidarity, compassion, mutual support, comradeship and a wider interest in one another's flourishing as full human beings.

The discussion above has highlighted some of the tensions and complexities of different approaches, at times critically. But the power and importance of activist sustainability – even when the attempt to achieve it 'goes wrong' somehow – arise because human beings will and do struggle to meet their needs in the most challenging circumstances. In this sense, activist sustainability is an irreducible aspect of any attempt to change the world.

Notes

1 Radicalism under this definition can of course be right-wing radicalism, in the sense of attempts to create a different, and more exploitative/oppressive/culturally hierarchical world. In the present context, however, I am only interested in those movements and communities which are pushing in the opposite direction: logically enough, their attempts at sustainability work very differently.

2 One of the defining features of social movements from above (Cox and Nilsen, 2014) is the way in which they draw on existing cultural hierarchies, forms of power and economic arrangements. The distinction between privileged leaders and useful idiots is often alive and well in these movements.

3 This section draws on the discussion in Cox (2009).

References

Bourdieu, P. (1977) *Outline of a Theory of Practice*. Cambridge: Cambridge University Press.

Cox, L. (2009) 'Hearts with One Purpose Alone? Mapping the Diverse Landscapes of Personal Sustainability in Social Movements.' *Emotion, Space and Society* 2: 52–61.

Cox, L. and Nilsen, A. (2014) *We Make Our Own History: Marxism and Social Movements in the Twilight of Neoliberalism*. London: Pluto.

Eley, G. (2002) *Forging Democracy: The History of the Left in Europe, 1850–2000*. Oxford: Oxford University Press.

Epstein, B. (1991) *Political Protest and Cultural Revolution: Non-violent Direct Action in the 1970s and 1980s*. Berkeley: University of California Press.

Ernst, S. and Goodison, L. (1993) *In Our Own Hands: A Book of Self-Help Therapy*. London: Women's Press.

Naples, N. (1998) *Grassroots Warriors: Activist Mothering, Community Work, and the War on Poverty*. New York: Routledge.

Nilsen, A. (2010) *Dispossession and Resistance in India: the River and the Rage*. London: Routledge.

Zibechi, R. (2010) *Dispersing Power: Social Movements as Anti-State Forces*. Oakland, CA: AK Press.

INDEX

Note: Page numbers followed by "n" denote endnotes.